June 10–14, 2017
Edinburgh, United Kingdom

Association for Computing Machinery

Advancing Computing as a Science & Profession

DIS'17

Proceedings of the 2017 ACM Conference on Designing Interactive Systems

Sponsored by:

ACM SIGCHI

Supported by:

Facebook, The MIT Press, Edinburgh Napier University, and CPI Conference Partners International

Association for
Computing Machinery

Advancing Computing as a Science & Profession

The Association for Computing Machinery
2 Penn Plaza, Suite 701
New York, New York 10121-0701

Notice to Past Authors of ACM-Published Articles
ACM intends to create a complete electronic archive of all articles and/or other material previously published by ACM. If you have written a work that has been previously published by ACM in any journal or conference proceedings prior to 1978, or any SIG Newsletter at any time, and you do NOT want this work to appear in the ACM Digital Library, please inform permissions@acm.org, stating the title of the work, the author(s), and where and when published.

ISBN: 978-1-4503-4922-2 (Digital)

ISBN: 978-1-4503-5601-5 (Print)

Additional copies may be ordered prepaid from:

ACM Order Department
PO Box 30777
New York, NY 10087-0777, USA

Phone: 1-800-342-6626 (USA and Canada)
+1-212-626-0500 (Global)
Fax: +1-212-944-1318
E-mail: acmhelp@acm.org
Hours of Operation: 8:30 am – 4:30 pm ET

Printed in the USA

DIS 2017 Chair's Welcome

Welcome to the historic, vibrant and beautiful city of Edinburgh. Scotland's capital is imbued with a rich tradition of creativity, design, innovation and research, making it a most fitting home for the 12th ACM SIGCHI Designing Interactive Systems (DIS'17) conference.

Running biennially since 1995, the Designing Interactive Systems (DIS) Conference is the premier, international arena where designers, artists, psychologists, user experience researchers, systems engineers, and many more, come together to debate and shape the future of interactive systems design and practice. DIS is owned by the ACM Special Interest Group on Computer- Human Interaction (SIGCHI). In the past, DIS has been held in Ann Arbor (1995), Amsterdam (1997), New York (2000), London (2002), Boston (2004), State College (2006), Cape Town (2008), Aarhus (2010), Newcastle (2012), Vancouver (2014), Brisbane (2016) and now, in 2017, moves to a new era of annual conferences.

The DIS'17 conference schedule starts with two days of pre-conference workshops and a doctoral consortium and continues with three main conference days into which we have packed 130 peer reviewed paper and pictorial presentations into 30 sessions across three parallel tracks, alongside which we have demos, provocations and works in progress, a lunchtime symposium held by Facebook and two invited keynote speakers. The social program includes a welcome reception on Sunday evening, a Demos & Posters Industry Reception on Monday night, the DIS conference dinner on Tuesday night, and a post-conference closing drinks party on Wednesday night.

The theme of DIS 2017 is bridging and connecting – across disciplines, practices, places and understandings. The most interesting things happen at edges and boundaries, and so the aim of the 2017 conference is to examine different approaches to framing knowledge about the design of interactive systems. As advancements in interactive technology continue to blur the demarcations between people and data, and between things and software, interaction designers and researchers are finding new ways to explore this evolving, interdisciplinary landscape. At DIS 2017 we shall consider the contrasts and commonalities that are central in shaping the landscape of emerging interaction paradigms.

I am very proud that we have been able to curate and assemble a stellar program, including two invited keynote presentations by Salvatore Iaconesi (ISIA Design Florence) and Di Mainstone (QMU), I am sure they and the program will encourage much thought, discussion and future endeavours.

DIS'17 is very much a team effort. I would like to thank all my colleagues on the organising committee, on the various program sub-committees, the student volunteers, our workshop and DC host, Edinburgh Napier University, our ACM sponsor, SIGCHI, and our generous corporate supporters.

I very much hope you enjoy DIS'17!

Oli Mival
DIS'17 General Chair
Centre for Interaction Design,
Edinburgh Napier University, UK

DIS 2017 Technical Program Chairs' Welcome

DIS 2017 centres on designerly approaches to creating, deploying and critically reflecting on interactive systems. It is an interdisciplinary conference that encompasses how such systems are built, introduced and employed in a wide variety of socio-cultural contexts. We welcome a broad engagement with the field by inviting submissions that consider the following, from a diverse range of researchers and practitioners within the field of interactive systems design:

- **Design Methods and Processes:** Methods, tools, and techniques for engaging people; researching, designing, and co-designing interactive systems; participatory design, design artefacts, research through design; documenting and reflecting on design processes.
- **Experience:** Places, temporality, people, communities, events, phenomena, aesthetics, user experience, usability, engagement, empowerment, wellbeing, designing things that matter, diversity, participation, materiality, making, etc.
- **Application Domains:** Health, ICT4D, children-computer interaction, sustainability, games/entertainment computing, digital arts, etc.
- **Technological Innovation:** Sensors and actuators, mobile devices, multi touch and touchless interaction, social media, personal, community, and public displays

The conference committees reviewed and accepted the following:

Venue	*Reviewed*	*Accepted*	%
Papers and Notes	487	107	22%
Provocations & Works-in-Progress	115	53	46%
Pictorials	59	13	22%
Demonstrations	20	14	70%
Workshops	25	12	48%
Doctoral Consortium	19	12	63%

This wide ranging and exciting program would not been possible had it not been for the work of the many contributing authors, the generous work of the reviewers, the organizational efforts of the Pictorals Chairs, Lone Koefoed Hansen and Andreas Unteidig, the Workshops Chairs, Augusto Esteves and Brian O'Keefe, the Provocations and Works in Progress Chairs, Shaun Lawson and Preben Hansen, the Demos Chairs, Ian Lambert and Erik Grönvall, and the Doctoral Consortium Chairs, David Benyon and Paul Dourish.

We thank everyone involved for all of their effort to make an amazing DIS 2017 program, and we are very much looking forward to this year's conference and engaging with the tremendous DIS community.

Michael Smyth
DIS'17 Program Chair
Edinburgh Napier University, UK

Peter Dalsgaard
DIS'17 Program Chair
Aarhus University, Denmark

Table of Contents

Session 4: Design Case Studies & Methods 2 (Technology)

Session 5: Spaces & Surfaces

Session 6: Pictorials 1

Session 7: Design Tools

Session 8: Health Studies

Session 9: Wearables & Materials

Session 10: Games

Session 11: Affect & Emotion

Session 12: IoT

Session 13: Futures

Session 14: Communication

Session 15: Quantified Self

Session 16: Children

Session 17: Robots

Session 18: Visualisation

Session 19: Creativity

Session 20: Pictorials 2

Session 21: Essays

Session 22: Human Relationships 1 (Design)

Session 23: Craft & Making 1 (Studies)

Session 24: Gesture Interactions

Session 25: Human Relationships 2 (Tech)

Session 26: Craft & Making 2 (Outputs)

Session 27: VR

Session 28: Prototyping

DIS 2017 Conference Organization

General Chair: Oli Mival *(Edinburgh Napier University, UK)*

Technical Program Chairs: Michael Smyth *(Edinburgh Napier University, UK)*
Peter Dalsgaard *(Aarhus University, Denmark)*

Pictorials Chairs: Lone Koefeld Hansen *(Aarhus University, Denmark)*
Andreas Unteidig *(Berlin University of the Arts, Germany)*

Demo Chairs: Ian Lambert *(Edinburgh Napier University, UK)*
Erik Grönvall *(IT University of Copenhagen, USA)*

Works in Progress Chairs: Shaun Lawson *(Northumbria University, UK)*
Preben Hansen *(Stockholm University, Sweden)*

Workshop Chairs: Augusto Esteves *(Edinburgh Napier University, UK)*
Brian O'Keefe *(Farmingdale State College, USA)*

Doctoral Consortium Chairs: David Benyon *(Edinburgh Napier University, UK)*
Paul Dourish *(University of California, Irvine, USA)*

Student Volunteer Chairs: Emilia Sobolewska *(Edinburgh Napier University, UK)*
Augoustinos Tsiros *(Edinburgh Napier University, UK)*

Publicity & Social Chair: Ingi Helgason *(Edinburgh Napier University, UK)*

Industry Engagement Chair: Dave Ward *(Create Future Ltd, UK)*

Treasurer & Registration Chair: Ollie Brook *(Conference Partners Ltd, UK)*

Steering Committee Chair: Steve Harrison *(Virginia Tech, USA)*

Steering Committee: John M. Carroll *(Penn State University, USA)*
Marcus Foth *(Queensland University of Technology, Australia)*
Kim Halskov *(Aarhus University, Denmark)*
Wendy Ju *(Stanford University, USA)*
Peter Wright *(Newcastle University, UK)*
Ron Wakkary *(Simon Fraser University, Canada)*

Sub-Committee Program Chairs:

Mark Blythe *(Northumbria University, UK)*
Licia Calvi *(NHTV, Holland)*
Steve Harrison *(Virginia Tech, USA)*
Sarah Kettley *(Nottingham Trent, UK)*
Wendy Moncur *(University of Dundee, UK)*
Floyd Muller *(RMIT University, Australia)*
Nuno Nunes *(University of Madeira, Portugal)*
Ron Wakkary *(Simon Fraser University, Canada)*

Associate Chairs:

José Abdelnour Nocera
Karthikeya Acharya
Ebtisam AlAbdulqader
Florian Alt
Kristina Andersen
Kristina Andersen
Rohit Ashok Khot
Madeline Balaam
Laurens Boer
Katharina Bredies
Margot Brereton
Jo Briggs
Daniel Buzzo
Rich Byrne
Jack Caroll
Diego Casado-Mansilla
Alan Chamberlain
Kenny Chow
Adrian Clear
Ashley Colley
Rob Comber
Paul Coulton
Leon Cruickshank
Sergiu Dascalus
Audrey Desjardins
Laura Devendorf
Tawanna Dillahunt
Graham Dove
Chris Elsden
Lars Erik Holmquist
Eva Erikson
Geremy Farr-Wharton
Melanie Feinberg
Tom Feltwell
Jonas Fritsch
Verena Fuchsberger
Marianne Graves-Petersen
Colin Gray
Dave Green Corina Sas
Erik Grönvall
Shad Gross
Jonna Hakkila
Kim Halskov
Chris Harrison
Ingi Helgason
Kieran Hicks
Christian Holz
Eva Hornecker
Steven Houben
Giulio Jacucci
Tom Jenkins
Ahmed Kharrufa
Reuben Kirkham
Ben Kirman
Boriana Koleva
Ilpo Koskinen
Nantia Koulidou
Jarmo Laaksolahti
Eulani Labay
Edward Lank
Shaun Lawson
Youn-Kyung Lim
Joseph Lindley
Steven Lindsay
Conor Linehan
Markus Löchtefeld
Kiel Long
Pedro Lopes

Associate Chairs (continued):

Andrés Lucero
Xiaojuan Ma
Lindsay MacDonald
Haley MacLeod
Jamie Mahoney
Scott McCrickard
Donald McMillan
Tim Merritt
Jussi Mikkonen
Ali Momeni
Hideyuki Nakanishi
Tek-Jin Nam
Valentina Nisi
Ian Oakley
Will Odom
Martin Porcheron
Janet Read
Jennifer Rode
Michael Rohs
Chiara Rossitto
Marco Rozendaal
Antti Salovaara
Thecla Schiphorst
Kakee Scott
Chaklam Silpasuwanchai
Gavin Sim
Chris Speed
Gunnar Stevens
Alistair Sutcliffe
Anthony Tang
Deborah Tatar
Nick Taylor
Lisa Thomas
Oscar Tomico
Manfred Tscheligi
Arno Verhoeven
Arnold Vermeeren
Jo Vermeulen
John Vines
Simon Voelker
Chat Wacharamanotham
Monica Whitty
Julie Williamsson
Diane Willow
Joyce Yee
Salu Ylirisku
John Zimmerman

DIS 2017 Sponsor & Supporters

Sponsor:

acm Association for Computing Machinery

SIGCHI

Supporters:

facebook

The MIT Press

Edinburgh Napier UNIVERSITY

cpi CONFERENCE PARTNERS INTERNATIONAL

The Third Infoscape: Opportunities for Design

Salvatore Iaconesi
Human Ecosystems Relazioni
Rome, Italy
salvatore.iaconesi@he-r.it

ABSTRACT

The Third Infoscape is a concept which originates from Soja's Thirdspace, Clèment's Third Landscape and Casagrande's Third Generation City. The Third Infoscape deals with the ruins of digital communication just as the Third Generation City deals with the ruins of the industrial city, the Third Landscape deals with ruins of gardens and Thirdspace deals with ruins of regulation and governance. Human beings and the environment ruin the city, and ruins are the city's syncretic maps, describing (in negative) usage patterns and, thus, becoming a form of knowledge of the life of the city. In the data-city, ruins are an open-source global that is progressively becoming the only one that can welcome transgressive behaviors. These are needed for radical innovation, and to host diversity. Floating between small data and big data, amidst the smart dust which circulates in the city, and in the emotions, expressions, desires, relations, interactions and imaginations expressed by humans, digital smart agents and network connected objects and environments, the Third Infoscape is the ruin of digital communication and interaction in the Industrial City.

What role is there for transgression in the Smart City? What form of governance for the Third Infoscape?

Gilles Clément, talking about the Third Landscape, wonders "what form does a gardener of a garden without a form have?" The answer is that it is a gardener with different tools and methods: not rake and shovel, but wind and knowledge.
This scenario holds great opportunities for Design, but requires the cultivation of such tools and methods, since Design Education, and what Massimo Canevacci defines as Methodological Indiscipline, and Elizabeth Grosz calls Excess Space.

DIS 2017, June 10–14, 2017, Edinburgh, United Kingdom.
ACM ISBN 978-1-4503-4922-2/17/06.
http://dx.doi.org/10.1145/3064663.3084178

ACM Classification Keywords

J. Computer Applications; J.4 Social and Behavioral Sciences; K. Computing Milieux; K.4 Computers And Society; K.4.0 General

Author Keywords

Information Philosophy; Interface Biopolitics; Data Biopolitics; Transgression; Innovation; Open Data, Big Data

BIOGRAPHY

Salvatore is an interaction designer, robotics engineer, artist, hacker. TED Fellow 2012, Eisenhower Fellow since 2013 and Yale World Fellow 2014.

He teaches Near Future Design and Multi Platform Digital Design at ISIA Design Florence and, in the past, at "La Sapienza" University of Rome, at the Rome University of Fine Arts and at the IED Design institute.

Salvatore has founded AOS in 2004, is President at HER (previously HE), and co-founder at Nefula.

His focus is at the intersection of Arts, Design, Technologies, Sciences and Business. He creates projects that are at the same time artworks, scientific research and business models, addressing fundamental issues in culture, inclusion, human rights, economy and access to knowledge and education.

Control and Being Controlled: Exploring the use of Technology in an Immersive Theatre Performance

Sarah Wiseman
Goldsmiths, University of London
London, UK
s.wiseman@gold.ac.uk

Janet van der Linden
Open University
Milton Keynes, UK
janet.vanderlinden@open.ac.uk

Ad Spiers
Yale University
New Haven, US
adam.spiers@yale.edu

Maria Oshodi
Extant
London, UK
maria@extant.org.uk

ABSTRACT
Immersive theatre is a growing trend within theatre entertainment: audience members can now wander around performances and choose how the story unfolds in front of them. Technology can be used to create novel, multi-modal experiences for audiences in these performances; but when the rules of such an experience are ill-defined, how do users react to this technology? We present an evaluation of 25 performances of an immersive, in the dark performance. Issues of control can arise in situations where technology becomes an important part of such a performance. Participants take and relinquish control in three key areas: navigation, exploration and attention during the performance, and this affects their perception of both technology and the piece itself. We discuss how technology can play a positive role in immersive theatre and other cultural settings, yet its use must be carefully choreographed to ensure the audience experience matches the intended goal.

Author Keywords
Immersive Theatre; User Experience; Navigation; Haptic; Audio; Visual Impairment.

ACM Classification Keywords
H.5.m. Information interfaces and presentation (e.g., HCI): Miscellaneous;

INTRODUCTION
Museums, galleries, theatres and places of historical interest are striving to engage their visitors in varied ways. Interactive audio guides have become a common service in most museums, which also often include interactive objects for hands-on learning and exploring [4]. Technology is becoming more important in cultural settings. Over the years HCI has extended its reach into this area by creating a range of more complex cultural user experiences where digital media, props, and physical locations are integrated [3,5,9,16]. Such visitor experiences are no longer characterized by passive absorption of facts and information, but are about active involvement, immersion and about creating moments that are of personal interest to the visitor [28].

Immersive theatre installations are an example of this trend [25]. No longer is the audience required to sit in assigned seats, at a distance far from the action of the play. Instead, the audience moves around freely and becomes part of the play, sometimes taking on roles and altering the course that the performance takes. In such performances previous boundaries can be blurred: the audience can directly influence and interact with the performance. As noted by Papaioannou, immersive theatre performances can be described as having a "choose-your-own-adventure" narrative in that audiences can pick which aspects of the performance they watch, engage with, or alter [18]. This approach however, can lead to unclear rules of engagement, with the audience unsure about what is "allowed" in the space and to what extent they are expected to push the apparent boundaries they are given [2].

In this paper we present an evaluation of the use of interactive haptic technology in an immersive theatre setting. The performance was set in complete darkness and centered around a play, based on the 1884 novella Flatland, about an imaginary world where hearing and feeling are the dominant senses. Alongside other interactive technologies, a hand-held shape-changing device was developed to be part of this performance, in order to guide the audience through the dark performance space, allowing them to find various places and objects of interest. The only human actors in the play were involved at the start and finish of the performance; for the majority of the time the audience were able to move around the open, dark space and find different "scenes" comprised of scenery and props which they could feel and listen to.

In this paper we explore the range of different user experiences that were had through an in-depth qualitative study of 25 performances. We explicitly aim to understand the breadth of user response compared with creative intention using a bottom-up evaluation approach based upon post-performance user discussion. We particularly explore how issues of control arose when asking audience

DIS 2017, June 10 - 14, 2017, Edinburgh, United Kingdom

ACM 978-1-4503-4922-2/17/06…$15.00
DOI: http://dx.doi.org/10.1145/3064663.3064694

members to interact with novel pieces of technology, and how this was affected by the overall sense of the unknown when experiencing an immersive theatrical performance.

RELATED WORK

Ubiquitous computing offers new opportunities to engage audiences in novel, engaging cultural experiences. Collaborations between artists, designers and engineers have created immersive theatre experiences where audience members take part in the performance by becoming an actual character in the play, or in the role of passers-by and witnesses to events. Well known examples of this approach are the performances by theatre group Punchdrunk, or the mixed reality games by Blast Theory. Benford at al. analysed the development of such user experiences, describing them as carefully orchestrated trajectories – where experiences unfold over space and time [6]. At appropriate moments the audience may be handed a variety of technologies to interact with – mobile phones to send SMS messages to characters in the play, swipe cards to open doors, or wearable sensors to capture the audience's emotional response to the performance – all carefully designed to provide complex user experiences, in which the digital and the physical are traversed in innovative ways. Benford et al.'s trajectories framework [6] aims to provide a lens to reflect on critical points in the development of such user experiences, particularly highlighting moments where transitions take place. Transitions could be moments at the beginning or end of the play, or issues to do with the sharing out of a limited set of physical resources. Managing such trajectories involves resolving the tension between participant trajectories and authors' intended canonical trajectories.

Discussions around how to resolve such tensions are not dissimilar to work by HCI researchers who have studied mental models, i.e. the user's understanding of the interaction and the way the designer had intended it, and how to minimize the distance between these two understandings [17]. Sengers [23] argues that while there may be disagreement on whose interpretation (e.g., the users' or the designers') should be privileged, there is general agreement that there should be a single, correct way to interpret an interactive product (e.g. how it works or the emotion it should exhibit or engender), and that the goal of the designer should be to convey that interpretation accurately to its users. Getting a certain interpretation across to users is often appropriate and useful. However, as argued by Sengers, we should also recognize, design for, and evaluate with a more nuanced view of interpretation, in which multiple, even opposing, views of interpretation co-exist. With this approach evaluation shifts from determining whether an authoritative interpretation was successfully communicated to identifying, stimulating, and analysing processes of interpretation in practice.

Guidance and control

The technology device used in the Flatland performance presented here was designed to support people navigating in a dark space. The issue of guidance versus instruction is central in the context of using navigation systems, as is the question about who is in control: the user or the technology?

Robinson et al [21] argue that for certain settings a person may not wish to receive precise instructions, as their main aim could be to wander and enjoy the journey itself, for example as a tourist visiting a foreign city. They developed a system where a user could request a reminder of whether they were still 'roughly' heading in the right direction (through a subtle squeeze on their phone), but otherwise move along on their accord. This method resulted in the user group taking a variety of paths between the same two points. This suggests that giving navigational control to the user, rather than the technology, can result in more "creativity" in path finding. However, this approach did result in users finding dead-ends during their navigation which can be highly frustrating, and is avoided by moving the locus of control back to the technology.

These issues demonstrate the large variety of demands on a navigation system: the need to get somewhere, the need for information and the need to enjoy the journey – all of which must be balanced. In an immersive performance there are also the demands coming from the narrative, where the creative team plan and anticipate a complex user experience to unfold in a particular way, including the places that are visited by the user. What level of control is most appropriate and "successful" in this situation?

Immersive Theatre

Immersive theatre allows audience members to have a more embodied experience of the performance they witness in comparison to the more traditional arrangement involving rows of chairs facing a stage. In immersive theatre, audience members are invited to view the performance whilst moving around the scenery and occasionally going beyond merely "observing" by interacting directly with actors. This level of interaction with a performance leads Reeves [20] to introduce the distinction between being an audience member and an active *participant* in such immersive pieces. Whereas an audience member spectates, watching the scene occur in front of them, the participant takes part in some way and has some control over the performance. This need not mean they control the narrative, or the actions of the actors, but means they can change what they see and how they respond to it.

A key aspect of such performances is that they often use "spatial" narratives rather than linear [15]. The audience are able to control the way that they engage with the narrative, choosing what order to encounter various elements of the performance. Such variations allows the audience members to choose whether they want to become "speca(c)tors" or remain "distanced theatre-goers" [18]. Papaionannou refers to a particular piece of immersive theatre as "a huge 'living' installation, or … an assemblage of tiny ones" [18] again highlighting the variable nature of the form.

Immersive theatre also offers an opportunity for a heightened sensory experience. Alston notes that although sitting in a theatre is a multisensory experience in itself, immersive theatre may purposefully create touch-, audio- and smell-based interactions [2].

Alston also highlights one of the aspects of immersive theatre that is most appealing for audience members: becoming an audience member in such a performance can feel "risky" but allows audience members to experience otherwise negative emotions such as fear or guilt in a positive or stimulating way [2].

Technology in Performance

Technology has been successfully used previously in immersive games [5,6]. In these instances, existing technology is utilized to create exciting mixed reality worlds, where players are able to interact in the city around them in a parallel game world. The ability of technology to heighten previously ordinary experiences to thrilling gaming arenas again highlights a trend in immersive performance. Often this technology is screen based or visual, for example asking participants to interact with characters using SMS messages [7].

Initial uses of technology in theatre allowed actors to augment their performance by interacting with visual displays on stage [22]. Modern uses of technology can allow drama groups to play with presence and multiple stages [26]. Technology can also be used to play with our senses in performances. In 2011, the immersive theatre performance 'The Question' used navigational technology to guide participants around a completely dark space with no visual input [14]. The research showed how technology had the ability to create a similar, yet not 'same' embodied experience for sighted and visually impaired users. The research highlighted how uncomfortable sighted users can feel in immersive experiences when they cannot rely on their sight, even if they have technology to support them.

In this paper we set out to evaluate the technology that was designed for an interactive, in-the-dark performance. We wanted to go beyond issues of usability and efficiency to understand how participants – many of whom had visual impairments – interpreted the technology as part of the performance. What did they feel were the capabilities and purpose of the device? How did that affect their confidence and enjoyment of the piece? How did the technology fit within the complex journey through Flatland?

THE RESEARCH APPROACH

The research approach involved the development of an immersive theatre performance in collaboration with a drama group and technologist. The drama group, a company of visually impaired people, have a particular interest in creating accessible performances. The show was therefore conceived to run in complete darkness, with participants hearing and feeling the various scenes in the performance. Throughout the piece, participants would be given instructions on where to move via a handheld device, and once at their target destination would find "scenes" to explore. These scenes comprised of audio narratives and haptic interactive technology.

A range of different data collection techniques were used throughout this project, generating both quantitative and qualitative data. Throughout the performances, the participants' locations were recorded and mapped, showing their paths through the space. This data showed both the moments when the participants were being given instructions by navigation technology on where to move, and when they were allowed to freely explore at each of the scenes without instruction. Notes taken by the technical team during performances also aided in understanding when the technology may have behaved erratically, thus altering that particular user's experience. For example, in a small minority of performances, some individual users lost audio information to their headphones, or their navigation devices became disconnected from the network.

Evaluations were run immediately following each performance to gather participants' reactions and responses to the piece. These were conducted in the form of a group discussion, led by a facilitator who aimed to follow a set of high-level questions relating to use of technology within the performance and reaction to the piece as a whole. These sessions lasted for approximately one hour. They were filmed and recorded.

By combining the multiple data sources, we were able to paint a rich picture of the user experiences throughout the piece. Our aim was to base our evaluation not just on the creative intent, but on the reported experience of all users. We highlight overall performance metrics, alongside more in depth response and expectations from the participants and discuss the themes that emerged from the data.

THE PERFORMANCE

The performance was based upon the book: *Flatland*, a novella by E. A. Abbott [1]. In the book, the inhabitants of the Flatland world exist in 2-dimensions, meaning every citizen is a flat shape. As the world is 2-dimensional, using vision to identify other people is not beneficial, as everyone appears as a line; for this reason, characters in the story use 'the Art of Hearing' and the 'Art of Feeling' to communicate with each other. These elements of the book map directly on to the immersive theatre performance that was produced: participants would move around in the dark, and would be asked to rely upon their sense of touch and hearing to understand the world around them. The storyline of the performance involved participants optimistically entering Flatland in order to witness the peaceful society but slowly discovering a world full of social oppression, fear and euthanasia.

The performance took place in a former church that had since been converted to a venue for cultural events. Four participants at a time were invited to attend the performance. After a brief, daylight training with the Animotus (the hand-held navigation device) the participants moved towards four individual corridors that led into Flatland and eventually, complete darkness. At this point, each participant was guided by the Animotus, to one of four scenes in the performance to be experienced individually, without the other participants. After arriving in a scene, the participant would put down their device (in their pocket) and explore the space around them. After they had interacted with the scene they would be asked to retrieve the Animotus and navigate to the next location (as determined by the Animotus). It was important to the artistic team that the participants feel like they were "exploring" and therefore the scenes were placed in various locations around the performance area and not in a linear fashion which could be easily navigable without the aid of the Animotus.

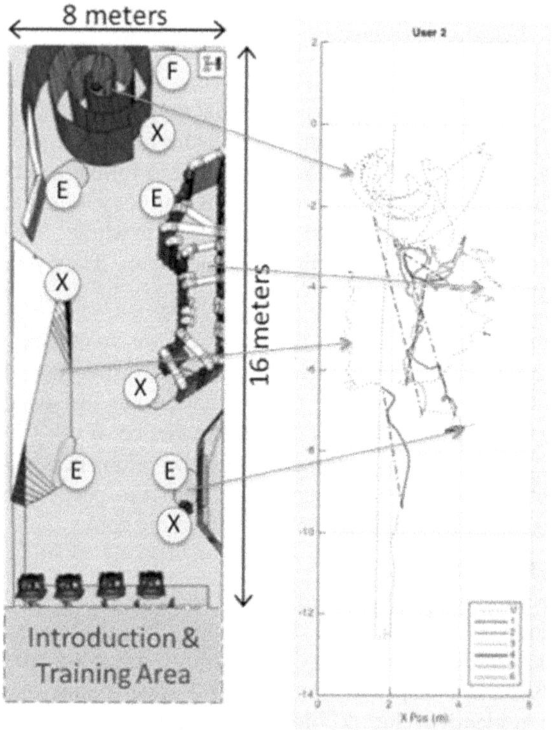

Figure 1. The left hand figure shows an over-head view of the performance space, with the four different scenes. The entrance to each scene is marked with E and the exit with X. On the right-hand side you can see the path a participant took through the space. Coloured lines show times that the participant was following guidance from the Animotus

The scene areas can be seen in Figure 1, which shows a view of the hall from above. The scenes were loosely based on an interpretation of the book, including zones such as (i) the 'university', where controversial lectures could be heard and people could physically move through a triangular pathway created using elasticated ropes (to the left of the figure); (ii) the church, a large velvet spiral construction playing an unnerving-sounding sermon (at the top of the figure); (iii) the hospital, a place of much cruelty in Flatland where a construction of pipes gave participants the impression they were overhearing conversations between doctors discussing the future of a child with uneven sides (a severe disadvantage in the Flatland society) (at the right of the figure); and finally, (iv) the domestic quarters, consisting of a brick wall and a soft "window" (fabric stretched across a frame) for the participants to feel. During this interaction, it was possible to hear the sounds of the women of Flatland (an oppressed people) crying out and moaning in abstract ways (lower, right of the left hand figure).

Each scene had an associated audio track which could be heard via headphones. Each participant heard a different track depending on which scene they were currently experiencing. Some audio provided a narrative, detailing the unrest within Flatland, whereas at other audio tracks provided a soundscape. Once several minutes had passed in each scene, an instruction was given to the participants via headphones to take their Animotus from their pocket and begin following it to leave and explore another scene.

THE TECHNOLOGY

Technology was required for three distinct roles within this piece: to guide the participants around the space performance, to provide audio narrative and ambient sounds, and to provide interactive haptic feedback when the participants began to explore the area around them.

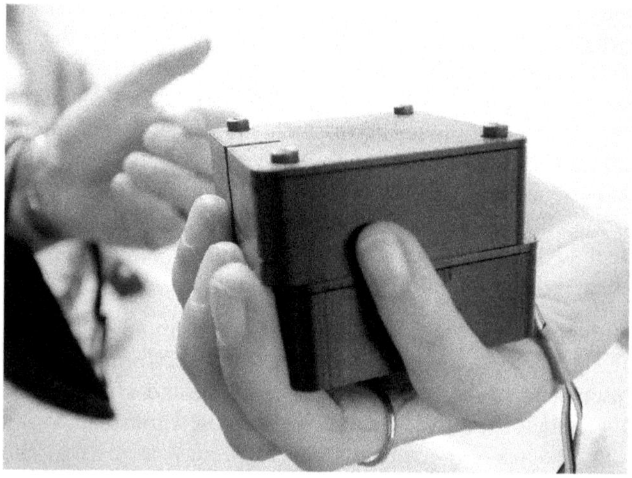

Figure 2. The hand-held "Animotus" navigation device. The top half of the cube extends slightly, an instruction for the user to move forward.

Navigation technology

During the performance, participants walked between locations in pitch black. This difficult task would be aided by a small piece of hand-held technology designed specifically for the performance. The "Animotus" device, a cube with dimensions 60x60x40mm, used novel shape-changing technology to guide its user on where to move (see Figure 2). The top half of the device could protrude (indicating the user should move forward) or rotate (indicating a move to the left or right was required). Combined with positioning technology, which used small radio tags to determine the user's location in the space, the Animotus was able to guide users to particular locations simply by changing shape. This location was determined by a technician controlling the destinations for all four participants during the performances. Further technical details can be found in [24].

The Animotus was the result of multiple iterations of testing, beginning with an array of alternative devices. While several designs were considered, some of which turned out to be too dangerous as they might hurt participants, or too complicated to use, two designs emerged as contenders for the immersive performance: one (device A) directed users to a specific location using left/right/forward commands and the other (device B) provided information about proximity alone, alerting the user as they got closer to their target. Device A therefore took control from the user whereas device B allowed the user remain in charge of their navigation by simply suggesting movement around the space. The designs were tested both in lab-settings and in the performance space itself. These tests firstly ensured that participants could use the device to successfully navigate between two locations without the aid of sight but secondly they allowed us to begin initial inquiries into how participants perceived the varying levels of control from both devices. When discussing the two devices with a pilot user with visual impairments, device A was likened to walking with a guide dog – the device "pulled" the user in various, specific directions. Device B on the other hand was likened to a cane – it was a tool that the user could use to explore the environment around them. After multiple rounds of testing, device A was chosen as the final Animotus design as it was most successful in terms of getting users to a specific point. It was clear though from this initial testing that this device would be perceived as more demanding by participants.

Audio Technology

During the performance, participants would be able to hear the narration of the play through bone-conducting headphones. These headphones sit just in front of the ear and allow the user to hear audio via facial bone vibration. In using this technology, the participants would be able to hear audio intended solely for them (through bone conduction) whilst keeping the ears free to listen to the ambient sounds in the performance space.

Interactive Technology

At various points of the performance the participants would be asked to explore the area around them. To make this experience richer, several haptic and audio technologies were introduced into the piece. In one instance, a stretchy piece of fabric with small, capacitive embroidered dots on it responded to touch by gently buzzing. This represented the women of Flatland moving to make themselves seen. In the University scene, elastic ropes stretched from ceiling to floor would cause small snippets of subversive conversation to play when touched and pulled (see Figure 3). Finally, in the church scene, a piece of velvet curtain would, when stroked, cause the sound of sharpening metal to play. The dissonance between the soft touch of velvet and grating noise of sharpening metal was intended to create an uneasy feeling for the participants. Each of these elements used technology to reward exploration – making elements of the performance world react to the participants' touch.

EVALUATION

By their nature, immersive theatre pieces are often non-linear, and as such the experience that each participant has differs. However, despite this variation between participants' journeys, the performance itself is carefully choreographed to create singular experience. For instance, in this piece the creative team hoped that the participants would move throughout the space with the aid of the Animotus, which would take them to the four individual scenes in different orders. At each of these locations, the participants would have a chance to hear the narrative, feel the world around them, and gain an understanding of the disconcerting situation in Flatland. One aim of the creative team was that participants should feel immersed in the experience – our definition of "immersion" here is not a formal measurement (as per [13] for example) but is instead self-reported by the participants themselves.

Figure 3. A participant touches the elastic ropes in the piece, causing sounds to play. (Taken with Infrared camera)

It is with this creative aim in mind that we evaluated how participants responded to technology in this immersive theatre production. Did their experiences match the intended outcomes? What successfully contributed to creative vision, and what hindered it? To answer these questions group discussions were held after each performance with the participants. Group discussions were chosen as they encourage deeper reflection and feedback on cultural stimuli [11]. A device was used to ensure that each member of the group was able to note their response to each question before beginning the discussion; this allowed the facilitator to ensure any varied opinions were brought up and were not lost in discussion.

The initial questions used to provoke discussion during the group sessions immediately after the performances covered a variety of topics, including control, immersion, emotional response to the Animotus to name a few. When analysing the data, a grounded theory approach was taken: each group discussion was transcribed and individual sentences coded. After the initial coding had been completed, the codes were grouped into themes. From these themes, it was clear that control was a key issue that audience members felt they wanted to express and had intriguingly differing opinions on. Lines of questioning which did not produce rich data were not reported.

Based upon observations, data from participant movements and this coded interview data, we focussed on the area of *control*. Control moved between participants and the technology around them at a number of points throughout the piece – for some these moments helped immersion in the performance, yet for others it felt constricting. Others made subconscious control decisions without being aware of them. In this section, we present an evaluation of three aspects of control that arose during the performance:

- Control in Navigation
- Control in Exploration
- Control in Attention

Control in Navigation

Within immersive theatre, participants and audiences are often required to move around a space between locations. This was the case in Flatland as participants moved between the interactive scenes. Rather than happening upon the scenes themselves, which may have resulted in overlap between participants, they were guided by handheld technology. The handheld technology required cooperation from its user, in the sense that the user had to follow its instructions in order to successfully guide them. Here we briefly discuss the ease of use of the Animotus before exploring participant reaction to the cooperative nature of using the device to explore the space.

Ninety-four participants took part in the experience as some performances ran with only three participants. Analysis of data after these performances do not suggest that this had an affect upon participants' experience. Navigational data was collected for all participants as they moved through the Flatland space. Each participant travelled several paths (usually five, one between each zone and a final path to the exit). The majority of participants were able to follow the guidance of the Animotus to some extent, and successfully found the scenes within Flatland.

The Flatland path data shows for each participant (i) the optimal paths and (ii) the travelled paths as guided by the device and (iii) the paths travelled without device. Figure 1 shows a participant who is well able to navigate their way to the various zones accurately, not straying far from the optimal path.

The majority of participants were able to navigate in the space with a middle to high degree of accuracy. Those who navigated accurately found the device easy to use *"I thought it was just so delightfully simple that I didn't have to worry about the device, and I could concentrate on thinking about my environment" (Performance2User4)*. Others mentioned the intuitiveness of the device, P10U4 (a visually impaired participant) explained that he didn't need to consciously think about his movements when following the device *"When it was actually starting to twist and things, I wasn't consciously thinking,* "I turn right or turn left"*. I just thought,* "Go with the flow"*".* P4U2 went further to say *"It sort of became really part of me"*. These experiences suggest that not only was it possible for the device to accurately guide its user, but the user could follow its commands without thinking, allowing them to focus on the experience as a whole.

The success of navigating with the Animotus meant that some participants were entirely happy to let go, and hand over all navigational control to the device *"I was just like,* "Fine, obviously it knows where it's going"*, and just walked straight wherever under the assumption that I wasn't going to fall down a hole or something" (P15U1)* others even found the hand-over of control to be exhilarating *"trusting the [Animotus] is the most dangerous thing there rather than trusting yourself. So that makes it more exciting" (P15U3)*. However, handing over control like this also came with an expectation that the device would look after the user; this caused tension when the user failed to understand what the Animotus was trying to convey *"I did very much kind of imbue it with a lot of responsibility to look after me and I was sort of cross with it when it felt like it was ... being tricksy or when it was wrong" (P14U4)*.

Interacting with the Animotus required the user to obey to the device, and willingly follow its guidance. For some this was counter to their expectations of an immersive theatre experience: *"A lot of the time, there was a temptation just to really put [the Animotus] away and just explore it that way.(P16U3)"* Another participant (P25U1) felt she was having to fight the urge to explore: *"I knew I really wanted to run around in the dark, but I couldn't"*. One participant even described herself as a puppet, being controlled from afar *"It sort of made me into a - it was like a sort of - it had a puppeteering quality to me" (P12U2)*.

Of those who expressed a dislike of how controlling the device was, the majority had identified as having visual impairments. One participant expressed that there were so many attention seeking things in her life that that she didn't appreciate having another piece of technology telling her what to do *"Being blind, I have so much technology. I have a talking GPS, you know, there's always vibrating canes or ... sunglasses that are giving you beeps in the world and it's just like, yet another tool to navigate and say, yes, I was just looking at it as yet another piece of technology" (P20U4)*. Another participant with visual impairments decided that the lack of control was too much for him. P12U4 began navigating in a highly accurate manner, but half way through the performance began to ignore the navigation device and started to explore on his own. This was a conscious decision on his part, he felt this performance was a chance to get away from the everyday experiences of lack of control: *"And actually in a place like that, as a blind person, you should be very free and incognito... unrecognised, because most of the time we're kind of shepherded from one place to another or you're taken to one place and then taken up to another place."* This reaction led to him trying to push the boundaries and take back control: *"And I spent the whole time very conscious that I was being watched and working out ways in which I could evade being watched. So I was always looking to go crossways"*. This sentiment is clear to see from the path he took, initially obeying the device and finally ignoring it in order to have his own experience.

Control in Exploration

Transitions during immersive theatre are an opportunity for the participants to experience a change in narrative, change roles or be exposed to new technology [6]. These moments are key, and require careful choreography to ensure that the participants do not become lost or confused, it is at these transition moments where engagement and immersion must be maintained.

During the Flatland piece, the Animotus technology was at the forefront of important transitions for the participants. These occurred when the participant had successfully navigated to their designated scene location, and were therefore asked through audio command in the headphones to put away their Animotus and explore the area until they were instructed to move on, at which point they would be asked to retrieve their Animotus from their pocket. On a physical level, this transition simply involved the participant changing from interacting with a piece of handheld technology (the Animotus) to interacting with the haptic and audio technology in the scene around them. However, from examination of the transcripts we see that a higher-level *cognitive* transition is also occurring at this point: the transition of being controlled, to being given freedom to explore.

When designing the experience, the artistic team had a clear vision of an "expected" experience. That is, an ideal trajectory through the space that a participant could take; the participant would navigate to and explore each of the four scenes. This is not to say that the participant was required to navigate the performance as though on a conveyer belt, the route they took to the scene could change as they desired, and if they wished they could have explored far beyond the scene they had navigated to, however ideally they would at least experience the elements that the director envisaged. This is similar to other theatrical performances as the creative team had a narrative they wished to convey to the participants as they moved round the experience with a beginning, middle and ending which all follow the journey of a key protagonist. From a technical perspective this journey, if taken as intended by the artistic team, would involve the participant interacting with the Animotus and the scenery interchangeably, requiring many elements of transition between control and free exploration. It is with this "minimal expected trajectory" in mind that we explore the various participant reactions to this control transition boundary.

For the bolder participants, the transition from following the Animotus to exploration was a welcome one: it represented a chance to explore freely, without having to obey the technology in their hand. When the Animotus was put away in their pocket, they felt they were able to immerse themselves fully, for example *"I quite liked putting it in my pocket and just going free-fall, not knowing what's going to be in front of me next. I quite liked that" [P22U2]*. Or P4U3 *"But I was always very glad to get rid of it."* These participants did not find the Animotus technology challenging, but its role in their experience of the performance was inhibitive. For them, this control transition boundary was a welcome one, allowing them to move from the strict guidance of the Animotus to a freer, exploratory experience with the performance.

For other participants however, this transition of control did not fully take place. After using the Animotus and obeying its instructions, at the point at which they were given the freedom to explore, they felt they were unable to be adventurous in their explorations: *"I didn't know what the boundaries of what I could explore were" (P15U1)*. This difference in exploration can be seen between two other participants, P20U1 and P20U2. Figure 4 shows their trajectories around the performance space. Both are able to navigate fairly accurately between the scenes (the coloured lines) whereas their exploration paths (the dotted lines) are very different. U1 wanders in many directions, looping around the space, whereas U2 seems static, unsure of where she is allowed to move. This sense is embodied particularly well in the interaction between two other participants discussing the experience after the performance. P14U4 spoke of kneeling down to feel the ground around her. When the other participant (P14U3) was asked to discuss whether she found the Animotus a useful guide, decided that it had restricted her too much, stating *"I think I'm divided by that question, because I think when [P14U4] was saying, whenever I knelt down, I [P14U3] was like,* "You were kneeling? You were like feeling around on the floor?" *And I think I was really unadventurous."* It appears the control transition was in some way stunted: the participant felt as though their experience obeying the device had hindered their ability to freely explore.

The control transition in the reverse direction was also occasionally problematic for the participants. The nature of the sound and Animotus control meant that at times the audio cue told the users to retrieve the Animotus from their pocket, with a lag of 5-10 seconds before the Animotus began moving again, ready to guide them to their next destination. As with all technology that does not respond within the time frame we expect, for some this transition was simply annoying, P5U1 explained that she *"definitely got frustrated with waiting sometimes"*. For this participant, the Animotus was similar to any "buggy" piece of technology she might encounter in her everyday life. However, for others, the fact that this problematic transition occurred during an immersive theatre piece caused concern regarding control. For sighted users who were unused to navigating without the aid of vision, this meant that the Animotus represented their best chance of moving around the space. Some sighted participants therefore found the lull before the Animotus began moving very unnerving, *"The times that I was most concerned when using it was after I was told to hold it again, it didn't move. He had stopped speaking to me and the cube wasn't moving, and I just felt very lost and like no one was looking after me" (P1U2).* This participant was particularly welcoming of the transition away from free exploration and specifically sought guidance from the Animotus. When that guidance and control was not forthcoming, she began to feel concerned and vulnerable.

Control in Attention

The multi-modal nature of the performance ensured that there were a wide range of stimuli for the participants to interact with throughout the piece: from ambient sounds, to audio narration, to tactile and responsive surfaces and even smell in some locations. This is highly unlike a traditional theatre experience, which presents a single, visual and audio experience which is intended to be consumed by the audience in a linear fashion. In Flatland, the audience were participants and therefore able to pick and choose the aspects of the performance that they wanted to engage with. This experience is perhaps more similar to browsing an art gallery: despite the immense array of art on offer, a visitor might choose their own path through the gallery, stopping to view only the pieces they want to.

Here arises another issue of control in immersive theatre productions – *control in attention.* With so many aspects of the performance demanding attention, how did the participants choose what to engage with? And to what extent was that choice a conscious one?

We sought to explore how aware the participants were of the narrative being presented to them and how that related to the touchable world around them. For some, the audio and haptic feedback balanced well, *"I felt like I was very aware, and directly making links between what I was hearing and what I was feeling" (P3U1)* and for others the sensory experience as a whole was very rewarding *"I stood at the centre and heard all that was happening. That was the deepest experience I had, when I was right at the centre, cuddled into this room" (P1U1).*

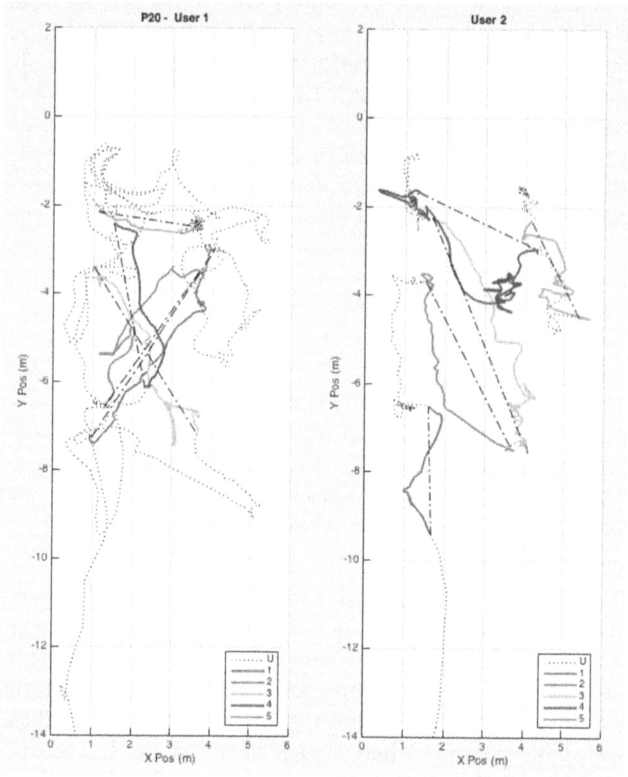

Figure 4. Paths for P20U1 and P20U2 in the performance. Both are able to navigate successfully between the scenes (coloured lines) but they explore in different ways. U1 moves freely (dotted line) whereas U2 barely moves when reaching a scene.

For some participants however, the audio and haptic stimuli were not working in harmony – some participants seemed to be experiencing them in isolation. We noted that some participants were more aware of the audio narration, whereas others were more focused on the tactile sensations. There was also a division between those who had *consciously* decided to focus on one sensory experience and those who had *subconsciously* made that choice.

Despite the constant narrative arc being played to participants through their headphones, for some people the narration passed them by due to either the experience as a whole (*"something more sort of primal takes over than paying attention to the narrative" (P6U3)*) or because they were more focused on what they were touching (*"I was having tactile overload and I realised I hadn't listened to anything" (P8U3)*). Yet this was not necessarily a negative experience for them *"I think it was so interesting to do that that I think maybe I didn't attach myself to the story as much as I should've done" (P18U2)*. This was a sentiment expressed by several participants – that in focusing on exploration with their hands, the narration through their headphones had become just sounds in the background.

In those instances, the participants were not making *conscious* decisions to shift their attention from the audio to the tactile experience, that act appeared more *subconscious*. However, for some participants, a more conscious decision was made *"I feel like I understand what the audio is telling me now so I'm just going to park that for a second and pay attention to something else" (P6U3).* Here the participant made an active decision to stop paying attention to the audio they were hearing, rather than accidentally letting it fade to the background as others had. Conversely, some gave the audio experience more of their attention whether they were aware of it (*"I just went back and just stood there for quite a while, just waiting until the story finishes, just not to miss something" (P8U1)*) or not (*"I think I retreated in just listening to an interesting story" (P14U3)*).

When reflecting on this apparent inability to focus on two different streams of sensory information, some participants felt they had learned an important lesson about their own lives. After the recorded interview, two museum employees expressed shock at how difficult it was to listen whilst touching and feeling objects. They realised that when explaining touchable objects to visitors with visual impairments that they may need to stay quiet at times so that the person exploring the object could have a chance to touch and listen separately.

DISCUSSION

Our findings have shown how technology can have a role in mediating the taking and giving of control in immersive theatre productions. We particularly discussed control in three distinct aspects of such a production – during moving around or navigation, while exploring and in dividing the attention between the senses.

As discussed in [2], the experience left the audience with mixed reactions: some were able to take the potentially negative sensations and turn them into positive, novel experiences whereas for others they remained less enjoyable. Further, these emotions were elicited both when the user and the technology had control. Figure 5 explores these spectrums and presents examples of each scenario.

In terms of control in navigation it appears that for many of the sighted participants who felt uncomfortable in the space because they had lost a sense that they were used to relying upon, they were highly reliant upon the device and welcomed the fact it took control over their navigation, and were thus annoyed when it did not provide the strict guidance that it promised. Others however, resented the lack of agency they had over their own movements. A sense of exploration is key in immersive theatre settings [25]. Despite offering the same level of guidance to all participants, the Animotus appeared to be able to both facilitate and inhibit this sense.

Participants similarly had mixed reactions to the amount of control during exploration during the performance. The transitions between using technology, and relying on self-guidance presented both opportunities, and causes for concern for participants. These transitional moments did not solely involve the physical process of switching technology, but represented a shift in control over one's own personal journey. For some, this was a welcome shift: they wanted the freedom to explore this novel space without constraint. However, for others these transitions of control were disconcerting: either they were unable to fully transition from obeying to exploration, or they felt unnerved when the control that they expected was not there to support them. Uncertainty when using technology has been noted in previous immersive experiences [5] and is sometimes seen as a positive. Alston comments on this ambiguity as a negative aspect of immersive theatre however, stating that the imbalance of experience in such circumstances "exacerbates inequalities" [2]. Whereas technology had the opportunity here to create equivalent but not replicated experiences for all audience members, it was still possible for inequalities to arise.

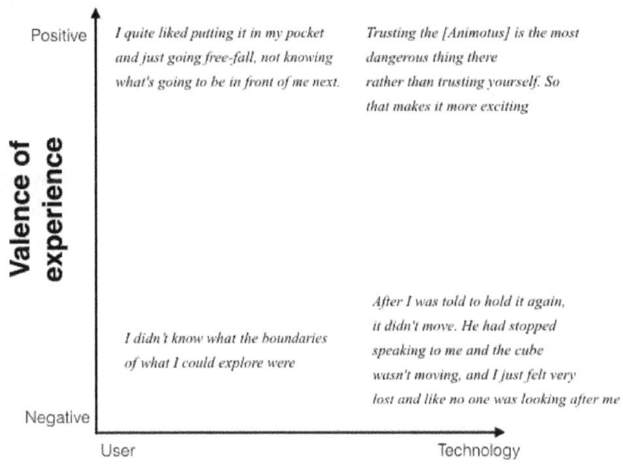

Figure 5. Example reactions to the differing levels of control, audience members experienced both positive and negative reactions to both levels of control.

These transitions of control also need to be carefully choreographed in order to ensure that these "seamful" moments [8] are positive or worthwhile experiences for the participant. In some instances, the control shift was welcomed, whereas for others this transition needed to be better defined and smoother in order for the participants to remain fully engaged in the experience around them.

The findings during this research suggest an interesting artistic use of control transitions with technology: it is possible that these transitions could be used consciously to create other narrative effects. For example, the sudden lack of control can create a feeling of loneliness, or a transition to a highly controlled state might evoke feelings of oppression and captivity. This work suggests that similar sensations that are created by actors in immersive theatre works can also be evoked by technology. That the Animotus at once appeared trustworthy and then occasionally stopped guiding its user created a similar level of broken trust as found in Ontroerend Goed's *Internal* (as reported in [2]) where performers elicit information from trusting audience members only to then broadcast this information to the group without explicit permission.

This research also highlighted that participants' control of attention on technology in immersive theatre settings can be problematic. Whether they are aware of it or not, participants may ignore certain sensory inputs in favour of others. This raises potential issues for future use of technology in this context: in multi-modal experiences, participants may need assistance in focusing on elements considered important by directors. If, for example, a key part of the narrative was being conveyed by audio technology, other haptic or visual technology may need to cease for the duration. However, if there is no such narrative constraint on a piece, the participants' tendency to exclude some sensory information may just add to the personalised experience that each participant receives during an immersive theatre performance: they can create and control their own individual narrative path.

Alternating between giving the participants freedom and taking control therefore can have a powerful effect upon their experience. The removal of control can be a positive experience for participants in immersive theatre – allowing them the chance to completely trust in a piece of technology that apparently knows better than they do, which can lead to a novel and exciting experience and can allow relationships with technology that would not occur in the real world.

Yet this sensation comes as part of a contract between the participants and those creating the performance. The participants relinquish control over their own journeys and in return expect a level of care. Whereas an apparently malfunctioning piece of technology can often be dealt with with little emotional toll by users in other situations, in an immersive theatre performance such an instance becomes a more worrying proposition. Any confusion in how the technology should be used, or any sign that the technology may be broken can instill concern and a sense of vulnerability in the participants. This could be used to dramatic effect, but in situations when that is not the intended outcome, the technology (and its creators) have a responsibility to convey a sense of certainty to the users.

This research has also highlighted the careful balance that needs to be achieved when presenting multimodal experiences to participants. A rich sensory environment can create a rich immersive experience for those walking through it, but does not guarantee that they will engage fully with every aspect of it. This may not be problematic, however when a particular message or interaction is particularly key for the performance, control may need to be taken from the participants to guide their attention.

We have shown that technology can help in creating an exciting, immersive experience, and what is more can be done without the aid of visual stimuli which is commonly the case in similar performances. In addition to this, we have highlighted an area of interest for creative teams aiming to use technology as a key part of future performances. It is important to ask questions about control in the performance. Can lessons be learned from the multitude of ways we use technology for navigation – should participants be given the choice between handing over full control or simply using technology as an assistant? How much do the participants in a performance need to know about the boundaries when exploring? Do participants need guidance in picking out the most important elements in a multisensory interaction?

This research has highlighted the dramatic role of technology in these settings. Every decision that is made can have a significant impact upon the narrative of the performance. Technology is not simply easy or difficult to use, successful or unsuccessful, but can be controlling, helpful, thrilling, ignored, overbearing, supportive, uplifting; all of which can ultimately contribute to the way participants experience immersive theatre.

CONCLUSION

This exploration of technology in an immersive theatre setting has shown how important it is to consider where control lies in a performance. Whereas experiences that involve live actors have the opportunity to adapt and reassure audience members as necessary, for technology with a pre-set range of interactivity, such adaption is not possible. Alternating control in immersive theatre performances between the participants and the technology around them has the ability to add dramatically to the experience – leaving people feeling empowered or alone. But when such an experience is not required, it is important that creative teams carefully choreograph the interactions, or else the participants may either retreat into themselves, thus missing key elements of the event, or may rebel against it, causing potential issues for others.

This area is an exciting stage for technology – audiences become participants and can explore surreal and novel new worlds in more embodied ways than traditional theatre experiences. In order to ensure the ideal immersive experience, creative teams need to take control over control.

ACKNOWLEDGEMENTS

Photos in this paper were taken by Terry Braun. We wish to thank Emilie Giles, Lyndsey Housden, Matthias Kispert and Tarim for their work on the Flatland project. We gratefully acknowledge the grant from NESTA. We would like to thank our colleagues for reading drafts of this paper and reviewers for their insightful comments And final thanks to all brave explorers who travelled through Flatland and gave their time to be interviewed.

REFERENCES

1. Edwin Abbott Abbott. 1884. *Flatland: A romance of many dimensions*. Princeton University Press.

2. Adam Alston. 2013. Audience Participation and Neoliberal Value : Risk , agency and responsibility in immersive theatre. *Performance Research* 18, 2, 128–138. http://doi.org/10.1080/13528165.2013.807177
3. Paul M Aoki, Rebecca E Grinter, Amy Hurst, Margaret H Szymanski, James D Thornton, and Allison Woodruff. 2002. Sotto Voce : Exploring the Interplay of Conversation and Mobile Audio Spaces. *Proceedings of the SIGCHI Conference on Human Factors in Computing Systems (CHI '02)*, ACM, 431–438.
4. Dominique Barni. 2011. The Handheld Museum. Retrieved from http://museumsandmobiledevices.wordpress.com/
5. Steve Benford, Andy Crabtree, Martin Flintham, et al. 2006. Can You See Me Now ? *ACM Transactions on Computer-Human Interaction (TOCHI)* 13, 1, 100–133.
6. Steve Benford, Gabriella Giannachi, Boriana Koleva, and Tom Rodden. 2009. From interaction to trajectories : Designing coherent journeys through user experiences. *Proceedings of the SIGCHI Conference on Human Factors in Computing Systems (CHI '09)*, 709–718. http://doi.org/10.1145/1518701.1518812
7. Steve Benford, Chris Greenhalgh, Gabriella Giannachi, Brendan Walker, Joe Marshall, and Tom Rodden. 2012. Uncomfortable Interactions. *Proceedings of the SIGCHI Conference on Human Factors in Computing Systems*, 2005–2014.
8. Matthew Chalmers and Areti Galani. 2004. Seamful interweaving: heterogeneity in the theory and design of interactive systems. *Symposium on Designing Interactive Systems*, 243–252. http://doi.org/10.1145/1013115.1013149
9. Steven Dow, Jaemin Lee, Christopher Oezbek, Blair Macintyre, Jay David Bolter, and Maribeth Gandy. 2005. Exploring Spatial Narratives and Mixed Reality Experiences in Oakland Cemetery. *Proceedings of the SIGCHI Conference Advances in Computer Entertainment (ACE '05)*, 51–60.
10. Tom Froese and Adam Spiers. 2007. Toward a Phenomenological Pragmatics of Enactive Perception. *Proceedings of the Conference on Enactive Interfaces (Enactive '07)*, 105–108.
11. Alison L. Grinder and E. Sue McCoy. 1985. *The Good Guide: A Sourcebook for Interpreters, Docents and Tour Guides*. Ironwood Press.
12. Nicholas A Guidice and Gordon E Legge. 2008. Blind navigation and the role of technology. In *The Engineering Handbook of Smart Technology for Aging, Disability, and Independence*. 479–500.
13. Charlene Jennett, Paul Cairns, and Andrew Epps. Measuring and Defining the Experience of Immersion in Games. 1–44.
14. Janet van der Linden, Yvonne Rogers, Maria Oshodi, et al. 2011. Haptic Reassurance in the Pitch Black for an Immersive Theatre Experience Conference Item Theatre Experience. *Proceedings of the 13th international conference on Ubiquitous computing*, 143–152. http://doi.org/10.1145/2030112.2030133
15. Paige Mcginley. 2010. Next Up Downtown: A New Generation of Ensemble Performance. *TDR/The Drama Review* 4, 54, 11–38.
16. Marc Mcloughlin. 2011. Design Interventions for Open-Air Museums : Applying and Extending the Principles of " Assembly ." *Proceedings of the SIGCHI Conference on Human Factors in Computing Systems (CHI '11)*, 553–556.
17. Donald A Norman. 1986. Cognitive Engineering. In *User Centred System Design*, Donald A Norman and Stephen W Draper (eds.). Lawrence Erlbaum Associates, 31–62.
18. Spyros Papaioannou. 2014. Immersion, "smooth" spaces and critical voyeurism in the work of Punchdrunk. *Studies in Theatre and Performance* 34, 2, 160–174. http://doi.org/10.1080/14682761.2014.899746
19. Lisa Ran, Sumi Helal, and Steve Moore. 2004. Drishti: An integrated indoor/outdoor blind navigation system and service. *Proceedings of IEEE Conference on Pervasive Computing and Communications (PerCom '04)*, 23–30. http://doi.org/10.1109/PERCOM.2004.1276842
20. Stuart Reeves. 2011. *Designing interfaces in public settings: Understanding the role of the spectator in Human-Computer Interaction*. Springer Science & Business Media.
21. S. Robinson, M. Jones, P. Eslambolchilar, R. Murray-Smith, and M. Lindborg. 2010. "I did it my way": moving away from the tyranny of turn-by-turn pedestrian navigation. *Proceedings of the International Conference on Human-Computer Interaction with Mobile Devices and Services (Mobile HCI '10)*, 341–344. http://doi.org/http://dx.doi.org/10.1145/1851600.1851660
22. David Z Saltz. 2001. Live Media : Interactive Technology and Theatre. *Theatre Topics* 11, 2, 107–130.
23. Phoebe Sengers and Bill Gaver. 2006. Staying

Open to Interpretation : Engaging Multiple Meanings in Design and Evaluation. *Proceedings of the 6th conference on Designing Interactive systems*, 99–108.

24. Adam Spiers, Janet van der Linden, Maria Oshodi, Sarah Wiseman, and Aaron M Dollar. 2015. Flatland : an immersive theatre experience centered on shape changing haptic navigation technology Conference Item. *IEEE World Haptics Conference 2015.*

25. Gareth White. 2012. On Immersive Theatre. *Theatre Research International* 37, 3, 221–235. http://doi.org/10.1017/S0307883312000880

26. Doug Williams, Ian Kegel, Marian Ursu, et al. 2015. A Distributed Theatre Experiment with Shakespeare. *Proceedings of the 23rd ACM international conference on Multimedia.*, 281–290.

27. Scooter Willis and Sumi Helal. 2005. RFID information grid for blind navigation and wayfinding. *Proceedings of International Symposium on Wearable Computers (ISWC '05)*, 34–37. http://doi.org/10.1109/ISWC.2005.46

28. Massimo Zancanaro, Elena Not, Daniela Petrelli, et al. 2015. Recipes for tangible and embodied visit experiences. *Proceedings of Museums and the Web (MW2015).*

Conceptualising Resourcefulness as a Dispersed Practice

Lenneke Kuijer
Eindhoven University of Technology, Industrial Design
Eindhoven, The Netherlands
s.c.kuijer@tue.nl

Iohanna Nicenboim
Delft University of Technology, Dept. of Industrial Design
Delft, The Netherlands
i.nicenboim@tudelft.nl

Elisa Giaccardi
Delft University of Technology, Dept. of Industrial Design
Delft, The Netherlands
e.giaccardi@tudelft.nl

ABSTRACT
In research on health and wellbeing, resourcefulness is seen as an important skill that can improve quality of life. In design and HCI literature, it has long been acknowledged that resourcefulness is about more than human skills and involves the adaptation, modification and reinvention of technologies in everyday life. In this paper we argue how certain aspects of resourcefulness have so far remained under-theorized, and present a new design perspective on resourcefulness that is grounded in practice theory. In this view, resourcefulness is conceptualised as the dispersed practice of dealing with everyday crises of routine. By elaborating on the complex interplay between means and purpose, we tease out resourcefulness as a practice of reconfiguration. The paper closes by discussing implications of this conceptualisation by zooming in on ways of capturing and designing for resourcefulness.

Author Keywords
Resourcefulness; practice theory; dispersed practice; thing ethnography.

ACM Classification Keywords
H.5.m. Information interfaces and presentation (e.g., HCI): Miscellaneous.

INTRODUCTION
Resourcefulness has been argued to reduce frustration, anxiety and depression among people facing challenging and stressful circumstances [34, 62]. When it comes to resourcefulness, older age is a particularly interesting phase of life because it is characterized by encountering challenges in daily activities due to diminishing physical and mental capabilities [40]. At the same time, research in science and technology studies shows how technologies designed for older people - an area of development referred to as gerontechnology - tend to be particularly closed to forms of situated reinterpretation and repurposing [1, 36, 52]. Such designs inhibit possibilities for innovation "in use" and adjustment to the varied and changing situations of use in which technologies are bound to end up [19]. Besides the ethical concerns regarding who decides what it means to live healthily and well that this tendency brings up [32], these highly scripted types of designs inhibit resourcefulness. New approaches are needed to design gerontechnologies that facilitate or even enhance resourcefulness.

Resourceful Ageing is a multidisciplinary design project that was set up to empower elderly people to live longer and more resilient lives. The aim of the project is to research how to design products and services that facilitate ageing resourcefully. The project uses a 'research-through-design' [77] process that enlists as participants a community of both elderly people and the mundane objects they ordinarily use and 'misuse' (from material artefacts to computational technologies).

We focus in particular on the understudied group of third age elderly, or young old. In contrast to what is commonly understood, Loe [46] describes the lives of the young old as in flux. Their bodies, roles, interests and responsibilities are changing. They have retired from work, but are active care givers, for parents, children and grandchildren. They are noticing signs of ageing more than before, but they are not governed by it. Instead, as Loe puts it, 'what lies before them is time, new family configurations and opportunities for reinvention' [46]. In spite of persistent prejudice of elderly as technologically less skilled, research has shown elders to creatively use and adapt artefacts and technologies in daily life [40].

In the project, we position the ageing society not as a problem but as an achievement [51] and view elderly not as dependent and technologically challenged, but as active participants in society, very well capable of making decisions about their own lives, and adjusting available means to their needs. Our approach is to learn from and work with ways in which elderly people creatively deal with the challenges they face as their body/minds age, in order to inform the design of products and services that facilitate and enhance resourcefulness. In this paper we report on our efforts within the project team to *jointly scrutinize and reframe the concept of resourcefulness* in order to inform our subsequent steps of capturing and designing for resourcefulness with a group of third age elderly households.

DIS 2017, June 10-14, 2017, Edinburgh, United Kingdom

ACM 978-1-4503-4922-2/17/06…$15.00
DOI: http://dx.doi.org/10.1145/3064663.3064698

We start the paper by offering an overview of conceptualisations of resourcefulness in HCI and design literature. We then introduce a revised definition of resourcefulness which is grounded in practice theory. To illustrate the application of this new framing, we discuss the implications for HCI of capturing and designing for resourcefulness, with a view on our collaboration with a group of third age elderly households. We continue the discussion by reflecting on how the conceptualisation of resourcefulness that we propose has implications also for other areas of HCI, beyond the specific application to matters of gerontechnology.

RESOURCEFULNESS IN DESIGN LITERATURE

Although 'resourcefulness' is not a widely used term in design literature, the practices by which users adapt, repurpose, and appropriate existing artefacts from their surroundings have been previously formulated with different notions. One of the earliest theoretical formulations is the term *adhocism*, coined by Charles Jencks and Nathan Silver in the 1970s, which describes the use of arbitrary objects in order to satisfy a momentary need in an improvised way [38]. The same process of spontaneous form-making was described by Christopher Alexander in the 1960s as *unselfconscious design*. In this process, users (or agents), exploit their immediate environment for resources, in order to consistently create well-fitting forms [2].

More contemporary terms for the same phenomenon found in design literature are *design-in-use* [50], and *non-intentional design* [5]. Design-in-use is defined as the 'ways in which users take over existing products according to personal needs, and practices beyond product design. It involves the emergence of unanticipated uses, and transformations in the structure and characteristics of the product'. Non-Intentional Design, similarly, describes the spontaneous changes people make to their environment through minor or major interventions once faced with a situational problem.

Function in and through use

What is clear from these conceptualisations is that people use objects in a different way than what designers have decided in advance, and thus its function cannot be defined by designers alone. Preston, for example, differentiates between two functions of objects: the *proper function* as opposed to the *system function*: The former is what a thing is designed to do, while the latter, is a purpose a thing may serve on occasion, without having been designed to do so [10].

Thus, we can say that the act of repurposing usually occurs when people use an object in a manner different from their 'prescribed' functional intention – or when the prescribed application is not 'honoured' in the new use [5]. For example, when a wheelchair is used as an office chair, or a walking stick to knock on the ceiling, whenever help is needed from the upstairs neighbour [21]. If we understand the function of an artefact as its *dispositions* [72], the 'normal' function of an artefact is a 'privileged' set of dispositions intentionally produced or selected by the designer of the artefact.

One way designers account for the unexpected use of objects, is to test and try out 'use' during the design process. In User-centred Design, this is described by Redström [61] as *use before use*, while *design after design* is the attempt to create a larger space of possibilities for acts of defining 'use through use' in which the definitions of use are meant to be in-/un-determinate. In the same way, Fischer and Giaccardi [19] claim that in order to be able to accommodate unexpected issues at use-time, systems need to be "underdesigned." In this view, instead of designing complete solutions for users, *underdesign* should provide users with the social and technical means to create the solutions by themselves at use-time.

Conditions for resourcefulness

Although we might use artefacts as resources without even thinking about their original functions, Vermaas and Houkes [72] explain that this is normally not due to a misinterpretation of their original function, but is rather rooted in our ability to see beyond the function and discover abstract or open forms [5]. Some people might be better than others in the skill of discovering new uses, but we can assume that the way artefacts are designed, perceived, or marketed, could affect whether it is easier or more difficult for users to look beyond their intended function. For example, factors which might influence the selection criterion for repurposing, include the object's material characteristics or *affordances*; the *time* to find a solution; and the *reversibility* of the object [5, 10]. Since misusing an artefact might imply that it becomes useless for its original function, the complexity of the object also plays an important role, and most high-tech appliances are not so well suited for misuse as low-complexity ones [5].

Another two important factors which can enable resourcefulness are *ambiguity and failure*. *Ambiguity* means allowing for multiple interpretations of objects, as it can invite adaptation and tinkering, and allow users to define their own meanings, rather than accepting those imposed by designers without question [25, 67]. In the same way, failure or breakdowns can release objects and their owners from a 'contract of use', offering an opportunity for the users to modify them. Furthermore, the reducibility of objects to their parts, can suggest the possibility of re-assembly in an alternative configuration [5]. Along these lines, Maestri and Wakkary [47] have shown that the repair of objects in the home can be not only an act of restoration, but also an act of creativity. While Brandes [5] believes that in the modification of products there is no impulse to consciously create, Mitchell [49] claims that these kind of actions can be highly self-reflexive. Moreover, he believes that modification practices can be transformative, and amplify consumer's agency: Since the designer's position of authority dictates the 'correct' use of the object, it divides the field of possible uses into authorized and unauthorized zones. For this reason, users are faced with a degree of resistance during the act of modification, which by overcoming it, challenges institutions or existing structures. Within this approach, conditions such as the material constraints and affordances of objects, as well as the cultural narrative or personal history, could be seen as a way to both assist and limit the acts of modification.

RESOURCEFULNESS IN HCI

A common term in HCI literature is *appropriation,* the process by which people adopt and adapt technologies, incorporating them into (working) practices. This might involve customization in the traditional sense, but also making use of the technology for purposes beyond those for which it was originally designed, to serve new ends [13]. In the same way, Wakkary and Maestri [73] describe appropriation as the remaking through use of designed artefacts and structures in ways that were often not intended, which lead to adaptation and evolution of unique design systems.

Maestri and Wakkary [47] have conducted research on *everyday design*, and shown evidence on how families appropriate artefacts and surroundings, leading to the design of everyday systems, which continually evolve through design-in-use [73]. These appropriations are described by them as *resourceful*, *adaptive*, and *emergent*: people appropriate artefacts and surroundings, adapting them and forming systems and routines through design in-use, which allows for emergent properties to arise [73]. These properties are crucial, because although resourcefulness is commonly understood as a temporary use, the authors show that it can also become part of a routine integral to daily life, and be combined to create ongoing systems. Taylor and Swan also suggest that technologies must be designed to accommodate the rich and diverse ways in which people organize their homes (and time), providing them with the resources to 'artfully construct their own systems' rather than enforcing ones that are removed from their experiences [71].

Eglash [16] distinguishes between three different stages in the appropriation of technology: *reinterpretation*, *adaptation* and *reinvention*. Reinterpretation is defined by a change in semantic association with little or no change in use or structure. Adaptation is a change in both semantic association and use, involving creativity to look beyond assumed functions and recognize new possibilities, but keeping the underlying structures unchanged. In reinvention, however, semantics, use, and structure are all changed: If adaptation requires the discovery of a latent function, reinvention is the creation of new functions through structural changes. The view that transformations in the structure and characteristics of the original product are necessary for design-in-use actions, is also mentioned by other authors [6, 50, 73].

Another framework that could be related to resourcefulness is *resilience* [22, 23], which identifies the intelligent ways in which systems go right despite adversity – due to poor behaviour, poor design, or poor circumstances. Resilience strategies, could include for example creating cues to remember things, separating similar objects and tasks so that there is less likelihood of confusion, and checking you have got the correct resources before committing to an action [22]. These strategies, together with the skills, and competencies that comprise a system's responses to threats and vulnerabilities, are part of a resilience repertoire, while resources, are the constraints that influence whether a strategy can be enacted [23]. This means that if the threat is too much for the system to handle, and its resilience repertoire insufficient or misapplied, then system performance will degrade or fail.

Lastly, similar concepts could be found in *domestication of technology* studies, which not only analyse the processes of acceptance, rejection, and use of technology, but also what technologies mean to us, how do we experience them and what are the roles they play in our lives [35]. The psychological dimension of objects, which reaches beyond their mere purpose, and mirrors the identity of their owners, has also been developed in the areas of sociology, ethnology, design and psychology (for a summary see [42]). It is argued that by endowing objects with meaning that reaches beyond their pure purpose, people take possession of them, providing them with emotional qualities [5]. This is especially important in the group of elderly and the field of assisted living, as certain objects could be stigmatizing to the users, which could be one of the reasons for misuse or lack of use at all. For example when a specially designed chair for showering is now used as a flower-bench [21] or when a hiking stick is preferred to a walking cane because it makes people feel sporty rather than old.

Digital resourcefulness

The modification of existing services and the collaborative re-design of existing products, has been widely developed within communities of software and Open Source projects in the past decades. In computer systems, the term *workaround* is often used to define what users do intentionally to evade designed limits in hardware or software [43]. Botero et al. [4], conceptualises the opportunities given to users as the *design space*: an area of possibilities for realizing new designs, which extends beyond the original area of designers, into the realm of design-in-use. However, until recently, people without particular technological expertise have had very limited possibilities to modify technologies. Currently, this is gradually changing with the emergence of new collaborative digital tools (such as blogs, wikis and feeds), which have made active participation in software development available to a wider audience, and have opened possibilities for contributions that are not limited to developers alone [4]. Prototyping platforms and digital fabrication spaces, like FabLabs [48]; as well as communities such as Ikeahackers.net, in which people share their modifications on commercial products.

More broadly, the framework of *meta-design* [19, 26, 27] explores the design space, and the opportunities at use-time, creating digital environments that allow end-users to act as designers. Rather than restricting users to just use a system, meta-designed environments provide end-users with opportunities, tools, and social reward structures to extend the system to fit their needs. In this process, the user becomes a co-developer, learning to operate a system and adapting to its functionality. In response, the system is modified to be adapted to the practices of its users. Thus, in this co-adaptive and reciprocal process, the system can evolve at use time, supporting more complex interactions than traditional, linear user-centred processes.

Within a similar approach, and drawing on Alexander's notion of *unselfconscious design* [2], Wakkary et al. [75] have developed the concept of *unselfconscious interactions*, a form of interaction with computational artefacts that is motivated by ongoing corrections and improvements of the fit among artefacts, environments and people within specific context of use. According to the authors, these interactions can act as catalysts to promote incremental engagements with artefacts, while the artefacts themselves serve as resources if they are purposely designed with non-existent or weak use goals.

In the previous chapters, we have recognized different notions which are related to resourcefulness, both in design, as well as in HCI literature. These notions conceptualise the way people adapt and repurpose objects in their everyday life, adding new functions or appropriating them into their own routines. Firstly, we have discussed how this phenomenon might affect our idea if function. Secondly, we have summarized some of the concepts that can be seen as the conditions that enable resourcefulness, such as reversibility, ambiguity and failure. Lastly, we have discussed how designers deal with this phenomenon and proposed different strategies in order to allow users to act as designers and use objects resourcefully.

In the next section we depart from these notions by introducing an alternative conceptualisation of resourcefulness as a dispersed practice, after which we will make the link back to this literature in discussing implications of this view for HCI research and design.

RESOURCEFULNESS AS A DISPERSED PRACTICE

Building on the practice turn in HCI [18, 45, 56], our research draws on theories of practice to frame resourcefulness. Theories of practice is a group of theories from sociology that take social practices as their fundamental unit of social analysis [60]. Practices are conceptualised as collectively shared ideas about normal and appropriate ways of proceeding in daily activities such as bathing, cooking, driving, playing, meeting, having a coffee and so on, that are recursively shaped and reshaped through repeated performances by people. In other words, all human activity is viewed as manifestations of socially shared 'blueprints' of normal behaviour, referred to by Schatzki as the 'organization dimension' of practices [65], and by others as the 'practice-as-entity' [7, 68, 76]. These 'entities' are in turn maintained, as well as modified by individuals adhering to or deviating from them when they act them out in the particular situations they face, i.e., when people are 'engaged in' [65] or 'performing' [64] the practice. The practice-as-entity consists of constellations of elements, for which the grouping into the categories of materials, competences and meanings proposed by Shove et al. [68] is the one most widely used in HCI. In everyday activities, individuals combine these elements into unique constellations that 'work' and 'make sense' in the particular situation at hand.

In HCI, practice theory has been drawn on in a diverse range of studies and theoretical reflections, including second hand interactions [55], reflecting on the effectiveness of energy feedback [54, 70], less resource intensive forms of bathing [44], sustainable behaviour [74] ecologies of artefacts [41], and material experience [29]. Theories of practice have been argued to present a new paradigm in HCI [45] that offers a spatially and temporally situated perspective on daily life beyond specific technologies and their (intended) use. This is particularly relevant in relation to resourcefulness, because it relates so closely to unintended and unanticipated forms of use, repurposing and reinterpretation. Such forms of use can be argued to be difficult to study using an 'interactions paradigm', as Kuutti and Bannon [45] describe the prevailing mainstream HCI paradigm, as they risk being labelled as misuse, or viewed as usability problems.

Everyday crises of routine

While resourcefulness does not feature explicitly in theories of practice, the concept can be positioned in relation to the practice theoretic framework. We argue that from a practice theoretic perspective, resourcefulness occurs in situations that are in some way exceptional, non-standard, non-routine or non-mainstream. Reckwitz [60] refers to these situations as 'everyday crises of routines', specified as 'constellations of interpretative interdeterminacy and of the inadequacy of knowledge with which the agent, carrying out a practice, is confronted in the face of a "situation".' (p255). The inadequacy of knowledge here refers to the issue that in such situations of crises, there is no tested, routinized, socially agreed way of proceeding in the practice. In relation to this idea of crises, Warde [76] adds that 'people in myriad situations adapt, improvise and experiment' (p141). In fact, therefore, people do know how to proceed in situations of crises because skills of adapting, improvising and experimenting are common human skills.

However, as discussed above, resourcefulness is about more than human skills, because it involves artefacts as well. Turning to Schatzki, these common skills could be considered as 'dispersed' practices [64]. Dispersed practices are agreed ways of proceeding that are common across many practices, such as for example having a conversation, writing, arguing, describing, etc. Schatzki positions this concept in relation to integrative practices [64], which are practices with a more particular form and social domain, such as bathing, cooking, driving a car, etc.

Conceptualising resourcefulness not as a human skill but as a dispersed practice brings materials back into the equation, because, although dispersed practices tend to rely primarily on know-how [76], coining them to be practices means that they can be viewed as constellations of interconnected elements, including materials. Writing, for example, is a dispersed practice that cannot be performed without the use of material artefacts (e.g., a pen) or computational technologies (e.g., a Word processor).

Importantly, this view also conceptualises meanings and purpose as part of the configuration. To further explain the implications of considering resourcefulness as a dispersed practice, we will now discuss relations between means and purpose in this practice in more detail. The discussion was inspired by, and uses examples from a small scale exploration conducted within the project team, which consisted of a homework assignment to collect examples of resourcefulness from our everyday lives and a workshop in which these examples were discussed and mapped on various scales.

Purpose and means in practices of resourcefulness

Roughly put, materials and competences together can be viewed as the means to achieve a purpose, each with particular, related meanings associated to them. For example, people may assign different meanings to the same purpose in different situations: having a cup of tea, or the cup and tea itself could be associated with relaxation, catching up, a break, an outing, being sick or warming up. In theories of practice, materials, competences, meanings and purpose are not seen as personal attributes but as elements or qualities of the practice in which an individual participates [60]. Crucially, this implies that the relation between means and purpose is recursive, and when focusing on implications of this view for design, Ingram et al. reiterate that while things tend to be designed to fit certain purposes, they 'also make the purposes for which they are fit' [37].

Resourcefulness can be a purpose for certain actions in itself, so we can speak of practicing resourcefulness. But while someone can be resourceful for the sake of being resourceful, being resourceful is generally directed at the integrative practice in relation to which it takes place. In the project we are looking at everyday life and therefore are dealing with mundane everyday practices and purposes, i.e., not purposes such as optimizing a production line, defeating an enemy, or winning an election, but everyday ones such as making a cup of tea, ordering groceries, taking a bath, meeting a friend, posting a photo, getting some exercise, going out, annoying the neighbours, disciplining the cat, and so on. In dealing with such mundane purposes, crises can occur one-off or repeatedly, and with more or less urgency. As such, different relations between means and purpose within resourcefulness can be described.

Adjusting means to purpose

Resourcefulness can be viewed as a form of adjusting means to purpose in crisis situations where designated means are not available for the purpose at hand. When viewed from the perspective of artefacts, this means that things that are at hand, or accessible with the skills and knowledge available are not appropriate for this particular situation.

Such a crisis may occur for two main reasons. One, because a 'solution' exists, but is not available in that situation, i.e., the person(s) involved are not aware it exists, do not have the means to obtain it, or skills to use it, or have it out of reach (e.g. using a handbag to fend a sudden downpour). Two, because an appropriate solution for this particular problem does not exist. For example, using chopsticks for pulling a small piece of bread out of the toaster (Figure 1). In such circumstances, resourcefulness entails the adjusting of available means to achieve the purpose at hand in a satisfactory manner. This does not mean however, that the original purpose can be fully maintained.

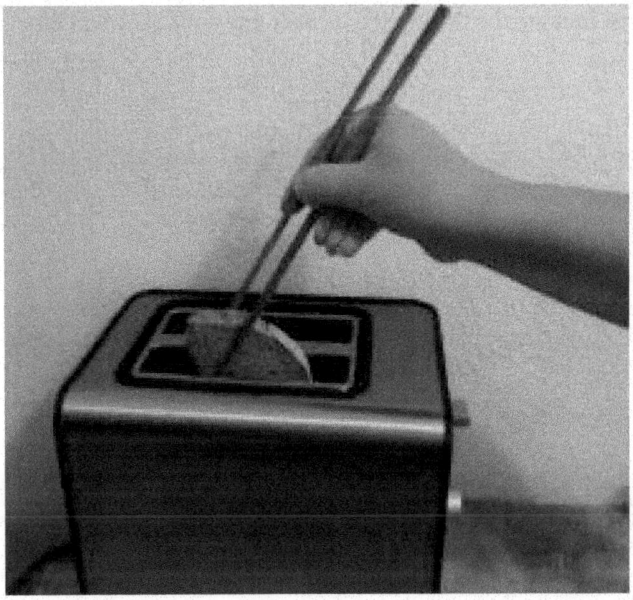

Figure 1. Pulling toast out of the toaster with chopsticks.

Adjusting purpose to means

In a practice paradigm, purposes are viewed as part of practices in which they are routinely shaped and reshaped through repeated performances, in relation to other elements, and to other practices. What it means and requires to make a proper piece of toast, for example, has a socially shared rough blueprint. If at some point the purpose is to have toast, but the piece of bread is too small for the toaster, then this can be considered a crisis. Ways to go about dealing with this crisis are to decide to have the bread untoasted, to wait until the bread is cooled down to pull it out, to hold the toaster upside down, to unplug the device and pull it out with a knife, or as in this case, to pull it out with wooden chopsticks.

Importantly, in all of these cases the original, blueprint practice of toasting cannot be maintained, because this would involve the bread popping up high enough to safely pull it out with ones fingers. So, in this type of crisis, all types of resourceful responses require at least some modification of the integrative practice. This modification can also be considered too extensive, for example when burning ones fingers. There is a fine line here, but in our view, *the response to a crisis ceases to be resourceful when it becomes a form of bearing with the situation. This is where the link between resourcefulness and wellbeing can be made.*

Deriving purpose from means

There is another type of crises where the purpose or problem is more exceptional and unique and arises from a particular situation without a simple matter of something lacking or failing. This can be explained using an example from our project that was gathered in our joint exploration of the concept of resourcefulness. In the example, sports gear was kept in an otherwise unused bathtub in a bathroom situated near the main entrance of the home (Figure 2). In this example, the unused bathtub that happened to be close to the entrance became a means for the thus far suppressed purpose of keeping the floor of the hallway free from sand and dirt.

Figure 2. Sports gear in the bathtub.

A crisis, a non-standard situation can be more or less urgent. On one end of the scale, something can hinder the normal course of living significantly, with an emergency or life threatening situation as the extreme example. A mild nuisance can be seen as the other end of the scale. In case of an emergency, resourcefulness can be lifesaving and any means available may be used for this purpose (e.g. a heavy object to break a window and get the neighbour's attention). On the other end of the scale, resourcefulness is likely to be much more subtle and will tend to occur when means are presenting themselves relatively obviously (such as in the case of the unused bathtub near the door). In these cases purpose is not explicit but rather derived from the means presenting itself in a situation. Between these two lie the responses to everyday crises of routine in which means and purpose recursively shape each other.

Resourcefulness in a practice paradigm

Considering resourcefulness as a practice and positioning it within the practice theoretic conceptual framework brings a new perspective to the concept compared to the ways in which it is currently considered and discussed in design literature.

Understandably, HCI literature approaches resourcefulness from the perspective of the qualities and characteristics of the computational technology, intended as a material artefact to interact with - thereby highlighting the importance of openness, ambiguity, modularity, and so on. In its definition of resourcefulness, this literature focuses on how artefacts are used by people – in ways different from those intended by their developers. There is also some attention for the ways in which artefacts are perceived and how the process of being resourceful requires not only skills of creatively looking beyond intended functions, but also skills of re-association and transforming the meaning of an artefact, but so far there is no theoretic framework to support this view.

Viewing resourcefulness as a dispersed practice shifts the perspective. Importantly, it positions resourcefulness as a form of reconfiguring the normal, (integrative) practice in relation to which it occurs. What this means is that being resourceful requires stepping outside of collectively established and tested frames. While in the design literature, resourcefulness tends to be viewed as something positive and desirable, this view highlights that it is also an inherently risky pursuit that requires courage to act out of the ordinary, and goes hand in hand with feelings of social uncertainty. As Scott et al. describe it, coming up with new configurations of elements 'requires creativity, courage, and the ability to envision something entirely new' [66].

Moreover, viewing resourcefulness as an act of reconfiguration also highlights how making one modification in the coherent configuration of elements that make up a practice can have a snowball effect on other aspects of that and other practices that also need change in order to continue to work and make sense. Moving from an interaction paradigm to a practice paradigm therefore allows a shift from a narrow focus on the qualities of the artefact to a horizontal view of ecologies of artefacts as part of webs of linked (or linkable) practices. We will return to this point in our discussion where we make the link between this conceptualisation and designing products that are digitally connected.

Finally, this view implies that if a resourceful reconfiguration that works becomes routine and spreads among other carriers of the practice, the modification becomes collectively accepted as normal and acceptable, and can therefore strictly speaking no longer be considered as resourceful.

Reframing resourcefulness

In summary, when viewing resourcefulness as a (dispersed) practice, being resourceful is about *using the materials (including other people) available in the situation as resources to solve problems or challenges arising from non-standard situations, i.e. (everyday) situations that are not part of common practice and for which there are neither commonly agreed nor widely 'tested' ways of proceeding*. This can mean that the situation is in that moment new to the person(s) involved and there is no agreed proper way of proceeding known to them. Or, the situation is familiar to the person(s) involved but not part of common practice. In these non-standard situations, *we identify resourcefulness as the adjusting of means to purpose, which inherently involves also adjusting purpose to means, up to the point where purpose becomes derived from means*. Being resourceful means that rather than bearing with the situation, artefacts and technologies are deployed in uncommon ways (as resources) to proceed in a satisfactory way in spite of more or less challenging circumstances. While this necessarily implies that purpose is to some extent adjusted to means, we identify resourcefulness when the person(s) involved are not feeling a victim of circumstances, but rather feel in control of the situation.

Resourcefulness can arise from uncommon configurations of elements that present themselves, are recognized and acted upon in a situation, and that turn out to work, and may then be repeated. *Resourcefulness, therefore, is not the same as everyday design*. Everyday design is about using artefacts in ways unintended by the designers and therefore has overlaps with resourcefulness, but forms of everyday design such as hanging your coat over a chair, an example used in [12], are in our view considered part of normal practice. Therefore, this is not considered as an example of resourcefulness in our view.

Resourcefulness as a configuration of elements

When considering resourcefulness as a practice, it can be described as a configuration of elements in itself. Our literature review and small scale exploration offer some clues as to how it may be configured.

Skills of resourcefulness in health research refer to 'a repertoire of coping strategies' for dealing with stressful situations [63]. Based on this view, Gonzales et al. [34] present a method for enhancing resourcefulness that contains six modules: problem identification, gaining confidence and motivation to solve it, brainstorming multiple solutions, comparing possible solutions and choosing the best one, implementing it, and evaluating it. This idea of resourcefulness as having similarity to a design process returns in HCI and design literature, where it has been conceptualised as everyday design or design-in-use. Other perspectives deformalize this process into more general skills of discovering abstract or open forms in objects, looking beyond assumed functions and more practical, technical skills of repairing, modifying and reprogramming.

These skills imply certain purposes and meanings involved in the practice, such as proceeding in the face of a challenge and avoiding stress, together with meanings of being resourceful as a challenge in itself, because somehow training is needed to practice it, including the building of confidence and motivation. This idea aligns with repurposing as a form of unauthorized use and our conclusion that being resourceful requires courage.

Regarding the material elements of resourcefulness, it becomes clear that the things used are somehow transformed either physically, or in terms of their intended or common meaning. The thing becomes *'something else'*, for which there isn't always a name: the bathtub a 'sports-gear-storage', the wooden chopsticks 'small-toast-removal-tools'.

This description of resourcefulness as a practice reveals that there are many caveats in existing knowledge about resourcefulness as a configuration of elements. Moreover, while any practice can be described in relatively general terms, understanding practices always requires empirical data on the particular practice under study. The following section will go further into how issues of data collection and interpretation might be further explored in our project and HCI more broadly.

CAPTURING AND ENHANCING RESOURCEFULNESS

Resourcefulness is of interest for HCI research and design in various respects. As argued in the introduction, resourcefulness is important for human wellbeing. Moreover, resourcefulness can be linked to technologies, and the way they are designed. Although there is always a case of people and artefacts coming together, there is a notion of artefacts being more or less open to repurposing and reinterpretation, and thus the way they are designed can either inhibit or enhance resourcefulness. Research in social gerontology moreover, has shown designs for elderly people to have a tendency to be particularly closed for resourceful repurposing.

In our project, we therefore focus on designing systems and devices for elderly people, and in particular the relatively understudied group of young old, that facilitate and enhance resourcefulness. However, because resourcefulness emerges from the ways in which people and artefacts work together in particular circumstances, this designing is not a simple matter of making ambiguous, open, modular or underdesigned systems and devices. To design for resourcefulness, insight is required into the particular circumstances, skills and broader ecology of artefacts involved in these situations.

Considering resourcefulness as a dispersed practice has implications both for gaining insight into its current manifestations in the everyday lives of people, and for designing artefacts to facilitate and enhance it. Questions arise like what strategies are used in situations of crises, what meanings are attached to uncommon reconfigurations and what makes reconfigurations that deviate from common practice and normal routines acceptable in that situation? How are new skills of resourcefulness acquired and how do they develop over time in interaction with new and existing things, other people and practices? This section touches upon a number of themes that begin to address these topics.

Capturing resourcefulness

We have reframed resourcefulness as the dispersed practice of adjusting and reworking the conventional relation between elements in normal practices—in particular the relation between means and purpose—to address unexpected or uncommon situations. During these reconfigurations, objects at hand are deployed in uncommon ways as resources, to proceed in a satisfactory way in spite of the challenging circumstances. As such, *we see resourcefulness as intimately linked to improvisation rather than already socially normed forms of everyday design*. The challenges and opportunities that such a conceptualisation of resourcefulness reveals for capturing resourcefulness concern primarily understanding how means and purpose come together to make a reconfiguration 'work'; this includes 'giving meaning' to an *improvised solution* that may ultimately lead to habituation and later to socially accepted, shared forms of everyday or even commercial design. This means orienting our methodology to gain insights on how and why the same object serves different purposes across different practices [28] – for example, at how a tub is used both for bathing *and* for putting away dirty sport gears. But also the reverse: how the practice of putting away, organizing objects makes a 'thing' such as stairs (Figure 3).

Figure 3. Stuff organized 'as stairs' to indicate where eventually items should be put away in the house.

When considering resourcefulness as a dispersed practice of dealing with everyday crises of routine in a variety of integrative practices, it becomes clear that because of its mundane, everyday character, resourcefulness is a practice that is relatively hidden from view and consciousness. Moreover, because of its characteristic of creating reconfigurations of normal practice, people may be insecure about the social acceptability of their particular solutions and inventions, or have trouble talking about it because no designated vocabulary exists to describe it. These characteristics make resourcefulness something that is particularly difficult to capture.

We believe that a thing-centred approach to research methodology may be suitable to address these challenges and opportunities, because it acknowledges the material and socio-cultural dimensions of artefacts in social practice, and see humans and artefacts relationally and symmetrically, in contrast to user-centred approaches conventionally more focused on human needs and wants.

A thing-centred approach

Our approach makes use of a 'living lab' of people *and* 'things' (i.e., artefacts that matter to our participants and have been instrumented with sensors) to loop qualitative ethnographic research in which artefacts record the world around them in the way ethnographers would try to record the world from a human's perspective, and quantitative insights from machine learning analysis.

As such, our approach links together several ongoing as well as recent developments in HCI, from living labs to thing ethnography and the use of machine learning in design research. We provide here a brief description of how these are understood and combined in our attempt of capturing resourcefulness.

Living labs form a diverse set of research methodologies that involve observing people's behaviour in real life settings [17]. Resourcefulness occurs in unexpected situations and can therefore not be realistically staged in a lab setting. It therefore has to be captured in real life situations. In the set-up of a living lab aimed to capture resourcefulness in a specific context, the characteristic of resourcefulness as a socially sensitive practice needs to be taken into account. When reconfigurations are acknowledged by the research team to be acceptable when they make sense to participants, as experts of their own situations, feelings of social insecurity might be turned into pride of creatively dealing with everyday challenges.

While research in the field must remain aware of and sensitive to what people feel and why they behave they way they do, a living lab for capturing resourcefulness must include artefacts too as 'participants' in the lab. To this end, thing ethnography [30] provides a methodology to establish a symmetrical feedback loop between people and things. Thing ethnography builds on the growing idea that artefacts have a different perspective on everyday life than people (e.g., Sensing the City [39], Davoli and Redstrom [11], BinCam [9], just to cite a few). From their particular perspective on daily life, artefacts 'see' what people cannot see, or would not notice [31]. Things cannot be directly interviewed, but developments in sensor technology, memory and wireless communication make it possible to obtain their point of view.

Equipping a number of carefully selected artefacts with sensors is therefore expected to be able to uncover some of the hidden events and actions involved in everyday resourcefulness. In addition, enabling these artefacts to talk to each other is expected to reveal links between different practices and how resourcefulness may be constructed across, and at the overlap, of these practices. For example, being able to observe that the same artefact is used as a different means, for a different purpose, within different situations, and as part of different practices, may render insights about relations and dependencies between artefacts and practices. It is at the crossover of these often unnoticed interdependencies that resourcefulness is expected to play a role, and using thing ethnography in a living lab set-up may help capture precisely such critical interdependencies (which designers often improperly refer to as misuse).

Putting machine learning in the loop

As introduced by Cila et al. [8], the main contribution of machine learning (ML) to the design field is expanding the processing of the data gathered by things beyond human capacity and skills. ML can be used as a way to identify novel patterns of use within the data that is streamed through the interaction between people and things, and things and things. Through a better understanding of what data can tell us about how we use things in practice, new understandings of use may emerge and inform the development of design concepts and prototypes. The identification of relevant patterns can also constitute an opening towards the radical ideation of new products and services in which different kinds of meanings and values are exchanged 'in use' [69].

When it comes to capturing resourcefulness from a thing-centred perspective, the way ML is performed requires careful consideration. Pattern recognition in ML can be classified as supervised and unsupervised [8]. Supervised learning can be used for discovering patterns by specifying for which attribute the patterns should be discovered. Any of the attributes could be at the center of the inquiry; e.g., toaster being on, type of bread inside, time of the day, and so on. Once the attribute is selected, the algorithm looks at other related attributes as to discover variety of patterns. For instance, in the case with the toaster being on, there might be patterns that include time of the day (everyday between 8am-9am), presence of certain individuals or objects (such as plates on the counter), and actions (such as opening the fridge). Supervised learning is particularly useful when there is a clear hypothesis to start with, but less applicable when interdependencies are hidden and may vary over time. In this case, unsupervised learning may prove more insightful. Unsupervised learning is a broader pattern search technique in which the algorithm decides for which attributes the patterns will be discovered. It uses an iterative process to identify patterns in the data, creating clusters on the basis of similarity on *emerging* categories. These categories and patterns can subsequently be used as a basis to identify outliers, exceptions and deviations from routines, which are the type of events that can then be investigated further within the living lab through interviews. These interviews can use the machine learning outcomes to help participants and the design team reflect and develop insights into people's everyday strategies of resourcefulness in the living lab.

By utilizing ML, a multitude of patterns could be discovered. However, many of the patterns might not be as meaningful. For example, ML may find a variety of obvious patterns for "the toaster being on": temperature increases when the toaster is on, toaster is on when the indicator light is red, toaster is on when a piece of bread was just inserted in the slot, toaster is on if it is not dark in the room. From the ML perspective all of these patterns are quantitatively very strong, yet in practice many might be of no value for designers. However, while most patterns might not be as interesting from a qualitative standpoint, some might provide an interesting insight that might not have been discovered otherwise (e.g., sometimes when the toaster has just been on, chopsticks are used in close proximity to it). Ultimately, by looping ethnography and ML, the multitude of patterns produced by ML could expose designers and participants to reflect and develop insights on a variety of aspects. In turn, feedback from examination of these patterns could be incorporated into the ML algorithms as to make the search for patterns more efficient and useful, and combine quantitative and qualitative forms of inquiry in a feedback loop [8]. Eventually, this work may provide deeper insights into the make-up of resourcefulness as a dispersed practice.

Designing for resourcefulness

Challenges in designing for resourcefulness relate to understanding diversity in skills, uncertainty about the use situations in which an artefact will end up, the norms and values that may facilitate the expression and construction of a resourceful identity. Therefore, while capturing resourcefulness may help identify design opportunities at the crossover of a unique web of practices, *it must be concerned also with learning how to keep the design open to appropriation in the variety of situations in which certain artefacts may end up.* By complementing qualitative data, the use of sensor data and machine learning algorithms serves here the goal of helping identify potential dimensions of openness of the digital artefact that will be offered to the elderly to facilitate and enhance resourcefulness in their everyday lives. A focus on understanding and supporting the dimensions of openness of the artefact is contrary to the way in which Internet of Things (IoT) infrastructures are commonly used for monitoring and optimization of existing products and functionalities.

But it is not at odds with the process of connecting houses to the internet, which is in itself a practice that requires skills of digital resourcefulness [53]. In contrast to the ideal and linear way in which IoT is often pursued by companies, it is actually expected that IoT will be highly heterogeneous, encompassing objects completely different in terms of functionality, technology and application fields [3, 14]. People will bring these different objects in different times and it will be a dispersed and discontinuous process. This phenomenon is defined by Edwards and Grinter [15] as the "accidentally" smart home: a home which contains technological components embedded in it but has not benefited from a holistic, ground-up approach to design and integration (which would necessarily require a pre-conceived, holistic idea of normal and acceptable household life).

In designing for resourcefulness the "accidentally" smart home is somehow embraced. In our design approach, data and ML are used as a means in the participatory set-up of the living lab for empowering both people and 'things' to act as co-ethnographers but also as co-designers 'in use'.

In this sense, the infrastructure for capturing resourcefulness might even form the beginnings of a design for resourcefulness in itself. After all, technologies like IoT are inherently "configurational technology" [20]—a platform, a form of open-ended systems that need configuration in specific contexts to work at all, that are not ready for use upon purchase [33]. By understanding how things and people work together, designers can expand their scope and begin to design entanglements, or ecosystems, rather than isolated products and services. For example, we could envision more dynamic 'families of objects', which share information among things that belong to the same temporal o spatial arrangement. New services could be spontaneously arranged and digital interfaces could adapt according to their proximity to other things. For example, when glasses are not around, the text in the tablet could suggest to be enlarged. Or, in the case of things that are always used together, the system could give cues to the user about the missing object and where to find it, and eventually suggest new objects to be added to or removed from families of objects that are initially defined by the user [24]. More speculatively, we can even explore how things could be bestowed with resourceful agency and identity themselves, and imagine what could they do in situations of crises, for example when facing ethical questions [58], or changes in their power relations [59]. In all these scenarios, the design would enable people or things to make use of the IoT underlying infrastructure as a configurational technology or platform, and to resourcefully improvise a novel assemblage of artefacts in response to a situation of crisis (i.e., I cannot find my glasses or I am faced with an ethical dilemma).

By understanding how things and people work together, and using IoT as a platform for design, designers concerned with resourcefulness may also expand their temporal framework and begin to design flows rather than fixed functionalities. Once able to observe how things are used over longer periods of time, designers could create systems that can be resourcefully adapted to new situations depending on how they are used and appropriated. Especially in the area of health and ageing, time is crucial, as changes happen at a slow pace. Thus, a system that is has been designed for change, could be able to adapt to new needs as life and circumstances change. For example, in a design for the elderly this could mean that the same system of exchanging newspapers that is used today to communicate messages within the family, could perhaps serve later as a gentle notification system when something is wrong. Additionally, designers could envision new kinds of design processes where things are aware of how they are used and misused, incorporating changes into the next generation of products, or rearranging services accordingly. Or, once objects know they are not used anymore, they could report back to their designers, or even demand to be moved to a new home where they are more needed [57].

CONCLUSIONS

In this paper we have presented a new conceptualisation of resourcefulness that is grounded in theories of practice, and illustrated how this conceptualisation has methodological implications for HCI research and design. Viewing resourcefulness as a dispersed practice that emerges in everyday crises of routine can be argued to reveal new challenges and opportunities that link to a wide range of existing concepts in HCI, as well as design opportunities for digital technologies, in particular IoT.

ACKNOWLEDGEMENTS

We would like to thank the reviewers for their thoughtful criticism, and all the colleagues – in particular the Resourceful Ageing team – that contributed to these ideas through previous projects and collaborations. This research is part of the project 'Resourceful Ageing' funded by STW under the Research through Design program (2015/16734/STW).

REFERENCES

1. Aceros, J.C., J. Pols, and M. Domènech, *Where is grandma? Home telecare, good aging and the domestication of later life.* Technological Forecasting and Social Change, 2014.
2. Alexander, C., *Notes on the Synthesis of Form*. Vol. 5. 1964: Harvard University Press.
3. Bassi, A. and G. Horn, *Internet of Things in 2020: A Roadmap for the Future.* European Commission: Information Society and Media, 2008.
4. Botero, A., K.-H. Kommonen, and S. Marttila. *Expanding design space: Design-in-use activities and strategies.* in *Proceedings of the DRS Conference on Design and Complexity*. 2010.
5. Brandes, U., S. Stich, and M. Wender, *Design by use: the everyday metamorphosis of things*. 2009: Walter de Gruyter.
6. Carroll, J., *Completing design in use: closing the appropriation cycle.* ECIS 2004 Proceedings, 2004: p. 44.
7. Chappells, H. and E. Shove, *Debating the future of comfort: environmental sustainability, energy consumption and the indoor environment.* Building Research & Information, 2005. **33**(1): p. 32-40.
8. Cila, N., et al. *Listening to an Everyday Kettle: How Can the Data Objects Collect Be Useful for Design Research?* in *Proceedings of the Participatory Innovation Conference*. 2015.

9. Comber, R., et al. *BinCam: Designing for engagement with Facebook for behavior change*. in *IFIP Conference on Human-Computer Interaction*. 2013. Springer.
10. Costall, A. and O. Dreier, *Doing things with things: The design and use of everyday objects*. 2006: Ashgate Publishing, Ltd.
11. Davoli, L. and J. Redström. *Materializing infrastructures for participatory hacking*. in *Proceedings of the 2014 conference on Designing interactive systems*. 2014. ACM.
12. Desjardins, A. and R. Wakkary, *Manifestations of everyday design: guiding goals and motivations*, in *Proceedings of the 9th ACM Conference on Creativity & Cognition*. 2013, ACM: Sydney, Australia. p. 253-262.
13. Dourish, P., *What we talk about when we talk about context*. Personal and Ubiquitous Computing, 2003. **8**(1): p. 19-30.
14. Dourish, P. and G. Bell, *Divining a digital future: Mess and mythology in ubiquitous computing*. 2011: Mit Press.
15. Edwards, W.K. and R.E. Grinter. *At home with ubiquitous computing: Seven challenges*. in *International Conference on Ubiquitous Computing*. 2001. Springer.
16. Eglash, R., *Appropriating technology: Vernacular science and social power*. 2004: U of Minnesota Press.
17. Eriksson, M., et al. *Living labs as a multi-contextual R&D methodology*. in *2006 IEEE International Technology Management Conference (ICE)*. 2006. IEEE.
18. Fernaeus, Y., J. Tholander, and M. Jonsson. *Towards a new set of ideals: consequences of the practice turn in tangible interaction*. in *Proceedings of the 2nd international conference on Tangible and embedded interaction*. 2008. ACM.
19. Fischer, G. and E. Giaccardi, *Meta-design: A framework for the future of end-user development*, in *End user development*. 2006, Springer. p. 427-457.
20. Fleck, J., *Learning by trying: the implementation of configurational technology*. Research policy, 1994. **23**(6): p. 637-652.
21. Forchhammer, H.B., A. Costall, and O. Dreier, *The woman who used her walking stick as a telephone: The use of utilities in praxis*. Doing things with things: The design and use of everyday objects, 2006: p. 131-146.
22. Furniss, D., et al., *A resilience markers framework for small teams*. Reliability Engineering & System Safety, 2011. **96**(1): p. 2-10.
23. Furniss, D., et al., *Unintentional non-adherence: can a spoon full of resilience help the medicine go down?* BMJ quality & safety, 2014. **23**(2): p. 95-98.
24. Fusaro, E., *Cues: Let your things take care of you.*, in *Industrial Design*. 2016, Delft University of Technology: Delft, The Netherlands.
25. Gaver, W.W., J. Beaver, and S. Benford. *Ambiguity as a resource for design*. in *Proceedings of the SIGCHI conference on Human factors in computing systems*. 2003. ACM.
26. Giaccardi, E., *Metadesign as an emergent design culture*. Leonardo, 2005. **38**(4): p. 342-349.
27. Giaccardi, E. and G. Fischer, *Creativity and evolution: a metadesign perspective*. Digital Creativity, 2008. **19**(1): p. 19-32.
28. Giaccardi, E., *A day in the life of things: How listening to things can help us innovate*, in *TEDx Delft*. 2015: Delft.
29. Giaccardi, E. and E. Karana. *Foundations of materials experience: An approach for HCI*. in *Proceedings of the 33rd Annual ACM Conference on Human Factors in Computing Systems*. 2015. ACM.
30. Giaccardi, E., et al. *Thing Ethnography: Doing Design Research with Non-Humans*. in *Proceedings of the 2016 ACM Conference on Designing Interactive Systems*. 2016. ACM.
31. GIACCARDI, E., et al., *Things as Co-Ethnographers: Implications of a Thing Perspective for Design and Anthropology*. Design Anthropological Futures, 2016: p. 235.
32. Giaccardi, E., Kuijer, L., Neven, L., *Design for Resourceful Ageing: Intervening in the Ethics of Gerontechnology*, in *Design Research Society 50th Anniversary Conference*, DRS2016, Editor. 2016, DRS: Brighton, UK.
33. Giaccardi, E., Speed, C., Netten, M. , *Things2Things: Reframing IoT as a platform for design*, D. United, Editor. 2016, Delft University of Technology: Delft, Netherlands.
34. Gonzalez, E.W., et al., *Enhancing resourcefulness to improve outcomes in family caregivers and persons with Alzheimer's disease: A pilot randomized trial*. International Journal of Alzheimer's Disease, 2014. **2014**.
35. Haddon, L., *The contribution of domestication research to in-home computing and media consumption*. The Information Society, 2006. **22**(4): p. 195-203.
36. Hyysalo, S., *Representations of use and practice-bound imaginaries in automating the safety of the elderly*. Social Studies of Science, 2006. **36**(4): p. 599-626.
37. Ingram, J., E. Shove, and M. Watson, *Products and Practices: Selected Concepts from Science and Technology Studies and from Social Theories of Consumption and Practice*. Design Issues, 2007. **23**(2): p. 3-16.
38. Jencks, C. and N. Silver, *Adhocism: the case for improvisation*. 2013: Mit Press.
39. Johnston, C. and H. Lorimer, *Sensing the city*. cultural geographies, 2014. **21**(4): p. 673-680.
40. Joyce, K. and M. Loe, *A sociological approach to ageing, technology and health*. Sociology of Health & Illness, 2010. **32**(2): p. 171-180.

41. Jung, H., et al. *Toward a framework for ecologies of artifacts: how are digital artifacts interconnected within a personal life?* in *Proceedings of the 5th Nordic conference on Human-computer interaction: building bridges*. 2008. ACM.
42. Kim, H. and W. Lee, *Everyday design as a design resource.* International Journal of Design, 2014. **8**(1).
43. Koopman, P. and R.R. Hoffman, *Work-arounds, make-work, and kludges.* IEEE Intelligent Systems, 2003. **18**(6): p. 70-75.
44. Kuijer, L., A. De Jong, and D. Van Eijk, *Practices as a Unit of Design: An Exploration of Theoretical Guidelines in a Study on Bathing.* Transactions on Computer-Human Interaction, 2013. **20**(4): p. 22.
45. Kuutti, K. and L.J. Bannon, *The turn to practice in HCI: towards a research agenda*, in *Proceedings of the 32nd annual ACM conference on Human factors in computing systems*. 2014, ACM: Toronto, Ontario, Canada. p. 3543-3552.
46. Loe, M., *Aging our way: Lessons for living from 85 and beyond.* 2011: OUP USA.
47. Maestri, L. and R. Wakkary. *Understanding repair as a creative process of everyday design.* in *Proceedings of the 8th ACM conference on Creativity and cognition*. 2011. ACM.
48. Menichinelli, M., *Business models for fab labs.* openp2pdesign. org, 2011.
49. Mitchell, S., *Objects in flux: the consumer modification of mass-produced goods.* 2011.
50. Nelson, J., S. Buisine, and A. Aoussat. *Design in use: some methodological considerations.* in *CIRP MS'09, 42nd CIRP Conference on Manufacturing Systems*. 2009.
51. Neven, L. *Innoveren voor actieve ouderen: zachte analyses als handreiking voor harde en hardnekkige problemen.* Inaugeral address, 2015. 64.
52. Neven, L., *By any means? Questioning the link between gerontechnological innovation and older people's wish to live at home.* Technological forecasting and social change, 2015. **93**: p. 32-43.
53. Peine, A., I. Rollwagen, and L. Neven, *The rise of the "innosumer"—rethinking older technology users.* Technological Forecasting and Social Change, 2014. **82**: p. 199-214.
54. Pierce, J., et al. *Some consideration on the (in) effectiveness of residential energy feedback systems.* in *Proceedings of the 8th ACM Conference on Designing Interactive Systems*. 2010. Aarhus, Denmark: ACM.
55. Pierce, J. and E. Paulos, *Second-hand interactions: investigating reacquisition and dispossession practices around domestic objects*, in *Proceedings of the 2011 annual conference on Human factors in computing systems*. 2011, ACM: Vancouver, Canada. p. 2385-2394.
56. Pierce, J., et al., *Introduction to the special issue on practice-oriented approaches to sustainable HCI.* ACM Transactions on Computer-Human Interaction (TOCHI), 2013. **20**(4): p. 20.
57. Rebaudengo, S., *The story of Brad the toaster*, in *Addicted Products*. 2012, Vimeo.
58. Rebaudengo, S., et al., *Ethical Things*, in *works*, automato.farm, Editor. 2015.
59. Rebaudengo, S., et al., *Politics of Power*, in *works*, automato.farm, Editor. 2016.
60. Reckwitz, A., *Toward a Theory of Social Practices: A Development in Culturalist Theorizing.* European Journal of Social Theory, 2002. **5**(2): p. 243-263.
61. Redström, J., *RE: Definitions of use.* Design studies, 2008. **29**(4): p. 410-423.
62. Rosenbaum, M., *Self-control under stress: The role of learned resourcefulness.* Advances in behaviour Research and Therapy, 1989. **11**(4): p. 249-258.
63. Rosenbaum, M.E., *Learned resourcefulness: On coping skills, self-control, and adaptive behavior.* 1990: Springer Publishing Co.
64. Schatzki, T., *Social Practices: A Wittgensteinian Aproach to Human Activity and the Social.* 1996, Cambridge: Cambridge University Press.
65. Schatzki, T., *„Introduction: Practice theory" in Theodore R. Schatzki, Karin Knorr Cetina and Eike von Savigny (eds.) The Practice Turn in Contemporary Theory.* 2001, London: Routledge.
66. Scott, K., C. Bakker, and J. Quist, *Designing Change by Living Change.* Design Studies, 2012. **33**(3): p. 279-297.
67. Sengers, P. and B. Gaver. *Staying open to interpretation: engaging multiple meanings in design and evaluation.* in *Proceedings of the 6th conference on Designing Interactive systems*. 2006. ACM.
68. Shove, E., M. Pantzar, and M. Watson, *The Dynamics of Social Practice: Everyday Life and How it Changes*. 2012, London: Sage.
69. Speed, C. and C. Barker, *New Domestic Locations: Reconfiguring the home through the Internet of Things.*, in *Paper presented at 20th International Symposium on Electronic Art*. 2014: Dubai, United Kingdom.
70. Strengers, Y.A.A., *Designing eco-feedback systems for everyday life*, in *Proceedings of the 2011 annual conference on Human factors in computing systems*. 2011, ACM: Vancouver, BC, Canada.
71. Taylor, A.S. and L. Swan. *Artful systems in the home.* in *Proceedings of the SIGCHI conference on Human factors in computing systems*. 2005. ACM.
72. Vermaas, P.E. and W. Houkes, *Use plans and artefact functions: An intentionalist approach to artefacts and their use.* Doing things with things: The design and use of everyday objects, 2006: p. 29-48.
73. Wakkary, R. and L. Maestri, *Aspects of everyday design: Resourcefulness, adaptation, and emergence.* Intl. Journal of Human–Computer Interaction, 2008. **24**(5): p. 478-491.

74. Wakkary, R., et al., *A sustainable design fiction: Green practices.* ACM Transactions on Computer-Human Interaction (TOCHI), 2013. **20**(4): p. 23.
75. Wakkary, R., A. Desjardins, and S. Hauser, *Unselfconscious Interaction: A Conceptual Construct.* Interacting with Computers, 2015: p. iwv018.
76. Warde, A., *Consumption and Theories of Practice.* Journal of Consumer Culture, 2005. **5**(2): p. 131-153.
77. Zimmerman, J., E. Stolterman, and J. Forlizzi, *An Analysis and Critique of Research through Design: towards a formalization of a research approach*, in *Proceedings of the 8th ACM Conference on Designing Interactive Systems (DIS '10)*. 2010, ACM: Aarhus, Denmark. p. 310-319.

Aesthetic, Functional and Conceptual Provocation in Research Through Design

Dimitrios Raptis, Rikke Hagensby Jensen, Jesper Kjeldskov, and Mikael B. Skov
Department of Computer Science / Research Centre for Socio+Interactive Design
Aalborg University, Denmark
{raptis, rjens, jesper, dubois}@cs.aau.dk

ABSTRACT
Recently within HCI, design approaches have appeared, which deviate from traditional ones. Among them critical design introduces deliberate provocations in order to challenge established perceptions and practices. We have engaged ourselves with this design approach out of interest in understanding how to use provocation in research through design. Towards this end, we report on a field study with four families that used an aesthetically, functionally and conceptually provocative future probe. The purpose of the probe was to challenge existing energy consuming practices through provocation and make its users reflect on them. The paper describes how all three provocative aspects were addressed, and our findings demonstrate how they were experienced in the real world, and how they impacted our research through design approach. We conclude by presenting reflections on how to design provocations, and reflections on the impact of provocations for research through design in general.

Author Keywords
Provocation; aesthetic; functional; conceptual; research through design; criticality; critical design; critical-technical practice.

ACM Classification Keywords
H.5.m. Information interfaces and presentation (e.g., HCI): Miscellaneous;

INTRODUCTION
We are currently witnessing a growing interest in research through design where the design itself is the means to explore and understand an area of interest [13, 21, 60]. Some of the previous research through design studies has revolved around designs where usually the purpose is to improve the utility of an artifact or a practice. There are designs though that move away from this example and are characterized as speculative [20], ludic [27], reflective [52], slow [32], counter-functional [48], value-sensitive [23], adversarial [15], as well as critical [18, 19]. These approaches are often called "provocative design approaches" [44], since they share a common goal. Provocative designs aim to challenge existing norms and attitudes, provoke discussion, and provide means for a constructive critique about the design itself, its impact, as well as the broader assumptions that characterize an area of interest. Towards this end, as suggested by [44], *"provocative design refers to design approaches that operate in a design space where asking questions is as important as solving a problem"*. For these reasons we treat provocative designs as an important element of our research work since they allow us to establish a critical-technical practice [2, 16] within the field of HCI; the split identity that we must have as researchers since we are engaged both in crafting designs as well as constructively critiquing them.

Our research in this paper investigates provocation as a means to conduct research through design. Provocation has been investigated before within Interaction Design and in particular within the DIS conference community. There has been substantial research work that relates provocation to critical design and critical theory [5], as well as, proposes ways to analyze critical designs [22]. In relation to research purposes, "provotypes" where proposed as ways to design for the future [7], and provocation was utilized to promote communal sustainability [8]. Following this stream of research our aim with this work is twofold. Firstly, we want to understand how provocation is experienced in the real world at three levels, namely aesthetic, functional and conceptual provocation [5]. Secondly, we want to challenge through provocation an existing everyday practice, the activity of washing clothes and consuming energy, and understand if and how it changes. Both aims contribute to understanding provocation under the frame of research through design. To do this we designed a provocative artifact, called The Box, and we conducted a field study with four families. Our interest stems out of curiosity for understanding provocation, from our previous work with sustainability, and from the fact that many existing solutions have had limited impact [e.g. 10, 14, 56].

DIS 2017, June 10-14, 2017, Edinburgh, United Kingdom
© 2017 ACM. ISBN 978-1-4503-4922-2/17/06...$15.00
DOI: http://dx.doi.org/10.1145/3064663.3064739.

Our paper is structured as follows. First, we discuss related work on provocation within HCI. Then we present in detail how we designed provocations. We continue by introducing our field study and by discussing our findings, which revolve around how provocation was experienced in use, and how it impacted our research through design approach. We conclude with reflections on designing provocations and using provocations for research through design.

PROVOCATION IN HCI

In order to contribute to better understanding the use of provocation for research through design, we got inspired from critical design. Critical design was coined in the work of Dunne [18, 19] and gained significant momentum within the Design Community. Critical design utilizes provocation as it tries *"to challenge the status quo"*, and as Dunne suggests, it is *"a form of social research to integrate critical aesthetic experience with everyday life"* [19]. A more theoretical discussion on what is critical design within Interaction Design has been initiated with the works of [3, 4, 5]. In these works, the authors highlight the importance of provocation, attempt to relate critical design to critical theory, and provide examples of critical designs. For the authors, the link between critical design and critical theory is somehow obvious, as critical theory aims in changing society in order to achieve *"human emancipation from slavery"* and *"create a world which satisfies the needs and powers of human beings"* [34]. At the same time though, and since critical design is a rather new concept for HCI, we observed a response from the Design community arguing that critical design is independent from critical theory, while highlighting that there is a danger that the new term may subsume all the other provocative design approaches, and thus narrow our field's point of view [49].

In this paper we will not attempt to define critical design, since there is an obvious need for more discussions among the communities until we reach an established definition. Our starting point in this paper is something that both sides agree on: critical designs critique the status quo and they challenge it through provocation. We believe there are three interesting questions that need to be addressed in order to understand the relation between provocation and interaction design. The first one is why to even bother to introduce provocation in an interaction design. We believe the reason is somehow simple. When an activity becomes an established practice then the involved artifacts in use, become 'invisible' [58], or taken for granted [42]. Provocation can be used to make them 'visible', thus questioned. The second question is related to how to produce a design that is provocative. Unfortunately, there are no methods and/or guidelines on how to be provocative. For example, in [4, 22] the authors suggest preliminary guidelines and tactics on how to analyze critical designs, but they also call for more research work towards this direction. Nevertheless, there are existing axes where provocation can be anchored. According to Bardzell et al. [5], an interaction design can be aesthetically, functionally and conceptually provocative. Aesthetic provocation is related to the visual look and the materials used for crafting the design. Functional provocation is related to the way it works and conceptual provocation to the idea that it tries to challenge/critique.

Finally, the third interesting question is related to the limits of provocation. How far can provocation go? Here we will attempt to make a rough distinction between two types of provocative designs based on their *purpose*. We propose that if their purpose is to challenge societal values through "provocation in first encounters" [7], then provocation may go to extremes, as it is the case with art. For example, the French artist Gustave Courbet painted in 1866 the 'L'Origine du monde' (The Origin of the World), in order to critique the hypocritical social conventions of his time in relation to the female body. Or the Australian-based performance artist Stelarc, who was a keynote speaker at the CHI 2002 conference, provoked the idea of a permanent human body architecture, by surgically constructing a full-sized ear on his forearm that had the ability to transmit the sounds it heard, and was also a remote listening device for people in distant places [54]. In comparison to art though, not so many critical studies in HCI focused on this way of challenging societal values and considered the broader impact of technology use on humanity, even though there are papers that clearly call for more research to be steered towards this direction [17, 30, 33].

There is though, a second type of provocative designs, whose purpose is to challenge everyday practices and these are the ones typically used for research through design ("provocation in use", [7]). We believe in these cases provocation cannot go to extremes, because the designs are domesticated and therefore need to be inconspicuous, otherwise they will be rejected [7]. For these cases *"a slight strangeness is the key - too weird and they are instantly dismissed, not strange enough and they're absorbed into everyday reality..."* [18]. These provocative designs can be used: a) for research through design with the aim to understand a specific, current practice, or b) for research through design aiming to explore future design possibilities. In the first case, the provocative design acts as a technology probe [35] that has some provocative characteristics. In the second, it acts as a provotype [7, 42, 43]. The difference between a provocative technology probe and a provotype is that the first focuses at the present, while the second focuses on design possibilities for the future [7]. In both cases the designs allow us to conduct research through design, as they force us to think of new ways of looking at the world, and stimulate discourse around a challenging topic [13, 21, 53, 60].

Within Interaction Design a few studies have acted as provocative technology probes and/or provotypes for research through design. For example, in Dawn Chorus [26] the authors designed a smart bird feeder that trained birds to sing users' favorite songs and provoked the idea of human dominance over animals. The Drift Table [27] is an interactive table without a specific set of tasks that challenges using task completion times and rates as a core metric to evaluate a product. In [5] they challenged the role of the male handyman through the design of the Significant Screwdriver, and the fact that spaces are often gendered through the design of the Whispering Wall. Furthermore, the Digital Music Box approached file sharing not from a legal point of view, but as an experience centered design challenge [6]. The Switch! project focused on the production of provotypes for exposing hidden norms and values in relation to sustainability [41], while in [8] the authors utilize provocation in order to bring forth the fact that energy consumption should be addressed at the communal level and not at the individual one. A similar area is also explored by [29] and their deployed Energy Babble. Finally, provocation has also been used in research approaches for studying participants' behaviors. For example, in [51] pedestrians encountered what appeared to be an autonomous car, while in reality a driver was hidden inside a seat costume, in an effort to explore how pedestrians would react to driverless cars in the future.

THE BOX

As we mentioned before our aim in this paper is twofold. To understand how provocation is experienced in the real world (*provocation in use* [7]), and how it may challenge existing practices. For this reason, we designed and implemented a provocative design called The Box, which aims to provoke domestic laundry practices.

We chose laundry in private households as the domain for our study inspired by existing critique within sustainability research. Here users are often seen as the problem, and HCI research in sustainability often does not aim to change users' lifestyles, but tries to improve their sustainable behavior on a small scale. In order to go beyond that, there is a call to study the everyday practices of our users [46, 47], to go beyond persuasion, and to shift from prescription to reflection and from behaviors to practice [10, 38, 56]. Furthermore, current sustainable HCI research often holds the assumption that users act rationally and make intentional decisions. This view about the user is beautifully described by the Resource Man, an archetype who *"in his ultimate imagined state, is interested in his own energy data, understands it, and wants to use it to change the way he uses energy"* [57]. This perception of energy consumers has also been criticized (see [10, 38, 56]) as it has led to limited results [10, 14].

The Box was designed with the purpose to challenge every day washing practices, to make its users reflect upon them, and even change them. It also attempts to go beyond the simple presentation of information and the idea that users are always rational, by combining information with provocative elements. The Box was deployed with a research purpose that lies in between a provocative technology probe and a provotype. The Box was used to understand an existing practice (as a technology probe), but this practice was also challenged by presenting to the users a provocative, future scenario. Therefore, we characterize The Box as a *provocative future probe*. In the following we present how The Box was designed to provoke conceptually, functionally and aesthetically [5].

Facilitating Conceptual Provocation

Conceptual provocation is about an idea/belief/concept that we want to challenge or critique through a design [5].

In relation to conceptual provocation we deliberately chose to focus on two issues: a) the quite dominant and western world belief that electricity is always available and cheap, and b) the idea that there is no need to reveal the energy's production origin to the consumers [8]. The Box categorizes electricity as green and red, and the way information is presented to the users is inspired by previous sustainability research, and in particular eco-feedback systems [25]. The Box forecasts the electricity type for the next 12 hours through a simple scenario. It relates the energy type to the local wind conditions. If there is a lot of wind, then the electricity is mostly produced from windmills and is characterized as green, otherwise as red. The type of electricity is materialized through a color-coded clock. When the electricity is red then The Box cuts off the electricity from the washing machine, and users are expected to "shift" their consumption [similarly to 9, 12, 36, 40, 46]. If, for example, the wind is not blowing, users may experience a clock like the one in Figure 1 (left side), where all the available slots are red. Thus, there is only red electricity for the next 12 hours and therefore they cannot use their washing machine (unless they override - details in the following section). With a bit of wind though, they may experience a clock that looks like Figure 1 (right side), where many slots are green.

Furthermore, conceptual provocation is also facilitated through the implemented price schema. The Box creates a savings account for its users. When they consume green electricity, then it is free and the money they save is added to their savings account. On the other hand, if they consume red electricity, then electricity is very expensive and the money they spent is deducted from their savings account. In Figure 2b we can see a numerical LED screen which materializes users' savings account: 239 Danish Kroner (equivalent to 36USD).

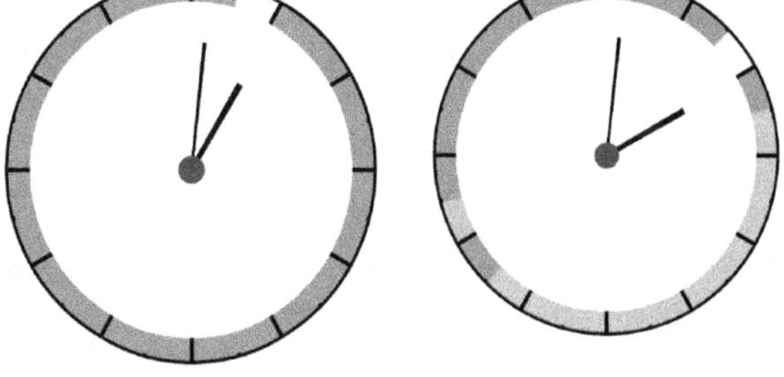

Figure 1. Examples of electricity status for the next 12 hours.

Facilitating Functional Provocation

Functional provocation deals with how far from the norm is the way a design works or operates [5].

Functional provocation was facilitated by imposing a dilemma to the users. According to [44], provocative dilemmas are triggered: a) by embodying symbols, b) by forcing users to make a choice, or c) through behavioral barriers. The Box imposes a forced choice to its users by cutting off the electricity when it is red, and providing only one physical interaction point in order to override this. For this, we adopted the emergency button metaphor that is often used in industrial equipment and the override button was placed on the bottom left corner of the box (Figure 2d). The button was purposefully selected to be red and fairly big in order to provoke a sense of reluctance, as it signals that it is something that should not be pressed accidently or without consideration. Inspired by [44], we believed that hesitation to press the button would make the users to slow down and reflect on their choices. In order to make the functionality even more provocative a second numerical LED screen was used to project how many times the override button was pressed, and thus the rules were violated (Figure 2c, 16 times in the current example).

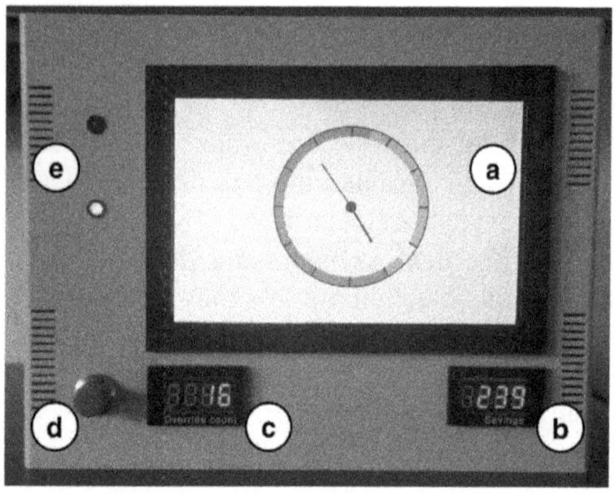

Figure 2. The Box: a) electricity status - 12 hour forecast, b) savings account, c) override button presses, d) override button, and e) electricity status at the moment.

Facilitating Aesthetic Provocation

Aesthetic provocation deals with how far from the mainstream is a design's visual look and the materials used for crafting it [5].

By browsing the sustainable HCI literature, we noticed that the majority of produced solutions are software applications either running on participants' existing mobile devices, e.g. [1, 24, 36, 40], or the mobile devices are provided as part of the study, e.g. [9, 11, 12, 40, 59]. In such studies, it is often stressed that the designs are beautiful, artistic, and conforming to the latest trends of simplicity and elegance. In a few cases, where the researchers did craft the physical form of their product themselves, e.g. [31, 37, 38, 45, 46], the majority or physical designs are also characterized as elegant as well as ambient, since their purpose was to reflect the calmness of the natural environment. Additionally, we investigated how off-the-shelf products look in terms of their physical design. Even though there are commercial products that have an industrial look, the majority of them can also be characterized as elegant and minimalistic (for example The Nest thermostat).

The Box attempts to provoke aesthetically by deviating from the norm in two ways. First, we decided to move away from the mobile application paradigm and design an actual physical probe. Second, we did not want to follow the style trends that we observed in most of related work and commercial products, namely simple, beautiful and minimalistic designs. Instead, we turned for inspiration to the past where such equipment was bulky. Several ideas were considered on how to design The Box. We experimented with different types of physical boxes, from old PC cases to even a military ammunition box. We also experimented with different layouts by attaching paper representations of the core functionality onto the boxes. In the end, we opted for an old, industrial case for electric equipment (Figure 2). Furthermore, in order to highlight the retro style of The Box instead of using nice, modern buttons and high-resolution screens, we visited various hardware stores in order to find components that had a retro look (override button and LED screens).

Creating The Box

The Box was crafted using the selected case (25 x 18 x 8cm) and by making the necessary modifications. A 7in screen was mounted and holes were drilled for the LEDs, the LED screens, and the override button. The black frames surrounding the screens were laser cut.

For the hardware, we used a Raspberry Pi with a GrovePi shield (Figure 3d) to control the override button, the LEDs (Figure 3c) and the numerical LED screens (Figure 3b). Furthermore, an off-the-shelf smart electrical plug (Energenie) was used to wirelessly control the power of the washing machine. In relation to software, we programmed in Python and used a variety of open source libraries to get real-time information about the wind conditions and for creating the interface.

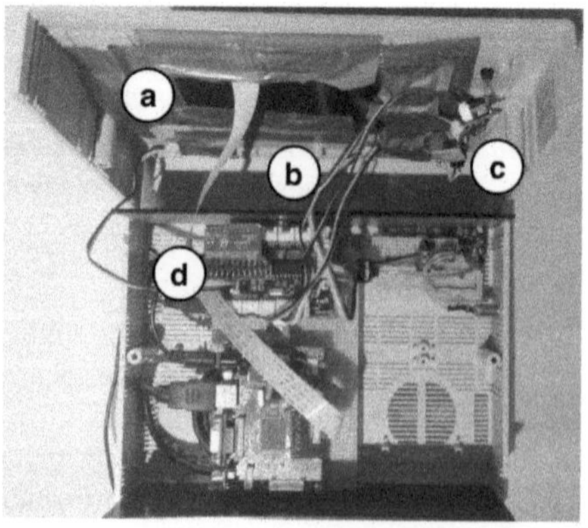

Figure 3. Internal components of The Box: a) 7in screen, b) numerical LED screens, c) LEDs and override button, d) Raspberry Pi and GrovePi shield.

FIELD STUDY

In the following subsections we present details on the results of our pilot study, the participants, the process we followed, and the data we collected in our field study.

Pilot Study

Before deploying The Box in the field, we conducted a pilot study with a five-person family for two weeks. They used their washing machine on average once per day. The primary purpose of the pilot study was to test The Box from an engineering perspective. Several software bugs were identified during those two weeks, which were addressed on the spot. Even though the pilot family used The Box for two weeks, we did not engage in deep discussions with them as the deployment period was often interrupted by software and hardware bugs and our interest was mainly in resolving them. Nevertheless, we gathered a few insights in relation to our design's provocativeness during these repairing sessions from the father. He informed us about its conceptual and functional provocativeness that *"he did not like it in the beginning but it made* him *think"*, and in relation to aesthetics that we *"could have done a better job because our design is very ugly and he wouldn't buy it if it was a real product"*. These findings provided indications to us that our design had indeed some provocativeness.

Participants

Four families participated in our field study. They all lived in Aalborg, Denmark and were recruited by snowballing within our social networks. In Denmark electricity blackouts are extremely rare and electricity prices are inflexible and cheap. Thus, in the context of the study, the perception that electricity is always available and cheap was common to the four families.

The first family was comprised by two adults (49 and 61 years old) and 3 children that were 16, 18 and 20 years old. The father was an electrical engineer, while the mother was a process coordinator at an energy company. They lived in their own relatively large house that extended into two floors. The washing facilities were located in the basement, in a utility room. The father was in charge of washing, drying, ironing and folding the clothes. They had *high* laundry needs since they were five and because they all physically trained almost everyday day. The father did at least one washing load per day, and often several during weekends (on average 10 laundries per week). We can characterize the level of environmental awareness of the first family as *medium*. They were recycling, bought a car with the main criterion of having a low fuel consumption, replaced most of the light bulbs at home with low consumption LEDs, all their new appliances were rated A+++ from a consumption point of view, and they were closely monitoring their water consumption too.

The second family consisted of a carpenter aged 51, a dental surgery assistant aged 46, and one 17-year-old boy. Two other teenagers, aged 14 and 19, were occasionally around. They also had a large dog that produced one load of washing per week. Together they had fairly *high* laundry needs (on average 7 loads per week). The family lived on a privately own rural property, where the washing machine was located in a hallway next to the entrance. The wife usually took care of laundry and she preferred washing in bulks during the weekend. The level of environmental awareness for this family can be characterized as *low*. They were mostly motivated by saving money, and thus they were buying A+++ appliances when replacing old ones, and recently changed all their light bulbs to LEDs.

The third family also consisted of two parents and three children. The father was 59 and the mother 49 years old, while the three kids were 6, 11 and 17 years old. The father worked as a surgeon at the local hospital and the mother was finishing her Master's degree in psychology while working at the same hospital too. They lived in a sizeable rural properly with the washing facilities located at one of the entrances. The father would usually wash his own work shirts and running clothes, while the mother would take care of the rest. Together they accumulated on average 7 loads a week, and they washed almost daily. We characterize the level of environmental awareness of this family as *high*. They mostly cooked with ecological food, recycled, bought energy efficient appliances and they had recently invested in a solar heat panel in an effort to *"support the environmental cause"*.

The fourth family was a young family consisting of only two adults aged 25 and 28. The boyfriend was a software engineer, while the girlfriend worked as a nurse. They had just bought a new semi-detached house, which they had recently moved into. Their washing machine was located in the bathroom. The girlfriend usually did the washing, but the boyfriend would occasionally do a wash if needed. Their laundry needs were *low* as they only washed on average 3 times a week. The level of environmental awareness for this family can be characterized as *low*. Like the second family, the main motivation for buying eco-efficient appliances and getting into the habit of turning the lights off was the prospect of saving money.

A summary of the most relevant demographic characteristics of the four families is presented in the following Table.

Family	Persons	Laundry needs	Environmental awareness	Additional details
1	5	High (~10 per week)	medium	washing machine in the basement
2	3+2	High (~7 per week)	low	washing machine next to the entrance
3	5	High (~7 per week)	high	washing machine next to the entrance
4	2	Low (~3 per week)	low	washing machine in the bathroom

Table 1. Relevant demographic characteristics.

Process

Each of the 4 families used The Box for 4 weeks. In each household The Box was placed on top of their washing machine in order to be closely related to the laundry activity. Eight, in-home, semi-structured interviews were conducted, two with each family, one before and one after the deployment of the probe. In the first interview we mainly focused on their existing laundry practices and their environmental awareness, and we introduced them to the purpose of the study.

Participants were presented with a future scenario that electricity companies are looking for ways to shift people's consumption away from carbon based sources and steer them to consume energy from windmills as much as possible. For this reason, electricity companies consider implementing different price policies (green = free and added to savings, red = double the price per KWh than the normal, and deducted from savings). Families were also instructed to use The Box in any way they thought suitable to their needs, and that their savings account would start at 100 Danish Kroner (equivalent to 15USD). Furthermore, we informed them that electricity is characterized as green or red based on the local wind conditions, but we did not exactly tell them how much wind should be blowing in order electricity to be green. We purposefully left this ambiguity in the scenario inspired by [7, 44], who suggest that some "mystery" should be maintained to allow for multiple interpretations to emerge. The second interview revolved around issues related to the usage of The Box, if and how it affected their washing practices, and their perception about its provocativeness in all three categories.

All data from the 8 interviews (each was on average 1 hour long) were transcribed (using interviewScribe) and the 4 concluding interviews were also coded (using NVivo). In all interviews both adults were present. In the families with children, we chose not to involve them in the interviews as we found out that they were not related to the laundry activity at all. We used the three provocation categories (aesthetic, functional and conceptual) as themes in order to guide the data analysis, which was conducted using a procedure known as 'explication de texte', or close reading, an analytical method that originated in the humanities [50]. Furthermore, all families' interactions with The Box were stored in a log file.

FINDINGS: EXPERIENCING PROVOCATION

Conceptual Provocation

With The Box we tried to challenge the idea of always available and cheap electricity, and that energy is often presented decoupled from its production source. We provoked the first by cutting electricity during the red, non-environmental friendly periods and by implementing a different price scheme, and the second by associating energy with local wind conditions.

In relation to the effect of the attempted conceptual provocation, we had mixed results. Families 1 and 3 informed us that had experienced in the past periods where electricity and water were scarce resources. Thus, they did not feel provoked. For example, the father in the first family informed us that he had *"experienced hot summers where you were not allowed to water your garden because there was a shortage in water"*, or that he remembered they *"were paying cheaper prices per KWh when consuming electricity in off peak hours"*. The other two families informed us that even though they did not enjoy that they couldn't use their washing machine during red periods, they chose to *"try it out"*.

In relation to the effect of conceptual provocation to their laundry practices, all the families eventually accepted the fact that electricity is not always available anymore, and they all perceived doing what they used to do before as "cheating". Three families used the word cheating to describe instances where they had a similar behavior as before the introduction of The Box. What was interesting though were the two reasons that drove them to change their practices. Families one and three, which pressed the button the least amount of times, told us that they hesitated to press the button as they wanted to *"take care of the environment"*, and *"have the feeling that you are actually doing something good"*. For them taking care of the environment was the motivating force. The second reason we identified, was the prospect of saving money. All families mentioned that saving money was an important factor, but for families two and four it was the strongest motivating force. Thus, even though they knew they saved the equal amount of *"two coffees"*, or *"a burger at McDonalds"* it was still enough for them, because *"if we do the same with other appliances we can save a lot"*, and *"it is the same as buying fuel for the car, it doesn't matter how much it is cheaper, just the fact it is cheaper is enough"*.

In relation to our decision to relate local wind conditions to the characterization of electricity and the ambiguity we introduced by not clearly defining the borders between green and red, we had two interesting findings. Since, wind is something that people can experience in the real world, for families one and three the wind conditions became a point of discussion. The father in the first family told us that he found very challenging the fact that he could not do a wash while the flag in their garden was moving: *"you know, we got a flag there and you can see its windy, and you think it should be green and it's not"*. The third family was also challenged by the fact they could see windmill farms from their living room: *"I have the feeling that your weather forecast is wrong or from another city, because a couple of times we could not wash, but we could see the turbines spinning"*. For those two families, provocation seemed to have an effect, as questions were raised in relation to how much wind is necessary in order to achieve 100% green consumption.

The second finding in relation to wind is more technical but it had important consequences for the families. In our implementation we decided to check the wind conditions and update the clock every 30 minutes. This decision resulted to situations where the families observed a green slot, for example 2 hours in advance, and when they went to wash, they found out that The Box had updated, and the slot was now red. We received a lot of critique about this and it was discussed for a long time by two families, even though the maximum reported number of times that this happened from all families was three (family one). Nevertheless, this perceived inability to properly plan became a discussion point for all families. For the example, the father in the first family informed us that he would *"immediately inform"* his wife *"whenever the bloody thing was red"*. They were annoyed by the update mechanism as *"it was impossible to plan"*, and because *"you get offended when it changes"*. Despite that, planning was also characterized by them as a *"mystery"*, *"a quite fun game"* and *"a funny race between* him *and the computer"* as he was *"sort of chasing the green slots"* as they were *"ahead of him"* and he *"constantly tried to pin them down"*. The same issue with planning was also pointed out by the second family, but more mildly as they told us that *"it should stay green"*. The third family somehow bypassed this issue, by characterizing it as a *"mischief"*, while the fourth family completely circumvented it, as they had observed patterns of long green periods between 2 and 6 o'clock in the morning and they tried to do their washing then. To this end, the boyfriend informed us that his girlfriend started getting *"up early very often to put a load on"*.

Functional Provocation

When we asked the families about the functionality of The Box, most reported that they felt a bit provoked but not challenged. The first family informed us that they felt provoked because that it *"governed"* whether they *"could or could not do a wash"*, but in the end they even got *"surprised that it has not been any inconvenience"*. In the end, they characterized The Box as *"practical"*, *"functional"*, and an *"instrument to be informed on what is going on.* The second family characterized The Box as *"smart"* and *"unsmart"* at the same time. Smart because it gave them information that made them *"more conscious"* about their consumption, and unsmart as it did not provide any kind of automation in order to schedule their laundry. The third family characterized The Box as *"rational"*, *"structured"*, and *"simple"*. They decided that they were going to *"be ruled by the box"* and that they would *"only wash in green slots"*. Overall it provided *"food for thought"* and it was characterized as *"a tool to take care the environment"*. Along the same lines, the fourth family characterized The Box as *"informative"* because it provided a *"really quick overview of when to wash"*.

Besides these positives comments, families also felt really provoked by the functionality of the override button and the counting screen, as they proved to be focal reflection points. Families one and three commented that the override button looked like industrial emergency equipment. The father from the first family, who was responsible for the laundry, told us that he didn't want to *"cheat and press the button, unless it was absolutely necessary"*. The Box was perceived as *"a game"*, and pressing the button felt like *"breaking the rules"*. Both parents expressed their strong disappointment that they had to press the button the last day of the deployment period, because they knew that we would pick The Box up at a specific time and thus *"they felt cheated cause he had to override, otherwise he would have worked around that ... he would have waited"*. They both insisted that the last press *"shouldn't count on their score"* (even though there wasn't one). In the second family, the mother told us that when she pressed the button she would *"swear at it, because it was not fun to press it"*, that *"it is bloody annoying when you have to do it"*, and that *"the screen should have stayed at zero"*. The third family informed us that they decided the first day that they would never press the button, and thus canceled from the beginning our imposed dilemma in an extreme way. They did that since the thought of pressing the button *"made* them *stubborn, so* they *just had to make it work"*. They approached the new laundry situation as a *"competition"* where *"the box and not the laundry basket is now in charge"* and they *"wanted to see if it is really feasible to be ruled by the box"*. Finally, in the fourth family they both perceived The Box as a game to beat, and breaking the rules was ok *"because it only happened when it was really necessary"*. Furthermore, the boyfriend informed us that he perceived The Box as rather *"boring"*, because its physical interaction was limited to *"one button to play with"*.

Aesthetic Provocation

We specifically discussed with the families about the physical design of The Box. First, we asked them to use three words to describe it and most characterized it as *"bulky"*, *"retro"*, *"industrial"*, and *"ugly"*. After being engaged in in-depth discussions about it, we have been told that they felt challenged since it is *"obviously not the finest design"*, and since it looks *"like something* we *have created from stuff we had available"*, *"like an old retro arcade game"*, and *"like an amperometer from a physics school class"*. Some also *"hoped the designer did not spend a lot of effort to come up with that"*. When we told the families that it was purposefully designed to look like this, most got surprised. The first family told us that they would prefer *"something smaller, something that looks like an Apple device"*, while the third informed us that *"it is ok as long as it stays in the utility room"*. This distinction between the utility room and other rooms within a home, was often highlighted as they told us that they wouldn't like to place something that *"looks like that next to designer furniture"*, or that *"people in general do not like cables and stuff in their living room and they even hide their internet boxes"*.

In relation to specific design elements, most of the discussions where positive. The two numerical LED screens that materialized *"how many times they cheated"* and their savings, were positively received. The mother in the first family specifically pointed out that The Box was very good at guiding them in saving money and reflecting on how to be more environmentally friendly because *"the screens put the information straight in your face"*. The boyfriend in the fourth family told us that it was good that the LED screen was there *"because if nobody is counting and I pressed the button 5 times, and then "forget" 4 of them –then it would be as bad"*. Interestingly, when we asked the families whether they would have had the same engagement if its design was more modern and all the information was presented on a single screen, or in a mobile application, we got different answers. Three families stated that they would have had the same level of engagement, while the first one told us that it wouldn't have been the same because right now they enjoyed that information was tangible.

In relation to the design of the color-coded clock, which we associated it with red and green energy, we had slight different perceptions about it. The first family told us that the clock was perceived as a traffic light that guided their washing activities, where *"green means Go, red means Forbidden"*. The second family associated the colors to sustainable behaviors and for them *"green means economical and sustainable, and red is wrong"*. The third family distinguished between *"rational"* and *"not rational behavior"*, and green color meant *"throw something in the washing machine now"*, and red *"no go"*. The same "go", "no go" approach was reported by the fourth family too.

FINDINGS: THE EFFECT OF PROVOCATION ON OUR RESEARCH THROUGH DESIGN APPROACH

Through The Box we did research through design. Thus, The Box should not be viewed as a product, but as a research tool that allowed us to have a better understanding of an area of interest, in this case electricity consumption. Since in studies like ours, the most valuable source of information are the participants, we want them to be highly engaged and as reflective as possible. The following subsections present findings in relation to those two issues.

Provocation increased participants' engagement

We view participants' engagement at three levels. The first is related to how much they got engaged with The Box, the second how much they got engaged with us during the interviews, and the third how much they related to our research purpose.

From the log files as well as the discussions with our participants, we understood that they got really engaged with The Box. All the laundry activities that took place in all households were conducted through The Box. Even though the participants knew that they could simply unplug it and go back to what they used to do before, none chose to do so. The Box was up and running throughout the duration of the study, except for a few instances were there have been some internet connectivity issues and it had to be reset. In detail, the first family pressed the override button 3 times, the second 19 times, the third 0 times and the fourth 3 times. They all saved money, according to our scenario, with the first family saving 6.5USD, and the rest 2.7, 3.4, and 3USD respectively. These results show that our probe was an overall success from a sustainable point of view as shifting did occur, even at extreme rates.

Furthermore, very often and with all four families, we experienced instances where we did not fully control the interviews, and the participants were so engaged that they started interviewing each other. Such instances were really useful for us, as they did not only give insights that were limited to the outcomes (e.g., how many times they pressed the button), but revealed to us their thinking behind their choices (e.g., what motivated them not to do a wash).

In relation to the third level of engagement, which is how interested they were to our research work, our findings also show a deep engagement. We experienced a similar situation as reported by Bardzell et al. [5], where our participants started behaving as researchers. Many asked questions about our research purposes and our study setup. When we informed them that we were interested in understanding provocation, we had interesting discussions in relation to its limits, and whether we did some things on purpose in order to provoke more. For example, the father of the first family told us that he *"knew there would be a green section in an hour's time, so I did go down at that time, and it was red again, so I couldn't do anything. So I began to wonder whether you did this on purpose"*. Then he asked us if we purposefully introduced these sudden changes from green to red in order to study extreme usage scenarios of The Box, since *"he would have done that"*. For him, provoking participants by making them experience extreme situations, was an interesting way to identify the limits of both provocation and interaction. Similar discussions occurred for all three provocation aspects. Finally, some of the participants shared their views on issues that went beyond our research interests in this study, such as privacy and security concerns, and existing research in electricity distribution.

Provocation strongly motivated reflection

All four families got deeply engaged with The Box and tried to reflect on their washing practices. These reflections went beyond what we anticipated in the beginning of the study, and occurred by both adults on every family, even though only one of them was responsible for the laundry. They even got diffused to other areas of their life, as most reported that they demonstrated The Box to visitors, and discussed about it with colleagues from work.

Firstly, we observed that the practice of doing the laundry became visible to our participants, it was deconstructed by them, and reflections and changes occurred to their practices on almost every aspect. Our participants reflected on the amount of clothes they washed every time, the temperatures they used to wash their clothes, even on the type of detergents they used, even though The Box was mainly designed for shifting. For example, the fourth family tried to fill up their washing machine with as many clothes as possible *"because when there is a green period we do not always have the time to wash two loads"*, while the father of the first family informed us about the washing temperatures that *"I mean, I suppose, I have been hypocritical about it in the past, because you can wash in 30 now with the detergents we have"*. In relation to shifting, we did also have unexpected results as most did shift their laundry times. In an extreme example, the third family that did not press the override button at all, sent their kids to school with day-old clothes a couple of times, and their teenage son *"was annoyed that we did not wash exactly the clothes he wanted. There have been complaints about it, but he has come to terms with it"*.

Furthermore, another very interesting finding was that our provocative future probe facilitated reflections that went beyond our scenario. For example, the mother in the second family told us that she *"often just caught myself thinking, well it is now green, so now it is a good time to run the dishwasher"*. Thus, our scenario got extended to other appliances, even though they were not part of the study. The families also reported that they started discussing energy consumption and sustainability issues in general. For example, the third family used The Box as an *"example of sustainable behavior"*, and as an *"educational tool"* to inform their children on why it is important to turn the lights off when no one is in a room. Finally, all families discussed and reflected about The Box itself as an artifact. We got suggestions on how to make it less energy consuming, how to combine it with a mobile app that would send *"service messages"*, discussed ways to make the laundry activity *"automated"* and *"remotely controlled"*, and talked about how to embed our functionality into an actual washing machine.

We treat all the above-mentioned instances as strong indications that provocation can facilitate strong reflections about existing practices, which may even lead to long lasting behavioral changes. Of course, at this point we can only speculate about such outcomes from studies like ours, but we would like to highlight that such instances could also be expected from other similar studies in the future.

DISCUSSION

Our discussion section revolves around two types of reflections. Reflections on designing provocations, and on using provocations in research through design.

Reflections on designing provocations

We identified two important issues on designing provocations.

Designing provocations is challenging but achievable

We started our design process by having in mind that our probe should by "slightly strange" [18] and a bit "mysterious" [7] in terms of aesthetic, functional and conceptual provocation. Since there are no specific methods for designing provocations, we understand that other researchers may experience the same difficulties we had during our design process. We will highlight three approaches that we found useful in dealing with this issue. Firstly, we strongly recommend to embrace *design authorship* [49] in order to design provocations. Design authorship highlights that not all designs need to be directly linked to specific requirements and users' needs, but can emerge out of the curiosity and the intuition of a designer. Design authorship should be combined with an iterative design process where the limits of provocation will be understood within the area of interest, and they will be instantiated through conceptual, functional and aesthetical elements. Secondly, we believe that often it is useful to involve users in the design process in order to define the provocation limits. In our study, we did not do that and we believe we might have missed some valuable input on provocation alternatives. Thirdly, we recommend to look for inspiration into existing provocative designs and identify aesthetic, functional and conceptual provocative elements that are successful. In order to do that we believe there is a clear need for "annotated portfolios" [28] within the Interaction Design community that will act as exemplars for future researchers and practitioners. According to Gaver [28], annotated portfolios are collections of designs that can act as an alternative to formalized theory, by explaining in detail the concepts behind a design, and the issues, values and themes which characterize them.

Provocations in use need to be experienced in the real world

As discussed before, we see a difference between "provocation in use" and "provocation in first encounters" [7]. In our study, we wanted to understand how provocation in use impacted everyday laundry practices. For studies with a similar purpose as ours, we believe it is important to have a deployment in the field, where the actual practices are realized. Otherwise, the participants will not easily make their practices visible, and reflect upon them. Also, since ambiguity and provocation go hand in hand [7, 44], we do not believe that we would have had these findings if our study was a laboratory experiment, which may be more suitable for studying provocation in first encounters.

Furthermore, it is also interesting for us that by introducing a probe into the real world, we may actually provoke more ideas/concepts than anticipated. For example, The Box did unintentionally provoke the idea that technology makes our lives more convenient in one of the families, as they had their washing machine located at their basement. The father told us that going up and down just to take a glimpse at the clock was *"annoying"*, but at the same time *"intriguing"*, and *"a good physical exercise"*. This openness in relation to what is provoked goes hand in hand with research through design approaches, as "designers can be *prepared-for-action*, but not *guided-in-action* by detailed prescriptive procedures" [55]. Therefore, we recommend to researchers that study provocations in use, not to be strict in their research plans, but to make them as flexible as possible [5].

Reflections on provocations & research through design

We will relate our reflections on using provocations for research through design, to the proposed model of interaction design research proposed by Zimmerman et al. [60], where researchers may assume three different roles within an interaction design process. The first is that of an engineer where they need to consider which technologies to use to make the design ("the *how* knowledge", [60]). The second role is the anthropologist, where researchers are interested in exploring the field by collecting data ("the *real* knowledge", [60]). Finally, the third role is being a behavioral scientist and integrate theory and models ("the *true* knowledge", [60]).

Designing provocations impacts all three roles. First, it impacts the role of being an engineer, as the decision of which technology to utilize in a design has to be filtered through conceptual, functional and aesthetic provocation. This is the reason, for example, that we did not materialize the savings account of The Box using software on the 7in screen, but we opted for an old-school, numerical LED screen. Second, it impacts the role of the anthropologist. Since provocations make the "invisible", "visible" [58] for a particular practice, as well as, increase the engagement and reflection level of the participants, they allow us to understand more of the "real" knowledge. We believe that this is really important for any research through design study that focuses on everyday practices. Finally, provocations also impact the role of the behavioral scientist, by facilitating unanticipated effects which may feed back to theories and models. For example, if we continue studying the energy consuming practices in private households, we might better model how to achieve behavioral change.

Another issue we will address is the notion of validity for using provocations in research through design. We will address the issue in two ways. The first is its relation to the notion of experimental setup. If someone considers our study as an experiment on provocation, then he might believe that we failed in our experimental setup since not all subjects received the same treatment – they did not perceive the imposed provocations the same way. We believe though that this way of viewing research through design studies is inherently wrong, as their purpose is to understand "what is real" and not on "what is true" like behavioral scientists [60]. Research through design studies and design theory in general, are unfalsifiable as their purpose is not to falsify a theory but to provide alternatives that confirm the theory [28]. Consequently, since The Box is a research tool and not a product, our study was successful since our purpose was not to solve a specific problem, but to understand different "realities" of practice. And these practices were uncovered in rich detail not because we had a rigid experimental setup, but because we did not have one.

The second way of approaching the notion of validity is related to provocation itself. Did we really design a provocative probe? Is there any criterion for evaluating its provocativeness? Again, we treat this discussion as irrelevant for research through design studies for the same reasons mentioned above. At the same time though we recognize that through more studies on provocation, through the creation of annotated portfolios [28], and through better understanding on what constitutes a good provocative design, we will be able to design better provocations. Towards this end, we do not believe we need strict definition on what provocation is, but a better understanding on what it is not.

Finally, we want to briefly touch upon the role that provocations can play for interaction design practitioners. We believe the decision to use provocations for the design of real products should be taken after careful consideration. The reason for believing this is that provocations may not fit well with all-in-one solutions that address the general public, since they may be experienced in vastly different ways. Therefore, they may facilitate negative experiences, when for example users believe that provocations went too far. With this we do not want to argue against embedding provocations into real products, but to simply highlight the challenges that such a decision might facilitate.

CONCLUSIONS

In this paper, we report on our efforts to understand provocation in research through design, through the design and deployment of a provocative future probe.

In short, our findings showed how provocation was experienced by our participants, how it affected their practices, and how it impacted our research through design approach. Overall, even though provocations may be experienced differently by participants, they can help them to better engage with a future scenario, as well as, to reflect and question their existing practices. This high level of engagement that provocations facilitate can be very useful for interaction design researchers in general, as they will allow them to better understand the "realities" they impose to users through their designs. Furthermore, provocations may impact all three roles interaction designers take within a research through design approach (engineer, anthropologist and behavioral scientist) and may guide them to discover more of the "real" knowledge.

In the future, we want to continue researching provocation. We want to study its long-term impact on domestic practices and do more research on how to define its limits. In relation to sustainability, we plan to extend this study and go beyond the individual, by studying provocation at the community level, and by researching its effect on resource consuming practices in general.

ACKNOWLEDGMENTS

We would like to thank the four families that participated to our study. This work is part of DiCyPS project (864703), funded by Innovation Fund Denmark.

REFERENCES

1. Alper T. Alan, Mike Shann, Enrico Costanza, Sarvapali D. Ramchurn, and Sven Seuken. 2016. It is Too Hot: An In-Situ Study of Three Designs for Heating. In *Proceedings of the 2016 CHI Conference on Human Factors in Computing Systems* (CHI '16), 5262–5273. http://doi.org/10.1145/2858036.2858222
2. Philip E. Agre. 1997. Towards a Critical Technical Practice. In *Bridging the Great Divide: Social Science, Technical Systems and Cooperative Work*, Geof Bowker, Les Gasser, Leigh Star and Bill Turner (eds.). Erlbaum.
3. Jeffrey Bardzell and Shaowen Bardzell. 2013. What is "critical" about critical design?. In *Proceedings of the SIGCHI Conference on Human Factors in Computing Systems* (CHI '13), 3297-3306. http://dx.doi.org/10.1145/2470654.2466451
4. Jeffrey Bardzell, Shaowen Bardzell, and Erik Stolterman. 2014. Reading critical designs: supporting reasoned interpretations of critical design. In *Proceedings of the SIGCHI Conference on Human Factors in Computing Systems (CHI '14)*, 1951-1960. http://dx.doi.org/10.1145/2556288.2557137
5. Shaowen Bardzell, Jeffrey Bardzell, Jodi Forlizzi, John Zimmerman, and John Antanitis. 2012. Critical design and critical theory: the challenge of designing for provocation. In *Proceedings of the Designing Interactive Systems Conference* (DIS '12), 288-297. http://doi.acm.org/10.1145/2317956.2318001
6. Mark A. Blythe. 2007. The digital music box: using cultural and critical theory to inform design. In *CHI '07 Extended Abstracts on Human Factors in Computing Systems* (CHI EA '07), 2297-2302. http://dx.doi.org/10.1145/1240866.1240997
7. Laurens Boer and Jared Donovan. 2012. Provotypes for participatory innovation. In *Proceedings of the Designing Interactive Systems Conference* (DIS '12), 388-397. http://dx.doi.org/10.1145/2317956.2318014.
8. Andy Boucher, David Cameron, and Nadine Jarvis. 2012. Power to the people: dynamic energy management through communal cooperation. In *Proceedings of the Designing Interactive Systems Conference* (DIS '12), 612-620. http://doi.acm.org/10.1145/2317956.2318048
9. Jacky Bourgeois, Janet van der Linden, Gerd Kortuem, Blaine A. Price, and Christopher Rimmer. 2014. Conversations with my washing machine: an in-the-wild study of demand shifting with self-generated energy. In *Proceedings of the 2014 ACM International Joint Conference on Pervasive and Ubiquitous Computing* (UbiComp '14), 459-470. http://dx.doi.org/10.1145/2632048.2632106
10. Hronn Brynjarsdottir, Maria Håkansson, James Pierce, Eric Baumer, Carl DiSalvo, and Phoebe Sengers. 2012. Sustainably unpersuaded: how persuasion narrows our vision of sustainability. In *Proceedings of the SIGCHI Conference on Human Factors in Computing Systems* (CHI '12), 947-956. http://dx.doi.org/10.1145/2207676.2208539
11. Enrico Costanza, Sarvapali D. Ramchurn, and Nicholas R. Jennings. 2012. Understanding Domestic Energy Consumption Through Interactive Visualisation: A Field Study. In *Proceedings of the 2012 ACM Conference on Ubiquitous Computing* (UbiComp '12), 216–225. http://doi.org/10.1145/2370216.2370251
12. Enrico Costanza, Joel E. Fischer, James A. Colley, Tom Rodden, Sarvapali D. Ramchurn, and Nicholas R. Jennings. 2014. Doing the laundry with agents: a field trial of a future smart energy system in the home. In *Proceedings of the SIGCHI Conference on Human Factors in Computing Systems* (CHI '14), 813-822. http://dx.doi.org/10.1145/2556288.2557167
13. Peter Dalsgaard. 2010. Research In and Through Design – An Interaction Design Approach. In *Proceedings of the 22nd Conference of the Computer-Human Interaction Special Interest Group of Australia on Computer-Human Interaction* (OzCHI '10), 200-203. http://dx.doi.org/10.1145/1952222.1952265
14. Carl DiSalvo, Phoebe Sengers, and Hrönn Brynjarsdóttir. 2010. Mapping the landscape of sustainable HCI. In *Proceedings of the SIGCHI Conference on Human Factors in Computing Systems* (CHI '10), 1975-1984. http://dx.doi.org/10.1145/1753326.1753625
15. Carl DiSalvo. 2012. *Adversarial Design.* MIT Press.
16. Paul Dourish, Janet Finlay, Phoebe Sengers, and Peter Wright. 2004. Reflective HCI: towards a critical technical practice. In *CHI '04 Extended Abstracts on Human Factors in Computing Systems* (CHI EA '04). 1727-1728. http://dx.doi.org/10.1145/985921.986203
17. Paul Dourish. 2010. HCI and environmental sustainability: the politics of design and the design of politics. In *Proceedings of the 8th ACM Conference on Designing Interactive Systems* (DIS '10), 1-10. http://dx.doi.org/10.1145/1858171.1858173
18. Anthony Dunne, and Fiona Raby. 2002. *Design Noir: The Secret Life of Electronic Objects.* Birkhauser.
19. Anthony Dunne. 2006. *Hertzian Tales: Electronic Products, Aesthetic Experience, and Critical Design.* MIT Press.
20. Anthony Dunne, and Fiona Raby. 2013. *Speculative Everything: Design, Fiction and Social Dreaming.* MIT Press.
21. Daniel Fallman. 2003. Design-oriented human-computer interaction. In *Proceedings of the SIGCHI Conference on Human Factors in Computing Systems*

(CHI '03). 225-232. http://dx.doi.org/10.1145/642611.642652

22. Gabriele Ferri, Jeffrey Bardzell, Shaowen Bardzell, and Stephanie Louraine. 2014. Analyzing critical designs: categories, distinctions, and canons of exemplars. In *Proceedings of the 2014 conference on Designing interactive systems* (DIS '14), 355-364. http://dx.doi.org/10.1145/2598510.2598588
23. Batya Friedman, Peter H. Kahn, and Alan Borning. 2008. Value Sensitive Design and Information Systems. In *The Handbook of Information and Computer Ethics*, K.E. Himma and H.T. Tavani (eds.). John Wiley & Sons. http://dx.doi.org/10.1002/9780470281819.ch4
24. Jon Froehlich, Tawanna Dillahunt, Predrag Klasnja, et al. 2009. UbiGreen: Investigating a Mobile Tool for Tracking and Supporting Green Transportation Habits. In *Proceedings of the SIGCHI Conference on Human Factors in Computing Systems* (CHI '09), 1043–1052. http://doi.org/10.1145/1518701.1518861
25. Jon Froehlich, Leah Findlater, Marilyn Ostergren, et al. 2012. The Design and Evaluation of Prototype Eco-feedback Displays for Fixture-level Water Usage Data. In *Proceedings of the SIGCHI Conference on Human Factors in Computing Systems* (CHI '12), 2367–2376. http://doi.org/10.1145/2207676.2208397
26. William W. Gaver and Heather Martin. 2000. Alternatives: exploring information appliances through conceptual design proposals. In *Proceedings of the SIGCHI conference on Human Factors in Computing Systems* (CHI '00), 209-216. http://dx.doi.org/10.1145/332040.332433
27. William W. Gaver, John Bowers, Andrew Boucher, Hans Gellerson, Sarah Pennington, Albrecht Schmidt, Anthony Steed, Nicholas Villars, and Brendan Walker. 2004. The drift table: designing for ludic engagement. In *CHI '04 Extended Abstracts on Human Factors in Computing Systems* (CHI EA '04), 885-900. http://dx.doi.org/10.1145/985921.985947
28. William Gaver. 2012. What should we expect from research through design?. In *Proceedings of the SIGCHI Conference on Human Factors in Computing Systems* (CHI '12), 937-946. http://dx.doi.org/10.1145/2207676.2208538
29. William Gaver, Mike Michael, Tobie Kerridge, Alex Wilkie, Andy Boucher, Liliana Ovalle, and Matthew Plummer-Fernandez. 2015. Energy Babble: Mixing Environmentally-Oriented Internet Content to Engage Community Groups. In *Proceedings of the 33rd Annual ACM Conference on Human Factors in Computing Systems* (CHI '15), 1115-1124. http://dx.doi.org/10.1145/2702123.2702546
30. Jan Gulliksen. 2014. Human computer interaction and societal impact: can HCI influence public policy making IT politics? In *Proceedings of the 13th Brazilian Symposium on Human Factors in Computing Systems* (IHC '14), 1-4.
31. Anton Gustafsson and Magnus Gyllenswärd. 2005. The Power-aware Cord: Energy Awareness Through Ambient Information Display. In *CHI '05 Extended Abstracts on Human Factors in Computing Systems* (CHI EA '05), 1423–1426. http://doi.org/10.1145/1056808.1056932
32. Lars Hallnäs, and Johan Redström. 2001. Slow Technology – Designing for Reflection. *Personal Ubiquitous Computing*, 5, 3: 201-212. http://dx.doi.org/10.1007/PL00000019
33. Harry Hochheiser and Jonathan Lazar. 2007. HCI and Societal Issues: A Framework for Engagement. *International Journal of Human–Computer Interaction*, 23, 3: 339-374. http://dx.doi.org/10.1080/10447310701702717
34. Max Horkheimer. 1972. *Critical Theory*. Seabury Press.
35. Hilary Hutchinson, Wendy Mackay, Bo Westerlund, Benjamin B. Bederson, Allison Druin, Catherine Plaisant, Michel Beaudouin-Lafon, Stéphane Conversy, Helen Evans, Heiko Hansen, Nicolas Roussel, and Björn Eiderbäck. 2003. Technology probes: inspiring design for and with families. In *Proceedings of the SIGCHI Conference on Human Factors in Computing Systems* (CHI '03), 17-24. http://dx.doi.org/10.1145/642611.642616
36. Rikke H. Jensen, Jesper Kjeldsov, and Mikael B. Skov. 2016. HeatDial: Beyond User Scheduling in Eco-Interaction. In *Proceedings of the 9th Nordic Conference on Human-computer Interaction: Game-Changing Design* (NordiCHI '16), Article No. 74. https://doi.org/10.1145/2971485.2971525
37. Li Jönsson, Loove Broms, and Cecilia Katzeff. 2010. Watt-Lite: Energy Statistics Made Tangible. In *Proceedings of the 8th ACM Conference on Designing Interactive Systems* (DIS '10), 240–243. http://doi.org/10.1145/1858171.1858214
38. Cecilia Katzeff, Loove Broms, Li Jönsson, Ulrika Westholm, and Minna Räsänen. 2013. Exploring Sustainable Practices in Workplace Settings through Visualizing Electricity Consumption. *ACM Trans. Comput.-Hum. Interact.* 20, 5: Article 31. http://dx.doi.org/10.1145/2501526
39. Jesper Kjeldskov, Mikael B. Skov, Jeni Paay, and Rahuvaran Pathmanathan. 2012. Using mobile phones to support sustainability: a field study of residential electricity consumption. In *Proceedings of the SIGCHI Conference on Human Factors in Computing Systems* (CHI '12), 2347-2356. http://dx.doi.org/10.1145/2207676.2208395

40. Jesper Kjeldskov, Mikael B. Skov, Jeni Paay, Dennis Lund, Tue Madsen, and Michael Nielsen. 2015. Eco-Forecasting for Domestic Electricity Use. In *Proceedings of the 33rd Annual ACM Conference on Human Factors in Computing Systems* (CHI '15), 1985-1988. http://dx.doi.org/10.1145/2702123.2702318

41. Ramia Mazé and Johan Redström. 2008. Switch! Energy Ecologies in Everyday Life. *International Journal of Design*, 2, 3: 55-70.

42. Preben Mogensen. 1991. Towards a provotyping approach in systems development. *Scandinavian Journal of Information Systems*, 3: 31-53.

43. Preben Mogensen. 1994. Challenging Practice – An Approach to Cooperative Analysis. PhD Dissertation, Computer Science Department, Aarhus University.

44. Deger Ozkaramanli and Peter M.A. Desmet. 2016. Provocative design for unprovocative designers: Strategies for triggering personal dilemmas. In *Proceedings of Design Research Society 50th Anniversary Conference* (DRS 2016), 1-16. http://www.drs2016.org/s/165-Ozkaramanli.pdf

45. James Pierce and Eric Paulos. 2010. Materializing Energy. In *Proceedings of the 8th ACM Conference on Designing Interactive Systems* (DIS '10), 113–122. http://doi.org/10.1145/1858171.1858193

46. James Pierce and Eric Paulos. 2012. The Local Energy Indicator: Designing for Wind and Solar Energy Systems in the Home. In *Proceedings of the Designing Interactive Systems Conference* (DIS '12), 631–634. http://doi.org/10.1145/2317956.2318050

47. James Pierce, Yolande Strengers, Phoebe Sengers, and Susanne Bødker. 2013. Introduction to the special issue on practice-oriented approaches to sustainable HCI. *ACM Trans. Comput.-Hum. Interact.* 20, 4: Article 20. http://dx.doi.org/10.1145/2494260

48. James Pierce and Eric Paulos. 2014. Counterfunctional things: exploring possibilities in designing digital limitations. In *Proceedings of the 2014 conference on Designing interactive systems* (DIS '14), 375-384. http://dx.doi.org/10.1145/2598510.2598522

49. James Pierce, Phoebe Sengers, Tad Hirsch, Tom Jenkins, William Gaver, and Carl DiSalvo. 2015. Expanding and Refining Design and Criticality in HCI. In *Proceedings of the 33rd Annual ACM Conference on Human Factors in Computing Systems* (CHI '15), 2083-2092. http://dx.doi.org/10.1145/2702123.2702438

50. Ivor Armstrong Richards. 1930. *Practical Criticism. A study of Literary Judgment*. Myers Press.

51. Dirk Rothenbücher, Jamy Li, David Sirkin, Brian Mok, and Wendy Ju. 2016. Ghost driver: A field study investigating the interaction between pedestrians and driverless vehicles. In *25th IEEE International Symposium on Robot and Human Interactive Communication* (RO-MAN 2016), 795-802. https://doi.org/10.1109/ROMAN.2016.7745210

52. Phoebe Sengers, Kirsten Boehner, Shay David, and Joseph 'Jofish' Kaye. 2005. Reflective design. In *Proceedings of the 4th decennial conference on Critical computing: between sense and sensibility* (CC '05), 49-58. http://dx.doi.org/10.1145/1094562.1094569

53. Phoebe Sengers and Bill Gaver. 2006. Staying open to interpretation: engaging multiple meanings in design and evaluation. In *Proceedings of the 6th conference on Designing Interactive systems* (DIS '06), 99-108. http://dx.doi.org/10.1145/1142405.1142422

54. Stelarc. Ear on Arm. Retrieved January 10, 2017 from http://stelarc.org/?catID=20242

55. Stolterman, E. 2008. The nature of design practice and implications for interaction design research. *International Journal of Design*. 2:1, 55-65.

56. Yolande A.A. Strengers. 2011. Designing eco-feedback systems for everyday life. In *Proceedings of the SIGCHI Conference on Human Factors in Computing Systems* (CHI '11), 2135-2144. http://dx.doi.org/10.1145/1978942.1979252

57. Yolande A.A. Strengers. 2014. Smart energy in everyday life: are you designing for resource man?. *Interactions*, 21, 4: 24-31. http://doi.acm.org/10.1145/2621931

58. Terry Winograd and Fernando Flores. 1986. *Understanding Computers and Cognition – A New Foundation for Design*. Ablex Publishing Corp.

59. Ray Yun, Azizan Aziz, Peter Scupelli, Bertrand Lasternas, Chenlu Zhang, and Vivian Loftness. 2015. Beyond Eco-Feedback: Adding Online Manual and Automated Controls to Promote Workplace Sustainability. In *Proceedings of the 33rd Annual ACM Conference on Human Factors in Computing Systems* (CHI '15), 1989–1992. http://doi.org/10.1145/2702123.2702268

60. John Zimmerman, Jodi Forlizzi, and Shelley Evenson. 2007. Research through design as a method for interaction design research in HCI. In *Proceedings of the SIGCHI Conference on Human Factors in Computing Systems* (CHI '07), 493-502. http://dx.doi.org/10.1145/1240624.1240704

Involving Autistics in User Experience Studies: A Critical Review

Doğa Çorlu[1], Şeyma Taşel[2], Semra Gülce Turan[3], Athanasios Gatos[2], Asım Evren Yantaç[1]

[1] KUAR, Koç University
Istanbul, Turkey
{dcorlu14, eyantac}@ku.edu.tr

[2] Koç University
Istanbul, Turkey
{stasel13, agatos15}@ku.edu.tr

[3] TU München
Munich, Germany
gulce.turan@tum.de

ABSTRACT

Autism spectrum disorder (ASD) is a neurodevelopmental disorder characterized by various sensory perceptual and cognitive issues that lead to far-reaching challenges in autistics' social and daily lives. Research in HCI is inclined to take an important role in providing support to autistic individuals. However, due to the sensitivity of this user population and the HCI research community's lack of experience in working with neurodiverse users, researchers struggle while conducting and reporting on user studies with autistics. Aiming at analyzing autistics' involvement in design processes and the struggles encountered, here we present a critical review of user experience studies with autistic users conducted between 2010 and 2016. Using qualitative and quantitative approaches together, we revealed common practices and major problems. We provide a two-fold contribution to the HCI field: A guideline for conducting studies with users with autism as well as suggestions on how to report these studies.

Author Keywords

Autism, neurodiversity; human factors; interaction design, user experience; design process; review.

ACM Classification Keywords

H.5.m. Information interfaces and presentation: Miscellaneous.

INTRODUCTION

Autism spectrum disorder (ASD) is a broad range of neurodevelopmental conditions that affect humans' sensory-perceptual and cognitive systems to varying degrees and throughout their lives. ASD is portrayed through problems in socializing, communication, sensory-perception as well as repetitive and restricted behavior patterns [2]. Although not much can be explained on the disorder's complete causation mechanism, an interaction of genetic, biological, developmental and environmental factors is thought to be the main reason [18]. The recent estimation of global ASD prevalence is 62/10000 [18] with a remarkable increase over the years.

DIS 2017, June 10-14, 2017, Edinburgh, United Kingdom
© 2017 Association for Computing Machinery.
ACM ISBN 978-1-4503-4922-2/17/06···$15.00
http://dx.doi.org/10.1145/3064663.3064771

With the increase in autism prevalence and the recognition of technology's benefits in autism intervention, involving this population in design processes has become a crucial part of developing products, systems and frameworks for autistics. However, involving this user group in design processes has emerged as a challenging issue mainly due to (1) socially demanding nature of design activities where autistics may struggle to interact with the researchers [24], (2) researchers' lack of experience in working with neurodiverse (ND) users, (3) lack of collaboration opportunities with autism schools or centers and (4) a general unwillingness among potential study participants within the population (including their caregivers) in taking part in such studies.

In HCI field, recent aim is to create models for including ND users and their contributions in design processes [9, 38]. Yet these studies mostly focus on the ND children or specific technologies. Contrarily, psychology studies involve ND population from varying ages, yet a considerably little amount report design practices. Besides, transferring the experiences in study conducting from one field to another may not always be suitable due to differing natures of the two fields.

We believe that bridging this methodological gap between HCI and psychology would be beneficial not only for the sake of better research conducting and documentation, but also for the target population's content both during their active involvement in and after the research. Deriving from this motivation, in this paper we present a critical review of user experience (UX) studies conducted with autistic users from any age group within the last 7 years. The primary focus of our research lies on the following questions:

- Why and when do researchers encounter problems during UX studies with autistics?
- How can researchers avoid these problems prior to conducting and/or during these studies?

To answer these questions, we extracted the following information from the publications we reviewed:

- How and when the autistics are involved in UX studies,
- What kind of problems researchers encounter while conducting UX studies with autistics,
- How the actors such as parents, teachers and caregivers are involved in these studies,
- How study participants interact with the prototyped, developed and/or tested products, and
- The existing guidelines and suggestions for involving autistics in design processes.

Before discussing our insights regarding each research question, we first summarize the current stand of leading research that focus on HCI studies involving autistic users.

BACKGROUND: NEURODIVERSITY AND HCI

Neurodiversity is a movement advocating different cognitive and perceptual capacities than what is normative, in other words, neurotypical. When the term was first coined in 1999 [51], the initial idea was to advocate autistic people's rights. Through the support of populations with other neurological conditions such as ADHD (Attention Deficit Hyperactivity Disorder) [17], Dyslexia and Tourette's Syndrome, the movement has become much diverse in the last two decades.

Recently, academics seek to create neurodiversity awareness in HCI both in terms of recruiting ND users in their studies and collaborating with ND researchers and practitioners in the field [17]. Several frameworks have been developed to engage ND individuals in participatory design (PD) through bringing out their creative potential by focusing on their strengths and supporting their difficulties.

Benton et al. [9] propose a guiding framework, named Diversity for Design (D4D), to adapt PD for ND children by taking their strengths and difficulties into account. They utilize previous structured teaching programs for autistic children and highlight the importance of adding minor situational modifications to the environment in order to meet each ND participant's individual needs for a better participation. They further suggest that both 'structuring the environment' and 'providing supports' should be realized after understanding the characteristics of the specific ND culture and tailoring both the environment and the support measures considering each participant's personality, abilities, interests, strengths and difficulties.

Makhaeva et al. [38] propose the concept of "Handlungsspielraum" and argue that creative spaces for PD sessions should be constructed within "structures" and "freedoms". They suggest that maintaining a balance between "structures" and "creative freedoms" will bring out the creative capacity of the participant. The term structures entails social, physical, mental and methodological structures in which participants feel comfortable and are able to participate. Creative freedoms accompany these structures through providing different kinds of possibilities that would encourage participants to contribute their ideas during the PD process.

These PD frameworks are useful, guiding and enlightening in terms of engaging ND participants in design processes and expanding their contribution limits. Yet we believe that there is also a need for better UX conduct with this population due to the variety in contexts, materials, techniques and roles in UX studies.

Apart from the PD frameworks, we identified four research works that deliver a review of studies conducted with ND participants (including autistics). All four research works center around designing for and with ND individuals. Benton and Johnson [7] attribute following process elements to a design process and expect to contribute within the sphere of these elements: technology, ND individuals, other actors (e.g. parents, caregivers, teachers), outcomes and reporting. The researchers analyze the roles and responsibilities ND children take over and assess the impact of these on the process outcomes along two dimensions: first, upon the designed product and/or system; second, on the children themselves – in other words, the intended users of the designed product and/or system.

Grynszpan et al. [26] focus on a single element in design process: technology. They measure the efficacy of chosen technologies and perform a meta-analysis among studies that entail computerized systems that allow for an active interaction with its users. The researchers excluded non-interactive systems such as video modeling from their analysis and provide recommendations on "developing technology-based applications for interventions with various goals for those with ASD".

Similar to Grynszpan et al. [26], Fletcher-Watson [22] focuses on technology and design process and defines her research objective around identifying best practices for the design, implementation and evaluation of computer-assisted learning systems (CAL) through evidence for CAL systems' value in autism education. It is important to note that CAL systems do not necessarily exclude training measures that enhance the life and/or social skills of individuals. Fletcher-Watson [22] draws attention to this aspect and excludes non-computerized systems (such as video modeling) like Grynszpan et al. [26]. In addition to video modeling, Fletcher-Watson [22] excludes systems including robotics in her review, arguing that users do not interact "in the traditional sense" with robots in robotics studies as the research field is "still in its infancy".

Börjesson et al. [12] let us zoom out and view the whole design process at a distance by giving an overview of research works that include recommendations for involving 'developmentally diverse' children during design.

To our knowledge, there is a lack of research that reviews empirical studies made exclusively with autistic participants. Besides, most work focusing on reviewing existing research conducted with ND study participants and formulating best practices based on them strive to cover a wide range of ND participants and refrain from focusing on autistics. With our research, we hope to contribute to the HCI research community's and our own understanding of conducting research for and with autistics by considering and carefully reviewing research conducted with autistic individuals. It is important to note that we are not excluding any studies made with any specific technologies and/or age groups from our review.

METHOD

The aim of this study is to reveal how autistic users from any age group, are involved in UX studies focusing on developing HCI solutions for this specific user population. We mainly focus on the methodological approaches and practices for conducting studies with autistic users and explore the nature of these studies. Following an iterative critical analysis approach comprised of 4 steps, we analyzed published studies from a wide range of disciplines. The first three steps were about data collection (searching the databases and elimination of papers) and the last step was for the data analysis using the selected papers.

Step 1: Retrieving Publications

Databases and Search Query: Publications from ACM Digital Library, IEEE and ScienceDirect (SD) were retrieved based on the search query illustrated in Table 1. Due to slight differences in search skills of the given databases, the following search procedure was applied respectively: 1) Combinations of the primary and secondary terms (See Table 1) were searched using the search engines, and 2) tertiary terms were scanned manually among the retrieved results of (1). In IEEE and ACM, the primary and secondary terms were searched in metadata (title, abstract, keywords). However, such a restriction was not provided by SD, so the primary and secondary terms were searched in whole text. The tertiary terms were searched only in titles in all databases (Table 1).

Timeframe: The HCI studies involving autistic users have prominently started increasing after 2010 (e.g. in Börjesson and colleagues' literature review of studies between 2003 to 2014 [12], 42 out of 55 papers including autistic users were published after 2010). So, the search was limited to seven years (from January 1st 2010 until October 31st 2016).

Primary term Searched in metadata (IEEE, ACM) or in whole text (SD)	*autism*
Secondary terms Searched in metadata (IEEE, ACM) or in whole text (SD)	*design, usability, UX*
Tertiary terms Manually searched in title (IEEE, ACM, SD)	*evaluation, participatory, presence, 3D, collaborative, virtual reality, augmented reality, mixed reality, develop, video, game, tool, app, iPad, case-study, application, system, user, interface, robot, interactive, device, mobile, technology, design, wearable, device, tablet*

Table 1. Search query using AND between rows, and OR between terms in each row.

Results: The search resulted in 606 publications (Table 2; ACM=238, IEEE=177, SD=191). All papers were imported in PDF format into a local drive accessible to all the authors for further elimination.

Step 2: Appropriate Papers

In this step, the papers that were not appropriate for the review were eliminated by one of the authors based on the exclusion criteria below:

- Papers written in another language than English
- Review papers, dissertations, thesis, demos and workshop calls
- Papers not including any studies with autistic users
- Papers not published even though they were already in press during the retrieval.
- Papers describing the same study including the same group of users or papers from the same project (paper and study duplications)

Result: The first elimination resulted in 258 papers (Table 2; ACM=182, IEEE=53, SD=23).

Step 3: Thorough Elimination

To ensure an unbiased selection, the remaining papers were scrutinized by two of the authors together based on the exclusion criteria below:

- Papers not describing the studies in enough detail and/or impossible to extract data regarding our study
- Papers not having explicit HCI implications for further studies, specifically in their discussion or conclusion sections
- Papers not focusing on the design of technologies and/or participatory methods for autistic users (e.g. medical studies).
- Papers not focusing on the autistic users primarily (e.g interface design for special need education teachers)

Result: The last elimination by two authors resulted in a final list of 98 papers (Table 2; ACM=62, IEEE=25, SD=11) to be included in the study we present here. The 98 publications selected for this analysis are listed in a document on: http://bit.ly/2obfRPK

Step 4: Analyzing the Papers

Quantitative and qualitative data were extracted from the papers and gathered in a database. The qualitative analysis of each substudy included the following information: (1) users (diagnosis, age and recruitment method) and (2) actors involved, (3) the roles they took, (4) the design phases in which a substudy took place, (5) substudy types, and (6) data collection techniques used, (7) where and (8) how long a substudy took place. We extracted the main intervention point of the studies and type of the product being designed as well. We will briefly mention the former in our analysis in the next section, however we leave the latter for our future studies. Qualitative data such as problems encountered and suggestions for further studies were analyzed using grounded theory methodology where the authors discussed emergent topics throughout the analysis.

Note that we separately extracted studies and substudies (the methods/techniques used within a study such as interview, think aloud etc.) from the papers to be able to see which substudies were used together in different studies. This process resulted in 153 studies and 253 substudies reported in 98 papers. In the following sections, we present statistical data based on the total number of substudies, not the papers.

User types and actors: To examine the involvement of the autistic users in the studies, we first specified the types of user groups and actors. We specified three different types of user groups: **ASD**, **TD** (typically developed) and **non-ASD** (conditions and disabilities other than ASD, e.g. ADHD, dyslexia and intellectual disability). A user group indicate the *primary users of a product* (any kind of design outcome, e.g. interface, PD framework) *or a control group* to compare the outcomes of a product primarily designed for the autistic users. Actors on the other hand, are the people surrounding the users such as their parents, teachers or the people who are involved in the process of product's design for autistics such as designers. Although in some cases actors are also the primary users of a given product, they are still defined as actors due to their *daily roles in autistics' lives.* We categorized the actors under two groups: **caregivers** (teachers, parents, psychologists, therapists, and other experts and workers in education and therapy of autistics) and **design experts** (product designers, interaction designers, experts from different areas of HCI). We keep the researchers in the studies as separate entities.

Age range: We examined user groups' ages in 4 stages: **preschooler** (age 0-4), **child** (5-12), **adolescent** (13-19), **adult** (20+). In few studies neither the users' age range nor the developmental stage was specified. We categorized them under 'not specified'.

Design phases: We examined users' involvement in 3 main design phases: (1) Requirements (R): where user requirements are elicited for designing a product. (2) Design (D): where ideation and prototyping took place. (3) Evaluation (E): where the product, as a prototype or product, is evaluated for further development (Fig. 1). In many cases, studies took place in more than one phase. So, we used combination of phases as well. We will mention design phases with their initials in the following sections (R, RD, D, DE, E, ER, RDE).

RESULTS

Here we present the results in two parts: (1) A state of the art section consisting of a statistical overview of the 253 substudies, an outline of what has been largely done, and what might need more attention in the field; (2) major problems encountered while conducting research with autistic users.

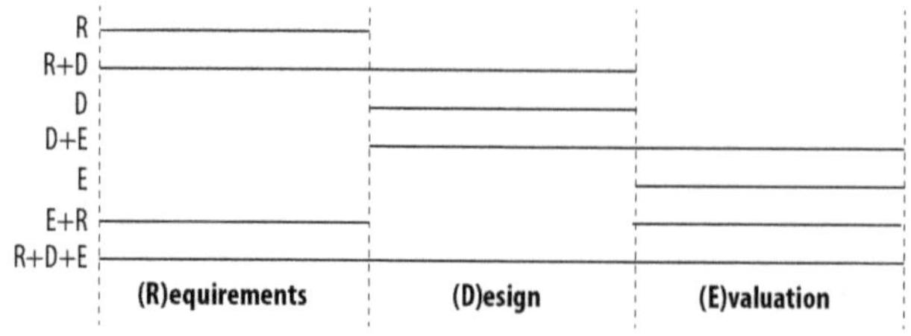

Figure 1: Design phases and their combinations we used in our analysis.

State of the Art

Our data collection resulted in 98 paper over 7 years. We observed a significant increase in publications including autistic users (Fig. 2).

Autistic Users' Involvement and User Sampling

Autistics were included in 173 out of 253 (68.4%) substudies and other user types (TD and non-ASD) involved only in 8 substudies (2.2 %). Actors, on the other hand, took part in 237 substudies (93.7 %). The reason why autistics were not present in all the substudies is that some substudies were conducted with actors or other types of users only. For instance, autistic kids can play with a product while their caregivers are present to observe kids' interactions. After the free play session, an interview session can be conducted with the caregivers. In such a case, first substudy is considered as conducted with autistics and caregivers whereas the second with caregivers only. And both substudies together form a study.

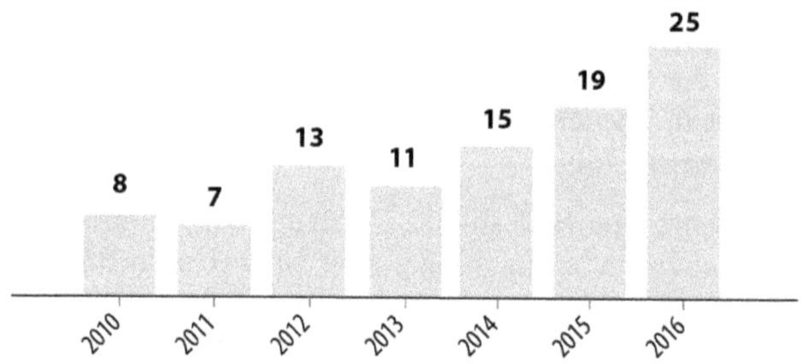

Figure 2: Number of papers per year until October 31st 2016.

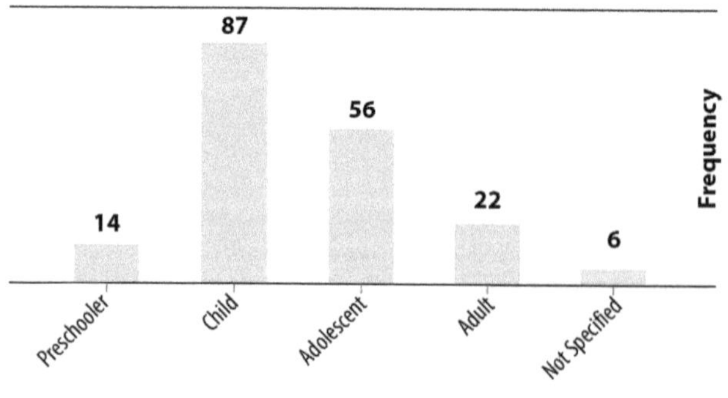

Figure 3: Age ranges of users with ASD

In most substudies (n=79), autistics are mentioned as 'user with ASD' [50], yet there are substudies where the degree of autism was specified as well: 43 substudies with high-functioning autistics (HFA) [44, 15], 20 with medium/low functioning (M/LFA) autistics [19, 11] and 5 with severe autistics [33]. Among autistic users, from all developmental stages, children (47%) and adolescents (30.3%) are the age ranges most often involved in UX studies (Fig. 3). Adults (11.9%) and preschoolers (7.6%) follow them with a considerably small involvement. In 3.2% of the studies, the developmental stage or age was unfortunately not specified.

In terms of intervention, 39 out of 98 studies predominantly aimed at overcoming issues related to social interaction such as emotion and expression recognition and reciprocal interaction (Fig. 4). Following this, learning (e.g. improving the learning capacity) (n=13) and communication (e.g. speech, word recognition) (n=12) were prominent intervention points.

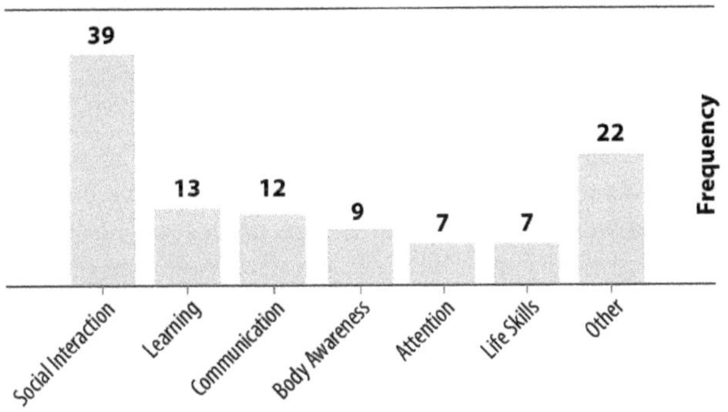

Figure 4: Intervention points of the 98 papers. Other includes intervention points such as attention, anxiety and routines.

The techniques that were the most commonly used in substudies with autistics were (Fig. 5): **(1) User testing & free-play** (n=78): In user testing the researcher follows a predefined procedure through which the user performs several tasks. In free play on the other hand, user is expected to interact with the product without any procedure or task [4, 5, 43]. Especially in substudies with preschoolers and children with autism, free play is a common technique; **(2) Post-test survey** (n=29): After these 3 techniques, users fill out a post-test survey which usually consists of a Smileyometer (a Likert-like scale to rate an experience with smileys ranging from sad to happy) [39] and/or simple questions. In some cases where the researchers develop PD models [8], users' experiences are elicited through post-test surveys regarding the PD session; **(3) Deployment** (n=25): Especially in educational settings [28, 20], product deployment for a long period is a common technique to be able to measure its effects on the students over time.

During the R phase, interviews (n=10) with autistics were commonly used. In interviews, evoking materials such as pictures of daily situations were used to facilitate users'

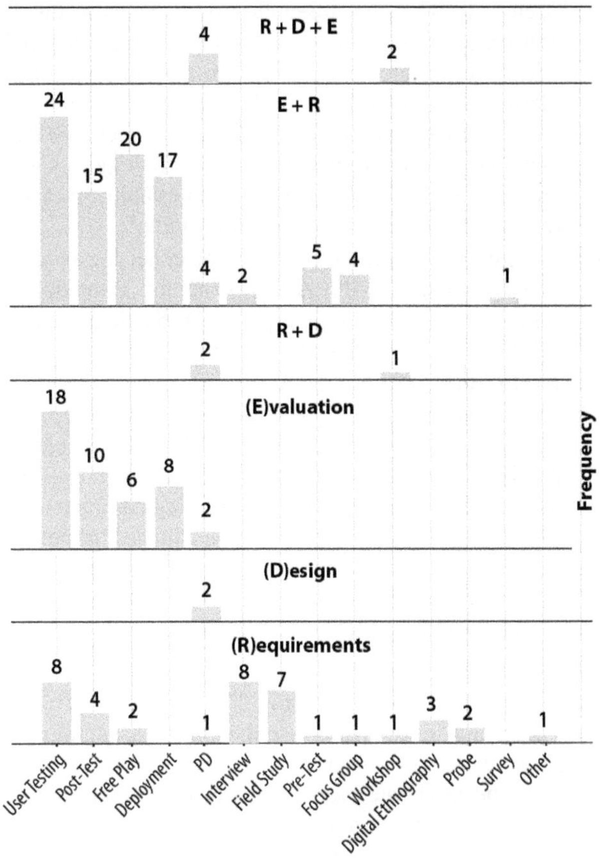

Figure 5: Techniques used in substudies including autistics, based on the design phases

ability to recall and express experiences [30]. Digital ethnography (n=3) and digital probes (n=2) were also presented by several studies as a fruitful information resource especially when investigating daily experiences and social networks [29, 31, 46]. In D phase, where the autistics were least involved, PD sessions (n=14), workshops and focus groups (n=9) took place [9, 21, 30, 49]. Most of the PD sessions were actually the studies where a model or concept was being established for including autistics in the design process [33, 38], but not a product for their direct use. We counted these studies in all RDE phases since they are used iteratively for the the model development throughout each session.

As discussed before, the way autistics were involved in design processes varied according to the phases and techniques used. The types of involvement we observed in our analysis is as follows:

- **Requirements: (1)** Talking about [30] or recording [31] their daily experiences and needs, regarding or regardless of a specific product. **(2)** Being observed by the researchers or the actors in a daily setting [46] or in a product use setting [52]. Observations can be done open (e.g. when the researcher participates in therapy sessions), or remotely (e.g. digital ethnography [46], when the researcher elicit information through online platforms) and with or without informing the user. Observations can be done. **(3)** Being recorded as a quantitative data source (video, physiological signals etc.) in order for the researchers can establish measures that will be used in their following studies.

- **Design: (1)** Developing a prototype either for a product they eventually will use [45] or for a model the researchers are developing [23]. **(2)** Ideating or giving feedback on a prototype to further develop it.
- **Evaluation: (1)** Using a product actively (e.g. in educational settings; where the product operates through user interaction) [11]. **(2)** Using a product passively (where the product operates without direct user interaction but with e.g. physiological input) [36]. **(3)** Being observed or recorded (open, remote or hidden). **(4)** Sharing personal or baseline information before product use [27]. **(5)** Sharing experiences after product use regarding self or the product [37].

Actors' Involvement

As mentioned, actors took part in 237 substudies (93.7 %). with changing roles within studies and throughout the design process. For instance, a teacher can collect data, facilitate and moderate product use, or convey information to the researcher throughout a deployment study. Similarly, parents of the autistic users can collect observational data [41], use a product together with their child [31] and develop prototypes [45] through R and D phases. In many cases, even if the overall study includes users, actors are involved in substudies (n=72) without users' involvement. This kind of single involvement mostly occurs in R in ER phases.

Actors' role were very similar to the users' when they were involved in the study as a user. The roles they took *differently than autistics* in each phase were:

- **Requirements: (1)** Providing information (e.g. general characteristics, daily experiences, needs, interests) about a group of autistics or a specific individual with autism, regarding or regardless of a specific product [25, 21]. **(2)** Facilitating data collection (e.g. using an app with the autistic so that the researcher can explore social interaction between the autistic and the actor [31]) or directly collecting data (e.g. observation).
- **Design: (1)** Facilitating autistics' design contributions in prototype development, and **(2)** developing prototypes [45].
- **Evaluation: (1)** Providing consents for autistics' participation in the studies [56]. **(2)** Conducting clinical assessment prior to studies where before and after conditions were measured. **(3)** Representing the autistics e.g. if they are non-verbal [53]. **(4)** Using a product with the autistic users [1]. **(5)** Moderating an e.g. user testing study with autistics. **(6)** Accompanying the autistics by being passively present or active only when needed [9].

Besides caregivers and design experts, a new actor emerged through our analysis: virtual therapist or robot therapist. We will discuss this in the following sections.

Environment, Tools and Materials

33 substudies were conducted in a place where the autistic users were not initially familiar with (e.g. research lab [50], gallery [48]). 30 of them didn't mention whether the autistic users were familiarized with the environment (or the people included in the setting) or not. Only in 3 of these substudies (e.g. [44]) familiarization process was explicitly mentioned.

Data collection

Data collection was mostly the researchers' (n=164) responsibility, yet there were cases where the actors or the physical setup itself (e.g. sensors, eye-tracking) collected data. Moreover, in rare cases the actors analyzed the data, especially when video annotation is needed. Regardless of the techniques, the most common data collection types were open observation (n=69), video recording (n=38) and log (sensors etc.) recording (n= 22).

Major Problems

Within 253 substudies, we spotted more than 50 problems which we think have a significant impact on data collection and analysis throughout the design processes. Following a grounded theory approach, we iteratively worked on the set of problems to spot the main problem spaces. To overcome the intertwined nature of the problems, we examine them with respect to the conventional parts of UX studies: (1) user sampling, (2) actors, (3) environment, tools and materials, (4) tasks, techniques and instructions, and (5) data analysis (Table 2).

User Sampling

The only problem regarding user sampling is the lack of continuous presence of the participants. Due to different reasons, the users may not participate in all the sessions in longitudinal studies, even if they exhibit engagement in the sessions they attended [10].

Actors

In cases where the researcher's presence is not appropriate (e.g. longitudinal deployments in schools), the caregiver becomes the researcher by moderating the procedure, facilitating the use as well as collecting data (e.g. [19]). The researcher takes the trainer role and teaches the caregiver how to utilize the given setting. The first advantage of transferring the research responsibility to an actor is that the research can take place where the product can be used in a natural and familiar environment. Secondly, data can be collected over a long time, without the researcher's direct involvement. However, depending on the novelty or complexity of the product and its technology, actors may struggle with facilitating its use. For example, in a study with Reactable (a musical tabletop interface with tangibles)

PART OF THE STUDY	PROBLEM SPACE	EXAMPLE
User Sampling	Physical participation [10]	The majority of children dropped out due to illness and absence although a few refused to continue to use ECHOES [10].
Actors	Facilitation [1, 53]	In general, the therapists appreciated the prototype and were able to use it without major problems. However, they most often used the prototype to engage the children in a description activity rather than in a storytelling activity [1].
		The therapist's difficulties with technology created a frustrated interaction with children in some cases [53].
	Obtaining consents [21]	In total 20 children (ASD) took part in these activities (...) but consent forms were returned for a sample of nine and so only their data are reported and analysed here [21].
Environment, Tools and Materials	Context of use [48]	At first most children were hesitant in approaching the plants because a gallery setting was not normal for touching plants [48].
	/ Expectedness Habituation [16, 58, 59]	One of the twin girls (...) was totally not interested and refused to enter the immersive room even with her parent's mediation [16].
		The sensation of wearing a watch was unpleasant for two children. C5's discomfort grew from the moment the watch was first strapped on his arm. He showed so much emotional distress at the beginning of the second session that we were unable to continue with the study [58].
		Two ASD children refused to sit in the experiment chair and thus did not start the experiment [59].
	Physical ergonomics [16, 32]	Some children with autism had problems with the 3-D glasses partially because that the active shuttering glasses used in this project are designed for adults [16].
Tasks, Techniques and Instructions	Understandability [3, 4, 13, 21, 27, 30, 55]	The investigator (...) asked them to rate each reward type using a simple visual voting system consisting of a smiling face, neutral face, and sad face (...) in a row. For some children, this system was too complex and so the investigator would instead present the three reward types side-by-side on three iPad screens and ask the child to indicate their preference. In some cases this needed to be further simplified, with options presented in pairs (with checking for consistency for preference across all 3 sets of pairs) [21].
		Similarly with the think-aloud, some participants struggled to talk as they remained focused and quiet whilst playing the game [27].
		He took instructions literally: when the researcher told asked him to write [type] his name in the profile he started looking for pen and paper [4].
	Engagement [3, 14, 35, 47, 54]	Some participants (n=5) only engaged with one aspect of SensoryPaint (...) [47].
		The children with ASD who did not complete the study stopped not because of the device but rather due to the monotony of the in-lab task [54].
Data analysis	Interpretetion / Result validation [23, 37]	As children speak little, they give their feedback using a cardboard chart with three different faces (I liked a lot, I liked a little, I didn't like). As the children in the study are not able to describe their experience in detail, there is no way of validating how well the evaluation results match children's subjective experience. While we had access to children's own overall evaluations of the gaming sessions, we do not know what aspects affected those evaluations [37].
	Record quailty [16, 40, 57]	Results from 3 participants from the ASD group were discarded due to poor calibration or data loss (too many head movements during reading), resulting in dramatic inaccuracies in more than 70% of the data collected from them [57].

Table 2: Categorization of major problems encountered in 98 papers.

[53], the autistic users' interaction with the product became a frustrating experience due to the caregivers' insufficient understanding of the product's functions. In [1], some of the caregivers could not fully utilize the product the way it was expected. Even though these findings provide insights regarding UX, the role transfer may also complicate the study structure. Another problem regarding the actors is obtaining consents from the caregivers. It is not possible to extract why caregivers refused to provide consents in the studies we reviewed, yet we feel the necessity of reporting that as a possibility to keep in mind while recruiting limited number of users.

Environment, Tools and Materials

Participants with ASD exhibit hesitant, distressed and anxious behavior when exposed to unfamiliar, unexpected contexts, environments and materials in UX studies. Habituation to the setting and materials may not be possible even with the parents' or other actors' presence and emotional support. For instance, there were cases where autistics exhibited refusal behaviors due to the study environment (e.g. the immersive room in [16]) or objects (e.g. the watch in [58] or the chair in [59]) used. These behaviors may result in irreversible situations leading to session cancellations.

Another problem derived from the inappropriate tools and materials chosen for the studies. Due to poor consideration of physical ergonomics, there were cases where the participant could not perform proper use of materials. For example, in a study conducted with autistic children [16], the 3D shutter glasses the children tried wearing, were designed for adults. Even though this case was independent from the ASD population, we've found it worth mentioning as a reminder for thinking about the physical ergonomics, particularly the unusual head orientations and body postures some autistics have, regardless of their age.

Tasks, Techniques and Instructions

Tasks, technique and instruction related problems were reported mainly due to the mismatch between users' cognitive and attentive capacities and the expected data to be collected. For example, think-aloud was reported in several studies (e.g. [3, 27]) as an improper mode of expression for individuals with ASD since they usually remained silent whilst using a product despite the instructions given by the researchers on how to think aloud. Similarly, use of personas was left for further consideration in [42] since it created confusing outcomes when applied in a PD session with autistics because some of them did not understand why they were designing something for someone who is not real.

Task simplicity and understandability were reported to impact the data collection as well. Autistic users may tend to take instructions and prompts literally and fail to perform the expected task. For example, in the usability study in [Bahiss2010], the participant was expected to fill in an online form and it resulted in an attempt of looking for a pen and paper once he was asked to *write* his name, instead of *typing* it. Some tasks which seem very simple to a typically developed researcher may actually be complicated for an autistic user [21]. Similarly, tasks that are engaging enough to be completed for a typically developed user, may seem too dull for an autistic user, or users may not be interested in all the aspects of the product under scrutiny. In an exploratory study on a working prototype [47] five of the fifteen users were interested only in a small portion of the functions available. Based on the five users' account, researchers reported that they got bored using the product. However, it was not clear whether the bored group of users was the same group with those who were not interested in all the functions available. Moreover, the researcher did not report what happened when they encountered such a disengagement.

In cases regarding understandability and engagement, commonly reported consequences were as follows: (1) the researcher simplifies the task according to the user's cognitive capacity by changing its content or order to be able to continue collecting data, or (2) user ends the study session. Or, as in the last example above, it remains unclear what happens when the disengagement occurs.

Data Analysis

Researchers reported struggle in interpreting the users' experiences. For instance, in a study with LFAs [37], the authors mention the challenges they faced while trying to extract meaning from the data they gathered through a simple questionnaire consisting of faces with different expressions (similar to Smileyometer). However, the children in that study had limited verbal skills and could not express their experiences verbally, so the reason behind why they chose a particular face in the questionnaire remained unknown.

DISCUSSIONS

Here we discuss what the previous studies involving autistic users in the UX design processes mean to HCI and present suggestions on how to design future studies in the domain. Then we propose a guideline on how to better conduct studies with autistics.

Our findings show that, based on the substudies that specified the degree of autism, *severe autistics'* involvement (n=5) in design processes was very limited in comparison to HFA and M/LFAs' involvement. The most probable reason behind this may arguably be the varying levels and types of environment awareness and self-expression capabilities of people with severe autism. In most cases where researchers managed to collect data from individuals with severe autism, interpreting and validating the collected data remained a strong challenge. This may also be a reason why severe autistics were never included in phase R, even through actors. And in phase E, data was mostly collected through interpreting physiological signals or counting on an actor's accounts - 72 substudies, predominantly for phases R and ER were conducted with actors only. This leads us to believe that actors have significant roles in defining and expressing the needs and experiences of autistic users. Thus, researchers either collect UX data quantitatively or largely depending on filtered information mainly structured by an actor. Both ways might prove beneficial in certain research settings, however, future research should focus on valid interpretation measures regarding how autistic people, particularly severe autistics, express their subjective experiences. We think UX researchers should challenge conventional methods to collect less actor-filtered information through a more systematical consideration of multiple sources of quantitative data such as physiological signals from autistics which can support and, to some extent, explain the reasons behind a specific experience.

Autistics involved in UX studies were mostly present during the phases E and RE. This means autistics' experiences were studied predominantly through product evaluations. Even though there were R and D studies involving autistics that did not incorporate any product evaluation, autistics were predominantly brought into the process once a product was designed based on literature findings. This relative late inclusion of autistics in the research process may be resulting from the challenges in recruiting autistic people and their caregivers for design studies. Alternatively, the needs and questions extracted from the literature may be found sufficient enough to inform the design process without any user input.

In total, 143 substudies were conducted with autistic children and adolescents, whereas adults were involved in 22 substudies. Numerous research shows that early intervention and special education in autism helps improving social interaction, communication, behavior management and independence. Yet, given that autism is a lifelong condition, HCI should not neglect adult autistics and extend its focus to (1) including and (2) assisting autistics from all ages, not only the young. The studies also showed that the products were primarily developed for educational settings aiming at better social communication skills. Even though social skills are one of the core deficit areas in autism [2], it should not be addressed as a problem which only the autistics should learn how to deal with. Rather, taking a neurodiversity-aware perspective and considering approaches that can bidirectionally mediate the social interaction between autistic and neurotypical users would be beneficial for both groups.

Prior to our study, we did not consider including virtual characters and robots as actors in the analysis, but in some cases, they took the human therapist's role as they gave instructions or prompts to the autistic user with therapeutic purposes [6, 59]. Besides, human-robot interaction studies in autism have been proving that robots' presence and guidance can be more efficient than humans' in educational and therapeutic settings [59]. Thus, their involvement in future studies may not only be based on how the users interact with them, but also how robots take roles in UX studies as actors.

Guidelines for UX Studies with Autistic Users

Given that people with autism have perceptual and cognitive sensitivities, failing to prepare the appropriate study settings and materials may lead to two undesirable consequences: (1) irritated, uncomfortable users, and (2) measurement error and data loss. Even though existing guidelines for clinical research with autistics [e.g 34] would help preventing these problems, UX studies require guidelines considering the interdisciplinary, reciprocal and multi-actored nature of UX. So, here we present a set of guidelines on how to conduct UX studies for autistic users informed by the recommendations proposed in the papers together with the autism literature. We gathered the guidelines under 4 categories, which also correspond to the steps that should be taken while conducting a user study:

Know your Users: *Understand your users' individual perceptual, cognitive and physical capacities by collaborating with their caregivers or directly interacting with them prior to conducting the study.* Beside their strengths and interests which were highlighted as cores for eliciting better design contributions in PD studies [23], learn what kind of environmental stimuli (e.g. certain sounds, textures) they cannot tolerate. Learn if they regularly use or are acquainted with any product similar to what you are working on. Get to know the users with the help of small interactions in their own settings without interfering with their routines. When it is not possible to be involved in their daily activities physically, use online platforms such as e-mail, instant messaging to remotely communicate. Getting to know each user individually may prevent most of the major problems we mentioned in the previous section.

Train the Actors: *Present the product to the actors prior to the study especially when they are to collect data.* Let them understand to what extent the product can be used, what kind of problems can emerge and how to handle the emergent issues during the study. If the study has multiple sessions, remind them the product features prior to each session. If data collection is via a device which the actors allow the autistics to use (e.g. when autistic kids use an app on their parents' tablet), let the actors know what kind of data they should set available to share with researchers. So, the data type obtained from different users can be balanced.

Familiarize your Users: *Let your users get to know you and the study environments.* If the study should be conducted in an unfamiliar setting, familiarize them with the setting, materials, tools and devices that will be used in the study. Let them ask you questions about what they are expected to use. Give them enough time to feel comfortable while e.g. wearing sensors or sitting on a chair. If familiarization is not appropriate due to the nature of the study, let them at least know the duration of the session and the steps to be followed. For longitudinal studies where the users and further actors actively take part (e.g. PD sessions), set meeting dates early enough – e.g. before the whole study starts.

Have a Plan B: *Think about cases where the data collection might fail, and come up with back-up plans accordingly.* Even if you take precautions regarding the users and actors, there can be situations you may not avert, e.g. you may have used a technique you think should have worked, but haven't. For example, using the think-aloud technique just because the users are verbal enough may not be efficient after thoroughly reconsidering the whole study concept. Having secondary data collection techniques and tools in mind prior to study may prevent measurement errors. Similar recommendations were proposed in different PD models as 'being flexible' [9] or providing 'creative freedoms' [38]. However, being flexible may not be precise enough where neat data collection is required. Instead of losing data completely or causing measurement errors by momentary decisions, preplanned techniques can be applied when needed.

Note that, this guideline set is not a PD model which forms a basis for capturing different participants' design contributions. Rather, it is a set of suggestions for researchers who conduct UX studies with autistics to design their research in better accordance with study participants.

Suggestions for Reporting UX Studies with Autistics

In numerous papers, participant and study details were not enough to have a clear idea about the setting, the users' characteristics and the way the actors participated in the study. So, we find it worth mentioning how to better report the study details, even though it's beyond this paper's primary focus.

Beside the common details such as age, sex and autism diagnosis (e.g. ASD, HFA), users' individual characteristics should be presented. Each individual's communication modes, motor capacities, prior experiences and interests regarding the product under scrutiny should be briefly described. Other than participant characteristics, facilitation details (when facilitation was needed, who facilitated what and how the facilitation was carried out), and if present, the familiarization process should be provided since they can directly affect the outcomes of the study. Moreover, researchers should report the problems they encountered during each task in detail in order to inform future studies to establish and develop suitable methods and techniques.

CONCLUSION

Through a qualitative and quantitative analysis of UX studies conducted between 2010-2017 that include autistic study participants, we identified frequent problems and commonly practiced solution approaches. Different than previous works of review research with similar research questions, we contribute to the field by examining the studies conducted with and primarily for autistic users of all ages. Additionally, we do not exclude any research based on the prototyped, developed and/or tested product's underlying technology. Deriving from the problems researchers encountered within the 98 reviewed papers, we propose guidelines on how to better conduct and report on UX studies including individuals with autism. We believe that these guidelines will help HCI researchers and reviewers. Also, researchers from related fields such as psychology and special education should benefit from our findings as well. Above all, we profoundly hope that, be it directly or indirectly, autistics will benefit from these guidelines the most.

Future Work

We will now work on evaluating and refining our guideline set through organizing empirical studies involving autistics. Other than that, we will continue analyzing the here reviewed paper set in order to generate design implications for future products developed for autistic individuals.

Limitations

Our study has several shortcomings. First, due to the page limit, we could not have mentioned all the papers we reviewed. Second, we have chosen the papers focusing on autistics as primary users and including design considerations at different levels. Meaning we ignored the papers focusing at topics other than design even if autistics were involved (e.g. psychological experiments). Our analysis is based on the authors' explicit accounts in the papers we reviewed. So, throughout our analysis we used names of techniques and diagnosis the way they reported. Lastly, we retrieved papers only from 3 databases and between the years 2010 and 2016.

REFERENCES

1. Andrea Alessandrini, Victor Loux, Gabriel Ferreira Serra, and Cormac Murray. 2016. Designing ReduCat: Audio-Augmented Paper Drawings Tangible Interface in Educational Intervention for High-Functioning Autistic Children. 463–472. https://doi.org/10.1145/2930674.2930675
2. American Psychiatric Association and others. 2013. Diagnostic and statistical manual of mental disorders (DSM-5®). American Psychiatric Pub.
3. Khadija Bahiss, Sally Jo Cunningham, and Tony Smith. 2010. Investigating the usability of social networking sites for teenagers with autism. In Proceedings of the 11th International Conference of the NZ Chapter of the ACM Special Interest Group on Human-Computer Interaction, 5–8.
4. Zhen Bai, Alan F. Blackwell, and George Coulouris. 2013. Through the looking glass: Pretend play for children with autism. In Mixed and Augmented Reality (ISMAR), 2013 IEEE International Symposium on, 49–58.
5. Laura Bartoli, Clara Corradi, Franca Garzotto, and Matteo Valoriani. 2013. Exploring motion-based touchless games for autistic children's learning. In Proceedings of the 12th International Conference on Interaction Design and Children, 102–111.
6. E. Bekele, J. Wade, D. Bian, J. Fan, Amy Swanson, Z. Warren, and N. Sarkar. 2016. Multimodal adaptive social interaction in virtual environment (MASI-VR) for children with Autism spectrum disorders (ASD). In Virtual Reality (VR), 2016 IEEE, 121–130.
7. Laura Benton and Hilary Johnson. 2015. Widening participation in technology design: A review of the involvement of children with special educational needs and disabilities. International Journal of Child-Computer Interaction 3–4: 23–40. https://doi.org/10.1016/j.ijcci.2015.07.001
8. Laura Benton, Hilary Johnson, Emma Ashwin, Mark Brosnan, and Beate Grawemeyer. 2012. Developing IDEAS: Supporting children with autism within a participatory design team. In Proceedings of the SIGCHI conference on Human factors in computing systems, 2599–2608.
9. Laura Benton, Asimina Vasalou, Rilla Khaled, Hilary Johnson, and Daniel Gooch. 2014. Diversity for design: a framework for involving neurodiverse children in the technology design process. 3747–3756. https://doi.org/10.1145/2556288.2557244
10. Sara Bernardini, Kaśka Porayska-Pomsta, and Tim J. Smith. 2014. ECHOES: An intelligent serious game for fostering social communication in children with

autism. Information Sciences 264: 41–60. https://doi.org/10.1016/j.ins.2013.10.027
11. Arpita Bhattacharya, Mirko Gelsomini, Patricia Pérez-Fuster, Gregory D. Abowd, and Agata Rozga. 2015. Designing motion-based activities to engage students with autism in classroom settings. 69–78. https://doi.org/10.1145/2771839.2771847
12. Peter Börjesson, Wolmet Barendregt, Eva Eriksson, and Olof Torgersson. 2015. Designing technology for and with developmentally diverse children: a systematic literature review. 79–88. https://doi.org/10.1145/2771839.2771848
13. Benoît Bossavit and Sarah Parsons. 2016. Designing an educational game for and with teenagers with high functioning autism. 11–20. https://doi.org/10.1145/2940299.2940313
14. Fatima A. Boujarwah, Hwajung Hong, Rosa I. Arriaga, Gregory D. Abowd, and Jackie Isbell. 2010. Training social problem solving skills in adolescents with high-functioning autism. In Pervasive Computing Technologies for Healthcare (PervasiveHealth), 2010 4th International Conference on-NO PERMISSIONS, 1–9.
15. Evren Bozgeyikli, Andrew Raij, Srinivas Katkoori, and Rajiv Dubey. 2016. Locomotion in Virtual Reality for Individuals with Autism Spectrum Disorder. 33–42. https://doi.org/10.1145/2983310.2985763
16. Yiyu Cai, Noel K. H. Chia, Daniel Thalmann, Norman K. N. Kee, Jianmin Zheng, and Nadia M. Thalmann. 2013. Design and Development of a Virtual Dolphinarium for Children With Autism. IEEE Transactions on Neural Systems and Rehabilitation Engineering 21, 2: 208–217. https://doi.org/10.1109/TNSRE.2013.2240700
17. Nicholas Sheep Dalton. 2013. Neurodiversity & HCI. In CHI'13 Extended Abstracts on Human Factors in Computing Systems, 2295–2304. Retrieved April 7, 2017 from http://dl.acm.org/citation.cfm?id=2468752
18. Mayada Elsabbagh, Gauri Divan, Yun-Joo Koh, Young Shin Kim, Shuaib Kauchali, Carlos Marcín, Cecilia Montiel-Nava, Vikram Patel, Cristiane S. Paula, Chongying Wang, Mohammad Taghi Yasamy, and Eric Fombonne. 2012. Global Prevalence of Autism and Other Pervasive Developmental Disorders: Global epidemiology of autism. Autism Research 5, 3: 160–179. https://doi.org/10.1002/aur.239
19. Lizbeth Escobedo, Catalina Ibarra, Jehu Hernandez, Mariana Alvelais, and Monica Tentori. 2014. Smart objects to support the discrimination training of children with autism. Personal and Ubiquitous Computing 18, 6: 1485–1497. https://doi.org/10.1007/s00779-013-0750-3
20. Charles Fage, Léonard Pommereau, Charles Consel, Emilie Balland, and Hélène Sauzéon. 2016. Tablet-Based Activity Schedule in Mainstream Environment for Children with Autism and Children with ID. ACM Transactions on Accessible Computing 8, 3: 1–26. https://doi.org/10.1145/2854156
21. S. Fletcher-Watson, H. Pain, S. Hammond, A. Humphry, and H. McConachie. 2016. Designing for young children with autism spectrum disorder: A case study of an iPad app. International Journal of Child-Computer Interaction 7: 1–14. https://doi.org/10.1016/j.ijcci.2016.03.002
22. Sue Fletcher-Watson. 2014. A Targeted Review of Computer-Assisted Learning for People with Autism Spectrum Disorder: Towards a Consistent Methodology. Review Journal of Autism and Developmental Disorders 1, 2: 87–100. https://doi.org/10.1007/s40489-013-0003-4
23. Christopher Frauenberger, Judith Good, Alyssa Alcorn, and Helen Pain. 2012. Supporting the design contributions of children with autism spectrum conditions. In Proceedings of the 11th International Conference on Interaction Design and Children, 134–143.
24. Christopher Frauenberger, Judith Good, Alyssa Alcorn, and Helen Pain. 2013. Conversing through and about technologies: Design critique as an opportunity to engage children with autism and broaden research(er) perspectives. International Journal of Child-Computer Interaction 1, 2: 38–49. https://doi.org/10.1016/j.ijcci.2013.02.001
25. Christopher Frauenberger, Julia Makhaeva, and Katharina Spiel. 2016. Designing Smart Objects with Autistic Children: Four Design Exposès. 130–139. https://doi.org/10.1145/2858036.2858050
26. Ouriel Grynszpan, Patrice L. Weiss, Fernando Perez-Diaz, and Eynat Gal. 2014. Innovative technology-based interventions for autism spectrum disorders: a meta-analysis. Autism 18, 4: 346–361.
27. Natalie Harrold, Chek Tien Tan, Daniel Rosser, and Tuck Wah Leong. 2014. CopyMe: a portable real-time feedback expression recognition game for children. 1195–1200. https://doi.org/10.1145/2559206.2581279
28. Sen H. Hirano, Michael T. Yeganyan, Gabriela Marcu, David H. Nguyen, Lou Anne Boyd, and Gillian R. Hayes. 2010. vSked: evaluation of a system to support classroom activities for children with autism. In Proceedings of the SIGCHI Conference on Human Factors in Computing Systems, 1633–1642.
29. Hwajung Hong, Gregory D. Abowd, and Rosa I. Arriaga. 2015. Towards designing social question-and-answer systems for behavioral support of individuals with autism. In Pervasive Computing Technologies for Healthcare (PervasiveHealth), 2015 9th International Conference on, 17–24.
30. Hwajung Hong, Jennifer G. Kim, Gregory D. Abowd, and Rosa I. Arriaga. 2012. Designing a social network to support the independence of young adults with autism. In Proceedings of the ACM 2012 conference on Computer Supported Cooperative Work, 627–636.

31. Hwajung Hong, Svetlana Yarosh, Jennifer G. Kim, Gregory D. Abowd, and Rosa I. Arriaga. 2013. Investigating the use of circles in social networks to support independence of individuals with autism. In Proceedings of the SIGCHI conference on human factors in computing systems, 3207–3216.
32. Xinlong Jiang, LouAnne E. Boyd, Yiqiang Chen, and Gillian R. Hayes. 2016. ProCom: designing a mobile and wearable system to support proximity awareness for people with autism. 93–96. https://doi.org/10.1145/2968219.2971445
33. Selvia Kuriakose and Uttama Lahiri. 2015. Understanding the Psycho-Physiological Implications of Interaction With a Virtual Reality-Based System in Adolescents With Autism: A Feasibility Study. IEEE Transactions on Neural Systems and Rehabilitation Engineering 23, 4: 665–675. https://doi.org/10.1109/TNSRE.2015.2393891
34. Anneli Kylliäinen, Emily J. H. Jones, Marie Gomot, Petra Warreyn, and Terje Falck-Ytter. 2014. Practical Guidelines for Studying Young Children With Autism Spectrum Disorder in Psychophysiological Experiments. Review Journal of Autism and Developmental Disorders 1, 4: 373–386. https://doi.org/10.1007/s40489-014-0034-5
35. Hoang H. Le, Rui CV Loureiro, Florian Dussopt, Nicholas Phillips, Aleksandar Zivanovic, and Martin J. Loomes. 2014. Soundscape and haptic cues in an interactive painting: a study with autistic children. In Biomedical Robotics and Biomechatronics (2014 5th IEEE RAS & EMBS International Conference on, 375–380.
36. Shu-Hsien Lin. 2012. Detecting hunchback behavior in autistic children with smart phone assistive devices. In Proceedings of the 14th international ACM SIGACCESS conference on Computers and accessibility, 293–294.
37. Susanne Mäkelä, Roman Bednarik, and Markku Tukiainen. 2013. Evaluating user experience of autistic children through video observation. In CHI'13 Extended Abstracts on Human Factors in Computing Systems, 463–468.
38. Julia Makhaeva, Christopher Frauenberger, and Katharina Spiel. 2016. Creating creative spaces for co-designing with autistic children: the concept of a "Handlungsspielraum." 51–60. https://doi.org/10.1145/2940299.2940306
39. Laura Malinverni, Joan Mora-Guiard, Vanesa Padillo, Lilia Valero, Amaia Hervás, and Narcis Pares. 2016. An inclusive design approach for developing video games for children with Autism Spectrum Disorder. Computers in Human Behavior. https://doi.org/10.1016/j.chb.2016.01.018
40. Laura Malinverni, Joan Mora-Guiard, and Narcis Pares. 2016. Towards methods for evaluating and communicating participatory design: A multimodal approach. International Journal of Human-Computer Studies 94: 53–63. https://doi.org/10.1016/j.ijhcs.2016.03.004
41. Chao Mei, Lee Mason, and John Quarles. 2014. Usability issues with 3D user interfaces for adolescents with high functioning autism. 99–106. https://doi.org/10.1145/2661334.2661379
42. Laura Millen, Sue Cobb, and Harshada Patel. 2011. A method for involving children with autism in design. In Proceedings of the 10th International Conference on Interaction Design and Children, 185–188.
43. José Carlos Miranda, Xenxo Alvarez, João Orvalho, Diego Gutierrez, A. Augusto Sousa, and Verónica Orvalho. 2012. Sketch express: A sketching interface for facial animation. Computers & Graphics 36, 6: 585–595. https://doi.org/10.1016/j.cag.2012.03.002
44. Joan Mora-Guiard, Ciera Crowell, Narcis Pares, and Pamela Heaton. 2016. Lands of Fog: Helping Children with Autism in Social Interaction through a Full-Body Interactive Experience. 262–274. https://doi.org/10.1145/2930674.2930695
45. Fnu Nazneen, Fatima A. Boujarwah, Shone Sadler, Amha Mogus, Gregory D. Abowd, and Rosa I. Arriaga. 2010. Understanding the challenges and opportunities for richer descriptions of stereotypical behaviors of children with ASD: a concept exploration and validation. In Proceedings of the 12th international ACM SIGACCESS conference on Computers and accessibility, 67–74.
46. Kathryn E. Ringland, Christine T. Wolf, LouAnne E. Boyd, Mark S. Baldwin, and Gillian R. Hayes. 2016. Would You Be Mine: Appropriating Minecraft as an Assistive Technology for Youth with Autism. 33–41. https://doi.org/10.1145/2982142.2982172
47. Kathryn E. Ringland, Rodrigo Zalapa, Megan Neal, Lizbeth Escobedo, Monica E. Tentori, and Gillian R. Hayes. 2014. SensoryPaint: a natural user interface supporting sensory integration in children with neurodevelopmental disorders. 1681–1686. https://doi.org/10.1145/2559206.2581249
48. Jinsil Hwaryoung Seo, Annie Sungkajun, and Jinkyo Suh. 2015. Touchology: Towards Interactive Plant Design for Children with Autism and Older Adults in Senior Housing. 893–898. https://doi.org/10.1145/2702613.2732883
49. Suleman Shahid, Jip ter Voort, Maarten Somers, and Inti Mansour. 2016. Skeuomorphic, flat or material design: requirements for designing mobile planning applications for students with autism spectrum disorder. 738–745. https://doi.org/10.1145/2957265.2961866
50. Leeseul Shim, Peipei Liu, Ioannis Politis, Paula Regener, Stephen Brewster, and Frank Pollick. 2015. Evaluating multimodal driver displays of varying urgency for drivers on the autistic spectrum. 133–140. https://doi.org/10.1145/2799250.2799261
51. Judy Singer. 1999. Why can't you be normal for once in your life? From a problem with no name to the

emergence of a new category of difference. Disability discourse: 59–70.
52. Vianey Vazquez, Carlos Cardenas, Franceli L. Cibrian, and Mónica Tentori. 2016. Designing a Musical Fabric-Based Surface to Encourage Children with Autism to Practice Motor Movements. 1–4. https://doi.org/10.1145/2967175.2967384
53. Lilia Villafuerte, Milena Markova, and Sergi Jorda. 2012. Acquisition of social abilities through musical tangible user interface: children with autism spectrum condition and the reactable. In CHI'12 Extended Abstracts on Human Factors in Computing Systems, 745–760.
54. Peter Washington, Catalin Voss, Nick Haber, Serena Tanaka, Jena Daniels, Carl Feinstein, Terry Winograd, and Dennis Wall. 2016. A Wearable Social Interaction Aid for Children with Autism. 2348–2354. https://doi.org/10.1145/2851581.2892282
55. Loo Weilun, Mohan Rajesh Elara, and Edgar Martinez Alonso Garcia. 2011. Virtual game approach for rehabilitation in autistic children. In Information, Communications and Signal Processing (ICICS) 2011 8th International Conference on, 1–6.
56. Pinata Winoto. 2016. Reflections on the Adoption of Virtual Reality-based Application on Word Recognition for Chinese Children with Autism. 589–594. https://doi.org/10.1145/2930674.2936001
57. Victoria Yaneva, Irina Temnikova, and Ruslan Mitkov. 2015. Accessible Texts for Autism: An Eye-Tracking Study. 49–57. https://doi.org/10.1145/2700648.2809852
58. Camellia Zakaria, Richard C. Davis, and Zachary Walker. 2016. Seeking Independent Management of Problem Behavior: A Proof-of-Concept Study with Children and their Teachers. 196–205. https://doi.org/10.1145/2930674.2930693
59. Zhi Zheng, Eric M. Young, Amy R. Swanson, Amy S. Weitlauf, Zachary E. Warren, and Nilanjan Sarkar. 2016. Robot-Mediated Imitation Skill Training for Children With Autism. IEEE Transactions on Neural Systems and Rehabilitation Engineering 24, 6: 682–691. https://doi.org/10.1109/TNSRE.2015.2475724

Exploring Design Opportunities for a Context-Adaptive Medical Checklist Through Technology Probe Approach

Leah Kulp[1], Aleksandra Sarcevic[1], Richard Farneth[2], Omar Ahmed[2], Dung Mai[1], Ivan Marsic[3], and Randall S. Burd[2]

Drexel University[1]
Philadelphia, PA 19104
{ljk58, aleksarc, dqm23}
@drexel.edu

Children's Nat'l Med Center[2]
Washington, DC 20010
{rfarneth, oahmed3, rburd}
@childrensnational.org

Rutgers University[3]
Piscataway, NJ 08854
marsic@rutgers.edu

ABSTRACT
This paper explores the workflow and use of an interactive medical checklist for trauma resuscitation—an emerging technology developed for trauma team leaders to support decision making and task coordination among team members. We used a technology probe approach and ethnographic methods, including video review, interviews, and content analysis of checklist logs, to examine how team leaders use the checklist probe during live resuscitations. We found that team leaders of various experience levels use the technology differently. Some leaders frequently glance at the checklist and take notes during task performance, while others place the checklist on a stand and only interact with the checklist when checking items. We compared checklist timestamps to task activities and found that most items are checked off after tasks are performed. We conclude by discussing design implications and new design opportunities for a future dynamic, adaptive checklist.

Author Keywords
Digital checklist; trauma resuscitation; technology probe; interactive systems for healthcare.

ACM Classification Keywords
H.5.m. Information interfaces and presentation (e.g., HCI): Miscellaneous.

INTRODUCTION
Trauma resuscitation is a dynamic, fast-paced medical environment where communication is a critical factor for efficient and error-free patient care. This team-based process requires careful coordination of tasks between seven to 15 medical providers during treatment of severely injured patients. To ensure safety, trauma teams follow Advanced Trauma Life Support or ATLS, an evaluation and management protocol standardized for this setting.

DIS 2017, June 10-14, 2017, Edinburgh, United Kingdom
© 2017 ACM. ISBN 978-1-4503-4922-2/17/06…$15.00
DOI: http://dx.doi.org/10.1145/3064663.3064715.

Trauma centers are also increasingly adopting resuscitation checklists, showing positive impacts on team performance [17]. These initial experiences have confirmed that checklists may play a critical role in emergency situations when the pressure to perform is high [3]. Despite the introduction of protocols and low-tech interventions like checklists, critical evaluation tasks are often delayed [11]. These delays may have minimal impact for less severely injured patients, but can contribute to adverse outcomes and even death in critically injured patients requiring life-saving interventions [11]. Many factors complicate medical emergencies, including the rapidly changing patient status, unreliable team communications and complex coordination of tasks in a short period of time. These factors also pose challenges to designing technologies for improving team performance during time-critical, medical work.

Checklists were created to assist with the performance of sequential steps, thereby reducing human errors and improving communication and collaboration [3]. Although paper-based checklists have improved healthcare safety, their digitization may lead to further advances by allowing faster access to data through integration with other hospital systems and sharing of information through common displays [21]. Digital checklists could also adapt to varying patient scenarios, a requirement for non-routine events where checklists could provide assistance for poorly recalled or necessary information. Attempts have been made to digitize checklists (e.g., Wu et al. [28]), but even a simple translation of tasks from analog to digital may compromise efficiency and user satisfaction, as evidenced in the domain of electronic health records. Selecting an appropriate approach to designing medical checklists, as well as "solving an interaction design problem" [10] for their continued success is therefore critical.

We conducted a mixed-methods study in a regional trauma center to understand how trauma team leaders use a digital checklist during trauma resuscitations. We used the technology probe approach [6] to collect information about the digital checklist use through logs and to identify new design opportunities. We compared 11 digital checklist resuscitations (or cases) to 10 cases with paper checklists to understand how the use of the checklist varied between the two formats. We also reviewed video records from paper and digital cases to gain insight about frequency of glancing at the checklist, checklist handling, and communication. Our results show that team leaders use the digital checklist differently than paper checklists. When using the digital checklist, leaders take fewer notes, but leave fewer items unchecked. They frequently glance at the digital checklist during task performance and before verbalizing directions. We use these results and participant feedback to discuss design implications for a future adaptive checklist, including improved note-taking abilities, customization of checklist layout for different team leaders, and adaptability of checklist information to varying patient contexts.

The context of medical emergencies offers new insights into the design and functionality of cognitive aids because these scenarios are more dynamic than routine situations, requiring new approaches to system design [10,28]. The resulting technology must support coordination of work in a time-pressured environment, while adapting to rapid changes in patient status. Context-adaptive checklists need to be simple to minimize cognitive load and ensure compliance, yet robust enough to reduce omissions, provide relevant information in changing contexts, and enhance individual performance [10]. Our contributions to the area of interactive systems design include:

- Application of technology probe in a dynamic, safety-critical medical context
- In-the-wild evaluation of an emerging technology
- Design implications for a future adaptive checklist

BACKGROUND AND RELATED WORK

Paper vs. Electronic Checklists in Medicine

Electronic checklists (e-checklists) are increasingly used in medical domains. These first-generation e-checklists are often either identical translations of paper checklists or their projections on large wall displays [4,16,19,20]. Although digital cognitive aids reduce omissions and improve team performance, these aids are facing the same design limitations as their paper counterparts [24,28]. Below we review studies of both paper and electronic checklists, their design, and their effects on team performance.

Paper checklists have been evaluated in several medical settings, including trauma resuscitation and operating rooms. Kelleher et al. [15] analyzed the completion and timeliness of tasks during pediatric resuscitations with and without a checklist, finding increased task completion and faster task performance when using a checklist. Hart and Owen [12] evaluated a verbal checklist for anesthesia administration. Although most participants found the verbal checklist useful, one third of the items were omitted. Paper is the simplest and most convenient medium for checklists [25], but it also has disadvantages. For example, paper checklists are static, limiting their adaptability to different patient scenarios. Also, they cannot exchange information with other medical systems or update automatically [19].

More recently, attempts have been made at making the digital aids more responsive to patient scenarios and user needs. Gonzales et al. [8], for example, evaluated the effectiveness of a projected shared display with two interaction modes, the Microsoft Kinect and a touchscreen, during acute care resuscitations. Despite an initial concern that a touchscreen display might create a distraction, it was perceived as more user-friendly than the gesture-based interaction. Christov et al. [5] introduced a smart checklist for blood transfusion, cardiac surgery, and infusion therapy that automatically generates a list of items based on predefined activities. Their design also supports adaptation of the user interface to different users, as well as dynamic updating of information based on the current activity. Wu et al. [28] analyzed the effectiveness of a dynamic procedure aid for operating rooms. The dynamic aid was found useful because it provided a step-at-a-glance layout, making the protocol steps easy to view and reducing provider cognitive load. We contribute to this body of work by designing and evaluating an adaptive checklist for medical emergencies, and by leveraging the technology probe approach in situ, during real trauma resuscitations with real users.

Several studies have compared the effects of paper and e-checklists on team performance [8,24,28], finding that e-checklists usually outperformed their paper counterparts. Thongprayoon et al. [24], for example, compared the use of a paper checklist to an identical e-checklist for intensive care unit providers. The e-checklist reduced provider errors and cognitive workload without increasing checklist completion time, showing the feasibility of checklists in emergency medical settings. In contrast, Watkins et al. [26] found no difference between the two formats. These studies are critical because they establish the importance of a proper design and appropriate use of cognitive aids, in addition to the format. In this work, our goal was not to compare how paper and electronic checklists perform in relation to protocol adherence or clinical measures (e.g., [16]). We were instead interested in comparing use practices and provider behaviors around interactions with the technology to identify issues with the electronic version and inform the design of a future adaptive checklist.

Methodological Approach: Technology Probes

A technology probe is an artifact designed to collect information around use, explore usability issues, and provide inspiration for a new design space. In several studies, technology probes were introduced into environments to elicit reflections from participants and to reveal technology needs and desires, supplementing other ethnographic methods [2,9,14]. Amin et al. [1], for example, introduced the probe as part of a participatory design exercise to derive design requirements for non-verbal messaging. Gaye and Holmquist [7] deployed probes to form an understanding of user environments and paths around a city for designing a system that uses the urban environment as an interface for real-time electronic music making. We have similarly deployed a digital checklist for

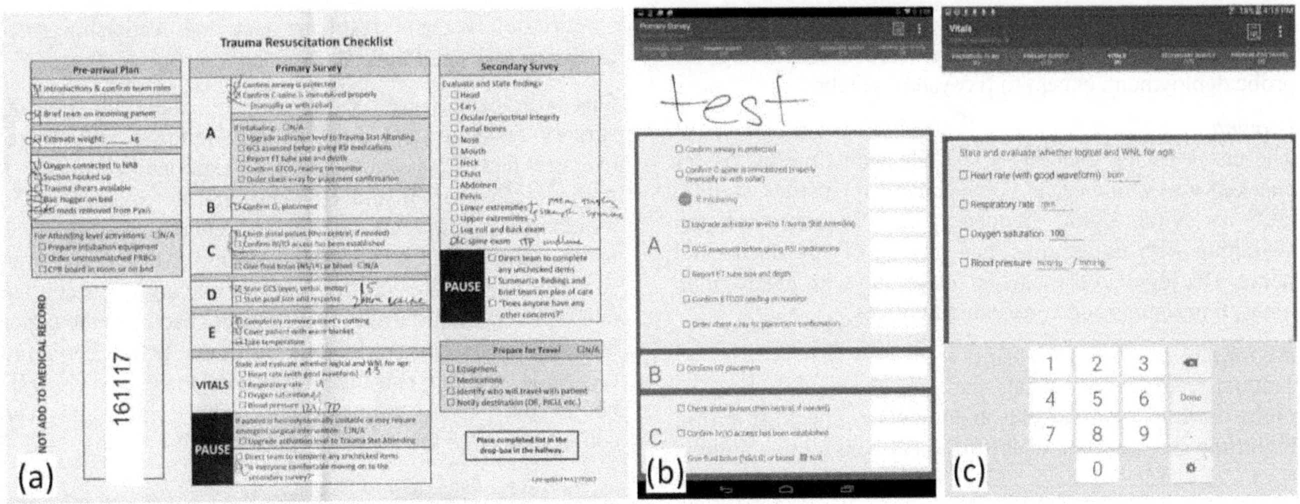

Figure 1: (a) Paper-based checklist. (b) and (c) Example pages of the digital checklist probe.

trauma resuscitation as a probe to gather contextual information about the environment and technology use, and to obtain new insights into the design and functionality of cognitive aids for medical emergencies.

A common approach to system design in HCI is to observe the environment to identify issues, create a prototype, and then test it in the lab. In previous studies, we worked with medical experts to design the checklist probe and evaluate for usability to stabilize the system [21]. In this study, we took the design out of the controlled usability setting and deployed it as a technology probe in the wild.

TRAUMA RESUSCITATION CHECKLIST PROBE

Our technology probe was an e-checklist that was designed and developed to (1) collect information about the checklist use during actual trauma resuscitations, (2) understand use practices around the technology, and (3) stimulate discussion about features that are needed for an adaptive checklist in this setting. The checklist probe is a mobile application based on its paper counterpart that has been in use at our research site since 2012 (Figure 1(a)). The probe allows its users—trauma team leaders—to prepare for patient arrival and ensure compliance with the patient evaluation protocol throughout resuscitation.

Hardware and Software

The checklist probe was implemented using the Android Studio IDE and was written in Java for the Android mobile operating system with a minimum support for platform version Android 4.2 with API level 17. The user interface was implemented using Android XML layouts. The system also uses the SQLite library as a SQL database engine. The design pattern for the checklist probe is Model-View-Controller. The hardware included a Google Nexus 10 tablet and an Adonit Jot Pro stylus for touchscreen devices.

Design

The initial design of the checklist probe and its features were informed by content analysis of 163 paper checklists collected during actual trauma resuscitations over four months [22]. To design the user interface, we used Google Material Design standards. Each section of the paper checklist—pre-arrival plan, primary survey, secondary survey, and prepare for travel—was designed onto its own tab on the digital checklist (Figure 1(b)). The pre-arrival plan includes preparatory steps for patient arrival. The primary survey focuses on major physiological systems like **A**irway, **B**reathing, blood **C**irculation and **D**isability or neurological exam (ABCDs), while secondary survey includes a head-to-toe evaluation to identify other injuries. The prepare for travel section includes the plan for care. We added a fifth tab for recording patient vital signs (Figure 1(c)). Each item from the paper checklist also appears as an item on the probe with a checkbox next to it. We observed in our analysis of paper checklists that trauma leaders take handwritten notes next to items and in margins. To provide them with a similar functionality on the probe, we implemented a white box next to each item, as well as a static margin at the top for taking handwritten notes. When items are checked off, the color of the text fades from black to grey. Optional, "If applicable" items from the paper checklist, like intubation, were implemented as collapsible sections that hide the items by default but are revealed by tapping the "+" symbol (Figure 1(b)). The user can tap the tabs or swipe between tab screens. A tab heading with the number of remaining items can be found at the top of each tab, providing a cognitive reminder for unchecked items. Several items, including patient weight, Glasgow Coma Score (or GCS, indicating the neurological status of the patient), and vital signs (Figure 1(c)) have input areas for typing numerical values on a keypad, which automatically checks off the corresponding item. Upon finishing the checklist, the user can review any unchecked items before pressing the "complete checklist" button and submitting the log. This action saves the log onto the tablet for internal review and analysis. The probe was first tested for usability [21] and then piloted by medical experts on our research team who shadowed trauma team leaders during 16 actual resuscitations. No design changes were made during the probe deployment, except to fix system glitches.

Logging

The checklist log contains a text file with timestamps for checked items, numerical notes entered for patient weight, GCS or vital signs, frequency and sequence of tab switching with timestamps, and the list of any unchecked items. The log also contains an image file with handwritten notes, timestamps and corresponding items.

METHODS

Trauma team leaders at our site used the digital checklist probe during daytime events and the paper checklist during nighttime and weekend events for three consecutive months (Oct. 1, 2016 – Jan. 5, 2017). During the deployment period, the checklist probe logs were collected from 11 events, and the paper checklist was used in 70 events. To understand the digital checklist use patterns and how they differed from the paper checklist use, we matched probe cases to cases with paper checklists based on case and patient characteristics. For each case, we then triangulated data from log analysis or paper checklist content analysis, live video review, and interviews with team leaders. The hospital's research ethics committee approved this study.

Study Setting

The study took place at a pediatric teaching hospital with a regional level 1 trauma center. Two adjacent resuscitation rooms, each with three beds, are used for assessing patients. Both rooms are equipped with video cameras and microphones, providing video records with multiple views of the patient area. The center treats an average of 600 patients per year, with injury mechanisms ranging from falls, to burns, to firearm- and motor vehicle traffic-related injuries. Patients are assigned one of three activation levels: low acuity (stat), high acuity (attending stat), and transfer. Activations are announced about 10 minutes before arrival, unless the patient arrives without notification (e.g., brought in by private vehicle or insufficient time to notify the hospital). Although resuscitation rooms lack information technology for data synthesis, there are tools and technologies that assist teams during resuscitations. These include paper-based flowsheets and checklists, sign-in boards, wall-mounted timers (to keep track of time), vital sign monitors, various wall charts with patient parameters, and the electronic health record (EHR) system.

Participants

Trauma teams consist of surgeons, emergency medicine physicians, nurses, critical care specialists, respiratory therapists, and anesthesiologists. Each team member has a specific role and a set of defined tasks. For example, anesthesiologists and respiratory therapists manage the patient's airway, while surgical residents or nurse practitioners examine the patient. Scribe nurses document the event, and bedside nurses establish intravenous access and administer medications and fluids. Attending surgeons, surgery fellows and residents take the leadership roles, assigning tasks and making decisions.

Our participants were six trauma team leaders: three senior surgery residents and three surgery fellows. Fellows, on average, had 7.2 years (SD: 2) of experience working in trauma resuscitation and residents had an average of 3.8 months (SD: 0.3). All participants reported confidence in using tablets and smartphones during work. Five were somewhat familiar with the Android operating system, and one was very familiar. Five participants had used the paper-based resuscitation checklist at least once before beginning this study, and one participant first used the digital checklist before ever using a paper checklist. Participants were compensated for the interview portion of the study.

Digital Checklist Training Session

Before deploying the checklist probe in live events, we ran an hour-long training session at the hospital with two residents and two fellows who at the time served as trauma team leaders. We also trained two research coordinators at the hospital to use the digital checklist and conduct training sessions with new residents at the start of their rotations. The session started with an introduction to the checklist features and functionalities and then users tested these features and familiarized with the checklist design. We also used this training session to address any issues or questions before moving forward with the study.

Probe Use Procedure

When a daytime trauma patient case came into the hospital, one of the research coordinators handed the checklist probe (tablet) to the team leader at the start of the resuscitation. The leaders were instructed to use the digital checklist as they would normally use the paper version. Upon concluding the resuscitation, team leaders were able to review any unchecked items and complete the checklist by pressing the "complete checklist" button. This action saved the log file locally on the tablet. The research coordinator then reviewed log files and removed any patient health information. The anonymized log files were transferred to a password-protected account on a cloud server to which only the research team has access.

Data Collection and Analysis

Our data included digital checklist logs collected via the probe, paper checklists, video records of live resuscitations, and interviews with trauma team leaders.

Digital Checklist Logs

Data from each anonymized checklist log file were first transcribed into a spreadsheet containing the following sections: checklist start and end times, time elapsed from when the checklist was started and completed, notes taken and their corresponding timestamps and checklist items (e.g., a note "2 mm bilateral" was written for the "State pupil size and response" item at 0:11:19), any unchecked items, items checked out of order and notes about the ordering (e.g., "1st pause completed at end of checklist"), tab switching sequence, and overall notes about the case

Experience Level	Activation Level	GCS	Age	Injury Type	Now Activation
Fellow	Stat	14	2y	Blunt	1
Fellow	Stat	14	1y	Blunt	0
Fellow	Stat	12	3y	Blunt	0
Fellow	Stat	13	1y	Blunt	1
Fellow	Stat	15	8y	Blunt	1
Fellow	Stat	14	8y	Blunt	1
Fellow	Stat	13	14y	Blunt	0
Fellow	Stat	14	13y	Blunt	0
Fellow	Stat	15	16y	Blunt	1
Fellow	Stat	15	14y	Blunt	0
Senior resident	Transfer	12	7w	No injury	0
Senior resident	Transfer	15	9m	Blunt	0
Senior resident	Stat	14	6m	Blunt	0
Senior resident	Stat	14	2y	Blunt	0
Senior resident	Stat	14	9m	Blunt	0
Senior resident	Stat	14	2y	Blunt	0
Senior resident	Stat	15	9y	Blunt	0
Senior resident	Stat	15	10y	Blunt	1
*Fellow	Attending	15	14y	Penetrating	0

Table 1: Probe case characteristics (grey rows) and their matching paper cases (white rows). For age, y = years, m = months, and w = weeks. *Case with no paper checklist match.

(e.g., "weight was checked, but no value typed in"). We then analyzed log transcripts using an open coding technique to identify patterns within notes, unchecked items, items checked out of order, or tab switching sequence. In addition, activity logs (e.g., start and end times for 37 most critical activities performed during resuscitations – three in the pre-arrival plan section, and all activities in the primary and secondary survey and vitals sections) were obtained through video review for six cases. We compared these activity logs to timestamps of checked items from corresponding checklist logs to determine the time difference between actual task performance and item checking. We also examined checklist use patterns among team leaders of different experience levels.

Paper Checklist Review

Paper checklists were used during nighttime and weekend resuscitations because the research coordinators were not present to hand off the probe and monitor its use for any troubleshooting. Seventy paper checklists were used during the study period, but only 49 were submitted for review. From this sample, we selected 10 checklists to match 10 of the 11 probe cases using systematic filtering based on several criteria (one probe case was unique and did not have an appropriate paper checklist case match). First, we filtered the checklists based on the experience of the leader, leaving two categories: surgery fellow and senior surgery resident. Next, we filtered the checklists based on activation level (stat, attending or transfer). We then matched the checklists based on the following criteria as closely as possible: patient age, type of injury (blunt, penetrating, no injury), and neurological score (GCS). Medical experts reviewed the match choices to ensure that any discrepancies in age or GCS were within reason (Table 1).

To analyze the paper checklists, we used a similar approach to that of the digital checklist logs. We first transcribed the handwritten notes and their location, unchecked items, team leader experience level, and case- and patient information (activation level, notification, injury type, patient age, and GCS). We then performed content analysis of notes, identifying common information types that were recorded. Note-taking patterns were also analyzed based on team leader experience levels and patient acuity.

Video Review

To better understand how team leaders used and interacted with checklists, as well as how checklist use affected teamwork, we reviewed 21 videos, 10 with the paper checklist and 11 with the digital probe. We transcribed any dialogue between leaders and other team members related to checklist items, and recorded observations pertaining to checklist use behaviors (e.g., "stepping closer to look over patient, glancing back to checklist"). Transcripts were then analyzed using open coding to identify patterns in use behaviors across both checklist formats. Due to ethics restrictions, we were not allowed to associate the resuscitation cases with individual team leaders, even though we could see them in the videos. We therefore report the results using the leaders' experience levels.

Interviews with Team Leaders

We conducted one-hour, semi-structured interviews with three team leaders who had used the probe at least twice. The interview focused on leaders' perceptions about the digital checklist, their needs, and on potential areas for checklist design improvement. Interview questions were categorized into: communication, decision-making, memory load, and checklist use behaviors. Example questions include, "Do you check items right after they are completed or information is verbalized, or wait for several items to be completed? Why do you use this method" and "At the end of a trauma event when summarizing, do you refer back to notes or items on the checklist?" Interviews were audio-recorded and transcribed for analysis.

FINDINGS

We present findings in four parts. First, we describe our general observations of the digital checklist probe use and how it differed from the use of paper checklists. We then describe the differences in probe use based on leaders' domain experience levels. Next, we present findings about note taking, checklist completion rates and item check off times. We conclude with the challenges our participants faced during the probe deployment.

General Observations: Paper vs. Digital Checklist Use
Through video review, we observed several trends in how team leaders used the checklist probe and paper checklist: (1) carrying the checklist around and checking off items on-the-go vs. leaving it on the stand and checking off items at the end; (2) frequently glancing at the checklists; and, (3) switching between checklist formats. We next describe these trends in greater detail.

Similar to paper checklists, the digital checklist in the form of a tablet afforded a great deal of mobility during team leaders' work. Although team leaders are usually hands-off—most of the time standing at the foot of the bed and monitoring a resident or nurse practitioner as they assess the patient—this mobility is important because team leaders sometimes need to approach the patient to confirm findings from physical assessment. In both paper and digital checklist cases, we observed team leaders moving around the patient to get a closer look at the injury, all while holding the checklist. Specifically, we saw leaders moving around with the checklist in their hands in three probe cases and two paper checklist cases. When walking around, they held the tablet in one hand with their palm facing up so they could glance at the checklist screen. For example, during the secondary survey in one digital probe case, the team was performing the log roll and back exam, during which the patient is rolled on one side and their back is examined. The junior resident is asking the patient if they are in pain while pressing various parts of the back. As the team turns the patient back to the supine position, the leader walks over to the side of the bed while holding the tablet, screen facing up. He leans over the bed and watches the respiratory therapist and junior resident remove the neck collar to perform the c-spine exam. The leader glances at one of the displays on the wall, then looks back at the checklist and checks off the corresponding "C-spine exam" checkbox. Our comparison of the activity completion times and timestamps from the log also showed that the leader first checked off "Log roll and back exam" step after this task was performed, and then walked to the bedside to check on the patient, stepped back, and checked off "C-spine exam." This leader explained during the interview that he uses the checklist in a check-as-you-go manner, or checking items after each task is performed. We observed similar behaviors with paper checklists; in one case, a team leader held the checklist with one hand while leaning in to look at the patient, and in another case, the leader tucked the checklist under his arm. The mobility that the checklists afford is a critical factor in allowing the leader to perform their job without being inhibited by the technology.

Not all leaders, however, kept holding the checklist probe during their work. In fact, we found that team leaders held checklists in different ways throughout resuscitations. In one digital checklist case and three paper checklist cases, various team leaders did not hold the checklist at all during the patient assessment and simply checked off items at the very end. In four paper-checklist cases, team leaders leaned on the scribe's stand at the foot of the bed while taking notes and checking off items. Team leaders in four other cases put the paper form on a clipboard or used their hand behind the paper as a support before switching to leaning on the stand. In one digital checklist case, the leader became upset when the checklist application stopped working, looked around for the research coordinator, but then put the checklist on the stand and pulled out a pen and blank piece of paper to take notes. Later in the event, this leader went back to the digital checklist, transcribed notes from paper into the probe and checked off the completed tasks. In three digital checklist cases, the leaders filled out the pre-arrival plan and then placed the checklist on the stand while waiting for the patient to arrive, but immediately picked the tablet up when the patient entered the room.

Team leaders tended to glance at the checklist often during resuscitations. In six paper checklist cases and seven probe cases, team leaders visually referenced the checklist at various points in the process: before they directed the team or clarified if tasks had been performed, as team members performed tasks, and after task completions. In one probe case, the junior resident asked if they could move on to the secondary survey. The leader first glanced at the checklist and then asked if a specific task had been completed:

JR: "Ready for secondary survey?"
TL: [glances at the checklist] "Did you check pupils?"
JR: "Pupils?"
TL: "Yeah."
JR: [checks pupils] "2 equal reactive."
TL: [checks off "State pupil size and response" item]

Team leaders also glanced at the checklist when providing the summary of the process and discussing the plan of care. One participant commented how retrieving information from the digital checklist was easier at a glance because it focused their attention on one section at a time, compared to the paper version that shows everything in one plane. The digital probe was also used as a reference point to check for incomplete tasks. One leader explained how they used the checklist if they noticed an item had been skipped:

"*If there's something I missed then I'll tell the second year [junior resident] to just go ahead [...] it's usually part of the secondary exam where we didn't look in the ears, so then we'll go back and do that.*"

Two paper checklist cases were unique in that they involved the use of both digital and paper checklists. In both cases, the leaders started by using the digital checklist, but they soon experienced issues so they put the digital checklist down and continued using the paper form. In both cases, the leaders were taking a note when the app malfunctioned; one was in the pre-arrival plan tab and the other in the primary survey tab. Both leaders became

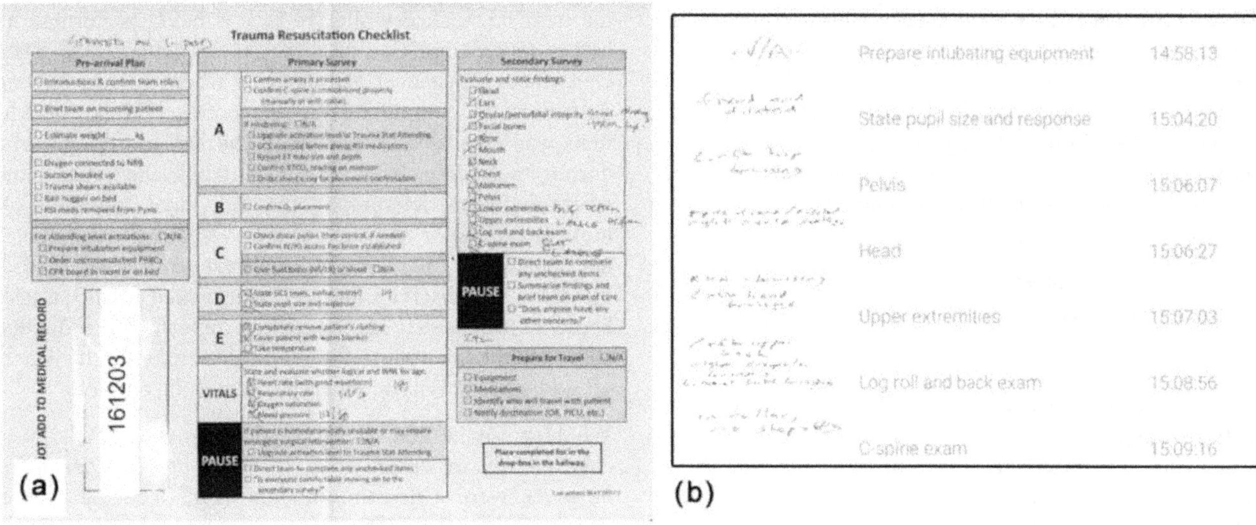

Figure 2: (a) Team leader's notes on the paper checklist after switching back and forth between the digital and paper version. (b) Example notes from the digital probe log, their corresponding items and timestamps.

frustrated with the probe, and one was even heard saying, "*Why is this not working?*" This team leader switched from probe to paper during step D, indicating this switch by leaving all items until step D unchecked and writing a note at the top that read "started on i-pad" (Figure 2(a)).

Checklist Use by Leaders of Different Experience Levels

We observed that team leaders of different experience levels used the checklists differently. Regardless of the checklist format, team leaders with less experience (senior residents) on average took more notes than surgery fellows (2.3 notes versus 1.5 for digital; 5.75 notes versus 0 for paper). We also observed surgery fellows, or more experienced leaders, placing the checklist on the stand and not referring to it in two probe cases and three paper checklist cases. Rather, they picked up the checklist and checked off items at the very end of the resuscitation. The fellows confirmed our observations during the interviews, reporting that they only take notes if there is something significant or abnormal about the patient. One participant elaborated: "*If there's something specific about the findings or the vitals, or if there's something relevant or abnormal about the exam, I just put it in the little comment section*". In contrast to fellows' behaviors, senior surgery residents tend to hold the checklist in their hands throughout resuscitations, checking off items as tasks are performed, both on paper and digital checklists. For example, one senior surgery resident was diligently glancing at the digital checklist, reading the items out loud and then checking them off immediately after they were performed:

"Do we have our oxygen hooked up? Trauma sheers available? Bair hugger... RSI meds pulled off there... [trailing off]" [...] "Do we have her covered with a warm blanket? Can we get a temperature?"

For more experienced leaders, the checklist served as a protocol reminder and as the information organizer, rather than a memory tool for taking notes: "*[The checklist] organizes the information gathering and then, in the sense that it expedites that and organizes it, it helps you come to a decision point more efficiently.*" To this end, both fellows explained that the primary survey steps are second nature to them and they have the checklist items memorized. Where they saw the checklist helpful, however, was in reminding them of the secondary survey, which has more steps in no particular order: "*For the secondary survey, you make sure that you're dotting your i's and crossing your t's.*" One fellow explained the usefulness of the checklist as a training tool for learning all steps of the ATLS protocol:

"If I were to have a checklist in residency, I probably would have gotten a lot better a lot faster at running traumas, just because hey there's a checklist, if I just put it to memory then most of the things I will not miss."

This reflection as a result of using the checklist probe showed the importance of having access to the checklist for team leaders of all experience levels, especially those who are in training or learning the ATLS protocol.

Note Taking on Paper vs. Digital Checklist

Content analysis of both paper and digital checklists showed several differences in the way these two formats were used for note taking. On average, the amount of notes taken on both paper and digital checklists was the same, but the deviations varied: 2 notes per paper checklist (SD 3.8) compared to 2 notes per digital checklist (SD 1.5). Vital signs were written down in two paper-checklist cases and typed in all digital checklist cases. In four digital checklist cases, notes were handwritten for pupil size. Notes were also handwritten for temperature in three digital cases. These findings suggest that, like for vitals, it may be more efficient to offer a typed note entry field for all numerical items (e.g., temperature or pupil size). Notes for the secondary survey items were taken in six digital cases, while only two paper cases had notes in this section of the checklist. The results of lab studies were written down in two paper checklist cases, and in one case the leader drew checkboxes next to the added lab items. The amount of notes on paper checklists during this study, however, was lower than what we found in our previous analysis of paper checklists [22], suggesting that the amount of notes may depend on individual preferences.

On paper checklists, most of the notes were written in the top margin section, vitals box, or secondary survey section, while the notes on digital checklists were often associated with specific checklist items, e.g., "fixed and dilated" for the item "State pupil size and response" (Figure 2(b)). Two team leaders reported that they use the digital checklist just like they use the paper checklist, taking notes only if a significant change in the patient's status or an abnormal finding occurs. One participant explained that handwriting on the tablet was more usable than taking notes on paper:

"There's more room to actually write something on the tablet, because on this sheet it's just clunky, where I would write something off to the side you have to write it in small print and it would run into other things."

To take notes on the digital checklist, the user must first click on a white box next to the checklist item, which opens up a large writing space for note taking. When the note is complete and the user presses the checkmark, the note minimizes back into the white box and shows up next to the related item (Figure 1(b)). The participant commented that this feature could be improved by enlarging the minimized notes so they are more readable for later referencing.

Digital Checklist Completion Rates and Check Off Times

Digital checklist logs showed that fewer items were omitted—3 items on average (SD 2.8) versus 17 items on paper checklists (SD 11.2). Most of the items omitted on paper checklists appear within sections with "N/A" checkboxes, relating to tasks that occur infrequently, like intubation. On the digital checklist, these "N/A" items are hidden by default (with the exception of the "Prepare for travel" section) and do not contribute to the number of unchecked items. Our analysis of timestamps for item check offs showed that a long delay averaging 10 minutes, occurred between when the last pre-arrival plan item and the first primary survey item were checked. We explain this delay by the fact that the pre-arrival plan is often completed before the patient arrival, and especially in cases with early notifications when the team assembles in the resuscitation room ahead of time. After comparing the digital checklist log timestamps with the task completion times from the activity log, we found that for about 20 tasks throughout the checklist, items were checked 3 minutes, on average, after the task was completed. In contrast, we calculated that about 5 to 6 times per checklist, items were checked an average of 1 minute and 39 seconds before the task was completed. Most of these "pre-checks" occurred in the primary survey where tasks may take longer to complete, so the item is checked while the task is being performed but before task completion is noted on the activity log. There were about 5 instances per checklist where the task was not performed to completion but the corresponding checklist item was checked. These "false checks" mostly occurred during multi-step tasks, like calculating the GCS score, which includes determining the individual score for eye movement, motor movement, and verbal behavior, but is not considered complete until the total score is reported. In the cases we observed, the leaders checked off these tasks because they received completion reports for individual task components, while the medical experts producing the ground truth activity log marked them as incomplete.

We also found that items on the digital checklist were checked out of order. Most of these out-of-order items, however, were within the same tab (e.g., secondary survey items checked out of order but not mixed with primary survey items). The interviews revealed that following the order within the primary survey is important, but less strict during the secondary survey, as long as all tasks are completed. When asked what they you do if one of the items is skipped, one of the participants responded:

"If it's in the primary survey, I stop them and I say you have to do this before you move on to anything else. If it's in the secondary survey, I'll let them finish what they're doing, then I'll say 'hey did you do this?' and go back. Once you've gone to the secondary survey I'm less concerned about it, but primary survey order matters so I stop immediately there."

The other items that were often checked out of order were the pause sections, which were checked after all other items, at the very end in four digital checklist cases.

Challenges in Using the Digital Checklist Probe

Team leaders described several challenges in using the digital checklist compared to the paper version. The first challenge was the need to setup the tablet upon arrival to the resuscitation room. This challenge emerged during the last few days of our study, after we installed a locking mechanism to secure the tablet. The team leaders needed to unplug the tablet from the charger, unlock the security lock, and then unlock the tablet screen. One participant commented that they would skip the tablet and go straight to the paper checklist if the patient was already in the room. We changed the probe access mechanism—from a research coordinator handing it to leaders at the beginning of resuscitations to storing it in the room—to allow for probe use and data collection during weekend- and night shifts, as we continue with the probe deployment. The leaders' comments, however, suggest that we need a different strategy to ensure the probe use in cases when the patient is already in the room and there is no time to prepare.

Another challenge was the lack of visibility for items that were left unchecked: *"I think it would be nice at the end to have the app tell you these were the fields that were missing.*" Unlike paper version that provides an at-a-glance overview of the entire checklist, the digital version separates items into tabs, making them visible only if the user goes to a particular tab. To address this design issue, we already had a feature implemented that provided a list of unchecked items to the user before they would submit the checklist log. It turned out this feature was not obvious to our users. Also, three team leaders had difficulties with using the stylus and the interface. In two of these cases, the application froze and the participants switched to using the paper checklist. Although most cases with the digital probe involved routine daytime events, there were several cases where environmental factors, like patient crying or delays in task performance, could have impacted the checklist use. In situations where the patient was crying, the team leader often had to request information from the junior resident more than once (e.g., JR: "*We'll roll once we get an IV.*" TL: "*Yep.*" [moments later, while patient is crying] TL: "*Did you get the IV?*" JR: "*Not yet.*" TL: "*Do we have IV access?*" JR: "*Yep*").

We next discuss the implications of our observations for designing a future, context-adaptive checklist to better support decision making and protocol compliance in a team-driven, time-critical and high-stress medical work.

DISCUSSION

Deploying the digital checklist probe allowed us to collect data about its use in actual trauma resuscitations by real users who will be using the digital checklist long term, and to determine if the new technology impacted the checklist use in any significant way. What surprised us was that behaviors around the probe use (e.g., carrying the probe around, leaving it on the stand, checking off on-the-go, or checking off all items at the very end) did not differ from those around the paper checklist use. This finding showed that the digital checklist could function as an appropriate replacement for the paper form within this dynamic and messy workflow. The challenges faced by users during the study period provided valuable information about future design directions, not only for short-term improvements, but also for "solving an interaction design problem" [10] to ensure the continued success of checklists in healthcare. Our goals are to make this technology dynamic and adaptable to different patient and user contexts, and with this study, we lay the groundwork for achieving these goals.

Adaptive Checklist Design for Medical Emergencies

A recurring theme in our findings was that of mobility—a technology affordance that is critical in collaborative work because it allows individuals to reconfigure themselves with regard to ongoing demands of the activity in which they are engaged [18]. As our results have shown, team leaders often moved around the patient bed to get a closer look at physical findings or to assist other team members. When team leaders moved to either side of the bed during patient assessment, they kept holding the probe in one hand while using the other hand to examine the patient. The probe implemented on a tablet was mobile enough to allow the leaders to freely move about the trauma room and quickly glance at the checklist when needed. Our participants commented that retrieving information at a glance from the digital checklist—quickly looking to see what items have previously been done and what items are next in the protocol, or quickly checking notes that have been taken—was easier than on paper because it only presented one section of the checklist at a time. This finding is somewhat contrary to the common belief that providing information on paper in one plane allows for an easy, at-a-glance access to all items [13,23]. When moving quickly about the room to access the patient, this ease of glancing makes an important difference and could make visual information retrieval more efficient. It is therefore important to take both of these issues—mobility and ease of glancing—into account when designing for the checklist adaptation. For example, it will still be important to keep the checklist sections (whether in tabs or through a different layout) small so that all items are visible at all times, and there is no need for scrolling, especially if the leaders are on the move. Showing all items for the current page or tab would also allow users to learn the relative positions of items and quickly localize them as they move about.

Our findings have also shown that items on the checklist are checked either on the go (often with a delay), or at the end of the patient assessment, which is often attributed to team leader preference. This discrepancy in checking behaviors could make the design of a context-adaptive checklist challenging because the system will not be able to detect when items are checked relative to task completion, especially if checking happens at once or at the end. Similarly, our analysis of the probe logs has shown that many items were checked out of order, or before and after task completions, further complicating the adaptive design. Three of the team leaders explained that the order of task performance matters on the primary survey, and if any items are left unchecked, they will immediately direct the team to complete those tasks. The secondary survey, however, is less strict about the order of tasks and our findings confirmed that out-of-order check offs most frequently occurred on the secondary survey tab. These findings have implications for making the checklist adaptable. On the one hand, linear presentation of the checklist items facilitates memorization and visual search for individual items, suggesting a layout with linear lists for all checklist pages. On the other hand, although following the order of steps for both surveys is recommended to avoid selection errors [27], the actual resuscitation workflow structure is often not linear. To balance these requirements, we could leverage adaptive design and visualizations to make the user aware when the sequential order of checking individual items is important but not critical, or to enforce a particular order when it truly matters. Similarly, to encourage timely check offs for completed tasks, the adaptive design could show incomplete tasks by moving checked items to the bottom of the page and populating the top area with unchecked items. Future studies are also needed to examine what tasks are associated with different patient scenarios, and which corresponding items are checked and when, to determine what kinds of checklist adaptations could be made.

Sometimes, items on the checklists were also left unchecked for various reasons, including user experience, skipped tasks, inability to perform tasks due to limited time or delays, or user negligence. This partial completion issue impacts the checklist adaptability in the same way as checking items out of order or at the very end. To address this issue, Christov et al. [5] for example, implemented an "X" button and an optional free-form notes field next to items on their smart checklist for nurses to indicate any problems with completing the process steps. A similar feature could also be designed for the resuscitation checklist to facilitate adaptation. A challenge in designing this feature, however, is that Christov et al. approach supports a single user or performer, whereas our goal is to support teamwork. With a single performer, there is a single thread of activity, making it easier to know the process status and reasons for incomplete tasks. With teamwork, there may be multiple activity threads in progress, making it difficult to immediately know what was done or not, and why.

Related to this issue is team leaders' domain experience. As we have observed in our study, more experienced leaders memorize the ATLS protocol steps without referring to the checklist or they take notes only when findings are abnormal. These observations suggest that checklist adaptation should tailor to user experience levels as well. This type of adaptation, however, should follow a different approach to allow team leaders to select features based on their individual preferences about note taking or checking items. For example, the system should allow users to take both handwritten and typed notes, depending on what works best for them. Users who "check-as-you-go" might prefer to only view tasks remaining within each tab, so checked items could automatically move to the bottom of the tab. If the patient's vital signs drastically change during the resuscitation, team leaders might want to record these trends for later reference, as expressed by our participants.

Increasing the system complexity, adding features, and making the checklist adaptive also increases the likelihood of system malfunctioning. As we have seen through the technology probe deployment, our users have already experienced issues with a relatively simple note-taking feature, when the app froze. These and other potential issues suggest that the design of an adaptive checklist must consider what this increasing complexity means for user interaction. We are taking several approaches as we continue with this work. First, our further extensive testing of the system will reveal different issues that future design iterations will resolve. Second, our goal is to keep the design simple and intuitive, without adding many obtrusive clicks or new screens. Third, it will be important to keep the user in the loop, especially as the system becomes "smarter" and less reliant on user input. Finally, the paper checklist will eventually be replaced by its digital counterpart, so the application will need a fallback mechanism, which could simply show the static checklist without interactive features.

CONCLUSION AND STUDY LIMITATIONS

In this study, we deployed a digital checklist in the trauma resuscitation environment using a technology probe approach. We collected information about the probe use through digital logs, video review and interviews. From these data, we compared how the use of the probe differed from using a paper checklist. We identified advantages and challenges to using the digital checklist in this setting, and discussed implications for designing an adaptive checklist.

Our study has several limitations. First, only six participants used the digital checklist probe due to resident rotations that are common at teaching hospitals. Residents at our study site rotate every four months, with current residents leaving and new residents joining the division of trauma and burn services. These rotations pose challenges for both the system and study design. For example, two residents left the hospital before the study period concluded, making it difficult to interview them. Additionally, the discontinuous nature of residents' schedules means that we cannot have users using the checklist probe over longer periods of time. Second, our initial deployment of the digital checklist probe focused on daytime resuscitations. We have recently implemented a locking mechanism to allow team leaders to access the tablet during off hours, nights and weekends. This ability will allow us to collect a more comprehensive sample of use cases. Third, the matching between paper and digital checklist cases was also challenging. For example, there were several cases with large discrepancies in patient age (e.g., 9 months versus 2 years), which could have an impact on some of the observed differences between cases.

Finally, this was a single site study, which could limit the generalizability of our results. However, because most US trauma centers use the same staffing and procedures, and follow the same resuscitation protocol, we believe that our results are at least generalizable to sites within the US. Additionally, it may be difficult to generalize from trauma resuscitation to generic medical care, and from medical care to other disciplines. Even so, trauma resuscitation alone is an important domain. Despite these limitations, we believe that researchers and designers will benefit from our results.

ACKNOWLEDGMENTS

This research is supported by the National Science Foundation under Award Number 1253285, and partially supported by the National Library Of Medicine of the National Institutes of Health under Award Number R01LM011834. We thank the medical staff at the research site for participating in this study.

REFERENCES

1. Alia K. Amin, Bram T. A. Kersten, Olga A. Kulyk, P. H. Pelgrim, C. M. Wang, and Panos Markopoulos. 2005. SenseMS: A user-centered approach to enrich the messaging experience for teens by non-verbal means. In *Proceedings of the 7th International Conference on Human Computer Interaction with Mobile Devices & Services* (MobileHCI '05), 161–166. https://doi.org/10.1145/1085777.1085804
2. Kirsten Boehner, Janet Vertesi, Phoebe Sengers, and Paul Dourish. 2007. How HCI interprets the probes. In *Proceedings of the SIGCHI Conference on Human Factors in Computing Systems* (CHI '07), 1077–1086. https://doi.org/10.1145/1240624.1240789
3. Thomas Boillat and Christine Legner. 2015. From paper-based to mobile checklists - a reference model. In *Wirtschaftsinformatik*, 106–120. https://doi.org/http://aisel.aisnet.org/wi2015/8
4. Amanda R. Burden, Zyad J. Carr, Gregory W. Staman, Jeffrey J. Littman, and Marc C. Torjman. 2012. Does every code need a "reader?" improvement of rare event management with a cognitive aid "reader" during a simulated emergency: a pilot study. *Simulation in Healthcare: Journal of the Society for Simulation in Healthcare* 7, 1: 1–9. https://doi.org/10.1097/SIH.0b013e31822c0f20
5. Stefan C. Christov, Heather M. Conboy, Nancy Famigletti, George S. Avrunin, Lori A. Clarke, and Leon J. Osterweil. 2016. Smart checklists to improve healthcare outcomes. In *Proceedings of the 2016 International Workshop on Software Engineering in Healthcare Systems* (SEHS '16), 54–57. https://doi.org/10.1145/2897683.2897691
6. Bill Gaver, Tony Dunne, and Elena Pacenti. 1999. Design: Cultural Probes. *interactions* 6, 1: 21–29. https://doi.org/10.1145/291224.291235
7. Lalya Gaye and Lars Erik Holmquist. 2004. In duet with everyday urban settings: A user study of sonic city. In *Proceedings of the 2004 Conference on New Interfaces for Musical Expression* (NIME '04), 161–164.
8. Michael J. Gonzales, Joshua M. Henry, Aaron W. Calhoun, and Laurel D. Riek. 2016. Visual TASK: A collaborative cognitive aid for acute care resuscitation. In *Proceedings of the 10th EAI International Conference on Pervasive Computing Technologies for Healthcare (Pervasive Health 2016)*, 1–8.
9. Connor Graham, Mark Rouncefield, Martin Gibbs, Frank Vetere, and Keith Cheverst. 2007. How probes work. In *Proceedings of the 19th Australasian Conference on Computer-Human Interaction: Entertaining User Interfaces* (OZCHI '07), 29–37. https://doi.org/10.1145/1324892.1324899
10. Eliot Grigg. 2015. Smarter clinical checklists: How to minimize checklist fatigue and maximize clinician performance. *Anesthesia and Analgesia* 121, 2: 570–573. https://doi.org/10.1213/ANE.0000000000000352
11. Russell L. Gruen, Gregory J. Jurkovich, Lisa K. McIntyre, Hugh M. Foy, and Ronald V. Maier. 2006. Patterns of errors contributing to trauma mortality. *Annals of Surgery* 244, 3: 371–380. https://doi.org/10.1097/01.sla.0000234655.83517.56
12. Elaine M. Hart and Harry Owen. 2005. Errors and omissions in anesthesia: A pilot study using a pilot's checklist. *Anesthesia and Analgesia* 101, 1: 246–250. https://doi.org/10.1213/01.ANE.0000156567.24800.0B
13. Christian Heath and Paul Luff. 1996. Documents and professional practice: "bad" organisational reasons for "good" clinical records. In *Proceedings of the 1996 ACM Conference on Computer Supported Cooperative Work* (CSCW '96), 354–363. https://doi.org/10.1145/240080.240342
14. Hilary Hutchinson, Wendy Mackay, Bo Westerlund, Benjamin B. Bederson, Allison Druin, Catherine Plaisant, Michel Beaudouin-Lafon, Stéphane Conversy, Helen Evans, Heiko Hansen, Nicolas Roussel, and Björn Eiderbäck. 2003. Technology probes: Inspiring design for and with families. In *Proceedings of the SIGCHI Conference on Human Factors in Computing Systems* (CHI '03), 17–24. https://doi.org/10.1145/642611.642616
15. Deirdre C. Kelleher, Elizabeth A. Carter, Lauren J. Waterhouse, Samantha E. Parsons, Jennifer L. Fritzeen, and Randall S. Burd. 2014. Effect of a checklist on advanced trauma life support task performance during pediatric trauma resuscitation. *Academic Emergency Medicine: Official Journal of the Society for Academic Emergency Medicine* 21, 10: 1129–1134. https://doi.org/10.1111/acem.12487
16. Heidi S. Kramer and Frank A. Drews. Checking the lists: A systematic review of electronic checklist use in health care. *Journal of Biomedical Informatics.* https://doi.org/10.1016/j.jbi.2016.09.006
17. Angela Lashoher, Eric B. Schneider, Catherine Juillard, Kent Stevens, Elizabeth Colantuoni, and William R. Berry. 2016. Implementation of the World Health Organization Trauma Care Checklist Program in 11 centers across multiple economic strata: Effect on care process measures. *World Journal of Surgery*: 1–9. https://doi.org/10.1007/s00268-016-3759-8
18. Paul Luff and Christian Heath. 1998. Mobility in collaboration. In *Proceedings of the 1998 ACM Conference on Computer Supported Cooperative Work* (CSCW '98), 305–314. https://doi.org/10.1145/289444.289505
19. Stuart D. Marshall. 2016. Helping experts and expert teams perform under duress: an agenda for cognitive aid research. *Anaesthesia.* https://doi.org/10.1111/anae.13707
20. Stuart D. Marshall, Penelope Sanderson, Cate A. McIntosh, and Helen Kolawole. 2016. The effect of two cognitive aid designs on team functioning during intra-operative anaphylaxis emergencies: a multi-centre

simulation study. *Anaesthesia* 71, 4: 389–404. https://doi.org/10.1111/anae.13332

21. Aleksandra Sarcevic, Brett Rosen, Leah Kulp, Ivan Marsic, and Randall Burd. 2016. Design challenges in converting a paper checklist to digital format for dynamic medical settings. In *Proceedings of the 10th EAI International Conference on Pervasive Computing Technologies for Healthcare (Pervasive Health 2016, 1-8).*
22. Aleksandra Sarcevic, Zhan Zhang, Ivan Marsic, and Randall S. Burd. 2016. Checklist as a memory externalization tool during a critical care process. In *Proceedings of the 2016 AMIA Annual Symposium (AMIA '16)* 2016: 1080–1089.
23. Abigail J. Sellen and Richard H.R. Harper. 2003. *The Myth of the Paperless Office*. MIT Press, Cambridge, MA, USA.
24. Charat Thongprayoon, Andrew M. Harrison, John C. O'Horo, Ronaldo A. Sevilla Berrios, Brian W. Pickering, and Vitaly Herasevich. 2014. The effect of an electronic checklist on critical care provider workload, errors, and performance. *Journal of Intensive Care Medicine*. https://doi.org/10.1177/0885066614558015
25. Emiel G. Verdaasdonk, Laurents P. Stassen, Prama P. Widhiasmara, and Jenny Dankelman. 2009. Requirements for the design and implementation of checklists for surgical processes. *Surgical Endoscopy* 23, 4: 715–26. https://doi.org/http://dx.doi.org/10.1007/s00464-008-0044-4
26. Scott C. Watkins, Shilo Anders, Anna Clebone, Elisabeth Hughes, Vikram Patel, Laura Zeigler, Yaping Shi, Matthew S. Shotwell, Matthew D. McEvoy, and Matthew B. Weinger. 2016. Mode of information delivery does not effect anesthesia trainee performance during simulated perioperative pediatric critical events: A trial of paper versus electronic cognitive aids. *Simulation in Healthcare: Journal of the Society for Simulation in Healthcare* 11, 6: 385–393. https://doi.org/10.1097/SIH.0000000000000191
27. Rachel Webman, Jennifer Fritzeen, JaeWon Yang, Grace F. Ye, Paul C. Mullan, Faisal G. Qureshi, Sarah H. Parker, Aleksandra Sarcevic, Ivan Marsic, and Randall S. Burd. 2016. Classification and team response to nonroutine events occurring during pediatric trauma resuscitation. *Journal of Trauma Acute Care Surgery* 81, 4: 666–673. https://doi.org/10.1097/TA.0000000000001196
28. Leslie Wu, Jesse Cirimele, Kristen Leach, Stuart Card, Larry Chu, T. Kyle Harrison, and Scott R. Klemmer. 2014. Supporting crisis response with dynamic procedure aids. In *Proceedings of the 2014 Conference on Designing Interactive Systems* (DIS '14), 315–324. https://doi.org/10.1145/2598510.2598565

Design Features in Games for Health: Disciplinary and Interdisciplinary Expert Perspectives

Christina Kelley[1], Lauren Wilcox[1], Wendy Ng[1], Jade Schiffer[2], Jessica Hammer[2]

[1]School of Interactive Computing
Georgia Institute of Technology
{christina.kelley, wilcox, ngwendy}@gatech.edu

[2]HCI Institute / ETC
Carnegie Mellon University
{jschiffe@andrew, hammerj@cs}.cmu.edu

ABSTRACT

Games for health (G4H) aim to improve health outcomes and encourage behavior change. While existing theoretical frameworks describe features of both games and health interventions, there has been limited systematic investigation into how disciplinary and interdisciplinary stakeholders understand design features in G4H. We recruited 18 experts from the fields of game design, behavioral health, and games for health, and prompted them with 16 sample games. Applying methods including open card sorting and triading, we elicited themes and features (e.g., real-world interaction, game mechanics) around G4H. We found evidence of conceptual differences suggesting that a G4H perspective is not simply the sum of game and health perspectives. At the same time, we found evidence of convergence in stakeholder views, including areas where game experts provided insights about health and vice versa. We discuss how this work can be applied to provide conceptual tools, improve the G4H design process, and guide approaches to encoding G4H-related data for large-scale empirical analysis.

Author Keywords

Health, games, G4H, serious games, game design

ACM Classification Keywords

H.5.m. Information interfaces and presentation (e.g., HCI): Miscellaneous; J.3. Life and medical sciences: Health

INTRODUCTION

Serious games—those designed for purposes beyond entertainment [14]—target a variety of topics from social issues [40] to higher-order science skills [29], and health is a common and growing area of focus. Sawyer describes health as a field of interest for serious games due to its deep research history in training and simulation and the large market for technological advances within the field; in addition, there is a prevalence of games already geared towards physical fitness, opportunities for scientists, medical professionals, and patients each to benefit directly, and the possibility of health markers to be used in evaluating game outcomes [41].

Growing evidence of the potential for games to produce positive health outcomes has led many in HCI and related fields to more closely examine the "active ingredients" of well-designed health games [7,13,24]. However, work on how specific game elements relate to health concepts has thus far been difficult to generalize, particularly in ways that serve both game designers and domain experts [11,49]. These disciplinary and interdisciplinary stakeholders [20,32] bring differing perspectives on the relevance of game features, how they instantiate health concepts, and even what counts as a feature in the first place. We therefore probed design phenomena surrounding G4H that can be understood only through collective perspectives, by enlisting experts with years of experience in game, G4H, or health intervention design. Through structured and semi-structured prompts, we collected rich and detailed sets of responses to specific games and game concepts from these experts. We draw on these responses to characterize how game design and health concepts are expressed and realized in G4H and to identify corresponding design attributes. We thus make the following contributions:

(1) We distill evidence of convergence as well as conceptual differences in how different stakeholder groups discuss design-related themes and features of G4H.
(2) We discuss how our research can be applied to provide conceptual tools and support interdisciplinary communication in the G4H design process.

RELATED WORK

Health Outcomes of G4H

Some games have been found to encourage and improve healthy lifestyles [13] and to increase disease knowledge for cancer patients [8] and people with diabetes [12]. Games also have shown positive effects on mental, physical, and social health in older adults [21]. However, many games for health have not been proven effective, and more and higher-quality clinical trials are needed to further understand the effects of different games on health outcomes [30,37]. Ideally, clinical studies of G4H should not just reveal *that* a particular game is effective, but also should

DIS 2017, June 10-14, 2017, Edinburgh, United Kingdom

ACM ISBN 978-1-4503-4922-2/17/06…$15.00
http://dx.doi.org/10.1145/3064663.3064721

help researchers understand *why* it is effective. This cannot be done without a foundational understanding of underlying game features.

Game and Health Frameworks

Many researchers have examined the current state of serious games in the health space through theoretical frameworks. The most prominent framework for health games, Sawyer and Smith's [42] taxonomy, categorizes games by their domain (*personal, professional practice, research/academia*, or *public health* –focused) and then by health activity (*preventative, therapeutic, assessment, educational*, or *informatics*). Mader et al. [34] further frame therapeutic games according to the three main foci of *player, game*, and *therapy* and the relationships between them. These frameworks provide important structural insights, such as helping identify areas where there is unexplored potential for G4H, but they do not extend to the level of specific game features. Conversely, game frameworks that are more specific regarding game features (e.g. [9]) do not address the challenges of embodying health theories in play.

Behavior Change Theories

Other researchers have focused on the application of health and behavior change concepts within games and gamified applications. Behavior change theories have influenced both the design and evaluation of serious games, particularly those focusing on health promotion and illness management (e.g., tobacco prevention [22], exercise [28], nutrition [19], physical therapy [39], and medication adherence [44]). Recent arguments against the application of purely cognitive models of behavior change (e.g., Transtheoretical Model [38], Health Belief Model [27]) point out their overemphasis on the individual [45] in modeling behavior. Such criticisms have prompted a more recent focus on adopting social models of behavior change (e.g., Social Cognitive Theory [5], Emergent Dialogue [45]) to promote observational learning or collective behavior change through design. Yet, particularly for health interventions, even these theory-driven approaches to design do not necessarily cohere with user-centered approaches [4]; moreover, research on the discovery and implementation of specific design decisions that incorporate elements and constructs of theoretical models is an open area.

Applying Behavioral Theory in Game Design

Content analysis of mobile apps for fitness and general health found that most apps did not contain much health theoretical content [10,50], and a review of fitness-focused console games found that concepts common in weight loss interventions were present in games but that no studies had yet tested the effects of these concepts in a game setting [33]. There is also a gap between evaluation of these outcomes and understanding of how best to incorporate them into the design of health games. For example, in the realm of exergames, Lieberman et al. [32] developed a model of mediating factors that should be considered in design—improvement of player self-concepts, self-efficacy, physical activity, and social support—which will enable the field to better evaluate the design of exergames and to improve their design and evaluation in the future. In parallel, Mueller and Isbister [35] developed principles for designing movement-based games and validated them with an audience of game designers. Themes from Lieberman's work appear in these design principles: for example, Mueller and Isbister propose giving players visualizations that support rhythmic movement, which connects to the concept of self-efficacy. However, these mediating factors have not been systematically linked to specific game features or design decisions.

This gap between game design and behavioral theory is mirrored in G4H design methodologies. Playmatics' five-point framework for health and science games emphasizes that, while scientists and game designers may be working on the same team, they have separate areas of expertise [49]. However, uniting game and health expertise is not a trivial task, as the limited replication of health-theoretical content in games suggests. Schell Games' Transformational Framework [11] for game design supports this process by providing workshops and discussion activities that help stakeholders collaborate; however, this framework is a broad approach to transformational games and does not focus specifically on health.

Game Mechanics and Features

Research is also limited on how to best design health games that incorporate established game mechanics, and experts in the field agree that more attention must be paid to such features in order to create successful games [6]. First, games must be engaging in order to encourage the play that moves the player toward the desired health and learning outcomes [31]; understanding successful game mechanics is important to this effort. Moreover, different game mechanics can encourage—or discourage—desired health outcomes in different ways (e.g., encouraging or limiting physical movement), and understanding the relationship is vital [6]. Furthermore, many game mechanics, such as multiplayer mechanics, are simply not well understood in the context of health games, which means that areas of promise are often overlooked [17].

However, we acknowledge that game mechanics are not the only types of features in games. For example, Bjork and Holopainen [9] include technical and social patterns in addition to game mechanical patterns in their taxonomy of game design patterns. While we expect to find game mechanics *included* in our experts' perspectives on game features in G4H, we do not expect expert discussion of features to be limited solely to mechanics. Game art, game narrative, and the context of play are other potential sources for features in G4H.

Values in G4H

Games can also embody points of view. In G4H, these views may focus on the health condition a game addresses; *Zombies Run!*, for example, reflects an inclusive, nonjudgmental notion of exercise [2], while other games are much more punitive about obesity [46]. Health games can also embody points of view about *how health behavior change works*, by incorporating elements of health and behavior change frameworks [20]. In *Values at Play*, Flanagan and Nissenbaum propose a conscious, reflective process for identifying the values that one wants to express in a game. These values can relate to health behaviors, to how the game treats users, or both. For example, the health game *Lit2Quit* addressed tobacco smoking; however, its stance is that the game should *support* players' pre-existing desire to quit, rather than attempt to *convince* them to quit [26]. This stance comes from value commitments on the part of the game designers, such as respecting the autonomy of smokers who better understand their own life circumstances; these values are in turn reflected in specific design decisions, such as helping reduce the urge to smoke in a process initiated by the player. A value-reflective process like this is especially important when the stakeholders involved in a game's creation come from different backgrounds, as is often the case in G4H, and understanding how these different stakeholders identify and interpret features and values is crucial to expressing them in games in more effective ways.

METHODS

We began our work by examining the current landscape of health games and aggregating these games into a G4H corpus. This helped us develop a deeper understanding of existing health games in both research and commercial settings, and provided a database from which to select games for use in our expert study sessions. We chose to create a corpus despite the existence of some G4H databases [47], as no current aggregation of health games followed our criteria (described below) or was fully exhaustive regarding games or game details.

Health Games Corpus

Our G4H corpus consists of 320 health games curated from a variety of sources, including previous publications, prior research databases [47], and Google, Android app store, and Apple app store searches (keywords: "games for health"; "games for health management"; "disease management games"). The corpus contains listings for each game with details (e.g., developer, platform(s), genre, health condition) and associated research where applicable. Health games fit our criteria and could be added to the corpus if they focused on disease prevention, health promotion, and/or disease management. We aimed to adhere to the designers' original intent: only games that promoted themselves as games were included, and applications with only minor "gamification" were excluded. Games designed for training medical professionals were also excluded. To assist with classification, games were required to have a *core loop* [43], or elements of feedback in which player actions affect the game and vice versa.

We selected 16 games from our corpus for use in all expert study sessions (see Table 1). We chose a random subset of playable games and evaluated them with replacement until we had a diverse, representative sample of the larger corpus that balanced research-based and commercial games, as well as game platforms. Selected games were either currently playable or had gameplay video accessible to our research team. For each, we constructed explanatory game cards for our study (with titles, sample images, and brief instructions for play).

Study Procedure

With IRB approval, we conducted individual study sessions with 18 expert participants (7M, 11F): game design experts (n=7), behavioral health experts (n=5), and health game experts (n=6). Participating experts must have completed or deployed one or more games, health interventions, or health games. Within each group, we also aimed to include experts from different backgrounds (e.g., both researchers and members of industry).

Game	Creator	Health condition
Re-Mission 2: Nanobot's Revenge	HopeLab	Cancer
Bronkie the Bronchiasaurus	Raya Systems	Asthma
Bubble Rubble	Playnormous	Physical activity
Chicken Farm	Nobel Media	Nutrition
Colorfall	Persuasive Games	Mental health, physical activity
Dex: Virtual Pet	Georgia Regents University	Diabetes
Elude	GAMBIT Singapore-MIT Game Lab	Depression
Escape from Diab	Achimage	Diabetes
Fix Frank	American Diabetes Association	Diabetes
Mindless Eating Challenge	Interaction Design Lab, Cornell University	Nutrition
Monster Manor	Ayogo Health, Sanofi	Diabetes
Packy & Marlon	Raya Systems	Diabetes
Rex Ronan: Experimental Surgeon	Sculptured Software, Health Hero Network	Smoking cessation
Snow World	University of Washington, Harborview Burn Center	Pain management
Squire's Quest II	Archimage, Baylor Children's Nutrition Research Center	Nutrition
Virtual Iraq	Virtually Better	PTSD

Table 1. The 16 games used in expert study sessions.

We recruited by word of mouth and snowball sampling, and conducted study sessions both in-person (for local participants) and remotely via Skype. All in-person participants gave informed consent and all remote participants signed waivers of consent, as approved by the IRB. Study materials for in-person sessions consisted of physical game cards, while remote sessions used digital "cards" in Google Slides (Phases I and II) [18] and OptimalSort (Phase III) [36]. All sessions were audio- and video- recorded and lasted approximately one hour. We provided a $25 Amazon gift card to each participant for completing the study. Study sessions consisted of three phases: an exploratory phase in which experts described an unknown game aloud based on images, a triading phase in which they compared groups of three games, and an open-ended card sort in which they categorized 15 games. These three phases, chosen to gather expert feedback in multiple ways—both structured and open-ended—are described in more detail below.

Phase I: Exploration
Participants first viewed images from a health game (Re-Mission 2: Nanobot's Revenge) and were asked what information they would need in order to understand the game; we used a think-aloud protocol to elicit—from the participant's perspective—what they understood from the photos, what information they would have liked to see, and what questions they would ask to understand the game to the best of their ability.

Phase II: Triading
In the second phase of the study, we conducted (with each participant) 15 rounds of *triading* [23], a technique borrowed from repertory grid technique (RGT), which aims to elicit domain-relevant constructs and the relationships between them [3]. We used the remaining 15 health games from our corpus in this phase; one game per card.

For each round of triading, participants viewed games in randomized *triads* of three cards at a time. For each of the first five rounds, we asked participants to decide which *two* games were most similar and which *one* was different, and then explain why. The following ten rounds included the addition of a concept card: in these rounds, participants again viewed randomized triads of games, this time presented alongside a randomized concept card (see Table 2 for a complete list of concepts). We asked experts to again identify which two game cards were similar and which one was different, but this time to compare the games according to the presented concept.

Phase III: Open Card Sort
In the final phase, participants conducted an open-ended card sort of all 15 health games from the triading phase. We asked each participant to sort the games however they thought best: giving no further instructions or limits on how many groupings should be created or what kind. When the card sort was complete, participants explained their sorting rationale to the researcher.

Concept	Explanation
Audience	Who this game is for
Behavior change	How players changed their behavior because of play
Context of use	When and how this game would be played
Core loop	How player actions influence the game, and how the game in turn influences player actions
Game challenges	Obstacles or difficult elements in the game
Game goals	In-game goals and objectives
Health motivation	Why players want to improve their health or change their health behavior
Outcome evaluation	How we know whether the intervention was successful or not
Play strategies	Strategies the player can use to be successful in this game
Preparation	What prior preparation the player needs for this health change

Table 2. Concepts used in framing triading rounds six through 15.

Data analysis
We analyzed quantitative triading and open-card-sort data through descriptive statistics and similarity matrices [1] to determine common game pairings. After transcribing spoken responses from participants verbatim, three researchers conducted an iterative, inductive thematic analysis [15] of triad comparison round results, using a constant comparative approach [22]. Multiple concepts were coded within each round. Through discussion among the research team, we used these concepts to derive seven higher-level themes.

FINDINGS & DISCUSSION
From 270 rounds of triading, we found 76 concepts mentioned a total of 761 times by experts (see Table 3 for a full list). These 76 concepts fell into seven higher-level themes, as follows: *player characteristics*, aspects of the player outside of their experiences with the game; *health model*, how the health subject matter is modeled, represented, and understood in and through the design; *game world*, fictional and experiential aspects of the game such as art and narrative; *game mechanics*, game rules and related features such as level design; *player behavior*, which includes physical and mental player activity in and around the game; *context*, or the way gameplay interacts with the real world; and *outcomes*, how players or the world around them are changed by their play experience.

In this section, we first examine the ways themes were understood differently by expert groups, beginning with a short overview before delving into specific results. We also offer further comparisons between expert groups, including comparisons by triading concept and by game. We end with implications of our work for design and for future research.

Game Design Experts

While game design experts did reference health concepts, they were unsurprisingly sensitive to the **game aspects** of G4H, tending to use language that referenced other games rather than other health experiences. They also frequently considered the **player as a person with autonomy and experiences**, rather than focusing solely on their health condition. Finally, game experts based their discussion of the relationship between game and health content on the **integration of game mechanics and health behavior**. We discuss these differences in more depth below.

Game aspects of G4H

Game design experts were most likely to conduct triading game comparisons based on game features. For instance, P2 compared Colorfall, Squire's Quest II, and Elude by explaining that *"[Elude] is about... moving a character around [and] Squire's Quest II] looks like a classical quest-based sort of thing... I think Colorfall is the most different one here [as] it has no main character and is more about stacking blocks, it's a more classical puzzle [game]."* Especially in the open-ended triading rounds, game design experts emphasized game-related themes and concepts. Experts compared games based on *narrative* (*"story-driven"* (P10)), *game goals* (*"changing things and seeing how they play out"* (P14)), *mechanics* ("firing" vs. "navigation" (P10)), *characters* (*"implied avatars"* vs. *"obvious avatars"* (P14)), and *aesthetic* (*"similar in art style and tone*" (P17)), among others. In these examples and many more, game experts compared the health games at hand but applied game "dialect" and referenced other games rather than health experiences when doing so. Despite ongoing debates in the field about the relative importance of mechanical and aesthetic elements in games, game design experts used both game-mechanical and game-world features to make these comparisons.

Despite this focus on G4H game aspects, game design experts did consider the player's *health goal* (a player characteristic) and the *health condition* represented by the game (part of the health model). For instance, P9 explained that *"[Escape from Diab and Dex] are very similar because they're both about diabetes... [but Elude] is exploring mood, which is completely different."* When comparing Monster Manor, Packy & Marlon, and Rex Ronan: Experimental Surgeon, P10 noted that *"Monster Manor and Packy & Marlon seem to be most similar... they're both about checking your insulin levels and diabetes... At the same time, Packy & Marlon and Rex Ronan seem to be pretty similar because there are these platforming levels, [and] at least mechanically they appear to have some similarities."* These experts frequently found that game triads could be characterized in multiple salient ways, often with one health-focused and one game-focused direction. As P10's response shows, the game and the health themes sometimes suggested different game pairings.

Player characteristics	
Cultural assumptions	Player health status
Gender	Player skills
Health goal	Preparation
Identity	Prior knowledge
Player cognition	
Health model	
Health condition	Similarity between game and target domain
Health subject matter	Simulation
Level of health-relatedness	
Level of seriousness	
Game world	
Abstraction	Game space
Emotion	Game text
Experiential	Narrative/story
Game analogies	Player role
Game characters	Point of view
Game clarity	Quests
Game classification	Rewards
Game dialogue	
Game mechanics	
Core loop	Game mechanics
Feedback	Game rules
Game challenges	Game speed
Game chokepoints	Game structure
Game complexity	Number of players
Game controls	Patterns
Game genre	Verbs
Game goals	Win condition
Game levels	
Player behavior	
Attention	Motivation
Caretaking	Player actions
Cheating	Player decision-making
Control	Progression
Exploration	Strategies
Interaction	
Context	
Audience	Modality
Context of use	Real-world interaction
Gamification	Repeated play
Length of game/engagement	Social
Outcomes	
Behavior change	Evaluation
Education	Health outcomes
Effectiveness	Reflection
Entertainment	Support/scaffolding
Escape/distraction	Tracking/logging

Table 3. High-level themes (*n* = 7) gathered from triading and open card sorting, with the corresponding concepts that make up each theme.

Player as Person with Autonomy and Experiences

Experts in this group were particularly sensitive to player characteristics, framing the player as a person with autonomy and considering their prior life experiences. P8 discussed the relevance of player experience when differentiating Escape from Diab, explaining that "*it seems based on a specific set of rules... this sort of game requires a very complex, logical thinking from the players, [some of whom] may have a great deal of experiences and knowledge for the circumstances.*" P17 described the relevance of potential differences in player experience for Virtual Iraq, noting that "*there [is] a stereotype about everybody [in the military] being a gamer... but half of them [can't use] the controls at all and spend thirty minutes just staring at a wall... Basically, you can't get the experience out of the game if you don't bring the ability to navigate the controls prior to the experience.*"

Additionally, game experts were the only group to consider that players may have goals that do not align with designer intentions: comparing Bubble Rubble, Chicken Farm, and Dex in the context of *game goals*, P2 said that *"I get the sense that there's going to be a big difference between what the designers of these games think that players are going to do and what the players are actually going to do... [for these two] I'm going to say the players are really going to be focused on score... and [Dex is] about keeping things alive over a long period of time, and not about the score but just about the character itself."* Even through the lens of game design and mechanics, there is room left for a disconnect between player and designer, which can affect a player's experience of the gameplay.

One game expert also framed player experiences in the context of gender and culture—the only expert in any group to mention either concept. The game expert who discussed gender did so during triading, in the context of *game aesthetic* and *audience*, noting that *"...this could just be poor design concept, but I feel like these two [Mindless Eating Challenge and Bronkie the Bronchiasaurus] could be more [geared towards] girls, or at least to a gender neutral sort of audience... I don't know if this is just the lack of consideration about aesthetics, but [Rex Ronan] definitely doesn't scream 'little girls'"* (P18). A few rounds later, the same expert touched on cultural assumptions isn the context of *game aesthetic* and *prior knowledge*, explaining that *"there's definitely cultural assumptions [in Monster Manor] about knowing what Frankenstein is [and] being able to interpret this aesthetic of the ghoulish kind of thing"* (P18).

While many experts in all groups discussed *audience* in terms of age (children vs. adults) or health status (diagnosed with a condition vs. general population), no other expert touched on the importance of sociocultural considerations in the design of health games. In fact, we expected to encounter this more frequently, given that the academic study of games often adopts analytical approaches that treat games as cultural texts and artifacts with a sociocultural context [16].

Integration of Game Mechanics and Health Behavior

When game experts discussed the health model of a game, they described game mechanics and health behavior as two equal, high-level concepts, working well together when they are integrated. In Phase III of the study, game design experts used *similarity between game and target domain* to group games, commenting frequently on this integration or lack thereof. P17, for example, explained groupings within the open card sort as *"[separating] games I thought [had] learning content very tightly integrated... [versus] games where I wasn't so sure how the learning content was even integrated at all... [and] then games where it seems that the learning content had an interactive component but [also] significant other non-learning scaffolding."* P14 also noted that *"[Escape from Diab] specifically has you making these changes that might be mirrored in real life."*

Meanwhile, other game design experts expressed concern about a lack of integration between game mechanics and health concepts in some games. P18, for instance, did not think Bronkie the Bronchiasaurus demonstrated adequate integration: "*I can't imagine that this could draw an analogy to any real-world behavior in kids, because it's like you're [just] little animals running through the jungle.*" P2 felt similarly about Nanobot's Revenge, explaining that "*it seems like they're borrowing a lot of mechanics from other games, without a clear sense of why they've borrowed those mechanics.*" For these game experts, such game–health integration was a frequent measure of comparison between games, and they saw a lack of such integration as an indicator that a game might be less effective as an intervention.

Behavioral Health Experts

Overall, behavioral health experts were most likely to reference concepts within the high-level theme of health model. Like game experts, behavioral health experts were also concerned with player characteristics, especially autonomy, but of a different kind: they focused on **player autonomy in relation to one's own health** and in relation to one's preparedness to take action and change behavior. These experts also differentiated **"fun"** in games as distinct from learning, monitoring, or other productive health activities. Finally, their understanding of the relationship between game and health content frames **game mechanics as a representation of the health model and content**, rather than two equally high-level concepts.

Player Autonomy in Relation to their Own Health

Much of this expert group's discussion of health concepts was based around player autonomy in relation to their health. Behavioral health experts most commonly compared game trios based on features of *health goals*, *health condition*, and *health subject matter*, but they did so in the context of outcomes, noting whether and how behavior change stages and preparedness for action were considered in the design. P11 compared multiple triads in these ways, explaining that *"[Escape from Diab and Squire's Quest II] both seem to be about nutrition [and] making healthy decisions"* and that *"[Bronkie the Bronchiasaurus and Elude] are more similar because they seem to be educational about understanding either yourself, having asthma or depression, or helping friends and family understand."*

Interestingly, some experts worried that the simple fact of playing a game might be interfering with player autonomy, or at least could have a negative effect on the player's real-life health experience: discussing Nanobot's Revenge in Phase I, P11 felt that, *"I don't want to say [the game] is making light of what they're going through, but you're already facing cancer, cancer is your life when you're going through chemo. Do you really want to play a game with cancer?"*

Behavioral health experts also contrasted games by mentioning aspects of context, especially *real-world interaction*. P15 explained that Monster Manor was different than Elude and Rex Ronan due to *"your individual behavior, you need to track that in order for the gameplay to be interesting"*, while P13 thought that *"Monster Manor and Packy & Marlon are similar because you're logging your personal information."* Other health experts discussed the interactivity and real-world context of both Mindless Eating Challenge and Dex: Virtual Pet. Additionally, in contrast with Fix Frank, P3 noted that, *"both [Monster Manor and Bubble Rubble] seem more grounded in what people's health behavior is in the real world."* Discussion of real-world context and related themes shows a focus on the player rather than the game—unsurprising from behavioral health experts— but in a way that still relates to player behavior and gameplay.

In Phase I of the study, behavioral health experts also tended to focus on how a player's real-world health could be affected by gameplay. P12 believed that Nanobot's Revenge's goal was to teach players how chemotherapy works and how it might affect them, while P15 was curious to learn more about the curriculum content of the game and how closely it hewed to reality, worrying that an actual simulation of chemotherapy might be disturbingly bleak. Interestingly, although many participants talked about the Nanobot's Revenge general audience, only one participant (P11) wondered if there was a more specific target audience than just "children with cancer." He asked, *"is this recommended to all patients, or [those] that are having extreme anxiety about getting chemo? [Is this supposed to] alleviate some of that anxiety, or is it just like a blanket 'Here. You're getting chemo. Play this game'?"* These sorts of questions and observations highlight this group's particular expertise, and demonstrate their interest in the player and his or her health autonomy both in and beyond the game.

"Fun" Games

Behavioral health experts also often discussed the *level of "seriousness"* of a game. In the open card sort, P12 categorized most of the games by health condition but grouped three games together as *"game-games"* that are just for *"fun"*. P13 also had a grouping called *"fun games"* that differentiated Snow World, Rex Ronan, Colorfall, and Squire's Quest II from other groupings of *"learning games"*, *"health monitoring games"*, and *"virtual games"*. There was frequent classification of "fun" as an outcome in opposition to learning, with P15 noting that *"on the entertainment versus education spectrum... [Nanobot's Revenge is] a little more entertaining than educational."* Other experts expressed similar sentiments during the triading phase, explaining that Fix Frank is *"just a game"* (P12) and that Colorfall and Snow World *"seem kind of pointless"* (P11). The concept of "fun" is not as simple as it sounds—it is in fact a concept so overloaded that game designers often avoid using the term [25]. This usage illustrates a particular disconnect between game and health experts: it reflects health experts' assumptions about how games are "supposed to" be: does the use of fun in this context imply that the other games are not fun, or shouldn't be fun? This question prompts additional ones about what these health experts perceive makes a game a game and whether they perceive an idealized dichotomy separating serious and non-serious games.

Game Mechanics as Representation of Health Content

Lastly, on the theme of *similarity between game and target domain*, behavioral health experts saw the relationship between health and game content as one in which game mechanics represent the health model. In the open card sort, in the context of *game mechanics*, P15 explained that *"the biggest group is the one where game mechanics are representative of the disease model... [games] like Packy & Marlon, Bubble Rubble, Escape from Diab, Squire's Quest II all kind of fit there."* In the triading phase, other experts noted how some games aimed to show the player how to change their behavior by *"modeling the effects of [behavior change]"* (P15) or *"reinforc[ing] the player doing things, [through repetition]... the mechanics bleed into player real life"* (P10). Health experts used game design terms such as "mechanics" to describe this similarity, but treated the health concept as a baseline model, which game mechanics can represent with varying degrees of fidelity and accuracy.

G4H Experts

G4H experts commonly discussed **context and interaction** during gameplay, considering when and how a game would be played and noting multiplayer mode and community as critical differentiators between games. G4H experts also frequently spoke about **outcomes and objectives** in both the game and in a player's health behavior. Finally, this expert group framed the relationship between game and health concepts as one in which **game mechanics produce health outcomes**.

Context and Interaction

While G4H experts, like behavioral health experts, were most likely to make triading comparisons based on *health goal* and *health condition*, G4H experts were much more focused on the context of use surrounding a game. P16 differentiated Monster Manor from other games by explaining that it *"stands out pretty clearly, just because it's a mobile game that's intended to be interwoven into a diabetic's life as they track their diabetes information, whereas the other two... [are] a separate event from the rest of the player's life."* Similarly, P15 found that "*Dex is the odd one out because it's supposed to be used over a period of time [and] you're earning daily rewards, whereas Virtual Iraq... you would do maybe once in a sitting and then talk about it, and Bronkie the Bronchiasaurus is similar, you could just play it once and get the lesson, it's not going to reward you for coming back the way that [Dex] does."* For many G4H experts, a discussion of the health games at hand was not complete without this focused discussion of the surrounding context.

Moreover, this notion of context was often framed more specifically in terms of *social context* by G4H experts. Interestingly, this was the only group to mention the social interaction within Nanobot's Revenge in Phase I. P1 asked whether or not clinicians get data from the game to help improve their interactions with a patient, and many G4H experts wondered if players are able to share game status and achievements through social media as a way for others to know how they are doing; for instance, "*the fact that she's at level five lets me know, 'Oh she must have had a chemo day today so she's probably feeling sick and I should reach out,'...[game results could allow her to share this information] without her having to type, 'I'm sick'*" (P1). In the triading comparisons, G4H experts also distinguished Squire's Quest II as a multi-player game and noted that Mindless Eating Challenge has both a multi-player and community component. P5 felt that Mindless Eating Challenge also requires that the player "*be judged by peers"* and have *"a willing audience."* While behavioral health experts discussed social relationships as outcomes of a game, G4H experts saw social interactions as something that happens during gameplay and is closely connected to the game context and the experience of the game itself [48].

Outcomes and Objectives

G4H experts in our study also discussed goals and outcomes both inside and outside the game. This group saw objectives as something that is inherent in the game rather than produced by the player, with P5 noting that *"kid-friendly games have simple objectives, [but the objectives are] less clear for Virtual Iraq."* P16 elaborated on game objectives as well, explaining that Packy & Marlon and Chicken Farm *"seem to have finite game play, a goal that you can reach, whereas [Monster Manor], because it's intended for behavior change and because of the social-mobile DNA there [is] much more infinite. The goals are more dynamic in terms of, I want to make it to the next level, or I want to find this particular monster... things like that. Then once one goal is completed, more goals become apparent, whereas the other two... look like the kinds of games that have an ending, where you reach your goal and you're done."* P1 compared another triad by saying that *"these two [Dex and Packy & Marlon] are alike because of their content, that they're for diabetes education... it seems like it's here to prompt them to have healthy habits and to educate them about their disease, whereas [Elude is] not really educating you about depression."* Other experts mentioned that certain games have a goal of teaching the player how to take care of themselves or others in real life (P5) or a prevention focus, in this case, prevention of diabetes (P7).

G4H experts also noted the possibility of negative game outcomes having a potential negative or demotivating effect on the player's real-world health, and they were the only expert group in Phase I to touch on possible concerns of the game for the target audience. P1 saw the game as an empowerment tool for children undergoing chemotherapy; however, she noted the importance of making sure the game wasn't too hard so that it didn't have this demotivating effect on the player. P5 echoed this concern, calling Nanobot's Revenge *"a bit of a touchy game"* given the content and audience. This concern for the physical and emotional health of the player, based on game mechanics and difficulty, demonstrates a critical understanding of the game, the player, and the powerful connection between them.

Game Mechanics Produce Health Outcomes

When discussing game mechanics and the health model together, G4H experts framed the relationship as one in which game mechanics produce health outcomes. They thought frequently about what happens outside the game, how the game can be incorporated into daily life, and how game skills can transfer to actual behavioral goals and outcomes. G4H experts considered *real-world interaction* in the context of *behavior change*, with one expert invoking real-life connections by differentiating Dex from other games because one's own management and real-life practices drive the virtual pet (P6). Likewise, P16 said that, *"the one I would call out as different here is probably the Mindless Eating Challenge because it explicitly asks you to complete tasks in real life. It is not purely endogenous, it's reaching outside the game to try and drive actual behaviors."* Later, P16 also discussed how Virtual Iraq is "*directly effecting a therapeutic intervention, [and] actively working on PTSD."*

G4H experts also referenced transfer to a real-world context in the open card sort, with P1 creating a grouping of games that were both educational and also included real-life content, while P6 characterized a subset of games as *"linking real behaviors to virtual games"* and another as *"behavioral rehearsal."* In Phase 1, P1 also found that the mechanics of Nanobot's Revenge helped to empower the player in their real-life health experience, as "*the goals of this game are to inform and possibly also to enhance their effect or locus of control: like, 'I can beat cancer. I can do this.'"*

Comparisons Between Expert Groups: Triad Themes

To better understand similarities and differences between game, health, and G4H experts, we next more closely examine their responses to the ten assigned triading concepts.

Expert group	Important results	Corresponding high-level theme(s)
Game design experts	Game aspects of G4H Player as a person with autonomy and experiences Integration of game mechanics and health behavior	Game world and game mechanics Player characteristics Game mechanics and health model
Behavioral health experts	Player autonomy in relation to one's own health "Fun" as outcome Game mechanics as a representation of the health model	Player characteristics and health model Health model Game mechanics and health model
G4H experts	Context and interaction Outcomes and objectives Game mechanics produce health outcomes	Context Outcomes Game mechanics and health model

Table 4. Overview of thematic analysis results, by expert group.

Within Phase 2 of the study, rounds six through 15 asked experts to compare game triads based on one of 10 assigned concepts. By varying the games being compared for a given concept, we observed common themes emerge. In the *play strategies* round, for instance, game experts were most likely to discuss game mechanics, especially *win/loss conditions*, differentiating games by explaining that *"[some games] are letting you play through... and you can lose, [but] over here you can die but you can't lose the game"* (P9). Health experts, on the other hand, were more likely to describe play strategies and game success in terms of the game world concept of *rewards*, noting that for some games *"you could come in with your knowledge and play to your strengths to get further points in the game"* (P11). This is an interesting distinction that demonstrates a key difference in framing: game experts are taking the frame of the game seriously in their assumption that winning and losing are valuable in their own right, while health experts seem to understand rewards as the main motivator for play irrespective of game outcomes.

There were further group differences in themes mentioned in the *audience* round. Game design experts talked about *game aesthetic*, intuiting, for example, that a game was geared towards children *"just from the interfaces and the colors and their choice of graphics"* (P10). G4H experts, however, more often discussed *health condition* and *health status*, differentiating audience between *"kids that probably have been diagnosed with something, with a chronic illness, whereas... this [other game] is just for anyone"* (P1). Finally, health experts most frequently discussed audience in the context of *health subject matter* and *motivation*, with P15 explaining that some games *"seem to be targeted at people who actually are looking to make an adjustment in their diet or physical activity"* (P15).

Some assigned concepts prompted similar themes across groups. *Game goals*, for instance, explained to participants as "in-game goals and objectives," still frequently led to discussion of *health goals* for experts in all groups. One game expert noted that in Dex *"the Tamagotchi format makes the goals align very closely with what the learning objectives would be"* (P17), while a health expert framed a comparison of game goals by explaining that *"the general goal is to be healthier... [make] food choices, and [improve] nutrition"* (P11). *Context of use* also saw all groups frequently discuss the same themes, namely *health goals* and *repeated play*. A G4H expert felt that Bronkie the Bronchiasaurus is the sort of game that you sit down and play once all the way through (P4), while a game expert thought that Mindless Eating Challenge *"is a bust out your phone from time to time, play with it a little bit, put it away [type of game]... connected to real time in some way"* (P14), and a health expert felt similarly that Dex is supposed to be played by logging data a little bit every day (P13). For these assigned concepts, the variance in responses further accentuate group differences, yet similarities offer promise for interdisciplinary understanding and communication.

Comparisons by Game

Finally, we examine discussion and comparison by game, both amongst and across expert groups. This is important for multiple reasons. First, there are real differences between the games in our study and we want to clarify the particular themes each game may have been more likely to elicit. Most importantly, though, since we are ultimately motivated by a desire to define and identify game features in ways that are useful to a range of stakeholders, it is crucial that we aim to understand individual games. This does not detract from the importance of comparing themes and features between expert groups; rather, it allows us an additional, more focused view of the games that our experts were comparing, and which instantiate the concepts explored to date.

Looking at the thematic results of the open card sort by game, we see that some games in our corpus were more likely to elicit particular themes across all expert groups: *health goal*, *health condition*, and *game genre* were the themes most commonly used to group 11 of the 15 games. For both Monster Manor and Mindless Eating Challenge, however, *real-world interaction* was most frequently used for characterization, with P15 calling this grouping *"real-world credit"* and P3 labeling these games as *"daily life"* and *"rewarding based on real behavior."* For Dex: Virtual Pet, *simulation* was the theme of choice, while for Snow World most experts mainly wondered about its *level of "seriousness"*. Similarly, Colorfall was often characterized by its *lack of health-relatedness*, with many experts saying that it *"doesn't fit with any categories"* and *"[I] can't tell what the health goal is"* (P16), or that it's a *"non-health"* (P7) or *"fun game"* (P14). This again serves to demonstrate a presumed dichotomy between games that are clearly serious and "useful" and other games that are not. These sorts of comments illustrate the challenges of subtly integrating serious content into games, and the tension between fun and education in creating and integrating serious health games.

We can also examine game trends by studying similarities and differences in how games were grouped together by participants from all three expert groups. During the open card sort, Fix Frank, Bubble Rubble, and Escape from Diab were grouped together by every participant in the health expert group, for instance, while each was grouped with the others far less frequently by both game and G4H experts. Within the health group, however, the three games were paired together for a variety of reasons: they were grouped as *educational*, *diabetes-related*, and as examples of *game mechanics as disease model.* It is interesting to note that while health experts fully agreed on the similarity of these games, they defined that similarity in very different ways; this clarifies the need to improve the understanding of game features to allow for easier communication *within* stakeholder groups as well as *between* them.

G4H: Beyond the Sum of its Parts

There are many implications of our work for the design and development of future G4H. First, an understanding of the perspectives of these different stakeholder groups can help us to improve interdisciplinary communication. We hypothesize that many G4H do not successfully embody health behavior change theory, as the literature shows, because game and/or G4H stakeholders are making many hands-on design decisions without the health perspective in mind. By improving conversations among collaborators during the design process, we can improve the design of G4H. For example, G4H-specific workshops could be constructed for existing design tools such as the Schell Games framework [11], but deliberately structured with our seven themes in mind to shape interdisciplinary communication.

Second, this work exposes the concepts and norms underlying G4H expertise, as distinct from the individual disciplines of game design and health behavior change. The themes and responses of the G4H expert group in our study were *not* simply the sum of the themes and responses of game design and behavioral health experts; for example, G4H experts were the only expert group to mention *number of players* or *game complexity* as themes. Now, for each stakeholder group, we have a list of concepts that they are likely to use in framing G4H—and also a list of concepts that they are likely to omit in their framing. We can create design "prompts" based not just on our high-level themes, but on specific concepts–for example, remembering players' prior experiences (commonly observed by only game designers), paying attention to their readiness to change behavior (only health experts), and considering the social context (only G4H). These prompts could be used during the G4H design process, to define research studies, and in G4H education, to encourage inclusivity of framings and features.

Finally, we hope that the lessons learned from our initial corpus creation and the foundational understanding of interdisciplinary G4H themes that we have gathered from our expert participants can help the field move towards computationally detecting and mining features of G4H and creating future data-driven G4H corpora. While computation will be key to this process, understanding stakeholder perspectives is a crucial first step to developing game corpora for use by G4H designers and researchers: G4H is such an interdisciplinary field that any attempt at a computational model must incorporate the viewpoints and expertise of a variety of groups, in order to most effectively identify G4H game features and provide the most value to future stakeholders. Our work offers a foundation for this process; future work will leverage this foundational interdisciplinary understanding by applying the identified G4H themes to new health games as we move towards computational creation of game corpora.

CONCLUSION

Our work provides a formative understanding of the similarities and differences in how game design, behavioral health, and G4H experts articulate G4H themes and features: an understanding that is central to improving the design and development of games for health. The need for improved communication and collaboration between stakeholder groups has been established, and our work elucidates the differing values and framings that experts and expert groups hold and provides a foundation for improving the G4H collaborative process. We aim to use our research to improve interdisciplinary communication, to formalize our understanding of the relationships between game design and health behavior change frameworks, and ultimately to move towards computationally detecting and mining features for encoding G4H corpora. Synthesizing expert perspectives gives us a more comprehensive and foundational understanding of G4H themes and features, and we can leverage this multidisciplinary expert knowledge to improve G4H design and research going forward.

ACKNOWLEDGMENTS

We thank our study participants, and Dave Culyba, Andrea Grimes Parker, Mark Riedl, and Jina Huh. This research was supported in part by the Okawa Foundation.

REFERENCES

1. William Albert and Thomas Tullis. 2013. *Measuring the User Experience: Collecting, Analyzing, and Presenting Usability Metrics*. Morgan Kaufman Publishers Inc, San Francisco, CA.
2. Naomi Alderman. 2015. There's no morality in exercise: I'm a fat person and made a successful fitness app. *Medium*. Retrieved from https://medium.com/matter/i-really-love-my-fat-body-eca64ca3ec78#.f9v23nswy
3. PM Alexander and JJ Van Loggerenberg. 2005. The repertory grid: "Discovering" a 50-year-old research technique. *Proceedings of the 2005 annual research conference of the South African institute of computer scientists and information technologists on IT research in developing countries*: 192–199.
4. Rosa I. Arriaga, Andrew D. Miller, Elizabeth Mynatt, Claudia Pagliari, Erika Shehan. 2013. Theory vs. design-driven approaches for behavior change research. *Extended Abstracts on Human Factors in Computing Systems (CHI EA '13)*: 2455–2458. http://doi.org/10.1145/2468356.2468801
5. A. Bandura. 1986. *Social Foundations of Thought and Action: A Social Cognitive Theory*. Prentice-Hall, Englewood Cliffs, NJ.
6. Moderator: Tom Baranowski, Participants: Debra Lieberman, Richard Buday, Wei Peng, Lukas Zimmerli, Brenda Wiederhold, Pamela M. Kato. 2013. Videogame mechanics in games for health. *Games for Health Journal* 2, 4: 194–204. http://doi.org/10.1089/g4h.2013.0617
7. Tom Baranowski, Richard Buday, Debbe I. Thompson, Janice Baranowski. 2008. Playing for real: Video games and stories for health-related behavior change. *American Journal of Preventive Medicine* 34, 1: 74–82. http://doi.org/10.1016/j.amepre.2007.09.027
8. Ivan L. Beale, Pamela M. Kato, Veronica M. Marin-Bowling, Nicole Guthrie, Steve W. Cole. 2007. Improvement in cancer-related knowledge following use of a psychoeducational video game for adolescents and young adults with cancer. *Journal of Adolescent Health* 41, 3: 263–270. http://doi.org/10.1016/j.jadohealth.2007.04.006
9. Staffan Bjork and Jussi Holopainen. 2005. *Patterns in Game Design*. Charles River Media.
10. Logan T Cowan, Sarah A Van Wagenen, Brittany A Brown, Riley J. Hedin, Yukiko Seino-Stephan, P. Cougar Hall, Joshua H. West. 2013. Apps of steel: Are exercise apps providing consumers with realistic expectations?: A content analysis of exercise apps for presence of behavior change theory. *Health Education & Behavior* 40, 2: 133–39. http://doi.org/10.1177/1090198112452126
11. Sabrina Haskell Culyba. 2015. A field guide for design leaders on transformational games. Retrieved from http://www.slideshare.net/SeriousGamesAssoc/sabrina-haskell-culyba
12. Jonathan DeShazo, Lynne Harris, Wanda Pratt. 2010. Effective intervention or child's play? A review of video games for diabetes education. *Diabetes Technology & Therapeutics* 12, 10: 815–822. http://doi.org/10.1089/dia.2010.0030
13. Ann DeSmet, Dimitri Van Ryckeghem, Sofie Compernolle, Tom Baranowski, Debbe Thompson, Geert Crombez, Karolien Poels, Wendy Van Lippevelde, Sara Bastiaensens, Katrien Van Cleemput, Heidi Vandebosch, Ilse De Bourdeaudhuij. 2014. A Meta-analysis of serious digital games for healthy lifestyle promotion. *Preventive Medicine* 69: 95–107. http://doi.org/10.1007/s12671-013-0269-8.Moving
14. Damien Djaouti, Julian Alvarez, Jean-Pierre Jessel. 2011. Classifying serious games: The G/P/S model. *Handbook of research on improving learning and motivation through educational games: Multidisciplinary approaches*, 2005: 118–136. http://doi.org/10.4018/978-1-60960-495-0.ch006
15. Jinjuan Feng, Jonathan Lazar, Libby Kumin. 2010. Computer Usage by Children with Down Syndrome : Challenges and Future Research. *Computer* 2, 3: 13. http://doi.org/10.1145/1714458.1714460.http
16. Clara Fernandez-Vara. 2014. *Introduction to Game Analysis*. Routledge, New York, New York, USA.
17. Alex Gekker. 2012. Health games: Taxonomy analysis and multiplayer design suggestions. In *Lecture Notes in Computer Science*. http://doi.org/10.1007/978-3-642-33687-4_2
18. Google. Google Slides. Retrieved from https://www.google.com/slides/about/
19. Andrea Grimes, Vasudhara Kantroo, Rebecca E Grinter. 2010. Let's play!: mobile health games for adults. *Proceedings of the 2010 ACM International Joint Conference on Pervasive and Ubiquitous Computing (UbiComp '10)*: 241–250. http://doi.org/10.1145/1864349.1864370
20. Stacey Guy, Alexandria Ratzki-Leewing, Femida Gwadry-Sridhar. 2011. Moving beyond the stigma: systematic review of video games and their potential to combat obesity. *International Journal of Hypertension* 2011: 1–13. http://doi.org/10.4061/2011/179124
21. Amanda K. Hall, Enmanuel Chavarria, Vasana

Maneeratana, Beth H. Chaney, and Jay Bernhardt. 2012. Health benefits of digital videogames for older adults: A systematic review of the literature. *Games for Health Journal* 1, 6: 402–410. http://doi.org/10.1089/g4h.2012.0046

22. Amanda K Hall, Rebeccah Mercado, Charkarra Anderson-Lewis, Gabrielle Darville, Jay M Bernhardt. 2015. How to design tobacco prevention and control games for youth and adolescents: A aualitative analysis of expert interviews. *Games for Health Journal* 4, 6: 488–93. http://doi.org/10.1089/g4h.2015.0013

23. Bruce Hanington and Bella Martin. 2012. *Universal Methods of Design: 100 Ways to Research Complex Problems, Develop Innovative Ideas, and Design Effective Solutions*. Rockport Publishers.

24. Kimberly Hieftje. 2013. Electronic Media–Based Health Interventions Promoting Behavior Change in Youth: A Systematic Review. *JAMA Pediatrics* 167, 6: 1. http://doi.org/10.1001/jamapediatrics.2013.1095

25. Robin Hunicke, Marc LeBlanc, Robert Zubek. 2004. MDA: A Formal Approach to Game Design and Game Research. *Workshop on Challenges in Game AI*: 1–4. http://doi.org/10.1.1.79.4561

26. Azadeh Jamalian, Jessica Mezei, Pazit Levitan, Adrienne Garber, Jessica Hammer, Charles K Kinzer. 2012. The Lit2Quit mobile app: Evoking game-based physiological effects that mimic smoking. *GLS 8.0 Games + Learning + Society Conference*: 484–485.

27. Nancy K. Janz and Marshall H Becker. 1984. The Health Belief Model: a decade later. *Health Education Quarterly* 11, 1: 1–47. http://doi.org/10.1177/109019818401100101

28. Mads Møller Jensen and Kaj Grønbæk. 2016. Design strategies for balancing exertion games: A study of three approaches. *Proceedings of the 2016 ACM Conference on Designing Interactive Systems (DIS '16)*: 936–946. http://doi.org/10.1145/2901790.2901843

29. Diane Jass Ketelhut, Brian C. Nelson, Jody Clarke, Chris Dede. 2010. A multi-user virtual environment for building and assessing higher order inquiry skills in science. *British Journal of Educational Technology* 41, 1: 56–68. http://doi.org/10.1111/j.1467-8535.2009.01036.x

30. Hadi Kharrazi, Amy Shirong Lu, Fardad Gharghabi. 2014. A scoping review of health game research: Past, Present, and Future. *Games for Health Journal* 1, 2: 1–23. http://doi.org/10.1089/g4h.2012.0011.A

31. Debra A. Lieberman. 2009. Designing serious games for learning and health in informal and formal settings. In *Serious Games: Mechanisms and Effects*. Routledge, 117–130.

32. Debra A. Lieberman, Barbara Chamberlin, Ernie Medina, Barry A. Franklin, Brigid McHugh Sanner, Dorothea K. Vafiadis. 2011. The power of play: Innovations in getting active summit 2011: A science panel proceedings report from the American Heart Association. *Circulation* 123, 21: 2507–2516. http://doi.org/10.1161/CIR.0b013e318219661d

33. Elizabeth Jane Lyons and Claire Hatkevich. 2013. Prevalence of behavior changing strategies in fitness video games: Theory-based content analysis. *Journal of Medical Internet Research* 15, 5: 1–11. http://doi.org/10.2196/jmir.2403

34. S. Mader, S. Natkin, Guillaume Levieux. 2012. How to analyse therapeutic games: the player/game/therapy model. *Entertainment Computing (ICEC 2012)*: 193–206. http://doi.org/10.1007/978-3-642-33542-6

35. Florian Floyd Mueller and Katherine Isbister. 2014. Movement-based game guidelines. *Proceedings of the 2014 ACM Conference on Human Factors in Computing Systems (CHI '14)*: 2191–2200. http://doi.org/10.1145/2556288.2557163

36. Optimal Workshop. OptimalSort. Retrieved from https://www.optimalworkshop.com/

37. Brian A. Primack, Mary V. Carroll, Megan McNamara, Mary Lou Klem, Brandy King, Michael Rich, Chun W. Chan, Smita Nayak. 2012. Role of video games in improving health-related outcomes: A systematic review. *American Journal of Preventive Medicine* 42, 6: 630–638. http://doi.org/10.1016/j.amepre.2012.02.023

38. James O. Prochaska, Wayne F. Velicer, Carlo C. DiClemente, Joseph Fava. 1988. Measuring processes of change: Applications to the cessation of smoking. *Journal of Consulting and Clinical Psychology* 56, 4: 520–528. http://doi.org/10.1037/0022-006X.56.4.520

39. Chad Richards and T.C. Nicholas Graham. 2016. Developing compelling repetitive-motion exergames by balancing player agency with the constraints of exercise. *Proceedings of the 2016 ACM Conference on Designing Interactive Systems (DIS '16)*: 911–923. http://doi.org/10.1145/2901790.2901824

40. Dana N. Ruggiero. 2014. Spent: Changing students' affective learning toward homelessness through persuasive video game play. *Proceedings of the 2014ACM Conference on Human Factors in Computing Systems (CHI '14)*: 3423–3432. http://doi.org/10.1145/2556288.2557390

41. Ben Sawyer. 2008. From cells to cell processos: The integration of health and video games. *IEEE Computer Graphics and Applications* 28, 6: 83–85. http://doi.org/10.1109/MCG.2008.114

42. Ben Sawyer and Peter Smith. 2008. Serious Games Taxonomy. Retrieved from https://thedigitalentertainmentalliance.files.wordpress.com/2011/08/serious-games-taxonomy.pdf

43. Miguel Sicart. 2015. Loops and metagames: Understanding game design structures. *Foundations of Digital Games.*

44. Katarzyna Stawarz, Anna L Cox, Ann Blandford. 2014. Don't forget your pill!: designing effective medication reminder apps that support users' daily routines. *Proceedings of the 2014 ACM Conference on Human Factors in Computing Systems (CHI '14)*: 2269–2278. http://doi.org/10.1145/2556288.2557079

45. Joshua G Tanenbaum, Alissa N Antle, and John Robinson. 2013. Three perspectives on behavior change for serious games. *Proceedings of the 2013 ACM Conference on Human Factors in Computing Systems (CHI '13)*: 3389–3392. http://doi.org/10.1145/2470654.2466464

46. Debbe Thompson, Tom Baranowski, Richard Buday, Janice Branowski, Victoria Thompson, Russell Jago, Melissa Juliano Griffith. 2010. Serious video games for health: How behavioral science guided the development of a serious video game. *Simulation & Gaming* 41, 4: 587–606. Retrieved January 17, 2016 from http://sag.sagepub.com/content/early/2008/12/24/1046878108328087.abstract

47. UCSB Center for Digital Games Research. Health Games Database. Retrieved from http://dev.cdgr.ucsb.edu/db

48. Kellie Vella, Madison Klarkowski, Daniel Johnson, Leanne Hides, Peta Wyeth. 2016. The social context of video game play. *Proceedings of the 2016 ACM Conference on Designing Interactive Systems (DIS '16)*: 761–772. http://doi.org/10.1145/2901790.2901823

49. Margaret Wallace. 2016. *5-point framework for making health and science games*. Retrieved from http://www.gamesforchange.org/2016/12/a-five-point-collaborative-framework-for-making-health-science-games/

50. Joshua H. West, P. Cougar Hall, Carl L. Hanson, Michael D. Barnes, Christophe Giraud-Carrier, James Barrett. 2012. There's an app for that: Content analysis of paid health and fitness apps. *Journal of Medical Internet Research* 14, 3: 1–12. http://doi.org/10.2196/jmir.1977

Participatory Design to Address Stigma with Adolescents and Young Adults with Type 1 Diabetes

Gillian M. McCarthy
School of Design, Victoria University of Wellington
Wellington, New Zealand
Gillian.McCarthy@vuw.ac.nz

Edgar R. Rodríguez Ramírez
School of Design, Victoria University of Wellington
Wellington, New Zealand
Edgar.Rodriguez@vuw.ac.nz

Brian J. Robinson
Graduate School of Nursing, Midwifery, and Health, Victoria University of Wellington
Wellington, New Zealand
Brian.Robinson@vuw.ac.nz

ABSTRACT

Adolescents and young adults with type 1 diabetes are required to use medical devices to test their blood glucose levels regularly. However, using these devices can be stigmatising in various everyday situations. This paper describes a participatory design workshop that explored six strategies for addressing product-related stigma with five young people with type 1 diabetes and five designers. The strategies were to strengthen the product's medical identity, to disguise the product as an accepted non-medical item, to make the device invisible or less confronting, to provide choice and opportunities for personalisation, to strengthen the product's brand identity, and to increase the social power of the device. The workshop resulted in five rapid prototypes for blood glucose monitoring technology that address stigma using a variety of strategies and a discussion of the advantages and disadvantages of each approach. This study elucidates young people's stigma-related user-requirements of blood glucose monitoring technologies.

Author Keywords

Type 1 diabetes; medical devices; participatory design; adolescents.

ACM Classification Keywords

D.2.10 Design; J.3 Life and medical sciences; H.5.2 User interfaces

DIS 2017, June 10-14, 2017, Edinburgh, United Kingdom

ACM ISBN 978-1-4503-4922-2/17/06...$15.00
http://dx.doi.org/10.1145/3064663.3064740

INTRODUCTION

Adolescents and young adults with type 1 diabetes are prescribed an intensive self-management regimen that includes frequent monitoring of blood glucose levels, diet and exercise, and calculation and self-administering of insulin [24]. Glucose monitoring has been described as adolescents' least favourite part of managing type 1 diabetes, with some adolescents not testing in social environments such as schools due to stigma and peer influences [4]. To test blood glucose levels, adolescents use a lancet to prick their finger and produce a drop of blood, which is transferred onto a test strip. The test strip is inserted into a blood glucose meter that displays the blood glucose level. Additionally, adolescents use syringes, insulin pens or insulin pumps to administer insulin, and often carry glucose sources, and consumables and backups such as extra needles or batteries.

Adolescents' self-management of type 1 diabetes should be considered in a social context, with disclosure of diabetes to friends associated with successful management [28]. However, self-managing in public spaces can be challenging, as it can draw unwanted attention and questions, at a life stage when social acceptance is important [27]. Product-related stigma around glucose monitoring aligns with Goffman's concept of the discreditable, whereby there is no noticeable stigmatising attribute until the person uses their medical equipment to test their blood glucose levels [12]. The act of managing health using medical devices is the same act that can trigger feelings of, or anxiety about stigma.

Social anxiety can result in poorer self-management and quality of life among adolescents with type 1 diabetes [8]. This study focuses solely on product-related stigma rather than, for example, stigma associated with a hypoglycaemic episode. While it is clear that medical devices can be stigmatising, it is less clear how to design devices that have more positive appraisals.

BACKGROUND

Addressing product-related stigma

A design review uncovered a number of medical and assistive device designs aimed to reduce the stigma of using these devices in everyday contexts. Designs include colostomy bags modelled on lingerie or tattoos [22], a catheter set that looks like common toiletries [7], scarves and accessories for storing and concealing insulin pumps [5,6] and sleek insulin delivery jewellery [13]. Interestingly, these approaches responded to stigma by hiding the medical device or disguising it as a consumer product. While some designs aimed to reduce negative attention, others increased positive attention.

While medical and assistive devices are commonly designed to be as discreet or unobtrusive as possible, this may convey an inherent message of shame in these devices [20]. It has been suggested that the stigma associated with disability cannot be ameliorated by hiding the disability, and that symbols that contradict the stigma should be employed (e.g., wheelchairs worn from high impact collisions in wheelchair rugby indicate the intensity of the sport, and contradict preconceptions of wheelchair user frailty) [3]. Other strategies for addressing product-related stigma include education, technological advances, mainstream characteristics, positive association with existing brands, adoption of stigmatised characteristics, and other groups desiring assistive device functions [23].

In addition, Jacobson proposed three strategies for addressing stigmatising features of assistive devices. These are to disguise, to shift attention away from, and to transform stigmatising features into prestigious features [14]. The current research draws on Vaes' Product Intervention Model for Stigma (PIMS), which builds on the strategies outlined above, setting out 17 strategies for addressing stigma through 'product interventions', 'user interventions' and 'culture interventions' [25].

Participatory design of medical devices

While there are clear benefits to involving young participants in the process of designing and developing medical devices, many medical device manufacturers report significant barriers and resultantly overlook adolescents [9,19]. However, research can effectively involve adolescent and young adult participants who can make important contributions to research and design [17].

Many methods are available for constructing and testing user requirements for medical devices. Scoping methods such as contextual inquiry, focus groups and ethnography can be used to determine user requirements with evaluative methods such as usability tests and cognitive walkthroughs to determine the success of a design in meeting these requirements [18].

Various methods can elicit different types of data. For instance, in designing medical technologies usability tests can elicit detailed requirements, whereas focus groups can elicit contextual requirements [11]. Accordingly, more than one method can be used where this is practicable.

Further, adolescents can be more active in design participation by taking on design roles and prototyping their ideas. A craft approach to participatory design can help young people to create personally meaningful health representations [1]. Paper prototyping has been a common method used in participatory design workshops with adolescents [10,16,26]. Importantly, participatory workshop participants with diabetes have been shown to develop original, innovative low-fidelity prototypes for medical technologies [15].

The workshop described in this paper followed participatory design principles, giving young people with type 1 diabetes a role in the design process, and allowing designers and users to collaborate and learn from each other [21].

METHODS

This paper describes a participatory design workshop to design medical technologies that might help young people with type 1 diabetes measure their blood glucose confidently in everyday situations.

Participants

Participants were five people with type 1 diabetes aged 15-24 and five designers aged 21-29. Three of the designers had a masters degree in design and were currently working in the industry, and the remaining two were currently completing a masters or PhD designing assistive technologies. Blind portraits participants drew of each other during the workshop are pictured in Figure 1. Young adult participants were included in addition to adolescent participants as they were comfortable reflecting on the diabetes-related challenges they had faced during adolescence, and how their self-management had changed since. Participants took part in either a morning or afternoon workshop comprised of designers and people with diabetes, with one designer participating twice.

Figure 1. Blind portraits drawn to ready participants for drawing activities and partner interaction.

Procedure

The designers were given pre-workshop materials outlining the aetiology, treatment regimen and medical devices used for self-managing type 1 diabetes. Each of the participants with type 1 diabetes had met with the researcher once or twice prior to the workshop to take part in other research activities such as interviews, a card sort task, cultural probe activities including writing and drawing, and giving feedback on students' design concepts. As such the facilitator had an established rapport with participants.

Before the workshop, participants perused quotes from prior interviews. Examples include, "It's kind of embarrassing having to inject myself in front of other people. Injecting yourself is gross for some people and that's weird... Sometimes, if I'm with lots of my friends, I go to the bathroom because there are so many people there." and, "You're wondering what people think about what you're doing, and then it's also thinking, 'I'm not normal, I have to do this'."

The aim of the workshop was "to design medical technologies that help people measure their blood glucose confidently in everyday situations." The facilitator explained that participants were free to design medical devices or any other products that would be helpful in completing this aim.

The workshop centred around 6 strategies for addressing stigma adapted from 17 strategies by Vaes [25]. Strategies that didn't pertain to the design of an object were eliminated for this workshop, and similar strategies were combined to suit the duration of the workshop. The six strategies used in the workshop were: to strengthen the product's institutional identity by reinforcing the medical role played by the device, to downplay stigma-sensitive features by disguising the product as an accepted non-medical item, to minimise stigma-sensitive aspects of the device by making it invisible or less confronting and minimise its presence when not in use, to strengthen the individual identity of the device by providing more choice and opportunities for personalisation so users value it as an extension of their personality, to strengthen the product's brand identity by creating or reinforcing positive brand associations, and to increase the device's social power by making the user more visually assertive. An image of a product that embodied each strategy from a different medical or assistive context was provided to ease explanation of the strategies to participants (e.g., a miniaturised hearing aid for the *make it invisible* strategy, and a sling with a pictogram showing how the user broke their arm for the *social power* strategy).

Participants brainstormed the advantages and disadvantages of each strategy in relation to blood glucose monitoring, and suggested how it could be achieved. Participants recorded ideas individually on sticky notes then shared these with the group as they attached them in clusters to a wall.

Figure 2. Participants sketching design concepts.

Following the brainstorm, participants were given stickers to represent three votes: one for a strategy that would be appropriate for a young person who was embarrassed managing type 1 diabetes in public, one for someone who was confident managing type 1 diabetes in public, and one for someone wanting a game-changing piece of technology.

Each participant then paired up with one or two designers for the remainder of the workshop. They rapidly sketched at least two ideas pertaining to blood glucose monitoring for three of the most popular strategies. After sharing these with the group, each partnership completed a storyboard and sketch for one idea, then created a rapid prototype, as seen in Figure 2. These were shared with the larger group, where each participant wrote one aspect they liked about each idea, and one aspect about which they were curious. By phrasing their feedback as 'I wonder' it was framed as an avenue for possible idea development rather than a critique. Finally, the group had a general debriefing session where they commented on the content and experience of the workshop. Priming activities to make participants comfortable included drawing and vocalising ideas. Breaks were also included throughout the three-hour workshop.

RESULTS

Exploration of strategies to address stigma

This section outlines participants' expected advantages and disadvantages of the six strategies to address product-related stigma, and also areas of non-consensus. Participants also suggested how strategies could be applied in relation to blood glucose monitoring. A selection of rapid sketches is included.

Strengthen the product's medical identity

Participants felt the main advantages of this strategy were that devices would be recognisable as medical devices rather than drug paraphernalia, easy and reliable to use, and that they would increase public awareness about type 1 diabetes and medical devices. Disadvantages were the stigma of the device being associated with a 'disability' or medical condition (as per the participants' words), a device that looked 'scary' and 'serious', not being user-friendly, and adding to misunderstanding and unwanted questions about self-care behaviours. Interestingly, participants were divided over whether medical looking devices were easy to use, and whether increased attention was an advantage or a disadvantage. Features that made a device feel 'medical' were white and grey colours, smooth plastic surfaces, exposed needles, medical wording and symbols, clunky and plain design with basic shapes, LEP displays, a futuristic look unlike consumer technologies, and having many unintuitive features.

Disguise the product as an accepted non-medical item

Benefits of disguising a medical device as a consumer device included making it less noticeable, allowing the user hide their 'disability', and self-care behaviours not being discernible. This strategy might allow the device to be incorporated into accessories the user wears, and to be wearable rather than carried. The overriding negative aspect of this strategy was that people may not know to help in an emergency if they didn't recognise the user had a medical condition, and non-standardised use. Not looking like a medical device was thought to be positive at many times,

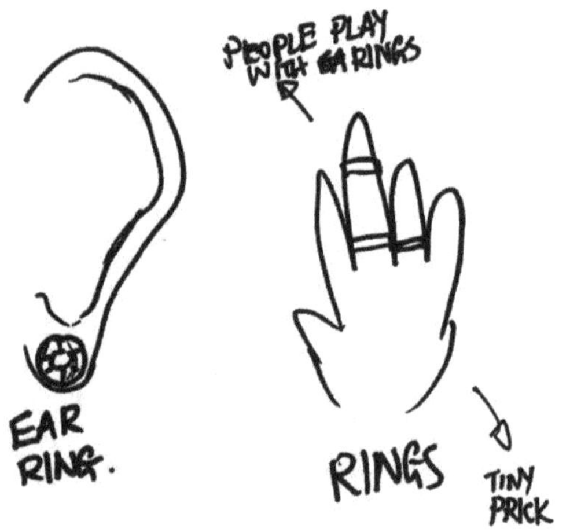

Figure 3. Earring and ring designs for glucose monitoring

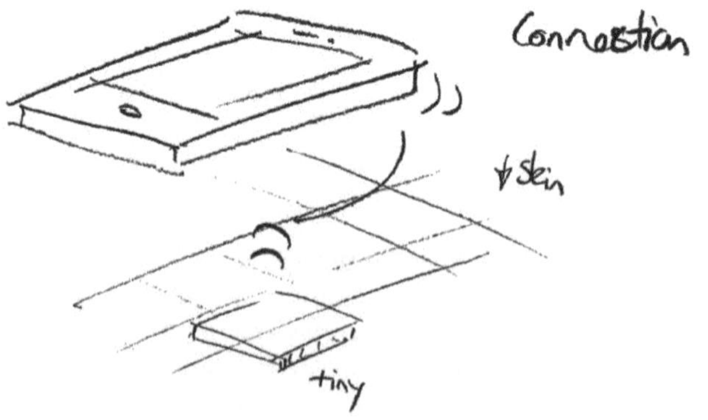

Figure 4. Sub-cutaneous chip and phone application for blood glucose testing

but negative in emergencies. Participants also added that a disguised device might be difficult to find. Implementation ideas included a blood glucose meter disguised as a handbag, toy, smartphone, tablet, watch, clothing, or jewellery using materials and forms that reflect these items. The profile could also be flattened to wear unobtrusively under clothes. Rapid sketches for jewellery concepts are pictured in Figure 3.

Make the product invisible or less confronting and minimise its presence when not in use

Advantages included the device being unobtrusive and consequently less embarrassing to use in public. Additionally, it might invite less 'social hassle' and unwanted questions from onlookers. It could also be ergonomically designed to fit to the body. Again, while diminishing the attention devices generated was sometimes an advantage, this could also result in less awareness and conversation of type 1 diabetes and result in acquaintances not knowing the user had the condition. Many participants felt it important for some peers or acquaintances to know that they had type 1 diabetes in case of an emergency. There were also opposing views as to whether a device that applied this strategy would encourage testing as it was able to be worn, or discourage testing as the device's reduced visibility would no longer act as a visual prompt for testing. Participants felt making the device less visible might make them feel more robotic, and as if the device should be hidden. Further, if it was slightly visible this may provoke more questions. Devices being less visible may also be less intuitive to use and easier to loose. Ideas for implementation were through use of colours that blend and transparent surfaces, making devices smaller, or developing clothing with integrated technology. Other ideas included placing the device on unexposed parts of the body, or using a site or subdermal element that connects to a smartphone, as seen in Figure 4. Participants also considered using more novel methods of testing glucose concentrations such as breath detection by animals, contact lenses, toilets, tattoos or human joey pouch.

Provide more choice and opportunities for personalisation

Benefits of increased choice or personalisation of glucose monitoring equipment were having a sense of control, feeling it was 'my device' and that it would reflect a user's personal style and function as an extension of them. Participants felt they would have pride in a device that felt personal and tailored to their condition. While some participants noted that this strategy gave people a choice to be discreet or flamboyant based on their personal preference, and thought it positive users would not be trying to hide the device, others were worried about the device drawing attention and that onlookers may not understand it was medical. The device could be 'trendy' or 'cool' and aid normalisation and implementation of frequent self-management, though they were wary of keeping abreast of fashion trends. The device could also be customised for

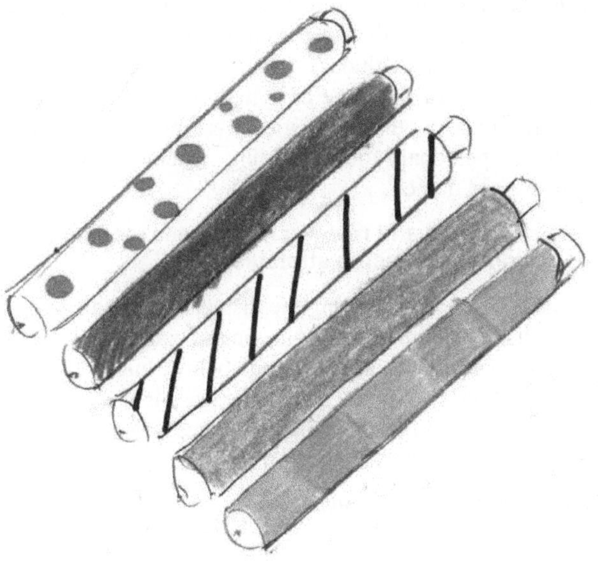

Figure 5. Personalising lancets with colourful skins

different environments and be comfortable to wear if it was made to measure. Participants worried that this approach might make devices more expensive, be taxing to customise for the user, and encourage choosing a device based primarily on how much the user liked the device rather than how efficient it would be. Strategies for personalisation included changes to the exterior with cases, accessories, attachments, stickers, programmable chameleon-like surfaces, colours, patterns and materials and skins, as seen in Figure 5. Changes could be made frequently to suit an outfit, or to garner or diminish attention. Additionally, changes to the core functions could be offered similar to modular phones and computers. Participants also felt users could be given the option of wearing the device over or under clothing. Participants suggested customisable options could be supplied or created individually, and 3D printing could be used. One participant suggested the device making her look like a cyborg would be 'awesome', while others wanted to adapt elements from toys or movies.

Strengthen the product's brand identity

Participants felt this could make the device fashionable and desirable, which in turn could boost their self-confidence and pride in the device, making self-management more acceptable in public spaces. The words 'luxury', 'cool', 'exclusivity' and 'loyalty' were associated with brands, and participants thought free samples might be provided to increase product competition. Possible downsides could be pressure to replace the device often, and not trusting the brand, and therefore the device. There was some concern that this strategy could commodify a medical condition, and consideration of whether people would notice product branding. Participants were divided whether branding and competition would increase or lower prices, and whether extra attention and associationg type 1 diabetes to a brand would be positive or negative. Additionally, one participant

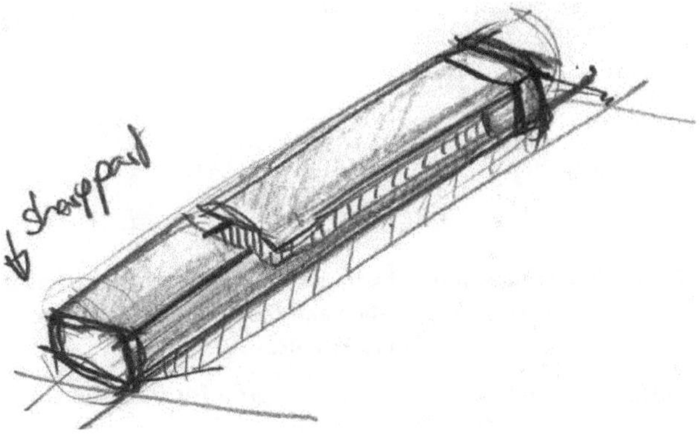

Figure 6. Lancet that borrows an aesthetic from consumer sports brands

felt that blood glucose technology needed to be functional but not appealing, whereas another participant disagreed, stating though devices must be functional, they could also be aesthetically appealing. Ways to associate the device with a brand would be to add a logo or to make the device look 'sporty' or 'classy' through the use of colours, materials, and patterns. A sporty device is pictured in Figure 6. Participants suggested a new medical brand could be created with marketing and aesthetics similar to a consumer brand. The phrase 'dazzling camouflage' was used to describe the potential of a branded device.

Increase the product's social power

Advantages of imbuing the device with greater social power would include avoiding repeated explanation of purpose, increasing awareness of type 1 diabetes and how to assist in an emergency. This strategy was thought to help in removing stigma and preventing users from hiding the condition, and providing a talking point to evoke positive conversations. Some participants felt that it was helpful to focus on distinguishing type 1 diabetes from type 2 diabetes, and that humorous conversations about the condition and medical devices eased social interactions. While some adolescents thought this strategy would help to communicate about diabetes management in a straightforward manner, resulting in the user receiving fewer questions, others thought it might create further misunderstandings as opposed to directly explaining the condition person to person. Participants considered that this strategy might also draw attention to and possibly make fun of their condition. Again, users do not want people to know they have the condition in all situations, and it could highlight their vulnerability. Strategies for increasing the social power of blood glucose equipment included using social media, advertisements, public service announcements, flash mobs (choreographed public events), placing explanatory comic strips or descriptions on devices, using QR codes to link to informative websites and diabetes awareness month, and having information printed on clothing or cards that could be given to people. A diabetes festival with themed rides and stalls was also proposed and is pictured in Figure 7.

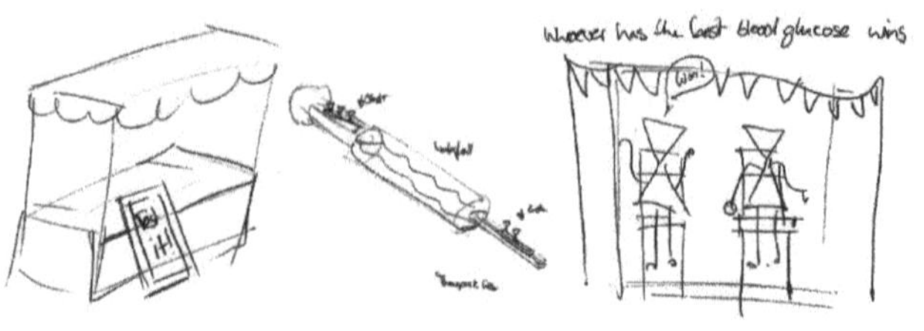

Figure 7. Diabetes festival with a stall with food shaped as a pancreas, syringe water slide and blood glucose guessing competitions.

Selecting strategies to address stigma for various users

Following the brainstorm detailed above, participants each voted for one strategy that would be appropriate for a young person who was embarrassed managing type 1 diabetes in public, one for someone who was confident managing type 1 diabetes in public, and one for someone wanting a game-changing technology (See Table 1). In previous interviews participants had talked of their own feelings about being embarrassed or not being embarrassed, but also noted that they knew of others with type 1 diabetes who felt or acted differently from themselves. They had also read quotes by other research participants at the beginning of the workshop to increase their awareness of other people's opinions about device-related stigma and embarrassment. The researchers chose to capitalise on their awareness of their own preferences and their knowledge of other individuals' preferences to ensure that the resulting designs catered for a wide spectrum of possible users. Further, this allowed participants to choose to design concepts that they would personally find helpful, or to design for others.

Each strategy could receive a total of 33 votes, however, votes were spread across strategies, with no strategy deemed appropriate for all user types, and no user type limited to one strategy. This reflects the differing needs and preferences of adolescents with type 1 diabetes, but is not currently reflected by the minimal range available in

Table 1. Voting by participants for strategies to address stigma for different types of users

Strategy	Embarrassed user	Confident user	Game-changing user	Total
Medical	0	0	0	0
Disguise	6	0	0	6
Invisible	5	0	4	9
Personalise	0	6	1	7
Brand	0	3	1	4
Social Power	0	2	5	7

medical technologies. Interestingly, no participants chose the medical strategy that is currently one of the commonly used strategies for glucose monitoring equipment. This strategy was seen by some as synonymous with the status quo. The most popular strategies were making the device invisible, personalisation, adding social power and disguising the device.

Design concepts and reviews for glucose monitoring using stigma addressing strategies

Five design concepts relating the disguise, medical, and personalisation strategies, and accompanying reviews by workshop participants are described below. Interestingly, while the strategy to make the device less visible was the most popular, and the social power strategy also ranked highly, no groups chose to design for these.

Phone attachment and application

The first pair chose to use the disguise strategy and create a blood glucose meter that could be attached to a smartphone and an application for viewing blood glucose and ketone levels (See Figures 8 and 9). They produced a storyboard of device interactions, including pressing separate buttons to measure blood glucose levels and ketones, inputting carbohydrate data, viewing data and graphs on the phone screen, having the phone communicate directly with an

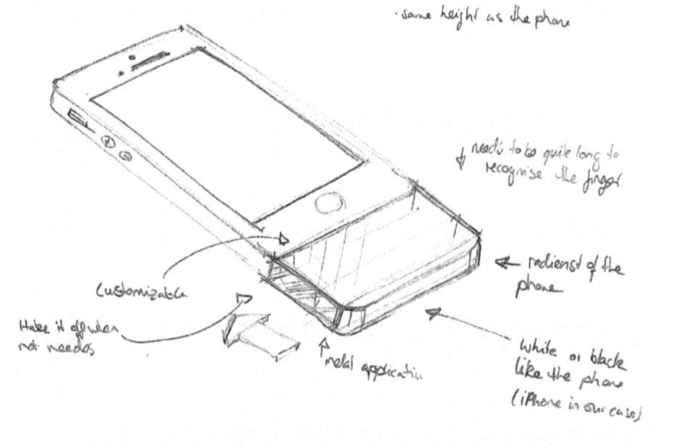

Figure 8. Smartphone attachment

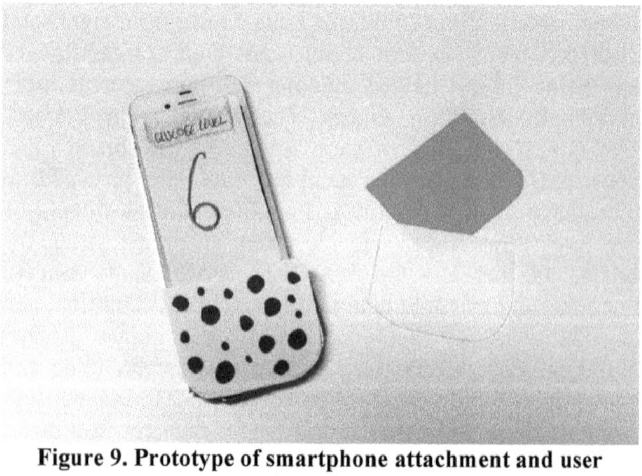

Figure 9. Prototype of smartphone attachment and user interface

Figure 10. Storyboard of functions including measuring blood glucose and ketones, displaying data and trends and communicating with an insulin pump and health professional.

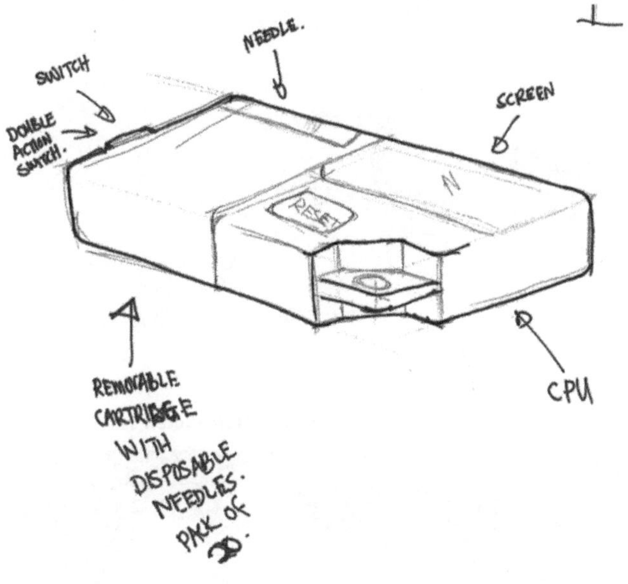

Figure 11. Miniature keyring blood glucose meter

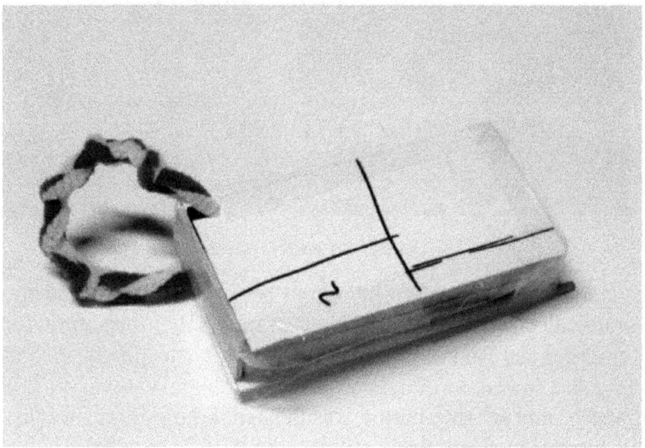

Figure 12. Keychain prototype at a larger scale

insulin pump, and being able to send data to a health professional (See Figure 10). The pair created different coloured and patterned sample attachments to demonstrate that it would come in a variety of styles.

Participants commented positively about the variety of styles and wireless connection to the phone, that this concept used existing technology that they already carried with them, eliminating the need for an extra device. They also valued that the application would help to educate new users and that it visualised data sets, allowing users to better understand trends in the data.

They suggested the attachment could be reshaped into a phone case, the application could provide reminders for testing and encourage data sharing and communication between the user and health professionals and wondered whether this would improve the standard of care. They also considered access for people without smartphones. Interestingly, all participants in the prior research with type 1 diabetes from age 13-24 had their own smartphones. They sometimes had access to phone prior to their peers as a safety precaution, and commonly used SMS messaging to communicate blood glucose levels and insulin doses with parents while at school before they were able to manage these decisions independently.

Keychain glucose monitor

The second group also used the disguise strategy to create a miniature keychain glucose monitor (See Figures 11 and 12). It had a cartridge of 20 lancets for finger pricking and a double action switch to stop users being pricked unintentionally. Although the keychain had a small screen, it also paired with a smartphone app complete with reminders to test and maps for nearby food locations.

Participants liked the small size of the device and that it contained the blood glucose meter, lancets and test strips within one device. They questioned whether the screen was necessary when it could sync to a smartphone, whether the casing could be customisable, how easy it would be to access the cartridge of lancets, and whether users might lose the small device.

Hologram watch

The third pair also chose to use the disguise strategy to create a blood glucose meter that looked like a watch, but

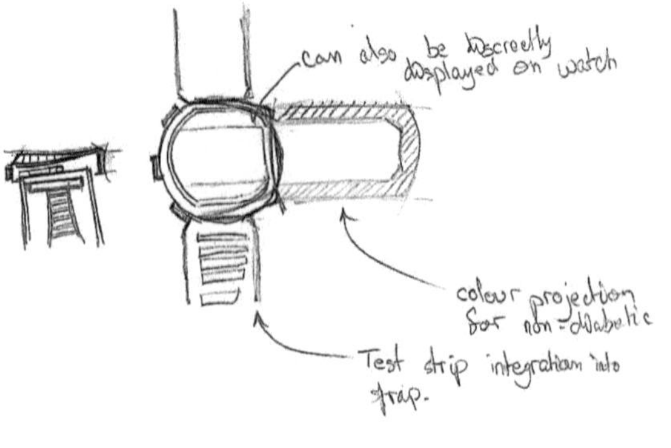

Figure 13. Hologram watch sketch

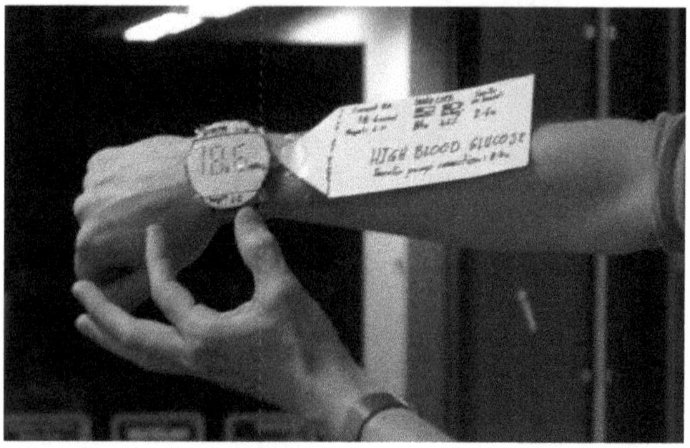

Figure 14. Hologram watch paper prototype

also had an innovative hologram feature that embodied the medical strategy, supplying clear medical information for emergencies and explaining the condition to others. Blood glucose level, target, time and date were shown on the watch, and when a button was pushed, a hologram showing information from the insulin pump and basic information for people who do not have diabetes e.g. 'type 1 diabetic', 'high blood sugar' was displayed. Test strips were housed in the watchstrap to be used with a traditional lancet (See Figures 13 and 14).

Participants commented that using a watch made the device accessible and was something people wore already. In addition, they liked that the watch projected detailed data and could be of help to people with diabetes while also educating others. They questioned whether the hologram would be legible and if there might be a better way to display this information. They wanted to ensure it was obvious in an emergency situation. Possible issues were the bulkiness of the watch, whether the test strips would be secure in the watch strap and if people might mistake it for a gaming device.

3D printed personalised blood glucose meter

The fourth pair chose to use the personalisation strategy. They created a software concept for creating custom blood glucose meters using a 3D printed casing. The software would provide basic shapes that could be adapted by users,

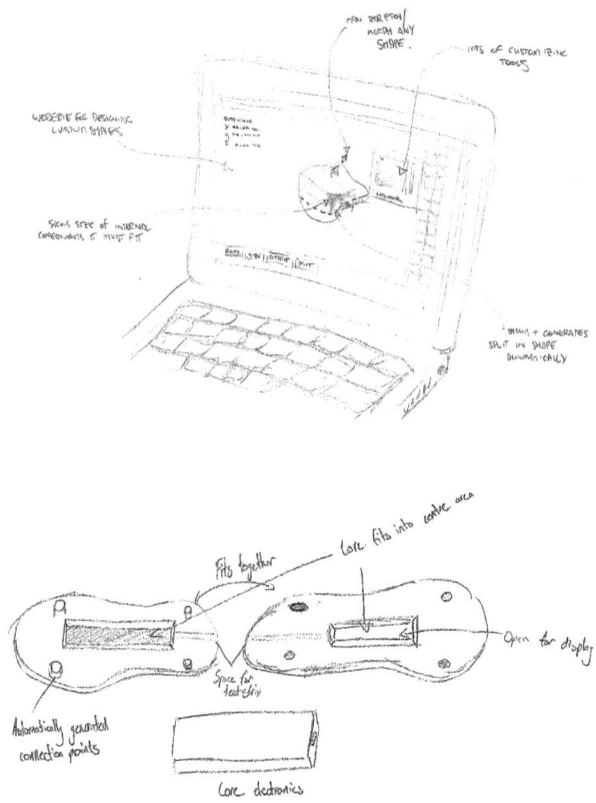

Figure 15. Concept sketch for software and 3D printed, customised blood glucose monitors

Figure 16. Prototype of a customised blood glucose monitor

and would automatically generate connections for assembly. Users could also choose colours and materials in the 3D printing process (See Figures 15 and 16).

Participants admired the simplicity of the idea and that it introduced an element of fun. They thought it important that the software would simplify aspects of the manufacturing process and also thought personalisation might result in more positive connections with devices. Participants wondered if some customisations might affect the core functions of the device, how accessible it would be, if materials other than those used in 3D printers could be introduced for texture and whether the software could aid the user in creating interesting designs.

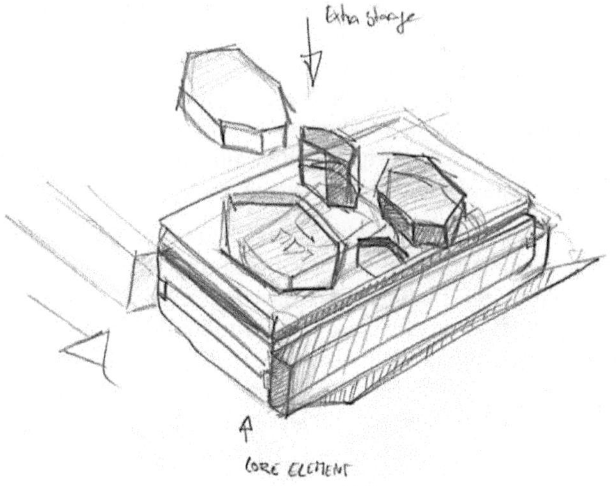

Figure 17. Sketch of a modular test kit with core element and extra storage

Figure 18. Large prototype of a modular test kit

Modular testing kit

The final pair also used the personalisation strategy, creating a modular test kit with a core compartment that fitted a lancet, blood glucose meter and test strips, with extra modular storage for insulin pump site changes, insulin pens, snacks, rubbish and such (See figures 17 and 18). They intended the core compartment and some extra storage to be used regularly, with more storage able to be added for occasions such as extended trips.

Participants liked the interesting modular design, and how it had capacity for extra equipment and long items. They thought it would fit many purposes and environments and would make transportation of the equipment easier. They wondered if hexagons were the most efficient shape and whether they would make it frustrating to pack, though these did make it look interesting. They questioned whether the case had enough space for all the equipment people might want to carry, and whether just having one larger case might be preferable for some people.

DISCUSSION

Addressing stigma

The workshop was themed around addressing medical-device related stigma, however participants with type 1 diabetes had varying opinions related to this. While some preferred people not knowing about their condition and managing privately, others were more open to managing publicly. There was debate during the workshop with one participant stating that devices need only be functional, while another thought that while the devices should be functional, any opportunity to make them aesthetically pleasing should also be taken, as this would make using devices in public settings more enjoyable. This aligns with literature stating functionality and aesthetics need not be mutually exclusive, especially when addressing stigma [2].

Diversity among participants allowed for a broad range of design outcomes, and was beneficial to the brainstorm activity. This diversity was demonstrated when there was no consensus for stigma-reducing strategies. In fact, this illustrated the requirement for multiple stigma-reducing strategies to be employed in the design of medical devices, as one strategy alone will not suit all users. This approach is contrary to currently accessible technologies.

Another area of non-consensus raised across multiple strategies was the advantages and disadvantages of medical devices that attract attention. Participants felt it important that others knew they had type 1 diabetes in case of a medical emergency. They also felt that talking about diabetes and using devices in public spaces could increase awareness and discussion, aiding disclosure of diabetes and normalising self-care behaviours. On the other hand, some described using medical devices in public settings as embarrassing or stigmatising, and device use often resulted in people asking undesired questions about their actions, devices and condition. Subsequently, there will be times be times when it is advantageous for medical devices to draw attention, and other times when users prefer discretion. In addition, for some users there is scope for devices to draw more positive forms of attention, even being desirable. This may be achieved through strategies such as strengthening the individual identity of the device by providing more choice and opportunities for personalisation, strengthening the product's brand identity, and increasing the device's social power.

While this workshop focused on stigma and embarrassment, a general frustration was also described from repeatedly having to explain diabetes and medical devices over the course of a lifetime. While this was related to the attention drawn by medical devices, it may need to be addressed through different strategies.

Participatory design approach

Participants responded positively to the participatory approach, describing the workshop as 'fun' and suggesting people with type 1 diabetes should be consulted in design processes. Though ethical processes for involving adolescents in medical research are stringent, sufficient participants were drawn in by the workshop method, easing the recruitment process. While previous research had identified 17 strategies for reducing product-related stigma, we limited this workshop to 6 strategies, and limited the time available for each task, creating a pace that was rapid and engaging.

Sketching and prototyping designs, rather than simply completing the brainstorm, resulted in additional, specific information being elicited. Examples include requirements for extended trips and what information needs to be communicated in medical emergencies. This points to the difference between this participatory approach in comparison to other methods such as focus groups.

For most of the designers, designing with a user was a rare and positive occurrence. Some pairs shared the ideation process equally, and other designers took a production role, leading drawing and prototyping activities but not contributing largely to ideation. However, such division in roles could make the tasks boring as pairs lacked synchrony in their activities. One designer conceptualised his role as helping to get his partner to articulate his needs, then collaboratively developing a concept based on these needs.

Although they were provided with pre-workshop materials, designers were nervous about their limited knowledge of diabetes and required participants to inform them of distinctions between more and less important aspects of self-management and device functions. While it is clear to many experienced designers that they must interact with many participants to elicit varying needs and opinions, it struck one designer that had he only been working with one user, he would not have uncovered the variety of needs elicited in the group brainstorm.

Designers were hesitant in critiquing participants' ideas, thought thought this workshop approach would be very helpful early in the research process to better understand the best design direction and user requirements. Designers were concerned, however, that if they developed these ideas in isolation, the original participants may be upset by how much the concepts would change.

Designers remarked that participants were surprisingly candid in discussing their personal experiences, and that this was beneficial to the design process. We suggest that the workshop facilitator having established rapport with the participants prior to the workshop facilitated this open sharing. Further, in one session some participants with diabetes knew each other, and conversation flowed easily. Additionally, the walls of the workspace were covered in quotes about embarrassment and stigma taken from earlier interviews with workshop participants. These honest disclosures possibly seeded the open discussions.

The industrial designers had biases about the strategies for design. Strategies to make the device invisible or increase its social power were not selected for the final designs although these both ranked highly in the voting task. Designers commented that these strategies were hard to implement. While increasing social power may not always relate to a device, designers also did not want to sketch products that would be barely visible.

While the participatory design workshop helped to refine adolescents' requirements for blood glucose monitoring technology, the findings were based on a small number of participants, some of whom were quite confident about self-managing in public. It is likely that there is a participation bias, with young people with diabetes who participate in research experiencing less social discomfort.

While the study showed that adolescents valued a range of the stigma-reducing strategies, further research is needed to determine how to design medical devices that do not create stigma for this group, and when different strategies may be appropriate. In particular, further research about context-based appraisals of whether it is advantageous for medical devices to draw attention should be conducted.

CONCLUSION

In this study ten participants took part in a participatory design workshop based on six strategies for reducing stigma of blood glucose monitoring technologies. Participants valued different strategies for various types of users (e.g., embarrassed users, confident users). All stigma-reducing strategies had advantages and disadvantages, and all except for strengthening the medical identity of the product were thought to be valuable. Participants with diabetes were unhappy that currently the medical identity strategy was most commonly used, though new possibilities for this strategy were not largely explored.

Vaes' strategies were successful in stimulating discussion and ideation among adolescents and designers, though to be usable in a workshop setting the number of strategies needed to be paired down [25]. Addressing stigma is a complex task, with differing opinions and experiences between users of medical devices. As such, this research suggests that a variety of stigma-reducing strategies must be employed to reflect the needs of differing users in various contexts. Further, it elicits context-dependent appraisals of whether device-based attention is advantageous or not.

The participatory design workshop method successfully facilitated open discussion of sensitive topics amongst adolescents and designers. This method resulted in detailed, contextual requirements, and also original design concepts for blood glucose monitoring including a smartphone attachment, all-in-one keyring, holographic watch, system for 3D printing customised devices, and modular test kit.

While medical devices can be stigmatising for adolescents with type 1 diabetes, this research has uncovered the benefits and drawbacks of six strategies for designing to minimise stigma, and begins to explore the context-dependent nature of product stigma.

ACKNOWLEDGMENTS

We thank all the participants, and gratefully acknowledge the support from the MedTech Centre of Research Excellence.

REFERENCES

1. Ananthanarayan, S., Siek, K., & Eisenberg, M. (2016). A Craft Approach to Health Awareness in Children. In *Proceedings of the 2016 ACM Conference on Designing Interactive Systems* (pp. 724–735). ACM.
2. Bichard, J.A., Coleman, R., & Langdon, P. (2007). Does My Stigma Look Big in This? Considering Acceptability and Desirability in the Inclusive Design of Technology Products. In *Universal Access in Human Computer Interaction. Coping with Diversity* (pp. 622–631). Springer, Berlin, Heidelberg.
1. Bispo, R., & Branco, V. (2011). Designing out stigma: a new approach to designing for human diversity. Retrieved from https://iconline.ipleiria.pt/handle/10400.8/456
2. Carroll, A. E., Downs, S. M., & Marrero, D. G. (2007). What Adolescents With Type I Diabetes and Their Parents Want From Testing Technology: A Qualitative Study. *CIN: Computers, Informatics, Nursing January/February 2007*, *25*(1), 23–29.
3. CNN, B. K. K. (n.d.). Physically challenged and fashionable - CNN.com. Retrieved January 16, 2017, from http://www.cnn.com/2012/08/03/living/disability-fashion/index.html
4. Core77 Design Award 2011: Hanky Pancreas, Notable for Soft Goods/Apparel. (n.d.). Retrieved January 16, 2017, from http://www.core77.com//posts/20185/Core77-Design-Award-2011-Hanky-Pancreas-Notable-for-Soft-GoodsApparel
5. Corydon, M. (2015). SpeediCath Compact Set. Retrieved from http://red-dot-21.com/design/speedicath-compact-set/speedicath-compact-set/
6. Di Battista, A. M., Hart, T. A., Greco, L., & Gloizer, J. (2009). Type 1 Diabetes Among Adolescents. *The Diabetes Educator*, *35*(3), 465–475.
7. Druin, A. (1999). Cooperative inquiry: developing new technologies for children with children. In *Proceedings of the SIGCHI conference on Human Factors in Computing Systems* (pp. 592–599). ACM.
8. Fitton, D., Bell, B. T., Little, L., Horton, M., Read, J. C., Rouse, M., & Toth, N. (2016). Working with Teenagers in HCI Research: A Reflection on Techniques Used in the Taking on the Teenagers Project. In *Perspectives on HCI Research with Teenagers* (pp. 237–267). Springer.
9. Garmer, K., Ylven, J., & Karlsson, I. M. (2004). User participation in requirements elicitation comparing focus group interviews and usability tests for eliciting usability requirements for medical equipment: a case study. *International Journal of Industrial Ergonomics*, *33*(2), 85–98.
10. Goffman, E. (1963). *Stigma: Notes on the Management of Spoiled Identity*. Englewood Cliffs: Prentice-Hall.
11. Heiss, L. (2013). Innovative forms of healing: new media art as a catalyst for lasting change in therapeutic settings. Retrieved from http://ses.library.usyd.edu.au/handle/2123/9737
12. Jacobson, S. (2010). Overcoming the Stigma Associated with Assistive Devices; *Proceedings of the 7th international conference on Design & Emotion*, Spertus Institute, Chicago, US.
13. Kanstrup, A. M. (2014). Design concepts for digital diabetes practice: Design to explore, share, and camouflage chronic illness. *International Journal of Design*, *8*(3), 49–60.
14. Kanstrup, A. M., Bertelsen, P., & Nøhr, C. (2015). Patient innovation: an analysis of patients' designs of digital technology support for everyday living with diabetes. *Health Information Management Journal*, *44*(1), 12–20.
15. Lang, A. R., Martin, J. L., Sharples, S., Crowe, J. A., & Murphy, E. (2012). Not a minor problem: involving adolescents in medical device design research. *Theoretical Issues in Ergonomics Science*, *15*(2), 181–192.
16. Martin, J. L., Murphy, E., Crowe, J. A., & Norris, B. J. (2006). Capturing user requirements in medical device development: the role of ergonomics. *Physiological Measurement*, *27*(8), R49.
17. Money, A. G., Barnett, J., Kuljis, J., Craven, M. P., Martin, J. L., & Young, T. (2011). The role of the user within the medical device design and development process: medical device manufacturers' perspectives. *BMC Medical Informatics and Decision Making*, *11*(1), 15

18. Pullin, G. (2009). *Design Meets Disability*. London: MIT Press.
19. Simonsen, J., & Robertson, T. (Eds.). (2013). *Routledge International Handbook of Participatory Design (Hardback) - Routledge*. New York: Routledge.
20. Stephanie Monty designs colostomy bag for intimate moments. (2016, July 25). Retrieved January 16, 2017, from https://www.dezeen.com/2016/07/25/stephanie-monty-colostomy-bag-intimate-moments-graduate-shows-2016-brunel-university-london/
21. Stockton, G. (2009). Stigma: Addressing Negative Associations in Product Design. The Design Society.
22. Strawhacker, M. (2001). Multidisciplinary teaming to promote effective management of type 1 diabetes for adolescents. *Journal of School Health*, *71*(6), 213–217.
23. Vaes, K. R. V. (2014). Product Stigmaticity: Understanding, Measuring and Managing Product-Related Stigma. Delft University.
24. van der Velden, M., & Machniak, M. (2014). Colourful Privacy: Designing Visible Privacy Settings with Teenage Hospital Patients, 60–65.
25. Wang, Y.-L., Brown, S. A., & Horner, S. D. (2010). School-based lived experiences of adolescents with type 1 diabetes: a preliminary study. *Journal of Nursing Research*, *18*(4), 258–265.
26. Wysocki, T., & Greco, P. (2006). Social support and diabetes management in childhood and adolescence: Influence of parents and friends. *Current Diabetes Reports*, *6*(2), 117–122.

Designing Contestability: Interaction Design, Machine Learning, and Mental Health

Tad Hirsch
University of Washington
Seattle, USA
thirsch@uw.edu

Kritzia Merced
University of Utah
Salt Lake City, USA
k.mercedmorales@utah.edu

Shrikanth Narayanan
University of Southern California.
Los Angeles, USA
shri@sipi.usc.edu

Zac E. Imel
University of Utah
Salt Lake City, USA
zac.imel@utah.edu

David C. Atkins
University of Washington
Seattle, USA
datkins@uw.edu

ABSTRACT
We describe the design of an automated assessment and training tool for psychotherapists to illustrate challenges with creating interactive machine learning (ML) systems, particularly in contexts where human life, livelihood, and wellbeing are at stake. We explore how existing theories of interaction design and machine learning apply to the psychotherapy context, and identify "contestability" as a new principle for designing systems that evaluate human behavior. Finally, we offer several strategies for making ML systems more accountable to human actors.

Author Keywords
Machine learning, psychotherapy, mental health, interaction design.

ACM Classification Keywords
H.5.m. Information interfaces and presentation (e.g., HCI): Miscellaneous; I.2.1. Artificial Intelligence: Applications and Expert Systems; J.4 Applications: Social and Behavioral Sciences: Psychology; Design.

INTRODUCTION
Mental health and addiction problems are among the most common causes of disability in the U.S. [31]. Psychotherapy – a goal oriented conversation between a patient and therapist – represents a class of effective treatments [17]. Performance based feedback is key to promoting the effectiveness of providers [29], but standard approaches that rely on direct observation by humans are slow, unreliable, and can't be offered at scale [22]. Recent work demonstrates that sessions can be evaluated by a machine learning (ML) system that provides summaries of different types of therapist interventions [3]. Such performance-based feedback is expected to assist skill development and retention, leading to better outcomes for patients [29].

However, designing interactive systems that rely on machine learning algorithms requires rethinking core assumptions about user control [2]. Accordingly, design researchers have begun to articulate new approaches to such systems. For example, Horvitz' principles for effective "mixed-initiative" systems include querying users for clarification about goals and preferences, and scoping system precision to match user needs [11]. Yang et al describe patterns for designing adaptive user interfaces [33].

Perhaps more provocatively, Allen argues that HCI's prevailing model of human-controlled systems needs to evolve to an interaction-based "dialogue" between people and machines [1]. Leahu similarly calls for fundamental shifts in how we think about relationships between people and machines [19], citing Taylor's observation that interaction designers typically assume that technologies are clearly delineated from and subservient to people [28]. In contrast, Suchman and Bødker have argued that agency resides in both human and nonhuman actors [26][4]. Machine learning algorithms would seem to further complicate this paradigm, presenting systems in which agency is clearly shared (and in some cases, weighted towards the machine). Accordingly, Verbeek suggests a hermeneutical approach to designing systems in which people and machines collaboratively interpret a seemingly inscrutable world [30].

Prior work on interaction design and machine learning systems has often focused on consumer applications, including various recommender systems. Much of the early thinking was necessarily speculative, conducted at a time when ML systems were relatively uncommon. In recent years, these systems have increasingly "become real" [10], finding widespread adoption and media attention. At the same time, they are finding their way into human service domains, including healthcare [32], public safety [8], and

DIS 2017, June 10-14, 2017, Edinburgh, United Kingdom

ACM ISBN 978-1-4503-4922-2/17/06...$15.00
http://dx.doi.org/10.1145/3064663.3064703

transportation planning. With these applications, they are being used not simply to predict user preferences, but to anticipate and evaluate human performance in contexts involving human life, livelihood, and wellbeing.

In this Note, we describe the design and implementation of a ML-based feedback system for psychotherapy to illustrate challenges in creating ML systems for such "high stakes" domains. As ML systems grow in popularity and expand the contexts in which they are employed, there is a greater urgency to articulate their attendant design challenges and patterns. Further, it is incumbent upon designers to develop principles that address social and ethical issues, in addition to pragmatic concerns. Our contribution is intended to advance this discourse.

CORE-MI

This paper discusses design issues that have arisen while developing CORE-MI, a system that uses speech and language processing to automatically generate evaluations of counseling sessions directly from session audio [14]. The system employs ML models trained on prior human ratings, whose reliability has been previously reported [5].

CORE-MI is designed for motivational interviewing (MI), which is an evidence-based psychotherapy focused on behavior change for substance abuse and health behavior problems [23]. The system uses machine learning algorithms to transcribe and evaluate the quality of therapy relative to best practices established in the research literature. The system provides an interactive report card-like, visual summary of counseling sessions.

CORE-MI is expected to be used for both provider training and supervision, and is currently being deployed in several clinics. We have employed a participatory, iterative design process in developing CORE-MI. Our research team includes designers, engineers, mental health researchers, and counselors. We have also conducted several information sessions with prospective users, which has enabled the design team to gauge user interest and identify early-stage concerns. This paper reports lessons learned through the design process to date. A formal user evaluation is currently underway, and will be reported in future publications.

DESIGN ISSUES

We have encountered three main interaction design challenges in developing CORE-MI. Two of these – incentives and transparency – are mentioned in the design literature, although not related to psychotherapy. We also identify "contestability" as a new class of concern, particularly relevant for systems that evaluate human performance.

Incentivizing Participation

Like many machine learning systems, CORE-MI relies on end-user input to train and improve its algorithms. As such, we must design appropriate incentives that encourage users to provide feedback on model predictions [16]. We identify two components of incentive system design: the reward model and the transaction model.

Reward model

Incentive systems typically employ intrinsic or extrinsic rewards to motivate user engagement [16]. Intrinsic rewards are inherently linked to the activity that a model is intended to support. For example, Amazon's recommender system solicits users' product ratings by promising better recommendations that will be more valuable to the user. By contrast, there is little or no logical connection between extrinsic rewards and user action. For example, researchers may offer micropayments [13] or "gamification" elements (points, badges, etc.) [20] in exchange for data labelling services.

Our design emphasizes intrinsic rewards. For example, we promise increased quality of care by offering accurate, inexpensive training and assessment. We are also developing features to automate session documentation, which should reduce counselor workloads. While not directly tied to session evaluation, these features are hoped to increase buy-in and encourage users to provide feedback.

We have been hesitant to explore extrinsic rewards. Ours is a specialized, professional user group with deep commitments to craft and patient outcomes. We are concerned that gamification-like approaches could alienate users and trivialize their work. That said, we recognize that incentives may appeal differently to various users – for example, students, early career therapists, and seasoned providers may respond differently to, say, receiving cash payments for coding transcripts.

Transaction model

The "transaction model" describes the mechanisms through which rewards are conferred. Some incentive systems reward users immediately following participation, in a quid pro quo manner. For example, reCAPTCHA [18] is a popular authentication service in which users provide semantic labels for images before they are allowed to access a desired website. Once a user provides a label, they immediately proceed to the desired content or service.

In contrast, other systems employ a promissory transaction model in which users are enticed to provide data with assurances of future benefit. While these models often appeal to user self-interest, some projects also make altruistic appeals that link user participation to others' benefit (typically at an unspecified future date). The Open Mind Common Sense project, for example, seeks to build a large, crowdsourced dataset of commonsense assertions that will benefit the artificial intelligence field generally, but makes little or no promise of direct benefit to individual contributors [6].

We expect to employ both immediate and promissory transactions. For example, automatically generated session transcripts will be updated in response to user corrections, which will immediately result in revised codes and summary reports for the session. At the same time, we promise improved models and feedback over time, based on user edits. More accurate ratings by the CORE-MI system are claimed to improve quality for current and future users, a mixing of selfish and altruistic encouragement.

Our assumption is that combining transaction models will lead to greater user buy-in and sustained, high-quality input. While it is expected that mixed approaches should be effective, there is limited research thus far ([12] is a notable exception).

From Transparency to Legibility

There is a longstanding principle in interaction design that users should have a conceptual model, or intellectual understanding of how systems work. With regard to machine learning algorithms, this is typically described in terms of "transparency", or of "opening the black box" (e.g.[15]) to reveal to users the inner mechanisms that drive computer prediction.

While transparency is an admirable goal, it may be unachievable for certain kinds of algorithms. In many cases, the interactions between large numbers of variables upon which predictions are made are so complex as to defy easy comprehension by non-expert users – consider economic forecasts, as one example. More challenging still are deep learning neural network approaches and other machine learning systems in which predictions result from thousands of hidden nodes and layers. Such systems are inherently obscure: while their behavior can be observed and evaluated, the precise mechanisms through which decisions are made are unknowable even to their designers, and thus cannot be made fully transparent to users.

Several approaches have been suggested to enhance user comprehension. Höök describes a "black box in a glass box," approach that enables users to query inputs and outputs, but does not provide insight into a system's inner workings [9]. Another method involves "inverting" models, prompting them to generate representative examples that provide insight into how their algorithms function [21] (cited by [19]).

Glass-box-in-a-black-box and inversion do more than make algorithms visible; they help people make sense of an algorithm's behavior. Emphasizing the degree to which a system can be deciphered and interpreted – its legibility – suggests an opportunity to enhance user understanding through "sandboxing" techniques that allow users to probe models with various inputs to investigate their effects on predictions. For example, we could allow users to manipulate percentages of therapist vs. patient talk time or edit sample transcripts to see their effects on overall efficacy scores. Or, we might experiment with having the system generate its own transcripts of what it considers to be high-quality therapy.

Importantly, legibility is linked to users' trust and willingness to adopt. For example, [25] found strong user preference for, and trust in, models that exhibit "sound" (i.e., human comprehensible) reasoning and "clear communication" about decision making. These models were also perceived as more accurate, which did not necessarily correlate with actual or statistical accuracy.

This points to an interesting tension for system designers. In some cases, human interpretable models may be preferable, even if they are less statistically accurate. We suspect that tradeoffs between legibility and accuracy will be particularly important in applications that evaluate human performance. For these applications, trust in a system's "soundness" – and by extension, its fairness – will be a crucial factor in people's willingness to abide by its edicts.

Our system employs a variety of algorithms and measures, of varying degrees of human-comprehensibility. On the one hand, summaries of types of therapist reflections and questions are broadly interpretable, and will be familiar to many of our users (although, the hidden Markov models that the system uses to identify reflections and questions may not be). Other measures are more complex. For example, we offer interpreted scores to indicate a users' overall adherence to MI "spirit." While users of an earlier version of our software expressed interest in interpreted measures [7], informal evaluation suggests that they struggle to understand how they are determined. Moving forward, one of our design challenges will be to provide adequate descriptions of these measures, or to consider dropping them despite their statistical accuracy.

Facilitating Contestation

CORE-MI is currently being implemented in several clinics, and we have already heard some counselors express concern about being "judged by a machine." We understand that such sentiments are bound up with concerns about evaluation more generally, and likely vary with professional status. Students, for example, expect to be evaluated during training, whereas this is exceedingly rare for therapists in private practice. Resistance to evaluation may be exacerbated by automated tools, because, unlike a human supervisor, a trainee cannot inquire about the ratings, nor engage the evaluator about their assessment.

The problem of contestation, of challenging machine predictions, becomes particularly acute when we recognize that our models are, and will continue to be, fallible, and the risks of "getting it wrong" can be quite high for therapists and patients alike.

Imperfect machine learning predictions can limit their appeal and misguide users. Providers may perceive correcting transcripts as a problematic addition to their workload. Perceptions of inaccuracy may also undermine confidence and suppress user interest, casting doubts on system credibility while also undermining its benefits. Equally troubling, overconfidence in model outcomes may lead to negative results for users. For instance, supervisors might weight model predictions too heavily in job performance evaluations, or trainees might adapt their practices to improve machine scores in ways that are ultimately detrimental to patient care.

We therefore must provide mechanisms for users to challenge model predictions. We already see this capability in small ways with recommender systems. For example, Netflix may predict that I'll love the film "Gigli," but I can override this suggestion with my own 1-star rating. Simple correction like this may work with discrete predictions; e.g. word errors from automated speech transcription should be easily correctable. But there the will also be a need for more nuanced and substantial argumentation.

Doing so may require users to marshal evidence and create counter narratives that argue precisely why they disagree with a conclusion drawn by an AI system. This becomes particularly important when the user cannot simply register disagreement with the system, but rather, must make arguments to powerful actors whose decisions are informed by those systems. Think, for example, of a mental health provider whose clinical supervisor relies on automated assessment technologies to evaluate performance, or an insurance company that employs machine learning algorithms in determining whether to cover an addiction treatment program. In cases like these, therapists and trainees will need to be able to access and annotate session transcripts, as well as provide additional contextual detail that might not be available to the algorithm. For example, a therapist who suspects that a patient is inebriated during a session might tailor her discussion in ways that lead to lower scores. Such contextual information would need to be included in any assessment of system performance.

DESIGN FOR CONTESTABILITY

In approaching contestability, we invoke Verbeek's ethical imperative [30] to anticipate and design for potential mediations that our system may embody. In our case, this means thinking beyond the experience an individual has while using our software, and recognizing that our technology can shape relationships between therapists, supervisors, insurance providers, patients, and other stakeholders. In particular, we recognize the potential for ML to be used as a blunt assessment tool by managers and businesses, to the detriment of therapists and patients. Indeed, we acknowledge that there will likely be significant financial and organizational pressures to do so, as our technology occurs at a time of increasing pressure to "rationalize" mental health care [24].

This concern is somewhat speculative, as systems like ours are fairly novel. Nonetheless, we identify several design strategies that can be put in place now, to help mitigate future misuse.

First, we strive to improve the accuracy of our models. This is achieved through phased deployment with expert users in training clinics and universities, and with students who are not expected to perform perfectly and who can be more easily incentivized to provide feedback. By running through thousands of sessions in education contexts, we hope to develop models that are reasonably accurate by the time they are released in broader healthcare settings.

Second, we strive to make our models as legible as possible. We provide detailed explanations of each measure, and highlight confidence scores to indicate the degree of certainty in each prediction. We will also provide mechanisms for users to unpack aggregate measures, tracing system predictions all the way down to the transcript level so that users can follow, and if necessary, contest the reasoning behind each prediction. At the same time, we recognize that certain measures defy human interpretation and will continue to evaluate the efficacy that these measures provide in light of their potential to foster distrust. Moving forward, we may decide that the value that some measures is outweighed by their cost in user confidence and trust.

Third, alongside technology development we anticipate designing training modules for therapists and supervisors that describe how the system works, including discussion of its strengths and limitations. These modules may include sandboxing features that allow users to experiment with inputs and outputs. By teaching users about the system's capabilities, we hope to discourage inappropriate use and interpretations of model output, and to create a shared understanding that can act as a basis for addressing inevitable disagreements.

Finally, we expect to remain vigilant about potential misuse and implicit bias. This includes providing mechanisms for users to ask questions and record disagreements with system behavior. It also means looking for aggregate effects that may not be apparent to individual users. For example, [27] has demonstrated racial bias in Google's AdSense system that were only made visible by looking at behavior across multiple users and sessions. We take this lesson seriously and hope to implement programs that can monitor for such effects on the behalf of vulnerable users.

The above suggestions arise from our experience designing and implementing a machine learning system for psychotherapy. However, we believe that the principles we describe will have wider applicability, particularly for ML systems that predict and evaluate human behavior in contexts that affect human life, livelihood, and wellbeing. That said, we offer these recommendations tentatively, as a step towards articulating a set of design principles and practices for this emerging area. We look forward to exploring and evaluating them more fully in future work.

ACKNOWLEDGMENTS

This work was supported by the National Institute of Health through grants AA018673, DA034860, and AA023814.

REFERENCES

[1] Allen, J.E. et al. 1999. Mixed-initiative interaction. *IEEE Intelligent Systems*. 14, 5 (Sep. 1999), 14–23.

[2] Amershi, S. et al. 2014. Power to the people: The role of humans in interactive machine learning. *AI Magazine*. 35, 4 (2014), 105–120.

[3] Atkins, D.C. et al. 2014. Scaling up the evaluation of psychotherapy: evaluating motivational interviewing fidelity via statistical text classification. *Implementation Science*. 9, 1 (Dec. 2014).

[4] Bødker, S. 1991. *Through the interface: a human activity approach to user interface design*. L. Erlbaum.

[5] Can, D. et al. 2016. "It sounds like...": A natural language processing approach to detecting counselor reflections in motivational interviewing. *Journal of Counseling Psychology*. 63, 3 (2016), 343–350.

[6] Catherine Havasi et al. 2010. Open mind common sense: crowd-sourcing for common sense. (2010).

[7] Cook, J. and Hirsch, T. 2014. Monologger: visualizing engagement in doctor-patient conversation. (2014), 37–40.

[8] Emerging Technology from the arXiv 2016. Neural Network Learns to Identify Criminals by Their Faces. *MIT Technology Review*.

[9] Höök, K. et al. 1996. A glass box approach to adaptive hypermedia. *User Modeling and User-Adapted Interaction*. 6, 2–3 (Jul. 1996), 157–184.

[10] Höök, K. 2000. Steps to take before intelligent user interfaces become real. *Interacting with Computers*. 12, 4 (Feb. 2000), 409–426.

[11] Horvitz, E. 1999. Principles of mixed-initiative user interfaces. (1999), 159–166.

[12] Huang, Y. et al. 2016. Combining contribution interactions to increase coverage in mobile participatory sensing systems. (2016), 365–376.

[13] Irani, L.C. and Silberman, M.S. 2013. Turkopticon: interrupting worker invisibility in amazon mechanical turk. (2013), 611.

[14] James Gibson et al. 2016. Developing an Automated Report Card for Addiction Counseling: The Counselor Observer Ratings Expert for MI (CORE-MI). (San Jose, CA, 2016).

[15] Jameson, A. 2003. Adaptive interfaces and agents. *The human-computer interaction handbook*. L. Erlbaum Associates Inc. 305–330.

[16] Kraut, R.E. et al. 2011. *Building successful online communities: evidence-based social design*. MIT Press.

[17] Lambert, M.J. 2013. *Bergin & Garfield's handbook of psychotherapy and behavior change*. Wiley.

[18] Law, E.L.M. and Von Ahn, L. 2011. *Human computation*. Morgan & Claypool Publishers.

[19] Leahu, L. 2016. Ontological Surprises: A Relational Perspective on Machine Learning. (2016), 182–186.

[20] Lindqvist, J. et al. 2011. I'm the mayor of my house: examining why people use foursquare - a social-driven location sharing application. (2011), 2409.

[21] Mahendran, A. and Vedaldi, A. 2015. Understanding deep image representations by inverting them. (Jun. 2015), 5188–5196.

[22] Proctor, E.K. et al. 2009. Implementation Research in Mental Health Services: an Emerging Science with Conceptual, Methodological, and Training challenges. *Administration and Policy in Mental Health and Mental Health Services Research*. 36, 1 (Jan. 2009), 24–34.

[23] Rollnick, S. and Miller, W.R. 1995. What is Motivational Interviewing? *Behavioural and Cognitive Psychotherapy*. 23, 04 (Oct. 1995), 325.

[24] Scheid, T.L. 2003. Managed Care and the Rationalization of Mental Health Services. *Journal of Health and Social Behavior*. 44, 2 (Jun. 2003), 142.

[25] Stumpf, S. et al. 2007. Toward harnessing user feedback for machine learning. (2007), 82.

[26] Suchman, L.A. 2007. *Human-machine reconfigurations: plans and situated actions*. Cambridge University Press.

[27] Sweeney, L. 2013. Discrimination in Online Ad Delivery. *Queue*. 11, 3 (Mar. 2013), 10.

[28] Taylor, A. 2015. After interaction. *interactions*. 22, 5 (Aug. 2015), 48–53.

[29] Tracey, T.J.G. et al. 2014. Expertise in psychotherapy: an elusive goal? *The American Psychologist*. 69, 3 (Apr. 2014), 218–229.

[30] Verbeek, P.-P. 2015. COVER STORYBeyond interaction: a short introduction to mediation theory. *interactions*. 22, 3 (Apr. 2015), 26–31.

[31] Whiteford, H.A. et al. 2013. Global burden of disease attributable to mental and substance use disorders: findings from the Global Burden of Disease Study 2010. *The Lancet*. 382, 9904 (Nov. 2013), 1575–1586.

[32] Yang, Q. et al. 2016. Investigating the Heart Pump Implant Decision Process: Opportunities for Decision Support Tools to Help. (2016), 4477–4488.

[33] Yang, Q. et al. 2016. Planning Adaptive Mobile Experiences When Wireframing. (2016), 565–576.

[illegible]

Attention from Afar: Simulating the Gazes of Remote Participants in Hybrid Meetings

Bin Xu[1, 2] **Jason Ellis**[2] **Thomas Erickson**[2]

[1]Information Science
Cornell University
Ithaca, NY14850 USA
bx55@cornell.edu

[2]IBM T. J. Watson Research Center
Yorktown Heights, NY 10598 USA
{jasone, snowfall}@us.ibm.com

ABSTRACT
Gaze is a powerful form of social feedback, providing cues about attention and interest, and boredom and distraction. We designed a working prototype that enabled remote participants in a collocated meeting to look around the local meeting space, and that showed local participants where the remote participants' "simulated gazes" (that is, their virtual cameras) were directed. Of course, pointing a camera is not the same as gazing, and so we conducted a study to understand how simulated gazes might be used, and to what extent they would be experienced as social cues. Findings range from the use of simulated gaze to signal attention, to ways in which local and remote participants experienced these simulated gazes. These findings illustrate the value of indirection and abstraction in presenting social cues; raise issues of privacy, visibility, and participation asymmetry; and suggest implications for design and further research.

Author Keywords
Hybrid meeting; gaze; computer-mediated communication.

ACM Classification Keywords
H.5.3. Information interfaces and presentation (e.g., HCI): Group and Organizational Interfaces: Synchronous Interaction.

INTRODUCTION
A hybrid meeting is a meeting in which several people are collocated in a meeting room, but that also has remote participants connected by phone or video. Although common, hybrid meetings are challenging for remote participants because of an impedance mismatch: the collocated participants can readily see and converse with one another, whereas remote participants are less visible to collocated participants and their options for signaling their engagement are more limited. In our view, enabling effective hybrid meetings is something of a grand challenge in designing tools for meetings. This is particularly true if one wishes, as we do, to avoid the use of high-end, dedicated video-conferencing rooms, and the need for remote participants to use specialized equipment. In this paper we report on formative design explorations that aim to reduce (but by no means eliminate) the impedance mismatch between collocated and remote participants.

DIS 2017, June 10-14, 2017, Edinburgh, United Kingdom
© 2017 ACM. ISBN 978-1-4503-4922-2/17/06…$15.00
DOI: http://dx.doi.org/10.1145/3064663.3064720

Specifically, we designed a working prototype with two features. It uses an omnidirectional camera in the meeting room to let remote participants independently look around (each participant using their own virtual camera). And it provides abstract representations that show those collocated in the meeting room where the remote participants have pointed their virtual cameras. Remote users only need a device that supports voice and a display to use the system.

In particular, we are interested in whether showing collocated participants where a remote participant is looking can function as a "simulated gaze." Gaze is a powerful social cue [6]. It can signal whether a person is interested or bored, and whether they are following a conversation or not. But of course, pointing a virtual camera is quite different from one human gazing at another, which is why we use the adjective "simulated," and do not assume that the benefits and uses of real gaze apply to simulated gaze. Since neither existing theory nor prior work seemed sufficient to suggest how simulated gaze might work, or how to use it in a design, we developed a working prototype to better understand its usefulness.

This paper describes the working prototype (Figures 1 and 2), the method, and issues and design implications. It begins by reviewing prior work, and then describes the working prototype. Next is the methodology, in which 19 participants used the prototype to carry out a discussion task, and then participated in a semi-structured interview. The results section describes the participants' experiences, their reactions to the system, and discusses our findings. The paper concludes with design implications and directions for further work.

RELATED WORK

Using Gaze in Collaborative Systems
Gaze is a powerful cue during face-to-face conversations [6]. It can silently trigger a conversation by capturing visual attention [4, 22, 26], refer to objects and persons [9, 30], coordinate turn-taking in a group [37], and indicate interest

in other persons [43]. Using gaze to communicate one's intentions is a part of human communication [e.g. 24, 25], as is our ability to use it to infer others' intentions [e.g.,1].

Research on collaborative systems has also explored the utility of gaze to support both conversation-oriented and task-oriented collaboration (e.g., [9, 26, 28]). Other work explores ways to allow virtual environment users' avatars to engage in mutual gaze [30], and to allow them to make eye contact in avatar-mediated virtual meetings [5] or an immersive virtual collaboration [19, 28]. Gaze was also studied in video-mediated collaborations. Monk et. al. designed a system to support awareness of gaze in video conferences and found that gaze awareness served as an alternative non-verbal channel for the development of common ground [33].

However, gaze in these systems differs from the real gaze that shapes face-to-face conversation. There, gaze was either captured by gaze-tracking devices (e.g., [9, 48]), or delivered through a 'transparent' interface that aligned users' viewing directions (e.g., [26, 28]). There are pros and cons to these methods. Although gaze-tracking devices are accurate, they must be calibrated before use and aren't ideal for daily use [44]. Solutions like [28] are less complicated, but are still limited to specially configured physical spaces.

Our aim is to explore approaches that are cheaper and less technically complex, and therefore have the potential to be broadly used. Our starting point was to deploy pan-tilt-zoom cameras [41] in a meeting room to empower remote users to look around, but these cameras provided a single shared view to all remote participants. As the number of users increases, control of such a camera is still limited to a single person and conflicts arise if there is disagreement about the direction it should be pointed. This limitation inspired us to use an omnidirectional camera [39], which uses wide-angle lenses to capture a sphere and, in this way, can "see in all directions at once". The camera streams this panoramic video and enables each remote participant to move a virtual viewport to a part of the panoramic image. This led us to wonder whether these individual virtual camera movements could stand in for the gazes of individuals, though the simulated gazes are not as accurate as what can be captured by eye-tracking devices.

Once gaze, real or simulated, is detected, we must consider how that gaze might be presented to others. One solution is to represent the gaze by animating the eyes of a users' avatar [5, 19]; another is to use a physical device whose orientation corresponds to the user's gaze, for example, by using a small rotating screen that depicts the remote person's face [31, 32], or a telepresence robot.

Our aim is to find an affordable way to present remote users' simulated gazes to local participants. While using avatar eyes and head movements to depict gaze has the advantage of mimicking natural behavior, we are not yet at a point where either virtual or augmented reality systems are being commonly used. Telepresence robots are somewhat more common, but are expensive and far from ubiquitous. Furthermore, availability aside, although telepresence robots can depict gaze, the use of telepresence robots does not scale to situations where there are many remote participants – physical meeting rooms can quickly become crowded, especially because maneuvering telepresence robots is still, at best, cumbersome. Inspired by [42], which shows how an abstract visual presentation can represent user status and activity, and following a discussion in [7], which cautions that a full and detailed presentation of remote person could be privacy sensitive and distracting, we decided to explore representing gaze with an abstract but hopefully legible visual representation.

Social Awareness in Collaboration

Awareness has been an important research theme in Computer Supported Collaborative Work (CSCW) since its early days [10]. Awareness in shared physical and virtual workspaces includes knowing who is present [e.g. 11], and other social factors [15], including knowing what others know [38], who they are connected to or their social network [53], and what they're doing (e.g., [47]). Research also shows the benefits that these kinds of awareness can provide, improving the performance of work [52], the coordination of tasks [29], the creation connections between employees [40], and team dynamics [8, 29].

Awareness is also important for distance collaboration. Early work like "Portholes" demonstrated the positive effects of having awareness of others when collaborating over distance [11]. Specifically, increasing a person's awareness of who the remote collaborators are provides an opportunity to enhance the presence of these remote users, even without embodied presence [42]. Approaches to supporting awareness across distance include sharing the video stream of a remote space and persons [11], sharing the planning and coordination activities of remote teams [40], and information about remote user activities [7], etc.

In hybrid meetings, local persons share a meeting space and are aware of each other's presence and attention, but remote participants have less access to this information. We expect that showing the simulated gazes of remote participants may be beneficial for awareness.

Social Translucence and Privacy

Making activities transparent has benefits and risks. The social translucence framework provides ways of thinking about how socially salient information can facilitate or inhibit social processes in collaborative systems [12, 13] and social media designs [21]. In a system that supports independent views of hybrid meetings, one question is whether all collaborators need to see the same things to build common ground. Limited work discusses this question in terms of gaze sharing. In this paper, we examine issues of social translucence by adopting a similar design.

Figure 1. The remote user's interface: The upper panning view allows users to look around the meeting room; the lower view shows a panoramic video of the entire room – and the green rectangles show what the panning window is viewing. The right margin contains thumbnails of the views from all sites – the meeting room (middle) and two remote users (above and below).

Because gaze indicates attention and interests [30], it may raise privacy concerns. For example, one study showed that employees felt their privacy was violated because they, their activities, or their data received unexpected attention [3]. Therefore, in hybrid meetings, it's possible that inferences based on the simulated gazes could lead to privacy problems, social pressure, or other forms of discomfort. We hope to gain insight into these issues.

PROTOTYPE SYSTEM

To support hybrid meetings, we developed a working prototype with two components: a Remote User Interface to allow remote users to view the meeting room, and a Gaze Simulation Interface to display remote 'gaze' to collocated users in the room. We also built a logging system to produce Usage Charts used to facilitate discussion during the study. These components are described in turn below.

Remote User Interface

To allow remote users to view the meeting room, we used an omnidirectional camera [39] to capture the space. The Ricoh Theta S camera [46] was chosen due to its low cost, popularity, and live streaming capabilities. The camera produces a 1280 x 720 live stream at 15 fps. We captured this video and streamed it using the WebRTC protocol.

The Remote User Interface (Figure 1) has three components: panning view, panoramic view, and remote participant thumbnails. The panoramic view (bottom) shows the entire image captured by the camera as a rectangle. This panoramic image is distorted at the top and bottom. We positioned the camera to make the faces of seated people fall along the equator of the image, so faces

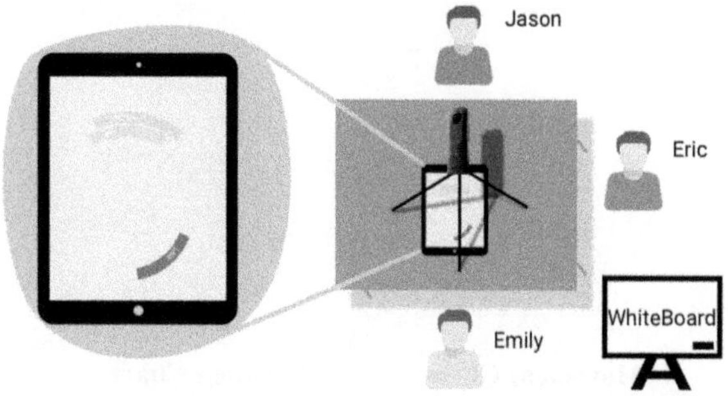

Figure 2. Gaze simulation as seen by local users. The gaze simulation interface sits on the table, adjacent to and aligned with the omnidirectional camera. Each arc shows where each remote person is looking using the panning view. Here, 2 users are looking at Jason and 1 at the whiteboard.

are typically recognizable, while higher (ceiling) or lower (conference table) objects tend to be distorted.

To compensate for this distortion, we provided a panning view (top in Figure 1) that shows an undistorted portion of the total video sphere. Users use their mice to control the direction of their viewports (aka virtual cameras). This functionality allows multiple users to look around the room in real time, independently and simultaneously. We call this ability to control the virtual cameras "simulated gazing" and use it to drive the Gaze Simulation (described below).

Lastly, the Remote User Interface captures video of the participant using her/her laptop camera and streams to the other remote users. Each of these video feeds is shown in a thumbnail along the right side of the user interface. When a user clicks on one of these thumbnails, the video expands to fill the large video window at the top left of the interface.

Gaze Simulation Interface

With the remote interface, the system captures where remote users point their virtual cameras. We also needed a way to display these simulated gazes in the meeting room. As discussed, we used an abstract representation to achieve this (Figure 2). This representation – or gaze interface – displays an arc for each remote user, the arc corresponding to the horizontal direction in which the virtual camera is pointed. As remote users change where they are looking, their arcs move accordingly. The simulated gazes were displayed on a 12.9" iPad on the table next to the camera. Local participants could view the gaze interface and see where remote users were looking by watching the arcs. Figure 2 illustrates a case where two remote users are looking at Jason and a third at the whiteboard. Note that the 'gazes' presented here are not perfect. To simplify the interface, only horizontal movement is represented. Thus, if a remote user looks up or down, this is not reflected.

Logging System and Usage Charts

For the purposes of the study, we also built a system to log each person's interaction with the panning window, including each time they changed their viewpoint and how

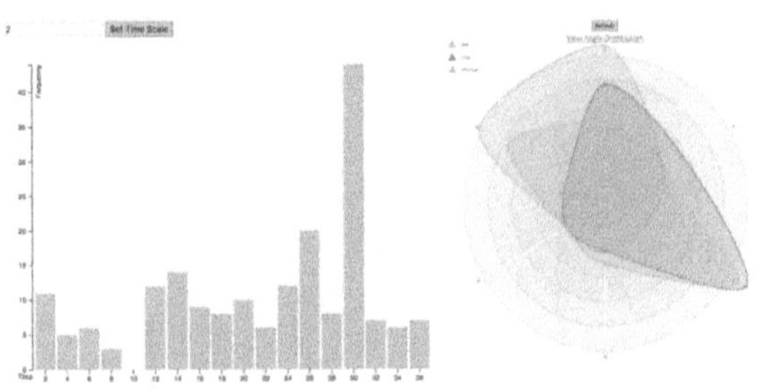

Movement Chart **Location Chart**

Figure 3. Usage charts. Movement chart shows how many times the remote user changed their perspective in the panning view. The location chart shows how long the user maintained a particular point of view in the panning view.

long they stayed at each viewpoint. These data are used to generate two usage charts – the movement chart and the historical location chart (Figure 3) – that were used in the study. The movement chart shows when and how many movements a user made during the study session, and the location chart shows the frequency with which a user looked in various directions. The logging mechanism was a Google Chrome web application, the client was built with HTML5, AnguarJS and D3, and server was Node.

METHDOLOGY

The Study

The purpose of this study was to determine how users used and experienced the various interface components, and to gather ideas for future design. In brief, 4 people (2 collocated and 2 remote) carried out a discussion designed to permit them to exercise the features of the technology. Afterwards a semi-structured interview, augmented by usage charts, was used to gather feedback. Details follow.

Setup

Because the aim was to understand both the experiences of those 'in the room' and those who were remote, each study session included two 'real' participants, P1, the local participant and P2, a remote participant (i.e. in a nearby room but connected only via the system). Each session also included two Experimenters: E1, who was in the room with P1, and E2, who was remote (but in a different location than P2). As noted in the description of the system, remote users E2 and P2 could independently control the direction of their views in the panning window of their user interface. A schematic of this setup is provided in Figure 4.

Task

Participants were told that they were members of a small group that had been asked to decide how to spend $100,000 to improve the social/work environment of the building in which they worked, for one of three groups (visitors, remote employees or regular employees). We designed this task to provide reasons for participants to both look at one another, and to look at objects in the room (e.g., a map). In addition to the design of the task itself, the 2 experimenters also acted in ways to encourage P1 and P2 to exercise

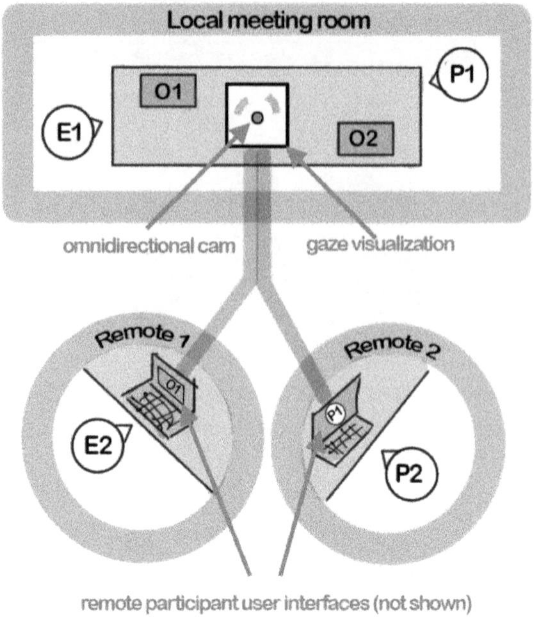

Figure 4. A schematic of the study setup: An experimenter (E1) and participant (P1) collocated in a room with an omnidirectional camera (center) and various objects (O1 and O2) on the table. A second experimenter (E2) is in one remote location, and a second participant (P2) is in a second remote location. E2 and P2 can independently adjust their views to look around the meeting room.

features of the interface. The first part of the discussion was guided by the two experimenters so that participants talked to (and optionally, looked at) the others. In this part, E1 acted as the coordinator of the discussion (and revealed himself as an experimenter), while E2 acted as a confederate who was a peer of P1 and P2. Typically, this discussion focused on which of the three groups should be supported. The second part of the discussion was guided to focus on changes that might improve the work environment. Here the E1 and E2 began referring to objects in the room, such as a large poster that showed areas of the site that might be suitable for alteration. After the first two sessions, other objects were added – e.g., a telepresence robot – to allow for a richer discussion of improvements.

Timeline

Participants P1 and P2 arrived at the study location and were introduced to one another by E1. The purpose of the study was described, the technology was demonstrated to both, and consent forms were signed. Next P2 was taken to a separate room and set up with the remote users' interface (Figure 1), reminded of how to use it and that the people in the room could see the direction in which the panning window was pointed. Third, E1 took the other participant, P1, into the meeting room. At this point, the discussion task began: it lasted 15-20 minutes, and followed the two-part discussion format already described. Fourth, the discussion was ended, and P2, the 'remote' participant, was brought back to the meeting room, and a group semi-structured interview was carried out with P1 and conducted by E1.

Semi-structured Interview
Each session concluded with a semi-structured interview. Initially, participants were simply asked to report on their reactions to the system; after about 10 minutes, they were shown the two Usage Charts (Figure 3). These charts were used as probes: first to extract more detailed accounts of participants' actions/reactions, and second as prompts to discuss privacy concerns.

In general, the interview covered the following topics:

- Meeting support technologies participants has used
- The remote user's experience of the remote UI (Figure 1)
- The local user's experience of the gaze simulation interface (Figure 2)
- Discussion with both users about when and why they made use of (or did not use) their portions of the UI
- Discussion with both users about the usage chart (Figure 3) and whether it should be private or shared
- A discussion about other uses for this sort of technology

Participants
Since the aim of the study was to gather reactions to the technology, and collect ideas for further development of the system, we sought technologically adept participants who had prior experience that could inform their comments. No attempt was made to recruit "average" participants to assess issues like ease of learning, usability, or likelihood of adoption. In our view, the prototype system was in too early a stage for this to be of value. Therefore, this study recruited employees from the Research division of the company in which the technology development was occurring. The company itself is a global information technology firm whose businesses range from hardware development to services provision, and which has on the order of a hundred thousand employees. Participants were recruited by approaching people in the cafeteria, who were later contacted by email to confirm availability; snowball sampling was used to expand the list of candidates.

We scheduled 10 sessions with 2 volunteers each. 1 volunteer did not show up, so in that session we only have the remote confederate as a remote participant. There were 19 participants (15 males and 4 females aged from 20 to 60+). All took part in the final interviews.

Data Analysis
Interviews were audio-recorded, transcribed and edited to remove identifiers and other references that may identify the participants and/or anyone they mentioned during the interview. Quotes from participants who served as "local users" are numbered (L#), and quotes from those who served as "remote users" are numbered as (R#).

After reading the transcripts to become acquainted with the data, transcripts were imported into the Dedoose qualitative data analysis tool and divided into meaningful units. Three of the authors did a close reading of the transcripts while identifying key points, as a part of an open-coding process in which we coded distinct concepts and categories in the data. After this, they examined relationships between key themes to refine categories, and to ensure close associations between participants' responses and emerging analyses.

RESULTS
Four categories emerged from participants' feedback: the usefulness of two different views in the remote interface; the meaning of the simulated gazes; the effects of asymmetry in interfaces and data; and the privacy concerns around collected data in system. We discuss each in turn.

Panning and Panoramic Windows Have Different Uses
Participants in the remote role saw two video views: the panning view that they could rotate to look around, and the panoramic view that showed a distorted but omnidirectional view of the conference room.

Panning view offers immersive perspective. First, the panning view was consistent with users' visual perception of space, as it "*is a pretty standard view that you get in any conference system* [and] *what I expected.* (R10)", and offers better *"spatial sense throughout the discussion* [that] *is very helpful.* (R7)" Especially when *"sometimes* [participants] *talked about some things in the room, the objects, and* [remote participant] *can definitely move around and focus and look at that object immediately.* (R7)" And it further increases remote's sense of belonging: "*It mostly helped me feel more included. It's not like we're talking and I have really no idea what's going on in the room.* (R6)"

Remote participants also found the panning view useful when there was significant turn-taking in the conversation in the local room, or those in the meeting room interacted with local objects: "*I changed the direction when there was a transition between speakers. And also when you point to a specific object in the room on the table then I tried to look at that object. I think that was an advantage.* (R7)"

Panoramic view offers navigating reference and overview. The panoramic window was used to "*follow what was happening there as people were pointing to, then you would want to look at that.* (R4)", and "*see overall who and what was there and sometimes I looked at that instead of moving the top camera to the person.* (R3)"

Regarding offering two views in one interface, participants reported it was beneficial to have reference/overview alongside a more detailed panning view: "*I think the combination of the views and helping with that, because ... When you have the* [panoramic view], *you see everything. If you just had the portal view* [panning view] *it's like, I'm looking at him but at the same time you're doing something which I'm totally unaware of because I don't see it.* (R6)"

However, other participants tended to prefer just one view. When there were fewer turns in the conversation, the panning window was less used, and they reported looking at the panoramic window briefly "*was sufficient to give an idea of what was, where you guys were, and what things were around and stuff* (R4)" because: "*all that was happening was people were talking. I could focus in on you* [in the panning view], *rather than on the bottom I could see you both, right? That doesn't really give you that much additional information.* (R4)" Some other participants preferred to have just the panning view (top) because it was not distorted and "*was very responsive and quick to just have a look around with it, and the lower* [panoramic] *one gives you that overview but it was a bit distorted.* (R3)"

Overall, the usefulness of being able to look around was highly related to whether there were *contents* located in the space, for example, an object of interest (e.g., pointed at by a local person), or *contexts* important to the conversation itself, for example, non-verbal cues of local people [49].

One way to understand the results is to think about how and when the two views provide information relevant to the conversation. The hyper-personal communication model [50] suggests that in digitally mediated communication, people are still able to achieve common ground without the non-verbal cues that face-to-face offers. This may explain why some remote participants expressed less interest in moving their viewpoint to the talking local person when the discussion was primarily verbal. When participants began referring to objects in the room, seeing the video became more important to following the conversation.

In summary, the panning view offers a non-distorted view of local room, which helped remote participants make sense of the space and focus on interesting activities and objects, which is hard to achieve through verbal conversations alone. The panoramic view is better for getting an overview and providing reference for the panning view, especially when there is a need to move the panning view. When participants were in a primarily verbal conversation, the panoramic window was quite effective on its own.

Simulated Gaze: An Indirect and Abstract Attention Representation Has Advantages and Disadvantages

During the discussion, participants paid occasional attention to the gaze UI, but did not concentrate on it as it "*was just* [in my] *peripheral vision* (L10)".

The movement of arcs in the gaze UI however did attract attention. Seeing an arc move led to "*inferences that maybe you* [remote person] *see this, and maybe you're following it, and that you made some attempt to move your camera around to look. That indicates some level of attention that you're doing something to look over in that direction* (L4)". Beside movement, "*if there is more than one person and they are looking in the same direction, then the people here can recognize that there is attention coming from the remote place as well.* (L7)"

Awareness of remote attention offered benefits to local participants. Besides being "*entertaining to watch* (L6)", "*it's not intrusive and it's easy to have in a situation. It doesn't necessarily always have a use, but when it doesn't have a use, it's not that annoying.*(L4)"

The simulated gazes also lead to the local person having a heightened sense of being visible and being paid attention to, or not: "*I think initially I was a little bit more exposed. People are turning, looking, and you're like, 'Oh, boy, better put on my best for the teleconference,' you know, I'll be eating granola bars and whatever else while the conference would be on, ... when the direction of the camera, of the focus, was being pointed away even though you've got that other overlay image at the bottom but it was pointed away, I sort of relaxed a little bit more.* (L6)"

Having a gaze simulation UI in conference room also increased the remote person's self-consciousness about their performance. They tended to adopt the norm that they should "*pay attention to be polite* (R2)", as well as to demonstrate their commitment to a meeting: "*if I was in a meeting that was an important meeting or a meeting with a lot of people, it's a way to show that I'm participating. That I'm awake and listening and following the conversation and not just off doing something else* (R3)". And such social pressures were also seen as a way to increase engagement: "*This is nice to give some feedback in terms of whether* [the 2 remote users] *were paying attention to what we were saying. They wouldn't be able to get away with pressing the button on mute at home and dancing around in their pajamas because if it's not moving and looking at where we're pointing to say, 'Hey, let's talk about this topic,' you knew that they're not paying attention. It puts pressure on everyone to be fully engaged* (L6)".

From a Goffmanian perspective [22, 23], making a remote person's attention visible brings the remote person more onto the front stage than a traditional video window that provides no gaze information (i.e., Mona Lisa Effect [34]). Being on the front stage stimulates the self-consciousness of performance and self-presentation, and increases social pressure to behave in particular ways. This also may explain why people in the conference room, who are already on the front stage, now get a better sense of attention from the remote audience and, thus, behave as if on stage. Without presenting simulated gazes, local persons may assume that remote audiences are always or never paying attention, which is a similar effect to that observed with self-presentation on the Facebook Newsfeed [2, 14].

However, the simulated gaze is not fully equivalent to real gaze, and local participants were aware of that: "*they* [remote persons] *might be looking at the lower window. Where they can see people at once and then they won't move* [the panning window to trigger arc movement]. (L3)" The ambiguity regarding whether the remote person was paying attention or not led to positive attributions when users were not following the norm of looking at people to be polite or show engagement: "*I could use this* [simulated gaze interface] *as an indicator of where people are looking and I saw* [remote person 1] *being much more active than* [remote person 3]. *I mean there's just something in the back of my mind wondering you know what's going on with* [remote person 3] *why aren't you looking around and the answer is you were just using the panoramic view.* (L9)"

Taking the perspective of the casual attribution theory [51], our prototype, as a socio-technical system, injects the ambiguity that simulated gazes do not always reflect what others' are attending to. This is similar to the finding in a machine translation mediated collaboration [20]: when there are two possible interpretations of communication errors, one due to system limitations and the other one to the human, communicators attribute errors to the system.

Finally, remote participants found that seeing simulated gazes helped improve their feeling of presence in the conference room: "*When I'm in the room, I can see, 'Oh, you know* [remote person] *is looking around,' and you can come in the room and say, 'Oh, hi* [remote person]*.' It's kind of nice. It's kind of sitting there. There's obvious value for remote people. ... Then also, for people coming in the room, they're kind of aware there might be these other people who are not there in person but who care about what's going on.* (R6)"

In short, the interface presenting simulated gazes is seen as an abstract view that provides a partial representation of the remote person's attention, and it has both advantages and disadvantages. The advantages are that it is less intrusive, it provides the local person with awareness of the remote person's attention, and it increases social presence by signaling the remote person's participation and activity. At the same time, it can increase social pressure on the remote person to pay attention, and may increase the local person's concern about receiving too much (or not enough) attention. Finally, the fact that the indication of attention is not entirely accurate, can lead to misinterpretation, but can also provide ambiguity that can support plausible deniability.

The Viewing Asymmetry Has Pros and Cons

As discussed, we were inspired by the social translucence framework to create an abstract representation of gaze. We chose not to show video of remote participants in order to let participants focus on the gaze interface rather than overwhelming them with multiple video streams. However, remote users were able to see video of the local room and other remote users. In contrast to the asymmetry in traditional meeting setting where local persons have more access than remote ones, our prototype introduced an asymmetry that limited local persons' access: "*I felt jealous of* [remote] *people who had cameras, who had a display. I could not see* [remote #1] *or* [remote #2] *and I felt a sort of asymmetry there. I felt blind where they could see so there was a kind of jealousy there of their ability to see more than I could* (L9)", or as a sense of inequality: "*People need to feel equal... and that's the best way I can describe it, otherwise it feels creepy.* (L7)" One solution the participants suggested was to integrate each remote person's video into the gaze interface: "*I really want to see the person, not just have their name. I mean the ideal thing would be if that was the image at the top.* (L10)" Although we deliberately designed the gaze simulation interface without the live video to probe reactions to simulated gazes, it would be useful to explore ways of combining gaze with video, etc., as we move towards a more functional design.

Despite the asymmetry, local participants experienced benefits from this design choice. First, by presenting remote's viewing behavior as an abstract visual cue to participants in the local room, the prototype required low cognitive load as the design "*makes it easier to understand out of the corner of my eye* [and] *this conveys less information and it requires way less cognitive bandwidth from me.* (L9)" Another potential benefit is that the gaze simulation is low fidelity and so avoids potential privacy issues or distraction often associated with live video: "*It's also good in some sense it's a low fidelity interface. It's more lively than, 'here are a list of people who are logged into the camera.' ... it's giving some sense of where people are looking, but it's kind of low fidelity. I don't think it's revealing a lot of stuff about you and I think it's a good thing to have.* (R6)"

Making Sense of Privacy, Making Sense of Data

Another asymmetry that the prototype introduced was in what data was collected. That is, remote participants' movements of the panning window are captured by the system, and potentially available for further use, unlike the collocated participants' gazes. Two usage charts (Figure 3) were used to demonstrate potential uses of the gaze data. They summarized the remote person's movements over time during the (movement chart) and the degree to which they looked in specific directions (location chart). The main purpose of visualizing these data was to let users to reflect what had happened in the meeting and help us examine to what extent this kind of data can help users understand the meeting and their own performance.

Remote participants felt that the two usage charts provided interesting insights on their own performance during the meeting: "*if my pattern was anomalous for me or different from most people and the system* [charts] *were to tell me that it might be an interesting: 'Are you OK, were you especially excited or bored by this meeting?' If it were an entree to a further exploration of why were you behaving in this way, it might be interesting.* (R9)" and there was value to "*understand my behavior a little bit better.* (L3)"

However, participants varied in their opinions about whether the charts should be shared. Some felt it was OK to share as the charts were just summaries of publicly observable activity, which "*is not really private because everybody saw it at the time, if they had been watching* (R3)". Others disagreed. The first concern is that there was insufficient context to allow others make sense of the gaze data: "*I don't know where they've moved to so there doesn't seem to be enough information there to care about this. It's not correlated with activity or anything* (L10)". Further, it also missed the important contexts like "*what was being said and who was saying it, what was being referred to and stuff like that.* (R7)" And the conversation itself "*is a context that is not being captured that is important to interpreting and giving you valuable insight.* (L4)" This in turn could result in misinterpretation and privacy concerns: "*If I interact with a person and that person never looked at me then I would say if that person really care about what we are talking about and so forth. It does have some implications, privacy implications.* (L3)"

Another concern was that sharing the usage chart would make remote persons self-conscious: "I am *going have to be self-conscious about where I look all the time and is this going to make it really obvious who talks and who didn't talk in the meeting and am I going to be the one person in the meeting that nobody points at?* (R3)" The same participant also suggested sharing the historical data might lead to behavior changes: "*I think I would probably behave differently if it was or wasn't shared.... If it's not shared the whole thing is more like a telephone call where you have a certain anonymity and you can do what you feel like and pay attention to what you. ... Where if it's shared people are going to draw conclusions from it.* (R3)"

One way to understand the importance of contexts is through the lens of Nissenbaum's context integrity framework [35, 36]. The attention, whether inferred from the simulated gazes or observed by others, co-occurs with a context of an episode of the meeting: the topic, the leader, and what has been discussed. The quantification of remote persons' simulated gazes, regardless its accuracy, loses the contextual and conversational information that supports interpretation. Later inspections of this data might use a default context – e.g., what a 'normal' meeting looks like – to interpret it. The potential for misinterpretation raises concerns on the part of data owners (remote persons). This is similar to what happens in Facebook: its sparse contexts, resulting from interface and access control features, tend to trigger violations of content sharing norms [27].

Participants had fewer privacy concerns regarding showing of simulated gazes in real time. One reason was that the gaze interface is not presenting historical data and *"because people aren't sitting there staring at it the whole time. ... I can just move it at some point and then when anybody looks at it they will see oh it did move since the last time I looked so she's still there.* (R3)*"*. The fundamental difference between the gaze interface and the two usage charts is that the simulated gazes are presented ephemerally: it only shows the present data in the current context, while the usage charts show historical data without context. The embedding of simulated gazes in the current context is similar to the way Snapchat's ephemeral communication design impacts the users' self-presentation [54]. Thus the real-time presentation of simulated gazes is more suited to the communication goals in the current context: *"As a participant in a discussion, what I'd really like is for the discussion to proceed as naturally as possible. For people that means knowing who is talking, who is paying attention to you, who is off doing their email or who is point where. In retrospect* [the usage chart] *is interesting to me but it is kind of a distraction and it is not going to help me towards the real focus of the meeting which is to address the goal of the meeting.* (L7)*"*

Figure 5. A multi-foci + context view of the local meeting environment.

Summary and Limitations

The aim of our study was to understand how the prototype, in general, and simulated gaze, in particular, will be used and experienced in hybrid meetings. Our findings were as follows: The ability to view remote spaces is more useful for seeing the space (and objects in it) than for tracking conversation. Simulated gaze is useful for signaling that remote participants are present and paying attention – all participants recognized this as helpful for increasing social awareness. Simulated gaze created some anxiety among producers and recipients of 'gaze,' – this is another indication that simulated gaze is a powerful cue, even as it indicates the need for more work. Users also agreed that their aggregated gaze data was useful for reflection and research, but were concerned about misinterpretation if it is more widely shared. Finally, we found that visibility and asymmetry of participation has both pros and cons, suggesting the need for more design work.

Our study had limitations. Because it was the first-time participants had used such a system, there might be novelty effects and, as participants mentioned, their understanding of simulated gaze, behavior, and norms might change over time. Also, the prototype was designed to support a hybrid meeting with a single collocated site (a hub), and distributed participants (spokes). Another limitation lies with methodology: although we collected some log data of their use of the system, and recorded participants' conversation as observational data for later content analysis, we chose to focus on qualitative analysis of interview data due to the limited participant sample size. A future study of a more mature system might involve more subjects in order to allow for quantitative analysis. These limitations suggest further research such as a long-term field study of a prototype with a more advanced design, with more data for both qualitative and quantitative investigation.

DESIGN IMPLICATIONS

The Panning and Panorama Windows

Most of our participants valued both windows, though when forced to choose one or the other their choices differed. What is significant is the reasons for their choices. They valued the panning window because it enabled them to focus on people and particularly on objects. Participants were dissatisfied with the panning window because it did not provide much better resolution than the full panorama window, and several commented on wanting to be able to zoom in, especially to read things written on the whiteboard during meetings. Participants valued the panorama window because it gave them a sense of the whole space (even though parts were quite distorted) and it served as a frame of reference for the panning window so they could see what part of the room they were viewing.

This suggests that a more mature design for supporting remote viewing should provide the following abilities:

- higher resolution images of people and objects
- the ability to zoom in (and out)
- the ability to see the larger context of the space to provide a frame of reference for the close-in views.

Higher resolution can be achieved by using a better camera system, and that would support zooming as well. The ability to see the larger context for the panning window is provided by the current two-window interface, but it also seems prudent to explore a more compact solution using the focus+context pattern as in [16] and [45].

Some participants also commented that in a very active discussion, where conversational turns are rapid, moving back and forth between participants could be cumbersome. This suggests another design implication:

- provide the ability for remote participants to follow rapid exchanges between local participants.

One approach to this would be to provide an automatic mode where the camera could identify who is speaking and shift the view point between people. This, of course, would introduce another form of 'indirection' to 'gaze', in that sometimes the remote participants would be shifting their 'gazes' and sometimes it would be automatically managed by the system. We favor a manual multi-focus + context solution, where remote users would be able to establish multiple foci (a sketch of this concept is shown in Figure 5).

Lastly, our participants saw the value of high resolution (e.g., for reading the whiteboard) but were also aware of the potential for privacy violations (e.g., zooming in to read someone's private notes). One solution would be to explore ways of automatically limiting high resolution viewing to certain zones; another would be give collocated participants a better sense of what remote participants were seeing, thus making remote participants more accountable.

Gaze Simulation and Presentation

As our findings suggest, simulated gaze is a useful and powerful social cue, even though it differs from real gaze. For the local participants, the simulated gaze provided useful indications of the presence and activity of the remote participants. Local participants were generally quite aware of the indirection involved – they understood that they were seeing the direction the camera was pointed, and that that did not necessarily mean that they were being gazed at by the remote participant. Local participants realized, for example, that remote participants might forget to shift their view, or that they might simply have stepped away from their computer. Some also realized that they could not detect the remote person's angle of view – whether they were looking straight at the participant, or down at something on the table, or even up towards the ceiling. This led to some discomfort – one participant seemed to find the ambiguity about whether they were being gazed at or not more uncomfortable than the certain knowledge they were the subject of gaze. This recalls Goffman's concept of "civil inattention," [23] in which strangers in close proximity demonstrate that they are aware of one another (e.g., exchange brief glances) without either staring or completely ignoring one another. While Goffman's concept was developed to explain how a person might have a sense of privacy even in the midst of a crowd, it would be interesting to further explore how it might be adapted to less anonymous events like meetings.

What local participants found most salient was when the simulated gaze moved. This was both because the movement attracted their attention and because it was then that participants were confident that the remote person was paying attention – especially if the movement made sense (e.g., moved to an object being discussed). Local users also wanted a better understanding of what the user gazing at them was doing, particularly when the gaze moved.

As noted in the findings, remote participants also had feelings about the visibility of their gazes. In addition to feeling more present and more involved, they also reported feeling more self-conscious. Some commented that they felt more accountable for their behavior, and that looking at the person who is speaking is the polite thing to do. Several had the experience of forgetting to shift their view and then feeling embarrassed for seeming to 'stare' at another person (another instance of a violation of "civil inattention"). Remote participants also weren't sure what to do when not using the panning window: the gaze indicator, taken literally, would show them staring fixedly at something.

These findings suggest other implications for the design of future versions of the gaze interface:

- distinguish between 'gazes' that have just moved, and those that have been still for a while
- provide a means to detect whether remote users are in front of or looking at their displays
- create a neutral point for the gaze interface, so that it is evident when the panning window isn't being used

One approach would be to enrich the simulate gaze interface. For example, a simulated gaze might brighten when moved, and then gradually fade out until moved again. If face recognition or gaze tracking were implemented on the remote participants' devices, their simulated gazes could be made more salient when they were present and watching. Additionally, or alternatively, if users did not move their gazes for a while, their views fade out, along with the corresponding simulated gazes.

Asymmetry of Functionality and Data Interface

The system we designed was deliberately constructed to provide asymmetric awareness – to allow remote users to see those in the room, but not to provide video in the other direction. This was because we wanted to isolate the impact of the abstract representation of simulated gaze, without conflating it with video feedback. However, as noted, some local participants were uncomfortable about being the subject of the gazes of people they could not see. This suggests one other implication:

- Provide a way for local participants to get a better sense of who is watching and what they are doing.

This would also address the desire of local participants to understand what the remote user was doing when he or she shifted her gaze to them.

This might be done by providing a small composite video of the audience, or perhaps by adding a transient video of the person who most recently shifted their 'gaze'. The sketch in Figure 6 depicts an enhanced gaze simulation UI where rays show the direction of five remote gazes, their length shows how recently each gaze direction was shifted (rays initially touch the periphery and then shrink), and an image of the user who most recently shifted their gaze is briefly shown. We suspect that this last feature would need careful adjustment to strike a balance between informing participants without being disruptive.

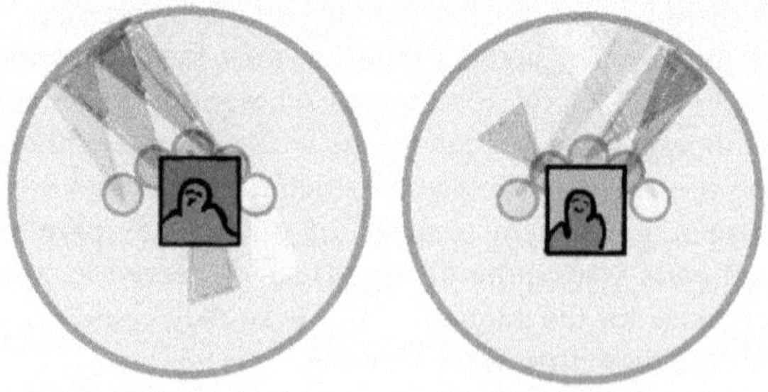

Figure 6. An enhanced gaze visualization. Rays show the direction of gazes, and their lengths reflect how recently each was changed (initially they reach the periphery, and then shrink). An image of the person who has most recently shifted their gaze is briefly shown.

While simulated gaze is useful to participants, it also offers the potential for tracking the fine-grained behavior of remote users. While, participants recognized the value of usage data for self-reflection and for research, they were concerned about privacy. In addition, they noted that the usage charts did not have sufficient context to enable full interpretation, and that other information about participants, interaction, meeting topics, etc., would be required for accurate interpretation. This suggests one more implication:

- Provide remote users with a private interface showing their personal gaze data with contextual information.

One approach would be to store users' data into a personal account that is private by default. The data would be saved with other information like the meeting topics (maybe from their calendar application), participants, and where the participants sat in the room (e.g. screen shot of the panoramic view in the remote interface as a reference for the direction of their accumulated gazes).

FUTURE WORK

We used an omnidirectional camera and system prototype to allow remote users to look around a meeting space, displaying their simulated gazes to those in the room. The accuracy of this approach to gaze differs from that provided by other methods (e.g., eye-tracking). It is not clear how much accuracy matters for providing social cues, without explicit comparison to other implementations, but the results suggest that it may have effects on interpretations of what the 'gaze' means. Thus, one area for future work is to extend our setup with more powerful cameras, and to employ eye-tracking and other methods to understand how other approaches to gaze capture impact its interpretation.

Participants also mentioned that the gaze interface was limited to showing only horizontal gaze. In the future, we are interested in exploring how we might provide a sense of vertical gaze in order to remove such ambiguity. However, care must be taken to avoid overcomplicating the presentation of simulated gaze and increasing the cognitive load required to make sense of it.

We are also interested how to attentions between remote participants, which could be a way to raise consensus between remote people.

CONCLUDING REMARKS

The work in this paper makes three contributions. First, it demonstrates a low-cost working prototype for allowing remote users to participate more fully in hybrid meetings, using virtual cameras to direct their 'gazes' at people and objects in the meeting. Second, using the prototype as a probe, the paper demonstrates that presenting "simulated gazes" can provide powerful social cues, in ways similar to that of real gaze. As with real gaze, our results show that simulated gaze can provide valuable information, or cause discomfort (or sometimes do both at the same time). Third, we draw upon our results to propose design implications, for improving the functionality of the prototype, and particularly for making the gaze simulation more helpful and less discomforting. Having verified the usefulness of simulated gaze, our future work will focus on creating a more robust and functional prototype for field deployment.

We hope that our work will provide a basis for others to pursue this line of research, as we see applications for this functionality not just to hybrid meetings but to areas like education (e.g., students remotely participating in a class) entertainment (e.g., a remote audience for a performance), and other domains.

REFERENCES

1. Geoffrey W. Beattie. 1981. A further investigation of the cognitive interference hypothesis of gaze patterns

during conversation. *British Journal of Social Psychology* 20.4: 243-248.

2. Michael S. Bernstein, Eytan Bakshy, Moira Burke, and Brian Karrer. 2013. Quantifying the invisible audience in social networks. In *Proceedings of the SIGCHI Conference on Human Factors in Computing Systems* (CHI '13). ACM, New York, NY, USA, 21-30. http://dx.doi.org/10.1145/2470654.2470658.
3. Jeremy P. Birnholtz, Carl Gutwin, and Kirstie Hawkey. 2007. Privacy in the open: how attention mediates awareness and privacy in open-plan offices. In *Proceedings of the 2007 international ACM conference on Supporting group work* (GROUP '07). ACM, New York, NY, USA, 51-60. http://dx.doi.org/10.1145/1316624.1316632.
4. Mark S. Cary. 1978. The role of gaze in the initiation of conversation. *Social Psychology*: 269-271.
5. Alex Colburn, Michael F. Cohen, and Steven Drucker. 2000. The role of eye gaze in avatar mediated conversational interfaces. *Sketches and Applications*, Siggraph'00.
6. Mark Cook. 1977. Gaze and Mutual Gaze in Social Encounters: How long – and when – we look others "in the eye" is one of the main signals in nonverbal communication. *American Scientist* 65.3: 328-333.
7. Laura Dabbish and Robert E. Kraut. 2004. Controlling interruptions: awareness displays and social motivation for coordination. In *Proceedings of the 2004 ACM conference on Computer supported cooperative work* (CSCW '04). ACM, New York, NY, USA, 182-191. http://dx.doi.org/10.1145/1031607.1031638
8. Daniela Damian, Luis Izquierdo, Janice Singer, and Irwin Kwan. 2007. Awareness in the wild: Why communication breakdowns occur. In *Proceedings of the International Conference on Global Software Engineering* (ICGSE'07), 81-90.
9. Deepak Akkil and Poika Isokoski. 2016. Gaze Augmentation in Egocentric Video Improves Awareness of Intention. In *Proceedings of the 2016 CHI Conference on Human Factors in Computing Systems* (CHI '16). ACM, New York, NY, USA, 1573-1584. DOI: https://doi.org/10.1145/2858036.2858127
10. Paul Dourish. 1997. Extending awareness beyond synchronous collaboration. *Position Paper for CHI* 97: 249-256.
11. Paul Dourish and Sara Bly. 1992. Portholes: supporting awareness in a distributed work group. In *Proceedings of the SIGCHI Conference on Human Factors in Computing Systems* (CHI '92), Penny Bauersfeld, John Bennett, and Gene Lynch (Eds.). ACM, New York, NY, USA, 541-547. http://dx.doi.org/10.1145/142750.142982
12. Thomas Erickson and Wendy A. Kellogg. 2000. Social translucence: an approach to designing systems that support social processes. *ACM Trans. Comput.-Hum. Interact.* 7, 1 (March 2000), 59-83. http://dx.doi.org/10.1145/344949.345004
13. Thomas Erickson, David N. Smith, Wendy A. Kellogg, Mark Laff, John T. Richards, and Erin Bradner. 1999. Socially translucent systems: social proxies, persistent conversation, and the design of "babble". In *Proceedings of the SIGCHI conference on Human Factors in Computing Systems* (CHI '99). ACM, New York, NY, USA, 72-79. http://dx.doi.org/10.1145/302979.302997
14. Motahhare Eslami, Aimee Rickman, Kristen Vaccaro, Amirhossein Aleyasen, Andy Vuong, Karrie Karahalios, Kevin Hamilton, and Christian Sandvig. 2015. "I always assumed that I wasn't really that close to [her]": Reasoning about Invisible Algorithms in News Feeds. In *Proceedings of the 33rd Annual ACM Conference on Human Factors in Computing Systems* (CHI '15). ACM, New York, NY, USA, 153-162. http://dx.doi.org/10.1145/2702123.2702556
15. Danyel Fisher and Paul Dourish. 2004. Social and temporal structures in everyday collaboration. In *Proceedings of the SIGCHI Conference on Human Factors in Computing Systems* (CHI '04). ACM, New York, NY, USA, 551-558. http://dx.doi.org/10.1145/985692.985762
16. George. W. Furnas. 1986. Generalized fisheye views. In *Proceedings of the SIGCHI Conference on Human Factors in Computing Systems* (CHI '86), Marilyn Mantei and Peter Orbeton (Eds.). ACM, New York, NY, USA, 16-23. http://dx.doi.org/10.1145/22627.22342
17. Susan R. Fussell, Leslie D. Setlock, and Elizabeth M. Parker. 2003. Where do helpers look?: gaze targets during collaborative physical tasks. In *CHI '03 Extended Abstracts on Human Factors in Computing Systems* (CHI EA '03). ACM, New York, NY, USA, 768-769. http://dx.doi.org/10.1145/765891.765980
18. Susan R. Fussell, Leslie D. Setlock, Jie Yang, Jiazhi Ou, Elizabeth Mauer, and Adam D. I. Kramer. 2004. Gestures over video streams to support remote collaboration on physical tasks. *ACM Trans. Hum-Comput. Interact.* 19, 3 (September 2004), 273-309. http://dx.doi.org/10.1207/s15327051hci1903_3
19. Maia Garau, Mel Slater, Vinoba Vinayagamoorthy, Andrea Brogni, Anthony Steed, and M. Angela Sasse. 2003. The impact of avatar realism and eye gaze control on perceived quality of communication in a shared immersive virtual environment. In *Proceedings of the SIGCHI Conference on Human Factors in Computing Systems* (CHI '03). ACM, New York, NY,

USA, 529-536. http://dx.doi.org/10.1145/642611.642703

20. Ge Gao, Bin Xu, Dan Cosley, and Susan R. Fussell. 2014. How beliefs about the presence of machine translation impact multilingual collaborations. In *Proceedings of the 17th ACM conference on Computer supported cooperative work & social computing* (CSCW '14). ACM, New York, NY, USA, 1549-1560. http://dx.doi.org/10.1145/2531602.2531702
21. Eric Gilbert. 2012. Designing social translucence over social networks. In *Proceedings of the SIGCHI Conference on Human Factors in Computing Systems* (CHI '12). ACM, New York, NY, USA, 2731-2740. http://dx.doi.org/10.1145/2207676.2208670
22. Erving Goffman. 1963. *Behavior in Public Places*. New York: Free Press.
23. Erving Goffman. 1984 [originally 1959]. *The Presentation of Self in Everyday Life*. Harmondsworth: Penguin.
24. Charles Goodwin, and John Heritage. 1990. Conversation analysis. *Annual review of anthropology* 19: 283-307.
25. Joy E.Hanna, and Susan E. Brennan. 2007. Speakers' eye gaze disambiguates referring expressions early during face-to-face conversation. *Journal of Memory and Language* 57.4: 596-615.
26. Keita Higuch, Ryo Yonetani, and Yoichi Sato. 2016. Can Eye Help You?: Effects of Visualizing Eye Fixations on Remote Collaboration Scenarios for Physical Tasks. In *Proceedings of the 2016 CHI Conference on Human Factors in Computing Systems* (CHI '16). ACM, New York, NY, USA, 5180-5190. DOI: https://doi.org/10.1145/2858036.2858438
27. Gordon Hull, Heather Richter Lipford, and Celine Latulipe. 2011. Contextual gaps: Privacy issues on Facebook. *Ethics and Information Technology* 13, 4: 289–302. http://dx.doi.org/10.1007/s10676-010- 9224-8
28. Hiroshi Ishii, and Minoru Kobayashi. 1992. ClearBoard: a seamless medium for shared drawing and conversation with eye contact. In *Proceedings of the SIGCHI conference on Human factors in computing systems* (CHI'92), Penny Bauersfeld, John Bennett, and Gene Lynch (Eds.). ACM, New York, NY, USA, 525-532. http://dx.doi.org/10.1145/142750.142977
29. Jeroen Janssen, Gijsbert Erkens, and Paul A. Kirschner. 2011. Group awareness tools: It's what you do with it that matters. *Computers in Human Behavior*27.3: 1046-1058.
30. Adam Kendon. 1967. Some functions of gaze direction in social interaction. *Acta psychologica 26*: 22-63.
31. Kana Misawa, Yoshio Ishiguro, and Jun Rekimoto. 2012. LiveMask: a telepresence surrogate system with a face-shaped screen for supporting nonverbal communication. In *Proceedings of the International Working Conference on Advanced Visual Interfaces* (AVI '12), Genny Tortora, Stefano Levialdi, and Maurizio Tucci (Eds.). ACM, New York, NY, USA, 394-397. http://dx.doi.org/10.1145/2254556.2254632
32. Kana Misawa, Yoshio Ishiguro, and Jun Rekimoto. 2012. Ma petite chérie: what are you looking at?: a small telepresence system to support remote collaborative work for intimate communication. In *Proceedings of the 3rd Augmented Human International Conference* (AH '12). ACM, New York, NY, USA, Article 17, 5 pages. DOI=http://dx.doi.org/10.1145/2160125.2160142.
33. Andrew F. Monk, and Caroline Gale. 2002. A look is worth a thousand words: Full gaze awareness in video-mediated conversation. *Discourse Processes* 33.3: 257-278.
34. Jens Edlund, Samer Al Moubayed, and Jonas Beskow. 2011. The Mona Lisa gaze effect as an objective metric for perceived cospatiality. In *Proceeding of International Conference on Intelligent Virtual Agents* (IVA'11). Springer Berlin Heidelberg, 439–440.
35. Helen Nissenbaum. 2009. *Privacy in context: Technology, policy, and the integrity of social life*. Stanford University Press.
36. Helen Nissenbaum. 2011. A contextual approach to privacy online. *Daedalus* 140, 4: 32–48.
37. David G. Novick, Brian Hansen, and Karen Ward. 1996. Coordinating turn-taking with gaze. In *Proceedings of Fourth International Conference on Spoken Language* (ICSLP'96). IEEE. 1888-1891.
38. Hiroaki Ogata , Kenji Matsuura, and Yoneo Yano. 1996. Knowledge awareness: Bridging between shared knowledge and collaboration in sharlok. In *Proceedings of Educational Telecommunications*: 232-237.
39. Omnidirectional camera. 2016. Retrieved January 12, 2017 from https://en.wikipedia.org/wiki/Omnidirectional_camera
40. Antti Oulasvirta, Mika Raento, and Sauli Tiitta. 2005. ContextContacts: re-designing SmartPhone's contact book to support mobile awareness and collaboration. In *Proceedings of the 7th international conference on Human computer interaction with mobile devices & services* (MobileHCI '05). ACM, New York, NY, USA, 167-174. http://dx.doi.org/10.1145/1085777.1085805
41. Pan–tilt–zoom camera. 2016. Retrieved January 12, 2017 from

https://en.wikipedia.org/wiki/Pan%E2%80%93tilt%E2%80%93zoom_camera

42. Elin Rønby Pedersen and Tomas Sokoler. 1997. AROMA: abstract representation of presence supporting mutual awareness. In *Proceedings of the ACM SIGCHI Conference on Human factors in computing systems* (CHI '97). ACM, New York, NY, USA, 51-58. http://dx.doi.org/10.1145/258549.258584
43. Christopher Peters, Catherine Pelachaud, Elisabetta Bevacqua, Maurizio Mancini, and Isabella Poggi. 2005. A model of attention and interest using gaze behavior. In *Proceeding of International Workshop on Intelligent Virtual Agents*. Springer Berlin Heidelberg, 229-240.
44. Alex Poole, and Linden J. Ball. 2006. Eye tracking in HCI and usability research. *Encyclopedia of human computer interaction* 1: 211-219.
45. Ramana Rao and Stuart K. Card. 1994. The table lens: merging graphical and symbolic representations in an interactive focus + context visualization for tabular information. In *Proceedings of the SIGCHI Conference on Human Factors in Computing Systems* (CHI '94), Beth Adelson, Susan Dumais, and Judith Olson (Eds.). ACM, New York, NY, USA, 318-322
46. Ricoh Theta S camera. 2016. Retrieved January 12, 2017 from https://theta360.com/en/about/theta/s.html
47. Markus Rittenbruch, and Gregor McEwan. 2009. An historical reflection of awareness in collaboration. *Awareness Systems*: 3-48.
48. Randy Stein and Susan E. Brennan. 2004. Another person's eye gaze as a cue in solving programming problems. In *Proceedings of the 6th international conference on Multimodal interfaces* (ICMI '04). ACM, New York, NY, USA, 9-15. http://dx.doi.org/10.1145/1027933.1027936
49. John C. Tang, and Ellen Isaacs. 1992. Why do users like video?. *Computer Supported Cooperative Work* 1.3: 163-196.
50. Joseph B. Walther, Brandon Van Der Heide, Artemio Ramirez, Judee K. Burgoon, and Jorge Peña. 2015. *Interpersonal and hyperpersonal dimensions of computer-mediated communication*. Wiley.
51. Bernard Weiner. 2001. Intrapersonal and interpersonal theories of motivation from an attribution perspective. *Student motivation*: 17-30.
52. Suzanne Weisband. 2002. Maintaining awareness in distributed team collaboration: Implications for leadership and performance. *Distributed work*: 311-333.
53. Timo Wolf , Adrian Schröter, Daniela Damian, Lucas D. Panjer, and Thanh HD Nguyen. 2009. Mining task-based social networks to explore collaboration in software teams. *IEEE Software* 26.1: 58-66.
54. Bin Xu, Pamara Chang, Christopher L. Welker, Natalya N. Bazarova, and Dan Cosley. 2016. Automatic Archiving versus Default Deletion: What Snapchat Tells Us About Ephemerality in Design. In *Proceedings of the 19th ACM Conference on Computer-Supported Cooperative Work & Social Computing* (CSCW '16). ACM, New York, NY, USA, 1662-1675. http://dx.doi.org/10.1145/2818048.2819948

Gaze-Adaptive Above and On-Surface Interaction

Barış Serim[1,3], Khalil Klouche[1,4], Giulio Jacucci[1,2]
[1] Helsinki Institute for Information Technology HIIT, Dept. of Computer Science, University of Helsinki
[2] Helsinki Institute for Information Technology HIIT, Aalto University
[3] Department of Design, Aalto University, [4]Media Lab Helsinki, Aalto University
firstname.lastname@helsinki.fi

ABSTRACT
We explore the combination of above-surface sensing with eye tracking to facilitate concurrent interaction with multiple regions on touch screens. Conventional touch input relies on positional accuracy, thereby requiring tight visual monitoring of one's own motor action. In contrast, above-surface sensing and eye tracking provides information about how user's hands and gaze are distributed across the interface. In these situations we facilitate interaction by 1) showing the visual feedback of the hand hover near user's gaze point and 2) decrease the requisite of positional accuracy by employing gestural information. We contribute input and visual feedback techniques that combine these modalities and demonstrate their use in example applications. A controlled study showed the effectiveness of our techniques for manipulation tasks against conventional touch, while the effectiveness in acquisition tasks depended on the amount of mid-air motion, leading to our conclusion that the techniques can benefit interacting with multiple interface regions.

Author Keywords
Eye tracking; gaze interaction; above surface interaction; multi-touch

ACM Classification Keywords
H.5.2. Information interfaces and presentation: Input devices and strategies

INTRODUCTION
Large multitouch screens allow designers to create wide workspaces that provide direct and concurrent access to UI widgets: users can access commands or information without any additional interaction steps. However, single-focus human visual attention remains a bottleneck for concurrent access. Although wide or distributed workspaces come with the benefit of displaying many UI elements, they can divide users' visual attention between distant interface regions where the cost of redirecting the gaze is high. This is especially the case for precise pointing tasks, as the positional accuracy of touch input depends on users visually monitoring their own motor actions [12, 25].

DIS 2017, June 10-14, 2017, Edinburgh, United Kingdom.

ACM 978-1-4503-4922-2/17/06...$15.00
DOI: http://dx.doi.org/10.1145/3064663.3064744

Previous research has shown that additional input modalities can decrease the need for positional accuracy by sensing more than the touch position. One such modality is *above-surface sensing* of hand posture, position and gesture. Above-surface information has been used to discriminate between different commands that a touch input could be intended for, thereby expanding the functional vocabulary of touch actions [7, 14]. Above-surface sensing also holds promise for decreasing the difficulty of pointing tasks on large screens by adapting the interface in anticipation of touch [2, 37]. In parallel, *eye tracking* has very recently been employed to address the challenge of limited visual attention on touchscreens. Previous work in this domain compensates the lack of visual monitoring through flexible input handling [12, 25] and gaze-adaptive visual feedback [25].

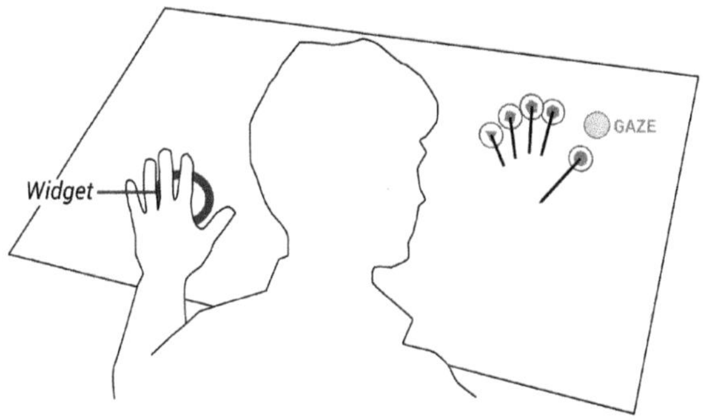

Figure 1. We use the combination of above-surface sensing and eye tracking to facilitate direct input, even when the user in not visually attending to the target. The system determines potential user actions through above-surface sensing, but defers their confirmation to touch input, accompanied by gaze-adaptive visual feedback between these two steps.

In this paper, we explore the combination of above-surface sensing with eye tracking to partly overcome the limitation of single-focus visual attention and facilitate concurrent interaction with multiple interface regions. Though each has shown individual promise, the combination of these modalities has not been studied. Our motivation for their combination is the new design possibilities they lend to supporting concurrent interaction. Together, above-surface sensing and eye tracking allow us to understand how users' hands and gaze are distributed across the interface and adapt the interface when the hands are further from user's gaze. Our interaction techniques address the aforementioned challenges of a) reliance on positional accuracy and b) limited visual attention under the two components of *input handling* and *visual feedback*.

Input handling: The interactive affordances of input widgets predispose hand posture and eye movements prior to the actual touch contact. Above-surface sensing and eye tracking allow the system to capture this pre-touch ([1, 14]) information, which we use to discriminate user actions (e.g. based on hand posture), without extensive reliance on input position.

Visual feedback: We utilize above-surface sensing and eye tracking to enable visual monitoring of multiple interface locations. This is accomplished by warping the interface contents hovered by hands to where the user's gaze is directed at, thus enabling interaction with distant interface locations without having to redirect the gaze. This allows for visual juxtaposition of a UI widget with an interface region.

Our main contributions are as follows:

- Our work contributes, to our knowledge, the first combination of above-surface sensing and eye tracking with touch. We formally describe the design considerations for the combination of these modalities to support concurrent interactions with multiple interface regions.
- We developed novel interaction mechanisms using these modalities. For input, we use hand posture to assign interactive widgets and finger-mapped touch actions for confirmation. These are complemented by visual feedback techniques that adapt the position, timing and visual aspects of the feedback using eye fixation coordinates and above-surface sensing. We demonstrate these techniques in example applications.
- Finally, we tested the efficacy of warped feedback for acquisition and manipulation tasks against a baseline condition of non-warped feedback that requires redirecting the gaze. The results show that for manipulation tasks, the performance of warped feedback was significantly better than baseline, while the results were comparable for within-widget acquisition tasks. On the other hand, the performance of warped feedback significantly suffered when the participants had to switch between widgets through midair movement.

Based on these findings we conclude that the proposed interaction techniques can be used to complement conventional visually-monitored motor actions, with warped visual feedback employed for inputs that require minimal midair movement and visually monitored motor actions employed for large midair movements by hand.

RELATED WORK

Touchscreens, which lack any tactile cues, require users to visually monitor their own action for positional accuracy. This has led to various strategies to support eyes-free input on touch surfaces, such as augmenting them with tactile widgets [34] or directing the finger to predefined locations using magnetic attraction [33]. In contrast, non-haptic solutions take advantage of the dynamic adaptation of motor and visual spaces afforded by touchscreens. In this section, we review the use of above-surface sensing and eye tracking as two modalities to decrease reliance on positional accuracy or visual monitoring during input.

Combining Gaze and Touch Input

The potential of gaze as a real-time input is being investigated in an increasing number of settings and in combination with other modalities. A common strategy is to take advantage of the rapid change of spatial context afforded by eye movements for gains in motor performance during selection. This has been the motivation for using gaze as a cursor on large and distant displays on which direct touch input is impractical [27, 29]. In these situations, eye fixations provide the input position whereas touch input on a handheld device confirms the action.

On the other hand, there has been a recent interest in combining manual input with gaze on the same surface. Common in this work, is the use of the distance between the gaze point and touch (or any other manual input type) for the flexible handling of touch. However, they differ in terms of how the situations in which touch and gaze misalign are handled. One approach is to utilize touch as an indirect and gestural input and use gaze point position for selection instead [18, 19]. This assumes visual attention on the location of input and has been motivated by the need to decrease the amplitude of motion (i.e. distance traveled by the hand), parallel to MAGIC pointing that cascades manual and gaze input [38].

Another approach to combining gaze and touch is preserving touch as a direct input but distinguishing between accurate and ambiguous touch actions by incorporating gaze point information. The main motivation in this approach has been facilitating input with decreased visual monitoring for concurrent access to multiple objects [25] or high-throughput interactions such as typing on a touchscreen while looking at the text field [12]. Both cases exemplify situations in which touch input is performed further from the location of visual feedback. They demonstrate flexible input handling mechanisms based on the level of visual monitoring with which the touch action is conducted. Decreased visual monitoring results in an expanded area for potential selection and subsequent delegation of control to the system for decision-making. The flexible input handling is accompanied by various techniques such as providing visual feedback at the periphery or translating the visual feedback coordinates to where the user's gaze is directed [25].

The aforementioned work also varies regarding how it operationalizes visual monitoring. The distance between the gaze and touch point can be utilized as a discrete distance threshold for classifying direct and indirect touch [18, 19] or as a continuous scale to determine positional uncertainty [12, 25]. However, common among them is input handling and visual feedback at the moment of touch contact. This poses a limitation because touch and gaze information at the moment of touch does not account for the complex hand-eye behavior that leads to a touch event.

Above and On Surface Interaction Continuum

Above-surface sensing promises to extend input handling and visual feedback processes to pre-touch. Earlier work used above-surface sensing in various ways, ranging from deliberate midair input actions [10, 13, 20] to implicit use of pre-touch movements by the system [14, 36]. Within previous work, we focus on a subset that use above-surface sensing in continuum with touch input [17] rather than in isolation. Research in this direction already targets relaxing the requirements of positional accuracy using various strategies.

One strategy for relaxing the requirements of positional accuracy has been adapting the motor space of the interface through target expansion [2, 37]. TouchZoom [37] uses the proximity of fingers to the screen to increase toolbar and icon target sizes before touch. Similarly, the proximity of the finger to the screen has been used to expand targets for in-vehicle interfaces that need to be operated with little visual monitoring, as visual attention is reserved for driving [2].

Above-surface sensing has also been used to extend touch functionality. Touch actions have been mapped to different interface commands based on various pre-touch or after-touch mid-air gestures [7]. The strategy that is most closely aligned with ours is that of Hinckley et al. [14] who utilize above-surface sensing (including grip) primarily as a pre-touch modality to provide anticipatory visual feedback and distinguish between the different commands a touch action can be intended for on a mobile device. However, instead of small and hand-held devices, we focus on interaction with large touch surfaces, which point to significantly different design considerations. We discuss these differences below.

Comparison to Previous Work

By combining gaze and above-surface sensing, we build on and advance the state of the art for these two input modalities.

When combining gaze and touch, we use touch primarily as a direct input, even in the cases where touch and gaze points misalign. This is in contrast to previous work that combines gaze with indirect manual input when touch is performed further away from gaze [18, 19]. We also further previous work that translates visual feedback near user's focus of visual attention [25]. In previous work, the visual feedback has been limited to the moment of touch contact and more importantly *does not leverage the multitouch capability of the human hand.* We use above-surface sensing to detect the proximity of not only the hand or a single finger tip, but multiple fingertips. In turn, this allows the system to visualize possible commands that can be triggered through touch with different fingers. This is achieved by showing a simplified representation of the hand that shows command-to-finger mapping near where the user is gazing.

In the domain of above-surface sensing, our main contribution is the extension of pre-touch to multifocus interactions on larger touchscreens. These interactions differ from handheld pre-touch [14] in at least three ways. First, hand grip becomes less relevant for larger screens, while the projected position of the hand over the interface (hover) gains relevance. Second, multifocus interaction on large screens causes the user's visual attention to be split between more distant interface regions, which can be detected through eye tracking for the purpose of input handling. Third, larger surfaces can accommodate the entire human hand, thereby allowing pre-touch visual feedback for all fingers.

Much effort in interaction techniques for large screens (e.g. [3, 16]) and gaze pointing [38, 18] has been directed to increasing the pointing performance for distant targets by decreasing the amplitude of motion. In contrast, we target situations in which the required motion by hand is not large but the cost of redirecting the gaze can be high. While the definitions of large touchscreen vary, the considerations of split visual attention and accommodation of both hands define the scope of our work. Indeed, previous work [12, 25] shows that input accuracy suffers when the gaze is away even for screens of 27" or smaller due to the very limited area where the vision is sharp. In the next section, we motivate our combination of these modalities and show how they enable interactions that are not possible with eye tracking or above-surface sensing alone.

DESIGN CONSIDERATIONS

Pointing to interface elements involves gradual alignment of fingertips to a visual target, a closed-loop control process that starts with midair motion and finalizes with the end of touch. Figure 2 summarizes this process and our design space by showing the progression of a command event in three modalities. It should be noted that our focus is on using the above-surface as a pre-command modality for selecting widgets and deferring the confirmation of action to touch. Thus, the figure excludes mid-air gestures that do not yield to a touch event as in gaze and gesture combinations [6] or after-touch gestures [7].

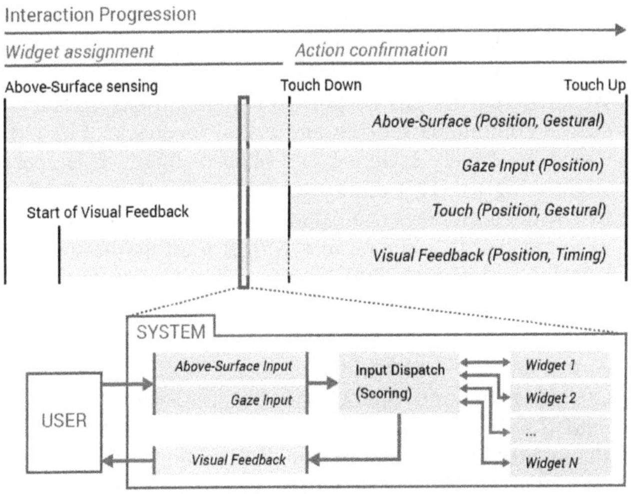

Figure 2. Continuous feedback control loop showing three input modalities during input. UI widgets are continuously ranked before a touch action, while the system provides the visual feedback of the selected widget (top). The widget assignment process (bottom) is modeled after Schwarz et al. [24].

To assign widgets to hands, we employ the uncertain input handling framework developed by Schwarz et al. [24], but adapt it to above-surface interaction. An event dispatcher continuously scores every widget-hand pair ($score_{ih}$) based on pre-touch information. Widgets can have multiple scoring criteria (j), such as position or hand posture, that are all scaled to a uniform range (0-1). Not all scoring criteria is equally relevant to a widget, which results in different scoring *weights*. As a preliminary method, we calculate the overall score of a widget by taking the weighted geometric mean of individual scores and assign the highest scoring widget to a hand (h):

$$score_{ih} = \left(\prod_{j=0}^{n} score_{jh}{}^{weight_j}\right)^{1/\sum_{j=1}^{n} weight_j}$$

The information of the assigned widget is communicated back to the user through visual feedback. The visual feedback differs based on the above-surface sensing and gaze conditions (Figure 3). *Minimal* refers to the visual representation in which a widget is unassigned and is minimally represented on the interface, to signify its location and current state. In *hover* condition, a hand or a finger is assigned to a widget at the same time as the user's gaze is directed to the widget. In this state the visual representation of the widget corresponds to the motor space. Finally, in the *warp* condition, a widget is assigned to a hand or finger, but the user's gaze is directed elsewhere. In this case, while the motor space remains the same, the visual feedback is warped to where the user's gaze is directed.

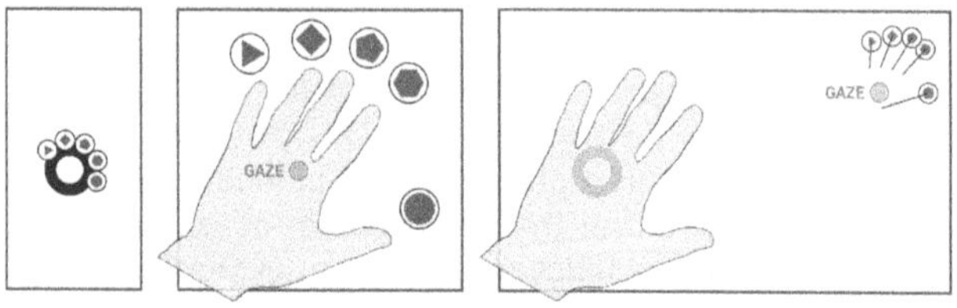

Figure 3. Three different visual states of a widget. Left: Minimal visual feedback in the absence of an assigned hand. Middle: Hover visual feedback when the widget is assigned and user gaze is directed on the widget. Right: Warped visual feedback at the gaze location when hands are above but gaze is directed elsewhere.

We made two design decisions to maintain robust interaction during continuous scoring and visual feedback. First, if a widget is already assigned to a hand or finger, it is scored slightly higher. This eliminates jittery alternations between two widgets in borderline situations. Second, when a hand or finger that is assigned to a widget touches the screen, it remains assigned to that widget until the touch is released regardless of its score.

Above and On-surface Input

Cognitive studies of motor control, distinguish between *proximal* (i.e. getting the hand near the target) and *distal* (i.e. shaping the hand in anticipation of the action) components of manual action [15]. In HCI, they correspond to the *positional* and *gestural* components of the user input. Figure 4 shows their breakdown into above- and on-surface modalities.

It is important to understand that the positional and gestural components are dissimilarly affected by low visual monitoring. Hand posture and relative finger positions are known to the user through proprioception, whereas positional accuracy requires the user to monitor where the hand or finger is located relative to the target. For input handling, the main design principle that guides the interaction techniques is replacing or complementing the positional component of input with the gestural component when possible.

Widget assignment based on hand posture

The interactive affordances of various touch actions favor certain above-surface hand postures, which we use for scoring widgets. For example, a widget that requires a pinch gesture can be scored higher for hand postures that feature the thumb and index as the only extended fingers. As we use

	Positional Component	Gestural Component
Above - surface	Projected position (x, y) Proximity to the surface (z)	Hand posture Hand / finger speed, direction
On - surface	Touch position (x,y)	Digit(thumb, index, ...) Touch gesture, touch duration

Figure 4. Breakdown of above and on-surface modalities into positional and gestural components.

above-surface sensing as a pre-touch modality, different finger configurations form the basis of various hand postures that we have defined (Figure 5). We use the data provided by a skeletal tracking software (Leap Motion) to calculate how bent each finger is and identify the best fitting hand posture (none if there is no fitting posture). The identification is done by assessing each finger for the designated range of the candidate posture.

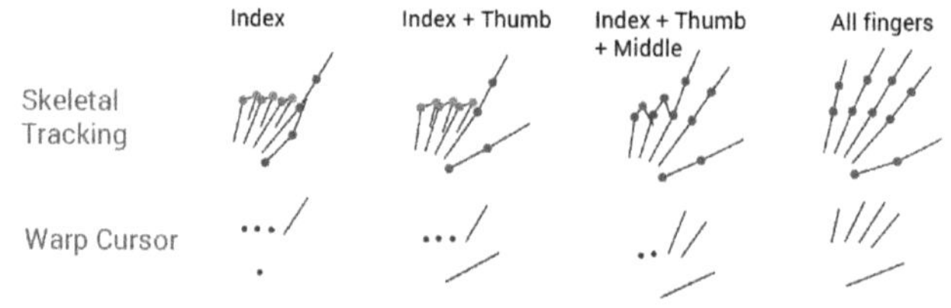

Figure 5. The system tries to match a predefined hand posture using skeletal tracking (above). The warped visual feedback shows a simplified representation of the hand (below).

An interface region can be populated with multiple widgets that favor different hand postures. In these situations, we use hand-posture information in addition to the positional component (i.e. proximity of the widget to the projected hand position) to score widgets (Figure 6). However, the same mechanism can also be applied to purely gestural interactions, in order to score widgets based on the gestural component alone.

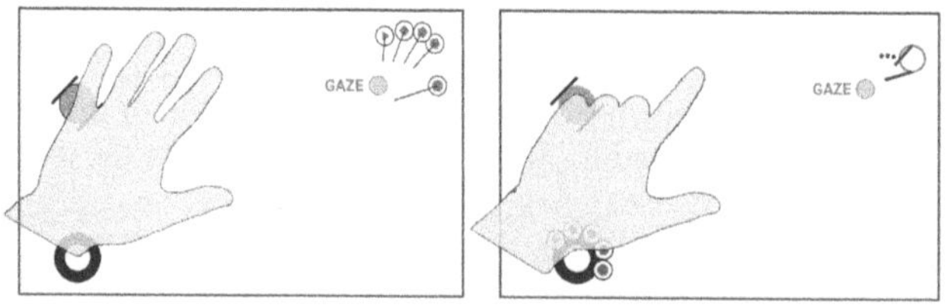

Figure 6. Hand posture can be used to discriminate between widgets in addition to the projected position of the hand or finger. Here, hand posture information is used to select between two widgets that are operated differently.

Finger-mapped touch actions

Another example of replacing positional component with the gestural component is finger-mapped touch actions. This interaction technique is accomplished in two steps. Once a widget is assigned to a hand, the system visually notifies the user by showing available command options that are mapped to individual fingers. At this stage, what determines action is the specific digit (e.g. thumb or index finger) that performs the touch action rather than the touch position (Figure 7).

This technique is related to previous efforts to design touch-screen interactions with the particular physical qualities of the human hand in mind, such as number of fingers [4, 9, 30]. For example, HandMark menus [30] provide access to menu elements upon resting the hand on the screen. The selection is then accomplished by tapping on the relevant item with the other hand. We use the above-surface modality to eliminate the need of confirmation by a second hand. Instead, available options are shown before the actual touch and are then confirmed through touch. More than a single command can be mapped to a digit. In this case, additional commands are accessed by dragging the finger to the additional commands before releasing it.

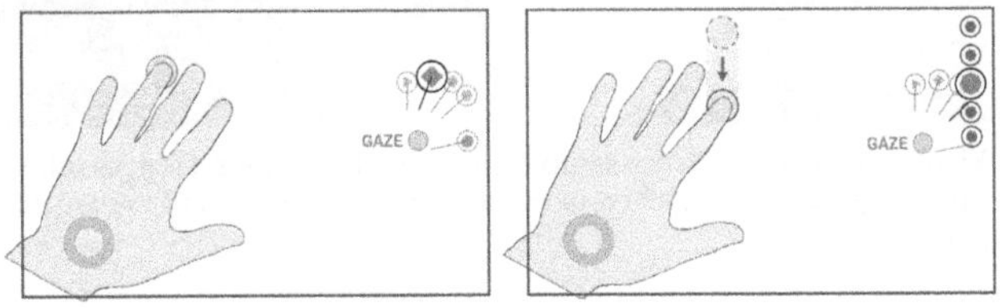

Figure 7. Various commands are associated with individual fingers when a hand is assigned to a widget. Available commands that correspond to fingers are visualized prior to the touch. Multiple commands that are mapped to the same finger can be accessed by dragging the finger (right).

Eye Tracking

We use eye tracking not only for determining the position of the visual feedback, but also for input handling. Eye tracking data is noisy and eye behavior is unstable, so we rely on fixation points as operational gaze points. The fixations are calculated with the commonly used dispersion-threshold identification algorithm, I-DT (implementation in [21]), with the minimum time window set to 90 milliseconds and the dispersion threshold set to 1°.

Determining the weight of the position score

We use gaze point information for scoring the widgets. When scoring widgets, positional and gestural components can *reinforce* each other, for example, when a thumb and index finger hand posture is in the proximity of a virtual knob. However, the two components can also *contradict* each other if the same hand posture is in the proximity of an interactive widget that is operated by tapping.

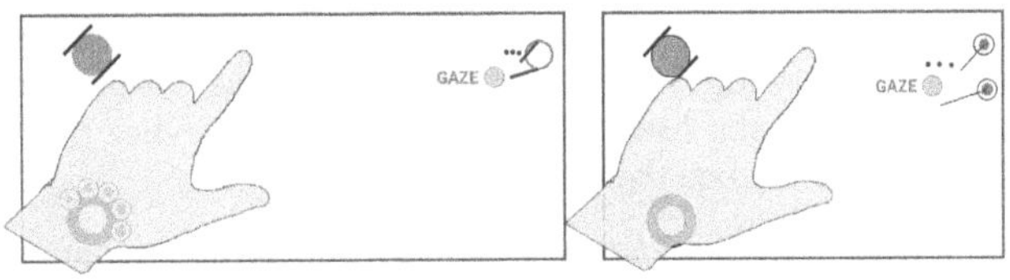

Figure 8. The weight of positional component is manipulated based on the degree the action is visually monitored. The relative weight of the gestural component (hand posture) increases when the user gaze is directed elsewhere.

In these cases, we employ eye tracking to determine the weight of the positional component for calculating the score (Figure 8). The weight is continuously re-evaluated based on the distance between the eye fixation and the projected position of the hand on the screen. The weight of the position is higher when the user's gaze is located near the widget and lower when it is further away.

Gaze as pointer interactions

The design space can also be extended to situations, in which gaze is used as a pointer for selection in combination with touch input (*gaze + touch interactions*). For example, a manipulation action on an object can be performed at a single step by keeping the gaze on the object and determining the action by touching on a widget. In other words, rather than following a sequential order for selection and manipulation, gaze and manual input are used concurrently. What distinguishes this technique from earlier work that combines indirect touch and gaze [18, 19] is the use of touch as a direct input and concurrent pointing by touch and gaze.

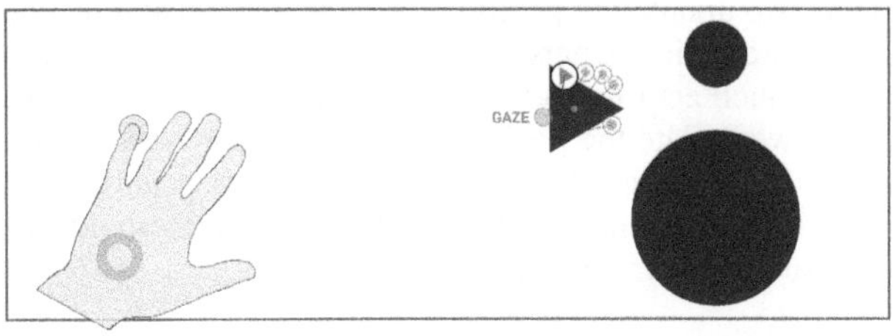

Figure 9. Gaze coordinates can be coupled with manual input to perform *gaze + touch* interactions. In the figure the hand is over a widget and the finger-mapped direct touch is used to modify the shape of an object.

Visual Feedback

Unlike hovering with a cursor, touch input lacks a pre-command notification stage. Above-surface sensing has been proposed as a modality for providing informative visual feedback prior to the actual touch [8, 17]. Input with low visual monitoring can benefit from the timely communication of the system's interpretation of the user input (assigned widget) back to the user. Above-surface interaction and eye tracking call for a reconsideration of design choices regarding the *timing* and *positioning* of the visual feedback.

Timing

While above-surface sensing enables pre-touch visual feedback, feedback that occurs earlier than expected can be intrusive. Similarly, appropriate withdrawal of the visual feedback is necessary when it is not needed. To prevent earlier-than-expected feedback, we use proximity to the surface (z) and hand velocity variables. Visual feedback is shown only when the hand is in the proximity of the screen (z) and the projected hand velocity (on x-y plane) is low.

We additionally rely on widget interaction events to correctly time the visibility of the feedback. As a principle, the system changes the visibility for continuous events gradually and for discrete events instantly (Figure 10). Assignment of a widget to a hand, or a touch-down action on a widget maximizes the visibility of the widget. The feedback starts fading out in case of inaction. Conversely, above-threshold hand movement causes the warped feedback to gradually gain visibility. The warped feedback is fully visible as long as the widget is being touched by a finger, whereas releasing all the fingers from a widget causes a sudden drop in visibility, followed by a gradual fade out. The visibility can be mapped to different visual channels such as opacity or size.

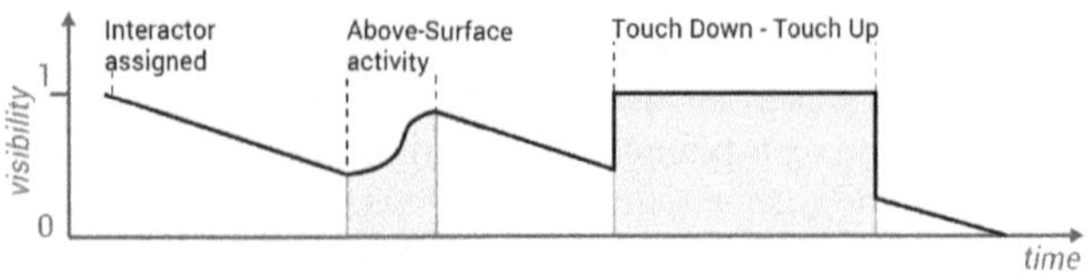

Figure 10. The relative visibility of a widget in relation to the interaction events. The visibility gradually decreases during episodes of inaction.

Position

We use eye fixation coordinates to determine the position of the warped visual feedback. However, eye fixations shift rapidly, and constant warping of the visual feedback can be intrusive. Thus, we update the position of the warped visual feedback upon interaction events (such as when a widget is assigned), upon touch actions and above-threshold mid-air movement. Also, we update the position of the feedback only when the distance between the current position of the visual feedback and the most recent fixation is above a certain threshold ($\approx 10^\circ$ of visual angle from eyes).

Summary

We described how gestural component can partially replace position during widget assignment and action confirmation. We also described how eye tracking can be used both for input handling and visual feedback. The next section describes example applications that demonstrate various combinations of the aforementioned techniques.

APPLICATION EXAMPLES

Apparatus

The applications were prototyped for a 10 finger multitouch screen (27", 2,560 × 1,440 pixels) that was tilted 30° to enable easier hand reach for touch input. For above-surface sensing, a commercial short range infrared sensor for skeletal hand tracking (Leap motion) was used. We mapped the coordinate system of above-surface depth sensing to screen coordinates using a 4 point calibration procedure. The eye tracking was performed by Pupil Labs binocular tracking glasses running at 60Hz. The applications consistently ran at 60fps, with the latest gaze data point synchronized at every frame.

Object Drawing and Manipulation

We prototyped an application that enables parametric manipulation of a group of objects or adding new objects on a canvas. Objects have multiple parameters, namely shape, fill color, border color, size and orientation. The application demonstrates how these parameters can be modified without redirecting the gaze between the toolbar and canvas areas through above-surface sensing and warped visual feedback. Besides allowing continuous fixation on the canvas, warped feedback allows for the juxtaposition of a widget with a specific region on the canvas. For example, warped feedback of the color selection tool on the canvas can facilitate easier visual comparison of the selected color with the already existing colors on the canvas. The application features the following widgets:

1) The shape selector allows switching between different geometric forms. Basic shapes such as triangle, square, pentagon and circle are selected through tap actions with different fingers. Additionally a larger set of polygons can be accessed by dragging the index finger on the surface. Given that all the fingers can be used for interaction, the widget is scored higher when all the fingers of the hand are extended.

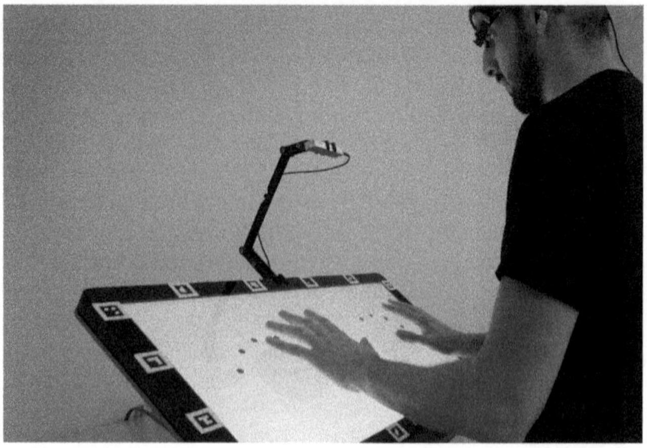

Figure 11. The hardware setup consisting of a touch screen, depth sensor (Leap Motion, attached to the upper screen edge) and eye tracking glasses.

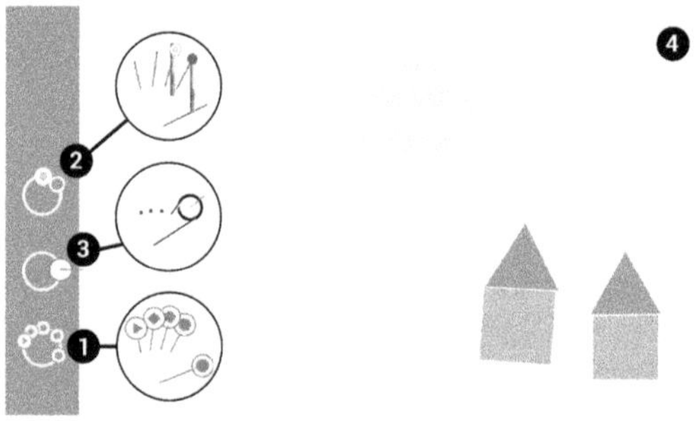

Figure 12. Drawing application featuring the shape selector (1), the color selector (2), the physical modifier (3) and the canvas (4). Warped feedback visuals of the widgets 1,2 & 3 are annotated.

2) The color selector selects or modifies object colors by dragging a finger on a two-dimensional color space. Index and middle fingers are mapped to fill and stroke colors, respectively. The widget is scored higher for hand postures that feature all or the first three (thumb, index, middle) fingers extended and when the hand is in the proximity.

3) The physical modifier manipulates the size and orientation of a group of objects through pinch and two-finger (thumb + index) rotation. Besides positional proximity, the widget is scored higher for hand postures that only feature extended thumb and index fingers.

4) The canvas allows users to add new objects to the scene. When the user's hand is hovering over the canvas, the system displays the shape that will be drawn upon touch. The canvas is scored based on the projected position and orientation of the hand. The widget is scored higher if the thumb is located to the left of the palm center. This allows for discrimination between other widgets on the toolbar in borderline conditions.

Real-time Video Manipulation

We prototyped a simplified VJ (video jockeying) tool that enables the user to apply a variety of visual filters to a video loop. Real-time video editing offers a relevant challenge, as the main feedback for most inputs results in real-time visual changes to the video picture away from the input location. In that case, being able to display essential interaction information at the gaze location allows users to keep their attention on the target when it is most critical. The different widgets either appear as soon as the user's hand is detected, or inconspicuously suggested on the sides of the display as perceived affordances. The application features the following widgets:

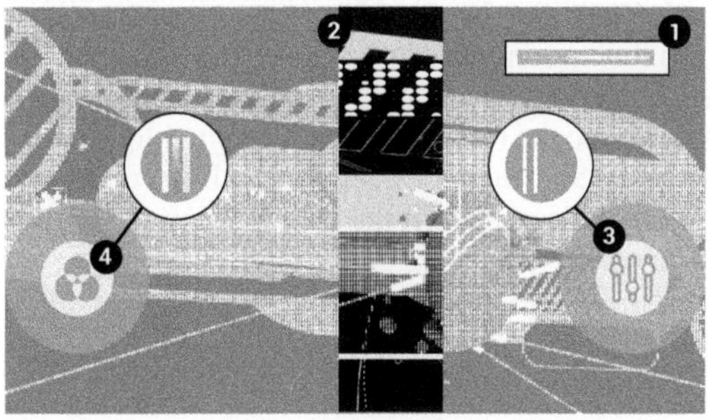

Figure 13. Vj application featuring loop control (1), the filter selector (2), the filter modifier (3) and the color modifier (4). Warped feedback visuals of the widgets 1,3 & 4 are annotated.

1) Loop control is a global widget that can be accessed from anywhere on the screen, as its score is solely based on hand posture. A pinch posture assigns the widget to the hand. Visual feedback of the playback information is shown near the gaze fixation. The loop ranges are then selected by dragging the index finger or the thumb.

2) The filter selector is scored based on the position information and appears when the user extends her hand towards the middle of the screen. The video picture then gets divided into multiple horizontal areas, each displaying a preview of available visual filters. The selection is then accomplished by touch.

3) The filter modifier and *the color modifier (4)* are located on the right and left sides of the screen and are scored based on position. The parameters are mapped to one specific finger each – i.e. index for parameter 1, middle for parameter 2, ring for parameter 3, and pinkie when a fourth parameter is needed. Approaching the widget with the hand will show gaze-adaptive feedback for the parameters, as vertical gauges, with cursors indicating the current value between the maximum and minimum allowed for each gauge. The locations of color and filter modifiers allow concurrent bimanual modification of both widgets.

STUDY: WARPED FEEDBACK AND DIVIDED ATTENTION

We set out to test the viability of warped visual feedback for situations in which attention needs to be divided between multiple interface regions. Previous work identifies two interaction stages, namely acquiring and manipulating a control device [11, 28]. Thus, we prepared a two-part experiment that involves acquiring a target on a touch surface and manipulating a widget through on-surface interaction. We were interested in seeing how the task completion times in these two stages vary for the conditions of:

1. Warped visual feedback condition, which facilitates continuous gaze fixation near the stimulus position using a smaller representation of hand (scaled down by a factor of 0.35 to be visible and less intrusive).
2. Baseline condition, which provides no specific support to facilitate continuous fixation.

Apparatus

The same hardware setup described earlier has been used, with a 27", tilted touchscreen (set to 1920×1080) for input. Additionally, The experimental setup involved a second, vertically positioned monitor of the same size placed on the upper edge of the first monitor (Figure 14). The combination of a horizontal input surface with a vertical monitor have been investigated before [5, 31, 32], and has the advantage of showing visual feedback at the eye level while providing arm support on the horizontal surface. In the experiments, the two monitor setup was used to display the target stimuli either in one of the following locations:

1. Near the left edge of the same tilted screen on which the input is performed (same screen condition). This resulted in a visual angle of around 50° degrees between the input and stimuli positions depending on the distance of eyes to the screen.
2. Near the upper-left corner of the vertical screen. This resulted in a visual angle of around 70° degrees between the input and stimuli positions.

The main motivation for using two screens was to compare the effect of different distances between target stimuli and input area expressed in visual angles. Different distances between the target stimuli and input area corresponds to different costs for redirecting the gaze, which can be be generalized to other display setups.

The experimental setup also controlled the warped feedback location by always displaying the warped feedback near the stimulus. This was implemented to prevent users from shifting their gaze to the input area (for warped feedback condition). However, eye tracking data was collected from participants for later analysis.

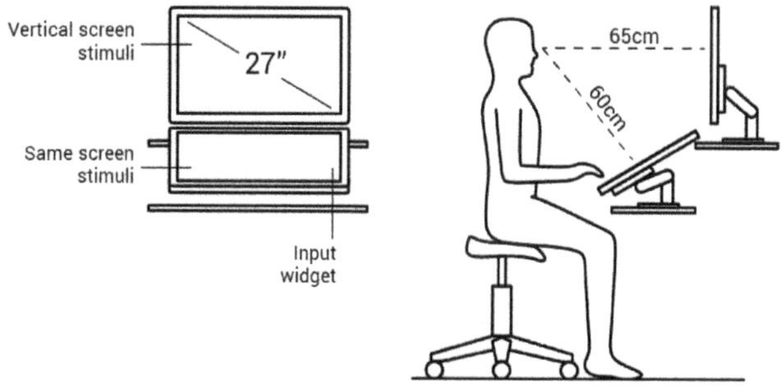

Figure 14. The front and right views of the experimental setup. The screens were positioned approximately 60 and 65 cms away from the eye.

Participants

Twelve participants (2 female), aged 20 to 33 (m=26.1, sd=3.4) were recruited for the study. Of the participants, eleven were right handed and all reported extensive familiarity with touch devices. The participants have been compensated with one cinema ticket and their informed consent has been collected for data logging.

Procedure

We performed a within-subject study of two interaction conditions (warped feedback and baseline) and two stimulus location (same or vertical screen) conditions. The order of the interaction and stimulus conditions alternated between participants using a Latin square design to counterbalance the potential effects of learning and fatigue. The participants were seated in front of the setup, with the input and vertical screens positioned approximately 60 and 65 cms away from the eye. The participants performed the acquisition and manipulation experiments in sequence. The participants had a chance to rest between experiments. The sessions lasted 40 to 50 minutes.

Analysis

The initial trials of each condition (1 block for acquisition tasks, 2 blocks for manipulation) were excluded from the analysis. The metric for evaluation is the task completion time, which we report as grand mean and the grand median, the latter being more robust to outliers. The baseline and warp conditions have been compared using Welch's t-test and normalized time completion values based on subtracting the means of each participant from the data divided by standard deviation. Error percentages represent the ratio of the erroneous touch releases to all touch releases.

Experiment 1: Widget Acquisition

With this task, we aimed to compare the combination of warped feedback and finger-mapped input versus regular direct touch actions. The experimental interface (Figure 15) consisted of 3 vertically arranged widgets (each with 4 targets "1,2,3,4", "A,B,C,D" and "+,-,*,/" from left to right).

Each widget covered a 400*120 pixel area of the screen. In the baseline condition this area was vertically divided into 4 pixel buttons that are each 100*120 pixels and selected through positional input. In contrast, for the warped feedback condition, the participants acquired a widget when their middle finger hovered within the 400*120 pixel area and selected any of the 4 targets respectively through thumb, index, middle and ring fingers rather than touch position. Thus, the spatial footprints of the widgets were the same for both input conditions, but the interaction differed regarding the selection of 4 targets within the widget (positional or finger-mapped) and the position of feedback (no warped feedback and warped feedback).

Each experimental block involved alternating between three widgets in randomized order and acquiring targets in the same widget in randomized order, which resulted in 12 trials (3 widgets × 4 targets). With this procedure, we aimed to observe the performance of acquisition task between-widgets (the first acquisition task after the widget is alternated) and for acquisition within-widgets.

We anticipated time savings by eliminating attention switches under warp condition. However, we also anticipated a decrease in motor performance in warped feedback condition due to lack of visual monitoring. Previous work reports a decrease in accuracy when the hand movement is not visually guided [26, 35]. More specifically, Schmidt et al. report decrease in performance for large amplitude bimanual tasks when visual feedback is separated from the motor space [23]. However, the cumulative effect of redirecting the gaze and motor performance has not been studied. Even we target relaxing the need for positional accuracy, we were interested in seeing the viability of positional input through warped visual feedback, which corresponds to between-widget acquisition tasks.

Each trial was completed upon a touch release on the correct target. The combination of 2 input methods × 2 stimuli positions × 10 blocks (excluding the training block) × 12 targets resulted in 480 trials per participant. Before the experiment the participants practiced the finger-mapped input condition with 60 trials.

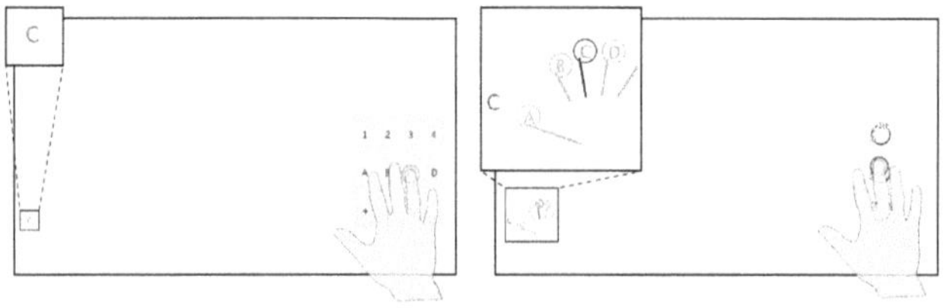

Figure 15. In the baseline condition (left) the target was acquired through touch position, while in the warped feedback condition (right) it was acquired through finger mapped input after the widget is assigned. Details are magnified. The stimuli character height was 9.3mm.

Results

Early in the analysis, we noticed time completion differences for between within-widget and between-widget tasks and analyzed them separately. For within-widget tasks, the mean completion times for warped feedback and baseline conditions were similar in both stimuli conditions (Table 1). A t-test comparison using within-subject normalized completion times did not show any significant effect for the same screen ($r = .03$, $p = .23$) and vertical screen ($r = .03$, $p = .17$) conditions. The error rates were higher for the warped feedback condition (Table 1). In few instances participants reported system failures for identifying the wrong finger, which might have affected the error rate for warped feedback condition.

However, the results were significantly different for between-widget acquisition tasks (Table 1). On average, participants spent significantly more time on the warp condition than on the baseline condition for both the same screen ($r = .42$, $p < .001$) and vertical screen conditions ($r = .54$, $p < .001$). This was accompanied by a much greater error rate for warped feedback condition (Table 1). Participant interviews suggested a few possible explanations for the difference in performance between the two input conditions. One is the mismatch between the distance traveled by the hand and its scaled down visual representation in warped visual feedback. During between-interaction tasks, we informally observed that in the baseline condition participants performed high-speed ballistic movements towards the touch target, while in the baseline condition,

Acquisition task *(within-widget)*				
Screen	Technique	Median(ms)	Mean(ms)	Error
Same	Warped	**902.75**	**1031.54**	6.41%
	Baseline	961.75	1068.36	**2.43%**
Vert.	Warped	**885.50**	1055.00	8.16%
	Baseline	986.25	**1021.88**	**3.31%**

Acquisition task *(between-widget)*				
Screen	Technique	Median(ms)	Mean(ms)	Error
Same	Warped	2094.00	2305.19	11.33%
	Baseline	**1164.50**	**1406.79**	**1.09%**
Vert.	Warped	2258.75	2342.36	9.09%
	Baseline	**1207**.5	**1415.19**	**2.17%**

Table 1. The grand median and grand mean completion times and overall error rates for two interaction and two stimuli conditions for the acquisition tasks. Emphasis (in bold) represents better performance.

they moved their hand parallel to the screen, keeping a tense hand posture. Participants also reported shoulder fatigue for warped feedback condition, which may have been caused by parallel arm movements.

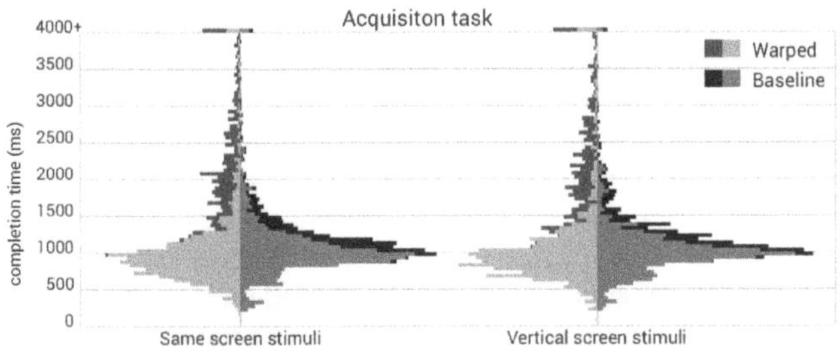

Figure 16. Distribution of acquisition task completion times (50ms bins) across all participants for two interaction and two stimuli conditions. The shades and tints respectively indicate between-widget and within-widget acquisitions tasks.

Experiment 2: Widget Manipulation

The manipulation task required participants to match the value of an interactive slider to that of the stimulus. To isolate manipulation from acquisition, the interactive slider was always assigned to the participant's hand. Each trial required the participants to manipulate the slider by dragging the index finger on the touchscreen. If the touch was released when the value of the slider matches with that of the stimulus, the task was counted as complete. The slider consisted of 5 steps (the targets being the numerals "1,2,3,4,5"), and 15 pixels of movement resulted in 1 step. Unlike the acquisition task, the only difference between the baseline and warped feedback conditions was the location of the visual feedback. In the warped feedback condition the feedback was displayed near the stimulus, whereas in the baseline condition it was displayed near the widget. We expected that eliminating visual attention switches in gaze-adaptive condition would result in shorter task completion times. The combination of 2 input methods × 2 stimuli positions × 20 blocks (excluding training blocks) × 5 targets (shown in random order) resulted in 400 trials per participant.

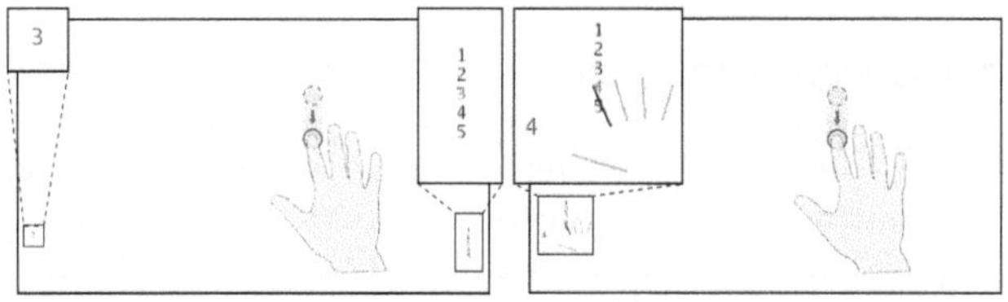

Figure 17. In the baseline condition (left) the visual feedback of the manipulated slider was shown at the widget location, while in the warped feedback condition (right) it was shown near the target. Details are magnified. The stimuli character height was 9.3mm.

Results

For both stimuli conditions participants spent more time on the baseline condition than on the warped feedback condition (Table 2). A t-test comparison of the same and vertical screen conditions using normalized data yielded a larger effect size for the vertical screen condition ($r = .19$, $p < .001$) than for the same screen condition ($r = .10$, $p < .001$), in line with the expectation that the higher cost of redirecting the gaze in vertical screen condition will result in more pronounced benefits when using warped feedback. The error rates were lower for the warped feedback condition in both screen conditions (Table 2).

Manipulation Task				
Screen	Technique	Median(ms)	Mean(ms)	Error
Same	Warped	**1387.25**	**1576.30**	**4.07%**
	Baseline	1530.25	1746.89	6.46%
Vert.	Warped	**1364.00**	**1509.06**	**3.69%**
	Baseline	1616.50	1770.58	6.54%

Table 2. The grand median and grand mean completion times and overall error rates for two interaction and two stimuli conditions for the manipulation task. Emphasis (in bold) represents better performance.

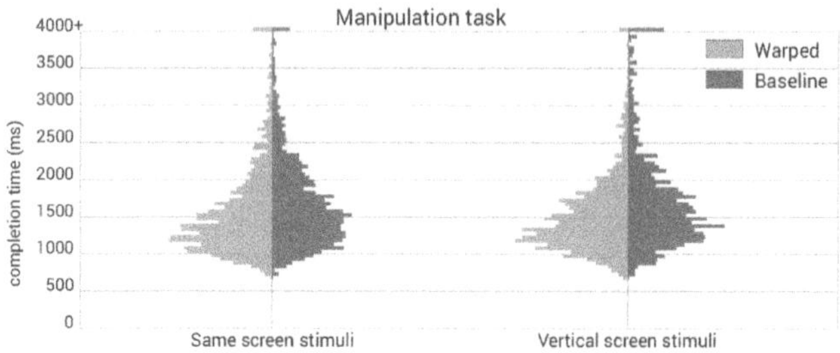

Figure 18. Distribution of manipulation task completion times (50ms bins) across all participants for two interaction and two stimuli conditions.

DISCUSSION

We combined above and on-surface modalities with eye tracking to decrease the need for positional accuracy for input on touchscreens. This is enabled by discriminating between potential user commands through the gestural component of input and visual feedback the near gaze point location. The controlled study evaluated a subset of the interaction techniques but gave us valuable insights about the viable scope of warped visual feedback. Here, we would like to discuss the strengths and weaknesses of the interaction techniques based on the outcome of the user study.

Midair Motion Amplitude

The performances of the warped feedback and baseline conditions were visibly different based on whether the task was manipulation, within-widget acquisition or between-widget acquisition. The performance of the warped visual feedback condition was higher for manipulation tasks that required no midair motion. The performance between warped feedback and baseline conditions were comparable for within-widget acquisition. However, the performance of warped visual feedback was significantly worse for between-widget acquisition tasks, in which participants had to acquire the widget through midair motion. Based on these results, we arrive at the following conclusions:

- The warped feedback was successful in decreasing the cost of redirecting the gaze, resulting in the improvement of task completion time for manipulation tasks.
- However, the warped feedback did not facilitate midair hand motion as effectively as direct visual monitoring, which resulted in a decrease in performance for between-widget acquisition tasks. Our results confirm earlier work by Schmidt et al. who reports lower performance and similar observations such as tense hand posture and parallel-to-screen hand movements when touch is performed without direct visual monitoring [23].

These conclusions also suggest that the interaction techniques described are strong in cases where the required midair motion is minimal and the task requires visual attention at a distant interface region. On the other hand, the conclusions suggest a weakness for inputs that require large amplitudes of midair motion. These have the following implications. First, in its current state, we see the role of warped feedback as complementary to conventional touch input. In these cases, the interface should allow for effortless transitions between warped feedback and conventional input modes by, for example, allowing acquisition of the widget through visual monitoring, but then transitioning to warped feedback for manipulation or within-widget acquisition. Second, for the interaction techniques presented, we see the main advantage of large touch surfaces in accommodating both of the user's hands to allow finger-mapped and bimanual concurrent input instead of expansive widget configurations.

Warped Feedback and Visual Search

Our primary reason for implementing warped feedback was decreasing the redirection of gaze and juxtaposing two different regions. Warping a color palette to a canvas area is a good example of this, as it enables comparison of the selected color with a region on the canvas. However, there can be cases in which it is more beneficial to see multiple input widgets rather than warping the interface widget. Visual search of a command in the toolbar area is a good example of such a use case in which the user needs to see widgets side by side. To support these use cases, the minimal representation of the widgets should facilitate visual search and interface learning.

Spatial and Motor Memory

Replacing positional accuracy with the gestural component (e.g. hand posture, or finger-mapped touch actions) also suggests an increased reliance on motor rather than spatial memory during interface learning. Although spatial and motor memories can be related (e.g. finger-mapped touch actions also correspond to different positions) the extent to which they are related is an open question in the research community [22]. Thus, the effects of spatial and motor memory for proficient use should be further investigated. Another important consideration is the number of interface position, hand posture and finger combinations that are both discernible and memorable.

Gesture Input

The interaction techniques we presented rely on both positional (proximity of hand to the widget) and gestural information (hand posture and digit). However, we see potential application cases for pure gestural interactions. Above-surface sensing can be used to anticipate the action in advance and provide visual confirmation at the gaze location to inform the user of the possible action a touch event can lead to, thereby addressing the problem of learning and memorization in gesture-based interfaces.

CONCLUSIONS

The limited nature of our visual attention stands in contrast to the concurrent action possibilities afforded by bimanual action. These concurrent action and sensing possibilities have been our motivation for supporting interactions that are distributed around multiple interface regions. We presented the design considerations for combining eye tracking with above- and on-surface modalities, in order to decrease reliance on positional accuracy during interaction. The system determined potential user actions midair, but deferred their confirmation to on-surface touch, accompanied by gaze-adaptive visual feedback between these two steps. The preliminary results from the controlled study suggest that warped visual feedback can complement conventional direct touch for manipulation tasks and acquisition tasks that require minimal midair motion, although future work can target improvements for increasing the viable scope. Besides immediate design implications, we identify these three modalities as a promising area for investigation, as their combination provides a fine-grained understanding of hand-eye coordination.

ACKNOWLEDGMENTS

This work has been partly supported by MindSee (FP7 - ICT; Grant Agreement #611570). We would like to thank Oswald Barral for his help with the data analysis, the anonymous reviewers for their comments and to the participants of the study.

REFERENCES

1. Michelle Annett, Tovi Grossman, Daniel Wigdor, and George Fitzmaurice. 2011. Medusa: A Proximity-aware Multi-touch Tabletop. In *Proceedings of the 24th Annual ACM Symposium on User Interface Software and Technology (UIST '11)*. ACM, New York, NY, USA, 337–346. DOI: http://dx.doi.org/10.1145/2047196.2047240

2. Ilhan Aslan, Alina Krischkowsky, Alexander Meschtscherjakov, Martin Wuchse, and Manfred Tscheligi. 2015. A Leap for Touch: Proximity Sensitive Touch Targets in Cars. In *Proceedings of the 7th International Conference on Automotive User Interfaces and Interactive Vehicular Applications (AutomotiveUI '15)*. ACM, New York, NY, USA, 39–46. DOI: http://dx.doi.org/10.1145/2799250.2799273

3. Patrick Baudisch, Edward Cutrell, Dan Robbins, Mary Czerwinski, Peter Tandler, Benjamin Bederson, Alex Zierlinger, and others. 2003. Drag-and-pop and drag-and-pick: Techniques for accessing remote screen content on touch-and pen-operated systems. In *Proceedings of INTERACT*, Vol. 3. IOS Press, 57–64.

4. Hrvoje Benko, T. Scott Saponas, Dan Morris, and Desney Tan. 2009. Enhancing Input on and Above the Interactive Surface with Muscle Sensing. In *Proceedings of the ACM International Conference on Interactive Tabletops and Surfaces (ITS '09)*. ACM, New York, NY, USA, 93–100. DOI:http://dx.doi.org/10.1145/1731903.1731924

5. Xiaojun Bi, Tovi Grossman, Justin Matejka, and George Fitzmaurice. 2011. Magic Desk: Bringing Multi-touch Surfaces into Desktop Work. In *Proceedings of the SIGCHI Conference on Human Factors in Computing Systems (CHI '11)*. ACM, New York, NY, USA, 2511–2520. DOI: http://dx.doi.org/10.1145/1978942.1979309

6. Ishan Chatterjee, Robert Xiao, and Chris Harrison. 2015. Gaze+Gesture: Expressive, Precise and Targeted Free-Space Interactions. In *Proceedings of the 2015 ACM on International Conference on Multimodal Interaction (ICMI '15)*. ACM, New York, NY, USA, 131–138. DOI: http://dx.doi.org/10.1145/2818346.2820752

7. Xiang Chen, Julia Schwarz, Chris Harrison, Jennifer Mankoff, and Scott E. Hudson. 2014. Air+Touch: Interweaving Touch & In-air Gestures. In *Proceedings of the 27th Annual ACM Symposium on User Interface Software and Technology (UIST '14)*. ACM, New York, NY, USA, 519–525. DOI: http://dx.doi.org/10.1145/2642918.2647392

8. Victor Cheung, Jens Heydekorn, Stacey Scott, and Raimund Dachselt. 2012. Revisiting Hovering: Interaction Guides for Interactive Surfaces. In *Proceedings of the 2012 ACM International Conference on Interactive Tabletops and Surfaces (ITS '12)*. ACM, New York, NY, USA, 355–358. DOI: http://dx.doi.org/10.1145/2396636.2396699

9. Daewoong Choi, Hyeonjoong Cho, and Joono Cheong. 2015. Improving Virtual Keyboards When All Finger Positions Are Known. In *Proceedings of the 28th Annual ACM Symposium on User Interface Software and Technology (UIST '15)*. ACM, New York, NY, USA, 529–538. DOI: http://dx.doi.org/10.1145/2807442.2807491

10. Bruno De Araujo, Géry Casiez, and Joaquim Jorge. 2012. Mockup Builder: Direct 3D Modeling On and Above the Surface in a Continuous Interaction Space. In *GI'12 - 38th Graphics Interface conference*. Canadian Information Processing Society, Toronto, Canada, 173–180. https://hal.inria.fr/hal-00687891

11. George W. Fitzmaurice and William Buxton. 1997. An Empirical Evaluation of Graspable User Interfaces: Towards Specialized, Space-multiplexed Input. In *Proceedings of the ACM SIGCHI Conference on Human Factors in Computing Systems (CHI '97)*. ACM, New York, NY, USA, 43–50. DOI: http://dx.doi.org/10.1145/258549.258578

12. Toshiyuki Hagiya and Tsuneo Kato. 2015. Probabilistic Touchscreen Text Entry Method Incorporating Gaze Point Information. *Journal of Information Processing* 23, 5 (2015), 708–715. DOI: http://dx.doi.org/10.2197/ipsjjip.23.708

13. Otmar Hilliges, Shahram Izadi, Andrew D. Wilson, Steve Hodges, Armando Garcia-Mendoza, and Andreas Butz. 2009. Interactions in the Air: Adding Further Depth to Interactive Tabletops. In *Proceedings of the 22nd Annual ACM Symposium on User Interface Software and Technology (UIST '09)*. ACM, New York, NY, USA, 139–148. DOI: http://dx.doi.org/10.1145/1622176.1622203

14. Ken Hinckley, Seongkook Heo, Michel Pahud, Christian Holz, Hrvoje Benko, Abigail Sellen, Richard Banks, Kenton O'Hara, Gavin Smyth, and William Buxton. 2016. Pre-Touch Sensing for Mobile Interaction. In *Proceedings of the 2016 CHI Conference on Human Factors in Computing Systems (CHI '16)*. ACM, New York, NY, USA, 2869–2881. DOI: http://dx.doi.org/10.1145/2858036.2858095

15. M. Jeannerod. 1984. The Timing of Natural Prehension Movements. *Journal of Motor Behavior* 16, 3 (1984), 235–254. DOI: http://dx.doi.org/10.1080/00222895.1984.10735319

16. Azam Khan, George Fitzmaurice, Don Almeida, Nicolas Burtnyk, and Gordon Kurtenbach. 2004. A Remote Control Interface for Large Displays. In *Proceedings of the 17th Annual ACM Symposium on User Interface Software and Technology (UIST '04)*. ACM, New York, NY, USA, 127–136. DOI: http://dx.doi.org/10.1145/1029632.1029655

17. Nicolai Marquardt, Ricardo Jota, Saul Greenberg, and Joaquim A. Jorge. 2011. *The Continuous Interaction Space: Interaction Techniques Unifying Touch and Gesture on and above a Digital Surface*. Springer Berlin Heidelberg, Berlin, Heidelberg, 461–476. DOI: http://dx.doi.org/10.1007/978-3-642-23765-2_32

18. Ken Pfeuffer, Jason Alexander, Ming Ki Chong, and Hans Gellersen. 2014. Gaze-touch: Combining Gaze with Multi-touch for Interaction on the Same Surface. In *Proceedings of the 27th Annual ACM Symposium on User Interface Software and Technology (UIST '14)*. ACM, New York, NY, USA, 509–518. DOI: http://dx.doi.org/10.1145/2642918.2647397

19. Ken Pfeuffer, Jason Alexander, Ming Ki Chong, Yanxia Zhang, and Hans Gellersen. 2015. Gaze-Shifting: Direct-Indirect Input with Pen and Touch Modulated by Gaze. In *Proceedings of the 28th Annual ACM Symposium on User Interface Software and Technology (UIST '15)*. ACM, New York, NY, USA, 373–383. DOI: http://dx.doi.org/10.1145/2807442.2807460

20. Henning Pohl and Roderick Murray-Smith. 2013. Focused and Casual Interactions: Allowing Users to Vary Their Level of Engagement. In *Proceedings of the SIGCHI Conference on Human Factors in Computing Systems (CHI '13)*. ACM, New York, NY, USA, 2223–2232. DOI: http://dx.doi.org/10.1145/2470654.2481307

21. Dario D. Salvucci and Joseph H. Goldberg. 2000. Identifying Fixations and Saccades in Eye-tracking Protocols. In *Proceedings of the 2000 Symposium on Eye Tracking Research & Applications (ETRA '00)*. ACM, New York, NY, USA, 71–78. DOI: http://dx.doi.org/10.1145/355017.355028

22. Joey Scarr, Andy Cockburn, and Carl Gutwin. 2013. Supporting and Exploiting Spatial Memory in User Interfaces. *Found. Trends Hum.-Comput. Interact.* 6, 1 (Dec. 2013), 1–84. DOI: http://dx.doi.org/10.1561/1100000046

23. Dominik Schmidt, Florian Block, and Hans Gellersen. 2009. A Comparison of Direct and Indirect Multi-touch Input for Large Surfaces. In *Proceedings of the 12th IFIP TC 13 International Conference on Human-Computer Interaction: Part I (INTERACT '09)*. Springer-Verlag, Berlin, Heidelberg, 582–594. DOI: http://dx.doi.org/10.1007/978-3-642-03655-2_65

24. Julia Schwarz, Scott Hudson, Jennifer Mankoff, and Andrew D. Wilson. 2010. A Framework for Robust and Flexible Handling of Inputs with Uncertainty. In *Proceedings of the 23nd Annual ACM Symposium on User Interface Software and Technology (UIST '10)*. ACM, New York, NY, USA, 47–56. DOI: http://dx.doi.org/10.1145/1866029.1866039

25. Baris Serim and Giulio Jacucci. 2016. Pointing While Looking Elsewhere: Designing for Varying Degrees of Visual Guidance During Manual Input. In *Proceedings of the 2016 CHI Conference on Human Factors in Computing Systems (CHI '16)*. ACM, New York, NY, USA, 5789–5800. DOI: http://dx.doi.org/10.1145/2858036.2858480

26. Will Spijkers and Simone Spellerberg. 1995. On-line Visual Control of Aiming Movements? *Acta Psychologica* 90, 1 - 3 (1995), 333 – 348. DOI: http://dx.doi.org/10.1016/S0001-6918(95)90000-4 Discrete and Continuous Information Processing.

27. Sophie Stellmach and Raimund Dachselt. 2013. Still Looking: Investigating Seamless Gaze-supported Selection, Positioning, and Manipulation of Distant Targets. In *Proceedings of the SIGCHI Conference on Human Factors in Computing Systems (CHI '13)*. ACM, New York, NY, USA, 285–294. DOI: http://dx.doi.org/10.1145/2470654.2470695

28. Philip Tuddenham, David Kirk, and Shahram Izadi. 2010. Graspables Revisited: Multi-touch vs. Tangible Input for Tabletop Displays in Acquisition and Manipulation Tasks. In *Proceedings of the SIGCHI Conference on Human Factors in Computing Systems (CHI '10)*. ACM, New York, NY, USA, 2223–2232. DOI: http://dx.doi.org/10.1145/1753326.1753662

29. Jayson Turner, Jason Alexander, Andreas Bulling, Dominik Schmidt, and Hans Gellersen. 2013. *Eye Pull, Eye Push: Moving Objects between Large Screens and Personal Devices with Gaze and Touch*. Springer Berlin Heidelberg, Berlin, Heidelberg, 170–186. DOI: http://dx.doi.org/10.1007/978-3-642-40480-1_11

30. Md. Sami Uddin, Carl Gutwin, and Benjamin Lafreniere. 2016. HandMark Menus: Rapid Command Selection and Large Command Sets on Multi-Touch Displays. In *Proceedings of the 2016 CHI Conference on Human Factors in Computing Systems (CHI '16)*. ACM, New York, NY, USA, 5836–5848. DOI: http://dx.doi.org/10.1145/2858036.2858211

31. Simon Voelker, Andrii Matviienko, Johannes Schöning, and Jan Borchers. 2015. Combining Direct and Indirect Touch Input for Interactive Workspaces Using Gaze Input. In *Proceedings of the 3rd ACM Symposium on Spatial User Interaction (SUI '15)*. ACM, New York, NY, USA, 79–88. DOI:http://dx.doi.org/10.1145/2788940.2788949

32. Malte Weiss, Simon Voelker, Christine Sutter, and Jan Borchers. 2010. BendDesk: Dragging Across the Curve. In *ACM International Conference on Interactive Tabletops and Surfaces (ITS '10)*. ACM, New York, NY, USA, 1–10. DOI: http://dx.doi.org/10.1145/1936652.1936654

33. Malte Weiss, Chat Wacharamanotham, Simon Voelker, and Jan Borchers. 2011. FingerFlux: Near-surface Haptic Feedback on Tabletops. In *Proceedings of the 24th Annual ACM Symposium on User Interface Software and Technology (UIST '11)*. ACM, New York, NY, USA, 615–620. DOI: http://dx.doi.org/10.1145/2047196.2047277

34. Malte Weiss, Julie Wagner, Yvonne Jansen, Roger Jennings, Ramsin Khoshabeh, James D. Hollan, and Jan Borchers. 2009. SLAP Widgets: Bridging the Gap Between Virtual and Physical Controls on Tabletops. In *Proceedings of the SIGCHI Conference on Human Factors in Computing Systems (CHI '09)*. ACM, New York, NY, USA, 481–490. DOI: http://dx.doi.org/10.1145/1518701.1518779

35. Jinglong Wu, Jiajia Yang, and Taichi Honda. 2010. Fitts' law holds for pointing movements under conditions of restricted visual feedback. *Human Movement Science* 29, 6 (2010), 882 – 892. DOI: http://dx.doi.org/10.1016/j.humov.2010.03.009

36. Haijun Xia, Ricardo Jota, Benjamin McCanny, Zhe Yu, Clifton Forlines, Karan Singh, and Daniel Wigdor. 2014. Zero-latency Tapping: Using Hover Information to Predict Touch Locations and Eliminate Touchdown Latency. In *Proceedings of the 27th Annual ACM Symposium on User Interface Software and Technology (UIST '14)*. ACM, New York, NY, USA, 205–214. DOI: http://dx.doi.org/10.1145/2642918.2647348

37. Xing-Dong Yang, Tovi Grossman, Pourang Irani, and George Fitzmaurice. 2011. TouchCuts and TouchZoom: Enhanced Target Selection for Touch Displays Using Finger Proximity Sensing. In *Proceedings of the SIGCHI Conference on Human Factors in Computing Systems (CHI '11)*. ACM, New York, NY, USA, 2585–2594. DOI: http://dx.doi.org/10.1145/1978942.1979319

38. Shumin Zhai, Carlos Morimoto, and Steven Ihde. 1999. Manual and Gaze Input Cascaded (MAGIC) Pointing. In *Proceedings of the SIGCHI Conference on Human Factors in Computing Systems (CHI '99)*. ACM, New York, NY, USA, 246–253. DOI: http://dx.doi.org/10.1145/302979.303053

Let's Talk About X: Combining Image Recognition and Eye Gaze to Support Conversation for People with ALS

Shaun K. Kane
University of Colorado Boulder
Boulder, CO, USA
shaun.kane@colorado.edu

Meredith Ringel Morris
Microsoft Research
Redmond, WA, USA
merrie@microsoft.com

ABSTRACT
Communicating at a natural speed is a significant challenge for users of augmentative and alternative communication (AAC) devices, especially when input is provided by eye gaze, as is common for people with ALS and similar conditions. One way to improve AAC throughput is by drawing on contextual information from the outside world. Toward this goal, we present SceneTalk, a prototype gaze-based AAC system that uses computer vision to identify objects in the user's field of view and suggests words and phrases related to the current scene. We conducted a formative evaluation of SceneTalk with six people with ALS, in which we evaluated their preference for user interface modes and output preferences. Participants agreed that integrating contextual awareness into their AAC device could be helpful across a diverse range of situations.

Author Keywords
Assistive technology; eye gaze; computer vision; augmentative and alternative communication; ALS.

ACM Classification Keywords
K.4.2. Social Issues: Assistive technologies for persons with disabilities; H.5.2. User Interfaces: Voice I/O.

INTRODUCTION
Augmentative and alternative communication (AAC) systems provide communication support for people with a range of physical, cognitive, and other disabilities [5]. Designing an effective AAC system requires balancing the user's expressive capability with their ability to quickly and reliably operate the device's user interface.

Creating effective AAC devices for people with neurodegenerative diseases such as Amyotrophic Lateral Sclerosis (ALS) is especially challenging, as these individuals typically retain their full linguistic abilities but often lose the ability to speak and use their hands entirely [2].

DIS 2017, June 10-14, 2017, Edinburgh, United Kingdom

ACM 978-1-4503-4922-2/17/06 $15.00
DOI: http://dx.doi.org/10.1145/3064663.3064762

Figure 1. SceneTalk is a gaze-based AAC system that uses the device's camera to recognize objects. Recognized objects are used to suggest relevant words and phrases as the user types. The prediction bar at the top of the keyboard combines contextual predictions detected in the image (in orange) with predictions from a language model (in white).

Many people with ALS use eye gaze to interact with their AAC systems [4]. Using gaze for real-time communication can be challenging, as eye-typing typically enables users to communicate at 10 to 20 words per minute (wpm) [18], while spoken conversation occurs at about 180 wpm [28]. Thus, improving the speed of AAC input has the potential to significantly improve quality of life for people with ALS.

One way to increase the speed of AAC input is to predict likely words and phrases as the user types. Predictions can be generated from a language model (e.g., [23]) or derived from knowledge of the user's context, such as their location (e.g., [7,12,26]). However, AAC systems may be able to infer context from other sources. For example, many conversations involve talking about nearby objects, such as when commenting on a friend's outfit, or requesting help with a door.

This paper introduces a new approach to improve the speed of AAC input: identifying objects in the user's environment and using information about those objects to generate contextual predictions. Our prototype system, SceneTalk, uses automated image recognition algorithms [8] to identify objects and suggest relevant words and phrases. We present findings from a formative study in which six people with ALS tested the SceneTalk prototype and provided feedback about the usefulness of this approach, as well as their preferences for integrating contextual data into an AAC user interface. Feedback from this study indicates that using objects in the local environment as contextual predictions may improve the user experience of gaze-based AAC.

RELATED WORK

Slow input speed is one of the most significant barriers to AAC adoption and use for people with ALS [21]. Prior approaches to speeding up AAC input include reducing dwell time [17,20], integrating word and phrase predictions [16], and supporting dwell-free eye-typing [15,22]. However, the theoretical maximum speed of any keyboard-based eye-typing method has been estimated to be only 46 wpm [14], well below the rate of spoken conversation. Alternative text entry methods such as Dasher [24,25] may offer improved performance, but learning an alternative text entry method requires extensive practice.

A common approach to improving AAC speed is to predict likely words using a language model and to suggest them as the user types [23]. Researchers have also explored how the user's context can be used to inform predictions. Higginbotham et al. [11] found that including task-specific predictions in an AAC reduced the number of key presses needed to discuss that subject. Marco Polo [7], TalkAbout [12], and GLAAC [26] offered predictions relevant to the user's location. AACrobat [10] introduced a secondary mobile device application that enabled conversation partners to suggest words and phrases as the AAC user typed. PhotoTalk [1] enabled individuals with aphasia to communicate by sharing photos rather than writing or speaking text. Our work introduces a new approach to generating contextual predictions: identifying nearby objects and suggesting words and phrases related to those objects.

SCENETALK: AN OBJECT-AWARE AAC SYSTEM

To explore the potential of object recognition for AAC word predictions, we developed SceneTalk, a prototype AAC application that identifies objects in the nearby environment and uses those objects to suggest relevant words and phrases.

User Interface

SceneTalk's user interface resembles a traditional character-based AAC system with a QWERTY keyboard (Figure 1). Targets are selected via an adjustable dwell time (defaulting to 500ms). A Play button speaks out the typed text. Word and phrase predictions are shown above the keyboard. A control panel at the top right provides controls for activating the device camera and retrieving contextual predictions, and shows the most recent image captured by the camera.

Interaction Modes

Because context-aware AAC has not been widely tested with users, and because activating the device camera may cause privacy issues if handled incorrectly, we developed three interaction modes for interacting with SceneTalk's contextual predictions. We designed these modes to explore users' preferences for automatic or explicit camera control, and to test whether users preferred contextual predictions to be integrated with linguistic predictions or shown separately. The three interaction modes are:

Always On. The camera captures images automatically at a regular interval. Contextual predictions are shown alongside linguistic predictions, but are presented in a different color and marked with a star symbol (Figure 1).

Click for Suggestions. The user interface is laid out identically to the previous mode. Linguistic predictions are updated as the user types. The user may activate the Camera button to capture an image and load contextual predictions.

Pop-Up Menu. The keyboard prediction row shows only linguistic predictions. The user retrieves contextual predictions by activating the Camera button. Predictions are shown separately via a full-screen overlay (Figure 2).

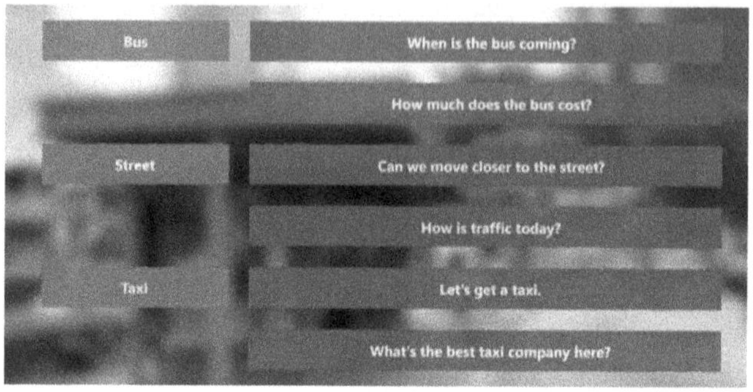

Figure 2. Suggested words (left) and phrases (right) are presented over the camera image in Pop-Up Menu mode.

Recognizing and Labeling Objects

SceneTalk captures images of the environment using the device's rear-facing camera. SceneTalk typically recognizes objects using automated computer vision, but supports crowd-based object labeling as a backup method.

Automated Recognition: SceneTalk uses computer vision to recognize objects in the image. Automatic image captioning has recently been used to provide alternative descriptions of images for blind users [27], but has not previously been used to support communication. SceneTalk uses the Microsoft Cognitive Services API [19], which is based on recent computer vision techniques [8], to identify objects. For each image, the API generates a list of nouns and adjectives describing the scene (e.g., table, café, sunny), along with a confidence value. To identify objects, SceneTalk extracts high-confidence nouns from the list.

Crowd-Based Labeling: SceneTalk also supports crowd-based object labeling using Amazon Mechanical Turk [3]. In this mode, the image is uploaded to a web server, which generates a set of Mechanical Turk tasks. Workers are asked to mark regions in the image corresponding to objects and to provide words or phrases describing each object. Crowd-based recognition may be useful when automated recognition is unavailable, for labeling objects that cannot be identified using current automated methods, and for identifying objects in low-quality images, such as images captured in bright or dim lighting. Crowd workers may also compose relevant phrases based on the identified object, which is not currently supported by automated approaches.

For example, if the user captured an image of a light switch, a crowd worker might suggest the phrase "Can you turn off the lights?" While crowd-based recognition is slower than automated recognition, crowd workers can be used to label images within minutes for a reasonable cost [6], which may still be faster than typing for many gaze-based AAC users, particularly for people with ALS, whose mobility restrictions may result in relatively infrequent changes of scenery.

Word and Phrase Predictions

SceneTalk presents word and phrase predictions as the user types, similar to many other AAC systems (e.g., [23]). SceneTalk's predictions combine linguistic predictions based on the user's prior text with contextual predictions derived from nearby objects.. Linguistic predictions use a word frequency model for determining the initial word and a bigram model for determining subsequent words.

SceneTalk's current interaction mode determines how predictions are displayed, as well as which types of predictions are shown. In *Always On* mode, linguistic and contextual predictions are interleaved and appear as the user types. In *Click for Suggestions* mode, the interface shows only linguistic predictions while typing. Activating the Camera button replaces the linguistic predictions with the top six contextual predictions. In *Pop-Up Menu* mode, only linguistic predictions are presented on the keyboard. Activating the Camera button causes the predictions menu to appear; this full-screen view shows a combination of predicted words and phrases (Figure 2).

SceneTalk can suggest both individual words and complete phrases. Phrases can be generated by crowd workers, but current automated techniques cannot generate relevant phrases. To compensate for this limitation, SceneTalk includes a set of stock phrases that can be attached to any recognized object. These phrases were identified during our formative research with AAC users who have ALS. The stock phrases include "Can you tell me about *X*?", "Can you help me with *X*?", "Can you give me *X*?", and "Can you move *X*?". Phrases are shown when the user begins a new sentence, or when the user selects the *Pop-Up Menu* mode.

FORMATIVE EVALUATION OF CONTEXT-AWARE AAC

Evaluating AAC systems with representative users presents many challenges. Eye-typing for people with ALS can be extremely slow and error-prone [4], making it difficult for participants to provide extended feedback, magnifying the frustration encountered when testing prototypes, and reducing the amount of data that can be collected and analyzed. Furthermore, eye-typing performance can vary significantly throughout the day due to sensor error, user fatigue, and side effects from medication [13]. These challenges make conducting performance evaluations especially difficult for people with ALS. Furthermore, people with ALS typically rely upon their AAC devices for most of their communication, including communicating about physical needs and even life-threatening emergencies. Given the critical importance of maintaining access to communication, we felt that a field deployment of our prototype was beyond the scope of the current work.

For these reasons, we chose to focus on collecting feedback about the usefulness of context-aware AAC, participants' interests and concerns regarding the use of context-aware AAC, and participants' preferences for accessing contextual predictions. We conducted two rounds of evaluation: preliminary interviews based on paper prototypes, and a demonstration and evaluation of our working system.

Paper Prototype Testing

Early in our design process, we collected feedback from six people with ALS (ages 48-54, 1 female). The research team showed participants a paper mockup of SceneTalk, and described how the system could detect and describe objects in the local environment. We asked participants whether the system would be useful to them, and asked them to list situations in which they might use such a system. We also asked participants whether they would prefer to use context-aware AAC predictions via a separate application on their communication device, as a mode in their current AAC device, or completely integrated into their current AAC.

Each of the six participants expressed enthusiasm about our paper prototype: five said that they would use context-aware AAC several times per day, and one said that he would use it several times per week. Participants stated that they would be interested in using context-aware AAC at the doctor's office, supermarket, pharmacy, and around the home. Participants were divided about how contextual information should be integrated into their existing AAC systems: two participants wanted contextual predictions to be integrated into the AAC's keyboard, one preferred to access contextual words and phrases via a separate application, and three said that they would need to try the application themselves before deciding. Feedback from this session was used to guide the design of the SceneTalk prototype and its interaction modes.

Prototype Demonstration and Feedback

After developing a functioning SceneTalk prototype, we presented it to six people with ALS (ages 39-60, 1 female). Three participants used a gaze-controlled AAC keyboard, one typed using a head mouse, and two still used speech as their primary form of communication. Three participants had previously provided feedback about the paper prototype. The SceneTalk prototype was deployed on a Microsoft Surface Pro 3 tablet placed on an adjustable mount. A Tobii EyeX tracker was used to track users' eye gaze.

Participants used the SceneTalk prototype during a single 30-minute session in their home or in our research lab. When possible, participants directly controlled the prototype themselves. However, participants sometimes encountered difficulties using our prototype device due to calibration issues [9], positioning, and fatigue. When tracking became difficult, one of the researchers demonstrated the user interface via the Surface Pro's touch screen. During the session, participants experienced each of SceneTalk's interaction modes (*Always On; Click for Suggestions; Pop-Up Menu*), presented in random order. Each interface was paired with a randomly-chosen scenario (bus stop, coffee shop, supermarket). For each scenario, pre-generated words and phrases were presented; the words were a subset of those automatically produced by the image recognition API, while the phrases were manually generated by the research team.

After the demonstration, participants answered three Likert-style questions about the prototype (Table 1), indicated their preferred interaction mode, and indicated whether they preferred word predictions, phrase predictions, or a combination of the two. Participants also provided freeform subjective feedback about their experience.

Question	Rating
Overall, how useful were the words and phrases suggested by this application? (1=Not at all useful, 5=Very useful)	3.7 (SD=0.8)
Overall, how likely would you be to use this application? (1=Not at all likely; 5=Very likely)	4 (0.9)
Assuming the camera can be turned off when needed, how do you feel about the application's ability to automatically capture images? (1=Very negative; 5=Very positive).	4.3 (0.5)

Table 1. Summary of Likert-style questions and responses.

Overall, participants rated their experience positively: all recorded Likert scores were 3 or higher. Participants were divided on their preferred interaction mode: two preferred *Always On*, two preferred *Click for Suggestions*, one preferred *Pop-Up Menu*, and one had no preference. Participants were also divided about whether they preferred contextual predictions as words, phrases, or a combination of the two. Four participants preferred an even balance of words and phrases, one preferred mostly phrases with some words, and one preferred only words (no phrases).

DISCUSSION

Because our participants had communication difficulties, they were unable to provide detailed verbal feedback. However, nearly all participants expressed frustration with the speed of their current AAC, and were enthusiastic about being able to more easily discuss items in their environment.

Participants differed in their preferred interface modes and prediction types. This divergence may be due in part to participants' varying abilities, as slower eye-typists may rely more heavily on suggested words and phrases. However, some design features were appreciated by the majority of participants: four of six participants who tested the prototype preferred interaction modes that showed predictions above the keyboard rather than in a separate window (one had no preference), and five of six participants preferred to receive both word and phrase predictions. Given the rapid changes in ability that can occur for people with ALS [4] and the challenges in using gaze-based AAC in certain environments due to ambient light and other factors [13], there may be some benefit in supporting multiple modes of interaction, or adapting the interaction mode to the user's context, such as presenting more predictions if the user appears to be experiencing difficulties using the eye tracker, or weighting contextual predictions more heavily if the user is in an environment in which they are more likely to discuss nearby objects, such as in a store or restaurant.

LIMITATIONS AND FUTURE WORK

A limitation of the present work is that the system has not been evaluated by representative users outside the lab. Testing AAC devices in the field presents many challenges, and these challenges are often amplified for our chosen population of people with ALS. Despite this limitation, we believe that our formative evaluation provides strong support for including contextual information in future AAC devices. Although it was not feasible to replace the AAC devices of people with ALS with a research prototype, publishing information about this novel interface design may bring these concepts to the attention of commercial AAC device makers, providing a route to improvements without requiring users to rely on a prototype AAC system.

While we have conducted this work in collaboration with people with ALS, our approach to providing contextual AAC predictions could be useful to people with a range of abilities. For example, people with aphasia could use SceneTalk to name objects, and foreign language learners could use SceneTalk to practice naming objects in a new language. Adapting SceneTalk to new user groups would likely require changing the user interface: for example, individuals with aphasia may prefer a more visually-oriented user interface, as in SceneTalk's *Pop-Up Menu* mode, rather than a keyboard-based user interface.

An additional area for future work is to improve SceneTalk's capability to generate relevant phrases. Currently, SceneTalk provides phrases from a pre-generated set. Future versions could leverage the crowd or a more robust language model to present more contextually relevant phrases. For example, when identifying a box of tissues, SceneTalk could suggest the phrase "I think I am getting a cold." SceneTalk could also identify groups of objects and infer information about the location (e.g., seeing pots and pans suggests the user may be in a kitchen), and could suggest phrases relevant to multiple detected objects (e.g., "Can you put the book in the bag?").

CONCLUSION

Leveraging information about a user's context to predict words and phrases can help to overcome the slow input speed and high error rate of gaze-based AAC. SceneTalk introduces a new source of contextual data for AAC, that of nearby objects. Our formative evaluation of SceneTalk with people with ALS indicates that objects in the environment can be a valuable source of context, and that these contextual predictions may be integrated into the everyday experience of typing with an eye-gaze based AAC device.

ACKNOWLEDGMENTS

We thank Margaret Mitchell and the Microsoft Research Enable team for their assistance with this project.

REFERENCES

1. Meghan Allen, Joanna McGrenere, and Barbara Purves. 2007. The design and field evaluation of PhotoTalk: A digital image communication application for people. In *Proceedings of ASSETS 2007*, 187–194.
2. ALS Association. Epidemiology of ALS and Suspected Clusters. *ALSA.org*. Retrieved May 25, 2016 from http://www.alsa.org/als-care/resources/publications-videos/factsheets/epidemiology.html
3. Amazon Mechanical Turk. Retrieved January 1, 2017 from http://www.mturk.com/
4. David Beukelman, Susan Fager, and Amy Nordness. 2011. Communication support for people with ALS. *Neurology Research International* 2011.
5. David Beukelman, Pat Mirenda, Kathryn Garrett, and Janice Light. 2012. *Augmentative and Alternative Communication: Supporting Children and Adults with Complex Communication Needs, Fourth Edition*. Paul H. Brookes Publishing Co, Baltimore.
6. Jeffrey P. Bigham, Chandrika Jayant, Hanjie Ji, Greg Little, Andrew Miller, Robert C. Miller, Robin Miller, Aubrey Tatarowicz, Brandyn White, Samuel White, and Tom Yeh. 2010. VizWiz: nearly real-time answers to visual questions. In *Proceedings of UIST 2010*, 333–342.
7. Carrie Demmans Epp, Justin Djordjevic, Shimu Wu, Karyn Moffatt, and Ronald M. Baecker. 2012. Towards providing just-in-time vocabulary support for assistive and augmentative communication. In *Proceedings of IUI 2012*, 33–36.
8. Hao Fang, Saurabh Gupta, Forrest Iandola, Rupesh K. Srivastava, Li Deng, Piotr Dollár, Jianfeng Gao, Xiaodong He, Margaret Mitchell, John C. Platt, C. Lawrence Zitnick, and Geoffrey Zweig. 2015. From captions to visual concepts and back. In *Proceedings of CVPR 2015*, 1473–1482.
9. Anna Feit, Shane Williams, Arturo Toledo, Ann Paradiso, Harish Kulkarni, Shaun Kane, and Meredith Ringel Morris. 2017. Toward everyday gaze input: Accuracy and precision of eye tracking and implications for design. In *Proceedings of CHI 2017*, to appear.
10. Alexander Fiannaca, Ann Paradiso, Mira Shah, and Meredith Ringel Morris. 2017. AACRobat: Using mobile devices to lower communication barriers and provide autonomy with gaze-based AAC. In *Proceedings of CSCW 2017*, 683–695.
11. D. Jeffery Higginbotham, Ann M. Bisantz, Michelle Sunm, Kim Adams, and Fen Yik. 2009. The effect of context priming and task type on augmentative communication performance. *Augmentative and Alternative Communication* 25, 1: 19–31.
12. Shaun K. Kane, Barbara Linam-Church, Kyle Althoff, and Denise McCall. 2012. What we talk about: Designing a context-aware communication tool for people with aphasia. In *Proceedings of ASSETS 2012*, 49–56.
13. Shaun K. Kane, Meredith Ringel Morris, Ann Paradiso, and Jon Campbell. 2017. "At times avuncular and cantankerous, with the reflexes of a mongoose": Understanding self-expression through augmentative and alternative communication devices. In Proceedings of *CSCW 2017*, 1166–1179.
14. Per Ola Kristensson and Keith Vertanen. 2012. The potential of dwell-free eye-typing for fast assistive gaze communication. In *Proceedings of ETRA 2012*, 241–244.
15. Andrew Kurauchi, Wenxin Feng, Ajjen Joshi, Carlos Morimoto, and Margrit Betke. 2016. EyeSwipe: Dwell-free text entry using gaze paths. In *Proceedings of CHI 2016*, 1952–1956.
16. I. Scott MacKenzie and Xuang Zhang. 2008. Eye typing using word and letter prediction and a fixation algorithm. In *Proceedings of ETRA 2008*, 55–58.
17. Päivi Majaranta, Ulla-Kaija Ahola, and Oleg Špakov. 2009. Fast gaze typing with an adjustable dwell time. In *Proceedings of CHI 2009*, 357–360.
18. Päivi Majaranta and Kari-Jouko Räihä. 2002. Twenty years of eye typing: systems and design issues. In *Proceedings of ETRA 2002*, 15–22.
19. Microsoft Cognitive Services. Retrieved January 1, 2017 from http://www.microsoft.com/cognitive-services
20. Martez Mott, Shane Williams, Jacob O. Wobbrock, and Meredith Ringel Morris. 2017. Improving dwell-based gaze typing with dynamic, cascading dwell times. In *Proceedings of CHI 2017*, to appear.
21. Joan Murphy. 2004. "I prefer contact this close": Perceptions of AAC by people with motor neurone disease and their communication partners. *Augmentative and Alternative Communication* 20, 4: 259–271.
22. Diogo Pedrosa, Maria Da Graça Pimentel, Amy Wright, and Khai N. Truong. 2015. Filteryedping: Design challenges and user performance of dwell-free eye typing. *ACM Transactions on Accessible Computing* 6, 1: 1–37.
23. Keith Trnka, Debra Yarrington, John McCaw, Kathleen F. McCoy, and Christopher Pennington. 2007. The effects of word prediction on communication rate for AAC. In *Proceedings of HLT 2007*, 173–176.
24. Outi Tuisku, Päivi Majaranta, Poika Isokoski, and Kari-Jouko Räihä. 2008. Now Dasher! Dash away!:

Longitudinal study of fast text entry by eye gaze. In *Proceedings of ETRA 2008*, 19–26.

25. David J. Ward and David JC MacKay. 2002. Fast hands-free writing by gaze direction. *Nature* 418.6900: 838.
26. Kristin Williams, Karyn Moffatt, Denise McCall, and Leah Findlater. 2015. Designing conversation cues on a head-worn display to support persons with aphasia. In *Proceedings of CHI 2015*, 231–240.
27. Shaomei Wu, Jeffrey Wieland, Omar Farivar, and Jill Schiller. 2017. Automatic alt-text: Computer-generated image descriptions for blind users on a social network service. In *Proceedings of CSCW 2017*, 1180–1192.
28. Kathryn M. Yorkston and David R. Beukelman. 1981. Communication efficiency of dysarthric speakers as measured by sentence intelligibility and speaking rate. *Journal of Speech and Hearing Disorders* 46, 3: 296–301.

"MyEyes": The Design and Evaluation of First Person View Video Streaming for Long-Distance Couples

Rui Pan, Samarth Singhal, Bernhard E. Riecke, Emily Cramer and Carman Neustaedter
School of Interactive Arts and Technology, Simon Fraser University
102 – 13450 102nd Avenue, Surrey, BC, Canada, V3T 0A3
[ruip, samarths, ber1, ecramer, carman]@sfu.ca

ABSTRACT
Couples in Long Distance Relationships (LDRs) often rely on the use of video chat systems to help maintain their relationship. However, designs are typically limited to only supporting face-to-face conversations or providing narrow fields of view. We designed and evaluated *MyEyes*, a First Person View (FPV) video streaming technology probe made with cardboard goggles and a smartphone. Distance-separated partners see each other's view on their screen where it can overlap their own view (Overlapped), be placed above it (Horizontal), or presented at the same time where each is seen with a different eye (Split). We compared the three different views with couples to explore the effect on social presence and body ownership. The Overlapped View was most preferred by couples and it provided the strongest feeling of co-presence, whereas a Horizontal View provided the greatest sense of mutual understanding. Our qualitative results showed couples valued performing synchronized acts together and doing activities 'in' the remote location.

Author Keywords
Long distance relationships; computer mediated communications; first person views; video chat systems; social presence

ACM Classification Keywords
H.5.m. Information interfaces and presentation (e.g., HCI): Miscellaneous;

INTRODUCTION
Long Distance Relationships (LDRs) involve couples who are geographically separated. LDRs are increasingly common due to various reasons such as school, work and travel [22,29]. Just like collocated couples, relationship maintenance is an important part of LDRs [30]. This includes being with one's partner, communicating with them, and empathizing [30]. Of course, this is hard to achieve when people are separated by distance; thus, many couples in LDRs rely on technologies such as video chat for mediating closeness [25]. The face-to-face metaphor offered in traditional video chat systems such as Skype and FaceTime allows people to see each other's face and to chat as though they are talking in-person [13,24,25]. Some couples also like to share activities together over video chat (e.g., eating, watching movies, parallel working) [25]. Yet this can be limiting since partners lack mobility in the remote space and are not able to touch one another [25]. Based on these limitations, our goal was to explore the design of richer video communication mediums that might allow LDR couples to more deeply immerse themselves in their partners' remote location.

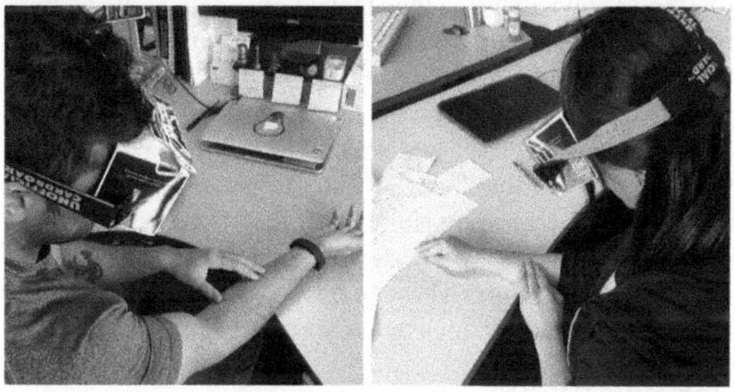

Figure 1. A couple uses *MyEyes* to share their first person views between two locations.

First person view (FPV) sharing (or first person video sharing) systems provide a feeling of seeing from another person's eyes [15,17,19,20]. Existing systems have revealed that FPVs are suitable for movement synchronization in distributed settings [12]. FPVs also give rise to an illusion of being within another people's body [15]. We were curious to know whether the features of FPVs could help LDRs to feel each other's physical embodiment, feel more deeply immersed in the remote location, and feel a greater sense of social presence. Such views might allow LDR couples to create new experiences to help them feel close. Yet designing FPVs that stream video between two partners raises interesting questions around how the video should be displayed and what effects it will have on the couple.

We first present our design of *MyEyes*, a FPV video streaming technology probe [11] made with cardboard goggles and smartphones. With MyEyes, partners exchange

DIS 2017, June 10 - 14, 2017, Edinburgh, United Kingdom
Copyright is held by the owner/author(s). Publication rights licensed to ACM.
ACM 978-1-4503-4922-2/17/06…$15.00
DOI: http://dx.doi.org/10.1145/3064663.3064671

first person views with each other to see exactly what each other sees (Figure 1). Distance-separated partners see each other's view on their displays where it can overlap their own view (Overlapped View), be placed above it (Horizontal View), or at the same time but each view is seen with a different eye (Split View). These views combine research from several past systems, which were designed for more general interactions and not LDRs [12,15–17]. We added a new type of view called Split View. We also focused on creating a low cost design that might be more easily adopted and used by couples in everyday situations, rather than being restricted to research labs or scripted environments [12,15–17].

We studied the technology probe using mixed methods with 12 couples—8 had been in a long distance relationship in the past and 4 had not. Couples compared the three different views for displaying video where we explored couples feelings of social presence—the feeling that you are in the same room as someone [3]—and body ownership—the ability to feel like you are in another person's body [7,23] as means to empathize with a person. We also explored how participants felt they might use the system as part of a LDR. Participants preferred the Overlapped View and it provided the most feelings of Co-Presence. Both Overlapped View and Split view provided strong feelings of 'body ownership', the feeling of being in another person's body. Horizontal View, however, received the highest score for 'mutual understanding' (e.g., feeling empathy for another) among the three interfaces. Couples enjoyed using MyEyes and wanted to use it as part of their relationship in the future. The FPVs were especially valuable for performing shared acts that were synchronized across locations, as well as activities that could be done 'in' the remote location. These were not always easy though and we suggest directions to circumvent the challenges.

RELATED WORK

Long Distance Relationships and Technology

Couples in LDRs need regular communication to maintain their relationship [22]. Here they rely on computer-mediated communication tools to overcome their physical separation [25]. A study of LDRs using video chat [25] describes the routines couples have for communicating over distance. Results show that couples highly value seeing their partner and sometimes use video chat to experience a sense of 'shared living' together [25]. Yet existing video chat systems (e.g., Skype) lacked mobility and support for conversing during shared and independent activities [25].

Recurring themes amongst communication systems designed for LDR couples are connectedness and playful interactions. For example, BreathingFrame [18] is an inflatable photo frame that enables couples to feel emotional connectedness by delivering a breathing signal to an inflatable surface. WearLove [14] is a wearable device for couples to stay connected through a tree-planning game. Gooch and Watts explored the design of systems to support touch and hand holding over distance [9,10]. Participants enjoyed a sense of personalization and playfulness [10]. They suggest designing for openness and flexibility [9]. Flex-N-Feel used a pair of interconnected gloves to allow couples to share touch over distance [27]. Again, couples enjoyed playful experiences with the prototype.

Similar to our study, Baishya and Neustaedter [1] studied a video technology probe called In Your Eyes for LDRs. The probe used smartphones with Skype in auto-answer mode and placed in shirt pocket to provide an 'anytime, anywhere' video chat experience, though it did not provide a true FPV as we do with MyEyes. One couple highly valued In Your Eyes because it allowed them to spontaneously interact with one another and be player [1]. A second couple felt the prototype infringed on each other's autonomy and privacy. Based on the aforementioned designs and studies, we aimed to similarly create playful experiences within the design of MyEyes while focusing on providing feelings of connectedness and social presence.

First Person View Sharing

FPV sharing utilizes devices like head mounted displays (HMDs) to provide a feeling of seeing from another person's eyes [15,17,19,20]. Researchers have studied FPVs in collocated collaboration and skill transition [5,15,17] and found FPVs to be valuable for enabling users to see from a remote perspective and create a physical embodiment in distributed spaces [15]. For example, Kasahara et al. [15] studied a four-view FPV system called Parallel Eyes for groups of people to investigate the difference of FPV in a one-way 'shooter-watcher' model (one user streams and the other watches the stream) compared to a mutual view sharing model (both users stream and watch both streams). A series of workshops explored activities such as shaking hands, drawing, and playing tag). They found a symmetric configuration such as first person view exchange could help people to understand complex information from multiple sides to enhance communication with people in a distributed setting [15]. Yet people sometimes lost their own sense of embodiment because they became overly focused on their partners' first person views [15]. While their system was similar to ours, Parallel Eyes was not evaluated for its ability to support specific relationship needs such as with long distance couples. We were interested to know whether the advantages of symmetric FPV exchange could help LDRs to feel a sense of social presence.

Similar to our study, Kawasaki et al. [17] and Iizuka et al. [12] designed and studied a system with a swapping view (users only see the remote view) and blended view (the scenes from local and remote side were merged in the same frame, similar to our Overlapped View). They found that merging the images from two sides on the same video frame could help users synchronize their movements easily. This inspired our interface design of MyEyes where we include a similar view as part of our design and evaluation.

Social Presence and Body Ownership

Researchers commonly study *social presence*—the feeling of being with someone in the same room—in mediated environments to compare media interfaces and understand user behavior [3]. The Networked Minds Measure [2] breaks down social presence into three sub-categories: Co-Presence, Psychological Involvement and Behavioral Engagement. It is considered to be a valid and reliable measurement for social presence and it has been used in other similar research. For example, JackIn Head was an omnidirectional wearable camera that streamed one-way video to a remote user [16]. The researchers discussed that their one-way FPV system could lead to higher Co-presence and Psychological Involvement for the person who receives FPV image and less social presence for the person who sends FPV image. Different from JackIn Head, our system provides two-way FPV exchange: one can see his/her own view and their partner's view at the same time.

Body ownership is the feeling that a body or body part is one's own [7,31]. Body representation consists of two significant factors, body schema and body image [7]. The body schema is an internal standard built based on people's sensory experience while body image is the visual perception of body appearance [7]. In some circumstances, such as the Rubber Hand Illusion [4], simulating a tactile or movement experience while changing the visual perception of the body can give rise to misunderstanding body ownership (e.g., feeling a rubber hand is my own hand) [26]. This can give rise to fascinating illusions of gender, race and age swapping [21,23,26]. By manipulating the chatting environment, we can utilize the 'rubber hand' illusion and let users feel as if they can 'touch' their partners' hands in an effort to strengthen intimacy. The study of Flex-N-Feel revealed that couples were interested in being able to touch each other remotely and that touch could impact couples' feelings of intimacy [27]. However, it is difficult for people to exchange a 'real' physical touching experience without sophisticated telepresence robots or vibrotactile technologies. As a result, we wanted to investigate whether our prototype could simulate a feeling of physical touch by manipulating one's sense of body ownership when using FPV video streaming.

THE DESIGN OF 'MYEYES'

Compared to traditional video chat systems, FPV video conferencing has typically required sophisticated and expensive equipment with pre-configured and scripted testing environments (e.g., [15,16]). Our design goal was to see if we could create a low-cost design that might be more easily adopted and used by couples in normal everyday situations rather than being restricted to research labs. Couples use video chat in various locations and at different times [25]; thus, portability and ease-of-use are critical factors for system design.

MyEyes is made with cardboard goggles and Android smartphones. We made a video chat app for web browsers with WebRTC. Local and remote video feeds show on the screen in real time. Users can wear the goggles on their head using the head strap and adjust lenses by pulling the 'ears' on the side of the cardboard. Our goal was twofold. First, we wanted to create strong feelings of social presence between partners. Thus, we wanted partners to feel like they were actually in the remote location and seeing through the eyes of one's partner. Second, we wanted to create a sense of body ownership. That is, we wanted partners see each other's body, almost as if it was their own. This might help to create feelings of connection, intimacy, and empathy with one's partner. We investigated what representations of visual information were suitable for creating feelings of social presence and body ownership by designing three interfaces: Split View, Horizontal View and Overlapped View (Figure 2). The first view has not been a part of existing systems, while the latter two views build on prior work. The views can be toggled by researchers remotely.

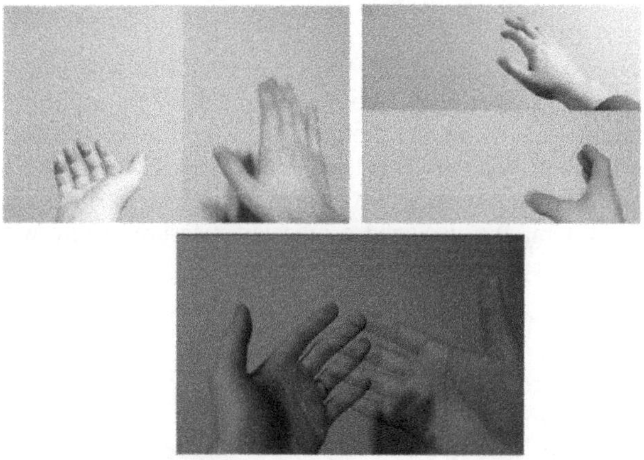

Figure 2. Split (top left), Horizontal (top right) and Overlapped (bottom) views.

Split View

In Split View, users' left eye and right eye see different video feeds: the left eye shows one's local view and the right eye shows the remote user's video feed. This allows users to filter the local or remote view by closing their left or right eye. Leaving both eyes opens allows users to see a merged view containing both video feeds. We designed this view as neuroscientists have found that visual information coming from one's left and right eyes are handled by different hemispheres of the brain but can be processed integrally [6,28]. Split View represents a flexible form to present visual information in FPV that enables users to choose which view to focus on—their own view or their partner's—and allows users to mix local and remote video feeds through brain processing. Yet we do not know if such a viewing mechanism would be an understandable and appropriate method for couples to feel a strong sense of social presence and body ownership with their partner.

Horizontal View

In Horizontal View, the local and remote video feeds are stacked vertically, one on top of the other. This is very similar to Parallel Eyes [15] which has four parallel videos shown at the same time. It is also similar to how Skype or Google+ Hangouts shows multiple video feeds tiled one above each other. Horizontal View is likely most familiar to people and so we wanted to see how this familiarity might merge with the ability to see the remote location through a FPV. Yet it is not clear whether this view can help couples feel a strong degree of social presence and body ownership.

Overlapped View

We merged two video feeds in the same frame in an Overlapped View, akin to the 'blended view' proposed by Iizuka et al [12]. They found this visual coupling style required less effort when people tried to synchronize their movements. We wondered if we could use the advantage of this interface to simulate a 'physical touch' without sophisticated telepresence robot or vibrotactile technologies. The answer could provide a new solution to help LDRs interact, experience and bond with each other.

METHODS

The goal of our study was to evaluate MyEyes to understand what visual representations of FPVs could help couples gain a stronger feeling of social presence and body ownership. We also wondered how couples would like to use a FPV and what activities they would like to share over the system. We designed a repeated measures study with three tasks and an exploratory session.

Figure 3. Two study rooms located on different floors. Each room has a whiteboard, a heart-shape sticker, a chair, a mirror, and an iPad.

Participants

We used online forums, posters, and in-class advertisements for the recruitment of 12 couples (N=24) through snowball sampling. The participants were marked from P1 to P24. The participants all lived in Vancouver, Canada and none were currently in a LDR. Four pairs were married. Most of participants had been in relationship for more than one year except for P21-P22 (four months) and P19-P20 (eight months). Eight couples had experienced long distance relationships before with the length from two months to three years. The age range was from 21–31 (M=25.83, SD=2.94). 11 couples were heterosexual, and one was homosexual. The occupation of the participants included college students, designer, engineers, sales person, and logistics coordinator. Participants signed consent forms prior to the study. Although couples were tested in pairs, they gave responses and were interviewed individually.

Experiment Design

We designed a within subject experiment with the three different interfaces. The independent variable (IV) is the interface style, which has three levels: Split View **(S)**, Horizontal View **(H)** and Overlapped View **(O)**. The dependent variables (DVs) are the responses from a questionnaire concerning social presence and body ownership. Our 11-item questionnaire was derived from previous experiments of other researchers on social presence and body ownership [2–4,8]. We gave each question a label for describing our results (Table 1). There were three rounds of testing for each pair of participants. For each IV, participants used MyEyes for three tasks followed by an exploratory session.

We hypothesized Overlapped View would do better than the other two views for social presence, especially for Co-presence and Behavioral Engagement because it provides an immersive experience and requires little effort for synchronization [12]. We also hypothesized that Overlapped View and Split View would receive higher ratings for "body ownership of partner" and provide a feeling of "I am touching my partner's hand" because these two views mix the perception of one's local hand and remote hand to provide an immersive feeling [26].

Procedure

We first asked participants to fill out a survey to get basic information of their age, occupation, and the relationship with the partner. The survey also includes the questions

Table 1. The 11-item (Q1-Q11) questionnaire used after each round of interface testing. Each question has a code. Q1-Q7 relate to social presence and others relate to body ownership.

Question 1: **Connectedness**	I felt more connected to my partner compared to a normal video chat like Skype when using the interface.
Question 2: **Mutual Awareness**	I felt as if I was in the same room with my partner when using the interface.
Question 3: **Isolation**	I sometimes forgot about my partner and concentrated only on doing my own task when using the interface.
Question 4: **Mutual Understanding**	I could easily understand what my partner was doing when using the interface.
Question 5: **Difficulty in Synchronization**	It was difficult for me to synchronize my movement with my partner when using the interface.
Question 6: **Seeing Through**	I felt like I was looking through my partner's eyes when using the interface
Question 7: **Similarity of Collocated Activities**	I felt like I was with my partner just like doing our daily activities (such as having dinner together, doing exercise together)?
Question 8: **More Hands**	I felt as if I had more than two hands when using the interface.
Question 9: **Hand Transition**	I felt as if my partner's hand changed to my hand when using the interface.
Question 10: **Stroking Partner**	I felt like I was stroking my partner's arm in Task 3 when using the interface.
Question 11: **Being Stroked**	I felt like I was being stroked by my partner when using the interface.

about their previous experience in LDRs, how frequently they use video chat, and if they have had motion sickness in virtual reality before. Then we gave a short demo of MyEyes. Next, we put couples in different rooms located on two different floors of the same building. The setting inside the rooms is shown in Figure 3.

In order to eliminate observer effect, researchers did not stay in either room. We sent all instructions through Skype on an iPad and video recorded participants' movement in the room. A switch on the system's web page was used to change the interface remotely so we did not have to enter the room. Participants then completed the study tasks.

Task 1: Aligning Shape.

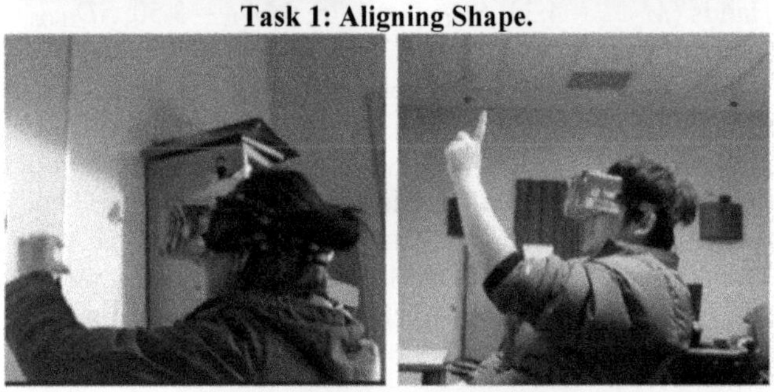

Task 2: Constructing Alphabet.

Task 3: Arm Stroking.

Figure 4. Study tasks performed with each MyEyes view.

Task 1: Aligning Shape - Participants sat on a chair, facing the white board. We asked participants to look at a heart-shape sticker on the whiteboard and make it overlap in each of their views. If they were using the Horizontal View, we asked them to make the shapes vertically aligned instead. This task requires view synchronization for couples. We imagined the heart shape to be a metaphor for the couple's relationship where the task could help participants quickly familiar themselves to using MyEyes at an entry level.

Task 2: Constructing Alphabets - Participants sat on a chair facing the white board. We asked them to draw three different English letters in the air using their hands at the same time as their partner. This task requires the coordination of hand movement and view synchronization. Gestures and body acts are typical and common in video communication [24]. The interaction of bodies provides couples with opportunities to express physical intimacy.

Task 3: Arm Stroking - We asked participants to stretch their left arm in front of their eyes and try to make the arm of both partners overlap in their view. If they were using the Horizontal view, we asked them to make the arms vertically aligned instead. Then we asked them to use their right hand to gently and slowly stroke the left arm of their partner synchronously. We imagined this might resemble a familiar intimate physical act. This task lasted for one minute. This task requires virtual touching, the coordination of hand movements in motion, as well as view synchronization.

Exploratory Session - Following the three structured tasks, participants completed an exploratory session that lasted for ~3 minutes. During the exploratory session, we did not give specific tasks to our participants. The goal of exploratory session was to observe what kind of activities couples might be interested in doing when using MyEyes.

The level of the difficulty for the tasks increased as they went because we assumed FPVs would be relatively new for participants. Seven participants did not have prior experience using head mounted displays or similar technologies. Hence, we setup the tasks to help them smoothly bridge into our experiment. The order of the interfaces was counterbalanced and we had 12 pairs of participants so all orders of testing were tested twice. The three tasks lasted for ~10 minutes in total. After each round of testing (each IV), we asked the participants to fill out the questionnaire. We used a 7-point Likert scale in the questionnaire. After three rounds of testing, we conducted one-on-one interviews that were audio recorded. A complete experiment for a couple took 50-60 minutes.

Individual interviews were conducted after participants completed all three rounds of testing (seeing all IVs). Here we asked them about their reactions to the views, what worked well or was challenging with the views, and how they felt they would use MyEyes in a LDR, if at all.

DATA ANALYSIS

We conducted a one-way repeated measure analysis since our participants were exposed to all three conditions. We applied a Shapiro-Wilk test for testing normality of our data. The results showed that none of the responses for the 11 questions were normally distributed ($ps < .0007$). We hence conducted Friedman tests as the nonparametric measure and Wilcoxon Signed Rank tests as post-hoc analysis comparing the effect of interface type on social presence and body ownership. There were three matched pairs for comparison (Horizontal–Split, Horizontal–Overlapped and Overlapped-Split), so we applied Bonferroni correction, resulting in a significance level at $p < .017$ in post-hoc tests. Statistical tests were run in SPSS.

We used thematic coding to find the main categories and themes in our interview transcripts and video recordings.

We finalized General Experience, Synchronized Activities, and Activities 'In' the Remote Location as the main themes.

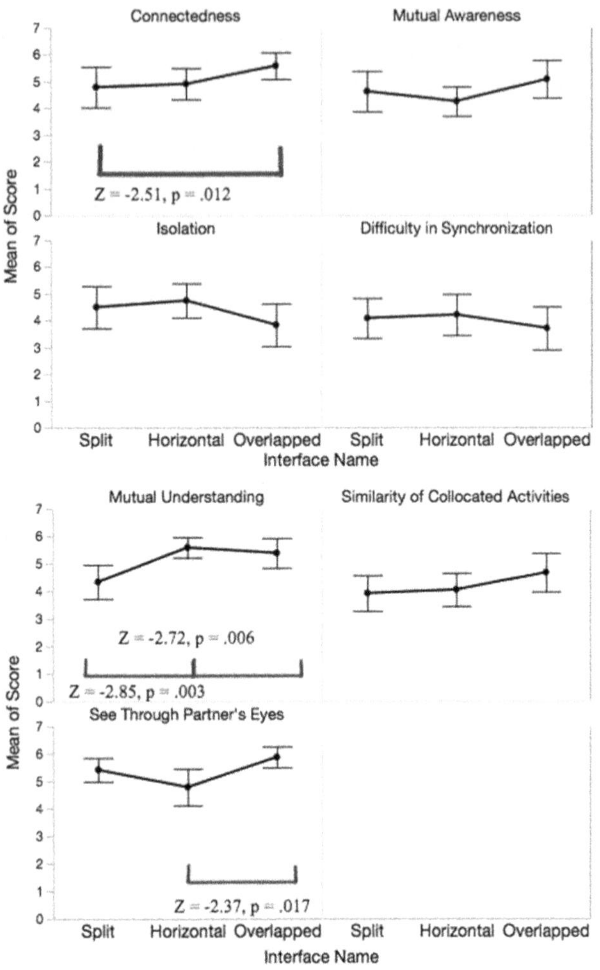

Figure 5. The line chart depicts the mean and confidence interval (*CI* = .95) of score for questions related to social presence across three interfaces. (Q1-Q7)

QUANTITATIVE RESULTS

Social Presence

Questions 1, 2 and 6 in our questionnaire related to Co-presence, questions 4 and 7 related to psychological involvement and questions 3 and 5 related to behavioral engagement. As shown in Figure 5, we calculated the means for every combination with a confidence interval bar. Freidman tests showed that there was a statistically significant difference in Connectedness ($\chi 2(2) = 6.86$, $p = .031$) and Mutual Understanding ($\chi 2(2) = 11.79$, $p = .002$) depending on which interface was tested for couples. Post-hoc tests revealed that Overlapped View had a higher score than Split View for Connectedness ($M_{O\text{-}Q1} = 5.58$, $SD_{O\text{-}Q1} = 1.18$, $M_{S\text{-}Q1} = 4.79$, $SD_{S\text{-}Q1} = 1.79$). Overlapped View also had a stronger feeling of Seeing Through a partner's eyes than Horizontal View ($M_{O\text{-}Q6} = 5.88$, $SD_{O\text{-}Q6} = .90$, $M_{H\text{-}Q6} = 4.79$, $SD_{H\text{-}Q6} = 1.59$). In terms of Mutual Understanding, the Horizontal View had the highest score amongst the three interfaces ($M_{H\text{-}Q4} = 5.58$, $SD_{H\text{-}Q4} = .88$, $M_{O\text{-}Q4} = 5.38$, $SD_{O\text{-}Q4} = 1.28$, $M_{S\text{-}Q4} = 4.33$, $SD_{S\text{-}Q4} = 1.47$), which indicated that Horizontal View was the easiest for couples to understand what their partner was doing. We could draw the conclusion from the Networked Mind Measure that the Overlapped View created a stronger feeling of Co-Presence (More Connectedness and feeling of Seeing Through a Partner's Eyes) whereas Horizontal View had better Psychological Involvement (higher score in Mutual Understanding).

Body Ownership

Our measure of body ownership was derived from questionnaires from researchers studying rubber hand illusions [4,7]. Figure 6 shows that for each question related to body ownership, Horizontal View had the lowest means. Freidman tests showed that there was a significant difference in Hand Transition ($\chi 2(2) = 10.23$, $p = .005$) and More Hands ($\chi 2(2) = 6.57$, $p = .037$). Wilcoxon Signed Rank tests showed that Split View had a higher score than Horizontal View for Hand Transition ($M_{S\text{-}Q9} = 5.08$, $SD_{S\text{-}Q9} = 1.70$, $M_{H\text{-}Q9} = 3.54$, $SD_{H\text{-}Q9} = 1.50$). Overlapped View had a higher score than Horizontal View in feelings of More Hands ($M_{O\text{-}Q8} = 4.33$, $SD_{O\text{-}Q8} = 1.76$, $M_{H\text{-}Q8} = 3.50$, $SD_{H\text{-}Q8} = 1.29$). Moreover, Overlapped View and Split View both had significantly higher scores for feelings of Stroking Partner ($M_{O\text{-}Q10} = 5.00$, $SD_{O\text{-}Q10} = 1.50$, $M_{S\text{-}Q10} = 4.92$, $SD_{S\text{-}Q10} = 1.64$, $M_{H\text{-}Q10} = 3.83$, $SD_{H\text{-}Q10} = 1.47$). In essence, both Overlapped and Split View provided higher body ownership of participants' partner than Horizontal View. The difference between Overlapped and Split View was not significant in the responses related to body ownership.

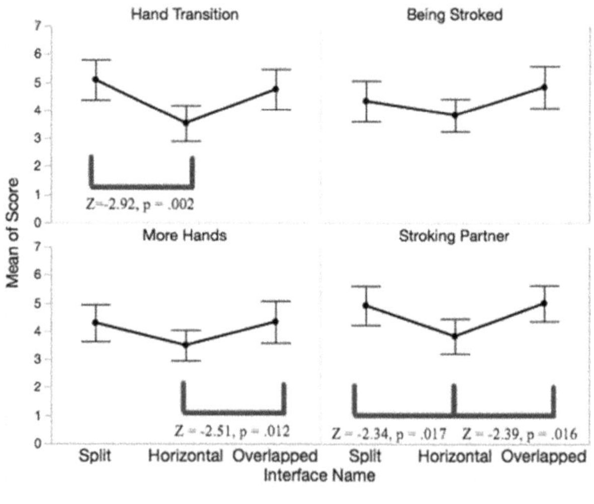

Figure 6. The line chart depicts the mean and confidence interval (*CI* = .95) of score for questions related to body ownership across three interfaces (Q8 – Q11).

Preference

We asked participants to rank their preferences for the three interfaces in the post-experiment interview. The results showed that 75% (18 out of 24) participants said that Overlapped View was their favorite. 62.5% (15 out of 24) participants said Split View was their least preferred. Thus, although Split View provided relatively higher body ownership than Horizontal View, participants did not like it.

Despite relatively lower scores in Mutual Understanding, Overlapped View still dominated couples' preferences. Figure 7 shows the distribution of participants' preference.

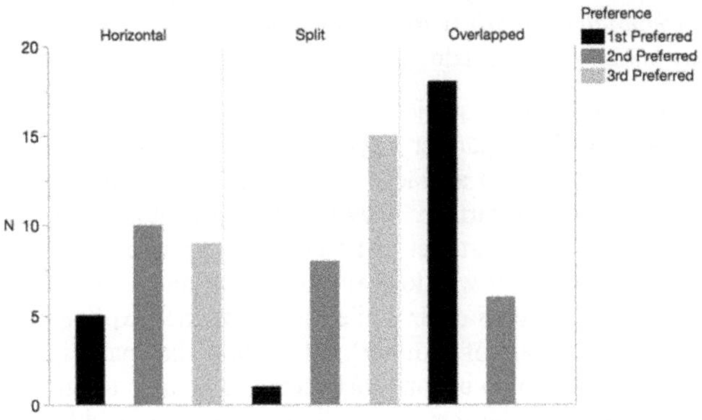

Figure 7. The bar chart showing participants' ranks of preference over three interfaces. ("1st Preferred" means "Favorite"). Overlapped View has zero "3rd Preferred".

QUALITATIVE RESULTS

We now describe our qualitative results from the post-study interviews, conducted individually with participants.

General Experience

Nearly all participants said they enjoyed the experiment and felt connected to their partner when doing the tasks. Descriptions like "cool idea", "novel experience" and "like the interactivity" were said about the system. Being able to see what one's partner was seeing was acknowledged by participants as an intriguing design characteristic. Many felt it was highly intimate.

"I found the idea of 'seeing through partner's eyes' was quite interesting." - P2, Female

"It was a different experience compare to Skype. You can see them in a more personal way. – P7, Male

"Very cool, very intimate!" – P23, Male

The design was not with its flaws though. Several participants said that they felt confused when doing tasks in Split View. This was largely because it was tiring to switch between one's left and right eye in order to see each view separately. Participants said that it was easy to understand what their partner was doing in Horizontal View, similar to our quantitative results.

"The Split View was very disorienting, my brain... I don't know what I want to see." – P23, Male

"The Horizontal View is easier for me. If I don't want to look at her screen I can do that but with the others I can't ignore. The split one made me really dizzy." – P19, Female

A few participants felt motion sickness when they or their partner moved too fast and it was difficult for them to quickly understand what was happening. Some participants mentioned that the network quality and the resolution could also affect their experience if used more regularly.

Synchronized Activities

In our post-experiment interviews, participants told us that one of the main benefits of MyEyes was the ability to synchronize movement and actions with their partner. This led to a sensation that they were actually touching their remote partner's hand because they could both be moving their hands at the same time, and this act was seen in their own view. In these cases, it was important to be able to focus on views from both locations at the *same time.*

"In Overlapped View, like the sensation is on my hand but because it was nicely aligned, I stroked my hand but I saw her hand. It was a good experience." – P5, Male

They told us that synchronization became especially salient in Overlapped View and Split View. This result echoed our quantitative results about their preference of interfaces and higher ratings for Overlapped and Split View in creating feelings of body ownership and social presence.

"And I really felt something like he was touching my hand or I was touching his in Split and Overlapped View. This gave me physical intimacy." – P2, Female

Participants said they wanted to use the synchronization from MyEyes to perform other acts with their partner that they felt traditional video chat systems were not capable of supporting in a rich way. For example, P14 said she would like to use MyEyes to work-out with her boyfriend:

"I would do some activities like push-ups together. My problem was that I was not going low enough. We tried to do push-ups over long distance before. We put the phone, Skype, do the push-up in front of it. Then he can see whether I am going low enough. Like video chat coaching. [But with MyEyes] I can see what he sees then we could coordinate to force to go as low as he does."–P14, Female

The benefits of synchronization were further elucidated during the exploratory sessions. More than half of our participants performed 'playful activities' where each of these acts leveraged the fact that body movements could be synchronized. For example, four couples played 'Rock, Paper, Scissors' with their hands (Figure 8) and one couple played a hand clap game (one tried to clap the other's hand remotely while the other was trying to escape). Other activities included high-fives, finger snaps, clapping, and forming heart shapes in the air with one's hands. For each of these activities, the activity benefitted from partners being able to do their hand movements at the same time.

"We tried a hand clapping game with our hands in overlapped view. The experience was good, I didn't play the same game in the other two interfaces because we can't." - P1, Male

"We played Rock Paper Scissors. And we tried to shape heart forms with our hands. Clapping, basically. The only

thing that I can see from her was her hand. So, do something with the hands. "– P5, Male

Some participants tried to overlap their shoes or feet (Figure 9). This revealed that although hand movements dominated the exploratory sessions, participants were also curious about the ownership of other parts of their body.

P21 and P22 played tic-tac-toe in both Split View and Overlapped View on the white board. They used markers to draw their moves so they were visible in the remote space. As they played, they took turns writing on the board. While their movements of drawing on the board were not synchronized, they had to pay careful attention to synchronize the game of tic-tac-toe on the whiteboard between the rooms or pen markings would be misaligned.

Figure 8. Rock Paper and Scissors in the exploratory session.

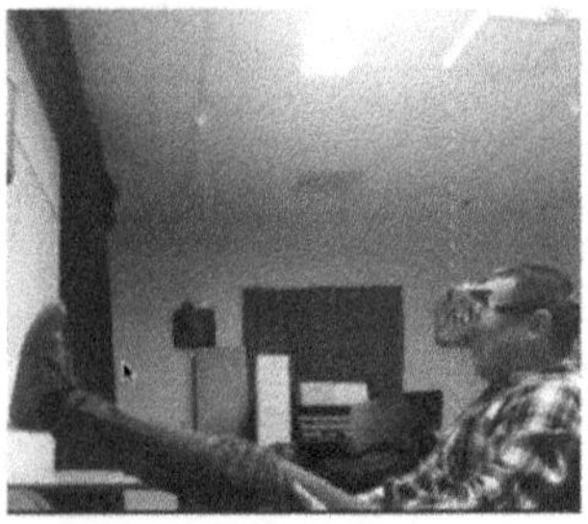

Figure 9. Participant looking at his feet.

Figure 10. Participant trying to pick up a chair at his partner's side.

While most participants agreed that the synchronization could help them feel like they were there together with their partner, P1 felt that sometimes the need to try and synchronize movements took away from the sense of feeling one's partner. That is, the task of trying to synchronize made one concentrate on it, rather than the associated feeling of social presence.

"When we were trying to synchronize our stroking, my efforts were on synchronizing the movement rather than to feel her. I would say when she stroked and I stopped, or when I stroked and she stopped, that feeling is better than do the stroking all together." - P1, Male

Activities 'in' the Remote Location

Participants also found it valuable to engage in activities with MyEyes 'in' the remote location where they focused on the view of the remote location and not their own. In these cases, it was not necessary to have synchronized movements.

"I think the best case is, I can see his surroundings but I can also merge only my hand movement or gestures in the surroundings to mix with his. Sometimes I don't need to see my side." – P2, Female

In the exploratory session, one participant tried to read a book through her partner's eyes. Some couples explored the rooms and showed artifacts (e.g., Lego blocks, snacks and pillows) to their partner. They usually came at a very close distance with the artifact and 'stared' at it while they were explaining what it was to their partner. In many cases, one participant sat on a chair while his/her partner explored the room 'on behalf of him/her'. We found that participants often wanted to go beyond just seeing to be able to interact with objects in the remote location, sometimes held by the remote partner. For example, a participant collaborated with his girlfriend to try to pick up a chair from his girlfriend's hand (Figure 10).

The environment sometimes made it difficult to perform the aforementioned activities. This involved challenges with lighting, the complexity of video backgrounds, and the speed at which one could move (moving too quickly could cause disorientation). Many participants said they could not easily differentiate the video feeds when backgrounds were dark or the background had too many artifacts and colors. This was especially the case for Overlapped view. Yet the ability to easily see only the remote view was essential for performing activities 'in' the remote location.

"When we were in Overlapped view, if my background was dark and her was bright, I can barely see my own view." - P1, Male

"I was by chance facing the white board against the wall and all I could feel was all his seeing. I suddenly felt a larger space in front of me although I was facing a wall." – P16, Female

Participants had workaround for overcoming environmental problems. Here they utilized lighting and different background colors to 'switch' between seeing the local view and remote view. For example, if one looked at a dark area in their room, it was easier to see the remote location because the view of their own space was dark.

"I was facing the white table on purpose." – P2, Female

Some participants talked about the transparency of remote and local images in Overlapped View. They felt it would be beneficial to be able to adjust the transparency of the images or be able to only show a particular part of one's body in the video such as only showing a hand interacting within the remote partner's location.

Participants imagined using MyEyes outside of the study room in other similar ways where one could focus on 'being' in the remote location. For example, P5 talked about his desire to use MyEyes to support virtual visits and share dinner at a restaurant with his remote partner.

"This (MyEyes) has more capability, like you go somewhere new and you wanna share the new place that you are seeing, or in the restaurant, show her the food. It has more capability than the current methods (Skype and Viber)." – P5, Male

Other participants wanted to cook, explore new places, and some even wanted to 'go to' a remote concert.

Privacy and Autonomy

When asked about how they would use MyEyes outside of the study context as a part of real life, two main privacy concerns arose. First, some participants worried that their partner would be able to see more of their environment than they might be comfortable showing because views would not be stationary, akin to a laptop pointing in a single, sometimes carefully selected, direction. Controlling where one looked at in a room could be quite difficult and glances in different directions might be easily seen by one's partner.

"But with this (MyEyes), she could probably see everything of what I am doing. It's not a good feeling that I have no control over what she can see." – P19, Female

"When we separate, if he goes out for a drink and he says he is studying at home, with Skype, he could just quickly pan the phone or ask his friends to go away. But with this, he will have nothing to hide from me. If I ask him to switch to back camera in Skype, he might not be willing to. But with this, by nature he has to switch it on." – P16, Female

Second, participants talked about not wanting to use MyEyes in a public environment where it could be seen by others. Some thought about and wanted to perform acts that might be more private in nature (e.g., touching). For example, two participants felt that it was socially awkward to use the system as part of a research study because touching another person was sometimes quite intimate.

"It's awkward (touching my hand in the study room). But I think it would be less awkward if you are at your own home."- P19, Female

We had posited that having a sense of body ownership over one's remote partner may cause privacy concerns (e.g., 'giving up' one's body to a partner); however, none of our participants brought this up as a concern.

DISCUSSION

In this section, we discuss: (1) The benefits and drawbacks of the three view styles for FPV systems; (2) Design implications for FPV systems; and, (3) Generalizability and limitations of our work.

First Person Views and Physical Intimacy

We measured social presence through the Networked Minds Measure, which breaks down social presence into Co-Presence, Psychological Involvement and Behavioral Engagement. Quantitative results show that the Overlapped View was the most preferred by our participants and it provided the strongest feeling of Co-Presence. However, contrary to our hypotheses, the Psychological Involvement score (feelings of mutual attention, empathy, mutual understanding) for the Overlapped View was not the highest. Yet Overlapped View provided a strong sense of "being with my partner" in a remote setting. This suggests that couples would value future designs that have an Overlapped View; however, such a view could be improved to better enhance feelings of empathy and mutual understanding (Psychological Involvement). The Horizontal View had the highest score for mutual understanding because people could easily distinguish their view from their partner's. This means that it might be possible to increase feelings of empathy in the Overlapped View by giving users clearer indications of which views are local vs. remote when they are merged in the same frame. Of course, this should be tested with further design work.

One of our study goals was to explore whether we could use a rubber hand illusion to create a sense of virtual touching between partners. Our results showed that Overlapped View and Split View *could* provide such a feeling. These results extend the work by psychologists and neuroscientists who have found that gender, age, and race swapping is possible by changing feelings of body ownership through the effect of a rubber hand illusion [8,21,26]. Previous work on FPVs showed that people sometimes lost the feeling of their own body and felt like they 'took on' the body of another person; this was reversed when they bumped into an object in their own location [15]. We extended these results to show that a similar feeling occurs when distance-separated couples are connected in FPVs. Moreover, given that couples in our study liked exploring a variety of different activities with FPVs, our results imply that FPV video systems could be a possible solution for offering physical intimacy between partners by simulating embodiment within a partner's body. Future FPV systems could focus on other intimate acts such as cuddling, kissing, or even sexual activities for LDRs. Our research suggests promise for such explorations.

Shared Activities over Distance

Our qualitative results showed that participants liked to do a range of *synchronized activities* together over distance. These benefitted from time-sensitive body movements and seeing both views. These activities involved very short reaction times and precise collaboration. A clear advantage for FPVs was the ease at which users could synchronize and coordinate their movements. These results show that couples could benefit from FPV systems for supporting such activities. However, future designs will need to pay careful attention to lighting and the complexity of backgrounds within the video feed as these can greatly affect users' experience when mixing perspectives from different sides. Participants also imitated the sound of clapping. It may be valuable to enable more sensing dimensions (e.g., smelling, hearing) in FPV systems.

Participants also found value in their ability to do activities 'in' the remote location where they would interact with objects that they could see in their remote partner's view. These activities did not require synchronization between partners in terms of what they were doing, though one partner would have to maintain a relatively fixed view during interaction. In these activities, users may not always focus on both views in a FPV system and users would find value in mechanisms that could allow them to filter out some or all of their own view. Split View provided such capabilities though the way users controlled it was tiring (closing and opening an eye). Such interactions would likely not be possible for activities that took place over a long period of time. Future work should explore how to augment views such as only displaying portions of a person's body in the remote view, e.g., showing only remote hand gestures in an Overlapped View. This would allow users to perform an action in the remote user's environment while only seeing their relevant body parts. Research could also explore other interaction techniques for toggling the visibility of views without using one's eyes, e.g., a toggle button as part of a smart watch.

Many long distance couples face time zone challenges and busy schedules; thus, it could be hard to find the time to have a shared activity [25]. One could imagine extending systems like MyEyes to provide forms of asynchronous video sharing where one partner might record a video from a first person viewpoint such that another could watch it from that same viewpoint later. This type of system would be difficult to use for the synchronized activities did in our study but could work well for activities focused on being 'in' the remote space and creating a stronger sense of mutual understanding and empathy.

Privacy

Like most video-based communication systems, privacy issues arose. People are not used to having views of remote locations where one can see everything that another person looks at. This caused concern for some participants in case something was shown that they were not comfortable with sharing. Participants said they did not want to show everything from their eyes to their partner and they desired greater control over what they streamed. This suggests being able to toggle one's own stream on or off in an easy way, or being able to blur out or block portions of the shared video view. Of course, it would be challenging to design interactions to regulate such views. A blurred portion of a video view, for example, may also raise more questions (e.g., why is that portion blurred?). Other techniques that replace background content may be more appropriate so that it is not obvious to the remote user that the video feed has been altered. Naturally, there are social ramifications to such designs and the honesty/trust that is found or expected within a LDR relationship.

Participants also said that the environment had an impact on how they would use MyEyes. This indicates that couples might use FPV systems differently in a home environment (more acceptable for intimate acts) than in a public space. In these situations, designers should consider designing for a larger range of activities than participants engaged in.

Limitations

Our research focuses on long distance couples though, for pragmatic reasons (e.g., it would be hard to study remote partners who might be in varied locations around the world), we had to conduct the study with couples who were not currently in a LDR. We tried to mitigate the effects of this difference by having eight pairs of participants who had previously been in a LDR before. Many of them compared the experience of using MyEyes with their previous experience of using Skype-like systems in a LDR. These comparisons were based on their real personal experiences. We did not have a large enough sample to quantitatively compare those who had been in a LDR in the past vs. those who had not; however, the qualitative reactions we received from participants did not reveal any obvious differences. Nonetheless, our research is limited by our participant sample. People presently in a LDR would likely not be able to see each other or have any physical interactions in person, which could cause different results to appear in a study like ours where they may have additional longing to be together. The other limitation in our study is that the age range of our participants fell within a young census (21-31 years old). Future research should explore participants within real LDRs and have diversity in different age groups.

CONCLUSION

MyEyes is a first-person view sharing video chat system for long distance couples. Users are able to exchange their first person view as if they are looking through their partner's eyes. We designed three different interfaces (Split View, Horizontal View and Overlapped View) and ran a mixed method study with 12 pairs of couples. Our quantitative results showed that most couples preferred Overlapped View and it provided the strongest feeling of co-presence. Both Split View and Overlapped View could help couples create a sense of body ownership with their remote partner. The qualitative results showed that couples found MyEyes novel and interesting where intimate experiences can be instantiated. We summarized the different type of activities that partners felt would be beneficial with FPV systems. Here we found that synchronized activities as well as those that allowed one to participate 'in' a remote location was highly valued. Future designs should carefully consider privacy concerns and how views can be controlled by users. Overall, FPV systems can be an intriguing way for couples to stay connected and build a strong relationship when they are geographically separated.

ACKNOWLEDGEMENTS

This research was funded by NSERC. We thank Song Qi and Jim Bizzocchi for their help. We thank all our participants for their time.

REFERENCES

1. Uddipana Baishya and Carman Neustaedter. 2017. In Your Eyes: Anytime, Anywhere Video and Audio Streaming for Couples. In *Proceedings of the 2017 ACM Conference on Computer Supported Cooperative Work and Social Computing* (CSCW '17), 84–97. https://doi.org/10.1145/2998181.2998200
2. Frank Biocca, Chad Harms, and Jenn Gregg. 2001. The networked minds measure of social presence: Pilot test of the factor structure and concurrent validity. In 4th annual international workshop on presence, Philadelphia, PA, 1–9.
3. Frank Biocca, Chad Harms, and Judee K. Burgoon. 2003. Toward a more robust theory and measure of social presence: Review and suggested criteria. *Presence* 12, 5: 456–480.
4. Matthew Botvinick and Jonathan Cohen. 1998. Rubber hands "feel" touch that eyes see. *Nature* 391, 6669: 756–756. https://doi.org/10.1038/35784
5. Philo Tan Chua, R. Crivella, B. Daly, Ning Hu, R. Schaaf, D. Ventura, T. Camill, J. Hodgins, and R. Pausch. 2003. Training for physical tasks in virtual environments: Tai Chi. In *IEEE Virtual Reality, 2003. Proceedings.*, 87–94. https://doi.org/10.1109/VR.2003.1191125
6. Michael C. Corballis. 1995. Visual integration in the split brain. *Neuropsychologia* 33, 8: 937–959. https://doi.org/10.1016/0028-3932(95)00032-X
7. Marcello Costantini and Patrick Haggard. 2007. The rubber hand illusion: Sensitivity and reference frame for body ownership. *Consciousness and Cognition* 16, 2: 229–240. https://doi.org/10.1016/j.concog.2007.01.001
8. H. Henrik Ehrsson, Nicholas P. Holmes, and Richard E. Passingham. 2005. Touching a Rubber Hand: Feeling of Body Ownership Is Associated with Activity in Multisensory Brain Areas. *Journal of Neuroscience* 25, 45: 10564–10573. https://doi.org/10.1523/JNEUROSCI.0800-05.2005
9. Daniel Gooch and Leon Watts. 2011. A Design Framework for Mediated Personal Relationship Devices. In *Proceedings of the 25th BCS Conference on Human-Computer Interaction* (BCS-HCI '11), 237–242. Retrieved January 16, 2017 from http://dl.acm.org/citation.cfm?id=2305316.2305360
10. Daniel Gooch and Leon Watts. 2012. YourGloves, Hothands and Hotmits: Devices to Hold Hands at a Distance. In *Proceedings of the 25th Annual ACM Symposium on User Interface Software and Technology* (UIST '12), 157–166. https://doi.org/10.1145/2380116.2380138
11. Hilary Hutchinson, Wendy Mackay, Bo Westerlund, Benjamin B. Bederson, Allison Druin, Catherine Plaisant, Michel Beaudouin-Lafon, Stéphane Conversy, Helen Evans, Heiko Hansen, Nicolas Roussel, and Björn Eiderbäck. 2003. Technology Probes: Inspiring Design for and with Families. In *Proceedings of the SIGCHI Conference on Human Factors in Computing Systems* (CHI '03), 17–24. https://doi.org/10.1145/642611.642616
12. Hiroyuki Iizuka, Daisuke Kondo, Hiroki Kawasaki, Hideyuki Ando, and Taro Maeda. 2011. Coordinated Behavior Between Visually Coupled Dyads. In *Proceedings of the 2Nd Augmented Human International Conference* (AH '11), 23:1–23:4. https://doi.org/10.1145/1959826.1959849
13. Kori Inkpen, Brett Taylor, Sasa Junuzovic, John Tang, and Gina Venolia. 2013. Experiences2Go: Sharing Kids' Activities Outside the Home with Remote Family Members. In *Proceedings of the 2013 Conference on Computer Supported Cooperative Work* (CSCW '13), 1329–1340. https://doi.org/10.1145/2441776.2441926
14. Yeong Rae Joi, Beom Taek Jeong, Jin Hwang Kim, Ki Hyuk Park, Taehyun Lee, and Jun Dong Cho. 2015. WearLove: Affective Communication via Wearable Device with Gamification. In *Proceedings of the 2015 Annual Symposium on Computer-Human Interaction in Play* (CHI PLAY '15), 559–564. https://doi.org/10.1145/2793107.2810337
15. Shunichi Kasahara, Mitsuhito Ando, Kiyoshi Suganuma, and Jun Rekimoto. 2016. Parallel Eyes: Exploring Human Capability and Behaviors with Paralleled First Person View Sharing. In *Proceedings of the 2016 CHI Conference on Human Factors in Computing Systems* (CHI '16), 1561–1572. https://doi.org/10.1145/2858036.2858495
16. Shunichi Kasahara and Jun Rekimoto. 2015. JackIn Head: Immersive Visual Telepresence System with Omnidirectional Wearable Camera for Remote Collaboration. In *Proceedings of the 21st ACM Symposium on Virtual Reality Software and Technology* (VRST '15), 217–225. https://doi.org/10.1145/2821592.2821608
17. H. Kawasaki, H. Iizuka, S. Okamoto, H. Ando, and T. Maeda. 2010. Collaboration and skill transmission by first-person perspective view sharing system. In *19th International Symposium in Robot and Human Interactive Communication*, 125–131. https://doi.org/10.1109/ROMAN.2010.5598668
18. Jina Kim, Young-Woo Park, and Tek-Jin Nam. 2015. BreathingFrame: An Inflatable Frame for Remote Breath Signal Sharing. In *Proceedings of the Ninth International Conference on Tangible, Embedded, and*

Embodied Interaction (TEI '15), 109–112. https://doi.org/10.1145/2677199.2680606

19. Hideaki Kuzuoka. 1992. Spatial Workspace Collaboration: A SharedView Video Support System for Remote Collaboration Capability. In *Proceedings of the SIGCHI Conference on Human Factors in Computing Systems* (CHI '92), 533–540. https://doi.org/10.1145/142750.142980
20. Hideaki Kuzuoka, Toshio Kosuge, and Masatomo Tanaka. 1994. GestureCam: A Video Communication System for Sympathetic Remote Collaboration. In *Proceedings of the 1994 ACM Conference on Computer Supported Cooperative Work* (CSCW '94), 35–43. https://doi.org/10.1145/192844.192866
21. Lara Maister, Mel Slater, Maria V. Sanchez-Vives, and Manos Tsakiris. 2015. Changing bodies changes minds: owning another body affects social cognition. *Trends in Cognitive Sciences* 19, 1: 6–12. https://doi.org/10.1016/j.tics.2014.11.001
22. Valerie Manusov. 2006. Maintaining long-distance and cross-residential relationships - by Laura Stafford. *Journal of Communication* 56, 3: 630–631. https://doi.org/10.1111/j.1460-2466.2006.00307.x
23. Antonella Maselli and Mel Slater. 2013. The building blocks of the full body ownership illusion. *Frontiers in Human Neuroscience* 7: 83. https://doi.org/10.3389/fnhum.2013.00083
24. Michael Massimi and Carman Neustaedter. 2014. Moving from Talking Heads to Newlyweds: Exploring Video Chat Use During Major Life Events. In *Proceedings of the 2014 Conference on Designing Interactive Systems* (DIS '14), 43–52. https://doi.org/10.1145/2598510.2598570
25. Carman Neustaedter and Saul Greenberg. 2012. Intimacy in Long-distance Relationships over Video Chat. In *Proceedings of the SIGCHI Conference on Human Factors in Computing Systems* (CHI '12), 753–762. https://doi.org/10.1145/2207676.2207785
26. Valeria I. Petkova and H. Henrik Ehrsson. 2008. If I Were You: Perceptual Illusion of Body Swapping. *PLoS ONE* 3, 12: e3832. https://doi.org/10.1371/journal.pone.0003832
27. Samarth Singhal, Carman Neustaedter, Yee Loong Ooi, Alissa N. Antle, and Brendan Matkin. 2017. Flex-N-Feel: The Design and Evaluation of Emotive Gloves for Couples to Support Touch Over Distance. In *Proceedings of the 2017 ACM Conference on Computer Supported Cooperative Work and Social Computing* (CSCW '17), 98–110. https://doi.org/10.1145/2998181.2998247
28. Charles Spence, Alan Kingstone, David I. Shore, and Michael S. Gazzaniga. 2016. Representation of Visuotactile Space in the Split Brain. *Psychological Science*. Retrieved December 16, 2016 from http://journals.sagepub.com/doi/abs/10.1111/1467-9280.00316
29. Laura Stafford and Daniel J. Canary. 1991. Maintenance Strategies and Romantic Relationship Type, Gender and Relational Characteristics. *Journal of Social and Personal Relationships* 8, 2: 217–242. https://doi.org/10.1177/0265407591082004
30. Laura Stafford, Andy J. Merolla, and Janessa D. Castle. 2006. When long-distance dating partners become geographically close. *Journal of Social and Personal Relationships* 23, 6: 901–919. https://doi.org/10.1177/0265407506070472
31. Manos Tsakiris. 2010. My body in the brain: A neurocognitive model of body-ownership. *Neuropsychologia* 48, 3: 703–712. https://doi.org/10.1016/j.neuropsychologia.2009.09.034

Design Techniques for Exploring Automotive Interaction in the Drive towards Automation

Ingrid Pettersson
Chalmers University & Volvo Car Group
Gothenburg, Sweden
ingrid.pettersson@chalmers.se

Figure 1. It seems counterintuitive, but automation in vehicles actually creates greater demand for interaction design and human-centered development.

ABSTRACT
Automotive interaction design is undergoing a major shift due to the disruptive forces of automation and information technology. This paper reviews current challenges in human vehicle interaction design and argues that these challenges demand that interaction become a primary consideration in designing automotive user experiences. We survey exploratory interaction design techniques for human vehicle interactions, showing examples from our research of each technique in action. The techniques are enactments, contextual inquiry, scale scenarios, Wizard of Oz, field experiments and video and animation prototyping. We reflect upon our experiences with these methods, and discuss as yet unmet needs in interaction design for the road ahead.

Author Keywords
Vehicle interaction design; autonomous vehicles; design method

ACM Classification Keywords
H.5.m. Information Interfaces and Presentation (e.g. HCI): Miscellaneous

INTRODUCTION
In recent years, new opportunities for automotive human machine interaction have been emerging. For instance, the development of technology for autonomous driving and active safety creates imperative challenges to the vehicle interaction as the relation between human and system fundamentally changes when the system gain agency [21, 41]. Also, the revolution in consumer electronics has fundamentally changed the users' expectations of interactions with in-car technology [60], especially for younger drivers [59]. Furthermore, the number of interactive services with a foothold in the car, such as in-car delivery, connected music services, conversational agents, or phone applications for remote car access, are increasing the complexity of vehicle interaction design.

DIS 2017, June 10-14, 2017, Edinburgh, United Kingdom

DOI: http://dx.doi.org/10.1145/3064663.3064666

The net effect of these changes is that our interactions with and in vehicles is fundamentally evolving. Previously, the vehicle was an extension of our selves, a mechanical apparatus which we continuously controlled to travel from one place to another. Now, more and more, the vehicle is becoming a separate entity with which we negotiate and share control. Furthermore, interactions in the vehicle are increasingly multifaceted, with the driver focused not only on the task of driving, but also on interactions with infotainment systems, brought-in devices, external services and, not least, on social interactions with others and the car itself [60, 24, 13].

As a result, the manner in which we design the interaction of the vehicle must evolve to adapt to the age of automation. In this complex environment, allowing the human-vehicle interaction to be the unplanned result of these disparate interfaces and services is unlikely to yield a coherent user experience. Even traditional interface design can fall short, because traditional designers have limited understandings of all of the cultures and social norms the vehicle will operate in. By starting automotive design with interaction as the central motivating consideration, we can better meet the specific challenges of interaction between human and vehicle in the age of automation.

In this paper, we discuss emerging trends in human-vehicle interaction, and present an interaction-centric approach towards designing automotive user experiences. We then move to argue that these forces that are moving to make interaction central in the automotive environment are also at work in products at large, and we should thus explicitly consider how interaction design practices address future trends in general.

BACKGROUND

While assessing trends in the automotive interaction community and the automotive industry as a whole in 2016, Kun, Boll and Schmidt noted a marked turn towards research interest in automation and autonomous driving, as well as advanced driver assistance systems [41]. In this new age, the user experience of interacting with in-vehicle devices is gaining prominence, and that means user experience and interaction design practice is gaining ground. They outlined four areas as research challenges to the larger community–Safety in the Age of Automation, Transforming Vehicles into Places of Productivity and Play, the Changing Meaning of Driving and Mobility, and Privacy and Security. Each one of these is associated with need for extensive reconsideration of what our experience with cars will be.

This transformation, of course, takes place amidst larger changes in the technology and interaction landscape. We have gone from an age where Gates' vision to have "a computer on every desktop" seemed ambitious to one where ubiquitous and multi-device landscapes are prevalent in the home [34] and workplace [69]. For those in the auto industry, the advent of smart phones and mobile tablet computers creates potential safety issues as people use these devices when they should be driving [77]. Even when automation enables people to drive less, the driver's hybrid experience with in-vehicle and brought-in technologies will be an important design area for the overall automotive experience [28].

These changes in the technology landscape also influence changes in the user landscape for automotive interaction designers. The runaway success of ubiquitous smart phone and tablet computers has dramatically changed the predominant interaction paradigms that users bring to their vehicles. In some cases, automotive companies can leverage user familiarity with such devices to make their interfaces easier to use. For examples, the Tesla Model S created a stir by using a 17" touchscreen module for its center console, a clear reference to tablet computing interfaces [66], and the recent Volvo Concept 26 focused solely on the in-car experience by exhibiting the concept without an exterior Apple and Google are developing CarPlay [31] and Android Auto [32] to make the bridge between brought-in devices and the car more explicit. However, while most automotive Original Equipment Manufacturers (OEMs) are making efforts to accommodate user's devices, they are also leery of passing over control of the automotive user experience to third parties; as Kun et al note [41], "the user experience of interacting with in-vehicle devices is gaining prominence, as vehicle manufactures realize its value in differentiating brands."

Interaction Design in Vehicles

In this pivotal moment, then, it is good to reflect on the role of interaction design in defining the intended use as well as roles and dynamics between humans and systems. It is particularly useful to consider context-specific aspects of interaction design in automobiles, to account for adaptations to general interaction design techniques that automotive interaction designers must create.

Interaction, not interfaces

Interaction design is distinct from interface design in that it, in the words of Michel Beaudouin-Lafon, "combines an understanding of the context of use with attention to the details of interaction, supported by a robust interaction architecture" [5]. Interaction in its nature is dynamic, both in terms of reactions, communication and actions between human and system.

In the car, the interaction between vehicle and the driver frames expectations, encourages or discourages actions, evokes emotional responses, triggers behaviors and eventually shapes adoption. It is central to the user experience, and forms a foundation for safe mobility.Interaction design, as a practice, helps to shape what could be an incoherent user experience into a well-crafted interactions, founded on theoretical and empirical knowledge, where self-explanatory and considerate organization and communication between vehicle and user is key.

Whole body experience

The car experience is an embodied experience; "people respond to the thrum of the engine, the smell of the interior, the feel of the car seat" [19] and Sheller [72] argues that the embodied emotional responses to driving are central to understanding the place of the car within different car cultures. Interaction design in vehicles is somaesthetic too–it engages the whole body [51]. For example, we are able to use feet for regulating speed, hands to control road position and now voice for commanding actions on the infotainment system. Input methods such as gesture recognition have been a recent research topic in human vehicle interaction [48, 55], adding one more technology to the mutli-modal opportunities of in-vehicle interaction [54].

Personal spaces

While the advent of car sharing might be changing the ownership model of vehicles, for now, the car is often an secluded and personal context where we are shielded from the outer world. Studies around driving cultures and in-car activity have explored the car as a personal space [47, 64]. Lyons and Urry [47] describe time in the car as a place not only for traveling, but for dwelling and inhabiting, thus constructing a home-like environment. The home-like environment is unlike public transport, and by being able to effect sound-scape, passengers, secondary activities etc., the atmosphere of the drive can be tailored to ones liking. As a secluded place the car is often valued as a good context for coaching, interviewing, etc. [49] as well as focused time with family members [24].

Long term interactions

Another interesting aspect of automotive interactions is that people have long-term relationships with their vehicles. In the US, the average age of cars on the road is 11.5 years [9]. People's experiences with car have been found to evolve overtime (see for example [81, 60]); users often form strong emotional attachments to their cars and carry strong mental models of cars and driving [72, 64]. Designing for human vehicle interaction means dealing with the tension between people's thoughts and feelings about cars with the rapid technological changes they are undergoing.

Changing roles of the car

With full and partial automation, the relationship between user and vehicle is transformed:the human is no longer always in control. Driving becomes a partnership with shared control [73]. Flemisch, et al. use the "H-metaphor" to capture shared control issues, likening the car and the driver to a horse and rider; the horse is able to walk and make decisions on its own, but the rider can exert more or less control based on whether the interaction is tightly or loosely coupled. [20] Ju proposes an alternate "H-metaphor" comparing interaction with automation to driving with her husband; she expects to have input on driving even if her husband is fully capable of driving on his own [35]. Meanwhile, many who are developing automation technologies have frame the vehicle as a robot [80], which suggests a less social and more independent and mechanical relationship. These various metaphors reflect many different possible roles, meanings and futures that could be addressed in future automotive interaction designs.

Adapting to different cultures

While the physical designs of automobiles have always been adapted to regional markets, the automotive OEMs have been pushing increasingly to develop common platforms across markets. [65] Many might assume that automated vehicles will dictate driving norms where they are deployed, but the experience from flight deck automation indicates instead that automation has to take into account differences in how people from different regions will interact with the automation. [74] Understanding these variations is important for interaction design of automation.

Existing surveys of automotive design techniques

While there are many works in interaction design that address how interaction designers can better understand the existing use and context of the car (see for example [52, 7]), as well as quantifiable evaluation of in-vehicle experience and issues related to driver assessment and distraction (see for example [39, 50, 58, 42, 45]), there is a wider gap in aiding designers when exploring and creating the future situations in vehicles, especially considering the increasing automation.

We believe that both the advent of automation and the multiplying of devices will make the future of automotive interaction quite different than what we are familiar with today, and so techniques used to explore future interactions are distinct from methods that designers might use to refine existing interfaces. We direct our focus to techniques that can lead to designs suited for facing future challenges. These address the specific needs we have discovered in design human vehicle interaction in the age of automation, but this collection of methods is also increasingly relevant to other domains facing similar developments.

DESIGN TECHNIQUES FOR HUMAN VEHICLE INTERACTION

We have been using a variety of techniques motivated by the unique opportunities of the human vehicle interaction. They are all in connection to the car context, but complement each other in exploring current situations, imagining new scenarios and exploring interaction ideas. The elements of flexibility and contingency of user/system communication have been especially important considering the car's increased interactive capabilities and agency to act independently. *Contingency* is a term borrowed from psychology and linguistics: one's utterances are semantically contingent if they continue topics introduced by the conversational partner's preceding utterances. [11, 76]

Enactment

Enactment of use of future technology presents a way to explore interactions of non-existing technology, giving a low-fidelity means for probing into future use [4, 56]. When the boundaries of artifacts are absent, enactment gives the possibility to be flexible and contingent to user and system actions and reactions. By role play, i.e. gesturing and expressing the actions of human and system, the technique can be used for rapidly showcasing ideas, co-jointly improvising new ideas [4] and early design evaluation [15]. The roots of enactment stem from participatory design practices, aimed at eliciting ideas and information from users in a system development setting [10, 68].

During enactments with simple, non-technical materials, the flow of contingent interactions can be followed and inquiries can go move in unexpected directions. This is in contrast to interactive prototypes, where the specific technologies can constrain the directions of the interaction. In a study exploring the differences between generative techniques for autonomous vehicle design, enactment vs. drawing + collaging, enactment contributed to a more grounded experience in the study participants own practices and situations connected to mobility [61]. Enactment has also been employed in vehicle settings for early evaluation of a interactive in-vehicle family games [15]

Figure 2. Enactment in a study of autonomous car interaction. As the scenario called for human control, the driver imagined the steering wheel smoothly moving towards his hands, and his reclined seat stretching towards an upright seating position.

and used to explore whole-body interactions [79]. Furthermore, enactment can also be used to explore interactions with groups of users, investigating, for example, the co-experience of vehicle systems [62]. Overall, enactments of future technology use requires little development time or technology and provide a rapid means for considering multi-sensory and full-body interactions.

Vignette: Setting the Stage for Autonomous Driving

Some of our studies used enactment as a way of addressing the interactions with autonomous vehicles early in the design process and with the input from potential users, probing into their expectations, emotions and reactions [53, 61]. One of the studies took place in an university parking lot, where people walking by, both solitary and in groups, were welcome to engage in the activity of enacting a commute to their next destination in a pretend autonomous car (see Figure 2) [61]. We used a basic representation of a car with four chairs and a drawn outline of the body as the study context.

The participants received a short introduction on the purpose of the study and on autonomous cars. Using a semi-structured interview, the participants were first asked about their current daily commute trips, then encouraged to envision future autonomous driving experiences, and asked to provide information regarding how their time would be spent during this future experience. We asked about what emotions this experience might bring, what value autonomous cars may have and how they expected the design of the car to change. We also used scenarios to elicit potential interaction models from users. One such scenario how drivers would take back control from partially autonomous cars at the end of the drive. Complementing enactments of future use, participants were also encouraged to draw future design elements, contributing to richer reflections and discussions.

From enactment sessions like this one, we have been able to access and ideate around factors for trust and comfort, as well as ideas for new features, gestures and movement in the car. We have continued our explorations, including a variety of artifacts, such as seats, steering wheels, and household items, building upon previous work suggesting that interacting with simple object early in the design phase can improve the design process [18, 43].

Contextual Inquiry

Understanding interactions situated in the specific context of driving is something that we consider extremely important for interaction design research. Techniques for understanding technology in the use date back to the 1980s when contextual factors of technology use were observed and given importance to [78]. The framework presented by Beyer and Holzblatt's Contextual Design [7] proves relevant for being able to observe users behaviors while also being able to interview them in the moment of action. Observing and interviewing in context rather than in the lab allows designers more tacit knowledge of the scenario. In vehicle design, with its need for globally successful products, it has been used as a tool to help designers understand specific driving situations and empathize with users [22]. Contextual inquiry can be used in combination with complimentary techniques such as user experience curves [40] and photo diaries for addressing the longitudinal aspects of the in-vehicle user experience [60].

In addition to using the vehicle space as a place for exploring current behaviors and experiences, it can also be used to probe into future situations and use of potential technologies. Examining naturalness of car interiors, Ramm et al emphasize the importance of subjective impressions of vehicles, especially as vehicles become more like agents. [63] They interviewed fifteen drivers in parked vehicles, surfacing insights about how individuals view the car as an agentic entity, and also how the driver-car-passenger relationship changes when autonomous driving is introduced. Meschtscherjakov [52] provided an overview of methods for conducting qualitative research in cars and suggested that contextual inquiry be used for the main driver space, which is similar to the methodology employed here.

Vignette: Contextual Interviews of Behaviors in Autonomous Vehicles

Contextual inquiry is often used to capture people in their native habitats, however, it can also be used to help people envision future settings. To help understand

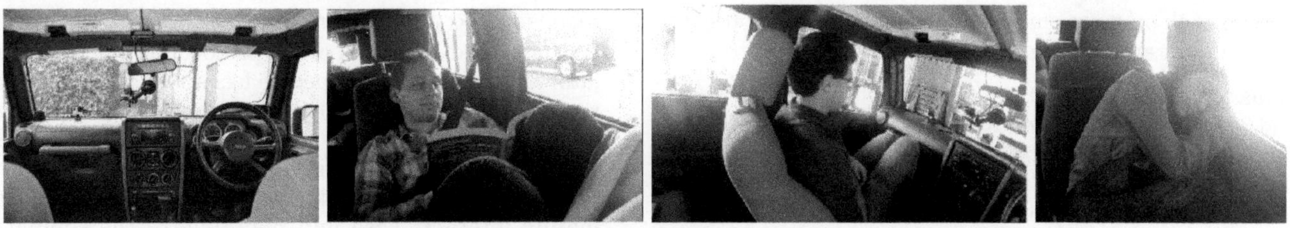

Figure 3. Contextual Inquiry of activities ad behaviors in autonomous cars.

how people might sit or orient themselves in automated vehicles, researchers conducted interviews and asked participants to imagine riding in an autonomous vehicle [33]. These interviews were in a right-hand drive Jeep Cherokee parked safely but with the engine running. This had the effect of immersing the participant in what feels like the drivers seat, but without the usual operator controls; at the same time, they are acting as a passenger, in what is not usually a passenger's seat. The capabilities of automation were left to the participant to define.

The study began with visualization and think-aloud exercise, where the experimenter guided the participants through an imaginary drive asked participants to close their eyes and verbalize their thoughts on being the driver in the car. Following the visualization exercise, participants were shown how to change and set the adjustable components of the seat, and were asked to describe and demonstrate the physical and social activities that they engage in as a passenger in non-autonomous cars today. They were then asked to demonstrate how they might engage in activities if this vehicle were autonomous. To encourage imagination and recall, participants were given props, like pillows, phones, tablets and computers. Hence, the contextual inquiry was used for prospective research, rather than capturing the existing context.

This investigation revealed that automation affords new social dynamics for passengers, with the ability to adjust seating to face away from or toward one another. This suggests that designers should look beyond ergonomic and safety considerations to develop ways to mitigate these possibly awkward and socially uncomfortable situations.

Scale scenarios

Designing for human vehicle interaction of autonomous vehicles is not an issue limited to the human machine interaction taking place in the vehicle interior. New challenges for on-road communication require consideration of the traffic scene as a whole, also addressing the systems communication with pedestrians, bicyclists, other vehicles etc. This requires making these situations tangible to researchers, designers as well as users in problem explorations, design ideation and evaluation. 3-D mock-ups of both system and scenarios scenarios of use have been employed as a participatory design technique [68, 10] to explore future interactions, and employed to uncover complex, multi-user interactions. It has for example been used in ship interaction design [57] and hospital design [2]. Bligård et al [8] found that using a small-scale overview of complex use scenarios can help in providing scenario overview, elicit in-depth group discussions, and create possibilities for rapid adjustments and rearrangements in a design process. To our knowledge, the technique has been less used for automotive interaction design, but we see a number of advantages for employing these approaches in the palette of techniques, as it give access to an helicopter view of different users behaviors and needs for information.

Vignette: Puppeting Pedestrian Car Interactions

One focus for us is to think about how autonomous vehicles can predict pedestrian trajectory to avoid collision. Traditional computer science approaches usually model the way that people walk on the road without considering the interaction between the car and the pedestrian [83], and yet we know from our own pedestrian experiences on the street that we try to establish communication and negotiate with drivers. To analyze and understand observations from our ethnographic studies, we often re-enact scenarios to enable discussion and analysis of the actions tactics, particularly in less-typical situations (see Figure 1, including a scale scenario).

In one of our sessions, we worked with researchers who work in human-robot interaction and human-vehicle interaction. We reviewed highlight video clips from our studies that demonstrated both common and most interesting patterns of behavior we observed, such as: when two parties are going to intersect in their trajectories, the faster-approaching party will likely make an adjustment further in advance to that intersecting point. We asked each group to improvise scenarios following our conditions for a variety of interactions. Videotaping from directly above each station, we captured the movements and gestures that the participants made with their objects on the diagram, as well as anything they said that added to the scenario.

We ran through different interaction conditions, which included oncoming interaction in the normal direction of travel, an oncoming interaction against the normal direction of travel, and a perpendicular interaction. After completing those structured but improvised scenarios, we asked the participants come up with their own condition and design a scenario from that condition. This opportunity led to many creative interactions where the robots took on more emotive personalities and expressive, human and animal behaviors.

This technique helped to move from ethnographic observations about current conditions to ways that future cars and robots might negotiate shared spaces safely. The grounding of scenarios in existing behavior and realistic road conditions made the exploration of novel features, interaction patterns and behaviors more productive.

Wizard of Oz

Wizard of Oz (WoZ) is a technique for prototyping and experimenting dynamically with a system's performance that uses a human in the design loop. It was originally developed by HCI researchers in the area of speech and natural language interfaces [38] as a means to understand how to design systems before the underlying speech recognition or response generation systems were mature.

We often involve users in a real-time collaborative design exploration using Wizard of Oz techniques. The incorporation of the human-in-the-loop allows for improvisation and spontaneous selection of different alternatives. It can inform system engineering, for example by identifying which features and gestures need to be recognized by a computer vision system [29], or which sensors best predict contextual needs [30]. It can also be used with built-in evaluation systems so as to automatically reach design outcomes.

The Wizard of Oz technique is commonly used in the automotive research community for the design and study of automotive user interfaces. It has been used by the designers of Virtual Intelligent Co-Driver (VICO) to evaluate user expectations [23], by developers of speech-based in-car entertainment systems, and by researchers at TU Munich [71]. This technique has also been used by researchers developing gesture- based interfaces for secondary tasks in a car environment [1], by researchers looking at different automotive interface input modalities [82] [70] and by researchers at Volkswagon ERL to examine speech in cars [44].

Unlike Wizard of Oz techniques employed in experimental studies, when it is applied to early stage interaction design exploration, the user of the system is often aware of the Wizard and interacts under a shared suspension of disbelief rather than under deception. For example, Lundgren et al. recently used this technique to autonomous vehicle functionality to observe emergent behaviors [46].

One way that we use Wizard of Oz is to find out how people feel about the operation of a car or different features of a car in real-time. This allows us to get reactions that are not colored by subsequent events in the course of driving or by memory effects. We can use a human "wizard" to act as the voice of the car, and engage drivers in natural language dialogue to engage in conversation and solicit feedback.

Vignette: Talking to the Car

We have used a Wizard of Oz protocol in a driving simulator to understand how people feel about transitions into and out of automated driving modes[53]. For this type of study we actually use two Wizards behind the screen: The Interaction Wizard is tasked with observing and interacting with the participant, while the Driving Wizard mainly interacts with and manipulates the simulation environment. The wizards can both hear the participant through the use of a small microphone hidden within the car. The wizards are also able to observe the participants and their context in real-time via video.

To understand how the automated vehicle should interact, we conducted a design research study inside the driving simulator and invited interaction and interface design experts to act as the participants. As these were design improvisation sessions, the participants were given more freedom to interact as they wanted. They were not provided with any instructional paradigms about the car and were allowed to make requests / ask questions at any time. Wizards interacted in real-time with the participant through the car's interface throughout the whole course.

The car would offer to take over driving at certain points throughout the course, and it would also request the participant to take over control at other times. The protocol around the pushing and pulling of information between the participant and the vehicle was intended to follow natural conversation norms, so this aspect of the study was not controlled. The wizards would be able to either freely offer explanations for the car's automated driving (pushing information to the driver), or respond to queries about the car's automated driving behavior (pulling of information by the driver). After the study, participants were interviewed to gather additional insights.

While everyone knows that transitions from autonomous to manual mode can be problematic, our use of this set up let us discover that participants found that transitions from manual and automated driving modes to also be filled with uncertainty. Even when the car used the phrase "I have control now," with a visual indicator on the dashboard changing afterwards, participants were still uncertain when they should actually relinquish control. After the transition, many of the participants still asked, "Are you driving the car now?" and, "Can I let go of the steering wheel now?" For more results from these studies please see [75, 53]

Field Experiments

Field experiments take the interactions from the lab or the design studio into the real-world setting in order to understand the impacts of technology [12]. In the automotive domain, naturalistic driving studies on real roads as opposed to labs and test tracks have been used for uncovering behaviors (see for example the well-known "100-car study" [16]) and evaluating systems (see for example [6]). Unlike other techniques such as enactment

Figure 4. People enjoyed giving the car feedback and encouragement in the WoZ set-up.

and video prototyping, which suspend reality, in field experiments we are often trying to leverage the naturalism, authenticity and spontaneous unplanned events offered by the real world. Study participants can go about their daily business as usual, and everyday experiences can be accessed. In some ways, this type of experiment is the best way to get at experiences where the particular phenomena of the car's private space, or the natural behavior of drivers and other road users on the road. Field experiments enable access to differing contexts of use, making it a suitable technique for accessing cultural aspects of human vehicle interactions.

To adapt the naturalism of the field to the novel possibilities introduced by future technologies and designs, mixes of Wizard of Oz and naturalistic field techniques can be performed [26].

Vignette: Exploring Pedestrian and Driver Need for Information from Autonomous Cars

One of our studies investigated the social situations emerging from autonomous cars and pedestrians co-existing on the road in a workshop format. [62] To explore situations of interaction between pedestrians and autonomous cars, we used a WoZ car setup with a right-hand drive vehicle (in a left-hand drive environment) as developed by Habibovic et al. [26], with the driver hidden behind a cover that resembled a seat. The WoZ car served as a tool for eliciting reactions to a supposedly autonomous vehicle.

Figure 5. Field Experiment with WoZ car.

In the workshop, seven researchers explored situations with lead from practitioners from the automotive industry employees and a research institute. The study took place at busy crossings with pedestrians and vehicles without traffic lights. The busy settings enabled researchers to explore specific behaviors of the car, and the reactions and experiences emerging from this situation. In contrast to what would have occurred if we had used a fully autonomous car, the situation could be explored quickly and in an agile fashion. Having access to the field meant we were able to observe pedestrians' reactions and behaviors. For example, we were able to try out different driving styles, and see how people reacted. It gave us the opportunity to study how the vehicle is experienced in social situations by groups of people and how we might mitigate the social "immaturity" of technology-driven concepts. In the continuation of the workshop, the field experiment was followed by further scale scenario explorations, as well as video prototyping based on these.

The research uncovered situations where the pedestrians may need of information from the autonomous car, as well as the rider in the autonomous cars need for information. From the exercise, conflicting scenarios and needs of pedestrians were identified, as well as research needs. The need from the pedestrians to be acknowledged were addressed in specific in following design proposals, as well as the need for the user of the autonomous car to receive feedback that the car has seen and understood the complex setting of a busy pedestrian crossing.

Video and Animation Prototyping

Video prototyping builds on all of the previous techniques by using recordings of enactment, scale scenarios, simple mock-ups, WoZ-functionality and more. The addition of video to the improvisational aspects of the above methods allows the designer to be more collaborative. Designers can more easily develop multiple alternatives to compare reflect, classify, categorize, and refine. Videos and animation can incorporate naturalistic and fantastic elements as are desired for the project at hand.

In comparison to field experiments, the video also allows more controlled experimentation, as designers can make sure that multiple people can experience the exact same material, or that the same people can evaluate varying versions of interaction [14]. Hendriks, Meerbeek, Boess, Pauws, and Sonneveld [27] interviewed participants who had just watched a video prototype to gain insights into user perception. Crowdsourcing has also been used to scale up the number of people giving assessment and feedback on interactions depicted in the videos [36].

In addition, video prototypes can be set in various environments. This is important in regarding contextual elements such as different driving situations. When using filmed video, as opposed to for example enactment, the designer is able to be more concrete in terms of context and flow of events. As a result the vehicle interaction is necessarily evaluated with relation to the context it is in, especially important in the driving context. Animation, on the other hand, allows designers to filter away stray elements that might detract from the interaction at hand, and also to introduce novel or fantastic elements as suits the exploration,

Vignette: Robot Car Seat

One recent project in which we used animated video prototypes was done in to explore how people might interact with a robot car seat. We began by engaging people from both the research community and the industry space, as well as movement experts from fields such as improvisational dance.

From there, we developed a set of motion we were interested in using, and developed animations of these movements in the 3D animation software Cinema 4D to test the more general reaction people might have of the intended expressions of the robot car seat movement. For example, we developed several animations around the idea of having the robot car seat greet people as they approach and entered the car. Because we were using animation, we were able to generate six different video prototypes of the car seat with moods or personalities–excited, cool, confident, aggressive, quirky and controlled.

The animated video prototypes allowed us to take hypotheses we developed during the course of our in-person enactment [75] into testing. We have deployed these studies online and used them to see how much people pick up on aspects of the car seat robot's personality that we intend to convey through motion, and also understand how they interpret these types of actions.

DISCUSSION

The techniques and case studies presented in this paper lay the groundwork for an interaction-centered approach towards vehicle design. By prioritizing the quality and communicative properties of interaction over pragmatic function or aesthetic form, we can give proper attention to the importance of interaction in human vehicle design.

In this discussion, we relate our work to the design of in-vehicle user experiences and suggest how this could benefit interaction design and automotive UI research.

Choosing Techniques

When performing user studies, there is always a tension in what people say, do and feel [67]. We find it useful in our research to use a variety of methods, such as interviews, observations and generative techniques, to advance our understanding of human vehicle interactions in terms of behaviors, motivations, emotions etc. By trying to access information about participant response iteratively, [37, 84] we strive to move between what users say, do and feel [67], in ways that are difficult to do all at once. Throughout our examples, we have when each technique has been preceded or followed by other techniques, to illustrate how these methods might be integrated.

The future orientation of our research presents a particular challenge to designers crafting interaction design approaches. We mentioned, for example, at the outset that one of the challenges that automotive designers are grappling with are the multi-device environments where the automotive designer has very little control over *what* other devices are introduced. To explore this type of scenario, designers might use contextual inquiry to profile what people carry with them, and then develop props that are like or extend these device categories in more fictional settings. These explorations can feed car-specific design requirements and tools for methods to explore complex multi-device environments [17]. The techniques mentioned need to be mindfully applied to address fully working human vehicle interactions.

The techniques offered here allow designers a range of perspectives–first person, over-head, through the eyes of the machine. They also enable designers to variably incorporate the authentic and surprising concerns of the real-world, or to suspend them and keep them at bay. We find that mixing techniques, with their different perspectives and constraints, allows us to explore a larger range of ideas in depth than dedicated adherence to one or the other technique alone.

Design Participation

Placing interaction as a primary consideration has expanding the designer's focus beyond the traditional driver. Our explorations help to raise the larger driving context, such as social settings in the car with multiple passengers. These are interaction aspects will become more interesting as the role of the driver dissolves, and the relationship of the car to its different passengers, and the relationship of the passengers to one another, and to people outside the car, become more prominent.

Much of this expanding of focus occurs because the techniques we use for exploration invite many perspectives.

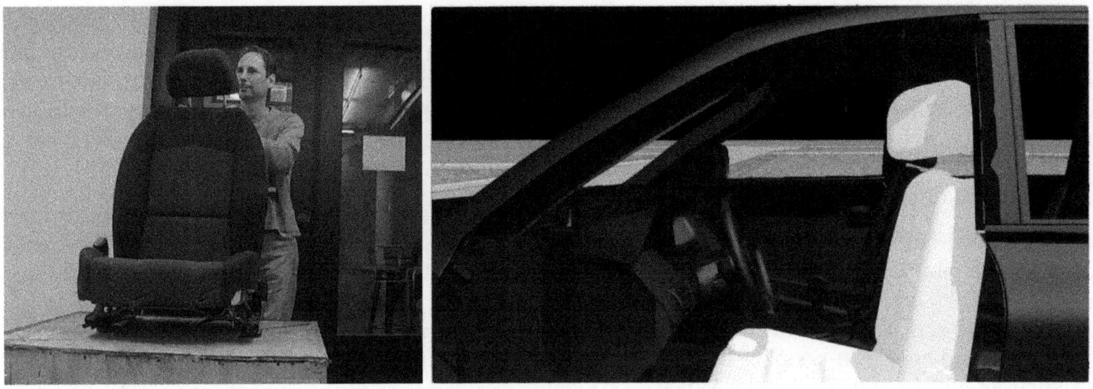

Figure 6. (a) Puppeted Enactments with Physical Car Seat, (b) Screenshot of Robot Seat Video Prototype.

Indeed, the techniques we surveyed may be easily recognized as participatory design techniques. This speaks to the importance in automotive user experience design of incorporating the viewpoints of many stakeholders, such as researchers, users and automotive industry designers and engineers. The participatory nature of many of the methods, when employed with people from different places in the world, also invites conversation about cultural norms and differences that are often invisible to designers working in more isolated contexts. This elicitation, discussion, and shared understanding is far more important than the specific design ideas generated over the course of these activities.

The Future of Interaction, and Interaction Design

The changes afoot in the automotive sector are but the leading edge of increased automation in the consumer product space. In this section, we discuss insights that we have gained through interaction design for the autonomous vehicle that in turn inform how we think that automation in general will change interaction design. These agents and automated systems can be designed to have a number of different roles with respect to users. And the right way for these automation technologies to act will depend not only on personal user preferences, but also larger societal norms.

Interactions, not interface

When the vehicle is a separate entity from the driver, it can take action on behalf of the driver, but it may also be a cause for mystery and confusion. This change motivates a need to move the design focus from interface to interaction; from an interaction paradigm perspective, the car has increasing capability to adopt a variety of roles beyond a mere mechanical vehicle.

The advent of AI agents such as Alexa, Siri and Cortana portend an age where people increasingly interact with products and services in a loosely coupled manner which requires delegation, oversight, trust and repair. One of the things gained by moving beyond traditional interfaces to consider interactions is the opening up of the consideration beyond the solo driver to the wider range of people who interact with the car–not only the person holding the steering wheel, but also the child sitting in the back seat, or the person crossing the street in front of the car. These are not mere "stakeholders" but also people in the periphery who will be implicitly interacting with vehicles as well, who need to be taken into consideration. This expansion of the definition of "user" will be an increasing trend in non-automotive automation as well.

Whole body experience

When automotive designers contemplate the bodily experience, we often think about the driving experience, the leather on the seats or perhaps the click-feel of the knobs. When we contemplate future scenarios, bodily communication [3] and situated cognition [25] come to the forefront as major themes.

Participants in pedestrian-vehicle experiments tell us what movements indicate that a car is likely to go or not, and sometimes are only able to show us how they signal who is going to go and who is going to yield if they set up a map of the scenario. Much is made, too, of things that are not bodily experiences, but still fit under the category of "the felt experience"–like the speeding up and slowing down of the sense of time in some scenarios, or the instinct for the proper timing of responses in our Wizard of Oz experiments.

Thus, the classic automotive concerns of ergonomics and craftmanship which tend to dominate discussions of bodily experience in cars are increasingly joined by concerns about how we use our bodies to communicate or know as well as act. When we ideate, prototype and experiment to explore the embodied space of the car–and other augmented spaces–we must address not only spatial and material concerns, but also interaction dynamics, attention and emotion.

Personal spaces

One of the interesting aspects of our various future user experience sessions is how people seek to preserve the isolated and personal nature of the automotive context. As much as information technologies serve to connect people anywhere they might be, it seems many cherish the space of the car for the personal time it affords them to think, and they perceive automation technologies to be a way to allow them more time to be alone, albeit with an information device to look at. We do find a willingness to dedicate this time to particular topics and tasks–health, or sleep therapy, or foreign language learning–but not to undo the dedicated and isolated nature of these activities.

The prospect of multi-device interaction can be a threat to this sense of the car as a bubble. In terms of interaction design practice, more techniques are needed to address the personal and isolated nature of the vehicle–and to other privileged spaces in people's lives. Adapting techniques such as contextual inquiry or Wizard of Oz so that they can take place in people's own spaces as they journey through their day-to-day–while incorporating future automation or interaction capabilities–might better help designers to address this solitary aspect of user experience, in ways that would be difficult with a traditional design ethnographer.

Long term interaction
Another aspect of interaction that our explorations indicate might be changing is the ability of vehicles to make more use of long-term interaction. The vehicle can observe driver's activity patterns and note trends and changes; it can act as a conversational agent that learns and remembers user patterns and preferences.

From the larger perspective of changing interaction design practices, interaction designers need to develop more ways to explore how interactions change and evolve over time. An interesting future direction would be to develop ways of applying these exploratory interaction design techniques explicitly to address scenarios which require a significant time dimension–learning or adaptation in interaction being one of the major promises of advanced interaction technology in the age of automation.

Changing roles of the car
Human vehicle interaction today, the communication is largely open-loop: the car assumes that warning signals etc. have been received and understood by the driver. The closed-loop communication that we use with other people, monitoring one another to check that what we said has been heard and understood, will be critical to improving the car's ability to adopt the role of a true interaction partner. The same machine learning technologies that make it possible for cars to recognize the environment to drive themselves down the road now need to be turned inward to recognize understanding and confusion, distraction and engagement. This recognition will allow the car to know when it should elaboration or repair. These new types of interactions will be critical to future efforts towards safe interaction with autonomy, not only in the car, but beyond.

In our enactment of future systems, both the user interaction as well as the system's interactions have been enacted, in order to gain an emphatic understanding of their mutual situations, needs for information and actions. Technology centered approaches leaves out the human aspects of interaction. Depending heavily on user centered approaches of current use situations leaves out understandings of upcoming, future interactions. We see the need for techniques where both the machine and human situation can be explored.

These aspects can be explored by the techniques we have highlighted above, but also others, and we look forward to continuing developments in the field.

Adapting to different cultures
Very often, people assume automation technologies will be designed the way that internet technologies have, with similar tools and interfaces beyond deployed with only small accommodations for regional language and laws. However, as we enact automotive interactions with people from different cultures, we have found that our participatory methods help elicit conflicts or differences in expectations that might require vehicles to behave differently in different cultures. Unlike the internet, autonomous vehicles and other automated technologies do not make their own space, but take place in ours, and hence need to be culturally situated and adapted. This requires greater cultural elicitation, understanding, prototyping, and testing.

CONCLUSIONS
By understanding how to design automotive interactions in the age of automation, we might better address the impending challenges. We have outlined an interaction-centered approach which focuses on the evolving partnership between technology and user, and discussed ways that we had to modify previous techniques to focus on communication and interaction rather than user needs and contexts, on prototyping as much as understanding.

Our applications of the techniques are oriented to the future, as well as to understanding both the users and the machines need for communication. Furthermore, they have served as arenas to approach complicated interaction situations with many viewpoints, such as those of researchers, users, automotive industry designers and engineers. We anticipate that as we continue to apply and adapt the design techniques for interaction design for applications involving automation that more distinct differences to the design practice will emerge.

ACKNOWLEDGMENTS
The methods described in this paper were developed and performed with a number of talented collaborators: David Sirkin, Nikolas Martelaro, Hamish Tennent, Page Ive, Brian Mok, Dirk Rothenbücher, Jamy Li, Catherine Smith, Heather Knight, MariAnne Karlsson, Dimitrios Gkouskos, Helena Strömberg, Jonas Andersson, Annie Rydström and Maria Klingegård. The research at Chalmers was supported by the VINNOVA FFI program. The research at Stanford was supported by the Center for Design Research Affiliates program.

REFERENCES

1. Micah Alpern and Katie Minardo. 2003. Developing a car gesture interface for use as a secondary task. In *CHI'03 Extended Abstracts on Human Factors in Computing Systems*. ACM, 932–933.
2. Simone Nyholm Andersen and Ole Broberg. 2015. Participatory ergonomics simulation of hospital work systems: The influence of simulation media on simulation outcome. *Applied ergonomics* 51 (2015), 331–342.
3. Michael Argyle. 2013. *Bodily Communication*. Routledge.
4. Mattias Arvola and Henrik Artman. 2007. Enactments in interaction design: How designers make sketches behave. *Artifact* 1, 2 (2007), 106–119.
5. Michel Beaudouin-Lafon. 2004. Designing Interaction, Not Interfaces. In *Proceedings of the Working Conference on Advanced Visual Interfaces (AVI '04)*. ACM, New York, NY, USA, 15–22. DOI: http://dx.doi.org/10.1145/989863.989865
6. Mohamed Benmimoun, Andreas Pütz, Adrian Zlocki, and Lutz Eckstein. 2013. Impact assessment of adaptive cruise control (ACC) and forward collision warning (FCW) within a field operational test in Europe. In *Transportation Research Board 92nd Annual Meeting*.
7. Hugh Beyer and Karen Holtzblatt. 1997. *Contextual Design: Defining Customer-centered Systems*. Elsevier.
8. Lars-Ola Bligård, Cecilia Österman, and Cecilia Berlin. 2014. Using 2D and 3D models as tools during a workplace design process–a question of how and when. In *The 11th Symposium on Human Factors in Organizational Design and Management (ODAM) and 46th Annual Nordic Ergonomics Society Conference (NES), Copenhagen 17-20 August, 2014*. Danmarks Tekniske Universitet, DTU, 799–804.
9. Nathan Bomey. 2015. Average age of cars on U.S. roads breaks record. (July 2015). http://www.usatoday.com/story/money/2015/07/29/new-car-sales-soaring-but-cars-getting-older-too/30821191/
10. Eva Brandt, Thomas Binder, and Elizabeth B-N Sanders. 2012. Ways to engage telling, making and enacting. *Routledge International Handbook of Participatory Design. Routledge, New York* (2012), 145–181.
11. Susan E. Brennan. 1991. Conversation with and through computers. *User Modeling and User-Adapted Interaction* 1, 1 (1991), 67–86. DOI: http://dx.doi.org/10.1007/BF00158952
12. Alan Chamberlain, Andy Crabtree, Tom Rodden, Matt Jones, and Yvonne Rogers. 2012. Research in the wild: understanding'in the wild'approaches to design and development. In *Proceedings of the Designing Interactive Systems Conference*. ACM, 795–796.
13. Chandrika Cycil, Mark J Perry, and Eric Laurier. 2014. Designing for frustration and disputes in the family car. (2014).
14. Kerstin Dautenhahn, Michael Walters, Sarah Woods, Kheng Lee Koay, Chrystopher L Nehaniv, A Sisbot, Rachid Alami, and Thierry Siméon. 2006. How may I serve you?: a robot companion approaching a seated person in a helping context. In *Proceedings of the 1st ACM SIGCHI/SIGART conference on Human-Robot interaction*. ACM, 172–179.
15. Scott Davidoff, Min Kyung Lee, Anind K Dey, and John Zimmerman. 2007. Rapidly exploring application design through speed dating. In *International Conference on Ubiquitous Computing*. Springer, 429–446.
16. Thomas A Dingus, Sheila G Klauer, Vicki L Neale, A Petersen, SE Lee, JD Sudweeks, MA Perez, J Hankey, DJ Ramsey, S Gupta, and others. 2006. *The 100-car naturalistic driving study, Phase II-results of the 100-car field experiment*. Technical Report.
17. Tao Dong, Elizabeth F Churchill, and Jeffrey Nichols. 2016. Understanding the Challenges of Designing and Developing Multi-Device Experiences. In *Proceedings of the 2016 ACM Conference on Designing Interactive Systems*. ACM, 62–72.
18. Pelle Ehn. 1988. Work-oriented design of computer artifacts. (1988).
19. Mike Featherstone. 2004. Automobilities An Introduction. *Theory, Culture & Society* 21, 4-5 (2004), 1–24.
20. FO Flemisch, CA Adams, SR Conway, KH Goodrich, MT Palmer, and MC Schutte. 2003. *The H-Metaphor as a Guideline for Vehicle Automation and Interaction Report No.* Technical Report. NASA/TM-2003-212672. NASA Langley, Langley.
21. Frank Flemisch, Matthias Heesen, Tobias Hesse, Johann Kelsch, Anna Schieben, and Johannes Beller. 2012. Towards a dynamic balance between humans and automation: authority, ability, responsibility and control in shared and cooperative control situations. *Cognition, Technology & Work* 14, 1 (2012), 3–18.
22. Andrew W Gellatly, Cody Hansen, Matthew Highstrom, and John P Weiss. 2010. Journey: General Motors' move to incorporate contextual design into its next generation of automotive HMI designs. In *Proceedings of the 2nd international conference on Automotive User Interfaces and Interactive Vehicular Applications*. ACM, 156–161.

23. Petra Geutner, Frank Steffens, and Dietrich Manstetten. 2002. Design of the VICO Spoken Dialogue System: Evaluation of User Expectations by Wizard-of-Oz Experiments.. In *LREC*.

24. Dimitrios Gkouskos, Ingrid Pettersson, MariAnne Karlsson, and Fang Chen. 2015. Exploring User Experience in the Wild: Facets of the Modern Car. In *International Conference of Design, User Experience, and Usability*. Springer, 450–461.

25. Charles Goodwin. 2000. Action and embodiment within situated human interaction. *Journal of Pragmatics* 32, 10 (2000), 1489–1522.

26. A Habibovic, J Andersson, M Nilsson, V Malmsten Lundgren, and J Nilsson. 2016. Evaluating interactions with non-existing automated vehicles: three Wizard of Oz approaches. In *Intelligent Vehicles Symposium*. IEEE, 32–37.

27. Bram Hendriks, Bernt Meerbeek, Stella Boess, Steffen Pauws, and Marieke Sonneveld. 2011. Robot vacuum cleaner personality and behavior. *International Journal of Social Robotics* 3, 2 (2011), 187–195.

28. Tobias Holstein, Markus Wallmyr, Joachim Wietzke, and Rikard Land. 2015. Current Challenges in Compositing Heterogeneous User Interfaces for Automotive Purposes. In *International Conference on Human-Computer Interaction*. Springer, 531–542.

29. Johanna Höysniemi, Perttu Hämäläinen, and Laura Turkki. 2004. Wizard of Oz prototyping of computer vision based action games for children. In *Proceedings of the 2004 conference on Interaction Design and Children: Building a Community*. ACM, 27–34.

30. Scott Hudson, James Fogarty, Christopher Atkeson, Daniel Avrahami, Jodi Forlizzi, Sara Kiesler, Johnny Lee, and Jie Yang. 2003. Predicting human interruptibility with sensors: a Wizard of Oz feasibility study. In *Proceedings of the SIGCHI Conference on Human Factors in Computing Systems*. ACM, 257–264.

31. Apple Inc. 2017. Apple CarPlay: The Ultimate CoPilot. (2017). `https://www.apple.com/ios/carplay/` (Date accessed 15-Jan-2017).

32. Google Inc. 2017. One app, two ways to use Android Auto. (2017). (Date accessed 15-Jan-2017).

33. Hillary Page Ive, David Sirkin, Dave Miller, Jamy Li, and Wendy Ju. 2015. Don't make me turn this seat around!: driver and passenger activities and positions in autonomous cars. In *Adjunct Proceedings of the 7th International Conference on Automotive User Interfaces and Interactive Vehicular Applications*. ACM, 50–55.

34. Tero Jokela, Jarno Ojala, and Thomas Olsson. 2015. A Diary Study on Combining Multiple Information Devices in Everyday Activities and Tasks. In *Proceedings of the 33rd Annual ACM Conference on Human Factors in Computing Systems (CHI '15)*. ACM, New York, NY, USA, 3903–3912. DOI: `http://dx.doi.org/10.1145/2702123.2702211`

35. Wendy Ju. 2015. The Design of Implicit Interactions. *Synthesis Lectures on Human-Centered Informatics* 8, 2 (2015), 1–93.

36. Wendy Ju and Leila Takayama. 2009. Approachability: How people interpret automatic door movement as gesture. *International Journal of Design* 3, 2 (2009).

37. MariAnne Karlsson. 1996. *User requirements elicitation-a framework for the study of the relation between user and artefact.* Chalmers University of Technology.

38. John F Kelley. 1983. An empirical methodology for writing user-friendly natural language computer applications. In *Proceedings of the SIGCHI conference on Human Factors in Computing Systems*. ACM, 193–196.

39. Moritz Körber and Klaus Bengler. 2013. Measurement of momentary user experience in an automotive context. In *Proceedings of the 5th International Conference on Automotive User Interfaces and Interactive Vehicular Applications*. ACM, 194–201.

40. Sari Kujala, Virpi Roto, Kaisa Väänänen-Vainio-Mattila, Evangelos Karapanos, and Arto Sinnelä. 2011. UX Curve: A method for evaluating long-term user experience. *Interacting with Computers* 23, 5 (2011), 473–483.

41. Andrew L Kun, Susanne Boll, and Albrecht Schmidt. 2016. Shifting Gears: User Interfaces in the Age of Autonomous Driving. *IEEE Pervasive Computing* 15, 1 (2016), 32–38.

42. Matti Kutila, Maria Jokela, Gustav Markkula, and Maria Romera Rué. 2007. Driver distraction detection with a camera vision system. In *2007 IEEE International Conference on Image Processing*, Vol. 6. IEEE, VI–201.

43. Morten Kyng. 1995. Making representations work. *Commun. ACM* 38, 9 (1995), 46–55.

44. Brian Lathrop, Hua Cheng, Fuliang Weng, Rohit Mishra, Joyce Chen, Harry Bratt, Lawrence Cavedon, Carsten Bergmann, Tess Hand-Bender, Heather Pon-Barry, and others. 2004. A Wizard of Oz framework for collecting spoken human-computer dialogs: An experiment procedure for the design and testing of natural language in-vehicle technology systems. In *Proceedings of Intelligent Transport Systems*.

45. John Lee, Jane Moeckli, Timothy Brown, Shannon Roberts, Trent Victor, Dawn Marshall, Chris Schwarz, and Eric Nadler. 2013. Detection of driver distraction using vision-based algorithms. In *Proc. 23rd Enhanced Safety Veh. Conf.*
46. Victor Malmsten Lundgren, Azra Habibovic, Jonas Andersson, Tobias Lagström, Maria Nilsson, Anna Sirkka, Johan Fagerlönn, Rikard Fredriksson, Claes Edgren, Stas Krupenia, and others. 2017. Will There Be New Communication Needs When Introducing Automated Vehicles to the Urban Context? In *Advances in Human Aspects of Transportation.* Springer, 485–497.
47. Glenn Lyons and John Urry. 2005. Travel time use in the information age. *Transportation Research Part A: Policy and Practice* 39, 2 (2005), 257–276.
48. Jun Ma, Maofei Xu, and Yuchun Du. 2016. *A Usability Study on In-Vehicle Gesture Control.* Technical Report. SAE Technical Paper.
49. Nikolas Martelaro and Wendy Ju. 2017. WoZ Way: Enabling Real-time Interaction Prototyping and On-road Observation. In *Proceedings of the 2017 Conference on Computer Supported Cooperative Work.* Portland, OR. DOI: http://dx.doi.org/10.1145/2998181.2998293
50. Stefan Mattes and Anders Hallén. 2009. Surrogate distraction measurement techniques: The lane change test. *Driver distraction: Theory, effects, and mitigation* (2009), 107–121.
51. Helena M Mentis, Kristina Höök, Florian Mueller, Katherine Isbister, George Poonkhin Khut, and Toni Robertson. 2014. Designing for the experiential body. In *CHI'14 Extended Abstracts on Human Factors in Computing Systems.* ACM, 1069–1074.
52. Alexander Meschtscherjakov, David Wilfinger, Nicole Gridling, Katja Neureiter, and Manfred Tscheligi. 2011. Capture the Car!: Qualitative In-situ Methods to Grasp the Automotive Context. In *Proceedings of the 3rd International Conference on Automotive User Interfaces and Interactive Vehicular Applications (AutomotiveUI '11).* ACM, New York, NY, USA, 105–112. DOI: http://dx.doi.org/10.1145/2381416.2381434
53. Brian Ka-Jun Mok, David Sirkin, Srinath Sibi, David Bryan Miller, and Wendy Ju. 2015. Understanding driver-automated vehicle interactions through Wizard of Oz design improvisation. In *Proceedings of the International Driving Symposium on Human Factors in Driver Assessment, Training and Vehicle Design.* 386–392.
54. Christian Muller, Garrett Weinberg, and A Vetro. 2011. Multimodal input in the car, today and tomorrow. *IEEE MultiMedia* 18, 1 (2011), 98–103.
55. Robert Neßelrath, Mohammad Mehdi Moniri, and Michael Feld. 2016. Combining Speech, Gaze, and Micro-gestures for the Multimodal Control of In-Car Functions. In *Intelligent Environments (IE), 2016 12th International Conference on.* IEEE, 190–193.
56. William Odom, John Zimmerman, Scott Davidoff, Jodi Forlizzi, Anind K Dey, and Min Kyung Lee. 2012. A fieldwork of the future with user enactments. In *Proceedings of the Designing Interactive Systems Conference.* ACM, 338–347.
57. Cecilia Österman, Cecilia Berlin, and Lars-Ola Bligård. 2011. Enabling end-user participation in ship design. In *Proceedings of the 43rd Annual Nordic Ergonomics Society Conference-Wellbeing and Innovation Through Ergonomics.*
58. J Östlund, B Peters, B Thorslund, J Engström, G Markkula, A Keinath, and others. 2005. Driving performance assessment-methods and metrics (EU Deliverable, Adaptive Integrated Driver-Vehicle Interface Project (AIDE) No. D2. 2.5). (2005).
59. Justin M Owens, Jonathan F Antin, Zachary Doerzaph, and Susan Willis. 2015. Cross-generational acceptance of and interest in advanced vehicle technologies: a nationwide survey. *Transportation Research part F: Traffic Psychology and Behaviour* 35 (2015), 139–151.
60. Ingrid Pettersson. 2016. *The temporality of in-vehicle user experience - exploring user experiences from past to future.* Institutionen för produkt- och produktionsutveckling, Design and Human Factors, Chalmers tekniska högskola,.
61. Ingrid Pettersson and IC MariAnne Karlsson. 2015. Setting the stage for autonomous cars: a pilot study of future autonomous driving experiences. *IET intelligent transport systems* 9, 7 (2015), 694–701.
62. Ingrid Pettersson, Annie Rydström, Helena Strömberg, Lena Hylving, Jonas Andersson, Maria Klingegård, and MariAnne Karlsson. 2016. Living Room on the Move: Autonomous Vehicles and Social Experiences. In *Proceedings of the 9th Nordic Conference on Human-Computer Interaction.* ACM, 129.
63. Simon Ramm, Joseph Giacomin, Duncan Robertson, and Alessio Malizia. 2014. A First Approach to Understanding and Measuring Naturalness in Driver-Car Interaction. In *Proceedings of the 6th International Conference on Automotive User Interfaces and Interactive Vehicular Applications (AutomotiveUI '14).* ACM, New York, NY, USA, Article 33, 10 pages. DOI: http://dx.doi.org/10.1145/2667317.2667416
64. Sarah Redshaw. 2012. *In the company of cars: Driving as a social and cultural practice.* Ashgate Publishing, Ltd.

65. Alan M Rugman and Simon Collinson. 2004. The regional nature of the world's automotive sector. *European Management Journal* 22, 5 (2004), 471–482.

66. Sonja Rümelin and Andreas Butz. 2013. How to make large touch screens usable while driving. In *Proceedings of the 5th International Conference on Automotive User Interfaces and Interactive Vehicular Applications*. ACM, 48–55.

67. Elizabeth Sanders. 2002. Special section: ethnography in NPD research. How 'applied ethnography'can improve your NPD research process. *Visions Magazine* (2002), 1–5.

68. Elizabeth B-N Sanders, Eva Brandt, and Thomas Binder. 2010. A framework for organizing the tools and techniques of participatory design. In *Proceedings of the 11th biennial participatory design conference*. ACM, 195–198.

69. Stephanie Santosa and Daniel Wigdor. 2013. A Field Study of Multi-device Workflows in Distributed Workspaces. In *Proceedings of the 2013 ACM International Joint Conference on Pervasive and Ubiquitous Computing (UbiComp '13)*. ACM, New York, NY, USA, 63–72. DOI: http://dx.doi.org/10.1145/2493432.2493476

70. Anna Schieben, Matthias Heesen, Julian Schindler, Johann Kelsch, and Frank Flemisch. 2009. The theater-system technique: Agile designing and testing of system behavior and interaction, applied to highly automated vehicles. In *Proceedings of the 1st International Conference on Automotive User Interfaces and Interactive Vehicular Applications*. ACM, 43–46.

71. Björn Schuller, Manfred Lang, Gerhard Rigoll, and others. 2006. Recognition of spontaneous emotions by speech within automotive environment. *Fortschritte der Akustik* 32, 1 (2006), 57.

72. Mimi Sheller. 2004. Automotive emotions feeling the car. *Theory, Culture & Society* 21, 4-5 (2004), 221–242.

73. Thomas B Sheridan and Raja Parasuraman. 2005. Human-automation interaction. *Reviews of Human Factors and Ergonomics* 1, 1 (2005), 89–129.

74. Paul J Sherman, Robert L Helmreich, and Ashleigh C Merritt. 1997. National culture and flight deck automation: Results of a multination survey. *The International Journal of Aviation Psychology* 7, 4 (1997), 311–329.

75. David Sirkin, Kerstin Fischer, Lars Jensen, and Wendy Ju. 2016. Eliciting Conversation in Robot Vehicle Interactions. In *2016 AAAI Spring Symposium Series, Palo Alto, Ca., AAAI Publications*. AAAI Press.

76. Catherine Snow. 1983. Literacy and language: Relationships during the preschool years. *Harvard Educational Review* 53, 2 (1983), 165–189.

77. David L Strayer and Frak A Drew. 2004. Profiles in driver distraction: Effects of cell phone conversations on younger and older drivers. *Human Factors: The Journal of the Human Factors and Ergonomics Society* 46, 4 (2004), 640–649.

78. Lucy A Suchman. 1987. *Plans and situated actions: The problem of human-machine communication*. Cambridge university press.

79. Jakob Tholander and Carolina Johansson. 2010. Design qualities for whole body interaction: learning from golf, skateboarding and BodyBugging. In *Proceedings of the 6th Nordic Conference on Human-Computer Interaction: Extending Boundaries*. ACM, 493–502.

80. Sebastian Thrun, Mike Montemerlo, Hendrik Dahlkamp, David Stavens, Andrei Aron, James Diebel, Philip Fong, John Gale, Morgan Halpenny, Gabriel Hoffmann, and others. 2006. Stanley: The robot that won the DARPA Grand Challenge. *Journal of Field Robotics* 23, 9 (2006), 661–692.

81. Sandra Trösterer, Daniela Wurhofer, Christina Rödel, and Manfred Tscheligi. 2014. Using a Parking Assist System Over Time: Insights on Acceptance and Experiences. In *Proceedings of the 6th International Conference on Automotive User Interfaces and Interactive Vehicular Applications*. ACM, 1–8.

82. Omer Tsimhoni, Daniel Smith, and Paul Green. 2004. Address entry while driving: Speech recognition versus a touch-screen keyboard. *Human Factors: The Journal of the Human Factors and Ergonomics Society* 46, 4 (2004), 600–610.

83. Harini Veeraraghavan, Osama Masoud, and Nikolaos P Papanikolopoulos. 2003. Computer vision algorithms for intersection monitoring. *IEEE Transactions on Intelligent Transportation Systems* 4, 2 (2003), 78–89.

84. Froukje Sleeswijk Visser, Pieter Jan Stappers, Remko Van der Lugt, and Elizabeth BN Sanders. 2005. Contextmapping: experiences from practice. *CoDesign* 1, 2 (2005), 119–149.

What Lies Above: Alternative User Experiences Produced Through Focusing Attention on GNSS Infrastructure

Christopher Wood
Media & Arts Technology,
Queen Mary University of London, UK
c.p.wood@qmul.ac.uk

Stefan Poslad, Antonios Kaniadakis
Electronic Engineering and Computer Science,
Queen Mary University of London, UK
{s.poslad; a.kaniadakis}@qmul.ac.uk

Jennifer Gabrys
Department of Sociology,
Goldsmiths College,
University of London, UK
j.gabrys@gold.ac.uk

ABSTRACT
This paper describes a study in which participants were made aware of the presence of Global Navigation Satellite Systems (GNSS) infrastructure (often colloquially known as GPS) through an exaggeration of its breakdowns and a defamiliarisation of its use. We found that, by drawing attention to satellites and their signals, participants began to feel part of a larger system and to reflect on their sociotechnical practices within that system. These reflections included playful exploration and an interrogation of power relations made invisible by the blackboxing of GNSS infrastructure. Despite these shifts from established practices, smartphone visual interfaces continued to be a powerful arbiter of how participants situated their experience. Drawing on the experience of this study, we suggest ways for designers and researchers using Location Based Services (LBS) to inspire critical relationships with infrastructure which circumvent dominant design inscriptions. We also offer these techniques for others working more broadly in the fields of participatory and critical design.

Author Keywords
Critical design; Location Based Services; Infrastructure; Inventive Methods; Human Factors

ACM Classification Keywords
H.5.m. Information interfaces and presentation (e.g., HCI): Miscellaneous;

INTRODUCTION
Although the first phones that supported a Global Navigation Satellite System (GNSS) appeared in the mid 1990s, we can trace the dramatic rise in everyday use of GNSS technologies and Location Based Services (LBS) to the introduction of 3G-enabled smartphones in the late 2000s. This shift allowed mobile devices to displace dashboard mounted satnav devices as the most common GNSS-enabled technology. Currently, it is extremely common for multiple applications on mobile devices to request access to the device's location. Such a request may be related to an app's functionalities, including navigation (*Citymapper* [14]), social media geotagging (*Instagram* [25], *Facebook* [21], *Foursquare* [22]), ordering a car and driver (*Uber* [47]) or gaming (*Pokemon Go* [37]). Equally, the establishment of location may be implicated in the ambient data-gathering performed by many applications during their use. Through these cases, we can say that the use of technologies which identify our location has become deeply embedded in our sociotechnical practices. Although many devices also use Wi-Fi and cellphone towers in supporting location capabilities, the best-known means of identifying device location is through Global Navigation Satellite Systems (GNSS), often colloquially known through the name of the longest standing GNSS, the American Global Positioning System (GPS). Currently, most mobile devices are equipped with a GNSS antenna and sensor, forming a vast collection of sensors which orient themselves using signals from the GPS satellite network operated by the US military, GLObal NAvigation Satellite System (GLONASS), a system operated by the Russian military, and, increasingly, the Chinese-operated service BeiDou. Besides user-facing consumer functions, GNSS is used in military operations and a diverse range of industries including logistics, high-frequency financial trading, earthquake prediction and weather forecasting.

DIS 2017, June 10-14, 2017, Edinburgh, United Kingdom
ACM 978-1-4503-4922-2/17/06.
http://dx.doi.org/10.1145/3064663.3064757

Our primary concern here is smartphone user driven cases. We note that for most users, the complex infrastructure which determines a device's location is frequently rendered invisible. For example, *Google maps* [35] shows a flashing blue dot which denotes 'You are here', not 'This device has received a minimum of four time-stamped signals from satellites in medium earth orbit and, despite the possibility of environmental disruptions, has estimated that you are here.' The infrastructure is blackboxed. Its existence and operation is concealed and thereby made invisible. Such blackboxing is by no means unique to GNSS technology, it is consistent with Mark Weiser's influential claim that, in ubiquitous computing, the user's attention should be on the task at hand rather than the tool [38, 51, 52]. However, while such a design approach may create smoother user experiences, it also works to determine the paths and aims of such experiences. Blackboxing may also conceal certain attendant operations and effects of a technology which are relevant to users. For LBS these may include on what terms nearby businesses are deemed relevant to a user or what is happening to their personal location information further up the data chain. In pursuing this line of research, we were interested in whether drawing attention onto the presence of GNSS infrastructure would make users critique their own sociotechnical practices. The ability to make such critiques and gain awareness of the ways practices are formed and maintained has benefits for both designers and users.

It should be noted that we deploy the term 'users' with a pinch of salt. This research argues that there is nothing fixed or rigid about such a term. Rather, users emerge from sociotechnical practices which are enacted in response to the uses inscribed by designers [2], often with strong measures of translation and friction [3]. However, we continue to use this term as a shorthand, while exploring how it and its attendant infrastructures are constructed and made durable.

As a technique to make infrastructure more visible and less naturalised, we take a lead from Bowker and Star's proposal for "infrastructural inversion" [11]. It should be noted that we do not focus on historical inversion approaches, where researchers study the development of a technology, exploring contingencies and how certain formations were made durable [10]. Rather, we concentrate on the phenomenological experience of having infrastructure revealed. This is done through exaggeration of points of infrastructural breakdown and defamiliarisation of sociotechnical practices during a task at hand. Through this, we create a more immediate sense of a participant's place within GNSS infrastructure as it acts.

In developing this technique, we also drew on art based walking practices, particularly the influential situationist proposal for derives (directionless walks which render a familiar cityscape new and unusual) [17].

We framed the inquiry with the research question: 'What alternative user experiences emerge when we foreground the infrastructure which supports LBS?' During the study, we found that participants were able, to some extent, to shift their familiar user position, and see themselves as part of a wider system in emotional, ontological, social and material terms. These new positions opened possibilities for playful interaction with GNSS technology and an ability to question the distribution of power within that system. We also note that established means for shaping sociotechnical practices remained strong, with the visual interface of the research app and ideas of mapping remaining powerful in forming experiences.

We begin the paper with a review of some theoretical understandings of infrastructure and blackboxing, along with our reasoning for challenging the established practices which lead to infrastructural invisibility. We then orient our methodology alongside some complementary practices. We describe our study; a series of walking workshops which took place around the Barbican Estate in London, a building complex with features which disrupt the smooth operation of GNSS. After describing the outcomes of the research, we discuss the alternative user experiences produced and consider their potential to inform surrounding research and design.

WHAT IS HIDDEN

It is difficult to pin down what an infrastructure 'is'. The term describes diverse formations of technical and organizational objects. In their influential article, Star and Ruhleder instead argue that "infrastructure appears only as a relational property, not as a thing stripped of use" [42: 113]. As such, we can understand it through "changes in infrastructural relations" rather than the causal agency of people or things. For Star and Ruhleder, infrastructures may vary in type and scale. Historic examples include the electrification of a town or the uptake of the file folder in the management of American industry. In these examples, both a power grid and a means of organising information are understood as infrastructures through the impact they make on surrounding relations. Infrastructures can be said to emerge with eight dimensions: Embeddedness; Transparency; Reach or scope; Being learned as part of membership; A link with conventions of practice; Embodiment of standards; Being built on an installed base; and becoming visible on breakdown [42]. In relation to our study of GNSS infrastructure, we reflect in detail on three of these dimensions: Embeddedness; Transparency and Visibility through breakdown.

Within the realm of this study, GNSS is embedded into the smaller, user-facing structure of the smartphone. The actions of the wider system are collected and re-interpreted by a sensor within the device. This sensor works with other structures to inscribe actions for users. Examples of such structures are the operating systems which support smartphone applications. The Android operating system (latest version at time of writing: Nougat 7.1) [4] allows developers to call a breadth of information from the device's GNSS sensor, including the number of satellites in view, the signal to noise ratio of their communications and the azimuth of their trajectory. Apple's iOS operating system (latest version at time of writing: 10.3) [26] on the other hand only allows developers to call information about the accuracy of the location fix. In this way, the presence of the infrastructure is embedded to the point of transparency. For Star and Ruhleder, transparency means that the infrastructure does not need to be reconstituted for each task, but rather "invisibly supports those tasks" [42:113]. This transparency is true of both Android and iOS's support of LBS, but something more radical is happening in

Apple's case. Here, invisibility becomes paramount because the presence and operation of the infrastructure is blackboxed. Even if they have need to, developers are unable to request information relating to operational components of the infrastructure. All they can tell is how well it is working (how accurate a fix can be established). This brings us to the dimension of visibility upon breakdown. In iOS development, the only pertinent information has been judged to be the degree of breakdown; in other words, to what extent has the tool become visible and, presumably, in turn, what solutions can the developer find to mitigate that visibility.

Blackboxing, or the making invisible of infrastructure, is frequently understood as something desirable within HCI. Weiser famously claimed that: "A good tool is an invisible tool. By invisible, I mean that the tool does not intrude on your consciousness; you focus on the task, not the tool" [52]. Bakke identifies a trend in HCI such that "the cultivation of an [information infrastructure] would benefit from hiding the infrastructural complexity beneath an easily comprehendable user-interface" both to make an interface easy to learn for new users and to offer quicker ways for experienced users to complete their tasks [7]. Weiser also argued for a type of ubiquitous computing which should recede into the background, ultimately becoming an ambient part of the environment [51]. Such invisibility, however, may emerge less from its physical placement and more through the aspects of its use. For Latour, blackboxing is understood as the way in which "scientific and technical work is made invisible by its own success" [28:304]. In the same way the use of a device like a refrigerator might become so widespread that we cannot imagine life without it, information infrastructures have the potential to "become tacit in thought and action for human users" [24]. When such developments become tacit they gain an aura of inevitability, as if their development could not have taken any other course [10].

Blackboxing may ultimately be realised by the proliferation of a particular infrastructure, but is also the result of a series of inscriptions from designers. Akrich notes that the affordances of a system or object work to try and define which tasks are possible, which in turn defines the nature of the user [2]. The complexity of this process has been emphasised in empirical studies of inscription in information infrastructures [1, 23]. At the same time as uses are inscribed by designers, alternative practices emerge through the ways in which those inscriptions are received [3]. GNSS infrastructure offers an interesting example of these processes because it has been leveraged by multiple communities of use. Besides familiar examples of finding your position on a map, or a route to your destination, practices such as weather forecasting leverage the relative speed of satellites' signals in different air humidities. High frequency financial trading uses the satellites' atomic clocks to synchronise trades. Establishing device location, while a more familiar use, also supports a complex set of practices including tracking pets and prisoners, finding potential sexual partners or providing metadata for photos or *Twitter* [47] posts. The emergent map of GNSS use shows it is not limited to any single practice. However, all these various uses rely on a shared material base, the largest parts of which are developed and maintained by the militaries of the United States and Russia. For Callon and Latour, blackboxing is a fundamentally asymmetrical process. It allows a micro-actor to become a macro-actor, which "bends space around itself, makes other elements dependent upon itself and translates [its] will into a language of its own" with a greater degree of success [12:286]. The crux of this power lies in invisibility; many actors become understood as one object or system. It therefore becomes more difficult to imagine how things could have developed in a different way. This process has implications for the way our surroundings are understood, both in spatial and political terms [34].

Stepping outside the historical inevitability which emerges through blackboxing is desirable for several reasons. For ethnographic research, which seeks to understand how sociotechnical practices are formed and enacted, it offers the possibility of a deeper level of engagement. Within participatory design practices, respondents and designers could be more empowered to think through how their sociotechnical practices are formed and could be reformed [43]. It would allow people (in various often overlapping roles as users and designers) to reflect critically on the unconscious values embedded in computing [8, 19, 41]. In more pragmatic terms, attention to the seams and points of breakdown in infrastructure may hold great potential for generating new and innovative designs [13]. Before these benefits can be reached, a way must be found to invert our usual practices and make what is hidden visible. In the following section, we describe the methodology we developed for making GNSS infrastructure visible by leveraging and exaggerating moments of breakdown

TURNING AN ICEBERG UPSIDE DOWN

Our aim in this project was to ask what alternative user experiences emerge when we foreground the infrastructure which supports LBS. To explore this question, we first needed to challenge the invisibility of blackboxed infrastructure. Our approach follows the principles of infrastructural inversion laid out by Bowker and Star. There are many ways to apply infrastructural inversion, but all share a drive to recognise "the depths of interdependence of technical networks and standards, on one hand, and the real work of politics and knowledge production on the other" [11:34]. This work is often done historically, unearthing the contingent preceding and parallel infrastructural conditions through which, "the initial claim came a posteriori to be seen as reasonable" [10:235]. In our case, rather than taking a purely historical approach, we chose to foreground "the sequencing of events in the present" [11:46]. We wanted to explore contemporary experience more directly to stage a more dramatic inversion of participants' usual practices.

This process is analogous to the taking the visible part of an iceberg and turning it upside down to expose its hidden, supporting depths. We brought this visibility about by defamiliarising GNSS technology through our experiment design, at the same time as using the affordances of a particular site to stage exaggerated moments of breakdown. Once the infrastructure is brought into focus in this way, we encouraged participants to explore it through movement and exploration, then to reflect on this experience through writing, drawing and discussion.

The act of making what has become naturalised strange and unfamiliar finds resonance in critical art practices going back at least a far as the situationists in the 1950s [17]. Here, practitioners would walk freely, without direction in the city, exploring what emerged when the familiar was made strange or 'detourned'. Indeed, situationist practices of re-configuring the city, or adding extra layers of meaning to it were influential in the first wave of locative media art projects that emerged in the early 2000s [46]. Such practices are, however, perhaps limited through the faith they put in distinct objects such as user and city. Such an understanding leaves little room for macro-actors such as blackboxed infrastructure to shape what lies around them [45]. Nevertheless, the principle of defamiliarisation has potential to be a useful one for critical work in design. Bell et. al. argue that such an approach "provides a lens to help us see our own design practices in a new light" [9:154]. We would go further and invoke critical design discourses [8, 19] to argue that it also has the potential to interrogate practices of use as they are experienced as well as designed. Such approaches may not uncover the totality of what is specific to the infrastructure in that moment, but rather provoke wider reflections on what lies beneath familiar tasks and what new understandings that knowledge can provoke.

The idea of making communications infrastructure visible also resonates through a number of contemporary design and art projects. Julian Oliver's *Border Bumping* project has interrogated moment of cellphone network switch and breakdown at national borders [36], while Martinussen, Knutsen and Arnall's *Satellite Lamps* installation uses lamps to alert people to the nearby presence of GNSS satellites [32]. Network visualization app, *The Architecture of Radio* uses static datasets to depict a realm of signals, including nearby cellphone towers, Wi-Fi routers and communications satellites [49]. These projects all share a desire to make communications infrastructures visible and thereby provoke reflection in the viewer.

Such reflection on the presence and operation of infrastructure can, in turn, generate new approaches for design. Chalmers and Galani argue that the disappearance of computing proposed by Weiser fails to recognise the everyday negotiations made at seams which become exposed during moments of breakdown or translation across different software or platforms. The negotiations which take place at such moments can be productive for designers to explore [13]. Infrastructural inversion, where one looks beyond those moments of breakdown to what they can reveal about the infrastructure, also has the potential to generate new systems or practices of use. While such approaches have not yet extensively explored in the literature, examples do exist of the generative potential of infrastructural inversion in digital humanities [27], sensors in field based scientific research [33] and climate science [20]. While the present study did not foreground the generation of new designs, we intend that it can be useful to critical design communities by providing techniques for making infrastructures visible and inspiration for designers to explore.

STAGING A STUDY

The experiments described here were undertaken as a series of three walks around the Barbican Estate in spring and summer 2016. We focused on the Barbican because its distinctive architecture often blocks GNSS signals, making breakdown more likely. An additional walk took place around Manchester city centre in August 2016. The walks were simultaneously understood as art and research projects, a formulation reinforced by their promotion with partner organisations. One Barbican walk was arranged with the Culture Capital Exchange, an organisation which focuses on "knowledge exchange, collaboration and wider engagement between the research base and the arts" [44]. Another was organised with Antiuniversity Now who aim to challenge existing structures of knowledge production "by inviting people to organise and share free learning events in public spaces" [5]. The event in Manchester was organised in association with the Loitering with Intent exhibition at Manchester Peoples' History Museum. The other walk around the Barbican was organised by the authors. Undoubtedly, as a result of our framing and choice of collaborators, the majority of our 26 participants identified as being from an arts or research background. For us this was an advantage. Respondents from these backgrounds had proven more willing to engage with the possibility of re-conceptualising GNSS in preliminary studies which also involved respondents from computer science and engineering backgrounds.

Figure 1. A Participant moves through the monolithic architecture of the Barbican Estate.

Besides attracting certain participants, the use of an art context to stage our research was motivated by a desire for the flexibility and freedom which art practices can provide for thought experiments [29]. By situating our study within this context, we also invoked a lineage of art practices around locative media and the act of walking. In this way, we acknowledge that we constructed a site in which to stage the research.

Interrogating what it means to site research, Dilley draws attention to the influence of the particular research questions being posed: "contexts are sets of connections constructed as relevant to someone, to something or to a particular problem, and this process yields an explanation, a sense, an interpretation for the object so connected." [18:2]. Law and Urry make a stronger claim that methods "can help to bring into being what they also discover" [30:395]. So, in this way, we are aware that we have made a conscious intervention in the participants' relationship with technical objects and the infrastructure which lies behind them, but we have done this to bring into existence a set of conditions which helps to probe our area of concern. This acknowledgement invites the kind of complexity described by Lindstrom and Stahl as "entanglements in multiple temporalities" [31]. We accept this and, in the analysis of our data, seek to include the attendant specificities of staging, site and technical tools.

After looking for an appropriate architectural site, we decided to stage the walks primarily in the Barbican Estate, a collection of concrete buildings, comprising a residential estate and an arts centre. The estate is built in the brutalist style and has many architectural features which block lines of sight with the sky (covered underpasses, extensive underground car parks, indoor public spaces (see figure 1)). These structures also have the potential to produce multipath errors as signals travel from satellite to device, bouncing off large-scale, reflective concrete surfaces on the way. Indeed, owing to its often obscure design, the complex is notoriously difficult to navigate, to the extent that *Googlemaps* offers an indoor navigation service for the arts centre. Our participants were given a commercial app developed by Chartcross called *GPS Test* which uses the affordances allowed by the Android operating system to plot a compass-style map of GNSS satellite positions in relation to the device (see figure 2). The app also offers a bar chart of relative signal to noise ratios for transmissions from the satellites in view (see figure 3) and information relating to the device's velocity and height relative to sea level. To give the participants some idea what they were seeing on the app, we gave them a brief explanation of the way location is established through the triangulation of time-stamped satellite signals and compared to the known trajectories of individual satellites within an almanac database.

We focused on the importance of lines-of-sight with the sky to allow reception of broadcast signals. We also gave them some very brief history of the development of the GPS and GLONASS systems. We ran the app on Yuntab K03-7 7-inch tablet devices using the Android 4.2 operating system. The app only takes GNSS signals into account, so there was no need to disambiguate from other modes a device may use to establish location. Participants walked freely around the Barbican site for 30 minutes during which time they were observed. After returning to the meeting point, they were given pens and paper and asked to reflect on their experience through drawing and writing. They did this for around 20 minutes after which the group came together for a discussion. Transcripts of the discussion formed the backbone of our data, while the drawn and written material was intended to allow participants to reflect individually before contributing to the discussion. Individual written and drawn responses were therefore read alongside the discussion as supporting material and to mitigate against the possibility of participants being shy or reserved in the discussion context.

We coded the data using grounded theory principles [16] to establish themes and then used the themes as part of a situational analysis [15] which also allowed for the influence of the physical site, art staging and surrounding sociotechnical practices. We chose this approach to be "accountable to the complexity" [15: 559] we were producing both through the conscious staging of our research and the problemetization of familiar technologies and practices. We would like to think that situational analysis also offers steps towards an infrastructural inversion of the research process itself, allowing us to probe what is assumed both in attendant sociotechnical contexts and our own theoretical assumptions.

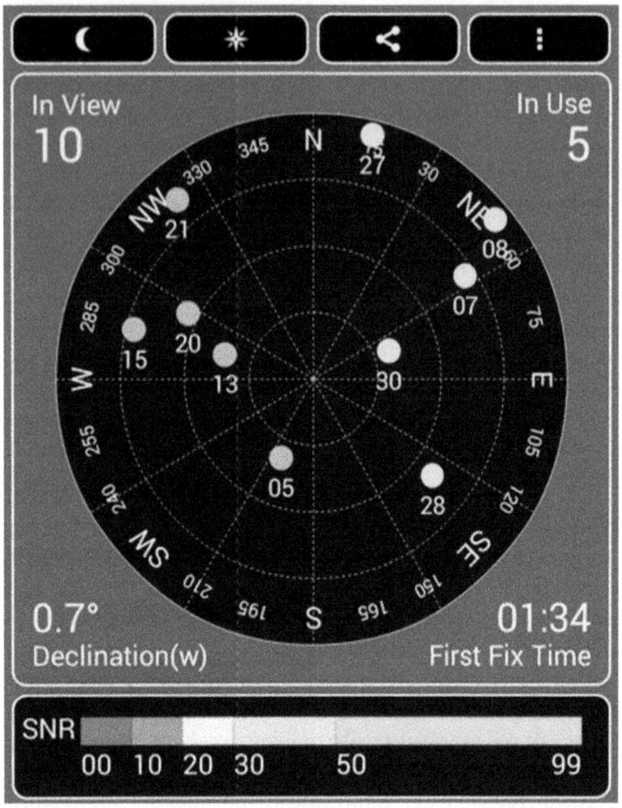

Figure 2. The compass-style display showing satellite positions in *GPS Test*. Here the device can only establish connections satellites to the east of its position.

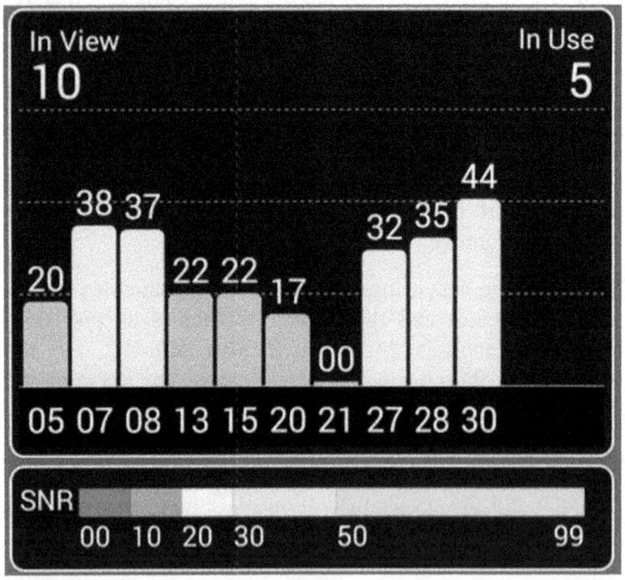

Figure 3. The bar chart display showing relative satellite signal to noise ratios in *GPS Test*.

ALIENATION / ENVIRONMENT / DYNAMICS

Our first question for the data generated by the workshops was whether we had succeeded in making GNSS infrastructure more visible. In three different workshops participants identified an "inversion" of the usual operation of the technology. The change was understood as a shift in what was being located by whom, so "you could see them [satellites] rather than being seen":

"I'm used to me on *Googlemaps* being a little blue dot, so in a strange way I thought there's something quite subversive about the satellites being located by me... locating the satellite rather than locating yourself was fun to play with".

The position of the satellites provided the point of contact with GNSS infrastructure. Other physical elements of GNSS infrastructure such as ground antennas and control stations remained concealed, as did the techniques and standards which fed into the design and testing of the satellites. These elements were embedded within the satellite, which was understood as a coherent and distinct object. This understanding was supported by the placement of satellites as separate dots of the visual interface.

Despite these caveats, the exercise did allow participants to think beyond conventional user experiences and, as we shall see, use satellites as prompts to reflect on their sociotechnical practices. This manifested in several ways. In the following section, we describe participants' responses beginning with alienation, moving through awareness of an infrastructural context, to reflection on some of the dynamics at work within that awareness. We conclude the section by noting the persistence of certain familiar aspects such as the power of a visual interface and the idea of GNSS as a tool associated with mapping.

Alienation

A sense of removal from usual tasks was experienced by several participants. This was felt through a re-orientation, where "the whole sense of direction became a bit more abstract and didn't seem to include me in it", or, in broader terms, everything on the site became "surreal". The participant who noted the "surreal" also stated that "this could be what it's like inside a computer game - a pixel slowed down to the speed of snails". This sense of disassociation was interpreted in terms of size and scale by another participant:

"The experience of reminding myself of the relationship between device and satellite had the same impact as when I'm in a space where I can see the stars. I often forget that I'm on a planet... one of many in a much bigger space, and whenever I see the stars it has an impact... so for me it's a slightly humbling experience... this experience has just reminded me of this scope of things, the ecosystem that is my life, the universe... and that came off very powerfully when I sat down and started to look up"

Here the scale of the infrastructure sparked a removal from everyday concerns and created reflection back on the profoundly large space and time of the universe. For him, stars acted as a point of comparison for the presence of satellites, indeed, the comparison also exists in the design nomenclature where an array of satellites is called a 'constellation'.

We would also reflect that, although the aspects specific to GNSS infrastructure (such as scale) certainly contributed to a sense of alienation, the staging of the exercise undoubtedly had an influence. One participant wrote that the exercise felt like a 'techno-derive', betraying knowledge of the work of the situationists. He described how wandering without a task emphasised his sensory experience:

"The thing was, not having to go from 'A' to 'B', it made me acutely aware of my body in relation to the temperature, humidity, sound. All of which could change with the pungent smells from the kitchen air extractors. The magnified distant booming of vehicles unloading, trolleys on prams bashing over textured flooring."

This enhanced sensory experience is similar to that which lead one participant to report an experience felt "at the speed of snails" and betrays the art staging of the experiment, especially to those in the know. Although it may be from a mix of causes, responses of alienation from usual practices were widespread, thereby laying the groundwork for more nuanced engagement with infrastructure.

An Environment of Signals

In taking their attention away from their usual practices, several participants were provoked to think about the presence of electromagnetic signals in their surroundings. This feature of the infrastructure was, again, partially driven by the experiment design and use of *GPS Test*. Through the app, the presence of satellites was revealed, but a secondary effect was the awareness of signal paths which allowed a given satellite to be designated 'in use'. The presence of GNSS signals made participants also consider how rich the air might be with Wi-Fi, cell phone and radio transmissions. Signals became a dominant theme in one of the discussions and appeared in two others. One participant "wonder[ed] what else was around", while another questioned the nature of those signals as a surrounding medium: "the question of how ethereal is this, it's like what are we actually moving through? What's the world that we're existing in and how much of it are we aware of?" For both these participants, the revealed presence of infrastructure raised questions, both of what was there and how it affects them. Another participant made a stronger claim, positing a whole ecosystem, which they, themselves were part of:

"So, you've got like universal background static all the way down to these super-precise signals and very short range signals which are probably coming from like Wi-Fi routers in the building or peoples' phones and it's this whole nested scale of like different kinds of signal which are penetrating your body, your phone, the building around you, and you're also part of that structure in a way, you know, you're accepting, receiving, deflecting all this stuff as well."

This understanding of oneself as a reflective and receptive body within a structure of signals marks something different from initial experiences of alienation. The participant has proposed an alternate system in which the user's body, phone, Wi-Fi and long-range signals are understood as an overlapping and interacting web. It is not clear in what sense this participant would or would not understand this structure as an infrastructure in the terms proposed by Star and Ruhleder [42], but the possibility of placing oneself within a system of ambient, ongoing interactions, leads us to think about what sociotechnical dynamics might emerge out of such an infrastructural awareness.

Dynamics

If it is possible to imagine a wider system of interactions between body, device, a scale of signals and technical objects, we can then ask what dynamics exist within that system. Those dynamics were surely experienced differently by each participant, but nevertheless some common themes emerged.

Every discussion exhibited a strong theme of play and experimentation. Participants chose to describe the activity variously as "hide and seek" or "like walking a puzzle". The process reminded another participant of "not stepping on the cracks when you're a kid". Within the app, when a location fix was possible, all the satellites in use would light up, when it was not, all the satellites would be greyed out. As a location fix provided strong visual feedback to participants, it is unsurprising that they would focus on this action. What does require more explanation, however, is that many of them understood this as play. In some ways, this aspect suggests a more open interaction with the infrastructure, one distinct from typical task-based practices. However, as a game, hide and seek does come with some basic roles and structures around the visibility of the participants.

This act of hiding can be understood in part as testing or, in the words of one participant, "probing" the infrastructure, but it also resonates strongly with another theme which was present throughout all the discussions; the position of GNSS infrastructure within a wider system of surveillance and privacy concerns. While it was noted in the workshops' technical introduction that the satellites themselves are merely emitting signals and they do not 'see' activity on the ground, the trope of spy satellites with observing eyes was persistent (see figure 4). Even without a direct link from satellite to surveillance, participants were aware of the collection of personal data by corporate and state actors further up the data food chain. The asymmetry of power implied by an infrastructure on such a scale did not escape the notice of one participant who referred to the satellite constellation as "the imperial grid" and "the all-seeing eye". While another described it as "kind of scary", reflecting on "possibilities for control and writers like Orwell and how it can be used for good or bad". Another participant voiced more specific concerns, stating that:

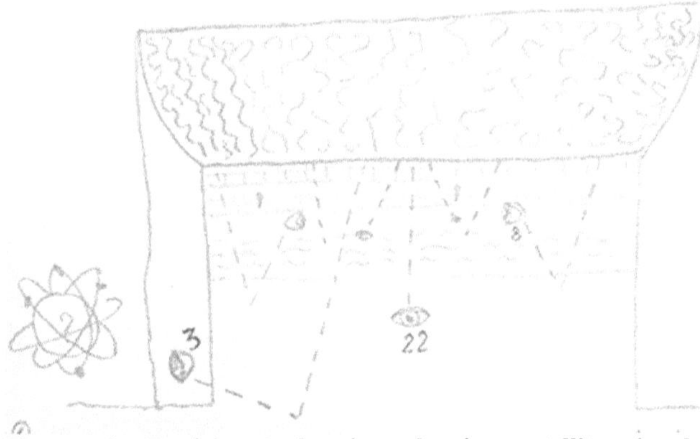

Figure 4. Participant drawing showing satellite signals descending as observant eyes.

"While I don't feel like I do anything where I would be surveilled for that thing, I know that information is used beyond its descriptive capabilities, and so that exercise of state or corporate power is not just in the hands of people who understand the specific limitations of the technology, but also people who have had it explained to them third hand… so I'd rather not leave a trail of breadcrumbs anywhere."

This comment betrays a lack of confidence in both the limits of explanatory power of location data and the ability of data-handlers to recognise those limits. Several other statements were made along these lines including one participant who described a privacy calculus she makes between giving up personal information and having the convenience of a locative service like *Googlemaps*. For her the experiment made her "think about it the other way", that "even though I'm using a service, the service is using me, just as… probably more than it's used by me." The trigger for this reflection was "the visual nature of having something like that in the sky… it brings it home to you, that they're really up there." Here, GNSS infrastructure acted as a stand in, an implicated composite part of a wider infrastructure concerned with tracking the movement of people and devices. The making visible of this infrastructure led her to reflect on the way she forms her usual practices around personal information.

Although this participant experienced the presence of GNSS infrastructure in an unsettling way, others responded to the satellites differently. During the Manchester study, several participants noticed that, despite their best efforts to "hide" from satellite signals, one satellite was more persistent than the others. Number 26 (named from its Pseudorandom noise (PRN) code) was described as "the plucky satellite that was still holding when all the others were vanishing". The persistence of this one satellite, while likely more the result of its position in the sky than any property specific to it, allowed the experience to "become personal", inspiring one participant to report:

"I was almost I don't know, really surprised about how it felt inside, rather than this kind of scientific gadget, cos I'm not a particularly gadget-y person, and I found myself completely transfixed by it."

What is perhaps most noteworthy here is that a "personal" relationship with a satellite can become possible. This is, in part, a result of the power of the visual interface which depicts satellites as distinct, numbered moving dots on a chart. While, strictly speaking, the satellites act primarily in concert, with four signals needing to be received to establish a reliable location fix, the design of the app presents satellites as discreet objects. This reveals the interface's continuing ability to inscribe user responses. Indeed, both the visual interface and other lingering established sociotechnical practices proved influential in other ways.

Visual Interface and Mapping

Features of the app's interface were recreated in several participants' drawn responses to the walk. In one case, the app's bar chart took on other potential meanings, with this participant likening it to a city skyline. Far more common was the presence of numbers in drawn responses. GPS Test's interface features a wealth of numbers, from the PRNs of individual satellites to the tickers for how many satellites are in view and in use. Numbers influenced user experiences to the extent that one participant wrote: "the space becomes a patchwork of numbers". This resulting space was variously understood as meandering (see figure 5) or part of a more ordered mapping process (see figure 6). Indeed, the mapping of space through the permeability of GNSS signals emerged in every discussion. This took slightly different forms, with some shift over whether the mapping would be done for the benefit of users who wanted to "escape" from GNSS signals or, perhaps, as a means for the satellites themselves to map and read the city. In this later case, one participant offered the concept of the "city as braille", a physical language to be read through the touch of signals. In practice this is not possible within the scope of current technology, but it does represent a very interesting dynamic where the user is removed and the focus of sociotechnical practice shifts to the possibility of GNSS infrastructure's actions on other, architectural infrastructures.

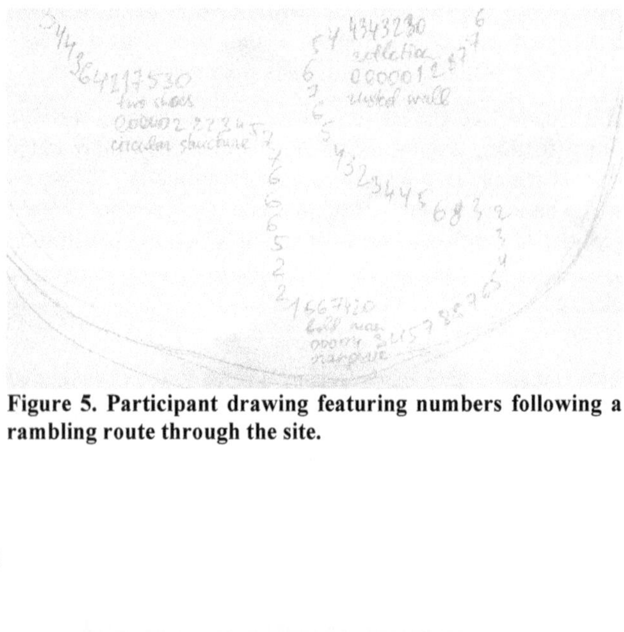

Figure 5. Participant drawing featuring numbers following a rambling route through the site.

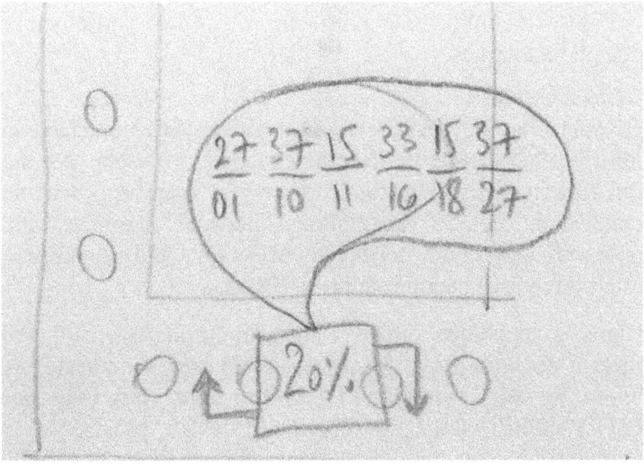

Figure 6. Detail of a participant drawing with an ordered use of numbers and a percentage sense of signal coverage.

DISCUSSION

Throughout the research activities, several alternative user experiences emerged. In this section, we briefly summarise them, reflect on the success of the experiments and discuss their implications for designers.

Firstly, the experiments did alienate participants from their usual sociotechnical practices, in the sense that it reversed the 'gaze' of the infrastructure. Typically, satellites and the technical objects which support them are concealed, but *GPS Test* allowed the satellites' presence to be revealed. This gave participants a new perspective on both the task at hand and the space around them. The experiment allowed participants to explore the effects of architecture on the functioning of GNSS infrastructure through moments of breakdown. As such, movement became a strong interaction mode, participants explored the site, testing different locations for signal strength, an interaction which was frequently described as a game of "hide and seek". This represents a type of the infrastructural inversion proposed by Bowker and Star, although it is limited by certain factors. The full infrastructure was not made visible. Rather, the app reported the presence of satellites and, through that visualisation, implied the presence of GNSS signals. The existence of ground antennas, control stations and the historical development of GNSS systems were not directly revealed through the experiment. Their existence was explained to participants in the introduction to the experiment, but they were certainly less present than other elements. The infrastructural inversion achieved here was, then, not complete, but was strong enough to create affective experiences of embeddedness within an ecosystem of signals and a profound sense of the scale of the infrastructure. Deeper and more wide-ranging infrastructural inversions would likely take considerably more time and commitment from participants. The use of a satellite-focused inversion is therefore incomplete, but offers a type of experiential immediacy which we found to be productive.

The inverted sense of space and practice achieved through the experiment allowed participants to begin to explore themes related to the process of blackboxing. The strongest among them was the idea of privacy. Participants were aware that "state and corporate" actors would be able to track them in their daily movements, but that knowledge had been parsed into the background. When participants stated "this really brings it home that they're up there", or drew a network of eyes coming down from the sky, they were referring to the satellites, but the satellites were acting as a symbol of wider interconnecting infrastructures of location tracking. Participants offered nuanced critiques of such infrastructures and the role their own practices play in them. They mentioned a privacy calculus between being provided with a service and giving up one's information. They also mentioned the ways in which the frequent use of such a technology can lead to "dependency", an interesting acknowledgement of the ways an infrastructure can become invisible through its successful adoption. Participants also acknowledged what Callon and Latour called the "asymmetries of power" [12] around macro-actors, while exploring the ways such asymmetries are negotiated by different groups in different contexts. One participant mentioned the work he undertakes as a researcher using GNSS to track migration patterns of birds, speculating on how the data models he develops could also be used to track humans. In response, another participant noted how, during the recent large-scale migration of refugees across eastern Europe, GNSS had proved very useful to allow people to navigate successfully through an unfamiliar environment. This discussion suggests that the experiment provided a successful prompt for critical engagement with themes generally made invisible by blackboxing. Participants could see the presence of macro-actors and reflect on their influence. As such, our findings suggest that practices which invert infrastructure would be useful in both "empowering" users in participatory design practices [43], while the staging aspect of the work may also provide inspiration for designers working with improvised theatrical approaches [39,50]. The project also points to ways through which designers can reflect on hidden critical issues at play in the design process [9, 41].

The experiment also points to the possibility of conceptualising experiences which do not centre around the user. Participants reflected on possible interactions between GNSS infrastructure and architecture, where, within an ecosystem of signals, the city emerged as "braille", a language of touch which could be explored by signal penetration. If we think of elements of the infrastructure as discreet entities, then satellites could not 'read' the city through this touch as no information is fed back to them. However, if we consider the process of knowing as something which can emerge across an infrastructure, then this proposition makes more sense, providing a way of conceptualizing practices which do not rely on users. The techniques to allow such a shift in thinking are likely to prove productive in fostering both critical reflection and inspiration as technologies develop which requires less human intervention.

Following Chalmers and Galani, we suggested that seams and moments of breakdown may offer generative potential for designers. From this work, we can offer some thoughts for designers of LBS interested in creating alternative and reflective experiences. We note that the visual interface remained extremely influential in participants' responses. In some cases, they copied elements for their drawings, and in many cases borrowed the trope of numbers to express the operation of GNSS. It may be that an experience design which takes the user away from the smartphone object and its visual interface would offer a more profound alternative to familiar user experiences. Indeed, another interaction dynamic which came through strongly was movement. Participants explored the site by moving between different locations. Nikki Pugh's *Landscape Reactive Sashes* project (discussed in [40]) may provide a useful counterpoint. Pugh had participants walk with two GPS devices. Owing to differences in site and sensor, each produces slightly different location readings. The readings are compared with a high-quality GPS sensor which has a clear view of the sky and participants are informed when accuracy drops by a vibrator attached to a sash hung over their bodies. This project leverages contingencies in the infrastructure to demonstrate that location is not a given and the processes used to establish it have a materiality formed variously from the nature of the sensor and the interplays between sensor, satellite and site. It also offers a promising alternative to the use of a screen. The use of vibration provides the user with less diagnostic information, but arguably offers an experience more distant from their usual practices.

Critical designers may also be interested to note the persistence of ideas of mapping. Participants suggested developing a graded topography of GNSS signal strength as a means of "hiding" from satellites. With dominant sociotechnical practices positioning GNSS as a spatial technology, mapping offers a useful point of leverage for critical designers interested in developing locative experiences which are challenging, yet contain a 'conceptual bridge' [6], to more familiar practices.

Finally, we acknowledge the specificity of our particular method to GNSS infrastructures. We hope however that our experiences will not just inform designers and researchers working with LBS, but rather provide encouragement to those working with other infrastructures. In particular we would reflect on the usefulness of casting attention onto infrastructure as a prompt for reflection on concealed aspects of the design and use of familiar technologies. We would like to see future work which applies and develops these techniques with a wider range of user groups than our useful, but narrow sample of artists and researchers, perhaps combining our approach with other participatory design techniques.

CONCLUSIONS

GNSS technology represents a pervasive, yet embedded and invisible infrastructure for the majority of users. As the infrastructure is blackboxed, power relations become concealed, design inscriptions become stronger and potential for both critical reflection and imagining alternative uses becomes more difficult.

Using a technique built on infrastructural inversion, we offer a potential route for designers and users interested in exploring what lies behind the veil of invisibility cast over GNSS infrastructure by dominant design processes. In applying our technique, we note the persistence of the visual interface in defining practices and modes of use. We also acknowledge practical limits to making extensive aspects of the infrastructure visible. In our case, we concentrated on the positions of satellites which were able to represent themselves and to act as a stand-in for attendant infrastructures already known to participants.

We conclude that, despite its limitations, our technique was successful in alienating participants from their usual practices and providing new perspectives and experiences. We note the specificity of our method to GNSS infrastructures, but encourage researchers and designers interested in exploring the hidden influence of infrastructures to leverage techniques of infrastructural inversion to their case-specific needs. In this spirit, we offer the limitations and successes we experienced as some signposts to all those interested in circumventing processes of infrastructural blackboxing.

ACKNOWLEDGEMENTS

We would like to gratefully acknowledge the contribution of the partner organisations and participants. This work is supported by the Media and Arts Technology programme, Engineering and Physical Sciences Research Council (ESPRC) Doctoral Training Centre EP/G03723X/1.

REFERENCES

1. Margunn Aanestad, & Tina Blegind Jensen. (2011). "Building nation-wide information infrastructures in healthcare through modular implementation strategies." *Journal of Strategic Information Systems*, 20(2), 161–176.

2. Madeline Akrich. 1992. The Description of Technical Objects. In *Shaping Technology / Building Society*, W. E. Bijker and John Law (eds.) MIT Press: Cambridge, MA. 205-224.

3. Madeline Akrich and Bruno Latour. 1992. A summary of a convenient vocabulary for the semiotics of human and nonhuman assemblies. In *Shaping Technology/ Building Society*. W.E. Bijker and J. Law (eds). MIT Press: Cambridge, MA. 259–264.

4. Android. 2017. Retrieved 3rd April 2017 from https://www.android.com/.
5. Antiuniversity Now. 2016. About. Retrived January 16, 2016 from http://www.antiuniversity.org/ABOUT
6. James Auger. 2013. Speculative design: crafting the speculation. *Digital Creativity*, 24, (1): 11–35.
7. Sturla Bakke. 2010. How principles of human-computer interactions could contribute in black- boxing complexities in information infrastructures. Presented at the *Information Systems Research Seminar in Scandinavia (IRIS 33)*
8. Shaowen Bardzell, Jeffrey Bardzell, Jodi Forlizzi, John Zimmerman, John Antanitis. Critical Design and Critical Theory: The Challenge of Designing for Provocation. *Proceedings of DIS 2012*. 288-297. http://doi.acm.org/10.1145/2317956.2318001
9. Genevieve Bell, Mark Blythe, Pheobe Sengers. 2005. Making by Making Strange: Defamiliarization and the Design of Domestic Technologies. *ACM Transactions on Human Computer Interaction* 12 (2): 149-173.
10. Geoffrey Bowker. 1994. *Science on the Run: Information Management and Industrial Geophysics at Schlumberger 1920-1940*. MIT Press: Cambridge, MA.
11. Geoffrey Bowker and `Susan Leigh Star. 1999. *Sorting Things Out: Classification and its consequences*. MIT Press: Cambridge, MA.
12. Michel Callon and Bruno Latour. 1981. Unscrewing the Big Leviathan; or How Actors Macrostructure Reality, and How Sociologists Help Them To Do So. In *Advances in Social Theory and Methodology*, Karen Knorr and Aaron Cicourel (eds.) Routledge: London.
13. Matthew Chalmers and Areti Galani. 2004. Seamful Interweaving: Heterogeneity in the Theory and Design of Interactive Systems. *Proceedings of DIS 2004*.
14. Citymapper. 2017. Retrieved 3rd April 2017 from https://citymapper.com/.
15. Adele Clarke. 2003. Situational Analyses: Grounded Theory Mapping After the Postmodern Turn. *Symbolic Interaction*. 26 (4): 553-576.
16. Juliet Corbin and Anslem Strauss. 1990. Grounded Theory Research: Procedures, Canons, and Evaluative Criteria. *Qualitative Sociology* 13 (1): 3–21.
17. Guy Debord. 1994. *The Society of the Spectacle*. Zone: New York.
18. Roy Dilley. 1999. Introduction: The Problem of Context. In *The Problem of Context*, Roy Dilley (ed.) Berghahn: New York. 1-46.
19. Anthony Dunne. 2008. *Hertzian Tales: Electronic Products, Aesthetic Experience and Critical Design* (2nd. ed.). MIT Press, Cambridge, MA.
20. Paul Edwards. 2010. *A Vast Machine: Computer Models, Climate Data and the Politics of Global Warming*. MIT Press: Cambridge, MA.
21. Facebook. 2017. Retrieved April 3rd 2017 from https://www.facebook.com
22. Foursquare. 2017. Retrieved April 3rd 2017 from https://foursquare.com
23. Ole Hanseth and Eric Monteiro. 1997. Inscribing Behaviour in Information Infrastructure Standards. *Accounting, Management & Information Technology*. 7 (4). 183-211.
24. Jeffrey Heer and Peter Khooshabeh. 2004. Seeing the Invisible. Presented at *Workshop on Invisible and Transparent Interfaces at Advanced Visual Interfaces*.
25. Instagram. 2017. Retrieved April 3rd 2017 from https://www.instagram.com/.
26. iOS 10. 2017. Retrieved 3rd April 2017 from http://www.apple.com/uk/ios/ios-10/.
27. Wolfgang Kaltenbrunner. 2015. Infrastructural Inversion as a Generative Resource in Digital Scholarship. *Science as Culture*. 24 (1): 1-23.
28. Bruno Latour. 1999. *Pandora's Hope*. Harvard University Press: Cambridge, MA.
29. Bruno Latour. 2004. From Realpolitik to Dingpolitik – An Introduction to Making Things Public. In *Making Things Public - Atmospheres of Democracy Catalogue of the Show at ZKM*. MIT Press: Cambridge, MA. 2-32.
30. John Law and John Urry. 2005. Enacting the Social. *Economy and Society* 33 (3): 390–410.
31. Kristina Lindström and Åsa Ståhl. 2014. Patchworking Publics-in-the-Making: Design, Media and Public Engagement. Ph.D Dissertation, Malmo University.
32. Einar Sneve Martinussen, Jørn Knutsen, & Timo Arnall. 2014. Satellite Lamps. *Kairos*. 19 (1). Retrieved April 3rd 2017 from http://kairos.technorhetoric.net/19.1/inventio/martinussen-et-al/index.html.
33. Matthew Mayernik, Jillian Wallis, Christine Borgman. 2013. Unearthing the Infrastructure: Humans and Sensors in Field-Based Scientific Research. *Computer Supported Cooperative Work*. 22 (1): 65 – 101.
34. Annemarie Mol. 2010. Actor Network Theory: Sensitive Terms and Enduring Tensions. *Kölner Zeitschrift Für Soziologie Und Sozialpsychologie* 50 (1): 253–69.
35. Maps. 2017. Retrieved 3rd April 2017 from https://play.google.com/store/apps/details?id=com.google.android.apps.maps&hl=en.
36. Julian Oliver. 2014. *Border Bumping*. Retrieved April 3rd 2017 from http://borderbumping.net/.

37. Pokemon Go. 2017. Retrieved on 3rd April 2017 from http://www.pokemongo.com/.

38. Stefan Poslad. 2009. Ubiquitous computing: smart devices, environments and interactions. Oxford; Wiley-Blackwell.

39. Merja Ryöppy, Salu Ylirisku, Preben Friis, Jacob Buur. 2016. Proceedings of the 20th International Academic Mindtrek Conference. 462-465. http://dx.doi.org/10.1145/2994310.2994361

40. Kim Sawchuk and Samuel Thulin. 2016. More Than Just a Pinpoint: Locative Media and the Chorographic Impulse. *Leonardo Electronic Almanac* 21 (1). 160–76.

41. Pheobe Sengers, Kirsten Boehner, David Shay, Jofish Kaye. 2005. Reflective Design. *Proceedings of the 4th Decennial Conference on Critical Computing: Between Sense and Sensibility*. 49-58. http://doi.acm.org/10.1145/1094562.1094569

42. Susan Leigh Star and Karen Ruhleder. 1996. Steps toward an Ecology of Infrastructure: Design and Access for Large Information Spaces. *Information Systems Research*. 7 (1): 111-134.

43. Cristiano Storni. 2015. Notes on ANT for designers: ontological, methodological and epistemological turn in collaborative design. *CoDesign*. 11 (3-4): 166-178.

44. TCCE. 2016. What We Do. Retrieved 16th January, 2016 from http://www.theculturecapitalexchange.co.uk/about-us/#horizontalTabs1.

45. Marc Tuters. 2012. From Mannerist Situationism to Situated Media. In *Convergence: The International Journal of Research into New Media Technologies* 18,3: 267–282.

46. Marc Tuters and Kays Varnelis. 2006. Beyond Locative Media: Giving Shape to the Internet of Things. *Leonardo*. 39 (4): 357-363.

47. Twitter. 2017. Retrieved on April 3rd 2017 from https://twitter.com.

48. Uber. 2017. Retrieved on April 3rd 2017 from https://www.uber.com/.

49. Richard Vijgen. 2015. *The Architecture of Radio*. Retrieved April 3rd 2017 from http://www.architectureofradio.com/.

50. John Vines, Tess Denman-Cleaver, Paul Dunphy, Peter Wright and Patrick Olivier. 2014. Experience Design Theatre: Exploring the Role of Live Theatre in Scaffolding Design Dialogues. *CHI '14 Proceedings of the SIGCHI Conference on Human Factors in Computing Systems*. 683-692. http://dx.doi.org/10.1145/2556288.2556960

51. Mark Weiser. 1991. The Computer for the 21st Century. *Scientific American* 265 (3): 94–104.

52. Mark Weiser. 1994. Creating the Invisible Interface (Invited Talk). presented at the *ACM Conf on User Interface Software and Technology (UIST)*. http://doi.acm.org/10.1145/192426.192428

Designing Intelligent Assistant through User Participations

Sang-su Lee
sangsu.lee@kaist.ac.kr

Jaemyung Lee
shurei@kaist.ac.kr

Kun-pyo Lee
kplee@kaist.ac.kr

Dept. of Industrial Design, KAIST
335 Gwahangno Yusung-Gu, Daejeon, Republic of Korea

ABSTRACT
Today, intelligent assistants, such as Apple's Siri, becoming a part of our everyday life. While there have been many studies focused on technologies, there are no studies dealing with design issues at the initial stage of the design, the stage prior to system implementation. Although the designers had a lot of questions in the design process, such as how the personality of virtual assistant should be, how users could discover the way of interacting, the designers had to rely on imagination. In this paper, we present a user-friendly way of designing intelligent assistant which allow designers and engineers to explore the possible design problems and solutions through user participation, before all the complex systems are ready to run. Through a low-tech approach involving two users, we could understand the behavior of users with intelligent assistants in an easy and fast way.

Author Keywords
Intelligent assistant; virtual assistant; design method; interaction design.

ACM Classification Keywords
H.5.m. Information interfaces and presentation (e.g., HCI): Miscellaneous.

INTRODUCTION
It is no longer the future that a computer understands what people say and responds appropriately to it. Today, computers (or smart devices) are becoming assistants, not just devices that perform a given command of the user. Intelligent assistants (or IA) or virtual assistants such as Apple's Siri, Amazon's Alexa, Microsoft's Cortana, or Google Assistant have become available to our everyday life [8]. Google believes that intelligent virtual assistants or the conversational user interface will largely supplant search engines and apps for many users. [1]

Although these intelligent assistants seem to be doing creative action based on 'intelligence', they are still results of careful design by engineers and designers with the help of technologies such as machine learning, natural language understanding, natural interaction recognition, and big data analysis. For example, if someone ask Siri and Cortana the same question, "Sing me a song", the result is quite different (Figure 1), and the difference is the result of what the designer intended. Therefore, many design problems arise in answering questions of how an intelligent assistant can support a user. However, while there have been studies on the technical aspects of implementing intelligence assistant and usability evaluation methods for completed systems, there has not been much research on the design method or trial to find answers to design problems in the early stage.

From the initial stages of IA development, there are many design areas that need to be carefully decided. Designers define a persona, such as the personality and profile of the virtual assistant that the user will be exposed to, and then define the talking style, voice tone, and detailed script accordingly. They also need to define the interaction details with the user, derive the expected user actions, and design the detailed reaction of the assistant according to the situation. During this process, compared to conventional interaction design, it is very difficult to do design iteration based on rapid prototyping and testing, which is important in design process.

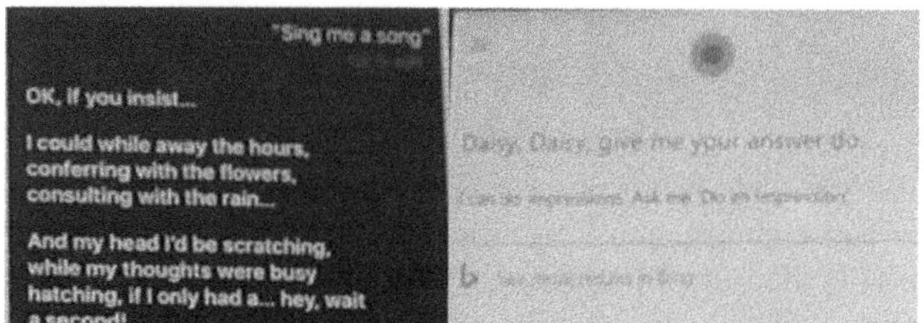

Figure 1. Different results between Siri and Cortana for the same question, "Sing me a song": at this point, while Siri just read the lyrics, Cortana actually sings a song.

DIS 2017, June 10-14, 2017, Edinburgh, United Kingdom
 ISBN 978-1-4503-4922-2/17/06...$15.00
DOI: http://dx.doi.org/10.1145/3064663.3064733

For implementing IA system, massive elements must be prepared at the same time, including techniques on natural language understanding and generating, rules and scripts for each situation that users can perform, server system, and so on. In many cases of IA development, after casting a voice actor to the planned voice and recording the language elements that are needed for generating natural language which takes several months, it is able to start the user test. Although the designers usually have a lot of questions in the design process, such as how the personality of virtual assistant should be, how users could discover the way of interacting, the designers have to rely on imagination. Also, once all the systems are set up and ready for testing, the basic design elements are often difficult to modify.

In this situation, we realized that we need a way to get design implications for developing IA from the early stage of design process before actual implementation. We devised a new method based on the fact that the design direction of most intelligent assistants today is to make users feel like they have a capable 'human-like' secretary. We recruited two participants as a team, and they were asked to perform a given task: one participant being the user, and the other being asked to interact with the user as if he or she were a virtual assistant built into the system.

In this paper, we present a user-friendly way of designing intelligent assistant which allow designers and engineers to explore the possible design problems and solutions through user participation, without waiting for the system to run. Then we discuss the value and limitations of the method through a simple exploratory case study.

RELATED WORKS

Spoken dialogue systems [11], which have been studied over the past two decades, are the origin of today's intelligent assistants (IA). The spoken dialogue systems understand and respond to the voice commands in a dialogue form. Intelligent assistants are different from traditional spoken dialogue systems in a way that IA understand user intent not only from the voice but also from various natural modalities and contexts [8], like a human does.

While most studies on intelligent assistants, personal assistants, or virtual assistants are mainly focused on technologies so far [13, 14], only few studies deal with IA in the user-centered design point of view.

Kiselev [8] described a user study that was designed to measure user satisfaction over a range of typical scenarios of use such as controlling a device and web search. Jiang et al. [7] focus on simulated tasks for controlling and chatting with device, and identify satisfactory and unsatisfactory elements of the spoken request.

Although these studies provided insights on improving user experience of voice-controlled intelligent agents, there have been no studies dealing with IA design at the initial stage of the design, which is the stage prior to system implementation. As many IAs today are aimed at mimicking human, we thought it would be possible for a person to pretend to be a virtual assistant.

There have been many studies that applied role play method in the design process [5, 6, 15]. Our study method can also be regarded as a kind of role play method in terms of creating idea in early phases of a project and enhancing the designers' understanding of the future context-of-use by giving roles to users. However, findings obtained through role play do not give direct implications since the interaction details as the actual system is omitted, thus the role play is not perceived as sufficient to create an overall understanding of a system. [17]

On the other hand, there have been studies on collecting interactions directly from users. [12, 10] For example, Wobbrock et al. [18] presented an approach to designing tabletop gestures that rely on eliciting gestures from non-technical users by first portraying the effects of a gesture, and then asking users to perform its cause. In those studies, they were convinced that preliminary explorations are possible before implementing any real interface device. These approaches, however, have limitations that the users cannot be provided feedback.

A Wizard of Oz approach [2, 3] is a solution to provide feedback regardless of technology. However, they were used to evaluate pre-defined interactions in the early design stages. The most directly inspired study we have is a modified user-driven Wizard of Oz method [9]. In that study, another non-technical user has been involved for providing feedback. In this way, it was possible to see not only how users performed input gestures but also how they created proper feedback. The biggest difference from our study is that they banned all communication except gestures, including dialogue, whereas we opened and encouraged all communication between the two participants.

METHOD

Conventional Wizard of Oz study is used to quickly prototype interactive system in the early design stages, by making the user believe that it is actually working. In this case, the role of the wizard performing the action is usually performed by the researcher. In this study, however, we recruited two participants as a team, then we gave each participant a role. One participant being the user, and the other being asked to interact with the user as if he or she were an intelligent agent of the computing system.

Each team was given a task goal from us. We wanted to be able to observe various interactions using IA in the process of achieving this goal, as naturally as possible. Participants in the user role received a task goal to select a destination for vacation with a friend or family, and document a timetable for delivery to them. Constraints include making a two-night, three-day schedule as a table, and attaching more than one image captured in Google Earth to the document. (Figure 2) Time limit was 30 minutes per team and allowing them to finish quickly so they can focus on the tasks and proceed in an efficient way.

Figure 2. Each team was given a task to create a document of vacation plan which includes a timetable and photo. (Result of Team 3)

The participant of assistant role did not act as planned, but as an 'intelligent assistant', she or he has to help the user's task most effectively based on understanding and thinking skills, while the participant of user role has to work with only natural interactions such as speech, motions, and gestures. There is no predefined command or interaction method, and the task is performed through communication between two participants. Through this process, we expect to be able to reproduce the various use case of the intelligent assistant system, by observing detailed tasks and interactions such as getting help for selecting a destination, launching and switching between programs such as Word and Google Map, writing and editing text, creating tables, zooming in and out, capturing and pasting.

Regarding the study environment, it is same as study setup in previous work [9]. Participants of the user role were seated to view the projected screen, while participants of the IA role were able to view the user behind and manipulate the computer accordingly.

Four teams, eight participants were involved in this case study, and they all have experience of using Word and Google Maps. An average of 24 minutes was spent per participating team, then around 10 minutes of interview was conducted after completing the task.

RESULTS AND DISCUSSIONS ON METHOD

Since every interaction feedback from the assistant was provided by a human, the fidelity of the feedback is low and unreliable [9]. Thus, quantitative analysis including the task performance could not be handled. Also, as an exploratory study, the size of our case study is not huge enough to generalize the results. In this section, therefore, rather than describing the detailed quantitative results of the case study itself, we focus on how the method has helped us with the parts we needed for designing intelligent assistant. Through this, we discuss how the method can be of help in this case as well as in general.

1. Get insights into defining the personality and persona of an intelligent assistant.

Although we did not recruit in consideration of the personality distribution of the participants, the participants who played the role of assistant showed different characteristics. (Team 1 was very cheerful and friend-like, Team 2 was introspective and quiet, and Team 3 was the lead for another participant) The various personality differences among the participants played a role in prototyping and testing various characteristics that the intelligent assistant could have.

We could see that the atmosphere and the interaction style between the user and the assistant are completely different due to the difference in personality. If the participant of the assistant role is friendly, the participant of the user role happily performed work and laughed a lot, however the time to complete was the longest. On the other hand, when the assistant was introverted, there was not much voice communication between the two. As a result of concentrating only on task, performance was highest. This result does not have any reliability since there are various variables other than personality in performance, and our sample size is not big enough. However, it is clear that the method provides insights on how to design an intelligent assistant to be viewed as a personal by investigating in advance how different characteristics an assistant can have are expressed in interaction with the user and how it makes a difference in the overall user experience.

By changing the profile of a participant who acts as an assistant as variables of the experiment, such as gender and age, the method may allow to observe how the user behaves for each 'intelligent assistant' before implementing real working system.

2. Collect user behavior and explore feedback.

We were able to collect the user behavior patterns against the IA and explore IA feedback on it. Participants in the user role liked the part where the participant of the intelligent assistant role automatically identified and automates the routine work during task execution. However, the intervention of the IA was not always welcomed by users. The automatic suggestion was made frequently according to the situation, users ignored or disliked it when are immersed in the current content. ("Do not zoom in automatically, just do as I say." [Team 1])

Another very interesting finding is that there was little voice feedback on confirming user input. This is in contrast to most existing commercial IAs that provide responses for every user commands. For example, if a user say "Show me the map", no participants in this study answer like "Opening the map" or "Okay, I got it".

3. Understand how to discover the way of interaction and avoid ambiguity.

From all the teams involved in the experiment, we were able to see the process of clarifying the intent by modifying the uncertainties through the repetitive dialogue between the two participants. (e.g. "Return to the state before." / "This state?" / "No, the state where Europe is visible before that." [Team 3])

The users may forget the gesture corresponding to the command during the task, then the user promptly asked the assistant for help. ("How did I do the Undo before?" / "I guess you had two fingers in X shape" [Team 2])

If there is a new command that is needed, the participants make the idea together to define new gesture that does not overlap with the existing one. ("Let's move to the default position if I clap like this." / "It seems that it is not different from the 'Stop' gesture." / "So how about twice?" [Team 2]

Since conversational user interface is lacking in visual affordance, one of the major challenges of designing intelligent assistant is figuring out how users discover and learn the way of interaction. Through the study, we were able to observe how the two participants naturally solved it, and how the user and intelligent assistant could improve the way of interacting, which was a great help in overcoming the design challenge mentioned above.

4. Understand the emotions that could go between the user and the intelligent assistant

Until technology is developed enough that the system actually has 'emotions', the emotional expression of the intelligent assistant and the way it responds to the user must be artificially created by the designer. Through this study, we were able to understand the emotions that could go between the user and the intelligent assistant, which provided implications on what emotional feedbacks could be designed.

On every team, as soon as the participant of the user role completed the given task, the participant of the assistant role praised it ("Oh, you are so great to find this!" [Team 2]), or enjoyed it together ("We did it!" [Team 4]).

Sometimes the user was blaming during task. The case of Team 1, which has the most intimate relationship, was interesting particularly. If a participant in the Assistant role does not understand the behavior well, participants in the user role have blamed it ("This was a reset gesture, you idiot!"). This emotional criticism has caused participant in the assistant role to suggest a different way of interaction ("It's like Rotation! That's too difficult to understand, how about doing this for reset?").

Since once the assistant system is commercialized, it receives not only simple commands from the user but also several emotional inputs including rough and aggressive one. Understanding how can react to this is a great help in designing intelligent assistant.

5. Explore creative design idea for IA design.

In the process of the two participants performing tasks, we could obtain unexpected design insights. Team 4 used facial expression to do some tasks such as undo. They also define shortcuts that only two knew: hand waving is for app switching, grasping a fist is for going to default position, for example. In team 3, participant of the assistant role suggested gesture improvement when he saw that the user had difficulty in performing a large gesture that use the arm: "Why don't you just use a index finger like this?") This shows that the methodology can also be used to generate novel design ideas.

LIMITATIONS

The intelligent assistant, implemented on a computing system, has capabilities that humans cannot do, based on massive amounts of big data analysis and fast computing power, and will become more powerful in the future. There is a limit to extend the approach introduced in this study, where human participants take the role of computer, to tasks that require massive data analysis and rapid processing. These limitations can be complemented by using the computer to provide the necessary information directly to the participant of assistant role.

Another limitation is that the participants who are in the role of user clearly recognize that the system they are dealing with are human rather than artificial intelligence. If the user has a distinct mental model with distinct behavior when interacting with a person and interacting with an assistant embedded in the system, the value of this method can be reduced. A systematic study of this part is going to be done as future works.

CONCLUSIONS

We devised a methodology for designing intelligent assistants based on our actual needs. Through a low-tech approach involving two users, we could understand the behavior of users with virtual assistants in an easy and fast way, before all the complex systems are ready to run. In addition, through the efforts of both participants to work effectively, we have seen this method not only work as a prototyping tool, but also work as a brainstorming tool to get novel design ideas. Although we have dealt with only a simple exploratory case study, we believe that the method can be applied to various area by adjusting the experimental setup according to various tasks and contexts, and this will continue through future works. We hope that this study will contribute to making HCI more human-centered even in the future where artificial intelligence has become commonplace.

REFERENCES

1. Computer World. Why google AI is the last user interface. 2016. Retrieved January 14, 207 from http://www.computerworld.com/article/3129098/artificart-intelligence/why-google-a-i-is-the-last-user-interface.html

2. Corradini, A. and Cohen, P.R. O the Relationships Among Speech, Gestures, and Object Manipulation in Virtual Environments: Initial Evidence. In Proc. of the International CLASS Workshop on Natural, Intelligent and Effective Interaction in Multimodal Dialogue systems, Copenhagen, Denmark, (2002).
3. Dahlbäck, N., Jönsson, A. and Ahrenberg, L. Wizard of Oz Studies: Why and How. In Proc. IUI 1993, ACM Press (1993), 193–200.
4. Gry Seland. 2006. System Designer Assessments of Role Play as a Design Method: A Qualitative Study. In Proceedings of the 4th Nordic Conference on Human-Computer Interaction: Changing Roles (Nordic CHI '06). 222-231. http://dx.doi.org/10.1145/1182475.1182499
5. Howard, S., Carroll, J., Murphy, J. and Peck, J., Using "endowed props" in scenario-based design. In NordiCHI 2002, ACM Press (2002), 1-8.
6. Iacucci, G., Kuutti, K. and Ranta, M., On the move with a magic thing: role playing in concept design of mobile services and devices. In Proc. DIS 2000, (2000), 193-202.
7. Jiang, J., Hassan Awadallah, A., Jones, R., Ozertem, U., Zitouni, I., Kulkarni, R. G., and Khan, O. Z.. Automatic online evaluation of intelligent assistants. In WWW, pages 506–516, 2015.
8. Kiseleva, J., Williams, K., Jiang, J., Awadallah, A. H., Crook, A. C., Zitouni, I, and Anastasakos, T, (2016). Understanding User Satisfaction with Intelligent Assistants. In Proc. CHIIR '16. 121-130.
9. Lee, S., Chae, J., Kim, H., Lim, Y., and Lee, K. Towards more natural digital content manipulation via user freehand gestural interaction in a living room. In Ubicomp 2013, ACM Press (2013), 617-626.
10. Lee, S., Kim, S., Jin, B., Choi, E., Kim, B., Jia, X., Kim, D., and Lee, K. 2010. How users manipulate deformable displays as input devices. In Proc. of CHI '10, ACM, 1647-1656, 2010.
11. McTear, M. F.. Spoken dialogue technology: enabling the conversational user interface. ACM Computing Surveys (CSUR), 34(1):90–169, 2002.
12. Morris, M.R., Wobbrock, J.O., Wilson, A.D. Understanding Users' Preferences for Surface Gestures. Proc. of Graphics Interface (GI '10) (2010), 261-268.
13. Myers, K., et al., An Intelligent Personal Assistant for Task and Time Management. AAAI Magazine, 2006.
14. Sano, S., Kaji, N., and Sassano, M. Prediction of prospective user engagement with intelligent assistants, Proceedings of the 54th Annual Meeting of the Association for Computational Linguistics, pages 1203–1212, Berlin, Germany, August 7-12, 2016
15. Sato, S. and Salvador, T. Playacting and focus troupes: Teather techniques for creating quick, intense, immersived, and engaging focus group sessions. Interactions, 6 (1999), 35-41.
16. Seland, G. 2006. System Designer Assessments of Role Play as a Design Method: A Qualitative Study. In Proceedings of the 4th Nordic Conference on Human-Computer Interaction: Changing Roles (Nordic CHI '06). 222-231. http://dx.doi.org/10.1145/1182475.1182499
17. Tür, G.. Extending boosting for large scale spoken language understanding. Machine Learning (ML), 69(1):55–74, 2007.
18. Wobbrock, J.O., Morris, M.R., Wilson, A.D. Userdefined gestures for surface computing. Proc. CHI 2009. ACM Press (2009), 1083-1092.

Guided Selfies using Models of Portrait Aesthetics

Qifan Li, Daniel Vogel
Cheriton School of Computer Science, University of Waterloo
{qifanli, dvogel}@uwaterloo.ca

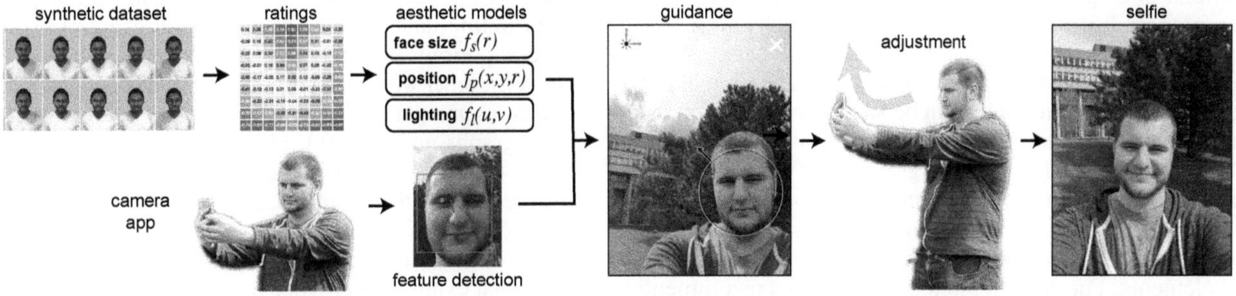

Figure 1: Methodology and techniques to enable interactive aesthetic guidance when taking a selfie on an unmodified smartphone.

ABSTRACT
We introduce techniques enabling interactive guidance for better self-portrait photos ("selfies") using a smartphone camera. Aesthetic quality is estimated using empirical models for three parameterized composition principles: face size, face position, and lighting direction. The models are built using 2,700 crowdworker assessments of highly-controlled synthetic selfies. These are generated by manipulating a virtual camera and lighting when rendering a realistic 3D model of a human to methodically explore the parameter space. A camera application uses the models to estimate the aesthetic quality of a live selfie preview based on parameters measured by computer vision. The photographer is guided towards a better selfie by directional hints overlaid on the live preview. A study shows the technique provides a 26% increase in aesthetic quality compared to a standard camera application.

ACM Classification Keywords
H.5.2 User Interfaces: Input devices and strategies

Author Keywords
mobile computing; computational photography;

INTRODUCTION
Smartphone self-portrait photographs, called "selfies", account for more than 30% of pictures taken by people aged 18 to 24 [15]. However, not everyone has photography skills, so these are often unsatisfying images. Visual aesthetics can be improved after a selfie is taken by editing and re-touching [8], but this requires extra effort, reduces realism, may degrade resolution, and aspects like face distortion and lighting direction are hard to correct. Using a "selfie stick" or a smartphone case with a built-in ring light [23, 24] can reduce distortion and improve lighting, but using accessories is not always convenient.

We introduce a methodology and techniques for interactive aesthetic guidance when taking a selfie on standard smartphone (Fig. 1). Instead of encoding rule-of-thumb photographic principles [26, 27, 33], we derive quantitative aesthetic models empirically. Rather than learning principles from a dataset of near-random images taken from the internet (e.g. [18, 10, 36, 9, 22, 38]), we generate highly-controlled synthetic self-portrait photographs using 3D rendering. This enables a methodical exploration and validation of underlying compositional features, in our case: face size, face position, and lighting direction.

Our dataset of synthetic selfies is used in 2,700 crowdworker assessments. These assessments are transformed into three quantitative models, each mapping a compositional feature configuration to an aesthetic score. We then describe a smartphone application to analyse the preview image with computer vision methods when taking a selfie. With this analysis, the configuration of each feature may be calculated and fed to our models to find the current aesthetic score and directions of improvement. Corresponding directional hints are then overlaid on the preview image, guiding the photographer to move the smartphone to improve one type of aesthetic quality. In a study, selfies taken with our system were rated 26% higher compared to those taken by a standard camera application. To make the problem tractable, our focus is on single-person selfies without a dominant background object. However, our system is designed so the photographer can selectively ignore some guidance to include other people or compensate for backgrounds like tourist landmarks. We make the following contributions:

- A systematic assessment of three features of selfie aesthetics: *face position, face size*, and *lighting direction.*
- Empirically-derived models to estimate the aesthetic score and *direction of improvement* for each feature.

DIS 2017, June 10-14, 2017, Edinburgh, United Kingdom.

DOI: http://dx.doi.org/10.1145/3064663.3064700

- A smartphone camera application to guide novice photographers to take better single person selfies using our models and a method to estimate dominant lighting.
- A controlled experiment validating the application's usability and capability to increase aesthetic quality.

BACKGROUND AND RELATED WORK

Although photography is an art form, rules-of-thumb have been proposed to make even casual photographs more aesthetically pleasing. Child [7] emphasizes that composition is important to attract and keep the viewer's attention and it complements the communication between the viewer and the photograph. One of the most common composition rules is the *rule-of-thirds* [31]. This is a 3×3 grid formed by dividing the image horizontally and vertically into nine equal portions. The grid line intersection points are called "power-points" which are commonly considered the best locations to place significant elements. For portrait photography, guides recommend how to use the rule-of-thirds to compose portrait styles such as "head-and-shoulders", "three-quarter", and "full-length" [17]. For example, placing the eyes in the top third for single person portraits [11]. A related compositional principle is the size of the subject [22, 25, 29]. In portraiture, some recommend filling the frame with the face [11], but face size is also dependent on the intended portrait style [17].

In addition to these spatial composition principles, Hurter [17] emphasizes the importance of lighting composition. Hurter argues light is the dominant factor to represent a three-dimensional reality in a two-dimensional space, "Just as a sculptor models clay to create the illusion of depth, so light models the shape of the face to give it depth and form." Different rules have been proposed for portraiture lighting. Some suggest a side-light so a pattern of light and shadow defines the face [7, 16], others recommend a frontal light to eliminate shadows and flatten the face [34].

Computational Aesthetics

Since such rules-of-thumb are imprecise and questionable, researchers have attempted to calculate the aesthetic quality of images using computational methods. One approach is to model aesthetic quality as a machine learning problem with an unconstrained number of features. A large corpus of images is rated by people to establish a ground truth for aesthetic quality. Many global and local features are extracted from the same images that were rated (typically image statistics related to colour, edges, contours, saliency, etc.). Then, machine learning algorithms are trained using the ratings and extracted features to automatically rate images for aesthetics. Most investigations use photographs acquired from an ad hoc online database [18, 10, 36, 9, 22, 38] since large amounts of data is needed for training. However, modelling using many features and with uncontrolled training images often spanning many classes (e.g landscapes, animals, groups, portraits, etc.) makes it difficult to find underlying aesthetic rules [25].

This general approach has also been applied to portrait photographs. Khan and Vogel [20] model aesthetic quality of individual portraits using a small set of features from photography tutorials, including face position and lighting. Males et al. [27] train on features they argue are used by professional photographers, including composition, face size, and features related to light, like contrast, lightness, and highlights. Redi et al. [33] use features inspired by photographic guides, including compositional rules. Chen et al. [6] develop a method to extract features of artistic lighting.

These works validates our focus on face position, face size, and lighting, but they still use highly variable training images from online databases. Although Redi et al.'s [33] results suggest portrait aesthetics are independent of age, gender, and ethnicity, other works suggest otherwise. Mazza et al. [29] find that dress and gender influence the perception of "head-shot" photographs and Xu et al. [37] found people rating photos for aesthetic quality often commented on non-compositional features like smile and mood. Also, Manovich et al.'s "Selfie City" [28] — a theoretic, artistic, and quantitative study of selfies — provides compelling evidence that age, gender, pose, and facial expression are linked to highly rated photographs.

This suggests that rating uncontrolled images to train models for compositional aesthetic quality is problematic. In addition to non-aesthetic confounds, precisely extracting high-level features like lighting direction is difficult for arbitrary images and many features change from image to image so understanding why a rater chose a certain image is difficult. Moreover, many of these works create features based on rules-of-thumb, but recent work suggests some rules, like the rule-of-thirds, may not improve aesthetic ratings [37, 2]. These factors all introduce errors and uncertainty into the aesthetic model.

Our highly controlled synthetic image corpus eliminates these potential confounds when rating aesthetics. In addition, our corpus isolates compositional features when rating, disentangling complex interactions resulting from comparative ratings when multiple features vary.

Realtime Aesthetic Guidance

The works above develop aesthetic models to evaluate existing images. Some explicitly use evaluated images as examples to teach amateur photographers methods to improve aesthetics [38], but they do not assist while taking a photograph. Our goal is to model aesthetics to create an interactive camera application with aesthetic guidance. This is complementary to guidance for low level features like exposure, luminance, and motion blur [30, 3].

Previous systems exist for realtime aesthetic guidance for photography and video. Ma et al. [26] develop an aesthetic model to suggest where to pose a person in a landscape photograph (visualized by a rectangle). However, the technique is not implemented on a smartphone or tested for interactive use. San pedro and Church [35] describe a smartphone camera application to guide photographers using 22 composition and 7 exposure features applicable to a wide class of images (proposed by Obrador et al. [31]). Feedback uses a musical composition mapped to feature scores, a small pilot study is inconclusive whether aesthetic quality is improved.

NudgeCam is a smartphone application to record product demonstration videos [4]. Text messages and a coloured box around the face indicate when there are problems with face size, face location, and scene brightness, tilt, and stability. A related system by Kumano et al. [21] uses icons to indicate when video motion is poor and to suggest when to zoom or pan the shot. These two systems encode existing videography rules-of-thumb, and neither is formally evaluated.

There are two direct precursors to our work. A commercial app called *Camera51* [1] "intelligently analyzes a scene and looks for lines, shapes, and people" [12] to provide guidance to a single, globally optimal composition. The underlying algorithms and aesthetic rules are unknown, and the user has no ability to selectively improve specific compositional principles while ignoring others.

Xu et al. [37] developed a realtime guidance system for portrait photographs. Face position and subject size are guided using a rule-based aesthetic model derived directly from the rule-of-thirds: the face should be on a grid line or power point, and the subject width should be one-third of the image. Their system requires a special laptop and external three-camera array. A study conducted outdoors evaluates whether the system improves aesthetics compared to a baseline system showing only a static rule-of-thirds grid. Unlike Xu et al., our system is specifically focused on self-portraits, it works on a standard smartphone, it considers lighting direction in addition to face position and size, our guidance is based on empirically-derived models derived from a synthetic dataset, and our final evaluation environment is highly-controlled.

DATASET AND AESTHETIC QUALITY RATINGS

Our goal is to help novice photographers take self-portraits that average people find more aesthetically pleasing. We accomplish this by rendering hundreds of synthetic portraits that systematically vary three key compositional features: face size, face position, and lighting direction. These portraits are used to gather aesthetic ratings in an online crowdsourcing experiment. We explain how these ratings are transformed into models to guide people when taking selfies in a later section.

3D Rendered Synthetic Selfie Dataset

All synthetic portraits are 3D renderings of realistic-looking 3D human models in front of a uniform 18% grey background. We use 3 female and 3 male models, with each gender pair having Caucasian, Asian, or Black ethnicity features. Models were selected to be consistent and "average" looking with neutral facial expressions, typical hair styles, no glasses, and similar poses. The arms of our 3D models are not poseable, so our synthetic selfies do not capture the subject though holding the smartphone. However, it is unlikely this small detail alters aesthetic ratings. By generating portraits across all six models, we eliminate confounds like background, gender, and smile when rated for aesthetic quality.

Renderings were generated using Blender (www.blender.com), an open-source 3D modelling program. Virtual camera properties were set to simulate the front camera of an iPhone 6 (focal length 45mm, field-of-view 54.2°, aspect ratio 3:4), and a parallel lighting source was configured to simulate the sun or dominant indoor light source. Ambient light was set to soften shadows and simulate typical lighting conditions outside or in brightly lit interiors. Using a Python API, the positions of the human model, virtual camera, and parallel light source were manipulated to explore each aesthetic feature as explained below.

Note that dataset generation and aesthetic quality ratings were interleaved as the three features were explored in sequence. First, portraits to explore face size were generated and assessed. These results established which face sizes to use when generating portraits to explore face position. After face position was assessed, the results were used to select face positions and sizes when exploring the lighting direction feature.

Face Size

Face size is an important feature because a face in a portrait should be large enough to be the centre of interest, but not so close that facial features distort [13]. We define *face size* as the ratio between the width of face — twice the distance between the eyes — and one-third of the image width. This ratio normalizes the feature and relates it to the rule-of-thirds guideline which suggests subjects should be sized to one cell in a rule-of-thirds grid. A face size of 1.0 matches this existing guideline.

To generate portraits exploring face size, we position the virtual camera and human model to render 19 images with face size ranging from 0.2 to 2.0 in steps of 0.1 (Fig. 2). The range of ratios is based on measuring real selfies taken as close as possible without face cropping and as far as possible using a standard "selfie stick." The face position and lighting direction are constant: face position is centred, and the light source shines straight onto the face.

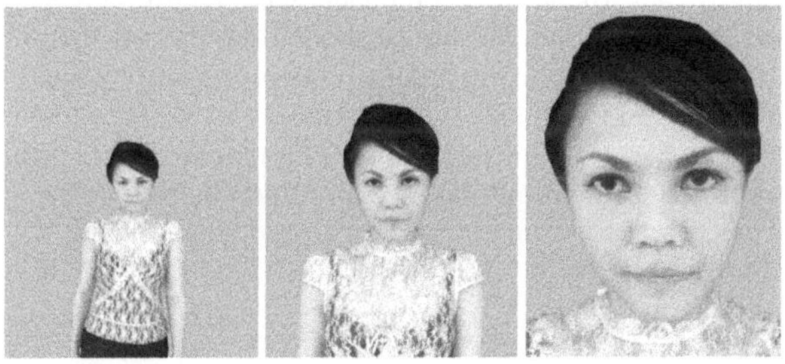

Figure 2: Example face size portraits: 0.4, 0.8, 2.0 using Asian female.

Face Position

The rule-of-thirds is commonly used to position subjects in photographs [7, 17] and previous research has employed it for aesthetic ratings [26, 9] and guidance [37]. We define *face position* as the 2D location of the centroid of the eyes and parametrize it using a subdivided 3×3 rule-of-thirds grid. Each grid cell is divided by 4 to construct a 12×12 grid with face position denoted as (x,y), where x and y are multiples of $\frac{1}{12}$ in terms of normalized image position. This way, face positions $(4,4)$, $(4,8)$, $(8,8)$, and $(8,4)$ correspond to rule-of-thirds "power points" assumed to be preferred positions [20].

Based on the distribution of face size aesthetic ratings (recall dataset generation and rating was interleaved), we explored face positions using 4 face sizes: 0.3, 0.5, 0.8, and 1.0. For each face size, 81 images were rendered with the virtual camera placed to create face positions ranging from (2,2) to (10,10) — a 9×9 subset of the 12×12 grid parametrization that avoids extremely cropped faces (Fig. 3). The face is kept oriented towards the camera by aligning the model's face direction (represented as the normal of a transparent plane) to the camera film plane. As in face size images, the light source shines straight onto the face.

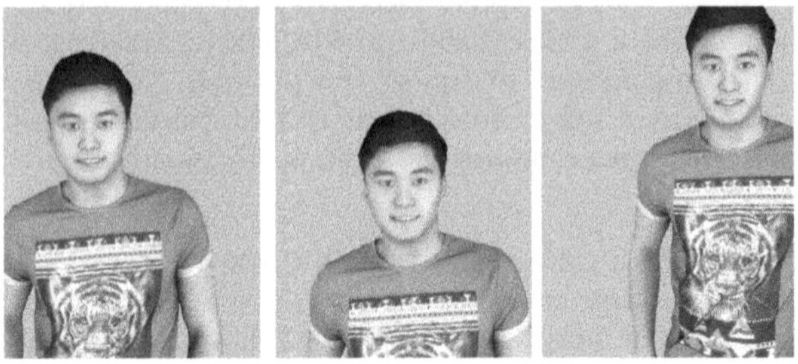

Figure 3: Example face position portraits: (4,4), (6,6), (9,2) using Asian male with face size 0.8.

Lighting Direction

The dominant light source is assumed to be omnidirectional with parallel rays like the sun. We define *lighting direction* as the light source position in spherical coordinates azimuth and polar angle (θ, ϕ), with the origin at the centre of the head. For example, the light is directly in front of the face at $(0°, 90°)$, to the right side and half-way above at $(-90°, 45°)$, and directly above at $(0°, 0°)$.

To reduce the space to explore, we assume light should not come from below or behind the face. This restricts the range of θ to $[-120°, 120°]$ and ϕ to $[0°, 90°]$. With step sizes of 30° for θ and 11.25° for ϕ, each component has 9 settings creating 81 total combinations. We use aesthetic rating results from face size and face position to create 4 sets of lighting images: size 0.3, position (6,2); size 0.5, position (6,3); size 0.8, position (6,4); and size 1.0, position (6,4). The virtual camera position was fixed to maintain the face size and position as the light source partially orbited around the head position (Fig. 4).

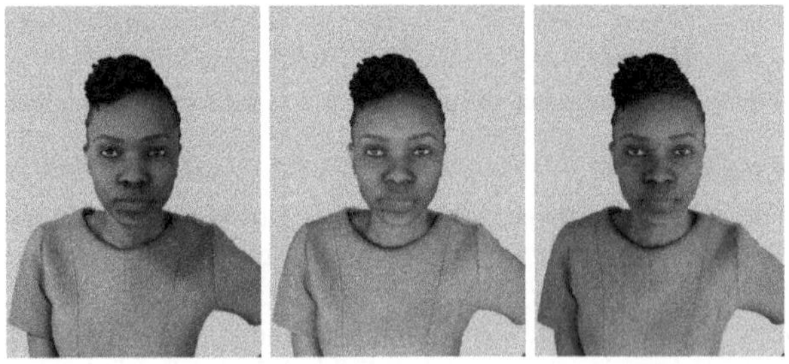

Figure 4: Examples of lighting direction portraits: (-60°,67°), (0°,90°), (90°,90°) using Black female with face size 1.0, face position (6,4).

Aesthetic Rating

These sets of synthetic selfies are rated for aesthetic quality on Amazon Mechanical Turk (AMT). Workers picked a multiple best and worst images for each set of images portraying a single 3D human model for each compositional feature.

Participants

We recruited 2,700 AMT workers without any experience, age, or location criteria (though the majority live in the United States). Our objective is to get aesthetic ratings from "average people." Workers were paid between $0.10 and $0.30 per task (called a HIT on AMT). The full protocol was approved by a research ethics board.

Task and Implementation

The task is to view a set of synthetic portraits of a single model exploring a single compositional feature, and pick at least N good and N bad images. For example, pick 8 good and 8 bad images among 81 portraits of the Caucasian male model with different face positions. Note that comparing two images at a time would not be practical — there would be 3,240 comparisons in just one face size image set.

User interfaces for AMT tasks must be clear and efficient to encourage workers to complete the task correctly and honestly [32]. We iteratively developed our interface with these goals (Fig. 5). Thumbnails of images are arranged in a 9×9 grid (for face position and lighting direction), or a 1×19 row (for face size). Clicking on a thumbnail displays it as a full image and selects it (when the task begins, a random thumbnail is selected). Thumbnails can be selected and viewed quickly by dragging the mouse or using cursor keys.

Clicking on a rating button, or using a shortcut key, classifies the selected image and indicates the decision with a colour outline: green for 'good' (shortcut key '1'), blue for 'undecided' (key '2'), and red for 'bad' (key '3'). An undecided decision is automatically assigned when a thumbnail is selected for more than 2 seconds, but no good or bad rating provided. The worker can change their ratings at any time. The remaining number of good and bad ratings are shown in the rating buttons. Once the minimum number of ratings is completed, a submit button is enabled. The task was implemented as a web application using AngularJS.

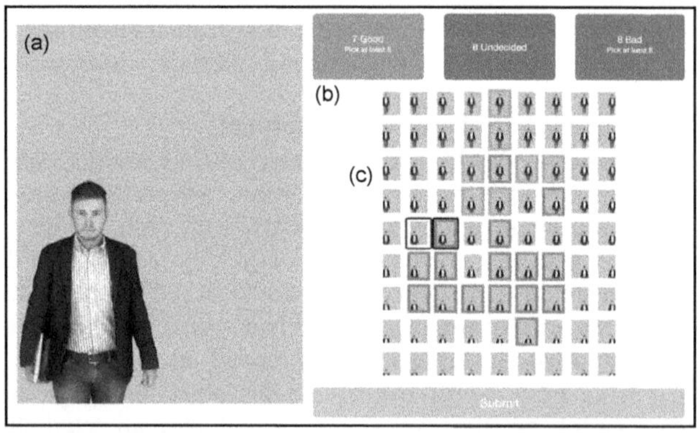

Figure 5: Aesthetic rating task interface (Caucasian male, rating face position): (a) large image view; (b) rating buttons; (c) thumbnails.

Design

Recall that we generated one set of images for face size, four sets of images for face position, and four sets of images for lighting direction, making nine sets in total. Each task rates images in one set for one human model: for face size, workers had to pick at least 3 good and 3 bad images; for face position and lighting direction, they had to pick at least 8 good and 8 bad images. With 9 sets and 6 human models there are

$9*6=54$ task variations. For each task variation, we recruited 50 workers, requiring 2,700 workers in total.

The procedure was a typical AMT HIT. When the HIT was accepted, the worker acknowledged a consent form and then viewed a video demonstrating the task interface. Instructions clarified that the goal is to "choose good and bad examples of images when considering them as selfies."

Results

To calculate the score of each image (representing a specific configuration for one of the principles being evaluated with a specific model), we summed all ratings using the following tally: +1 for each 'good', -1 for each 'bad', and 0 otherwise. Each image tally is then divided by the number of times that image was rated (regardless if 'good', 'bad', or 'undecided') to normalize scores to a range between -1 and 1.

To examine the consistency of scores and actual sample size for each image, we calculated the standard error of the mean (SEM) and percentage of tasks each image was rated. Rating scores were consistent, all SEMs are less than 0.05. Actual sample sizes were excellent for face size, with all images rated by at least 74% of workers, and good for face position and lighting direction with all images rated by at least 30% and 45% of workers respectively.

Face Size

Figure 6 illustrates the results. The preferred face sizes are 0.8 (score 0.33) and 0.5 (score 0.32). The score dips to 0.22 between those peaks and down to 0.13 for the smallest face size 0.2. However, all face sizes less than 1.4 have a positive rating. In contrast, scores for large face sizes fall sharply, decreasing to -0.6 for face size 2.0.

This suggests people prefer faces to be 50% of a rule-of-thirds-grid cell (16% of image width) or 80% to 90% of a rule-of-third grid cell (27% to 30% of image width). Note that faces very far from the camera, approximately less than 30% of a rule-of-thirds grid cell (10% of image width), are rated lower. Most pronounced are low ratings for faces very close to the camera, with negative scores when faces are larger than 130% of a rule-of-thirds grid cell (43% of the image width).

Face Position

Figure 6 illustrates the results. A mass of positive scores 0.7 or greater can be seen when the face is roughly horizontally centred. This positive mass moves vertically up the image as the face size becomes smaller. Positions near the bottom and sides are negative, most below -0.3, likely due to cropping.

Higher aesthetic ratings for a centred faces break from the accepted rule-of-thirds principle [9]. Rows and columns labelled 4 and 8 represent rule-of-thirds "power lines", and cells at positions $(4,4)$, $(8,4)$, $(4,8)$, and $(8,8)$ represent rule-of-thirds "power points." There is no indication of higher ratings for power-lines or power points. This adds empirical support to Xu et al.'s [37] informal observations.

Lighting Direction

The pattern of scores for the four sets of lighting direction scores appear very similar. Figure 6 illustrates the scores for the four sets and the aggregated results. A mass of positive scores can be seen when θ is between $-30°$ to $30°$ and ϕ is between $67.5°$ to $78.75°$, with a notable positive extension down to $\phi=90°$ at $\theta=0°$, and out to $\theta=\pm60°$ at $\phi=78.75°$.

Higher aesthetic ratings for lighting shining directly (or nearly directly) on the face reduces shadows and evenly lighting the entire face. This is exactly the result when using a smartphone cases with a built-in ring light [23, 24], but it contradicts some past work [20, 6] suggesting that lighting a face from one side is preferable.

Summary

These ratings suggest clear preferences for face size, face position, and lighting when taking selfies: faces should not be too big, faces should be centred and near the top without getting too close to the edge, and lighting should shine from the front. Although these may appear elementary, they have not been derived empirically before. Moreover, having matrices of scores will enable our guidance system to suggest local directions of improvement (i.e. "move your face right") which is more flexible for users than simply suggesting the globally preferred location (i.e. "move your face here").

AESTHETIC MODELS

In order to use the ratings for real-time guidance, we transform the matrices of scores into three models. Each model estimates an aesthetic score and direction of improvement for one compositional feature given the current state of compositional feature parameters. The main challenge is how to transform empirically known scores at discrete parameter settings into continuous functions that return a score for any measured face size, face position, and lighting direction.

The general form of each model is $(s,\boldsymbol{d})=f(\omega_0,\omega_1,...,\omega_n)$. It is a function f which accepts compositional feature parameters $\{\omega_0,\omega_1,...,\omega_n\}$ to calculate a score s and a vector $\boldsymbol{d}$ describing the *direction* in compositional feature space that will improve the score.

The specific models are:

- Face Size: $(s_s,\boldsymbol{d_s})=f_s(r)$

  The model uses an interpolated lookup into the 1×19 row matrix of face size scores. Given the detected face size ratio r, the score s_s is a linear interpolation between the two known scores at face sizes defining the interval where r lies. If r is outside the 1×19 row matrix, the s_s is extrapolated using the two closest known scores. The one-dimensional direction of improvement $\boldsymbol{d_s}$ is the direction towards the largest interval score.

- Face Position: $(s_p,\boldsymbol{d_p})=f_p(x,y,r)$

  Recall there are four 8×8 matrices of face position scores for four face size ratios (0.3, 0.5, 0.8, 1.0). The model uses a two-step interpolated lookup into these four matrices. The detected face size ratio r is used to construct an 8×8 matrix by linearly interpolating corresponding elements of matrices forming the interval around r. If r is outside all matrices, elements are extrapolated. Then the score s_p is a bilinear interpolation (or extrapolation) of the elements

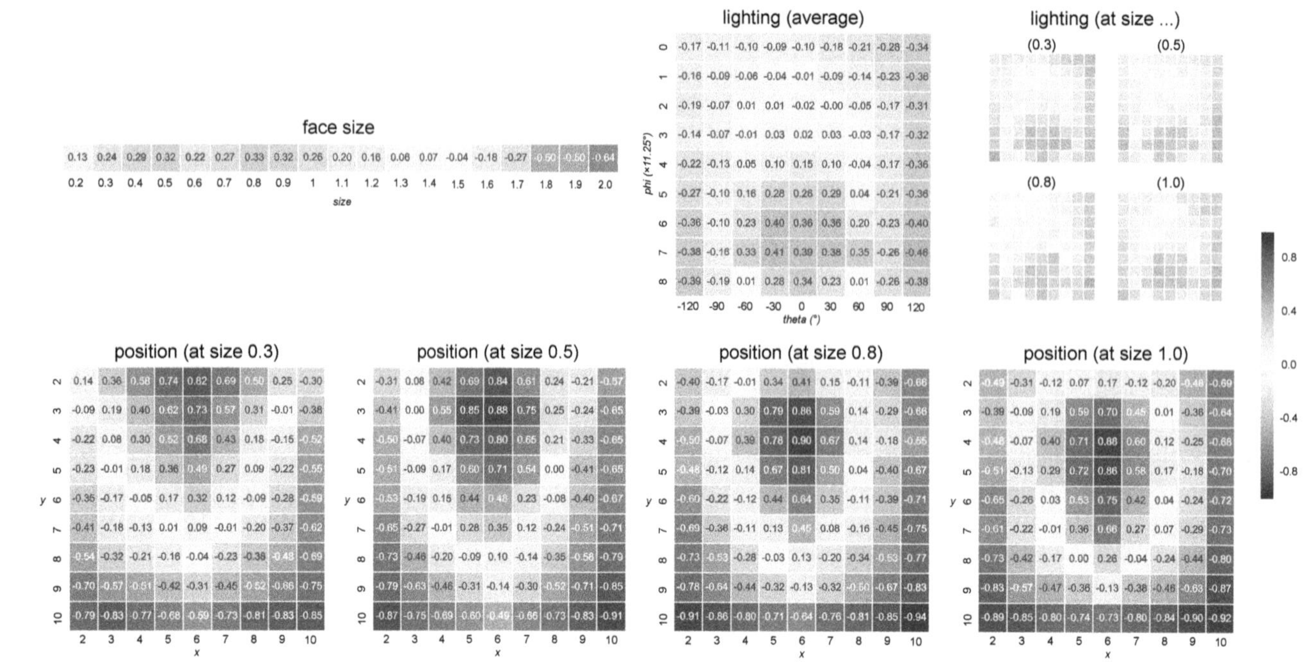

Figure 6: Visualizations of aesthetic ratings for size, position, and lighting. Note lighting is averaged across size given similar patterns for specific sizes.

surrounding the 2D interval where the detected position (x,y) resides in the interpolated matrix. The direction $\boldsymbol{d_p}$ is the 2D direction towards the surrounding element with the highest score.

- Lighting Direction: $(s_l, \boldsymbol{d_l}) = f_l(u,v)$

  Unlike face position or face size, we cannot directly measure 3D lighting directions Θ and Φ from a 2D image. Instead, the model uses (u,v), vector components to represent the direction and magnitude of the brightest patch of skin around the nose. We describe our algorithm to compute (u,v) later. These lighting direction components are transformed into the best estimate for Θ and Φ by finding the nearest neighbour to a set of canonical components (u^*, v^*) computed using the 3D human models and known Θ and Φ. With Θ and Φ, the corresponding score can be found in the single aggregated 8×8 lighting score matrix. The direction $\boldsymbol{d_l}$ is the 2D direction towards the surrounding matrix element with the highest score.

SMARTPHONE APPLICATION

We created a smartphone “app” that detects the current face size, face position, and lighting direction using computer vision techniques and passes these to the aesthetic models. The results are used to provide interactive guidance by suggesting how to move the smartphone to improve aesthetics. Our app runs on an iPhone 6 with iOS 9.3 using OpenCV 2.4.10 for computer vision.

Feature Detection and Calculation using Computer Vision

Each frame of the camera preview is captured and downsampled to 240×320 pixels. The native IOS `CIDetector` is used to find the bounding box of the face, mouth, and eyes. An OpenCV Haar classifier is used to detect the nose, but to improve speed and robustness, only the region bounded by the eyes and mouth is searched. Face and eye detection run at 12 FPS and nose detection at 8 FPS, acceptable for real time photo guidance. These detected features are used to compute model parameters as follows.

Face Size (r) and Face Position (x,y)

Recall face size and face position are expressed relative to a rule-of-thirds grid. The current face size (r) is the ratio of twice the distance between the detected eye positions to one-third of the width of the preview image. The current face position (x,y) is the centroid of the eyes expressed in twelfths of the preview image width and height. A low-pass filter [5] is applied to stabilize the face size and face position ratio across frames.

Lighting Direction (u,v)

To calculate the lighting direction, we examine the pattern of luminance on and around the nose. The protruding nose geometry produces local shadows and highlights that capture the global lighting information. Previous work used the pattern of light on the nose for 2D tracking [14].

The detected nose region-of-interest (ROI) is downsampled to 100×100 px and converted to HSV colour space. Eight 9×9 px patches are defined radially around the centre of the nose ROI, each with a corresponding patch direction vector $\boldsymbol{v_i}$ from nose ROI centre to patch centre (Figure 7a). The ratio of the median luminance of each patch l_i to the luminance at nose ROI centre l_c is used to scale each corresponding direction vector: $(l_i/l_c) \times \boldsymbol{v_i}$. For robustness, the steps above are repeated for patches at radii from 9 px to 45 px. The final lighting direction vector component (u,v) is the sum of the scaled vectors from all iterations. A low-pass filter [5] is also applied to stabilize (u, v) across frames.

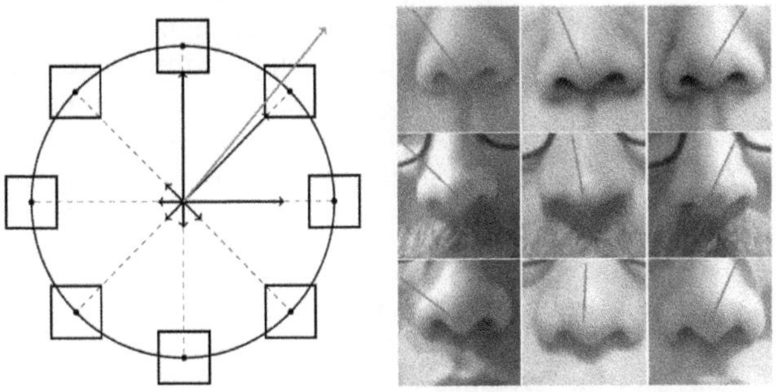

Figure 7: Lighting direction detection: (a) algorithm illustration; (b) test examples.

We informally tested this algorithm in two stages. First, we ran the algorithm on the synthetic images used for the lighting direction ratings. To prevent a confound from imperfect nose detection, the nose region was defined in Blender by rendering a rectangle. A comparison of the calculated lighting directions with known lighting directions for different values of Φ and Θ suggest the algorithm works well when the face is lit from the front ($\Theta \in [-90°, 90°]$), but becomes noisy when lit from behind ($\Theta \in [-120°, -90°] \cup [90°, 120°]$) or top ($\Phi = 0°$).

Second, we ran the algorithm on real photos (1 female and 2 males) taken at different orientations to the sun (examples in Figure 7b). The calculated lighting directions were consistent for all three sets with similar noisy measurements when lit from the top and behind. It also appeared to be robust to the presence of eyeglasses and facial hair.

In practice, we found it works well inside as well, long as there is a reasonably dominant light source. Diffuse lighting or very low light introduces some noise, but in those conditions light direction has no effect. The noisy estimates when lit from behind or above will likely guide people towards some better lighting position, albeit in a less consistent direction.

User Interface Design

The primary interface components are the guidance icons for the three compositional features. When a face is detected, a circle surrounding the face indicates tracking is working and guidance icons are overlaid for each feature.

Face Size Guidance – The direction of small radial arrows indicates whether the face should be made larger (by moving the phone closer) or smaller (by moving the phone farther away) (e.g. Figure 8-a). The transparency of the arrows reflects the difference between the current face size score and the highest possible face size score. This means the arrows are very opaque when the score is poor, so face size adjustment appears more strongly suggested. If the arrows disappear, the score is near optimal.

Face Position Guidance – The direction of a large arrow emanating from the tracking circle indicates the direction to move the face. The direction is constrained to 8 cardinal compass directions for simplicity. Face movement is accomplished by slightly tilting the phone, for example, if the arrow points NW, then slightly tilting the phone SE moves the face up (N) and left (W). Like face size, arrow transparency reflects the relative difference between the current face position score and the best possible score.

Lighting Direction Guidance – Arrows are drawn around a sun icon located in the top-left corner. Horizontal arrows indicate the phone should be orbited around the head to adjust side-lighting (azimuth, Θ) and vertical arrows indicate an up or down tilt to adjust polar-angle (Φ), In practice, these motions are accomplished by fixing both the camera and the face and rotating or bending the body. For example, arrows pointing up and right indicate that the smartphone should be tilted up and orbited right to improve lighting (Figure 8-b). As before, the transparency of the arrows indicates how close the current lighting score is to the optimal score.

Once the face is positioned, the picture is taken by tapping a circular shutter button (or pressing either volume button for convenience). A debug mode, activated by double-tapping, is used for testing and demonstration. In this mode, the guidance visualization is augmented with tracked positions for the face, eyes, mouth, and nose, the estimated lighting direction vector, as well as the numeric scores for all three features.

Since guidance provides *directions of improvement* for each feature rather than a direct path to a single *global maximum*, the application indirectly handles selfies other than simple self-portraits. For example, when taking a self-portrait in front of a tourist landmark like a statue or building, the photographer can ignore the position guidance to keep that object in frame, but still optimize the size and lighting of the face.

Figure 8: Guidance user interface: (left) inward arrows suggest making the face smaller and arrows around sun icon suggest rotating up and right to improve lighting; (right) transparent inward arrows indicate face size is optimal, lighting is near optimal with some right rotation possible, and position can be slightly improved indicated by nearly transparent upward arrow at the top of face circle.

EVALUATION

We evaluated our app from two perspectives: usability and effectiveness at improving selfie photograph aesthetics. In our study, participants took selfie photos without and with our app in an indoor controlled setting. Usability was evaluated by examining logged usage patterns and subjective ratings. Aesthetic effectiveness was evaluated by asking AMT workers to rate the best photos taken by each participant without and with our app.

Although Xu et al.'s [37] system was not designed for selfies, we considered using it as a baseline. Since it ran on a landscape-oriented "Ultrabook PC" with a 3-camera array, this would have required re-designing the visual guidance to work in portrait aspect ratio and creating a simplified version suitable for a smartphone with a single-camera. This would have significantly altered the goal and fidelity of their system, but more importantly reduced the comparison to one between their rule-of-thirds model and our data-driven model. Xu et al. already discuss how rule-of-thirds did not correlate with better photo aesthetics and our empirical results already provide further evidence of this. For these reasons, we used a standard camera app as our baseline.

Participants

We recruited 20 participants from a university campus (mean age 24.4, 11 female). Recruitment was limited to people who could view a smartphone screen without eye glasses (since the eye detection algorithm is less reliable with dark-rimmed eye wear). Our participants exhibited visible diversity in terms of skin pigments and facial features. Participants had a range of experience: 7 took selfies daily or weekly, 10 monthly or yearly, and 3 almost never. Only 1 participant had taken a course in photography.

Apparatus

Participants used the smartphone app described above, configured to run without and with visible guidance. Regardless whether guidance was shown, the app ran the full compositional feature analysis and computed the scores and directions of improvement. These were logged, even when invisible to the user. This ensured the refresh rate of the preview mode was the same regardless of guidance, and most importantly, provided quantitative data to test whether aesthetic ratings (as determined by our models) were improved using guidance. A *launch* button provided a timestamp that together with a shutter button or volume button timestamp, enabled calculation of picture-taking time.

Instead of conducting the study outdoors with natural sunlight, we built an indoor studio so that lighting and background are controlled and consistent (Fig. 9-a). A 2.7 m wide roll of grey backdrop paper was hung from the ceiling like a curtain to create a circular space 4m in diameter. A bright light simulating the sun was placed high at one end and 5 additional bulbs were spaced around the circle for ambient fill light. To keep participants at the centre of the circle, they sat on a swivel office chair throughout the study. Note this made lighting direction adjustments by swivelling somewhat more convenient than turning once body while standing.

Task

The task was to take ten selfie photos. First, five without guidance (BASELINE condition) and then, five *with guidance* from our app (GUIDED condition). The presentation order was fixed due to strong carry-over effects if GUIDANCE was performed first. After both parts were completed, the participant selected their best BASELINE photo and their best GUIDED photo separately.

Design and Protocol

At the beginning of the session, participants were asked to focus on three compositional principles, face size, face position, and lighting direction, but the optimum configuration for those principles was not conveyed. In each part, they were told to take the five best photos they can and that they would pick the best one afterwards. To avoid other factors like smile affecting their choice or aesthetic quality, we specifically asked participants to use the same neutral expression in all photos.

At the beginning of the second part using the GUIDED condition, participants were told they would now be using a camera application with guidance (they did not know this before). The meaning of the guidance icons were explained without any hint of what the best settings were for the three compositional principles. In fact, they were told they could follow or ignore the guidance to make the evaluation realistic — if they were told to always follow guidance, everyone would end with global optimum settings determined by the model.

Finally, A post-experiment questionnaire gathered subjective scores for GUIDED (only) regarding *Ease of Learning*, *Ease of Use*, *Accuracy of Guidance*, *Operation Speed*, and *Hand Fatigue*. All scores were on a continuous scale from 1 to 5, with 1 being worst and 5 being best.

This is primarily a within subjects design. Dependent measures for usability are photo-taking time and compositional feature scores for BASELINE and GUIDED, as well as subjective scores for GUIDED. The study took 30 mins on average. The dependent measure for aesthetic effectiveness is a score assigned by AMT workers to the best BASELINE and GUIDED photos.

Results

Given only two-level independent variables, and all dependent variables are continuous, interval, and ordinal, a t-test with .05 critical value is used for statistical tests.

Photo-Taking Time

The photo-taking time is the duration between pressing the "launch" button until the moment the photo is taken. The average time for taking photos with BASELINE was 20 s (SD 22), significantly lower than 33 s (SD 27) with GUIDED ($t(198) = -3.72$, $p < .001$). These long times may be an effect of the study setting. Regardless, the relative difference indicates following guidance has a time cost. Perhaps because more time is spent considering composition options before taking a photo. The average picture-taking time when participants took their single "best" photos supports this theory: the average time to take the best BASELINE photo was 28 s (SD 28) compared to 36 sec (SD 36) for GUIDED. A significant difference $t(38) = -0.821$, $p < .042$, but smaller in magnitude.

Subjective Ratings of User Experience

Since participants rated user experience qualities on a continuous scale from 1 to 5, we examine mean values (Table 1). All ratings are positive, ranging between 3.7 and 4.3. Participant comments indicate that *Ease of Use* and *Accuracy of Guidance* were negatively affected by flickering arrows for lighting guidance. The score for *Hand Fatigue* was affected by the need to hold the arm still to read and follow guidance.

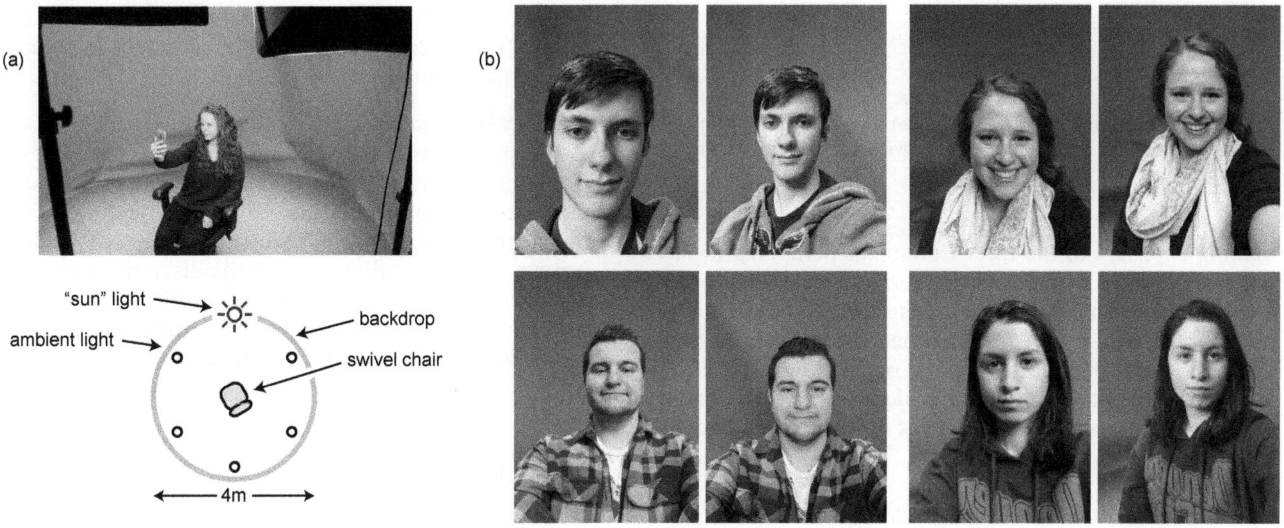

Figure 9: Evaluation: (a) controlled environment used for study; (b) examples of "best" photo pairs, left BASELINE, right GUIDED.

Ease of Learning	4.2 (±0.18)
Ease of Use	4.0 (±0.19)
Accuracy of Guidance	3.7 (±0.24)
Operation Speed	4.3 (±0.21)
Hand Fatigue	3.8 (±0.26)

Table 1: Mean user experience ratings (± SEM) for GUIDED

	BASELINE	GUIDED	t-test
Size	0.170 (±0.027)	0.245 (±0.023)	t(198)=-2.05, p<.05
Position	0.714 (±0.037)	0.723 (±0.022)	t(198)=-0.20, n.s.
Lighting	-0.019 (±0.012)	0.049 (±0.024)	t(198)=-2.46, p<.02

Table 2: Mean feature scores (± SEM) for BASELINE and GUIDED.

Note that although participants only rated GUIDED, there is an implied comparison to BASELINE, since GUIDED was completed second and BASELINE represents a real-world baseline familiar to participants.

Feature Scores

We compared mean feature scores for the best GUIDED and BASELINE photos selected by each participant. The scores for face size and lighting direction are significantly higher for GUIDED (values and t-tests in Table 2). This indicates that our app was successful in guiding participants to improve those two features according to our aesthetic models. This suggests that an increase in overall aesthetic quality, when the photos are rated in the following section, may be attributed to our app providing useful guidance. Similar face position feature scores is likely the result of people instinctively placing their face near the centre of the frame.

Aesthetic Effectiveness

To measure aesthetic effectiveness, we recruited 100 AMT workers to rate each pair of best photos taken by the participants. We did not specify any experience, age, or location criteria for the workers (though the majority live in the United States). Xu et al. [37] report ratings by AMT and expert photographers follow the same pattern, and our focus is on aesthetic attractiveness to the general population.

The task interface was modelled after the one used by Xu et al. A pair of photos is displayed with the best photos presented randomly on the left or right. The worker selected a rating between 0 and 100 for each photo using a slider. They were also instructed to consider the aesthetic quality of the face size, face position, and lighting direction, similar to the synthetic photo rankings described earlier. A text box was available for additional feedback.

We removed five participants from the set to be rated because they used very different expressions or poses in their pair of photos. For example, they were smiling in one and frowning in the other, or they turned their head to the side in one and looked straight at the camera in the other. The concern is that these pairs introduce a "pose and expression confound" that could alter a worker's aesthetic judgement. In all, 15 pairs of photos were rated by each worker, totalling 3,000 ratings.

Results

Table 3 summarizes mean ratings. Overall, selfie photographs taken with GUIDED have significantly higher ratings; $t(2998) = 17.37$, $p < .0001$. The average rating for GUIDED is 68.9 compared to 54.8 for BASELINE, an absolute difference of 14.1 — a 26% improvement in aesthetic quality. The low Standard Error of the Mean (SEM) and the relatively large absolute difference show this is a large and stable effect. The pair with the most improvement for GUIDED (the "highest pair") improved by 71% and the pair with the least improvement (the "lowest pair") decreased by -1%. The SEMs across all pairs is low, suggesting consistency among workers. The SEM of 2.4 for the "lowest pair" is among the highest across all pairs, suggesting this was the most difficult pair to judge.

In their additional feedback, workers often cited a central face position and a face lit with even, bright light as reasons for higher ratings. Some workers commented that photos appearing "washed out" were less attractive, and this was sometimes caused by frontal lighting encouraged by the guidance system. This could be remedied with more attention to the overall

	BASELINE	GUIDED	Improvement
All Pairs	54.8 (±0.6)	68.9 (±0.5)	26%
Highest Pair	45.4 (±1.6)	77.6 (±2.0)	71%
Lowest Pair	61.5 (±2.6)	61.1 (±2.4)	-1%

Table 3: Mean aesthetic ratings (± SEM) for BASELINE and GUIDED. "highest" is the pair with greatest mean improvement, "lowest" is the pair with least mean improvement.

lighting exposure of the face. Comments pertaining to face size were less consistent: some preferred a larger face, others a smaller one. This may be related to the two-peaked distribution for face size discovered by the synthetic selfie ratings. Overall, worker feedback supports our findings in the first rating experiment and provides evidence that workers were focusing on compositional principles for their assessment.

DISCUSSION

Our results show that our methodology to build highly-controlled aesthetic models, our computer vision algorithms, and our guidance interface, combine into a system that is effective at helping people take better selfies.

Limited Aesthetic Style

It is important to note that system encourages a symmetric and plain aesthetic style, no doubt due to the limited range of synthetic selfies used for aesthetic quality measurements. People also appreciate selfies with asymmetric compositions, dramatic lighting, or a tightly cropped face [19, 28]. Similarly, the neutral grey background may have affected how people rated the synthetic selfies. Generating and evaluating a wider range of synthetic selfies could diversify our system to guide people also to these more artistic types of selfies.

Implications for Human-Computer Interaction

Our aesthetic rating methodology relies on a fast, usable, and accurate interface for rating a large set of related images. We believe our solution for rating a synthetic dataset has applications in other fields such as rating options for visual design or ground truth dataset creation in machine learning.

Our system relies heavily on effective guidance visualizations packaged in a usable and responsive system. Using arrows for guidance was effective, but also makes the camera preview more cluttered and partially obscures the subject. An interesting future direction is to evaluate how subtle this style of feedback can be, while still being effective at communicating directions of improvement.

Learning about Aesthetic Preferences from the Models

When pondering what the models suggest, one may conclude that the recommendations are obvious: do not make the face too big or too small, put it near the top-centre, and make sure it is bright. Before passing judgement, recall that centering the face contradicts the commonly referenced rule-of-thirds and there are competing rules-of-thumb for lighting that suggest using side-lighting to create shadows. Moreover, stretching the arm to keep the size from being too large is not natural, but sometimes such awkward movements are necessary to produce a better quality photograph. After all, our goal was to discover, and empirically validate, what the optimum compositional rules are for self-portrait photographs as determined by "normal people."

Technical Limitations

Our system is restricted by computer vision capabilities. Face detection is constantly improving, but tracking is lost under extreme lighting or cropping. While our lighting estimation algorithm was successful at providing guidance, the lighting arrows sometimes flicker when the discretized model is at a threshold position. This creates oscillation between two different recommended directions. Adding anti-hysteresis methods and increasing the resolution of the lighting model (more scores at intermediate angles) would correct this small issue.

CONCLUSION

Our work contributes a systematic assessment of three basic features of selfie aesthetics using synthetic photographs and thousands of ratings. We transform these ratings to create interpolation-based models to estimate the aesthetic score and direction of improvement for each feature. With the help of a computer vision algorithm to estimate the dominant lighting direction in a person's face, we designed a smartphone camera application to guide novice photographers to take better selfies. A controlled experiment validated the usability of the application and its capability to increase aesthetic quality.

We see our three compositional features as an initial test of our methodology and guidance interface. Other compositional features like colour, texture, and balance could be included, as well as features like head tilt, facial expression, and background contrast. We think scaling our model to more features is possible. There is likely some inter-feature independence allowing some features to be evaluated independently. If not, the same "pipeline" approach that we used for position and lighting can be used: the results of one feature reduce the search space of the next. Note that although alternative machine-learning regression techniques can handle high dimensional data, they result in a black box preventing us from learning about aesthetics based on the final models.

Currently, if a photographer wishes to take a selfie in front of a background object (such as a tourist landmark) they have the option to ignore some of our system's guidance (such as position). An enhanced system could recognize salient background objects and alter the guidance accordingly. Models which consider the compositional relationship between the face and the object could be empirically generated using the same methodology used here. Synthetic selfies could be generated with a generic background object (perhaps a sphere) in different compositional positions relative to the person and the photograph frame. Finally, our methodology could be applied to photos of two or more people, specific classes of people (e.g babies, athletes), picture-taking settings (e.g. restaurant, beach), or entirely different subjects (e.g. cars, landscapes).

We hope our work demonstrates how a methodical and controlled study of aesthetics can lead to usable and useful applications which can increase aesthetic quality.

ACKNOWLEDGMENTS

This work was made possible by funding from NSERC Discovery Grant (#402467) and a Google Focused Award project on context-aware mobile computing.

REFERENCES

1. ArtInCam LTD. 2014. Camera51. (2014). https://www.camera51.com
2. Subhabrata Bhattacharya, Rahul Sukthankar, and Mubarak Shah. 2010. A Framework for Photo-quality Assessment and Enhancement Based on Visual Aesthetics. In *Proceedings of the International Conference on Multimedia (MM '10)*. ACM, New York, NY, USA, 271–280. DOI: http://dx.doi.org/10.1145/1873951.1873990
3. Stephen A. Brewster and Jody Johnston. 2008. Multimodal Interfaces for Camera Phones. In *Proceedings of the 10th International Conference on Human Computer Interaction with Mobile Devices and Services (MobileHCI '08)*. ACM, New York, NY, USA, 387–390. DOI: http://dx.doi.org/10.1145/1409240.1409295
4. Scott Carter, John Adcock, John Doherty, and Stacy Branham. 2010. NudgeCam: Toward Targeted, Higher Quality Media Capture. In *Proceedings of the 18th ACM International Conference on Multimedia (MM '10)*. ACM, New York, NY, USA, 615–618. DOI: http://dx.doi.org/10.1145/1873951.1874034
5. Géry Casiez, Nicolas Roussel, and Daniel Vogel. 2012. 1€ filter: a simple speed-based low-pass filter for noisy input in interactive systems. In *Proceedings of the SIGCHI Conference on Human Factors in Computing Systems*. ACM, 2527–2530.
6. Xiaowu Chen, Xin Jin, Hongyu Wu, and Qinping Zhao. 2015. Learning templates for artistic portrait lighting analysis. *IEEE Transactions on Image Processing* 24, 2 (2015), 608–618.
7. John Child. 2008. *Studio Photography: Essential Skills*. Focal Press.
8. Casio Computer Co. 2016. Life Style Digital Cameras. (2016). http://www.casio-intl.com/asia-mea/en/dc/lineup/ Hardware: Digital Cameras.
9. Ritendra Datta, Dhiraj Joshi, Jia Li, and JamesZ. Wang. 2006. Studying Aesthetics in Photographic Images Using a Computational Approach. In *Computer Vision – ECCV 2006*, Aleš Leonardis, Horst Bischof, and Axel Pinz (Eds.). Lecture Notes in Computer Science, Vol. 3953. Springer Berlin Heidelberg, 288–301. DOI: http://dx.doi.org/10.1007/11744078_23
10. S. Dhar, V. Ordonez, and T.L. Berg. 2011. High level describable attributes for predicting aesthetics and interestingness. In *Computer Vision and Pattern Recognition (CVPR), 2011 IEEE Conference on*. 1657–1664. DOI: http://dx.doi.org/10.1109/CVPR.2011.5995467
11. Christina Dickson. 2009. 6 Tips for Perfect Composition in Portrait Photography. (Sept. 2009). http://digital-photography-school.com/6-tips-for-perfect-composition-in-portrait-photography/
12. Felix Esser. 2014. Camera51 Android app makes you a master photographer by guiding your framing. (Oct. 2014). http://www.digitaltrends.com/photography/camera51-android-app-makes-master-photographer-guiding-framing/
13. Ohad Fried, Eli Shechtman, Dan B. Goldman, and Adam Finkelstein. 2016. Perspective-aware Manipulation of Portrait Photos. *ACM Trans. Graph.* 35, 4, Article 128 (July 2016), 10 pages. DOI: http://dx.doi.org/10.1145/2897824.2925933
14. Dmitry O Gorodnichy and Gerhard Roth. 2004. Nouse 'use your nose as a mouse'perceptual vision technology for hands-free games and interfaces. *Image and Vision Computing* 22, 12 (2004), 931–942.
15. Melanie Hall. 2013. Family albums fade as the young put only themselves in picture. (June 2013). http://www.telegraph.co.uk/technology/
16. Darlene Hildebrandt. 2013. Lighting Ratios to Make or Break your Portrait. (2013). http://digital-photography-school.com/lighting-ratios-to-make-or-break-your-portrait/
17. Bill Hurter. 2007. *Portrait Photographer's Handbook* (3 ed.). Amherst Media.
18. Wei Jiang, A.C. Loui, and C.D. Cerosaletti. 2010. Automatic aesthetic value assessment in photographic images. In *Multimedia and Expo (ICME), 2010 IEEE International Conference on*. 920–925. DOI: http://dx.doi.org/10.1109/ICME.2010.5582588
19. Mahdi M Kalayeh, Misrak Seifu, Wesna LaLanne, and Mubarak Shah. 2015. How to take a good selfie?. In *Proceedings of the 23rd ACM international conference on Multimedia*. ACM, 923–926.
20. Shehroz S. Khan and Daniel Vogel. 2012. Evaluating Visual Aesthetics in Photographic Portraiture. In *Proceedings of the Eighth Annual Symposium on Computational Aesthetics in Graphics, Visualization, and Imaging (CAe '12)*. Eurographics Association, Aire-la-Ville, Switzerland, Switzerland, 55–62. http://dl.acm.org/citation.cfm?id=2328888.2328898
21. Masahito Kumano, Kuniaki Uehara, and Yasuo Ariki. 2006. Online training-oriented video shooting navigation system based on real-time camerawork evaluation. In *Multimedia and Expo, 2006 IEEE International Conference on*. IEEE, 1281–1284.
22. Congcong Li and Tsuhan Chen. 2009. Aesthetic Visual Quality Assessment of Paintings. *Selected Topics in Signal Processing, IEEE Journal of* 3, 2 (April 2009), 236–252. DOI: http://dx.doi.org/10.1109/JSTSP.2009.2015077

23. LuMee LLC. 2016a. LuMee Phone Case. (2016). https://lumee.com/collections/all [Hardware: Phone Accessory].

24. Ty-Lite LLC. 2016b. Ty-Lite Phone Case. (2016). https://ty-lite.com [Hardware: Phone Accessory].

25. Wei Luo, Xiaogang Wang, and Xiaoou Tang. 2011. Content-based photo quality assessment. In *Computer Vision (ICCV), 2011 IEEE International Conference on*. 2206–2213. DOI: http://dx.doi.org/10.1109/ICCV.2011.6126498

26. Shuang Ma, Yangyu Fan, and Chang Wen Chen. 2014. Finding your spot: A photography suggestion system for placing human in the scene. In *2014 IEEE International Conference on Image Processing (ICIP)*. 556–560. DOI: http://dx.doi.org/10.1109/ICIP.2014.7025111

27. M. Males, A. Hedi, and M. Grgic. 2013. Aesthetic quality assessment of headshots. In *ELMAR, 2013 55th International Symposium*. 89–92.

28. Lev Manovich. 2014. SelfieCity. (2014). http://selfiecity.net

29. Filippo Mazza, Matthieu Perreira Da Silva, Patrick Le Callet, and IEJ Heynderickx. 2015. What do you think of my picture? Investigating factors of influence in profile images context perception. In *IS&T/SPIE Electronic Imaging*. International Society for Optics and Photonics, 93940D.

30. Christopher McAdam, Craig Pinkerton, and Stephen A. Brewster. 2010. Novel Interfaces for Digital Cameras and Camera Phones. In *Proceedings of the 12th International Conference on Human Computer Interaction with Mobile Devices and Services (MobileHCI '10)*. ACM, New York, NY, USA, 143–152. DOI: http://dx.doi.org/10.1145/1851600.1851625

31. P. Obrador, L. Schmidt-Hackenberg, and N. Oliver. 2010. The role of image composition in image aesthetics. In *Image Processing (ICIP), 2010 17th IEEE International Conference on*. 3185–3188. DOI: http://dx.doi.org/10.1109/ICIP.2010.5654231

32. Bahareh Rahmanian and Joseph G Davis. 2014. User interface design for crowdsourcing systems. In *Proceedings of the 2014 International Working Conference on Advanced Visual Interfaces*. ACM, 405–408.

33. Miriam Redi, Nikhil Rasiwasia, Gaurav Aggarwal, and Alejandro Jaimes. 2015. The Beauty of Capturing Faces: Rating the Quality of Digital Portraits. *CoRR* abs/1501.07304 (2015). http://arxiv.org/abs/1501.07304

34. Patrick Rice. 2005. *Professional Techniques for Black & White Digital Photography*. Amherst Media, Buffalo, NY.

35. Jose San pedro and Karen Church. 2013. The Sound of Light: Induced Synesthesia for Augmenting the Photography Experience. In *CHI '13 Extended Abstracts on Human Factors in Computing Systems (CHI EA '13)*. ACM, New York, NY, USA, 745–750. DOI: http://dx.doi.org/10.1145/2468356.2468489

36. Lai-Kuan Wong and Kok-Lim Low. 2009. Saliency-enhanced image aesthetics class prediction. In *Image Processing (ICIP), 2009 16th IEEE International Conference on*. 997–1000. DOI: http://dx.doi.org/10.1109/ICIP.2009.5413825

37. Yan Xu, Joshua Ratcliff, James Scovell, Gheric Speiginer, and Ronald Azuma. 2015. Real-time Guidance Camera Interface to Enhance Photo Aesthetic Quality. In *Proceedings of the 33rd Annual ACM Conference on Human Factors in Computing Systems (CHI '15)*. ACM, New York, NY, USA, 1183–1186. DOI: http://dx.doi.org/10.1145/2702123.2702418

38. Lei Yao, Poonam Suryanarayan, Mu Qiao, James Z Wang, and Jia Li. 2012. Oscar: On-site composition and aesthetics feedback through exemplars for photographers. *International Journal of Computer Vision* 96, 3 (2012), 353–383.

Reef: Exploring the Design Opportunity of Comfort-Aware Eco-Coaching Thermostats

Chuan-Che (Jeff) Huang, Sheng-Yuan Liang, Bing-Hsun Wu, Mark W. Newman
School of Information, University of Michigan, Ann Arbor
{chuanche,plantain,bhwu,mwnewman}@umich.edu

ABSTRACT
Smart thermostats have been proposed as a way to reduce energy consumption in the home. While occupancy-based thermostat control and scheduling has been shown to provide energy savings, more recent work in comfort-aware thermostats promises to provide even greater savings. Comfort awareness and adaptive thermal comfort models, combined with the mixed-initiative *eco-coaching* approach to thermostat control, offer a promising approach to optimizing savings by offering both schedule and setpoint recommendations and actionable plans. In this paper, we investigate the design space of *comfort-aware eco-coaching thermostats*. Through a user enactment study wherein 11 participants encountered fifteen design probes covering various design attributes and interaction scenarios, we uncover insights on how to design such thermostats in a way that respect people's values relating to comfort, sustainability, control, convenience, and allocation of agency while also encouraging more energy efficient behaviors.

Author Keywords
Sustainability; Thermostat; Energy Savings; Smart Home

ACM Classification Keywords
H.5.m. Information interfaces and presentation (e.g., HCI): Miscellaneous.

INTRODUCTION
In the U.S., the domestic sector consumes more than 20% of the total energy produced, and half of this is consumed by heating and cooling usage [35]. The high level of usage can be reduced. Researchers have pointed out that consumption is highly dependent on occupants' behaviors [29], as well as the inefficient use of existing manual and programmable thermostats [20,33].

Over the past decade, numerous intelligent thermostats have thus been proposed to mediate temperature control, helping people to save energy while maintaining comfort (e.g., [12,18,21,28]). Such thermostats may have occupancy-responsive control (e.g., [17]), learning capability (e.g., [1,36]), and/or eco-coaching features (e.g., [25]). However, there are still two problems with these thermostats that limit the energy savings that can be achieved.

First, the majority of intelligent thermostats assume occupants have a fixed temperature preference at home while in reality this can be quite dynamic, changing depending on occupants' activities and other contextual factors [22]. While researchers have recently explored comfort-aware thermostats—thermostats that can react to people's changing preferences by predicting their comfort based on sensed conditions (e.g., [9])—such thermostats have been principally studied in office settings, and are not suitable for the home due to the sensors used and low accuracy [15].

Second, a fundamental assumption underpinning most smart thermostat development is the view that occupants are primarily receivers of comfort (i.e., comfort is given by the heating and cooling system), rather than active agents that can utilize other means, such as changing clothes, to maintain their comfort. Researchers like Clear et al. [5] have therefore proposed to investigate approaches based on *adaptive thermal comfort* [16], an approach that emphasizes occupants' agency in performing adaptive behaviors to achieve comfort, and challenges the notion that comfort and controlled indoor temperatures exist in a fixed relationship.

Our work in this paper proceeds from the observation that a comfort-aware approach can be combined with *eco-coaching* [25,34] to provide additional opportunities for reducing heating- and cooling-related energy waste. In the eco-coaching approach, an intelligent system models user behavior and produces recommendations for energy-saving actions that can be taken by users. Recent work has shown that eco-coaching can save 5-12% of energy expended for cooling when recommending thermostat control schedules [25], and that users find eco-coaching to ease the selection and execution of more energy-efficient actions [34]. Previous work, however, only examined recommendations based on occupancy schedules—the opportunity for gaining efficiency by optimizing temperature setpoints was not explored. By including knowledge of users' comfort preferences and recommendations derived from the adaptive thermal comfort model, additional savings can be realized.

Thus in this paper, we report our initial steps in exploring the design space of *comfort-aware eco-coaching thermostats*,

DIS 2017, June 10-14, 2017, Edinburgh, United Kingdom.

ACM 978-1-4503-4922-2/17/06...$15.00.
DOI: http://dx.doi.org/10.1145/3064663.3064685

i.e. thermostats that seek to synthesize comfort-awareness, adaptive thermal comfort, and the eco-coaching approach.

Our work makes two contributions: 1) We illustrate the design space of comfort-aware eco-coaching thermostats by systematically mapping the design space and producing fifteen diverse prototypes representing key points in the space; 2) By further carrying out User Enactments [6,23,24] wherein we engaged 11 thermostat users in scenarios involving the prototypes we had developed, we were able to uncover underlying values and tensions that are likely to drive user reactions to different design directions if and when they are encountered in the wild. Our work provides a critical first step towards the realization of comfort-aware eco-coaching thermostats, and provides valuable insights for future system development and field deployments.

RELATED WORK

Many researchers have developed smart thermostats to help reduce energy consumption and increase comfort [2,9,12,17,18,21,25,28]. These smart systems have achieved their goals in various ways, including the ability to: react to residents' occupancy status (e.g., [28]), adapt to building characteristics or user preference (e.g., [36]); and respond to people's thermal comfort (e.g., [9]).

Occupancy-based thermostats [12,17,18,28] focus on reducing the heating or cooling time when people are away from home. Most of these systems make a simplistic assumption that people are satisfied with a fixed temperature when they are at home. While occupancy-based thermostats have been shown to be successful in reducing energy usage, this simplistic assumption misses a chance for both further energy savings and increased comfort, as in reality people's temperature preference at home is dynamic according to their activities and other context [13].

Preference-based thermostats may be able to cope with people's dynamic preferences, for example, by learning the desired setpoints at different times of day (e.g., [36]) or at different pricing conditions (e.g., [1]). However, users still struggle to understand the smart features of such thermostats, leading to suboptimal use or abandonment [33]. In addition, current preference-based thermostats only scratch the surface of how smart thermostats can interact with their users. While this work largely focuses on thermostats that learn people's preferences passively, more recent work on *eco-coaching* [25,34] finds that thermostats that provide actionable recommendations based on their learning capability are more promising in reducing energy consumption.

Comfort-aware thermostats, although a less explored alternative, provide the potential of reacting to people's changing temperature preferences. Such thermostats infer occupants' thermal sensation in real-time using wearable and indoor sensors and predictive models to map environmental conditions and user activity onto inferred thermal sensation [9]. While this approach seems promising [15], the imperfection of comfort inference means that full automation is infeasible. Researchers have proposed employing mixed-initiative design in creating smart thermostats [25,33], emphasizing the collaboration between machines and humans to reach a shared goal. *Eco-coaching* [25,34], employs a mixed-initiative approach wherein the system offers suggestions for actions to take and users are held responsible for finalizing the decisions. Although this approach is helpful for dealing with misprediction, it has not yet been applied to design *comfort-aware thermostats*, as previous implementations were constrained to suggesting timing for setbacks (energy-efficient *away* and *sleep* temperatures) rather than alternative temperature settings for times when the home is occupied.

While researchers have demonstrated that occupancy-based and comfort-aware thermostats can reduce energy consumption by 7-57% (e.g., [9,28]), the fundamental design philosophy that underpins such thermostats has been criticized on the basis that it limits the potential to reach more sustainable ways of living [4,5,16]. Past work on smart thermostats assume *comfort as a product*, something that is delivered to us by the indoor environment. However, recent research on adaptive thermal comfort has proposed to reconsider *comfort as a goal*, a view that emphasizes the role of human agency: occupants can leverage different adaptive behaviors such as adjusting their clothing level to reach comfort in addition to cranking their thermostats up or down. In alignment with this view, Clear et al. [5] have proposed to create systems that facilitate adaptive behaviors and temperature variations, yet limited work has been done in exploring this design opportunity.

In this work, we therefore explore comfort-aware thermostats' potential in reacting to occupants' dynamic temperature preferences while accommodating mispredictions by leveraging eco-coaching. We also broaden the concept of eco-coaching to include the view of *comfort as a goal* rather than just *a product*. Therefore, rather than only suggesting to users how to control their temperature setpoints, we explore thermostats that might also encourage adaptive behaviors such as changing clothing or drinking warm beverages. We call such thermostats *comfort-aware eco-coaching thermostats*.

METHOD & DESIGN

The aim of our study was to advance understanding of how to design comfort-aware eco-coaching thermostats. While others have explored technologies that seek to challenge or overturn people's expectation or values around thermal comfort (e.g., [4]), we sought to explore more subtle approaches that work within the existing constraints of people's cultural expectations of mechanically-mediated thermal comfort. We thus pursued designs that encourage more efficient behaviors through being adaptive while respecting people's expectation on thermal comfort.

To illuminate the design space and understand how people would react to possible design approaches, we chose user enactments as our method [6,24]. User enactments allow researchers to rapidly explore how potential users' values, expectations, and social identities inform their reactions to different design possibilities. Through simulating real world scenarios involving potential technological futures, researchers gain insights into how users might react to technology designed with different attributes, as well as the values users bring to bear when assessing design alternatives. While prior thermostat work has employed field deployments to validate the effectiveness of various designs (e.g., [1,25]), our designs require significantly more complex technology (e.g., personalized comfort prediction and room-level localization) which makes deployment a less reasonable action to take as a first step. Applying user enactments in understanding users' values is essential to ensure that costly system development and field deployment efforts are well-grounded and more likely to succeed.

Our study involved three main steps. First, through synthesizing prior literature and conducting multiple rounds of brainstorming, affinity diagramming, and expert review, we delineated the design space of comfort-aware eco-coaching thermostats. We distilled three key design dimensions (Table 1) that guided our later designs and summarized the technology constraints of state-of-the-art smart thermostats and comfort prediction approaches. Second, we operationalized our concept through iterative prototyping. We generated numerous ideas and low fidelity prototypes before creating fifteen design probes (D) in the form of high fidelity interactive prototypes (Figure 1). Third, we conducted user enactments to qualitatively probe our target users' opinions: how they perceive the different design concepts and how these designs might encourage or impede users from reaching higher energy savings.

Reef: Thermostat Designs

We first identified the key technology constraints of state-of-the-art smart thermostats and comfort prediction, focusing on constraints that are likely to persist for the foreseeable future. We used such constraints to guide the design of Reef, a hypothetical thermostat that can predict people's comfort, react, and encourage energy savings. First, we assumed Reef employs a sensing approach similar to Huang et al. [15], namely, it relies on wearable devices that detect activity level and near body temperature (e.g., [37]), as well as in-home sensors that capture humidity and temperature (e.g., [38]). Second, we assumed that Reef is able to detect and predict people's house occupancy status, room-level location and sleep status, which have been demonstrated feasible in prior research [19,25]. Therefore, Reef can use its users' status to determine whether to trigger an Away, Asleep or Awake mode (i.e., users are at home but not sleeping). Third, Reef can learn personalized comfort preferences by soliciting feedback from users, ultimately generating comfort predictions on a five-level scale ranging from uncomfortably cold to uncomfortably warm [15]. Fourth, due to limited sensing and inference capabilities, Reef will sometimes make mispredictions (e.g., predicting occupants are comfortable while they are slightly cold) [15]. Finally, as the smartphone-based control has emerged as a common approach for interacting with smart thermostats (e.g., [36]), we expected users to interact with Reef through a smartphone application. Our interfaces were therefore all designed for mobile screens.

Eco-Coaching Style	Persuasive Strategy	Timing of Interaction				
		Real-time Control	Short Engagement	Plan.	Mis-pred.	Refl.
Informative	NA	D1				
	RT			D7		D13
Advisory	NA		D4	D8	D10	
	RT	D2				D15
Proactive	NA					
	RT		D5	D9	D11	
Adaptive	NA					D14
	RT	D3	D6		D12	

Table 1: The key design dimensions and the corresponding prototypes. NA: Norm-Activation, RT: Rational Thinking.

Through prior literature, we identified three key design dimensions for smart thermostats (see Table 1). These dimensions facilitated the systematic generation of fifteen distinct interface prototypes. The three design dimensions we chose include *eco-coaching style*, *persuasive strategy*, and *timing of interaction*. Here we will describe these three design dimensions in detail as well as their relationship with the various prototypes we created.

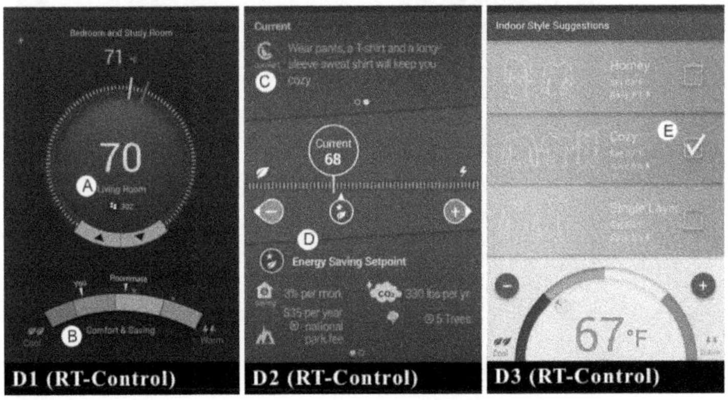

Ⓐ Show the number of Reef users using this setpoint to provoke reaction about norms.

Ⓑ Show the predicted current and future comfort levels for both residents in white and red.

Ⓒ Suggest the clothing needed if the temperature is set at 68°F.

Ⓓ Suggest a personalized energy saving setpoint, 70°F, with benefits as well as recommended clothing in the next card.

Ⓔ Provide three options of clothing with the corresponding setpoints and benefits. Users can click on one option to change the setpoint.

Figure 1: Selected interfaces for our 15 prototypes. We skip D11 as it looks the same as D5 but was tested in a different scenario.

(F) Track comfort history and only recommend short-term adjustments when users have been feeling comfortable for five days.

(G) Show the benefits if the user and 30 others accept this recommendation.

(H) Automatically adjust the setpoint for its users if they've been comfortable lately.

(I) Suggest users to drink a cup of tea and lower the setpoint briefly.

(J) Automatically activate a personalized energy saving plan without asking users' permission. It shows the benefits and the clothing needed for this plan.

(K) Users can easily switch the thermostat schedule by choosing different plans.

(L) Users can assign different days to different energy saving plans.

(M) Show the benefits as well as friends of the users who use this setting.

(N) Explain how to be rated as "energy saving". Users need to manually adjust the setpoints themselves.

(O) Users need to manually create their own schedule. They can view the effect of different setpoints on comfort and the temperature differences in different rooms.

(P) Reef first sends a notification to recommend users to lower their setpoints. If they don't accept, Reef reveals it's sensing limitations.

(Q) Recommend an immediate activity (walk around) to warm themselves up and lower the setpoint.

(R) Show data-driven suggestions. For example, Reef recommends that users could lower their setpoint in the morning since they usually leave home soon after they wake up.

(S) Offer other adaptive thermal comfort tips (e.g., change to stay in a warmer room.)

(T) Show data to support the tips, including people's sleep pattern and when they are usually at a warmer or cooler room.

(U) Show adaptive behavior suggestions shared by people living in the similar area.

(V) Show current usage before the month ends, to give opporuntiies for changes.

(W) Provide reasons for increased heating usage and actionable items (e.g., encouraging users to only fully heat up their home 30 minutes after arrival).

Eco-coaching style refers to the approach Reef takes to communicate with users. At one end of the spectrum, Reef seeks to be *informative* by showing useful eco-feedback to help decision-making, letting users remain in control [11,14,26]. This information might include comfort level prediction, estimated financial savings, and environmental impact. While respecting users' agency was one reason that we explored such a hands-off approach, this approach also handles inaccuracy. Due to the inevitability of imperfect prediction, it may not be most favorable for Reef to automatically change the temperature according to its comfort prediction [8]. One prototype that implements such an approach is D1, which shows the predicted comfort of different household members at home in four colors. Similarly, D9 shows users the predicted comfort level in different rooms at different settings while requiring them to manually create their temperature schedules. At the other end of the spectrum, Reef can be *proactive* [6,27], making decisions for users and only informing them about the benefits. In some situations users might feel that the benefits of automation outweigh the cost of minor mispredictions. D5 and D7 are two prototypes that implement the proactive approach. In D5, Reef identifies that the user has been comfortable for a few days and therefore automatically lowers the setpoint for an evening. It only informs the user about the decision and the benefits without first asking permission. Similarly, in D7, Reef automatically generates and activates an energy-saving schedule after observing occupants' behaviors and comfort level for a month.

A third approach lies in the middle of these extremes, offering suggestions to users and letting them make the final decision [25,34]. Here we probed two possible design directions: one is to offer suggestions directly related to temperature settings (*Advisory*), the other is to encourage adaptive behaviors [5] *(Adaptive)*. For the former type, two different saving suggestions were implemented in Reef's prototypes, namely, personalized saving modes and short-term variation. D2, D4 and D8 are examples that implement such strategies. Inspired by ThermoCoach's [25] saving suggestion design, Reef offers four similar modes: high energy saving, energy saving, regular and warm. Each mode has a corresponding temperature when people are at home and awake (i.e., the Awake setpoint). This temperature is determined by Reef's learning of occupants' comfort. In winter, for example, when running in regular mode Reef will pick a temperature that the user mostly feels comfortable with, and in energy saving mode Reef will find an Awake setpoint that is likely to feel slightly cold. The second strategy is short-term variation, meaning that Reef might suggest users to lower their setpoints for only a short period of time (e.g., a night or a day). The rationale is that while people care about their own comfort, they might be willing to lower their expectation shortly for saving energy. Whereas in some prototypes Reef suggests users to directly change thermostat settings, in others Reef encourages *adaptive* behaviors. One of the adaptive behavior Reef encourages is to change indoor clothing style. The suggestions are made in different ways. For example, in D2 Reef shows the appropriate clothing to wear at different setpoints; In D3 Reef makes the suggestion more salient—users can pick a clothing option and Reef will adjust the setpoint to a corresponding temperature. Besides clothing level, we also explored other adaptive behaviors suggestions such as drinking a hot beverage (D6), walking at home for a few minutes (D12), lowering the setpoint in the morning when users are leaving soon for work (D13), and delaying the time to heat up one's home after arrival (D15).

Persuasive Strategy refers to the approaches used to promote energy-saving behaviors [7,10,11,14,26]. Froehlich et al. [11] highlighted two major strategies: *Rational Thinking (RT)* and *Norm-Activation (NA)*: While some people might respond better to analytical insights, others might be more easily persuaded by emphasizing cultural norms and leveraging social influence.

In our study, we probed different persuasive strategies to encourage saving. Besides information about financial savings, we explored the use of environmental impact framed under a 2015 U.S. government's policy to reduce CO_2 emission by 17% [31] (e.g., D2 and D4). In other prototypes, we showed users about friends that use a similar saving mode (e.g., "Mark and 33 others also use this mode" in D8), as well as adaptive behavior tips shared by households similar to the user (D14). These are also two examples demonstrating how we combined the eco-coaching style dimension with persuasive strategy to create the final prototypes.

Timing of Interaction refers to the various situations in which users might interact with thermostats. We chose to explore five situations and created one user enactment scenario for each (as shown in Figure 2), including *real-time control*, *short engagement*, *planning*, *misprediction* and *reflection*. Although timing of interaction is slightly different from other design dimensions—in the sense that the options in this dimension are not mutually exclusive and can be supported by one thermostat—this dimension helps us understand if a particular approach that works well in one situation also works well in another. Here we briefly explain the first three situations while discussing *misprediction* and *reflection* in more depth. Note that all of our scenarios were created for winter settings.

Real-time control (UE-RT) refers to the situation when one feels uncomfortable and wants to change the setpoint. In our scenario, a participant encounters this situation when watching TV in the living room. He feels cold and opens up Reef to see if he can make any adjustment. *Short engagement* (UE-ShortEngage) refers to the situation that a notification is sent from the thermostat to the user to encourage energy saving. In our scenario, a participant faces this situation when reading books in their study room. Reef recalls that she has been comfortable for a few days thus sends a message to encourage saving. *Planning* (UE-Planning) refers to the situation when one is thinking about next week's plan and checking the thermostat schedule. In our scenario, a participant does this on Saturday night before going to bed or another self-selected time that the participant usually plans his next week's schedule.

Misprediction (UE-Mispred) refers to the situation that the thermostat inaccurately predicts an occupant's comfort and makes an inappropriate decision or suggestion. In our scenario, while the participant feels cold and sick, Reef inaccurately predicts she is comfortable, thus suggesting her to lower the setpoint. From previous literature [15] we already knew that comfort prediction is not perfect, especially when people are sick, wear extra clothes, or are affected by other local factors that are challenging to track by sensors [15]. We were curious to explore how to work around technology constraints regarding comfort prediction. For example, a thermostat might apologize [30] and inform its users about its limitations when it makes mistakes (i.e., a form of incidental intelligibility suggested by Yang et al. [32]). We therefore created a prototype, D10, to present an implementation of incidental intelligibility and compared it with other designs (D11, D12) that do nothing when mispredictions happen.

Reflection (UE-Reflect) refers to the situation when users are thinking about their long-term usage of the thermostats, reflecting on their practices, and reassessing actions they took. We designed a scenario where the participant has just finished checking their energy bill and becomes curious about the heater usage. We explored different ways to support reflection. This includes strategies to support data-driven reassessment proposed by Yang et al. [34]. For example, in D13, Reef allows reassessment by tracking people's in-home behaviors and their schedules. It shows a visualization depicting when the user is likely to go to bed based on behavior tracking. In some prototypes, Reef supports reassessment by considering other real-world factors. For example, in D15 Reef explains how colder temperatures cause additional heater usage, potentially helping users understand why their actions may not lead to the expected outcomes. In addition to supporting reflection by data-driven reassessment, we also explored the inclusion of a discussion board, D14, which helps users share and learn from peers about different ways to maintain their comfort while not turning their thermostat up.

User Enactments Study

Our interactions with study participants involved three steps: an initial interview, a diary study, and the user enactment sessions. The purpose of the initial interview was to understand how participants currently used their thermostats. This interview also shed light on how participants chose their default setpoints, their attitudes toward climate change and sustainability, and how they viewed the relationship between comfort and energy-saving. We then conducted a diary study lasting three to seven days. The purpose of this study was to raise participants' awareness of their own temperature preferences, facilitating better feedback during the user enactments. We installed an experience sampling app, PACO [39], onto participants' phones and gave them two thermometers to place in their homes. Participants were asked to report their comfort and the corresponding indoor temperature three times a day. On average each participant created 13 reports (min: 7, max: 24).

After the diary study we then conducted the user enactments in our two-story smart home testbed (a.k.a. the first author's home). Inspired by Rodden et al.'s [27] approach to ground participants, we presented a series of storyboards to 1) illustrate the current energy problem, 2) envision the future and introduce Reef, and 3) offer the context of enactment.

We first introduced the problem—the high energy usage of heating systems at home and the variation in consumption caused by different usage practices [29]. We showed each participant an estimate of their potential financial savings using the average household size in our region of study. By factoring in the energy sources, we also illustrated the potential environmental impact a participant could make in terms of CO_2 reduction. Finally, to offer a frame of reference for a possible environmental impact goal, we introduced the policy announced by the U.S. government in 2015 [31], which is to reduce 17% of CO_2 emissions by 2020. We made a simplistic assumption that the domestic sector should contribute equally by reducing 17% of energy use.

Afterward, we asked participants to envision the year 2020, four years in the future from the time of the study, and a new thermostat product, "Reef," has been released. We described the key characteristics of Reef, namely its use of wearable and in-home sensors for predicting people's comfort; the ways it learns from its users; its capability to predict whether residents are sleeping or away from home; and its support for user-defined Away, Awake and Asleep temperatures.

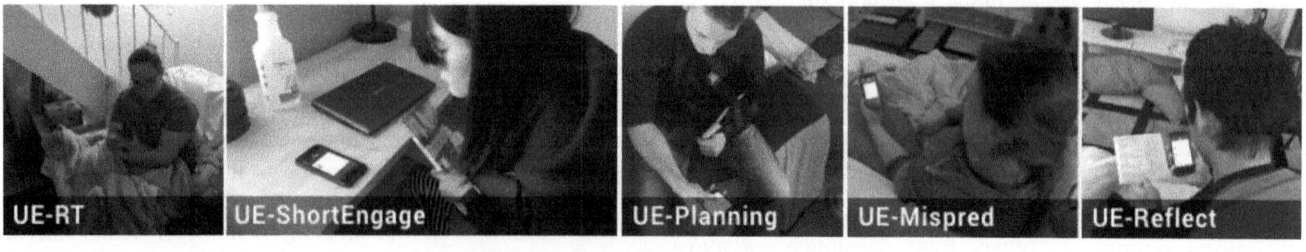

Figure 2: Participants reacted to our prototypes in five different scenarios. From left to right: real-time control; short engagement; planning; misprediction and reflection. Note that each UE took place in a different part of the home.

We asked participants to imagine living in a smart home in February 2020, and gave them a simulated calendar showing what their daily schedules might look like at the time. They were also provided with a simulated weather app interface showing the "current" week's weather ranging from 21 °F to 55 °F. We also asked them to imagine living with another person in the house, either a partner or a roommate. After showing them this information, we asked them to walk through the scenarios we designed.

As described earlier, we developed five scenarios and created three prototypes for each scenario. To ensure the session time was bounded in two hours, we let each participant experience a subset of 3-4 scenarios (thus each design was experienced by 7-8 participants and each participant experienced 9-12 designs). We showed one prototype at a time in a scenario, and we repeated the subset of scenarios three times to show all the design variations. In each scenario we first briefly explained the interface of the prototype and asked participants to interact with it. To increase realism, we tried to match the indoor temperature of our smarthome testbed with what was depicted on our prototype thermostat displays (within 1°F difference). At the end of the session, we then displayed all the 9-12 selected prototypes together for participants to compare. All of the user enactment sessions were video recorded for later analysis by the study team.

Participants & Data Analysis

We conducted our study with 11 participants. We recruited participants through emails, online forums, and social networking sites. Participants were compensated with $50 for completing the interview, diary and UE study. Six males and five females participated in the study, representing a range of occupations including teacher, midwife, finance manager, school administrator, software engineer, among others. Most of them were between ages of 26-35 except for U6 (36-45), U7 (>55) and U11 (46-55). Only U8 owned a smart thermostat with the rest using either manual or programmable thermostats. The study was conducted from the end of April to the beginning of May 2016 where the average temperature in the region of the study was 52 °F (max: 79 °F, min: 28 °F). Thus people were still using their heaters at the time, though the outdoor temperature was somewhat warmer than the simulated temperatures depicted in the study.

To analyze the data we conducted a debriefing session for each enactment within 48 hours. During the debriefing, three of the authors reviewed the whole video and discussed emerging patterns and questions to probe during later sessions. After all the UE sessions, we transcribed all the videos and conducted a thematic analysis [3] to identify common patterns in participants' reactions and understand the underlying expectations and values.

FINDINGS

In the following section, we present three major themes that emerged in our thematic analysis: the desire for comfort and its relationship with sustainability; the desire for control and its tension with the desire for convenience (e.g., the desire to have the system make decisions); and the importance of careful allocation of agency while being pertinent.

Comfort & Sustainability

In this section we present findings related to short-term variation, adaptive suggestions, comfort visualization, and personalized saving modes which helped us uncover participants' values regarding comfort and sustainability.

Our design probe (D4) that encouraged short-term variation based on prior comfort history received polarized responses. Before user enactments, we expected participants to be fairly open to this suggestion because the suggestion was only triggered when they had been "comfortable" for five days. However, some participants felt that being comfortable now didn't imply they should compromise their comfort in the future. According to U1, *"That does not make any sense. If I feel comfortable in the past five days, then what I should do is just keep the same temperature, so that I can keep feeling comfortable."* Others were fine with compromising their comfort for a limited time. U2 said, *"That's fine [for me to live less comfortably for a day]. That's reasonable and just for tomorrow. I think it's like, five days I use temperature I like, and one day I lower it. It sounds OK. ... Because I am not constantly sacrificing my comfort level, so it's just temporary."* We suspect this discrepancy is due to differences around how our participants valued comfort. Although they all desired to be comfortable, some perhaps viewed comfort more as a necessity while some others viewed it as something more like a luxury. Participants who viewed comfort as more of a luxury might be more willing to compromise their comfort, as long as it's temporary and as long as their comfort needs had been reasonably satisfied.

In addition to short-term variation, some of our adaptive suggestions also shed light on the dynamic nature of comfort. Participants had different expectations of comfort at certain times of the day, such as in the morning when they are leaving home soon (e.g., it would be OK to lower the setpoint in the morning slightly earlier) or when they come back home (e.g., delaying the time to fully heat up home upon arrival.). U3: *"I don't mind waking up a little chilly"* (D13); U9: *"Well as long as it's warmer than outside. [In February] it's going to feel better than what we just came from. I think that would be a great solution that I heat up halfway and heat up rest of the way [after] I get home."*(D15) This suggests that although they valued comfort, their perception of comfort varied within a day. Thermostats designed to fit this dynamic expectation may increase the chance for savings.

Most participants had a strongly positive reaction to the design (D1) that allowed them to view the comfort level of their roommate or partner. Three participants who currently lived with their partners specifically said they were willing to sacrifice their own comfort to keep their partner comfortable. U9: *"I would probably just grab a blanket and leave how it is ... I think a lot of changes in the thermostat is the regulation between my wife and myself and the baby honestly. But if I could see that me trying to get more comfortable would [de]crease hers that much ... then I wouldn't do it."* These participants valued some household members' comfort more than their own.

In UE-Planning, participants were shown a design (D8) that suggests three different energy-saving modes (e.g., "energy saving" and "regular") that were personalized according to inferred comfort preferences. While we expected that such saving modes would encourage participants to explore a slightly more energy efficient setting, three of our participants raised a similar concern with this design. U6 explained: *"There [is] something interesting to me about describing the level as high saving, energy saving, very comfortable, ... Because being very comfortable, is like a qualitative statement about my own personal experience of the temperature, these two levels describing high saving and energy saving feels distant from me. It shifts the priority from my comfort to external energy savings and so even though I'm motivated by it ... it seems like to put [me] in a conflict: saving energy or being comfortable."* Whereas these participants valued both comfort and energy saving, and thought they could achieve both—*"I can be quite comfortable in the colder [mode, i.e.] in the energy saving to high saving [mode] with proper [clothing], like having a blanket, that to me is comfortable, I'm more comfortable in cooler environment anyway"* (U6). It seems that rendering energy saving and comfort in a mutually exclusive relationship created a conflict where none need exist.

Control & Convenience

A major question explored in our study is what types of eco-coaching styles better fit participants' values regarding control and convenience. We were especially interested in the intersection of eco-coaching style and the timing of the interaction.

As we expected based on prior research, participants valued user control and favored a more advisory and informative (as opposed to proactive) approach when presented with short-term saving opportunities in UE-ShortEngage. However, in the UE-Planning scenario, the majority of them preferred a more proactive Reef, even though in this prototype (D7) Reef activates an energy-saving schedule without asking participants' permission. U6: *"I don't mind [Reef acting on my behalf] ...I think it's why people engage with smart devices in general. I think that's part of the payoff. [That] is, you have this intelligent device using the data to make data-driven decisions, but does not maximize unless it's making the decision. So I want it to go ahead and use the data that is collected and I would have the real world experience of feeling it. And so if I don't agree ... [like] 'oh gosh that was way too far to being cold' then I know I can adjust it."* This indicates that participants' values regarding comfort and convenience may shift based on interaction context. This openness to Reef's proactivity was also contingent on their trust in the system's capability to capture behavioral information, the value placed on convenience, and the ease of control.

Prototypes (e.g., D8) featuring short-term variation also helped us uncover insights relating to the differing weighting of control and convenience among our participants. Our participants' reactions toward short-term variation were polarized. Some favored consistency rather than variation. U7: *"I guess that is [like] my eating philosophy, I have two days when I eat less and the other day I get [what] I want so. I can see that. But it seems like for the temperature I would rather find the lowest temperature during [a] day that are still comfortable. Try maximize that [aspect] as opposed to being uncomfortable on days."* This could be related to valuing convenience—they didn't want to fiddle with the thermostat—, or could be related to the challenges of planning ahead. U6: *"I don't think I would pick two days a week [to be more energy-saving] ... because I wasn't sure what will make these two days [more] special than the rest of the days."*

However, some participants thought it was possible to set some days to be more energy-saving than usual. U5: *"I would consider [lowering the setpoint for a day every 6 days]."* Interestingly, this willingness to compromise comfort and convenience is also fluid and negotiable depending on different conditions. U5: *"I think it also depends on, again, like, the temperature outside. If it's going to be significantly colder, and then it asks me to lower the temperature tomorrow, I [would] probably say no. ... If I perceive it's going to be colder, even though the inside temperature theoretically should stay the same... I don't want be colder".*

Whereas the prototypes mentioned above were probed under the situations where Reef made accurate predictions, we also explored participants' attitudes and values when mispredictions happened. We expected our "incidental intelligibility" [32] design (D10, UE-Mispred) to receive positive feedback from participants. In this enactment, we told participants to imagine that Reef had misjudged their comfort, and suggested lowering their setpoints while they were sick and cold. If they chose not to, Reef then showed a sample interface attempting to explain why it may have made that mistake. However, almost all the participants expressed that they didn't even want to look at Reef's explanation when they were sick and when Reef made a misprediction. U1, for example completely dismissed the explanation, saying that, *"I don't' want to debug it."* Participants' first reactions were to just increase the temperature to a comfortable point—they didn't necessarily want to fix Reef. This finding suggests that for some people, understanding the system models and capabilities is not as highly valued as we expected based on prior work (e.g., [32]). To them, convenience and error recovery are more important.

However, some participants found that Reef's transparency made it more considerate. U5: *"I like this one better [D10] because it's more honest..., it makes me feel like it does understand like you are a human, you are doing different things, different things might affect you, and we are an app, and we might not be able to get that all the time... It feels kinder, doesn't feel quite as harsh"* (U5). This transparency could also help users trust the thermostat more by mitigating the negative perception that might result from mispredictions. U4: *"If I never knew that Reef knew that [i.e., its limitations], and I came to my own [conclusion] and said like 'oh, Reef is terrible at figuring out when I am sick' then that makes me lose faith in the device."*

Impertinence, Irrelevance & Allocation of Agency

By engaging participants through different scenarios and prototypes, we were able to gain insight into participants' attitudes about the appropriate allocation of responsibility between a thermostat and its users. Finding the boundary between what is and isn't appropriate for a smart thermostat to ask of its users is critical for mixed-initiative design, and more generally for designing technology that will be perceived as appropriate.

Participants' responses toward designs that suggest alternative indoor clothing were polarized (e.g., D3 and D7). Some expressed negative feedback on these designs because they thought they knew how to dress already. For some, such suggestions were seen as impertinent as they felt indoor clothing was a personal domain that the thermostat should not be involved with. U11: *"It's OK [for Reef to change] the temperature but I'm not very excited about it picking what clothes I want to wear. I find that's more personal... part of yourself. Temperature, you know, in your house, that's not part of you. What you wear, it's part of you. If I want to feel comfortable today, I'll wear this, if I don't, if I want to wear shorts around, I will wear what I want to" (D7)."* For others, clothing suggestions were acceptable but they were not enthusiastic about it as they had been wearing more layers of clothes at home already and viewed it mainly as reminders. Clothing selection, including what to wear at home, emerged as an area of personal choice incorporating lifestyle choice and personal expression, in addition to comfort preferences. The difference in reaction may be partly attributed to participants' views of the role of the thermostat, e.g., as a passive instrument versus a cooperative agent.

Besides clothing, the majority of participants reacted negatively to adaptive suggestions that required them to change their routines and living styles (e.g., D13, D14). Suggesting a move to a different room or exercising at certain time of the day to reduce heater usage are examples of such suggestions. Most of the user-generated tips we prototyped fell into this category. Participants hoped to see tips and suggestions that fit their current lifestyle. For example, U10 mentioned a tip he would like to share on the Reef forum (D14). After describing how warm he had to keep the house in order to keep his baby comfortable since safety guidelines prevent the use of blankets on infants, he added: "*It's like impossible. And we are on Amazon, and we found a wearable blanket that they can like clip on and zip into it, it's like a sleeping bag, that's attached to them, which then let us... keep us house colder,... If I was on this [forum], that would be a tip I would have."* This tip reflects a useful adaptive behavior tip that similar users would be more likely to accept. However, participants felt that tips that were irrelevant to them failed to resonate with their identity (e.g., as "parents") and damaged their trust in the system.

DISCUSSION

Our findings allowed us to gain a deeper understanding of how various designs of comfort-aware eco-coaching thermostats might align with or oppose people's values with respect to comfort, sustainability, convenience, control and agency. Here we discuss how our study extended or challenged insights produced from prior research, specifically in terms of coordinating comfort and sustainability, balancing control and convenience, and allocating of agency while avoiding impertinence.

Coordinating Comfort & Sustainability

While prior systems have incorporated comfort sensing for temperature automation in offices [9], there has been limited work investigating how people value comfort-aware systems in the home. Although we knew that people desire to be comfortable and hope to be environmentally responsible [33], it was unclear if people are open to smart thermostats that actively encourage sustainability while considering their comfort. Our study explored this question by surfacing comfort in different ways, including showing sensed comfort in visualizations (D1), suggesting short-term variation only when people have been comfortable for a few days (D4), suggesting adaptive behaviors when people may have a lower expectation on comfort (e.g., D15), and offering personalized saving modes (D8).

First, our findings point out that for some people, the comfort of certain others is more important than individual comfort. Interestingly, while prior research [9] resolves multi-user conflict around comfort through automatically identifying a middle ground, our findings point to the possibility that in small households, visualizing comfort or using an important person as a reference might also be a solution, even a better outcome in some cases. In addition, our findings suggest that some people might value their comfort more as a necessity while others view it more as luxury. People who view comfort more as a luxury are more likely to compromise their comfort, and respond more favorably to recommendations of short-term variation. Furthermore, we found that while people desire comfort, their expectation and perception of comfort change throughout the day. This finding challenges previous measurements of comfort for smart thermostats: For example, PreHeat [28] aimed to optimize comfort by minimizing "MissTime", which the authors define as the amount of time where the users are at home but the temperature does not reach the target temperature. Our findings point out that this measurement of thermostat efficiency is not in line with people's changing expectations of their comfort. Finally, our design of saving modes raised some concerns. Inspired by the success of prior research [25,34], we chose to use a similar framing of saving mode suggestions (i.e., "energy saving", "comfortable"). However, our findings point out that this framing renders energy saving and comfort in a mutually exclusive relationship. This implicitly highlighted conflict may steer people to weight their comfort as more important their adaptive potentials.

Balancing Comfort & Convenience

We knew from prior work that leaving users in control is essential, yet in a situation like thermostat scheduling, people appreciate some degree of automation [1,32]. However, these prior insights were produced from reactions to smart thermostats that take a passive stance on energy savings (e.g., Nest). We were unclear whether these insights would still hold for eco-coaching thermostats that actively probe comfort boundaries by lowering the setpoint. It was also unclear whether implementing incidental intelligibility would help strike a balance between convenience and control, making them more tolerant to a proactive design even in the face of mistakes.

Our findings related to eco-coaching styles suggest that due to people's value of convenience, many people are accepting of a proactive design when doing temperature scheduling. This is of course contingent on people's trust in the system's capability to make data-driven decisions, and the perceived ease of control if adjustments need to be made. Although people might still adjust the temperature back if they feel uncomfortable, this brings up an opportunity to view eco-coaching as a negotiation process. Prior work has only explored eco-coaching in a more passive way [1,25,34], but our findings point to the potential for smart thermostats to negotiate a more energy-saving configuration by setting a first reference point.

Our findings also point out that incidental intelligibility [32] was helpful for some participants, although error recovery was even more important when mispredictions happened. For these people incidental intelligibility helped them sustain their trust in the system. However, some other participants didn't value intelligibility as highly as we expected. We suspect there are multiple factors that contribute to the observed reactions. These factors include context (i.e., participants were asked to imagine being sick), the nature of interaction (i.e., system-initiated push notification), and the presentation (i.e., verbal explanation). More research is still needed to see whether implementing incidental intelligibility in user-initiated actions, and with other forms of presentation, might yield better results.

Being Pertinent & Respecting Allocation of Agency

Researchers [4,5] have already proposed to incorporate adaptive thermal comfort into the design of energy-saving systems. However, it was still unclear to us how to operationalize this concept in an appropriate way that can result in a useful system. Our findings suggest the importance of making adaptive suggestions that are pertinent and relevant to people's identity and situations.

Our findings point out that supporting appropriate user agency in making personal decisions at home is critical. Indoor clothing suggestions, even for passive designs like D3 and D7, might step into some people's private domain and be perceived as impertinent. Our findings also point out that many people already engage in adaptive behaviors. Suggesting these already-familiar adaptive behaviors without bringing in new insights comes across as ignorant and does not represent an effective approach to impacting behavior. Further, it is important to offer adaptive suggestions that fit people's lifestyles and routines. People are usually quite resistant to changing their lifestyle or routines. Many of the common adaptive behaviors mentioned in prior adaptive thermal comfort work (e.g., drinking hot beverages) elicited negative responses from our participants due to their highly user-dependent nature.

LIMITATIONS

The insights from our study were obtained through User Enactments, which involve short-duration engagements with possible future designs. We expect that users' reactions to the designs proposed in our study would evolve during a longer engagement. Our prototypes were also all probed in a single-participant setting. While we did ask participants to envision co-habitation, and we designed our interfaces with multiple users in mind, our study did not capture the complex social dynamics that may emerge in a longer field deployment. Given the early stage of design for both comfort-aware and eco-coaching thermostats, however, we felt that an important first step would be to survey a broader set of potential design directions using an approach that gives us insight into the underlying expectations and values that would drive responses to different approaches, as such values would influence both immediate and longer-term reactions. We look forward to future research that addresses the evolution of usage and complex social dynamics at home in a long-term deployment.

CONCLUSION

This work represents the first attempt to explore the design opportunity of *comfort-aware eco-coaching thermostats*: smart thermostats that can understand occupants' thermal comfort while persuading them to save energy. To research this opportunity, we created fifteen prototypes covering a diverse set of design attributes and conducted a user enactment-based study with 11 participants. Our study provides insights into how different designs of comfort-aware eco-coaching thermostats might align with or against people's values related to comfort, sustainability, control, convenience and allocation of agency.

ACKNOWLEDGMENTS

This work was funded in part by NSF grant 0905460. We thank our participants and also Tawanna Dillahunt and members of the Interaction Ecologies group for their thoughtful comments on this work.

REFERENCES

1. Alper T. Alan, Mike Shann, Enrico Costanza, Sarvapali D. Ramchurn, and Sven Seuken. 2016. It is Too Hot: An In-Situ Study of Three Designs for Heating. In *Proceedings of the 2016 CHI Conference on Human Factors in Computing Systems* (CHI '16), 5262–5273. https://doi.org/10.1145/2858036.2858222
2. Alex Beltran, Varick L. Erickson, and Alberto E. Cerpa. 2013. ThermoSense: Occupancy Thermal Based Sensing for HVAC Control. In *Proceedings of the 5th ACM Workshop on Embedded Systems For Energy-Efficient Buildings* (BuildSys'13), 11:1–11:8. https://doi.org/10.1145/2528282.2528301
3. Virginia Braun and Victoria Clarke. 2006. Using thematic analysis in psychology. *Qualitative Research in Psychology* 3, 2: 77–101. https://doi.org/10.1191/1478088706qp063oa
4. Adrian Clear, Adrian Friday, Mike Hazas, and Carolynne Lord. 2014. Catch my drift?: achieving comfort more sustainably in conventionally heated buildings. 1015–1024. https://doi.org/10.1145/2598510.2598529
5. Adrian K. Clear, Janine Morley, Mike Hazas, Adrian Friday, and Oliver Bates. 2013. Understanding Adaptive Thermal Comfort: New Directions for UbiComp. In *Proceedings of the 2013 ACM International Joint Conference on Pervasive and Ubiquitous Computing* (UbiComp '13), 113–122. https://doi.org/10.1145/2493432.2493451
6. Scott Davidoff, Min Kyung Lee, Anind K. Dey, and John Zimmerman. 2007. Rapidly Exploring Application Design Through Speed Dating. In *UbiComp 2007: Ubiquitous Computing*, John Krumm, Gregory D. Abowd, Aruna Seneviratne and Thomas Strang (eds.). Springer Berlin Heidelberg, 429–446. https://doi.org/10.1007/978-3-540-74853-3_25
7. Tawanna R. Dillahunt and Jennifer Mankoff. 2014. Understanding factors of successful engagement around energy consumption between and among households. 1246–1257. https://doi.org/10.1145/2531602.2531626
8. Povl Ole Fanger. 1970. *Thermal comfort. Analysis and applications in environmental engineering*. Danish Technical Press.
9. Mark Feldmeier and Joseph A. Paradiso. 2010. Personalized HVAC control system. In *2010 Internet of Things (IOT)*, 1–8. https://doi.org/10.1109/IOT.2010.5678444
10. B. J. Fogg. 2002. Persuasive Technology: Using Computers to Change What We Think and Do. *Ubiquity* 2002, December. https://doi.org/10.1145/764008.763957
11. Jon Froehlich, Leah Findlater, and James Landay. 2010. The Design of Eco-feedback Technology. In *Proceedings of the SIGCHI Conference on Human Factors in Computing Systems* (CHI '10), 1999–2008. https://doi.org/10.1145/1753326.1753629
12. Manu Gupta, Stephen S. Intille, and Kent Larson. 2009. Adding GPS-Control to Traditional Thermostats: An Exploration of Potential Energy Savings and Design Challenges. In *Proceedings of the 7th International Conference on Pervasive Computing* (Pervasive '09), 95–114. https://doi.org/10.1007/978-3-642-01516-8_8
13. E. Halawa and J. van Hoof. 2012. The adaptive approach to thermal comfort: A critical overview. *Energy and Buildings* 51: 101–110. https://doi.org/10.1016/j.enbuild.2012.04.011
14. Helen Ai He, Saul Greenberg, and Elaine M. Huang. 2010. One Size Does Not Fit All: Applying the Transtheoretical Model to Energy Feedback Technology Design. In *Proceedings of the SIGCHI Conference on Human Factors in Computing Systems* (CHI '10), 927–936. https://doi.org/10.1145/1753326.1753464
15. Chuan-Che (Jeff) Huang, Rayoung Yang, and Mark W. Newman. 2015. The Potential and Challenges of Inferring Thermal Comfort at Home Using Commodity Sensors. In *Proceedings of the 2015 ACM International Joint Conference on Pervasive and Ubiquitous Computing* (UbiComp '15), 1089–1100. https://doi.org/10.1145/2750858.2805831
16. Michael A. Humphreys, J. Fergus Nicol, and Iftikhar A. Raja. 2007. Field studies of indoor thermal comfort and the progress of the adaptive approach. *Advances in building energy research* 1, 1: 55–88.
17. Christian Koehler, Brian D. Ziebart, Jennifer Mankoff, and Anind K. Dey. 2013. TherML: Occupancy Prediction for Thermostat Control. In *Proceedings of the 2013 ACM International Joint Conference on Pervasive and Ubiquitous Computing* (UbiComp '13), 103–112. https://doi.org/10.1145/2493432.2493441
18. Jiakang Lu, Tamim Sookoor, Vijay Srinivasan, Ge Gao, Brian Holben, John Stankovic, Eric Field, and Kamin Whitehouse. 2010. The Smart Thermostat: Using Occupancy Sensors to Save Energy in Homes. In *Proceedings of the 8th ACM Conference on Embedded Networked Sensor Systems* (SenSys '10), 211–224. https://doi.org/10.1145/1869983.1870005
19. Dimitrios Lymberopoulos, Jie Liu, Xue Yang, Romit Roy Choudhury, Vlado Handziski, and Souvik Sen. 2015. A Realistic Evaluation and Comparison of Indoor Location Technologies: Experiences and Lessons Learned. In *Proceedings of the 14th International Conference on Information Processing in*

Sensor Networks (IPSN '15), 178–189. https://doi.org/10.1145/2737095.2737726

20. Alan Meier. 2012. How people actually use thermostats. *ACEEE Summer Study on Energy Efficiency in Buildings. Pacific Grove, Calif.: American Council for an Energy Efficient Economy.* Retrieved December 14, 2014 from http://escholarship.org/uc/item/3vd5q0cp.pdf
21. Michael Mozer, Lucky Vidmar, and Robert H. Dodier. 1996. The Neurothermostat: Predictive Optimal Control of Residential Heating Systems. In *Neural Information Processing Systems*, 953–959.
22. J. Fergus Nicol and Michael A. Humphreys. 2002. Adaptive thermal comfort and sustainable thermal standards for buildings. *Energy and Buildings* 34, 6: 563–572. https://doi.org/10.1016/S0378-7788(02)00006-3
23. William Odom, John Zimmerman, Scott Davidoff, Jodi Forlizzi, Anind K. Dey, and Min Kyung Lee. 2012. A Fieldwork of the Future with User Enactments. In *Proceedings of the Designing Interactive Systems Conference* (DIS '12), 338–347. https://doi.org/10.1145/2317956.2318008
24. William Odom, John Zimmerman, Jodi Forlizzi, Hajin Choi, Stephanie Meier, and Angela Park. 2014. Unpacking the Thinking and Making Behind a User Enactments Project. In *Proceedings of the 2014 Conference on Designing Interactive Systems* (DIS '14), 513–522. https://doi.org/10.1145/2598510.2602960
25. Devika Pisharoty, Rayoung Yang, Mark W. Newman, and Kamin Whitehouse. 2015. ThermoCoach: Reducing Home Energy Consumption with Personalized Thermostat Recommendations. In *Proceedings of the 2nd ACM International Conference on Embedded Systems for Energy-Efficient Built Environments* (BuildSys '15), 201–210. https://doi.org/10.1145/2821650.2821671
26. Zachary Pousman, John T. Stasko, and Michael Mateas. 2007. Casual information visualization: Depictions of data in everyday life. *Visualization and Computer Graphics, IEEE Transactions on* 13, 6: 1145–1152. https://doi.org/10.1109/TVCG.2007.70541
27. Tom A. Rodden, Joel E. Fischer, Nadia Pantidi, Khaled Bachour, and Stuart Moran. 2013. At Home with Agents: Exploring Attitudes Towards Future Smart Energy Infrastructures. In *Proceedings of the SIGCHI Conference on Human Factors in Computing Systems* (CHI '13), 1173–1182. https://doi.org/10.1145/2470654.2466152
28. James Scott, A.J. Bernheim Brush, John Krumm, Brian Meyers, Michael Hazas, Stephen Hodges, and Nicolas Villar. 2011. PreHeat: Controlling Home Heating Using Occupancy Prediction. In *Proceedings of the 13th International Conference on Ubiquitous Computing* (UbiComp '11), 281–290. https://doi.org/10.1145/2030112.2030151
29. Robert C. Sonderegger. 1978. Movers and stayers: The resident's contribution to variation across houses in energy consumption for space heating. *Energy and Buildings* 1, 3: 313–324. https://doi.org/10.1016/0378-7788(78)90011-7
30. Vasant Srinivasan and Leila Takayama. 2016. Help Me Please: Robot Politeness Strategies for Soliciting Help From Humans. In *Proceedings of the 2016 CHI Conference on Human Factors in Computing Systems* (CHI '16), 4945–4955. https://doi.org/10.1145/2858036.2858217
31. OAR US EPA. Clean Power Plan. Retrieved September 2, 2016 from https://www.epa.gov/cleanpowerplan
32. Rayoung Yang and Mark W. Newman. 2013. Learning from a Learning Thermostat: Lessons for Intelligent Systems for the Home. In *Proceedings of the 2013 ACM International Joint Conference on Pervasive and Ubiquitous Computing* (UbiComp '13), 93–102. https://doi.org/10.1145/2493432.2493489
33. Rayoung Yang, Mark W. Newman, and Jodi Forlizzi. 2014. Making Sustainability Sustainable: Challenges in the Design of Eco-Interaction Technologies. In *Proceedings of the SIGCHI Conference on Human Factors in Computing Systems* (CHI '14), 823–832. https://doi.org/10.1145/2556288.2557380
34. Rayoung Yang, Devika Pisharoty, Soodeh Montazeri, Kamin Whitehouse, and Mark W. Newman. 2016. How Does Eco-coaching Help to Save Energy? Assessing a Recommendation System for Energy-efficient Thermostat Scheduling. In *Proceedings of the 2016 ACM International Joint Conference on Pervasive and Ubiquitous Computing* (UbiComp '16), 1176–1187. https://doi.org/10.1145/2971648.2971698
35. Total Energy. Retrieved from http://www.eia.gov/totalenergy/
36. The Nest Thermostat. Retrieved from https://nest.com/thermostat/
37. Basis B1. Retrieved from http://www.mybasis.com/
38. AeoTec MultiSensor. *Aeotec*. Retrieved February 10, 2015 from http://aeotec.com/z-wave-sensor
39. Paco. Retrieved September 2, 2016 from https://www.pacoapp.com/

Prototyping Ubiquitous Imaging Surfaces

Kyle Montague[1], Daniel Jackson[1], Tobias Brühwiler[2], Tom Bartindale[1], Gerard Wilkinson[1], Patrick Olivier[1], Otmar Hilliges[2], Thomas Ploetz[3]

[1]Newcastle University, Newcastle upon Tyne, United Kingdom
{firstname.surname}@ncl.ac.uk, g.wilkinson@ncl.ac.uk

[2]ETH Zurich, Zurich, Switzerland
brutobia@student.ethz.ch, otmar.hilliges@inf.ethz.ch

[3]Georgia Institute of Technology, Atlanta, USA
thomas.ploetz@gatech.edu

ABSTRACT
Mass adoption and innovation in the field of the Internet of Things has transformed the environments we live in, from stale siloes of technologies into rich interactive playgrounds. Nevertheless, the vast majority of surface area in these spaces are being overlooked and under-utilized in today's research. Surface imaging provides the means to extend and include typically out-of-reach, disconnected objects into these playgrounds. However, existing surface imaging technologies are impractical to embed in everyday environments, restricting researchers from exploring the design and interaction opportunities they can afforded these spaces. In this paper, we propose IRIS, a modular surface imaging prototype capable of providing scalable, low-cost, high-resolution surface imaging. We describe a real-world case study where IRIS is used to identify and track fresh fruit produce being prepared – a task that is typical infeasible with existing technologies. Through IRIS, we hope to enable the community to exploit these under-explored surface areas and enhance the rich, interactive, connected environments we inhabit.

Author Keywords
Surface Imaging; Modular Sensing; Internet of Things.

ACM Classification Keywords
H.5.2 User Interfaces: Input devices and strategies.

INTRODUCTION
It was predicted, that in the future all of the spaces in which we work, live and play will be rich with interaction and ubiquitous sensing woven into the environment [17]. Today, we are already experiencing digital sensing and interaction embedded into many aspects of our daily lives. We have connected smart homes that monitor and learn our daily routines with seemingly autonomous control over an entire arsenal of IoT (*Internet of Things*) devices. With each new *Thing* added to the network the sensing capabilities and interaction opportunities grow exponentially. Despite the tremendous efforts to make everything part of IoT, there are a wealth of objects that remain disconnected – and therefore invisible to our connected worlds. For objects where it is impractical or infeasible to embed the required digital identification and communication means, we need alternative strategies to include them in our networks and IoT environments.

DIS 2017, June 10-14, 2017, Edinburgh, United Kingdom
ACM 978-1-4503-4922-2/17/06.
http://dx.doi.org/10.1145/3064663.3064688

We believe surface-based imaging in conjunction with Computer Vision hold the key to expanding what is possible within these interactive playgrounds. Nevertheless, we are currently limited by existing imaging technologies, which fail to support the pixel density, form factors and scalability required to achieve truly ubiquitous imaging surfaces. It is undeniable that new interactions can be made possible in spaces where every surface is capable of imaging objects placed onto it; where the physical form of objects can be linked with their provenance and history through time and space. However, it is unclear what this new paradigm of interaction will look like without first embedding the technology – which can be infeasible due to the aforementioned constraints. To investigate the design space and interaction possibilities of ubiquitous imaging surfaces, we developed a modular imaging surface prototype, made with off-the-shelf components. Our modular design enables multiple units to be connected together, supporting the creation and reconfiguration of arbitrary-shaped imaging surfaces, to accommodate a diverse range of surface imaging scenarios.

In this paper, we present IRIS, a practical implementation of ubiquitous imaging surfaces – using cheap, readily-available components. Our hardware designs and software are Open Source and have been made available as a platform to support other designers and researchers exploring ubiquitous imaging environments. Finally, through a case study, we explore the potential application of IRIS for food identification without RFID markers.

RELATED WORK
The identification and tracking of real-world objects in a space can be valuable in many contexts. Office [13,14], home and social [2] environments all present rich interaction spaces for ubiquitous surface imaging. Historically, single [5,11] and multiple [1] high-resolution cameras

mounted behind surfaces have been demonstrated as valid approaches to surface imaging, and LCD based technologies such as PixelSense [9], FiberBoard [3] and cameras placed on surface edges [7] have demonstrated how flat form factors can be utilized for optical imaging in low pixel density imaging tasks. However, these solutions are single units which constrains the capture resolution and physical size, and ultimately limits the shape that an imaging surface can be, typically conforming to rectangular or circular forms. In addition, installation often requires significant depth behind or underneath individual units.

Using smaller, individual units combined together is a viable alternative [15], but this work has been limited to large collaborative interaction and display spaces, rather than ubiquitous environmental sensing. As existing surfaces include integrated displays, these technologies typically rely on infrared vision, where the limited spectrum would restrict their ability to differentiate real-world objects.

Computer Vision based tracking has traditionally been performed using video of the environment [8], however surface occlusion becomes a significant issue when identifying objects placed on surfaces being used by people. Some objects can often be 'tagged' in advance using RFID [12] or visual marker [4,6] technologies; however, RF methods do not track orientation, and both techniques fail with objects that cannot be tagged. Moreover, it is not always desirable or possible to embed cameras in an environment, as they capture more than the intended interactions and impose on individuals' privacy. While, surface imaging approaches can rely on embedded cameras, it is possible to maintain privacy by limiting focus and diffusing light to obfuscate anything beyond the imaging surface.

UBIQUITOUS IMAGING SURFACES

Connected environments need to be aware of objects out of reach of current IoT infrastructure. Surface imaging has the potential to support this need. However, due to technical constraints the design space of imaging surfaces has been limited to traditional form factors. To explore the interaction opportunities and design challenges of truly ubiquitous imaging surfaces, we need functional prototypes that can be embedded into real world environments, with diverse spatial, contextual and privacy demands.

To ensure our approach could support a wide range of imaging surface scenarios, we adopted the following conceptual principles:

Configurable and Malleable

The world we live in is not comprised of solely rectangular surfaces – nor is it likely that surface imaging will impose these rules in the future. Therefore, we must be able to easily create arbitrary-shaped imaging surfaces that conform to the environment.

Scalable

Our environments consist of surfaces large and small. The dimensions of a surface can restrict or promote behaviors and interactions. Ubiquitous imaging surfaces must be suitable for the same dimensional configurations as used in our existing environments.

Spatial Reconfiguration and Extensibility

The transient nature of surfaces within environments can lead to changes in their spatial configuration. For example, as one table is moved adjacent to another, the physical interactions often extend to occupy the new space. Ubiquitous imaging surfaces should respond appropriately, e.g. by exchanging local surface knowledge with each other. These surfaces are prime locations for interaction and collaboration, therefore it is vital that ubiquitous imaging surfaces can respond to this demand of spatial reconfiguration and extensibility.

Self-Organizing

Furthermore, the spatial configuration of objects, such as grouping or clustering, can hold an intrinsic meaning to interactions. As such, at the unit level, the spatial configuration of imaging of surfaces must be known.

Acceptability

A fundamental barrier to the adoption of technology is its acceptability within society. The appearance and privacy norms of environments should be reflected in the form and function of ubiquitous imaging surfaces.

IRIS DESIGN

We approach the challenge of creating a ubiquitous imaging surface by moving away from the notion of a single imaging device per surface, to a collection of smaller devices working cooperatively. U-Texture demonstrated a similar approach, using inter-connecting touchscreen displays, to created smart objects [16]. Distributing a surface between multiple cameras allows a high pixel density while minimizing the overall depth required, and yet the scale is still limited in two important ways. Firstly, at some magnitude, camera bandwidth and image computation will exceed a single processing unit's capabilities – indicating a need to distribute the processing. Still, at some scale, distributed processing using a single physical medium for communication between

Figure 1. The modular design of an IRIS surface showing the interlocking, tessellating units.

nodes (e.g. a wireless network or un-switched Ethernet connection) would saturate that channel – indicating that a non-global network topology must be used.

In response to these challenges, IRIS uses a modular design, which allows larger surfaces to be composed from multiple smaller IRIS units, each with a single camera and processor for local surface imaging. This decentralized approach – where each module has its own processing ability and direct, local communication with neighboring modules – frees the modular construction from shape and scale limitations.

Hardware Components

Each IRIS unit (Figure 1 and 2) is an identical, self-contained imaging surface. A unit is compact (160 × 105 × 73 mm) and designed to be connected to form a larger surface, supported by power and data coupling along each edge. A camera (Raspberry Pi Camera 2) with a wide field of view (5MP 160° FOV) is used to obtain a high pixel density image of the local surface (1944 × 1458 pixel color, after correcting for distortion yields 170–300 dpi). The image is processed locally by the embedded computer (Raspberry Pi 3 Model B). A four-channel UART (FT4232H mini module) provides bi-directional serial communication with adjacent boards via sprung *pogo pins* and contact pads mounted on the sides of the unit, which also distribute power. Optional LED rear-illumination to improve color and contrast is switched through a Darlington array (ULN2803). Finally, a battery allows the devices to continue to continue to operate and maintain state during brief periods of disconnection (e.g. rearrangement of devices).

The unit enclosure is an inter-locking, tessellating design made from laser-cut acrylic sheets with an acrylic top surface and plywood base. This configuration allows the units to quickly be snapped together or extended to create larger surfaces, as illustrated in Figure 3. Power transfer and local communication is achieved via the physical contact made by units when connected together. IRIS units determine their local topology and are hot-swappable, allowing imaging surfaces to be reconfigured and individual units to be replaced as required.

The top surface can be diffused so that objects away from the surface are blurred. This configuration offers better privacy for people otherwise within the camera's field of view, without impairing the high-resolution imaging of objects placed directly on the unit. An additional benefit is that the diffusion allows for more robust image segmentation. Furthermore, we ensure that objects remain visible when the unit has little or no ambient light by using a backlight diffuser with white LEDs to illuminate the subjects from below.

Image Processing

IRIS units capitalize on the available hardware acceleration within the processor by directly delivering the camera image to the GPU (via a CSI bus). The units use a wide-angle camera lens to reduce the depth of the device, yet this produces an image that suffers from strong barrel distortion.

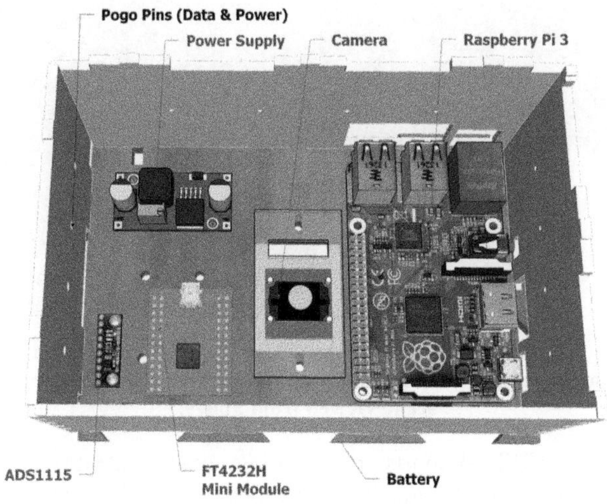

Figure 2. The internal layout of a single IRIS unit with components labelled.

We create an un-distortion map, tailored to each device with a semi-automated calibration procedure, loaded into the GPU to allow efficient correction of the incoming images.

The system uses two schemes of object classification: recognition of object type, and identification of unique objects. Using the un-distortion map, we extract a low-resolution (256 × 192 pixel) image and segment the foreground from the background by thresholding the saturation channel to create an image mask. From the resulting image, we can perform object recognition by processing the image for contours. We then match these contour features to recognize the type of object. With the bounds of the resulting object candidate contours, we extract high-resolution (up to 1944 × 1458 resolution) patches from the original image. Each patch is processed for *Speeded-Up Robust Features* (SURF) to perform object identification using a brute force matcher.

Communication between units

As objects can be freely placed on the IRIS surface, and particularly given the small surface area of a single unit, objects can be expected to be positioned across multiple

Figure 3. A coffee table created from 16 IRIS units.

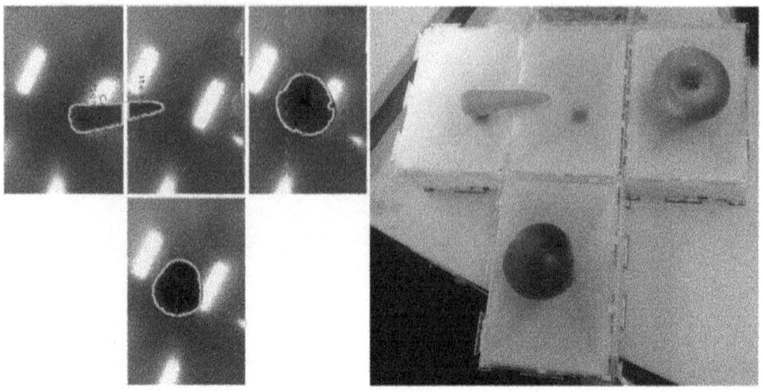

Figure 4. IRIS surface identifying fresh food. Left: the composite image as seen and labelled by the surface, right: the scene viewed from above.

units. IRIS supports determining object identification between multiple units by exchanging extracted features and object definitions with connected neighbors. When a contour patches lies along the border of two units, their features (object contour and SURF extracted points) are automatically communicated to the adjacent unit; this reciprocal action allows both devices to independently process the features for object candidates.

Networking is achieved via a physical connection to the immediately attached neighboring units. When the devices are snapped together, four pogo pins and pads make contact from adjoining edges. Two connections provide common power rails (positive voltage and ground), and two provide bidirectional serial communication (transmit and receive).

A collective catalogue of objects known to the surface is maintained through each unit recursively sharing object definitions and features with their neighbors. This approach is beneficial because it allows any unit to extend the object catalogue; additionally, as new units are introduced to the surface to extend it, they too are notified of the existing object catalogue and can immediately begin contributing to the imaging tasks.

CASE STUDY: FOOD IDENTIFICATION

Radio Frequency identification (RFID) tags revolutionized large-scale commercial product identification and tracking by enabling individual goods to be assigned unique identities; thus, supporting persistent and historical tracking of their life-cycle. While a large proportion of consumer goods are already being shipped with some form of identification marker, it is not always physically possible or sustainably viable to embed electronic tags in goods such as fresh foods. For these items, we are currently unable to take advantage of the interaction opportunities such identification can afford, rendering these goods invisible to today's IoT and connected environments. Work has proved, however, that surface image recognition of these items can be successful given appropriate image information [10].

We conducted a case study to explore the interaction opportunities of uniquely identifying these objects. Using our IRIS prototype platform, we built an RFID alternative for identifying and tracking fresh foods. IRIS is capable of distinguishing between multiple types of fresh foods (including apples, carrots, oranges, onions and peaches), moreover IRIS can uniquely identify specific instances of fresh food. Each piece of fresh food was assigned its own unique identification number; by placing it on to the IRIS surface. Once added to the surface's catalogue of objects, the fresh food could be successfully moved around and identified anywhere across the surface.

In initial testing, object feature descriptors included a total of 38 active variables extracted from the SURF algorithm, this configuration produced a recognition accuracy of 97.2% (five categories, three instances of each category). While this case study used a relatively small catalogue of objects, the results were promising and demonstrate the potential for this type of ubiquitous imaging application, shown in Figure 4.

CONCLUSION AND FUTURE WORK

In this paper, we have discussed the technical challenges and design opportunities of ubiquitous imaging surfaces to enhance our connected environments. Recognizing the need for functional technologies to enable designers and researchers alike to explore this exciting interactive space, we created IRIS, an Open Source imaging surface prototype. IRIS is a modular high pixel density surface that can be scaled and physically reconfigured to create arbitrary shaped planar imaging surfaces. IRIS contributes a practical approach towards extensible, ubiquitous imaging surfaces using off-the-shelf components.

We acknowledge our solution is a stepping stone to true ubiquitous imaging surfaces, and as camera, battery and networking technologies improve, so will the form-factor and availability of this type of sensor. We envision a world where imaging surfaces are like stickers, cameras are consumables and can be placed anywhere, without preparation, by anyone. Using currently available technology, we have demonstrated the potential for IRIS to extend the IoT, and connected environments to include previously excluded everyday objects through high resolution imaging to support object identification.

Our contribution stands as a practical and cost-effective solution for creating scalable imaging surfaces. We encourage the community to build upon this platform to explore the design space and create increasingly connected environments using ubiquitous surface imaging.

ACKNOWLEDGEMENTS

This project was funded by EPSRC award number DERC EP/M023001/1 (Digital Economy Research Centre). All source code and hardware designs are available at: https://github.com/digitalinteraction/iris

REFERENCES

1. YoungSeok Ahn, HyungSeok Kim, Mingue Lim, Jun Lee, and Jee-In Kim. 2010. A slim tabletop interface based on high resolution LCD screens with multiple

cameras. In *ACM International Conference on Interactive Tabletops and Surfaces - ITS '10*, 241. http://doi.org/10.1145/1936652.1936696

2. Till Ballendat, Nicolai Marquardt, and Saul Greenberg. 2010. Proxemic interaction. In *ACM International Conference on Interactive Tabletops and Surfaces – ITS '10*, 121. http://doi.org/10.1145/1936652.1936676
3. Daniel Jackson, Tom Bartindale, and Patrick Olivier. 2009. FiberBoard: compact multi-touch display using channeled light. In *ACM International Conference on Interactive Tabletops and Surfaces – ITS '09*. 25–28. http://doi.org/10.1145/1731903.1731908
4. Mark Fiala. 2005. ARTag, a fiducial marker system using digital techniques. In *IEEE Computer Society Conference on Computer Vision and Pattern Recognition 2005 (CVPR '05)*, vol. 2, 590–596. http://doi.org/10.1109/CVPR.2005.74
5. Christian Holz and Patrick Baudisch. 2013. Fiberio. In *Proceedings of the 26th annual ACM symposium on User interface software and technology - UIST '13*, 41–50. http://doi.org/10.1145/2501988.2502021
6. Martin Kaltenbrunner and Ross Bencina. 2007. reacTIVision: a computer-vision framework for table-based tangible interaction. In *TEI*, 69–74. Retrieved from http://portal.acm.org/citation.cfm?id=1226969.1226983
7. Otto Korkalo and Petri Honkamaa. 2010. Construction and evaluation of multi-touch screens using multiple cameras located on the side of the display. In *ACM International Conference on Interactive Tabletops and Surfaces - ITS '10*, 83. http://doi.org/10.1145/1936652.1936667
8. Girish Kulkarni, Visruth Premraj, Sagnik Dhar, et al. 2011. Baby talk: Understanding and generating simple image descriptions. In *CVPR 2011*, 1601–1608. http://doi.org/10.1109/CVPR.2011.5995466
9. Microsoft. 2012. The Power of PixelSense™. Retrieved November 12, 2012 from http://www.microsoft.com/en-us/pixelsense/pixelsense.aspx
10. Cuong Pham, Daniel Jackson, Johannes Schoening, Tom Bartindale, Thomas Ploetz, and Patrick Olivier. 2013. FoodBoard. In *Proceedings of the 2013 ACM international joint conference on Pervasive and ubiquitous computing - UbiComp '13*, 749. http://doi.org/10.1145/2493432.2493522
11. Johannes Schöning, Jonathan Hook, Nima Motamedi, et al. 2009. Building Interactive Multi-Touch Surfaces. *Journal of Graphics, GPU, and Game Tools* 14, 3: 35–55. http://doi.org/10.1080/2151237X.2009.10129285
12. Roy Want, Kenneth P. Fishkin, Anuj Gujar, and Beverly L. Harrison. 1999. Bridging physical and virtual worlds with electronic tags. In *Proceedings of the SIGCHI conference on Human factors in computing systems the CHI is the limit - CHI '99*, 370–377. http://doi.org/10.1145/302979.303111
13. Pierre Wellner and Pierre. 1991. The DigitalDesk calculator. In *Proceedings of the 4th annual ACM symposium on User interface software and technology - UIST '91*, 27–33. http://doi.org/10.1145/120782.120785
14. Danicl Wigdor, Gerald Penn, Kathy Ryall, Alan Esenther, and Chia Shen. 2007. Living with a Tabletop: Analysis and Observations of Long Term Office Use of a Multi-Touch Table. In *Second Annual IEEE International Workshop on Horizontal Interactive Human-Computer Systems (TABLETOP'07)*, 60–67. http://doi.org/10.1109/TABLETOP.2007.33
15. Multitaction. 2016. Multitaction – Collaboration Made Easy. Retrieved September 21, 2016 from https://www.multitaction.com/
16. Naohiko Kohtake, Ryo Ohsawa, Takuro Yonezawa, et al. 2005. u-Texture: Self-Organizable Universal Panels for Creating Smart Surroundings. In *UbiComp 2005: Ubiquitous Computing*. Springer, Berlin, Heidelberg, 19–36. http://doi.org/10.1007/11551201_2
17. M Weiser. 1995. *The computer for the 21st century.* Scientific American. 265(3):94–104.

Evaluating Interface Characteristics for Shared Lighting Systems in the Office Environment

Thomas van de Werff **Karin Niemantsverdriet** **Harm van Essen** **Berry Eggen**
Department of Industrial Design
Eindhoven University of Technology
{t.c.f.v.d.werff; k.niemantsverdriet; h.a.v.essen; j.h.eggen}@tue.nl

ABSTRACT
IoT developments make shared systems, such as lighting systems, increasingly connected. From an interaction perspective, this offers opportunities for personal control. Especially for lighting, the benefits of personal control have been underlined by research. However, how to design interfaces that realise these potential benefits is much less investigated. This paper presents a long-term qualitative study in which three interfaces for a shared lighting system are evaluated by 17 people working in an open plan office. The interfaces are designed to vary on a number of characteristics, including the distribution over space, interaction modality, and sequence of interaction. Based on the results, we provide new insights in the impact of interface characteristics on lighting use and experience. We find, i.a., that having an interface on a personal multi-purpose device or on a central interface solely dedicated to lighting, influences whether people make individual or more collective lighting adjustments and decisions.

Author Keywords
Interface Characteristics; Shared Interaction; Connected lighting systems; Personal control; Internet of Things (IoT); Work environment; Open plan office; Interaction Design.

ACM Classification Keywords
H.5.2. Information interfaces and presentation (e.g., HCI): User Interfaces – Interaction styles / User-centred design

INTRODUCTION
The Internet of Things (IoT) paradigm has been rapidly gaining ground in our daily lives, resulting in systems becoming increasingly connected. This brings many advantages for personalization of an environment, service provision and system management. One of the most evident recent examples are connected lighting systems for office environments. This development offers potential benefits, including cost and energy savings in both installation and operation; adaptation of other building systems for (remote) building management, facility services, security provision and data management; and – most interestingly – personal control for office workers over their environment [44]. The benefits of personal control over lighting have been studied widely, especially in the office environment. Personal control can decrease energy consumption [6,7,46], increase work comfort [38] and appraisal of the work environment [43], and improve job satisfaction [42]. These are clearly desirable benefits, especially with the increasing number of open plan offices where people share space and desks with co-workers [23]. However, *how* to design lighting interfaces that realise these potential benefits is a much less explored area.

Traditionally people interact with office lighting through switches, turning light on or off. However, developments in LED technology give more detailed control possibilities, thus requiring a new interaction paradigm [25,32]. Most commercially available connected lighting systems currently present mobile phone applications to interact with the light, both in the home environment [5,13,33,35] and in the office environment [10,34,36]. The reasons for doing so are understandable: mobile phones are a widely available and highly advanced platform, applications are relatively cheap and endlessly scalable, and people are getting used to this means of interaction. Nevertheless, their suitability for lighting interaction has also been questioned. Taking the phone out of your pocket, locating and activating the app takes effort and time [4,32]. Also, usually not everyone has access to the application or network connection; e.g., [29]). Moreover, mobile phones offer highly personalized interaction styles – often based on personal preferences and presets – while the resulting light setting is likely to influence multiple people that share the lighting output [29,30]. In research, an array of alternative lighting interfaces has been proposed (e.g., [1,4,9,18,24,29,40]) but they have rarely been evaluated in use. Hence, the impact that interface characteristics have on the user experience of these systems is not fully known.

The study that we present in this paper has two main aims: to investigate (1) how different user interface characteristics influence use and experience with lighting systems and (2) how a representation of social information in the interfaces can help people to take each other into account while

DIS 2017, June 10-14, 2017, Edinburgh, United Kingdom
ACM 978-1-4503-4922-2/17/06.
http://dx.doi.org/10.1145/3064663.3064749

interacting with the lighting system. We expect that insights from this study guide the design of interfaces for shared lighting systems. Since both aims require a separate detailed analysis, this work focuses on the first aim by investigating the influence of interface characteristics on use. To address this aim, we take an explorative research-through-design approach [47]. We design three interfaces that offer the same control over the light but that vary in distribution over space, being single- or multi-purpose, and ownership; interaction modality; sequence of interaction; representation of the light in a preview; and social information. The resulting three interfaces – the Floorplan, Pointer, and Canvas – are evaluated for approximately a month each with 17 participants working in an open plan office. Based on the results, we provide new insights in the impact of interface characteristics on lighting use, and we argue to carefully consider these characteristics in the design process.

RELATED WORK

Personal control (beyond the traditional light switches) in the professional work environment is a relatively new development but several systems have recently become commercially available. Philips connected lighting [36] and Osram Lightify Pro [34] offer office workers a mobile phone application to control the light intensity and room temperature. Connected lighting systems are more common for the home environment (e.g., [5,13,33,35]). Most of these systems offer interaction through mobile phone, tablet, and smart watch applications. In some cases, dedicated switches or remotes are added [22,37]; or connection to home automation systems [2,17,48] can be made to open up a range of alternative interaction styles, including connection to sensors and speech.

In research, a large range of lighting interfaces has been presented for the home environment. Tangible lights [40] present in-air gestural controls over lighting that is inspired upon giving a light beam physical qualities. The Reality Editor [18] maps graphical user interface elements on top of a real-time video capture of the lamp through augmented reality techniques. Bakker and Niemantsverdriet [4] present four tangible and tangible-gestural interfaces for domestic lighting systems that can potentially be interacted with in the periphery of attention – i.e., without attending to explicitly [3]. The case for peripheral lighting interaction had been made before by Aliakseyeu et al. [1], since lighting is usually not a goal in itself but more *"a means to an end"* ([1], p. 219). To our knowledge, there are much less interface proposals in research for personal lighting control in office environments. Magielse and Offermans [27] present a range of interfaces for a breakout area within the office, consisting of a preset-cube for atmospheric light, a touchpad to control direct light, and multiple screen-based apps for more detailed lighting control [27]; described in more detail in [1]. The Bolb [26] is a portable handheld device for workers in shared office spaces that lets people create a personal 'light bubble' that follows them around. While all interfaces present interesting possibilities, many are one-off designs and many are not evaluated.

A more systematic evaluation of interface characteristics is presented by Brumitt & Cadiz [9]. They compare a number of different lighting interactions: plain text computer displays, graphical user interfaces, voice control, and gestural interactions; all worked out into Wizard of Oz interfaces [11]. The evaluation sessions were done in a smart home lab. Less related to specific interface proposals, ethnographically inspired probes have aimed at finding overarching interaction requirements for lighting interaction at home. Lucero et al. [24] studied interactive lighting opportunities in bathrooms and concluded that opportunities are limited by people's concerns about the potential complexity of the interaction. Offermans et al. [32] investigated people's current everyday interaction with lighting systems. They found that lighting needs are mainly latent and highly dependent on context. Overall, the ethnographic studies present interesting insights but they are not based on actual interaction designs and therefore more difficult to implement directly.

INTERFACE CHARACTERISTICS AND DESIGNS

In this work, we aim to systematically evaluate how variations of five interface characteristics influence the use of a shared lighting system in an office environment. In this section, we first explain the characteristics and their variations when implemented in interface designs. We then present three lighting interfaces that each embody a different combination of such variations (see Table 1).

	Floorplan	Pointer	Canvas
Ownership and distribution	On a personal device	Distributed per table group	One shared, central interface
Purpose	Multi-purpose	Dedicated	Dedicated
Interaction modality	Graphical user interface	Tangible-gestural interface	Tangible interface
Sequence of interaction	Starting from the location	Starting from light parameters	Combining parameters and location
Represen-tation of light	Screen-based graphics	Light-based (LED)	Printed graphics
Social information	Intention	Identity	Preference

Table 1. An overview of the interface characteristics represented in the three interfaces.

Interface Characteristics

1. Ownership over the interface, Distribution over space, and Single-/Multi-purpose devices.

Choosing for a mobile device for interaction with a lighting system defines characteristics such as distribution, ownership, and purpose. Since mobile devices (e.g., laptops, smart phones, smart watches and tablets) are generally personal, they are unlikely to be shared with others, resulting in a fine-grained distribution of interfaces over space. Also, such a device is not dedicated to lighting control only, as it is used for more purposes (such as work, communication, or entertainment). Characteristics as the location and the number of people that share an interface need to be carefully considered when designing a dedicated lighting interface. For example, Offermans et al. [32], found that the location of the interface greatly influences effort, and thus the willingness to interact – people often do not bother to move in order to adjust the light. In this sense, personal devices present an interesting paradox in availability of lighting control. Personal devices are mobile and at hand but finding and opening an application still requires effort and time, which is expected to lower availability [1,32].

In this study, we aim to make three distinct combinations of distribution (at hand, at the table, centrally in the space), ownership (personal, shared with a small group, and shared with everyone), and purpose (single- or multi-purpose).

2. Interaction Modality

Applications are screen-based *graphical user interface* (e.g., [13,34–36]), but other interaction modalities can also be considered. Two examples are *tangible* [19,41] and *gesture-based* interaction styles [21], which *"rely on embodied interaction, tangible manipulation, physical representation of data and embedding in real space"* ([19], p.437). Tangible interaction is known to have potential advantages over screen-based interaction styles. For example, tangibility can lead to increased directness and better understanding of mapping between input and output, since the state of the system can generally be directly read from the manipulated object [20,41]. Moreover, tangible interaction appeals to people's perceptual-motor skills, rather than focusing only on cognitive skills [12,20]. Because of this last quality, tangible and embodied interactions are seen as a valuable approach to design interaction in the periphery of attention [3,4]. Tangible gesture interfaces have good embedding in space, which can be useful when addressing individual lamps. Advantages of screen-based approaches are the ability for higher complexity in feedback [20]. Also, interaction elements in digital interfaces are more scalable (e.g. the number of individually addressable lamps). Lastly, people are accustomed to this type of interaction nowadays, as screen-based interfaces are omnipresent.

In this study, we compare three types of modalities: a tangible, a tangible-gestural, and a screen-based graphical user interface, to investigate how the benefits of the different modalities apply to lighting interaction.

3. Sequence of Interaction

One should carefully consider how light parameters are presented to the user of the interface, as people are generally unfamiliar with detailed lighting control [24,25,32]. Even without variations in the number of controllable parameters, different layers of control can be offered. Offermans ([31], p.134) describes a model consisting of three levels of light parameters: *context*, *lighting*, and *lamp* parameters. For example, *ambient presets* (as recommended by [24]) regard context parameters, where *lamp parameters* refer to technical settings of individual lamps (intensity, hue, saturation). However, which of these control parameters (light parameters, location in space, or lamps in a group) is a starting point in the sequence of the interaction, and how their relations are visualized still make an important design consideration. For example, the Philips Hue application [35] the sequence of interaction starts with the *location* of lamp groups: the main menu shows the areas to which lighting settings can be applied. But on a deeper interaction layer, the *lamp parameters* are central: lamps can be placed on a field of hue and saturation.

In this study, we make use of Offermans' *lighting layer* in the three interfaces, where we let people control parameters such as colour temperature and intensity of groups of lamps pertaining to a certain area in the space. We aim to compare three different sequences of interaction, presenting different mappings of lighting, lamps and space. In the first interface, the location for the adjustment is first selected after which light settings can be applied to that location. In the second interface, first a light setting is made that can then be applied to specific lamps. And in the third interface, lamps can be placed in a field of light settings.

4. Representation of the Light in the Interface (Preview)

In general, people are not acquainted with technical light parameters [25]. Control over intensity is more or less known because of conventional dimmer controls, but parameters like colour temperature, hue, or saturation are relatively new. Therefore, it might be challenging to find the right light setting instantly. An interface can support people in estimating the effect of an adjustment on the context, before the light setting is applied [45]. But the appropriateness of the medium in which this representation is expressed is unknown. The prediction accuracy of lighting representations of photographs and renderings have been studied (e.g., [14,39]), but such representations are much more detailed than the abstracted representation we envision.

In this study, we compare different media for previewing the light adjustment: digital graphics (on a backlit OLED or LCD screen, as is the case in most applications), an LED light source, and printed graphics that do not involve light.

5. Social Information

The final characteristic for the interfaces is the social information about other people in the space that is represented in the interface. Making socially salient information *visible* in order to make people *aware* of each other's needs, wishes, and motivations, resulting in *accountability* over an interaction; is known as *social translucence* [16]. We have previously emphasized the

Figure 1. Photos of the interfaces: (A) the Floorplan interface displays a map of the space were light can be adjusted; (B) the Pointer as remote control for the light; and (C) the Canvas interface with tokens that can be moved around to change the light.

importance of social translucence in interfaces for shared systems [29,30], and we have presented first ideas on how this information could be presented in lighting interfaces [29,45]. But the relevance of the *type* of social information is yet unknown. Therefore, we vary three different types of social information in the interfaces: (1) *intention* with the new light setting; (2) *identity* of the person that made the last lighting adjustment; and (3) *preference* of the people in the space. As mentioned in the introduction, the evaluation of this characteristic is outside of the scope of this paper.

Interface Designs

We iteratively designed three interfaces* that combine variations of the characteristics: The Floorplan, Pointer, and Canvas interface (figure 1). These interfaces vary on their designed characteristics, not on the level of control they offer. Therefore, all three interfaces can be used to control intensity (0 to 3800 lm) and colour temperature (1700-8000K) of four clusters of lamps. While the interfaces are one-off prototypes, they are robust and fully functional.

The Floorplan interface

The Floorplan interface (figure 1A) is a graphical user interface that can be installed on a personal device and is available on a tablet located centrally in the space (figure 5). Central in the interface is a map of the space, indicating the layout of the tables and the four clusters of lamps. To start the interaction, users can select one or more clusters by drawing on the map (figure 2A). Next, the user can control sliders to adjust intensity and colour temperature within the selected area (figure 2B). The circle in the centre of the controls gives a representation of the new light setting (the preview). Only by pressing the preview circle, the setting is applied to the space. After setting the light, the user can select an activity to indicate their intention with that light setting to others (figure 2C). The icon and the light setting itself remain visible on the interface for other people in the space. Active instances of the application are synced without noticeable delay, and thus always display the current status of the luminaires (figure 2D).

The application is made with Processing [49] and exported as an application for Windows, Apple OS, and Android devices. The application communicates with the local server PC over Wi-Fi. The server uses broadcast messages to make sure all Floorplan apps are in sync with each other.

Pointer Interface

The Pointer interface (figure 1B) is a tangible-gesture interface, which can be used as a remote control for the light. A remote control, or sender, is positioned on each table area in the space. Above each table area, a receiver is installed in the ceiling, which is visible from every position in the space. Every table area is given a colour. The senders and corresponding receivers have a colour corresponding with their respective table. The sender has two sliders that can be used to adjust intensity and colour temperature (figure 3A). A button with an integrated RGB LED shows a preview of the new light setting. By pointing the sender to an area and pressing the button, the light setting is applied to the lamps in that area (figure 3B). The indication light in the targeted receiver briefly flickers to confirm that it received a message, and takes on the colour of the sender that made the adjustment. This indication light shows the colour until it is targeted by a different sender. In this way, people can always see who set the current light setting. By pointing at other areas and pressing the button again, the setting can be applied to multiple areas (figure 3C).

When the button is pressed on the sender, the ID of the sender is transmitted to the targeted receiver using a coded infrared (IR) signal. The sender comprises an IR LED (TSAL6100), 2 analogue linear slider potentiometers, a Lithne board [28], and a button with an integrated RGB LED, in a laser cut MDF casing with acrylic cover. The receiver comprises an IR receiver (TSOP32438), a Lithne board [28], and an RGB LED with diffuser, integrated in a cardboard ceiling tile.

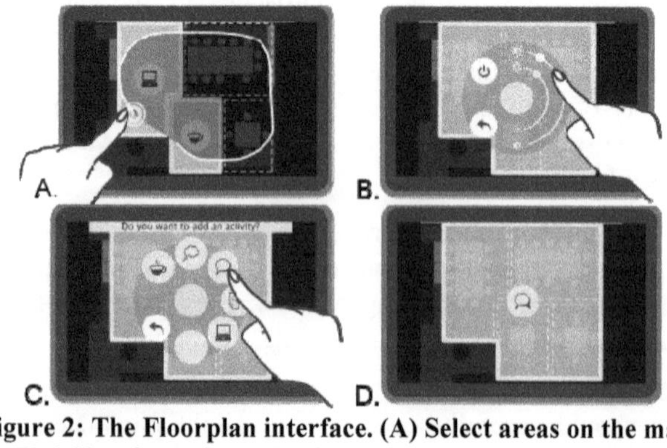

Figure 2: The Floorplan interface. (A) Select areas on the map. (B) Adjust intensity and colour temperature and press the preview to apply. (C) Select an activity to show intention (optional). (D) The interface shows the current status.

* Video of the interfaces: vimeo.com/twerff/sharedlighting

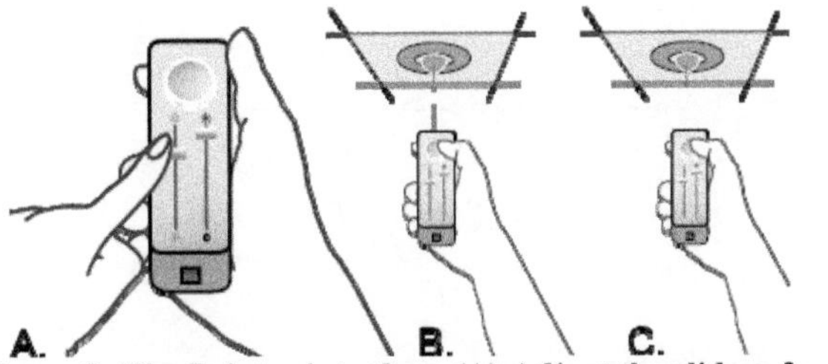

Figure 3: The Pointer interface. (A) Adjust the sliders for intensity and colour temperature. (B) Point to an area and press the button. The indicator shows the sender's colour. (C) Point and click to other areas to apply the same setting.

Canvas Interface

The Canvas interface (figure 1C) is a tangible user interface located in a central location in the space. The four areas are represented by tokens with a colour and an icon in the shape of the corresponding table group. Tokens can be moved around on a gradient map with two axes: the colour temperature on the horizontal axis, and intensity on the vertical axis. The gradients are printed on the canvas to provide a preview of the light adjustment. To adjust the light, a token can be repositioned on the map. The new values for colour temperature and intensity of the token's position are applied directly to the lamps in the cluster corresponding with that token (figure 4A). By drawing a line around one or more tokens with the boundary stylus, the user can show to others how much change to the light is accepted (figure 4B). Boundaries thus show light preferences of people in the room. Boundaries can be removed by briefly tapping them with the stylus or by moving the token(s) out of the boundary.

The Canvas interface comprises passive physical tokens, made of MDF and magnets, on a photo frame with a semi-translucent print between two layers of acrylic. Markers on the back of the frame are connected by magnets to the tokens on the front of the frame. Sliding a token over the Canvas makes the magnetic marker follow. The position of the markers is detected by a webcam connected to a PC running a Processing sketch [49]. The boundary stylus is a laser pointer that is tracked through pixel colour detection. The boundaries are projected again from the back onto the Canvas. The interface is placed in an open doorframe to hide the projector, webcam and computer from sight.

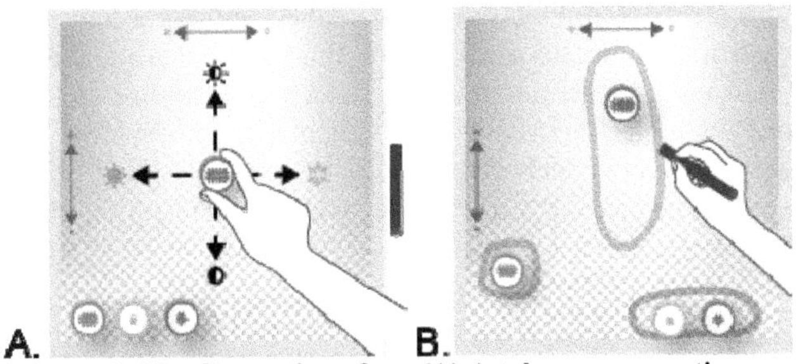

Figure 4: The Canvas interface. (A) A token, representing an area, can be moved freely over the canvas: vertical to adjust intensity; horizontal for colour temperature. (B) A boundary can be drawn with the stylus, indicating preference to others.

Figure 5. A map of the office with the lamps (grey) in 4 areas (dashed lines), the tables, the position of the central tablet (Y) and the Canvas (Z). The photo is taken from position X.

EVALUATION SETUP

To make sure that the insights on how interface characteristics affect daily use represent real life interaction, it is important to evaluate the interfaces longitudinally and in a real work environment. Since connected lighting systems are not widely available yet, we equipped an open plan office at the Eindhoven University of Technology (figure 5) with a connected lighting system. This system is the only light source, apart from little daylight from north-facing windows. The office measures 88m^2 and provides space for up to 28 people. It is occupied daily by students from the department of Industrial Design, and is used for a variety of activities. The space can be easily observed, allowing for a quick response to (technical) issues.

The connected lighting system is a prototype system developed by the Enlight consortium [15] and comprises 22 custom LED luminaires. Each luminaire has integrated logic and sensing (motion, light level, and temperature) and its light output can vary in intensity (0 - 3800lm) and colour temperature (1700K - 8000K). The luminaires can be addressed and controlled individually by the server, using the ZigBee protocol for wireless communication. As said, for this study control was restricted to four groups of luminaires. The groups are predefined to match the four table groups in the space (see figure 1). In any given moment, the groups can differ in light setting, but individual luminaires cannot be addressed and luminaires cannot change group. A server PC runs a Processing sketch [49] that processes incoming messages from the lighting interfaces to usable commands for the luminaires. The Floorplan and Canvas interfaces communicate with the server through UDP messages over Wi-Fi. The senders and receivers of the Pointer interface communicates with the server over a second ZigBee network.

Method

The three interfaces were deployed in the living lab for 4 to 5 weeks each. The 14-week study was conducted during the university semester from September to December as these are dark months in the Netherlands, ensuring a need for artificial lighting in the space. Participants were recruited during an introductory presentation for bachelor and master students involved in a project on lighting interaction at the faculty of industrial design. Participation was voluntarily and not a part of the educational process. The performing researchers had no formal role in the educational project and assessment. A total of 18 participants signed up for the study. One person stopped participation in the first 4 weeks and was therefore not included in the results. The fact that all participants (age 20-30, F=5) were involved in a project about lighting interaction helped in sensitizing them for study. The office has flexible workplaces and is open to all students of the department. Therefore, the interfaces were used not only participants, but by others (visitors) as well. To facilitate use, we spread manuals for the interfaces over the space. We cannot distinguish participant's interactions from the interactions of visitors in the gathered log-data.

Figure 6 shows a schematic setup of the study. The Floorplan was implemented first as the screen-based application was expected to correspond with people's experience and expectations of interacting with a connected system. The Canvas was implemented last as the tokens representing areas were expected to be most complex to learn. The Pointer as second, introduced the colour coding.

Data was collected in three ways. First, every incoming message from the interfaces was logged, including time and date, the sender of the message (interface or participant ID), and the adjusted light parameters (the adjusted area, colour temperature, and intensity). Second, a weekly data sampling survey was sent out to each participant via email (the circles in figure 6). The survey requested motivation and a description of context for a specific moment of interaction. In this way, the survey was a weekly reminder of the ongoing study and triggered reflection upon peoples' experiences. Third, three semi-structured interviews were conducted with each participant individually during the last week of each interface use-period (blue lines in figure 6).

The interviews included questions about general use of lighting and space, specific interactions with the interface (referring back to the results from the data sampling surveys), and evaluation of the interfaces. To fuel the conversation on evaluation of the interfaces, we presented the interviewees with a five-point Likert scale survey on specific features (e.g., 'How enjoyable was the interface?', and 'How much effort did interaction take?'). We concluded the third and final interview with an extra 20-minute part where participants compared their experiences with the three interfaces by positioning magnetic images of features of each interface (e.g., 'quality of the preview', 'precision of control', 'invitation to interact') on 5-point scales (figure 7). All interviews were audio-recorded with permission. 15 out of 17 participants participated in all interviews, one person missed the second interview and one missed the concluding interview.

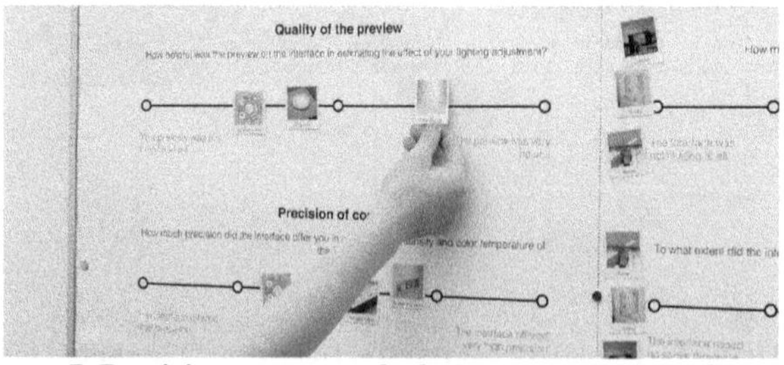

Figure 7. Participants were asked to compare certain features of the three interfaces on a number of 5-point scales.

The setup was piloted with seven PhD students that were asked to work in the living lab for one week. During this week, they used the Floorplan interface to control the light and received three data sampling surveys. At the end of the week, five participants received a closing questionnaire and two were interviewed. Next to minor adjustments in the interface and the resolving of stability issues, the introduction and explanation of the interface was refined and the concluding questionnaire was replaced by a semi-structured interview with the Likert scales.

Analysis

Quantitative data was used to analyse and demonstrate general use during the study of the space, lighting, and interfaces. This includes the log data from the interfaces and self-reported number of interactions and presence in the space from the three interviews. Log data from the first two days of each period was excluded as technical fine-tuning happened during those days. Since one interaction can comprise of multiple separately logged messages (because of, for example, fine-tuning), the separate messages were clustered where applicable.

We based most of our results presented in this paper on the analysis of qualitative data. This data includes the recorded audio from the concluding section of the final interview, since this part focused most directly on the comparison of the characteristics of the interfaces. The remaining qualitative data from the weekly surveys and the other interviews is to be used in a later, more extensive analysis, focusing on the social information and multi-user interaction. The results from the Likert scale questionnaires in the interviews were used to make subjective evaluation of the interfaces comparable amongst participants.

The audio recordings were transcribed verbatim, and then used in a thematic analysis [8]. First, quotes from the 16 interview transcriptions were selected, resulting in 173 unique quotes (between 5 and 21 quotes per interview). The quotes were collaboratively coded and clustered using qualitative analysis software MaxQDA [50], resulting in the following themes: general use (29 quotes), interface

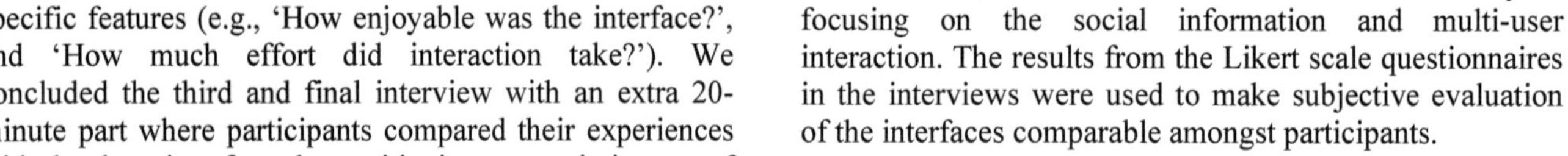

Figure 6. An overview of the study, including the log data collection period of three interfaces (black line), the data sampling questionnaires (circles), and the interview weeks (blue line)

evaluations (43 quotes), and the four interface characteristics (74 quotes on *distribution, dedication, and ownership*, 17 for *interaction modality*, 54 for *sequence of use*, and 32 for *representation of light*). Within each theme, we iteratively reviewed the quotes to identify recurring patterns, especially looking for effects of the characteristics on user experience and use of the lighting system. The identified effects within characteristics were compared amongst each other, resulting in five distinct effects: *Sharedness* of an interaction, *Effort*, *Reminder* to interact, *Engagement,* and feeling of *Control*. Figure 10 displays a visual overview of the relation between characteristics and effects, which is further elaborated in the next section.

RESULTS

In this section, we first describe how the space, the lighting, and the interfaces were used during the period of the study. Second, a brief evaluation of each interface by the study participants is described. Third, the effects of the interface characteristics on user experience are described per characteristic. The findings are illustrated with example quotes and quantitative results.

General use

During the test period, participants interacted 290 times with the Floorplan, 413 times with the Pointer and 351 times with the Canvas (see figure 8 for an overview of the number of interactions per interface per day). There was a noticeable decrease in usage over time for each interface, as it became more familiar to the participants. All interfaces were used at least once each day.

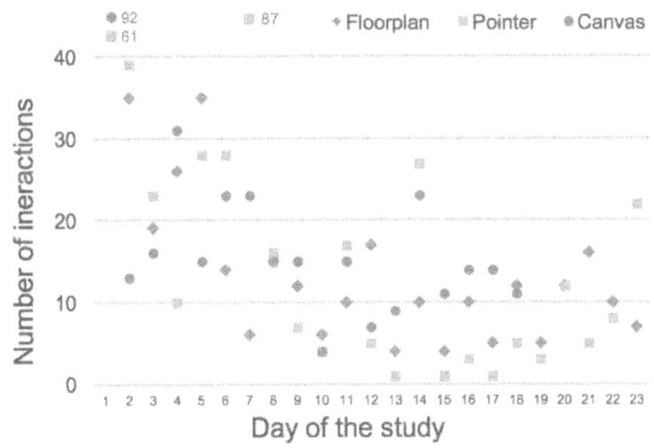

Figure 8: Number of interactions per day, per interface.

Since the Floorplan interface can identify each user through his/her IP address, we know the number of interactions per person for this interface. There were between 1 and 25 interactions per person with the Floorplan during the five-week period (see figure 9). This difference can be explained by interpersonal differences on how important good lighting is, as well as by the variance in presence. Over the whole study period, 67% of the participants was in the space at least a couple of times per week. On average, when people were present they interacted with the interfaces at least once. This seems to be the same for all three interfaces, judging from self-reported presence and use of the Canvas and Pointer.

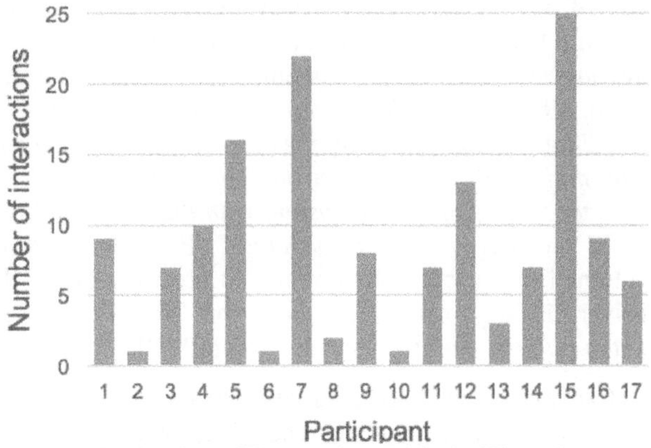

Figure 9: Number of Interactions with the Floorplan per participant. An additional 143 interactions were done by non-participating visitors.

In most interactions, people adjusted the lighting in one area (54%), or in all four areas in the space at once (24%). In the interviews, participants explained that most of the time they only adjusted the lighting in the area that they were located in. *"I would only, mainly, adjust light above the table where we sat. I didn't really think about changing it above the other tables because there were people there and I didn't know their preferences."* (P14). When no other people were present, they would consider making adjustments to the whole space: *"Suppose I was sitting in an empty space in the dark. I would not change only my own lamps; I would change everything. Otherwise it feels weird."* (P11). We noticed a slight difference between interfaces: with the Floorplan, 41% of the interactions adjusted one area, while this is 66% and 52% respectively for the Pointer and Canvas. With the Floorplan, in 40% of the interactions the whole space was adjusted; much more than with the Pointer (12%) and Canvas (25%).

General Evaluation of the Interfaces

The Floorplan was understandable: it matched people's experience of interacting through applications. *"[The Floorplan] is not hard to interact with [...] Because you use applications and stuff all the time, so it's not hard. It is just less fun."* (P6). People generally valued the possibility of controlling light on a personal device: 12 participants installed the Floorplan on their laptop, of which 10 also used the application on their laptop. And 9 out of 10 participants that installed the application on their phone, used the application on their phone. 59% of the participants (10/17) used the application on the central tablet. The interface had some stability issues, which resulted in a decreased feeling of control. *"Since the system was down and the response was sometimes a bit late, the feeling of control was lost sometimes."* (P14). For some participants, the area selection through drawing on the floorplan gave the illusion of control over individual lamps instead of the predefined clusters. Also, most participants found the sliders too small on their phone application.

Most of the participants enjoyed the Pointer interface, especially because of its physical presence and availability. Directing and clicking – 'shooting' – was enjoyable and playful. *"You could shoot with it, which was fun. [...] Personally, I liked the Pointer the best, because it was there in the middle of the table: anyone could take it easily. It was clear what you were adjusting with that preview light, and it was not overly complicated."* (P17). Participants mentioned that it could be difficult to precisely target the receiver, leading to some trial and error: *"Sometimes [...] I had to press the button a number of times."* (P1).

The Canvas was well received with all participants. It was described as surprising and engaging, and participants enjoyed playing with the physical tokens. The size and location of the interface made it visible from anywhere in the space. *"I enjoyed the [Canvas] most. It did take a bit more time but it invites you to play, to change something. It also gave a bit more precision; or maybe not precision but it is more visual."* (P4). We observed that many participants presented and explained this interface to visitors and colleagues. Most participants mentioned that walking up to the interface was effortful, especially in comparison with the Pointer that was closer by, but few refrained from interacting because of this extra effort.

Interface characteristics

The interfaces were designed to vary on several characteristics. Figure 10 provides an overview of the four characteristics (left) and the five effects on people's experience with the lighting (right) that we identified in the thematic analysis. The arrows show the relations we identified between characteristics and effects. Next, we describe these relations for each interface characteristic.

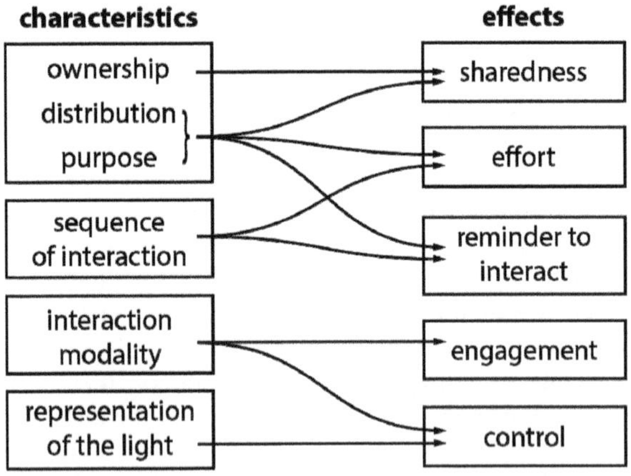

Figure 10. Relational overview of characteristic and effects.

Ownership/Distribution/Purpose

The interfaces differ in their distribution over space: The Canvas is placed in a central location, the Pointer is located per table group, and the Floorplan is both distributed (on laptops and phones) and on a central tablet. In all cases, people mentioned that if an interface is not within reach, this costs *effort* and raises the threshold to interact. *"[The Canvas] did invite, but it had that barrier of getting up and going to it. So, it was easier to say: 'OK, it is fine as is'."* (P12). In line with findings of Offermans et al. [32], we found that taking out a phone and starting an application also requires effort, even though the phone is usually within reach. *"It is funny that I find it more difficult to get my phone than to walk across the room. I just don't like getting my phone out at all."* (P6).

The three interfaces also differ in ownership: The Floorplan is personal, the Pointer is shared per table, and the Canvas is shared with all people in the room. We observed an effect on the feeling of *'sharedness'* of a lighting adjustment. People felt that the adjustment was an individual or a collective decision: *"I always consulted others, except with the [Floorplan]. I did say something to others, but in the end, you do it alone. And with [the Pointer and Canvas] you do it together."* (P17). With the non-personal interfaces, people engaged others more in the adjustment and they wanted to be engaged when others interacted, leading to more conversations about the light. *"[With the Canvas], everyone notices you walking to the interface, and thinks: 'that person is going to change the light, we need to pay attention.' With the [Pointer] the same, but it is only visible to a smaller group of people."* (P13). A requirement for this collective decision making (or sharedness) is visibility of one's actions, making people accountable for them, as also stressed by [16]. Naturally, the location of the interface is important to achieve this visibility, as well as the interface being dedicated solely to lighting interaction: *"If you pick up the Pointer, other people at the table notice that right away, which makes it easier to start a conversation. With the Floorplan application, other people do not see that you are interacting with the light, which makes it awkward to start a conversation about the light."* (P11). A second effect of this visibility is that the interface can become a *reminder to interact*: *"I just forgot about the [Floorplan] because I didn't see it. Even though it is in my pocket, I don't always check my phone. And even if I do, I still forget that I have an application for that."* (P5).

Interaction Modality

The interfaces implement three different interaction modalities: The Floorplan is a graphical user interface, the Pointer is tangible-gestural, and the Canvas is tangible. Many participants preferred tangible interfaces to screen-based applications in general: *"I'm not really fond of using an app"* (P16). This might be explained by a bias in the participant group consisting of interaction design students. However, in most cases tangibility was experienced as more *engaging* and fun: *"I think I would rather use the [Canvas] than a web application, even though I have always said that I prefer web interfaces. [...] but I like using the tokens way more."* (P4). When asked how enjoyable interaction was, 75% of the participants rated the Floorplan 3 or higher (means: 3.6), while 75% scored a 4 or higher for the Pointer (means: 3.9) and Canvas (means: 4.3), on a scale of 1 (not enjoyable at all) to 5 (highly enjoyable).

The physicality of controls in the tangible interfaces made it easier for participants to reach a feeling of control; both with the tokens on the Canvas and, to a lesser extent, with the sliders on the Pointer. On a scale representing *precision of control*, ranging from 1 (low precision) to 5 (high precision), participants rated the Canvas higher with a smaller spread in ratings (avg: 4.2, range: 2.0) than the Floorplan (avg: 3.4, range: 3.8). This finding is in line with Bakker et al. [3], who state that tangible interaction potentially requires less attention. However, it might be an effect of the digital sliders being quite small in the Floorplan.

The gestural expressivity of the Pointer was expected to increase visibility of the interaction, which can be important for the previously described sharedness. However, this was not mentioned by participants, even though the physicality of both the Canvas and the Pointer was used for this purpose: *"[With the Floorplan] there is no way to communicate that this is my light. But [with the] Pointer, placing it close to me would make me feel like the owner of the area. So, someone reaching out and taking it to control the light would feel like an intrusion in my area."* (P12).

Sequence of Interaction

The interfaces vary in interaction sequence. In the Floorplan, areas are selected after which a light setting is made and applied; in the Pointer, a light setting is created and then applied to an area; and in the Canvas, areas are placed on a field of light parameters, making selection of location and parameters a combined action. All three interfaces provided an understandable sequence of interaction. The overview of the map in the Floorplan was valued: *"It feels nice to have the little map, saying do this and this. It's like playing age of empires."* (P14), although orientation on the map could take some participants time to learn. Also, as explained earlier in this section, people mainly adjusted their own area, making the map less appropriate: *"Actually, I never felt the urge to adjust more than my own area. [...] The [Floorplan] provides an easy way to do this, but I just don't need the option."* (P11). The directness of pointing in the space with the Pointer was easier to learn but again, since people hardly adjusted other areas than their own, people regarded the pointing action needlessly effortful. Participants were surprisingly positive about the area-tokens on a grid of light parameters in the Canvas. The relation between tokens and table areas was expected to be difficult for people as it is a cognitive connection. Some participants mentioned this took time to learn. However, this mapping seemed to fit the general lighting use better: *"Of course you need distinct token colours, it would be difficult if they become too similar. But after a few days, I knew my table was orange, and from then on you know that is the one you need to use."* (P4). Overall, it seems that one sequence of interaction is not inherently better than another but that it should be carefully designed to fit context, the controllable parameters, and use of the system.

Next to the order of parameters, the interfaces also differ in the number of actions required to make an adjustment. In the Floorplan, an area is selected, then parameters are adjusted, the setting is applied, and an activity is selected (optional), leading to a multi-step sequence. The Pointer has two steps: adjusting parameters and applying the setting (with an additional step for each area). With the Canvas, the user adjusts the parameters and apply the setting in one action. Most people valued this directness of the Canvas, as it cost less *effort*. The decreased effort lead to more fine-tuning of the light during the interaction: *"The light changes immediately when moving [the token on the Canvas]. [With the Floorplan] you need to change the light a bit and apply the setting again if you are not satisfied with [the light setting]. That is easier with [the Canvas]"* (P11).

The two-dimensional field of light parameters that the Canvas shows (due to the chosen sequence of interaction) was used as a way to estimate the added value of starting an interaction. People estimated whether engaging with the interface was worth the effort, as they could assess how much the light could still be changed by looking at the position of the token in relation to the canvas. In this way, the overview formed a *reminder to interact*: "*The [Canvas' printed preview] was my favorite because I could just glance up at it and see not only the current state as in the LED [preview of the Pointer], but the current state in relation to the possibilities. So, 'it's quite warm', for example. Or 'it could be warmer', or 'this is as warm as it can go'."* (P6). Also, people could remember the position of the token for light settings they liked, thus forming sorts of presets in their memory. *"I just knew: on the top right, is nice and bright."* (P7). Theoretically, this was also possible with the other two interfaces by looking at the position of the parameter sliders but this was not mentioned by participants. Possibly because of the lower visibility of the Floorplan and Pointer.

Representation of light

Each interface uses a different medium to show a representation of the envisioned lighting adjustment, based on colour temperature and intensity). The Floorplan uses screen-based graphics, the Pointer uses an LED light, and the Canvas has printed graphics. Our findings show that a preview is a necessary form of feedback upon interaction, which increased the feeling of control. *"Of course [a preview] is necessary, otherwise you won't know what you are doing."* (P11). However, the preview was used to understand the functionality of a slider, rather than as a preview of the actual output of the lighting. *"I did not use it as main reference of how the light was supposed to be. I think I usually just changed it and if I didn't like it I changed it again."* (P16). This made accuracy of the representation less important, as long as adjustments could be made easily. *"After using the thing twice you kind of know what to expect from it. [The preview] is not super important. It is necessary, but it is not a big deal if it deviates a bit [from the lighting]."* (P11).

In the Floorplan, the preview was often not noticed as such by participants, because it blended in with the other digital graphics. *"Did the button change during interaction with [the Floorplan]? I didn't notice that. I guess a preview is useful but it's very cartoonish [in the Floorplan interface]. I think the LED preview is better."* (P8). The light-based preview of the Pointer was generally liked because it is the same medium as the output system. However, the RGB-LED did not accurately represent the resulting light, which was generally seen as a downside. Surprisingly, on a scale representing quality of the preview from 1 (low quality) to 5 (high quality), the digital print of the Canvas scored very high (75% rated 3.9 or higher, means 4.3), in spite of its low accuracy. This is partly because of the previously described overview that the mapping of light parameters gives: all possible colours can be previewed at once. This is also because of its abstraction: accuracy was not expected in the printed graphics, while it was expected in the light-based representation. *"I like [the printed preview] because it was an analogy. I know it is not giving me this red or this blue, but it is easier to learn how it would affect it."* (P12).

Overall, none of the media (screen-based, light-based, or print) is generally better. It is important to have a representation as feedback on an action to increase the feeling of control, and to make the preview stand out from the rest of the interface. High accuracy is not always necessary as long as people's expectations of accuracy for the chosen medium are met.

CONCLUDING REMARKS

In this paper, we presented a long-term qualitative evaluation of three interfaces – the Floorplan, Pointer and Canvas – to investigate the influence of interface characteristics (*ownership, distribution, and purpose, interaction modality, sequence of interaction* and *representation of light*) on the user experience and use of a shared lighting system in a living lab office environment.

During the study, the living lab was occupied daily and each interface was used at least once every day. While the frequency of interaction differed per person, there were multiple interactions per day. The qualitative and quantitative results of the study show that participants were positive about all three interfaces. Moreover, we can conclude that the variations on interface characteristics were successfully represented in the three implementations, as participants were able to recognize and evaluate them.

The variations in the interface characteristics clearly affected people's experience and use of the lighting system. We found that the distribution, ownership and purpose affect how *shared* the interface and interaction feels to participants, and how much people include others in their lighting adjustments. Visibility of the interaction is a requirement for this sharedness. Distribution and purpose influence the effort that an interaction takes: having to walk to, or having to locate an app raises a threshold to interact. Moreover, a visible interface reminds people of the possibility to interact. The modality of the interaction can affect engagement with the system and the feeling of control over the light: the interfaces with more tangibility were scored higher on both factors. The sequence of interaction has to fit the context and common use patterns. Since people mainly adjusted the lamps in the area they were located themselves, an emphasis on the location of the adjustment (as the Floorplan and Pointer gave) was sometimes experienced as superfluous. Lastly, having a preview, or representation of the light, increases the feeling of being in control. However, this preview helps more with understanding the interface and light parameters than with estimating the impact of an adjustment on the lighting and the room. Surprisingly, the medium of that representation does not seem to matter much, as long as the accuracy lives up to the expectations people have of the chosen medium.

The identified effects of interface characteristics upon experience and use show that the characteristics represent important decisions when designing interfaces for a shared lighting system, and shared systems in general. What the most suitable alternative is for each characteristic depends on the context, controllable parameters, and intended use, and should therefore be considered carefully. The overview of the relations between characteristics and effects (figure 10) can fuel these considerations. However, one should be careful to use the identified relations as design guidelines, for three reasons. First, we combined design decisions on five characteristics in only three interfaces, which makes it difficult to clearly parse out the contribution of each design choice to the outcome. Second, the participants of the study were interaction design students and thus more knowledgeable on the subject than regular office workers. Third, the findings are based on one group of participants – with their own group dynamics –that used three interfaces in a fixed order. So, based on our results, we identified relevant design considerations, and we present promising hypothesis on the relations between characteristic and effect that require further research.

There are several future steps we aim to take ourselves. To exclude effects of group dynamics and order, we plan to conduct the study again with a new group of participants and a different order of interfaces. Next to this, we aim to do a more extensive analysis (including all qualitative data) that focuses on the social aspects of shared lighting interaction. In this way, we expect to contribute to a better understanding of the relevance of design choices regarding interface characteristics for interaction with shared systems.

ACKNOWLEDGEMENTS

We thank our participants for their effort and openhearted accounts. This work was performed within the joint research program on Intelligent Lighting between TU/e and Koninklijke Philips N.V. and within the OpenAIS project, which has received funding from the European Union's Horizon 2020 research and innovation programme under grant agreement No 644332.

REFERENCES

1. Dzmitry Aliakseyeu, Bernt Meerbeek, Jon Mason, Remco Magielse, and Susanne Seitinger. 2016. Peripheral Interaction with Light. In *Peripheral Interaction, Challenges and Opportunities for HCI in the Periphery of Attention*, Saskia Bakker, Doris Hausen and Ted Selker (eds.). Springer International Publishing, 207–235. http://doi.org/10.1007/978-3-319-29523-7
2. Apple. The smart home just got smarter. Retrieved March 31, 2017 from http://www.apple.com/lae/ios/home/
3. Saskia Bakker, Elise Van Den Hoven, and Berry Eggen. 2012. Acting by Hand: Informing Interaction Design for the Periphery of People's Attention. *Interact. Comput.* 24, 3, 119–130. http://doi.org/10.1016/j.intcom.2012.04.001
4. Saskia Bakker and Karin Niemantsverdriet. 2016. The Interaction-Attention Continuum: Considering Various Levels of Human Attention in Interaction Design. *International Journal of Design* 10, 2, 1–14.
5. Belkin. WeMo Home Automation. Retrieved March 31, 2016 from http://www.belkin.com/us/Products/ home-automation/c/wemo-home-automation/
6. Peter R. Boyce, Neil H. Eklund, and S. Noel Simpson. 2000. Individual Lighting Control: Task Performance, Mood, and Illuminance. *Journal of the Illuminating Engineering Society* 29, 1, 131–142. http://doi.org/10.1080/00994480.2000.10748488
7. Peter R. Boyce, Jennifer A. Veitch, Guy R. Newsham, et al. 2006. Occupant use of switching and dimming controls in offices. *Lighting Research and Technology* 38, 4, 358–376. http://doi.org/10.1177/1477153506070994
8. Virginia Braun and Victoria Clarke. 2006. Using thematic analysis in psychology. *Qualitative Research in Psychology* 3, 2, 77–101. http://doi.org/10.1191/1478088706qp063oa
9. Barry Brumitt and Jonathan J. Cadiz. 2001. "Let There Be Light" Examining Interfaces for Homes of the Future. *Proceedings of IFIP INTERACT01: Human-Computer Interaction*, 375–382.
10. Cisco. Cisco Digital Ceiling. Retrieved March 31, 2017 from http://www.cisco.com/c/en/us/solutions/ workforce-experience/digital-ceiling.html
11. Nils Dahlbäck, Arne Jönsson, and Lars Ahrenberg. 1993. Wizard of Oz studies - why and how. *IUI '93 Proceedings of the 1st international conference on Intelligent user interfaces*, 193–200. http://doi.org/10.1145/169891.169968
12. Tom Djajadiningrat, Stephan Wensveen, Joep Frens, and Kees Overbeeke. 2004. Tangible products: Redressing the balance between appearance and action. *Personal and Ubiquitous Computing* 8, 5, 294–309. http://doi.org/10.1007/s00779-004-0293-8
13. Elgato. Avea. Retrieved March 31, 2017 from https://www.elgato.com/en/smart/avea
14. Ulrich Engelke, Mariska G.M. Stokkermans, and Michael J. Murdoch. 2013. Visualizing lighting with images: converging between the predictive value of renderings and photographs. *Proc. SPIE 8651, Human Vision and Electronic Imaging XVIII.* http://doi.org/10.1117/12.2008465
15. Enlight consortium. Enlight: Energy efficient and intelligent lighting systems. Retrieved March 31, 2017 from http://www.enlight-project.eu
16. Thomas Erickson and Wendy A. Kellogg. 2000. Social Translucence: An Approach to Designing Systems That Support Social Processes. *ACM Transactions on Computer-Human Interaction* 7, 1, 59–83. http://doi.org/10.1145/344949.345004
17. Google. Get to know Google Home. Retrieved March 31, 2017 from https://madeby.google.com/home/
18. Valentin Heun. 2015. Reality Editor. Retrieved March 31, 2016 from http://www.valentinheun.com/portfolio/ reality-editor-smarter-objects/
19. Eva Hornecker and Jacob Buur. 2006. Getting a Grip on Tangible Interaction: A Framework on Physical Space and Social Interaction. *CHI '06*, ACM, 437–446. http://doi.org/10.1145/1124772.1124838
20. Elise van den Hoven, Evelien van de Garde-Perik, Serge Offermans, Koen van Boerdonk, and Kars-Michiel H. Lenssen. 2013. Moving tangible interaction systems to the next level. *Computer* 46, 8, 70–76. http://doi.org/10.1109/MC.2012.360
21. Elise van den Hoven and Ali Mazalek. 2011. Grasping gestures: Gesturing with physical artifacts. *Artificial Intelligence for Engineering Design, Analysis and Manufacturing* 25, 3, 255–271. http://doi.org/10.1017/S0890060411000072
22. Ikea. IKEA TRÅDFRI Connected lighting. Retrieved March 31, 2017 from http://www.ikea.com/se/sv/ catalog/categories/departments/living_room/36812/
23. Arjan de Kok. 2016. The new way of working: Bricks, bytes, and behavior. *The Impact of ICT on Work*, 9–40. http://doi.org/10.1007/978-981-287-612-6_2
24. Andrés Lucero, Tatiana Lashina, Elmo Diederiks, and Tuuli Mattelmäki. 2007. How probes inform and influence the design process. *Proceedings of the 2007 conference on Designing pleasurable products and interfaces - DPPI '07*, August, 377. http://doi.org/10.1145/1314161.1314195
25. Andrés Lucero, Jon Mason, Alexander Wiethoff, Bernt Meerbeek, Henrika Pihlajaniemi, and Dzmitry Aliakseyeu. 2016. Rethinking our interactions with light. *Interactions* 6, October, 54–59. http://doi.org/http://dx.doi.org/10.1145/3003334
26. Remco Magielse, Bart Hengeveld, and Joep Frens. 2013. Designing a light controller for a multi-user lighting environment. *Proceedings of the 5th International Congress of International Association of Societies of Design Research (IASDR 2013).*
27. Remco Magielse and Serge A. M. Offermans. 2013. Future lighting systems. *CHI '13 Extended Abstracts on Human Factors in Computing Systems on - CHI EA '13*, 2853. http://doi.org/10.1145/2468356.2479545

28. Remco Magielse and Serge A. M. Offermans. 2013. Lithne - A Platform for Interaction Designers to Develop Interactive Networked Environments. *Proceedings - 9th International Conference on Intelligent Environments, IE 2013*, 137–144. http://doi.org/10.1109/IE.2013.14
29. Karin Niemantsverdriet, Mendel Broekhuijsen, Harm van Essen, and Berry Eggen. 2016. Designing for Multi-User Interaction in the Home Environment: Implementing Social Translucence. *International Conference on Designing Interactive Systems (DIS'16)*, ACM, 1303–1314. http://doi.org/10.1145/ 2901790.2901808
30. Karin Niemantsverdriet, Harm van Essen, and Berry Eggen. 2017. A perspective on multi-user interaction design based on an understanding of domestic lighting conflicts. *Personal and Ubiquitous Computing* 21, 2, 371–389. http://doi.org/10.1007/s00779-016-0998-5
31. Serge A.M. Offermans. 2016. Interacting with Light. Doctoral thesis. Eindhoven University of Technology, Eindhoven, The Netherlands.
32. Serge Offermans, Harm van Essen, and Berry Eggen. 2014. User Interaction with Everyday Lighting Systems. *Personal and Ubiquitous Computing* 18, 8, 2035–2055. http://doi.org/10.1007/s00779-014-0759-2
33. Osram. LIGHTIFY - smart connected light. Retrieved March 31, 2017 from https://innovation.osram.com/ connected-lighting-en/
34. Osram. LIGHTIFY Pro - intelligent, networked light for offices, lawyers' and doctors' practices and shops. Retrieved March 31, 2017 from
35. Philips. Hue. Retrieved March 31, 2016 from http://www2.meethue.com/en-XX/
36. Philips. Connected lighting for Offices. Retrieved March 31, 2017 from http://www.lighting.philips.co .uk/systems/system-areas/office-and-industry/ offices/connected-lighting.html
37. Philips. Hue Tap. Retrieved March 31, 2016 from http://www2.meethue.com/en-us/productdetail/philips-hue-tap-switch
38. Seyed Amir Sadeghi, Panagiota Karava, Iason Konstantzos, and Athanasios Tzempelikos. 2016. Occupant interactions with shading and lighting systems using different control interfaces: A pilot field study. *Building and Environment* 97, 177–195. http://doi.org/10.1016/j.buildenv.2015.12.008
39. Bart Salters, Michael Murdoch, Dragan Sekulovksi, Shih-Han Chen, and Pieter Seuntiens. 2012. An evaluation of different setups for simulating lighting characteristics. *Proc. SPIE 8291, Human Vision and Electronic Imaging XVII*, 1–13. http://doi.org/10.1117/12.912107
40. Tor Sørensen, Oskar D. Andersen, and Timothy Merritt. 2015. "Tangible Lights": In-Air Gestural Control of Home Lighting. *Proceedings of the 9th International Conference on Tangible, Embedded, and Embodied Interaction - TEI '15 Work-in-Progress*. http://doi.org/10.1145/2677199.2687909
41. Brigg Ullmer and Hiroshi Ishii. 2000. Emerging frameworks for tangible user interfaces. *IBM Systems Journal* 39, 3&4, 915–931.
42. Jennifer A Veitch. 2011. Workplace design contributions to mental health and well-being. *HealthcarePapers* 11 Spec No, 38–46. Retrieved January 16, 2017 from http://www.ncbi.nlm.nih.gov/pubmed/24917255
43. Jennifer A. Veitch, Guy R. Newsham, P. Boyce, and C. Jones. 2008. Lighting appraisal, well-being and performance in open-plan offices: A linked mechanisms approach. *Lighting Research and Technology* 40, 2, 133–151. http://doi.org/10.1177/1477153507086279
44. Thomas C. F. Van de Werff, Harm A. Van Essen, and Berry Eggen. 2017. The Impact of the Internet of Lighting on the Office Lighting Value Network. *Journal of Industrial Information Integration*, accepted for publication. http://doi.org/10.1016/j.jii.2017.03.002
45. Thomas van de Werff, Karin Niemantsverdriet, Harm van Essen, and Berry Eggen. 2016. Designing Multi-user Lighting Interfaces : Four strategies to implement Social Translucence. *DIS '16 Companion Proceedings*, 137–140.
46. Alison Williams, Atkinson Barbara, Karina Garbesi, and Page Erik. 2012. Lighting Controls in Commercial Buildings. *LEUKOS: The Journal of Illuminating Engineering Society of North America* 8, 3, 161–180. http://doi.org/10.1582/LEUKOS.2012.08.03.001
47. John Zimmerman, Jodi Forlizzi, and Shelley Evenson. 2007. Research through design as a method for interaction design research in HCI. *Proceedings of the SIGCHI conference on Human factors in computing systems - CHI '07*, 493–502. http://doi.org/10.1145/1240624.1240704
48. Amazon Echo. Retrieved March 31, 2017 from https://www.amazon.com/Amazon-Echo-Bluetooth-Speaker-with-WiFi-Alexa/dp/B00X4WHP5E
49. Processing.org. Retrieved March 31, 2017 from https://processing.org/
50. Qualitative Data Analysis Software | MAXQDA for Windows & Mac - MAXQDA. Retrieved March 31, 2017 from http://www.maxqda.com/

Supporting Cultural Heritage Professionals Adopting and Shaping Interactive Technologies in Museums

Laura A. Maye
Department of Computer Science
Aalto University
Espoo, Finland
laura.maye@aalto.fi

Dominique Bouchard
National Army Museum
London, UK
dsb31@columbia.edu

Gabriela Avram
Interaction Design Centre
University of Limerick
Limerick, Ireland
gabriela.avram@ul.ie

Luigina Ciolfi
CCRC,
Sheffield Hallam University
Sheffield, UK
l.ciolfi@shu.ac.uk

ABSTRACT

Increasingly, cultural heritage professionals (CHPs) (including curators, museum directors, and education officers) are becoming more involved in designing interactive technologies. Specifically, growing access to and availability of digital technology enables CHPs, who may have limited experience with interactive technologies, to create content for and integrate these technologies into their museums. With these developments, there is a growing importance in investigating how CHPs build understandings of these tools in context; this is particularly since curators aim to learn how those tools can support their audiences. In this paper, we highlight how CHPs formed understandings for integrating an interactive tool to support an intended visitor experience into the museum environment through experimentation. Inspired by lessons learned, we propose design recommendations for interaction designers and HCI experts in designing tools and resources that support CHPs to experiment with various ways these technologies could service their interpretation goals.

Author Keywords

Cultural heritage; interactive technology; case study; action research

ACM Classification Keywords

H.5.m. Information interfaces and presentation (e.g., HCI): Miscellaneous.

INTRODUCTION

The role that cultural heritage professionals, including curators, museum directors, and education officers, are playing in creating interactive technologies in museums is evolving. Particularly, in HCI, there is an increased interest in providing toolkits and resources for enabling cultural heritage professionals (CHPs) to create content for, and configure, interactive technologies [16,8,22]. These developments blur the boundaries between the designer, technologist, and the CHP. However, as indicated by much of the existing HCI research in the domain of cultural heritage, integrating interactive technologies in museums requires a great deal of understanding in terms of how those tools can serve visitors in engaging with heritage artefacts and stories [28,15,17]. Thus, investigating how CHPs build new understandings surrounding the ways these interactive technologies can support the visitor experiences they intend to design and addressing how CHPs can be aided in forming these understandings becomes a timely and salient challenge in HCI.

However, HCI research seldom investigates how CHPs discover in what way interactive technologies can support their goals through active experimentation in context and in depth. Indeed, some studies investigate CHPs' involvement in the design of these tools [1,27] and, to some extent, how CHPs build understandings of an interactive tool over time to become effective co-designers [8]. Nonetheless, in these cases, the researchers are the ones who determine the type of experience to design and guide CHPs based on these decisions. In this paper, we reveal how CHPs at a particular museum took control of designing content and narratives to be enhanced by an interactive tool; in turn, we illustrate how they formed new understandings of this interactive tool to aid visitor interpretation and engagements with heritage artefacts. The findings from this study reveal important design considerations for supporting CHPs integrating interactive technologies into their practices in creating and adapting tours, exhibitions, and other museum activities.

This study involved a partnership between the Interaction Design Centre at The University of Limerick and The Hunt Museum in Limerick, Ireland. The first author was, at the time of the study, active as interaction design researcher at the University of Limerick, and also an active volunteer at the museum since February 2013. The second author was the education curator at The Hunt Museum during most of that period. During the study, the CHPs were involved in shaping a portable interactive technology –The Loupe– to support the visitor experience they aimed to design. The Loupe is a magnifying glass-shaped tool for revealing

DIS 2017, June 10-14, 2017, Edinburgh, United Kingdom
© 2017 ACM. ISBN 978-1-4503-4922-2/17/06…$15.00
DOI: http://dx.doi.org/10.1145/3064663.3064753

stories surrounding museum artefacts. As well as forming the intended visitor experience, the CHPs were also responsible for creating the narrative and the content. As facilitator of the project, the researcher was responsible for supporting the introduction of the technologies, making suggestions for the content, and documenting the design process as it unfolded.

While the museum had a record of incorporating interactive technologies, the participating CHPs had seldom been heavily involved in the design of these technologies and integrating them as part of their practice in forming museum activities. We illustrate here how different methods for experimenting with the tool enabled them to consider different opportunities and challenges in creating and shaping a particular interactive tool to support visitor engagement. Reflecting on lessons learned from this project, we provide recommendations for designing tools and resources that support CHPs in identifying suitable technology and integrate those tools as part of their practices in designing visitor activities. As we argue later in this paper, it would be beneficial if CHPs were supported in building these understandings from the onset of the project. The case study was completed as part of a larger, 4-year project, supported by The Material EncounterS with Digital Cultural Heritage project (meSch) [22] and Irish Design 2015 [13].

DESIGNING INTERACTIVE TECHNOLOGIES FOR MUSEUMS

HCI has a long tradition of investigating how interactive technologies can be used to support visitors in engaging with museum artefacts. For instance, interactive tools have been introduced to enable visitors to make their own interpretive contributions to museum objects. At the *Re-tracing The Past* exhibition held at The Hunt Museum, Limerick, Ireland, visitors were encouraged to record and share their opinions surrounding 'mystery' objects within the museum collection [4]. Moreover, museums nowadays are now encouraging visitors to use their own smart devices to form and share their own interpretations to others beyond the museum walls using applications such as Instagram [29].

In addition, interactive technology can be used to support enhanced social interactions within the museum's walls. For example, the design of the *Ghost Ship* exhibition was intended to provoke surprise, interaction, and chance discovery between groups of visitors [10]. Grinter et al. [7] reveal indicate how audio guidebooks can be designed to support interactions between small groups of people.

Considerations in Integrating Interactive Technologies

As long noted in HCI research, the integration of technology in museums is complex: it requires understanding how those tools can serve the museum, the narrative, and the overall intended experience. As indicated by Hornecker [11], if interactive tools are difficult to use or the interactions are inappropriate, they can distract visitors from embracing the narrative or engaging with heritage artefacts.

In addition, HCI research has also indicated the impact that the medium has on engaging visitors in museum stories and objects. In a later study, Hornecker [12] further describes how two different installations designed to engage visitors in a dinosaur exhibition provoked diverse responses from visitors. Collectively called *The Jurascopes*, one installation included a telescope-like device (the Tele-Jurascope) for overlaying animations on the artefacts in the exhibition; the other installation incorporated a large horizontal screen for viewing animations. While the visitors who used the Tele-Jurascope appeared to be more immersed in the exhibition, those who interacted with the screen were more likely to engage in social interaction.

In HCI, most cases have revealed that the content and technology used should effectively maintain, where appropriate, connections with artefacts, stories, and other people. Some of the design case studies have defined sensitivities and frameworks for supporting visitor engagements using handheld devices [28,25] and static devices [28,5]. In these instances, the authors argue that the interactive technologies, as well as the content provided, should complement each other to support visitor engagement.

The Shifting Role of CHPs in Designing Interactive Technologies in Museums

Indeed, as can be seen from the above literature, the design and integration of interactive technologies require a great deal of consideration. Traditionally, interactive exhibits are created by a team of design experts, technologists, and CHPs. Large museums may have staff in-house with the design expertise to build these installations [17]. In other cases, CHPs may commission the task to external companies that also have the relevant expertise to design interactive technologies for museums. While CHPs may be involved heavily in designing interactive exhibitions in-house, they are usually rather minimally involved in the case of commissioned exhibitions [2].

Within the frame of HCI, there are other approaches for designing interactive exhibitions; for example, through using user-centred approaches, visitors and other stakeholders may be involved as informants of the design [4]. HCI researchers and design experts may formulate design requirements for creating interactive technologies through these approaches. Using co-design, various stakeholders, such as children [23,3], students, and CHPs [14,27], may be involved in the design and integration of interactive tools. However, in these cases, little attention is given to how CHPs build understandings surrounding interactive exhibitions.

There is an increased interest in enabling CHPs to take control of designing interactive tools, thus blurring the distinction between the designer, technologist and CHP role. In particular, HCI has focused on the development of toolkits aimed to design, for example, augmented reality tools [16], location-based multimedia guides [6], and tangible interactive technologies [22]. However, the focus has been on the usability of these toolkits [6] or on how they are used to construct narratives outside of the context of the museum [16]. The design of such toolkits is no longer done by researchers only; the emergence of commercially available toolkits, such as OpenExhibits [21] for creating multi-touch, multi-user tabletop devices and Tap/TourML [26] for creating virtual tours, increase the opportunities for CHPs to take control of the design of interactive technologies. With the growing interest of involving CHPs in the design of interactive technologies, further emphasis needs to be placed on understanding how curators take control of their emerging role in designing interactive tools to support their intended interpretation goals.

Several co-design studies have focused, to an extent, on learning about the curators' involvement in designing interactive technologies. In creating the digital natives exhibition, Bossen et al. [1] highlight that the curators were inspired by the methods used in the co-design and chose to experiment with them in their own practice. Halloran et al. [8] detail the participation of curators in creating a personalised tour guide experience for visitors. The authors focus on how these curators developed understandings of a particular interactive technology over time through co-design. While this study provides insights into how curators built understandings of this technology, the intended visitor experience has been defined by the researchers coming in; these researchers had the goal of demonstrating to the curators how their tour activities could work differently.

In the above studies, we learn to some extent how curators respond to their involvement in designing interactive tools. However, due to the curators' limited participation in constructing the visitor experience and designing the content in context, little is known regarding the opportunities and challenges that CHPs face when taking control of and building understandings of interactive tools to support their own interpretive goals.

THE HUNT MUSEUM

As mentioned in the introduction, this research involved CHPs working at The Hunt Museum, a small museum that hosts a range of artefacts gathered by a family of collectors. The selection of objects and artworks was not guided by a particular theme, period or culture; rather, the artefacts are a reflection of the interests and curiosities of the collectors. The interpretive layout of the museum was originally designed by the son of the collectors, with the goal of provoking a sense of reflection and discovery in the visitor. Therefore, the objects are not, nor were they intended to be, grouped strictly either thematically or chronologically. In saying that, many objects are grouped into general themes: for example, Early Christian Art, Bronze Age and Egyptian. In addition, there is little interpretive material in the gallery space: labelling in the museum is kept at a minimal level, so as to encourage visitors to form their own meanings of the collection. For visitors who desire further interpretive information, the museum offers several guided tours to help them comprehend the collection in general, or with a focus on a specific theme.

There are four full-time CHPs employed at the museum. The rest of the staff are volunteers. Some volunteers take the roles of docents, while others are interns. The docents are long-term volunteers of the museum who specialise in a particular activity: this could be delivering tours in the gallery, hosting workshops or trails, or cataloguing the museum's collection. The docents are highly valued because of their knowledge and expertise on the collection. Interns join the museum for 2 - 12 months with a broad but common goal of gaining experience. Interns are selected for their multi-cultural and multi-disciplinary backgrounds: they travel from other countries across Europe and the USA and have backgrounds in a variety of disciplines including museum studies, digital media and marketing. Some interns work in the Care of Collections and Exhibitions department, where they assist the Head of Collections in setting up and administering exhibitions, while others work in the Education Department, where they gain experience in administering, creating and delivering tours, workshops and other education activities in the museum. The museum also regularly hires a marketing intern who is responsible for the museum's promotional activities.

METHODOLOGY

Our project took place over a 15-month period (October 2014 – January 2016). An action research approach was adopted for this study: action research involves an iterative process of planning, acting, observing and reflecting upon a particular change. In this case, the change involved designing a visitor activity in the museum to be supported by an interactive technology. Those conducting action research can observe how change affects a particular situation or environment and adapt their research plans in response to lessons learned [9].

The project described in this paper was divided into three cycles (Figure 1 – next page). Each cycle represents a new iteration of creating and shaping tours to be delivered on an interactive device the CHPs chose. 15 CHPs were primarily involved in creating and shaping the tour assisted by this device called The Loupe. Out of the 15 CHPs, three had, to some extent, experience in creating and integrating interactive digitally enriched exhibitions. These three included two of the curators. As seen in Figure 1, these CHPs were involved at different stages of the project; this was due to their roles in the project and, particularly for the interns, the time of the year when they joined the museum.

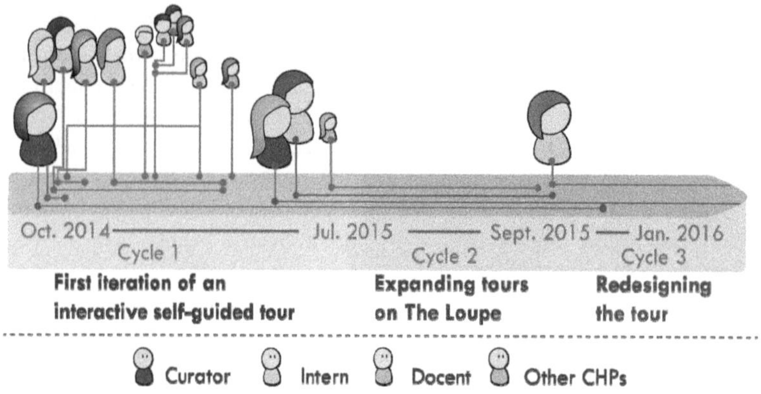

Figure 1. CHPs involved in creating tours for an interactive device during all three cycles

Over the course of the project, 30 meetings were organised to discuss the progress on developing these tours and to agree on the next action points. Participant observation and informal conversations were used during these meetings. The meetings lasted between 19 minutes and 2 hours. During all of these meetings, the researcher took detailed notes that were further elaborated upon once the meeting had ended. Most of the meetings were audio recorded; however, in some cases, on the request of the CHPs or because some meetings were spontaneous and not planned in advance, no recordings were made. The meetings that were recorded were transcribed verbatim.

At the end of the first cycle, the tour was tested internally by 13 CHPs. 17 museum visitors participated in evaluating the tour as supported by the device at the end of the second cycle. Both of these studies involved a mixture of observations of the participants using the device as part of a self-guided tour and interviews directly after the tour. The researcher in the project was responsible for conducting these studies, analysing the feedback, and sharing this feedback with the CHPs for further analysis and discussions.

At the end of the third cycle, the researcher conducted interviews with 12 CHPs who were, in some way, involved in the project in order to gain insights into the CHPs' viewpoints on their involvement in the project. The data gathered is presented in the form of excerpts and vignettes extracted from the meetings and interviews conducted with the CHPs. All names were replaced with pseudonyms.

The CHPs involved in the project were responsible for designing the intended visitor experience: they formed the narrative, the content (using PowerPoint and Google Slides), and chose the interactive device to be integrated. The researcher's role in the project was to suggest software for creating the content, to introduce the technologies and to provide advice on shaping the content.

At the beginning of the project, the CHPs formulated objectives for introducing an interactive tour at the museum. Curator Pascale's intentions for introducing an interactive device were to:

- Enhance the visitor experience by providing content that is not available through other modes of delivery;
- Widen the appeal of the collection; and
- Provide access to the collection to as many visitors as possible.

She specifically opposed introducing an interactive that would provide little to no educational value or was a distraction on the intended visitor experience.

Curator Pascale was interested in providing an alternative avenue for delivering themed tours currently on offer at the museum. These themed tours were designed to enable visitors to learn about the collection from different perspectives. A series of these themed tours are on offer in the museum, including *Queer Tour*, *Gross and Gruesome*, and *Architectural Perspectives Tour*; these tours are delivered either by a docent or self-guided with a booklet. The tour that the CHPs decided to focus on was *The History of Ireland in 10 Objects*. This is a themed tour of the collection that explores the history of Ireland through ten objects, spanning the three floors of the museum.

CYCLE 1: FIRST ITERATION OF AN INTERACTIVE SELF GUIDED TOUR

Upon deciding on the interpretive goals and the kind of experience they wanted to design for, the meetings focused on determining how an interactive technology may be able to complement these goals.

Based on Curator Pascale's intention for supporting a self-guided tour, the researcher presented the CHPs with four interactive concepts that were relevant for supporting their goals; these tools were designed by a multi-disciplinary international team as part of meSch project. They have different functionalities and they are designed to reveal content in diverse ways. The designer presented these concepts in the form of a video [20]; following this, the CHPs were provided with written scenarios that demonstrated how the interactive concept could work to support visitors.

Figure 2A shows The Way Detector, an egg-shaped interactive that follows a hot-cold metaphor: the visitor holds The Way Detector in her hand, and as she moves closer to the object, The Way Detector vibrates at a faster rate to inform her she is close to an object of interest. When placed on a platform next to the target point of interest, the Way Detector triggers media (such as sound or visuals) on an external device. Figure 2B presents The Plinth, upon which replica objects can be placed. Information is projected from above on each of the six sides of The Plinth. As the visitor moves closer to one of the sides, further information is revealed about the object. Figure 2C presents The Belt. The visitor chooses a theme by placing a card inside the belt. When the visitor is close to a point of interest, he hears an alert sound coming from the point of interest and after that hears a story.

Figure 2D presents The Loupe. Shaped as a magnifying glass, The Loupe aims to instil a sense of discovery and exploration, giving visitors the freedom to see details on objects and unfold layered narratives. It operates through scanning a point of interest, which leads to presenting the first screen of content on The Loupe. The visitor reveals the next screen of content relating to the same point of interest by tilting The Loupe right. Tilting left moves back to the previous content. The Loupe also supports other interactions, such as moving forward and shaking.

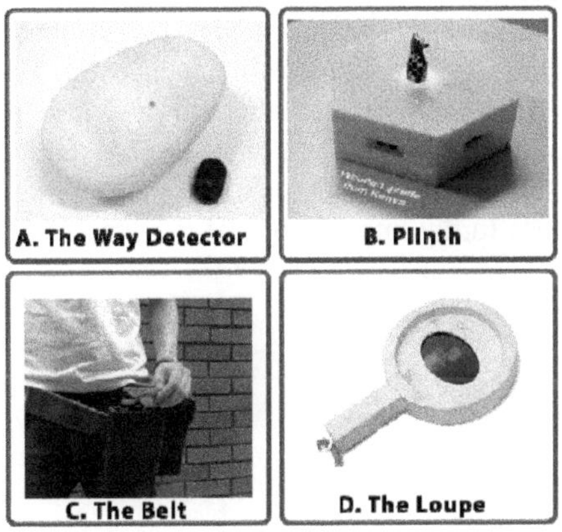

Figure 2. The Four Interaction Concepts

In the following excerpt, the CHPs were describing potential interactions that may be suitable for engaging visitors with the museum's objects as part of a tour. At this stage, the CHPs had not seen or chosen the interactive device they had wanted to use for the tour. During these discussions, Pascale was adamant to ensure that the team kept in mind how the actions could enhance visitor engagement and support interpretation:

> *Curator Pascale: Rather than thinking about an action, interrogate why that action appeals. Some more ideas will be able to come and you'll be able to think of things in a more coherent way across the whole tour.*

Following this, Pascale continued:

> *Curator Pascale: If the story is good and the interpretation is rigorous and has integrity, then everything that descends from it will also have integrity because its genesis will have come from an intelligent place. If it's 'let's do this gimmicky thing for the sake of having a gimmick, then it's going to feel gimmicky at the time. But if there's something relevant to it... there's that plate in the Captain's Room of the guy who's sort of singing up to the tower lady, what is it about that object that's compelling?*

From these excerpts, it appears that the CHPs felt that all interactions were an element of the interpretation and required a great deal of thought. This suggests that understanding the relationship between the interactions and the overall interpretive goals is an important consideration when choosing to integrate new interactive tools into their practice of designing guided tours.

Following this, the researcher presented the CHPs the videos and written scenarios describing the potential interactive tools. In the following vignette, we see the discussion that unfolded after presenting these scenarios to the CHPs. Here, the CHPs focused on understanding the differences between these interactives, and how they may affect the visiting experience:

> *Intern Mark: The castle you [Intern Nora] were at, where they had all of the interactives in a room and the sounds, that almost adds to the experience. When you're walking in the castle, you could imagine there would be a lot of sound. Whereas in somewhere like this, you appreciate silence to immerse yourself in [looking at] an object.*

> *Intern Leeanne: Even then, if [The Way Detector] is vibrating, or if it's giving a heartbeat... would that not be annoying to others? That's a sound as well.*

> *Intern Nora: This is a very quiet museum. There'll never be a huge amount of people in it at the same time in the collection area. There might be a couple coming in off the street and maybe a small group or something... that couple doesn't want to be distracted by the school going around doing sounds or anything. So something like this [looks at The Loupe image on the scenario sheet] this doesn't make sound, does it?*

> *Researcher: No it doesn't make sound.*

> *Intern Nora: This is my personal favourite.*

> *Curator Pascale: It's a nice idea that there is a particular detail like a thumbprint that you can scan an object and that thumbprint would be there and you could say 'thumbprints are often found on ancient objects'...*

Through discussing the tools, the CHPs were able to build some understandings on what those technologies could do and how they could support or impede upon the intended visitor experience. As Intern Nora had mentioned, the video really: *"brought it to life"*. The CHPs were able to compare the different tools and discuss their potential in the museum. For instance, the CHPs knew that sound should be kept minimal in the museum. Moreover, Curator Pascale discussed the interpretative potential of The Loupe, highlighting how the action of scanning could be related to uncovering more information about a particular story behind an object: for example, a thumbprint. This is what attracted the CHPs to The Loupe and drove them to choose this device. This suggests that the CHPs were able to, on some level, discuss how the interactive technology could support the intended visitor experience through viewing video and written examples.

On the initial version of The Loupe, the content supporting the object was triggered by the shape recognition of the artefact. However, implementing object recognition was not appropriate for a self-guided tour of this museum. There are many objects, often small, close to each other and in dimly lit spaces. Therefore, the target content on this version of The Loupe is triggered by NFC tags placed on labels. NFC is wireless communication protocol that enables short distance communication between two compatible devices. NFC tags can store and send information when an NFC-enabled device is very close (typically within 5cm).

However, at this stage, the CHPs felt that further experimentation was required to understand what The Loupe could do to support their goals. For this reason, they chose to reuse and experiment with existing text content that was created and tested already for *The History of Ireland in 10 Objects* tour brochure. Their goal was to experiment with what the tool could do to serve their intended visitor experience. As the CHPs wanted to integrate The Loupe to support a self-guided tour, they decided to add wayfinding to guide visitors to the next object. The CHPs provided the content, which the researcher then arranged and prepared for The Loupe. Following this, the researcher deployed the content on The Loupe. Figure 3 shows a sample flow of content.

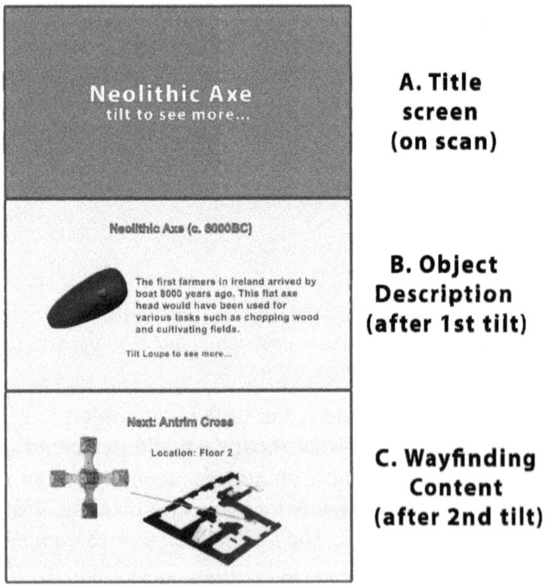

Figure 3. Flow of content (cycle 1)

Following the transfer of this content to The Loupe, the tour was evaluated internally in situ by CHPs. While the exercise was brief, this was the first time the tour was tested on the device from start to finish and in context. Two CHPs (Curator Sarah and Intern Ciara), who had recently joined the project at this time, also participated in the evaluation. Both had the opportunity to familiarise themselves with The Loupe beforehand. However, the evaluation was their first time viewing the content on The Loupe.

As expected, the evaluations with CHPs had revealed challenges concerning how The Loupe supported the tour and the presentation of the content. In particular, the feedback highlighted the need to:

- Further support visitors using The Loupe in scanning the labels;
- Form stronger connections with the objects; and
- Experiment further to better understand the presentation space of The Loupe, in terms of its size, how the content should be designed, and how the narrative should be structured to support the intended experience and narrative.

CYCLE 2: EXPANDING TOURS ON THE LOUPE

Overall, testing The Loupe helped the CHPs to learn the challenges of using this tool to support interpretation and identify potential solutions for shaping the narrative to address these issues. In response, the CHPs were more confident to place further effort in the content. For example, further understandings of the presentation space on The Loupe led the CHPs to explore alternative ways of presenting the wayfinding content. As well as redesigning the floor plans, the CHPs decided to provide written directions in response to the implications of the screen size (figure 4).

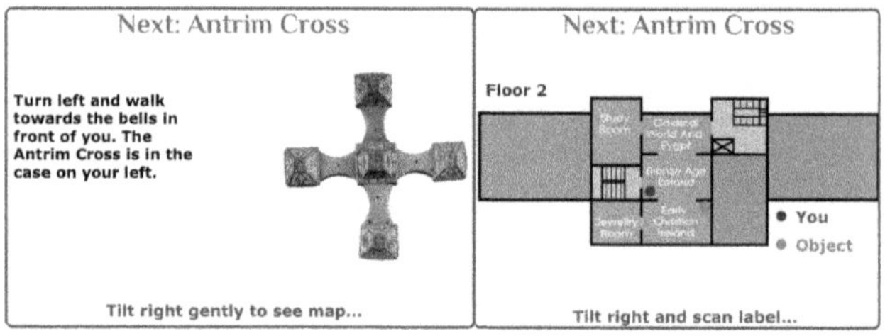

Figure 4. Left – sample written directions; right – sample map.

However, the CHPs felt there was still more to learn and understand regarding what The Loupe could do. In the following vignette, Curator Sarah indicates that she was aware that further work was needed for structuring the narrative on this tool; however, their limited time availability and limited experience in using the device was hindering these efforts:

> *Curator Sarah: The booklets that you're taking it from - when you read the booklet, it has a picture and a paragraph of text. But when you're here, you're in front of the object and you are getting half of the text and you move on to the other half of the text. So, sometimes it jars. You read this [screen] as one thing and then you go on and you read [the next screen] as another thing. Then you go on and you read*

this [next screen] as another thing. So when the information has to go across two [screens], it's the link sentences that need to be worked on properly. It's not a big thing, but it will probably take a bit of thinking about.

Researcher: It definitely takes an awful lot of thinking, because I was trying to look through this content myself and figure out... there's simple things you can do like, "look at X". But I think that's... "you must do this".

Curator Sarah: Yeah, and there's things that we can do here that we can't do with a guided tour, it would be nice in the future to have all of [the images] not to be photographs. That they're just outlines. As you were saying, you've got everything that you need on the screen, so what's the point of them being in front of the object? [...]

Researcher: Or a certain detail...

Curator Sarah: Or a close up [...] There's things that can be taken advantage of [on The Loupe] that I just don't think we've had enough time to really get into because we just don't have enough time. It's literally just a time thing, and using it as well, and the more we use it, the more things we will go "oh, wouldn't it be cool if we did that", getting the interaction between this [the target image] and the object, you know with the shamrock [the target image], lining it up, and stuff like that we could do a bit more with.

Sarah indicated several features of The Loupe could be used more creatively. While she did acknowledge this, her response also indicated that she felt there was more to learn and discover, particularly with relation to the interactive and behaviours supported by the device that could complement their goals in supporting visitor interpretation.

In September 2015, the content on The Loupe was evaluated with visitors; the findings enabled the CHPs to identify further implications of adopting the device in the context of this museum. In the following subsections, we will describe how further understandings gathered from the visitor feedback led subsequently to them shaping their approach in supporting a self-guided tour using a portable interactive tool. The vignettes presented in the following sections are taken from meetings where the feedback gathered from the visitor evaluation was shared and discussed between the researcher and the CHPs.

Responding to Visitor Feedback

One of the main comments shared by the visitors related to the structure of the tour. Particularly, many visitors did not realise the tour they were taking was themed around *The History of Ireland in 10 Objects*. In the vignette below, it can be seen how the CHPs, in collaboration with the researcher, responded to the feedback:

Researcher: I think it definitely needs to be highlighted throughout the tour that this is the History of Ireland in 10 Objects. Because a couple of people, when I interviewed them afterwards, didn't realise it was the History of Ireland in 10 Objects. Even though it was said [on The Loupe] at the beginning.

Curator Sarah: It doesn't go chronologically, doesn't it not? Because [the interpretive layout makes this very difficult to implement]...

Curator Pascale: I have an idea. I mean, this is a lot more design work, what you would want is some sort of...

Curator Sarah: Timeline...

Curator Pascale: Timeline. But you would want to say, 'History of Ireland in 10 Objects' and then you would say 'Object 1' and then you have a circle... you have everything in a trendy circle. Then you scan the object, then the timeline comes up, and it shows you where on the timeline... maybe like '3000 BC'...

Overall, the visitor feedback provided guidance on what further steps to take with the content. In response, the CHPs were more confident in investing further effort into its design and presentation than at the beginning of the project. This suggests that it is important for CHPs to have a good understanding of how the behaviour and functionality of the device affect the presentation of the content and the intended visitor experience they intend to design.

Up until this point, the CHPs felt they needed to further understand The Loupe as an interpretive tool in the context of their museum, particularly in terms of its functionality. When discussing the feedback, it emerged that the CHPs did not see the relevance of the tilting gestures in supporting the experience they intended to design for visitors. In the next vignette, Curator Sarah asked the researcher if the tilting gestures were a relevant feature of The Loupe; she was especially interested in learning what they could do to enhance the content and story:

Researcher: The idea - from the guys who created The Loupe - of using the gestures [the tilting] was so you didn't touch the screen. It is basically part of the discovery process. There's also other features for being able to zoom into different objects, and seeing things from the back [of the objects], for example, having a high resolution image which you can explore, and pan around through it. So there are other options.

Curator Sarah: I mean it's convenient. If this is your design, it is easier to [tilt] than to get involved with the screen. I want to know is it a convenience thing or is it 'ssscchhhhhhhwwwoooo! Forward in time! Zoom in!'

Curator Pascale: If that kind of gesture can be translated into additional content, which is intuitive, like zooming in, then I think it's worth it. If it's a constraint we just have to deal with, that's fine, I agree, we should figure it out.

For the CHPs, it was important that the behaviour of the device and the content complemented each other. The researcher followed by further discussing the intentions of the tilting gestures:

Designer: The idea of having the gesture was so that you didn't have to touch the screen. Basically trying to follow as much as possible the metaphor [of discovery] and going past through content.

> *Curator Pascale: Right. And the idea of the magnifying glass is that you move it, you don't touch the Loupe.*
>
> *Curator Sarah: So we need to incorporate [the tilting] into the way that we are presenting our text.*

The feedback of the evaluation aided the CHPs in further understanding the opportunities and constraints of the device they had chosen for supporting visitor engagement. In their view, the behaviour of the interactive tool needed to enhance the narrative. To ensure that the content and the behaviour complemented each other, the CHPs felt that the content needed to be shaped further.

Overall, testing The Loupe with visitors provided the CHPs with necessary feedback for understanding how the interactive device could support visitor interpretation. In addition, the feedback helped the CHPs to identify the subsequent steps to ensure the narrative and content was clear. Following this, the CHPs redesigned the tour structure and content in the third iteration of the tour.

CYCLE 3: REDESIGNING THE TOUR

In response to the CHPs' enhanced understandings gathered on The Loupe from the previous iterations, the content had changed significantly. From the CHPs' point of view, the story needed to have a tight structure to support a self-guided tour. In implementing this change, the CHPs had divided the tour into five subthemes (see Figure 5). The CHPs' intention for adding the subthemes was to suggest the experience of moving through different parts of Irish history.

Figure 5. Dividing the tour into five subthemes

While the CHPs were more aware of the opportunities and constraints of the tool, some challenges remained especially since the CHPs felt that its behaviour may pose distractions. It was through actively shaping the content of the tour that the CHPs identified this challenge. For instance, as presented in the following vignette, Curator Sarah was adamant to portray a complex story surrounding a particular painting in the museum. While the story could theoretically be revealed using the tilting gestures on The Loupe, she felt too many tilts would be a distraction:

> *Curator Sarah: This is the verse from Romeo and Juliet from which the title of the [Sean Keating] painting is taken. And this is Sean Keating explaining the title of the painting. So it makes sense to have both of them. But I don't want people to have too many... swinging The Loupe around so there's that as well. Getting enough content in, but not breaking their arms in a sense. If there's too much content, it's better than not enough because we can take it out.*
>
> *Researcher: One of the major comments during the [visitor evaluation] was that the text was quite small on [The Loupe] as well. And even though [the text] was bolded as well, you couldn't really see that it was bolded on The Loupe because the screen is quite small.*
>
> *Curator Sarah: And if we can't have a(n) [animated] scrolling... then it's a case of tilting. We could do a little gif animation of this [points at letter on left of content – figure 6] comes up, then it comes in and then it fades into this quote [points at the Sean Keating's quote on right of content – figure 6]. I don't really know how to do that, which is why I haven't done that! But I know there's a website or something called giphy... which I'm sure, we can learn how to use!*

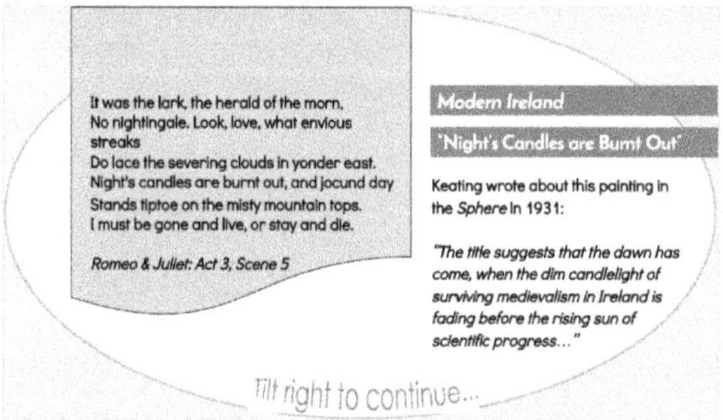

Figure 6. Sarah wanted to present this story on The Loupe

Indeed, the CHPs were limited to the behaviours available on The Loupe. However, further experimentation enabled the CHPs to develop solutions that could help them "workaround" these constraints. In this case, working around these constraints required the CHPs to use skills that they currently did not have: creating GIF animations.

When shaping the content during this cycle, the CHPs felt it was important that they reminded themselves of how The Loupe worked. However, when the CHPs had changed the content, they could not test it on The Loupe directly because they required assistance from the researcher to deploy the content to the device. In her interview, Intern Deirdre describes how simulating the way The Loupe worked with the printed content helped her with further understanding the opportunities and constraints of the tool (see excerpt below). This is similar to the bodystorming method often used in HCI and Interaction Design projects. Deirdre had recently joined the project during the third cycle of iteration of the Loupe-assisted tour. While she had used The Loupe once before, she did not have enough experience to fully understand how it worked:

> *Intern Deirdre: We printed it [the content] off because it's easy to forget the screens that come and go. So the ones that say like 'tilt right to continue' it's easy to forget that was there. But when you have it on the paper, you have to pretend to do that! Turn it over or something like that!*
>
> *Researcher: Did you actually pretend to do the tilt [with the paper]?*

Intern Deirdre: Yeah! Let me go around to the next one and scan the labels!

[We continued to discuss this, until Deirdre commented]:

Intern Deirdre: Because it gets you into the head of like 'would you do that?' [...] Because, for some of them when we reformatted it, we'd accidentally take off 'now scan the label'. And then when you take the piece of paper around, you'd be like 'ok, now what am I doing?' And in your head you're like 'there's the label; I should be scanning it' but it's not telling you to do that? So you have to be like ok, I need to add that bit back on 'now scan the label'! 'Cause they don't know to do that. And that way [by printing it], we could write loads of notes on and stuff as well, which was really handy when you go back to Drive [Google Slides], because you've got notes... like I wrote all over the first one that I did, just saying like 'this needs to be here, that needs to be added in, this content and this date and stuff needs to be checked'.

Deirdre identified an important consideration when designing tours incorporating novel interactives: it is easy to forget how the interactive works. Specifically, it is important to acknowledge its functionality when structuring the narrative. Through experimentation, Intern Deirdre highlighted that simulating the tour was adequate for gaining further understandings of the way the device could support the intended visitor experience. Noting that Deirdre was new to the project, this suggests that methods for simulating the functionality of the tool may work are adequate for building fundamental understandings of these tools.

DISCUSSION AND CONCLUSION

From the beginning of the project, it was clear that CHPs needed to know how different interactive technologies could support their intended visitor experience. While it is long known in HCI literature that understanding how technology can complement the visitor experience is important [27], little is known about how CHPs build understandings and could be supported in this practice. In this section, we reflect upon the findings presented. We further discuss how Interaction Designers and HCI experts could use these findings for designing tools and resources to aid CHPs in understanding how these tools can help support their goals.

CHPs have interpretation goals that need to be met to satisfy their visitor goals. In this case, when making the decision to use technology in supporting a self-guided tour, the CHPs always referred to what, in their view, the interactive tools were capable of doing and what they could do to complement their goals. Their concerns for integrating these tools into museums were similar to those described in previous studies [17,18]. While CHPs collectively agree that technology should serve a meaningful purpose, the findings from this project suggest that understanding the implications of adopting those tools in context requires further, hands-on experimentation and experience. Thus, to support CHPs as co-designers of interactive exhibits, it could be useful to provide adequate resources and tools that enable them to engage in these experimentations.

While the availability of toolkits for the purpose of shaping and configuring interactive technologies is increasing (see for example [8,22]), the extent to which they can be reconfigured is limited for those with little technical skill. These constraints may result in CHPs designing workarounds to present the narrative. However, these workarounds could require CHPs to build additional skills (as seen in this case) or make compromises between the narrative they intend to portray and the available behaviours provided by the functionalities of the interactive technology. These points suggest that it is not enough to build these understandings over time once the technology is adopted; the CHPs also need to be given adequate support from the onset of the project to have some understanding of what those tools can do for aiding visitor interpretation. While having this understanding may be considered more important in situations where there is a financial cost for adopting these technologies, a lot of time and effort is required to create the intended visitor experience. Therefore, regardless of the cost of these devices, resources that help CHPs in building these understandings from the onset could help CHPs comprehend what those tools can do for supporting the experience they intend to design for.

In some sense, visual and written scenarios were a useful resource in aiding the CHPs to learn how the tools functioned. On a small level, these scenarios provided some information for the CHPs to identify how those tools could support or impede upon the intended visitor experience and determine whether the technologies could fit into the context of their museum. They may have been able to grasp these understandings because they were clear about the goals they wanted to meet from the onset of the project. By the time CHPs decide to use toolkits to explore different technologies, they may already have some interpretation goals in mind. Many toolkits provide templates to enable CHPs to alter content and reconfigure interactive technologies. Those designing these templates could provide examples (and, if resources are available, video examples) that explicitly demonstrate how the features and behaviours of those interactive technologies could be used to enhance the intended visitor experience. These resources would be beneficial for CHPs to build some understandings on how those technologies can support visitor interpretation.

Nonetheless, visual and written examples may not be sufficient for building adequate understandings of the opportunities and constraints of using those tools for both portraying stories and supporting visitor interpretation. It appears that hands-on experimentation with these tools is necessary to build those understandings, as also recommended by [17,18]. However, beyond experimenting with how the tool physically functions as described by the above authors, our study suggests that CHPs could benefit from exploring how those tools and their associated behaviours could support different activities in the museum. Providing examples could help CHPs in these experimentation activities, with a particular focus on 1) how different technologies could facilitate the presentation of the narrative and 2) how the features and behaviours of those interactive devices could enhance interactions with the artefacts, stories, and other people.

Due to financial costs, it may not be feasible for CHPs to experiment with the actual technologies. However, encouraging experimentation with low fidelity prototypes could help in building further understandings on how to structure the content and narrative to support interpretation. For instance, bodystorming was shown to be an effective method for visualising the flow of the narrative, as well as identifying and overcoming potential obstacles and constraints of using the technology for supporting visitor interpretation. Indeed, it is possible that CHPs may not be familiar with these design simulation methods, as indicated by Bossen et al. [1]. Therefore, resources could be made available for CHPs to create connections with local designers. These designers could help in facilitating the development and experimentation of these low fidelity prototypes; for instance, they could host design workshops featuring low fidelity prototypes of interactives that CHPs are considering integrating into the activities they offer. CHPs could prepare content in advance. During the activity, the CHPs could be encouraged to enact in context how the content may be revealed using those technologies. CHPs can then shape the content as appropriate. Indeed, this activity could be time-consuming and may require a great deal of time for both designers and CHPs to prepare for. However, we argue that such activities could help CHPs in building necessary understandings of the interactive devices they are considering using without needing to purchase them beforehand.

Nonetheless, it may not always be feasible to have designers facilitating such design sessions. In these cases, it could be useful to provide CHPs with resources to experiment on their own with low-fidelity prototypes using these methods, independent of designers. While providing these resources as part of toolkits may not be practical, toolkits could provide links to already existing resources for assisting CHPs in taking the first steps in creating and experimenting with low-fidelity versions of the tools provided. An example of such a resource was created by the meSch project, one of the projects funding this study [19].

While these tools and resources may be helpful for supporting CHPs in understanding what interactive technologies could do to support their goals, it is important to note that unforeseen challenges could still arise. Without testing the chosen interactive device in context, it would be difficult to determine how it could support visitor interpretation. In saying that, we believe that providing these resources will help CHPs build sufficient understandings of the implications of adopting interactive tools within the context of their own museums.

We are fully aware that there are some limitations to this research. Due to the scope of the project, which was focused on one small museum, generalisation is difficult. However, we believe these findings could be transferred to relate to CHPs in other contexts. For instance, CHPs need to know how the interpretive tools that they integrate can be used to support visitors in engaging with stories and artefacts. Moreover, here the CHPs chose to focus on a particular kind of narrative experience: a guided tour. As already demonstrated in HCI research, different challenges may emerge when incorporating technology to support other types of experiences: for example, games [15] or free explorations visits [9]. Therefore, the question as to whether these co-design methods could help CHPs in understanding how those tools could aid them in supporting the intended visitor experience remains open. In addition, this case study did not consider that there are various types of museum visitors (such as tourists and specialists); the intended visitor experience was defined the same way for all visitors. However, each visitor type has different motivations and interests, and knowledge [24]. While the goal of this project was to aid CHPs in taking first steps to incorporate new interactive technology, future research could involve identifying different visitor types to formulate interaction concepts and narratives personalised to these different visitor groups.

In this paper, we have discussed how CHPs took control and built understandings of an interactive tool to support interpretation. This study has been inspired by existing HCI research, which focuses on enabling CHPs to create content for and configure interactive technology. Furthermore, we provided recommendations for designing tools and resources to aid CHPs in experimenting with and building understandings of different interactive technologies. Indeed, this study revealed some insights into the challenges of supporting CHPs of shaping and integrating interactive tools into their practices. However, further work is needed to explore possible ways of supporting CHPs in understanding how those tools are relevant for enhancing the experience they intend to design for visitors.

ACKNOWLEDGMENTS

This study was supported by the Material EncounterS with digital Cultural Heritage (meSch) project and Irish Design 2015. meSch (2013-2017) received funding from the European Community's Seventh Framework Programme 'ICT for access to cultural resources' (ICT Call 9: FP7-ICT-2011-9) under the Grant Agreement 600851. Irish Design 2015 was a year-long programme exploring, promoting and celebrating Irish Design in just about every form. We are also grateful for the participation of the CHPs at The Hunt Museum, Limerick, Ireland.

REFERENCES

1. Claus Bossen, Christian Dindler, and Ole S. Iversen. 2012. Impediments to User Gains: experiences from a critical participatory design project. In *Proceedings of the 12th Participatory Design Conference: Research Papers - Volume 1 (PDC '12)*, 31–40.
2. Tim Caulton. 1998. *Hands-on Exhibitions: Managing Interactive Museums and Science Centres*. Routledge, London, UK.
3. Christian Dindler, Ole S. Iversen, Rachel Smith, and Rune Veerasawmy. 2010. Participatory Design at the Museum: inquiring into children's everyday engagement in cultural heritage. In *Proceedings of the 22nd Conference of the Computer-Human Interaction Special Interest Group of Australia on Computer-Human Interaction (OzCHI 2010)*, 72–79.
4. Kieran Ferris, Liam Bannon, Luigina Ciolfi, Paul Gallagher, Tony Hall, and Marilyn Lennon. 2004. Shaping Experiences in The Hunt Museum: a design case study. In *Proceedings of the 5th Conference on Designing Interactive Systems: Processes, Practices, Methods, and Techniques (DIS '04)*, 205–214.
5. Ben Gammon and Alexandra Burch. 2008. Designing Mobile Digital Experiences. In *Digital Technologies and the Museum Experience: Handheld Guides and Other Media*, Loic Tallon (ed.), AltaMira Press, Plymouth, UK, 35–63.
6. Giuseppe Ghiani, Fabio Paternò, and Lucio D. Spano. 2009. Cicero Designer: An Environment for End-User Development of Multi-Device Museum Guides. In *2nd International Symposium on End-User Development (IS-EUD '09)*, 265–274.
7. Rebecca E. Grinter, Paul M. Aoki, Margaret H. Szymanski, James D. Thornton, Allison Woodruff, and Amy Hurst. 2002. Revisiting the Visit:: understanding how technology can shape the museum visit. In *Proceedings of the 2002 ACM Conference on Computer Supported Cooperative Work (CSCW '02)*, 146–155.
8. John Halloran, Eva Hornecker, Geraldine Fitzpatrick, G., Mark Weal, David Millard, Danius Michaelides, Don Cruickshank, and David De Roure. 2006. Unfolding Understandings: co-designing ubicomp in situ, over time. In *Proceedings of the 6th Conference on Designing Interactive Systems (DIS '06)*, 109–118.
9. Greg Hearn, Jo Tacchi, Marcus Foth, and June Lennie. 2009. *Action Research and New Media: concepts, methods and cases*, Hampton Press, Cresskill, NJ, USA.
10. Jon Hindmarsh, Christian Heath, Dirk vom Lehn, D., and Jason Cleverly. 2002. Creating Assemblies:: aboard the Ghost Ship. In *Proceedings of the 2002 ACM Conference on Computer Supported Cooperative Work (CSCW '02)*, 156–165.
11. Eva Hornecker. 2008. "I Don't Understand it Either, but it is Cool": visitor interactions with a multi-touch table in a museum. In *Horizontal Interactive Human Computer Systems, 2008: TABLETOP 2008*, 113–120.
12. Eva Hornecker. 2010. Interactions Around a Contextually Embedded System. In *Proceedings of the Fourth International Conference on Tangible, Embedded, and Embodied Interaction (TEI '10)*, 169–176.
13. Irish Design. Irish Design. 2015. Retrieved 30 Mar., 2017 from http://www.irishdesign2015.ie/
14. Ole S. Iversen and Rachel C. Smith. 2012. Connecting to Everyday Practices: experiences from the Digital Natives exhibition. In *Heritage and Social Media*, Elisa Giaccardi (ed.), Routledge, London, UK, 126–144.
15. Eric Klopfer, Judy Perry, Kurt Squire, Ming-Fon Jan, and Constance Steinkuehler. 2005. Mystery at the Museum: a collaborative game for museum education. In *Proceedings of the 2005 Conference on Computer Support for Collaborative Learning: Learning 2005: The Next 10 Years!*, 316–320.
16. Boriana Koleva, Stefan R. Egglestone, Holger Schnädelbach, Kevin Glover, Chris Greenhalgh, Tom Rodden, and Martyn Dade-Robertson. 2009. Supporting the Creation of Hybrid Museum Experiences. In *Proceedings of the SIGCHI Conference on Human Factors in Computing Systems (CHI '09)*, 1973–1982.
17. Laura A. Maye, Fiona E. McDermott, Luigina Ciolfi, and Gabriela Avram. 2014. Interactive Exhibitions Design: what can we learn from cultural heritage professionals? In *Proceedings of the 8th Nordic Conference on Human-Computer Interaction: Fun, Fast, Foundational (NordiCHI '14)*, 598-607.
18. Fiona McDermott, Loraine Clarke, Eva Hornecker, and Gabriela Avram. 2013. Challenges and Opportunities faced by Cultural Heritage Professionals in Designing Interactive Exhibits. In *Proceedings of NODEM*, 19–26.
19. Fiona McDermott, Gabriela Avram, and Laura Maye. Co-Designing Encounters with Digital Cultural Heritage. 2014. Retrieved on 8 Jan., 2017 from http://codesign.website/wp-content/uploads/2016/01/meSch_CoDesign_Booklet.pdf
20. meSch. November 2013 meSch workshop at WAAG Society. 2013. Retrieved on 8 Jan., 2017 from https://www.youtube.com/watch?v=q8NdtIYZgw8
21. Open Exibits. Open Exhibits: A Free Multitouch & HCI Software Initiative. 2017. Retrieved 8 Jan., 2017 from http://openexhibits.org/
22. Daniela Petrelli, Luigina Ciolfi, Dick van Dijk, Eva Hornecker, Elena Not, and Albrecht Schmidt. 2013.

Integrating Material and Digital: a new way for cultural heritage. *Interactions* 20, 4: 58–63.

23. Maria Roussou, Elina Kavalieratou, and Michael Doulgeridis. 2007. Children Designers In The Museum: applying participatory design for the development of an art education program. In *Proceedings of the 6th International Conference on Interaction Design and Children (IDC 07)*, 77–80.
24. Maria Roussou, Akrivi Katifori, Laia Pujol, Maria Vayanou, Stefan J. Rennick-Egglestone. 2014. A life of their own: museum visitor personas penetrating the design lifecycle of a mobile experience. In *Extended Abstracts on Human Factors in Computing Systems (CHI EA)*, 547–552.
25. Yao-Ting Sung, Kuo-En Chang, Huei-Tse Hou, and Pin-Fu Chen. 2010. Designing an Electronic Guidebook for Learning Engagement in a Museum of History. *Computers in Human Behavior* 26, 1: 74–83.
26. Tap/TourML.TAP into Museums. 2017. Retrieved on 8 Jan., 2017 from http://www.tapintomuseums.org/
27. Gustav Taxén. 2004. Introducing Participatory Design in Museums. In *Proceedings of the Eighth Conference on Participatory Design: Artful Integration: Interweaving Media, Materials and Practices-Volume 1 (PDC 2004)*, 204–213.
28. Dirk vom Lehn and Christian Heath. 2005. Accounting for New Technology in Museum Exhibitions. *International Journal of Arts Management* 7, 3: 11–21.
29. Alexandra Weilenmann, Thomas Hillman, and Beata Jungselius. 2013. Instagram at the Museum: communicating the museum experience through social photo sharing. In *Proceedings of the SIGCHI Conference on Human Factors in Computing Systems (CHI 13)*, 1843–1852.

The Evolution of a Scale Model as an Impromptu Design Tool

Dorothé Smit
University of Salzburg,
Salzburg, Austria
dorothe.smit@sbg.ac.at

Martin Murer
University of Salzburg,
Salzburg, Austria
martin.murer@sbg.ac.at

Vincent van Rheden
University of Salzburg,
Salzburg, Austria
vincent.vanrheden@sbg.ac.at

Thomas Grah
University of Salzburg,
Salzburg, Austria
thomas.grah@sbg.ac.at

Manfred Tscheligi
University of Salzburg,
Salzburg, Austria
manfred.tscheligi@sbg.ac.at

DIS 2017, June 10-14, 2017, Edinburgh, United Kingdom
© 2017 ACM. ISBN 978-1-4503-4922-2/17/06...$15.00
DOI: http://dx.doi.org/10.1145/3064663.3064797

Abstract
The use of generative design tools for collaborative design tasks has been common practice in the fields of HCI and Design. In this pictorial, we present the evolution of an open-ended design tool: a scale model of a car showroom, used to investigate collaborative interactions in spatial environments. The features of the scale model evolved through several impromptu usage scenarios. With this contribution, we share our observations about the use of the prototype as a means of communication, as well as a means of inspiration, and argue for the use of non-prescriptive design tools in collaborative design projects.

Authors Keywords
Generative design tools; cooperative design tasks; multi-stakeholder projects; non-prescribed use; ideation

ACM Classification Keywords
H.5.m. Information interfaces and presentation (e.g., HCI): Miscellaneous

Introduction
The use of generative design tools in cooperative design processes is well established in the fields of Human-Computer Interaction and Design [12]. Generative design tools, often visual and tangible representational artefacts, are a compelling way to gather and create insights in the design process, and for stakeholders to become integral players in projects [13]. Examples of generative tools

for design are plentiful (see, for example: [2,9,12,14]). Prototypes can be seen as part of the design tools designers use to influence the way they think [3]. In fact, any artifacts that are used in the design process shape cognition and collaboration [16].

We consider mock-ups of spatial, often architectural, projects a subset of prototyping tools that architects and designers use to grasp, evaluate and communicate the impact of their ideas on the physical space in which they are situated [10,15]. These scale models are often used in collaborative, creative processes, and to communicate ideas to clients or other external parties [1,11]. Advantages of building physical scale models include the ability to quickly and cost-effectively iterate on certain aspects of a space (e.g., layout, facilities, decoration), either individually or in a collaborative setting.

The use of tools for design is not static, i.e., the way an artifact is used is contingent on properties that go beyond the material and functional characteristics of the artifact as it was once designed [6]. The evolution of design tools in this context can be considered as a design process in itself: 'design in use' [5], which accentuates the incompleteness of any tool or prototype. The use of a design tool is then not an inherent property of the artefact, but something that is developed over time by any user of the artefact.

In this pictorial, we present the evolution of a prototype used as a generative design tool. The prototype, a miniature model of a car showroom (1), was used in a number of different contexts and situations. Several of different users and stakeholders, with different backgrounds used it in (often) collaborative creative processes; and as a presentation tool. It was constructed in an impromptu manner, without clearly defined properties. The only guidelines were the scale of the model (i.e., 1:43

1

to match the size of the miniature cars that would be placed inside of the model), and the material the model would be made out of (i.e., acrylic glass, so that white-board markers could be used in and on the model without permanent marking). No specific usage scenarios were defined for the scale model, other than its use as a presentation tool for the stakeholders at the start of the project.

The scale model was used over the span of seven months in a large scale research project that aims to improve and innovate the experience of the car showroom. We illustrate the evolution of the (uses of) the prototype by means of several usage scenarios that took place – mostly spontaneously – over the course of the project. We share our observations about the use of the prototype as a means of communication, as well as a means of inspiration and ideation. We reflect on our observations of the features of the scale model as they developed and conclude with arguments for the use of the spontaneous, non-prescriptive prototype as a design tool in complex, multi-stakeholder design projects.

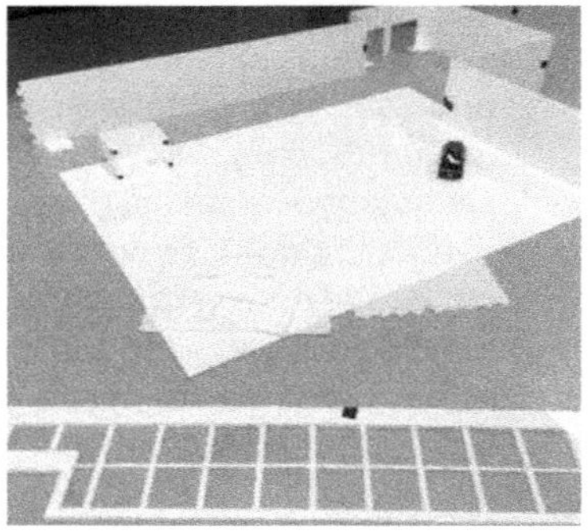

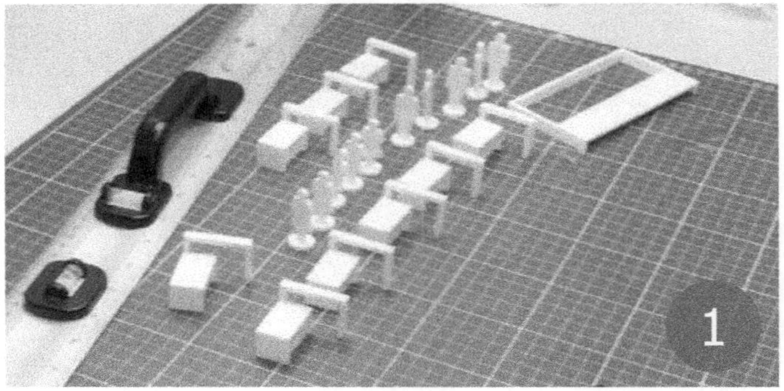

The Scale Model

The subject of this pictorial is a 1:43 scale model of an existing car showroom. The model – with the exception of the windows – is completely constructed out of 3mm thick white acrylic, which was lasercut to size. The interior of the scale model was filled with a combination of furniture ❶ (desks, office spaces) of the same material, and existing 1:42 scale models of cars. Small puppets ❶, to function as sales-people and customers, were also constructed.

The showroom model is accompanied by a light box ❷, placed below the acrylic floor plate of the model. The light in the box is created by a 16x16 grid of RGB LEDs ❸, and controlled by an Arduino.

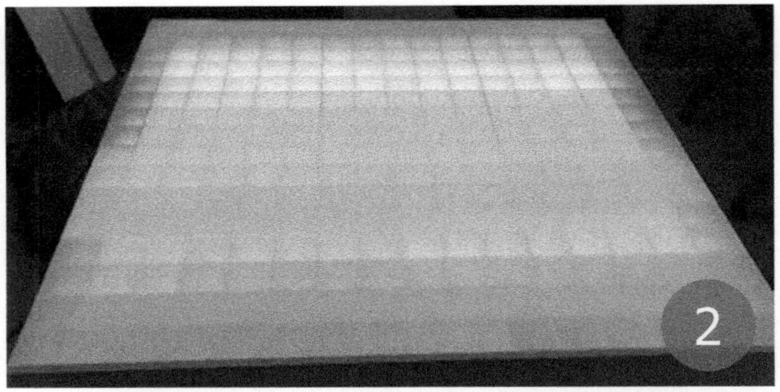

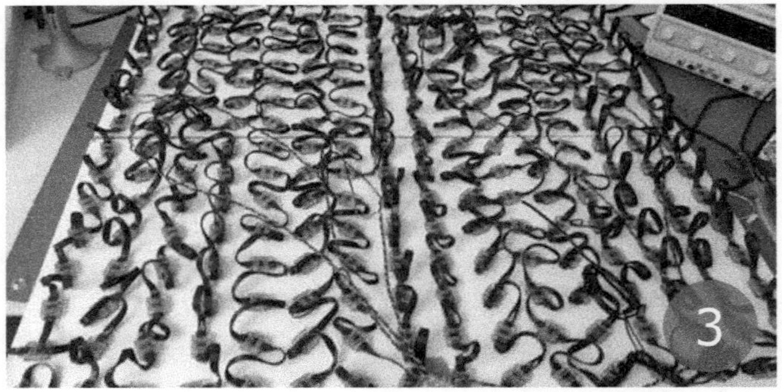

The model was constructed over the course of three days (with some preparation in advance, such as ordering the materials and preparing the CAD files for the lasercutter). Many of the design decisions made during the building process were made on a 'whim', so to say. The necessity of puppets in the showroom, the way the windows were sandwiched between the walls ❹, the design of the entrances and garage doors – the way the showroom model is shaped by these details was not necessarily planned beforehand. Spontaneously deciding on these factors fostered an atmosphere of creativity and improvisation towards the scale model and the research project that it supports.

Observation:

shaping the scale model after a familiar tool like a whiteboard,

created a **low threshold tool** for designers, researchers and stakeholders to **appropriate in their design processes**.

Features of the model

Using the scale model, we noticed that its use can be articulated in two categories. The scale model is an informant – it communicates project goals and design ideas to stakeholders and unwitting out-siders. The scale model is also an inspirer – it supports ideation and creativity among its (multi-disciplinary) users. Sometimes, the scale model functions as a combination between these two categories, both informing and inspiring its users. In the legend (top-right corner on each page), an indication of where each usage scenario of the miniature showroom took place in the scale model can be found.

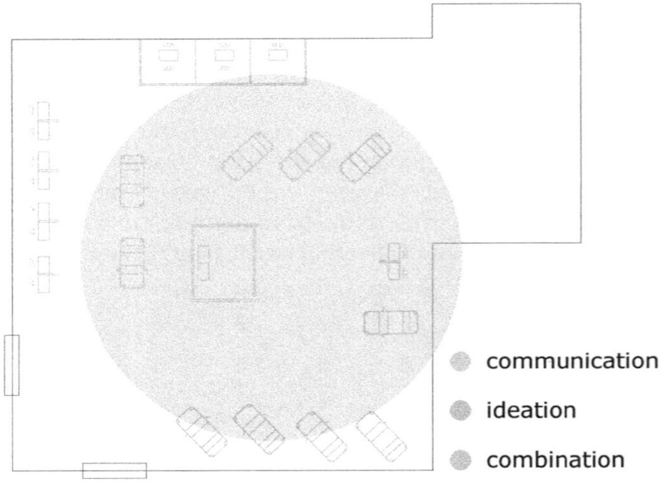

The scale model as a 3D whiteboard. One of the few features of the model defined beforehand, was the material out of which it was constructed. We opted for white acrylic glass for both practical and conceptual reasons. The material is easily cut to size by lasercutter and constructed by hand, but more importantly, one of the initial goals for the scale model was for it to function as a 3D whiteboard 1, allowing users to discuss and draw concepts and ideas right in the showroom, were the ideas would actually take shape in reality.

Observation:

the combination between **physical experimentation** and an **improvisational atmosphere** led to **new applications and features** of the scale model.

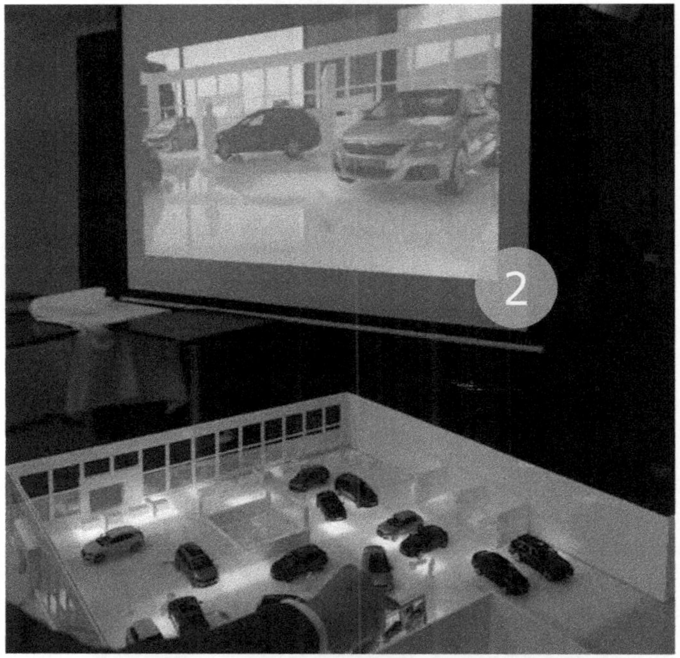

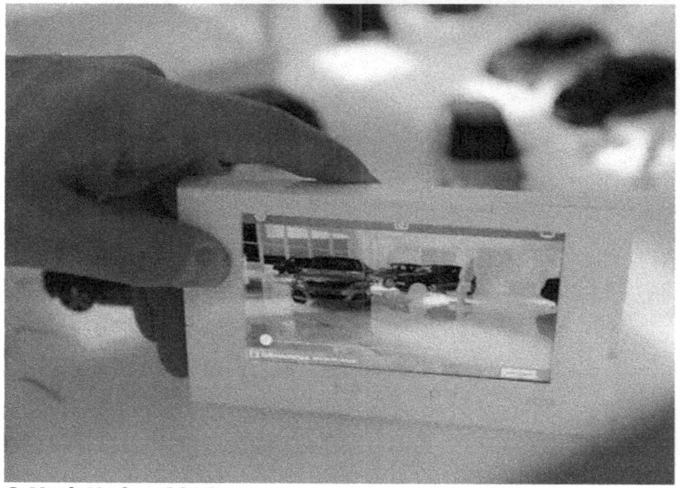

The scale model as a creative stimulus. The spontaneous nature of constructing the scale model left plenty of room for impromptu ideas about the features of the showroom model. Physically building and experimenting with the constraints of the miniature showroom, and documenting the process with a smartphone, led us to a new perspective on the showroom. From placing a phone as a massive 'tv screen' (1) in the model, we were inspired to create a live connection between the phone's camera and an external screen (2), allowing viewers and users an 'immersed' perspective in the showroom.

Observation:

a physical tool helps

the uninitiated and shy

to **share ideas and**

even criticism.

© Mark Hader, 2016

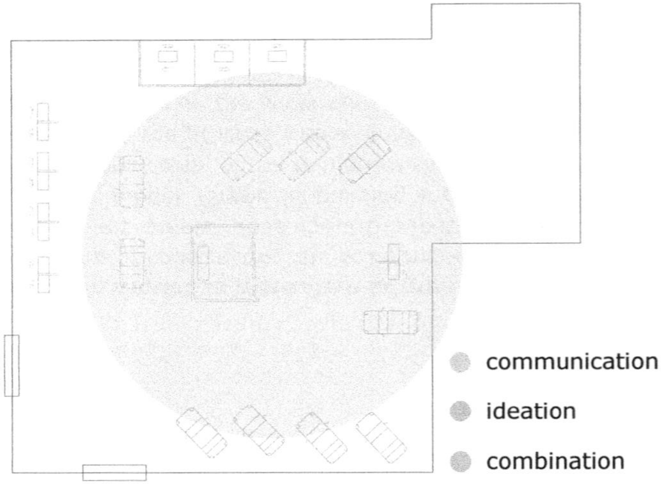

The scale model as a presentation tool. One envisioned feature of the scale model was its suitability to be used as a presentation tool at various events, at which partners and stakeholders would be present. As such, the scale model has proved invaluable. The *lightweight* [7] (i.e., low-commitment, accessible and straightforward) means of tangibly manipulating objects in a space enticed many non-designers to interact with the scale model, and, subsequently, offer feedback on the project and design problem.

Observation:

the scale model

provided a **perfect**

playground to

quickly build and

communicate

new ideas.

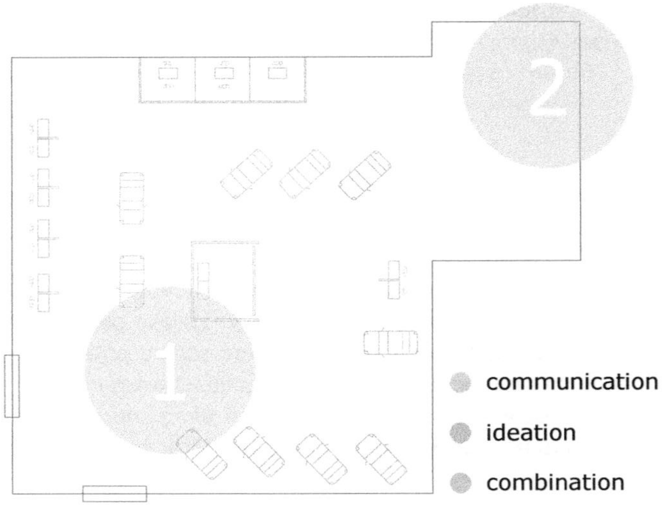

The scale model as a communicator of design concepts. The scale model itself also proved to be a good stage to create communicative materials to share with stakeholders and others involved in the process. Examples of this are two videos that were filmed in the miniature showroom. The first video was a stop motion video to introduce the scope of the project to partners ①. Shooting the video in an actual car showroom would have been a major logistic and financial hassle, which was avoided by using the scale model. The second video was a means to communicate several concepts to be executed within the project ②. Using the scale model, it was straightforward to visualize these concepts in a miniature scale with tangible solutions in the miniature showroom, as well as digital solutions in post-processing.

Observation:

during creative sessions, the scale model was used as a stage for **physical scaffolds** [8] that illustrate ideas, leaving **traces** [8] to discuss with other participants.

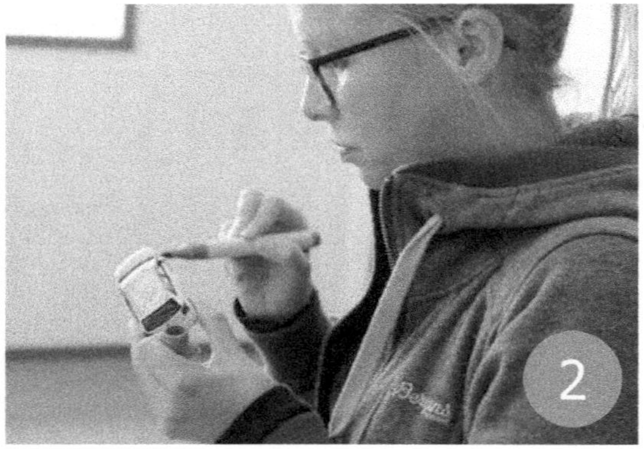

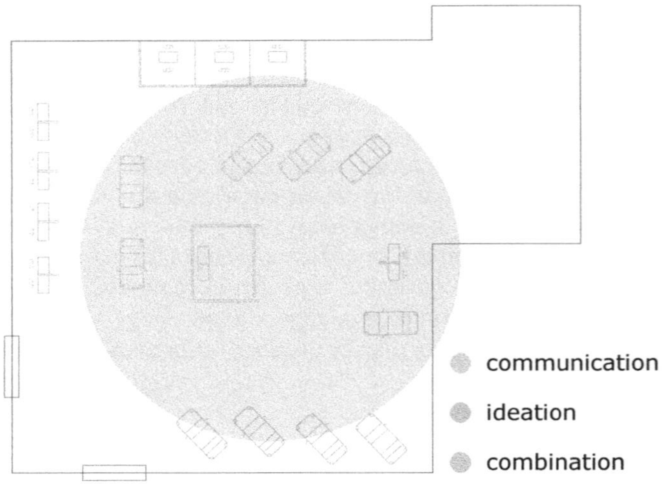

The model as a generative design tool. The miniature showroom has been used in several creative workshops, as well. In these scenarios, the scale model was complemented by the light box, on which a program was running that allowed users to easily 'draw with light' (1) on the floor of the showroom. The users could use software like Photoshop or Illustrator to use the floor of the scale model as a 16x16 pixel canvas, to draw shapes and lines to clarify their ideas, or highlight areas. The same program could also be used to cast other visual elements (colored backgrounds, videos, etc.) to the lightbox.

Additionally, tools like whiteboard markers, post-its, LEGO® and old magazines (2) were provided. During these sessions, multidisciplinary groups (including sociologists, computer scientists, communication scientists and designers) brainstormed about technological interventions and solutions in the showroom. The scale model was also used to communicate the results of the brainstorms with the rest of the team (3) (e.g., by acting out, constructing or drawing the solutions in the scale model).

Observation:
in the context of the scale model, prototyping became **a collaborative process** in which researchers from **many different backgrounds** could participate.

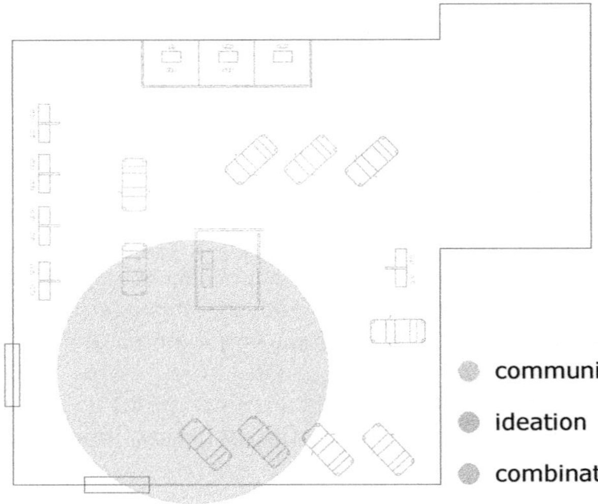

The model as a prototyping tool. The scale model of the showroom, a prototype in itself, also functioned as a tool for prototyping in the project. In the model, a video prototype [4] was filmed for one of the concepts of the project. This video prototype will be used to assess the context of customers visiting the showroom, with a focus on social norms. Shooting a stop-motion video in the scale model (a cost effective and efficient solution, as mentioned before), enabled the researchers to iterate on, and assess multiple variations of the video prototype (e.g., female character vs. male character) before deploying it to the target group for feedback and input.

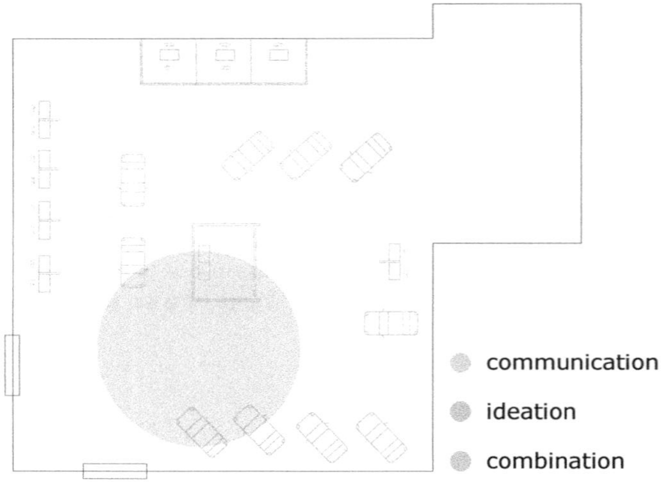

The model from a different perspective. Inspired by the image captured by the phone camera placed in the model, we further developed an augmented reality solution to create a fully immersive, first-person perspective on the model. For this, we placed a camera ① in the model, directly connected to a VR headset ② that allowed one user to view the scale model from the perspective of one of the puppets inside the showroom ③. This *first-person perspective* was then used in an ideation session about the customer journey in a car showroom. In this session, three people participated, of which one participant was immersed in the first-person perspective in the scale model via a VR headset. During the ideation session, we noticed an interesting shift in the creative roles of the participants in comparison to a 'normal' ideation session, as the wearer of the VR headset became more of an informant, rather than an active participant, during the creative session, while the other participants behaved as 'executers' or 'creators' of the informants' suggestions and ideas.

Reflection
We reflect on the use of the scale model as a design tool in the context of collaborative interactions in spatial environments, were the physical and digital meet. We extrapolate our observations on communicative and creative use of the scale model to this context when applicable.

Communication
The scale model proved to be a catalyst of conversation on many occasions, engaging business men and children alike. The strength of this feature of the scale model, we argue, lies in the physical properties of the showroom, and the terminology connected to it. We have always called the scale model a 3D whiteboard, emphasizing on properties of the 2D whiteboard that everyone is familiar with: you can freely write, and wipe away again. This invited people to be creative with the markers provided, but also enticed them to consider the 3D properties of the scale model in a more inventive way, especially when additional familiar tools, like clay or LEGO® were provided. The input from many people, with many different backgrounds, has been invaluable throughout the process. *Tools for collaborative, interactive efforts should invite adventurous, creative interaction in both their physical form and the terminology connected to them.*

Ideation
Creating a design tool that allowed people to build their ideas directly in a representation of the space the ideas were meant for, led to realistic and decisive conversations. The non-rigid (and often non-existent) rules about how to use the scale model, encouraged the users to appropriate the tool to their use. The traces [9] of creative sessions were often not immediately removed after using the scale model. They therefore unintentionally informed the next users about the creative and spontaneous ways to use the tool, and inspired them by what was done before.

Tools for collaborative, interactive efforts should not ask users to adhere to (m)any rules, but instead be designed to attract new ways of use.

Combination of Communication & Ideation
The scale model often functioned at its best as a design tool when it toed the line between being an inspirer and an informant. The concepts, prototypes, videos and other outputs created with the scale model were easily communicated to anyone involved in the project, due to the aesthetic coherence between all of these outputs. As everyone involved in the project was familiar with the scale model and its physical properties, a basic referential 'design language' was established for communication about the different facets of the project. *Applying a specific tool for design consistently throughout a project may improve coherence and mutual understanding in multi-disciplinary design teams.*

Conclusion
Over the course of seven months, the scale model – initially constructed as a representational prototype – evolved into a physical playground for researchers, designers and stakeholders in the project to appropriate and deploy at will in the process of designing collaborative interactions in a spatial environment.

As stated in the introduction, the properties of design tools change through use. The tools we build during our design processes continuously influence *how* we use them – sometimes in ways that are planned, but often in ways that are unplanned. Reflecting on the evolution of this particular design tool, we argue that its growth was in fact stimulated by the fact that the tool did not prescribe any 'fixed' use scenarios: users were free to appropriate the tool to fit their needs, and, for that reason, may have been more likely to use the design tool to support their processes.

Additionally, technological additions that intended to combine the digital with the physical, e.g., the integration of the first-person perspective, quite literally forced users of the tool to take a different perspective on the showroom and its environment. It influenced the way people worked together: a clear divide appeared between the 'first-person user' as an informant, and the other users as executers of the first-person user's ideas.

An inverse of this effect was noticed when the drawing program was introduced on the light box during ideation sessions: the user executing the drawing of shapes, lines and highlights on the lightbox was instructed by the other users standing around the scale model. These technological interventions thus caused an artificial shift in the roles users took on in creative sessions, by limiting some freedoms of the users, while also creating new ones. The shift in roles and perspectives can stimulate users to take a fresh look at both the challenge before them, as well as the people with whom they are working to solve it.

We argue that the construction of impromptu prototypes as non-prescriptive, generative design tools is good practice for multi-stakeholder projects, both in the realm of architectural, spatial projects; and in the general fields of HCI and Design.

In this project, the advantages of the representational, architectural mock-up, the well-known whiteboard and additional creative tools came together, supported by practical technological interventions. The presented design tool is incomplete and still evolves.

We will continue to use the scale model as a generative design tool in many different scenarios throughout this project, and study the relation between the evolution of the project and the evolution of the tool. Particularly, we will focus on the technical development of the virtual first person perspective by increasing the quality of integration - i.e., higher resolution imagery, greater field of view, lower latency.

Additionally, we intend to provide more autonomy to the wearers of the VR headset, by giving them tools to manoeuvre themselves through the scale model without the help of others. We will evaluate the influence of these improvements on both the creative process, as well as the described artificial roles of executive and informant in the creative process.

Acknowledgements

We gratefully acknowledge the support by the Automotive Retail Lab (hci.sbg.ac.at/ARL).

References

1. Eva Brandt. 2007. How tangible mock-ups support design collaboration. *Knowledge, Technology & Policy* 20, 3: 179–192.
2. Tim Brown and Jocelyn Wyatt. 2010. Design Thinking for Social Innovation. *Stanford Social Innovation Review 8*. Retrieved January 12, 2017 from https://gwht.pratt.duke.edu/sites/gwht.pratt.duke.edu/files/u7/Design%20Thinking%20for%20Social%20Innovation%20copy.pdf
3. Marion Buchenau and Jane Fulton Suri. 2000. Experience prototyping. In *Proceedings of the 3rd con-ference on Designing interactive systems: processes, practices, methods, and techniques*, 424–433. Re-trieved January 4, 2017. DOI: 10.1145/347642.347802
4. Beant Dhillon, Peter Banach, Rafal Kocielnik, Jorge Peregrín Emparanza, Ioannis Politis, A. Pączewska, and Panos Markopoulos. 2011. Visual fidelity of video prototypes and user feedback: a case study. In *Proceedings of the 25th BCS Conference on Human-*

Computer Interaction, 139–144.
5. Yvonne Dittrich, Sara Eriksén, and Christina Hansson. 2002. PD in the Wild; Evolving practices of Design in Use. In *PDC 02 Proceedings of the Participatory Design Conference.*
6. Clint Heyer and Margot Brereton. 2010. Design from the Everyday: Continuously evolving, embedded exploratory prototypes. In P*roceedings of the 8th ACM Conference on Designing Interactive Systems:* August 16-20, 2010, Aarhus, Denmark. DOI: 10.1145/1858171
7. Eva Hornecker and Jacob Buur. 2006. Getting a grip on tangible interaction: a framework on physical space and social interaction. In *Proceedings of the SIGCHI conference on Human Factors in computing systems,* 437–446. DOI: 10.1145/1124772.1124838
8. Caroline Hummels and Jelle van Dijk. 2015. Seven Principles to Design for Embodied Sensemaking. In *Proceedings of the Ninth International Conference on Tangible, Embedded, and Embodied Interaction* 21–28. DOI: 10.1145/2677199.2680577
9. Alison James. 2013. Lego Serious Play: a three-dimensional approach to learning development. *Journal of Learning Development in Higher Education.*
10. Andrea Mina. 2009. intimate immensity, an interior architecture. Retrieved August 30, 2016 from http://researchbank.rmit.edu.au/view/rmit:6161
11. Mark Morris. 2006. *Models: Architecture and the Miniature.* Academy Press.
12. Elizabeth B-N. Sanders. 2000. Generative tools for co-designing. In *Collaborative design.* Springer, 3–12. DOI: 10.1007/978-1-4471-0779-8_1
13. Elizabeth B-N. Sanders and Pieter Jan Stappers. 2014. Probes, toolkits and prototypes: three approaches to making in codesigning. *CoDesign* 10, 1: 5–14. DOI: 10.1080/15710882.2014.888183
14. Elizabeth B-N. Sanders and Colin T. William. 2003. Harnessing people's creativity: Ideation and ex-pression through visual communication. *Focus groups: Supporting effective product development:* 137.
15. Albert C. Smith. 2004. *Architectural model as machine: a new view of models from antiquity to the present day.* Architectural Press, Oxford.
16. David D. Woods. 1998. Designs are Hypotheses about How Artifacts Shape Cognition and Collaboration. *Ergonomics* 41: 168–173.

Cairn: A Tangible Apparatus for Situated Data Collection, Visualization and Analysis

Pauline Gourlet
Paragraphe - C3U, Université Paris 8
& EnsadLab, Paris
pauline.gourlet@gmail.com

Thierry Dassé
Universcience, Cité des sciences
et de l'industrie, Paris
thierry.dasse@universcience.fr

DIS 2017, June 10-14, 2017, Edinburgh, United Kingdom

ACM 978-1-4503-4922-2/17/06 $15.00
DOI: http://dx.doi.org/10.1145/3064663.3064794

Abstract
In this pictorial, we present the design process and the functioning of *Cairn*: a tangible apparatus that enables data collection, visualization and analysis. Designed within a community of practice of a French FabLab, *Cairn* aims at understanding the variety of practices within FabLabs. *Cairn* explores tangible alternatives to questionnaires and other traditional evaluation techniques, and stressed the aesthetic and affective dimensions to create an engaging experience. It invites Fablab visitors to reflect on their practices by materializing their activities using small colored wooden-tiles. Interacting individually with *Cairn*, people contribute to create a collaborative and meaningful sculpture, upon which they can reflect collectively. We discuss the opportunities that this prototype opens for future situated HCI research.

Authors Keywords
Dataphysicalization; Data Collection; Communities of practice; Situated Analysis; Reflective Design

ACM Classification Keywords
H.5.m.

CAIRN, closeup.

CAIRN, in the FabLab, day 8. (Carrefour Numérique^2-Paris)

CAIRN, [kairn], noun.

A cairn is a human-made pile (or stack) of stones. It comes from the Scottish Gaelic: càrn (plural càirn). They have been used for variety of purposes, from prehistoric times to the present. In modern times, cairns are often erected as landmarks.

source Wikipedia

INTRODUCTION Conducting a research through design on FabLab practices—focusing on sharing and documentation processes within maker environments—, we worked within a Parisian FabLab for three months. Together with the FabLab managers and some regular makers, we addressed the assumptions we had on makers' practices and specifically, on people that were visiting this particular FabLab. Located inside a famous Parisian museum, this FabLab is a crossroad where a large and diverse audience passes by. The tools used by the FabLab managers to understand and assess the FabLab use are traditional surveys. Unsatisfied with these evaluation tools, we looked for ways to 1) create an apparatus that would not be completed only by frequent FabLab regular members, 2) find ways to engage people in answering it and design an experience, and 3) create a collective inquiry about the meaning of the collected data.

In this first version, the apparatus took the shape of a table, which looks like a big board game with a myriad of colored wood-tokens displayed on the tabletop. After a brief overview of our inspiration sources, we present the design principles of Cairn and detail our participatory design process.

INSPIRATIONS To design Cairn, we were inspired by many different sources, from ancient traditions to construction systems with a focus on their aesthetic properties such as touch, shape and color. We also looked at some visualization and physicalization projects and articles [e.g. 9, 10].

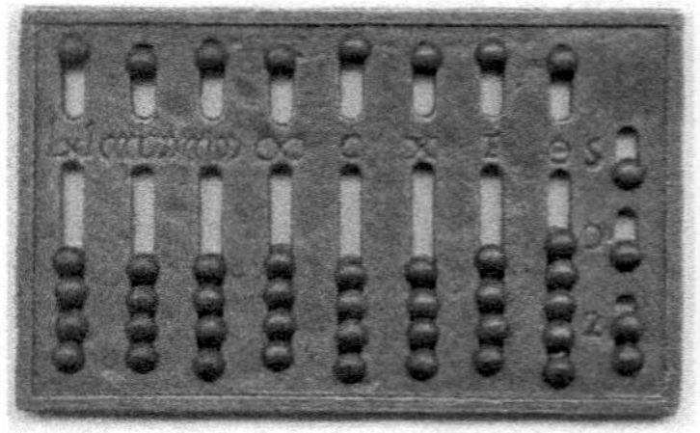

Abacus

Cairn

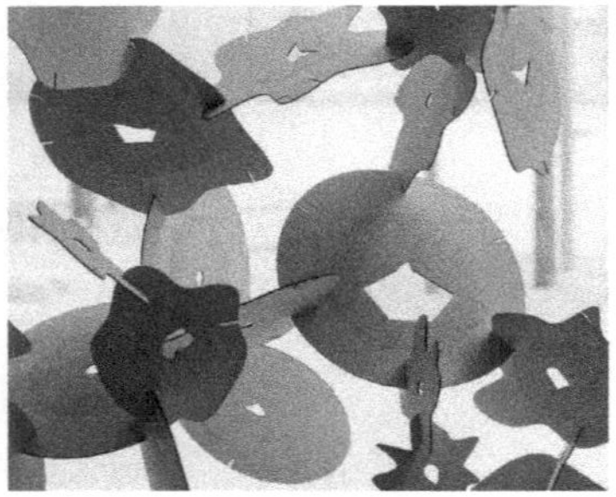

Que la force soit avec toi
Nolwenn Maudet, Thomas Thibault, Arthur Richard and Langevinium (ESPCI). [1]

Magnetic Bisymmetric Hendecahedrons
Walter Hsiao [2]

Table Ronde (1949)
Jean Prouvé

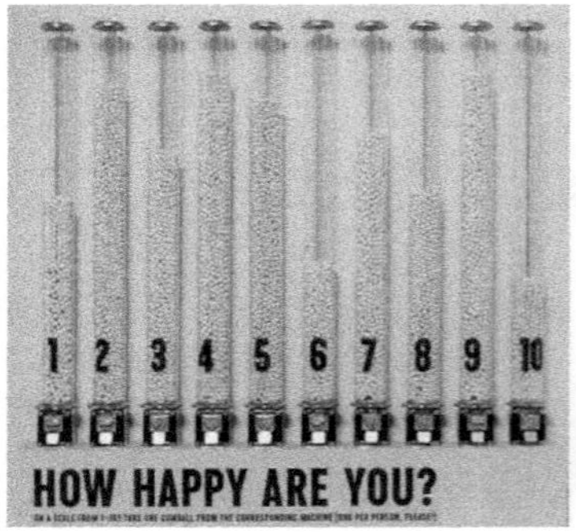

The Happy Show (2012)
Stefan Sagmeister [4]

MoMa Poll (1970)
Hans Haacke [5]

Bit Planner (2012)
Vitamins [6]

VoxBox (2015)
Golsteijn, et al. [7]

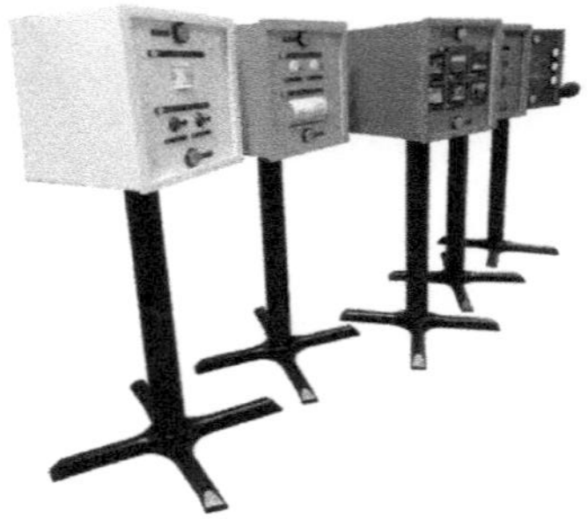

SmallTalk (2016)
Gallacher, et al. [8]

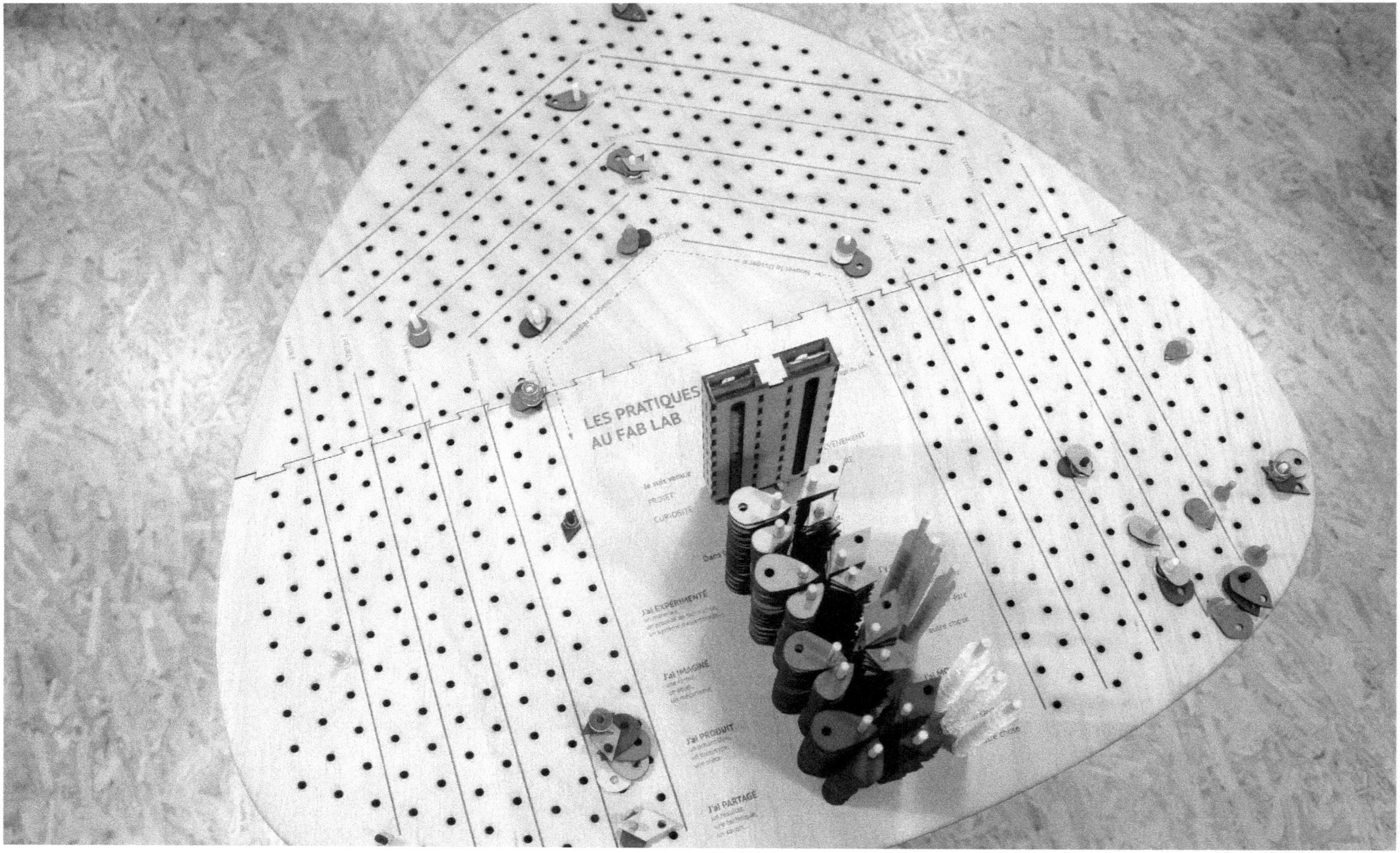

CAIRN, top view, day 1.

WHAT IS IT? A tangible apparatus that enables situated data collection, visualization and analysis.

COMPONENTS

◇ a table with a table-top regularly drilled
◇ colorful tokens of different shapes and sizes
◇ wood-pins

CAIRN, close up.

HOW DOES IT WORK?

Data Collection | Data Visualization | Data Analysis

DESIGN PROCESS Description of the collaborative process of enquiry to define the design principles and the physical properties of Cairn.

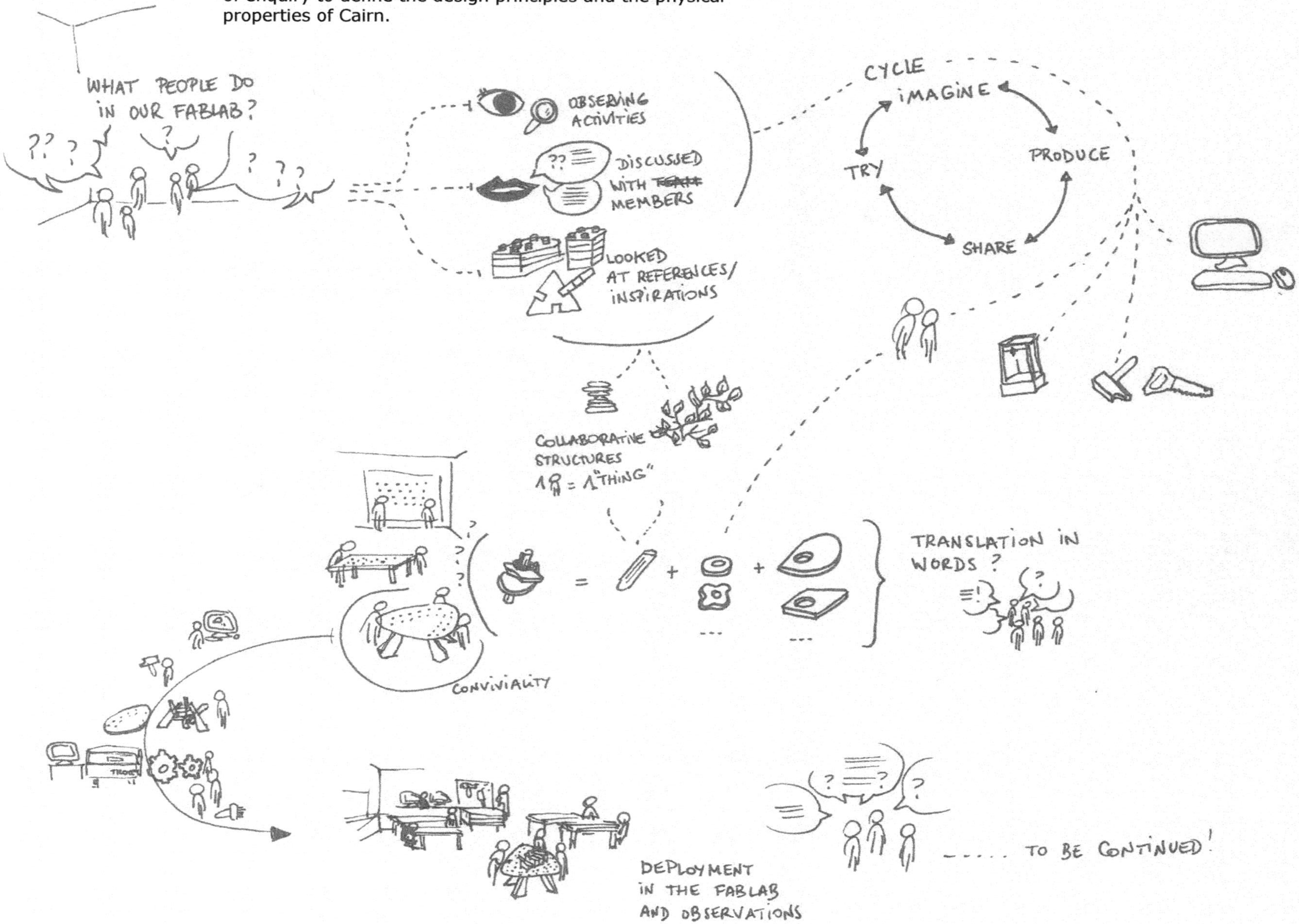

CAIRN, diagram of the design process.

FABRICATION PROCESS The fabrication takes from 3 to 4 days for a person alone. All the files are accessible and open-source *(CC license — http://carrefour-numerique.cite-sciences.fr/fablab/wiki/doku.php?id=projets:table_t35)*

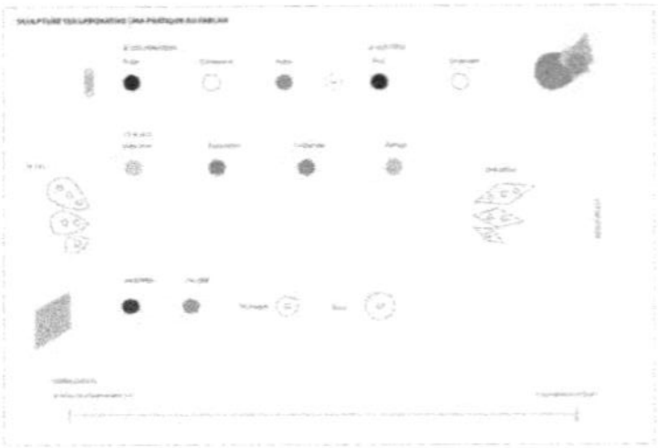

Preliminary drawings, used to discuss between the FabLab members.

First tokens, testing color tones.

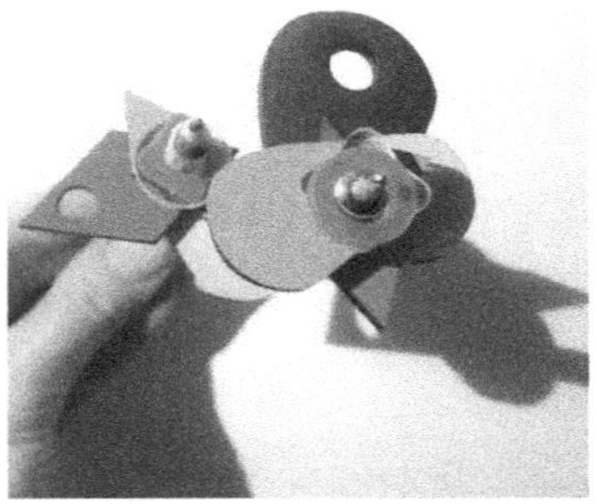

First assemblies, testing constructions principles.

Modeling the structure of the table.

Producing all the tokens (laser-cutting).

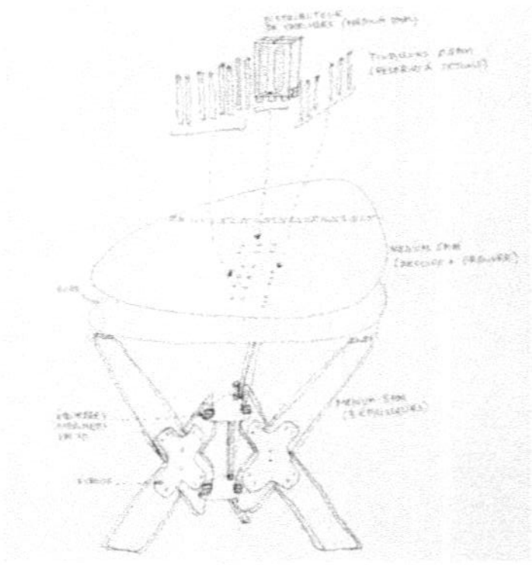

The complete assembly manual.

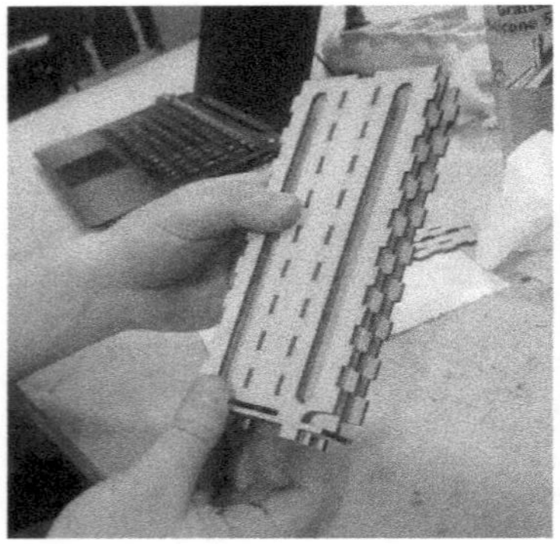

Assembling the wood-pins distributor.

Assembling the table together (structure and table-top).

Mounting all the tokens on bars.

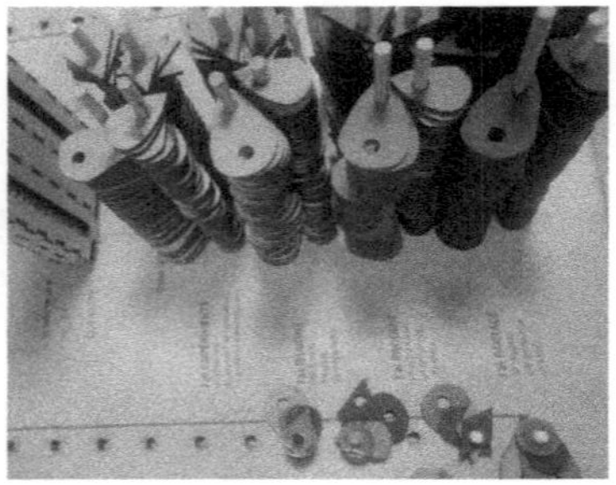

Final assembly of all bars and wood-pin distributors on the table top.

THE VARIABLES After several back-and-forth with different fablab members (see process diagram), we ended up with an encoding system engraved on the table top.

The position of each "little cairn" on the table encodes time and visit frequency values. Wood pins & tokens encode visit's motives, activities and learning practices.

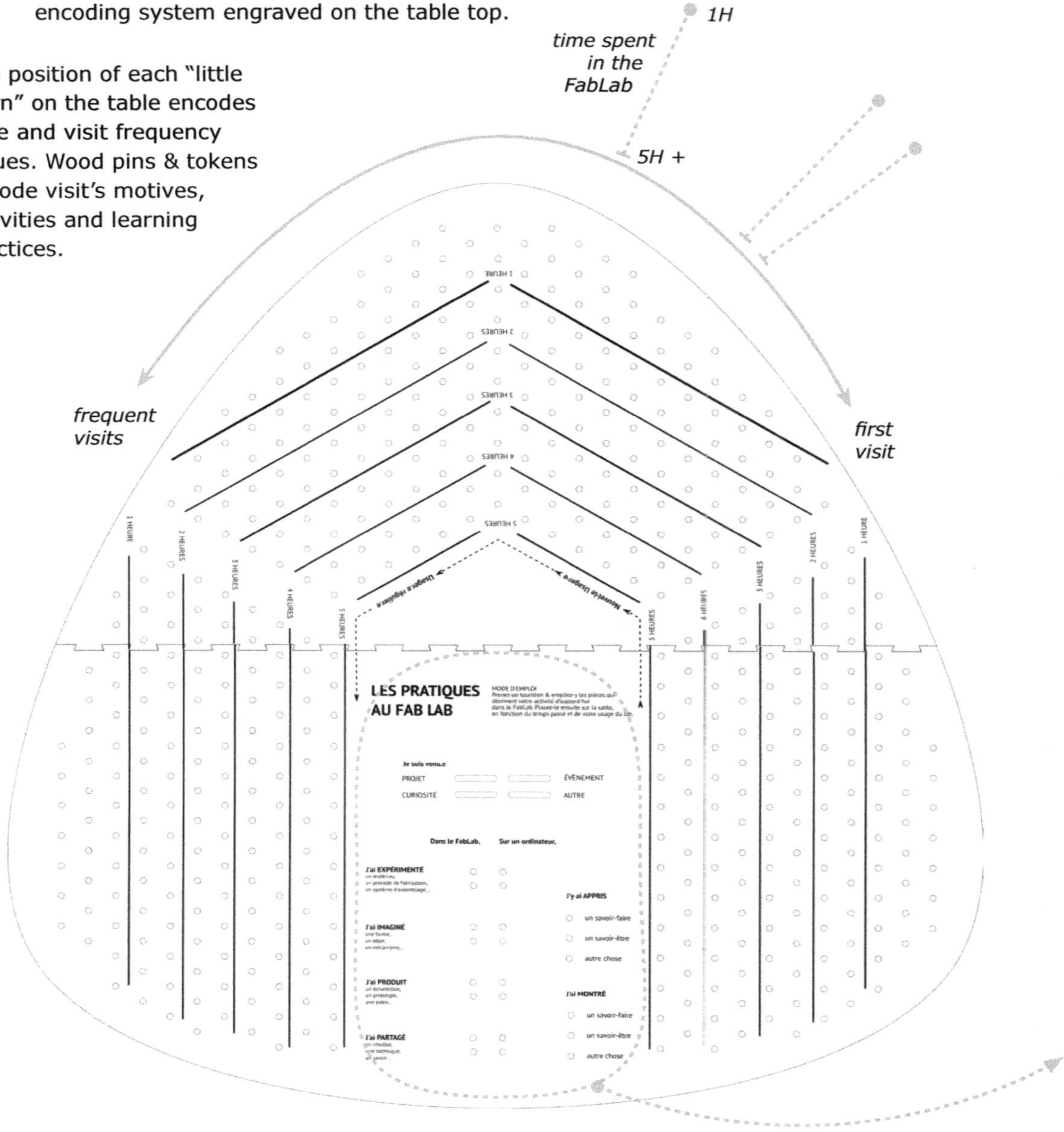

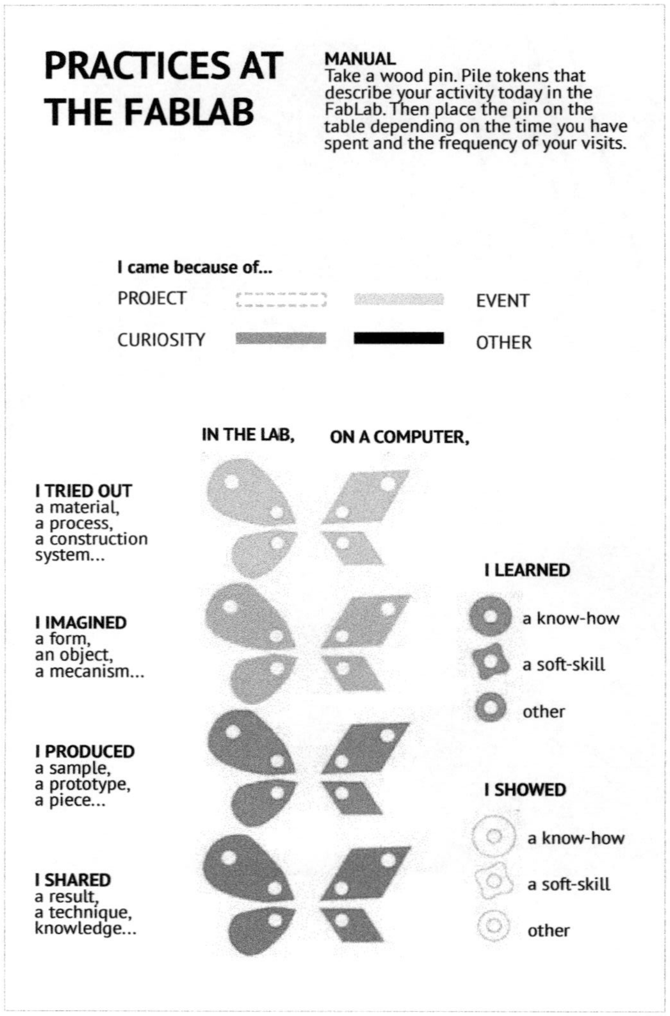

CAIRN, table top (Inkscape file), and details of the code (english translation / by authors).

EXPERIENTIAL OUTCOMES According to the people who used *Cairn*, the experience differs from answering an oral or written survey. Here are some dimensions people noticed as valuable while interacting with Cairn:

- ◇ **PRACTICING** A CODE
  Making an artifact that encodes meaning as a trigger to think.
- ◇ THE **AESTHETIC** DIMENSION
  The colors and the general appearance of the apparatus is appealing.
- ◇ THE **PLAYFUL** DIMENSION
  The display is reminiscent of board games and makes people want to play with it.
- ◇ THE **COLLECTIVE EFFECT**
  Being able to situate oneself in many.
- ◇ A MEANINGFUL **REFLECTION**
  The act of replaying and qualifying all steps of one's activity as a true reflective experience.
- ◇ NEW **COLLECTIVE REFLECTIONS**
  Discussing what "we are" as a community in front of a landscape that describes our practices and with an experienced, thus, negotiable code.

CAIRN, in use.

VISUAL OUTCOMES After a first experimentation that lasted 10 days, we present here the main visual cues that were discussed between participants. (NB, this is not an analysis of our results).

1 *INVERTED BAR CHARTS*
The amount of tokens left on each bar let us see the aggregate proportion of activities being conducted in the FabLab by all participants.

2 *INDIVIDUAL CAIRN*
This person is a regular member of the FabLab and this time, he came for a project and stayed 2hours. He mainly produced using the tools something and he also shared with other makers and tried out something new on his computer. During his time in the Lab, he has learned a new skill.

3 *CLUSTERS*
We identify clusters. For example, regular members spend more than 5hours in the FabLab when they come and do a lot of different activities each time.

4 *OUTLIERS*
We notice some outliers, such as this person you is a regular member and came only for an hour to experiment something.

LIMITS One of the main limits of our design is the large number of variables and their display. People sometimes encoutered difficulties reading/seeing the code. This deserves consideration for later improvement. Another limit concerns the reliability of the collected data. One cannot take for granted statistical results derived from its use, mainly due to token displacements. This was not our goal, but this can be problematic for someone aiming statistical reliability.

CAIRN, in the busyness of the FabLab.

CONCLUSION We described the design process and design principles of an apparatus, aiming at exploring individual and collective reflective potentials through data collection, visualization and analysis. We discussed the experiential and visual outcomes of our apparatus vis-à-vis this goal. These insights on people's experiences both while interacting and while discussing the results together are worth some more in-depth examinations. One aspect we particularly found fascinating was the potential of this apparatus to trigger discussions within the FabLab, among people from diverse backgrounds. These discussions concern both people's introspective experience when interacting with Cairn, and broader questions about the FabLab community. The verbal code that was proposed to categorize and qualify people's activities was subject to negotiations and redefinitions (e.g., what is learning? Can I say that talking to you is sharing in a FabLab context?, What is a soft-skill?, etc.). Displayed in the FabLab for five months, we observed the development of unexpected uses (a tool to present the FabLab, a discussion spot, an incentive for newcomers, etc.) We plan to conduct finer analyses on these outcomes. We also will also propose Cairn to other FabLabs for comparative enquiries. We also gained insights on its use as a methological tool to conduct qualitative interviews as an experience sample tool after an activity, as it supports externallization and verbalization. We believe this work opens a great research agenda for pluridisciplinary work, as it is at the crossroad of visualization, HCI, design, psychology and social sciences.

Acknowledgements

We thank the staff from the Carrefour Numérique[2] for creating the opportunity for this experience. We thank Bumblebee for letting us use some of his beautiful pictures. We also thank all the FabLab community for giving us feedback on this project.

References

1. Retrieved from http://www.nolwennmaudet.com/quelaforcesoitavectoi.php
2. Retrieved from http://www.thingiverse.com/thing:784951
3. Retrieved from http://www.minieco.co.uk/i-mathematics-platonic-solids-garland/
4. Retrieved from http://sagmeisterwalsh.com/work/all/the-happy-show/
5. Retrieved from http://dataphys.org/list/moma-poll-haackes-participatory-bar-chart/
6. Retrieved from http://www.bit-planner.com/
7. Golsteijn, C., Gallacher, S., Koeman, L., Wall, L., Andberg, S., Rogers, Y. Capra, L., 2015. VoxBox: A Tangible Machine that gathers Opinions from the Public at Events. *Proceedings of the ACM Conference TEI 2015*. Stanford, USA.
8. Gallacher, S., Rogers, Y. Capra, L., Eustace, S., Golsteijn, C., 2016. SmallTalk: Using Tangible Interactions to Gather Feedback from Children. *Proceedings of the ACM Conference TEI 2016*. Eindhoven, Netherlands.
9. Bertin, J. 1967. La sémiologie graphique. Paris, Mouton/Gauthier-Villars.
10. Wesley Willett, Yvonne Jansen, Pierre Dragicevic. Embedded Data Representations. IEEE Transactions on Visualization and Computer Graphics, Institute of Electrical and Electronics Engineers, 2017, pp.461 - 470.

[X]Changing Perspectives: An Interactive System for Participatory Sensemaking

Philémonne Jaasma
Eindhoven University of Technology
LaPlace 32, 5612 AP Eindhoven,
The Netherlands
p.g.jaasma@tue.nl

Evert Wolters
Necker van Naem
evert@necker.nl

Joep Frens
Eindhoven University of Technology
LaPlace 32, 5612 AP Eindhoven,
The Netherlands
j.w.f.frens@tue.nl

Caroline Hummels
Eindhoven University of Technology
LaPlace 32, 5612 AP Eindhoven,
The Netherlands
c.c.m.hummels@tue.nl

Ambra Trotto
RI.SE Interactive & Umeå School of Architecture
Östra Strandgatan 32
SE-903 33 Umeå, Sweden
ambra.trotto@ri.se

DIS 2017, June 10-14, 2017, Edinburgh, United Kingdom
 ISBN 978-1-4503-4922-2/17/06...$15.00
DOI: http://dx.doi.org/10.1145/3064663.3064796

Abstract
Public issues are complex: they concern many different stakeholders who have conflicting stakes and are involved from their unique perspective. Working on public issues requires an open process that allows stakeholders to not only contribute to decision-making but also to take up a role in the process. We propose [X]Changing Perspectives, a product service system that stimulates participatory sensemaking: the joint construction of meaning between individuals that could not have been reached on their own.
We visually demonstrate the designed materials and service elements and discuss the promise of our approach to [X]CP for complex design challenges in public issues.

Authors Keywords
Multi-stakeholder collaboration; Product Service System; Participatory Sensemaking; Embodied Sensemaking.

ACM Classification Keywords
H.5.m. Information interfaces and presentation; H.5.3. Group and Organization Interfaces.

Introduction
Societies are faced with complex issues, from the refugee crisis, to the availability and the cost of urban housing, to youth unemployment or affordable health care. These are public issues that are characterised by different stakeholders with conflicting perspectives. Recently, Norman et al. [6] observed that designers are increasingly working on complex socio-technical issues

that they call 'DesignX problems'. Public issues present examples of DesignX problems because as they are characterised by 'Multiple Disciplines and Perspectives' and 'mutual incompatible constraints' [6, p.86].

Focusing on innovation, Buur and Larssen [1] argue that innovation emerges from interactions between people with different stakes as their 'crossing intentions' can create new insight and new ways of thinking and doing. They call for designers to develop "new formats of collaboration for large, complex contingents of stakeholders" [1, p.12] beyond common workshops and for design-facilitators to address the role of conflict and crossing intentions.

Norman et al., [6] emphasise that implementation is often the biggest challenge in socio-technical issues (DesignX problems). In local governance, multi-stakeholders like municipalities, entrepreneurs, citizens, companies and organisations work together on local solutions for complex public issues. Such collaborations require open processes that shed light on different perspectives and open forms of participation that allow all different stakeholders to take a role in the process.

Within this context, we take on the challenge of designing for constructive interactions in multi-stakeholders dynamics around public issues. More specifically, we aim to design for participatory sensemaking: the collaborative generation of meaning in and by interactions between multiple agents in a social encounter [4]. Participatory sensemaking finds its roots in enaction, the principle that sees cognition as a continuous, active process of perception and action to make meaning in the world [7]. It emphasises that cognition is embodied and not a separate computation in the head, and participatory sensemaking adds to that that people can make meaning together.

In this pictorial we introduce [X]Changing Perspectives ([X]CP): a product service system (PSS) that invites participatory sensemaking between multi-disciplinary stakeholders in a participation setting around public issues.

We start with a graphical outline of the design space in terms of theoretical lenses and practical contexts. We continue with a visual overview of the [X]CP system and its technological and material specifications. Then we elaborate on the service elements of the PSS. This is followed by a photographic scenario of the PSS in use and observations of interactions in screenshots from video recordings of real-life sessions. Finally we discuss the value of our proposal of [X]CP for complex design challenges in public issues.

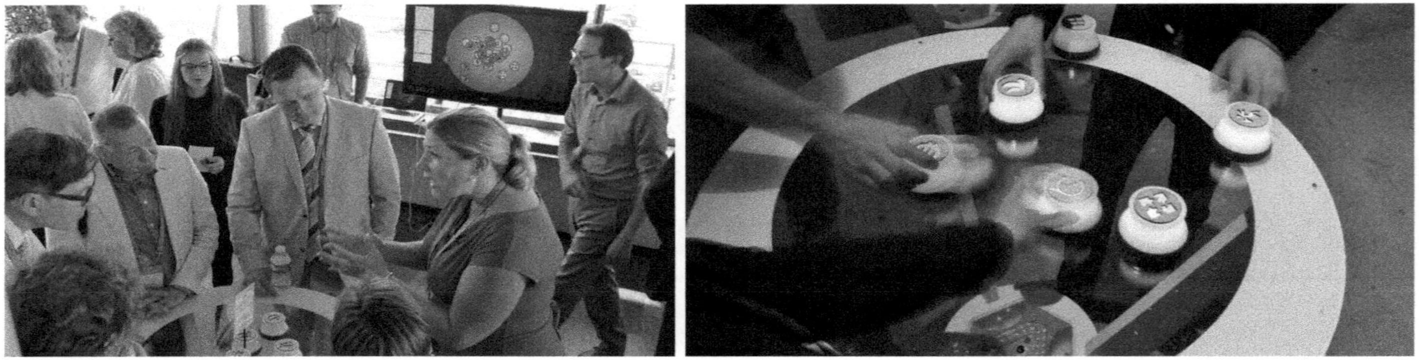

[X]Changing Perspectives in use (left) in a multi-stakeholder discussion and demonstrated at a congress (right).

DESIGN SPACE

In the foregoing we have introduced the design challenge. In this section we sketch out the theoretical and practical design space and position our design intervention in it.

CONTEXT: SYSTEM & LIFEWORLD

In the context of multi- stakeholder collaborations around public issues, this work focuses on interactions between local governance and citizens. Recognising their differences, Habermas [3] described a dichotomy of System and Lifeworld, respectively: guided by rules and regulations (*instrumental rationality*) and the messiness of interrelations in everyday life (*communicative rationality*). These two paradigms meet when public issues need to be discussed, in the Public Sphere. This is a zone where a *critical-rational* debate can take place.

It must be noted that in our work we value Habermas' theory as a contextual framework. We move away from his emphasis on rationality and instead take an embodied approach to sensemaking.

EXPERIMENTAL SPACE

Our design intervention is implemented in the Public Spere.

We designed [X]Changing Perspectives, an interactive system that invites participatory sensemaking [4] between different stakeholders. Participants move and relate tokens on the table, in order to discuss the central question, at the centre of the table, that introduces the public issue at hand.

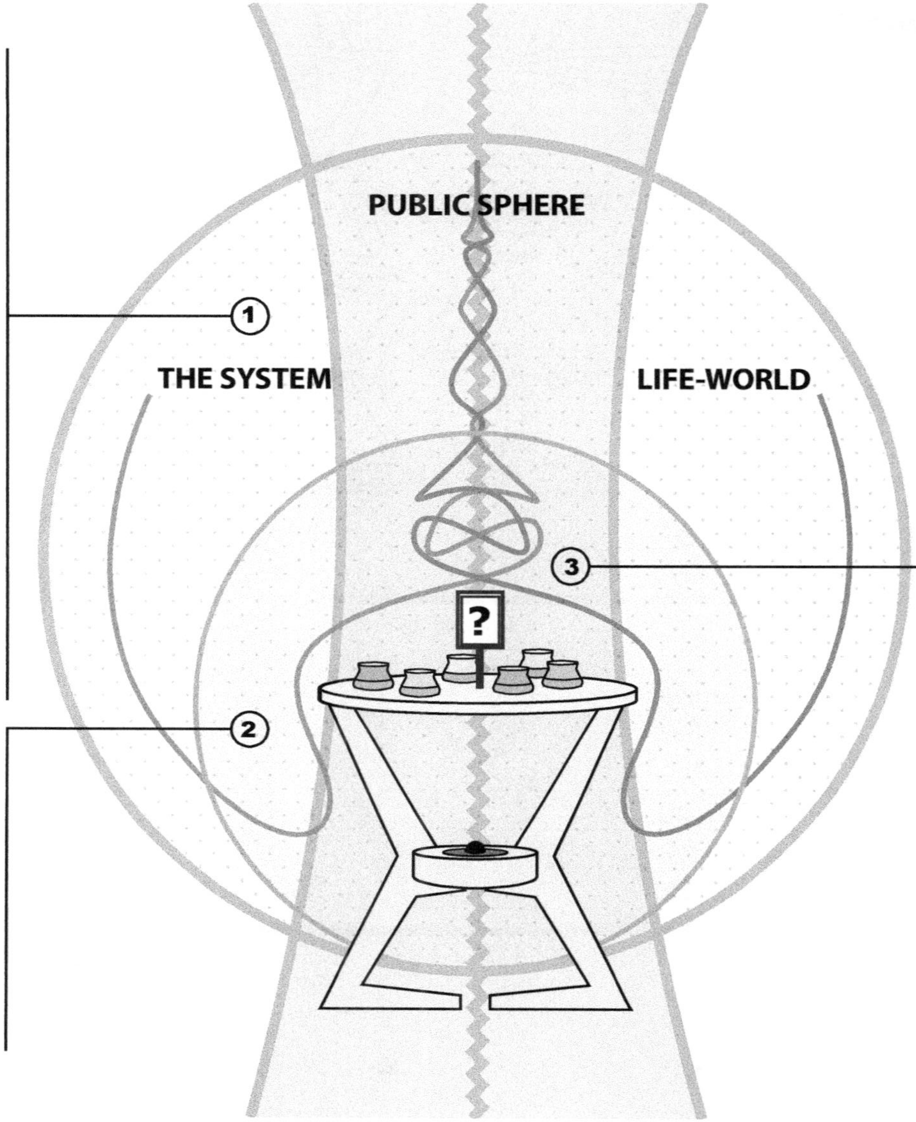

MULTI-STAKEHOLDER INTERACTIONS

Stakeholders interact with the tokens and with each other around the table, creating an intimate setting for personal exchange.

Their discussions gain physical shape through the tokens. The tokens act as phsyical scaffolds [2] that enrich the discussion, as they invite people to interact with them- and thus play into the cognitive loop of action and perception through which meaning is generated [7]. The design of [X]CP speaks to the bodily senses of people and enables them to talk through materials.

We explain the designed materials in detail in the next session.

Moreover, the [X]CP system allows for scaling up from an intimate setting of interpersonal thought exchange to the mass expected to reach a democratic decision.

SYSTEM

In the foregoing we sketched the design space. In this section we explain the designed system: [X]Changing Perspectives.

SETTING: [X]CP SYSTEM IN USE

The [X]CP system consists of 15 tables each with 6 tokens and one real-time online visualisation of the token movements.
Participants are distributed over the tables so that all different perspectives are represented at each table. Six to eight participants group around a table. In total, the system enables 90 - 120 participants to discuss a public issue simultaneously.

SCALING UP: REAL-TIME DATA VISUALISATION

The movements of all tokens are visualised in real-time and projected on a screen.
The moderator of the session can use filters (select specific tables or tokens) to find patterns in the movements. For example, the visualisation could show a clutter of yellow lines, indicating that the Puzzle icon (yellow token) has been moved around a lot on most tables.
During an intermezzo, the moderator uses these patterns to collect stories from different tables and opens up a dialogue acrosss the tables.

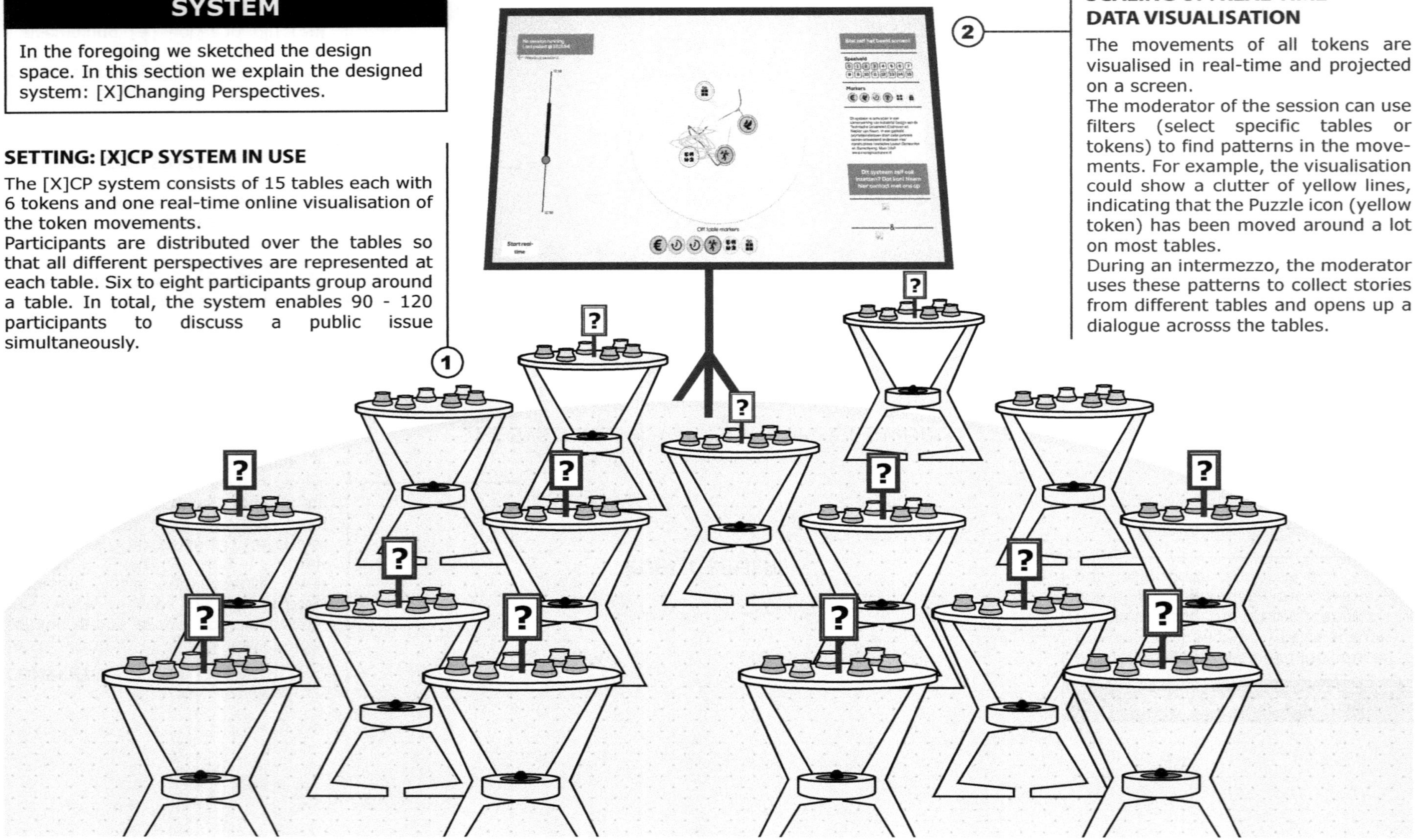

SPECIFICATIONS

In the foregoing we introduced the [X]CP system and in this section we explain its technological and material specifications.

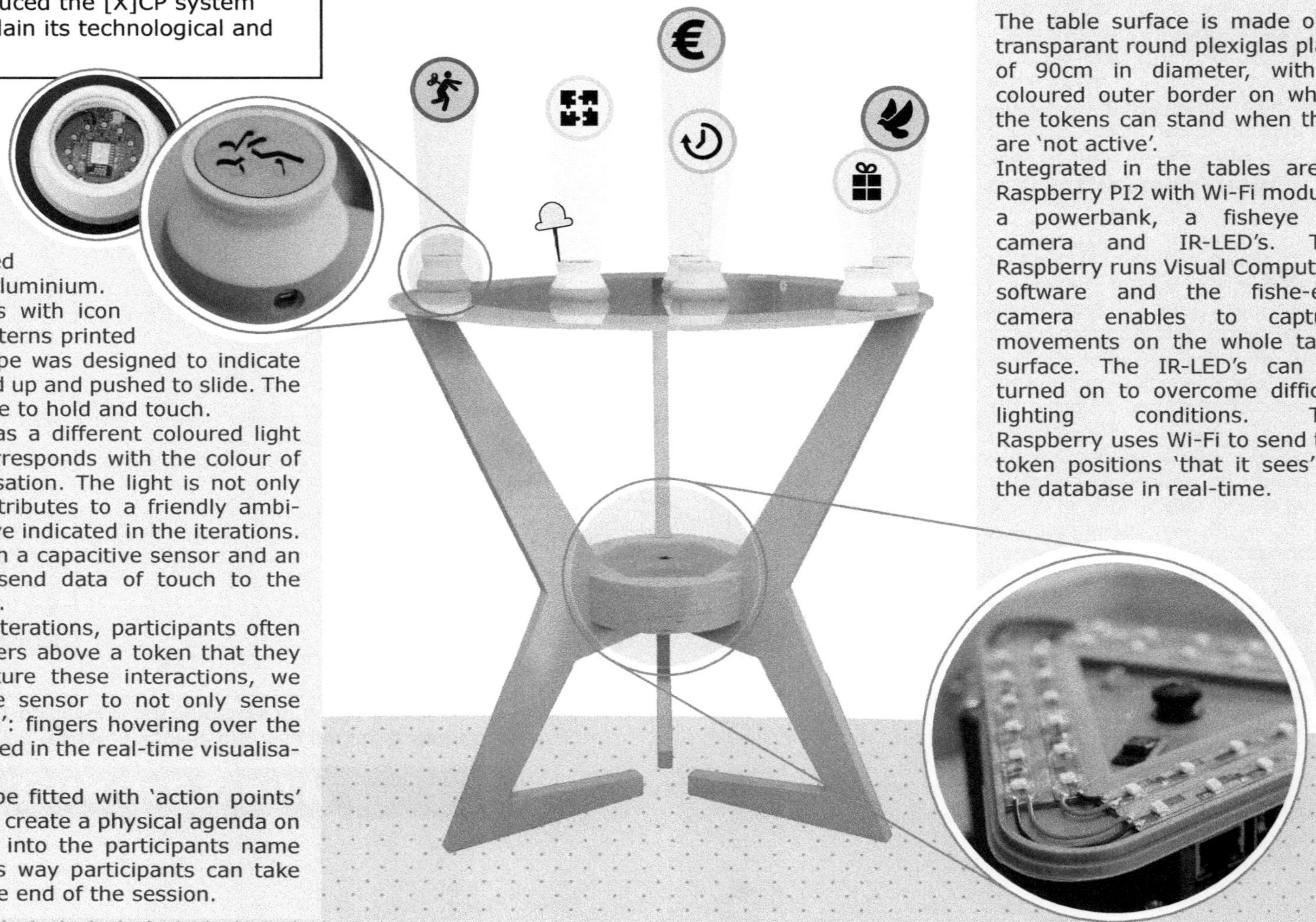

TOKENS

The tokens are 3D printed of white plastic and aluminium. They have wooden tops with icon cut-outs and marker patterns printed on the bottom. The shape was designed to indicate that tokens can be picked up and pushed to slide. The materials are comfortable to hold and touch.
Each of the 6 tokens has a different coloured light (neopixel LEDs) that corresponds with the colour of the token in the visualisation. The light is not only functional, but also contributes to a friendly ambience, as participants have indicated in the iterations. Tokens are equipped with a capacitive sensor and an ESP WiFi module and send data of touch to the visualisation in real-time.
As we observed in the iterations, participants often point or circle their fingers above a token that they are discussing. To capture these interactions, we calibrated the capacitive sensor to not only sense touch, but also 'pointing': fingers hovering over the token. This data is included in the real-time visualisation.
Finally, the tokens can be fitted with 'action points' (yellow notes on pins) to create a physical agenda on the table. The notes fit into the participants name tags as well, and in this way participants can take home action points at the end of the session.

TRACKING TOKEN MOVEMENTS

The table surface is made of a transparant round plexiglas plate of 90cm in diameter, with a coloured outer border on which the tokens can stand when they are 'not active'.
Integrated in the tables are a Raspberry PI2 with Wi-Fi module, a powerbank, a fisheye IR camera and IR-LED's. The Raspberry runs Visual Computing software and the fishe-eye camera enables to capture movements on the whole table surface. The IR-LED's can be turned on to overcome difficult lighting conditions. The Raspberry uses Wi-Fi to send the token positions 'that it sees' to the database in real-time.

PRODUCT SERVICE SYSTEM

The [X]CP system is not only a research vehicle but also part of a service provided to partners (project owners) & stakeholders of public issues.

[X]CP SESSION

An [X]CP session lasts between 1,5 and 2 hours. Within this time, there are two discussion rounds of 15-20 minutes and two intermezzos of 15-20 minutes. The session consists of up to 120 participants around up to 15 tables.

EXPECTATION MANAGEMENT

We collaborate with the partner to create suitable media to invite participants (different media for different stakeholder groups) and to develop a central question and follow-up strategy to work with the input from participants in a meaningful way and to keep participants in the loop.

The invitation for the [X]CP session is important to generate willingness to participate and to manage expectations. It is sent out up to 4 weeks prior to the session and includes the cental question.

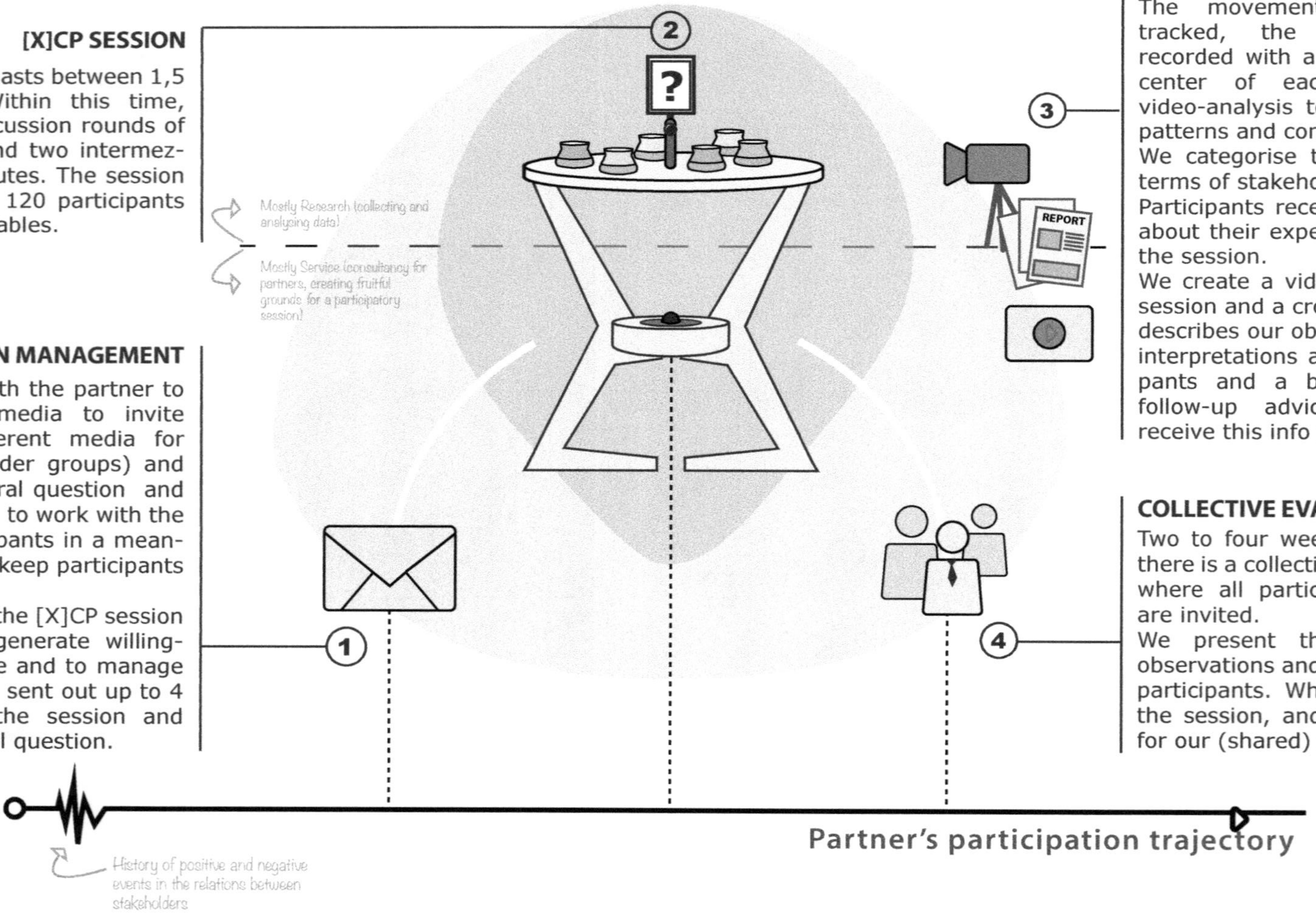

DATA COLLECTION & ANALYSIS

In order to approach the richness of the sensemaking that occured around the tables, we use mixed qualitative methods to capture and analyse data. The movements of tokens are tracked, the conversations are recorded with a 360º camera in the center of each table. We use video-analysis to explore interaction patterns and conent of conversations. We categorise the 'action points' in terms of stakeholder group and topic. Participants receive an online survey about their experiences directly after the session.

We create a video impression of the session and a cross-media report that describes our observations, the broad interpretations and stories of participants and a brief translation into follow-up advice. All participants receive this info per email.

COLLECTIVE EVALUATION

Two to four weeks after the session there is a collective evaluation session where all participants and partners are invited.

We present the report and our observations and trigger reflections of participants. What was the value of the session, and what does it mean for our (shared) next steps?

SCENARIO

In the foregoing we have introduced the product service system.
In this section we illustrate the PSS through a step-by-step scenario with pictures.

1 | Invitation: The partner invites (sometimes selects) the participants, via e-mail and flyers that are, when possible, co-created with the researchers. We stimulate a broad invitation of stakeholders. Sometimes an online survey is set out before the session to gather input.

2 | Central Question: The topic of the discussion is formulated as a question that allows prioritisation, e.g. "what is needed for / most important when..."
The question is developed in co-creation with the researchers and formulated such, that it invites different views and an open discussion.

3 | First Token: The participants are distributed over the tables so that the different perspectives (stakeholder groups) are represented at each table. The youngest person at each table starts by placing the token that they relate most with the question on the table, and motivating their choice.

4 | (Re)Positioning:
The participants (re)position the other tokens on the table, while sharing ideas, opinions, knowledge and experiences.

5 | Collective reflection: During this intermezzo, the visualisation is used to discover patterns and relations among the tables.

6 | (Re)Positioning: The participants (re)position the tokens on the table, reflecting on their landscape whilst taking into account the stories of the other tables.

7 | Action Points: In order to realise the landscape they created, the participants attach action points to each token. Finally they take action points with them or give them to others, which unlocks a discussion about roletaking and responsibilities.

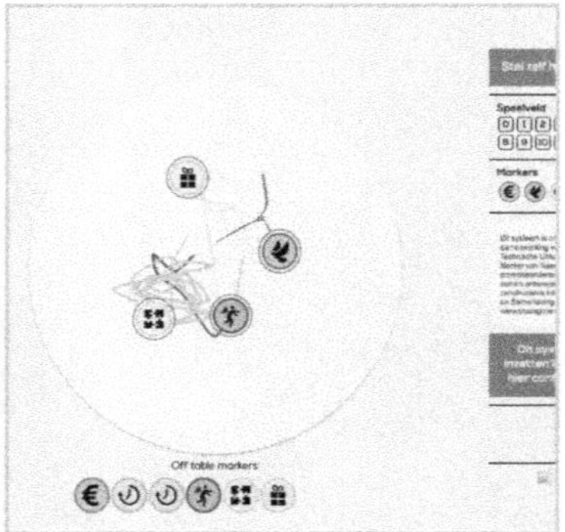

8 | Evaluation: We analyse the token data, observations and recordings, and visually report it to all participants. We present and reflect on the insights with all participants in an evaluation session. The partner presents the next (participatory) steps.

IMPLEMENTATION

The [X]CP system was developed in three iterations. In each iteration, the prototype system was implemented in real-life settings, in a total of 10 sessions that present pilot user studies for our research.
The final [X]CP PSS was implemented in three sessions, of which two were commercial settings.

Impressions of five [X]CP sessions implementing three iterations of the system.

[X]CP sessions in real-life contexts
Over the course of one year, the different iterations of [Name] have been implemented in 9 real-life contexts wherein stakeholders discussed about their roles concerning public issues. The topics for these pilot sessions ranged from "What do you need in order to collaborate on pleasurable living in the village?" to "What is important when refugees are housed in your neighbourhood?" to "What is needed to become a data-driven municipality in a good way?'. The partners of the sessions were municipalities, housing corporations or congress organisers. The stakeholders and thus participants of the sessions varied from citizens, aldermen, entrepreneurs, social welfare professionals to caretakers, consultants and policymakers.

PSS implementation
Additional to the 9 pilot studies, the [X]CP system was implemented in two commercial settings and one full scale research study. The commercial implementation was based on the product-service-system as outlined on page 6. Additionally, we developed a moderation manual and trained prospective moderators for [X]CP sessions. Main points of attention were the use of the visualisation and handling the scale (10-15 tables). Finally, we created checklists and an IKEA-inspired manual to physically set up the [X]CP system. Using these materials, and with our on-site assistence, partners were able to moderate their own [X]CP sessions for their clients.

Feedback loop
The insights from the analysis of each session were presented and reflected upon in a participatory evaluation with all participants and partners. In these reflections and in the questionnaires, participants indicated that during [X]CP sessions the tokens provided conversation starters and helped to express conflicting stakes and viewpoints that in turn led to opening up their horizons regarding the public issue at hand. Partners remarked the conflict-free atmosphere as a unique contribution of the [X]CP system. Critical participants said that the tokens felt childish and stood in the way of expressing their rational arguments as they could normally do.

OBSERVATIONS: TOKENS

In order to illustrate the potential of [X]CP to contribute to participatory sensemaking we highlight some observations of interactions with the [X]CP system. To avoid comparing different settings and iterations, we use the video-analysis for one of the sessions. The session was organised by a (social) housing corporation and their consultants, tenants and members of the city council and representatives of the tenant association participated. In this section we share our observations of participants's interactions with tokens.

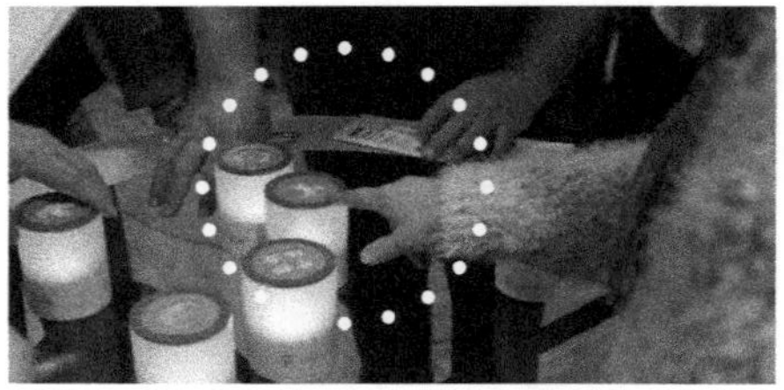

1 | Tapping:
Tapping onto the icon while emphasising its role & holding a token whilst someone else is talking to indicate that one wants to speak next.

2 | Pointing:
Pointing at a token (with middle finger) without touching it, while giving his interpretation of the token that someone else had placed.

3 | Stacking:
Indicating that two tokens are equally important and directly linked to one another, the participant stacks them on top of each other- making it invisible for the tracking system. The new cone shape of the token makes it harder to stack them, and the visalisation melts together tokens that are side to side for 3 minutes.

4 | Gesturing around the token:
Describing association with the token, whilst holding it close to the body in one hand and gesturing with the other hand, before placing in on the table.

5 | Gesturing around the token:
Floating above the token with both hands, while carefully describing its importance.

6 | Manipulating tokens during second time use:
After the man on the right (upper picture) picked up and repositioned a token, the woman in the middle (lower picture) placed it back and slid it to the same place. She had participated once before, and knew about the tracking system. She thought that only sliding worked, so she felt that she had to show the others how to use the tokens. Her 'prior knowledge' of [X]CP therefore created unequal roles in participation around the table.

OBSERVATIONS: ACTIONS

The previous observations were focused on the interactions with tokens. In this section we highlight some observations of interactions with the action points of the [X]CP system.

1 | Taking on action points:
Taking action point for oneself and pinning it onto nametag: "This is so much fun!".
After the session she volunteered to roll out the idea in collaboration with the partner.

2 | Handing out action points:
Participant gives an action point to another participant, and, playfully, even pins it onto her name tag for her.

3 | Capturing physical agenda (of action points):
One of the iterations included reflection booklets wherein participants could stick their action points. They were experienced as a hassle: we observed that participants prefer to take pictures with their smartphones in order to capture and share their memories of the session.

4 | Handing out action points:
Giving action point to other participants: the man on the right reacheds over to the man opposite him, to give him the action point. However, that man is not inclined to accept that action point. He left the man hanging for two seconds, and then the woman on the left stepped in and volunteered to take the action point.
It seems that a sense of common owenership and responsibility emerged at the table.

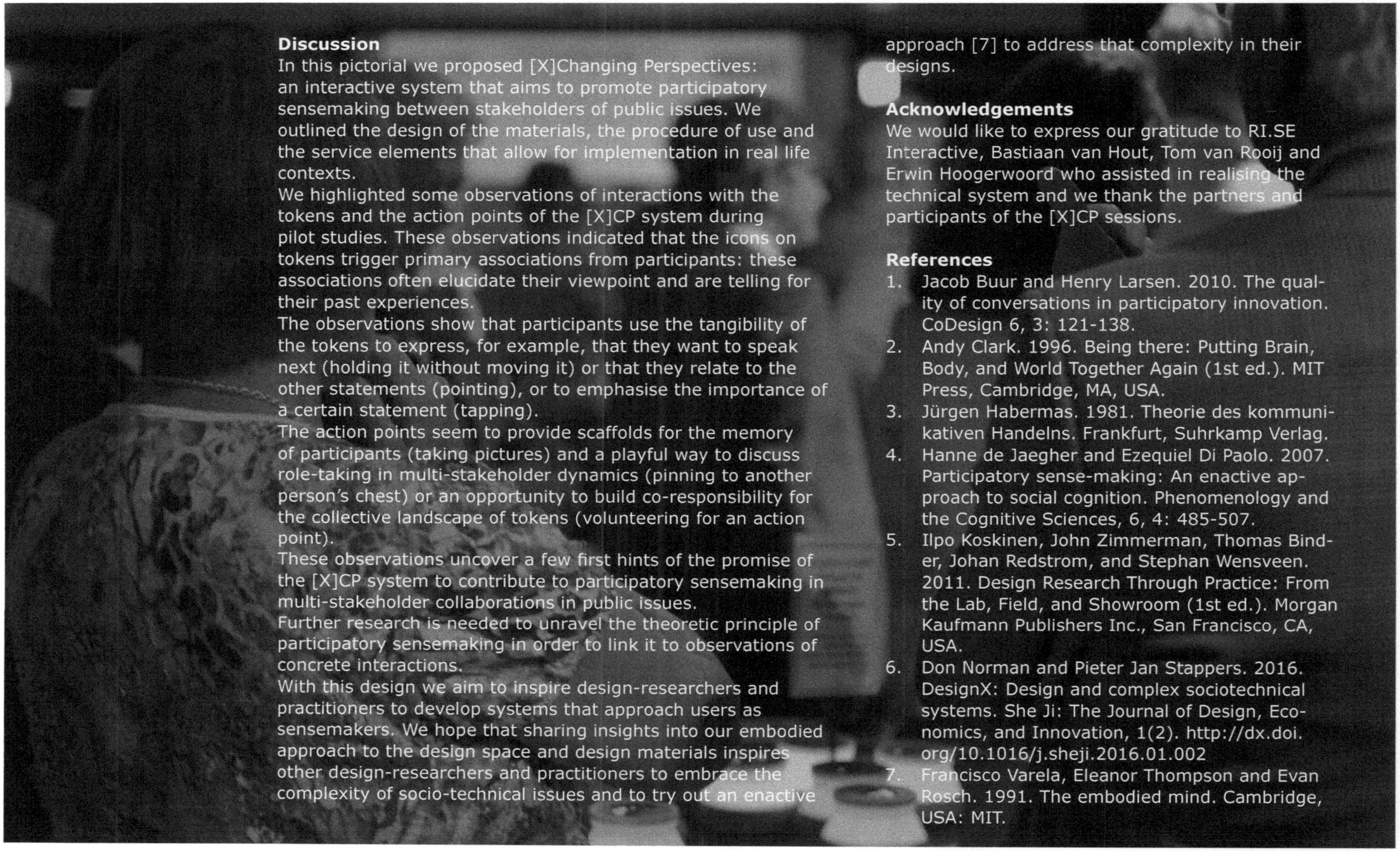

Discussion

In this pictorial we proposed [X]Changing Perspectives: an interactive system that aims to promote participatory sensemaking between stakeholders of public issues. We outlined the design of the materials, the procedure of use and the service elements that allow for implementation in real life contexts.

We highlighted some observations of interactions with the tokens and the action points of the [X]CP system during pilot studies. These observations indicated that the icons on tokens trigger primary associations from participants: these associations often elucidate their viewpoint and are telling for their past experiences.

The observations show that participants use the tangibility of the tokens to express, for example, that they want to speak next (holding it without moving it) or that they relate to the other statements (pointing), or to emphasise the importance of a certain statement (tapping).

The action points seem to provide scaffolds for the memory of participants (taking pictures) and a playful way to discuss role-taking in multi-stakeholder dynamics (pinning to another person's chest) or an opportunity to build co-responsibility for the collective landscape of tokens (volunteering for an action point).

These observations uncover a few first hints of the promise of the [X]CP system to contribute to participatory sensemaking in multi-stakeholder collaborations in public issues.

Further research is needed to unravel the theoretic principle of participatory sensemaking in order to link it to observations of concrete interactions.

With this design we aim to inspire design-researchers and practitioners to develop systems that approach users as sensemakers. We hope that sharing insights into our embodied approach to the design space and design materials inspires other design-researchers and practitioners to embrace the complexity of socio-technical issues and to try out an enactive approach [7] to address that complexity in their designs.

Acknowledgements

We would like to express our gratitude to RI.SE Interactive, Bastiaan van Hout, Tom van Rooij and Erwin Hoogerwoord who assisted in realising the technical system and we thank the partners and participants of the [X]CP sessions.

References

1. Jacob Buur and Henry Larsen. 2010. The quality of conversations in participatory innovation. CoDesign 6, 3: 121-138.
2. Andy Clark. 1996. Being there: Putting Brain, Body, and World Together Again (1st ed.). MIT Press, Cambridge, MA, USA.
3. Jürgen Habermas. 1981. Theorie des kommunikativen Handelns. Frankfurt, Suhrkamp Verlag.
4. Hanne de Jaegher and Ezequiel Di Paolo. 2007. Participatory sense-making: An enactive approach to social cognition. Phenomenology and the Cognitive Sciences, 6, 4: 485-507.
5. Ilpo Koskinen, John Zimmerman, Thomas Binder, Johan Redstrom, and Stephan Wensveen. 2011. Design Research Through Practice: From the Lab, Field, and Showroom (1st ed.). Morgan Kaufmann Publishers Inc., San Francisco, CA, USA.
6. Don Norman and Pieter Jan Stappers. 2016. DesignX: Design and complex sociotechnical systems. She Ji: The Journal of Design, Economics, and Innovation, 1(2). http://dx.doi.org/10.1016/j.sheji.2016.01.002
7. Francisco Varela, Eleanor Thompson and Evan Rosch. 1991. The embodied mind. Cambridge, USA: MIT.

Video Prototyping for Interaction Design Across Multiple Displays in the Commercial Flight Deck

Axel Roesler
University of Washington
Division of Design
Interaction Design Program
Art Building, Room 102
Box 353440
Seattle, WA 98195 USA
roesler@uw.edu

Barbara Holder
Advanced Technology
Honeywell Aerospace
Barbara.Holder@Honeywell.com

Dan Ostrowski
University of Washington
OstrowskiDesign@gmail.com

Nate Landes
University of Washington
natelandes@gmail.com

Stephen Minarsch
University of Washington
stephenminarsch@yahoo.com

Daniya Ulgen
University of Washington
daniyaulgen@gmail.com

Erin Murphy
University of Washington
erin.m.murphy@jpl.nasa.gov

Haeree Park
University of Washington
hairiprac@gmail.com

DIS 2017, June 10-14, 2017, Edinburgh, United Kingdom
 ISBN 978-1-4503-4922-2/17/06…$15.00
DOI: http://dx.doi.org/10.1145/3064663.3064800

Abstract
The commercial flight deck is a workspace with more than a century of knowledge in human-machine interaction, pioneering the transition from direct analog displays to computerized screens. The flight deck is a collaborative workplace where pilots interact with automated systems and flight information that is distributed across an array of screens that present information in spatial alignment to tasks and flight situation. This pictorial examines new Interaction Design video prototyping techniques for spatially aligned and collaborative interactions across multiple screens for a next generation commercial flight deck.

Authors Keywords
Interaction Design; Design Methods; Design Prototyping Techniques; Video Prototyping; Flight Deck Design

ACM Classification Keywords
H.5.m. Information interfaces and presentation

Introduction
The commercial flight deck is a rich interaction environment that is based on a century or research. The flight deck has been the birthplace of complex human-machine interaction, a work setting that connects human perception and cognition with advanced technological systems that mediate the environment of flight with the reasoning and decision making capabilities of pilots to control the aircraft [1]. Early flight was direct as pilots reasoned about flight conditions and the route ahead using their vision, as well as audible and tactile feedback from the airplane.

Flight controls were directly coupled with the airplane engine and control surfaces on the wings. Today's airplane flight systems mediate pilot awareness and control across automated control systems [2]. Flight deck instrumentation augments the view out of the window and pilots can rely on the instrument's representation of flight conditions and navigation when the view conditions are poor. During instrumentation-based flight at night displays replace the view into the world ahead. The flight deck also provides a rich collaborative work setting [3] where two pilots interact with each other and jointly interact with the automated systems that fly the airplane (Figures 1-4). Single pilot operation of commercial airplanes is still a vision of the future as complex work tasks during high pressure work sequences require the distribution of workflows across the captain and the first officer. On the other hand there are low work load periods, for example during cruise between take-off and landing when the automation flies the plane without pilot intervention [2]. During this period that can last many hours, pilots become supervising agents that monitor the automation [4].
Outside the flight deck, commercial interactive technology has rapidly developed and has in many aspects surpassed the technological state-of-the-art of the commercial flight deck [5]. We set out to explore how the current state-of-the-art for consumer interactive devices could affect the design of flight information displays and control of the aircraft in future commercial flight decks. Together with pilots, human factors researchers, cognitive scientists, ethnographers, and engineers, our team of interaction designers set out to explore the future of interactions in the flight deck in a concurrent design approach [6] to ground design in observation and use design ideas to probe and contextualize knowledge at the intersection of people, technology, and work. Design ideas were based on ethnographic studies of pilots at work and thorough process traces of flight operations. In aviation, flight operations are designed sequences of action that are driven by checklists and communication and interaction protocols that pilots learn during flight training [7, 8]. The trends were apparent: screens would become larger and pilots would bring mobile devices on board.

Figure 1. A typical gauge- and dial-based flight deck pre-1984 comprised of an array of analog displays for the different flight data components

Figure 2. A current glass cockpit with the main flight display suite of large integrated digital displays.

Figure 3. Captain and first officer engaged in take-off and landing calculations. Thrust levers are in the foreground, centered in front of the Flight Management System.

Figure 4. Collaboration between Captain (right) and First Officer. Notice that there isn't workspace in the center console. Exchange of information takes the form of conversations and paper.

What are the expectations of tomorrow's pilots when they enter the flight deck? How could flight operations unfold given that rich visual interaction would become the norm in commercial flight decks—screens would continue to increase in size and resolution, new interaction techniques such as touch screens and direct surface interaction would be integrated in the visual displays? [9, 5]. How could these new interaction models be integrated in future concepts? How would the new interaction sequences play out during operational scenarios? [10, 7] How would these new interactive systems have to be designed to support the collaboration between pilots? [11] How could the collaboration between pilots be improved using new types of visualizations that would provide more transparent representations of flight systems and better navigation and planning support? [1] Our design of the new interaction concepts for the commercial flight deck took the form of three design efforts: 1) Design of a new suite of flight displays that is based on the traditional display set in glass cockpit airplanes 2) Design of physical control interfaces 3) Design of flight interactions that are contextualized in the flight deck workspace.

Flight Displays

Currently, the main flight display set (Figure 5) is comprised of a primary flight display, a navigation display, and an engine and crew altering system display. The primary flight display shows the attitude of the plane—its pitch, roll, and yaw relative to a horizontal plane and lateral axis. The navigation display shows a map-like top down view of the airplane with the location of the plane in the center at the bottom of the display. The engine-indicating and crew alerting system displays engine performance and flight systems notification and alerts. The flight management system programming and control panels are used to program flight route and adjust course. We took a radical design approach to the visual displays when we adapted current display content to the much larger 19" panels we explored. We also introduced two large displays in

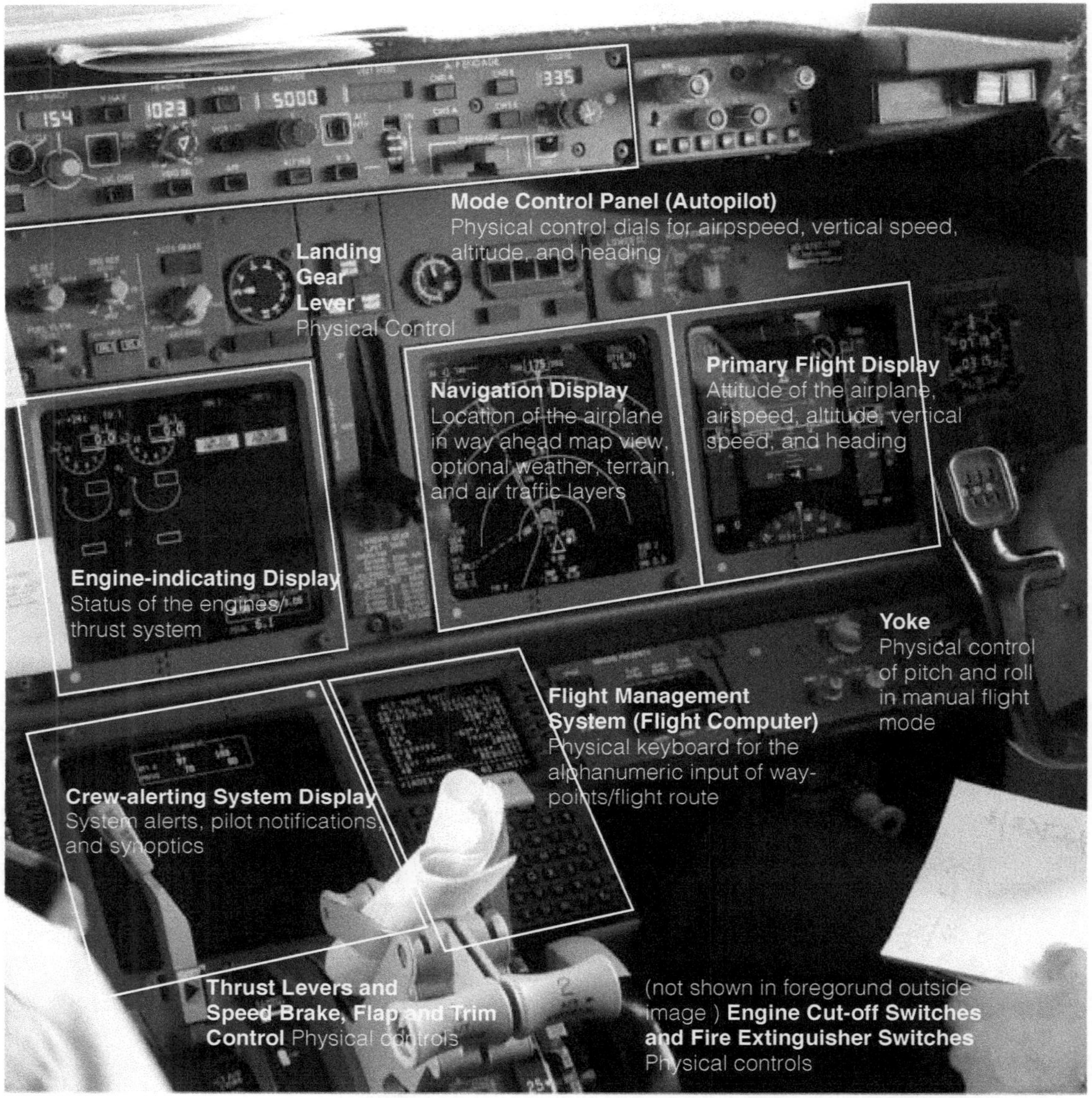

Figure 5: Current pilot display suite in the commercial glass cockpit with call-outs of key instruments and physical controls.

the center main panel and center console that would expand the collaborative display work space between the two pilots (Figure 7). The center console display is a touch screen used for strategic flight planning tasks along a flight mission timeline. The center panel screen is an external view of how the automaton is flying the airplane. Left and right main panel displays show primary flight display, navigation display, and/or flight timeline in combined views. Instead of adding more information into the larger screen spaces, we reduced the amount of numerical information and focused the design on large and open visualizations of maps, diagrams, timelines, and alignment geometry in order to provide big picture views on the relationships between flight data [12]. We also reduced the current 31-hue color coding of the aviation displays to black and white [13] in order to experiment with a minimal display approach.

Flight Deck as Physical Workspace

All digital flight displays and physical controls in the commercial flight deck are located in specific locations relative to the pilots, their work tasks, and in alignment with the airplane, flight direction, and view out of the window (Figure 5). Most flight controls and display views are replicated so that both pilots have access to them during flight to distribute work tasks and hand over control of the airplane. In order to redesign interaction flows we had to carefully examine the relationships between display content and the location where information would be presented. We conducted process traces of typical normal and non-normal flight operations [7] with pilots and technical ethnographers. We examined which flight controls would remain physical and which one could be integarted as display interaction. Pilots use primarily physical flight controls to provide tactical input for the plane. The yoke is a hand interface that controls the attitude of the airplane: A pilot can pull it back to pitch up the nose, push it forward to point down the nose, rotate it to roll the plane in order to change the lateral direction of flight. The thrust lever is used to control the airplane engines. Foot pedals are used to rotate the plane around its vertical axis to counter cross winds. Other physical switches and levers are used to control the landing gear, extinguish engine fires, control systems on the overhead systems panel, and control the magnification scope of maps in the Navigation Display. The main interface input elements for the automation are the alphanumeric keyboard of the Flight Management System and the physical dial knobs for airspeed, vertical speed, altitude, and heading on the flight management control panel (Figure 5).

(Below left) Figure 6. Early design sketch of the new physical flight deck layout as four-panel large screen arrangment with new main panel and center console displays.

(Below right) Figure 7. New four-panel layout of the main flight deck panel and enter console. Vector illustatration with display designs. The mission planning screen in the center console provides a new collaborative workplace for both pilots.

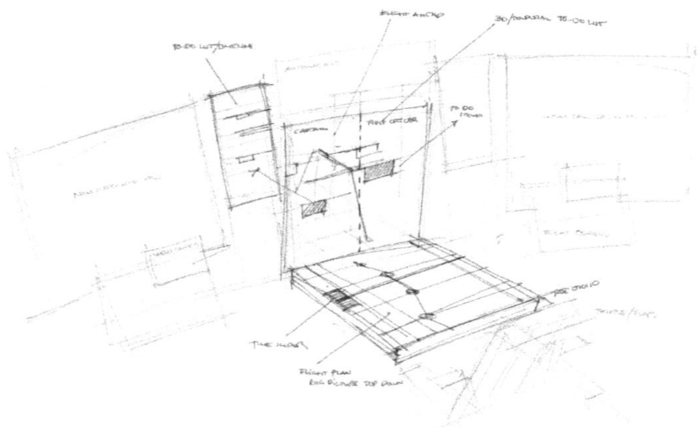

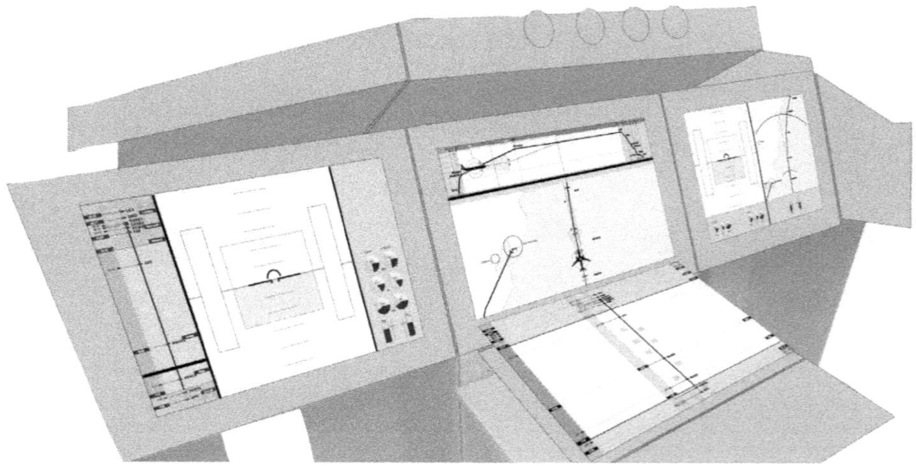

Figures 8-10. Hand sketching (Figure 11, right) and 3-D computer modeling (below) alternated: We used 3-D modeling in Rhino to adapt our flight deck panels to the actual flight deck space of a Boeing 787-size airplane.

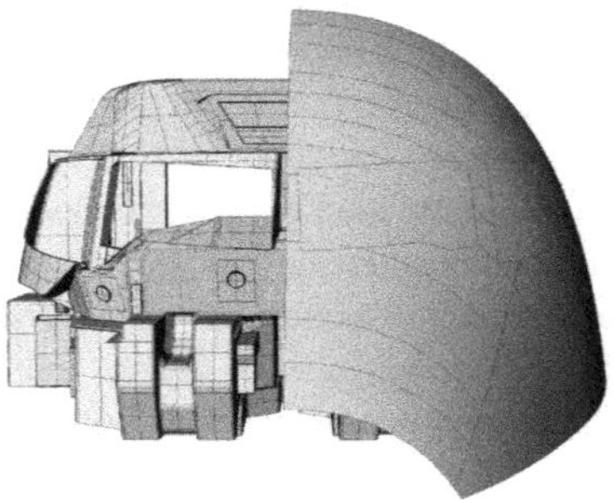

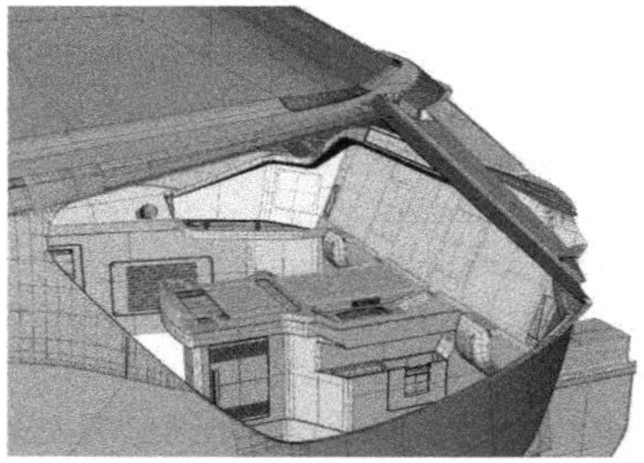

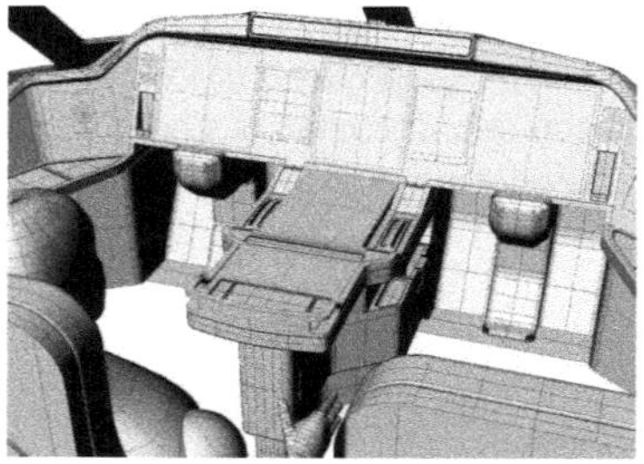

From the moment when we moved from process tracing to design development it became clear to us that in order to present and share design concepts of interaction flows, display content, and display locations in the flight deck effectively, we had to move beyond traditional presentation formats such as sketches, illustrations, and slide shows. Flat, static and partial representations turned out to be insufficient to share a big picture of an integrated design concept for the flight deck as workspace, as images showed either individual displays and decontextualized them from relationships with other displays, or they flattened out the display space by showing all displays in the same plane. We began to build full scale cardboard mock-ups of the flight deck [14, 15] and used paper print-outs of display screens at full size, positioned in their respective screen locations in the flight deck mock-up to discuss interface concepts during meetings (Figures 13-17).
To capture envisioned interaction flows during flight operations we began to experiment with video prototyping techniques [16, 17].

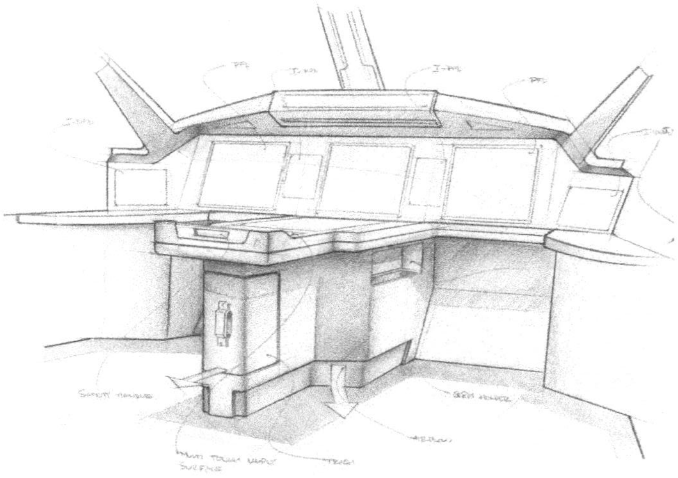

Figure 11. Design sketch of the physical flight deck design.

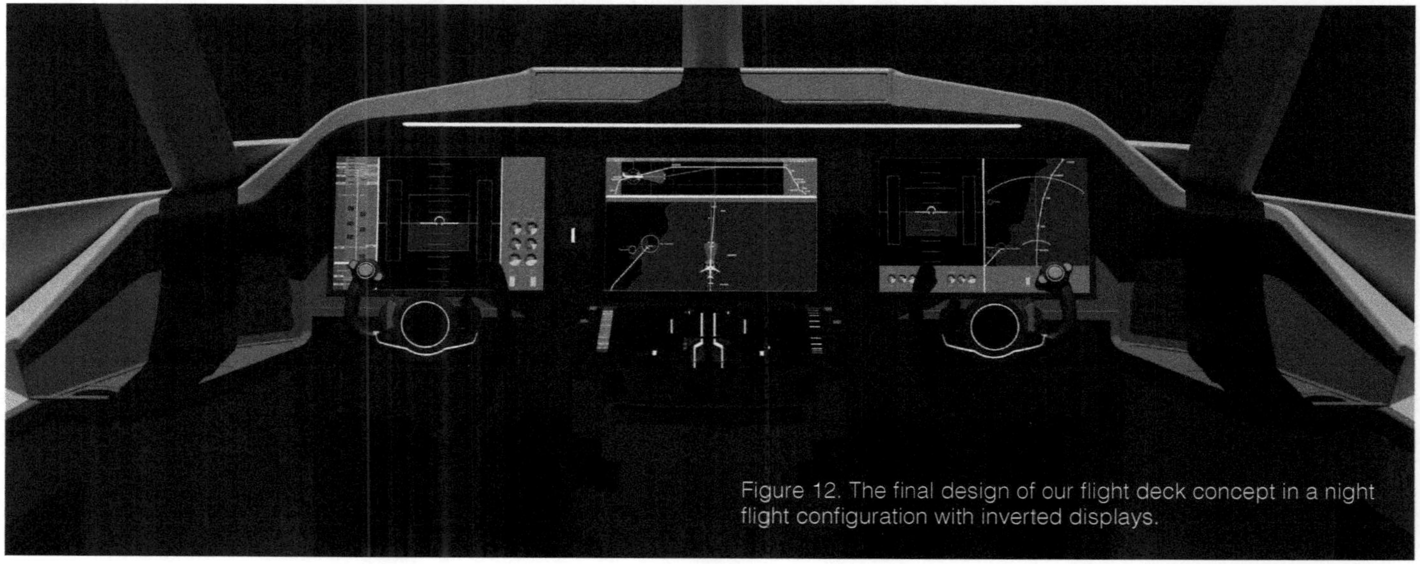

Figure 12. The final design of our flight deck concept in a night flight configuration with inverted displays.

Video prototyping of interaction sequences was introduced in the early 1990's to capture future design scenarios [9,18, 19, 20, 21], but its application for detailed interface scenarios was limited due to constraints of earlier video technology, in particular the low resolution of video in 640x480 standard definition. We used full HD 1920x1080 resolution and multiple camera angles to capture mock-ups of screen content, pilots, and physical flight deck layout during realistic operations scenarios that reflect current flight procedures. Capturing this information rich environment was key for reviewing interaction design and physical design of the flight deck with pilots in context during participatory design sessions.

Paper Video Prototype

For our first video prototype experiment, we used our full scale cardboard flight deck mock-up as stage (Figure 17), and working with the full scale screen print outs in 17x11" we developed continuous display screen flows and used a stop-motion video technique to simulate direct screen interactions (Figures 18-21). Our pilots would point at a button in the paper print-out, hold the position, we would replace the print out with a new interface screen print out, and continue interaction gestures from there; the transitions would be edited out during digital video post production later (watch the video at https://vimeo.com/213371977). The paper video prototype was great for sketching out interaction sequences.

(Above) Figures 13-16. We set up weekly meetings in our lab adjacent to the Interaction Design studios of the University of Washington's Division of Design in the School of Art + Art History + Design to meet with airline pilots, human factors specialists, ethnographers, engineers and designers involved in current flight deck design to conduct hands-on design sessions and reviews of our design concepts and scenarios. These check-ins were instrumental in developing realistic operations scenarios [7, 8, 10] for workflows that would shape the Interaction Design of the flight deck.

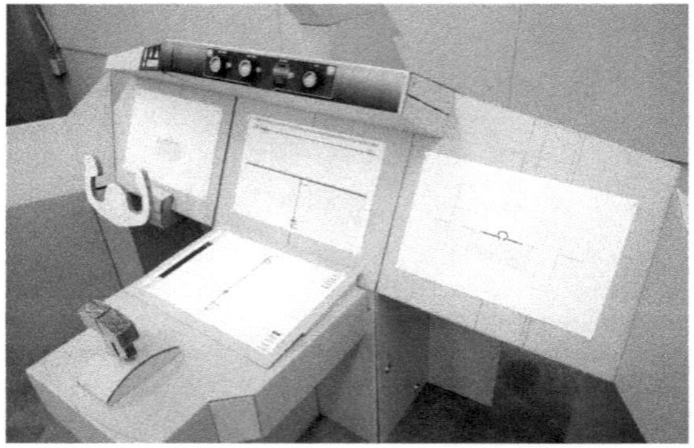

(Right) Figure 17. The full scale cardboard mock-up provided common ground during discussions. We pinned screen printouts in their respective locations and were then able to annotate the interface designs with hand sketches, ideas, and suggestions directly on the paper print-outs.

Shooting in stop motion manner was quick but required significant preparation as hundreds of screens needed to be designed, printed, and organized sequentially. This preparation work oftentimes revealed gaps in the screen sequences such as screen states, transitions, and continuity elements that we had not considered. In hindsight we look at this as a benefit as the paper video prototype served as an effective test bed for the completeness and flow of interaction concepts. From the point of view of the actors, another strength of the paper video prototype was that all screens and gesture touchpoints were visible to them during filming. This made hand/eye coordination straight forward and turned out to help evaluate the physical ergonomics of touch gestures: When gestures felt clumsy because of their location and orientation in relationship to the operators we were able to sketch out new touch locations that felt better suited directly on the paper print-outs and then adapted the digital display design files accordingly.

Figures 18-21: Video prototyping was an effective prototyping technique to identify gaps in the interaction model. We scripted operations scenarios in real time and developed key frame screen sequences that were drawn in Illustrator, then laser printed in black and white at the size of the envisioned displays. The aesthetic of the video left a good space for feedback, as attention was focused on content rather than form.

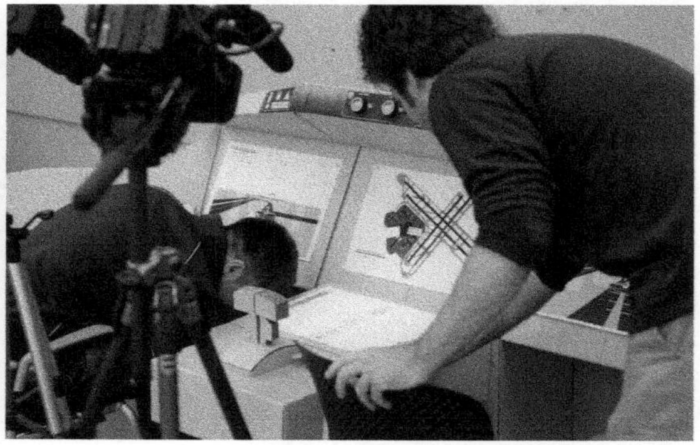

Green Screen Video Prototype

We moved to the next level of fidelity for video prototyping by capturing all surface interactions in a green screen compositing approach (Figures 22-24). We gestured interactions on screen areas of the displays that were masked out in green during video shooting, and then timed an animation of all six screens in an After Effects file to synchronize it with the timing of the screen gestures captured in the video. We then matched the scale and perspective of the animated screen sequence with the captured video and composited both videos together using chromakeying so that the screen animations would appear in the green masked areas of the camera video and hand and finger pointing over the green screened display areas would occlude the display beneath. The result was a fairly realistic video prototype from the perspective of a jump seat observer in the flight deck (watch the video at https://vimeo.com/213372407). The green screen video prototype allowed us to demonstrate fluid screen transitions and swipe gestures with motion elements. This would have been very production intense in the paper video prototype approach, as it required several in-between paper print-outs. A challenge that we discovered was that touch locations wouldn't be visible to the actors during filming as the screens were added later during post production.

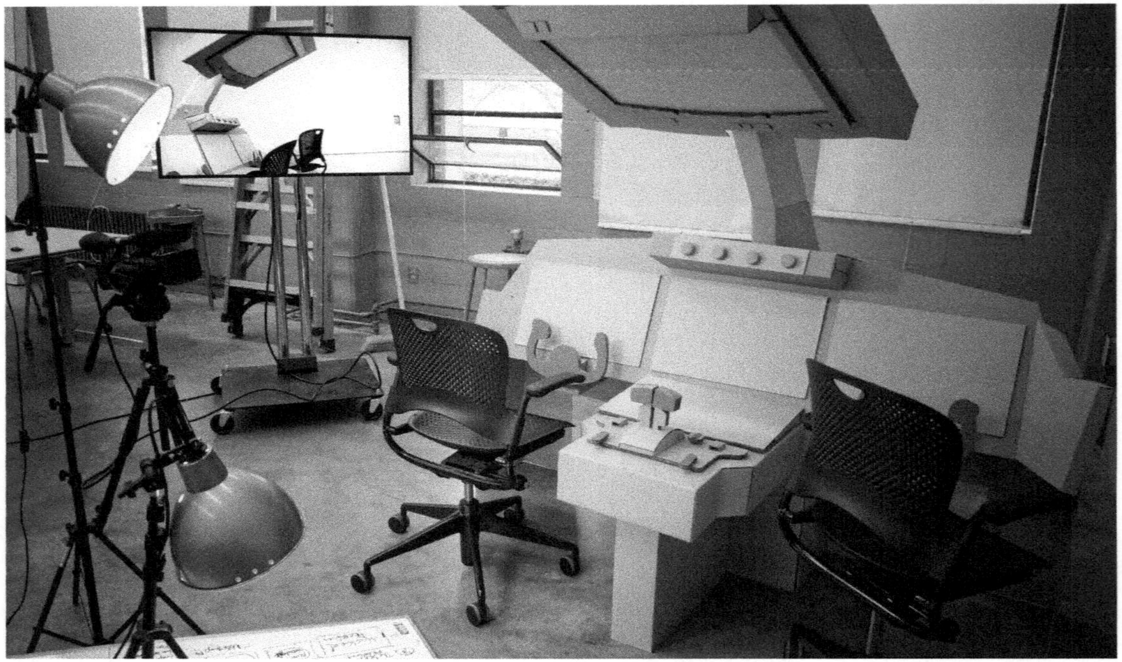

(Top right) Figure 22. Green screen video prototype shooting set-up.

(Bottom left) Figure 23. Frame from the green screen video prototype. In this scene the first officer monitors the airplane slowing down to a new air speed setting.

(Bottom right) Figure 24. Transfer of paper screen print-out to a hand gesture trace on the green mask for the overhead panel. The marks were used to identify touchpoints on the screens during the green screen video shooting.

To provide our actors with view and touch targets, we had to mark touch locations and swipe tracks on the green screen masks using push pins to transfer location points from the paper prototype screens into the green masks and then add annotations to identify the push pin marks using green pencil (Figure 24). Our actors then followed the annotations to synchronize finger gestures with the progression of the screen animations. This approach required paper print outs of key screens that we already had from the previous paper video prototype. Overall, the production of the green screen prototype turned out less time consuming than the paper prototype because the entire interaction sequence was developed and the timing was down as result of prior paper prototyping. Digital files for screen design were linked to the animation file. This provided a great organization framework. Where needed, screen design adjustments could be made directly in the Illustrator source files (visual design) or the After Effects animation sequence (timing and motion design) and didn't require print-outs and sequential file and paper organization.

(Below) Figure 25: Screen array status for a scene in checklist step 7.1. Excerpt from the screen state rehearsal script that our actors used to familiarize themselves with upcoming screen transitions that they would follow with screen gestures.

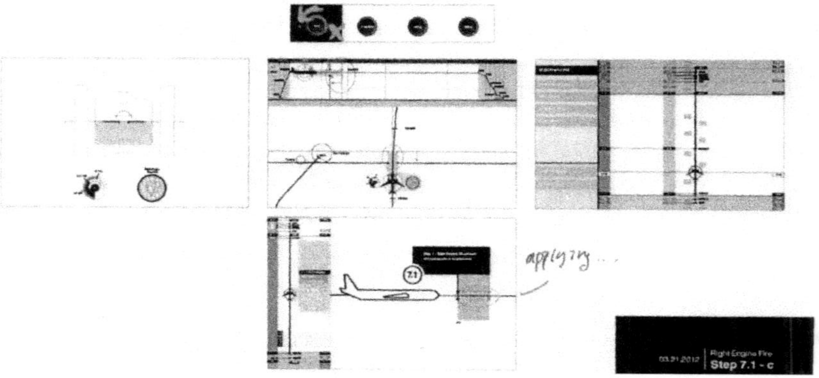

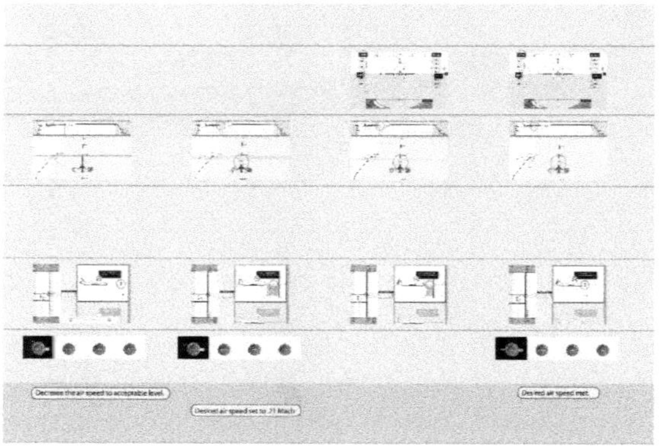

(Above) Figure 26: Full scale flight deck mock-up equipped with six 19" LCD displays for the six-panel video prototype.

(Bottom Center) Figure 27: Notation of the screen sequence for the three main panel and center console screens.

Six Panel Video Prototype

For our final video prototype we built a new physical flight deck prototype that was equipped with six 19" LCD displays (Figure 26). Our intent for this video protoype was to produce a promo-style video that incorporated dramatic camera angles and narrative-driven editing between camera views (you can watch the video at https://vimeo.com/213372846). We were able to use the same screen animation files we had produced for the green screen video prototype and ran these in a split-up version via six video cards from a single computer on six separate displays. Members of our design team then rehearsed finger point gestures, touch locations, and changing screen states to follow the various screens with interaction gestures as they were filmed. At any time during the shooting we were able to stop the playback of all six screens to adjust camera angles or run re-takes. After serving as stage for the six panel video prototype, the second flight deck mock-up was used to present live demos.

The six panel video prototype (Figures 25-39) provided freedom for camera placement and although we used cameras on tripods, fixed viewpoints weren't a constraint as there wasn't a critical post production step that required perspective matching. Even hand held camera work would be possible. The most significant time investment for the six panel video prototype went into the rehearsal of the screen sequences and gesture interaction steps that needed to be performed during acting to synchronize interaction gestures with the animated screen content.

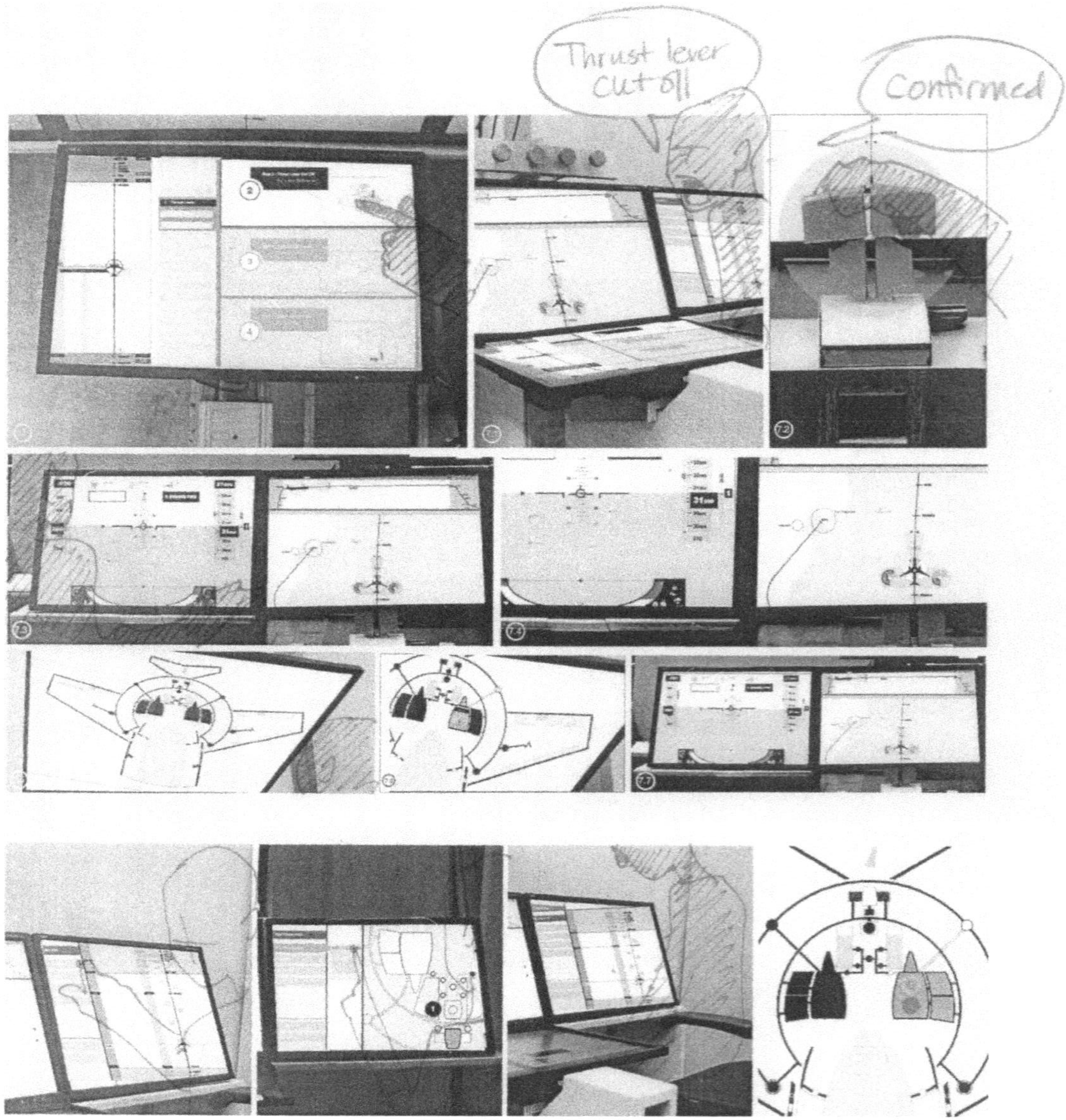

Figure 28. For the six panel video prototype we filmed the engine fire response scenario from multiple camera angles and edited it for a dramatized, points of interest oriented visual storytelling style. In order to determine story flow and camera angles, we storyboarded the video to control the composition of each scene and continuity between edits. By documenting the interactions between the pilots in response to the non-normal event of the engine fire, the video scenario captures the key features of our design of the display suite and flight deck work space.

What we discovered during this process was that the six panel prototype really was a full scale physical demonstration set-up that showcased the integration of work environment and screens. All screens and display content were presented in full size and situated in their actual physical location to another, all this in relationship to the pilots. The unfolding scenario could be experienced by taking the seat of a pilot. Instead of just serving as a stage prop for video prototyping, the six panel display set-up could be used to evaluate display element sizes and placement, viewing distances, and the physical ergonomics of screen gestures. This allowed us to demonstrate flight deck and display scenarios to pilots who could now observe the design concepts in action from their familiar point of view in the pilot seat. Or they could sit in the jump seat, a seat behind the pilot that flight that instructors use to assess pilots. Pilots and aviation researchers are familiar with the perspective from this seat and shared with us observations of current flight operations and how these relate to the new interaction concepts presented.

Figures 29-38. Screen shots from the six-panel video prototype of an engine fire response scenario. The sequence unfolds as follows:

1. Flight operations are normal
2. Engine fire alert appears, autopilot disengages, captain takes over manual control, electronic engine fire response checklist appears in center console.
3. First officer throttles down the affected engine.
4. First officer activates fire extinguishing system.
5. After a waiting period of 30 seconds, the first officer checks in the overhead systems panel if the fire has been successfully extinguished.
6. The checklist moves to the next step and calls for a reduction of airspeed.
7. Captain dials in new airspeed.
8. First officer monitors airplane slowing down to new airspeed setting.

Full six panel video prototype: **https://vimeo.com/213372846**

Discussion

We set out to explore new Interaction Design opportunities in the commercial flight deck setting. We based display design and physical workspace design on the Interaction Design for key operations scenarios. To communicate our design concepts with pilots, human factors specialists and engineers, we captured the operations as video prototypes at various levels of fidelity. The video prototypes captured the collaboration between pilots, their interactions with the automated flight systems, and the spatial and operational context of the flight deck as distributed cognition [22]. Camera angles in the video prototypes resembled the perspective of pilots and flight observers. Physical flight deck mock-ups in combination with the video prototypes provided us with an effective demonstration and test platform for design reviews with pilots and engineers. Our video prototypes enabled us to record, annotate, and communicate concepts to gather feedback during the design process.

We intentionally choose a sketch-like aesthetic for the video production, using corrugated cardboard props and black and white laser print-outs as interface displays to encourage deep-level feedback that was targeted on the interaction flows, visual design and usefulness of the information displayed. The various video prototypes were extremely successful in capturing the contextual aspects of the interactions, such as the ensemble of flight information that resulted from multiple views on the flight mission across several screens, and interactions between the two pilots and their collaboration with each other during layered work tasks that required the monitoring of different screens and physical interactions, often situated in locations outside the displays. The video prototypes effectively presented workload and work setting aspects of the presented scenarios and proposed design concepts.

The paper video prototype was a great tool during the design process that helped us reveal gaps in interaction sequences. The green screen video prototype provided an effective presentation platform to share semi fidelity design concepts in realistic appearance. This was a very helpful presentation format to share the design work with pilots and aviation researchers for feedback.

The six panel video prototype provided a demonstration set-up where the flow of interactions could be experienced from the perspective of pilots with authentic timing, screen sizes, and viewing distances, potentially suitable to obtain early measurements for design evaluation.

Video prototyping enabled us to validate design concepts and improve various aspects of the design based on feedback from pilots and other design stakeholders. It also provided an effective platform to capture and document display design, interaction flows, and experience of new interaction concepts for the future commercial flight deck.

Acknowledgements

We would like to thank Mark Nikolic, Paul Snow, Tony Parkington, and Pamela Munro of the former Boeing Flight Deck Concept Center for their invaluable feedback during the process. We would also like to thank our extended team at the University of Washington's Division of Design, Interaction Design Program: Sergei Larionov, Kari Gaynor, Shweta Grampurohit, Josh Nelson, and Adriel Rollins for their valuable contributions to this project.

References

1. Hutchins, E. (1995) How a cockpit remembers its speeds. Cognitive Science. 19, 265-288.
2. Sarter, N.B., Woods, D. D., Billings, C.E. (1997) Automation Surprises. Handbook of Human Factors & Ergonomics, second edition, G. Salvendy (Ed.). New York: Wiley
3. Hutchins, E & Klausen, T. (1996) Distributed Cognition in an Airline Cockpit. In Y. Engeström and D. Middleton (Eds.) Cognition and Communication at Work. New York: Cambridge University Press. pp. 15-34.
4. Hollnagel, E. and Woods, D. D. (2005). Joint cognitive systems: Foundations of cognitive systems engineering. Boca Raton, FL: Taylor and Francis.
5. Avsar, H., Fischer, J.E. and Rodden, T., 2016, September. Designing touch screen user interfaces for future flight deck

operations. In: Digital Avionics Systems Conference (DASC), 2016 IEEE/AIAA 35th (pp. 1-9). IEEE.
6. Roesler, A. and Woods, D. D. (2005). Inventing the Future of Cognitive Work: Navigating the 'Northwest Passage' in Design, in: Jonas, W., Chow, R., and Verhaag, N. (eds.): Design—System —Evolution—The Application of Systemic and Evolutionary Approaches to Design Theory, Design Practice, Design Research and Design Education. Proceedings of the 6th International Conference of the European Academy of Design, University of the Arts, Bremen, Germany, March 29–31, 2005. https://www.researchgate.net/publication/228668738
7. Degani, A. & Wiener, E.L. (1994). On the design of flight deck procedures. NASA Ames Research Center. NASA Contractor Report 177642.
8. Degani, A. & Wiener, E.L. (1990). Human Factors of Flight Deck Checklists: the Normal Checklist. NASA Ames Research Center. NASA Contractor Report 177549.
9. Buxton, W. (2008). Sketching User Experiences. San Francisco: Morgan Kaufman.
10. Carroll, J. (2000) Making Use: Scenario-based design of Human-Computer Interactions. Cambridge, MA: MIT Press.
11. Roesler, A. (2011). Interaction design in high stakes domains: The impact of design at the intersection of expertise and technology. Design Principles and Practices: An International Journal, Volume 5, Issue 5, pp.37-52. Champaign, IL: Common Ground.
12. Roesler, A. (2009). Lessons from Three Mile Island: The Design of Interactions in a High-stakes Environment. Visible Language 43.2/3, Special Issue on Communication Design Failure, pp. 170–195.
13. Christ, R.E. (1975) Review and Analysis of Color coding Research for Visual Displays. Human Factors, 17(6), 542-570.
14. Dreyfuss, H. (2003). Designing for People. New York: Allworth Press.
15. Butter, R. (1989). Putting Theory into Practice: An Application of Product Semantics to Transportation in: Design Issues: Vol. V, Number 2, Spring 1989; Cambridge, MA, 1989
16. Mackay, W.E. (2002) Using Video to Support Interaction Design [Video DVD, ISBN 1-58113-516-5], New York: ACM.
17. Mackay, W.E., Ratzer, A.V., Janecek, P. (2000). Video Artifacts for Design: Bridging the Gap between Abstraction and Detail. Proceedings of DIS '00. Brooklyn, NY: ACM Order 608026
18. Dubberly, H & Mitch, D. (1987). The Knowledge Navigator [Video]; Cupertino, CA: Apple
19. Tognazzini, B. (1994). The Starfire Video Prototype Project: A Case History. Proceedings of CHI '94. New York: ACM
20. Tognazzini, B. et al. (1992) Starfire Videoprototype [Video, http://www.asktog.com/starfire/starfire.mp4] Sun Microsystems/SunSoft.
21. Arnowitz, J., Arent, M., Berger, M. (2010). Effective Prototyping for Software Makers. San Francisco: Morgan Kaufman.
22. Hutchins, E. (1995). Cognition in the Wild. Cambridge, MA: MIT Press.

Referenced video files:
Paper Video Prototype: https://vimeo.com/213371977
Green Screen Video Protype: https://vimeo.com/213372407
Six-panel Video Prototype: https://vimeo.com/213372846

Design Guidelines for Web Readability

Aliaksei Miniukovich[*], Antonella De Angeli [*,#], Simone Sulpizio[$], Paola Venuti[^]

[*] DISI, University of Trento, Italy
[#] School of Computer Science, University of Lincoln, UK
[$] Faculty of Psychology, Vita-Salute San Raffaele University, Milan, Italy
[^] DiPSCo, University of Trento, Italy

{aliaksei.miniukovich, antonella.deangeli, paola.venuti}@unitn.it, sulpizio.simone@hsr.it

ABSTRACT
Reading is fundamental to interactive-system use, but around 800 million of people might struggle with it due to literacy difficulties. Few websites are designed for high readability, as readability remains an underinvestigated facet of User Experience. Existing readability guidelines have multiple issues: they are too many or too generic, poorly worded, and often lack cognitive grounding. This paper developed a set of 61 readability guidelines in a series of workshops with design and dyslexia experts. A user study with dyslexic and average readers further narrowed the 61-guideline set down to a core set of 12 guidelines – an acceptably small set to keep in mind while designing. The core-set guidelines address reformatting – such as using larger fonts and narrower content columns, or avoiding underlining and italics – and may well aply to the interactive system other than websites.

Author Keywords
Web; readability; accessibility; dyslexia; WCAG 2.0.

ACM Classification Keywords
H.5.2. Information interfaces and presentation (e.g., HCI): User Interfaces – Style guides.

INTRODUCTION
Reading is a major part of almost every task on the Web. High readability makes the tasks substantially easier, which reduces users' frustration and time wasting. High Web readability and its positive outcomes may be a luxury for the regular users, but become almost a necessity for the users with reading difficulties. For these users, reading and understanding text requires more time and effort than for regular users. Unless website designers are ready to neglect them – which many government and non-profit websites are forbidden to do – they should design for high readability.

Dyslexics are a notable group among the users with reading difficulties, as they – unlike, for example, low-literacy users – have no problem comprehending complex concepts, only decoding concept presentation. This quality of dyslexics might help researchers disentangle poor concept presentation from genuinely high concept complexity: re-design would address presentation and design practice would want to have recommendations about presentation.

DIS 2017, June 10-14, 2017, Edinburgh, United Kingdom

ACM ISBN 978-1-4503-4922-2/17/06… $15.00
http://dx.doi.org/10.1145/3064663.3064711

Psychology has accumulated a formidable amount of theoretical knowledge on dyslexia and readability, but little of it has reached design practice. Abstract models and theoretical findings cannot be directly applied in design practice, and intermediate-level tools [39] – such as design guidelines – are needed to bridge theory and design practice. However, HCI research has given insufficient attention to the development of readability guidelines: They still require much improvement before they are finalized and taught to future Web designers: many of them lack clarity or empirical support, contradict each other, or are poorly formulated.

This paper adopted a systematic approach for developing an actionable set of Web readability guidelines. We pooled, reviewed and reduced a large number of existing guidelines in a series of workshops with dyslexia experts and designers. This activity resulted in a set of 61 non-composite, concise, and actionable guidelines based on psychological evidence. Applying all 61 guidelines, however, might take too much time and effort for some projects, so we attempted to define a preliminary sub-set of core guidelines. For this purpose, we triangulated three datasets: (a) webpage readability evaluation by 13 dyslexic and 23 average readers, (b) expert opinion of 14 trained evaluators (designers and dyslexia experts); and (c) automatic evaluation of webpage compliance with the WCAG 2.0 (Web Content Accessibility Guidelines) [33] and selected readability guidelines. The study highlighted 12 guidelines that affected reading for either dyslexic or non-dyslexic users, or for both of them.

In the remainder of the paper, we review the readability and dyslexia related literature, and list and analyze a big set of readability guidelines. We then describe guideline selection in the workshops and user study. The paper concludes with several implications for future research and design.

RELATED WORK
Dyslexia affects a large group of users, up to 10% of population [10], and have been addressed in both psychology and HCI.

Dyslexia

Individuals with dyslexia have difficulties in accurate or fluent word recognition, poor spelling and decoding abilities; at the same time, these individuals have adequate instruction, intelligence, and sensory abilities [3]. Several typical errors that dyslexics tend to make include letter inversion (e.g. b for d, p for q) or reversal (e.g., m for w), letter transposition (e.g., felt and left), word reversal (e.g., tip for pit). Apart from these specific errors, individuals with dyslexia generally struggle to recognize, spell and decode written words. Reading becomes more difficult, which further undermines text comprehension.

Although cross-linguistic differences exist in terms of easiness of learning to read – which is easier in transparent languages, such as Italian where the letters (graphemes) are in most instances uniquely mapped to each of the speech sounds (phonemes), than in non-transparent languages where this mapping is more ambiguous (like English or French, [27]) – it seems that developmental dyslexia has a similar rate of occurrence across languages [10], and has universal basis in the brain that are independent of the spoken language [14].

A prominent theory of dyslexia etiology argues that developmental dyslexia is caused by a deficit in visuo-spatial attention and originates in the mechanisms responsible for the attentional shifting [31]. Issues with attentional shifting may then result in crowding [8,34] – a perceptual phenomenon occurring when an object becomes more difficult to detect or discriminate from its surroundings, if it is presented in isolation. Compared to typical readers, individuals with developmental dyslexia are abnormally affected by crowding [32,12,28].

Readability Guidelines

Past research advocated using design guidelines instead of other means to tackle Web accessibility issues [7]. The guidelines concisely summarize good design practices, fit well in design classes, and thus, can increase awareness of accessibility solutions. Such awareness would address accessibility issues in a more robust fashion than, for example, specialized accessibility tools [35,25] Furthermore, guidelines also decrease reliance on specific technological platforms.

However, most of the accessibility guidelines addressing reading focused on the need of blind [29,16] or elderly users [11], with scant attention given to dyslexic readers. Other studies focused on accessibility in general [7,33], which make it difficult to understand what guideline helps which category of users. However, some specific set of guidelines targeting dyslexic users exist. For example, Santana et al. [24] surveyed web accessibility and dyslexia, proposing a set of guidelines set aimed at developing dyslexia-friendly websites. Jackson [9] assembled a similar guideline set, focusing on typographic issues (e.g., font size, inter-letter space) that could help dyslexic readers.

Yet, building a comprehensive set of readability guidelines remains a challenge, mostly because past studies tested only few guidelines at a time and are hard to compare due to their methodological heterogeneity (e.g., [2,6,37,20]). Further, different guideline sets include recommendations that contradict each other, e.g., the guideline *Line spacing of 1.5 is preferable* was supported in [20,37], but not in [22,26]. In other cases, a guideline may contradict empirical findings from psychological studies. For example, *Avoid capital letters* [1,5] contradicts the finding of dyslexic children recognizing words in upper-case better than in lower-case [15]. Finally, some guideline sets included recommendations lacking empirical validation, as in the case of *Avoid splitting words at the end of a sentence, i.e. do not use hyphens*, or *Use bullet points and numbering rather than continuous prose* [18,1].

GUIDELINE REVIEW

We reviewed existing readability guidelines in four rounds. The first round assembled an initial guideline set; the other three rounds – initial guideline analysis, workshop with dyslexia experts, and workshop with user interface experts – reviewed and iteratively excluded guidelines from the initial set. We considered only the guidelines related to both readability – the effort spent on reading a text – and dyslexia. Our review aimed at assembling a manageable-size set of concise and potentially useful guidelines to be tested in a user study.

Guideline Collection

In November 2015, we queried Google Scholar for the papers mentioning "dyslexia" and "guidelines" and searched through the 50 first pages of the search output. We further looked through the references of the retrieved papers for other possible sources of guidelines for dyslexia. In this way, we collected a total of 10 documents with guidelines on how to design dyslexia-friendly web or book pages [1,5,24,4,9,13,18,20,30,36,19]. The sets of guidelines partially overlapped. Some recommendations appeared in most of the documents (e.g., *Use left-justified with ragged right edge*, [18,24,4,1,30]) while other guidelines were unique (e.g., *Use single space after period* [30]). We removed the duplicates, retaining the more concisely formulated one. After pooling the guidelines from all the documents and filtering out duplicates, we ended up with 138 potentially helpful guidelines. We also considered 61 W3C-recommended WCAG 2.0 guidelines [33], as they are widely perceived as the standard set of guidelines about accessibility issues, including dyslexia. The WCAG set was treated separately as we wanted to look at the overlap between the dyslexia-related and WCAG guideline sets. This would let us conclude how well dyslexia is addressed in the WCAG 2.0 guidelines.

Guideline Analysis

Two authors reviewed the entire corpus of guidelines and excluded those belonging to one of three categories. The first category included the text-to-speech webpage adaptation guidelines (e.g., "*Use the <abbr> tag to explain* *abbreviations and acronyms*" [18] helps the text-to-speech software parse the website, but does not improve the readability of website). The second category included dyslexia-unrelated guidelines (e.g., "*Avoid green and red/pink combinations as these can cause confusion for colour-blind users*" [18]). The third category included guidelines with an extremely broad and unfocused scope (e.g., "*Colour preferences vary*" [5]). During the coding, the two authors independently analyzed all guidelines, flagged those belonging to one of the three categories, and discussed eventual coding discrepancy till a consensus was reached.

Many of the guidelines included composite statements: they reported several independent pieces of information, each of which could be considered a guideline on its own. During the analysis, we split these composite guidelines in simple, one-instruction recommendations. For example, the guideline "*Consider short paragraphs. Avoid complicated language/jargon. Use short, simple, and direct sentences…*" [24] was divided into three separate recommendations. Many of the guidelines were then re-worded to make them more actionable and concise. For example, "*Very large graphics make pages harder to read*" [5] became *Avoid very large graphics that make pages harder to read*; whereas "*Whenever possible, structure index pages considering a logical order involving tasks sequence or structure (e.g., when involving information that can be structured as part-whole), without requiring exclusively the alphabetical ordering*" [24] became *Arrange the items on index pages in a logical order (e.g., by function); avoid exclusively using the alphabetical order.* The total number of guidelines became 98, with 17 of them extracted from WCAG 2.0. Overall, we noticed the WCAG 2.0 predominantly addressed website use and functionality; text structure and appearance were largely ignored.

Dyslexia Experts

The first workshop addressed three issues. First, 12 guidelines about five design aspects contradicted each other (e.g., Rainger [18] called for using bold text for highlighting keywords and concepts, whereas [1] advocated against having bold anywhere on a page). Second, some guidelines lacked empirical evidence directly supporting their validity, though they could be inferred from the expert-level knowledge of dyslexia. Third, the connection of selected WCAG guidelines to dyslexia remained to be checked.

Method

Three experts in dyslexia – two practicing psychologists and one academic – were invited to resolve contradictions and review the validity of guidelines. Participants were invited in a quite room, introduced to the study and handed over the guidelines. Each guideline was printed on a card; the cards also included an id for easier identification. The WCAG-extracted guidelines were printed on yellow paper, while the other guidelines were printed on white paper, so the experts could clearly differentiate the two sets. We first asked the experts to individually review contradicting guidelines, and then to discuss and select the guidelines that they thought had more supporting empirical evidence. We then asked them to link the Dyslexia guidelines to the WCAG guidelines that addressed the same reading-related phenomena. Such analysis would check if the selected WCAG guidelines were indeed related to dyslexia. Finally, experts rated each guideline considering "*How much the complete violation of a guideline will degrade webpage readability for dyslexics, relative to the full adherence to the guideline*", using a 7-point Likert scale (from *not at all* to *completely*).

Results

Table 1 presents the results of dyslexia experts resolving the contradictions among the guidelines. One guideline was chosen and retained for each of five design aspects, which solved the first issue. To solve the second issue, experts' scores of guideline impact were converted into z-scores and averaged per each guideline. The total of 12 guidelines with average scores below -1 (i.e., with the impact more than one standard deviation below the average) were excluded from further analysis, as they were deemed unlikely to have an impact on readability. Addressing the third issue, the experts linked 16 of selected 17 WCAG-based guidelines to between 21 and 33 dyslexia guidelines (the experts did differ in the criteria they used to count two guidelines as linked; the workshop lasted for over two hours and we could not delay the experts for any longer to reach consensus). Finally, based on experts' feedback and additional analysis, we further excluded several guidelines that the experts failed to find meaningful (e.g., the advice of avoiding digressive hyperlinks [18]). WCAG-based and dyslexia guidelines were merged, with 67 guidelines remaining in total.

Design aspect	Guideline
Line Spacing	*- Line spacing of 1.5 point is preferable.*
Color combination	*- Use an off-white color for your background, like light gray or tan; use dark gray for text instead of pure black.*
Bold	*- Use bolding to highlight in order to emphasize keywords and concepts.*
Underline	*- Avoid underlining large blocks of text as it makes reading harder.*
Font Size	*- Use a minimum of text size 12pt or 14pt.*

Table 1. Webpage aspects and corresponding guidelines that dyslexia experts chose as the most effective.

Design Experts

The second workshop revised the guidelines with web designers, who the guidelines are ultimately aimed for. The workshop intended to address three issues: to check the clarity of guidelines, to exclude the guidelines that were less-relevant for webpages, and to categorize the guidelines in groups.

Method
Three experts with working and/or teaching experience in web design or development participated in the workshop. All 67 guidelines were printed on same-size paper cards and placed on a large empty desk in three groups, one for each expert (Figure 1). The front of each card featured a number and the guideline text. The back was empty. We introduced the experts to the study, asked them to look through the guidelines and indicate those that required further explanation or re-wording. This addressed the issues of clarity and relevenace. To address the issue of categorization, we administered two rounds of single-criterion card sorting [23], with a few adaptations. In the first round, the experts were given no pre-defined sorting criteria; they defined themselves the sorting criteria they would adopt and the resulting categories, and finally sorted the guidelines. In the second round, the experts were given three pre-defined sorting categories – *appearance*, *content*, and *functionality*, cf [4] – and also instructed to use the *other*, *not sure* or *not applicable* categories if needed. After individually sorting the guidelines in the pre-defined categories, the experts discussed and tried to resolve eventual differences in sorting.

Figure 1. Card sorting during the workshop with web experts. Each expert was assigned to a desk with a set of 67 guideline cards; yellow masking tape was used to split each desk in sections; each section provided space for one card group.

Results
Six guidelines were excluded from further analyses because experts indicated them as duplicates (e.g., *Avoid using long and dense paragraphs* and *Consider using short paragraphs*), as inapplicable to a general webpage (e.g., *Use flow charts to explain procedures and diagrams to explain spatial concepts*), or as overly vague (e.g., *Consider that people may not be able to distinguish background from foreground in images and may be distracted*). The number of guidelines in the set was thus reduced to 61.

In the first round of card sorting, each of the three experts suggested six categories for the guidelines. Little consistency was present in these categorizations, with 16 unique category labels used. Instead of choosing one of categorizations and discarding others, we tried to detect a configuration that would rely on all three experts' categorizations. We created 18 (3 experts * 6 categories each = 18) dummy variables for each guideline. The possible variable values were one (a guideline was in a category) and zeros (not in the category). We then calculated the L_1 pairwise distances among the guidelines and used the distances to conduct a hierarchical cluster analysis. The resulting tree-like hierarchy of guidelines was cut in n clusters. The cutting was repeated nine times, for n = 3 to 12 clusters. Each time we reviewed the resulting clusters for the consistency of their member guidelines. The five-cluster configuration seemed the easiest to interpret, and we retained it (Table 2, 1st column). The emerged five clusters emphasize the important aspects of design, and could be treated as the general readability dimensions in future studies and for readability-guideline presentation.

In the second round of card sorting, the experts individually sorted all guidelines in the three pre-defined categories (none of the *other*, *not sure* or *not applicable* categories were used). When later asked to compare their categories and resolve differences, the experts could not agree on a single categorization in a reasonable amount of time, arguing about almost a half of all guidelines. For example, each of them assigned *Limit the amount of content on a page to avoid scrolling* to a different category and they all had a strong justification for their choice as they claimed that the guideline could influence any of the webpage *appearance*, *content*, and *functionality*. These three categories appeared to semantically overlap, which was sub-optimal and we dropped the pre-defined category data from further analyses.

USER STUDY
The three rounds of review reduced the initial set of 199 guidelines down to 61 guidelines, which were still too many for the use in design practice. To further reduce the set down to a few core guidelines, we conducted a study, collecting three types of data: ground-truth readability data by dyslexics and average readers, compliance with guideline data by experts, and automatic readability evaluation data.

Study Sample
We opted for sampling and studying *multiple* real-life webpages. The other, classical-psychology approach would be sampling *few* webpages and carefully manipulating their appearance to a possibly unrealistic extent. Such approach would allow for definitively validating the guidelines, but would be sub-optimal for the main goal of the study: finding the core guidelines that applied to most of realistic webpages.

The sample included 36 full-page screenshots (1185 pixel wide) of Italian webpages from three domains, *local government*, *health*, and *education*. The websites in such domains should comply with accessibility standards: government and education websites were subject to the disability-discrimination laws, whereas health websites often specifically targeted people with disability, including reading disabilities.

Category	Guideline	Scope	Excluded
Visual appearance	*Use left-justified text with ragged right edge.* [1,30,5,18,4,24]	A	
	Use an off-white color for your background, like light gray or tan; use dark gray for text instead of pure black. [24,1,18,20,4]	A	
	Use a plain, evenly spaced sans serif font such as Arial and Comic Sans. [18,30,5,1,24,4,9]	A	
	Avoid using italics in the main body of the text. [30,5,1,24,4,9]	A	Lr
	Use bolding to highlight in order to emphasize keywords and concepts. [5,4]	A	
	Avoid underlining large blocks of text as it makes reading harder. [18,30,5,1,4]	A	Lr
	Avoid using more than one whitespace after period. [30]	A	Lr
	Use a minimum of text size 12pt or 14pt. [18,5,1,24,36,20]	A	
	Avoid capital letters, apart from the beginning of sentences, abbreviations, and where it is grammatically correct. [18,5,1,24,20]	A	
	Ensure navigation menus use a text size that allows for comfortable reading. [24]	E	
	Whenever text highlighting is needed, consider using boxes, border, and background color to call user attention. [18,24,5]	M	Na
	Keep the between-line spacing of 1.5 point. [5,18,1,24,4]	A	
	In the body of text, always underline hyperlinks as users expect to be able to recognise hyperlinked text or images. [18,24]	A	Na
	Avoid the fonts in which letters like b-d or p-q are perfectly mirrored letters. [4]	A	
	Ensure navigation menus differ visually from the main body of webpage. [24]	E	
	Avoid fonts with unusually shaped letters. [18]	A	
	Avoid splitting words at the end of a sentence, i.e. do not use hyphens. [18,1]	A	Lr
	Use enough white space between webpage elements. [5,18,24,36]	A	
	Ensure high luminance contrast between text and background, with the luminance of one 7 times the luminance of the other. The rule doesn't apply to low-relevance, decorative visual elements. [18,5,24,36,33]	A	
	Ensure webpage elements (buttons, links, icons, etc.) that have the same function also have the same look. [33]	E	
	Keep the white space between paragraphs of at least 1.5 times the space between text lines. [33,24,20]	A	
	Avoid formatting texts in large-width columns, especially Asian logogram texts. [18,33,24,20]	A	
	Ensure visited links are visually distinct from unvisited links. Visited links are often given in a purple colour. [24,5,18]	W	
	Avoid using blinking or moving text. [24,18,5,13]	W	
	Avoid dynamic menus or menus that use transparency, because users with dyslexia may find hard to contrast them with the background partially visible. [24]	W	
Structure of content	*If appropriate, use bullets or numbers rather than continuous prose.* [18,5,1,24,20]	M	
	Use graphics, images, and pictures to break up text, whilst remembering that graphics should be relevant to the material and not distract from the content. [18,30,24,36,4]	M	
	Use short, simple sentences in a direct style. [18,30,5,24]	M	
	Use active rather than passive voice. [5,1]	M	
	Avoid complex language and jargon. [1,24,36]	M	
	Consider using short paragraphs. [18,30,24,5]	M	
	Avoid images that are 'busy', cluttered, include irrelevant or too much extra detail. [1]	M	
	Avoid placing images above text or text around images. [1]	A	
	Place the main point at the very top of page. Place any other important information above the fold, to minimize the risk of users losing their place after scrolling. [5,13]	E	
	Place important content in a single main column, so users don't have to scan the page and pick out design elements in a two-dimensional layout. [13]	M	
	Be conscious of where sentences begin on the page. Starting a new sentence at the end of a line makes it harder to follow. [5,18,20]	M	
	Provide clear intuitive categories for menus and links. [18,24,36]	E	
	Put the main point of sentence or paragraph into the beginning of the sentence or paragraph. [1]	M	
	Always put the search box in a clear obvious position, usually the top of the page. [18]	E	
	Limit the amount of content on a page to avoid scrolling. [18,24,13]	E	
	Ensure Web pages have titles that describe their topic or purpose. [18]	E	

	Ensure the purpose of each link can be determined from the link text alone, without reading much text before the link. [24,36,33]	M	
	Ensure headings and labels concisely describe the topic or purpose of page sections and elements. [18,33]	M	
	Use section headings to organize the content. [18,33]	M	Na
	Arrange the items on index pages in a logical order (e.g., by function); avoid exclusively using the alphabetical order. [24]	W	
	When building a site index, use visualizations revealing hierarchy of website pages. [24]	W	
	Provide a printer-friendly version of webpage. [18]	W	
	Let the user change text and background colors, and enlarge text. [33]	W	
	Provide users enough time to read and use content; avoid setting time limits on reading. [33]	W	
Navigation	*Embed in Webpage texts the hyperlinks to the pages with the text-related concepts.* [24,36]	M	
	Use text and symbolism for navigational elements that are truly representational or a well-known concept e.g. a house for home. [18]	M	
	Use a breadcrumb trail (e.g., "Home page > section 1 > sub-section 1.1") to let the user understand their location on a website. [18]	E	
	Ensure navigation menus group information by function. [18,24,36]	E	
	Avoiding nested menus (e.g., containing items, sub items, sub-sub items, etc.); opt for broader one-level menus. [13]	W	
	Allow the user to go back and re-read information. [4,33]	W	
Functionality	*Include in your website common "helper" pages, such as homepage, contact us, site map, references and links, copyright and disclaimer, and accessibility statement pages.* [18,5,24]	E	
	Offer internal search on a website; provide self-completion, and orthographic verification to point errors and ease correction. [5,18,24]	W	
	Avoid horizontal scrolling on webpages. [33]	W	
	Ensure navigation buttons and links that are repeated on multiple pages of a website occur in the same relative order and similar position across the webpages. [33]	W	
Simplification	*Use the lists of dos and don'ts, which are more useful than continuous text to highlight aspects of good practice.* [18]	M	Na
	Provide a version of regular texts, which doesn't require reading ability more advanced than the lower secondary education level. [33]	W	

Table 2. The list of guidelines after 3 rounds of review. Guideline category was automatically derived from the expert-based categorization. *Scope* describes the area of guideline effect: W – applies to entire website; E – applies to an entire webpage; A – applies to all webpage elements; M – applies to the main body of content. *Excluded* describes the guidelines excluded during statistical analyses due to limited range (Lr) or non-applicability (Na).

The selected webpages featured one of six types of information: *rules & regulations, service being offered, piece of news, public announcement or public event, health-related article,* and *educational course information.* The webpages were unrelated to the region our participants were based in, which should have reduced familiarity biases. All webpages had to feature a complete article requiring no specific expertise to comprehend.

The authors collected an initial large sample and reduced it to satisfy a set of requirements. We strived to represent well the present-day Web and ensured retaining both poorly and well-designed webpages. The webpages that looked broken or abandoned were omitted from the sample. The webpages with an excessive amount of text were also omitted – too much text to read could needlessly burden our participants. Finally, our sample did not include the webpages featuring too much advertisement or dubious content, such as alternative teaching techniques or alternative medicine.

Data Collection

Data were collected in three separate rounds. First, we collected the baseline readability scores for each webpage: dyslexics and average readers read the webpages and rated their readability. Second, dyslexia- or design-experienced reviewers rated the webpages on their compliance with the subset of 47 out of 61 guidelines. Lastly, the expert-based evaluation was complemented with automatic measures: we created automatic measures for several guidelines and computed measure estimates.

User Ratings

An online user study collected the baseline ratings of webpage readability. We emailed the link to the study website to a local dyslexia association that we collaborated with in a number of research projects. The greeting webpage contained a study description and instructions (e.g., how to maximize a browser window), and asked for participants' consent to the use of their data.

Participants. A total of 36 people completed the study; 13 of them reported having been certified with dyslexia (7 female) whereas 23 (11 female, 1 refused to specify a gender) did not. We call these two groups as dyslexics and average readers. Dyslexics reported spending 4.65h a week on reading; average readers reported spending 6.20h a week on reading. Dyslexic users were slightly younger than average readers: no dyslexics were older than 40y, whereas five out of 23 average readers were (we collected the age data using age brackets).

Procedure. After reading the instructions and agreeing to their data being used in research, each participant read and rated 10 webpages using a 7-point semantic differential scale (“*reading this webpage was very simple/very difficult*”), cf., [17]. This measure has been successfully used in past psychological research [38, 40, 41]. To ensure that participants carefully read the pages, we asked three content-related questions: two multiple-choice questions (“*Choose a category that describes the website genre the best*” and “*Choose a category that describes the webpage content the best*”) and one open question (“*Describe the webpage info using up to 5 keywords*”). At the end of the study, participants filled in a brief demographic questionnaire. For each webpage, we recorded two types of data: readability rating and time to read a webpage (time between a webpage appearing on the screen and user clicking a ‘proceed’ button).

Expert Ratings

To evaluate the webpages on their conformity to guidelines, we conducted a study with designers and dyslexia experts.

Participants. We sought participants that could fluently speak both Italian and English, since the evaluated webpages were in Italian and the guidelines were in English. We also required participants to be experienced in either web development or dyslexia, or in both. In total, 14 experts (5 female; mean age = 29.9y, SD = 5.1y) working for or with the university (graphic designers, developers, and research personnel) participated in the study; their reported design and dyslexia expertise ranged from basic to substantial, which represented the whole spectrum of people who might need to apply the guidelines in practice.

Guidelines. Out of the total of 61 guidelines that were previously selected, 14 guidelines (Table 2, column *Scope* values of W – website) could not be tested on screenshots, as they would require fully functional websites as stimuli. The remaining 47 guidelines (Table 2, column *Scope* values of E, M and A) were applicable to entire webpages (E), main body of text (M) or all webpage elements (A), and could and were tested.

Procedure. The experts participated in the study individually. After reading instructions and agreeing to the use of their data, each expert rated seven webpages on their compliance with the 47 guidelines. A webpage screenshot was shown on the left of the screen; the guidelines were reported on the right (Figure 2). We used a 7-point Likert scale, with the question “*the webpage complies with the guideline* [guideline text]” and anchors “*not at all*” and “*completely*”. For each question, the experts could also select on of two extra answers, “*The guideline doesn't apply to the webpage*” and “*I don't understand the guideline*”.

The guidelines were presented in 3 clusters based on their scope: applicable to the entire webpage as a unit, applicable to the main body of content, and applicable to all individual visual or textual elements of webpage. Each group was accompanied by a short instruction on how to apply the guidelines. Experts had no time limit to complete the experiment, which on average lasted 85 minutes. The experts did not report fatigue. For each guideline, we recorded three types of data: compliance rating (1 to 7), if applicable to a particular webpage (binary), and if understood (binary).

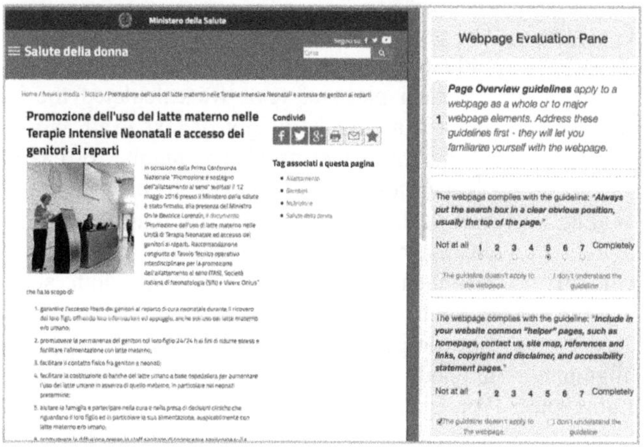

Figure 2. The set-up of expert evaluation of webpage compliance with guidelines.

Automatic Measures

The compliance of each web page with the WCAG 2.0 accessibility guidelines was automatically measured. First, we queried the API of online WCAG 2.0 validator *Achecker*[1] and recorded the number of accessibility *errors*, and *likely errors*. Each webpage size in bytes and in number of HTML elements was also recorded. We expected the numbers of errors to depend on both webpage accessibility and webpage size (larger webpages had more room for error) and needed to normalize error numbers by page sizes, i.e., we would calculate the number of errors per unit of page size.

In addition, we operationalized several of the guidelines to be automatically measured (Table 3). One might have expected algorithms to evaluate low-level aspects of webpages (e.g., the amount of italics on a page) better than human experts could: expert-based evaluation should have been supported with algorithmic evaluation. To compute the measures for the guidelines, we implemented a plugin for the Mozilla Firefox v.30 browser. This solution allowed accessing webpage content exactly how it looked in the browser, after all CSS were applied and JS scripts executed on the webpage. The plugin also let us exclude from the analyses all invisible webpage parts.

[1] http://achecker.ca/checker/index.php

Page aspect	Measure	Guideline
Amount of text	The number of characters of visible text.	*- Limit the amount of content on a page to avoid scrolling.*
Headers	The proportion of text taken by headers.	*- Use section headings to organize the content.*
Text style	The proportion of text formatted as italic, bold, or underlined.	*- Avoid using italics in the main body of the text.* *- Use bolding to highlight in order to emphasize keywords and concepts.* *- Avoid underlining large blocks of text as it makes reading harder.*
Font size	For each font size, we counted the number of characters, weighed by font size, and normalized by the number of all characters.	*- Use a minimum of text size 12pt or 14pt.*
Font type	The proportion of text styled with serif, sans serif, cursive, and fantasy fonts.	*- Use a plain, evenly spaced sans serif font such as Arial and Comic Sans.*
Line spacing	For each piece of text, we calculated the height of text element minus the height of text itself and normalized by the height of text itself. The number of characters in each piece of text was weighed by the calculated index.	*- Keep the between-line spacing of 1.5 point.* *- Keep the white space between paragraphs of at least 1.5 times the space between text lines.*
Width of text column	For each piece of text, we calculated the number of characters that fit in one line. The size of each piece of text was then weighed by the column width, summarized, and normalized by the number of all page characters.	*- Avoid formatting texts in large-width columns, especially Asian logogram texts.*
Text alignment	The proportion of webpage text that was styled as left-aligned.	*- Use left-justified text with ragged right edge.*
Luminance contrast	For each piece of webpage text, we calculated the text-background luminance contrast. The length of text pieces was weighed by the contrast, summarized, and normalized by the length of all page texts.	*- Ensure high luminance contrast between text and background, with the luminance of one 7 times the luminance of the other. The rule doesn't apply to low-relevance, decorative visual elements.*
Color difference	For each piece of webpage text, we calculated the Euclidian distances between text color and background color. The number of characters in the text pieces was weighed – large and small color distances received smaller weight; medium distances received bigger weight – summarized, and normalized by the length of all page texts.	*- Use an off-white color for your background, like light gray or tan; use dark gray for text instead of pure black.*

Table 3. The automatic measures for several readability guidelines.

Table 3 lists the implemented automatic measures and associated guidelines. All measures (except Text Amount) returned a single numeric value ranging from 0 to 1, which would indicate *how much* a webpage complied with a guideline. Out of many different elements on the same webpage (e.g., headers, buttons or paragraphs), some elements complied with a guideline; others did not. The effect of all elements needed to be aggregated in a single score per webpage, which made only meaningful answering how much a webpage complied with the guideline.

Study Results

The study collected three types of data: baseline readability scores, experts' scores of webpage conformity to guidelines, and computed scores for some of the guidelines.

User Data Review

We reviewed readability data for irregularities and excluded the data of three average readers because they used only a narrow sub-scale (e.g., one participant gave 2 to all webpages) or strongly deviated from other participants (e.g., the mean of one participant ratings was 6.3, more than double the average of all others).

The review of the expert-based data suggested that they could understand all guidelines, with a minor issue with "*Place the main point at the very top of page. Place any other important information above the fold, to minimize the risk of users losing their place after scrolling*" and "*Avoid formatting texts in large-width columns, especially Asian logogram texts*". Two experts found these guidelines difficult to understand, but we still kept them since the other 12 did not report any problem. We then reviewed the guidelines that the experts indicated as non-applicable to a webpage. Four guidelines that applied to less than a half of webpages were excluded from further analyses (Table 2, column *Excluded*). Finally, we reviewed the score histograms for each guideline and excluded four more guidelines due to their scores varying in a very limited range (e.g., mostly 7 and some 6). Such limited variance indicated that all webpages fully followed a guideline, rendering the guideline not relevant for typical webpages.

Readability Validation

Dyslexics' readability ratings moderately correlated with non-dyslexics' ratings ($r(33) = .33$, $p = .05$), suggesting both groups experienced similar, but not identical reading difficulties. Dyslexics appeared to spend longer time reading webpages than average readers (83s vs 72s, $t = 1.53$, $p = .06$). However, inspection of reading-time histograms revealed a number of outliers: the participants would get distracted and come back to the task after a pause. In such case, a comparison of means was still possible (the t-test above), but the reading-time data could not be used in correlational analyses and we focused on the readability ratings instead.

We correlated the readability scores with the expert scores of compliance with guidelines. For 15 guidelines, the compliance scores did not satisfy the normality requirement for the Pearson product moment correlation. We used Spearman correlation coefficients instead. The correlation between compliance scores and readability scores was significant for five guidelines (Table 4), suggesting that following these five guidelines could improve readability.

Guideline	Dysl	Avg R	Corr
- Use short, simple sentences in a direct style.	$-.39^{*}$	$-.35^{*}$	P
- Avoid complex language and jargon.	$-.50^{**}$	$-.35^{*}$	P
-Consider using short paragraphs.	-.15	$-.35^{*}$	P
- Put the main point of sentence or paragraph into the beginning of the sentence or paragraph.	$-.46^{**}$	-.30	P
- Use section headings to organize the content.	$-.36^{*}$	.20	S

$^{**}p < .01$; $^{*}p < .05$

Table 4. Correlations between readability scores and guideline compliance scores. The last column shows the correlation method (S – Spearman's; P – Pearson's).

The readability ratings of both dyslexics and non-dyslexics did not correlate with any WCAG-based automatic measures, neither with the number of detected accessibility errors nor with the number of errors per unit of webpage size. We used Spearman's rank correlation since the number of errors was not normally distributed.

The automatic measures of the guidelines (Table 3) performed better than the WCAG-based measures. Table 5 shows correlations between the measure scores and readability scores. The scores for two measures – text style and text alignment – were not normally distributed, which forced us to use Spearman's correlation coefficients instead of Pearson's coefficients. A review of Font Type scores revealed that most webpages used almost exclusively sans-serif fonts, ruling out a correlational analysis. Instead, the numerical scores were converted in a factor: webpages with >30% of texts in Serif fonts were marked 'serif'; others 'sans-serif'. A t-test revealed a difference between the two webpage groups for dyslexics ($t = -1.65$, $p = .07$), but not for average readers ($t = -.36$, $p = .37$), which implied dyslexics struggled to read texts in serif fonts.

Measure	Dyslexics	Avg Readers	Corr
Amount of text	.18	.35*	P
Headers	$-.46^{**}$	-.13	P
Text style: bold	-.01	.08	S
Text style: italic	.37*	-.03	S
Text style: underline	.38*	-.09	S
Font size	-.35*	-.11	P
Font type	--	--	--
Line spacing	.06	-.11	P
Width of text column	.34*	.14	P
Text alignment	.16	-.12	S
Luminance contrast	.10	.33*	P
Color difference	-.07	-.39*	P

Table 5. Correlations between readability ratings and automatic measures. The last column shows the correlation method (S – Spearman's; P – Pearson's).

Table 6 combines the guidelines that received empirical support from Table 4 and Table 5, except for *Luminance Contrast* (Table 5). The measure correlated positively with readability, implying higher contrast would increase reading difficulty, which contradicted the underlying guideline "*Ensure high luminance contrast between text and background, with the luminance of one 7 times the luminance of the other*". The contradiction could stem from people disliking black-on-white text, as said in "*Use an off-white color for your background, like light gray or tan; use dark gray for text instead of pure black*".

DISCUSSION

The research reported in this paper started from a large set of readability guidelines that could not be readily applied in Web design: they were too many and some of them were poorly formulated, too obscure, not validated, contradicted each other, or focused on text-to-speech software instead of reading behavior per se. We iteratively filtered out irrelevant guidelines and improved the others until the guideline set contained 61 actionable guidelines (Table 2).

We further reduced this 61-guideline set down to 12 core guidelines (Table 6) that our study indicated as effective. Interaction designers could rely on the validated 12 guidelines to quickly evaluate and iterate designs: 12 guidelines are relatively few and easy to follow, and at the same time, should suffice for a substantial improvement in webpage readability. The guidelines also bear implications for teaching. They give concise, actionable, and validated advice, which might ease learning design and accessibility, and help spread awareness of good design practices.

	Guideline	Dyslexics	Avg Readers
E	*- Use short, simple sentences in a direct style.*	x	x
	- Avoid complex language and jargon.	x	x
	- Consider using short paragraphs.		x
	- Put the main point of sentence or paragraph into the beginning of the sentence or paragraph.	x	
B	*- Use section headings to organize the content.*	x	
A	*- Limit the amount of content on a page to avoid scrolling.*		x
	- Avoid using italics in the main body of the text.	x	
	- Avoid underlining large blocks of text as it makes reading harder.	x	
	- Use a minimum of text size 12pt or 14pt.	x	
	- Avoid formatting texts in large-width columns.	x	
	- Use an off-white color for your background, like light gray or tan; use dark gray for text instead of pure black.		x
	- Use a plain, evenly spaced sans serif font such as Arial and Comic Sans.	x	

Table 6. The guidelines that received empirical support, based on experts' scores (E) or on automatic measures (A) or on both (B).

The research indicated that the experts could not evaluate with sufficient accuracy the low-level detail of webpages: none of the guidelines that the expert-based evaluation found helpful (Table 6, E) addressed such low-level visual detail. On the other hand, the algorithms could evaluate the low-level visual detail with sufficient accuracy (Table 6, A). Such observation may suggest the experts – all of whom were non-dyslexics – viewed the 'acceptable' levels for the low-level design detail differently from dyslexics and even from average readers. The experts may have failed to empathize with the user. This reinforces the participatory-design idea of actively involving the user in design process, but also suggests that the algorithms may act as a stand-in for the users, particularly for the user with accessibility disabilities.

The research also indicates that the WCAG 2.0 hardly addresses readability: from the core 12 guidelines, WCAG 2.0 seem to only include two, "*Use section headings to organize the content*" and "*Avoid formatting texts in large-width columns*". The next iteration of WCAG should include additional guidelines that specifically address reading. The automatic measures we developed in this paper (Table 3) could help to improve the next iterations of WCAG: they detail some of the guidelines and make them non-generic, which WCAG favors. These measures could also be used to develop an automatic validation approach

The study suggested that the readability issues of dyslexics differed from the readability issues of average readers: out of 12 core guidelines, only two applied to both dyslexic and average readers (Table 6). However, no guideline that helped dyslexics harmed average readers and vice-versa. All 12 guidelines can be applied to improve readability for all user groups and designers do not have to prioritize designing for one group at the expense of the other.

The study may also benefit fundamental dyslexia research, as some of 12 guidelines that we propose had not had empirical support. For example, three guidelines – avoiding underlining, using section headings, and putting the main point as the first sentence – were neither tested nor actively discussed in the psychological research on dyslexia. Two more guidelines – avoiding wide text columns and avoiding italics – were tested [20] but without a control group, which would not let one conclude if the guidelines affected both dyslexics and average readers, or only dyslexics. Contrasting what phenomena affected dyslexics and what phenomena affected regular readers (Table 6) may help future research to better understand dyslexia and its outcomes.

The study contained several limitations that future research should address. First, future research will use more ecologically valid stimuli (e.g., websites instead of screenshots) and more realistic tasks (e.g., search instead of reading). Such stimuli and tasks may reveal the reading shortcuts that users might take (e.g., using a search function may let the user avoid reading an entire page). Second, future research will sample more webpages. Studying more webpages might reveal additional guidelines that should be included in the core set. Finally, future research will validate our results and conclusions, relying also on non-subjective data such as reading speed and number of errors or eye-tracking data.

CONCLUSION

This paper contributes two sets of Web readability guidelines. The first set (Table 2) includes 61 guidelines that have passed all three rounds of our guideline review. These 61 guidelines can potentially improve readability, but may be too many to be practical in many design settings. The second set (Table 6) includes 12 core guidelines that the study has highlighted as significantly effective for typical webpages. However, the 12 guidelines address design aspects present in many interfaces, and we expect them to apply to other-than-webpages interactive systems.

ACKNOWLEDGMENT

The work was funded by Fondazione Cassa di Risparmio di Trento e Rovereto, and Italian Ministry of Education, University and Research (project CTN01_00034_393801).

REFERENCES

1. A. Ailesgain, O'Connor S., D. O'donoghue, A. Quinn, and G. Tinney. (2011) Make it Easy: A guide to preparing Easy to Read information. [Online]. http://www.walk.ie/userfiles/file/Make%20It%20Easy%20-%20A%20guide%20to%20preparing%20Easy%20to%20Read%20Information.pdf
2. A. Al-Wabil, P. Zaphiris, and S. Wilson, "Web navigation for individuals with dyslexia: an exploratory study," in *International Conference on Universal Access in Human-Computer Interaction*, 2007, pp. 593-602.
3. American Psychiatric Association, *Diagnostic and statistical manual of mental disorders*, 5th ed. Washington, D.C: American Psychiatric Association, 2013.
4. F. A. Aziz and H. Husni, "Interaction Design for Dyslexic Children Reading Application: A Guideline ," in *Knowledge Management International Conference (KMICe)*, 2012, pp. 682-686.
5. British Dyslexia Association. (2012) Dyslexia style guide. [Online]. http://www.bdadyslexia.org.uk/common/ckeditor/filemanager/userfiles/About_Us/policies/Dyslexia_Style_Guide.pdf
6. C. J. Chen, M. W. Y. Keong, C. S. Teh, and K. M. Chuah, "Web text reading: what satisfy both dyslexic and normal learners?," *Journal of Computers in Education*, vol. 3, no. 1, pp. 47-58, 2016.
7. M. G. Friedman and D. N. Bryen, "Web accessibility design recommendations for people with cognitive disabilities," *Technology and Disability*, vol. 19, no. 4, pp. 205-212, 2007.
8. S. He, P. Cavanagh, and J. Intriligator, "Attentional resolution and the locus of visual awareness," *Nature*, vol. 383, pp. 334-337, 1996.
9. J. E. Jackson, "Towards Universally Accessible Typography: A Review of Research on Dyslexia," in *29th Annual International Technology and Persons with Disabilities Conference*, 2014.
10. T. B. Kirkwood, J. Bond, C. May, I. McKeith, and M. M. Teh, "Foresight mental capital and wellbeing project.," The Government Office for Science, 2008.
11. S. Kurniawan and P. Zaphiris, "Research-Derived Web Design Guidelines for Older People," in *7th ACM Conference on Computers and Assessibility*, 2005, pp. 129-135.
12. M. Martelli, G. Di Filippo, D. Spinelli, and P. Zoccolotti, "Crowding, reading, and developmental dyslexia," *Journal of Vision*, vol. 9, no. 4, pp. 1-14, 2009.
13. J. Nielsen. (2005) Lower-Literacy Users: Writing for a Broad Consumer Audience. [Online]. https://www.nngroup.com/articles/writing-for-lower-literacy-users/
14. E. Paulesu et al., "Dyslexia: cultural diversity and biological unity," *Sience*, vol. 259, no. 5511, pp. 2165-2167, 2001.
15. M. Perea and V. Panadero, "Does Viotin Activate Violin More Than Viocin?," *Experimental Psychology*, vol. 61, no. 1, pp. 23-29, 2014.
16. H. Petrie and O. Kheir, "The relationship between accessibility and usability of websites," in *SIGCHI conference on Human factors in computing systems* , 2007, pp. 397-406.
17. E. Pitler and A. Nenkova, "Revisiting readability: A unified framework for predicting text quality," in *Conference on Empirical Methods in Natural Language Processing*, 2008, pp. 186-195.
18. P. Rainger. (2003) A Dyslexic Perspective on e-Content Accessibility. [Online]. https://users.dimi.uniud.it/~giorgio.brajnik/dida/psw/galleria/05/vallega/relaz-1/03-04-01_dyslexic.pdf
19. L. Rello and R. Baeza-Yates, "Good fonts for dyslexia," in 15th International ACM SIGACCESS Conference on Computers and Accessibility, 2013.
20. L. Rello, G. Kanvinde, and R. Baeza-Yates, "Layout guidelines for web text and a web service to improve accessibility for dyslexics," in *International cross-disciplinary conference on web accessibility*, 2012.
21. L. Rello, M. Pielot, and M. C. Marcos, "Make it big! The effect of font size and line spacing on online readability," in *CHI'16*, 2016, pp. 3637-3648.
22. L. Rello, M. Pielot, and M.C. Marcos, "Size Matters (Spacing Not): 18 Poionts for a Dyslexic-friendly Wikipedia," in *10th International Cross-Disciplinary Conference on Web Accessbility*, 2013.
23. G. Rugg and P. McGeorge, "The sorting techniques: a tutorial paper on card sorts, picture sorts and item sorts," *Expert Systems*, vol. 22, no. 3, pp. 94-107, 2005.
24. V. F. Santana, R. de Oliveira, L. D. A. Almeida, and M. C. C. Baranauskas, "Web accessibility and people with dyslexia: a survey on techniques and guidelines," in *International Cross-Disciplinary Conference on Web Accessibility*, 2012.
25. V. F. Santana, R. Oliveira, L. D. A. Almeida, and M. Ito, "Firefixia: An accessibility web browser customization toolbar for people with dyslexia," in *10th International Cross-Disciplinary Conference on Web Accessibility*, 2013.
26. M. H. Schneps et al., "Shorter lines facilitate reading in those who struggle," *PloS one*, vol. 8, no. 8, 2013.

27. P. H. K. Seymour, M. Aro, and J. M. Erskine, "Foundation literacy acquisition in European orthographies," *British Journal of Psychology*, vol. 94, pp. 143-174, 2003.
28. D. Spinelli, M. De Luca, A. Judica, and P. Zoccolotti, "Crowding effects on word identification in developmental dyslexia," *Cortex*, vol. 38, no. 2, pp. 179-200, 2002.
29. M. F. Theofanos and J. Redish, "Guidelines for accessible and usable web sites: Observing users who work with screen readers," *Interactions*, vol. 10, no. 6, pp. 38-51, 2003.
30. A. Tseng. (2012) uxmovement.com. [Online]. http://uxmovement.com/content/ 6-surprising-bad-practices-that-hurt-dyslexic-users/
31. T. R. Vidyasagar and K. Pammer, "Dyslexia: a deficit in visuo-spatial attention, not in phonological processing," *Trends in Cognitive Sciences*, vol. 14, no. 2, pp. 57-63, 2010.
32. D. Whitney and D. M. Levi, "Visual crowding: A fundamental limit on conscious perception and object recognition," *Trends in cognitive sciences*, vol. 15, no. 4, pp. 160-168, 2011.
33. World Wide Web Consortium. (2008) w3.org. [Online]. https://www.w3.org/TR/WCAG20/
34. Y. Yeshurun and E. Rashal, "Precueing attention to the target location diminishes crowding and reduces the critical distance," *Journal of Vision*, vol. 10, no. 10, pp. 1-16, 2010.
35. C. H. Yu and R. C. Miller, "Enhancing web page readability for non-native readers," in *the sIGCHI conference on human factors in computing systems*, 2010, pp. 2523-2532.
36. V. Zarach and JISC CETIS. (2002) Ten Guidelines for Improving Accessibility for People with Dyslexia. [Online]. http://wiki.cetis.ac.uk/Ten_Guidelines_for_Improving_Accessibility_for_People_with_Dyslexia
37. M. Zorzi et al., "Extra-large letter spacing improves reading in dyslexia," *Proceedings of the National Academy of Sciences*, vol. 109, no. 28, pp. 11455-11459, 2012.
38. Braun, C. C., Mine, P. B., & Silver, N. C. (1995). The influence of color on warning label perceptions. *International Journal of Industrial Ergonomics*, *15*(3), 179-187.
39. K. Höök and J. Löwgren. Strong concepts: Intermediate-level knowledge in interaction design research. *ACM Transactions on Computer-Human Interaction (TOCHI)*, *19*(3), 23, 2012.
40. E. Pitler and A. Nenkova. "Revisiting readability: A unified framework for predicting text quality." In *Proceedings of the Conference on Empirical Methods in Natural Language Processing* (pp. 186-195). Association for Computational Linguistics, 2008.
41. N. C. Silver and C. C. Braun. "Perceived readability of warning labels with varied font sizes and styles." *Safety Science*, *16*(5-6), 615-625, 1993.

Translating Texture: Design as Integration

Melanie Feinberg
School of Information and Library Science (SILS)
University of North Carolina at Chapel Hill
mfeinber@unc.edu

Daniel Carter, Julia Bullard, Ayse Gursoy
iSchool, The University of Texas at Austin
carter.daniel.w@gmail.com;
julia.a.bullard@gmail.com; agursoy@utexas.edu

ABSTRACT

This conceptual essay uses the notion of *texture* to articulate the relationship between data infrastructure (the attributes and value parameters that give data its shape) and data environment (the mode of implementation in which data is stored and manipulated). We take experimental datasets that we authored with unorthodox, weird data infrastructure and translate those datasets from one data evironment to another. In performing these translations, we surface integration as a design activity. Integration work is often tedious, mundane, and technical—but it is nonetheless design. We show how texture arises from the integration of material components, demonstrating the effects of integration work upon user experience.

Author Keywords

Data; infrastructure; metadata; materiality; critical design

ACM Classification Keywords

H.5.m. Information interfaces and presentation (e.g., HCI): Miscellaneous.

INTRODUCTION

Last summer, I moved to a new university and into a new office. The new office had many similarities to the old one: it had similar furnishings (bookshelves, filing cabinet, work surface, desk chair, visitor's chair) and was a similar size and shape. Both offices had a window on one wall and were painted a similar off-white color, with similar beige berber carpet. All my belongings—books, papers, photographs, brightly colored rug—traveled with me. It should have been pretty much the same as my old office. But the new office was terrible. Why?

My new office is on the garden level, or half basement. While the window is decently sized, it's higher up the wall than my old office, and trees in front of the building block the sun. An artificial light source is necessary at all times of the day. But the overhead lights in my new office are harshly fluorescent.

DIS 2017, June 10-14, 2017, Edinburgh, United Kingdom
© 2017 ACM. ISBN 978-1-4503-4922-2/17/06...$15.00
DOI: http://dx.doi.org/10.1145/3064663.3064730

The change in light most affected the function of that brightly colored rug. In my old office, the rug integrated with the light to draw people in. Nothing else in my old office was special, but people would refer to the rug as they remarked how the office seemed so warm and inviting. In the new office, the rug changed. Its colors seemed harsh and abrasive, and the office too felt grating and prickly. I tried moving the furniture in all sorts of combinations, but that didn't help. Finally I got some lamps, and some Marimekko wall hangings, and turned off the overhead lights. I tried to recreate the warm texture of the old office by changing the character of the light, not its intensity.

With these changes, the office now feels more like the old one. But visitors don't mention the rug anymore. Although the new office experience now approximates the old one's warmth, the function of the rug has permanently changed.

My rug story is not unusual. Many of us can point to similar experiences, where initially the integration of components in a new environment seems like it will be a mundane matter of technical implementation—just unpacking. But then you unpack, and something is off: the composition is out of balance. The design situation has shifted, and the relationships between components must be renegotiated. Still, although common, integration work is not often remarked upon as a design activity, except when the new environment is radically different from the original: designing for a Web-based application instead of a desktop one, or for mobile instead of the Web. When the environment change is more subtle, like moving to another office—or when migrating data to another database, or replacing one data source with another—integration seems closer to implementation, with less effect on experience.

But as "computer" interaction continues its turn towards data, integration requires more direct attention as a design activity. Infrastructural components that might have once seemed tangential to user experience—outside the core work of design—increase in importance. Here's an everyday example: when Netflix simplified the "altgenre" categories displayed on its main page, simplifying complex categories like "Visually-striking cerebral crime thrillers in Japan" to "Cerebral" or "Crime" or "Thrillers," the whole experience changed for me, even as the filmstrip-style interface and content remained the same. I had much less interest in scrolling down or across. Previously, I might have said that the filmstrip interface encouraged browsing, but after the change in data infrastructure, I realized that the *relationship between* the filmstrip interface, intriguingly complex categories, and available video selections encouraged browsing, not one or the other in isolation. Similarly, if you had asked me before the move, I'd have said that my rug itself was warm and welcoming. The old office was not exceptional, and I did not think that the environment itself had anything to do with the experience of the rug. Moving to the new office showed that the rug itself was not warm: it was the integration of the rug in the office that produced that feeling of warmth.

This paper examines integration and design through the lens of *texture*. As introduced to the HCI community by Robles and Wiberg, texture describes the "the intersection of surface and structural form" that arises through the integration of material components [14]. The relation between components in my office produces its texture. Here, my co-authors and I use texture to understand the relationship between data infrastructure (the attributes and value parameters that give data its shape) and data environment (the database implementation in which data is stored and manipulated). We take experimental datasets that we had authored with unorthodox, weird data infrastructure and translate those datasets from one database implementation to another. Performing these translations enables us to critically examine the design work of integration. It also enables us to reflect upon the interaction between data infrastructure and data environment, and to describe the resulting effects on texture. Although our ruminations on texture arise through empirical work, however, this paper is a conceptual essay, not a report on study findings. We use our design work to explore ideas, not to evaluate a hypothesis or to demonstrate the utility of a particular design approach.

This paper makes several contributions. First, we surface the work of integration—work that, because it may seem tedious, mundane, and technical, is often marginalized as mere implementation, incidental to the primary work of design. Second, we show how texture arises from the integration of material components, demonstrating how integration work bears directly upon user experience. Third, we extend recent conversations on digital materiality and design. Our project provides evidence for the view that materiality arises from relationships between components, rather than from components themselves.

Although integration work has always been a necessary element of software development, the increasing role of data in *constituting* experience makes the relationship between integration work and experience design particularly salient at this historical moment. We challenge the notion that data is merely an input to design. We believe that design must integrate data—that it must concern itself with data infrastructure and data environments—and not merely provide access to data by creating interfaces on top of those components.

Our paper proceeds as follows. First, we situate this essay within conversations about digital materiality, focusing on the notion of texture. Next, we describe our translation project, where each co-author integrated data infrastructure that we had created for one data environment into a different data environment. We describe two of these translations in detail, focusing on the challenges posed by the original designs, the integration work we undertook to meet those challenges, and the effects of our integration work on texture. We conclude by reflecting on texture as the product of integration work.

RELATED WORK

We draw on a body of interdisciplinary scholarship that seeks to understand the qualities of digital artifacts and how those qualities emerge through the integration of materials, people, and practices [8]. In these studies, the work of design serves to locate, express, and accentuate qualities such as playability and suppleness in digital artifacts [11, 17]. Similar accounts describe the work performed to create properties in physical materials, as when furniture designer David Pye proposes that materials such as walnut are "made" through the activities of workmanship, and not "found" in nature [12]. In HCI, research emphasizes how material qualities emerge through complex relations between materials, designers, users, and activities. For example, Dourish and Mazmanian consider how digital and film photography structure different activities and focus attention on different material qualities of photographs, even as the content of an image might remain the same in both modalities [3]. Rosner, likewise, illustrates how materials in a bookbinding workshop reveal themselves situationally [15]. Redström describes how some aspects of design occur in use and not prior to it, as with customizing a personal computing device [13]. These explorations within HCI complement work from other disciplines. For example, archeologist Christopher Tilley argues that prehistoric rock art in Norway must be understood as the relationship between image, environment, and viewer [18].

Similarly, Paul Dourish unpacks digital media scholar Lev Manovich's contention that "databases" employ a different expressive logic than "narrative" by noting that Manovich's "database" is understood at a very high level of abstraction [2]. Dourish argues that database models, such as a relational model and a noSQL model, may emphasize very different properties. While one might implement a conceptual model in both a relational database and a noSQL database, this is not a trivial mapping exercise. Moreover, the affordances assumed by a particular logical model affect the development of a (theoretically abstract) conceptual model. Relational databases, in their requirements to develop systematic data structures prior to, and separate from, the capture of data values, foreground operations of sorting, splitting, and recombining according to well-defined, consistent structural parameters. NoSQL databases, which do not use an external schema, do not suggest such operations. The material properties of data emerge differently within the representational infrastructures of different database models.

Robles and Wiberg propose *texture* as a design quality that is produced through the integration of material components [14]. While we might speak of a material as having a texture—of wool as being rough or silk as being liquid—the texture of an artifact emerges from the manipulation of all its materials, from their relationships to each other. The texture of a wool rug might be warm and enveloping rather than rough, or it might be hard and firm, depending on the integration of materials in the composition. (While Robles and Wiberg introduce the notion of texture to HCI, texture has been used similarly in the arts and humanities; in referring to the texture of a symphony, for example, a music critic indicates the quality that emerges through the integration of each instrument's part into the whole.)

Robles and Wiberg emphasize that texture does not exclusively refer to tactile sensations or to tangible objects. They articulate texture as having equal application across digital and tangible domains. For us, texture provides a means of generalizing Dourish's observations about database implementations. Substituting wool for silk in a rug might produce an artifact that looks similar, but the texture, and the experience, will be different. To maintain a similar texture with different materials, the relationships between components may need to be redesigned. This recalibration might involve significant changes to the composition. Obtaining a liquid texture in a wool rug might involve using intricate weaving patterns to create the appearance of fluidity by a visual mechanism, rather than tactile sensation. Similarly, maintaining texture between a relational database and a NoSQL database may involve more than technical recalibration.

TEXTURE AND TRANSLATION

Robles and Wiberg frame their discussion of texture around their own translation project [14]. They introduce the Swedish Icehotel, a seasonal structure built in a sparsely populated area of the Arctic Circle. The Icehotel comprises guest rooms, furnishings, public areas, and other common hotel features, all created from ice. Robles and Wiberg's project, Icehotel X, was to maintain the texture of the Swedish Icehotel in an indoor environment in the cosmopolitan city of Copenhagen. Robles and Wiberg articulated the texture of the Swedish Icehotel as the integration of ice, structure, and environment: the texture was produced from a particular use of ice in a time and place in the Arctic Circle, not just from creating an ice building. Accordingly, Robles and Wiberg created Icehotel X as a multimedia installation: not actually an ice building at all. Icehotel X fused ice, light, and low-fidelity digital projection to produce a texture similar to that of the Icehotel, indoors in Copenhagen.

The basic structure of our translation project was similar to that of Robles and Wiberg. We took a design that employed a mundane material in an unusual way to create a distinctive texture, and then we attempted to maintain that texture in translating the design to a new environment.

In our project, the original designs comprised small libraries of videos about the U.S. state of Texas, made with purposefully ambiguous data infrastructure, or metadata. While creating Texas-themed video libraries out of ambiguous metadata is much less spectacular than creating a hotel out of ice, our goals were similar. It seems absurd and worse than useless to create a hotel out of ice, but doing so enables us to think about ice, and hotels, and user experience, in new ways. The experience of staying in the Icehotel is clearly not about getting a good night's sleep, but it's still a valuable—if challenging—experience. Moreover, the process of designing and building a hotel out of ice enables us to understand the texture of that new experience and the material relations that produce it.

Similarly, it seems absurd and useless to structure a collection of information resources with purposefully ambiguous metadata. We typically design metadata to enforce cleanly delineated categorical divisions between resources, and so to facilitate reliable, predictable retrieval, filtering, and sorting. But there is an intractable problem with typical metadata design. The world is dynamic, unstable, ambiguous, and unruly, and it inevitably bursts through any category boundaries we might devise. Metadata is *inherently* ambiguous (even if computers are the agents collecting the data).

Star and Bowker use the idea of *residuality* to describe this phenomenon [16]. Star and Bowker assert that there's always something outside, insufficiently articulated, or split among a set of categories. Nonetheless, best practices for metadata design continually attempt to define and enforce category boundaries in a consistent, reliable way [19].

The Swedish Icehotel took an inevitable phenomenon that we would typically attempt to minimize—the severity of winter in the Arctic Circle—and exploited that phenomenon as a design resource. We did the same. We took an inevitable phenomenon that we typically attempt to minimize—residuality in data infrastructure—and exploited that phenomenon as a design resource. In our original project, each co-author created our own system of data infrastructure (metadata) that accentuated and made use of residuality, instead of trying to suppress it. We used our data infrastructure to separately organize the same small set of Texas-themed digital videos in the same data environment, a digital library system called the Open Video Digital Library Toolkit (OVDLT) [7]. (In other words, each co-author used our unique data infrastructure to organize the same videos in the same environment, so that each design differed only in its metadata.) [Findings from our experiences building these original designs appear in 4, 5.]

In creating these original designs, we learned some things about ambiguous metadata and the kinds of experiences that ambiguous metadata might support. The Swedish Icehotel might be terrible for a good night's sleep, but what kinds of experiences does it enable? Thinking about such questions can help us think about other kinds of experiences for hotels, in addition to restful sleep: the hotel as immersive sensory environment. Similarly, our original designs were terrible at facilitating retrieval. But we proposed that our designs also enabled other kinds of experiences with data [4]. Following Tim Ingold, we described the form of experience supported by ambiguous metadata as wayfaring, or exploring a landscape [10]. If typical metadata is supposed to support retrieval of items, ambiguous metadata supports understanding the relationships that make up a collection of items. If typical metadata is supposed to have a lucid, clean, articulated texture, like clear plastic pipes, ambiguous metadata has an organic, layered, interconnected, shaggy texture, like roots of a plant.

The Swedish Icehotel is rebuilt every winter in the same location by different designer teams. Each winter's Icehotel is different, but the textural similarity between designs enables the Icehotel Web site to articulate a coherent general experience that spans the years [9]. We also rebuilt our metadata designs with new designer teams, who used a different set of videos on a different theme, and the texture of the designs—organic, layered, interconnected—was similar [5]. At that point, just like Robles and Wiberg, we found ourselves pondering texture. Robles and Wiberg had asked themselves if it was possible to recreate the texture of the Icehotel outside of its original environment in the winter of the Arctic Circle. In turn, we asked ourselves if it was possible to recreate the texture of our original designs in another data environment. Robles and Wiberg translated the original rural, Arctic Icehotel to the urban, indoor Icehotel X. We translated our original video libraries from the OVDLT, which operated like a relational database, to a new data environment, Scalar, which operates using a "rhizomic," graph-based paradigm.

In subsequent sections, we'll describe two translations in detail, focusing on challenges posed by the original designs, integration work we undertook to meet those challenges, and effects of that work on texture. First, though, we compare the OVDLT and Scalar. In Robles and Wiberg's translation, differences between their two environments are readily apparent: empty snowy landscape and cosmopolitan city. In our case, the differences between the OVDLT and Scalar require a somewhat technical explanation. But part of our contribution arises from confronting this thicket of detail: although the particularities of the OVDLT and Scalar might seem mind-numbingly specific, texture emerges from these particularities, just as it does from snow and city.

Comparing Two Very Different Data Environments: The OVDLT and Scalar

The OVDLT and Scalar are as different as the rural Arctic of the Swedish Icehotel and the cosmopolitan Copenhagen of Icehotel X. The OVDLT experience is modeled around actions typically enabled through relational databases—filtering, sorting, selecting, searching. In contrast, Scalar operates around a network paradigm where "anything can do everything to anything" [1]. (While there is now a 2.0 interface for Scalar, our translations were developed using the original 1.0 version.)

The following comparison between Scalar and the OVDLT helps us to subsequently explain how the material quality of texture emerges through what appear to be tedious, specific details of particular data environments. Our translation project demonstrated the extent to which texture was ultimately dependent on integration work with these environmental particularities. These details are tedious and complicated, to be sure, but they have a direct relationship to texture. Materiality emerges through the boring details!

To begin, we'll compare describing a video in the two systems (see Figure 1 for a visual representation). The OVDLT is a digital library system for a single kind of entity: videos. The OVDLT provides features for designers to define different kinds of metadata to apply to videos, to add videos, and to catalog videos according to the metadata structure that the designer has specified. Each video in the library has its own catalog record that displays the video's metadata in a standardized interface.

OVDLT users browse, search, filter, sort, and select between videos in a collection via the metadata infrastructure. For example, a user can browse the videos associated with a particular descriptor (a descriptor is a designer-defined label, or tag) and then select between videos in that category by viewing other metadata associated with each video. Or users can browse thematic playlists annotated by the library designer. (OVDLT designs in Figures 2 and 4 display some of these features.)

In the OVDLT, controlled descriptors are defined in sets, using an administrative interface. For example, a designer might create a descriptor set called Location, with associated descriptor values (typically just called *descriptors)* such as Austin, Dallas, and Houston, or a descriptor set called Characters, with descriptors such as Mavericks and Believers. A descriptor, such as Austin or Believers, can then be applied to videos in a separate cataloging interface. As presented to users, descriptors are associated with their sets. On the home page, a user opens a menu called Characters and clicks Believers to obtain the videos associated with the Believers descriptor. This process aligns with a relational model of an attribute/value pair assigned to an entity.

In contrast, "everything" in Scalar is conceptualized as a "page," where a page operates as a node in a network. Pages are empty containers, initially represented in Scalar as a blank display area. The Scalar designer fills pages by adding content such as text and embedded media. A "tag" in Scalar is a relationship between pages: a page displays links to the other pages that "tag" it. The Scalar implementation of tags is different from most tagging systems; a tag is not a different "thing" from the resource it describes. In Scalar, a tag is relationship between functionally equivalent pages.

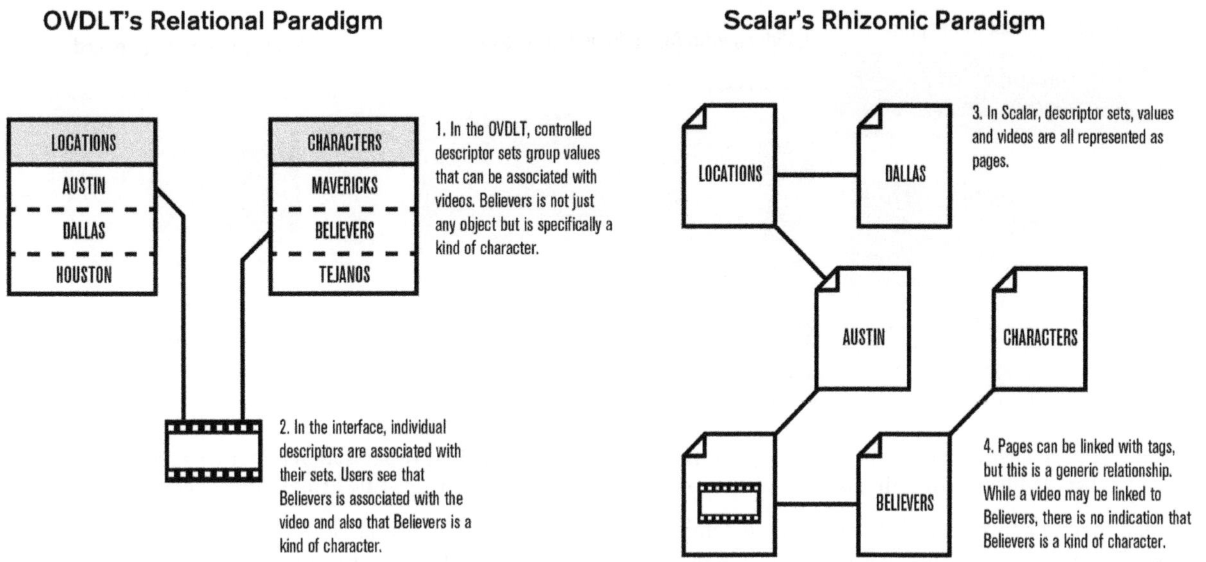

Figure 1. Differences in data structure as perceived by designers working with the OVDLT and Scalar.

Scalar does not predefine a mechanism to recreate the idea of a video (entity) associated with a Character (attribute) called Believers (value). One can create pages for all of these constructs: a page for the video, a page for Characters, and a page for Believers. From the perspective of Scalar, however, there is no conceptual difference between a page with an embedded video and pages meant to represent concepts like Characters or Believers. While a page called Believers could have a tag relationship to both Characters and to a page with an embedded video, there is not a native mechanism to indicate that Believers are Characters, or that the relationship between "Believers" and a video and "Believers" and Characters is conceptually distinct.

Comparatively, the OVDLT constrains design choices. Beyond the customizable metadata elements, nothing in the user experience can be changed. Videos are the only allowable resource type. User operations are limited to those enabled by the OVDLT: users can access a list of all videos, they can use menus to filter by descriptor values, they can create sets via text search, and they can access playlists. From within an individual video's metadata page, users can click descriptor links to access other videos associated with that descriptor. Designers cannot create additional means to discover and and arrange resources.

In contrast, while a Scalar "book" (the name for a collection of pages in Scalar terminology) can describe and enable access to media resources, expression of that functionality to users requires extensive designer intervention. In Scalar, designers determine content and arrangement for each page individually. Pages can be "tagged" to other pages; pages can be connected via embedded Web-like links; pages can be set in a linear order in a grouping structure called a "path." Pages can also be listed in a persistent "main menu" that appears to the left of the page display. The final structural element in Scalar is the annotation. Annotations are a form of relationship similar to tags, except they link a page to a specific point within a media file (a whole-part relationship instead of a whole-whole relationship). For a video, annotations link another page to a particular point or duration within the video. The 30-second appearance of a cowboy in a video might be annotated with a page that discusses cowboy symbolism, for example. If that video were then embedded within a subsequent page, the Cowboy Symbolism annotation would accompany the video.

Using tags, embedded links, paths, and annotations, the creator of a Scalar book determines its unique navigational structure. All page content is individually specified and can combine any number of media elements with embedded text. Custom JavaScript can be added to adapt the visual design of each page beyond a set of provided themes. The user experience of a Scalar implementation is thus specific to each design. Although the navigational features of tags, annotations, links, and paths are limited, they can be deployed by the designer in flexible, diverse ways.

The differences between Scalar and the OVDLT facilitate our exploration of texture through translation well. Scalar presents itself to both designers and users through a network model, while the OVDLT presents itself through a set-based, relational model. One can make a digital video library in Scalar, but Scalar doesn't prescribe a structure to present such functionality. Set-based filtering operations are built into the OVDLT interface; this is not the case in Scalar. The OVDLT clearly separates resources (videos) from attributes and values (descriptors and their sets). In Scalar, everything operates as a page. But Scalar's flexibility enables an approximate representation of everything in the OVDLT to be expressed in a Scalar book, although the mode of that representation might vary extensively depending on the book designer. For example, an OVDLT descriptor might be represented as a tag,

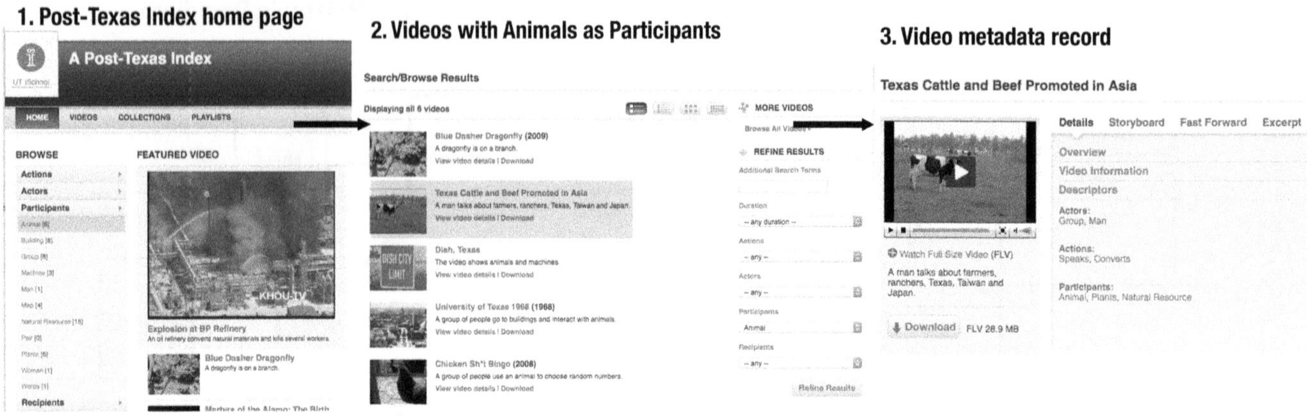

Figure 2. Post-Texas Index in the OVDLT. (1) is the home page. By clicking Animals under Participants in the Browse menu, a list of videos with Animals as Participants (2) appears. Clicking a video title brings up its metadata record (3).

annotation, path, or link in Scalar—or as some combination of these. In the next sections, we describe our project to translate the OVDLT designs in Scalar. We explain our integration work to manipulate the data environment—Scalar—and maintain the material quality of texture in the translated designs. As with the descriptions of the OVDLT and Scalar, the details of our manipulations may seem tediously specific, but our project shows how texture depends on such mundane integration activities.

TRANSLATING TEXTURE

Each of the four coauthors translated their own OVDLT design into Scalar. In formulating this act of translation, we emphasized conceptual integrity of the original texture. We were not interested in reproducing formal and functional details from one environment to another, but in understanding the integration work to renegotiate relationships between data infrastructure and environment.

We describe two of our four translations in detail, focusing on the challenges posed by the original designs, the integration work we undertook to meet those challenges, and the effects of our integration work on texture. We limit our discussion to two examples in order to present their interpretive analyses in greater depth, although we did use all four designs to develop our overall account of the work. Because the other two translation strategies align with the included examples, this omission simplifies our discussion without changing our argument.

These translation descriptions include nitty-gritty details of integration work to express the texture of a particular data configuration in a new environment. For designers who focus on visual or physical designs, and not the design of data itself, the work we describe may seem unfamiliar. The operations that we describe—changing a descriptor to an annotation, a set to a path—are the design work of data infrastructure, as implemented in each data environment.

TRANSLATION 1: POST-TEXAS INDEX

In this section, we describe the integration work we performed to translate one of our original designs from the OVDLT to Scalar. First, we introduce the original design and characterize its texture. Next, we describe how we integrated the data infrastructure of the original design into the new Scalar environment. We conclude by assessing the texture produced through that integration work.

The Original Design and Its Texture: Post-Texas Index

Post-Texas Index, the original design in the OVDLT, employed its descriptors at an unnaturally high level of abstraction, focusing description on the basic action of identified entities in the videos (see Figure 2). The human significance of the video content was not engaged. Descriptor sets included Actions, Actors, Participants, and Recipients; descriptors in the latter three were identical. Actions values included generic verbs such as Speaks and Converts; Actors, Participants, and Recipients values included generic, abstract nouns such as Animal, Group, Machine, and Man. Sentence summaries for each video repeated the banal, abstract metadata of the descriptors. A video documenting an oil rig explosion might be summarized, for example, as "A man speaks." (In fact, fifteen videos are summarized as "A man speaks.")

We've previously discussed our initial characterization of ambiguous metadata as having a layered, interconnected, organic texture. In Post-Texas Index, the metadata is layered, interconnected, and organic—the metadata is not, for example, applied consistently to each video—but the texture of the overall design is that of an artificially generated meshwork, not a natural one. The conceit motivating Post-Texas Index was that of an alien life-form from sometime in the future attempting to make sense of humans as a type of specimen, and the highly abstract description *is* alien; while it is accurate and objective to describe a video's contents as a man speaking, it is not how people describe things. From a human perspective, this objective and accurate metadata is arbitrary and absurd.

The design technique used to convey this idea in the OVDLT relied on the repetition of individual metadata statements (such as the Actor in a video being "Man" and the Action being "Speaks"). Texture in Post-Texas Index

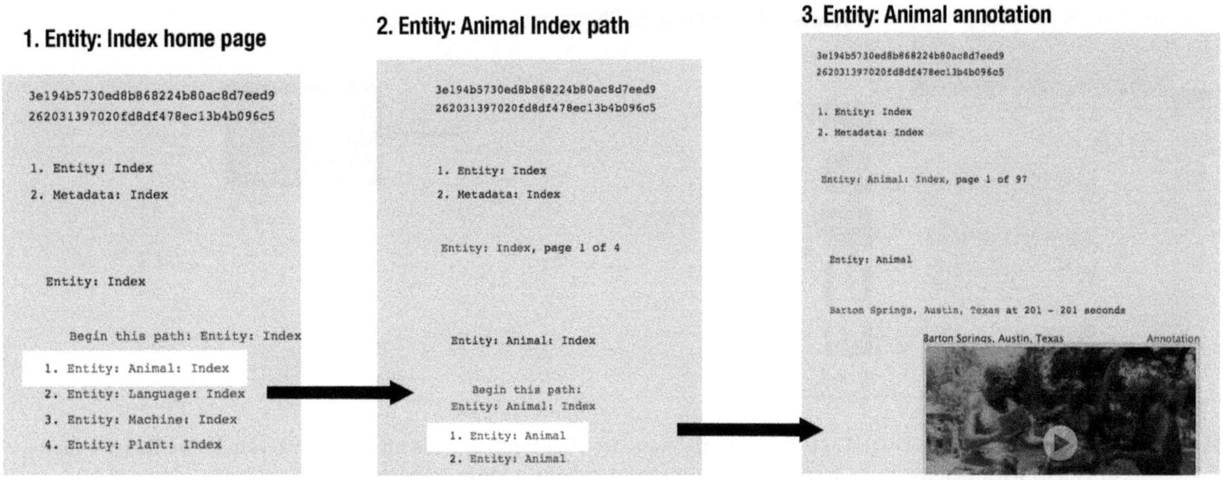

Figure 3. Entity: Index Scalar translation. (1) Entity: Index home page. (2) 97 identically named pages appear in a linear "path" when Entity: Animal: Index on (1) is clicked (only the first 2 pages in the path are in the figure). (3) appears when the first Entity: Animal page is clicked on (2). This page annotates a segment of a video (Barton Springs, Austin, Texas) with Animals in it.

arose from the continual rediscovery that structural sense (a Man is indeed a type of Actor in the videos) can lead to conceptual nonsense (this is true but useless for purposes of understanding what each video means, in human terms).

Integration Work: Translating the Data Infrastructure of Post-Texas Index into the Scalar Data Environment

The repetition strategy did not align well with the Scalar environment at the same scale as it did in the OVDLT. In the OVDLT, one could create a descriptor with the same label (Man) in multiple descriptor sets (Actor, Participant, Recipient), and the OVDLT provided facilities to keep these separate and distinct. In Scalar, one could create multiple pages titled Man, but there was no easy mechanism to maintain distinctions between these pages. We found it impossible to keep duplicate descriptor pages (Man, Group, Woman, Animal, and so on, in Actor, Participant, and Recipient variations) straight in Scalar. Our situation was like trying to replicate an actual ice hotel in Copenhagen: it would be a terrific effort to accomplish, and the relationship between components and environment—the material quality of texture—would shift anyway.

Accordingly, to maintain the texture of alien, artificial interconnection in the translation to Scalar, we dramatically narrowed the data infrastructure in the translation, Entity: Index (see Figure 3). We eliminated the OVDLT descriptor sets (Actors, Participants, Recipients, Actions), along with most of the other metadata elements (such as sentence summaries). Indeed, any sense of the design as a collection of discrete videos was eliminated. Instead, Entity: Index has a hugely limited function: users progress linearly through all the video segments where four "entities" appear: animals, language, machines, and plants. (Humans are a type of animal in this classification.)

The Entity: Index home page presents a list of these four "entity" types. Upon clicking one of the four, a list of all annotated appearances of that entity are arranged in linear order. Each annotation has the same name. For example, clicking Entity: Animal leads to a path with 97 identically named annotations. Clicking an annotation in the list retrieves the video cued where that entity (e.g., an animal) appears. The "database," such as it is, no longer represents videos at all, and the notion of Texas has likewise disappeared. Entity: Index merely lists all the video segments where the four "entities" appear.

The Texture of the Translated Entity: Index

Reading about the scale of the integration work performed for this translation, it might seem as if Entity: Index was unrelated to Post-Texas Index. Post-Texas Index was, recognizably, a collection of videos about Texas. Entity: Index is not even clearly a collection of videos, and nothing in Entity: Index mentions the location of Texas. But although videos were important to the OVDLT as a data environment, and Post-Texas Index had to accomodate that in its original design, the texture of Post-Texas Index arose primarily from its strategy of abstract repetition.

In the OVDLT, repetition was enabled through manipulation of diverse metadata elements. The same abstract information—that there was a Man in a video, for example—was repeated in multiple ways across different metadata elements (different descriptor sets, sentence summaries, and so on). This *breadth* of repetition was not replicable in Scalar. Scalar, however, enabled *depth* of repetition that wasn't possible in the OVDLT. In using the Scalar annotation feature to associate "entities" with video segments instead of entire videos, Entity: Index heightened interconnection by focusing user attention on the web of entity appearances, rather than discrete videos. In Scalar, moreover, user action could be constrained to enforce repetition. Unlike the Post-Texas Index, the Entity: Index user can only progress through entity annotations (traverse the network in a linear fashion) and cannot filter, sort, or

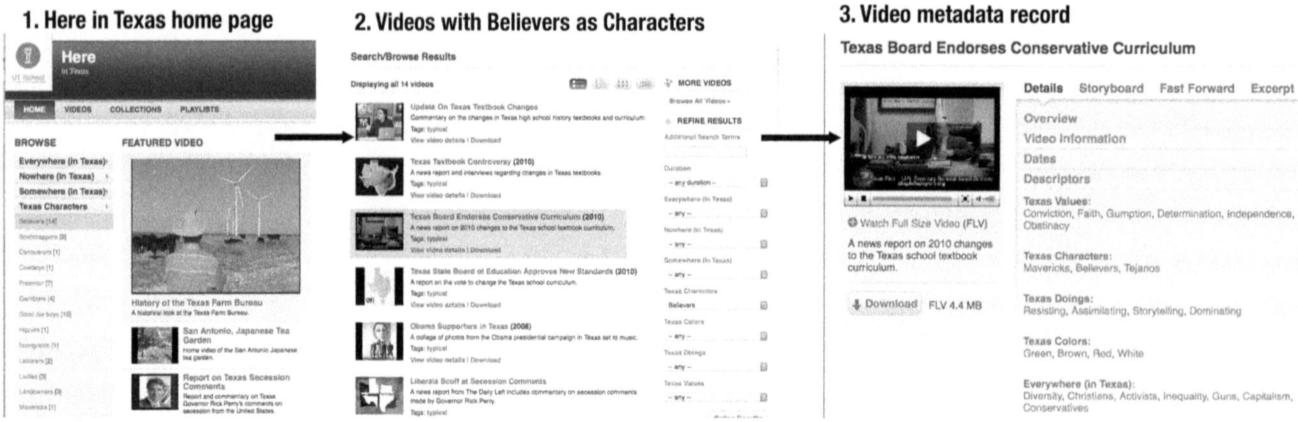

Figure 4. Here in Texas in the OVDLT. (1) is the home page. By clicking Believers under Characters in the Browse menu, a list of videos with Believers as Characters (2) appears. Clicking a video title brings up its metadata record (3).

otherwise compare or analyze them (the user cannot create or manipulate entity sets).

Although repetition is implemented quite differently in the original design and in its translation, the two designs feel similar: the texture of alien interconnection is maintained. The result is like that achieved by Robles and Wiberg in Icehotel X; while the material components of the original and translated design are very different, their integration maintains similar relationships, and the texture reflects this.

TRANSLATION 2: HERE IN TEXAS

In this section, we describe the integration work we performed to translate another of our original designs from the OVDLT to Scalar. The structure of this section is identical to the previous one. First, we introduce the original design and characterize its texture. Next, we describe how we integrated the data infrastructure of the original design into the Scalar environment. We conclude by assessing the texture produced through that integration.

The Original Design and Its Texture: Here in Texas

The strategy of abstraction and repetition employed in Post-Texas Index could have been applied to any dataset: it wasn't particularly important that the data infrastructure created for Post-Texas Index (descriptor sets of Actors, Participants, Recipients and Actions) was employed to structure a set of videos about Texas. In contrast, this original design, called Here in Texas, relied on a much deeper integration of infrastructure and environment with the data content. Here in Texas used the application of its data infrastructure to the video data to simultaneously endorse, reject, and question perceptions of "Texas" as a distinctive place and of "Texan" as an identity.

Some Here in Texas descriptors reflect popular images of Texas. For example, in the Characters descriptor set, such values include Good Ole Boys, Bootstrappers, and Mavericks. Other Here in Texas descriptors comment upon the insufficiency of these popular images. In the same Characters descriptor set, such values include Unfortunates, Immigrants, and Laborers. Moreover, these descriptors are applied to videos in ambiguous ways that reflect conflicted thoughts and feelings. The Character descriptor Believers is a representative example. Believers on its own implies the religious belief of fundamentalist Christians, a group often associated with Texas. In Here in Texas, Believers is often applied to videos that endorse the secession of Texas from the United States to be its own sovereign country, a position sometimes held by extreme political conservatives. However, Believers is also used as a descriptor for videos of politically liberal commentators who scoff at secession. As employed in Here in Texas, Believers suggests similarities of faith and dedication in groups with disparate, strongly opposed views. The stereotypical image of Texan Believers is not as simple as it first appears. (See Figure 4.)

As implemented in the OVDLT environment, the texture of Here in Texas relies on a strategy of directed, but flexible movement through the video content. To understand Believers, users must employ available actions of browsing, filtering, and sorting to traverse the database, creating and comparing sets of videos with different descriptors, interpreting how Believers is applied across the collection in conjunction with other metadata choices. (What kinds of Values do Believers tend to be associated with, for example)? In Post-Texas Index, the texture of alien interconnection was achieved by a user's merely observing the repetition of extreme abstraction. But in Here in Texas, the texture required a more active user engagement. Users had to find, and then follow, different paths associated with a descriptor like Believers to feel the more organic (as opposed to alien) interconnection of this design.

Integration Work: Translating the Data Infrastructure of Here in Texas into the Scalar Data Environment

To maintain the texture of organic interconnection produced in the OVDLT version of Here in Texas, we attempted to enact directed, yet flexible movement in the translation. This combination was difficult to achieve in Scalar, where everything is implemented as a page: descriptor sets (like Characters) descriptor values (like Believers) and the videos themselves (see Figure 1).

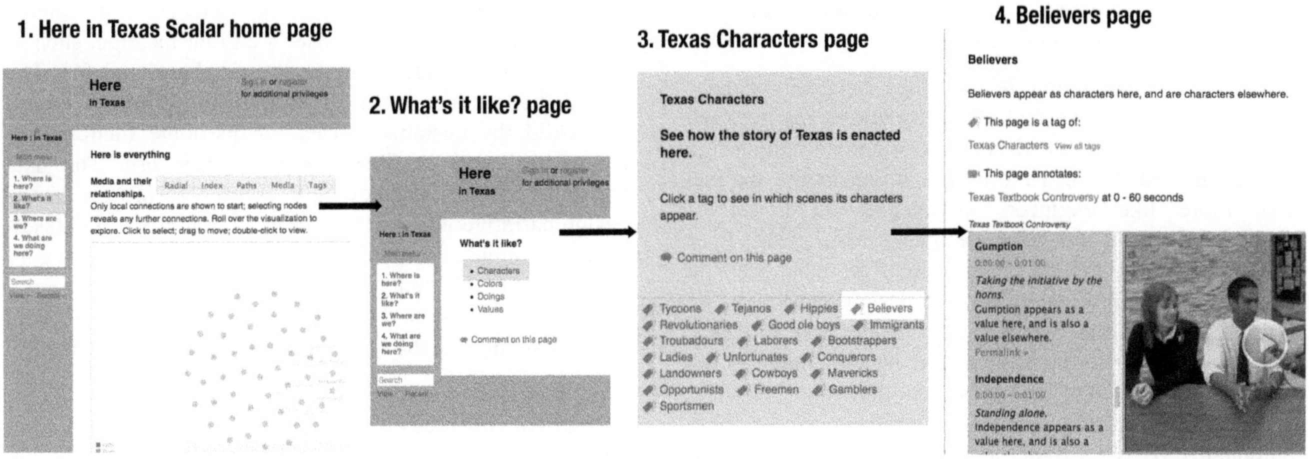

Figure 5. Here in Texas Scalar translation. (1) is the home page. (2) provides access to descriptor sets (such as Characters) via *internal links.* (3) displays descriptors (such as Believers) as *tags.* (4) includes all videos *annotated* with Believers. Each video lists all its additional annotations (other descriptors, such as Gumption and Independence). The annotation caption gives a sense of what the descriptor signifies (Gumption is "taking the initiative by the horns") and clarifies the descriptor set (Gumption is a Value; Independence is also a Value). Clicking Permalink under Gumption opens a page with all the videos annotated with Gumption.

To establish distinctions between descriptor sets, descriptors, and videos, we imposed our own artificial constraints on three types of Scalar linking mechanisms. We used the Scalar tag feature *only* to relate descriptors (like Believers) with their higher-level categories (like Characters). We used the Scalar annotation feature *only* to link descriptors and videos. We created additional pages with internal links *only* to provide access to descriptor sets (such as Characters, Doings, and Values). With these constraints, we hoped to manipulate Scalar (the new data environment) to maintain the compositional relations—texture—of the original data environment (the OVDLT).

But although these constraints—using tags, annotations, and internal links *only* for one kind of relationship—were necessary to establish distinctions between descriptor sets, descriptors, and videos, they were not sufficient. The differentiation between these three mechanisms in Scalar was too subtle. Moreover, the function of a Scalar page with *only* a linking mechanism as its content (such as a page called Characters with no content other than its tags to descriptor pages such as Believers) was not apparent. We resorted to explanatory text to clarify the function of different pages. For example, the Characters page tells users to "click a tag to see in which scenes its characters appear" (the tagged pages are the descriptors, such as Believers). To invoke that organic texture, we also included slightly more indirect and evocative text, such as "see how the story of Texas is enacted here." (The flow from page to page is documented in Figure 5.)

The Texture of the Translated Here in Texas

While Entity: Index looks very different from the original Post-Texas Index, the translation of Here in Texas appears quite similar to the original design. All of its many descriptor sets and descriptor values have been instantiated in the translation, and users can travel between sets of videos for each descriptor (from the videos annotated with Believers to the videos annotated with Gumption, for example). It's clear that the Scalar Here in Texas is a collection of videos about Texas that tells a story about a place, which can be unravelled by following the descriptor annotations. We successfully made Scalar mimic a kind of database. In many ways, the Scalar translation replicated the OVDLT version with surprising fidelity.

However, despite the painstaking effort we took to manipulate Scalar features in the service of our design goals, we did not recreate the texture very well. While the Scalar translation of Here in Texas maintains its layered interconnections, it does not feel organic. We had to force Scalar into submission, enacting our own artificial constraints and then writing explanatory text to tell users what to do and what to think. As we constrained Scalar, we also constrained the design's ability to reveal itself, organically, through interaction. Yes, one might come to understand all the different applications of a descriptor like Believers in the Scalar translation, and see how Believers can be conservative or liberal, dogmatic or inspirational. But this understanding would come because the data infrastructure said so, not because the data infrastructure supported its potential discovery. We had done exactly the wrong thing: metaphorically speaking, we had built a replica of the Swedish Icehotel in Copenhagen, exactly the approach avoided by Robles and Wiberg with Icehotel X.

DISCUSSION

When we were finishing our translations and beginning to reflect on our activities, some of us were more satisfied with the integration work in the Here in Texas project. We had retained all the primary elements of data infrastructure and data content in the Here in Texas translation, and we had manipulated Scalar (a system whose functions aligned with a graph-type database) to mimic the OVDLT (a system whose functions aligned with a relational database). This seemed like quite an achievement.

However, in maintaining relationships between primary design components, we had altered relationships between those components and the data environment, and the design texture changed. In the Here in Texas translation, we had acted more like engineers in keeping to a set of specifications, and not like designers responding to a changed situation. As an engineering feat, what we had done was indeed impressive. But as a design translation, we were focusing on the wrong things. In the Here in Texas translation, we put tremendous effort into maintaining the integrity of the data infrastructure and data content, performing convoluted technical maneuvers to get these components to "work right" in Scalar. But in focusing our attention on the components, we neglected the relationships between infrastructure, content, and environment, and the texture changed around us.

Like Robles and Wiberg, our translation project involved speculative designs, to set the notion of texture and the role of the data environment into high relief. We needed to work with atypical metadata to perceive how texture emerged from the integration of data infrastructure with data environment, because in everyday applications, the textural relations are more subtle. But the basic situation that we found ourselves in with the Here in Texas translation is very typical. We were trying to "plug in" data infrastructure and data content as prefabricated components, merely changing the environment in which the data was stored and accessed. We were treating data infrastructure and data content as mere inputs to design, and not as objects of design. As a consequence, our attempt to recreate a particular design texture was almost sure to fail.

To return to my rug story from the beginning of this paper, with Here in Texas, we were trying to recreate the warmth of the old office by moving around the furniture in the new office, trying to find the best place for the colorful rug. But although it was the "same" rug, it was different in the light of the new office, and moving it around was an exercise in futility. In the rug story, I needed to change the light itself (the data infrastructure) and get some wall hangings (adjust the data content) in order to maintain the texture, and even then, the function of the rug in the overall composition changed. With Here in Texas, we may have found the "best" possible configuration of Scalar without altering the data infrastructure and data content—and yet, even though we kept them perfectly intact, the data infrastructure and data content nonetheless changed, just like the rug did. Within the altered balance of the new composition, the data itself had changed, even though we did nothing to it. The change in design texture made this clear.

It's not uncommon practice for design projects in HCI to treat data infrastructure and data content as replaceable inputs that might be swapped out with minimal effects on user experience. As one example, Gaver and colleagues describe the design of 150 "datacatchers" to convey socioeconomic data about a user's current location, such as the employment percentage in the neighborhood [6]. The datacatcher project involved tremendous effort to design and build the custom devices, to distribute them in the community, and to film stories of their use. The data conveyed through the device is much less present in the design narrative: the devices "draw on hundreds of datasets from 14 online sources." Data in numerical or category form is transformed into sentences with "templates." Beyond this reformatting, the researchers portrayed data itself as an input to the design, not the object of design.

This was exactly our miscalculation in our Here in Texas translation. Our focus on manipulating Scalar to work with our existing data—on redesigning the data environment, but not the data infrastructure or content—resulted in significant changes to the design texture. We did not adequately approach the integration work of this translation as a design problem, and our engineering approach to integration dimished the resulting user experience. In contrast, the Entity: Index translation treated all design components—data infrastructure, data content, and data environment—as design objects. In the Entity: Index translation, integration work was design work, and the experience texture was more effectively maintained.

With data, perhaps more than with other design materials, it can be easy to miss how its character can change from one environment to another, even as the data itself is kept apparently pristine. For example, rainfall totals in a spreadsheet should be the same as rainfall totals in a database...right? Integration work between spreadsheet and database would be likely to focus on the display of the data, and not on the data itself. The rainfall amounts aren't changing!

The heightened perspective of our translation projects helps to understand this everyday situation in a new way. By translating our strange data from one environment to another, we can see more clearly what happens in all such cases: that manipulating only the data environment and not the data infrastructure and data content affects design texture. In the case of rainfall, precipitation totals wouldn't change from one environment to another. To maintain the texture from one design composition to another, however, the size and complexity of the total dataset might *need* to change. (A database with few, simple records seems, in its own way, as impenetrable as a spreadsheet with an excess of columns and rows—a database needs enough data in it so that query results aren't empty.) Our projects demonstrate that using data must involve translating it. Whenever you integrate data into a new environment, you might need to redesign the data as well. An engineering approach to force the new data environment to act like the old one—to make a database act like a spreadsheet—affects compositional balance. *Texture* provides a means to calibrate the design work of such integration.

REFERENCES

1. Alliance for Networking Visual Culture. Scalar. Available at http://scalar.usc.edu/ (We used version 1 of Scalar; a 2.0 version was released in September, 2015.)
2. Paul Dourish. 2014. NoSQL: The shifting materialities of database technology. *Computational Culture* 4.
3. Paul Dourish and Melissa Mazmanian. 2011. Media as material: information representations as material foundations for organizational practice. Third international symposium on process organization studies, Corfu, Greece.
4. Melanie Feinberg, Daniel Carter, and Julia Bullard. 2014. Always somewhere, never there: using critical design to understand database interactions. In *Proceedings of the SIGCHI Conference on Human Factors in Computing Systems* (CHI '14). ACM, New York, NY, USA, 1941-1950. DOI=http://dx.doi.org/10.1145/25562
5. Melanie Feinberg, Daniel Carter, and Julia Bullard. 2014. A story without end: writing the residual into descriptive infrastructure. In *Proceedings of the 2014 conference on Designing interactive systems* (DIS '14). ACM, New York, NY, USA, 385-394. DOI=http://dx.doi.org/10.1145/2598510.2598553
6. William Gaver, Andy Boucher, Nadine Jarvis, David Cameron, Mark Hauenstein, Sarah Pennington, John Bowers, James Pike, Robin Beitra, and Liliana Ovalle. 2016. The Datacatcher: batch deployment and documentation of 130 location-aware, mobile devices that put sociopolitically-relevant big data in people's hands: polyphonic interpretation at scale. In *Proceedings of the 2016 CHI Conference on Human Factors in Computing Systems* (CHI '16), 1597-1607. http://dx.doi.org/10.1145/2858036.2858472
7. Gary Geisler. Open Video Digital Library Toolkit. Retrieved September 9, 2015, from www.open-video-toolkit.org/
8. Elisa Giaccardi and Elvin Karana. 2015. Foundations of materials experience: an approach for HCI. In *Proceedings of the 33rd Annual ACM Conference on Human Factors in Computing Systems* (CHI '15), 2447-2456. http://doi.acm.org/10.1145/2702123.2702337
9. Icehotel Web site. 2017. Retrieved January 10, 2017 from http://www.icehotel.com/
10. Tim Ingold. 2007. *Lines: A brief history.* London: Routledge.
11. Jonas Löwgren. 2007. Pliability as an experiential quality: Exploring the aesthetics of interaction design. *Artifact* 1,2: 85-95, 2007.
12. David Pye. 1968. *The nature and art of workmanship.* Cambridge, UK: Cambridge University Press.
13. Johan Redström. 2008. RE: definitions of use. *Design Studies* 29, 4, 410–23.
14. Erica Robles and Mikael Wiberg. 2010. Texturing the "material turn" in interaction design. In *Proceedings of the fourth international conference on Tangible, embedded, and embodied interaction* (TEI '10), 137-144. http://dx.doi.org/10.1145/1709886.1709911
15. Daniela K. Rosner. 2012. The material practices of collaboration. In *Proceedings of the ACM 2012 Conference on Computer Supported Cooperative Work* (CSCW '12), 1155-1164. http://doi.acm.org/10.1145/2145204.2145375
16. Susan Leigh Star and Geoffrey Bowker. 2007. Enacting silence: residual categories as a challenge for ethics, information systems, and communication. *Ethics and Information Technology* 9: 273–280.
17. Petra Sundström and Kristina Höök. 2010. Hand in hand with the material: designing for suppleness. In *Proceedings of the SIGCHI Conference on Human Factors in Computing Systems* (CHI '10), 463-472. http://doi.acm.org/10.1145/1753326.1753396
18. Christopher Tilley, with the assistance of Wayne Bennett. 2008. *Body and image: explorations in landscape phenomenology 2.* Walnut Creek, CA: Left Coast Press.
19. Marcia Lei Zeng and Lois Mai Chan. (2009) Semantic interoperability. In Bates, Marcia, and Mary Niles Maack (eds). *Encyclopedia of Library and Information Sciences.* 3rd ed. CRC Press.

The Moving Context Kit: Designing for Context Shifts in Multi-Device Experiences

Katie O'Leary[1] *, Tao Dong[2], Julia Katherine Haines[2], Michael Gilbert[2], Elizabeth F. Churchill[2], Jeffrey Nichols[2]
[1]The Information School, University of Washington | DUB Group, Seattle, WA, USA
[2]Google Inc., Mountain View, CA, USA
kathlo@uw.edu; {taodong; juliahaines; mdgilbert; echurchill; jwnichols}@google.com

ABSTRACT
Multi-device product designers need tools to better address ecologically valid constraints in naturalistic settings early in their design process. To address this need, we created a reusable design kit of scenarios, "hint" cards, and a framework that codifies insights from prior work and our own field study. We named the kit the **M**oving **C**ontext **Kit,** or McKit for short, because it helps designers focus on *context shifts* that we found to be highly influential in everyday multi-device use. Specifically, we distilled the following findings from our field study in the McKit: (1) devices are typically specialized into one of six roles during parallel use—*notifier, broadcaster, collector, gamer, remote,* and *hub,* and (2) device roles are influenced by context shifts between private and shared situations. Through a workshop, we validated that the McKit enables designers to engage with complex user needs, situations, and relationships when incorporating novel multi-device techniques into the products they envision.

Author Keywords
Multi-device experiences; design process; design tools; field study; privacy; device use; context of use

ACM Classification Keywords
H.5.2 User-centered design

INTRODUCTION
People interact with many devices in everyday life, but face challenges managing multiple platforms, form factors, and applications. For example, it is difficult for users to manage attention across many screens, learn different interface and interaction conventions, and sync content [9,20,34]. Novel multi-device interaction techniques have been proposed to relieve these pain points by helping users migrate information across device screens [16] and allowing users to combine computing resources from many devices [43].

DIS 2017, June 10-14, 2017, Edinburgh, United Kingdom

ACM ISBN 978-1-4503-4922-2/17/06.
http://dx.doi.org/10.1145/3064663.3064768

While users find these new interaction techniques useful in lab-based studies (e.g.,[16,31]), it is unclear whether the conclusions drawn about these designs are ecologically valid. In the design of interactive systems, ecological validity means how users might appropriate these techniques in their everyday lives [4]. One of the major challenges to the ecological validity of multi-device systems is that sophisticated multi-device *systems* (consisting of devices designed to collaborate with one another in a particular ecosystem), and ad hoc multi-device *collections* (consisting of devices a person uses together in specific situations) co-exist in users' everyday life. This makes it difficult to envision and test new multi-device interactions in the context of users' existing device collections and behaviors, which is one reason that few of these techniques are tested outside of the controlled environment of the lab, with the exception of Chen et al.[6]. Moreover, research has shown that technology adoption and use are influenced by many contextual factors, including the physical and social setting [30], privacy considerations [19], and local values and norms [42], yet these factors are not currently well-represented in existing multi-device design tools [7,8,31]. Thus, our goal in developing a design kit was to help designers address ecological validity by considering contexts of use grounded in field research when envisioning multi-device experiences.

Specifically, we created the **M**oving **C**ontext **Kit,** or McKit for short, to help designers consider shifts in privacy needs, device roles, and device relationships that we found to be particularly influential on the use of multiple devices in everyday settings. Our design kit is both lightweight and reusable, suitable for use in envisioning workshops, design sprints, and reflective design processes (e.g., [17,22,36]). It provides product teams with familiar design aids and prompts, including scenarios and personas, to engage with complex and rich field data on multi-device use. The McKit is composed of several components[†]:

- A set of context-shifting scenarios from our field research

* This work was done while the first author was an intern at Google.

[†] The McKit is at: https://sites.google.com/view/mckit/

- Three sets of "hint" cards that remind designers of various multi-device interaction patterns, potential device roles, and known user burdens
- A framework that sensitizes designers to shifts in contexts, tasks, and relationships we found especially important in multi-device use
- Worksheets that scaffold the process of combining the design kit components

To develop these context-rich materials, we followed a 4-step process. First, in the **analytical step**, we analyzed insights from prior work related to multi-device design and use, and used these to inform our design kit components. Second, in the **empirical step**, we went to the field to collect rich examples of technology use in naturalistic settings. Our methods included experience sampling and field interviews with 25 participants from four diverse U.S. regions (Detroit, Boston, Miami, and the Bay Area). While some of our findings echo prior studies [20,21,34], our inquiry also yields new insights into multi-device use. We found that participants specialized their devices to perform six roles—*notifier, broadcaster, collector, gamer, remote, and hub*—in related and unrelated parallel use. We also found that device privacy and sharing considerations influenced device roles. In particular, when devices shifted from private use to shared use, users shifted the roles and relationships of their devices within a multi-device configuration. In the third step, the **codification step**, we distilled these insights in scenarios that force context shifts, cards that represent device roles, and in dimensions of a framework that map a multi-device design space with privacy and sharing on one axis, and multipurpose and specialized roles on the intersecting axis.

Finally, in the **validation step**, we evaluated the McKit in a one-day design workshop with nine members of a product team at a large technology company. Workshop participants had backgrounds in design, engineering, and research. The participants were focused on envisioning designs of a product under development that features multi-device experiences. The results of the workshop demonstrate that the design kit helps designers to consider contexts and constraints of situated use of multiple devices. It also provides a common language and framework to critique one another's designs from the standpoint of ecological validity (i.e., how might this work in the real world?).

In the rest of the paper, we show our approach to creating the McKit in detail and demonstrate its utility for addressing ecological validity early in the multi-device experience design process. This paper makes three contributions to research on multi-device experiences:

1. A reusable design kit that allows designers to consider ecological validity and consume insights derived from our field study and literature review, specifically for multi-device experience design;
2. Insights into six device roles that we found in everyday multi-device use, and the ways in which these roles are influenced by shifts in contexts of use; and
3. A generalizable approach to making field research more accessible and useful to design practitioners.

ANALYTICAL STEP: DRAWING ON RELATED WORK

In this section, we describe related work that influenced our empirical inquiry and codification of design kit materials.

Multi-device Theories and Frameworks

The design space of multi-device experiences is rich in theoretical foundations and frameworks, including works on ecologies of interactive artifacts, a perspective rooted in theories such as information ecology [30]. Understanding people's device ecologies emerged from Jung et al.'s [21] work on how people categorize their artefacts based on relations, and Forlizzi's [11] work on how aesthetic, symbolic, and functional aspects of robots influence their relations within the home. These ideas were expanded upon by Bodker and Klokmose [1] who developed the notion of dynamic device ecologies that change over time. Note that the term "ecology" used in this line of work is not in the same sense of "ecological validity" which speaks to the utility and feasibility of a design in the real world.

Other frameworks are more technical in focus, aimed at guiding concrete design decisions. For example, Sorensen et al [37] describe a framework representing the "4Cs" of multi-device interaction design: communality, collaboration, continuity, and complementarity. The authors show how this framework can guide heuristic evaluation of existing technologies and concrete design ideation of new concepts. Waljas et al [41] proposed an initial framework for cross-platform web services based on their findings from a field study investigating user experiences across PCs and mobile devices. The themes represented in their framework prompt designers to consider: appropriate system composition, fluency in content and task migration, and service consistency. Paterno and Santoro [33] present a logical framework for understanding, analyzing, and comparing features of multi-device user interfaces (UIs) that reveals dimensions of multi-device UI design that are underexplored. One of the underexplored areas of multi-device research that they identified, that we address in our field study, is users' attitudes towards multi-device UIs when the context is shared with other users. A framework by Lundgren et al [26] helps to map this underexplored design space, through consideration of spatial, temporal, social, and technical perspectives of mobile collocated interactions. Our work adds to this literature by offering a framework that helps designers to explore tradeoffs in technical and social considerations (i.e. seamless integration versus privacy needs) that we found to be highly salient in multi-device use in our field study.

Multi-device Interaction Techniques

Design practitioners might be familiar with multi-device interaction patterns that have been widely used in commercial products such as mirroring content between screens, but it is important for them to be aware of the technologies on the horizon and consider how users might adopt them. Many novel interaction techniques have been proposed to seamlessly move content across multiple devices to optimize task flow and information display, such as those exemplified in Pick-and-Drop [29], Conductor [16], and Pass-them-Around [25].

Five typical multi-device interaction patterns emerged from our analysis of the literature, including: (1) *mirroring* information from one display to another (e.g., Chromecast‡); (2) providing *overview + detail*, with an overview of information on one device and more detailed information on another device (e.g., Display Stacks [14], United Slates [5] and Conductor [16]), (3) displaying *related information* for a single task on multiple devices, such as writing the response to an email on the tablet while having the email being replied to on a smartphone (e.g.,XDBrowser [31]); (4) *stitching* information across multiple displays to maximize real estate (e.g., Pass-them-around [25] and TableTalk [10]), and (5) providing *alternative views* of information (e.g., the dual map views example in Panelrama [43]). These five patterns are by no means exhaustive, but their technical feasibility has been demonstrated. We believe including these patterns in our design kit, described later in the paper, can inspire designers in their ideation process.

Studies of Multi-device Use

Empirical studies of how people use multiple devices have yielded several insights about device roles, patterns of use, and workarounds. Early work by Oulasvirta and Sumari [32] identified challenges and workarounds of multi-device use experienced by workers at a large IT company. Workers had difficulty synchronizing data across devices and often resorted to carrying around "mobile kits." Jung et al. [21] found that users group digital artifacts according to purpose of use, context of use, and subjective meanings that motivate different device configurations. In particular, they found that multipurpose devices, like smartphones and tablets, had many interconnections with other devices, making them central in personal device kits. Multipurpose devices are often specialized within parallel multi-device configurations. Dearman and Pierce [9] studied academic and industry professionals, and found that users assign specialized roles to devices to support complex tasks (e.g., writing and testing code), conduct a secondary task (e.g., monitoring email on a device other than the one being used for the primary task), and to cope with hardware and software constraints. Santosa and Wigdor [34] also found that industry professionals assign specific roles to devices in multi-device configurations, especially for performing related tasks in parallel. In addition, Jokela et al. [20] found these types of parallel uses in a diary study of everyday users in Southern Finland: resource lending (of device input/output capabilities), related parallel use, and unrelated parallel use. We add to this prior work new examples of the specialized roles that devices take on, especially during *unrelated* parallel use of many devices for multitasking, in a sample of lay users from four diverse regions in the U.S.

Particularly relevant to findings in our field study are empirical studies focusing on the use of shared devices such as [2,27,28]. These studies yield insight into the privacy and sharing behaviors that characterize everyday use of devices. For example, Matthews et al [27] showed that device sharing in households is common and upsets the private and personal nature of device collections. Ion et al [19] found that people are wary of storing data on the cloud, a major barrier to cross-device integration, and Mazurek et al [28] found that sharing devices in the home led to complex privacy rituals for access control. Suh et al [38] showed that privacy considerations are a core user burden influencing adoption and use of technologies. However, these studies did not have an explicit multi-device focus, lacking implications for designing multi-device experiences across many tasks and settings.

Overall, prior work suggests the importance of device role specialization within device ecologies, device sharing and privacy across different settings, and challenges of managing data across many devices. It also reveals several interaction patterns aimed at relieving multi-device pain points. Our analysis of this prior work led to the codification of multi-device interaction patterns, and user burdens into paper-based design tools that we refer to as "hint" cards. Beyond offering key insights, prior literature also raised several questions about multi-device use that we sought to answer in our "empirical step," i.e., field study, including: how device sharing influences multi-device configurations in everyday settings, how lay users configure many devices across many settings, and what new patterns of multi-device use may be observed with frequent daily experience sampling. Below, we show our empirical step wherein we investigated multi-device use in the wild, and then detail how we codified insights in the design kit.

EMPIRICAL STEP: INVESTIGATING MULTI-DEVICE USE

We drew data from a large, ongoing field study of people's everyday technology use. The study method is based on trace ethnography [13], and combines several streams of data about users' digital interactions and contexts through logging device and app usage, experience sampling method (ESM), and field interviews. This situated approach enabled us to explore the daily routines, habits, and challenges that shape everyday multi-device use. To create the McKit, we used two data sources: experience sampling and field interviews.

Participants

We selected a sample of 25 (17 male; 8 female) participants drawn from the large, ongoing study described above, who exhibited frequent multi-device use in the ESM and/or

‡ Chromecast: https://www.google.com/intl/en_us/chromecast/

	N	P#	Age range	Gender	Education	Household income
Boston	6	P01-P06	18-50	4M; 2F	HS (1); College (4); Masters (1)	$9,999 or less to $249,000
Detroit	6	P07-P12	25-50	3M; 3F	HS (1); College (2); Masters (3)	$9,999 or less to $99,999
Bay Area	7	P13-P19	18-60	6M; 1F	College (5); Masters (1); PhD (1)	$50,000 to $250,000+
Miami	6	P20-P25	25-50	4M; 2F	HS (1); College (3); Masters (1); PhD (1)	$10,000 to $74,999

Table 1. Participants. N=number of participants, P#=participant id, Age range in years, M=male, F=female, HS=high school.

interview data. These participants were from four U.S. regions: Detroit, Miami, Boston, and the Bay Area from a participant database at a large technology company. Potential participants were sent a screener, then selected for diversity on a range of criteria, including: gender, age, employment, education, household income, and device ecosystem (i.e., Apple and Android) (Table 1). Participants were required to be 18 years or older. Each participant received $75 for responding to experience sampling moments, and $100 for the interview conducted in their home or office.

Procedures

Participants were enrolled in the study for 5 days. Each day, participants responded to prompts about their activities 5 times at random times within a fixed time period (8 AM to 9 PM). . These momentary states provide a "dense record of quality of experience at each point" [35]. Participants were asked to report their primary and secondary activities, devices in use, who they were with, and location. Data was collected Wednesday through Sunday to get a picture of their digital habits during weekdays and weekends. After the 5-day period, the third and fourth authors went to each participant's home or office to conduct the interviews. Interviews included questions about daily routines, device use, and digital privacy concerns. Interviews lasted for about one hour, and they were transcribed for analysis.

Analysis

To analyze interview data on multi-device use, we coded responses to two questions: (1) Can you tell me about some typical ways you use your devices together? (2) Do you ever share your devices with anyone? If so, what are some examples?" We coded for instances of parallel, sequential, and shared device use. We also coded for frictions in using many devices, including mentions of privacy burdens and difficulty of use. Using the ESM data, we identified 136 moments with multiple devices reported, and then counted the number and types of devices and digital activities reported in each of those moments. The first author completed the coding, and all authors worked together to synthesize the outcomes of the interview and ESM analyses.

Device role	Description
Notifier	Notifies the user of tasks
Broadcaster	Broadcasts or displays information
Hub	Is a hub of activity for multiple tasks
Remote	Controls or streams content to a display or speakers
Collector	Collects data, like pictures, video, or fitness activity
Gamer	Enables user to play games

Table 2. Six device roles within parallel multi-device use.

Findings

Here, we present the findings from our field study (i.e. the *Empirical step*) that led to the creation of design kit components. We found that (1) participants specialized their devices to perform one of six roles—*notifier, broadcaster, collector, gamer, remote, and hub*—in related and unrelated parallel use, and (2) device privacy and sharing needs influenced the roles that participants wanted to assign to their devices in the moment.

Six device roles during multi-device use

In contrast to previous work, our field study revealed that participants often used many devices in parallel for *unrelated* tasks. In other words, many participants had the experience of multi-tasking with several devices. Over half (52%) of the moments involving more than one device reported in the ESM data involved the use of multiple devices for two or more unrelated tasks. Jokela et al [20] called this type of multi-device use, "unrelated parallel use," but did not find many examples through diary studies. Below, we show how this type of device use was common among our participants. Moreover, we demonstrate that devices can take on *separate but complementary* roles to support multi-tasking in everyday contexts. Specifically, from the ESM data we found six different roles of devices to support multi-tasking: *notifier, broadcaster, hub, remote, collector, and gamer* (Table 2). Overall, we found that laptops were often "hub" devices that our participants typically combined with notifiers and broadcasters to support both related and unrelated parallel use in everyday situations. As an example of paralleled unrelated use of multiple devices, P02 described a typical evening routine: "*I'll watch TV, have the laptop open, and I'll be playing on my phone. So, I'll have Netflix; I'll have like House [TV show] was on. That's background noise. [...] So, I'm cooking, too. But then I'm looking on my phone, making sure I got it going for the right amount of time. And then I'll have my laptop up, and when I have nothing else going on over there, I'll browse around on the Internet.*" In this case, his TV was *broadcasting* media, his phone was *notifying* him of the cooking time, and his laptop was a *hub* for web surfing activity. Five of his sixteen multi-device moments captured in the experience sampling also featured a console for *gaming*, in addition to the phone, TV, and laptop. Having different devices play different roles helped P02 switch attention between activities which were distributed across devices as information became more or less important (e.g., timing of cooking), or interesting (e.g., content on TV).

The role of a device was to some extent constraint by its capabilities. For example, P03 used her phone to view an app, kept the radio on in the background for *broadcasting* media, and her laptop as a *hub* of activity: "*Sometimes I'll have a radio on and be using an iPhone app and be sort of casually monitoring something on my laptop. [On] the laptop itself, I am one of those people with multiple programs, multiple tabs open on a website doing personal e-mail and work e-mail sort of all in one and you know with sort of major projects open and also just killing time tabs [...]*" In this case, the radio was a natural broadcaster and the laptop was a hub because of its capability of handling different tasks.

What was more interesting was that some multi-purposed devices could be artificially limited to specialized roles to separate different types of tasks. For example, P20 temporarily used his smartphone to *broadcast* videos while he used his laptop as a *hub* for work: "*Let's say I'll just be watching a YouTube video, and then I have to do something on my laptop. I would literally have the phone open while I'm doing work.*" Some participants exercised such role specialization of multi-purposed devices on a more permanent basis. For example, P19 had very clear separations between his devices for specific tasks on a more permanent basis. He explained: "*If I am in bed, and we have something streaming from the iPad to the TV, through Chromecast, then I will most likely either use my phone or the laptop to do that other task. I want this [iPad] to remain the remote control, so if I need to pause it, I can do it right there with that. I kind of don't like to multi-task on a single device as much as I like to have the availability of two devices or multiple devices to do that. So I can have different apps pulled up in different devices.*" P19 used his iPad as a *remote control* and TV to *broadcast* media, and his laptop as a *hub* for, in his words, "*more intense*" activities like email and web surfing.

The role assigned to a device could also be influenced by the personal relationship the user had with the device. For example, P05 said, "*My computer, I don't let it have any notifications, like, they made me mad. My computer is my device. It's not my master. My phone on the other hand, we have a different relationship.*" This example points to how the subjective value of a device—an important factor identified by Jung et al [21]—can influence its role in multi-device experiences.

These device roles were important in *related* parallel use of multiple devices as well. P10 gave an example when she described using her phone to "update" her of work to follow through with on her laptop. She was a full-time blogger who used her laptop as a *hub* of digital activity to switch between different social media accounts and photo editing, using the phone to *notify* her of tasks to prioritize in the moment: "*Well I use the phone and the laptop all the time at the same time. [...] My phone alerts me to all those -- you know, whatever, like, little updates. So I'm able to look at whatever, and then go on the laptop and follow through. Like, if somebody sends me a message on that Facebook page, then I'd go on the laptop usually.*" In contrast to the examples of unrelated parallel use, P10's routine exemplifies related parallel use for work. Her ad hoc set up of relations between a *notifier* and *hub* was not explicitly supported by technology design, presenting an opportunity to enhance these relations through more seamless integration. Next, we show how context shifts had an important influence on everyday device role specialization.

Shifts in context influence device roles

We found that participants' use of devices were influenced by two types of shifts in context: 1) from using devices in a private setting to a public setting, and 2) from having exclusive control over a device to sharing that device. When such shifts occurred, participants often wanted to specialize their devices into roles that could enable discrete use, enable separation of private and public activities, or protect their data and task state on a device. However, that required effort and was not always successful.

The following two examples demonstrate how shifting the usage setting from private to public can influence device roles within multi-device experiences. P01 explained a situation where he needed to share his laptop to present information to colleagues, which made it necessary to temporarily specialize his phone in the role of notifier in that context: "*Sometimes when we do customer calls, if I'm presenting on my laptop, I will shut off, like, Slack and Gmail and all that stuff, because people will post the craziest things and notifications will slide up. So, I want that stuff off the screen, so I'll just do all that stuff on my phone at the same time.*" Similarly, P18 had begun a new job and used affordances of his phone and smartwatch to be discrete: "*I'm new to the job so I don't want to leave a bad impression of the phone and stuff. [...] If I'm waiting on a call, or a text, I might put my watch to vibrate so that if you have an alert for some reason or another. I try not to, at least now, spend too much personal time on the computer.*"

In P01's case, his laptop was no longer suitable as a hub in a public setting, so he transitioned his laptop to a "broadcaster" role and used his phone as a "notifier." For P18, his need to be discrete at his new job made his work desktop unsuitable for personal messages, so he dedicated his smartwatch as a private notifier for that content.

The second type of context shift—from exclusive to shared device control—was more common within households than work settings among our participants. Participants described situations of device sharing that enabled household members to take advantage of each other's devices. P08 borrowed her husband's phone when she wanted to play karaoke because it had better sound: *"I use his [phone] for the karaoke apps, because I think it sounds better. [...] It makes you feel like you might be slightly in the studio."* P01's wife often borrowed his desktop to take advantage of the large monitor: *"She likes the large monitor. [...] She's an urban planner, so she has to sometimes, like, wrestle with gigantic spreadsheets, and it's nice to have a largescale thing to work on, as opposed to a small little window."* These examples suggest that participants desired the ability to opportunistically use others' devices to temporarily optimize a task, whether for leisure or work. This device sharing was an explicit form of *resource lending* [20] in which a personal device collection was temporarily enhanced by the resources of a shared device to perform a very specific role.

Nonetheless, participants lacked technical means to preserve their privacy and reduce the risk of losing task state and device configuration when they lent their devices to other members of their household. Parents who lent devices to their children felt these challenges most acutely. For example, P14 did not usually allow his daughter to use his phone, but sometimes gave in: *"From time to time I'll let my kid watch a YouTube video if something in the car, if they're crying, but for the most part nobody uses my phone but me."* P10 routinely allowed her children to borrow her laptop with Bluetooth mouse to play certain games for which it was better suited than their small tablets: *"The kids use my laptop for a limited amount [of time] for, like, ABC Mouse and things that it's easier to go on a computer for. Plus, I want them to learn how to use the mouse and not just be stuck learning a tablet."* In such a situation, P10 did not have a convenient mechanism to restrict a multi-purpose device to a specific role such as a gamer. P10 would lend her entire laptop, upon which she relied for her livelihood as a blogger, to her children.

The burden of privacy in sharing devices with children was sometimes motivation to buy a new device and dedicate it for a specific role. For example, P09 valued having the Fire TV in his device collection for his kids, taking the burden off of sharing his personal phone for broadcasting media: *"Actually that is probably what gets used the most at my house, because it comes with a remote control, so the kids can use it. You don't have to, you know, hop on the phone. It would be hard, which they could probably figure out [how to use it], but you don't necessarily want them to."* Being able to share devices on the basis of specific roles, such as *broadcaster* or *remote*, could be valuable for ensuring better privacy and for enabling users to shift device roles to adapt to shifts in context. Overall, we found the interrelationship between context shifts and device role specialization highly salient to multi-device use among our participants across both work and home situations.

CODIFICATION STEP: DISTILLING KEY INSIGHTS

We distilled our insights into the McKit with several components. The Shift framework is the central component that represents a multi-device design space wherein device roles *shift* across private and shared contexts. To support the use of this framework for designing multi-device experiences that hold up under ecologically valid constraints, we created supportive materials based on some familiar design tools: personas and scenarios [3,15], the action-reflection design model [44], and paper-based cards [12,18]. These supportive materials distill insights from our analytical and empirical steps that can help designers to reflect on implications of traversing the multi-device design space represented in the framework.

Overall, we developed a framework, 3 scenarios, 3 personas, 3 types of "hint" cards, and worksheets to put all the materials together in an ideation process. Below, we describe each of these materials as part of a comprehensive multi-device design kit.

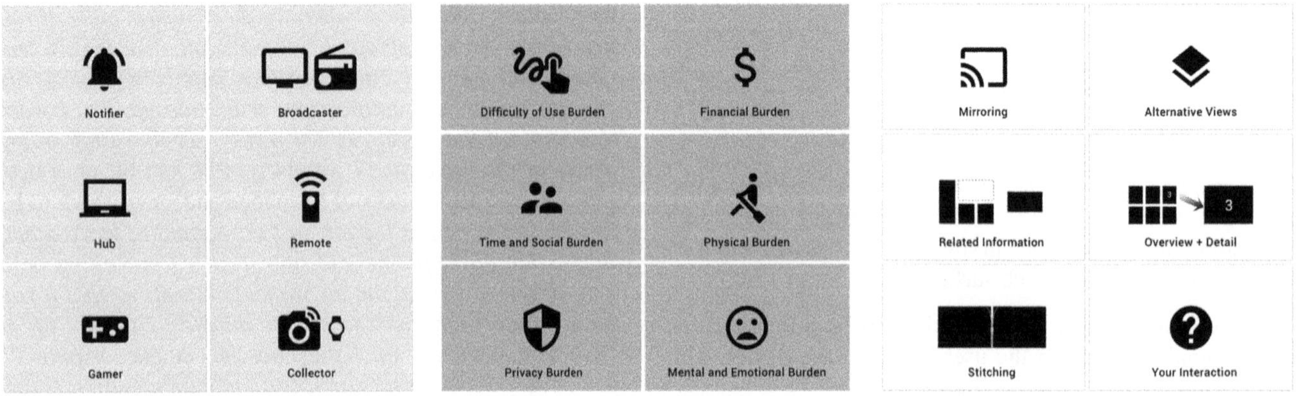

Figure 1. "Hint" cards: (a) Device role cards; (b) User burden cards; (c) Interaction pattern cards.

Hint Cards

There are three sets of "hint" cards (Figure 1) for exploring and reflecting on design ideas: (1) a set of interaction pattern cards for inspiring feasible technical solutions, (2) a set of device role cards for examining role-based relations between devices, and (3) a set of user burden cards for provoking reflection on how different technical solutions relieve and/or introduce burdens for users. Each card has an icon on the front, and description of the pattern on the back with examples. The interaction pattern cards and user burden cards are based on our review of the literature; the device role cards were drawn from our "empirical step," i.e. fieldwork.

Multi-device interaction pattern cards

Our design kit distills five common interaction patterns from existing products and innovations in recent research, described in greater detail in the analytical step earlier in the paper. These five patterns include *mirroring*, *alternative views, related information, overview + detail*, and *stitching.* We also offer a "Your interaction" card to encourage inclusion of additional techniques.

Device role cards

To help designers consider various device roles in multi-device configurations, we included a set of six device roles identified in our empirical study, described in depth above: *notifier, broadcaster, hub, gamer, remote,* and *collector*.

User burden cards

In addition, we include the six types of user burdens identified by Suh et al [38] as another set of cards to sensitize designers to the burdens that users might experience in multi-device use: (1) the *privacy burden* of managing the risk that a system will reveal confidential information, (2) the *difficulty of use burden* of a system that does not fit with the abilities of the user, (3) the *mental and emotional burden* of undue demands on attention or managing anxiety, (4) the *time and social burden* of managing interference with personal time and social relationships, (5) the *financial burden* of paying for costly technology, and (6) the *physical burden* of coping with technologies that are uncomfortable. To our knowledge, this is the first instance of the user burdens from Suh et al [38] being used as design prompts for ideation.

Part 1: Routine event

Marissa needs to be really productive in the evenings. She has several tabs open on her laptop so that she can switch between email, social media accounts, and a photo editor. Her central task is to create a blog post, so she needs to choose pictures, edit them, and create content. She needs her phone to notify her of incoming messages, so that she can follow through with them on her laptop, using the keyboard. She likes having the TV on in the background set to Jeopardy.

Part 2: Context shift

One evening, Marissa's son came into the room because he couldn't sleep. He wanted to play ABC Mouse on her laptop. So, she gave her son full access to her laptop. She tried to work with a bunch of tabs open on her phone while monitoring her son to make sure he didn't mess with any of her work tabs open on her laptop.

Figure 2. Marissa's scenario

Context-shifting Scenarios

We created three scenarios that explicitly feature a *context shift* that provokes changes in privacy needs and device role specializations (see one of them in Figure 2). Each scenario is synthesized from data reported by a single participant referred to by a pseudonym: "Marissa" (P10), "Seth" (P01), or "Alex" (P18). The events did not necessarily occur in the time span in which they appear in the scenarios; however, they are based on actual events reported by participants. Each scenario has two parts. Part 1 is a *"routine event"* in which the character is combining many devices as part of an everyday routine. Part 2 is a *"context shift"* that necessitates the character to adapt the devices she uses and the way she uses those devices in response to sharing needs and/or privacy concerns. Thus, each context shift in the scenarios can be mapped onto the design framework (described below) to aid reflection and ideation (Figure 3). Each scenario is accompanied by a persona of the main character that details their everyday routines and devices.

The Shift Framework

Our finding that context shifts influence device roles, led us to create a framework that represents these two interrelated dimensions: *private* versus *shared* contexts, and *specialized* versus *multipurpose* roles (Figure 3). This framework can be used to map multi-device flows across contexts and to

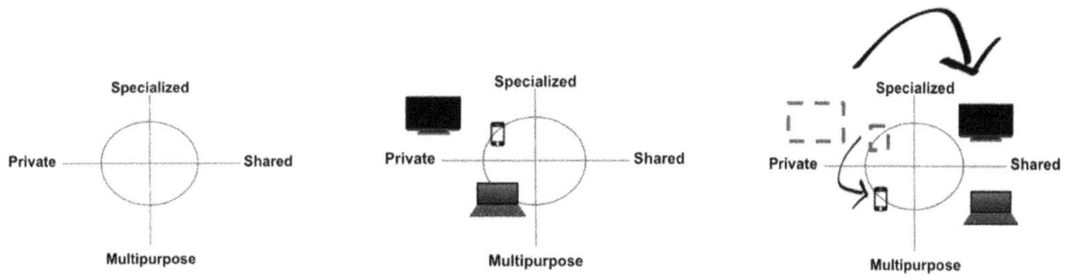

Figure 3. Using the framework to map devices in Marissa's scenario on the dimensions of role specialization and device sharing and then demonstrating how that mapping changes as her context shifts.

reflect on how shifts in context, from private to shared influences device role specialization. In addition, we represent the *relationship* between devices—the extent to which devices are explicitly joined in a related task—as a circle in the middle of the intersecting axes. The framework can be used to analyze scenarios to gain an understanding of how people shift devices across contexts, and in turn, how those shifts might influence multi-device design.

VALIDATION STEP: EVALUATING THE UTILITY OF THE DESIGN KIT

To investigate the usefulness of our multi-device design kit, we conducted a one-day workshop with a product team at a large technology company. From the team, we recruited nine participants (2 females) involved in multi-device product design. Participants from this product team were diverse in terms of expertise (4 designers, 3 engineers, and 2 user experience researchers), and cultural background (Chinese, Canadian, American, Italian, Japanese). After the workshop, we conducted follow-up interviews with the four designer participants about the benefits and drawbacks of using the kit to stimulate their design ideas. We analyzed participants' design work, and video recordings of the workshop, and transcripts of the follow-up interviews.

Action-reflection Process

The worksheets included in the McKit guided the use of the scenarios, cards, and framework in an action-reflection process—a process in which designers use prompts based on empirical field data to aid reflection on design choices [44]. Each worksheet contains prompts for using kit materials to design for one of the three scenarios: "Alex," "Marissa," or "Seth." We divided the participants into three groups, each focusing on one of the three scenarios.

The participants used the worksheets to combine the design kit materials in a three-step action-reflection process. First, participants focused on the "routine event" in the *scenario*, and mapped the devices described onto the *framework* according to privacy, specialization, and relatedness. They used the *user burden cards* to reflect on the burdens the particular user faced when using multiple devices in his or her situation. Second, participants focused on designing a solution for their user. They used the *interaction patterns cards* and *device role* cards to ideate and create a multi-device design that addressed the user burdens they identified in the previous step. Lastly, participants focused on the "context shift" in the scenario and re-mapped, or *shifted*, the devices across the framework to represent changes in the multi-device experience (see Figure 3). They reflected on how the context shift affected device roles and user burdens, and adapted their designs. At the end of the workshop, each participant presented his or her design work. Below, we demonstrate how the design kit sensitized workshop participants to privacy needs, device roles, and user burdens, as they envisioned multi-device features of a product. Due to the proprietary nature of the product, we reserve some details of the designs in our report of findings. We use "WP" as a prefix for workshop participant IDs.

Findings: Towards Ecologically-valid Design

We found that the McKit helped product stakeholders consider a wide range of devices roles, situations of use, and multi-device behaviors that helped address ecological validity in their design work. The focus on context shifts in the semi-structured design process (provided in the kit), triggered critical points of reflection on ecologically valid constraints and opportunities in multi-device experiences.

For example, in explaining his design for Marissa (see Figure 4a), WP01 described how the context shift provoked reflection on his design: *"It evolved into this situation where Marissa had to cede her laptop to somebody else, so then it was like, oh, okay, now we have to think about how the roles of this hub device [laptop] can be re-assigned to these other devices"* Similarly, WP03 found that his initial design was *"not such an ideal of a solution"* for Alex's scenario due to the context shift that Alex routinely experienced: going from a youth center where he volunteers, to an office where he works, that made the designer's initial solution *"a lot less discrete."* WP03 then adapted his design to anticipate his user's privacy needs.

We found the kit's emphasis on privacy burdens and the shared nature of many devices helped participants to explicitly consider those factors in design. WP02 sketched a "device control center" (see Figure 4b) and "user identity

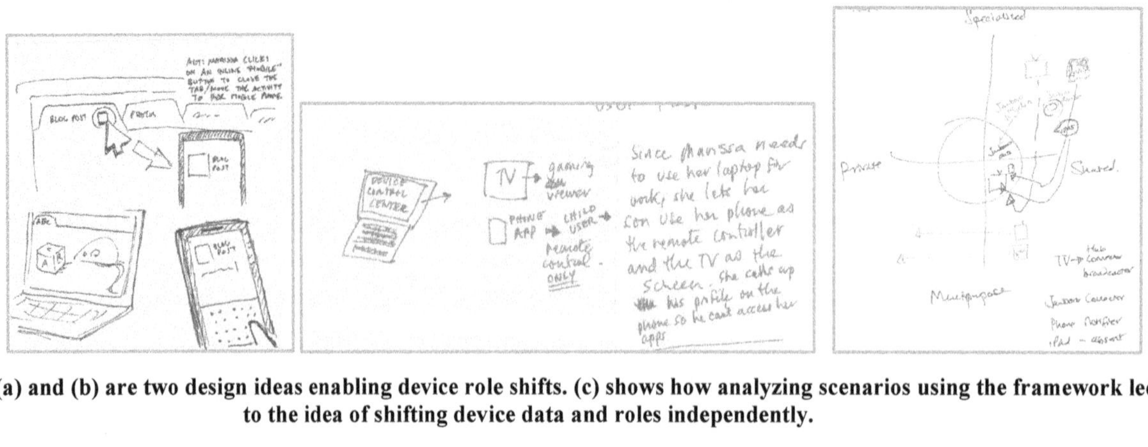

Figure 4. (a) and (b) are two design ideas enabling device role shifts. (c) shows how analyzing scenarios using the framework led to the idea of shifting device data and roles independently.

platform" that enabled Marissa to shift her private device configuration (TV, laptop, phone), to accommodate her son's shared use of her devices to play games: *"From her laptop, from the device control center, she assigns her TV as a gaming viewer, and she puts the phone into the child identity mode, so that her son can use that as a remote control, so he can play a game on the TV while she gets work done on the laptop."* This example shows how this designer engaged extensively with the device roles while considering the influence of privacy burdens.

Participants also showed sensitivity to the relationship between context shifts and device roles. WP04, WP05, and WP06 used the Shift Framework to analyze the roles and relationships of devices in "Seth's" scenario (see Figure 4c). These participants used the kit materials to identify a design requirement that devices should be discovered by services based on the roles they can perform (e.g., *notifier, collector, broadcaster*) without needing to share the data generated when in use by a service. WP06 talked about the value of the role cards especially, and how this design idea was directly tied to them: *"That idea came out exactly because I saw these [role] cards and I thought 'Oh wait a second we can actually take a device and change, temporarily, its role.'"*

In addition to the value participants found in the cards, they felt that the scenarios helped them better understand the problems faced by real users. WP08 commented on the value of the data-driven scenarios for testing a specific product vision: *"This let me exercise in a really meaningful way what that [vision] would feel like to a specific person and that was really useful."* WP01 commented that, overall, the kit helped "*making sure that we're not losing sight of making computing a more human experience.*" These comments highlight the importance of developing lightweight and reusable design tools, such as personas and scenarios, specifically to support multi-device product teams to ground their envisioning process.

We found that some scenarios offered better support for ideation than others. For example, Seth's scenario and Marissa's scenario featured complex social relationships that provoked interesting tradeoffs in design. The groups working with these scenarios were highly engaged in developing solutions to resolve the complex privacy and sharing needs across the different social relationships depicted. For example, Marissa's context shifted when her son entered the room and wanted a device to play games, and Seth's context shifted when his mother took on primary use of the iPad and the baby camera when he was absent. In contrast, Alex's scenario contained a context shift from volunteer center to work that did not introduce as much social complexity. Thus, Alex's group had less heterogeneity among their designs than other groups whose scenarios inspired more divergent design thinking.

Participants also told us a few ways to make the kit more effective. One suggestion is to spend more time introducing the content of the cards. WP05 said: *"I feel we could spend a little bit more time to understand what the cards are."* Another suggestion was to provide concrete examples of the burden cards. WP06 had trouble applying the user burden cards: *"I think it was a bit more difficult to use the burdens, mostly because I think the categories, I mean these make sense, but they're still somehow a bit too broad."*

To sum up, the design kit supported a collaborative multi-device design process, across diverse stakeholders on a product team. We have demonstrated some ways that participants utilized the cards, scenarios and the Shift Framework to help formulate and reflect on design ideas, and some ways in which these materials could be improved. We learned that, similar to other types of design cards (e.g., [12,18,24]), designers in our workshop considered the cards useful in building a common ground and getting informed of the technological possibilities. Moreover, the scenarios from our fieldwork helped designers situate their designs in the actual use of devices, and that is an important step towards ecologically valid design.

DISCUSSION

New tools for data-driven ideation can help designers understand the everyday needs and burdens that influence multi-device use. Both sophisticated multi-device *systems* and ad hoc multi-device *collections* will co-exist in users' everyday life. Most of the existing multi-device design tools and frameworks focus on technical aspects of multi-device systems design (e.g., continuity of information across screens) [23,33,37,39–41]. Few frameworks address contextual factors of multi-device experiences in naturalistic settings, with the exception of Lundgren et al.'s [26] framework for designing collocated mobile interactions that account for spatial, temporal, social and technological perspectives. These factors are important, as various HCI theorists have vocally advocated attention to different aspects of human-artifact relationships and contexts [1,11,30]. Our Shift Kit helps designers of multi-device experiences to test design moves using ecologically valid constraints, tasks, and needs.

Our findings from the workshop demonstrate that designers benefitted from the process of using the design kit materials for explicit consideration of context shifts, user burdens, device roles, and privacy needs in multi-device product design. The design insights that emerged from the workshop were clearly derived from our empirical findings (e.g., devices roles should be able to shift flexibly according context), or built upon them (e.g., data should be decoupled from devices that might be shared). Thus, the design kit successfully helped designers to interact with complex data in a relatively short amount of time (*i.e.,* one day). Our design materials supported conscientious and rigorous design ideation based on a shared understanding of core concepts, similar to other techniques for "designing with cards": Lucero et al.'s [24] PLEX cards and Inspiration Card Workshops, IDEO Method Cards [18] for inspiring the use of diverse design methods, and the Envisioning Cards [12] for prompting designers to reflect on the long-term influences of their technologies.

Our process for creating the design framework and supporting materials followed four steps: analytical, empirical, codification, and validation. Our empirical step, detailing a field study of multi-device use across four U.S. regions, yielded novel insights about everyday use of devices. We contribute insight into device roles in multi-device use, especially for multitasking, that adds to existing notions of parallel usage patterns (e.g., Jokela [20]). We found that users in everyday settings compose multi-device experiences that support parallel related and unrelated tasks. We also found that as users change context, they shift their device roles to adapt to different privacy and sharing needs. These findings contrast with previous field studies on multi-device use that have reported little privacy concerns [20,34]. In contrast, we found that, not only do people switch device configurations to suit different tasks and environments [9,20,32], they do so to preserve privacy and sharing.

One reason that our empirical findings differ from previous field studies on multi-device use is that we explicitly focused on practices of device sharing in our data collection and analysis. Another reason, is that we used the experience sampling method to gather in-the-moment reports of using many devices throughout the day, that enabled us to observe patterns of unrelated parallel use that have not been deeply explored in prior work.

Overall, we contribute a reusable design kit that allows design practitioners to consume insights derived from our field study and related work; insights into six device roles that we found prevalent in everyday multi-device use; evidence of the ways in which device roles are influenced by shifts in device sharing and privacy; and a generalizable approach to make field research more accessible and useful to design practitioners. Through sharing our empirical insights and design kit, we hope to support designers to consider ecologically valid constraints when envisioning multi-device experiences.

Limitations

The sample we chose was biased toward people who exhibited a lot of multi-device use in our field study. Non-use or minimal use was not explored in this analysis. Due to time and organizational constraints, the follow-up interviews with the four design participants were conducted by the same person who ran the workshop, potentially biasing designers' reflections on the kit.

FUTURE WORK

The design kit is not definitive; rather it is a version of a kit that can be extended and customized to suit different needs. In fact, as a design tool, the kit should evolve as multi-device interactions become more common and better supported. For example, components of the kit could be replaced with different data and updated as new interaction patterns are developed. We provide a template and process for researchers to distill field research into actionable resources for designers. We hope that future work will build on this design kit as the technological landscape changes. Further validation through use of the kit with different stakeholders and settings is an important next step. We plan to conduct more workshops using the design kit within our organization and offer a printable version of the kit for other researchers and designers to try it.

CONCLUSION

Designers of multi-device experiences need tools to better address situated contexts of use early in their design process through ideation and reflection. To address this need, we created and tested a reusable design kit, called the **M**oving **C**ontext **Kit,** or McKit for short, that contains scenarios, cards, and a framework for understanding tradeoffs of multi-device innovations in realistic contexts of use. In a workshop, we demonstrated that the design kit makes it easier for designers to build on prior work and insights from our field study on everyday multi-device use. The McKit can help designers explore a large design space of sequential, related, and unrelated parallel device use by focusing on the ways in which context shifts force changes in everyday multi-device experiences. Our design kit, and the process of creating it, can support ecological validity in the design of multi-device computing for everyday life.

ACKNOWLEDGMENTS

We thank Peter Hamilton for his help with identifying examples of multi-device interaction patterns, our workshop participants, our colleagues for their feedback and encouragement, and the reviewers for their helpful suggestions for improving this paper.

REFERENCES

1. Susanne Bødker and Clemens Nylandsted Klokmose. 2012. Dynamics in artifact ecologies. *Proceedings of the 7th Nordic Conference on Human-Computer Interaction: Making Sense Through Design*: 448–457. http://doi.org/10.1145/2399016.2399085
2. A.J. Brush and Kori Inkpen. 2007. Yours, Mine and Ours? Sharing and Use of Technology in Domestic Environments. *Proceedings of the 9th international conference on Ubiquitous computing (UbiComp '07)*, 109–126. Retrieved September 20, 2016 from http://dl.acm.org/citation.cfm?id=1771592.1771599
3. John M. Carroll. 1999. Five Reasons for Scenario-Based Design. *Hawaii International Conference on System Sciences*.
4. Scott Carter, Jennifer Mankoff, Scott R. Klemmer, and Tara Matthews. 2008. Exiting the Cleanroom: On Ecological Validity and Ubiquitous Computing. *Human–Computer Interaction* 23, 1: 47–99. http://doi.org/10.1080/07370020701851086
5. Nicholas Chen, Francois Guimbretiere, and Abigail

Sellen. 2012. Designing a multi-slate reading environment to support active reading activities. *ACM Transactions on Computer-Human Interaction* 19, 3: 1–35. http://doi.org/10.1145/2362364.2362366

6. Nicholas Chen, François Guimbretière, and Abigail Sellen. 2013. Graduate student use of a multi-slate reading system. *Proceedings of the SIGCHI Conference on Human Factors in Computing Systems - CHI '13*, ACM Press, 1799. http://doi.org/10.1145/2470654.2466237
7. Pei-Yu (Peggy) Chi, Yang Li, and Björn Hartmann. 2016. Enhancing Cross-Device Interaction Scripting with Interactive Illustrations. *Proceedings of the 2016 CHI Conference on Human Factors in Computing Systems - CHI '16*, ACM Press, 5482–5493. http://doi.org/10.1145/2858036.2858382
8. Pei-Yu Chi and Yang Li. 2015. Weave : Scripting Cross-Device Wearable Interaction. *Proceedings of the 2015 CHI Conference on Human Factors in Computing Systems - CHI '15*, ACM, 3923–3932. https://doi.org/10.1145/2702123.2702451
9. David Dearman and Jeffrey S Pierce. 2008. It's on my other computer!: computing with multiple devices. *Proceedings of the SIGCHI Conference on Human Factors in Computing Systems*: 767–776. http://doi.org/10.1145/1357054.1357177
10. Hasan Shahid Ferdous, Bernd Ploderer, Hilary Davis, et al. 2016. TableTalk: Integrating personal devices and content for commensal experiences at the family dinner table. *Proceedings of the 2016 ACM International Joint Conference on Pervasive and Ubiquitous Computing - UbiComp '16*, ACM Press, 132–143. http://doi.org/10.1145/2971648.2971715
11. Jodi Forlizzi. 2007. How Robotic Products Become Social Products : An Ethnographic Study of Cleaning in the House. *Proceedings of the ACM/IEEE international conference on Human-robot interaction (HRI '07).*, ACM, 129–136. http://doi.org/http://dx.doi.org/10.1145/1228716.12287 34
12. Batya Friedman and David G. Hendry. 2012. The envisioning cards: A toolkit for catalyzing humanistic and technical imaginations. *Proceedings of the 2012 ACM Annual Conference on Human Factors in Computing Systems - CHI '12*: 1145–1148. http://doi.org/10.1145/2207676.2208562
13. R Stuart Geiger and David Ribes. 2011. Trace Ethnography: Following Coordination through Documentary Practices. *2011 44th Hawaii International Conference on System Sciences*, IEEE, 1–10. http://doi.org/10.1109/HICSS.2011.455
14. Audrey Girouard, Aneesh Tarun, and Roel Vertegaal. 2012. DisplayStacks: Interaction techniques for stacks of flexible thin-film displays. *Proceedings of the 2012 ACM annual conference on Human Factors in Computing Systems - CHI '12*, ACM Press, 2431. http://doi.org/10.1145/2207676.2208406
15. Jonathan Grudin and John Pruitt. 2002. Personas, Participatory Design and Product Development: An Infrastructure for Engagement. *PDC*, 144–152.
16. Peter Hamilton and Daniel J. Wigdor. 2014. Conductor: Enabling and Understanding Cross-Device Interaction. *Proceedings of the 32nd Annual ACM Conference on Human Factors in Computing Systems - CHI '14*: 2773–2782. http://doi.org/10.1145/2556288.2557170
17. Björn Hartmann, Scott R. Klemmer, Michael Bernstein, et al. 2006. Reflective physical prototyping through integrated design, test, and analysis. *Proceedings of the 19th annual ACM symposium on User interface software and technology - UIST '06*, ACM Press, 299. http://doi.org/10.1145/1166253.1166300
18. IDEO. 2003. IDEO Method Cards: 51 Ways to Inspire Design.
19. Iulia Ion, Niharika Sachdeva, Ponnurangam Kumaraguru, and Srdjan Čapkun. 2011. Home is safer than the cloud!: Privacy concerns for consumer cloud storage. *Proceedings of the Seventh Symposium on Usable Privacy and Security - SOUPS '11*, ACM Press, 1. http://doi.org/10.1145/2078827.2078845
20. Tero Jokela, Jarno Ojala, and Thomas Olsson. 2015. A Diary Study on Combining Multiple Information Devices in Everyday Activities and Tasks. *Proceedings of the ACM CHI'15 Conference on Human Factors in Computing Systems* 1: 3903–3912. http://doi.org/10.1145/2702123.2702211
21. Heekyoung Jung, Erik Stolterman, William Ryan, Tonya Thompson, and Marty Martin Siegel. 2008. Toward a framework for ecologies of artifacts: how are digital artifacts interconnected within a personal life? *Proceedings of the 5th Nordic conference on Human-computer interaction: building bridges*: 201–210. http://doi.org/10.1145/1463160.1463182
22. Jake Knapp, John Zeratsky, and Braden Kowitz. 2016. *Sprint: How to solve big problems and test new ideas in just five days*. Simon and Schuster.
23. M Levin. 2014. *Designing Multi-device Experiences: An Ecosystem Approach to User Experiences Across Devices*. O'Reilly.
24. Andrés Lucero, Peter Dalsgaard, Kim Halskov, and Jacob Buur. 2016. Designing with Cards. In *Collaboration in Creative Design*. Springer International Publishing, Cham, 75–95. http://doi.org/10.1007/978-3-319-29155-0_5
25. Andrés Lucero, Jussi Holopainen, and Tero Jokela. 2011. Pass-them-around. *Proceedings of the 2011*

annual conference on Human factors in computing systems - CHI '11, ACM Press, 1787. http://doi.org/10.1145/1978942.1979201

26. Sus Lundgren, Joel E Fischer, Stuart Reeves, and Olof Torgersson. 2015. Designing Mobile Experiences for Collocated Interaction. *Proceedings of the 18th ACM Conference on Computer Supported Cooperative Work & Social Computing - CSCW '15*: 496–507. http://doi.org/10.1145/2675133.2675171
27. Tara Matthews, Kerwell Liao, Anna Turner, Marianne Berkovich, Robert Reeder, and Sunny Consolvo. 2016. "She'll just grab any device that's closer": A Study of Everyday Device and Account Sharing in Households. *Proceedings of the 2016 CHI Conference on Human Factors in Computing Systems - CHI '16*, ACM Press, 5921–5932. http://doi.org/10.1145/2858036.2858051
28. Michelle L. Mazurek, Brandon Salmon, Richard Shay, et al. 2010. Access control for home data sharing: Attitudes, needs, and practices. *Proceedings of the 28th international conference on Human factors in computing systems - CHI '10*, ACM Press, 645. http://doi.org/10.1145/1753326.1753421
29. Robert C. Miller and Brad A. Myers. 1999. Synchronizing clipboards of multiple computers. *Proceedings of the 12th annual ACM symposium on User interface software and technology - UIST '99*, ACM Press, 65–66. http://doi.org/10.1145/320719.322584
30. Bonnie A. Nardi and Vicki O'Day. 1999. *Information ecologies : using technology with heart.* MIT Press.
31. Michael Nebeling and Anind K. Dey. 2016. XDBrowser: User-defined Cross-device Web Page Designs. *Proceedings of the 2016 CHI Conference on Human Factors in Computing Systems - CHI '16*, ACM Press, 5494–5505. http://doi.org/10.1145/2858036.2858048
32. Antti Oulasvirta and Lauri Sumari. 2007. Mobile kits and laptop trays: managing multiple devices in mobile information work. *Chi '07*: 1127–1136. http://doi.org/10.1145/1240624.1240795
33. Fabio Paternò and Carmen Santoro. 2012. A logical framework for multi-device user interfaces. *Proceedings of the 4th ACM SIGCHI symposium on Engineering interactive computing systems - EICS '12*, ACM Press, 45. http://doi.org/10.1145/2305484.2305494
34. Stephanie Santosa and Daniel Wigdor. 2013. A field study of multi-device workflows in distributed workspaces. *Proc. of UbiComp '13*. http://doi.org/10.1145/2493432.2493476
35. Norbert Schwarz, Ed. Diener, Daniel Kahneman, and Project MUSE. 2013. *Well-being : the foundations of hedonic psychology*. Russell Sage Foundation.
36. Phoebe Sengers, Kirsten Boehner, Shay David, and Joseph "Jofish" Kaye. 2005. Reflective design. *Proceedings of the 4th decennial conference on Critical computing between sense and sensibility - CC '05*, ACM Press, 49. http://doi.org/10.1145/1094562.1094569
37. Henrik Sørensen, Dimitrios Raptis, Jesper Kjeldskov, and Mikael B Skov. 2014. The 4C Framework:Principles of Interaction in Digital Ecosystems . *Proc. Int. Conf. on Ubiquitous Computing*: 87–97. https://doi.org/10.1145/2632048.2636089
38. Hyewon Suh, Nina Shahriaree, Eric B. Hekler, and Julie A. Kientz. 2016. Developing and Validating the User Burden Scale: A Tool for Assessing User Burden in Computing Systems. *Proceedings of the ACM Conference on Human Factors in Computing Systems (CHI 2016)*: Under Review. http://doi.org/10.1145/2858036.2858448
39. Lucia Terrenghi, Aaron Quigley, and Alan Dix. 2009. A taxonomy for and analysis of multi-person-display ecosystems. *Personal and Ubiquitous Computing* 13, 8: 583–598. http://doi.org/10.1007/s00779-009-0244-5
40. Mejdi Trimeche and Tomi Aarnio. 2005. Enhancing End-User Experience in a Multi-Device Ecosystem. *Design*: 19–25. http://doi.acm.org/10.1145/1149488.1149492
41. Minna Wäljas, Katarina Segerståhl, Kaisa Väänänen-Vainio-Mattila, and Harri Oinas-Kukkonen. 2010. Cross-platform service user experience. *Proceedings of the 12th international conference on Human computer interaction with mobile devices and services - MobileHCI '10*: 219. http://doi.org/10.1145/1851600.1851637
42. Jill Palzkill Woelfer, Amy Iverson, David G. Hendry, Batya Friedman, and Brian T. Gill. 2011. Improving the safety of homeless young people with mobile phones: Values, form, and function. *Proceedings of the 2011 annual conference on Human factors in computing systems - CHI '11*, ACM Press, 1707. http://doi.org/10.1145/1978942.1979191
43. Jishuo Yang and Daniel Wigdor. 2014. Panelrama: Enabling Easy Specification of Cross-Device Web Applications. *Proceedings of the 32nd Annual ACM Conference on Human Factors in Computing Systems - CHI '14*: 2783–2792. http://doi.org/10.1145/2556288.2557199
44. Daisy Yoo, Alina Huldtgren, Jill Palzkill Woelfer, David G. Hendry, and Batya Friedman. 2013. A value sensitive action-reflection model: Evolving a co-design space with stakeholder and designer prompts. *Proceedings of the SIGCHI Conference on Human Factors in Computing Systems - CHI '13*, ACM Press, 419. http://doi.org/10.1145/2470654.2470715

Thoughts and Tools for Crafting Colors: Implications from Designers' Behavior

EunJin Kim
KAIST
Daejeon, Republic of Korea
kejkim8@kaist.ac.kr

Hyeon-Jeong Suk
KAIST
Daejeon, Republic of Korea
color@kaist.ac.kr

ABSTRACT
Despite the substantial changes made in the platforms to create graphic works, it is hard to clarify the improvement of authoring tools to manipulate design components such as colors, text, and images. In this regards, this paper presents empirical findings from designers' behavior and suggests preliminary ideas to develop graphic tools that support the visual design process. In particular, this paper focuses on the articulation of colors and images in the context of graphic design. Through experiments with designers, we investigated how designers perceive images and colors and how they create integrated aesthetics of images and color components. Based on the findings, we characterized a general color design process and derived implications for graphic tools to support image comprehension, color craft, and archiving design changes. As a primitive attempt, we expect this study can provide insights to advance the way of manipulating a variety of design components.

Author Keywords
Graphic design; color design process; visual content; image-color combinations.

ACM Classification Keywords
H.5.2. Information interfaces and presentation (e.g., HCI): User Interfaces.

INTRODUCTION
Due to the rapid growth in its popularity and importance, the use of the visual content is now prevalent throughout media and platforms. A variety of visual contents such as images and videos are now engaged in the communication process to convey informative and/or emotional messages. Accordingly, a variety of services has been introduced in the market in order to support users who want to create personalized and aesthetic visual contents.

DIS 2017, June 10-14, 2017, Edinburgh, United Kingdom
 ISBN 978-1-4503-4922-2/17/06...$15.00
DOI: http://dx.doi.org/10.1145/3064663.3064769

For instance, Canva [1] is a platform that enables users to generate a wide range of two-dimensional graphic works utilizing pre-designed templates. Similarly, Magisto [10] and Shakr [9] provide automatic video editing services based on video templates and editing algorithms. Wix [7] and WordPress [5] are well-known platforms to publish a website, and these platforms significantly reduce the barrier that has obstructed novice users who do not own sufficient knowledge and skills to design and build a website. In general, these services are characterized by a large body of pre-designed templates and automation of a certain part of design tasks. Due to the aid of these services, the design activities of novices now become proliferated throughout various domains including web publishing, application development, and multimedia production.

There have been considerable changes in the tools and interfaces for experts as well. One of the distinctive trends is the embodiment of crowdsourcing technology. Sharing design resources in the crowdsourced platform is now prevailing among professional designers. Such platforms also function as a public archive and portfolios of professional designers to promote themselves [6, 8].

Although significant development has been made in the macroscopic systems to generate visual content, it is hard to notice changes in microscopic tools to manipulate design components including text, colors, and visual content. In particular, the authoring tool to manipulate colors is rarely changed or improved despite its prevalence and importance on the design process. Figure 1 compares the color picker of Adobe Photoshop version 1.0 (released in 1990) and version CS 6 (released in 2012). Except for the Lab color values, the interfaces almost remains constant for more than 20 years.

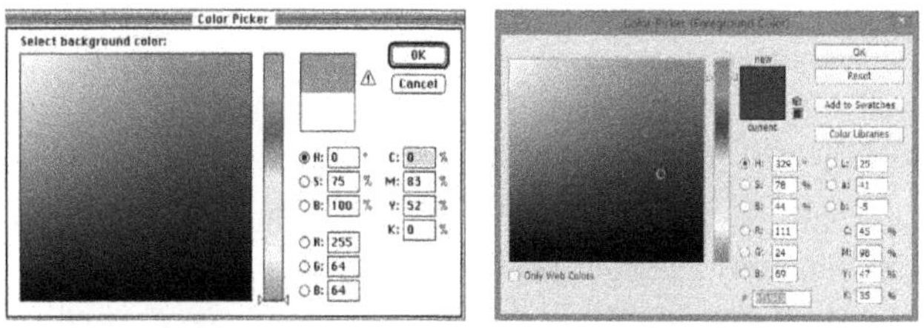

Figure 1. Comparison of color pickers of Adobe Photoshop version 1.0 (left, released in 1990) and version CS6 (2012).

In this regard, this paper aims at investigating the way that people uses graphic tools and suggesting implications for visual design tools in particular interest of color manipulation. In a more detail, the goal of this study is understanding the creative nature of color design process and presenting implications for a graphic tool to promote creative and reflective authoring activities of general users. To achieve the goal, we conducted experiments with designers to understand their color design process. Along with their design outcomes, we analyzed verbal protocols in order to understand their latent thoughts. Note that this study explores the designers' process not because we target the expert group, but because the trained people are more fluent and familiar to demonstrate their thoughts and intention regarding design creation explicitly. Thus, the implications proposed in this paper are not restrained to tools for a professional usage. It rather argues its implication to ease the visual design process of general users in a wide range of tools and interfaces.

The rest of the paper is structured as follows. We first overview the related research that deals with color design. We then introduce experiments with designers to understand their color design process in the context of visual content creation. Based on the findings from qualitative analysis, we present practical implications for color manipulation tools and suggest prospective topics to be investigated further. The paper concludes with a broad discussion and limitation of the study.

RELATED WORK

In relation to the aim of this study, we have identified two fundamental topics that have been widely investigated by researchers. One topic is related to the perception of color and the other introduces tools that support the color design process.

Perception of Colors

Color is one of the most important factors that have a strong influence on human perception. Hence understanding the perception of colors was long been an interest of researchers. For instance, Osgood et al. [1, 23] revealed the cross-cultural similarities in the affective perception of colors. They associated colors with perceptual aspects including as evaluation, activity, and potency, and specify the emotions each color is related. The study of Valdez and Mehrabian [35] reported the strong and consistent effects of saturation and brightness on emotions. A more recent of study by Suk & Irtel [38] also supported the major influence of tone upon the emotion.

Not only the perception of single color, but also the color combinations have been studied by several authors. Ou and Luo [25] developed a three dimensional color-emotion space defined by activity, weight, and heat of colors. By positioning single colors and color combinations on the same space, they revealed that emotion of two-color combinations can be estimated by the mean of single color emotions. Addition to emotion of color combinations, color harmony has long been an interest of researchers. The early studies [13, 16, 28] has suggested universal and global principles, while more recent studies [32, 34] have differed the emotions that colors can convey. Like Goethe [13], Munsell [28] viewed balance as a key to creating harmony among colors. Matsuda [22] suggested a hue template that defines harmony among colors. Similar to the Matsuda's study, various color harmony principles were suggested, and a quantitative measure developed by Moon and Spencer [25] was one of them. A more recent study of Ou and Luo [33] also emphasized the great influence of hue on color harmony.

Although these studies have supported a better understanding of the perception of colors and color combinations, there is little information available on how the knowledge engages in the design practice. In this manner, we believe that this study can contribute to the understanding of the knowledge and tactics embedded in the color design process.

Tools for Color Design

Inspired by the findings of color harmony research, a number of tools have been suggested to support the generation of harmonious color combinations and its applications to certain design contexts [15, 23, 27]. For instance, Meier et al. [23] developed a toolset, Interactive Palette Tools (IPTs) that enables various activities including browsing, breeding, displaying of color palettes. Hu et al. [15] presented a tool that helps users to generate color themes based on the principles of familiarity and rhythmic span. Studies by Hsiao et al.[14] and Jahanian et al. [17] both utilized the image colors to construct a color theme and applied the theme for graphic and product design. Compared to the tools that only generate color schemes, the tools developed by Hu et al., Hsiao et al. and Jahanian et al. provide a more situated and extensive ability by allowing a direct utilization of a color theme in design practice [14, 15, 17]. A recent study by Jalal et al. [18] suggested a color interaction tool based on five key color manipulation activities they identified. Among commercial tools, Adobe Color CC [3] and Colourlovers [4] are well-known services due to the academic contribution of their database [19, 29]. Both services provide a tool to generate color themes and a platform to share the color resources. Adobe Capture CC [2] is another notable applications that support the color design process. In addition to color theme generation, it covers a wide range of design applications based on the platform of Adobe systems.

Although these tools have assisted an easier way of tailoring colors, their applications are limited to color combinations instead of the integration of colors and visual contents. In the present study, we thus tried to provide a novel and practical insights by investigating implications for graphic tools used in the integrated color design process.

EXPERIMENT WITH DESIGNERS

We performed experiments with designers to understand the process of manipulating colors in the context of visual content generation.

Method

Participants

A total of 15 designers participated in the individual experiment. All of them hold a bachelor's degree in an industrial or graphic design major and are currently enrolled in a graduate school of industrial design. The participants' mean age was 28.6, ranging from 26 to 31.

Materials: Images and Keywords

For the experiment, we prepared a set of 1000 by 1000 images and style keywords that deliver a certain emotion or affective image. Images were pictures that portray various topics including people, objects, animals, plants, and landscapes. Although the main objective of this study was understanding how designers create an aesthetic image-color combinations, we have specified the desired style of each image-color combination to observe multifaceted tactics and strategies of designers. The style keywords have been adopted from both of PAD theory [36] that suggested three dimensions of emotion and Color Image Scale [20] which investigated the emotion that colors can deliver.

Table 1 summarizes the information of stimuli of all three experiments. Instead of providing the same stimuli to every participant, we prepared three different set of images and style keywords. As a result, five designers received the same stimuli. In the stimuli, some images were presented more than once with different style keywords. This experimental design allowed us to investigate how designers' color choice could be differed according to the changes of design contexts.

Set	Style keywords	No. of images / keyword
1	4 keywords: Active, Afraid, Depressed, Relaxed	30
	120 image-color combinations / designer	
2	10 keywords: Chic, Clean, Enjoyable, Intellectual, Modern, Pastoral, Peaceful, Placid, Sporty, Youthful	5
	50 image-color combinations / designer	
3	10 keywords: Cheerful, Fresh, Friendly, Graceful, Healthy, Polished, Restful, Simple, Tender, Wholesome	5
	50 image-color combinations / designer	

Table 1. Stimuli for three experiments. Each experiment utilizes a distinctive set of keywords and images.

Procedure

The experiment was conducted individually in an isolated room that disguised as an office environment with a desk, a chair, and a desktop computer. Figure 2 shows a brief look of the experimental setting. When the experiment began, one of the images was presented with a style keyword. The designers were instructed to decide a color that is harmonious with the image as well as delivers the style suggested by the keyword. As a design outcome, they asked to present an image-color combination by filling the selected color into a rectangle located under the images (Figure 2). The size of the rectangle was 1000 pixels wide and 350 pixels tall, and the entire design process was performed with Adobe Photoshop® CS6. The color-selection task was described as a part of graphic design, but we did not specify its use in order to explore general and unbiased behaviors of designers that could be applied to a wider range of applications.

Throughout the experiment, we also asked them to think-out-loud their thoughts and concerns as much as they can. However, we did not strongly enforce them to keep speaking in order to minimize its influence upon the design activities. Instead, we conducted a thorough posthoc interview to retrieve the details of their thoughts by reviewing the design outcomes together.

Data Analysis

Through the experiments, we obtained design outcomes - 1,100 image-color combinations - and verbal protocols from think-aloud and posthoc interviews. To understand the designers' latent thoughts, we began with the analysis of the protocols and utilized the design outcomes as supplementary quantitative data.

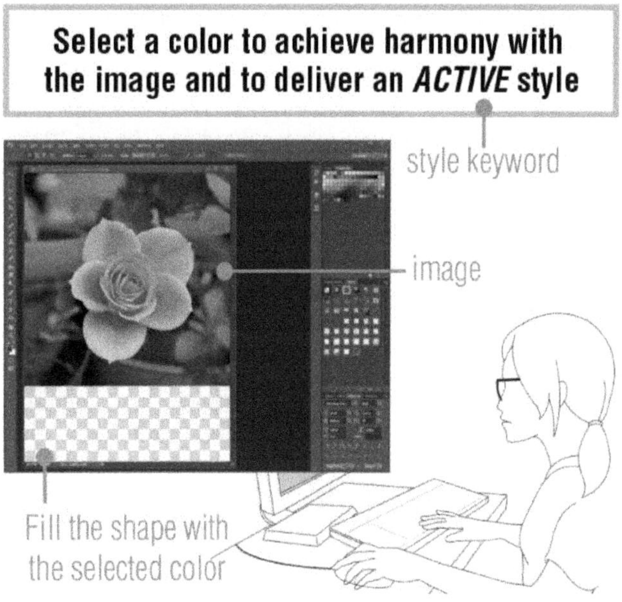

Figure 2. Settings and exemplary task of the experiment

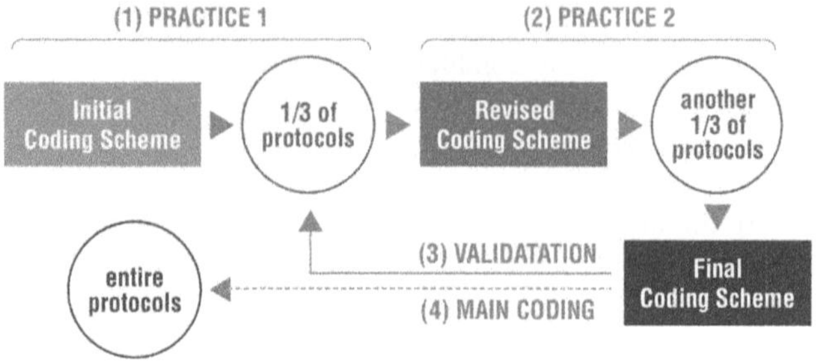

Figure 3. The entire coding procedure

The protocols were transcribed verbatim, and the transcripts were used for the analysis. Since we had a sound perspective on the objects of investigation, we conducted a closed coding with a predefined coding scheme. The initial coding scheme was developed based on our research question as suggested by Miles and Huberman [24] and had revised and confirmed during the two repetitive pre-coding practices. Figure 3 shows the entire coding procedure. The pre-analysis consists of two phases of coding practices to develop a solid and comprehensive coding scheme. With an initial coding scheme, one of the researchers analyzed one-third of the protocols and revised the coding scheme. During the first practice (Figure 3, (1)), a code that comprehends image, color and style were added to the scheme. In the second practice, the researcher coded another one-third of protocols using the revised scheme (Figure 3, (2)), and developed layers of the final coding scheme by specifying the subcategories of Image code. At last, the final coding scheme was validated by revisiting the protocols that have analyzed in the first practice (Figure 3, (3)). In the validation process, an external coder, who has more than three years of experience in qualitative studies, was invited to review the final coding scheme along with the protocols.

Figure 4 shows the structure of the final coding scheme. According to the factor that designers mainly considered, we classified the segments of protocols into one of the seven codes (A~G). The categories from A to C include verbal expressions that participants solely designate an individual factor such as Style keyword (A), Image (B) or Color, respectively. In the cases of Image (B) and Color (D), subcategories were utilized in order to discern the intricate changes in designers' perspective. The rest of four categories encompasses designers' cognitive activities regarding interactions between Style-Image, Style-Color and Image-Color as well as the holistic view of Style-Image-Color.

The qualitative analysis enables us to understand cognitive process of designers to create integrated aesthetics using images and colors. The results were interwove with the design outcomes which visualize the last decision of designers. In the following sections, we will discuss the findings that have been revealed and confirmed by both qualitative and quantitative analysis.

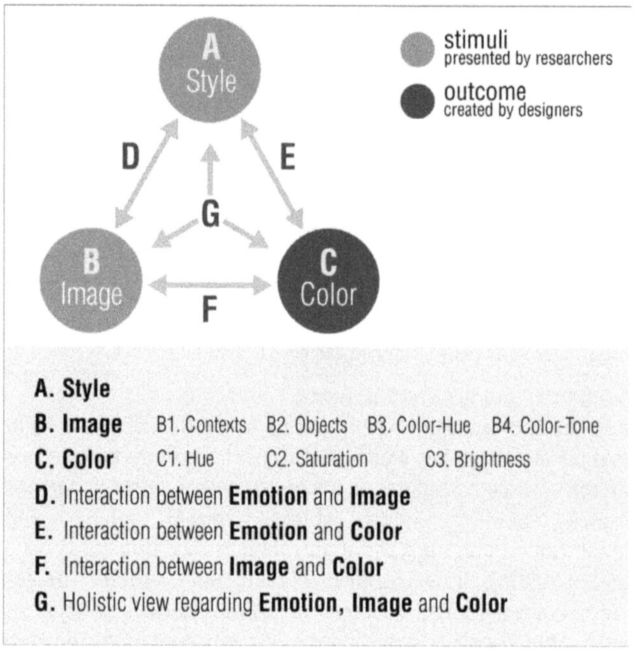

Figure 4. Structure of the final coding scheme

FINDINGS FROM DESIGNERS

Through the observations during the experiments, we noticed that the procedures of generating desired colors are much alike among designers. In short, it consisted of three activities. They have started the practice by identifying representative one from a mass of colors in an image. In most cases, designers employed the Eyedropper tool for the sorting-out activity. Once they identified a good starting point to proceed, they moved to articulating the initial color. In this step, the Color Picker has been mainly explored to identify better alternatives. While selecting a proper color for the image, they also considered the integrated visual effect generated by the combination of the image and the color they selected. Figure 5 (next page) is a diagram that summarizes the color design process by locating principal cognitive activities in parallel with the use of design tools. We visualized the process as a linear flow for its clarity though the reality was a mixture of parallel and synchronous activities.

How designers perceive images

The analysis of the protocols revealed two different perspectives that designers perceive and understand given images. The first perspective was color-focused perspective and the second one was semantic-focused. When a new image was presented to them, designers tended to deploy one of the perspectives predominantly, while both engaged in the perception of images mutually in most cases. Following sections provides the descriptions of each perspective with supportive instances from both verbal protocols and design outcomes.

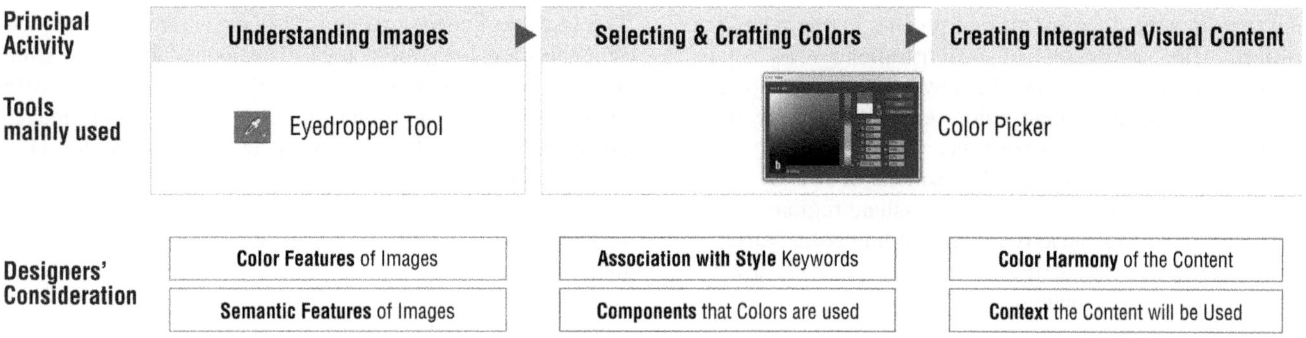

Figure 5. Color design process in general. It comprises three principal activities, of which has distinctive considerations.

Color-focused: Image as a Collection of Hues

Since the design task was generating a color for an image-color combination, designers naturally exhibited a primary focus on the color features of images. A majority of descriptions of a new stimulus – an image and a keyword - has begun with stating noticeable color features that an image possesses. We compiled the descriptions of images and unfolded two characteristics in relation to designers' perception of colors in an image.

First, the nomenclatures appeared in the descriptions attested designers' intent and delicate views on the hue rather than the brightness or saturation of an image. To be specific, terms related to hues were identified far more than those of saturation or brightness. Table 2 provides the average percentage of the terms used per designer, and representative expressions for each category. Throughout the transcripts of 15 designers, 87.10 % of denotations were selected in consideration of hues, while the terms regarding tones only took 12.90 %. Since the hue feature has more definitive nomenclatures to describe its condition than tone, it is difficult to directly compare the quantity of comments. Despite the difficulties of the direct comparison, it is considered that the frequent mentions of hue features implies the rich and exquisite capacities of designers in hue perception.

Then, we moved to a profound analysis to understand how designers comprehend an image and incorporating its features into design process selectively. By discerning the color features involved in the color generation process, we identified two distinctive measures which are devised by designers, that is, **color-dominance** and **color-saliency.** Figure 6 shows images and all colors selected by designers in consideration of different style keywords. Depending on the color distribution of images, designers tended to selectively devise one of the two measure in the perception of images.

The measure of **color-dominance** was typically devised when an image is perceived as a single color feature that holds the global tone or hue of the image. The upper part of Figure 6 is an exemplary that illustrates the apparent color-dominance and its impact upon the color selection of a designer. As shown, the images are recognized in relation to blue or yellow respectively, and the majority of designers' colors follows the dominant hue in general. The verbal protocol of designers supported the involvement of color-dominance measure. Words such as *'Bluish Gray', 'Light Blue' 'Blue tone'* were utilized to depict the left picture while *'Yellowish'* and *'Lemon'* were repetitively appeared in the comments regarding the right one.

	Expressions of Hue	Expressions of Tone
Examples	Yellow, Red, Brown, Blue.. (color names), Warm, Cool, Blu*ish*, Green*ish*, *Nuance* or *Hint* of ~, *Shades* of ~...	Monotone, Neutral, Pastel, Vivid, Dark, Dull, Lightness...
Average % of its Frequency	87.10 %	12.90 %

Table 2. Expressions used to describe color features of images. The average proportion is calculated based on frequency.

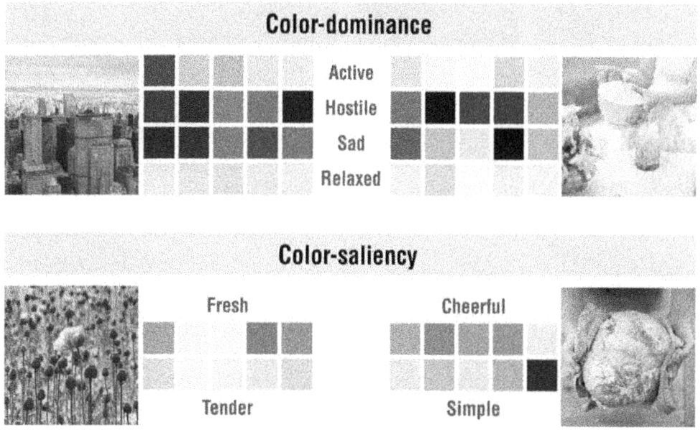

Figure 6. Images and selected colors demonstrating the semantic-focused perspective in perception of images

Contrary to such decision-making process, participants also utilized the measure of **color-saliency** to grasp representative colors. Like the lower cases of Figure 6, several images had salient color segments that are much more distinctive and noticeable than the rest. In these cases, participants tended to refer the salient colors by using specific color names. Opposite to the salient region, the rest often described as a background. Regarding color selection, however, designers exhibited a comparable use of background color depending on their intention or desired styles.

Semantic-focused: Meanings of Objects

The *semantic-focused* perspective is related to the **object-semantics** that describe the properties and/or sentiments of objects in given images. The focus of object-semantics is local and individual instead of embracing the entire features of an image, and exhibits interactivity with the color features of the object.

Figure 7 shows four image-color combinations that have been mentioned by designers with the view of object-semantics. The first image was presented with keyword *Cheerful* in experiment 3, and D11 described, *"In this image, yellow-green or the color of the rail load is dominant, but I'd like to use the red from the train. Somehow I can feel cheerfulness from the train, such as an excitement of a journey."* The designer related the perceived semantic of the train with cheerfulness. In the case of second images, D8 thought of the sunshine as the most *Pastoral* thing of the image. Hence she utilized the color of the sunlight to represent Pastoral mood in her image-color combination.

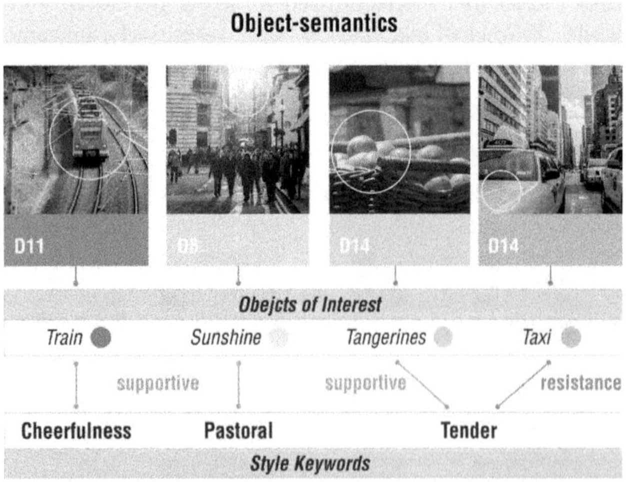

Figure 7. Examples that demonstrate the engagement of object-semantics in color design process. Three examples from the left shows that colors of the objects of interest support the style keywords. The right case is conflicting case that the object-semantic does not match with the style keyword.

The last two images of Figure 7 demonstrates how object-semantics can vary the perceived meanings of colors. Both images have similar color distribution – main objects with yellow color and grayish background. When the two images presented individually with the same keyword *Tender*, D14 made different choices. Yellow was selected for the picture of tangerines while light gray was picked for the street picture. During the posthoc interview, the designer plainly mentioned the influence of object-semantics: *"I think.. it relates to impressions of each object. I recognized the similarity in color features, but it was hard to associate the tenderness with a car, I mean a taxi. However, I can sense soft and warm feelings from fruits."*

The evidence of object-semantics was observed frequently and commonly among designers throughout diverse stimuli. Though its influence was strong enough to overwhelm other factors, it broadly interacted with the given keywords and colors of the object during the color selection process. In qualitative analysis, the view of object-semantics was mainly identified in concordance with the code G (Figure 4) which encompasses the holistic view regarding image, style, and color. This result suggests that object-semantics have supported the integration of image, style, and color. Thus it contributes to a semantic structure among them which provides a persuasive rationale for designers' selection.

In addition to the role of object-semantics, we identified another interesting trait originated from individual designers. Even with the same image and keyword, sometimes the perceived semantic upon an object was highly personal and idiosyncratic. Figure 8 highlights the outcomes of two designers who made unique interpretations on meanings and relationships between objects and the given keyword. As shown, the mood of presented picture is quite distant from the desired style *Enjoyable*. The perceptual distance made the task fastidious, and all designers commented its difficulty. As a result, three designers did not deploy any of semantic-focused perspectives, but D7 and D10 brought their personal impressions into the design process. For instance, D7 mentioned about a warm and delectable tea time to support his color choice from the golden teacup. On the other hand, D10 related the *Enjoyable* feeling with books: *"I wanted to convey the pleasures of reading since there are books in the image."*

Figure 8. Personalized interpretation of object-semantics regarding the style keyword.

As mentioned previously, we did not make a minute observation on the results of the code A (Figure 4) which is solely related to given style keywords. A preliminary analysis suggested characteristic differences of designers in the perceiving and interpreting the style keywords. This indicates the possibility of other factors that encourage designers to disclose their distinct characteristics. Hence it is hard to argue that object-semantics is a major factor that enforces the expression of personal identities during the design process. Considering the role of object-semantics, however, we believe that understanding the view of object-semantics has a significant relationship with the understanding of the way that designers express their identity. Designers constantly endeavor to provide meanings and values toward their design. Throughout the endeavoring, object-semantics offer opportunities to build compelling narratives behind the design by integrating multiple design components. Although there have been attempts to utilize the outcomes of designers [21, 30], the tactics and strategies embodied in the color selection process are still veiled. As an initial step, investigating the utilization and implication of object-semantics could contribute to understanding a hidden facet of designers' tacit knowledge.

Furthermore, the view of object-semantics also implies design-oriented potential of advanced techniques in other disciplines, for instance, an object detection technology which identifies objects in images. Due to the continuous efforts made in computer vision domain, the technology is now capable of detecting objects rapidly with a high detection rate [12, 39, 41]. However, the technology has yet been applied to construct a meaningful narrative that delivers a sentiment and intent. By incorporating these techniques in further studies, we expect novel insights that trigger prospective applications are suggested and demonstrated.

To summarize, examining the color features of images seems the prior and major perspective of designers to perceive an image (color-focused perspective). Specifically, designers selectively focus on either of the dominant colors or salient colors depending on the color distribution of an image. In addition to color features, designers also perceive semantics from the image (semantic-focused perspective). In general, object-semantics broadly engages in the interpretation and configuration of the entire design components – image, color and a keyword.

How designers craft a color

In the earlier stage of color design, designers exhibited a tendency to discover colors that represent given images. Once a satisfactory color is identified, designers moved to craft the color to make it aesthetically and purposefully proper for design usage. In such crafting activities, we identified two distinctive factors that designers considered. The first factor is the style keyword we provided in the experiment, and the second one is a design component designers assumed that the color would be applied.

In general, designers identified multiple representative colors. Thus they had to select one among them since a single color was the solution we asked. We found that style keywords are frequently used to prioritize the representative colors according to their perceptual congruity with the given style. Figure 9 shows two sets of a design outcome along with representative colors that have been discovered during the design process. The left set of Figure 9 derived from outcomes and verbal protocols of D11, the participant of experiment 3. He said, *"This image is quite complicated. There are several salient colors - yellow, red, and purple... Among them, I think, yellow fits to the Fresh feeling."* His description explicitly displays the role of style keyword to select the most suitable color from the representatives.

Through prioritization, designers were able to narrow down their choices into a single color feature. Thus it was one of the most significant decision-making activities throughout the color selection process. In addition to the selection, the style keywords were also highly engaged in the articulating process. D8 who designed the right set of Figure 9 said, *"Ugh... this was a truly knotty case. For me, this image is something opposite to Chic mood. Among yellow, red and green, I looked for a color that is likely to be Chic. Green was chosen and I deliberately change its tone to the dark one."* This partial protocol clearly demonstrates the act of color selection and the further elaboration of the selected color according to the style keyword.

The other factor that designers considered in the articulation stage is the component that the color will be used. Even we did not specify the usage of the color selected, designers frequently assume or imagine its usage by themselves to assist their decision making. The most notable consideration is whether the color will be used for text or not. Seven designers have considered the text component when they design the color, and articulate the color in order to make it more proper to be used for a text color. It is highly related to the functional aspect of the design outcome that determines its readability and clarity.

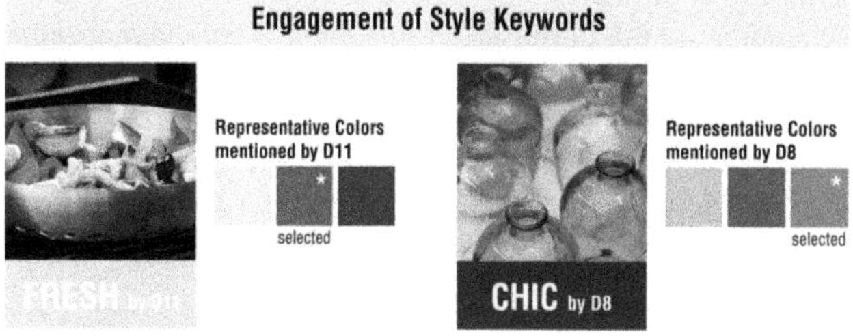

Figure 9. Engagement of style keywords in selecting and crafting colors. The left example demonstrates the role of the style keyword in the selection of colors and the right one demonstrates both selection and crafting of a color.

Additionally, there were instances that a color is considered as a background or a dominant color of the design. Since we asked designers to fill a rectangle, it is somehow natural to assume a background color to present an image or texts. In this case, designers often exhibit their prior knowledge about the area effect, which means that a larger area makes the color looks more saturated [26].

How designers create integrated aesthetics

At last, we observed two viewpoints that help us to envisage the designers' perception upon image-color combinations. The findings were mainly extracted from the segments belong to the code F (Figure 4) which signify the interaction between an image and a color. In terms of their properties, the viewpoints are not compatible with each other, but each provides valuable insights and implications towards potential applications.

The first viewpoint is considering the image-color combination as a two-color combination. We observed multiple cases that designers devised their prior knowledge upon the color harmony and emotion. Words such as *'contrast' 'rhythm'* and *'balance'* frequently appeared in their descriptions. They also referred to the general emotion and perception they had obtained from various color combinations. For instance, D6 commented, "For me, a strong contrast between complementary colors looks dynamic and active." D7 also mentioned that the use of analogous colors looks not only harmonious but also calm and *Peaceful*. In relation to this viewpoint, we identified that designers considered the color as a liberal design component that is not subsidiary, but equivalent to the image. Especially when designers had a clear intention or design direction, the color often became a leverage to steer the look and feel of the entire image-color combination. They strived for unified and synergetic visual impressions by manipulating the color.

The second finding covers a wider and practical view of designers. Although the use of image-color combination was not prescribed purposely, nine out of 15 designers mentioned a specific use of the image-color combination more than once. For example, D11 said, *"If I'm gonna use this for a perfume package..."* The comments of D12 indicates a possibility of different color selection criteria depending on the purpose: *"If this is for a calendar, I think this color can be a good alternative, but for a book... I'd rather use a heavier color."* Throughout the protocols, *a book cover, a calendar, a package* and *a poster* were mentioned, and *a perfume package* and *a travel guide* were specific cases with the detailed application.

DISCUSSION: IMPLICATIONS FOR TOOLS

Based on the insights and thoughts identified through the experiment, we explored their implications upon the development of tools and further studies to support visual design process of both novices and experts. The implications are classified into three categories: how to support the utilization of images, how to improve the ways of color manipulation, and how to provide a better way to explore alternatives.

Supporting Comprehension of Image Colors

Although an image has a bunch of color features, only a few attracted designers' attention and involved in the design process. In general, dominant or salient color features were mainly considered, and hues received more interests than the features of tone. The Eyedropper tool was the one and only tool that designers utilized to explore and simulate the color of an image.

Considering the repetitious actions of designers using the Eyedropper tool, it seems like that there is a disagreement between the purpose of the task and the capacity of the tool. The Eyedropper tool is suitable to extract a single color from few pixels but does not fit to extract multiple colors from a broader range. In the perspective of color perception, designers' main interest was the distribution of the color in order to identify dominant or salient colors. Instead of the eyedropper tool, an instrument that displays the distribution of colors or summarizes the color features of a broader space could be an alternative.

A function that automatically extracts several colors and presents them along the image could be one of the solutions that minimize the designers' effort to identify representative colors. Fortunately, Adobe Capture CC [2] provides the function that allows users to extract five-color themes and utilize the theme throughout the Adobe platform. However, the prime features of the service are not sufficient to aid the perception and utilization of image colors. To better represent an image, the number of colors in a theme could be flexible. In addition, the size of color swatches can be differed depending on their dominance or saliency in order to represent the importance of each color.

In addition to the color features of images, designers frequently devised semantic-focused perspectives. Advanced technologies related to object detection may replace a part of designers' ability within an automatic design system. However, the semantics that designers reflect upon an object or a context is significantly complicated and yet fully investigated. Further research is required to understand the way that designers deploy the semantic perspective and the tactics utilizing the semantics to construct a compelling narrative. Moreover, its relevance and values should be investigated more profoundly in prior to introducing such technology into the graphic tools for designers.

Providing Flexibility to Color Manipulation Interfaces

Regarding the tool used, the crafting of a color was mainly performed on the plane of Color Picker. When designers explore the multiple colors and try to prioritize them, it seems the Color Picker provides an adequate amount of usability. It has a hue slider that alters the hue value only and this offers easy transitions among distant hues. Since designers depicted a greater interest on hue features rather than the brightness or saturation, providing an independent instrument seems like a good strategy. As design process proceeds, designers rarely made a huge movement on color features. Instead, they kept simulating alternatives with minimal differences and tried to identify the most satisfactory color. In this stage, the Color Picker has shown limitations on assisting the delicate manipulation of colors. The easy transition benefited from a hue slider shifts to a limitation which discourages a further elaboration of the hue feature. Few designers made attempts to adjust the numerical values of a color, but a majority of designers prefers to utilize the graphical user interfaces. Even a designer (D15) who used the numeric values commented that manipulating numbers do not provide any sense of perceiving and elaborating a color. He also mentioned that it is almost impossible to correlate the changes in color values with the ones in the appearance of a color.

Considering these issues, GUI (Graphic User Interface)-based color tools seem to be preferred by designers, because of its conceptual coherence as well as its usability. On the basis of the current interface, providing a zoom-in or magnifying ability would be a good strategy to flexibly respond to designers' needs upon color manipulation.

In a more radical way, providing a three-dimensional representation of a color space could be a significant change that breaks the limits of two-dimensional space. In general, colors are designated by three-dimensional color spaces such as RGB, HSB, and Lab. Thus, a three-dimensional representation could be more natural and intuitive to understand the relationship among color features and the distance between two colors. By granting a controllability over the entire features of a color, the final elaboration color could be largely smooth and fluent.

Archiving Design Moves for Alternative Exploration

In general, we also identified that there is no sufficient space to review the changes made and compare several alternatives generated from such changes. In particular, there was a limitation to compare multiple image-color combinations together in the middle of the design process. Because of this limitations, designers inevitably chose to narrow down their alternatives into two, and compare them by switching between two colors. This caused repetitive operations since designers were not able to compare even two alternatives together.

Considering the iterative nature of design process, providing a repository to save and retrieve their design movements can aid designers to effectively manage the entire design process. Even in the Color Picker, designers made a number of trials to pick a color. However, none of the trials are recorded or successively displayed during their actions. By recording the traces and presenting them properly, the tool can promote the reflection of designers that increases the design-driven activities and brings new insights [35, 37].

It also would be useful to provide a space to juxtapose several alternatives to compare and evaluate the integrated design outcomes. In the case of our experiment, an image-color combination was a design outcome for each of the task. Thus, it was important for designers to view the image and the color together. In general, graphic design practice often incorporates different types of resources and elements. Enabling parallel comparison among various combinations of multiple resources could improve the compatibility of a graphic tool and enlarge the design space of designers. There also have been several studies related to the benefits and advantages of providing alternatives in parallel [11, 31, 40]. Based on the knowledge from these studies, a future study can be advanced further in order to suggest a novel tool for graphic design practice.

CONCLUSION

The present study has conducted to understand the intricate aspects of color and image manipulation in the context of visual design and to provide practical implications for the development of graphic tools. Through the experiments with designers, we investigated how designers perceive images and colors and how they create integrated aesthetics of colors and images based on the capacity of current graphic tools. The findings revealed a comprehensive color design process which comprises three activities – understanding images, crafting colors, and creating integrated visual of an image and a color. For each activity, we also identified factors that influence the decision making of designers. In particular, the engagement of object-semantics and personal interpretation regarding the object-semantics provided a probable explanation about how designers make their design distinctive and idiosyncratic. Based on the findings, implications for graphic tools were suggested to support image utilization, color manipulation, and alternative comparison during the design process. Although it provides relevant findings, this study has limitations including its context confined to a color selection task. The suggested ideas for graphic tools are also needed to be implemented and verified. As a primitive attempt, we expect this study brings forth in-depth studies to understand constituent characteristics of the design process and inspires further investigation to develop better tools for the creation of creative aesthetics.

REFERENCES

1. 2017. All Your Designs - Canva. Retrieved January 15, 2017 from https://www.canva.com/
2. 2017. Capture color themes with Adobe Capture CC. Retrieved January 15, 2017 from https://helpx.adobe.com/mobile-apps/how-to/capture-color-theme.html
3. 2017. Color wheel | Color schemes - Adobe Color CC. Retrieved January 15, 2017 from https://color.adobe.com/
4. 2017. COLOURlovers: Color Trends + Palettes. Retrieved January 15, 2017 from www.colourlovers.com/
5. 2017. Create a site with WordPress - Easy SetUp, Outstanding Design. Retrieved January 16, 2017 from https://wordpress.com/com-vs-org/
6. 2017. Discover graphic design ideas & inspiration - 99 designs. Retrieved January 15, 2017 from https://99designs.com/discover
7. 2017. Free Website Builder | Create a Free Website | WIX.com. Retrieved January 16, 2017 from http://www.wix.com/
8. 2017. Online Portfolios on Behance. Retrieved January 15, 2017 from https://www.behance.net/
9. 2017. Shakr | Online Video Maker & Video Ad Creator. Retrieved January 15, 2017 from https://www.shakr.com/
10. 2017. Video Editing By Magisto | An Automatic Online Video Editor. Retrieved January 15, 2017 from https://www.magisto.com/
11. Steven P Dow, Alana Glassco, Jonathan Kass, Melissa Schwarz, Daniel L Schwartz, and Scott R Klemmer. 2012. *Parallel prototyping leads to better design results, more divergence, and increased self-efficacy*. Springer, 127-153.
12. Pedro F Felzenszwalb, Ross B Girshick, David McAllester, and Deva Ramanan. 2010. Object detection with discriminatively trained part-based models. *IEEE transactions on pattern analysis and machine intelligence* 32, 9: 1627-1645.
13. Johann von Wolfgang Goethe. 1971. *Goethe's Color Theory*. Van Nostrand Reinhold, New York.
14. Shih-Wen Hsiao and Cheng-Ju Tsai. 2014. Transforming the natural colors of an image into product design: A computer-aided color planning system based on fuzzy pattern recognition. *Color Research & Application.*
15. Guosheng Hu, Zhigeng Pan, Mingmin Zhang, De Chen, Wenzhen Yang, and Jian Chen. 2014. An interactive method for generating harmonious color schemes. *Color Research & Application* 39, 1: 70-78.
16. Johannes Itten and Faber Birren. 1970. *The elements of color*. John Wiley & Sons.
17. Ali Jahanian, Jerry Liu, Qian Lin, Daniel R Tretter, Eamonn O'Brien-Strain, Seungyon Lee, Nic Lyons, and Jan P Allebach. 2013. Automatic design of colors for magazine covers. In *IS&T/SPIE Electronic Imaging*, 86640B-86640B-86649.
18. Ghita Jalal, Nolwenn Maudet, and Wendy E Mackay. 2015. Color Portraits: From Color Picking to Interacting with Color. In *33rd Annual ACM Conference on Human Factors in Computing Systems*, 4207-4216.
19. EunJin Kim and Hyeon-Jeong Suk. 2016. Key Color Generation for Affective Multimedia Production: An Initial Method and Its Application. In *Proceedings of the 2016 ACM on Multimedia Conference*. 2964323, 1316-1325.
20. Shigenobu Kobayashi. 1981. The aim and method of the color image scale. *Color Research & Application* 6, 2: 93-107.
21. Sharon Lin and Pat Hanrahan. 2013. Modeling how people extract color themes from images. In *SIGCHI Conference on Human Factors in Computing Systems*, 3101-3110.
22. Y Matsuda. 1995. *Color design*. Asakura Shoten, Tokyo.
23. Barbara J Meier, Anne Morgan Spalter, and David B Karelitz. 2004. Interactive color palette tools. *Computer Graphics and Applications, IEEE* 24, 3: 64-72.
24. Matthew Miles and Michael Huberman. 1994. *Qualitative data analysis: An expanded sourcebook*. Sage.
25. Parry Moon and Domina Eberle Spencer. 1944. Aesthetic measure applied to color harmony. *JOSA* 34, 4: 234-242.
26. Parry Moon and Domina Eberle Spencer. 1944. Area in color harmony. *JOSA* 34, 2: 93-101.
27. Giovanni Moretti, Stephen Marsland, and Paul Lyons. 2013. Computational production of colour harmony. Part 2: Experimental evaluation of a tool for gui colour scheme creation. *Color Research & Application* 38, 3: 218-228.
28. Albert H Munsell and Faber Birren. 1969. *A grammar of color*. Van Nostrand Reinhold.

29. Peter O'Donovan, Aseem Agarwala, and Aaron Hertzmann. 2011. Color compatibility from large datasets. In *ACM SIGGRAPH 2011*. 1964958, 1-12.

30. Peter O'Donovan, Aseem Agarwala, and Aaron Hertzmann. 2014. Collaborative filtering of color aesthetics. In *ACM Workshop on Computational Aesthetics*, 33-40.

31. Peter O'Donovan, Aseem Agarwala, and Aaron Hertzmann. 2015. DesignScape: Design with Interactive Layout Suggestions. In *33rd Annual ACM Conference on Human Factors in Computing Systems*, 1221-1224.

32. Li-Chen Ou, M Ronnier Luo, Andrée Woodcock, and Angela Wright. 2004. A study of colour emotion and colour preference. Part I: Colour emotions for single colours. *Color Research & Application* 29, 3: 232-240.

33. Li-Chen Ou, M Ronnier Luo, Andree Woodcock, and Angela Wright. 2004. A study of colour emotion and colour preference. part II: colour emotions for two-colour combinations. *Color Research & Application* 29, 4: 292-298.

34. Li-Chen Ou, M Ronnier Luo, Pei-Li Sun, Neng-Chung Hu, Hung-Shing Chen, Shing-Sheng Guan, Andree Woodcock, José Luis Caivano, Rafael Huertas, and Alain Treméau. 2012. A cross-cultural comparison of colour emotion for two-colour combinations. *Color Research & Application* 37, 1: 23-43.

35. Horst WJ Rittel and Melvin M Webber. 1973. Dilemmas in a general theory of planning. *Policy sciences* 4, 2: 155-169.

36. James A Russell and Albert Mehrabian. 1977. Evidence for a three-factor theory of emotions. *Journal of research in Personality* 11, 3: 273-294.

37. James Self, Mark Evans, and Eun Jin Kim. 2016. A comparison of digital and conventional sketching: implications for conceptual design ideation. *Journal of Design Research* 14, 2: 171-202.

38. Hyeon-Jeong Suk and Hans Irtel. 2010. Emotional response to color across media. *Color Research & Application* 35, 1: 64-77.

39. Minghui Tian, Shouhong Wan, and Lihua Yue. 2010. A color saliency model for salient objects detection in natural scenes. In *International Conference on Multimedia Modeling*, 240-250.

40. Kashyap Todi, Daryl Weir, and Antti Oulasvirta. 2016. Sketchplore: Sketch and Explore Layout Designs with an Optimiser. In *Proceedings of the 2016 CHI Conference Extended Abstracts on Human Factors in Computing Systems*, 3780-3783.

41. Paul Viola and Michael Jones. 2001. Rapid object detection using a boosted cascade of simple features. In *Computer Vision and Pattern Recognition, 2001. CVPR 2001. Proceedings of the 2001 IEEE Computer Society Conference on*, I-511-I-518 vol. 511.

StressTree: a Metaphorical Visualization for Biofeedback-assisted Stress Management

Bin Yu, Mathias Funk, Jun Hu, Loe Feijs
Industrial Design Department
Eindhoven University of Technology
{B.Yu, J.Hu, M.Funk, L.M.G.Feijs}@tue.nl

ABSTRACT
In today's highly competitive environment, chronic stress is one of the main reasons for a health problem. To address this, biofeedback techniques have been used to assist in relaxation training and stress management. In this paper, we present 'StressTree,' a metaphorical visualization of heart rate variability (HRV) biofeedback system. StressTree aims to present HRV data in a more evocative, meaningful way in the context of stress management. The HRV biofeedback system consists of a heartbeat data acquisition unit, a data analysis unit, and a visualization unit. The feedback from interviews in the evaluation shows that StressTree could display different growth pattern during a stressful work or a relaxation training. The participants suggested that the biofeedback interaction through StressTree is explicit and engaging, and brings them a strong motivation to regulate their breathing pattern for a 'healthy-looking' tree.

Author Keywords
Biofeedback; Metaphor; Visualization; Stress; Heart Rate Variability

ACM Classification Keywords
H.5.1 [Information interfaces and presentation]: Multimedia Information; H.5.2 [Information Interfaces and Presentation]: User Interfaces

INTRODUCTION
In modern society, fierce social competition leads to an increasing number of people suffering from chronic stress. Excessive stress that persists over an extended period may result in serious health problems including anxiety, insomnia, muscle pain, hypertension, and a weakened immune system [1]. The hazard of chronic stress is closely associated with the imbalance of the autonomic nervous system (ANS). The conditions will get worse the longer this imbalance persists.

DIS 2017, June 10-14, 2017, Edinburgh, United Kingdom
© 2017 ACM. ISBN 978-1-4503-4922-2/17/06…$15.00
http://dx.doi.org/10.1145/3064663.3064729

It is important to for individuals to realize their negative stress and cope with stress proactively.

As one of the most promising markers of ANS activity [2], Heart Rate Variability (HRV) is often visualized and presented to individuals, enabling them to be aware of the internal ANS activities related to stress responses. This process is commonly known as HRV Biofeedback. HRV biofeedback can be categorized into two classical approaches: representation of calculated HRV and representation of successive beat-to-beat intervals. In the first approach, biofeedback serves as a 'mirror' to improve the user's awareness of their stress levels. The calculated parameters of HRV, such as the ratio of LF/HF, can reflect the balance between the sympathetic and parasympathetic branches of ANS, indicating the stress level [3]. In the second approach, biofeedback serves as a 'crutch,' which assists the user's self-regulation in a relaxation training. For instance, the successive beat-to-beat intervals (also referred to as RR intervals or respiratory sinus arrhythmia, RSA) is widely used as the content of HRV biofeedback, which assists the users in learning resonant respiration for relaxation [4].

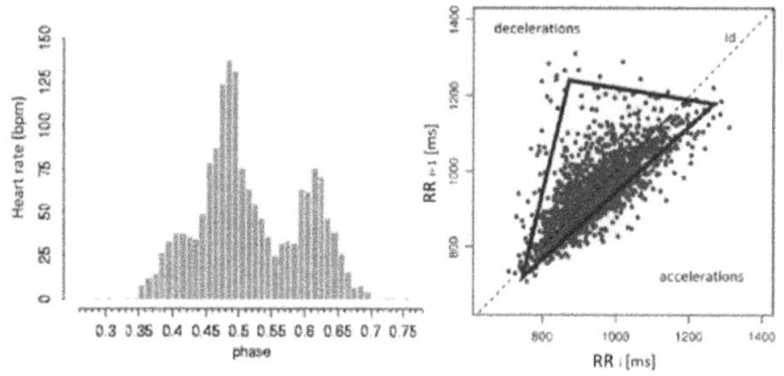

Figure 1. The clinical biofeedback visualizations of HRV data

Since the early 1970s, biofeedback techniques have been used in clinical settings[5], as a special intervention or treatment in cognitive or behavioral therapy. With the ubiquitous computing has been addressed in recent years[6], biofeedback devices become increasingly portable and affordable. Biofeedback information becomes easily accessible to casual users. Thus, biofeedback is not only the treatment of severe stress disorders[7] but also a tool for facilitating self-regulation in our daily life. These 'casual' biofeedback systems form a new branch of the biofeedback field: Ubiquitous Biofeedback (U-Biofeedback) [8]. In most clinical biofeedback systems, the visualizations of bio-data use 'medical' style that is designed for clinical staff, such as the RR intervals wave and Poincaré plots shown in Fig 1. In our view, the bio-data visualizations in U-biofeedback field should be more understandable, engaging, and more persuasive for casual users to use every day.

In this paper, we present a metaphorical visualization of heart rate variability (HRV) data for biofeedback. In the visualization of StressTree, the parameters of HRV data is mapped to the attributes of the abstract visual form (i.e. thickness, length, and direction of the bar) in real-time.The abstract visual form is then transformed into a metaphorical visual presentation that can present a slowly growing accumulative effect of stress responses or self-regulations. Metaphorical visualizations in biofeedback aim to present bio-data in a more evocative, meaningful and thought provoking way in the context of stress management. Our hypothesis is that the use of metaphor in visualization could translate the obscure bio-data into an image that is easy to understand and the biofeedback interaction through the metaphorical visualizations might be more motivated and engaging.

DESIGN OPPORTUNITIES

This study is initiated by problems arising during the design of the 'output' part of the HRV biofeedback system. In clinical biofeedback systems, HRV visualizations tend to be 'medical' and 'serious.' Most of the classical systems utilize numeric or graphic displays. *StressEraser* [4] guides the user to practice resonant breathing by presenting the RSA waveform back to the user, as shown in Fig 2(a). With the manual, this type of simple graphic display tend to be easy to understand, but it might also easily become boring and less attractive. More casual visualizations appear in ubiquitous biofeedback field. They become more 'playful' by gamification, or more 'artistic' by focusing on the amplification of the bodily experience. *Chill-Out* [9] is a casual biofeedback game for relaxation training. It is adapted from the game of Frozen Bubble by mapping the breathing rate to the game difficulty, see Fig 2(b). Many artists are also devoted to creating various biofeedback visual artworks. They focus on creating a new bodily experience with an abstract visualization through an immersive display. For instance, *Cardiomorphologies* [10] visualizes the breath and heartbeat data into a series of colorful rings, see Fig 2(c).

In our previous studies, some new presentations of HRV information have been explored, such as using circle maps [11] or ambient lighting [12]. Through those explorations, we learned that aesthetic qualities of visualizations are important to how the users 'feel' during biofeedback-assisted relaxation. We also found that the health-related information and meanings contained in physiological data are of the same importance, but not well expressed in most biofeedback visualizations. To solve this, here we turn to the use of metaphors in biofeedback visualization design.

Metaphorical visualizations map the characteristics of some well-understood visual images/patterns to a more poorly understood data source so as to render aspects of the target understandable[13]. Analogy and metaphor are considered as key aspects of human cognition [14]. Metaphors enable us to understand abstract information with familiar and well-understood images [15]. Visual metaphors not only help to present information but shape a specific meaning. A right visual metaphor can increase the expressiveness of information and define the context for correct interpretation of information and its meanings.

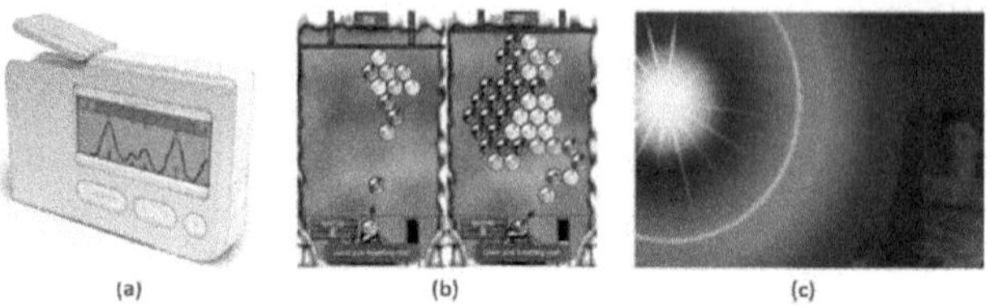

Figure 2. The visual interfaces in U-biofeedback design

In many literary works, trees are used as images typically associated with life and health, such as 'the Tree of Life.' A lush tree is often a symbol of a healthy person, in contrast; a withered tree represents an unhealthy state. Here, we use the image of the tree as a metaphor in visualization design, aiming to add a layer of meaning regarding the stress and health. In previous studies [16, 17], the metaphor od tree has been used in visualization of bio-feedback. In this study, we embarked on an interesting design journey, taking hints from understandings gained through the study of the autonomic nervous system, stress, and health, drawing metaphors into our design, ending up with a new interactive visualization of HRV named StressTree.

DESIGN CASE: STRESS TREE

The initial concept of StressTree was to transform the stress-related HRV data into an image of a tree, which metaphorically represents the health of the user, as shown in Fig 3. When a user suffers from excessive stress at work for a long period, the tree will become increasingly fragile and show a sub-healthy pattern. When the user is in the right balance of stress in life, the tree will grow up strong and looks more healthy. During the growth of the tree, the growing pattern can be affected by users' stress state, and it is possible for the user to manipulate the way the tree develops by relaxation training, such as deep breathing.

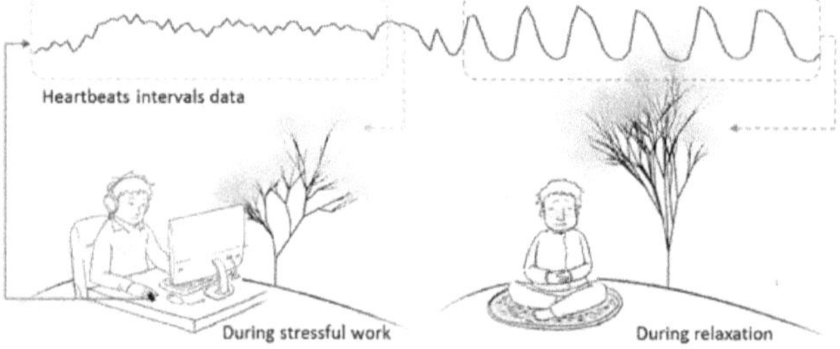

Figure 3. The concept of StressTree

Two approaches are experimented in the design of the 'StressTree.' The first one is the static L-system-based tree, which is generated by the calculated HRV data over a period, showing a long-term stress state. The second one is an interactive growing tree generated with the individual's real-time RR intervals data. It is designed as an alternative of the graphic display of RR intervals data shown in Fig 2(a).

Biofeedback System

Figure 4 shows the framework of our HRV biofeedback system. The pulse signal is measured by a PPG sensor placed on the left index finger. The sensor is connected to an *Arduino* board as a unit for data acquisition. The program on Arduino processes the raw pulse signal into beat-to-beat intervals (RR intervals), and then transmits the data to the PC through a USB serial port. The PC runs the visualization program (developed based on the *Processing* programming environment), transforming the RR intervals data and calculated HRV data into an image of a tree in real time.

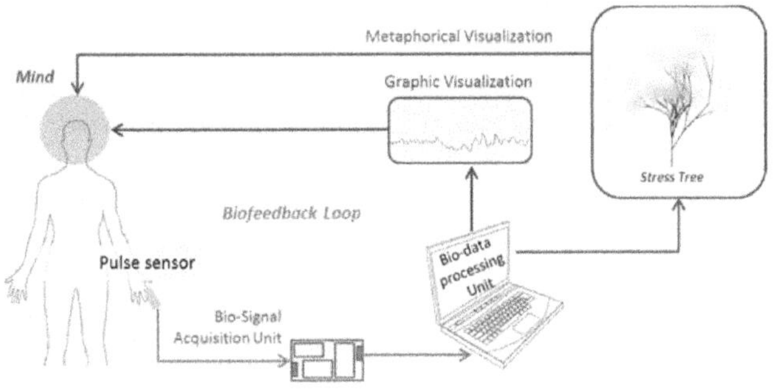

Figure 4. The framework of HRV biofeedback system

L-system based StressTree

Lindenmayer systems (L-systems) have been used as a foundation for plant modeling since the early 1970s. According to the theory of L-systems [18], tree development can be controlled by one production or a set of productions that describe the fate of plant components over discrete time intervals. Productions replace all modules of the predecessor tree in parallel derivation steps. This parallelism is intended to reflect the simultaneous progress of time in all parts of the modeled tree. The development of StressTree begins with a single segment and is modeled using one simple production: $A \rightarrow A\ (-A)\ (+A)$ with A as the initial state. The symbols '+' and '-' mean that the next move should turn right and left by an angle.

The shape of L-system StressTree represents the overall stress state over a period. In this study, we use the basic HRV analysis in the time domain as the indicator of user's stress level. The *SDNN* (the standard deviation of RR intervals) is calculated over a 10-minute period. According to the literature [19], the normal reference range of *SDNN* is from 100 to 180 *ms*. *SDNN* value is mapped to three parameters of the visualization: the thickness of the initial structure, scale factor and rotation angle of each new segment. The range of the initial thickness is 5 to 10 pixels, and the scale factor ranges from 0.6 to 0.8. The branches turn left or right in an angle between the ranges from $\pm PI/8$ to $\pm PI/4$. Thus, the larger the *SDNN* contributes to the thicker and longer branches with more straight and upward growing direction. In an iterative procedure, subsequently generated branches will be scaled down and rotated. The number of iterations is fixed at ten. As shown in Fig 5, with a low HRV ($SDNN$<60 *ms*), the StressTree looks small twisted and fragile; in contrast, a high HRV ($SDNN$>120 *ms*) makes the tree thrive, growing tall and lush.

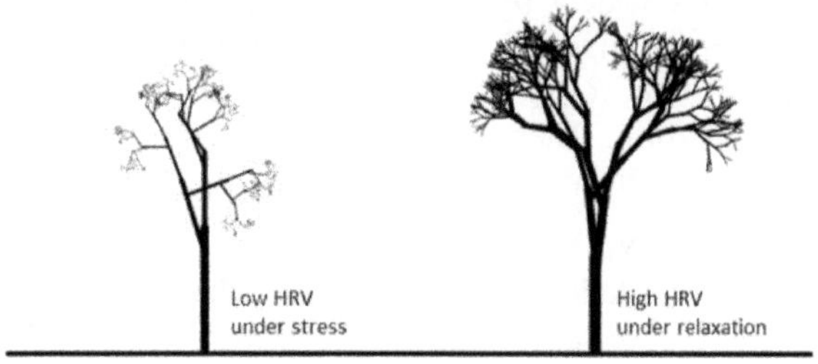

Figure 5. The L-system based StressTree

Interactive growing StressTree

To assist the user's relaxation training, an interactive StressTree was designed to present the RR intervals data in real time. Thus, the users could control the growth of StressTree through self-regulation, such as deep breathing exercises. The growth of StressTree also visualizes the process of relaxation training and its cumulative effect on stress reduction.

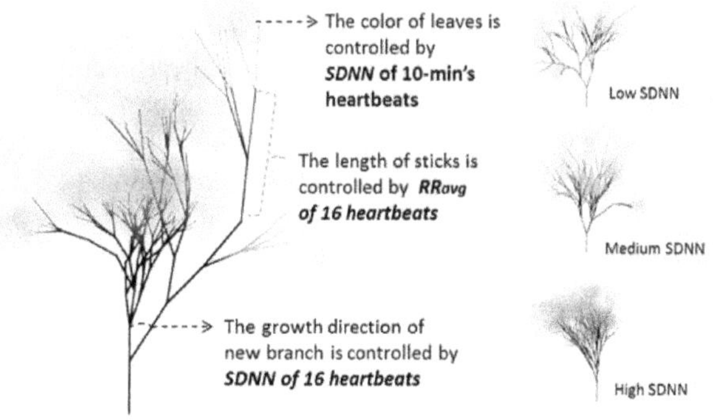

Figure 6. The interactive StressTree

Two parameters of HRV (RR_{avg} and $SDNN_{16}$) are calculated based on a moving window of 16 heartbeats. RR_{avg} denotes the average of RR intervals in the window; the formula is as follows: $RR_{avg} = (15 \times RR_{avg} + RR)/16$. In the calculation of real-time $SDNN_{16}$, we use the following formula: $SDNN_{16} = ((15 \times SDNN_{16} + |RR - RR_{avg}|)/16)$. The *SDNN* of the whole measurement over the 10 minutes is calculated for rendering the color of leaves at the end of visualization. The normal reference range of RR_{avg} and $SDNN_{16}$ are selected as 600-1000 ms and 100-180 ms respectively [19]. The rules in the generation of the tree are shown in Fig 6.

The growth of StressTree is triggered by the user's heartbeat. The attributes (length, thickness, and direction) of the new branch is updated by the HRV parameters of the coming heartbeat data. Each heartbeat brings one growth opportunity in one node, and the number of the split, the length, and direction of the branch in one growth depends on the updated $SDNN_{16}$ and RR_{avg}. Specifically, $SDNN_{16}$ data determines the number of the split at one node. When $SDNN_{16}$ is less than 60 ms, no new branches is sprouted. Instead, higher $SDNN_{16}$ gives more opportunities of sprouting (up to 3 at each node). The RR_{avg} is mapped to the length of branches. Under long-term stress, an individual's RR_{avg} rarely changes (e.g. around 650 ms); by contrast, RR_{avg} varies widely (e,g, ranging from 600 to 1200 ms) when the individual is relaxed. Especially during deep breathing, the RR_{avg} will change in an approximately sinusoidal form. Therefore, a sequence of flexible RR_{avg} yields a much richer hierarchy of branches.

Besides, $SDNN_{16}$ is also mapped (via the map function) to the range of rotation of each branch. In the initial stage of growth (here we set to 4 minutes), bigger $SDNN_{16}$ makes a smaller angle of branch's spread (*-PI*/8 to *PI*/8), making branches growing upward. In middle and last stages, bigger $SDNN_{16}$ makes large rotation angle (*-PI*/4 to *PI*/4), making branches spread out widely. At the end of the period, the overall *SDNN* of the whole period determines the color used for the leaves rendering. The color ranges from yellow-green to dark green, and the deeper the color represents, the higher average HRV level, the better state of relaxed.

INITIAL EVALUATION

To test the feasibility of StressTree to present stress state under different situations, we did the initial evaluation with ten participants. For each participant, the heartbeat data was measured and visualized in two conditions: 10-minute stressful work and 10-minute relaxation. The evaluation was conducted in a simulated working environment. To not interrupt participants' regular work, the StressTree was projected onto the office's wall, as shown in Fig 7. At the end of the study, we conducted the follow-up interviews with a focus on the following questions: *"Can you discern the information about your stress level through StressTree? Do you think StressTree is helpful to inform you of your stress level during the work? Do you think StressTree is helpful during the relaxation training?"*

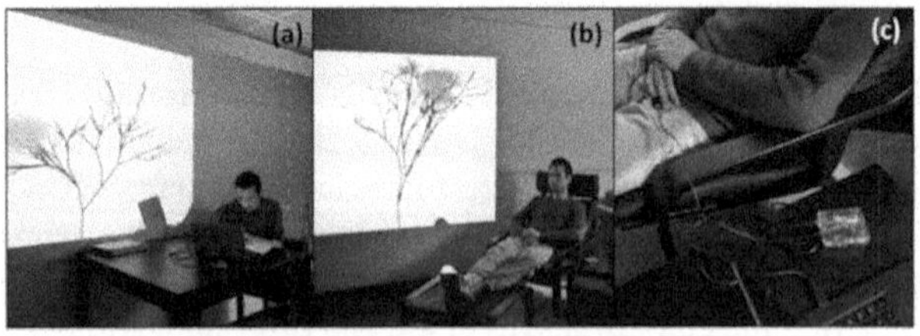

Figure 7. User evaluation (a). during the work (b). during relaxation (c). the pulse sensor on the finger

Fig 8 shows the StressTrees from 9 participants collected during stressful work activities and during the relaxation training. The shape of the collected StressTree varies from a small and crooked tree to a tall and upward-growing one with more branches and dark green leaves. The comparison between these two groups of StressTrees shows the impact of the chronic stress on our health in a more meaningful way. The feedback from interviews shows that StressTree has the potential to be a visual representation of stress level but also a real-time feedback of RR intervals data for biofeedback-assisted relaxation training.

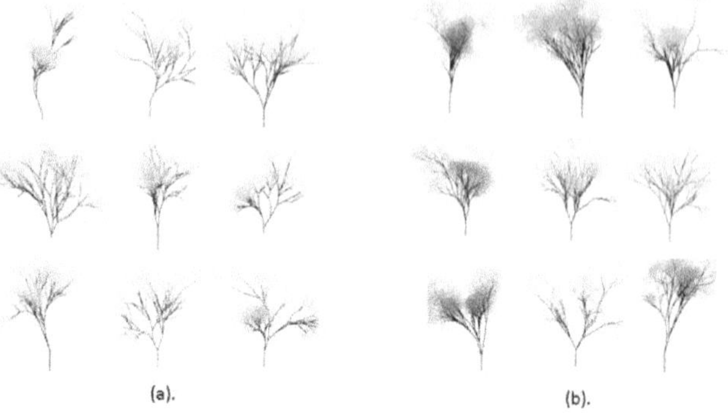

Figure 8. The collection of StressTrees (a). during a stressful work (b). during a relaxation training

Firstly, the participants reported that the visualization of StressTree was easy to understand. It is natural to link the 'health' of the tree to their stress level. Secondly, most participants thought that the projection of StressTree on the wall is an acceptable way of stress intervention. However, they were also concerned about the privacy of personal data visualization. They suggested that StressTree might be more suitable for visualizations on a smartphone, especially for a long-term stress management. Thirdly, the participants thought the feedback through StressTree during the relaxation training helped them to focus, reduced negative thoughts and clear the mind. They expressed that "*watching the StressTree growing is a relaxing thing.*" Besides, some participants also mentioned that the StressTree brought them a strong motivation to regulate their breathing pattern for a 'healthy-looking' tree. Some participants also reported that the shape and color of the StressTree promote their self-reflections on their behaviors and experience during the experiment.

CONCLUSION AND FUTURE WORK

In this study, a tree-shaped metaphorical visualization was designed to present individuals' heart rate variability data for stress management. Our explorations have shown that it is very promising to visualize physiological data in the form that can express health-related meanings by using a well-fitting metaphor. For future research, we are considering two main directions. StressTree is our first attempt to present bio-signals into a more natural form. Based on the features of different bio-signals, various objects or processes in nature could be used in the creation of visualization to express specific meanings of the physiological information. Secondly, more parameters could be extracted from the raw physiological data based on more methods of data analysis. As mentioned above, HRV analysis in frequency domain also yields much information about autonomic balance. In a future study, we will visualize more aspects of stress using the approach of metaphorical visualization we explored in this study.

ACKNOWLEDGMENTS

We thank all the participants of the experiment, and all colleagues in Designed Intelligence group for their support and help with the study. We would also like to thank China Scholarship Council for support with the research.

REFERENCES

1. Baum, A., & Posluszny, D. M. 1999. Health psychology: mapping biobehavioral contributions to health and illness. *Annual review of psychology*, 50,1: 137-163.
2. Appelhans, Bradley M., and Linda J. Luecken. 2006. Heart rate variability as an index of regulated emotional responding. *J. Review of general psychology* 10,3: 229.
3. J. A. Healey and R.W. Picard. 2005. Detecting stress during real-world driving tasks using physiological sensors. *IEEE Trans. Intell. Transp. Syst.*, 6, 2:156–166
4. Moore, S. K. 2006. Calm in your palm: Biofeedback device promises to reduce stress. *IEEE Spectrum*, 43,3: 60.
5. Hauri, P. P. 1975. Biofeedback and self-control of physiological functions: clinical applications. *The International Journal of Psychiatry in Medicine*, 6,1-2: 255-265.
6. Weiser, Mark. 1993. Some computer science issues in ubiquitous computing. *Communications of the ACM* 36,7: 75-84.
7. Zucker, T. L., Samuelson, K. W., Muench, F., Greenberg, M. A., & Gevirtz, R. N. 2009. The effects of respiratory sinus arrhythmia biofeedback on heart rate variability and posttraumatic stress disorder symptoms: A pilot study. *Applied psychophysiology and biofeedback*, 34,2: 135-143.
8. Al Osman, H., Eid, M., & El Saddik, A. 2014. U-biofeedback: a multimedia-based reference model for ubiquitous biofeedback systems. *Multimedia Tools and Applications* 72,3: 3143-3168.
9. Parnandi, A., Ahmed, B., Shipp, E., & Gutierrez-Osuna, R. 2013. Chill-Out: Relaxation training through respiratory biofeedback in a mobile casual game." In *Proceedings of the International Conference on Mobile Computing, Applications, and Services*, 252-260.
10. Muller, L., Turner, G., Khut, G., & Edmonds, E. 2006. Creating affective visualisations for a physiologically interactive artwork. In *Proceedings of the Tenth International Conference on Information Visualisation*, 651-657.
11. Feijs, L., Langereis, G., & Van Boxtel, G. 2010. Designing for heart rate and breathing movements. In *Proceedings of the Conference on Design and semantics of form and movement,* 57-66.
12. Yu, B., Hu, J., & Feijs, L. M. 2014. Design and Evaluation of an Ambient Lighting Interface of HRV Biofeedback System in Home Setting. In *Proceedings of the Conference of UCAmI*, 88-91.
13. Ziemkiewicz, Caroline, and Robert Kosara.2008. The shaping of information by visual metaphors. *J. IEEE Transactions on Visualization and Computer Graphics* 14,6: 1269-1276
14. Gentner, Dedre, Keith James Holyoak, and Boicho N. Kokinov. 2001. *The analogical mind: Perspectives from cognitive science.* MIT press
15. Blackwell, Alan F.2006. The reification of metaphor as a design tool. *J. ACM Transactions on Computer-Human Interaction* 13,4: 490-530
16. Rajanna, V., Lara-Garduno, R., Behera, D. J., Madanagopal, K., Goldberg, D., & Hammond, T. 2014. Step up life: a context aware health assistant. In *Proceedings of the Third ACM SIGSPATIAL International Workshop on the Use of GIS in Public Health*, 21-30.
17. Al Osman, H., Dong, H., & El Saddik, A. 2016. Ubiquitous biofeedback serious game for stress management. *IEEE Access*, 4, 1274-1286.
18. Prusinkiewicz, P., & Lindenmayer, A. 2012. *The algorithmic beauty of plants.* Springer Science & Business Media.
19. Marina Medina, C., Blanca de la Cruz, T., Alberto Garrido, E., Marco Antonio Garrido, S., & José, N. O. 2012. Normal values of heart rate variability at rest in a young, healthy and active Mexican population. *Health,* 4, 7: 377-385.

Turned On / Turned Off: Speculating on the Microchip-based Contraceptive Implant

Sarah Homewood
IxD lab, IT University of Copenhagen
Copenhagen, Denmark
shom@itu.dk

Clint Heyer
K3, Malmö University
Malmö, Sweden
clint.heyer@mah.se

ABSTRACT
For over 50 years, hormone-based contraceptives have allowed women to control their fertility, thus reconfiguring society and how women relate to their body. On the horizon are long-life microchip-based implanted contraceptives that can be turned on and off, which may further the societal disruptions of 'the pill'. Framed as interactive technology, we speculate on the design space of controllable implanted contraceptives. We explored existing implanted contraceptives through a performance ethnography of their implantation. Inspiration from this process informed a speculative video of living with controllable implants and a guide for healthcare professionals. These materials, along with expert presentations, backgrounded a design workshop in which participants unpacked issues around controllable contraceptive implants. Participants created and roleplayed physical mock-ups of controllers, manifesting discussions around security, relationships and hormones. Drawing from the outcomes of the workshop, we produce a speculative design in the form of a film and physical mock-ups.

Author Keywords
Implant; hormone; performance ethnography; contraception

ACM Classification Keywords
J.3 [Computer Applications]: Life and Medical Sciences—*Medical information systems*

INTRODUCTION
Implantable microchips that allow controlled, micro-dose drug delivery over several years are currently under development and human trial [5,13]. The implant consists of hundreds of sealed micro-reservoirs which are electronically managed by a chip, which itself can be controlled via short-range radio. One of many potential application areas for this technology is female contraception [8]. Two advantages over current non-digital hormone-based implants is that the microchip can last 16 years (rather than five), and women can turn it on or off [9]. The tension between the advantages resulting from the 'technological fix' [12 p122] that the implant represents, and the political and societal implications of this new form of contraception provides the motivation behind this research.

† Work was conducted while first author was affiliated with Malmö University

DIS 2017, June 10-14, 2017, Edinburgh, United Kingdom
© 2017 ACM. ISBN 978-1-4503-4922-2/17/06…$15.00
DOI: http://dx.doi.org/10.1145/3064663.3064726

The stakes for this new form of contraception are high. 'The Pill' allowed women to decouple sex from reproduction [4], to control their natural hormonal cycles, thus refiguring how they relate to their own body. Implantable, controllable contraceptives are expected to be on the market in 2018 [9], but little is published about how the controller might look or function, and its manufacturer declined to participate in this research. Interaction design is well-placed to investigate the design space of 'insertables' [7] such as this. Because of the implications of this technology, we suggest this investigation should begin now, albeit in a speculative manner, rather than awaiting its general availability. In the present paper, we begin this work using design, embodiment and performance techniques with an emphasis on the emotions and narratives surrounding interactions [3 p244, 10] in order to draw out findings and speculate on the design of controllable contraceptives.

BACKGROUND
As implanted devices become more common - for medical reasons or otherwise - so too are the risks of their unauthorised control or access [1]. This is particularly problematic for life-critical implants such as pacemakers, already shown to be vulnerable [2,6]. Implanted microchips pose new security challenges. Unlike pacemakers, which are wirelessly controlled by medical practitioners in a clinical setting, the contraceptive microchips are intended to be controlled by consumers at home.

While some work has investigated the possibilities of interacting through the skin with different kinds of input technologies [7], our work concerns indirect interaction with the implanted device, using a kind of remote control. In general, there has been little exploration of the design opportunities and challenges for controlling implanted devices, especially so in this domain.

PERFORMING IMPLANTATION
To begin our exploration into future implants, we considered the case of existing non-digital hormone-based contraceptive implants. Drawing on the first author's background in dance

performance, and the goal of drawing out the emotional and physical experience of receiving an implant, performance ethnography [11] was the primary method.

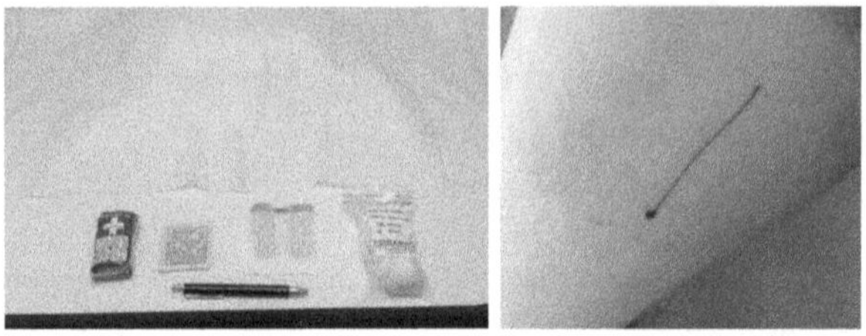

Figure 1. Re-enactment props (L), implant insertion mark made on designer's body by participant (R)

We used four participants, between the ages of 25-32, studying at university, two were personal acquaintances of the first author. Two of the participants currently have the hormonal implant, while the other two had it previously. Sessions were conducted one-on-one, lasted between 30-90 minutes and held at a location convenient for the participant. Following the session, participants were interviewed.

Following Laurel [11], we used props, improvisation and re-enactment to empathise with participants and gain our own bodily experience of their procedure. Simple staging was used to set the scene of a doctor's surgery, laying down a medical sheet on a table or bed, and furnishing medical props such as bandages, surgical gloves, disinfection wipes, and a pen to represent the implant applicator (Figure 1).

Upon arriving at the staged doctor's surgery, participants were told that they were to play the role of the medical practitioner, and that the researcher (the first author) was to play them. Together they were to re-enact the participant's implantation procedure. The participant was asked to direct the researcher in how to move and position themselves according to the participant's experience of their procedure.

Without prompting, all participants engaged with the props to support the re-enactment, two participants using the pen as both the implant applicator as well as a pen to mark the insertion point. Participants alternated between recounting events in the first-person and third-person, telling the researcher how to react. The researcher maintained a relatively passive state during the procedure, instigating no movement of her own accord, and holding posture only as to not fall over. Participants could then take charge of her body and direct her movements physically by moving her limbs (as two did), or through verbal commands.

Although there were few participants, it became clear they had rather different experiences of their implantation. For some, the procedure was straightforward, with little in the way of tension. For others, it was a frightening experience, bordering on traumatic. Although the re-enactment was based in the physical procedure, participants readily expressed their remembrance of emotional state as the session progressed. One participant directed the researcher (as she herself was directed) to pinch the skin on her stomach to distract her from the thought of the applicator entering her body. This action represented her fear and the coping strategies employed to manage it.

IMAGINING THE CONTROLLABLE IMPLANT

We resisted deep analysis of the performance ethnography and ensuing discussion with participants. Instead, we used these impressions to inspire the scripting and production of a short film (Video Figure 1). Briefly, the film is set in a couple's bedroom, and makes reference to security, transhumanism, new rituals, sex, pregnancy and hormonal side effects. The audience is given the female character's first-person perspective, with her male partner talking directly to camera.

To probe into people's concerns of the product, a 90-minute design workshop was held. It was publicly advertised online and with posters around campus, attracting 20 participants, 9 of whom studied interaction design. 11 participants self-identified as female, 9 as male. The speculative film, a presentation on the product and presentations by two female health experts, introduced participants to the technology and topic. One of the experts professionally advised women on natural forms of contraception (such as the Fertility Awareness Method), the other was a practitioner from the campus sexual health clinic with thirty years of experience of prescribing hormonal contraceptives.

Participants were asked during the workshop to complete parts of a questionnaire, including the question "what is your initial reaction to the contraceptive microchip?" Security and control were concerns of 13 participants, relating mostly to who would be able to control the chip and under what circumstances. One woman noted, for example *"what is interesting is the question of control, which is supposed to be the woman's but it could be someone else. I think I would check compulsively if it's turned 'on'"*. The issue of an invisibly implanted chip's accountability was brought up by four other participants. These reactions were used to produce a speculative leaflet for healthcare professionals to introduce them to the product and sensitise them to the perceived concerns of potential users.

DESIGNING THE IMPLANT CONTROLLER

The second stage of the design workshop was a turn toward the design of a remote control for the microchip. Participants were asked to model controllers in white clay and to annotate the controller on a piece of paper, describing how it worked (Figure 2). After this activity, participants were invited to form pairs for a roleplay exercise. One person took the role of the healthcare professional introducing their controller to the other, who acted as the patient, about to take the controller home after the implant procedure. Roles were then rotated so all controllers were introduced. Participants were asked to show (and ask about) how it was used, its appearance (since the clay material lacked clues of material and finish), where it might be kept and who might use it.

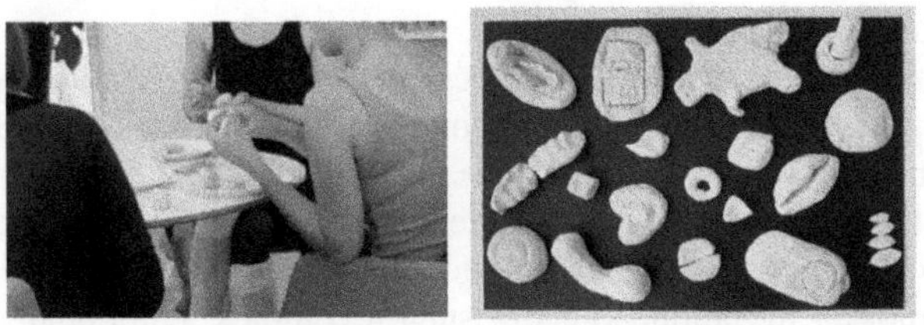

Figure 2. Design workshop and created controllers

Following the workshop, we attempted to identify the issues embodied in participants' designs. The controllers tended to reflect the themes from the prior stage of the workshop, several controllers for example reflected the issue of accountability by providing visual feedback of the microchip state. Two participants chose to observe rather than create controllers themselves. Roleplaying and discussion was useful for the participants to clarify and develop their ideas. In the below exchange, an idea occurs to P7 in the course of discussing with P1:

P7: Oh yes, to the crazy idea. I made it look like a baby. And if you, if you choose... I don't know why but uh, it could also be, afterwards I thought maybe you could choose when you buy the implant you could have either a very nice baby looking very nice or a warning, like something "urghh"... this is what happens if you...
P1: To be honest I imagine this as something more as a teddy bear collection, like when you have something as a teddy.
P7: Yeah, well could be. Well then I thought about also, if you already have a kid what if they find it and start playing with it, also the same thing with that (gesturing to P1's remote). And I was thinking if it were for men too, I don't think it is at first, but if it were for men too, that is a question I think. I think it could be quite revolutionary.
P1: Yeah I don't know why really there is no conversation happening really for these things for males.
P7: Now I got an idea. What if, it could be, both have an implant, what if there is a need of some mutual... pushing together (laugh) so you could both (conceive?).

Doing it together

Surprisingly, only one controller explicitly related to sex. It took the form of a sex toy, based on the assumption that the chip would be placed inside the vagina. Controlling fertility was thus intertwined with the stimulation and penetration of the body. This raises questions of the circumstances of fertility control: in some cases, the penetration might provide erotic stimulation, and in other situations might be considered a violent physical invasion.

For three other participants, their controllers reflected mutual control over the chip through some form of two-part controller. Each party keeps their own part of the controller, which only functions when brought together to form a whole. One participant imagined a ritual around the creation of the parts – each controller would be moulded to each other's hand shape, and there would be a ceremonial gifting of the man's part of the controller by the woman: "*this you can give as a gift for someone who will take part in your pregnancy,*" noted one participant. Interestingly, three out of the four controllers that related to mutual control of the chip used a split design. Joining the parts when it is time to turn the chip on or off could be a moment of significance in a relationship. We also interpret their forms as a tangible 'keepsake' or memento of the intimate relationship they share.

Form

Most of the controllers seem to have a neutral form, with little to indicate their significance to sex or fertility. Four participants made non-descript buttons, perhaps fitting a plain clinical aesthetic, that could have easily been any sort of internet-connected button. A contrary example is participant P7's *'crazy idea'* controller described opposite.

Security

Several participants designed controllers with security in mind, for example with in-built fingerprint readers, code entry or the ability to locate a lost controller. Participants seemed to frame the controller as the 'key' to the microchip. To some extent the split controllers also provide a mechanism of accountability and security in the use of the controller. Even though there are stories in the mass media about the risks of passports and cash cards being manipulated by unauthorised devices, participants didn't register the same threat to the implanted chip itself. This suggests a worrying naivety – even on the part of participants that stated they were concerned with hacking – that designers should consider.

Hormones

Although nine participants expressed health concerns over hormone-based contraceptives, only three created controllers that directly related to the hormones delivered by the microchip. Two of the controllers modulated the amount of delivered of hormones, perhaps, for example, in relation to experienced side-effects. Another participant considered a companion app for registering self-reported mood and weight so side effects can be monitored and hormone levels automatically adjusted.

CONTRACEPTION IN A RELATIONSHIP

Drawing from the outcomes of the workshop, we decided to further elaborate on the notion of mutual control of contraception in the context of a stable relationship. We also wanted to incorporate suggestions of rituals for entering into mutual control and eventual shared use.

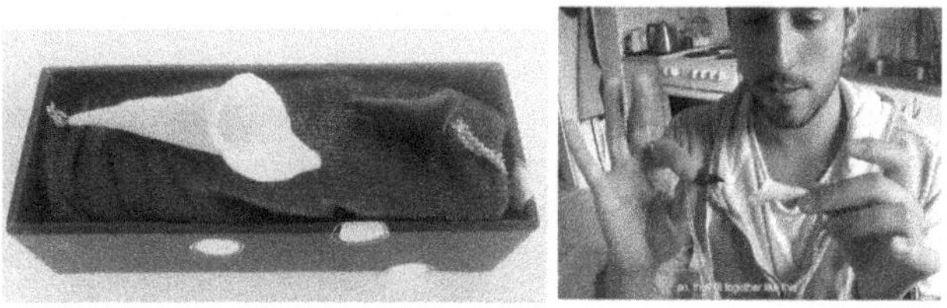

Figure 3. Controller necklaces in their presentation box, and a still from Video Figure 2.

Inspired by the symbolism of commitment in exchanging and wearing engagement rings, we designed a two-part controller in the form of necklaces, white for the female, black gifted to the male (Figure 3). For the male, wearing it publicly expresses a commitment to his partner, that one day they will attempt to conceive a child together. The design makes a demand of the male, reflecting our finding during the performance ethnography that some women resent having to bear the greater burden for avoiding pregnancy. The female partner would likewise keep and wear the other part, signifying her commitment of shared parenthood with her partner. The form of the jewellery was inspired by common fertility symbols. Inserting the male part into the female likewise references the joint act of penetrative sex. Several low-fidelity prototypes were made of the jewellery and presentation box. We also scripted a scene concerning the jewellery, speculating on its role in a relationship, and drawing on the experiences and findings of our investigations. Actors were hired and the film was shot, again from a first-person perspective (Video Figure 2).

PERFORMANCE AND IMPLANTABLES

Nine months after the initial implantation performance ethnography, we interviewed our four participants again to understand their experience of the session. The approach seemed to open up alternative reflections and perspectives unavailable through classic techniques such as contextual interviews. As one participant noted *"to be asked to re-enact it allowed you to remember physical parts – [to] go into the memory in another way. The memory was more alive"*. In the design of body-centric technologies – such as wearables and insertables – being able to draw out recollections and reflections of bodily experiences would seem highly valuable.

This also raises ethical concerns. While none of our participants had a negative experience from the research session, two wondered whether it was because their actual implantation procedure was not negative. The method risks revisiting traumatic experiences also in a way that makes them *"more alive"*. Notwithstanding, for one participant, for whom *"all the memories around contraceptives are negative"*, the re-enactment proved positive: *"...it felt good to discuss it with you – a bit therapeutic."* The re-enactment would seem to be an intimate experience, by both revisiting and sharing an otherwise private experience, and, we believe, because of the bodily contact involved between participant and researcher. Dialogue with participants seemed to reflect this, with participants expressing their emotions more readily than with the other forms of inquiry. That said, each inquiry had quite different aims which does not support direct comparison. In our case, personal relationships with some participants lowered barriers to intimacy that might otherwise preclude this mode of inquiry with unknown participants.

The performative nature of the method places demands on participants. The process of acting out and acting on another person isn't an everyday activity for most, and one participant reported feeling uncomfortable with this, since she is *"not an actress"*. Further refinement of these approaches is needed to lower participants' performance anxiety.

CONCLUSIONS

In this paper we describe our method and results of exploring a speculative design space of controllable, implanted female contraceptives. This paper aims not only to bring the subject to light, but we hope that this research will make visible the value in performance-based and speculative methods when exploring the implications of such a complex, emotionally weighted and political application of technology. The contribution of this paper is firstly in the novelty of bringing this domain to the interaction design table. The introduction of this technology will potentially have a transformative effect on society, and women in particular. Although described in the popular press and articles in the medical field, the technology needs to be critically examined from the perspective of how we will interact with it, and the role it may play in our lives. This work is our own modest attempt at doing so.

Secondly, we use performance ethnography to uncover bodily experiences and narratives through re-enactments, and report on its potential. We used performance to understand how women experience the process of implanting existing contraceptives. This technique was critical for drawing out the lived experiences of our participants in order to ground the following research. Interestingly, it allowed participants to re-enact their experience through the researcher's body, seeing and touching in the third person as they themselves were seen and touched during the process. In doing so, the typical power of the designer was shifted, as the designer themselves becomes a manipulatable prop for the re-enactment.

Thirdly, the findings of the design workshop point to several issues for the design of controllable implanted contraceptives, suggesting opportunity for design as well as what people may take for granted about it. Participants' controllers reflected the *mechanism* of hormone-based contraceptive, *control* over the microchip's functioning, the *implications* of fertility and sex, and the *role* within relationships. Amongst concerns of security, form and hormones, was the notion of mutual control over contraception, which we further developed.

Fourth, we produced two films, informed by our research, which ground the ideas and give accessible form to some of the issues present and facilitating their propagation. The films question gender and sex roles within contraception and how new forms of contraceptive technologies can mediate conversations of parenthood and our sexual relationships.

ACKNOWLEDGEMENTS

We would like to thank all research participants and Susan Kozel for her feedback.

REFERENCES

1. Wayne Burleson, Shane S. Clark, Benjamin Ransford, and Kevin Fu. 2012. Design challenges for secure implantable medical devices. In *Proc. DAC'12*, p12–17.

2. Tamara Denning, Alan Borning, Batya Friedman, Brian T. Gill, Tadayoshi Kohno, and William H. Maisel. 2010. Patients, pacemakers, and implantable defibrillators: Human values and security for wireless implantable medical devices. In *Proc. CHI'10*, 9p17–926.

3. Eric Dishman. 2002. Performative In(ter)ventions: Designing Future Technologies through Synergetic Performances. _Teaching Performance Studies (ed) Stucky, N. and Wimmer, C. Southern Illinois UP, p235–46.

4. Carl Djerassi, 2014. The Divorce of Coitus from Reproduction. [online] The New York Review of Books. Available at: http://www.nybooks.com/articles/2014/09/25/divorce-coitus-reproduction/ [Accessed 24 Apr. 2016].

5. Robert Farra, Norman F. Sheppard, Laura McCabe, et al. 2012. First-in-Human Testing of a Wirelessly Controlled Drug Delivery Microchip. *Science Translational Medicine* 4, 122: 122ra21-122ra21.

6. Daniel Halperin, Shane S. Clark, Kevin Fu, et al. 2008. Pacemakers and implantable cardiac defibrillators: Software radio attacks and zero-power defenses. In *Proc. IEEE Symposium on Security and Privacy*, p129–142.

7. Kayla J Heffernan, Frank Vetere, and Shanton Chang. 2015. Insertables: I've got IT under my skin. *interactions*, 52–56.

8. Microchips Biotech Inc. 2016. Microchips Biotech, Inc. Retrieved September 11, 2016 from http://microchipsbiotech.com/about.php

9. Gwen Kinkead. 2014. A Contraceptive Implant with Remote Control. *MIT Technology Review*. Retrieved September 11, 2016 from https://www.technologyreview.com/s/528121/a-contraceptive-implant-with-remote-control/

10. Lone Koefoed Hansen and Susan Kozel. 2007. Embodied imagination: a hybrid method of designing for intimacy, *Digital Creativity*, 18:4, p207-220.

11. Brenda Laurel. 2003. *Design Research: Methods and Perspectives*. MIT Press, Cambridge, MA.

12. Soheir Morsy. 1997. Biotechnology and the Taming of Women's Bodies. *Processed Lives: Gender and Technology in Everyday Life* (ed) Terry, J. and Calvert, M., New York: Routledge, p165-173.

13. John T. Santini, Michael J. Cima, and Robert Langer. 1999. A controlled-release microchip. *Nature* 397, 6717: p335–338.

Mindfulness and Technology: Traces of a Middle Way

Yoko Akama
Design Futures Lab,
RMIT University, Australia
yoko.akama@rmit.edu.au

Ann Light
University of Sussex
Falmer, UK
ann.light@sussex.ac.uk

Simon Bowen
Open Lab, Newcastle
University, UK
simon.bowen@newcastle.ac.uk

ABSTRACT
We contemplate paths between *form* and *formlessness* as a middle way between digital technology for mindfulness, and mindfulness without digital technology, thereby inviting alternative departure points with interactive systems. In doing so, we step into a contested yet potentially fertile arena to challenge the handling, analysis and reporting of the relationship between mindfulness and technology and the methods used to interrogate it. Through the documenting of the authors' own creative practices (video, photography, and gardening), material traces and written vignettes of our experiments are presented to stimulate resonances and evoke mindfulness with readers. We also question the form of conference papers to consider how we can best share formless states of being in discussing their relevance for design.

Author Keywords
Mindfulness; form; formlessness; interrelatedness; creative practice; Zen Buddhism; design; awareness; technology.

ACM Classification Keywords
H.5.m. Information interfaces and presentation (e.g., HCI): Miscellaneous;

INTRODUCTION
We present here thoughts about how we might design with an awareness of mindfulness that develops existing but fragmented work in this area [14,22,26]. While the dominant rational frame of technology design research can be problematic for mindfulness, we attempt to engage with it rather than avoid or criticise it, using this essay to wonder what relationships are possible between technology and mindfulness, while contemplating the interrelatedness of designing for interaction, use and wider life.

A considerable challenge is that our topic draws attention to states of being and how we might describe and aspire to them, both as a starting point for designing tools and in what we design. States of being are not traditionally associated with words or images, and we deliberately struggle with this relation – between what we mean and what we can show and can discuss. Although much of this essay is taken up with representing the conditions we are talking about, we also devote part of the paper to reflecting on how we represent such intangible facets of being.

DIS 2017, June 10-14, 2017, Edinburgh, United Kingdom
ACM 978-1-4503-4922-2/17/06.
http://dx.doi.org/10.1145/3064663.3064752

The work reported here comprises explorations into how we configured technologies in our mindfulness practices and how we developed a collaborative methodology to analyse this together. From this, we put forward three contributions:

1) We offer thoughts on mindfulness to help others speak about this concept constructively and imaginatively in design terms, drawing on the work of philosophers and the spirituality (e.g. Zen and Buddhism) that informs it.

2) We build on Zen and Taoist frameworks to speak about technology in a novel way: *giving form to formlessness*; *immersing in formlessness through form*; and *sharing form to evoke formlessness* provide three ways that technology and mindfulness interrelate.

3) We question the suitability of existing publication formats for sharing design knowledge of concepts born outside positivist conventions (such as mindfulness) to continue work done by creative practice research [e.g. 6,16] in innovating presentation methods.

This leads us to propose a relationship between technology and mindfulness, not in service of one another, but through their processual engagement, to find out what we might learn about ourselves, about one another, our relationships to the world and how we accommodate openness, interpretation and, additionally, awareness, within the structures of technology design.

BACKGROUND
We give an introduction to existing work on mindfulness, methods of collective research, and work on formal aspects of aesthetics and design, to help situate our arguments.

While for academic rigour and knowledge advancement, definitions may be desirable, when it comes to mindfulness, we partly resist such logical constructs. We do so to respect and acknowledge the history of mindfulness and its spiritual and philosophical roots in India, China, Tibet and Japan. When we trace these origins, it becomes apparent that deploying mindfulness towards an end outcome has been questioned and rejected [11,13,24,28]. Meditation is like a 'technology' (to use the language of our field), 'designed' over thousands of years to short-circuit the mind, which discriminates, analyses and divides the world into objects, and bring mind, body and spirit into holistic alignment. Looked at with the wisdom of such teachings, the Cartesian separation is an unfortunate legacy that pervades interaction design; a separation which may go some way to explain why mindfulness is often framed in functional ways, quipped to be "an instrumental tool almost on a par with aspirin and accorded no respect as an on-going state of being" [2:626]. A conflation of mindfulness and meditation can exacerbate the issue, leading to a misunderstanding that a method (like meditation) can be undertaken as a guarantee for certain outcomes (like mindfulness). Instead, here, we consider how to accommodate openness, interpretation and awareness within the structures of technology design, making such tensions in worldview explicit.

Mindfulness and Living Life

Interest in mindfulness in interaction design and HCI has increased in recent years. Designers have always been motivated by a desire to solve real-world problems including the design of technology for the 'betterment' of people's lives. Such intentions are admirable, but the instrumentality with which design and technology is approached and deployed, can be problematic when mindfulness enters this paradigm. Existing work often emphasizes usefulness, like enhancing work performance [5,15] or reducing stress [29], reflecting the positivist epistemology in HCI. Such deployment of mindfulness echoes remarks by the authors of seminal book *The Embodied Mind* [28], Varela, Thompson & Rosch, who note that the folk understanding of mindfulness in America has a tendency to emphasize states of altered consciousness (increased concentration, trance-like dissociation and medically beneficial ways to relax) as means to get away from "mundane, unconcentrated, unrelaxed, nondissociated, lower state of reality" [28:23]. This is the opposite to mindfulness informed by Buddhism and Zen. Celebrated Zen scholar and practitioner Nhat Hanh [18:4] elucidates differences between a goal-driven activity and bringing aliveness to every moment: "There are two ways to wash the dishes. The first is to wash the dishes in order to have clean dishes and the second is to wash the dishes to wash the dishes". To have clean dishes is to be "sucked away into the future"; we are "incapable of realising the miracle of life while standing at the sink" [18:5] if we only focus on outcomes. Zen-informed mindfulness is to "recognize the fact of living in the midst of life as it is lived" [15:45], even in the most mundane, dreary, rainy day (see Yoko's 'rain video' at vimeo.com/ 211613276).

Technology and Mindfulness

In seeking mindfulness, modern tools can be part of the problem. Mental distance from what surrounds us, i.e. not being present in the moment, can be a chronic symptom of technology use, aggravated by the ubiquity of technology in our lives. This has led some to believe that the only way to be mindful is to switch off one's mobile device(s) as an act of resistance to its intrusiveness and distraction [3].

Instead, we build on previous work [2] where Yoko and Ann explored mindfulness as a means to enable a reflective and collective awareness with and through technology. In their earlier work, they posit that "our daily lives are already implicated relationally to all other constituents of the world" and that technology might disrupt *mindlessness* through "portals and detours to a changed state and the moments when a different consciousness beckons" [2:631]. They note that technology cannot enable mindfulness unless the user is disposed to being mindful in the first place and describe examples of pre-digital forms of technology used in religious practice as aids for contemplation and inner development (e.g. a Buddhist prayer wheel, a Catholic rosary). The view of technology here, similarly extends beyond using interactive applications to consider a broader starting point. This is juxtaposed with work that focuses on apps [e.g. 14,22,26], where there is a growing trend to use neuro-biology, VR and other sophisticated tools to measure and give feedback on body functions with a view to quietening them.

METHODOLOGY: Methods to Research Mindfulness

An immediate challenge to experimental and ethnographic processes is that we subscribe to a mindfulness practice that cannot be measured or explicitly observed as a visible state of being. Following Suzuki [25], to be self-conscious about mindfulness is also problematic because mindfulness has then been forfeited to some inner reflection on how one is processing the world. Therefore, the authors innovated a method, inspired by other non-standard pieces of research, such as the collaboration between Watts, Ehn and Suchman (in which letters about thinking and emotional states were sent and mutually influenced each partner in the research) [30]. As with their work, our friendship and shared interest evolved into a practice of research. We liken the evolution of our shared understanding, with its growing body of relevant work, to a collaborative auto-ethnography, where material builds through collaboration with others [4]. More detail of our collecting, sharing and reporting processes is discussed below, interwoven with accounts of what we began to learn. We note that sharing of significant objects appears in other work in our field, for instance, Petrelli et al.'s time capsules [21] or Odom et al.'s teenagers' digital objects [19]. While these are not drawn from similar inquiries, they do exhibit the power of artefacts (both physical and digital) to provide stimulus for reflection and emergent discussions among those working with them.

How We Came to Share Practices

Our collaboration grew from a conversation immediately following Yoko and Ann's presentation [2], which inspired a common interest in mindfulness and possible interrelationships with technology and design. Whilst none of us profess to be experts, we practice mindfulness in unique ways in different locations in our personal time. Such diversity, evident in our subsequent communications, sparked intrigue to learn more about each other's varied experiences and orientations to mindfulness, so we embarked on this endeavour as remote colleagues with a mutual curiosity. That the form of this work grew out of friendship and dialogue is not surprising when it is considered. We are design researchers and acted as practitioners taking a leap of faith collectively, without too much rational fortification [10]. Personal meanderings are not only allowed to feature, but are exemplary of form following meaning. It is doubtful if our explorations would have been so compelling had we planned and rationalized our approaches for the reasons given by Suzuki and Nhat Hanh. Our rigour exists in honesty and conviction.

Our process was largely self-directed and independent. We could not practice together in one location – we live and work in Australia and UK (south and north-east England). However, we aimed to share our accounts regularly through email, Skype, Dropbox etc., as aids in disclosure.

There was no agenda to use technology in our practices other than being open to experiment. While such online technologies did not create our practices of mindfulness, they helped us overcome challenges to our communication over distance and time zones. More importantly, the desire to share with each other – and the role of technology to share – became clearer as we conversed, reflected and were mutually inspired by each other's creations. This fuelled our explorations in how various technologies such as smart phone, video, and digital camera already accompanied or could accompany our mindfulness practices. Visual media became a means and focus for our sharing, rather than something imposed on our conversation. Our discussions trace how these technologies configured our sharing and came to have more significance as time went on.

Our accounting here is drawn from materials created during 2015-16, and our reflection on our method of exploration, improvised serendipitously through sharing materials. This account is, thus, supported by a curated and reflexive interweaving of video stills, photographs, quotes and reflective writing, mutually shaped by our collaboration. This partly captures our discussions and poetic descriptions of personal practices complement the images. Due to space, only the most salient examples we discussed and explored are shown, drawn from a broader collection of work (see Yoko's videos on vimeo.com/user51424305/videos; Simon's photography www.flickr.com/photos/simonbowen/ and Ann's garden blog boundaryobjects.tumblr.com).

Avoiding Analysis Through Text, Images and more

As noted, our orientation to mindfulness is informed by Buddhism and Zen. Ironically for us, Zen teaching avoids manuals and definitions because, as the Zen scholar Daisetz Suzuki cautions, they can over-emphasize the analytical brain that "in spite of its practical usefulness … goes against our effort to delve into the depths of being" [24:271]. From cognitive psychology, Bortoft [7] explains the analytic orientation as a selective perception, distinguishing one thing from the other to immediately separate oneself and to stand outside of phenomena. Building on Goethe's science, he suggests foregrounding sensory, holistic, intuitive, non-verbal and non-linear modes as a way to turn one's awareness from the singular object and to encounter the whole. Likewise, the images and videos here are traces of sensory, non-linear and immersive forms explored to "encounter the whole" [7] in places we inhabit. Echoing Bortoft, Varela et al. further observe that mindfulness meditation leads to an awakening of "how disconnected humans normally are from their very experience" [28:25]. Disconnect is a habit that can be broken. Mindfulness meditation can prevent the practitioner from being lost in mindless habits and to realise "the meaning of what we are doing, if we can be what we do" [27:38]. Thus, the authors' practices of mindfulness, as well as the routes toward it, are as diverse as life itself, providing glimpses of their personal environments, urban settings and daily routines. The plurality of expression and practices, as well as the multiple interpretations of mindfulness, offers another challenge to formal reporting. What we cannot convey through words alone, we assemble through juxtaposition of forms over the next few pages.

We observe that the form of the analytic academic paper is particularly hostile to the commitments of mindfulness observed by these masters, but in order to find a 'middle way', we explore how both text and images can make a contribution to share our ways of thinking, not just to explain and analyse, but to evoke and invite hermeneutical participation by the readers. While this cannot make readers mindful, we present our examples as experiments to connect with readers to see if we can meet somewhere in the "in-between" [1] that emerges in mindfulness, as categories (e.g. image/text) and boundaries are eroded.

We use form to play with form and formlessness as an essential ingredient in complementing the linearity and narrow formatting of traditional papers. This is not a *pictorial* submission, because *pictorial* criteria emphasize visual over written forms [5], which would also be limiting for our paper. We seek to extend what is possible with a paper submission to play with the configuration of these elements as a sensorial fulcrum in communicating our routes towards mindfulness. We learn from graphic design, where meaning and communicative power come from composition, hierarchy, contrast, movement, tension and balance of white space, which, combined, constitute visual literacy [17]. By exploring how text and image can be used flexibly and interrelationally, with neither given explicit preference, we aim to inject a different tempo and purpose into the reading here.

The following four pages comprise the authors' (henceforth Y, A, S) verbal and material conversations, illustrating how we grew more responsive and sensitive to our environment and to one another, and how we made sense of our experience of mindfulness by connecting with and through technology and how, in turn, the technology fed our practices of mindfulness and reflection upon it.

I'm not a film-maker. My iPhone has a good, easy-to-use video function so in moments when I felt I was in a mindful state, I used it as a way of accompanying what I was doing. I followed the crested pigeons peck around for food - I like their pointy quiff. I was taking a walk in the park, and the rustling sound of the leaves was really delightful. I was waiting for my train to come so I watched the Melbourne Star from the station platform pulse its lights. I don't think these clips 'capture' mindfulness, I don't believe mindfulness can be captured this way, but I am curious as to what role these traces perform. And when I watch these videos again, they draw me back to that moment in a powerful, embodied way. I feel it. I know it's not just a cognitive recall thing, and can't really put a finger on how to describe it.

These clips aren't precious. They're low-quality, home-made videos. All I did was three actions with the camera ... Because it's so simple, it wasn't distracting to do in those moments. I wasn't carefully composing, framing, adjusting lighting etc., which would've brought another kind of attentiveness and focus, but towards an outcome, perhaps, rather than on the act of doing.

Video still and quote by Y, 23/7/2015

Photography and quote by S, 24/7/2015

I was at a train station, waiting for a train to Liverpool. We'd had heavy rain showers since late afternoon, including during the drive to the railway station. The rain had paused and the sky was very dramatic. I could have spent the time checking emails, but instead decided to simply watch the clouds moving across the sky. I realised that I had my DSLR camera with me, so made a couple of photos. The sky was changing all the time - layers of clouds moving past each other, the light breaking through and between, constantly morphing.

Y's video recording practice sprang to mind - would it work in a similar way for me in accompanying a moment of mindfulness? Not quite. I think I became occupied with the technicalities of video recording too much - framing the view, bracing my iPhone against a wall to get a steady shot... But, watching it again now, the resulting recording does evoke that moment.

I wander into my garden. Sometimes it is with the intention of doing some gardening. But there is another type of visit. I am going outside to check on the outside world: What has grown since I last visited? I have long known that it is of emotional importance for me to be able to wander out into a green space and tend something. There are at least two temporal scales operating here and both are important.

One is long term: I started building my current garden in 2008, leaving an apple tree and a few shrubs that predate my arrival in the house. Everything else is new, put where I wanted it and has been growing fast or slowly, meekly or aggressively, ever since. Different plants dominate each season and which will change each year. Making the garden is a balancing act: training and pruning, encouraging and clearing. Soft fronds meet the hard edges of the lawn. Bronzes are cut with bright green and deep reds. Seed heads are left to age and provide shape into autumn. Sweet scents are placed near the house in the hope they will waft in. The work is never quite finished.

This is one scale and it progresses over the seasons (or longer) and a good example of the tempo is the way that some self-seeding flowers creep into the garden, across it and on to the neighbour's over the course of several summers. The movement is only visible over years.

At another scale is the garden's mood. This is not about managing and tending, though it might be to tuck a tendril into a lattice, like pinning back a lock of unruly hair. It is looking in the pond to see if the tiny black goldfish of the new generation will come to the surface if I am quiet. It is about smelling every rose in the garden, rubbing the sage and sniffing my fingers.

This tempo is affected by the season, but it also relates to weather, light and time of day. The moment is caught in the curl of a petal or the hot pinks, reds and oranges of what happens to be flowering. It is the sharpness of a ripe raspberry and the acid smell of cutting rhubarb. It is the sweet low scent of honeysuckle in the evening. In the space of a few moments I can reverse the stress of a day.

Photography and quote by A, 12/12/2015

I crept out of the holiday cottage before 6am, needing to get to the shore before the sun rose. This meant that preparation was important to increase my chances of making the kind of image I envisaged – checking the weather forecast for clearer skies, using the ephemeris app to plot the direction of sunrise and therefore, along with a map, from where I could watch this light hitting the castle. I parked at the beach car park closest and walked quickly through the dunes, around the golf course, and behind the castle to my chosen spot. Lugging my camera bag and tripod whilst anxiously watching the sky to the east, and my watch.

So far, so mindless. I was certainly cleaning rather than washing the dishes. But then I get to the rocky shore with half an hour until sunrise and everything changes. I am here and I must slow down and observe. The preparation might indicate how the light will illuminate the castle but, in the wide vista I am seeking to create, this is a background point of interest, something to draw the eye. Now, I must find my foreground, the essence of this place at this time that roots the castle to its surroundings. I must look. I must feel.

I know this section of coast from previous visits so wander along the shore looking for where the sea scoops in and the rock thrusts out – a spot from where the sea and rock vie for attention in front of the castle. I move down onto a such a candidate and, my camera still in its bag, spend more time at that spot looking at how the sea moves over the layers of rock, noticing which rock pools are touched by the waves and which are still, and finding the greens and oranges of the seaweed a welcome contrast to the harsh dark rock. I crouch and shift, seeking the exact spot at which these elements combine into an arresting whole. Only then do I unpack my tripod and camera. After a flurry of activity, most of it on auto-pilot (I know my gear from much practice), there is more waiting. Waiting for the sun to rise. Watching the light as it changes and develops. Pressing the shutter release when appropriate. I am calmer in those moments, happy to be in that place at that time witnessing the sunrise with my camera.

Photography and quote by S, 24/7/2015

I like how they [photographs by S, A, Y] *work, even though they're different ...*[each] *describes ways of being present in the moment, and opening up to the wonderment of the surroundings.*

An outcome can evoke this for others - whether they call it mindfulness, is then academic. Technology, landscape, weather, our presence 'assembled (?)' or 'opened up' in that moment...

Quote by Y, 14/9/2015

There is something about who these images are for. Or, rather, to what degree the images are made intentionally for self or others at all. My landscape photographs are strongly towards the intended audience end of the scale - I want others to appreciate the feelings these landscapes evoke in me, as well as re-connect with them myself. Much of the technical practice of photography serves this - the composition, the timing, the adjustment of camera parameters, post-processing. This is almost to exaggerate what was observed and experienced through the technical and stylistic quality of the image.

But this is clearly not the only way to practice photography/videography, as Y's account demonstrates.

So-called snapshot photographs also can be hugely evocative and meaningful. Perhaps because, for those viewing them, they are a connection to a personal moment and the friends and family present. Similarly Y's videos spoke to me and A (I think) because they evoke parallel moments of mindfulness of our own (and because we appreciate the practice that they accompany).

Y- I wonder, then, given that the recordings draw you back to those moments so strongly, whether your practice of making them has changed? Are they still an accompaniment, or is there some intentionality beyond 'doing alongside' appearing? And, again, does it matter? It may be a distraction, it may be a further focussing of mindfulness through the iPhone.

Quote by S, 24/7/2015

... I wonder if there is a projection to a future state when mindfulness is possible with ones' media efforts. Can we horde mindfulness? If we are making images for ourselves, does this happen with a sense that even if we are busy with technology now, perhaps, later, there will be a reflective moment for consuming our work and being mindful then?

Quote by A, 14/9/2015

... Maybe we travel through these photos/videos, or there's something that invites us to do so. Instead of 'future' states, perhaps 'possible' states? I think we are taken somewhere to meet in the in-betweens of 'imagined' moments and we believe they are also 'ours'. There's something really powerful and emotional about this 'we-ness' through artefact, in the sense, S took the video, and the video Y and A watches alters our states in ways we can 'meet' with S's state of being.

Quote by Y, 14/9/2015

Photography by S

DISCUSSION

We have shared some ways in which technology and mindfulness relate for us, and it is clear from these accounts that neither technology nor mindfulness feature in instrumental ways, but might enable different meaning, quality and purpose in the authors' lives.

Mindfulness with and through Technology

We see a blurring as we consider our tools as platforms for scaffolding something as formless as mindfulness. Our tools can act as a path to mindfulness or a distraction. When S picks up his camera, he is embarking on a form of mindfulness-to-come in his expectations of what it enables him to do. By contrast, Y's iPhone is a response to circumstances and has immediacy, both in recording and replaying (Fig. 1).

Fig. 1 A still from Y's video (https://vimeo.com/163898238)

We note here that the technology described – a DSLR, an iPhone, a garden – cannot be interchanged, because our practices of mindfulness are distinct - engaged with in highly personal ways - and thus our relationship to technology is also different. This is most apparent in the story shared by S, who, inspired by Y's video, then films the storm clouds when waiting for a train: *"Y's video recording practice sprang to mind - would it work in a similar way for me in accompanying a moment of mindfulness? Not quite. I think I became occupied with the technicalities of video recording too much"*. Yet, his preparation of photography equipment is described as *"auto-pilot (I know my gear from much practice)"* and his intuitive, well-rehearsed knowledge of his equipment enables him to be 'in the moment' to watch the light and landscape unfold through the camera lens.

In contrast, Y's equipment (iPhone) accompanies her mindfulness moments because it is always there in her handbag. Filming via iPhone is not her usual practice in the way S speaks of his camera, but the iPhone's ease-of-use makes it unobtrusive. Familiarity with tools is a part of moving past awareness of them, as phenomenologists have told us. Settling in with our tools is a part of welcoming them into a more nuanced relationship with broader ambitions, even when that ambition is to abandon our ambitions for a while.

Form and Formlessness

In this section, we show how we can cohere our practices and explorations through a Zen construct of *form* and *formlessness* (sometimes also referred to as *being* and *nonbeing*).

The interrelatedness *form* and *formlessness* is well articulated by Thomas Kasulis [11], an American scholar of Zen philosophy. When Kasulis visits a Japanese temple, he sees a giant suspended iron bell and asks a priest how old it is. The priest replies "This is about five hundred years old, but... [pointing to the void within the bell] the emptiness within – that's eternal." The priest then proceeds to strike the bell and the tone "permeates the area from the distant mountains across the valley, beyond the tops of the cedars". The priest smiles, turns to Kasulis and asks: "Now please answer *my* question. Where did the sound come from?" [11:34].

This *mondo* – an oblique, dialogic puzzlement between a master and student [31] – is a common structure in Zen teaching to avoid deliberate instructions. Kasulis is dumbfounded by the question, but then comes to make sense of it, thus: "think of the casting of the bell as Being [form] and the hollow center as Nonbeing [formlessness]. ...Without the hollow interior, the bell would be a metal slab that might clang but never emit music. On the other hand, the hollowness without the casting could only produce the rushing echo of silence. For the bell to resound, both the Being and Nonbeing of the bell are necessary ... the bell is *both* the casting *and* the emptiness within" [11:34]. We see how the priest's question draws out the limitations of Kasulis' perception, which fixates only on the form (bell), to provoke a way to accommodate formlessness (emptiness) as well. Focussing just on the bell is to omit the eternity of emptiness. Formlessness does not just refer to the spatial hollowness of the bell, but encompasses a holistic totality of interrelatedness – a resonance with the world around – through the striking of the bell. "Nonbeing itself is timeless and unchanging; only through its interrelatedness with Being does it become specific ... and meaningful" [11:35].

Technology, bell, incense, chanting, and breathing used in meditation are examples of form, all potentially bringing one's presence in resonance and interrelatedness with the world. As the priest reminds us, there is significant difference between focusing only on form, thus ignoring formlessness, or viewing form and formlessness as discrete. If we apply this insight in designing interactive technology, it means we must always consider technology (form) *with* formlessness, and be vigilant about what is omitted. Looked at from this position, the life-force of nature that permeates and constitutes our universe is already part of our technologies – but we have been conditioned to disregard this relationship by our fixation on form alone. Our explorations thus could be considered to be *mondo*-like, like the conversation between the priest and Kasulis: the technologies we are using and materials shared 'talk back' to question us through our exploration and reflection [8,13].

To give more definition to this account, we offer three types of interrelatedness between form and formlessness.

Giving form to formlessness

This paper shares traces of our making as part of our respective mindfulness practices. This sharing would not have been possible without the aid of digital and interactive technology like a camera or a smart-phone. S's photography practice reveals how his camera constitutes his encounters with the awe and beauty of his surroundings. Visiting the location, preparing the equipment and waiting for the right moment are rituals of S's preparation towards mindfulness as much as the photos he takes in the moment: *"Waiting for the sun to rise.... Pressing the shutter release when appropriate. I am calmer in those moments, happy to be in that place at that time witnessing the sunrise with my camera"* (Fig. 2). Here we see how the camera crystalizes as well as constitutes his presence and embodiment in the landscape. The camera becomes a portal that heightens and attunes his awareness to "the pulsation of Reality" [14:9] in resonance with the awe and beauty of the surrounding.

Fig. 2: S's photography (https://flic.kr/p/pdmZS6)

Immersing in formlessness through form

Structured use and assemblage of artefacts (e.g. pre-digital technology) can also catalyze mindfulness practice. This is strongly pronounced in A's accounts of her garden (Fig. 3) as a place for immersion into moments of mindfulness, having significance and personal meaning. If we see A's garden as a form of pre-digital technology (in the same vein as a prayer wheel), she has assembled and structured various materials – grass, pond, trees, fish, plants, paths – that invite, remind and immerse her in a sensory ebb and flow of life, energy and decay. This assemblage of materials is not dissimilar to that of Zen gardens (*kare-sansui*), composed of rocks and raked pebbles to invite meditation and immerse in an imagined vastness of oceans, islands and currents through its deliberate emptiness [9]. In other words, we can contrast recording one's wonder at the world with shaping one's own world to wonder at. A's wandering, checking, pruning, clearing, planting, eating and smelling are rituals that parallel Zen meditation by 'stripping off all the artificial wrappings humanity has devised' [24:271] and 'wip[ing] off the mental dust' [24:277]. Being in her garden is a way to find moments of connection and contemplation in nature and harmony, while calibrating her mood and cultivating a heightened sensorial aliveness. A uses her words and camera to make a representation of a way of structuring and being with living things, to share these aspects, but the key artefacts are the growing ones.

Fig. 3: Photo of A's garden

Sharing form to evoke formlessness

Technology, like the iPhone, features as accompaniment to Y's mindfulness practice. It is not central to it. For Y, mindfulness practice takes place with or without a recording of it, whereas S and A use technology as part of their practice. This distinction highlights a different role that interactive technology can perform: replaying and sharing to evoke a moment: *"...when I watch these videos again, it draws me back to that moment in a powerful, embodied way. I feel it. I know it's not just a cognitive recall thing..."*. Y's videos are quotidian in their snapshot, low-res quality. A view from a train station (Fig. 1), walking (Fig. 4), regarding pigeons or watching rain cascade down the window are almost uneventful scenes of the everyday. Suzuki calls these "sensitivity for the small things of Nature", in contrast to the grandness of the sun, moon, mountains and rivers, yet "these insignificant and ignoble creatures are in intimate relationship with the grand totality of the cosmic scheme" [24:238]. In fact, these mundane activities are an entry point that connects Y to the 'grand totality' of her urban environment. And, perhaps, due to their ordinariness, they are accessible to S and A. For instance, A remarks that she loves to rustle leaves too. The images and sounds on Y's video are able to conjure sensations and smells of Autumn to resonate with the pleasures of this activity, even if, in reality, it is springtime in the UK when it is watched by A and S (Fig. 4). The memory evokes both pleasure and tranquility.

Fig. 4: A still from Y's video (https://vimeo.com/163897911)

Developing this thought, we could say the traces of our imagery, video and texts act upon the authors in ways that help us also create and meet in the in-between of our imagination. The traces can invite others to travel through them: *"we are taken somewhere to meet in the in-betweens of 'imagined' moments and we believe they are also 'ours'. There's something really powerful and emotional about this 'we-ness' through artefact, in the sense, S took the video, and the video Y and A watches alters our states in ways we can 'meet' with S's state of being."* The 'in-betweens' collapse boundaries, merge distinctions and heighten a relational sensitivity. This resonates with Akama's [1] discussion of 'in-between' as *Ma* from Japanese philosophy. People who encounter *Ma* (between-ness) "can no longer feel part of a world of predefined boundaries that seek to distinguish self-other, object-subject, human-non-human, time-space" (p24). In other words, the very acts of distinguishing and naming "collapses and becomes an 'opening or emptying of oneself into the immediacy of the ever changing moment', and [can] be taken to a 'boundary situation at the edge of thinking and the edge of all processes of locating things' " (Akama quoting Pilgrim [1:24]).

The three relationships we offer between technology and mindfulness are presented to invite speculation as to how interactive technology might support a middle way between instrumental use and non-use. When we *give form to formlessness*, we can be open to wonderment, find the spectacular in the most mundane and carry the spectacular with us, sometimes, through our technologies. *Immersing in formlessness through form* is to make one's own world to wonder at, reminding us to awaken and attune to the pulsation of broader ecologies. *Sharing form to evoke formlessness* invites others to travel through technology to meet in the in-betweens of mindful and evocative moments.

IN CONCLUSION

Calling on Bortoft, we have attempted to encourage sensory, holistic, intuitive, non-verbal and non-linear modes of perception as a way to turn awareness from the singular object (form) and to encounter the whole. Such attempts present another *mondo* in sharing knowledge in academia – what need be explicated and what is better left incomplete? And in sharing such work, is it perhaps the *fluid* and *sensitive* use of written and visual forms that is more important than the weighting given to each? If the technology of writing papers is one kind of form, what forms can we pursue as a design community to also acknowledge and foreground formlessness? The emergent and exciting ways research is being undertaken in creative practices might offer a way. Our goal in delivering an unconventional paper format for our theme is to attempt to evoke in the reader some of the exploration of form and formlessness that is personal, profound and compelling to us. Cognitive and theoretical understanding will only go so far.

Finding a middle way is a timely challenge as "human activity recognition" [e.g.12] informs the design of the systems around us, and computers are asked to interpret further aspects of what humans do. As such, the insights we offer here are not about how we improve, or better design, current or future technology for everyday contexts, or even for mindfulness. While readers in HCI may desire such instruction, that cannot be our purpose here. The constructs that separate form and formlessness lead to a disconnect with the world and with ourselves, as a "spacesuit" padded with "habits and preconceptions, the armor with which one habitually distances oneself from one's experience" [28:25]. A significant stepping stone is the effort required to unlearn and erode entrenched constructs to fully immerse and re-engage with oneself and the world anew [28].

Designing interactive technologies or advancing research on technology and mindfulness requires a similar unlearning. If the technologies we have designed have, in any way, made us more destructive, more isolated and more fearful, then we must take this as a warning that we need a profound reorientation in this community. The compassion underlying the evolution of the philosophies and spiritual teachings we draw upon here would seem to serve well in addressing destruction, isolation and fear. Practicing mindfulness is to embark on a different starting point in considering human-world interaction, as well as considering the smaller subset of human-technology interactions that is normally our community's concern.

ACKNOWLEDGEMENTS

We thank the reviewers for their comments, which have helped us clarify and refine our arguments presented in a somewhat novel format for academic conferences. This work was partly funded by a UK AHRC KE Hub for the Creative Economy (ref: AH/J005150/1 Creative Exchange).

REFERENCES

1. Yoko Akama. 2014. Attuning to Ma (between-ness) in designing. PDC '14, ACM , 21–24.
2. Yoko Akama and Ann Light, 2015. Towards Mindfulness: Between a Detour and a Portal. CHI EA '15, ACM Press, 625– 637.
3. Sam Anderson. 2009. In Defense of Distraction: Twitter, Adderall, lifehacking, mindful jogging, power browsing, Obama's BlackBerry, and the benefits of overstimulation, in New York Magazine.
4. Theresa D. Anderson, and Ina Fourie. 2015. Collaborative autoethnography as a way of seeing the experience of care giving as an information practice. In *Proceedings of ISIC, the Information Behaviour Conference, Leeds, 2-5 September, 2014: Part 2*, (paper isic33). Retrieved from http://InformationR.net/ir/20-1/isic2/isic33.html
5. Beatriz Bernárdez, Amador Durán, José Parejo, and Antonio Ruiz--Cortés. 2014. A controlled experiment to evaluate the effects of mindfulness in software engineering. Proceedings of the 8th ACM/IEEE International Symposium on Empirical Software Engineering and Measurement, ESEM '14, ACM, 1–10.
6. Eli Blevis, Sabrina Hauser and William Odom. 2015. Sharing the hidden treasure in pictorials. interactions 22, (3), 32–43.
7. Henri Bortoft, H. 1996 The Wholeness of Nature: Goethe's Way of Science. 1996, New York: Floris Books.
8. Andrew. M Dearden. 2006. Design as conversation with digital materials. Design studies, 27 (3), 399-421.
9. Kenya Hara. 2011. *White*. Zurich, Switzerland: Lars Müller.
10. Brad Haseman and Daniel Mafe. 2009. Acquiring Know How: Research Training for Practice-led Researchers, in Practice-led Research, Research-led Practice in the Creative Arts, R.T. Dean and H. Smith, Editors. Edinburgh University Press: Edinburgh. 211-228.
11. Thomas P Kasulis. 1981. Zen Action/Zen Person. University of Hawai'i Press, Honolulu, USA.
12. Kim, E., Helal, S., and Cook, D. 2010. Human Activity Recognition and Pattern Discovery. IEEE pervasive computing / IEEE Computer Society [and] IEEE Communications Society 9, (1), 48.
13. Yasuhiko G. Kimura. 2004. The Book of Balance: Lao Tzu's Tao Teh Ching. New York: Paraview.
14. Ilkka Kosunen, Mikko Salminen , Simo Järvelä , Antti Ruonala , Niklas Ravaja , Giulio Jacucci, 2016, RelaWorld: Neuroadaptive and Immersive Virtual Reality Meditation System, Proceedings of the 21st International Conference on Intelligent User Interfaces, March 07-10, Sonoma, California, USA
15. David M. Levy, Jacob O. Wobbrock, Alfred W. Kaszniak, and Marilyn Ostergren. 2012. The effects of mindfulness meditation training on multitasking in a high-stress information environment, 45–52.
16. Ann Light, Lone Malmborg, Jörn Messeter, Eva Brandt, Joachim Halse, Per-Anders Hillgren and Tuuli Mattelmäki. 2016. Writing Participatory Design – A Workshop on Interpreting, Accounting and Novel Forms of Reporting, PDC '14, ACM.
17. Katherine McCoy. 1988. Graphic design: Sources of meaning in word and image. Word & Image: A Journal of Verbal/ Visual Enquiry, 4(1), 116-130.
18. Thich Nhat Hanh. 1976. The Miracle of Mindfulness. Beacon Press, Boston, USA.
19. William Odom, John Zimmerman, and Jodi Forlizzi. 2011. Teenagers and Their Virtual Possessions: Design Opportunities and Issues. *Proc. of CHI '11*, 1491-1500.
20. Daniela Petrelli, Steve Whittaker and Jens Brockmeier. 2008. Auto Topo-graphy: what can physical mementos tell us about digital memories? *Proc. of CHI '08*, 53-62.
21. Daniela Petrelli, Elise van den Hoven and Steve Whittaker. 2009. Making History: Intentional Capture of Future Memories, CHI'09
22. Corina Sas and Rohit Chopra. 2015. MeditAid: a wearable adaptive neurofeedback-based system for training mindfulness state, Personal and Ubiquitous Computing,19(7), 1169-1182.
23. Donald Schön. 1983. The reflective practitioner: how professionals think in action. New York: Basic Books.
24. Daisetz T. Suzuki. 1958 Zen and Japanese Culture. Princeton University Press., New York, USA.
25. Daisetz T. Suzuki. 1969. An Introduction to Zen Buddhism. London: Rider and Company.
26. Anja Thieme, Jayne Wallace, Paula Johnson, John McCarthy, Siân Lindley, Peter Wright, Patrick Olivier, Thomas D. Meyer. 2013. Design to promote mindfulness practice and sense of self for vulnerable women in secure hospital services. In: Proceedings of the SIGCHI conference on human factors in computing systems (CHI `13). ACM, 2647-2656.
27. Thich Thien-An. 1975. Zen Philosophy, Zen Practice. Dharma Publishing, Berkley, CA, USA.
28. Francisco J. Varela, Evan Thompson and Eleanor Rosch. 1993. The Embodied Mind: Cognitive Science and Human Experience. MIT Press, Cambridge, Massachusetts, USA.
29. Jay Vidyarthi, Berhard E Riecke and Diane Gromala. 2012. Sonic Cradle. Proceedings of DIS '12, ACM, 408.
30. Laura Watts, Pelle Ehn and Lucy Suchman. 2014. Prologue, in Making Futures: Marginal Notes on Innovation, Design, and Democracy. Editors Pelle Ehn, Elisabet M. Nilsson, Richard Topgaard. Cambridge MA, MIT Press
31. Liuning Zhou. 2003. "Koan as Ritual: The Role of Language in Zen Discourse." annual meeting of the International Communication Association, San Diego, California, USA, May 27.

Examining Localization Approaches for Community Health

Aditya Vashistha[†] Neha Kumar[§] Anil Mishra[‡] Richard Anderson[†]
[†]University of Washington {adityav, anderson}@cs.washington.edu
[§]Georgia Institute of Technology neha.kumar@gatech.edu
[‡]PATH amishra@path.org

ABSTRACT
We present a mixed-methods study that compares and contrasts two distinct localization approaches for imparting video-based health education to rural Indian populations. Prior research efforts in the Human-Computer Interaction for Development (HCI4D) community have emphasized the value of localization of educational content. Our research uses a combination of focus groups, interviews, and knowledge retention tests to deconstruct what localization means and how it might be incorporated. Our findings highlight how characteristics of localized videos shape the participants' viewing experiences. For development-focused organizations that leverage video-based learning, our study provides insights regarding the costs and benefits of distinct localization approaches, and offers design recommendations for producing videos that yield greater traction and higher information absorption.

Author Keywords
Health; Video-Based Education; Localization; HCI4D

ACM Classification Keywords
H.5.m. Information Interfaces and Presentation: Miscellaneous

INTRODUCTION
Rural, socioeconomically disadvantaged, and disconnected communities in developing regions face a complex array of socioeconomic barriers, literacy constraints, and infrastructural challenges that impede their access to physical, print, and online sources of information. In India alone, 58% of the population earns less than USD 3 a day [1], 26% of the adult population is illiterate [2], and over 72% of the population does not have smartphones and Internet access [3, 27]. The Human-Computer Interaction for Development (HCI4D) community attends, in large part, to the challenges in imparting new information and inculcating new practices in these resource-constrained communities, frequently in the domain of global health, but also in the realms of education, agriculture, financial literacy, and repair, among others [11]. Recently, many HCI4D researchers have explored video-based storytelling approaches for disseminating information and increasing audience engagement across communities with consistently low literacy rates [24, 25, 28, 32, 34].

DIS 2017, June 10–14, 2017, Edinburgh, United Kingdom

DOI: http://dx.doi.org/10.1145/3064663.3064754

Several video-based HCI4D interventions have variously prioritized the situating of language, content, characters, and spatial context [8, 17, 18, 23, 33, 34]. Similarly, there are also examples of large-scale interventions that have been administered across multiple geographic regions without particular emphasis on customization for language and content [4, 5, 6]. Our research aims to unpack the tradeoffs involved in employing these different localization approaches. For example, 'hyper-localizing' a video such that it features the neighborhood of individuals [18, 23] that it targets might lead to effective reception and information absorption, but scaling up this approach could prove expensive. On the other hand, approaches that target larger populations at once might be scalable, but they are frequently criticized for their *one-size-fits-all* approach [15]. In this paper, we aim to understand how two distinct localization processes operate, and break down the notable elements of these design processes for effective uptake of video-based learning. Our final research goal is to leverage this knowledge towards careful design of video-based HCI4D interventions.

To achieve these objectives, we examine the case of *video-based maternal health education* in rural India, a country with persistently high maternal and infant mortality rates. We identified and compared two public health videos: one was produced by Projecting Health (PH), a maternal and newborn health project running in rural Uttar Pradesh [23], while the second was produced by a UNICEF program for a much larger target audience [7]. PH promotes a 'hyper-local' approach to video production, where rural community-based organizations produce videos locally and feature community members discussing health messages in rural areas. UNICEF employs a different approach, where videos with high production aesthetics are produced with professional actors who discuss health information in a high-quality studio set mimicking rural areas. PH focuses on generating a sense of place with its videos, while UNICEF creates a setting that is at once nowhere and everywhere. PH uses the local dialect popular in the targeted villages (Awadhi), while UNICEF uses the dialect of Hindi spoken by higher-income households across several Indian states, also known as the prestige dialect. PH videos feature esteemed community members endorsing the key health messages, while UNICEF videos leverage the appeal of renowned Bollywood celebrities. Despite apparent differences in their approaches to localization, the projects have much in common; both employ frontline health workers to leverage these videos in facilitated group sessions with women and men, have common goals, and serve similar target populations. We examine the nature of these similarities and differences in our study.

Prior research in HCI4D literature has emphasized the value of localization [18, 23]. Our research questions how far we might go with this approach, as we consider the dimensions that make videos *local*. Our comparative study indicates that out of 168 rural participants, a significant majority of 74% chose UNICEF's video over PH's video. Deconstructing their responses revealed that high production quality, a well-formed story, use of demonstrations, the prestige dialect, 'shareability', and a focus on infotainment were all factors that drew participants to the UNICEF video. Those who preferred the PH video did so due to the presence of a local doctor, information on home remedies, and characters and context they could relate to. Our quantitative findings indicated, in addition, that the UNICEF video resulted in a statistically higher knowledge gain among targeted women. We discuss the lessons learned from our analysis, and offer design recommendations for global development initiatives that engage in localized approaches to video-based learning.

RELATED WORK

We now situate our research in a body of related work on HCI4D and public health, video-based approaches to maternal health education, and localization approaches in HCI4D.

HCI4D and Health

The field of HCI has increasingly begun to focus on understanding diverse, under-represented populations across the globe and designing technologies to improve their lives in meaningful ways, as discussed in Dell and Kumar's account of HCI4D [11]. Research efforts in HCI4D have leveraged growing technology penetration in the developing world to design interventions in the health [21], agriculture [10], education [37, 20], governance [19], journalism [29], and social media [26, 35] domains, among others. In health alone, HCI4D research target various application areas, such as data collection, access to information, training, disease surveillance, and monitoring of health services [13]. For example, Perrier et al. studied the use of mobile messaging for maternal health in peri-urban Kenya [31]. DeRenzi et al. designed a mobile phone tool that guided Tanzanian health workers step-by-step through the IMCI treatment algorithm [14]. Kumar and Anderson explored the use of mobile phones for disseminating maternal health information [22]. This is a growing body of work that recognizes the importance of a situated, localized approach to design solutions for global health. HCI4D researchers working in other domains also grapple with when and how to localize their intervention.

Video-based Maternal Health Education

Prior research on video-based maternal health education has drawn on the wide penetration and usability of mobile technology. For example, Ramachandran et al. [32] experimented with the creation of short *ad hoc* videos by health workers using mobile phones to persuade village women to utilize state-provided health services. Fiore-Silfvast et al. [16] studied the use of mobile videos by midwives for patient education during postnatal care examinations. Molapo and Marsden [28] designed a tool to aid rural health trainers in creating instructional videos for training low-literate community health workers in Lesotho. Ladeira and Cutrell [24] highlighted the instructional value of digital storytelling that combines motivational content with narrative framing. Many of these works are motivated by the desire to reduce text dependence and increase audience engagement in communities with low literacy rates. Our work extends existing research by examining how two localization approaches to video-based maternal health education affect users' engagement and knowledge gain.

Localization Approaches in HCI4D

Several research initiatives target low-resource environments for dissemination of locally relevant content. For example, Frohlich et al. [17], Reitmaier et al. [33], and Bidwell et al. [8] have studied local mobile audio and video content creation for digital storytelling in rural communities of South India, Kenya, and South Africa, respectively. Digital Green [18] — an agricultural non-profit operating in over 7000 villages in India — advocates leveraging locally-produced videos to improve adoption of agricultural best practices among farmers. Similarly, Projecting Health (PH) — a public health project deployed across five blocks in the state of Uttar Pradesh (India) — uses community-led video education model [23] to leverage community resources for local generation, dissemination, and assimilation of visual media. Patel et al. examined the influence of authority on agricultural information dissemination in India, and found that the farmers acted upon the information more when it was provided by locals than by scientists [30].

Several practitioners have also leveraged top-down approaches at scale to provide health information to beneficiaries. For example, *Mobile Kunji* [6] — a health system deployed by BBC Media Action across Bihar, India — provides well-illustrated cards with image- and text-based life saving information to frontline health workers. The government of Uttar Pradesh uses an Interactive Voice Response system to monitor its midday meal program in 75 districts covering 150,000 schools [4]. UNICEF also employs a top-down approach to produce high quality instructional videos for community health that feature the 'Indian Village' [7], but makes its decisions on content in collaboration with state and industry level actors instead of community actors.

For resource-constrained global development projects that leverage video-based learning, the costs and benefits of different approaches to video production naturally become of high relevance. We extend prior research by examining localization approaches employed by two video-based health education projects mentioned above: PH and UNICEF videos. A study of these projects affords us an enriched understanding of localization given that the projects have similar goals, target demographically similar populations, but employ different localization approaches. By reflecting on the tradeoffs involved and deconstructing the dimensions of localization, our research also allows us to make design recommendations for video-based HCI4D interventions that aim to use localized content. We outline the takeaways of our study so that these projects may take a more informed approach.

METHODOLOGY

We now present our methodology for conducting the comparison study. First, we describe how we selected the videos that formed the basis of our study. We then describe our qualitative and quantitative approaches.

Video Selection

UNICEF produced a video series titled *Kyunki Ammaji Kehti Hain*[1] to provide maternal and child health information to parents and caregivers in rural India. Our research team did a rigorous inspection of 42 UNICEF and 80 PH videos, and used several layers of filtering to identify two comparable videos. First, we discarded seventeen videos from the UNICEF repository that addressed topics not covered by PH videos. We then discarded two videos that were not relevant to both women and men in rural settings (*e.g.*, menstrual hygiene) or included sensitive information (*e.g.*, family planning). We then discarded sixteen videos that offered information that was commonplace in rural India (*e.g.*, breastfeeding) so that it is easier for us to measure comparative knowledge gain for both approaches. We then matched the remaining seven UNICEF videos with an equivalent PH video. We discarded six video pairs where the number or content of key messages, or video length were different. The final two videos focused on treatment for diarrhea and were roughly 11 minutes long.

Qualitative Methods

Our primary instruments for this study were focus groups and interviews (see Table 1). The focus groups and interviews took place at eight locations, such as community health centers, homes, and school buildings, in an area of 205 square miles in rural Uttar Pradesh[2]. In India, states are divided into multiple levels of hierarchy for administrative purposes: villages, *Gram Panchayats* (GP), blocks, and districts. For example, a GP in Uttar Pradesh includes roughly three villages, a block has 63 GPs, and a district has 11 blocks. We conducted research activities at each of these levels to examine the definition of *local* and the impact of localization on people's perceptions.

The first author (male, 30 years, native Hindi speaker) conducted focus groups and interviews in Hindi. Since people in the study area also speak Awadhi (a local dialect of Hindi), a three-member support team fluent in the local dialect accompanied the first author. We selected participants who were previously unaware of the existence of PH- and UNICEF-produced videos in an effort to mitigate bias. To ensure that participants do not associate us with one of the two videos and give biased feedback [12], we explicitly stated that we produced both videos and wanted feedback to understand which one is better and why. We framed our questions to compare the videos with each other than to elicit individual feedback on any. This mitigated the response bias even when participants associated us with both videos. We randomized the order in which participants viewed the videos and requested them to observe differences between the videos. We asked them to report their preferences verbally during interviews and by show of hands during focus groups. We used a set of pre-defined questions and followed-up with specific questions on topics that emerged during the discussion.

[1]"Kyunki ammaji kehti hain" is a Hindi phrase meaning "because the elderly woman says so"

[2]See http://bitly.com/studyarea.

	Stakeholders	Total sessions	Total participants
Focus groups	Women	8	97
	Men	2	25
	MSOs	2	12
	ASHAs	2	10
	Video team	2	12
Interviews	Women	x	12

Table 1. Description of focus groups and interviews.

Figure 1. A focus group session with women in a rural village.

Focus groups: We conducted 16 focus group discussions: eight with low-income women in remote rural areas, two with low-income men, two with community health workers, two with mobile shop owners (MSOs) in rural areas, and two with staff of video production agencies. The number of participants in these focus groups varied. Since low-income women are the direct beneficiaries of videos produced by PH and UNICEF, we conducted focus groups with 97 women (see Figure 1) who were 30 years old, on average. Ninety of them were married, 32 were new mothers, and seven were pregnant. Almost half of them were completely illiterate. We also conducted focus groups with 25 low-income men since prior works have identified men as key decision makers for family health [32, 23]. A majority of them were farmers and laborers. Twenty men were married, and ten had a pregnant woman or a new mother in their family. The mobile phone penetration among women and men was 50% and 80%, respectively. Almost a quarter of them watched videos on their phone.

Because both projects distribute these videos through a network of community health workers, we conducted focus groups with 10 Accredited Social Health Activists (ASHAs) — local women trained to disseminate health information — who were also 30 years old, on average. All of them owned a phone and seven watched videos on their phone. We conducted focus groups with 12 MSOs to understand which video could be more appealing for the target beneficiaries since previous research has identified them as experts with a deep understanding of media needs of rural communities [22, 36]. All of them were male (24 years old, on average) and tech-savvy; they

Groups	Age (years)	Education					Family size	Family Occupation			
		Illiterate	Primary	Middle	High	Bachelors		Farmer	Laborer	Other jobs	Unemployed
PH	29	4	1	6	6	3	6.8	12	5	3	0
UNICEF	31	5	2	7	3	3	6.4	8	7	4	1

Table 2. Demographic information for knowledge gain study participants.

owned a smartphone and laptop, and used the Internet. We conducted focus groups with 12 staff members of PH's video production team to examine how they perceive the benefits and limitations of the two localization approaches. All of them lived in villages or small towns in our study area, had completed their bachelor's degree, and used the Internet. Each focus group lasted around 75 minutes.

Interviews: After we completed all focus groups, we conducted 12 interviews with low-income women in rural areas to investigate the high-level themes that emerged during the focus groups. All women participants (38 years old, on average) were married. Two women were illiterate, three had completed primary school, four had completed middle school, one had completed high school, and another had a bachelor's degree. Two women worked as laborers, one in a private job, and the remaining were homemakers. They came from families of laborers, farmers, shop owners, and auto drivers with an average family size of 5.7 people and average monthly family income of USD 110. One woman was pregnant while four were new mothers. Eight women owned a mobile phone and five watched videos on their phone. Each interview lasted around 45 minutes.

Analysis: To analyze the data collected during our focus groups and interviews, we engaged in regular discussions to make sense of findings and iterate on our questions. Interview transcripts were translated to English and analyzed along with our field notes. We subjected our data to thematic analysis as outlined in [9]. All authors analyzed the data and iterated through the findings as a group.

Quantitative Methods

To measure the effect of localization approaches on knowledge retention, we used a pretest-posttest-retention test control group design. We designed the experiment with two balanced groups – the first group was shown the PH video and the second was shown the UNICEF video. At each focus group session with women, we requested attendees to (voluntarily) take a pretest and posttest. The first five volunteers were assigned to one of the two experiment groups randomly. We worked with three veteran health experts to design a knowledge pretest to include 12 objective questions that could be answered by watching either video. For the posttest, we randomized the order of questions and responses in the pretest. Each experiment group took the pretest, watched the video assigned to it with all focus group participants, and then took a posttest. Literate participants completed the test on paper while our support team conducted an oral test for illiterate participants. Once the five participants finished the posttest, we showed the second video to all focus group participants and conducted the session.

We recruited 40 women to participate in the pretest-posttest-retention test control group design. We controlled for age, family size, and education. Table 2 shows participants' demographics. The majority of women who volunteered to participate in our knowledge retention test had studied at least until middle school. They were thus more likely to understand the prestige dialect than less literate women, which may have biased our findings in favor of the UNICEF video.

FINDINGS

Among 168 participants of 16 focus groups and 12 interviews, a high majority of 74% (N=124) preferred the UNICEF video while only 26% (N=44) found the PH video more appealing. Table 3 presents the number of participants at each geographic level, and their preference between the two videos conveyed during the focus groups and interviews. The UNICEF video was preferred by all stakeholders at each geographic level except the GP where the PH video was produced. We now present video characteristics that were considered salient in our participants' responses, how they were localized, and how they affected participants' perception, preferences, and knowledge.

Local Dialect vs. Prestige Dialect

PH used Awadhi, a local dialect of Hindi popular in the study area, with the intent that these videos would be relatable for as many in the target blocks as possible. UNICEF, on the other hand, used the prestige dialect of Hindi, generally used by literate people in middle- and high-income households across several states in India. Over 80% of participants found dialect to be the key difference between the videos. Though a majority of them could understand both dialects, we found a significant preference for the prestige dialect (N=93) over the local dialect (N=39). Table 4 shows that all stakeholders preferred to watch videos in the prestige dialect.

Women who preferred the prestige dialect did so because they found it clear and easy to understand. They believed that everyone, including *"city dwellers as well as village dwellers, the literate as well as the illiterate,"* understood the prestige dialect, and attributed this to the popularity of Hindi soap operas. Several MSOs stated that a majority of their customers demand movies and songs in the prestige dialect. A few women considered themselves to be *"city people who are misfits in a rural community"* and found it natural to use the prestige dialect. Others felt that the local dialect used in the PH video is spoken by *"unsophisticated and uneducated people"*. One of them stated:

> *"It appeared that literate people like us are having a conversation with each other in the UNICEF video. Anyone can easily understand Hindi. But women in the PH video were speaking like illiterates and villagers."*
>
> P1 (Women interviewee, different block)

Several participants recommended us to produce new PH videos in the prestige dialect. They believed that produc-

Activities	Location: Same GP	Location: Different GP	Location: Different block	Location: Different district	Summary
Women focus groups	PH 11, UNICEF 5	PH 3, UNICEF 20	PH 3, UNICEF 25	PH 7, UNICEF 23	PH 24, UNICEF 73
Men focus groups	PH 4, UNICEF 2	x	x	PH 4, UNICEF 15	PH 8, UNICEF 17
MSOs focus groups	x	PH 3, UNICEF 4	UNICEF 5	x	PH 3, UNICEF 9
ASHAs focus groups	x	PH 3, UNICEF 2	UNICEF 5	x	PH 3, UNICEF 7
Video prod. team focus groups	x	PH 4, UNICEF 2	UNICEF 6	x	PH 4, UNICEF 8
Women interviews	x	PH 1, UNICEF 5 (6 interviews)	PH 1, UNICEF 5 (6 interviews)	x	PH 2, UNICEF 10 (12 interviews)
Summary	PH 15, UNICEF 7	PH 14, UNICEF 33	PH 4, UNICEF 46	PH 11, UNICEF 38	PH 44, UNICEF 124

PH UNICEF

Table 3. Number of participants who preferred the PH video and the UNICEF video during focus groups and interviews conducted at different geographic levels. *Same GP* column refers to the focus groups and interviews conducted in the Gram Panchayat (GP) where the PH video was produced, *Different GP* column refers to the activities conducted in another GP in the same block where the PH video was produced, and *Different block* and *Different district* columns presents the activities conducted in a different block and district, respectively, in relation to where the PH video was produced.

Stakeholders	Local Dialect	Prestige Dialect	No preference
Women FGs	23	41	33
Men FGs	5	18	2
MSOs FGs	4	8	0
ASHAs FGs	1	9	0
Staff FGs	3	8	1
Women interviews	3	9	0

Table 4. Preferences of participants for the local and prestige dialect indicated during focus groups (FGs) and interviews.

ing videos in the local dialect would be unscalable and have diminishing returns on users' traction. A woman participant warned that PH would have to produce innumerable videos on the same subject, since variations in the local dialect appear every 20 kilometers.

Nine ASHAs preferred the prestige dialect and reported receiving responses in it even when they speak to young women in the local dialect. MSOs and staff members concurred that young rural residents feel a sense of accomplishment in speaking the prestige dialect, and associate it with education, knowledge, sophistication, and higher social status. A staff member reasoned:

"People in villages want their children to speak the prestige dialect. Several women speak Hindi while conversing with their children so that the children don't get into the habit of speaking Awadhi. Some women learn Hindi from their kids. Prestige dialect speakers are idolized."

P2 (Male, project coordinator, different GP)

Several staff members preferred the prestige dialect since they believed that its use would motivate people to watch health videos more carefully.

We also found some support for the local dialect. Though many illiterate and old women could understand both dialects, assimilating information in the local dialect was effortless for them. They found the local dialect more relatable and entertaining. They believed that their neighbors would find it difficult to understand the prestige dialect, primarily because of their limited education. In a focus group session, the first author was unable to understand an old woman speaking in the local dialect. When the author requested help from the support team, the woman exclaimed: *"When you are unable to understand what I am saying in a dialect unfamiliar to you, how would I be able to understand what women in the [UNICEF] video are saying."* Three staff members concurred that older people enjoy watching PH videos predominantly because of the use of local dialect in them. Other reasons also contributed to the preference for the local dialect. Some participants associated the local dialect with their culture and history, and felt an obligation to conserve and promote it. Others believed that designing videos in the prestige dialect defeats the purpose of the intervention. An ASHA stated:

> *"If I speak in Hindi with women who speak Awadhi, they say 'From where has this madam come? Does she not live in the village?' Old women and low-literate women still like to converse in the local dialect. Literate people already go to a hospital. That's why the local dialect should be used to increase awareness of illiterate people."*
>
> P3 (ASHA, different GP)

Four MSOs and a staff member suggested using a combination of the local and prestige dialects. They wanted videos to mimic the real world where the illiterate use the local dialect, and doctors, nurses, and literates speak the prestige dialect.

Aspirations vs. Association

Both PH and UNICEF aspired that their beneficiaries feel an association with their videos. Since both projects use different localization approaches, the videos inherited distinct properties which influenced participants' perception and preferences.

Our thematic analysis revealed that 42 women, nine men, nine ASHAs, and two MSOs labeled the PH video *"rural video"* and the UNICEF video *"urban video."* They could discern that the PH video was shot in an actual village, while the UNICEF video was shot in a studio. Several participants felt a sense of association with the women, surroundings, and story in the PH video. They found the UNICEF video too manicured and reported never seeing *"such a clean bowl, spoon, and water jug"* or *"fancy pots and chairs"* in their community. A woman stated:

> *"I could see cows and farms in the PH video. The health center in the UNICEF video is so different from ours. It looks like a set used in TV serials."*
>
> P4 (Women focus group session, different GP)

Several participants also perceived differences in actors' appearances (see Figure 2). They noted that women in the PH video were from villages and women in the UNICEF video were from urban areas — a clear effect of the localization approach. Others noticed differences in age and education. They found women in the UNICEF video to be young and educated, and women in the PH video to be low-literate and middle-aged. Some participants termed the PH video *"rural"* because it prescribed home remedies and used the local dialect. Other participants attributed differences in storylines to the rural-urban distinction. A woman stated:

> *"Women in a village take their sick children first to neighbors and ASHAs. But children are taken to a hospital in the cities. This is what is shown in the two videos."*
>
> P5 (Women focus group session, different block)

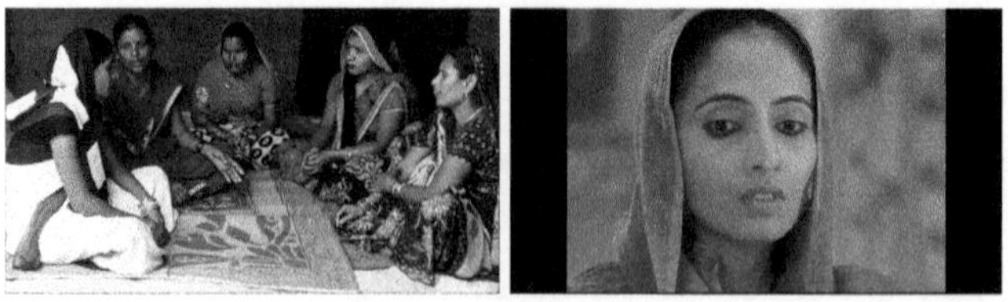

Figure 2. Images from the PH video (left) and the UNICEF video (right).

Nine participants observed differences in production quality and labeled the two videos as *"hi-tech vs. lo-tech."* The PH video was seen as a workable solution, inferior to the UNICEF video in quality, resources, and final outcome. Six participants distinguished between the two videos in terms of *"old vs. young."* They found the PH video to be more suitable for older people and the UNICEF video for the young. Five participants termed the videos as *"illiterate vs. literate"* because of the dialects used in the videos.

Though the participants could relate more to the surroundings, actors, and storyline in the PH video, we did not find a strong correlation between association and video preference. The 'state-of-the-art' understanding regarding localization in the HCI4D domain claims that information from community members is valued more than information from experts due to the association factor [18, 23, 30]. Despite high association with the PH video, many participants still preferred the UNICEF video because they found it unique, entertaining, and aspirational. Several (women) participants found the women in the UNICEF video to be *"educated and sophisticated,"* and aspired to appear and speak like them. An MSO stated:

> *"My customers will prefer the UNICEF video. It is more entertaining, just like a movie or TV show. People in the villages feel jealous when their friends come back from a city and start speaking the prestige dialect. They want to see and share content in the prestige dialect."*
>
> P6 (MSO, different block)

Aspirations and drive to access entertainment trumped association to play a key role in affecting video preferences, but not always. Some participants preferred the PH video because they could relate to women featured in it due to the similarity in their dressing style and mannerisms. A woman stated:

> *"Women in the PH video were dressed like me. The way they called the meeting, how they were sitting and talking, the place it was conducted, all seemed familiar. Women in the UNICEF video wore heavy make-up and looked like actors. They were wearing a salwar kameez. That's weird. No married women wear such attire here."*
>
> P7 (Women focus group session, same block)

Locally Sourced vs. High Production Quality

Participants found stark differences in the technical production quality of the two videos. They strongly preferred the UNICEF video because of its high production aesthetics. Thirty-nine participants found the audio and video quality of the UNICEF video far superior, almost akin to a Bollywood film. The staff members considered video quality to be the key factor that affected people's preferences in rural regions. They believed that people would willingly replay the aesthetically shot UNICEF video and thus, would hear the key messages repeatedly. Some participants reported sound mixing issues in the PH video that worsened their experience with it. MSOs were concerned that the low-quality PH video would be pixelated on smaller form factor feature phones, which are ubiquitous in rural areas.

Participants also found differences in the acting skills of artists. While UNICEF had the resources to hire trained actors, the PH video featured unexperienced local residents-turned-actors. Forty-seven participants explicitly expressed their admiration for actors in the UNICEF video and found them engaging. Compared to the UNICEF video, several participants found the dialogue delivery of the PH video's actors to be fast, monotonous, and unclear. A staff member reported:

> *"The expression and body language of actors is fantastic in the UNICEF video. They are confident, expressive, act naturally, and know what they are doing. They are well-dressed and have also put on make-up. The PH video has a straight dialogue delivery."*
>
> P8 (Female, video production team, different block)

The high production aesthetics also impacted the story and entertainment value of the UNICEF video. UNICEF hired professionals to produce videos that were informative, engaging, and entertaining. PH, on the other hand, hired local talent with a solid understanding of the rural context but limited exposure to screenwriting skills. Though the PH video's storyline was more grounded in the local culture, it was replete with health information. For this reason, 13 participants found the PH video to be overwhelming, and preferred the UNICEF video that found a balance in offering useful information and entertainment. Fifty-two participants preferred the story of the UNICEF video, while 21 participants preferred the PH video's storyline. The PH video showed an enterprising ASHA conducting a mothers' group meeting. Several participants saw a reflection of their ASHA in her, and thus could relate to the story. They appreciated that women in the PH video assembled for a group discussion with ASHA and were taking preemptive actions to prevent diarrhea. An elderly woman who liked the story stated that showing such group discussions will set a precedence and awareness for women's group meetings.

Ninety-four participants found the UNICEF video more entertaining because of effective use of drama, facial expressions, and variations in dialogue delivery and background score. Many described the UNICEF video as a *"television serial with important health messages."* On the other hand, 27 participants found the PH video more entertaining because it was shot in a village similar to theirs and had people speaking the local dialect. Nineteen of them were locals in the GP where the PH video was produced.

The content and presentation style were also affected by the choice of localization approach. The high-skilled UNICEF production team used demonstrations to make the key messages more salient. Thirty-five participants preferred the UNICEF video because it demonstrated how to give ORS solution and zinc tablet, while the PH video merely offered a theoretical discussion. Several participants reported that the demonstration not only increased their understanding of the treatment, but also boosted their confidence that they could do it themselves if and when necessary. The staff concurred that people adopt health practices when they see it rather than when they hear or read about it. A woman participant stated:

> *"After watching the PH video, no one knows how a zinc tablet should be given. However, the demonstration in the UNICEF video leaves nothing to imagination."*
>
> P9 (Woman interviewee, different district)

The localization approach used by the PH video leveraged information on home remedies that use ingredients available in the region. Thirteen participants preferred the PH video for this reason. The access to information for use in the local context made the video more appealing to them. Four women stated that the treatment using home remedies seemed more achievable in rural areas. Five staff members considered the information on home remedies as a key strength of the PH video.

Local Experts vs. Famous Celebrities

While the UNICEF video chose the endorsement of a famous Bollywood actress, the PH video leveraged the popularity and expertise of a local male doctor to engage a wider audience. The differences between the two endorsers were noticed by several participants. Over a hundred participants recognized Raveena Tandon but only 38 participants recognized the doctor. Despite the high popularity of the actress, 91% of participants (N=142) preferred the doctor to repeat key health messages. Many participants understood the information from the doctor better because he shared home remedies in the local vernacular. Unlike the actress, he was perceived as a trustworthy resident health expert. A woman reasoned:

> *If I want any information, if I need consultation, if I need medicine, I can always go to a doctor. How will I go to Raveena Tandon if I have any questions?"*
>
> P10 (Women focus group session, same GP)

Many participants felt that the actress lacked expertise to deliver health information and was repeating what was asked by the director. They saw her as an outsider and could not connect with her at a personal level. They also believed that she would be unable to empathize with them and understand their problems. A woman stated:

> *"What Raveena Tandon is saying is not wrong. But we don't know her. She does not live here. We haven't met her in person and that is why I trust her opinion less."*
>
> P11 (Women focus group session, different GP)

A few male participants preferred the actress because they were her fans. They believed that any health information shared by the actress has to be accurate. Others preferred her delivery style to the doctor's. Two participants initially thought that the actress was a doctor and preferred her over the doctor in the PH video because of her speaking skills. However, they changed their vote soon after realizing that she was an actress. Three women participants preferred the actress because they wanted a woman to share maternal and child health information with them.

Given the strong preference for the doctor, we explored whether participants saw any benefits of featuring celebrities in health videos? MSOs believed that several people would watch the videos repeatedly only to see their favorite celebrities and thus, would indirectly get exposed to important health information. A staff member concurred that people in rural India are greatly influenced by celebrities and may adopt new health behaviors if a celebrity says so:

> *"If a celebrity endorses hair gel, then people will use it even if they lose hairs. New generation believes in celebrities more than doctors."*
>
> P12 (Female, project coordinator, different block)

We asked participants who they would *trust* more: Raveena Tandon or a doctor they have never seen before? Though some people voted for the actress, the majority still preferred an unknown doctor. On several occasions, we heard sentiments like *"a doctor is the one who saves lives and an actress is the one who acts."* A staff member expressed:

> *"People associate comedy, dancing, and acting with an actress rather than health expertise. A person wearing white coat, even if s/he is not a real doctor, is taken more seriously than anyone else when it comes to health."*
>
> P13 (Male, project coordinator, different GP)

An MSO and three staff members highlighted the importance of endorsements from local celebrities rather than local people known only in their village or mainstream celebrities known all across India. A staff member stated:

> *"The best is to feature people who are popular even in nearby villages and are approachable. People should be able to make a personal connection with them unlike the Bollywood actors. Such local celebrities can be a village head or local doctor or social activist."*
>
> P14 (Male, project manager, different block)

Shareability

We asked participants to select one of the two videos they would like to share with their friends and family. We then compared it with their preference for themselves. Surprisingly, more participants preferred to share the UNICEF video with their social connections (N=133) than those who preferred it for themselves (N=124). This further attests that participants found the UNICEF video more engaging.

The comparison revealed that 25 participants selected a different video to share with their friends and family than the one they preferred for themselves. Fifteen of them changed their vote to share the UNICEF video since they wanted to share content that has high 'infotainment' value and demonstrations, and is new and relatively difficult to access. A woman stated:

> *"We can always see the PH video or go to meetings. However, we will not get access to the UNICEF video, produced outside the village. The content in it is not what people normally see so they will like it more."*
>
> P15 (Women focus group session, different district)

Two participants opted to share the UNICEF video, since they wished to augment their social reputation by sharing a high quality video in the prestige dialect. They wanted to project themselves as more knowledgeable and sophisticated in their community. A woman expressed:

> *"I would like to share the UNICEF video with my friends so that they will easily understand it and also because they like to watch videos that are in Hindi."*
>
> P16 (Woman interviewee, different block)

Among the participants who changed their vote, eight opted to share the PH video with their friends and family. Three of them believed that the local dialect would make it easier for their social connections to understand the information. One participant wanted to share information on home remedies. Another participant wanted to show the acting skills of familiar local doctor to her family members. Since the PH video showcased rural women discussing health issues in a public space, a woman wanted her family to realize that she should go out and have discussions with others. Two ASHAs opted the PH video because it featured an enterprising ASHA dispensing her responsibilities. The ASHAs wanted their family to appreciate the importance of their work.

Knowledge Retention

Since both videos had identical key health messages, we conducted a pretest-posttest-retention test control group design to measure the effect of both localization approaches on short-term knowledge retention. To evaluate if videos were effective in increasing participants' knowledge, we treated the pretest score and posttest score for both groups as a within-subjects design intervention with video as the factor with two levels — before watching the video and after watching the video — and score as the dependent variable. We used a paired samples t-test to analyze the result and found a significant difference in the pretest score ($M = 6.65$, $SD = 1.95$) and the posttest score ($M = 9.1$, $SD = 1.89$) for women who saw PH video; $t(19) = -4.71$, $p < 0.001$. We also found a significant difference in the pretest score ($M = 6.4$, $SD = 2.87$) and the posttest score ($M = 10.5$, $SD = 1.88$) of women who saw the UNICEF video; $t(19) = -6.952$, $p < 0.001$. These results suggest that both videos were individually effective in increasing participants' short-term knowledge.

To understand which video is more effective in increasing knowledge, we compared the difference in the pretest score and the posttest score (*i.e.,* gain score) for both groups. We used an independent samples t-test for analysis where video was the factor with two levels — PH video and UNICEF video — and the gain score was the dependent variable. We found a statistical difference in the gain scores for the PH video ($M = 2.45$, $SD = 2.33$) and the UNICEF video ($M = 4.05$, $SD = 2.60$), $t(38) = -2.048$, $p = 0.0475$ ($p < 0.05$). These results suggest that the UNICEF video resulted in higher knowledge gains than the PH video.

DISCUSSION

Our work compares and contrasts two video-based education approaches that prioritize localization along different dimensions, as emphasized in our findings. Almost 74% of all participants preferred the UNICEF video, 78% found the UNICEF video more entertaining, 71% preferred the prestige dialect of Hindi over the local dialect, and 91% preferred endorsements from the local celebrity rather than the Bollywood celebrity. We examine these preferences below, discuss the challenges with local approaches, and present recommendations for localization of video-based HCI4D interventions.

Local is Relative

Local approaches for video production focus on adapting features, including content, actors, characters, language, surroundings, and culture, to a community or region. However, the definition of *local* is nebulous and continually evolving, depending on what it is being compared with. To some participants in our study, *local* meant their village, while to others it meant their block, district, state, and some perceived anything they were familiar with as *local*.

Since a majority of the participants preferred the UNICEF video, we narrowed the definition of *local* to understand the effects of hyperlocality. We asked participants which video they would prefer: the UNICEF video or a hyperlocal video that is shot in their village with familiar people sharing health information in their dialect? Sixty-five participants (49%) preferred the hyperlocal video because they valued the ability to seek clarifications on key health messages anytime, especially when people from their village were part of the video production process. They placed more trust in health information coming from neighbors and wanted to see them in videos. They believed that the hyperlocal video would be a delight to watch, and the production process would provide additional socializing opportunities for women. An ASHA felt that the hyperlocal video would increase her social status in the village, and thus people would take her advice more seriously:

> *"When I share information with people in my village, they don't always listen carefully. But now when they will see me in a video, they will know that ASHAs are doing important work and are featured in the videos to give information. This will increase our motivation."*
>
> P17 (ASHA, different block)

Fifty-one participants (38%) reported that it did not matter to them where the video is produced and what local attributes it has as long as the video is entertaining, easy to follow, uses familiar dialect, and offers useful information. Seventeen participants (13%) stated that the hyperlocal video would still be less appealing than the UNICEF video because it would be impossible for it to match the quality of the UNICEF video. They preferred the UNICEF video because it was divergent from their daily lives. They believed that the excitement of seeing familiar faces from their village in a video would wear off easily. A participant stated:

> *"If familiar faces are there in the video, people might see it a couple of times. However, I think, the excitement to see familiar faces will wear off easily and then all that would matter is the quality and content of video, in which the UNICEF video is a clear winner."*
>
> P18 (MSO, different block)

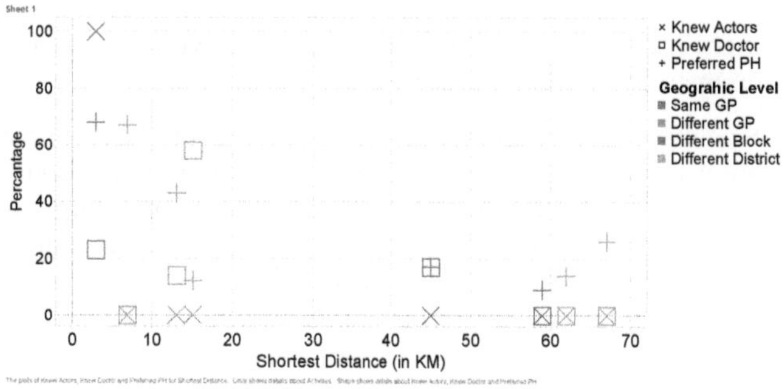

Figure 3. Understanding the effects of localization

To assess the meaning of localization for both videos, we analyzed three attributes of the PH video — video preference, participants who knew any local actor, and participants who knew the local doctor — across all geographic levels where we conducted our activities. Figure 3 plots the attributes spatially based on the shortest distance (in Kilometers) of study locations from the village where the PH video was locally produced. The percentage of participants who preferred the PH video and participants who could recognize an actor dropped drastically as we moved farther away from the *Gram Panchayat* (GP) where the PH video was produced. Similarly, the percentage of people who knew the local doctor also dropped as we moved away from the block where the PH video was produced. This indicates that the effect of localization is the most within the radius of a GP.

We also found qualitative evidence for the scope of locality to be defined as a GP. Seven staff members and three ASHAs concurred that hyperlocal videos are very popular even among other villages in the vicinity, since people often know others in their GP through interactions in local elections and social functions. They believed that once a video crosses the boundary of a GP, it doesn't matter where it is made, provided people can understand the language. We call on the analogy of wedding videos here – while these are valuable for those in the wedding party, the *local* nature loses its value beyond this group. We acknowledge that this definition of local may only be relevant in the Indian context, but encourage researchers working in alternate geographies to assess for themselves what *local* means, as they embark on projects that uses video-based education.

Challenges with Local Approaches

We found wide disparity in the resources available to both projects. Several PH staff members complained about the lack of resources. They found it challenging to get local people to act and get approval from their family. They reported that community members had no prior training and limited time for rehearsals. Though initially rural residents are keen to act, their enthusiasm wanes as the shoot proceeds. The staff members expressed interest in experimenting with monetary incentives, make-up, and finer costumes to improve the production quality and motivation of local actors rather than relying on their enthusiasm or *pro bono* actions. They believed that access to more resources will allow them to produce videos of quality comparable to the UNICEF video.

Scalability is an important consideration when the resources are scarce. The hyperlocal approach requires tremendously more resources to build and maintain grassroots setup, and to replicate video production efforts in multiple geographic locations. Therefore, it is important for local approaches to not only improve their production aesthetics, but also maintain the balance between scalability and localization.

Implications for Community Health Video Design

Our study has several implications for video production approaches seeking to provide community health in rural settings. We found that presentation style and content, driven by the localization, plays an important role in increasing the appeal of health videos. In addition to providing standard medical advice, the videos could feature home remedies and demonstrations. To yield higher information absorption, a ten-minute video should include no more than three key health messages.

Several participants did not want only information akin to the PH video or entertainment akin to a television soap opera. They wanted infotainment — a mix of information and entertainment — which the UNICEF video offered. Since local approaches may have limited production skills, training workshops for local scriptwriters could be organized by street theater artists to improve storytelling skills. The screenplay could be made more engaging by seeking feedback from community members. Our study revealed that people preferred videos that have high production aesthetics. Though the constrained availability of high quality video production equipment and skilled talent might make it difficult for local approaches to improve technical production quality, they could provide monetary compensation, certificates and finer costumes to motivate people from villages to act well. We encourage researchers to examine intrinsic and extrinsic motivations that could improve participation of rural residents in community-led video education interventions.

We observed that PH videos feature people who are generally unknown outside their village and UNICEF videos feature television actors and Bollywood celebrities. Several participants highlighted the importance of featuring local celebrities — local people who are approachable, popular in nearby villages, and with whom people can associate — rather than either local people less known outside their village or mainstream celebrities. For future video production employing local approaches, we suggest identifying local celebrities to act in these videos to make the videos more appealing across several villages. Though endorsements by Bollywood actors certainly attract a larger audience, participants exhibited a deep trust in local celebrities and strongly preferred endorsements from a medical practitioner. Thus, we recommend that local doctors and/or nurses must be included in future videos. We also encourage researchers to examine how the popularity of local and global celebrities could be leveraged together to increase the appeal and adoption of health practices.

Hindi is spoken by more than 422 million people in India. However, this includes tens of millions of people who consider their language to be a dialect of Hindi. The region of our study speaks Awadhi (a local Hindi dialect) that has an estimated 35 million speakers throughout India. Even for Awadhi, there are variations in the dialect within blocks and districts, making it difficult to truly localize the dialect without seriously sacrificing scalability. We found Awadhi to be more inclusive of people who are old and/or less literate. However, several participants preferred Hindi because of its association with higher social status, knowledge and education. The use of local dialect may reap more benefits when it is significantly different from the mainstream dialect. For future video productions, we recommend a careful assessment of whether using the local dialect would truly be beneficial, given the value attached to the prestige dialect by many among the target population.

LIMITATIONS OF OUR WORK

We were able to examine various elements of localization but for the role played by community engagement in both cases. It is likely that PH has greater enrollment among the rural residents because it is a project several in the community have participated. In selecting participants who were unfamiliar with PH, we might have unintentionally introduced bias, for it is likely that those familiar with PH's history would feel a greater sense of ownership towards PH, which is not a factor we assessed. Additionally, identifying equivalent videos for our study was a non-trivial exercise. We were constrained to carefully select existing videos from PH and UNICEF repositories that focused on the same health topic and had identical key messages. We also needed to avoid videos on topics that the community was overly familiar with or sensitive topics. Our results are therefore based on a comparative analysis of two videos. Future work could bring additional localization approaches to the fray.

CONCLUSION

For resource-constrained global development organizations that leverage video-based learning, our study provides insights regarding the costs and benefits of diverse aspects of localization approaches for imparting knowledge. By examining audience response to two videos targeting identical population groups but utilizing disparate approaches to localization, we were able to analyze receptivity to a host of video-making decisions, including choice of settings, actors, language, pedagogical tools, and more, also highlighting the difference in resultant learning gains. We believe that the enriched understanding our study provides will aid the choices that future approaches make, modulo budget constraints.

Our qualitative findings indicated that most of our rural Indian participants preferred high production quality, a well-formed storyline, the use of the prestige dialect, pedagogical techniques, ability to share content, and a high infotainment quotient. Those who liked PH's localization approach appreciated the presence of a local trusted authority (the doctor), information on home remedies, and characters and set-up they could relate to. Our quantitative results indicated that the UNICEF video led to statistically significant knowledge gain among participants.

REFERENCES

1. 2011. Poverty & Equity Data I India I The World Bank. (2011). http://povertydata.worldbank.org/poverty/country/IND.
2. 2011. State of Literacy. (2011). http://censusindia.gov.in/2011-prov-results/data_files/india/Final_PPT_2011_chapter6.pdf.
3. 2015a. *Internet in India 2015*. Technical Report. Internet and Mobile Association of India and IMRB International.
4. 2015. IVRS âĂŞ Daily Monitoring System of Mid-Day Meal Scheme. (2015). http://www.upmdm.in/.
5. 2015. mDiabetes. (2015). http://arogyaworld.org/mdiabetes/.
6. 2015b. Mobile Kunji Usage and Engagement Study. (2015). http://www.rethink1000days.org/publication/.
7. 2016. UNICEF: Ammaji Kehti Hain. (2016). http://www.healthphone.org/ammaji/index.html.
8. Nicola J Bidwell, Thomas Reitmaier, Gary Marsden, and Susan Hansen. 2010. Designing with mobile digital storytelling in rural Africa. In *Proceedings of CHI*.
9. V. Braun, V. Clarke, V. Braun, and V. Clarke. 2006. Using Thematic Analysis in Psychology. *Qualitative Research in Psychology* 3, 2 (2006), 77–101. http://dx.doi.org/10.1191/1478088706qp063oa
10. Sebastien Cuendet, Indrani Medhi, Kalila Bali, and Edward Cutrell. 2013. VideoKheti: Making video content accessible to low-literate and novice users. In *Proceedings of CHI*.
11. Nicola Dell and Neha Kumar. 2016. The Ins and Outs of HCI for Development. In *Proceedings of CHI*.
12. Nicola Dell, Vidya Vaidyanathan, Indrani Medhi, Edward Cutrell, and William Thies. 2012. "Yours is Better!": Participant Response Bias in HCI. In *Proceedings of CHI*.
13. Brian Derenzi, Gaetano Borriello, Jonathan Jackson, Vikram S. Kumar, Tapan S. Parikh, Pushwaz Virk, and Neal Lesh. 2011. Mobile phone tools for field-based health care workers in low-income countries. *The Mount Sinai Journal of Medicine, New York* 78, 3 (2011), 406–418.
14. Brian DeRenzi, Neal Lesh, and T Parikh. 2008. E-IMCI: Improving pediatric health care in low-income countries. In *Proceedings of CHI*.
15. Paul Dourish and Scott D. Mainwaring. 2012. Ubicomp's Colonial Impulse. In *Proceedings of Ubicomp*.
16. Brittany Fiore-Silfvast, Carl Hartung, Kirti Iyengar, Sharad Iyengar, Kiersten Israel-Ballard, Noah Perin, and Richard Anderson. 2013. Mobile Video for Patient Education: The Midwives' Perspective. In *Proceedings of DEV*.
17. David M Frohlich, Dorothy Rachovides, Kiriaki Riga, Ramnath Bhat, Maxine Frank, Eran Edirisinghe, Dhammike Wickramanayaka, Matt Jones, and Will Harwood. 2009. StoryBank: mobile digital storytelling in a development context. In *Proceedings of CHI*.
18. Rikin Gandhi, Rajesh Veeraraghavan, Kentaro Toyama, and Vanaja Ramprasad. 2009. Digital Green: Participatory Video and Mediated Instruction for Agricultural Extension. *ITID* 5, 1 (2009).
19. Mohamed Gulaid and Aditya Vashistha. 2013. Ila Dhageyso : An Interactive Voice Forum to Foster Transparent Governance in Somaliland. In *Proceedings of ICTD*.
20. Kurtis Heimerl, Janani Vasudev, Kelly G. Buchanan, Tapan Parikh, and Eric Brewer. 2010. Metamouse: Improving Multi-user Sharing of Existing Educational Applications. In *Proceedings of ICTD*.
21. Anirudha Joshi, Mandar Rane, Debjani Roy, Nagraj Emmadi, Padma Srinivasan, N. Kumarasamy, Sanjay Pujari, Davidson Solomon, Rashmi Rodrigues, D.G. Saple, Kamalika Sen, Els Veldeman, and Romain Rutten. 2014. Supporting Treatment of People Living with HIV / AIDS in Resource Limited Settings with IVRs. In *Proceedings of CHI*.
22. Neha Kumar and Richard J. Anderson. 2015. Mobile Phones for Maternal Health in Rural India. In *Proceedings of CHI*.
23. Neha Kumar, Trevor Perrier, Michelle Desmond, Kiersten Israel-Ballard, Vikrant Kumar, Sudip Mahapatra, Anil Mishra, Shreya Agarwal, Rikin Gandhi, Pallavi Lal, and Richard Anderson. 2015. Projecting Health: Community-led Video Education for Maternal Health. In *Proceedings of ICTD*.
24. Ilda Ladeira and Edward Cutrell. 2010. Teaching with Storytelling: An Investigation of Narrative Videos for Skills Training. In *Proceedings of ICTD*.
25. Indrani Medhi and Kentaro Toyama. 2007. Full-context videos for first-time, non-literate PC users. In *Proceedings of ICTD*.
26. Indrani Medhi-Thies, Pedro Ferreira, Nakull Gupta, Jacki O'Neill, and Edward Cutrell. 2015. KrishiPustak: A Social Networking System for Low-Literate Farmers. In *Proceedings of CSCW*.
27. Mary Meeker. 2015. *2015 Internet Trends*. Technical Report. KPCB. http://www.kpcb.com/blog/2015-internet-trends
28. Maletsabisa Molapo and Gary Marsden. 2013. Software Support for Creating Digital Health Training Materials in the Field. In *Proceedings of ICTD*.
29. Preeti Mudliar, Jonathan Donner, and William Thies. 2012. Emergent Practices Around CGNet Swara, A Voice Forum for Citizen Journalism in Rural India. In *Proceedings of ICTD*.

30. Neil Patel, Kapil Shah, Krishna Savani, Scott R. Klemmer, Paresh Dave, and Tapan S. Parikh. 2012. Power to the Peers: Authority of Source Effects for a Voice-based Agricultural Information Service in Rural India. In *Proceedings of ICTD*.
31. Trevor Perrier, Nicola Dell, Brian DeRenzi, Richard Anderson, John Kinuthia, Jennifer Unger, and Grace John-Stewart. 2015. Engaging Pregnant Women in Kenya with a Hybrid Computer-Human SMS Communication System. In *Proceedings of CHI*.
32. Divya Ramachandran, John Canny, Prabhu Dutta Das, and Edward Cutrell. 2010. Mobile-izing health workers in rural India. In *Proceedings of CHI*.
33. Thomas Reitmaier, Nicola J Bidwell, and Gary Marsden. 2010. Field testing mobile digital storytelling software in rural Kenya. In *Proceedings of the 12th International Conference on Human Computer Interaction with Mobile Devices and Services*.
34. Piya Sorcar. 2009. *Teaching taboo topics without talking about them: An epistemic study of a new approach to HIV /AIDS prevention education in India*. Ph.D. Dissertation. Stanford University.
35. Aditya Vashistha, Edward Cutrell, Gaetano Borriello, and William Thies. 2015. Sangeet Swara: A Community-Moderated Voice Forum in Rural India. In *Proceedings of CHI*.
36. Aditya Vashistha, Neha Kumar, Anil Mishra, and Richard Anderson. 2016. Mobile Video Dissemination for Community Health. In *Proceedings of ICTD*.
37. Susan Wyche, Charles Steinfield, Tian Cai, Nightingale Simiyu, and Martha E. Othieno. 2016. Reflecting on Video: Exploring the Efficacy of Video for Teaching Device Literacy in Rural Kenya. In *Proceedings of ICTD*.

In Harmony: Making a Wearable Musical Instrument as a Case Study of using Boundary Objects in an Interdisciplinary Collaborative Design Process

Clint Zeagler
clintzeagler@gatech.edu

Maribeth Gandy
maribeth.gandy@imtc.gatech.edu

Scott Gilliland
scott.gilliland@gatech.edu

Delton Moore
delsomo@gmail.com

Rocco Centrella
roccocentrella@gmail.com

Brandon Montgomery
montgomery.bradon@gmail.com

ABSTRACT
Working on a wearable technology interdisciplinary project team can be challenging because of a lack of shared understanding between different fields, and a lack of ability in cross-disciplinary communication. We describe an interdisciplinary collaborative design process used for creating a wearable musical instrument with a musician. Our diverse team used drawing and example artifacts/toolkits to overcome communication and gaps in knowledge. We view this process in the frame of Susan Leigh Star's description of a boundary object, and against a similar process used in another musical / computer science collaboration with the group Duran Duran.

Author Keywords
Design Process; Musical Garment; E-Textile Interface; Boundary Objects

ACM Classification Keywords
H.5.m. Information interfaces and presentation (e.g., HCI): Miscellaneous.

Figure 1: Rhó interacting with the 'Hood' a musical garment developed through interdisciplinary collaboration.

DIS 2017, June 10 - 14, 2017, Edinburgh, United Kingdom

ACM 978-1-4503-4922-2/17/06…$15.00
DOI: http://dx.doi.org/10.1145/3064663.3064678

INTRODUCTION
This short case study explores the deliberate use of a "boundary object" as a prescriptive device for aiding interdisciplinary collaborative design. Many expected themes and observations about interdisciplinary design and group work also emerge, however our focus here is on the pilot investigation of using the framework of boundary objects within the context of design process.

Over the course of one week an Italian musician named Rhó, an architect, a computer scientist, a fashion designer, an engineer, and a digital media expert came together to create one wearable musical instrument "the Hood". There were communication and ideation challenges to overcome in a team with such diverse skill sets. Wearable technology is a unique working space, allowing for, and often requiring diverse participants who may have fundamental differences in their formal training. A fashion designer has a different thought process, different product goals, and even a different vocabulary than a computer scientist. A musician has a very creative process and his/her time scale for creation might diverge from all other design fields. On top of disciplinary differences there are also cultural (American and Italian) variances in process, which this multicultural team also highlights. These conflicts must be reconciled for true collaboration to take hold. We cannot expect everyone on the team to learn the skills of the other team members, especially over such a short time frame. This paper describes the use of drawing and artifacts framed as disciplinary boundary objects [41] allowing for discussion and shared understanding, leading to a productive creative team process.

"This is an analytic concept of those scientific objects which inhabit several intersecting social worlds and satisfy the informational requirements of each of them. Boundary objects are objects which are both plastic enough to adapt to local needs and the constraints of the several parties employing them, yet robust enough to maintain a common identity across sites" [41]

RELATED WORK
Much of the value of this work comes in the framing of how an interdisciplinary team might view their creative

process. However we also need to know about the specific interdisciplinary context within which the team is working.

Work Related to Wearable Technology and Musical Instrument Interfaces

While we are interested here in discussing interdisciplinary teams and the unique opportunities boundary objects afford the design process for wearable technology, it is important to note that there have been numerous projects that look at wearable technology for musical instruments. Serafin, Mitchel, and Heap describe the evolution of a very successful glove instrument used by Imogen Heap in her performances and music creation [31, 40]. An interest in interactive textiles can also be seen in projects such as the music textile seen on talk2myshirt.com and the devices which stem from the Musical interaction and e-textile workshop developed on the RHYME platform [32, 33]. Many glove-based wearable systems are also described in the archive of NIME New Interfaces for Musical Expression [14, 21]. There has also been wearable technology research into how gloves may help teach musical abilities. Markow and Huang created a set of gloves with vibration motors which they found help participants learn piano through passive haptic learning [22, 29].

Within the larger community of wearable technology and specifically electronic textile applications much work has been done over the years. It was 1997 when Post and Orth described the use of interactive textiles and e-broidery [36, 37]. Jayaraman and colleagues also worked on incorporating technology with fabric to produce their "wearable motherboard" smart t-shirt [20, 28]. Zeagler and colleagues also researched the use of such embroideries and textile techniques for on-body interfaces, including material and wash-ability studies [18, 24, 25, 43–45]. Buechley has focused much of her e-textile work on the democratization of technology within education, and using wearable tech as a way to make inroads with typically non-tech-enthusiast communities [7]. Buechley's work has lead to the very popular Lilypad Arduino microcontroller, making designing and working on wearable technology easier and more inviting [27].

Dunne and Profita look into the social acceptability of textile based on-body interactions [12, 13, 38], which could be important to designers when thinking about placing on-body interfaces. Within the context of a performance garment the social acceptability of body touch, and presentation of self within a social group become very important aspects of design. Goffman would say that it is the presentation of ourselves that gives others cues as to how to interact with us [19]. He goes on to explain that most people take this inferential information as a fact of whom one is and act accordingly. "The others find, then, that the individual has informed them as to what is and as to what they *ought* to see as the 'is'"[19]. Fashion designers on the team will find this expression of self at the heart of their discipline, where as an engineer might not.

Work Related to Interdisciplinary Design Process

Martin et al. speak to both the need for interdisciplinary teams while working on wearable technology projects and the nature of the current educational system producing engineers and designers. *"Practitioners in these fields gain their interdisciplinary team experience by trial-and-error and sheer luck, if at all. The deeply disciplinary nature of universities does not prepare students for working on the types of design teams that are required for successful wearable computing systems."*[30].

When asked "Why work on performance led research in the wild" Benford et. al give three reasons [4]. First among them is that *Artists' uses of emerging technologies are often highly innovative and unusual, stretching the technology in unforeseen ways, highlighting new design values and approaches that are sometimes contrary to received wisdom in HCI (e.g., ambiguity or discomfort as we discuss later), and opening up new areas of application* [4]. The use of boundary objects hopefully magnifies the creative nature of ambiguity through their flexible and plastic nature.

Many could see this wearable musical device case study as a participatory design workshop. Placing the artists in the role of participator, and the computer scientist in the role of facilitator. Much valid and celebrated work has been completed under this framework. Disalvo eloquently states "*In this light, design, inclusive of both the process of making artifacts and the artifacts made, can be considered a discursive activity and participatory design can be cast as using design to enable people to take part in public discourse in new or more effective ways.*" [11]. We could also view our project as a participatory corporative prototyping case study. "*Prototyping: the construction of the future through the preliminary and iterative design of potential systems enabling concrete experience and modification by prospective users.*" [6, 10]. Rhinow et al. describe a prototype as a way to converge thinking stating that "the prototype as a model helps to visualize the focus of exploration" [39]. These are certainly well founded ways of framing our work. However, the spirit of our collaboration wasn't to enable (technological advancement, or to give agency to the artist in directorial notion), but to truly work together in an interdisciplinary collaboration. All of us learning and acting on and with technology. All of us adding to the process by being creative and expressive. Pobiner might understand our meaning of this inclusive design process when he argues "*Design in many cases comes from intuition, which is not a quantitative factor and there is often no (or little) rationale that can be associated with why something is the way it is, or how one derived a specific idea. Such an experiential model may be flawed in its construct but may work better in the real world – mostly because our existences are, thus far, infinitely more complex than current models for human interaction provide. Perhaps it is time to, once again, revise the notion of 'Design' in order to incorporate other disciplines that encounter and apply its values."* [35]. Baker and Gandy discuss this form of inclusive participatory design in their work on incorporating policy within the methodology of the design process. By thinking about how design will affect the community, and thus policy, at the onset and throughout the design process. Baker poses that innovative interdisciplinary teams begin design 'use case ideation and visualization' with the broader community in mind, and this also helps the diverse teams communicate across disciplines more effectively [2, 16]. Working through the guidelines of this proposed collaborative policy/design framework could in itself be seen as a boundary object bringing together the methodology of different disciplines, and creating a way for them to work together more effectively.

One example project that seems to exemplify the use of what could be described as a boundary object for design collaboration is Gandy's DART. Gandy explains the development and use of an augmented reality (AR) toolkit (DART) for designers new to the medium [17]. Many of the choices made for DART came from an effort to allow easy entry to designers and performers, such as working on top of a well-known platform for media (at the time Macromedia Director). DART's success in part shows the importance of toolkits speaking to different and new communities in a local way, while holding onto a common identity for all communities. In this way a toolkit can act as a boundary object, allowing for artists to work directly on design iterations with technologists. DART was in part informed by work Gandy did previously with a team building AR experiences for Duran Duran (a well known rock band) performances, this was a collaborative process with many different stakeholders including members of the band. Based on the comments from the Duran Duran interviewees it was clear that a significant challenge in creating AR applications with diverse teams is the need to *convey ideas and technical constraints to other contributors so that they may participate effectively*. In working with Duran Duran there was a critical initial step, which was helping the non-technical collaborators to fully understand the affordances and technical constraints of AR. It was important to build their enthusiasm for the project and to get to the point where they could actively contribute to the design and development process. As a member of the Duran Duran team (project manager) described, the system was improved in an iterative process (taking place over several live performances) due to the contributions of the other stakeholders. An authoring ecosystem for this type of project must accelerate and improve this process. Communication and collaboration among a diverse team is challenging, yet it is imperative that everyone be able to contribute to early ideation. However, for non-technology focused collaborators to be able to contribute effectively they must have a solid grasp of the *affordances and constraints* of augmented reality. For example, in the Duran Duran project they urged the band members to test the boundaries of marker tracking with technology prototypes so as to set realistic expectations and to inform their brainstorming activities. So authoring ecosystems that either convey this information and/or guide the team towards appropriate design choices are ideal. [15]

In relation to working on wearable technology in interdisciplinary teams Cochran and Zeagler described the use of a LED calibration system as a boundary object for teamwork. *"Such interdisciplinary artifacts can act as boundary objects and the process of making these tools can create a shared meaning that facilitates product development."* [9]. Gilliland and Zeagler created an interdisciplinary e-textile toolkit of sorts in developing the E-Textile Interface Swatch Book [18]. Zeagler went on to use the ESwatchBook to run a series of workshops with teams of fashion designers and computer scientist [34, 42], and while he did not describe the ESwatchBook as a boundary object at the time it is clear that it was used as such an artifact.

HOOD DESIGN PROCESS

Day one – Understanding and Ideation

Using a copy of Gilliland et al's ESwatchBook [18] we began the collaboration by allowing the musician and architect to explore the possibilities of sensing with fabric. The ESwatchBook also be came a launch point for a discussion about what was possible using this sensing technique. Here just as with Gandy's work with Duran Duran, the artists were able to quickly figure out the *affordances and constraints* of the e-textile interface medium. The ESwatchBook allowed each of the team members to build a *shared understanding* of how the technology worked, including a platform to create ideas about textile based interactions. It was less effective in helping provide inspiration for the aesthetic design of the garment.

Figure 2: Gilliland et al's ESwatchBook [18] **became a boundary object** [26, 41]**, creating shared understanding.**

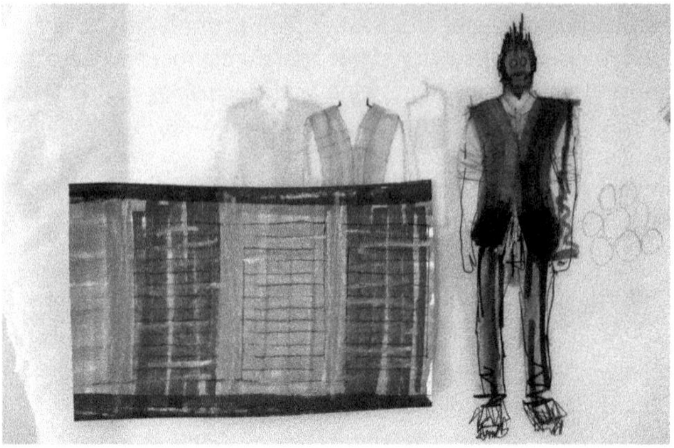

Figure 3: Drawings by the fashion designer and architect on the team investigating textile texture, color, and mood.

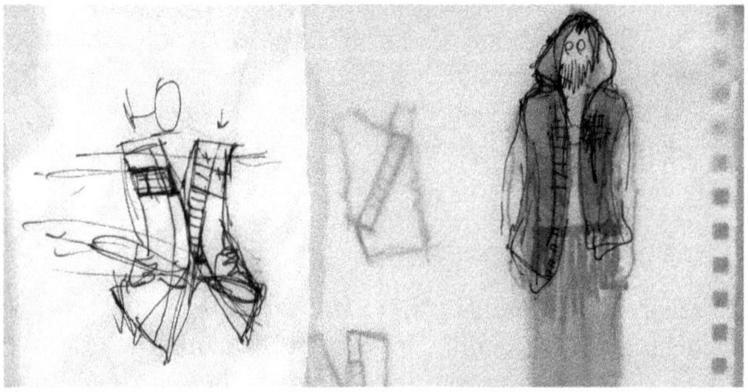

Figure 4: Drawings by the fashion designer exploring silhouette and interactive textile placement.

Just as Zeagler found in his E-textile workshops, drawing became a medium through which designers and non-designers could explain and communicate. *Drawings like these were mandatory to overcome points at which the technical requirements of practitioners from one domain were not clear to those from another* [42]. The act of drawing and specifically sketching actively together as a team can be viewed as creating a boundary object together. A schematic, or aesthetic plan created together can have the shared meaning and plasticity needed for true collaboration to take hold. It also gives the group some since of shared timescale (for instance an electrical schematic is just simple lines and shapes, but it might take some thought while sketching, thus adding time to a simple drawing, and therefore imparting weight or importance beyond the perceived simplicity of the schematic). The Architect on the team was familiar with the musician's self-presentation [19], style and music. While the musician focused on how he would play the garment, the CS and HCI experts were drawing to explain to the fashion designer how circuits might work and needed to be connected. The fashion designer was also working in tandem with the architect and musician to pick fabric and develop the touch sensitive textile's appearance (Figures 3&4). The musician wanted the ability to don and doff the garment with ease, so a vest like silhouette was chosen. The musician, architect, and fashion designer, liked the dramatic element of adding a hood, as the architect put it "story telling through dress", a musical vestment of sorts, "taking the formalism of the past and moving it to the present". The designers were also shown research about the social acceptability of male on-body interaction [38] so they could plan the best place on the body for the touch sensitive textile.

Day two & three – Prototyping and Iteration

In research through design, researchers make prototypes, products, and models to codify their own understanding of a particular situation and to provide a concrete framing of the problem and a description of a proposed [46]. In prototyping the touch sensitive textile, and LEDs the team became excited to see the signals show up on the computer screen, even if they were not yet making music. This explorative iterative process allowed the team to begin to understand the scope, abilities, and timescales of the incongruent disciplines involved. The garment muslin was also created and fitted to Rhó, and the team liked the shape.

Day four & five – Construction and Troubleshooting

Initially, the technologist on the team did not know how the system would be connected to the software Rhó was accustomed to working with for live performances. They started with the assumption that the hardware could provide access to the sensor input via HID joystick, and that Rhó's software could handle it accept these inputs. We quickly discovered that Rho's software was designed for MIDI input only, and we sought out a laptop-side software to help convert our joystick input to MIDI.

Rhó believed that the engineers, computer scientists and HCI professionals would know how to hook the garment up to his software easily. On the contrary the engineers thought Rhó (who specializes in musical composing using computer programs) would be able to take what they gave him and make it connect. Each group did not quite understand the scope of the others knowledge, this is a reoccurring theme in interdisciplinary work. Team members often had a hard time understanding what the others knew, and more specifically in estimating the amount of time tasks outside their personal disciplines would take. The digital media designer was instrumental in helping bridge this gap in knowledge when it came to connecting the finished garment to Rhó's software.

Description of Use:

The 'Hood' is played by touching the interactive textile portion of the garment that is separated into six touch pads. The top touch pad cycles through three different states allowing for the bottom five touch pads to act as 15 selection points. These touch pads act as a MIDI controller turning on and off preprogramed sounds in a program called Abelton Live [1]. The distance sensor acts as a volume control for each selection, saving the volume of the sound/beat at release. To control the volume the wearer pulls his hand towards or away from his chest at the location of the sensor.

Day five & six –Playing and Composing

After the garment was working Rhó took the 'Hood' and learned to play. He also used the garment to create new music for the concert. During the process it was evident to the team that Rhó was very interested in the concept of wearable technology and the tactile nature of interacting with fabric textures. However, he and the architect on the team were hunting for a reason, some authentic need, for the instrument to be on the body instead of on sitting on a stand like a keyboard. When Rhó had the prototype to use he found that he could make grand gestures to activate the touch surfaces. Because the touch activated areas made selection on release, Rhó decided to use release from his chest as a theatrical aspect to accentuate musical additions selected through the Hood.

Figure 5: Rhó in concert using the 'Hood'

Day seven - Concert

Rhó used the 'Hood' in concert for 100 people. There was only one mishap right before he began his set. He left the stage to hug a friend, breaking his Bluetooth connection. Rhó states "I forgot". The team sees this as a testament to the clothing like nature of the 'Hood'. Rhó would have set down a guitar before leaving the stage, but as he was wearing the instrument he forgot about its digitally connected characteristics. Benford explains another reason why doing performance led research in the wild is useful, in that "*the public deployment of artworks offers a test-bed for putting emerging technologies into the hands of users in a "realistic" situation, meaning a situation in which the technology needs to be made to work and is treated in some sense a professional product - this is the "in the wild" aspect of the approach*"[4]. Here the pressure of performance and the public nature of the presentation heightens the "real" or "in the wild" nature of HCI research, the stakes are higher when everyone is watching.

PERFORMANCE PROTOTYPE CONSTRUCTION

The hardware consists of a microcontroller to drive the system, a Bluetooth module to communicate with a laptop. On the front of the garment, 'smart LEDs' were included for visual feedback, sewn-in wiring was used to make touch points for discrete input, while a proximity sensor was included for continuous input. The entire system runs from a rechargeable lithium-ion battery, charged via USB.

Figure 6: Interactive touch sensitive textile.

Thin un-insulated wire is used to create interlacing touch points much like the pattern for selection points chosen in Komor et al.'s "is it gropable" study [24] only at a much larger scale. The wire was chosen over conductive thread used in the ESwatchBook because the 'Hood' needs to be made more robust for performance. Conductive thread used in the ESwatchBook has proven to not stand up to repeated use and cleaning as of yet [43]. The wire was hand stitched onto yarn and fabric and then sewn down with a domestic sewing machine.

Enameled magnet wire was chosen for leads to the touch points due to its size and malleability as compared to other insulated wiring, thus interfering less with the drape of the garment figures 7 & 8. The leads were soldered to a connector so that the micro controller and battery could be removed easily from the garment. Because we decided to incorporate LED display of interaction this means this performance prototype cannot be washed or submerged in water. The Hood is to be worn on the outermost layer only during performance so as a team we were not too concerned with durability for cleaning, but again were more concerned with durability for performance.

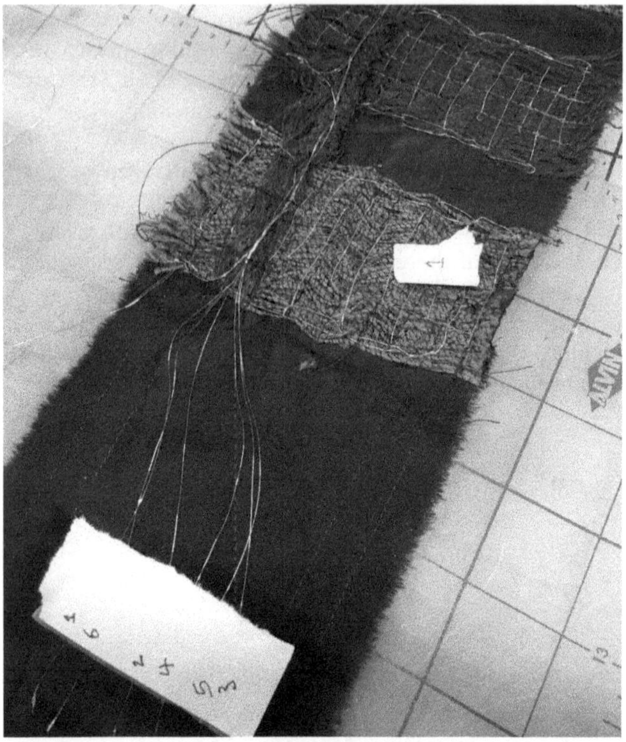

Figure 7: Incorporating the conductive touch points and connecting the enameled lead wires.

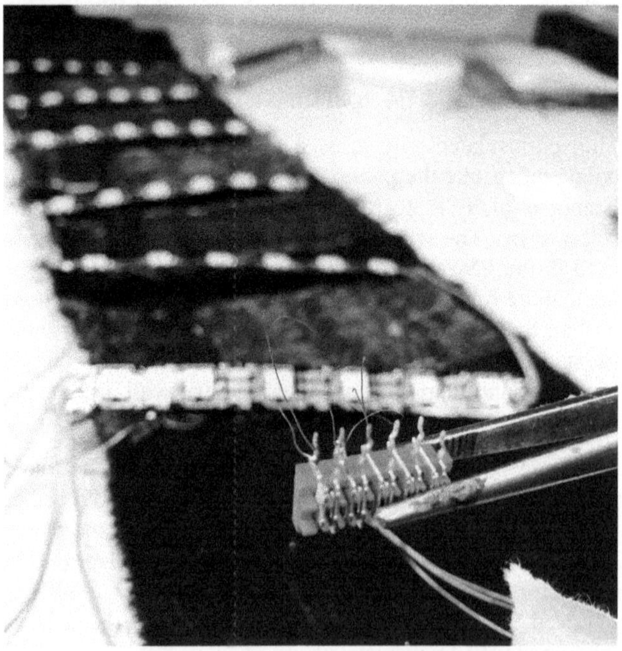

Figure 8: wiring the conductive elements to the connector used to attach the microcontroller.

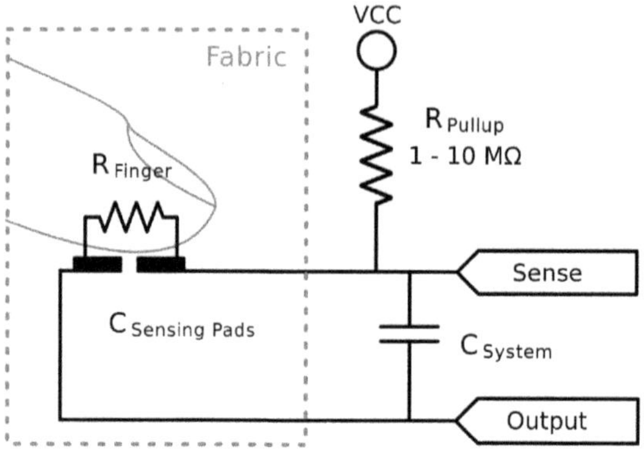

Figure 9. Resistive-capacitive technique used for all other touch sensitive swatches. ***From*** [18]

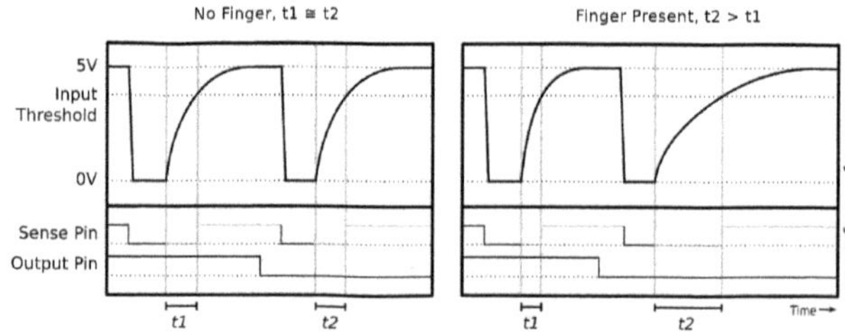

Figure 10. When the fingertip is not present, t1 = t2 (left). Otherwise, t2 > t1 (right). ***From*** [18]

The touch points utilized hybrid capacitive sensing, as described by Gilliland for the ESwatchBook [18]. For a simple capacitive sensor, one general-purpose input/output (GPIO) pin is needed on a microcontroller, which we will call the 'sense' pin. We connect this pin through a high resistance to the system's power supply (labeled as Rpullup), and begin by driving the pin to GND using the microcontroller. This fully discharges the capacitor formed between the pin and the GND of the system. We then switch the pin to input mode, and continuously sample it until it reads 'high'. As the resistor charges the line to higher and higher voltages, the pin eventually reads as a digital 'high', with the time determined by the capacitance of the line.

To make this into a hybrid resistive-capacitive sensor, we use a second GPIO pin, labeled as 'output' in figure 9. We run the sense pin and the output pin out to pads in the fabric such that a user's fingertip can contact both at the same time. When a fingertip is present, it behaves as a very high resistance between the two pins, labeled as Rfinger. When we drive the output pin high, this acts like a second Rpullup, causing the capacitance charge time (t1) to be slightly faster. When we drive the output pin low, this acts against Rpullup, causing the capacitance charge time (t2) to be slightly slower. By taking two capacitance readings, one with the output high and one with the output low, we can take the delta between the two times and determine if there is a finger contacting both pads.

The main advantage of this sensing technique is that it can be done with any embedded processor with GPIO pins. It also allows for many connections using relatively few GPIO pins, as multiple sense and output lines can be connected in a matrix.

The proximity sensor was an ST VL6180X, a time-of-flight IR distance sensor. The VL6180X was chosen for its ability to measure distance to an object up to 100 mm away, with accuracies of <5mm. Also ambient lighting and the reflecting object's color/tone do not overly affect this proximity sensor. This means that we could get a reliable and accurate measurement of the distance that Rho's hand was held from his chest, without concern for the dynamic environment.

A custom ARM Cortex microcontroller development board is used running the ChibiOS real-time OS. That board also contains a Laird BTM441 bluetooth module, chosen to provide the flexibility of several Bluetooth profiles. While initially used as a Bluetooth Serial Port Profile (SPP) device, we ended up using the BTM441 as a Bluetooth Huan Input Device (HID) device with a custom HID descriptor. This allowed the device to appear to any computer as a joystick with 'buttons' representing the touch points, and linear axes corresponding to the proximity sensor.

We also implemented a stateful interface on the device: the top touch point was used to cycle through three 'sets', allowing to five remaining touch points and the proximity sensor to show up as 15 buttons and three sliders. This also lined us up for using the color LEDs to indicate the state to Rho while he was using them, although we did not get the LEDs completely working in time for the live performance.

OUTCOMES AND DISCUSSION

The HCI expert on the Hood project noted that "People like me are not going to invent the future of this medium, we need all of the creative people from different domains and expertise."

On looking back over the process Rhó states: "*My time on the project was exciting and inspiring, but also hard. It stressed me in a way, when I got here I did not know how to deal with the guys (engineers / computer scientist), I thought they were really talented people, so I had to prepare myself to learn. When I met them, I had to deal with a new language, new stories, with a new environment, which is not a usual one for a musician. It's not only about using one software or another, but it's how to translate a process, something artistic, to people who come from technology, and how to transform a technology process in to music.*"

Boundary Objects used in the Creative Design Process. Star's original description of boundary objects [41], and many subsequent use cases focus around interdisciplinary work, but not necessarily design work. Carlile [8], Barrett and Oborn [3] enumerate how to view boundary object in use. Carlile makes a clear point valid to our work. "*First, knowledge in new product development is localized around particular problems faced in a given practice. The effective development of knowledge in organizations demands that individuals specialize or localize around different problems. To say localized does not mean that knowledge is limited to only one situation or location; rather, knowledge can be quite similar across practices if it is localized around a similar set of problems; knowledge is local in character, not global.*" [8] But in his description of product he talks more of engineering, and Barrett and Oborn are focused on software development teams. This type of teamwork might need cross-cultural and interdisciplinary collaboration, but are very different from the creative design process of disciplines closer to the arts. Bergman, Lyytinen, and Mark do describe the use of boundary objects within design. *Through a synthesis of design they formulate four essential features viable for design boundary objects. First is the capability for common representation* [5]. We also found this to be true, especially within the context of drawing to create boundary objects. Drawing can also exhibit the second and third of Bergman's features *the capability to transform design knowledge and the capability to mobilize for action* [5]. Drawing acts as means to plan and exchange knowledge after a shared meaning is developed. *The capability to legitimize design knowledge* [5] might arrive from the combined acceptance of a design schematically drawn, which through an iterative drawing process now contains understandable elements from all disciplines collaborating.

We agree with Johansson et al. "*In a collaborative design session bringing together a diverse group of professionals, each with their own practices of framing and representing their respective design games, it is not obvious how such a conversation can become a collaborative endeavor, and the alternation between participation and reification has to be taken into account.*" [23]. Johansson also advocates for the use of design materials "so rich in content" that they act as a boundary object. In our work here we hoped to show the use of the ESwatchBook as an effective boundary object, but it is important to note that the ESwatchBook itself was insufficient and drawing methods were also needed to bridge this gap between disciplines.

One substantial characteristic of boundary objects, which we believe make them effective tools in collaborative interdisciplinary design of artistic creative outcomes, is their plasticity in nature. Just as Benford et al. explained that the ambiguity and discomfort between HCI researchers and artists can act as a proving ground and springboard for innovation [4] . The plastic and flexibility in shared meaning of boundary objects used in bridging knowledge between artists/designers and HCI/engineers can create wonderfully opportunistic misunderstandings. When designing a product in terms of an aircraft component, this type of misunderstanding could be disastrous. When designing fashion, performance, or other artistic leaning endeavors this could lead to truly unique and innovative solutions, which neither individual discipline or expert would have developed while working within their isolated standard working process. The EswatchBook we used was designed with this plasticity of meaning in mind [18]. The interface was purposefully designed without direct use cases foregrounded, meaning that when a user interacts with an e-textile swatch the computer screen shows a square which changes colors depending on types of interaction (Figure 2). Gilliland, Komor, Starner, and Zeagler designed the device in this way as to not point to specific use cases, hoping to inspire designers while leaving them free to come up with their own uses for e-textile technology. The original ESwatchBook contains somewhat aesthetically sterile e-textile swatches mimicking standard GUI gestures. We would argue that the ESwatchBook could use an overhaul and include some swatches with more influence form designers and trend forecasters. This could make the ESwatchBook more effective as a boundary object, pushing the balance of shared meaning closer to design and closer to the fulcrum between the disciplines it wishes to connect.

Formalizing and labeling artifacts and materials as boundary objects within the creative design process can have a number of beneficial outcomes. As a prescriptive measure, in planning to work with boundary objects, prepares a creative interdisciplinary team (researchers, technologists, and designers) to know that they speak different languages and have different processes before they even start working. By using or creating boundary objects the team also accepts up front the flexible nature of the terminology, which surrounds these objects, aiding in opportunistic misunderstandings. Star notes in her later writing on boundary objects that they "became almost synonymous with interpretive flexibility" [26].

Star used her description of a boundary object as a framework for explaining collaborative work around which consensus of meaning was seldom reached, but work was effectively completed. This descriptive use of the boundary object can help frame collaborative work process after the work is completed. If at the start of collaborative group work, we set out to use boundary objects, the framework of boundary objects can also help build a design process which is inclusive and participatory. When we consider boundary objects by Star's definition we should also consider the scale and scope of the object [26], which in turn would reflect on the scale and scope of the project.

By starting the 'Hood' project with an understanding that the ESwatchBook and drawing were to act as boundary objects, we also appropriately scaled the work to be accomplished. If we had considered language a boundary object, the scale of our project could have been too grand, or too broad [26]. By having a clear set of technology and a boundary object starting point that was flexible in use and understanding, we were able to scale our work to the appropriate time frame. Thus we arrived at a functional, aesthetically, and socially appropriate prototype.

Usefulness of Boundary Objects in Time Constrained Collaborative Work.

In our work here on the 'Hood' and in other work described by Gandy [15] and Zeagler [42] tools such as DART and The ESwatchBook have acted as boundary objects between disciplines. The usefulness of these boundary objects is highlighted in case studies like the 'Hood' and the E-textile interface workshops, where the time frame of the project is constrained and expedited. Forced timeframes and pressure to complete a prototype can lead to solutions without compromise, weakening at least one discipline's participation. Boundary objects allow for quicker translation of information through the shared meaning within the object. This stress of process translation echoes back to Gandy's work with Duran Duran, and how it helps when all team members have a solid grasp of the affordances and constraints of the task at hand early in the process [15]. The time constraint of one day within the e-textile interface workshops along with the pressure to perform by showing final ideation prototypes parallels the one-week time frame and musical performance of the 'Hood'. Both the time constraint and pressure of performance necessitate a timely understanding between parties so creativity and ideation can take hold. In the future it might be possible to use time constraints and qualitative methods to tease out the effectiveness and scale considerations embedded in the shared meanings created through boundary objects such as DART and the ESwatchBook.

ACKNOWLEDGMENTS

The authors would like to thank the Wearable Computing Center and the GVU Center at the Georgia Institute of Technology for encouraging the project and supporting the performance.

REFERENCES

[1] Abelton Live: *https://www.ableton.com/en/live/*. Accessed: 2016-12-29.

[2] Baker, P.M.A., Gandy, M. and Zeagler, C. 2015. Innovation and Wearable Computing: A Proposed Collaborative Policy Design Framework. *IEEE Internet Computing*. Sept.-Oct. 2015 (2015), 18–25.

[3] Barrett, M. and Oborn, E. 2010. Boundary object use in cross-cultural software development teams. *Human Relations*. 63, 8 (2010), 1199–1221.

[4] Benford, S., Greenhalgh, C., Crabtree, A., Flintham, M., Walker, B., Marshall, J., Koleva, B., Egglestone, S.R., Giannachi, G., Adams, M., Tandavanitj, N. and Farr, J.R. 2013. Performance-Led Research in the Wild. *ACM Transactions on Computer-Human Interaction*. 20, 3 (2013), 14:1-14:22.

[5] Bergman, M., Lyytinen, K. and Mark, G. 2007. Boundary Objects in Design: An Ecological View of Design Artifacts. *Journal of the Association for Information Systems*. 8, 11 (2007), 546–568.

[6] Bødker, S. and Grønæk, K. 1991. Cooperative Prototyping -. *International Journal of Man-Machine Studies*. 34, 3 (1991), 453–478.

[7] Buechley, L. 2006. A Construction Kit for Electronic Textiles. *2006 10th IEEE International Symposium on Wearable Computers*. (Oct. 2006), 83–90.

[8] Carlile, P.R. 2002. A Pragmatic View of Knowledge and Boundaries : Boundary Objects in New Product Development. *Organization Science*. 13, 4 (2002), 442–455.

[9] Cochran, Z., Zeagler, C. and McCall, S. 2015. Addressing Dresses: User Interface Allowing for Interdisciplinary Design and Calibration of LED Embedded Garments. *ISWC '15 Proceedings of the 2015 ACM International Symposium on Wearable Computers* (2015), 61–64.

[10] Crabtree, A. 1998. Ethnography in participatory design. *Proceedings of the 1998 Participatory design ....* (1998).

[11] DiSalvo, C., Nourbakhsh, I. and Holstius, D. 2008. The Neighborhood Networks project: a case study of critical engagement and creative expression through participatory design. *Proceedings of the Tenth Anniversary Conference on Participatory Design* (2008).

[12] Dunne, L., Profita, H. and Zeagler, C. 2014. Social Aspects of Wearability and Interaction. *Wearable Sensors: Fundamentals, Implementation and Applications*. E. Sazonov and M. Neuman, eds. Elsevier Inc. 25–43.

[13] Dunne, L.E., Profita, H., Zeagler, C., Clawson, J., Gilliland, S., Do, E.Y. i L. and Budd, J. 2014. The social comfort of wearable technology and gestural interaction. *Annual International Conference of the IEEE Engineering in Medicine and Biology Society. I* (2014), 4159–4162.

[14] Fels, S., Pritchard, R. and Lenters, A. 2009. ForTouch : A Wearable Digital Ventriloquized Actor. (2009), 274–275.

[15] Gandy, M. 2012. *Creating augmented reality authoring tools informed by designer workflow and goals.* Georgia Institute of Technology.

[16] Gandy, M., Baker, P.M.A. and Zeagler, C. 2016. Imagining futures: A collaborative policy/device design for wearable computing. *Futures*. (2016).

[17] Gandy, M. and MacIntyre, B. 2014. Designer's augmented reality toolkit, ten years later: implications for new media authoring tools. *Proceedings of the 27th annual ACM symposium on User interface software and technology - UIST '14.* (2014), 627–636.

[18] Gilliland, S., Komor, N., Starner, T. and Zeagler, C. 2010. The textile interface swatchbook: Creating graphical user interface-like widgets with conductive embroidery. *Proceedings - International Symposium on Wearable Computers, ISWC* (2010).

[19] Goffman, E. 1959. *The presentation of self in everyday life.*

[20] Gopalsamy, C., Park, S., Rajamanickam, R. and Jayaraman, S. 1999. The Wearable MotherboardTM : The First Generation Responsive Textile Structures Medical Applications. (1999), 152–168.

[21] Han, Y., Na, J. and Lee, K. 2012. FutureGrab : A wearable synthesizer using vowel formants. *Proceedings of the International Conference on New Interfaces for Musical Expression.* (2012), 491–494.

[22] Huang, K., Starner, T., Do, E., Weinberg, G., Tech, G., Kohlsdorf, D., Ahlrichs, C. and Leibrandt, R. 2010. Mobile Music Touch : Mobile Tactile Stimulation For Passive Learning. (2010), 791–800.

[23] Johansson, M., Fröst, P., Brandt, E., Binder, T. and Messeter, J. 2002. Partner Engaged Design New Challenges For Workplace Design. *Participatory Design Conference*. (2002).

[24] Komor, N., Gilliland, S., Clawson, J., Manish, B., Garg, M., Zeagler, C. and Starner, T. 2009. Is It Gropable?–Assessing the Impact of Mobility on Textile Interfaces. *International Symposium on Wearable Computers, ISWC* (2009), 71–74.

[25] LEE, H.S., Shin, H.C., Starner, T.E., Gilliland, S.M. and Zeagler, C. 2016. Sensor for measuring tilt angle based on electronic textile and method thereof. US Patent 9316481. 2016.

[26] Leigh Star, S. 2010. This is Not a Boundary Object: Reflections on the Origin of a Concept. *Science, Technology & Human Values*. 35, 5 (2010), 601–617.

[27] Lilypad Arduino: *https://www.arduino.cc/en/Main/ArduinoBoardLilyPad*.

[28] Marculescu, D. and Marculescu, R. 2003. Electronic textiles: A platform for pervasive computing. *Proceedings of the ...*. 91, 12 (2003), 1995–2018.

[29] Markow, T., Ramakrishnan, N., Huang, K., Starner, T., Schooler, C., Tarun, A., States, U. and States, U. Mobile Music Touch : Vibration Stimulus in Hand Rehabilitation.

[30] Martin, T., Kim, K., Forsyth, J., McNair, L., Coupey, E. and Dorsa, E. 2011. An interdisciplinary undergraduate design course for wearable and pervasive computing products. *Proceedings - International Symposium on Wearable Computers, ISWC*. (2011), 61–68.

[31] Mitchell, T., Madgwick, S. and Heap, I. 2012. Musical Interaction with Hand Posture and Orientation: A Toolbox of Gestural Control Mechanisms. *Proceedings of the International Conference on New Interfaces for Musical Expression*. May (2012), 21–23.

[32] Musical interaction and e-textile: *http://musicalfieldsforever.com/rhyme/?page_id=1234*. Accessed: 2016-07-26.

[33] Musical Textile: *http://www.talk2myshirt.com/blog/archives/164*. Accessed: 2017-03-20.

[34] Pobiner, S., Zeagler, C., Profita, H., Gilliland, S., LEE, H.S., Audy, S., Shin, H.C. and Starner, T. 2012. The Electronic Textile Interface Workshop: Scaffolding Communication Across Disciplines. *Designing Interactive Systems DIS* (Necastle, UK, 2012).

[35] Pobiner, S.G. and Mathew, A.P. 2007. Who killed design?: addressing design through an interdisciplinary investigation. *Proceedings of ACM CHI 2007 Conference on Human Factors in Computing Systems*. 2, (2007), 1925–1928.

[36] Post, E.R. and Orth, M. 1997. Smart fabric, or "wearable clothing." *Digest of Papers. First International Symposium on Wearable Computers* (1997), 167–168.

[37] Post, E.R., Orth, M., Russo, P.R. and Gershenfeld, N. 2000. E-broidery: Design and fabrication of textile-based computing. *IBM Systems Journal*. 39, 3.4 (2000), 840–860.

[38] Profita, H., Clawson, J., Gilliland, S., Zeagler, C., Starner, T., Budd, J. and Do, E.Y.-L. 2013. Don't mind me touching my wrist: a case study of interacting with on-body technology in public. *Proceedings of the 17th annual International symposium on wearable computers - ISWC '13*. (2013), 89–96.

[39] Rhinow, H., Köppen, E. and Meinel, C. 2012. Design Prototypes as Boundary Objects in Innovation Processes. *Conference on Design Research Society*. July (2012), 1–10.

[40] Serafin, S., Trento, S., Grani, F., Perner-Wilson, H., Madgwick, S. and Mitchell, T. 2014. Controlling Physically Based Virtual Musical Instruments Using The Gloves. *Proceedings of the International Conference on New Interfaces for Musical Expression*. July (2014), 521–524.

[41] Star, S. and Griesemer, J. 1989. Institutional Ecology, Translations' and Boundary Objects: Amateurs and Professionals in Berkley's Museum of Vertebrate Zoology. *Social studies of science*. (1989).

[42] Zeagler, C., Audy, S., Pobiner, S., Profita, H., Gilliland, S. and Starner, T. 2013. The electronic textile interface workshop: Facilitating interdisciplinary collaboration. *International Symposium on Technology and Society, Proceedings*. (2013), 76–85.

[43] Zeagler, C., Gilliland, S., Audy, S. and Starner, T. 2013. Can I Wash It?: The Effect of Washing Conductive Materials Used in Making Textile Based Wearable Electronic Interfaces. *Proceedings of the 17th annual international symposium on International symposium on wearable computers - ISWC '13* (Zurich, Switzerland, 2013), 143.

[44] Zeagler, C., Gilliland, S., Profita, H. and Starner, T. 2012. Textile interfaces: Embroidered jog-wheel, beaded tilt sensor, twisted pair ribbon, and sound sequins. *Proceedings - International Symposium on Wearable Computers, ISWC*. (2012), 60–63.

[45] Zeagler, C., Starner, T., Hall, T. and Wong Sala, M. 2015. *Meeting the Challenge: The Path Towards a Consumer Wearable Computer*. Georgia Institute of Technology.

[46] Zimmerman, J. and Forlizzi, J. 2008. The Role of Design Artifacts in Design Theory Construction. *Artifact*. 2, June 2008 (2008), 41–45.

Interioractive: Smart Materials in the Hands of Designers and Architects for Designing Interactive Interiors

Sara Nabil[1], David S. Kirk[2], Thomas Plötz[3], Julie Trueman[2], David Chatting[1], Dmitry Dereshev[2], Patrick Olivier[1]

[1]Open Lab, Newcastle University
Newcastle upon Tyne, UK
{s.nabil-ahmed2, david.chatting, patrick.olivier}@ncl.ac.uk

[2]Northumbria University
Newcastle upon Tyne, UK
{david.kirk, julie.trueman, dmitry.dereshev}@northumbria.ac.uk

[3]School of Interactive Computing
Georgia Institute of Technology
Atlanta, GA, USA
thomas.ploetz@gatech.edu

ABSTRACT

The application of Organic User Interface (OUI) technologies will revolutionize interior design, through the development of interactive and actuated surfaces, furnishings and decorative artefacts. However, to adequately explore these new design landscapes we must support multidisciplinary collaboration between Architects, Interior Designers and Technologists. Herein, we present the results of two workshops, with a total of 45 participants from the disciplines of Architecture and Interior Design, supported by a group of HCI researchers. Our objective was to study how design disciplines can productively engage with smart materials as a design resource using an evolving set of techniques to prototype new interactive interior spaces. Our paper reports on our experiences across the two workshops and contributes an understanding of techniques for supporting multidisciplinary collaboration when designing interactive interior spaces.

ACM Classification Keywords

H.5.m. Information Interfaces and Presentation (e.g. HCI): Miscellaneous; J.5 Computer Applications: Arts & Humanities – Architecture

Author Keywords

Organic User Interfaces; smart materials; e-textiles; Interactive Architecture; Interior Design.

INTRODUCTION

Over several centuries the architectural movements that have impacted our built environments have adopted varying levels of reference to nature. It is not uncommon to see architectural forms that try to mimic the flowing lines and natural references of the living environment. This was evident (arguably) in the gothic, baroque, rococo and art nouveau periods [36] and then more recently and literally in 'Biophylic Design'. Since the art deco and modernist periods however, buildings have adopted increasingly abstract and metaphorically static shapes. That is not to say however that buildings are static and non-dynamic. As Brand [3] astutely illustrates buildings change over time. They have a patina, that develops through use and they age ostensibly, through weathering and other effects of time. It is also true to say that interiors, the artefacts and furnishings we have within our buildings, are moved, age and are replaced over time, shaping a dynamic environment within the buildings themselves [9]. However, these dynamic features of buildings often sit outside of the temporal flows that make them readily perceivable to the average occupant. We are aware of change over time, but the time-scales at play often mean we do not actively attend to it (beyond specific demarcated points of transition). Within environmental psychology there has long been a discussion around the restorative benefits of the natural environment, and concern for how this might be installed within the built environment [18]. One area of research Attention Restoration Theory (ART) [19] posits that dynamic, moving and possibly interactive elements of the built environment might support inhabitant well-being along a number of dimensions. From this we believe that our built environment should be designed to have the capacity for dynamic interactive change, at a time scale that is more perceptible to inhabitants. Not only could our homes morph as we grow old in them, and thus be more adaptable to our experiences and comforts over a lifespan, but also be more responsive to our daily needs and moods.

Research already exists in the area of Interactive Architecture [6, 22] but with limited understanding of Interactive interiors that does not really address matters of interior design in many kind of ways. However, deeper study and research for Interactive Interiors will help and support the vision of ubiquitous computing. In various ways researchers are beginning to think about more dynamic and adaptable living and working spaces [28, 14]. Organic User Interfaces (OUIs), including the use of smart materials offer a rich potential to 'retrofit' [22] interactivity in to domestic artefacts and surfaces. OUIs are defined as non-flat multi-touch interfaces that can exist in both rigid or flexible forms, can take any shape, and can -actively or passively- change this shape [35]. This kind of flexible and dynamic sensing and actuation is more feasible and affordable than ever. Smart materials such as shape-changing alloys (SMAs), colour-changing paints (thermochromic pigments), conductive materials (conductive fabrics, conductive

DIS 2017, June 10-14, 2017, Edinburgh, United Kingdom

DOI: http://dx.doi.org/10.1145/3064663.3064745

Figure 1. Examples of Interactive Interiors: (Left) Light-Form [Daniele Gualeni Design Studio, 2010] [31], (Right) Engaging Retail Space [Dalziel & Pow, 2015] [7]. Images reproduced with permission.

paints, metal powders) and other flexible sensors all form an interesting medium for embedding both actuation and sensing capabilities into everyday objects and surfaces.

For the practical and aesthetic qualities of these materials to be fully exploited within interior architecture and design however, the materials must be brought to the attention and understanding of those who work most prevalently in the design of the built environment, namely architects and interior designers. To date however, there has been no significant exploration of how such communities can be supported in working with these new kinds of new materials in interior design projects. Evidently, there is a need to understand the processes through which designers can come to understand and work with such smart materials, in collaboration with technologists, if we wish to see visions of smart environments fully realised.

In this paper therefore, we discuss our study of interdisciplinarity between HCI and Interior Design. We explore the use of embedded smart materials to support new interactions in interior designs. In particular, we critically reflect upon our efforts to scaffold interior designers and architects, as two specific communities, learning to design with smart materials through hands-on exploration.

Below we first introduce some related work, which grounds some of our key understanding of interactive architectures and OUIs. We then unpack two case studies, as two workshops conducted with architects then interior designers respectively, which brought them in to collaboration with an HCI team who scaffolded their prototyping with new interactive materials, whilst designing novel interactive interior spaces. In each case we were utilising techniques for supporting their exploration (with smart materials) of 4D interaction. We conclude the paper with reflections on the process of supporting interior designers and architects to design with new materials and in doing so try to tackle some of the proposed challenges of Interactive Architecture [22], namely Radical Interdisciplinarity, Appropriation and Retrofitting, and Scalability.

RELATED WORK

Interactive Architecture that used shape-change as means of reflection and interactivity with users has been subject to a few HCI studies [6, 22] and prototypes, such as ExoBuilding [32] a physiologically driven Adaptive Architecture prototype, the MuscleTower [24] another prototype of an interactive/ proactive architectural structure and the Kinetic Interactive Architecture [27] that explores bodily interactions with different dynamic interior surfaces. But when we observe the design of any of these examples, we can't seem to picture them as architecture to live with. The interactivity, adaptivity, and proactivity researchers introduced in these previous examples were basically kinetic. Other research looked into the possibilities of designing entire building facades as digital displays [11, 33].

On the other hand, architects took kinetic and adaptive architecture to another level where scalability essentially triggers new forms of dynamic behaviours, capabilities and challenges. The most basic type would be the Kinetic sun-shade facades that take a variety of shapes and motion axes, from the very early examples such as the Institut du Monde Arabe in Paris (Jean Nouvel, 1987) [23] to the modern recent buildings such as the Kolding Building of SDU in Denmark (Henning Larsen Architects, 2014) [16], Al Bahr Towers in Abu Dhabi (Aedas Architects, 2012) [1], and the Kiefer Technic Showroom (Giselbrecht, 2010) [12]. Other kinetic architecture may transform the entire structure such as the shape-changing Hoberman's Arch (Hoberman, 2004) [17]. Current Interactive Architecture - other than being kinetic - often include colour-changing LED displays such as the Luminous Interactive Public Art Platform in Darling Quarter, Sydney [8].

A primary aspect of interior architecture is lighting and finding creative ways of manipulating lighting with other forms of kinetic actuations to realise user interaction. In interior design practice, interactive design firms are starting to create interactive spaces to engage and react to users or the ambient environment as well, using light and sound. Examples of interactive interior designs are the Engaging Retail Space (Dalziel & Pow, 2015) [7] that responds to touch using capacitive paint on wood wall panels and reacts through audible sounds and projected graphical animations, and the Aegis Hyposurface kinetic wall (Mark Goulthorpe, 2000) [13] that actuates its shape-changing mechanism either autonomously (pre-programmed) or responding to ambient sounds or noise. Other examples that involve LED interactivity are Light-Form (Francesca Rogers, 2010) [31] and the Philips Luminous Patterns [26]. More immersive experiences can be also found in some novelists' work such as Nicolas Schoffer's Spatiodynamic Luminodynamic & Chromodynamic Space [34]. All these examples were designed and built to extend the user experience in the space by pushing the boundaries and adding a dynamic nature to the interior design instead of being just static as traditional designs (see Figure 1).

OUI materials leverage these possibilities from being mechanical into organic in terms of the nature and effect of the actuation's interaction and materialism. Such smart materials have the physical changeable properties that are reversible and repeatable, responding by changing their shape (morphogenic), skin texture, opacity or colour (chromogenic) or other morphological forms [29] reacting to external stimuli such as heat (thermo-), light (photo-), electricity (electro-), pressure, water/humidity (hydro-/hygro-), magnetism or chemical reactions [30]. Other smart materials may have sensing qualities rather than actuating ones. For example: conductive fabrics, conductive paints and flexible sensors that allow a range of manipulative and tactile sensing (from light touch to pressure) onto other normal materials. Previous research has looked into how OUI materials in Interactive Architecture can be used to create prototypes for both skin-changing OUIs such as Morphing Lumina Architectural Skins [20], Morphogenic Adaptive Building Skins [2], and OUI Interiors such as the LivingSurface [37], LivingWall [4] and the playful home interior Squeeze [25].

Therefore, interactive interiors based on OUI smart materials have great potential to create immersive enriched user experiences within interior spaces in a range of contexts. Some may be designed as a conversation starter, for storytelling or to stand out from the crowd and/or overcome temporal blindness [5]; while others may be driven by the need to use technology in a way that redefines the identity of the space or the service being presented and practiced within. Other motivations for OUI interactive interiors includes visualizing the unseen [37], yielding pleasure [21] and uplifting emotions and feelings of people through adding new dimensions to the spatial context such as discoverability, revealing, playfulness and temporality.

EXPLORING INTERACTIVE INTERIORS

Our review of related work identified two barriers to the transfer of research into practice. First, previous HCI research does not emphasize the 'design' of the prototypes, in large part due to the computing approach that tends to frame the challenge as one of functional problem-solving nature that is primarily concerned with system performance. That is, an emphasis on functionality and operational aspects of their design rather than the visceral and aesthetic qualities and values it creates and imposes. The second issue is that interactive interior practitioners are rarely concerned with deeper and long-term examinations of how people will interact, perceive and live with such designs for lifetime. Consequently, if we want to explore the design space of different interactive spaces and unwrap the potentials of smart materials in designing interactive interiors and objects, HCI researchers need to engage professional interior designers and architects in a multi-disciplinary exploratory process.

In our study we held two workshops with a total of 45 participants from both disciplines: Architecture and Interior Design, together with a group of supporting HCI researchers to develop concepts and designs for interactive interior spaces. Our objective was to get design disciplines to engage with and explore smart materials using an evolving set of techniques.

INTERIORACTION: CASE STUDY 1

The first case study was a hands-on workshop for a group of architects to get them to experience interactive materials and explore together ways of utilizing and embedding them into building fabrics as a means for designing interactive interior spaces, or as we term 'interioractives'.

Method

The first case study was with the School of Architecture, Newcastle University, UK in which we had 9 participants (3 undergraduate students, and 6 postgraduates in different programs: MArch and MSc in Experimental Architecture) out of which there was 1 male and 8 females. The workshop was held over a full week and was located within our research lab, facilitated by three researchers, and participants signed up willingly as a part of a pre-teaching 'Design Week'. The objective was to collaborate together in groups to ideate and design a interactive interior spaces. Participants were first briefed about the concepts of OUI Architecture and interaction design, then introduced to an array of OUI materials (sensing and actuation) and controlling them using Arduino programming. Several group discussions and brainstorming sessions took place in between their learning sessions to allow them (and us) to evaluate, and critically reflect upon concepts of Interactive Interiors. The smart materials used included shape-memory muscle wires, thermochromic paints, conductive materials and flexible pressure and bend sensors. Participants had a goal to design an interactive interior space that could potentially make use of these novel technologies.

Activity 1: Material Exploration

Participants had the opportunity and time to not only examine the smart materials but to use them in the form of well prepared kits by themselves. We introduced the basics of Arduino electronics and programming to facilitate their hands-on prototyping of different interactive OUIs. They wired different capacitive materials (fabric, thread, fibre, paint, ink and metals) and flexible pressure, tilt, squeeze, bend and stretch sensors as input, and SMA (Shape-Memory Alloy) muscle wires and controllable heating pads for colour-changing thermochromic paints as actuations/output.

Activity 2: Ideation

After the exploring and playing with the materials, participants were asked to work in groups discussing different applications of sensing and actuating interior architectural spaces on four different categories: spaces, surfaces (walls, floors, ceilings, windows, etc), furniture, decoration and accessories. Eventually, few ideas were generated for both the 'spaces' (the whole) and 'accessories' (the detailed), but rather participants focused on 'structural surfaces' and 'furniture'. The ideation activity led to 39 different applications ranging from the simple obvious "window regulating indoor ventilation according to weather or pollution" to the creative and immersive "show warmest place in the house using thermochromic paint" or "lighting sculpture that glows more the more the WiFi-connected number of users in the building". We then analyzed

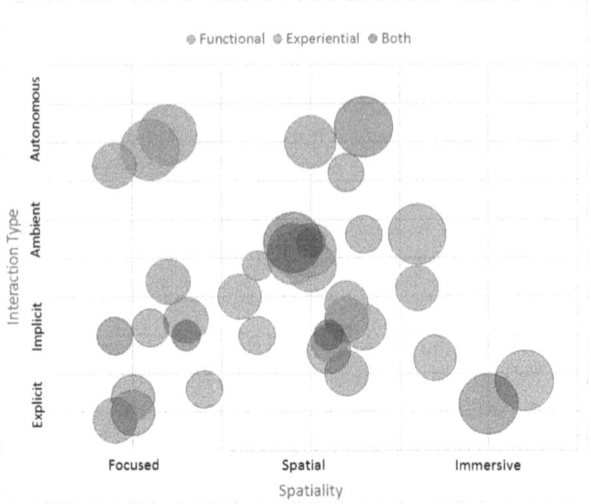

Figure 2. Visualization of data analysis of Case Study 1 Ideation Activity using different dimensions: (a) Spatiality (x-axis), (b) Interaction Type (y-axis), (c) Engagement (diameter), and (d) purpose (colour).

these ideas to unwrap the inherited features and attributes these applications incorporated. Their ideas were (unexpectedly) equally distributed among three types of interaction: (1) Explicit Deliberate Interaction (hand manipulation i.e. touch, press, in-air gestures, speech control); (2) Implicit Motion (motion: proximity/ moving around, posture: sitting down/ laying/ standing, displacement: moving/dropping objects); (3) Ambient and Autonomous: surrounding environment (weather: temperature/ humidity), ambient conditions (sound, light, time, heat) and based on external network feed.

We analyzed these ideas by coding key aspects of each idea/ application according to the type of interaction, spatiality, engagement dimensions, purpose, legibility and re-adaptability. We rated the level of spatiality (over a spectrum from focused to spatial to immersive) and the interaction type (from deliberate explicit control to implicit user actions to ambient conditions recognition and finally autonomous behaviour). We also considered the dimensions of user engagement as: 1D: linear, 2D: planar, 2.5D: planar with an object, 3D: spatial/bodily, 3.5D: building-scale, and 4D: adds the effect of temporality to the 3D engagement. Then we identified the purpose of each application to be either functional, experiential or aiming both function and experience. The result of this analysis is shown in Figure 2 as plotted data points on scales of spatiality and interaction, with the size indicating the dimensions of engagement, for functional (blue), experiential (red) and combined (purple) purposes. Through this approach we only intend to visualize data in a meaningful way that shows the spectrum on a qualitative scale with no emphasis on any particular numerical value so no quantitative rating is considered. As shown in Figure 2, we concluded these findings:

- The average dimension or level of engagement (size of circles) of applications or ideas increases with the increase of the spatiality and/or the interaction getting less intentional i.e. implicit and ambient.
- The average dimension or level of engagement (size of circles) of applications or ideas that has both experiential and functional purposes (purple) is larger than that of those introducing functions only or experience only.

Activity 3: Design Challenge

The whole group then moved from the lab to the wild, with the aim of designing an interactive interior space, in a gallery room around 6m x 4m. The resulting design concept was: creating a playful experience in the form of an 'enchanted' interior, a cave-like dark room with hidden maze-like qualities, themed as 'Alice in Wonderland', and augmented with interactive installations and clue(s) leading to the location of a treasure (a magical object). Based on the sensing and actuation techniques they had learnt about, they split themselves into smaller groups to design and build six interactive installations to augment their interior walls with interactivity:

1. A tactile wallpaper/poster that used conductive fibre and paint to display audio feedback for users playing with it.
2. A touch-sensitive wood wall-panel using capacitive paint manipulating LED lights that shows an arrow for the right way in the maze.
3. A 2D cardboard light switch based on conductive paint, that activated a far away lighting sign showing users what to do next.
4. A haunted/actuated curtain that moved flipping cut-outs using SMA reacting to proximity sensing.
5. A hidden clue painted with thermochromic paint on a wall that only revealed the invisible treasure code when a connected corresponding pressure-sensitive chair was sat on.
6. A treasure (i.e. actuated object) designed as a mushroom model that activated (bounced cap using SMA wire and lights up LEDs) when a user entered the right code by dipping a finger in capacitive connected tea cups.

All designs were then installed and the room was opened for public visitors as part of a bigger architecture gallery event.

Data Analysis

Our gathered data consisted of 8 hours of audio data, recorded during the workshops, to which we chose to perform selective audio transcription of 2.5 hours that formed the entire length of group discussions and presentations after each group activity. The collected data was also supplemented by participants' sketches, schematic architectural drawings, textual written descriptions of their ideas and designs, and most importantly our observational notes made throughout the sessions.

During this workshop, we not only empowered these designers with brief knowledge on new frontier possibilities of dynamic designs and embedded interactions, but we also had the opportunity to to; (1) investigate how they perceived OUI Architecture; (2) examine their views on appropriation and applicability; (3) unwrap new ideas and potentials of such OUIs; (4) discuss and raise new challenges and considerations; (5) design and implement six different interactive artefacts using OUI smart materials; (6) create an Interactive Interior space with an enchanted theme; (7) capture visitors' user experiences with the OUI interior developed, and (8) observe user reactions and interaction behaviours of novice users (i.e. exhibit visitors) with OUI artefacts.

Findings

The results of our data analysis can be articulated in three main themes, describing the unwrapped ideas, potentials and challenges of interioractives. For anonymity, we refer to participants as P1 to P9.

Spatio-Autonomy & Context-Awareness

Participants mainly ideated around different context-aware functional uses for interactive interiors, rather than their aesthetics. For example, P4: *"proximity activates lights leading the way to get somewhere"*, P4: *"curtains change opacity whether it was heated up or it was more brighter outside, the curtains' back would become more or less opaque so the space would be more comfortable inside"* and P5: *"if you walk by, chairs pop out so it reacts to you wanting to sit down."* Other functional purposes were also proposed for interioractive objects such as furniture with context-aware ergonomics such as P3: *"more comfortable furniture that shape your body"*, P6: *"reading chair checks and regulates the surrounding ambient lights"* and furniture responding to noise in the space or supporting space comfort: P5: *"chairs would heat up or become more comfortable and soft the colder you are and then also get rather sturdy and colder if you're too hot"*. Throughout the sessions, we observed how designers started thinking of and referring to interior objects as living things that have minds of their own e.g. P6: *"when bins feel full they can tell us they need to be put out at the night before"*, P6: *"plant pot that moves to stay in the sun"*.

Playfulness vs. Calmness

Temporarily Playful: participants expressed how they feel interioraction can be more appropriate for non-permanent installations (e.g. museum seasonal exhibits, shows, tourist sculptures/ attractions, retail stores, temporary entertainment). For instance, P2: *"a lot of this is about the novelty, it's great when you've never seen it before and it's the first time, fantastic, but if that's on your wall forever, it kinda loses its novelty."* and P6: *"it has to be things that are consistently useful rather than being sort of transiently entertaining"*. So for exciting engagement, sequential interaction was discussed. For example: P2: *"you would touch something then it would tell you something to do next and then that does something else, for example it lights up and when you touch it, it tells you to jump around then when you jump around something else happens."* On the other hand, architects suggested residences and permanent spaces should be designed with "calmness" in mind i.e. designing for permanent settings should be carefully considered to avoid boredom and/or frustration through creating hidden and/or calm interaction scenarios. Alternatively, participants pointed out how interior interaction can not only be pleasurable but provoking as means for promoting physiological wellbeing P1: *"what else could get people moving, for example, if you sat too long on a seat it would get really cold or really warm so that it would help you move like a little provocation somehow so not always pleasurable"*. Still, the design challenge showed how participants kept considering these two paths as an interaction 'double-edged sword' where designing a simple logic is too obvious, unimpressive and therefore not quite playful, while the complicated scenario is unintuitive and often incomprehensible to users. At the end, however, they succeeded in designing their enchanted exhibition in a way where visitors were observably enjoying the playful experience, commenting how it was a *"curious, "surprising"* and a *"wow"* experience (see Figure 6). Although, unexpected user interaction behaviour for exhibit visitors was not uncommon, for example, some visitors were observed repeatedly touching everything as if playing a musical beat with interactive sounds and lights.

Design Constraints and Limitations

Scalability issues bring limitations to some designs; P5: *"probably anything that is out in the rain but needs to be controlled by an electric current would become way more difficult to construct it and also would break much easier.* Other aspects such as the expectations of users were also raised; P2: *"you don't want to make people lazy, you still want them to want to interact with things, but if everything is constantly being done for you, if you have sensors that tell you what the weather is like outside"*, P6: *"what if you want it to be brighter, what if you want to sit in the dark"*, P2: *"when you want the design to stop being intuitive and for you to then as the user to take over that"*. Designs were also constrained by the simple but delicate materials that are quite easy to use/prototype but lack the resilience required for a public installation, so careful considerations needed to be taken (e.g. transparent coating, tight fixing, soldering, etc.).

Critical Reflections

Collaborating with architects yielded a productive framework to design interactive spaces. Architect participants successfully: *(1)* understood how to use smart materials in their designs, *(2)* learnt basic programming and electronics essentials to connect/ build their own circuits with sensors and actuators, *(3)* were able to design and create a playful theme of an interactive interior space in a sequential interaction approach, and *(4)* build an interactive space from raw materials of conductive and electronic products we provided. Although not structurally dynamic or adaptive, the space they designed and constructed was context-aware with embedded interactions within the walls, furniture (sensitive seat) and interior objects (enchanted treasure: cups and center piece) using Arduino microcontrollers controlling motion sensors, tactile conductive, shape-changing and colour-changing materials. What slowed down the design process at the beginning was their need to visit and check the physical location, which wasn't ready from Day 1. We have learnt how the site visit is a crucial starting point for interior architects to be able to conceptualize any design. This should be considered by interaction designers wishing to collaborate with architects to create an interactive space i.e. having the physical space ready before hand and scheduling the site visit at the very beginning. Another lesson we have learned from this case study regards the visitors' reaction and behaviour within the exhibit: not all people should be expected to act in the same normal way. For instance, some visitors were overly cautious while gently touching the touch-sensitive walls, while others were too intense and rough (consumption of wine was involved!). A good interaction design should therefore take such different kinds of users into account.

INTERIORACTION: CASE STUDY 2

Method

The second case study was in the School of Interior Design where 36 students (7 male and 29 female) in their final year of three-year undergraduate program, participated in a full day workshop in their own studio space, together with 3 HCI researchers to facilitate the planned activities. Our research goal was to explore with them the potentials of OUI materials in Interior Design as a means of designing interactive interior spaces in different contexts and using different traditional finishing materials such as Wood, Metal, Paint, Acrylic, Glass, Ceramics, etc. Participants were briefed as part of a module they were attending to develop an interior space for a theatre set for a production of 'Pan's Labyrinth', which we incorporated into our workshop plan to investigate what interesting interaction designs might be employed in such an unusual exciting interior.

Activity 1: Material Exploration

For demonstrating interactive materials to interior design students who are accustomed to material samples from different suppliers, we prepared four sample models that would show tactile and flexible input and colour-change and shape-change output each embedded in standard interior design materials that students may be more familiar with. For example, we designed a tactile palette to demonstrate to designers a variety of possible embedded capacitive-sensing in the form of wood sheet, wood engraving, fabric, leather, fibre, thread, paint, glass, acrylic and ceramic tile, using flexible conductive materials underneath such as capacitive paints, fabrics and metal powders (see Figure 3). These ready made models we prepared helped in rapid learning, exploration of physical interaction and how such materials can be weaved into their normal interior designs.

Figure 3. Tactile Palette: a design tool created for Case Study 2 for introducing capacitive-sensing embedded within different interior finishing materials (e.g. wood, fabrics, leather, glass, acrylic, ceramic).

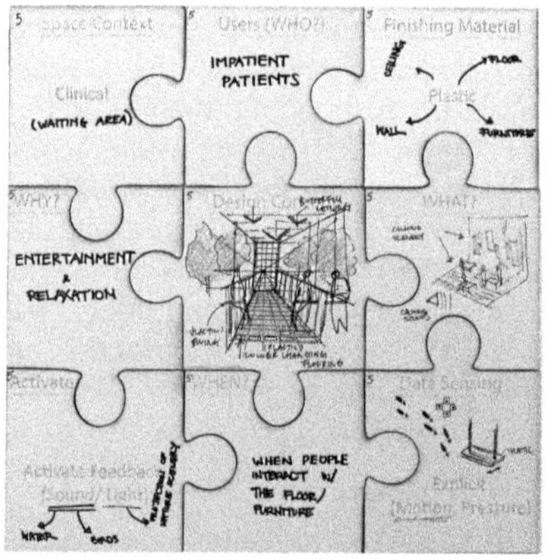

Figure 4. Ideation Jigsaw: a design tool created for Case Study 2 for supporting the development of design concepts to interactive interiors.

Activity 2: Ideation

This group activity was designed in a way that is closer to how interior designers work. Their methodology is mainly about how a design concept would be developed based on a series of fixed constraints such as space or building typology, in addition to a set of parameters which allow for creative exploration. As we wanted to explore designing different interactive spaces, we had a set of space contexts (educational, clinical, entertaining, retail, residential and an eatery). We also wanted to explore the possibilities of embedding a variety of the normal interior finishing materials (wood, metal, paint, acrylic, glass and fabrics) with sensing and actuation capabilities. Data sensing may include Explicit hand manipulations or air-gestures, Implicit motion or pressure, Bio-sensing, Environmental conditions, and Ambient sounds or lights, while actuation may include change in physical shape, colour, skin or style, pattern or texture, and activating feedback such as sound, light/shadow or motion. Consequently, we designed six 3 by 3 jigsaw puzzles each containing four pieces (from the set of space contexts, finishing materials, data sensing and actuation effects) that are pre-defined as means of constraining the design with some boundaries, and four other pieces left as variables they can decide (who are the users, what is the interactive surface or object, when will it transform or trigger reaction, and why will it do that). With four constraints and four variables, plus a main middle piece for the design concept, each group would have random nine pieces to help define their interactive interior idea (see Figure 4). This method resulted in a variety of ideas with different combinations of interaction attributes (users, inputs, outputs, context, usability and user experience).

The result was impressive as using this technique proved to be a rapid ideation allowing creativity yet bounded to some constraints. After a few minutes, each of the six groups developed a creative idea of an interactive interior design as following:

1- Shopping in Space: glowing footprints of retail customers would appear on the pressure-sensitive wood floor near key areas (entrance, stairs/lifts, changing rooms) visualizing their flow as they step-in and wander in the shop, could direct them also to area they want, then fading over time. Hangers could also glow to direct customers to their size reacting to speech, all for creating a memorable experience in shopping.

2- 4D Cinema: hall that changes colours/ patterns of sound-proofing fabric covering walls, floors based on ambient sounds/ light of movie scenes creating immersive story moods for enhancing people's movie experience, or even seats that could have glowing seat numbers for late audience.

3- Campus Navigator: a wayfinding/ outdoors map navigation system embedded across a university campus that stores and shows students and visitors different routes and paths on opacity-changing glass panels that are touch-sensitive to allow users to point to where they want to go and it shows the path on the interactive glass panel in front of thc map background board offering information for lost visitors or students on open days directing them to classes, refreshments, toilets, etc.

4- Sensory Assisted Living: texture-changing (uplifting) and colour-changing (associated to emotions) residential object (water cube sculpture/ wall covering/ floor/ toy tunnel) responding to bio-sensing and facial expressions of special needs (impaired/ blind/ child patients) when different moods detected (through heart rate, etc) by kinetic changing patterns and textures to turn their bad days into good ones, motivate, encourage positivity, optimism, inclusion, normality and playfulness.

5- Healthy Smoothies Bar: an eatery for children designed with organic installations (trees) that moves branches, glows LEDs and transforms colour when heated based on busy rate and day and night temperature for educating kids (healthy nutrition awareness, sustainability) and an interesting feature that when moves unleashes a story.

6- Butterfly Clinic: a clinical waiting area designed as a butterfly garden for impatient patients where pressure-sensitive floor panels (hanging bridge), walls or furniture could produce nature sound effects (birds, grass stepping, waterfall) and display calming nature sceneries, responding to user interactions such as moving around and sitting on motion-sensitive swings and passing underneath ceiling butterflies will move their wings, for relaxation and entertainment while waiting for their turn or stressful waiting for their relatives.

Activity 3: Design Challenge

During the design challenge, participants were split into five groups where they worked on theatre set designs that use smart materials and interaction technology to achieve two main goals: 1) immerse the audience within different scenes and 2) create changing scenery through dynamic shape-changing SMA and colour-changing materials. See Figure 5.

Group1: (War Scene) Use conductive fabric integrated in a sand bag to trigger different effects within the scene such as explosions and light effects, creating an integrated way of performing. Using light and photochromic fabric to change atmosphere of the scene from colourful to dark dingy scene or descending mist on stage activating hydrochromic fabric changing colour of the uniforms from crisp clean to military style gear which is important within that scene. Trees in the scene actuated using muscle wire instead of being a static object. Use photochromic foot prints illuminating way-

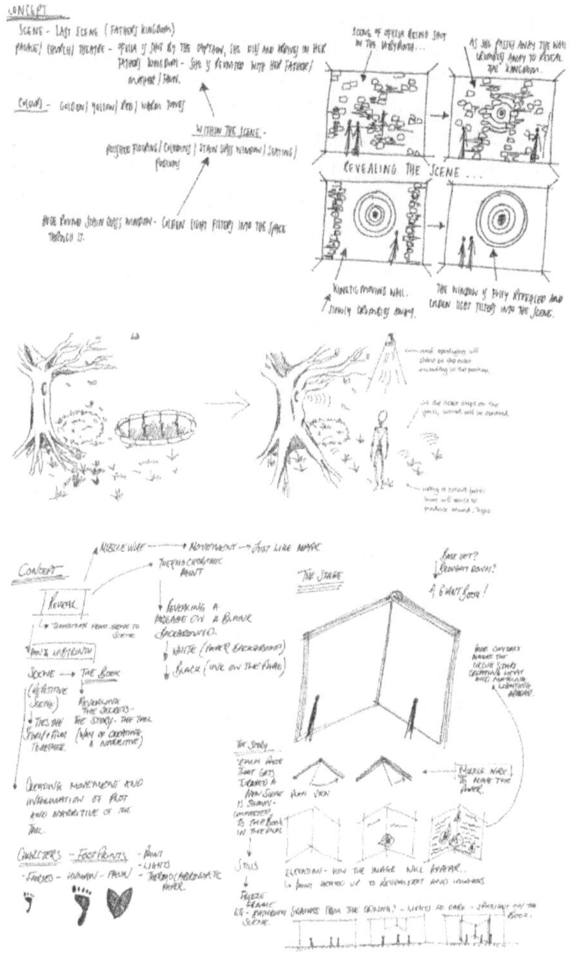

Figure 5. Some sketches from Case Study 2 drawn by participants during the Design Challenge.

finding within the dark theatre. Back-seat panels to produce special effects like smells and gust-air to simulate different senses.Group2: (Last Scene: Death) Use revealing concept to create a scene of stages where the prominent circular back window that lets a lot of light in would react to her death by turning dark once she's shot, colours would be dark, gloomy and dingy. The back wall will use SMA to crumble like rocks break away piece by piece then the wall would reveal another appearance for the next scene, then colours would convert to reveal the golden heaven kingdom. Ink that appears when she opens the book with narrative aspect could be a giant book that reveals the story using thermochromics when pages flip, and footprints of different characters (fairies, etc) would appear to make it magical.

Group3: (Start Scene) When she enters and steps on the grass, it will react to produce sound and spot light to shine on her and follow her as she walks in through the stage, and hidden pressure-sensitive buttons activates the curtain rolling down. The scene where she draws a doorway with a chalk will reveal the perspective view through thermochromics. Similarly, when she reads the book, it reacts by revealing pictures of her future when she touches it.

Group 4: (Labyrinth Pit Scene) when she enters and moves across the stage it will look like she's descending into the pit without actually moving down, using two interlocked circular slanted structures starts off both inline then create focus transition effect between two spaces. SMA hanging from the ceiling creating moving leaves of the forest, and changes the shadows behind it as it moves, as if the sunlight is coming through. Pressure-sensors on stage spark the noise of the forest at night.

Group 5: (Crawling under Tree Scene) getting the audience to make assumptions on what will happen in advance. Create a tree that had dead leaves and flowers that would come to life and open up using SMA to open and close thermochromic fabric flowers and leaves so that when it opens it starts slowly changing colour as well. As she crawls on the sensitive floor will glow beneath her in the dark stage, reflecting the frog scene, creating that sense of mystery. Mapping what is on the stage sets off another response in the cafe or box office, such as glowing footprints of actress, frog, fairies, etc.

Data Analysis

Our gathered data consisted of 6 hours of audio data, recorded during the workshop, to which we chose to perform selective audio transcription of 1.5 hours that form the entire length of group discussions and presenting back after each group activity. The collected data is also supplemented by participants' sketches, schematic architectural drawings and textual written descriptions of their ideas and designs. Again, the notes of our observations of activities constituted a significant part of the gathered data.

This data was then subjected to a process of thematic analysis. Initial codes were generated and refined through iterative analysis to produce coherent themes that were then refined to establish meaningful findings that contribute to the future research of interactive interior architecture and design. Thematic analysis was chosen to reflect the complexity of the research initiative and the desire to retain the generative possibilities of data analysis to support future interactive interior designs. As we had five groups in the Design Challenge activity, we will be referring to them as G1, G2, to G5 from hereafter. The result of thematic analysis process was four main themes described in detail below:

Findings

Special Effects: Light/Shadow, Sounds and Smell

One of the main themes that was clear throughout the data gathered was how designers focused on embedding special effects when asked to design for interactivity. Four out of the five groups used sound and light as means of output feedback/ interaction. Other effects such as smoke and smell (odour) were also used for a more immersive experience. Light was used in the form of both spot-lights and illuminating objects and floors as means of grabbing attention and/ or changing focus from one area or action to another. Personal light was also created to follow the user by G3: *"to shine on her and follow her as she walks"*. Sound effects were often triggered by implicit actions such as walking, stepping and approaching something or somewhere as means of immersive experience engaging different senses. Controlling both sound and light together was a clear theme across different designs with response to motion and other implicit user input, and were considered a bold mix of actuation effects that instantly captures user attention. Shadow was also manipulated with light to create a sense as per G4: *"as if the sunlight is coming through with a dappled shadow-lighting effect"*. Sound and light were also used separately as inputs to trigger other actions; G2:*"once she's shot, .."*, not just an output interaction. In this sense, one interaction can open the way to another, allowing the interior space to conceal and reveal interactions, unfolding as the user digs up embedded sensation/ interactivity and get exposed to hidden discoverability within the space.

Exploring Materiality through Tactile Sensations

All six groups were clearly enthusiastic about embedding sensation within the fabric of their interior design, using both capacitive materials and pressure sensors. Pressure-sensitive floor tiles seamed popular as four groups designed them in different ways considering them a form of G3: *"hidden buttons"* that can control/ activate some features. Apparently they all wanted their interior to have motion detection as means of implicit input that is either deliberate or not, such as walking, approaching or entering somewhere; G3: *"when she enters and steps on the grass"*, G4: *"when she gets to the center"*, G3: *"As she crawls on the sensitive floor"*. Others embedded pressure-sensing as weaved into the fabrics of soft decorative objects; G1: *"conductive fabric integrated in sand bags can trigger explosions and light effects of the war when stood on creating an integrated way of performing"*. Other designs of embedded sensing included manipulating interior objects such as: G3: *"when she holds it"*, G3: *"when she touches it"*. An interesting code was found as: G2: *"would react to her death by turning dark"* meaning that death can be sensed and can trigger the aesthetic death of the interior space of its owner for a mourning time.

Communicating Through Colour-Change

Realizing their disparate properties, participants used a variety of colour-changing materials in their designs to be triggered at different conditions/inputs. Photochromic footprints (triggered by light in the dark) on the floor was repeatedly thought of as means of immersiveness leaving a glowing mark behind to be faded over time, even that of imaginary or distant characters/users who do not necessarily exist within the same space; G5: *"creating that sense of mystery"*, G2: *"would appear to be magical"*. Hydrochromic dyed fabric was used to respond to mist, and thermochromic paints and dyes were used on walls, fabrics and decorative artefacts. Two main reasons were behind using colour-changing interaction in the six designs: 'revealing' and 'reversing'. 'Revealing' a hidden story, text, picture or view was a noticeable objective behind embedding colour-change in different interior elements and composed an essential part in designing discoverability within the space; G2: *"ink that appears to give a narrative aspect to the hanging book that reveals the story using thermochromics when pages flip"*, G3: *"it will reveal the perspective view through thermochromics"*, G3: *"it reacts by revealing pictures of her future when she touches it"*. On the other hand, 'reversing' was the aim of integrating colour-changing materials to change the atmosphere, the feeling and appearance of the space between three states normal/default, cheerful/colourful, and dark/gloomy on both the background (walls) and the foreground (objects) accounting on the psychological effects and social-norm interpretations of different hues of colour schemes; G1: *"to change the atmosphere of the scene from colourful to a dark dingy scene"*, G2: *"once she's shot, colours would be dark, gloomy and dingy.. then colours would convert to reveal the golden heaven kingdom"*. Although not designed, but during the discussions, colour-changing materials were considered appropriate to show the unseen such as mapping distant unseen actions or conditions.

Shifting Focus Through Shape-Change

SMA was mainly used to add dynamics to decorative objects that already exist in their designs and was explicitly justified by adding automated vibrance to the interior; G1: *"trees in the scene are actuated using muscle wire instead of being static"*, G2: *"The back wall will use SMA to crumble away like rocks break away piece by piece without anyone moving anything"*. Kinetic actuation in general was also used to allow a focus-shifting effect between two spaces, scenery transition, revealing a hidden appearance. Another usage of kinetic actuation was to create an illusion of spatial movement; G4: *"it would look like descending into the pit without actually moving down"*. SMA muscle wire was not just used for shape-change but to activate ambient subtle motions that could manipulate light shadows underneath; G4: *"as it (SMA) moves it would change the shadows behind it, as if sunlight is coming through with a dappled shadow/lighting effect"*. However, SMA was mostly considered for an organic actuation effect due to its linear lift and bend nature that resembles a subtle breath motion, so most groups embedded SMA within artificial flowers and tree leaves for ambiance. When integrated within thermochromic fabric the combined effect of shape-change with colour-change attributed to creating a living scenery; G5: *"dead leaves and flowers would come to life and open up using SMA to open and close thermochromic flowers and leaves so that when it opens it starts slowly changing colour as well"*. This technique actually utilized the same energy source/ wiring that heats up the SMA to implicitly heat up the thermochromic fabric triggering colour-change as well, so a flower would blossom and brighten at the same time, as if alive.

Critical Reflections

As much as they succeeded in designing with the concept of 'Revealing', other findings included difficulty of designing for 'Reflection, Speculation, Legibility (Indirectness) & Para-Engagement (Extra-involvement)'. For example, G5 mentioned that during their brainstorm: *"we thought getting the audience to make assumptions on what will happen next in advance"*, then they tried to frame it in other ways *"like mapping, so what is on the stage sets off another response in the cafe or box office"* and even *"get the audience to be part of the play, so what they do reflects on the stage or what actors perform can be projected around the audience, reflecting what happens in the scene"*. These 'para-engagement' types of designs create a deeper meaning of involving the users within a public space and takes engagement and interactivity to a level

Figure 6. Capturing visitors response with the interactive wall-paper at Workshop 1 Exhibition: 'Enchanted Architecture'.

that is beyond the traditional direct interaction that is obvious, discoverable and legible. However, they did not actually design much of these insightful preliminary ideas. Perhaps due to their complexity, deepness and unconventional nature.

While designers in Case 1 expressed more elaboration and interest on the 'structural' scale of surfaces (walls, floors, ceilings) and furniture, designers in Case 2 had a perspective of the 'ambient' scale joined both ends of the holistic view of the 'space' and the decorative details/ accessories that essentially contribute to their conceptual design identity and experience. This is mostly the result of the 'theme' at which each particular case study was framed upon. Therefore, we recommend clear and careful consideration of the setting and subject of collaboration with interior architects and designers to yield both 'functional' and 'experiential' applications and domains to enable the emerge of a new level of 'interioractive' designs.

DISCUSSION

From the observations in both workshops and our architects' and interior designers' efforts to understand and work with the smart materials, in addition to the visitors' feedback during the exhibit (see Figure 6), we have developed three considerations for the design of interactive interior elements. We explicate these below, before turning to discuss how our work is contributing to the developing challenges of 'Interioraction'.

Discoverability and Legibility

The discoverability of an interactive interior space ranges from fully discoverable and understandable to being hidden. By discoverability we mean the property or an interface that describes the extent to which a space is designed to express or hide its interactivity. That is; how quickly can people uncover interactive elements within a space and how an interior can unfold as users start interacting with it, either through implicit or explicit interactions. On the other hand, legibility defines how easily users can make a connection between the cause and effect i.e. input and output of interactions. Some spaces can be deliberately designed in a way that appears disconnected to urge users to systematically act within the space in order to reason what is happening. While we may not need or want to be reasoning about the legibility of some spaces, others should be designed in a way to reveal cause and effect relationships in dynamic environments.

	Fully Discoverable	Undiscoverable *(Hidden Interaction)*
Fully Legible	Obvious and Consistent	Hidden and Playful
Not Legible *(Hidden Logic)*	Spatio-Temporal and Autonomous	Mysterious and Magical

Table 1. Combinations between ranges of discoverability and legibility of an interactive interior space

In this sense, there is a clear relationship between discoverability (clarity of how to interact) and legibility (clarity of why it reacts). Table 1 shows how combining different ranges of discoverability and legibility can result in different space interactivity features and qualities. For example, a fully discoverable (flat) space that is fully legible (intuitive) with simple logic is understandable, obvious and consistent such as a regular light switch. An undiscoverable (unfolding) space that is also fully legible will be more playful (as it unfolds hidden interactions) depending on its learning curve as it still holds a 1-to-1 legible constant reaction, such as the Engaging Space [7] and the History Tablecloth [10]. On the contrary, a fully discoverable illegible interactive space is one that reacts to complicated logic/ scenarios that often use more variables in the interaction equation such as number of users/tangibles, their position/ roles within the space as well as variable time, distance/proximity or a composition of more variables creating spatio-temporal responses, sequential or accumulative interactions over time. This combination results in an autonomously-perceived space or object with no clear idea of why it is changing or behaving in a certain way, e.g. shape-changing bench [15]. Finally, a space that doesn't immediately show how to interact with it or why it is changing creates a mysterious atmosphere and can in the right circumstances then be perceived as a magical object or an enchanted space.

Revelation and Coherent Dynamics

How the interior space can conceal hidden appearances, and hidden personality of its own and be able to slowly reveal them through user interaction is an interesting aspect of an interactive interior. Although it is not necessarily always the case, a space that entirely transforms its interior elements together playing one symphony creates an immersive experience with its coherent dynamics. For example, colour-change and/or texture-change of an interior's wall paint, curtain, sofa cushion, flower vase, rug and wall art can create an impression of a whole new space or reveal a different feeling or mood. This can be achieved by wirelessly networking each of these soft decorative interfaces and playing with the options of appearance-changing in a coherent theme that can unfold together showing the veiled mystery beneath, designing for both the playfulness and aesthetics of interaction [25].

Spatio-Temporality and Spatio-Autonomy

An actual immersive experience is the one that takes interaction into 4-dimensions (rather than just 3D) by adding temporality as a key player in the user spatial interaction. An interior element can change its appearance as a result of interactions done over a week, capturing all the dynamics of the space within that period of time rather than instantaneous reactions developed in previous work [20, 37, 4] that relied on a direct and prompt action-reaction approach. Once we design interactive spaces that can change over time or possess some autonomy of their own, our environment can start communicating 'self-expression' through their unfolding interaction.

INTERIORACTION CHALLENGES

Through this exploratory study we aimed at tackling some of the key challenges of Interactive Architecture [22]. Primarily, 'Radical Interdisciplinarity' through engaging relevant design communities i.e. architects and interior designers. Our engagement -as interaction designers- with interior architecture designers has taken a shape that is beyond the traditional researcher-participant relationship. But was rather a co-designer and co-author interrelationship where we all worked together in collaborative ideation, exploration and design group activities and discussions. This yielded a unique and productive experience that should specifically be applied to research around interactive spaces which is inherently multi or interdisciplinary. Other challenges we tried to exploit included 'Appropriation and Retrofitting', where we succeeded in embedding interactivity into standard finishing materials and decorative objects with simple, affordable and available materials that are paintable, printable and programmable. Whilst a delicate and tricky task, the new techniques we have introduced (e.g. the jigsaw, tactile palette, etc), helped simplify the ideas and forms of retrofitting such normal materials and real-world objects in a way that keeps -and extends- the aesthetics of the interior space and does not jeopardize the social and emotional associations people have with daily physical objects and surfaces. However, with regards to 'Scalability', we faced numerous obstacles related to embedding them in room-sized scale, but found iterative design methods and special material considerations to be helpful.

CONCLUSION

Not only did we *i)* engage architects and interior designers in 'interaction design' for creating interactive spaces, but also, through this collaboration, we have *ii)* explored the design space of interioraction, usages and limitations, *iii)* explored the potentials of affordable interactive materials in designing and prototyping interioractives, *iv)* developed new design techniques to do so, *v)* designed six different interactive spaces with a holistic experience, and built an actual interactive interior space (with reactive walls, furniture and decorative objects), *vi)* addressed some of the challenges identified for interactive architecture, and finally *vii)* tested and captured user responses to interactive spaces of novice users (in the wild) who were visiting our 'enchanted' exhibition. As we intend to continue such engaging and inclusive studies, we encourage the community to carry on similar collaborations and investigate new possibilities and potentials of 'Interioraction'.

ACKNOWLEDGMENTS

This research was funded by Newcastle University SAgE DTA scholarship programme. We would like to thank all of our participants, from Newcastle University and Northumbria University, who generously contributed their time and skills so willingly, and actively participated in this study.

REFERENCES

1. Aedas Architects. 2012. Al Bahr Towers. Abu Dhabi, UAE.
2. Nimish Biloria and Valentina Sumini. 2007. Performative Building Skin Systems: A Morphogenomic Approach Towards Developing Real-Time Adaptive Building Skin Systems. *International Journal of Architectural Computing* 07, 04 (2007). DOI: http://dx.doi.org/10.1260/1478-0771.7.4.643
3. Stewart Brand. 1995. *How buildings learn: What happens after they're built.* Penguin.
4. Leah Buechley, David Mellis, Hannah Perner-Wilson, Emily Lovell, and Bonifaz Kaufmann. 2010. Living Wall: Programmable Wallpaper for Interactive Spaces. In *Proceedings of the international conference on Multimedia.* Firenze, Italy, 1401–1402. DOI: http://dx.doi.org/10.1145/1873951.1874226
5. Nicholas S Dalton, Emily Collins, and Paul Marshall. 2015. Display Blindness? Looking Again at the Visibility of Situated Displays using Eye Tracking. In *CHI'15.* ACM, Seoul, Republic of Korea. DOI: http://dx.doi.org/10.1145/2702123.2702150
6. Nicholas S Dalton, Holger Schnadelbach, Mikael Wiberg, and Tasos Varoudis. 2016. *Architecture and Interaction.* Springer.
7. Dalziel & Pow. 2015. Engaging Space. In *Exhibited at the Retail Design Expo (RDE) in 2015.* Exhibited at the Retail Design Expo (RDE) in 2015, London, UK.
8. DARLING QUARTER. 2016. Luminous | Darling Quarter. (2016). http://www.darlingquarter.com/luminous/
9. Simon Dodsworth. 2009. *The Fundamentals of Interior Design.* 184 pages. https://books.google.co.za/books/about/The
10. William Gaver, John Bowers, Andy Boucher, Andy Law, Sarah Pennington, and Nicholas Villar. 2006. The History Tablecloth: Illuminating Domestic Activity. *Dis 2006* (2006). DOI:http://dx.doi.org/10.1145/1142405.1142437
11. Sven Gehring, Elias Hartz, and Markus Löchtefeld. 2013. The Media Façade Toolkit: Prototyping and Simulating Interaction with Media Façades. In *UbiComp'13.* Zurich, Switzerland. DOI: http://dx.doi.org/10.1145/2493432.2493471
12. Ernst Giselbrecht. 2010. Kiefer Technic Showroom. Styria, Austria.
13. Mark Goulthorpe. 2000. Aegis Hyposurface. Cambridge, Massachusetts, USA. http://www.hyposurface.org/
14. Jens Emil Grønbæk, Henrik Korsgaard, Marianne Graves Petersen, Morten Henriksen Birk, and Peter Gall Krogh. 2017. Proxemic Transitions: Designing Shape-Changing Furniture for Informal Meetings. In *Proceedings of CHI '17.* Denver, CO, USA.
15. Erik Grönvall, Sofie Kinch, Marianne Graves Petersen, and Majken K. Rasmussen. 2014. Causing Commotion with a Shape-Changing Bench. In *Proceedings of CHI'14.* Toronto, ON, Canada. DOI: http://dx.doi.org/10.1145/2556288.2557360
16. Henning Larsen Architects. 2014. Kolding Building of SDU. Universitetsparken Kolding, Denmark.
17. Chuck Hoberman. 2004. Hoberman's Arch. Salt Lake City, Utah, USA.
18. Yannick Joye. 2007. Architectural Lessons From Environmental Psychology: The Case of Biophilic Architecture. *Review of General Psychology* 11, 4 (2007), 305–328. DOI: http://dx.doi.org/10.1037/1089-2680.11.4.305
19. Stephen Kaplan. 1995. The Restorative Benefits of Nature: Toward an Integrative Framework. *Journal of Environmental Psychology* 15, 3 (1995), 169–182. DOI: http://dx.doi.org/10.1016/0272-4944(95)90001-2
20. Chin Koi Khoo and Flora D. Salim. 2013. Lumina: A Soft Kinetic Material for Morphing Architectural Skins and Organic User Interfaces. In *Proceedings of UbiComp'13.* Zurich, Switzerland, 53. DOI: http://dx.doi.org/10.1145/2493432.2494263
21. Nadia Mounajjed and Imran A Zualkernan. 2011. From Simple Pleasure to Pleasurable Skin: An Interactive Architectural Screen. In *DPPI '11.* Milano, IT. DOI: http://dx.doi.org/10.1145/2347504.2347537
22. Sara Nabil, Thomas Plötz, and David S Kirk. 2017. Interactive Architecture: Exploring and Unwrapping the Potentials of Organic User Interfaces. In *Proc. of TEI'17.* Yokohama, Japan, 89–100. DOI: http://dx.doi.org/10.1145/3024969.3024981
23. Jean Nouvel. 1987. Institut du Monde Arabe. Paris, France.
24. Kas Oosterhuis and Nimish Biloria. 2008. Interactions with Proactive Architectural Spaces. *Commun. ACM* 51, 6 (2008). DOI:http://dx.doi.org/10.1145/1349026.1349041
25. Marianne Graves Petersen. 2007. Squeeze: Designing for playful experiences among co-located people in homes. In *Proceedings of the ACM 2007 Conference on Human Factors in Computing Systems.* San Jose, CA, USA, 2609–2614. DOI: http://dx.doi.org/10.1145/1240866.1241050
26. Philips Lighting. 2016. Philips Luminous Patterns. (2016). http://www.lighting.philips.com/main/systems/packaged-offerings/retail-and-hospitality/luminous-patterns.html
27. Ingrid Maria Pohl and Lian Loke. 2012. Engaging the Sense of Touch in Interactive Architecture. In *Proceedings of the 24th Australian Computer-Human Interaction Conference on - OzCHI '12.* Melbourne, VIC, Australia, 493–496. DOI: http://dx.doi.org/10.1145/2414536.2414611

28. Larissa Pschetz and Richard Banks. 2013. Long Living Chair. In *CHI '13 Extended Abstracts on Human Factors in Computing Systems*. ACM, Paris, France, 13–14. DOI: http://dx.doi.org/10.1145/2468356.2479590

29. Carolina Ramirez-Figueroa, Martyn Dade-Robertson, and Luis Hernan. 2013. Adaptive Morphologies: Toward a Morphogenesis of Material Construction. In *ACADIA 2013 Adaptive Architecture*. Cambridge, ON, Canada, 21–23.

30. Axel Ritter. 2015. *Smart Materials in Architecture, Interior Architecture and Design*. Vol. 1. Birkhauser. DOI: http://dx.doi.org/10.1017/CBO9781107415324.004

31. Francesca Rogers and Daniele Gualeni Design Studio. 2010. Light-Form. In *Designed for ILIDE (Italian Light Design) and Exhibited at the Milan Design Week in 2010*.

32. Holger Schnadelbach, Ainojie Irune, David Kirk, Kevin Glover, and Patrick Brundell. 2012. ExoBuilding: Physiologically Driven Adaptive Architecture. *ACM Transactions on Computer-Human Interaction* 19, 4 (2012). DOI:http://dx.doi.org/10.1145/2395131.2395132

33. Odilo Schoch. 2006. My Building is my Display. In *Proceedings of the the 24th Conference on Education and Research in Computer Aided Architectural Design in Europe: Communicating Space(s) (eCAADe'06)*. Volos, Greece, 610–616.

34. Nicolas Schöffer. 2005. Spatiodynamic, Luminodynamic & Chronodynamic. In *Nicolas Schöffer's Précurseur de l'Art Cybernétique Exhibition*. Paris, France.

35. Roel Vertegaal and Ivan Poupyrev. 2008. Organic User Interfaces. *Commun. ACM* 51, 6 (2008), 26. DOI: http://dx.doi.org/10.1145/1349026.1349033

36. Richard Weston. 2003. *Materials, Form and Architecture*. Yale University Press.

37. Bin Yu, Nienke Bongers, Alissa van Asseldonk, Jun Hu, Mathias Funk, and Loe Feijs. 2016. LivingSurface: Biofeedback through Shape-changing Display. In *Proceedings of the TEI '16*. Eindhoven, Netherlands, 168–175. DOI: http://dx.doi.org/10.1145/2839462.2839469

Exploring Interactions and Perceptions of Kinetic Wearables

Hsin-Liu (Cindy) Kao[1], Deborah Ajilo[2], Oksana Anilionyte[3],
Artem Dementyev[1], Inrak Choi[4], Sean Follmer[4], Chris Schmandt[1]

[1]Media Lab, MIT, Cambridge, MA
[2]Mechanical Engineering, MIT, Cambridge, MA
[3]Fashion Design, Royal College of Art, London, UK
[4]Mechanical Engineering, Stanford University, Stanford, CA

{cindykao, dmajilo, artemd, geek}@mit.edu[1,2], oksana.anilionyte@network.rca.ac.uk,[3]
{irchoi, sfollmer}@stanford.edu[4]

ABSTRACT
Jewelry and accessories have long been objects for decorating the human body; however they remain static and non-interactive. This work explores the role of accessory-like kinetic wearables in relation to personal style: What does it mean to wear kinetic accessories and why would one be motivated to do so? We developed Kino, a kinetic accessory system which enables both aesthetic and functional clothing-specific design possibilities. We engaged fashion designers and non-designers to investigate how they would integrate the platform into their design practice or personal wardrobe. Participants viewed the devices not as gadgets but as companions due to their close proximity to the body. They envisioned a wide range of usage scenarios, highlighting the complexity of mobility in relation to personal style. We observe how mobility offers opportunities for fluid representations of self, which is unachievable though static clothing and accessories. We also outline how personalized aesthetics is important for the meaning making of novel on-body devices.

ACM Classification Keywords
H.5.m. Information Interfaces&Presentation (e.g.HCI): Misc.

Author Keywords
Fashion; Wearable Technology; Robotics.

INTRODUCTION
Jewelry and accessories have long been objects encoded with social, cultural, and personal meaning for ornamenting the body. While there have been numerous explorations with the aesthetic form of jewelry, they largely remain analog and non-interactive. Recently, there has been a rise in computational jewelry [24], i.e., adornment artifacts that function both as jewelry and as a computational device. However, they are often limited to output in the form of alpha-numerical displays or LEDs. In this work, we incorporate movement into static accessories so they become mobile objects on the body. They reconfigure location and complete functions beyond decoration. Movement opens the design space for dynamic interactions between device, clothing, and the body. Through mobility, the device can alter the appearance of one's outfit for increased fluidity in self-expression. It can also configure between location-specific roles, shifting between technical gadget and object of ornamentation according to location.

DIS '17, June 10-14, 2017, Edinburgh, United Kingdom
ACM 978-1-4503-4922-2/17/06...$15.00
DOI: http://dx.doi.org/10.1145/3064663.3064686

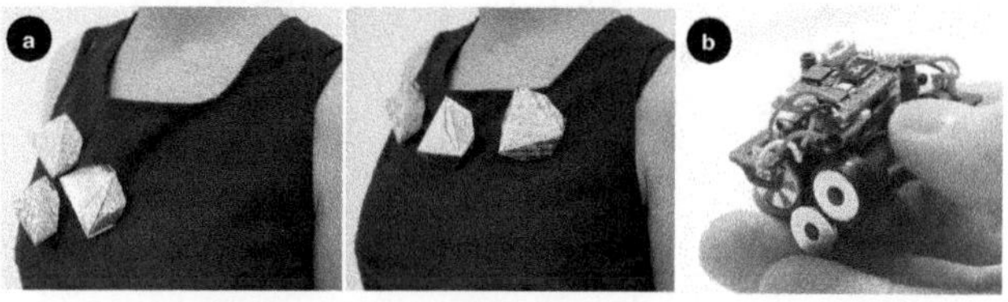

Figure 1. (a) Example of kinetic wearables transitioning from brooch to necklace (b) the robot without a cover.

In this paper, we aim to explore the future of kinetic wearables and its meaning for interaction and personal style. We build upon an existing on-body robot platform, [8], which we previously developed, to create Kino, a mobile accessory system. We describe the design space of Kino, and created several garment applications that explored clothing-specific design possibilities. We engaged fashion designers and participants with no fashion design experience to unpack the personal meanings and social functions dynamic accessories foster within personal style.

BACKGROUND AND RELATED WORK
Smart Jewelry: The emerging trend of smart jewelry seeks to transition gadgets into fashionable body-wear. However, interactions are limited to visual [6, 22] and tactile [12] output, or input through touch screens [12, 21]. Kino incorporates movement as a novel interaction modality.

Shape-changing Clothing: The fashion industry has explored adaptive clothing: Hussein Chalayan's animatronic dresses [27] reconfigure with motors and pulleys. ZipperBot [28] is a motorized zipper. Pneumatics [10, 18, 20] and shape

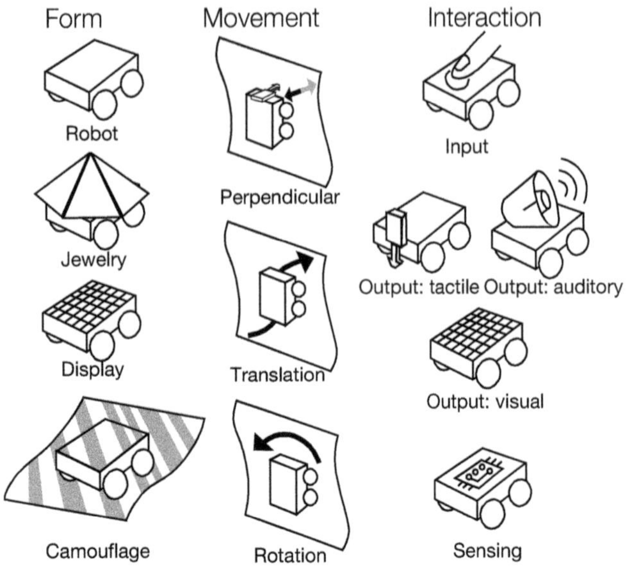

Figure 2. Design Primitives.

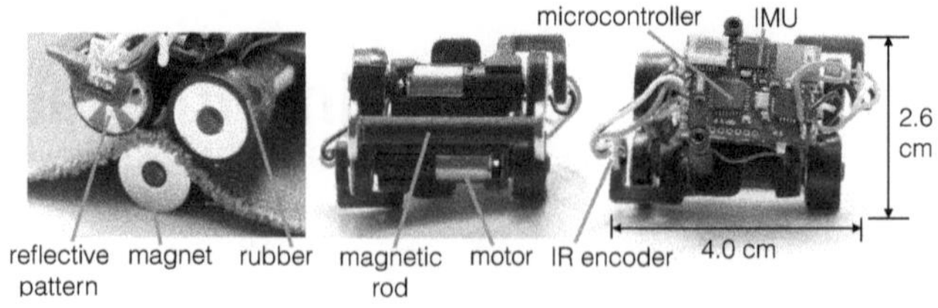

Figure 3. Mechanical and hardware implementation.

memory alloys [2] have also been used for shape change. However, the work in this area is mostly task specific and does not realize a generalized platform. Moreover, the technology is often integrated into the clothing itself, while Kino can be fabricated outside of the soft goods realm and incorporated on top of existing garments.

On-body robots: The robotics field has realized systems which grip onto folds [5, 16] or penetrate into cloth [3] for vertical movement. Parasitic Mobility [14] sensor nodes jump from one human host to another. Saga et al. [23] created a mouse-like robot that moves on a arm-mounted rail. Nixie [7] is a wearable drone that can detach from the wrist and take selfies. Additional works explore actuation in fixed locations [15, 17, 19]. While these works demonstrate functional capabilities, applications and user perceptions are under-explored.

DESIGNING KINO

Mechanical and Hardware implementation

As shown in Figure 3, the main drive system consists of motors connected to magnetic wheels on top and underneath the fabric. This holds the robot in place regardless of its orientation. The robot is untethered with a custom circuit board and on-board battery. The robot's size is 4cm by 2.6cm. Additional details can be found in [8].

Design Primitives

To use Kino for on-body design, we outline the design primitives which consists of form, movement, and interaction.

Form. There is tension with computation jewelry seen as a gadget versus an object for decoration [24]. Individually, the form of the robots can enable different purposes.

- Robot. The bare structure is an on-body robot.
- Jewelry. Material and geometry are important design elements constituting a piece of jewelry. With the addition of an overlay cover on top of the structure, various materials and geometric designs can be explored. The material choice can enable a gem-like jewelry piece, or fabric-like and integrated with the garment.
- Display. With a LED matrix, it becomes a digital display for information presentation.
- Camouflage. These devices can become camouflaged with cover designs that blend in with the underlying fabrics. They become hidden, only drawing attention when in movement.

Movement.

- Perpendicular. The addition of a linear actuator can create motion perpendicular to the fabric. It can create tactile feedback on the skin or attach to objects
- Translation. Moving on fabric plane from point A to B.
- Rotation. The device can turn and rotate to navigate in different directions. Turning in a fixed location can enable fabric manipulation, providing visual feedback.

Interaction. The addition of various sensors and actuators can expand the interactive capabilities of the device.

- Input. The addition of a touch sensitive add-on transitions it to an input device.
- Output. Providing graphical output through displays and non-graphical output such as tactile and auditory feedback.
- Sensing. Integrating specific sensors, the device can detect environmental signals (light, temperature, proximity) or body movements (accelerometer, gyro).

Application Examples

Building on the design primitives, we present two types of applications (demos in accompanying video): (1) aesthetic-driven which alters the appearance of clothing for aesthetic presentation, and (2) function-driven which completes a task for the wearer. Function and aesthetics are not mutually exclusive, and we highlight opportunities for both.

Aesthetic-Centric Applications

Shape-changing jewelry. Multiple devices can become building blocks to form jewelry design. With its mobility, the individual pieces can form various shapes and designs. We present an application of a jewelry set that starts as a minimalistic brooch for going to work, and when the wearer later goes to a dinner outing, it is activated to shift into a necklace statement piece (see Figure 1a).

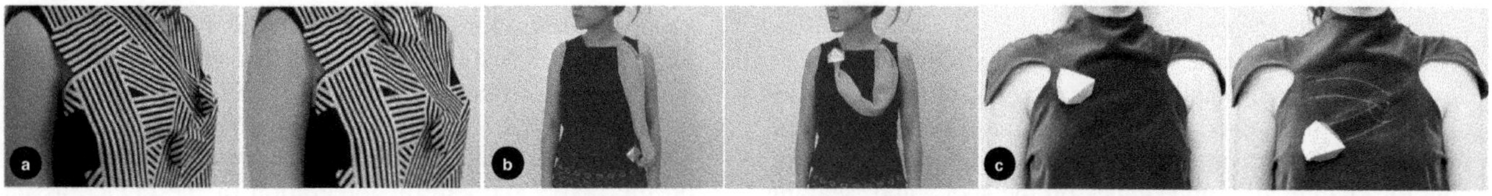

Figure 4. Aesthetic-centric applications: (a) pattern changing, (b) shape changing clothing for aesthetics, (c) pattern etching.

Pattern changing. Cover designs camouflaged with the underlying textile can morph between unique patterns effects. We present an example of a stripe pattern with matching device covers (Figure 4a). By shifting its location on the body, the device creates different aesthetic effects.

Shape changing clothing for aesthetics. By attaching the robots to open ends of a garment, the robots can pull, flip, and shift the ends to alter clothing appearance. We present a shawl which shape-changes into a scarf according to how the wearer wishes to present herself (Figure 4b).

Etching patterns. When moving, the devices can etch into specific fabrics and "draw" patterns. On fabrics such as velvet, the robots leave visible tracks during movement - the clothing becomes a canvas to etch designs. The traces are temporary and therefore new patterns can be generated (Figure 4c).

Function-Centric Applications

Mobile on-body microphone. With addition of a microphone and speaker, the robot is a bluetooth microphone/speaker to receive phone calls when the wearer's hands are full. It normally sits as a decorative brooch, and when the wearer receives a phone call, it shifts close to the neck for the wearer to talk to the device (Figure 5a).

Shape changing clothing for function. The robots can trigger clothing to actively adapt based on the climate or comfort needs of the wearer. We created a coat and connected each drawstring of the hood to a device. Upon detecting an increase in temperature, the devices move downwards to unfold the hood (Figure 5b).

ENGAGING DESIGNERS AND WEARERS

To study how mobility relates to one's perception of personal style, we used the system as a material probe [13] for material-centric modes of design and analysis [9, 26, 29]. We engaged wearers to understand how everyday people would integrate the system in their wardrobe, and fashion designers as "experts" of the symbolism of clothing and its design practice. We seek to understand:

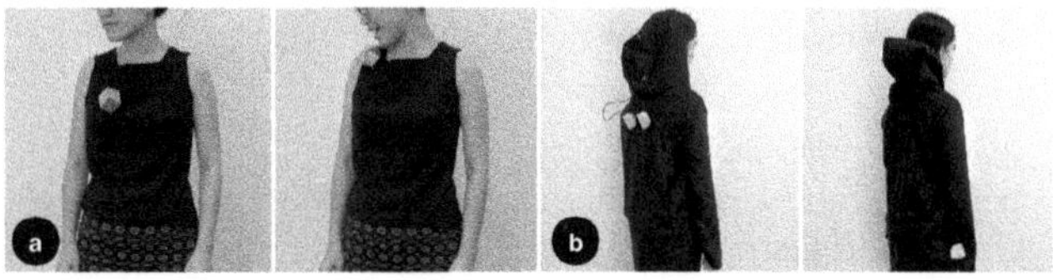

Figure 5. Function-centric applications: a) bluetooth microphone, b) climate reactive clothing.

- What associations shape one's perceptions towards kinetic wearables? As a novel device, Kino lacks historical reference of its own and must be understood in association with existing objects and experiences.
- How do people envision a kinetic wearable system to shape their everyday interactions?

We conducted 60-min semi-structured interview sessions where participants were first introduced to the system, and then invited to wear and control the device. The researcher then demonstrated the functional and aesthetic applications described in the previous section. Participants were asked to select interactions they were likely to integrate into their wardrobe or design practice, and describe at length how they would design/wear the device and interact with the system socially and personally. To understand the symbolism of such a system, we asked participants to compare and contrast the system with alternatives which might serve similar functions, such as wearable devices, clothing, or jewelry.

17 individuals: 11 wearers (aged 20 to 31, M=25.5, 5M, 6F) and 6 designers (aged 23 to 33, M=28.3, 2M, 5F) participated in our study. The designers had a vast range of experience and worked for large brands or as independent designers. All sessions were video recorded and transcribed for analysis using grounded theory approach [4].

Findings

Symbolism of Kino: Personal Companion

Participants described the device as a "companion", "pet", or "living animal." They compared it to a heart rate monitor or health tracker, but felt it was much more personal and possessed animalistic qualities. P2, a wearer, said it felt like "a dog licking my face" when it moved close to her neck. P10, a designer, compared it to ornamented beetles in Mexico which people would wear as a "living brooch." The fact she could "feel it moving" and "gripping to my clothes" made it "a living gadget." P8, a wearer, and P12, a designer, imagined developing a relationship with the robot by naming it and assigning it personalities. P8 imagined "talking to it all the time" and asking it to help her complete tasks. While many participants welcomed the experience, others described the initial encounter as "eerie", "creepy", or "foreign." P3, P7, wearers, and P9, a designer, compared it to "a bug crawling on my shirt." However, if its movement served a specific purpose and was not "aimless", they would then see it as "a little assistant" and not just "a random bug" over time. They suggested miniaturizing the device to the size of a button, and reducing the gear noise for a more seamless experience.

Envisioned Interactions

1) Many outfits in one. P1, P6, P8, wearers, and P12, a designer, imagined enabling representations of "various sides of self." P12 mentioned how "clothing in the morning, now, is the same when you put it back at night." He imagined being able to "change your appearance on the spot," and "leaving with one outfit in the morning, yet coming home with another." Specifically, P1 imagined altering between a "minimalistic classic look" where she could wear to class, versus a "loud statement piece" for going out at night. P8 and P6, wearers, imagined how the system might change their hairstyles by altering between long and short hair.

2) Personal assistant. P1, P4, P6, wearers, and P12, a designer, imagined the system as a personal assistant which performs just-in-time, specific tasks. P4 talked about his frustration with the "generic and never ending" notifications from mobile phones. He imagined being able to personalize and "assign meaning" to notifications. For instance, it would move towards his face to notify of a phone call, whereas it would move towards his legs to notify of yoga time. The "freedom" to program "specific" nudges shifted his perception of the device from "gadget" to "assistant." P10 contrasted how with the device, "you do get to choose what its doing" whereas "the smartwatch at the end of the day is just watch." The capability to designate its function made it "like your little helper."

3) Remote communication device. P4, P5, P11, wearers, imagined the platform for intimate communication between remote loved ones. P11 mentioned how it embodied the presence of a family member or significant other, "the fact it touches my skin [...] makes it feel human." P5 expressed he would like to "let it be controlled by someone that has a connection with me." For instance, when it tapped him, it would communicate presence or a playful interaction.

4) Active, functional garments. P13, P15, P17, designers, and P8, a wearer, imagined garments which actively engage with the wearer's body. P13 described it as a "wearable Nest thermostat" that would "learn your patterns." For instance, it would tighten his jacket according to temperature, and clinch it to the exact fit of his preference. P15, a designer, described an ultra-form fitting garment that could "move between a size 4 and 6" for a more professional or casual fit.

5) Fashion that moves. Participants described movement as a new aesthetic. P8, a wearer, saw the system as "fashion that moves", and "fashion that is alive." She imagined the devices fully integrated into the textile, and creating a "magical feeling" through slow, subtle movement. Both P8 and P3 contrasted this with LED-laden garments and found it to be "less frighteningly techy" and somehow "naturally integrated" with things they already wear. It "looked normal but with a pleasant twist." P16, a wearer, saw the "slowly, ambiguously changing" pattern as "a playful agency, a new fashion."

Discussion

Meaningful coupling of aesthetics with function

From the study, the unique individual preferences highlight the complexity of personal style. While some participants were function-inclined and others more aesthetic-centric, we observe a desire for the coupling of both for a truly wearable experience. The function provided reason to wear such a device as it assisted in the completion of a task unachievable by current devices, accessories, or clothing. Aesthetics, on the other hand, provided means for making sense of the object on the body: the careful integration of the device as part of the garment assigned it meaning. P8 mentioned she felt uncomfortable with "wearing a robot so close to my body," yet when she could "dress it up" her perspective shifted: "it's a wearable, but it's more integrated as part of my clothing [...] something that is part of who I am." Roland Barthes [1] noted, "Fashion is play, with the most profound of human questions: Who am I?" The action of "dressing up" links to our play with identity; being able to integrate the device with their clothing seemed to enable participants to carve out an identity for the novel, foreign device, which then made it easier to accept and embrace as a part of their everyday dress. The ability to personalize device appearance is also an emerging necessity in the wearable technology market [25]. Seemingly as technology moves ever closer to the body, assigning meaning is increasingly critical for its adoption.

Fluid representation of self

P9 described the system as "an aesthetic change of more than one state," and compared the system to "designing for a video versus a photograph." The addition of movement enables fluidity in presenting multiple states of self which was previously unachievable. As noted by Goffman's [11] theatrical representation of social interaction: "we all take different parts given the situations we give ourselves to be in" and "we adapt who we are based on who we interact with." Many participants seemed to want to seamlessly adjust between different aesthetic appearances or technical functions to represent their various roles, states and needs. To this end, mobility becomes an enabler for rapidly shifting representations of self.

CONCLUSION AND FUTURE WORK

This paper draws out ways kinetic wearables can function within the complex and meaning-laden landscape of personal style. We developed Kino as a material probe to elicit associations that shape perspectives towards wearable mobility. Assigning identity and meaning to the foreign, mobile object was achieved in the same way we craft our own identity though fashion: by "dressing up" and personalizing the appearance of the device. Mobility enabled more fluid representations of self, suggesting a dynamic future of the things we wear, and the multitudes of identities we can project. We extend mobility as an additional vocabulary for this possible future of personal style. In future work, we seek to overcome current technological constraints (e.g., size) to increase wearability, iterate the design with further user feedback, with all this leading to autonomous deployment in the wild for everyday usage.

ACKNOWLEDGEMENTS

We thank undergraduate researchers Karla-Sofia Zapata-Garcia and Daphne Lin for help with prototyping, and Seth Avecilla for screen printing and garment construction support. This project was supported in part by the MIT Council of Arts Grant and the Bill Mitchell++ Fund.

REFERENCES

1. Roland Barthes. 1967. *The Fashion System*. University of California Press.
2. J. Berzowska and M. Coelho. 2005. Kukkia and Vilkas: kinetic electronic garments. In *Ninth IEEE International Symposium on Wearable Computers (ISWC'05)*. 82–85. DOI:http://dx.doi.org/10.1109/ISWC.2005.29
3. P. Birkmeyer, A. G. Gillies, and R. S. Fearing. 2011. CLASH: Climbing vertical loose cloth. In *2011 IEEE/RSJ International Conference on Intelligent Robots and Systems*. 5087–5093. DOI: http://dx.doi.org/10.1109/IROS.2011.6094905
4. Kathy Charmaz. 2006. *Constructing Grounded Theory: A Practical Guide Through Qualitative Analysis*. Pine Forge Press.
5. G. Chen, Y. Liu, R. Fu, J. Sun, X. Wu, and Y. Xu. 2013. Rubbot: Rubbing on flexible loose surfaces. In *2013 IEEE/RSJ International Conference on Intelligent Robots and Systems*. 2303–2308. DOI: http://dx.doi.org/10.1109/IROS.2013.6696678
6. CNET. 2014a. Kovert connected jewellery is high-tech and high fashion. (4 July 2014). https://www.cnet.com/news/kovert-connected-jewellery-is-high-tech-and-high-fashion/.
7. CNET. 2014b. Nixie lets you wear a selfie-taking drone on your wrist. (26 September 2014). https://www.cnet.com/news/nixie-wear-a-selfie-taking-drone-on-your-wrist/.
8. Artem Dementyev, Hsin-Liu (Cindy) Kao, Inrak Choi, Deborah Ajilo, Maggie Xu, Joseph A. Paradiso, Chris Schmandt, and Sean Follmer. 2016. Rovables: Miniature On-Body Robots As Mobile Wearables. In *Proceedings of the 29th Annual Symposium on User Interface Software and Technology (UIST '16)*. ACM, New York, NY, USA, 111–120. DOI: http://dx.doi.org/10.1145/2984511.2984531
9. Ylva Fernaeus and Petra Sundström. 2012. The Material Move How Materials Matter in Interaction Design Research. In *Proceedings of the Designing Interactive Systems Conference (DIS '12)*. ACM, New York, NY, USA, 486–495. DOI: http://dx.doi.org/10.1145/2317956.2318029
10. Ying Gao. 2006. Walking City Dress. (2006). http://yinggao.ca/interactifs/walking-city/.
11. Erving Goffman. 1959. *The Presentation of Self in Everyday Life*. Anchor.
12. Intel. 2014. Intel MICA Intelligent Bracelet Stays Alert with Style. (17 November 2014). http://iq.intel.com/micaintelligent-luxury-fashion-bracelet-stays-alert-\withstyle/Intel.
13. Heekyoung Jung and Erik Stolterman. 2011. Material Probe: Exploring Materiality of Digital Artifacts. In *Proceedings of the Fifth International Conference on Tangible, Embedded, and Embodied Interaction (TEI '11)*. ACM, New York, NY, USA, 153–156. DOI: http://dx.doi.org/10.1145/1935701.1935731
14. Mathew Laibowitz and Joseph A. Paradiso. 2005. Parasitic Mobility for Pervasive Sensor Networks. In *Proceedings of the Third International Conference on Pervasive Computing (PERVASIVE'05)*. Springer-Verlag, Berlin, Heidelberg, 255–278. DOI: http://dx.doi.org/10.1007/11428572_16
15. Sang-won Leigh and Pattie Maes. 2016. Body Integrated Programmable Joints Interface. In *Proceedings of the 2016 CHI Conference on Human Factors in Computing Systems (CHI '16)*. ACM, New York, NY, USA, 6053–6057. DOI: http://dx.doi.org/10.1145/2858036.2858538
16. Y. Liu, X. Wu, H. Qian, D. Zheng, J. Sun, and Y. Xu. 2012. System and design of Clothbot: A robot for flexible clothes climbing. In *2012 IEEE International Conference on Robotics and Automation*. 1200–1205. DOI: http://dx.doi.org/10.1109/ICRA.2012.6224620
17. Diana MacLean, Asta Roseway, and Mary Czerwinski. 2013. MoodWings: A Wearable Biofeedback Device for Real-time Stress Intervention. In *Proceedings of the 6th International Conference on PErvasive Technologies Related to Assistive Environments (PETRA '13)*. ACM, New York, NY, USA, Article 66, 8 pages. DOI: http://dx.doi.org/10.1145/2504335.2504406
18. Mashable. 2011. The Futuristic Fashion of Diana Eng. (26 March 2011). http://mashable.com/2011/03/26/diana-eng-fashion/.
19. Masayasu Ogata, Yuta Sugiura, Hirotaka Osawa, and Michita Imai. 2012. Pygmy: A Ring-like Anthropomorphic Device That Animates the Human Hand. In *CHI '12 Extended Abstracts on Human Factors in Computing Systems (CHI EA '12)*. ACM, New York, NY, USA, 1003–1006. DOI: http://dx.doi.org/10.1145/2212776.2212371
20. Laura Perovich, Philippa Mothersill, and Jennifer Broutin Farah. 2013. Awakened Apparel: Embedded Soft Actuators for Expressive Fashion and Functional Garments. In *Proceedings of the 8th International Conference on Tangible, Embedded and Embodied Interaction (TEI '14)*. ACM, New York, NY, USA, 77–80. DOI:http://dx.doi.org/10.1145/2540930.2540958
21. PopSuger. 2014. Tory Burch and Fitbit Just Released Their Chicest Collaboration Yet. (15 July 2014). https://www.popsugar.com/fitness/Tory-Burch-Fitbit-35249877.
22. Ringly. 2014. Smart Jewelry and Accessories. (2014). https://ringly.com/.
23. Tamami Saga, Nagisa Munekata, and Tetsuo Ono. 2014. Daily Support Robots That Move on the Body. In *Proceedings of the Second International Conference on Human-agent Interaction (HAI '14)*. ACM, New York, NY, USA, 29–34. DOI: http://dx.doi.org/10.1145/2658861.2658882

24. Yulia Silina and Hamed Haddadi. 2015. New Directions in Jewelry: A Close Look at Emerging Trends and Developments in Jewelry-like Wearable Devices. In *Proceedings of the 2015 ACM International Symposium on Wearable Computers (ISWC '15)*. ACM, New York, NY, USA, 49–56. DOI: http://dx.doi.org/10.1145/2802083.2808410

25. TechRepublic. 2014. Wearables and fashion: Blending the two will be a key to success. (25 April 2014). http://www.techrepublic.com/article/wearables-and-fashion-blending-the-two-will-be-a-\key-to-success/.

26. Anna Vallgårda and Johan Redström. 2007. Computational Composites. In *Proceedings of the SIGCHI Conference on Human Factors in Computing Systems (CHI '07)*. ACM, New York, NY, USA, 513–522. DOI:http://dx.doi.org/10.1145/1240624.1240706

27. VOGUE. 2006. Hussein Chalayan, Spring/Summer 2007 Ready-to-wear. (2006). http://www.vogue.co.uk/shows/spring-summer-2007-ready-to-wear/hussein-chalayan/.

28. Adam Whiton. 2013. *Sartorial Robotics: Electronic-textiles and fiber-electronics for social soft-architecture robotics*. Ph.D. Dissertation. Massachusetts Institute of Technology, Cambridge, MA.

29. Mikael Wiberg, Hiroshi Ishii, Paul Dourish, Anna Vallgårda, Tobie Kerridge, Petra Sundström, Daniela Rosner, and Mark Rolston. 2013. Materiality Matters—experience Materials. *interactions* 20, 2 (March 2013), 54–57. DOI: http://dx.doi.org/10.1145/2427076.2427087

AnimSkin: Fabricating Epidermis with Interactive, Functional and Aesthetic Color Animation

Yanan Wang[1], Shijian Luo[1], Yujia Lu[1], Hebo Gong[1], Yexing Zhou[1], Shuai Liu[1], Preben Hansen[2]
[1] NO.38 Zheda Rd, Zhejiang University, Hangzhou, China
[2] Borgarfjordsgatan 12, Kista, Stockholm University, Stockholm, Sweden
{wangyanan1120, sjluo, luyujia, gong_hb, zhouyexing, shuaidesign}@zju.edu.cn
preben@dsv.su.se

Figure 1. AnimSkin is a thin-film and multi-layer structure on body interface, which will emit aesthetic and dynamic color animation by using thermochromic paint, such as (a) Email Reminder, (b) Light control system; individuals could also customize their own graphic designs (c); all processes are manipulated by an accessible and low-cost fabrication method.

ABSTRACT
Human epidermis, as the largest organ on body, has become a new design platform for wearable computing. The availability of miniature electronics makes more possibilities for on-skin designs. In this paper, we present *AnimSkin*, a thin-film interface, which will emit dynamic color animations directly on skin. This is done by using thermochromic material embedded with transparent electrode acting as a capacitive sensor. Moreover, an accessible and low-cost fabrication method is introduced. Individuals could also customize aesthetic graphic designs by following the detailed fabrication process to achieve personalized patterns. We propose four different dynamic types of color animation by applying certain voltage to the heating circuitry. With two examples, Email Reminder and Light Control System, we demonstrate how *AnimSkin* can be integrated into everyday life, and specifically, we show how *AnimSkin* can benefit areas such as on-skin design, thin-film interface and beauty technology.

Author Keywords
Wearable computing; on-skin interfaces; beauty technology; hybrid material; color animation; fabrication;

DIS 2017, June 10-14, 2017, Edinburgh, United Kingdom
© 2017 ACM. ISBN 978-1-4503-4922-2/17/06…$15.00
DOI: http://dx.doi.org/10.1145/3064663.3064687

ACM Classification Keywords
H.5.m. Information interfaces and presentation (e.g., HCI): Miscellaneous

INTRODUCTION
Wearable computing is aiming to extend human capabilities, and Robert Hooke proposed the concept of "artificial organ" for improving our "hearing, smelling, tasting, and touching" [16]. Today, an increasing number of researchers are devoting themselves to designing seamless interfaces on body and with its accessories, causing a rethinking between electronics and human body. As can be seen in Project Jacquard [17], NailO [5] and Hairware [12]. Recently, body surface has been a new design platform for wearable computing. Scientists have developed ultra-thin electronics on human skin for the measurement of bio data. Hammock et al. provides a brief history of e-skin [3]. However, to build such system, expensive materials and equipment is needed. Previous researches have utilized skin for touch input [9, 14]. Through a perspective of beauty technology, a new subfield of wearable computing [11], aesthetics of body decoration has emerged. DuoSkin and ChromoSkin [6, 7] inspired from digital cosmetics, create on-body decorations. However they still have a long response time for thermochromic material to react.

Developments in smart materials are improving the ease of use of the digital technologies, making more possibilities for electric-responsive materials or flexible displays. Researchers also pursue multi-layer but thin hybrid material for extended behaviors [4, 10, 15]. Thermochromic materials can be used in e-textiles, Ebb and Mosaic modules combining thermochromic paint with conductive fabric for smart textile display [2, 13]; very slow animation textiles can be framed [1]. Muksit presented the temperature-actuated properties of such thermochromic system on textiles in detail within coloration society [8]. However, questions like what's the explicit response time to create more real-time feedback, what different types of color animation can be framed, and how can this kind of material be embedded with other materials within on-skin are still open questions within the HCI research field.

In this paper, we consider thermochromic, a non-emissive and heat-actuated material, and used together with dynamic color animation embedded with heating circuitry and touch sensing modules. They could form a new direction for wearables and body decoration. And as such, they could be merged into individual's everyday life.

In summary, we list our four significant contributions:

1. A multi-layered and thin-film material structure is proposed to achieve interactive, functional and aesthetic color animation.
2. By introducing thermochromic material as the aesthetic layer, four basic predefined dynamic color animation patterns could be framed: a) breathing, b) moving, c) internal succession, 4) graphics changing.
3. We articulate an initial, accessible and low-cost fabrication approach, which is easy to copy for individuals in order to be customized according to own designs.
4. A technical evaluation on the 1) behavior of ITO covered with silicone overlay acting as a capacitive sensor; 2) skin-friendliness and durability of *AnimSkin.*

DESIGN CONSIDERATIONS AND CHALLENGES

Accessibility: The fabrication method proposed, intended for both designers and customers, is novel, accessible and economical, can of course be improved. The materials of *AnimSkin* can be bought from on-line shop, and the average cost for one is around 7 RMB in China, approximately equal to $1.01 USD.

Skin Safety: Silicone, has a good insulating property from electricity, heat and water. The body glue bonding to surface of the skin is on a medical level and will not cause problems like skin irritation. We choose 38°C actuated thermochromic powder mixed with silicone for avoiding skin burns from higher temperature.

Heating Module: We use X-Silver silver coated nylon conductive yarn as the heating material for its flexibility and durability by comparing with other material (e.g. silver ink, conductive ink). For avoiding unnecessary color change from circuitry, we connected conductive thread with copper wire (lower resistance compared with conductive thread) directly at the back of the thermochromic layer for shaping a certain pattern (Figure 2). So within the same current in one circuitry, there will not cause the redundant color change in our system.

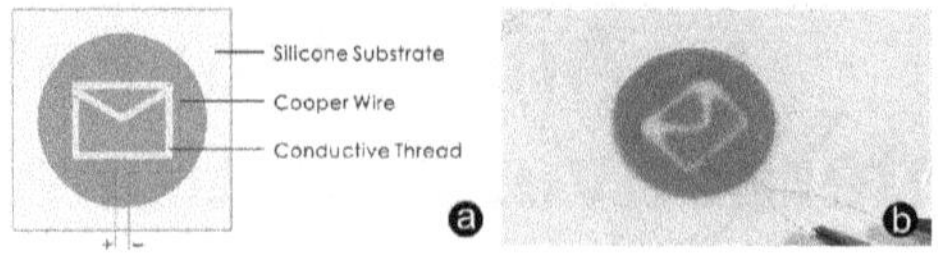

Figure 2. Heating module: (a) circuitry system design; (b) display as an envelope.

- **Interactivity and Aesthetics:** To achieve various color-changing patterns and interactive, aesthetic functions, we propose a collection of different materials for a thin multi-layer structure (Figure 3).

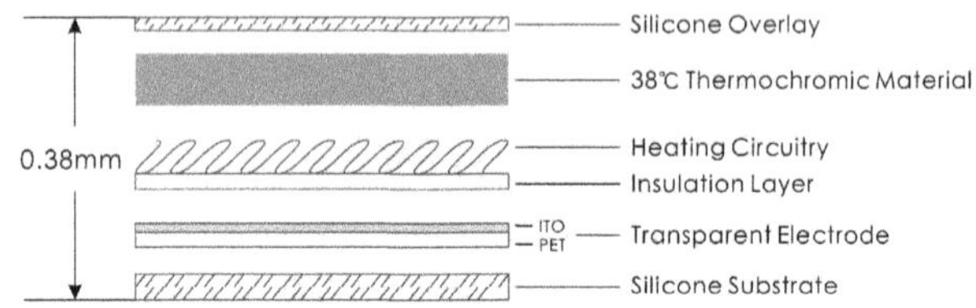

Figure 3. Multi-layer structure

From top to bottom: a transparent water proof silicone overlay; TK-CHEM SDS 38°C heat sensitive thermochromic pigment acting as a color-changing and aesthetic layer that will be actuated within 0.5~1s by applying a 0.08A current, much faster than similar designs. Individuals also could customize their own designs with different shapes and colors; soft conductive thread (6Ω/cm) with a thickness of 0.02mm binds with the second transparent silicone level for insulation; Indium Tin Oxide (ITO) is a transparent conducting material coated on a thin polymer layer, for aesthetic and safe consideration, we place ITO with 0.05mm thick for analogous capacitive sensor under heating layer, and ITO (2.5cm^2) with a silicone overlay less than 0.45mm thick which can still be sensed through technical evaluation; silicone substrate for binding with skin. The overall thickness can be as thin as 0.38mm.

COLOR ANIMATION PATTERN

In order to explore how the thermochromic material can be controlled, and what effects how it can be displayed, we designed four basic color animation patterns, which DuoSkin and ChromoSkin [6, 7] still fall short on. We did this by arranging predefined heating circuitry, using a 38°C red thermochromic silicone film with a thickness of 0.12mm (Figure 4). The room temperature was 25°C, and the air temperature 17°C. Every effect could be envisioned in different applications as a on-skin display and touch feedback:

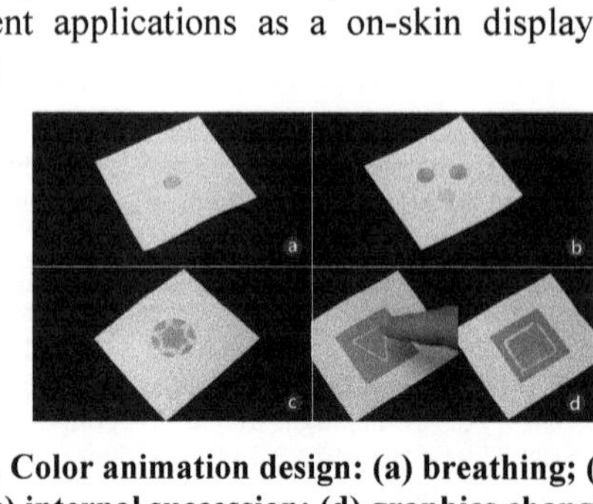

Figure 4. Color animation design: (a) breathing; (b) moving; (c) internal succession; (d) graphics changing.

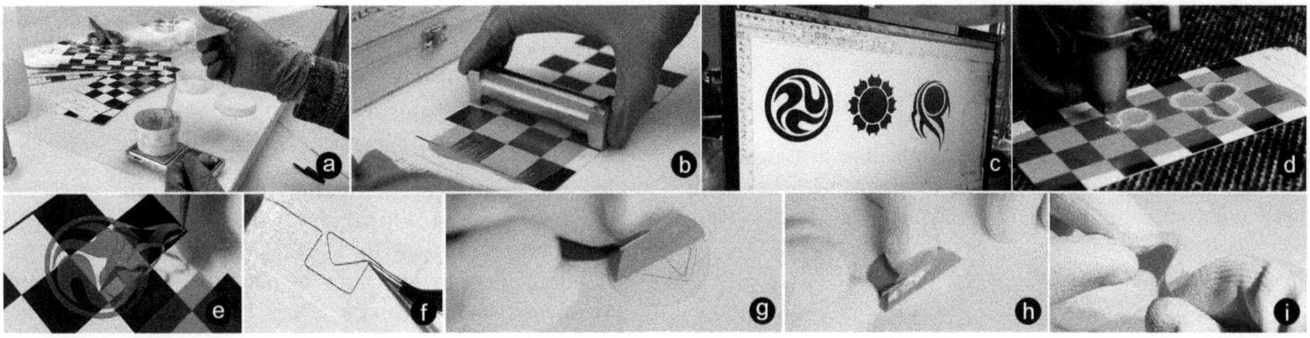

Figure 5. Fabrication approach: (a) mix thermochromic powder with silicone and curing agent; (b) thermochromic layer and transparent layer made by a thin-film applicator; (c) graphic design; (d) target design pattern by CNC; (e) removing the unnecessary part; (f) making heating circuitry; (g) apply thermochromic layer; (h) apply transparent electrode; (i) thin-film design.

1.Breathing as a surface (Figure 4a): the breathing time for once is around 1~1.5s powered with 3.3V DC; this color animation can be connected with a "*notification*" or a certain "*status*".

2.Moving as a whole (Figure 4b): the round surface can be moved from one spot to another within 7s, connecting with the "*time*", "*place-changing*", or "*direction*".

3.Internal succession (Figure 4c): dynamic line pattern changing in one surface within 5s, can be designed and can be associated with the "*progress*" of a certain activity, such as file transfer, achievement achieved in a game

4.shape change (Figure 4d): the triangle can be changed to a square, two different shapes can represent different "*camps*", such as a strategy game playing for two.

FABRICATION APPROACH

For making thin-film on-skin interface, we decided on an affordable and low-cost fabrication method, which is inspired from iSkin [14] and Strechis [15]. All processes were manipulated as lab experiments (Figure 5). Here we present a set of several basic steps for crafting an AnimSkin as an Email Reminder.

Thin-film making

First, we mix the silicone with curing agent and 38°C red thermochromic powder according to the proportion 100: 3: 9. Then we used the SZQ thin-film applicator with thickness of 30, 60, 90,120μm to form a silicone film. The red film is for the aesthetic layer, and the transparent film is made for the overlay, insulating and substrate layer (Figure 5a and 5b).

Graphic design

We customize various vectograms based on the common software CorelDraw, and cut the target design by laser cutting machine (Figure 5c and 5d). Remove the unnecessary part of thermochromic layer, and glue the needed part with transparent silicone overlay (Figure 5e).

Integrate layers

This stage involves wrapping the conductive thread binding with copper wire on the insulating layer according to the wireframe of an email (Figure 5f). Then position them under the thermochromic layer, ensuring that the conductive thread contacts with themochromic material tightly to achieve the color change within the shortest time. Finally, attach the transparent electrode and the substrate at the back of silicone insulating layer in order (Figure 4f to 4h), then flat each layer and we could achieve the thin-film as a soft and flexible design. The overall thickness is largely determined by the silicone overlay and the substrate.

ENVISIONED INTERACTION

Email Reminder

We crafted a flower shape of Email Reminder (Figure 1a), placing the heating circuitry in the center of the flower, and then applied the flower with 0.08A current and a 3.3V Lithium battery. Email Reminder could then be connected with your mobile phone. In general, it is acted as a kind of body decoration and will not change color. When you receive an email, the heating circuitry will be activated, and the thermochromic material begins to breathe by displaying an envelope. And it won't stop until you notice and touch the surface. The time for breathing is around 1~1.5s. In this case, the breathing color-changing animation plays a role as a "*notification*", just like a ring tune or vibration of a mobile phone.

Light Control system

For a light control system (Figure 1b), we fabricated three different components for controlling the LED independently by applying 0.08A and 1.44V DC: for the first touch, a white round color animation comes up and with one LED lights; for the second touch, the thermochromic material will breathe as a line together with the LED; touching it for the third time, the animation disappears and led turns off. If they were touched one by one, a successive animation will show on the skin to represent the light control "*progress*". In this system, the successive color animation will simulate the "*status*" of dynamic light changing system and display the different feedback for users to control.

TECHNICAL EVALUATION

In this paper, we also conducted a technical evaluation experiment, including: 1) behavior of ITO acting as an analogous capacitive sensor when covered with silicone overlay, and 2) of the skin-friendliness and durability of *AnimSkin.*

Behavior of Analogous Capacitive Sensing of ITO

For the aesthetic and safety considerations, we choose transparent electrode and place it under the heating layer. We then tested the analogous capacitive sensing behavior of ITO with silicone overlay of different thickness when placing them on skin.

Session structure: We prepared 5 pieces of ITO with different area: 2cm^2, 2.5cm^2, 3cm^2, 3.5cm^2, 4cm^2, and six 5.5cm^2 pieces of silicone overlay with thickness: 120μm, 210μm, 240μm, 330μm, 360μm, 450μm. Each this ITO is soldered with copper wire to an Arduino controller. In this experiment, we set the initial value of ITO putting on skin without an overlay and touch is 1 (≈0.090 nF).

We recruited 10 participants (4 female), ages 24 to 35 years (M= 27.5 years). All participants tested each ITO with six different silicone overlay. For each test, the participants were required to place the first piece of ITO (2cm^2) on the back of left hand and cover it with six silicone surfaces one by one, touching every silicone surface with his right index finger three times, and then repeated the processes with the remaining four ITOs. The average time spent for one participant is around 10 minutes.

S(cm²) / δ(μm)	2	2.5	3	3.5	4
120	4	6	7	8	8
210	4	6	6	7	7
240	4	4	6	6	6
330	4	4	6	6	6
360	3	4	6	6	6
450	3	4	4	6	6

Figure 6. Experimental results for analogous proximity sensing (each unit ≈ 0.003 nF)

Results: Figure 6 summarizes the average value of the experiment results. Firstly, once the ITO covered by silicone overlay, the initial value will be 3 (≈ 0.096 nF), which means that sensing values higher than 3 will be sensed; secondly, as figure 6 shows, for more precise sensing we'd better choose the ITO of the area ≥ 2.5 cm^2. The key finding is that the value of capacitive sensing is indeed influenced by the thickness of the silicone overlay, however, there is still enough precision for the system to do basic touch recognition.

Test of Skin-friendliness and Durability of *AnimSkin*

In this experiment, we evaluated the *AnimSkin*'s friendliness and durability, including the ease of application and removal, comfort with the heating element, skin sensitivity of wearing silicone for a long time, and the durability when exposed to daily wear (e.g., water, sweat).

Session structure: The test consisted of 8 participants (5 female) with age range from 19 to 31 years (M = 26 years). We prepared eight 3.5x3.5cm *AnimSkin* samples, each with an email-shaped heating element by applying 0.08A and 3.3V DC controlled by Arduino. Each sample's back was painted with body glue for binding with skin. And the room temperature is 23°C. All sessions were hand recorded.

First, the participants were allowed to attach the *AnimSkin* onto their exposed skin wherever they want, then removed it, and repeated it for three times. Second, we tested the heating element by attaching the material onto participants' left forearm and hand back. Then, let participants rank the comfort level from 1 to 5 (1= most negative, 5= most positive) based on our questionnaire. Finally, four participants were allowed to wear *AnimSkin* for 6 hours on the backside of their left hand, the others on the left forearm. After the 6 hours, they returned back to our lab. We recorded their activities and tested the circuitry with a multimeter. Finally, we removed the sample to observe if it will cause skin sensibility.

Results: *AnimSkin* was easy enough for participants to attach and removal, it did not leave any residue of glue that could cause skin discomfort. Through questionnaires, participants could feel the tepidity from the heating element on the back of the hand, stronger than the forearm, but without any skin discomfort. Besides, after 6 hours wearing, all tests performed well without disconnection of circuitry. There was no detachment of wearing it on the forearm, but one sample of the backhand-wearer tilted in two corners. No skin sensibility was caused among our 8 participants after wearing *AnimSkin* for a long time.

DISCUSSION AND FUTURE WORK

In this paper, we build four basic animations for dynamic on-skin display. More color-changing effects and input methods should be developed and tested based on present structure. It is possible that *AnimSkin* will be activated inadvertently if the air temperature > 38°C. We will next try a closed-loop approach by adding additional sensing, like cooling techniques, to improve this system. Finally, a more comprehensive user study needed to be conducted involving the user experience and the product usability.

CONCLUSION

We proposed *AnimSkin*, a thin-film multi-layer design for pursuing interactive and aesthetic color animation on skin. We connect the color animation with different scenarios in everyday life, and also developed a novel and inexpensive fabrication approach for individuals to customize personalized designs. Our technical evaluation supports the feasibility of ITO touch sensing and also the durability and skin-friendliness of *AnimSkin* for everyday use. We hope our work could benefit the area of wearable computing, thin-film interface and the beauty technology area.

ACKNOWLEDGMENTS

The research and development described in this paper have been funded by the National Natural Science Foundation of China (No. 51675476 and No. 51175458).

REFERENCES

1. Berzowska J. Very slowly animating textiles: shimmering flower[M]. ACM, 2004
2. Devendorf L, Lo J, Howell N, et al. "I don't Want to Wear a Screen": Probing Perceptions of and Possibilities for Dynamic Displays on Clothing[C]// CHI Conference. 2016:6028-6039
3. Hammock M L, Chortos A, Tee B C, et al. 25th anniversary article: The evolution of electronic skin (e-skin): a brief history, design considerations, and recent progress.[J]. Advanced Materials, 2013, 25(42):5997-6038.
4. Heibeck F, Tome B, Silva C D, et al. uniMorph: Fabricating Thin Film Composites for Shape-Changing Interfaces[C]// The, ACM Symposium. ACM, 2015:233-242.
5. Kao H L, Dementyev A, Paradiso J A, et al. NailO: Fingernails as an Input Surface[C]// ACM Conference on Human Factors in Computing Systems. ACM, 2015:3015-3018.
6. Kao H L, Holz C, Roseway A, et al. DuoSkin: rapidly prototyping on-skin user interfaces using skin- friendly materials[C]// ACM International Symposium. 2016:16-23.
7. Kao, Hsin Liu, et al. "ChromoSkin: Towards Interactive Cosmetics Using Thermochromic Pigments." CHI Conference Extended 2016:3703-3706.
8. Muksit A Chowdhury, Bhupendra S Butola, and Mangala Joshi. 2013. Application of thermochromic colorants on textiles: temperature dependence of colorimetric properties. *Coloration Technology* 129, 3 (2013), 232–237.
9. Ogata, Masa, et al. "SenSkin: adapting skin as a soft interface." ACM Symposium on User Interface Software and Technology ACM, 2013:539-544.
10. Olberding S, Wessely M, Steimle J, et al. PrintScreen: fabricating highly customizable thin-film touch-displays[C]// ACM Symposium on User Interface Software and Technology. ACM, 2014:281-290.
11. Vega K C, Fuks H. Beauty Technology: Designing Seamless Interfaces for Wearable Computing [M]. Springer Publishing Company, Incorporated, 2016.
12. Vega K, Cunha M, Fuks H. Hairware[C]// The, International Conference. 2015:89-92.
13. Wakita A, Shibutani M. Mosaic textile: wearable ambient display with non-emissive color-changing modules.[C]// International Conference on Advances in Computer Entertainment Technology, Ace 2006, Hollywood, California, Usa, June. DBLP, 2006:48.
14. Weigel, M., Lu, T., Bailly, G., Oulasvirta, A., Majidi. C., and Steimle, J., iSkin: Flexible, Stretchable and Mobile Computing. In Proc. of CHI '15. 2991-3000.
15. Wessely M, Tsandilas T, Mackay W E. Stretchis: Fabricating Highly Stretchable User Interfaces[C]// Symposium on User Interface Software and Technology. ACM, 2016:697-704.
16. Wolbarsht M L. Micrographia or Some Physiological Descriptions of Minute Bodies Made by Magnifying Glasses with Observations and Inquiries Thereupon. by Robert Hooke[J]. 2003.
17. Poupyrev I, Gong N W, Fukuhara S, et al. Project Jacquard: Interactive Digital Textiles at Scale[C]// CHI Conference. 2016:4216-4227.

Left Them 4 Dead: Perception of Humans versus Non-Player Character Teammates in Cooperative Gameplay

Rina R. Wehbe[1,2,5]
rina.wehbe@uwaterloo.ca

Edward Lank[1,4]
lank@uwaterloo.ca

Lennart E. Nacke[1,2,3]
lennart.nacke@acm.org

Cheriton School of Computer Science[1]
HCI Games Group, The Games Institute[2]
Department of Drama and Speech Communication[3]
University of Waterloo, Waterloo, ON, Canada[1,2,3]
CRIStAL, University of Lille, Lille, France[4]
University of Ontario Institute of Technology, Oshawa, ON, Canada[5]

ABSTRACT

Why do we care if our teammates are not human? This study seeks to uncover whether or not the perception of other players as human or artificial entities can influence player experience. We use both deception and a between-participants blind study design to reduce bias in our experiment. Our qualitative results show that people do care about the perceived nature of other players, even though they are not always able to correctly identify them as human or as non-player character teammates. Interview data suggest believing that one is playing with other humans can positively affect a player's subjective experience. Furthermore, our qualitative results indicate that players view their non-player character teammates as humanized entities, but adopt a neo-feudalistic (i.e., an unequal rights) view of them. Based on our results, we establish game design guidelines for non-player character teammates leading to stronger, emotional human-computer relationships in video games.

ACM Classification Keywords

H.5.m. Information Interfaces and Presentation: Miscellaneous; K.8.0 Personal Computing: Games

Author Keywords

Cooperative Games; Sociality; User Experience; Games User Research (GUR)

INTRODUCTION

Major publishers of next-generation console games are focusing on the development of multiplayer, multicharacter gaming experiences. Consequently, players engage more often with both human and computer-controlled opponents and partners. Regardless of the proximity and number of human players, computer-controlled characters are an important part of video games. They add depth to the player experience (i.e., the experience of interacting with human players and virtual characters during play).

A character we encounter in a gaming environment may be a human-controlled character, i.e. an avatar [20, 15, 25, 27] or a computer controlled character, i.e. a Non-Player Character (NPC). The term NPC covers many virtual characters—opponents, acquaintances, collaborators—and the player's relationship with each of these may range from non-existent to highly valuable. The specific focus for this research is to explore how NPC Teammates [33] or NPC-Ts—a sub category of NPCs that we define for this paper—are perceived and valued in comparison to human teammates. Unlike other NPCs, a player's NPC-Ts assist, support, and cooperate with them. NPC-Ts sometimes replace human players entirely. Sometimes, game missions are impossible without NPC-Ts, which makes them valuable to the player. However, when NPC-Ts replace human teammates, players have a clear preference for human teammates [42, 24, 20].

Two research opportunities follow from this dissatisfaction with NPC-Ts. First, one could continue to seek improving in-game Artificial Intelligence (AI) so that NPCs—in particular NPC-Ts—reach a sophistication level where humans feel NPC-Ts are as competent as human teammates [38]. However, we also have to ask a related question about NPC competency: Will NPCs—regardless of their sophistication—ever be perceived on par with human-controlled characters in a game? Said differently, imagine the only way to tell AI apart from a human-controlled character is if you are told your teammate is an NPC: How similar or different would the interaction with a human player be?

Answering this question depends on context. At present, people approach AI in games, especially NPCs, with biases and expectations triggered by the limitations of AI. While acknowledging present-day limitations, research seeking to understand current perspectives and practices regarding NPC-Ts and human-controlled teammates is worthwhile on two fronts: First, it may help us understand *a priori* biases that condition reactions to AI, which contextualizes what users report when they evaluate NPC-Ts in particular, NPCs in general, and AI in games overall. There is psychological evidence that pre-conceived biases are hard to overcome: For example, the

DIS 2017, June 10-14, 2017, Edinburgh, United Kingdom

ACM 978-1-4503-4922-2/17/06...$15.00
DOI: http://dx.doi.org/10.1145/3064663.3064712

Pygmalion Effect (i.e., higher expectations lead to higher performance) is well-established in psychological research [45]. Second, understanding the effects that improved AI has on players can reveal how enhancements to NPC behaviour affect human perception of these characters. In particular, we want to understand how our perspectives change when we fully grasp the 'lived experiences' of players interacting with these characters.

While researchers are aware that human players prefer other humans and look down on NPCs, understanding the rationale for value judgments of NPCs warrants more research, particularly for NPCs with whom players collaborate (i.e., NPC-Ts). To explore these questions, we designed a single-blind, qualitative, deception experiment to examine attitudes toward NPC-Ts and human collaborators in games. First—to explain the deception part—we occasionally deceived human players in our experiment about the nature of their teammates, indicating they were AI when they were humans playing with the participant, or indicating they were human when they were AI. Alongside deceiving participants, the experiment was conducted by a facilitator, and during the multiplayer experience, both the player and a research assistant (interacting with and observing the player during the experiment) were not aware they were being deceived. This ensured that, during gameplay, no one was aware of the presence of absence of human players. The truth was revealed during post-experiment debriefing and interviewing by a second researcher.

Overall, two primary theories arise from an inductive analysis of our interview data. First, regarding power dynamics of in-game relationships, we compare tendencies toward NPC-Ts with the social-contract negotiated power dynamics between human teammates

[13, 18, 63]. Within these dynamics, it is important to recognize that, as with any power structure, human players can be better or worse at collaborating with other humans as peers and the same holds true for NPC-Ts. Second, regarding perception, we look at issues of humanization and competence with respect to discursive interactions between participants and NPC-Ts and human teammates. We observed a double standard: when viewing teammates as human, compassion is given for errors; however, NPC-Ts are judged on their humanness based on competency.

RELATED WORK

Much literature is focused on improving NPC behaviour through development of AI [64]. Techniques such as evolutionary learning [39] and scaling for difficulty [46] are common. Research has sought to improve AI including attempting to create believable movements and behaviours [3, 21, 29, 35, 34, 40], design of characters [19, 18, 23], and programming reactions to the environment [17].

The literature spans diverse topics including machine consciousness [1] and imitation of human players [41]. In addition, programming game AI has been the focus of books and edited volumes [6, 5]. The goal of improved AI is making NPCs in a game more believable; thus, development of AI for control of NPCs, especially for conversational interactions with players resembles the Turing test [52, 37]. Livingstone [28] reviewed literature about creating more believable computer characters. Assuming characters have a sufficient level of believability to enhance player experience, an emerging question—particularly in co-operative games—is the socialization with NPCs: if and whether this socializing differs from socializing among human players [57, 58, 56].

Outdoor games as well as board and card games are considered a social activity. Stenros *et al.* [47] argue that even single-player computer games are social because of the surrounding social interactions, including discussing the content of the game. Leveraging this understanding of games as a social interaction, researchers including Szentgyorgyi *et al.* [50], Voida and Greenberg [55], and Linderoth et. al. [26] discuss social aspects of multiplayer, in-person gaming.

Some game types, including many handheld and console games, are skill tests where the social experience is not core to the game itself [50, 55]. The social components in these games improve player experience, but other games require socialization and communication among participants to successfully play. These latter games are called cooperative games and plenty of them exist and are popular among players. The goal of our research is to explore this field of cooperative gaming, particularly in an online gaming context. When judging the effectiveness of a cooperative game, it is important to understand the sociability of the game. Sociability depends on the players. We must understand the characteristics of video game players as well as the design of NPC-Ts when investigating NPC-Ts. Lastly, the attitudes of players towards their computer-controlled teammates or Non-Player Character (NPC) teammates, commonly referred to as AI, is an important component of cooperative games—particularly when cooperation with NPCs is necessary.

One main difference between human and NPCs is how they socialize. Many researchers have studied social aspects of gaming [47, 50, 55]. Many studies have investigated socialization in games: We learn game techniques from other humans [60] and enjoy couch-cooperation. We find that people's co-presence and attention to the same stimulus changes our experience [61]. Additionally, we are encouraged by on-looker feedback [22]. Overall, the literature on cooperative gaming is extensive and accounts for many different game types (e.g., exergames [36]).

Generally, we accept the intuitive idea that differences between human-human and human-AI gaming exist. Disentangling whether these differences are because of AI efficacy or other social factors is challenging. In a study by Lee *et al.* [24], *Flow*, the optimal experience characterized by the feedback of the task as the reward [9], was found to be higher when playing with other people cooperatively, as opposed to playing alone. DeKort *et al.* [10], reviewed video game sociability and human interaction in games. They state that players can be influenced by a feeling of involvement in another player's social group, or by social affordances allowed by the interaction. Both DeKort *et al.* [10] and Stenros *et al.* [47] discuss the differences between conditions of co-location and mediated interaction (i.e., whether or not the players are in the same place), for example, if the players are co-located, but not situated in a traditional face-to-face interaction model.

While characterizing human-to-human engagement tells us much about social gaming, much of this work is orthogonal to distinguishing differences between human-human and human-AI sentiment. It is acknowledged that NPCs are valuable for player experience. NPCs populate the world and increase the frequency of interactions available to players [16]. NPCs are also valuable in console gaming [55] where—without NPCs—one could only player with another human player, and in handheld gaming [50] where many games are primarily designed with NPC opponents in mind.

More recently, games such as Pokemon Go are based primarily around the collection of 'living' in-game characters. We hypothesize that differences in value may not solely be caused by NPCs not being 'real' people: Players often assign meaning and value to game objects [51, 65]. Research also demonstrates players have emotional emphatic reactions to works of fiction [32, 31], which can extend to game narratives [4] and players' relationships with in-game avatars [2, 27].

When comparing playing with humans versus playing with NPCs, prior research has leveraged physiological measures to try to determine if there are distinctions and what those physiological distinctions might be [30, 42, 20]. Recent results in this area [20] found playing with humans increased relatedness (i.e., relation to others) and increased brain activity in the alpha, beta, and theta bands. The researchers believe playing with human players was therefore more work which they referred to as *'mentalising'*. In contrast, video game players tended to elicit greater feelings of competence. The researchers concluded that flow was higher in this condition. This work echoes earlier work by Weibel *et al.* [62] reporting that—compared to playing with computers—playing online with humans increased presence, flow, and enjoyment.

Given past work—particularly using physiological measures—existing differences seem indisputable. Alongside quantitatively measured differences, we have conducted analyses that argue for higher levels of engagement and flow during human-human gaming, providing guidance as to what those differences are between human-human and human-NPC gameplay. *Why* these differences exist remains less clear to us in our exploration of past work. We lack knowledge on what motivates different engagement and flow. It could be the efficacy of the AI alone. Whether it is or it is not, is solely a question of AI efficacy, but how do these differences manifest with respect to perspective on game characters?

METHODOLOGY: ATTITUDES TOWARD NPC-TS

Our interest is in probing the attitudes and experiences of players working collaboratively with computer-controlled characters to understand how perspectives toward human teammates and NPC-Ts differ. To begin answering this question, we need both a context of study and an experimental design which will allow us to compare these factors while controlling—to the extent possible—confounds associated with *a priori* biases that arise when one knows the nature of one's teammate. In this section, we describe the study design setup, the gaming environment chosen, and the experimental methodology. We justify each in turn with respect to our study design.

Setup and Deception

We evaluated three possible study scenarios to determine differences in attitudes toward human versus toward computer-controlled collaborators. First, we considered providing full awareness of whether one is playing with a human or a computer and then elicit a reaction. The challenge was that preconceived biases may play a role in the assessment of the game and of the interaction with in-game characters, a casual "human primacy". The next option was to simply not tell users and allow them to play with an undefined collaborator which may be human or computer. The problem with this setup is that issues of competence and efficacy of AI within the game may come to dominate perspectives. Players may also be tempted to ascertain whether they are playing with humans or AI through on-going evaluations of interactions, a form of quasi-Turing-testing. Our third option, and the one we adopted was to leverage deception to understand whether differences in treatment arise from an awareness that it is the AI or from the efficacy of the AI making decisions for computer-controlled collaborating in-game characters (i.e., NPC-Ts).

We studied 30 participants divided into two groups. Half of the participants played with the human confederate team, the other half played with the NPC-T. We deceived one third of participants (five from each group) by falsely informing them that they were playing in the opposite condition. This study design allowed us to see if they were reacting to their perception (who they were told they were playing with) or the true condition (who they actually played with). In summary, ten people played with humans and were informed they were playing with humans, ten played with NPC-T and were told they were playing with NPC-T. Finally, ten were deceived into believing they were playing with the opposite condition.

Game and Modification

We used *Left4Dead2 (L4D2)*[G3] played on Steam (Valve Corporation) as a stimulus. The game is a first-person shooter (FPS) that involves four players escaping from a Zombie apocalypse. The game is rated M for violence, and only participants 18 years and older were invited to participate. The level played was titled "No Mercy", a level echoing the original *Left4Dead* [G2]; as a result, the original game characters were used.

The researchers added modifications [1] to ensure that the game protocol did not reveal the social environment (i.e., to preserve the unawareness of the deception). These modifications included the prevention of game end upon death of the participant's character. Additionally, the characters' names were always their default names (no Steam user names were used).

Our choice of L4D2 was motivated by several characteristics of the gameplay. L4D2 is a game where teammates are required to rely on each other to complete tasks, meaning coordination and collaboration are important. This coordination and collaboration peaks when a teammate—near the end of the

[1] Dziggy (2013). Improved Bots (Advanced) http://www.l4dmaps.com/details.php?file=15461

game—is required to sacrifice themselves so that the mission can be completed.

Participants

Overall, 30 participants completed our experiment, 15 males and 15 females. All participants were older than 18 years (Mode = 20-24 years; Range = 18-45+ years). Skill level or experience with the game was not an exclusion criterion.

Out of the 30 participants, two identified themselves as complete beginners, four as novice players, four as moderate, nine as intermediate, eight as advanced, and three as skilled. Twenty-five participants were PC gamers, and twenty-five claimed to have at least one game console in their household that they use regularly for games. Sixteen participants had played a first-person shooter game before, and twenty-four participants played at least one other genre of games. Fourteen of the participants had previously played *Left4Dead1*, while another fourteen, with some overlap, also played *Left4Dead2* prior to participating in the study.

Study Structure with Deception

Our 30 players were divided into two groups, one an AI group and one a human group (15 players each, with near gender parity or 8/7 within groups and with skill parity between groups). Players were informed, if in the AI group, that they would be playing with AI and, if in the human group, that they would be playing with humans on their team. To incorporate deception, one third of the players in each group were deceived (i.e., 1/3 of players in the AI group were actually playing with human teammates, and 1/3 of the players in the human group were actually playing with AI teammates).

Controlled Experimental Setup and Communication

Participants were unaware of the deception involved in the study. As a result, we used human confederates during gameplay in every condition to ensure that AI and human conditions were as similar as possible. Human (confederate) players were of different skill levels. One player acted as a beginner, one as an intermediate, and one as an advanced player. They were told to activate game events at specific points, such as triggering certain enemies. They were asked to stay within reasonable range of the player because of the team-like nature of the game. Confederates were also instructed not to communicate with the participant in any way. At the same time, within game they were told to play competently to their ability. In other words, they should react as their human responses dictated to in-game events.

A blind facilitator, unaware of the deception, conducted the study. This ensured that the blind experimenter could not subtly bias conditions of the study. Further precautions were taken to ensure the blind facilitator could not observe confederate gameplay; the blind facilitator was asked to stay near the participant, observe gameplay and note significant game events (e.g., the appearance of "special infected" unique enemy variants in the game).

The study proceeded as follows. Players were introduced to the confederates during the walk-through of the study by the blind facilitator and informed on whether they were playing

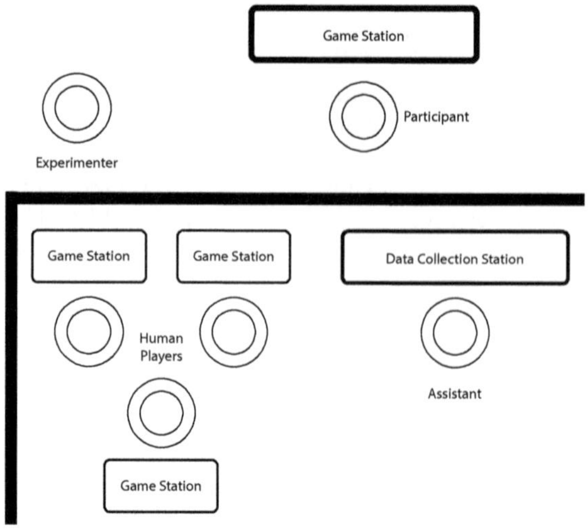

Figure 1. The experimental room layout

with our L4D2 team or with AI depending on whether they were playing with human teammates or AI teammates. Upon consent, players were informed (correctly or incorrectly) of the condition in which they would play for their first game. No verbal, messaging, or out-of-game exchanges were allowed between players and confederates and the environment was physically configured to prevent the blind facilitator or participant from peeking at confederates' screens to prevent revealing the placebo condition (see Figure 1). Major in-game events were scripted, such as triggering main enemy waves, activating special encounters. This was done to ensure consistency of basic game progression across participants.

All players, including confederates, were asked if they were ready before playing. The human confederates were needed in all conditions to control the environment, preventing differences in audible player activity or number of co-located individuals from affecting the participant perceptions. To control between conditions (e.g., sound of mouse and keyboard, observation of the game, presence of the human players), human confederates always played a game; if the condition was truly a computer-controlled condition, the confederates played a game individually.

Data and Measures

We collected the following data: Observations of the blind experimenter to gameplay, video of gameplay and reactions, and an interview of players post-treatment. The interview focused on the thoughts and feelings of the player regarding the social experience as well as their perceptions of fellow players. Once the deception was revealed to the deceived players, the interviewer asked about their thoughts and feelings following the reveal of the condition in the placebo group. The purpose of this line of inquiry was to determine if the debriefing would change the players' retrospective views of their player experience. For example, two of the areas of questioning explored whether players had any awareness of the deception and—in light of the deception—whether the identity of their teammates affected their enjoyment of the game. Participants indicated they were unaware of the deception involved in the study.

DEBRIEFING THE BLIND FACILITATOR

One challenge with any study based on deception is the need to ensure the deception was effective. While deception may be effective in a discrete case for any one participant, different study conditions could not be sufficiently similar to provide a true measure of masked differences. Fortunately—alongside participants—in our study the facilitator of the experimental session was unaware of the deception.

To evaluate the success of our experimental design with respect to similarity of conditions, the blind facilitator was interviewed and debriefed. The interviewer asked the facilitator if he was able to differentiate between human and computer-controlled conditions after repeated exposure to the game and questioned his perception of the true hypothesis.

The blind experimenter was not aware of the presence of deception, but was able to identify points of suspicion in retrospect:

> "I may have suspected something, but I always thought that they played AI and I didn't know any different."

In discussion, the blind experimenter notes, in particular, post-hoc suspicions based on aspects of competency, suggested in the preceding quote and expanded upon as follows:

> "I remember a few occasions where I thought, the AI; why are they spreading out so much? Because I thought this is what humans do, but I don't know the game that well, so I don't know what the AI is really capable of. [...] You told me AI and I thought it was AI but they would just go off to the next screen and start shooting people and I thought well ok whatever. Sometimes, you told me humans and there were some of these [participants] who got stuck and they may have needed a little pushing in a certain direction and then I thought 'why are the guys not helping her?'"

RESULTS

In our attempts to understand the in-game experiences associated with NPC-Ts, a consistent negative bias toward NPCs as confederates was observed. We found an immediate preference for human-controlled players, among all participants in the studies. Then—with respect to beliefs, behaviours, and outcomes—we wanted to understand the different perspectives applied to NPC-Ts and human confederates, especially the behaviours that are valued in both characters.

Interview data, field notes, and video observations were analyzed using open coding to extract low-level themes from the data [49, 48, 8]. Low-level clusters were agglomerated collaboratively by the researchers into ten central clusters: Negative Sentiment to AI, Anthropomorphism, AI Skill, Communication, Leadership, Teamwork, Social Expectations, Variable Human Skill, Playful Interaction, Romanticized View, Gameplay Behaviour, Person-Display Discourse.

From these thematic clusters, collaborative axial coding produced two over-arching constraining themes that unify the data: Power Dynamics and Social Obligations; and Humanism, Anthropomorphism, and Competency. We discuss each of these in turn in this section.

From our results, we combine our themes into two theories. One theory emerged from the players' attitudes towards the NPC-Ts. To the players, NPC-Ts were both valuable and disposable. Players perceived themselves as more important and we can see this power dynamic emerge from the data. In contrast, with human-teammates, players felt a need to negotiate more carefully. The second emerging theory is that of humanization of the NPC-Ts and the expectation of competence. Incompetence from NPC-Ts and humans was treated differently by the players. For an NPC-T to be perceived as human, competence was needed; however, when the participants were expecting a human player, they were more forgiving. The double standard of human versus NPC-T players was interesting because of the deception built into the study design.

Power Dynamics and Social Obligations

The most obvious way humans distaste for NPC-Ts is articulated is the innate value assigned to these different characters in the game. In this subsection, we argue that NPC-Ts are viewed as a resource to be exploited whereas human confederates are viewed as collaborators. In analyzing these concepts, the view of NPC-Ts as resources reminds us of the social ranking perceived by players towards one another based upon skill. Mediating against this perception in human-to-human player relationships, the negotiation and compromise required by human confederates evolves into a social contract for players.

Power Dynamics in Gaming

Power dynamics have been discussed within social structure of game communities. Social relationships between players in game can be influenced by this differential [19, 18]. The results of the study highlight the power differential between human and NPC-Ts, where NPC-T's are subordinate to the human player and their status as non-person negates the tools human players can leverage vis a vis other human players to mitigate against these different perceptions.

When analyzing players attitudes toward NPC-Ts, there are many positive aspects that NPC-Ts bring to the gaming experience. NPC-Ts provide shelter and protection, i.e. they can "watch your back". Given this idea of protection, the existence of NPC-Ts circumvents the trepidation experienced by players. Players essentially feel that, with their protectors willing to die for the sake of their goals, they can be more effective and aggressive in pursuit of those goals. In essence, the game is populated by human players with agency and NPC-Ts which are perceived to be a valuable resource for human players to exploit support and utilize to accomplish their ultimate mission. While NPC-Ts were viewed as a valuable resource, they were not viewed as peers and were not invested with decision-making authority.

We characterize behaviour toward NPC-Ts as nuanced benevolence because, while NPC-Ts were viewed as a resource, this is not to say that human players treated them completely as disposable. Many players adopted the perspective that it was useful to support NPC-Ts, and, in particular, to try to keep them alive as long as possible.

> "If you tell me 'Oh there's no people playing!' I still feel kind of obligated to pretend they're people because I'm

> thinking that they're my allies and they're probably going to help me out later; because if I get hurt they help me out, right."

> "Objectively they're not going to help you that much, and essentially they are just walking ammunition boxes. But for a sense of character, or atmosphere, they're people right. Sure they are controlled by AI, but they're not completely devoid of any meaning. So I'm going to kind of keep them alive or whatever."

However, there remains a distinction. Players may feel varying levels of obligation to help human-players versus computer-controlled players, essentially expressing more willingness to leave computer-controlled players for dead. Human players exhibited a willingness to sacrifice a NPC-T where they would feel guilt taking the same actions were the player human.

> "A couple times I reflected on the game, and I'm like: 'Oh this is just so generic that I'm playing a level with AI for some data collection.' But if I would've known they were people I probably would've felt more like [...] you know the team needed me, like I needed to actually [...] I guess you could say play more seriously."

While this nuanced benevolence exists, the fact that NPC-Ts are not human results in some subtle differences in how these characters are perceived. Consider the following statement from a discussion on NPC-Ts:

> "They're programmed to help you, which your friends would probably do I assume."

A superficial analysis of this statement might seem, at first, to articulate a similarity between NPC-Ts and human confederates. However, a second read of even this single quote highlights a profound difference. NPC-Ts are programmed to help you; friends "probably" would. Friends, human players, have agency and choice about helping you. This distinction between choice and obligation came up in many interviews around the difference between human and computer-controlled teammates. We probed this difference to understand why the distinction was important even with low-skilled teammates, and users highlighted the experience of their co-players.

> "If you were to say there's just AI playing, I still feel the obligation, just not as strongly. If there's an actual human player, I'm ruining someone else's experience."

This, in turn, led us to examine how the larger obligation to other human players evolved.

Social Obligations

The concern with other players' experiences noted above for human teammates highlights the obligation that exists between human confederates within a game, the negotiated compromise needed to preserve in-game experience for others. This obligation was expressed clearly by one participant in our study.

> "So, again, having teammates to help you out[...] It kind of feels the same as when I go into a match of Battlefield with AI teammates. Like where I don't really know much about them, 'Oh there's somebody over there doing their own thing.' I kind of feel the same thing with Left 4 Dead, in a situation at least. If I was playing with people it would be much different. [With AI] it was kind of like[...] They're a separate entity. Okay, I'm here, but you know, I'm going to be doing my own thing, maybe get into trouble, and they're probably going to help me out because they're nice." "I guess if you have other people around you, especially in an atmospheric game like that, [...] I feel kind of safer. You know somebody else can screw up and you're like oh I feel good I helped them. Then if you screw up it's like ok that helps it's all good, somebody helped me out."

Between human players, there exists a social agreement that describes expected behaviours. Essentially, to continue working together, compromise between parties is necessary, be that compromise one that arises via discourse and consensus or one that arises through the will of the majority. There is an expectation that human confederates must be collaborators, not solely confederates.

While all players perceived the connection with and mediation required between human players, there were challenges. These challenges included the obligation placed on a player by other human players (and the potential benefit to playing with NPC-Ts when players perceived their skill as being insufficient), and the desire to occasionally violate social norms to create disruption.

First, mismatched skill levels were a significant challenge when navigating the obligation to human confederates. Players who felt their own skills were not comparable felt that social expectations on them were too high. They worried about feeling judged for their skills. They felt others would resent their errors. They also perceived a need to seek forgiveness when an error was made.

> "It's fun to play on your own and feel that 'Oh my gosh I can be the best one that I can be!' With my friends it's like, yeah no, I'm not the best one here."

Insufficient skill articulated itself as a benefit to NPC-Ts for those players who felt their skills were too low.

> "Because then if I mess up, the computer doesn't get mad at me [...] People get mad at me if I mess up! So you don't have to answer to [computers]."

In contrast, more skilled players found that the lack of ability to create social obligation on the part of NPC-TS hurt the game experience, leaving them feeling unable to punish, pressure, or yell at the NPC-Ts in an effort to improve their performance.

> "Uh, if I was playing with people I would've yelled at you more because yelling is part of the fun."

A second challenge observed in our data regarding the social contract between players involves a practice colloquially known as "trolling". Humans are not always good collaborators. When playing a game with a human teammate and setting up the social contract, the player must remember there is a negotiation that is involved to set up collaboration but there is a trepidation that the player faces: Will this human cooperate with me? Humans are not as biddable as computer-controlled teammates, they may play pranks, act unexpectedly, or be silly.

> "[I prefer] multiplayer with friends. Um, multiplayer with friends and single-player are kind of tied, it's just that usually I like to play with friends. And the reason I like that more than playing with strangers or many people online is just because I have a good kind of relationship with my friends so it's always fun to just be ridiculous."

> "Humans are always more chaotic and a bit more silly so I feel the unpredictable factor, like what makes humans a bit unpredictable. I like that."

One participant trolled players in our experiment. This participant believed that they were playing with humans and made certain by looking at the 'pings' to other players, despite the instructions that communication tools were **not** allowed by the experimental protocol. Afterwards, they disrupted gameplay and ditched the team. When interviewed, they stated that 'pings' are only done with human players. The person checked because with AI they would not have taken the same actions. This participant prefers to play with humans because they enjoy creating chaos among human players; they would not derive the same enjoyment from doing so with the AI:

> "I saw that the people were human, so I wanted to [mess] with you guys[...] Bots you know, they're not real. People are real, so when you mess with people it's funnier."

The fact that our study was a deception study also provides for interesting insight into the behaviour of human players with respect to NPC-Ts. As one example, one participant was informed that they were playing with a NPC-T, despite the fact that they were playing with a human confederate. This player rejected NPC-Ts, freely overlooking, abandoning, or shunning the NPC-Ts. In debriefing the participant reacted to the reveal that they were playing with human confederates with an acknowledgement that their behaviour was incorrect, "Uh, I just assumed. Go figure!". Others, particularly in the case where they were told AI but were actually playing with humans, expressed similar sentiments, using terms like "oops" and "oh well" to express post-hoc acknowledgement that they would have behaved differently. Participants deceived in the inverse direction (told human, actually AI) also noted how the perception that teammates were human altered interpretation of behaviour of NPC-Ts in gameplay.

> "Because they were supporting their team members [...] It didn't seem like they were out for themselves. They seemed more like a team kind of."

Overall, this acknowledgement further illustrates the quid-pro-quo expected between human-controlled confederates versus the relatively reduced value that can be ascribed to NPC-Ts.

Humanization and Competence

> "It was still like a person, right? It still stood out as behaviour of what a person would do instead of AI who knows where people are and just *he gestures a motion of shooting something*"

Determining the humanness of a player's teammate was difficult for our participants. In part we see this through the success of our study design; participants rarely questioned whether their teammates were computer-controlled or human confederates, despite the fact that in one third of gameplay, players were being deceived. However, alongside the success of our deception study, we also saw that players anthropomorphized or humanized computer-controlled teammates.

On the other hand, while players humanized NPC-Ts, they did not expect competence from their NPC-Ts. As a further result, when computer-controlled teammates demonstrated any competence or skill they were regarded as more human. The perception (and, indeed the reality) is that NPC-Ts lacked the subtly of a human-controlled player, demonstrated by their typical inability to lead and work in a team.

Within our data, we perceive a hierarchy of engagement. At the lowest level, NPC-Ts are not perceived of as people, but may have human-like qualities, a phenomenon known as Anthropomorphism. Some characters perceived to be NPC-Ts were actually human confederates playing in the game (because of our double-blind study). The sophistication of these NPC-Ts did, at times, lead participants to humanize their AI-controlled confederates. Finally, levels of gameplay skill with regards to strategy and leadership/teamwork were perceived to more fully indicate a human confederate was playing collaboratively with the gamer. We expand on this theme as follows.

Humanization

Humanization of NPC-Ts was frequently observed in our experiment. Aspects of NPC-Ts such as the pre-programmed speech of the characters—statements of thanks, negative or positive reactions to game events, or encouragement to hurry through the game—enhanced the tendency of participants to humanize NPC-Ts, (i.e., made players feel more connected to the NPC-Ts). We were surprised that the pre-programmed speech was cited by some players as causing the feelings of humanness and not actual actions taken by humans. More specifically, rather than the actions of teammates, the reactions or interactions between participants and their teammates were most effective at encouraging humanization of NPC-Ts.

Because we were preserving parity between human and NPC-T conditions, there was no voice communication. Participants often cited the lack of voice communication as a factor that reduced the sociality of the gaming experience. The lack of voice communication made it hard to feel that either condition was different. Even in human-to-human play, however, the pre-programmed textual speech of the characters which may include statements of thanks, negative or positive reactions to game events, or encouragement to hurry through the game made players feel more connected to the NPC-Ts.

> "The fact that there was some dialogue in there I think was a big one. So I could hear someone telling me to get into a room that I couldn't get into. And reminding me, I think that they heard things around the corner..."

Alongside anthropomorphic attributes, the fact that NPC-Ts were teammates provided a further encouragement for participants to humanize the NPC-Ts. For example, multiple participants felt that the computer-controlled and human teammates had personalities and play styles; In one case, one participant in our study felt that one player was defensive, one was aggressive, and one held back.

> "I could almost see which behaviour they were acting in. Like Zoey had the aggressive behaviour, Louis had the whole defensive behaviour and was constantly behind, and Bill [he means Francis] was kind of in the middle there. So[...] like I could definitely tell who was showing which characteristic."

In this case, the participant was deceived. Initially she was told that the NPC-Ts in the game were human players. At the end of the game, after the truth was revealed, that they were actually AI (and would not have different tendencies), the same participant stated, "I still hold to my point that Zoey knew where she was going, Francis was in the middle, and Louis kind of held back."

Some players spoke aloud to the NPC-Ts. Interactions ranged from a short-lived "Hi Francis" or "Aww Zoey" when observing teammates, to laughter and guilt when NPC-Ts complained about incidents of friendly fire. One participant was healed by a computer-controlled ally, at which point they turned and said, "Thank you" to the experimenters. The participant was aware they were playing with computer-controlled teammates, yet was still compelled to direct their gratitude towards someone. This same participant expressed shock while nearly shooting their teammate in the process of learning the game's controls.

Participants would also react to dialogue spoken by avatars in the game. In one example, a NPC-T character in the game said, "Let's do it", prompting the participant to reply, "Wait what are we doing? Ok what do you people want me to do? I'm just going to start following you around", despite the fact that the participant was told (accurately) that they were playing with computer-controlled players.

Competency Makes it Human

The study design calls for the deception of the participant, allowing us to determine their opinions on human versus computer-controlled teammates. When their assumption that the blind-experimenter gave accurate information about their teammate was pressed, participants revealed information about the nature of their assumptions.

We found that humanness was determined based on levels of competence. Where computer-controlled teammates may have been humanized or anthropomorphized, they still did not reach the level of thought and subtly and richness in behaviour typical of humans. The more skill and competency playing the game a character demonstrated, the more likely a player was to begin to infer human tendencies.

Competency is a multi-faceted concept for our players. At the simplest level, players make the negative assumption that computer-controlled teammates are useless in times of need.

> "[Humans are] the best, because at times I really needed saving, so I'm really glad I had a team of people and not like computers or robots or whatever; because yeah they really saved my ass."

However, alongside this low-level attribute of skill, more complex issues of self-preservation indicated a higher likelihood of human control for our players.

> "Well I noticed sometimes they would move away from a dangerous area, which seemed a little weird. Like the thing that shot green stuff like they would move away from it after so they wouldn't get injured. Which I thought was a kinda unusual for an AI. [AI] just sort of 'Oh I'm getting shot now, might as well just die."'

At the highest level, issues of skilled teamwork and leadership were significant indicators participants were playing with a human. NPC-Ts were perceived as being poorer team players with respect to working with others. Participants also looked to their companions for leadership. When given a leadership position, some participants felt this was proof that their teammates were not human. In other words, being ceded control leads participants to believe they were the only human—particularly when that control is ceded too easily.

Alongside skill within the game and skill at teamwork and leadership, communication was a large determining factor in the humanness and competency of a teammate. Instructions given by another player, reactions to the in-game actions (e.g., accidentally shooting another teammate), caused players to feel more sociable towards the teammate. Players cited speech as the determining factor towards feel sociable, despite the fact that this dialogue was pre-programmed and present in both human and computer-controlled conditions.

> "Someone in there sounded like they had a crabby attitude, so that was kind of more real. It wasn't just that they all acted the same. They used names a lot so it seemed a little more personal."

Communicative competency, however, remains a big indicator for our participants of when they might be playing with human confederates. In particular, sarcasm and bile were perceived to be less likely from NPC-Ts than from humans, and when characters exhibited this type of speech, it increased the likelihood for deceived participants of post-hoc rationalizations that NPC-Ts were actually humans (i.e., participants could identify these actions as being indicative post-hoc of the deception though they did not identify the deception during gameplay).

DISCUSSION

Better AI in games does matter, but can we answer the question whether it changed the relationship to NPCs within games, particularly NPCs who are our collaborators? We suspect the relationship will not change any time in the near future. To understand the limits of playing alongside NPC-Ts requires an understanding of the social dynamics of gaming and gamers.

There is a significant body of work that has studied gamer communities and the social dynamics of these communities both with respect to online interactions [13, 18, 63] and real-world perceptions [7, 43] of gamers toward each other. This past work has included studies of the dynamics of power and prestige within these communities. While some authors have focused on specific actions within the community [7], much of the writing on status focuses less on specific acts of dominance and more on perceptions of pervasive empowerment.

Obviously, notions of pervasive empowerment are not new; they have simply been applied within the study of social structures in gamer communities. Historically, Foucault writes extensively on power structures and their maintenance, beginning with notions of power being perceived of as a "right" ascribed to specific individuals. He also comments extensively on the instability of power structures that are maintained by specific actions of individuals:

> In certain societies, of which the feudal regime is only one example, it may be said that individualization is greatest where sovereignty is exercised and in the higher echelons of power. The more one possesses power or privilege, the more one is marked as an individual .... [However], neither the residual forms of feudal power nor the structures of the administrative monarchy, nor the local mechanisms of supervision, nor the unstable, tangled mass they all formed together [can maintain these pre-specified social hierarchies].

His argument culminates with the claim that societies maintain these hierarchies less through explicit action and more through pervasive interactions between people – discourse, common knowledge, pervasive behaviours. These results align well with studies of power dynamics within many communities, including gamer communities [7, 43].

Our work, however, is not about human-to-human conceptions of power; instead it focuses on distinctions between NPC-Ts and human confederates. We find that NPC-Ts have both similarities and differences with human teammates. From the perspective of similarity, we find issues of competence that promote NPC-Ts as more closely considered peers by human players. Competence is also an important aspect of status and value within online communities, as explored by Duchenaeaut et al. [13] in World of Warcraft guilds. However, players also noted the differences, including an inability to yell at or bully NPC-Ts in contrast to human players. In other words, with ranking between human players comes a need to preserve those ranks or ascendant individualism, and the mechanisms by which it is maintained. Mitigating against this social stratification—biasing the game too heavily toward one player or another—are issues of social contract that arise between human players. Human players know they need to preserve the enjoyment of other players to ensure they have teammates who continue to help them and play the game.

One significant difference between NPC-Ts and human teammates is the lack of need for a maintenance of power imbalance. When one's teammates are NPC-Ts, there is an obvious expectation that the human player matters and the NPC-Ts serve a subservient role. Alongside this, because social hierarchy is automatically maintained, the interactions become more autocratic, more feudal, between human player and NPC-Ts. In our data, NPC-Ts were both cared for and disposable to players. This has similarities to the power structures of feudalism or monarchies as noted by Foucault, with the added reinforcement that the power imbalance does not need to be preserved through specific action. The fact that the NPC-T does not resist makes these power differentials stable. We characterize this overall impression of interaction between human player NPC-Ts as quasi-feudalistic. The primary characteristic that differentiates role is a distinction in control and agency. In some ways, our observation of feudalistic impressions of NPCs aligns with results on utility characters, or alts, by Livingston *et al.* [27] in World-of-Warcraft. These alts were considered ephemeral, existing to satisfy a specific goal, whether short-term—for a raid, to quest with another—or long term—as a bank to store items of value. Rather than representations of self, alts were tools.

Can we and should we moderate these quasi-feudalistic aspects of the relationship between human players and NPC-Ts? We do note that the (lack of) humanness of the computer-controlled teammate was moderated by a hierarchy of humanization extending from NPC-Ts with anthropomorphic tendencies through to higher levels of competence leading to a greater likelihood of acceptance as a collaborator. Underlying all of these observations is the sense, throughout our data collection, that NPC-Ts matter: They enhance the gaming experience and add realism; they protect and support the human player; they respond and interact in ways that create atmosphere. This observation drives a set of design recommendations.

Design Implications

We now leverage our observations of NPC-T behaviour to drive design implications and recommendations.

Encourage altruistic quasi-feudalism toward NPC-Ts by rewarding humanization of the computer-controlled characters. Players want to feel central to the game. Recognizing and celebrating altruistic feudalism can significantly enhance the centralization and importance of the human player. In the same way that fictional protagonists care for the "others" written into their stories without parity existing between parties [12, 44], games can reward behaviours where NPC-Ts are managed, guided, and valued. We hypothesize that magnifying the benefits of effective interaction between NPC-Ts and human player can foster attachment between human and NPC-Ts. For example, designers could make the NPC-Ts better collaborators depending on the positive interactions with the player. NPC-Ts could be more aware of their surroundings and provide better information, for example, if well treated.

Simulate a social contract between NPC-Ts and human players. Game designers could also simulate the development of a social contract between NPC-Ts and the human player. Obviously, the question of who will lead is already decided between NPC-Ts and humans, but justifying the decision based upon in-game actions makes the NPC-Ts appear to have more agency. Alongside the negotiation of social dynamics with NPC-Ts, one can further emphasize the relationship between NPC-Ts and each other during emotional in-game decisions. As one example, strategies involving sacrifice of a NPC-T could affect other NPC-Ts.

Support Anthropomorphism and humanization of Computer-controlled teammates by encouraging reactive actions towards the narrative of the game. We found that players want to humanize NPC-Ts. Supporting this humanization tendency by making the computer-controlled teammates react to the situation in the games—shots taken by players, the need to hurry through a stressful area—connects the computer-controlled teammates to the player. In our data we see that these naturalistic reactions enhance the narrative of the game. Furthermore, games could seek to preserve information on past interactions or past missions that NPC-Ts have participated in with the human player. NPC-Ts who are killed could be replaced by new recruits. Overall, developing a shared history with a team of NPC-Ts could make more subtle the line between human-controlled and human-like.

Encourage self-efficacy through supportive NPC-Ts. The NPC-Ts and player's avatar in *Left4Dead2* converse with each other to indicate direction, healing of teammates, (im)polite exchange, and strategic planning. In this sense, the AI are creating the simulated feeling of togetherness. Participants reported feeling as if they were being supported or part of a group, even in the AI conditions. From the results of the study, we note that company of AI in a game setting can emotionally affect players, empowering and encouraging them. Supportive NPCs reduce trepidation and influence perceived difficulty. NPC-Ts could provide an engaging alternative to traditional methods of challenge mitigation; rather than weakening enemies or strengthening the human player, more competent NPC-Ts could serve the purpose of difficulty adjustment. A simplified form of this technique to empower the player has been used in the fitness game Zumba Fitness [G1]: Increased effort allows one to increase background dancers on one's screen. In this sense, as a player's skill progresses, their character and their adversaries do not change; instead, their team changes. Perhaps they have fewer teammates, for example, requiring increasing efficacy on the part of the human player.

Consider lying by omission about the nature of teammates. In the field of dynamic difficulty adjustment, DDA, one recent result notes that, if one uses dynamic difficulty to increase the parity between players, it is best to not directly inform players of its use [11]. Players can react negatively both when DDA is applied to their actions (because of the assumption of their incompetence) and when DDA is applied to their opponents (because it makes the playing field not level between competitors). This is true despite the fact that parity of skill enhances the playing experience. It seems that, most importantly, the parity of skill—from the perspective of both parties—must be an accurate reflection of actual skill levels.

Similarly, one open question for future work is whether ignorance of the nature of teammates as NPC-Ts or as human teammates matters as much as we sometimes think it does. Perhaps games can be less explicit in communicating the nature of teammates. In a virtual world, there are significant advantages to leveraging NPC-Ts to complete game teams, particularly early in the game. Over time, the nature of the different teammates will undoubtedly become clear, but, given the fact that our participants simply accepted the nature of the teammates and reacted accordingly during truncated gameplay argues that discretion may not be exceedingly negative.

LIMITATIONS AND FUTURE WORK

This study did not test communication between players, but the primary goal of this study was to understand differing perceptions of human and NPC players. A large collection of literature already exists on side channel communication between human players and pre-existing relationships [54, 53, 55], and it may be interesting to leverage these studies to understand how we can leverage side-channels in future work.

Alongside communication, any game study is limited by the fact that only a finite number of game environments can be tested. We leveraged L4D2 because it requires close collaboration with teammates, whether human or NPC-T. Collaborative games provide the best opportunity to bond with NPC-Ts and to develop positive impressions. Given the goals of our study, we feel our platform choice was appropriate. Although some of the design guidelines are hypothesized to apply to competitive or single player games, further research is necessary.

CONCLUSION

Why do we care if our teammates are human or not? Superficially, one can simply say players are aware that the world they are in is artificial, but—with human-controlled characters—the game intersects the real world. This intersection means impressions created in-game can persist when playing with human collaborators. In other words, humans are just protecting their potential social capital, whereas with NPC-Ts that altruism will never be repaid intentionally. Of course, this perspective ignores the observations of trolling, of variable competency, and of altruism toward NPC-Ts on the part of some of our participants.

More aptly, generalizing from our themes of quasi-feudalism and social obligation, or humanization and competence, what we found could perhaps best be grouped under an assumption of human primacy in games [14], which recognizes the need for negotiation with humans and a valuing of striving with and against humans more than "others" in the game. Overall, given the transient nature of NPC-Ts, there is nothing wrong with this belief; we advocate in our design implications that celebrating the quasi-feudalistic tendencies of human players could be encouraged through game designs that placed effective collaboration and support of NPC-Ts as a more explicitly rewarded aspect of game design.

ACKNOWLEDGEMENTS

We thank our participants, the L4D2 confederate team, research assistants Eddie Shearer and Jens Johannsmeier, and Elisa Mekler for editorial feedback. Thanks to Mike Ambinder at Valve Corporation for providing the games. Funding for this work was provided by the Natural Science and Engineering Research Council of Canada (NSERC), the Canadian Fund For Infrastructure (CFI), Mitacs, and the Social Sciences and Humanities Research Council of Canada (SSHRC). This research was approved by the University of Ontario Institute of Technology's Research Ethics Review Board as part of the first author's M.Sc. dissertation [59].

REFERENCES

1. Raul Arrabales, Agapito Ledezma, and Araceli Sanchis. 2009. Towards conscious-like behavior in computer game

characters. *CIG2009 - 2009 IEEE Symposium on Computational Intelligence and Games* (2009), 217–224. DOI:http://dx.doi.org/10.1109/CIG.2009.5286473

2. Jaime Banks and Nicholas David Bowman. 2016. Emotion, anthropomorphism, realism, control: Validation of a merged metric for player-avatar interaction (PAX). *Computers in Human Behavior* 54 (2016), 215–223. DOI: http://dx.doi.org/10.1016/j.chb.2015.07.030
3. Anton Bogdanovych, Simeon Simoff, Marc Esteva, and John Debenham. 2008. Teaching autonomous agents to move in a believable manner within virtual institutions. *IFIP International Federation for Information Processing* 276 (2008), 55–64. DOI: http://dx.doi.org/10.1007/978-0-387-09695-7_6
4. Julia Ayumi Bopp, Elisa D. Mekler, and Klaus Opwis. 2016. Negative Emotion, Positive Experience? *Proceedings of the 2016 CHI Conference on Human Factors in Computing Systems - CHI '16* (2016), 2996–3006. DOI: http://dx.doi.org/10.1145/2858036.2858227
5. David M Bourg and Glenn Seemann. 2004. *AI for game developers*. O'Reilly Media, Inc.
6. Mat Buckland. 2005. *Programming game AI by example*. Jones & Bartlett Learning.
7. Shira Chess and Adrienne Shaw. 2015. A conspiracy of fishes, or, how we learned to stop worrying about# GamerGate and embrace hegemonic masculinity. *Journal of Broadcasting & Electronic Media* 59, 1 (2015), 208–220.
8. Juliet M Corbin and Anselm Strauss. 1990. Grounded theory research: Procedures, canons, and evaluative criteria. *Qualitative sociology* 13, 1 (1990), 3–21.
9. Mihalyi Csikszentlmihalyi. 1990. *The Psychology of Optimal Experience*. Harper and Row, New York.
10. Yvonne A. W. De Kort and Wijnand A Ijsselsteijn. 2008. People, places, and play. *Computers in Entertainment* 6, 2 (2008), 1. DOI: http://dx.doi.org/10.1145/1371216.1371221
11. Ansgar E Depping, Regan L Mandryk, Chengzhao Li, Carl Gutwin, and Rodrigo Vicencio-Moreira. 2016. How Disclosing Skill Assistance Affects Play Experience in a Multiplayer First-Person Shooter Game. *Proceedings of the 2016 CHI Conference on Human Factors in Computing Systems* (2016), 3462–3472. DOI: http://dx.doi.org/10.1145/2858036.2858156
12. Stephen R Donaldson. 1986. Epic Fantasy in the Modern World. *Kent, OH: Kent State University Libraries* (1986).
13. Nicolas Ducheneaut, Nicholas Yee, Eric Nickell, and Robert J. Moore. 2007. The Life and Death of Online Gaming Communities: A Look at Guilds in World of Warcraft. In *Proceedings of the SIGCHI Conference on Human Factors in Computing Systems (CHI '07)*. ACM, New York, NY, USA, 839–848. DOI: http://dx.doi.org/10.1145/1240624.1240750
14. M. E. Ellithorpe, D. R. Ewoldsen, and K. Porreca. 2015. Die, Foul Creature! How the Supernatural Genre Affects Attitudes Toward Outgroups Through Strength of Human Identity. *Communication Research* September (2015). DOI:http://dx.doi.org/10.1177/0093650215609674
15. Jesse Fox, Sun Joo Ahn, Joris H Janssen, Leo Yeykelis, Kathryn Y Segovia, and Jeremy N Bailenson. 2015. Avatars versus agents: a meta-analysis quantifying the effect of agency on social influence. *Human–Computer Interaction* 30, 5 (2015), 401–432.
16. Johan Hagelbäck and Stefan J. Johansson. 2010. A study on human like characteristics in real time strategy games. *Proceedings of the 2010 IEEE Conference on Computational Intelligence and Games, CIG2010* (2010), 139–145. DOI: http://dx.doi.org/10.1109/ITW.2010.5593362
17. Kiran Ijaz, Anton Bogdanovych, and Simeon Simo. 2011. Enhancing the believability of embodied conversational agents through environment-, self- and interaction-awareness. *Conferences in Research and Practice in Information Technology Series* 113, Acsc (2011), 107–116.
18. Katherine Isbister. 2006. *Better Game Characters by Design: A Psychological Approach (The Morgan Kaufmann Series in Interactive 3D Technology)*. 368 pages. DOI: http://dx.doi.org/10.1016/B978-1-55860-921-1.50012-0
19. Katherine Isbister, Hideyuki Nakanishi, Toru Ishida, and Cliff Nass. 2000. Helper agent. *Proceedings of the SIGCHI conference on Human factors in computing systems - CHI '00* January (2000), 57–64. DOI: http://dx.doi.org/10.1145/332040.332407
20. Daniel Johnson, Peta Wyeth, Madison Clark, and Christopher Watling. 2015. Cooperative Game Play with Avatars and Agents: Differences in Brain Activity and the Experience of Play. In *Proceedings of the 33rd Annual ACM Conference on Human Factors in Computing Systems - CHI '15*. 3721–3730. DOI: http://dx.doi.org/10.1145/2702123.2702468
21. Lilian Juma. 2008. The Role of secondary emotions in Action Selection and its Effects on the Believability of a Character. (2008), 137.
22. Dennis L. Kappen, Pejman Mirza-Babaei, Jens Johannsmeier, Daniel Buckstein, James Robb, and Lennart E. Nacke. 2014. Engaged by boos and cheers. In *Proceedings of the first ACM SIGCHI annual symposium on Computer-human interaction in play - CHI PLAY '14*. Toronto, Canada, 151–160. DOI: http://dx.doi.org/10.1145/2658537.2658687
23. Petri Lankoski and Staffan Björk. 2007. Gameplay design patterns for believable non-player characters. In *Situated Play: Proceedings of the 2007 Digital Games Research Association Conference*. 416–423.

24. Christopher Lee, Peta Wyeth, Daniel Johnson, and Joshua Hall. 2015. Flow during Individual and Co-operative Gameplay. *Proceedings of Computer-human Interaction in Play - CHI Play'15* (2015), 103–107.

25. Sohye Lim and Byron Reeves. 2010. Computer agents versus avatars: Responses to interactive game characters controlled by a computer or other player. *International Journal of Human-Computer Studies* 68, 1 (2010), 57–68.

26. Jonas Linderoth, Staffan Björk, and Camilla Olsson. 2012. Should I stay or should I go?-Boundary maintaining mechanisms in Left 4 Dead 2. In *Proceedings of.*

27. Ian J. Livingston, Carl Gutwin, Regan L. Mandryk, and Max Birk. 2014. How Players Value Their Characters in World of Warcraft. In *Proceedings of the 17th ACM Conference on Computer Supported Cooperative Work & Social Computing (CSCW '14).* ACM, New York, NY, USA, 1333–1343. DOI: http://dx.doi.org/10.1145/2531602.2531661

28. Daniel Livingstone. 2006. Turing's test and believable AI in games. *Computers in Entertainment* 4, 1 (2006), 6. DOI: http://dx.doi.org/10.1145/1111293.1111303

29. Linbo Luo, Suiping Zhou, Wentong Cai, Malcolm Yoke, Hean Low, Feng Tian, Yongwei Wang, Xian Xiao, and Dan Chen. 2008. Agent-based human behavior modeling for crowd simulation. *Computer Animation And Virtual Worlds* 19, August (2008), 271–281. DOI: http://dx.doi.org/10.1002/cav

30. Regan L. Mandryk, Kori M. Inkpen, and Thomas W. Calvert. 2006. Using psychophysiological techniques to measure user experience with entertainment technologies. *Behaviour & Information Technology* 25, 2 (mar 2006), 141–158. DOI: http://dx.doi.org/10.1080/01449290500331156

31. Raymond A. Mar and Keith Oatley. 2008. The Function of Fiction is the Abstraction and Simulation of Social Experience. *Perspectives on Psychological Science* 3, 3 (2008), 173–192. DOI: http://dx.doi.org/10.1111/j.1745-6924.2008.00073.x

32. Raymond A. Mar, Keith Oatley, Jacob Hirsh, Jennifer dela Paz, and Jordan B. Peterson. 2006. Bookworms versus nerds: Exposure to fiction versus non-fiction, divergent associations with social ability, and the simulation of fictional social worlds. *Journal of Research in Personality* 40, 5 (2006), 694–712. DOI: http://dx.doi.org/10.1016/j.jrp.2005.08.002

33. Tim Merritt and Kevin McGee. 2012. Protecting Artificial Team-mates: More Seems Like Less. In *Proceedings of the SIGCHI Conference on Human Factors in Computing Systems (CHI '12).* ACM, New York, NY, USA, 2793–2802. DOI: http://dx.doi.org/10.1145/2207676.2208680

34. Maxim Mozgovoy and Iskander Umarov. 2010. Building a believable and effective agent for a 3D boxing simulation game. *Proceedings - 2010 3rd IEEE International Conference on Computer Science and Information Technology, ICCSIT 2010* 3, 2 (2010), 14–18. DOI: http://dx.doi.org/10.1109/ICCSIT.2010.5564876

35. Maxim Mozgovoy and Iskander Umarov. 2011. Behavior Capture: Building Believable and Effective AI Agents for Video Games. *International Journal of Arts and Sciences* (2011). http://web-ext.u-aizu.ac.jp/

36. Florian Mueller, Martin R. Gibbs, and Frank Vetere. 2010. Towards understanding how to design for social play in exertion games. *Personal and Ubiquitous Computing* 14, 5 (jan 2010), 417–424. DOI: http://dx.doi.org/10.1007/s00779-009-0268-x

37. Clifford Nass, Jonathan Steuer, and Ellen R. Tauber. 1994. Computers Are Social Actors. In *Conference Companion on Human Factors in Computing Systems (CHI '94).* ACM, New York, NY, USA, 204–. DOI: http://dx.doi.org/10.1145/259963.260288

38. Magalie Ochs, Nicolas Sabouret, and Vincent Corruble. 2009. Simulation of the dynamics of nonplayer characters' emotions and social relations in games. *IEEE Transactions on Computational Intelligence and AI in Games* 1, 4 (2009), 281–297.

39. Marc Ponsen and Pieter Spronck. 2004. Improving Adaptive Game AI with Evolutionary Learning. *Proceedings of the Computer Games: Artificial Intelligence, Design and Education Conference* Manslow 2002 (2004), 389–396. DOI: http://dx.doi.org/10.1.1.109.6055

40. Mike Preuss, Nicola Beume, Holger Danielsiek, Tobias Hein, Boris Naujoks, Nico Piatkowski, Raphael Stüer, Andreas Thom, and Simon Wessing. 2010. Towards intelligent team composition and maneuvering in real-time strategy games. *IEEE Transactions on Computational Intelligence and AI in Games* 2, 2 (2010), 82–98. DOI: http://dx.doi.org/10.1109/TCIAIG.2010.2047645

41. Steffen Priesterjahn. 2007. Imitation-based evolution of artificial game players. *ACM SIGEVOlution* 2, 4 (2007), 2–13. DOI: http://dx.doi.org/10.1145/1399962.1399963

42. Niklas Ravaja, Timo Saari, Marko Turpeinen, Jari Laarni, Mikko Salminen, and Matias Kivikangas. 2006. Spatial presence and emotions during video game playing: Does it matter with whom you play? *Presence: Teleoperators and Virtual Environments* 15, 4 (2006), 381–392.

43. Gabriela T Richard. 2015. Intersecting vulnerabilities in game culture: the effects of inequities and stereotype threat on player confidence, identification and persistence across gender and race. In *Proceedings of DiGRA.*

44. Adam Roberts. 2002. *Science fiction.* Routledge.

45. Robert Rosenthal. 1973. The Pygmalion Effect Lives. *Psychology Today* (1973).

46. Pieter Spronck, Ida Sprinkhuizen-Kuyper, and Eric Postma. 2004. Difficulty scaling of game AI. *Proceedings of the 5th International Conference on Intelligent Games and Simulation (GAMEON'2004)* (2004), 33–37.

47. Jaakko Stenros, Janne Paavilainen, and Frans Mäyrä. 2009. The Many Faces of Sociability and Social Play in Games. In *Proceedings of the 13th International MindTrek Conference: Everyday Life in the Ubiquitous Era (MindTrek '09)*. ACM, New York, NY, USA, 82–89. DOI: http://dx.doi.org/10.1145/1621841.1621857

48. Anselm Strauss and Juliet Corbin. 1994. Grounded theory methodology. *Handbook of qualitative research* 17 (1994), 273–85.

49. Anselm Strauss and Juliet M Corbin. 1997. *Grounded theory in practice*. Sage.

50. Christine Szentgyorgyi, Michael Terry, and Edward Lank. 2008. Renegade Gaming: Practices Surrounding Social Use of the Nintendo DS Handheld Gaming System. In *Proceedings of the SIGCHI Conference on Human Factors in Computing Systems (CHI '08)*. ACM, New York, NY, USA, 1463–1472. DOI: http://dx.doi.org/10.1145/1357054.1357283

51. Gustavo F. Tondello, Rina R. Wehbe, Zachary O. Toups, Lennart E. Nacke, and Nicole K. Crenshaw. 2015. Understanding Player Attitudes Towards Digital Game Objects. In *Proceedings of the 2015 Annual Symposium on Computer-Human Interaction in Play (CHI PLAY '15)*. ACM, New York, NY, USA, 709–714. DOI: http://dx.doi.org/10.1145/2793107.2810292

52. Alan M. Turing. 1950. Computing machinery and intelligence. *Mind* 59, 236 (1950), 433–460.

53. Deepika Vaddi, Zachary Toups, Igor Dolgov, Rina Wehbe, and Lennart Nacke. 2016. Investigating the Impact of Cooperative Communication Mechanics on Player Performance in Portal 2. In *Proceedings of Graphics Interface 2016 (GI 2016)*. Canadian Human-Computer Communications Society / Société canadienne du dialogue humain-machine, 41–48. DOI: http://dx.doi.org/10.20380/GI2016.06

54. Deepika Vaddi, Rina R. Wehbe, Zachary O. Toups, Samantha N Stahlke, Rylan Koroluk, and Lennart E. Nacke. 2015. Validating Test Chambers to Study Cooperative Communication Mechanics in Portal 2. In *Proceedings of the 2015 Annual Symposium on Computer-Human Interaction in Play*. ACM, 721–726.

55. Amy Voida and Saul Greenberg. 2009. Wii All Play: The Console Game As a Computational Meeting Place. In *Proceedings of the SIGCHI Conference on Human Factors in Computing Systems (CHI '09)*. ACM, New York, NY, USA, 1559–1568. DOI: http://dx.doi.org/10.1145/1518701.1518940

56. Henrik Warpefelt. 2016. *The Non-Player Character : Exploring the believability of NPC presentation and behavior*. Ph.D. Dissertation. Stockholm University, Department of Computer and Systems Sciences.

57. Henrik Warpefelt, Magnus Johansson, and Harko Verhagen. 2013. Analyzing the believability of game character behavior using the Game Agent Matrix. In *Proceedings of DIGRA*. 70–81.

58. Henrik Warpefelt and Björn Strååt. 2013. Anti-heuristics for maintaining immersion through believable non-player characters.. In *FDG*. 455–456.

59. Rina R. Wehbe. 2014. *Evaluating Social and Cognitive Effects of Video Games using Electroencephalography*. Ph.D. Dissertation. University of Ontario Institute of Technology (UOIT). http://hdl.handle.net/10155/460

60. Rina R. Wehbe, Dennis L. Kappen, David Rojas, Matthias Klauser, Bill Kapralos, and Lennart E. Nacke. 2013. EEG-based assessment of video and in-game learning. *Proc. CHI'13 Extended Abstracts* (2013). DOI: http://dx.doi.org/10.1145/2468356.2468474

61. Rina R. Wehbe and Lennart E. Nacke. 2015. Towards Understanding the Importance of Co-Located Gameplay. In *Proceedings of the 2015 Annual Symposium on Computer-Human Interaction in Play (CHI PLAY '15)*. ACM, New York, NY, USA, 733–738. DOI: http://dx.doi.org/10.1145/2793107.2810312

62. David Weibel, Bartholomäus Wissmath, Stephan Habegger, Yves Steiner, and Rudolf Groner. 2008. Playing online games against computer- vs. human-controlled opponents: Effects on presence, flow, and enjoyment. *Computers in Human Behavior* 24, 5 (sep 2008), 2274–2291. DOI: http://dx.doi.org/10.1016/j.chb.2007.11.002

63. Dmitri Williams, Nicolas Ducheneaut, Li Xiong, Yuanyuan Zhang, Nick Yee, and Eric Nickell. 2006. From Tree House to Barracks. *Games and Culture* 1, 4 (2006), 338–361. DOI: http://dx.doi.org/10.1177/1555412006292616

64. Geogios N. Yannakakis. 2012. Game AI Revisited. *Proceedings of the 9th Conference on Computing Frontiers* (2012), 285–292. DOI: http://dx.doi.org/10.1145/2212908.2212954

65. Rina R. Wehbe Gustavo F. Tondello Zachary O. Toups, Nicole K. Crenshaw and Lennart E. Nacke. 2016. "The Collecting Itself Feels Good": Towards Collection Interfaces for Digital Game Objects. In *Proceedings of the 2016 Annual Symposium on Computer-Human Interaction in Play - CHI PLAY '16*. ACM, Austin, TX, USA. DOI: http://dx.doi.org/10.1145/2967934.2968088

LUDOGRAPHY

1. Majesco, 505 Games. 2008. *Zumba Fitness*. Game [Wii]. (2008). Majesco Entertainment, Edison, New Jersey, USA.

2. Valve Corporation. 2008. *Left4Dead*. Game [Windows, Xbox 360, OS X]. (2008). Valve Corporation, Bellevue, Washington, USA.

3. Valve Corporation. 2009. *Left4Dead*. Game [Windows, Xbox 360, OS X], Linux. (2009). Valve Corporation, Bellevue, Washington, USA.

Touchomatic: Interpersonal Touch Gaming In The Wild

Joe Marshall
Mixed Reality Lab, School of Computer Science
University of Nottingham, UK
joe.marshall@nottingham.ac.uk

Paul Tennent
Mixed Reality Lab, School of Computer Science
University of Nottingham, UK
paul.tennent@nottingham.ac.uk

ABSTRACT
Direct touch between people is a key element of social behaviour. Recently a number of researchers have explored games which sense aspects of such interpersonal touch to control interaction with a multiplayer computer game. In this paper, we describe a long term, in-the-wild study of a two-player arcade game which is controlled by gentle touching between the body parts of two players. We ran the game in a public videogame arcade for a year, and present a thematic analysis of 27 hours of gameplay session videos, organized under three top level themes: control of the system, interpersonal interaction within the game, and social interaction around the game. In addition, we provide a quantitative analysis of observed demographic differences in interpersonal touch behaviour. Finally, we use these results to present four design recommendations for use of interpersonal touch in games.

Author Keywords
Interpersonal touch; game; in the wild; arcade.

ACM Classification Keywords
H.5.2. *Input devices and strategies*

INTRODUCTION
Touch between people is a key part of social communication, being part of everything from early bonds of caring touch between parent and child, to the many uses of touch in later life, communicating friendship, aggression, physical attraction and physical competition [39]. However, as Marshall et al. [25] note, interpersonal touch is largely unused in computer entertainment, with most games designed for some form of 'parallel play', where all interaction between multiple players is mediated via computer systems and increasingly via remote network connections.

In this paper, we present a study of a two-player game which senses nuances of pressure in gentle interpersonal touch in order to provide control to an airship flying through a mountainous landscape. To achieve a high score in the game, players must collaborate and negotiate to adjust their touching behaviour in order to fly the airship accurately. We believe this kind of gentle, extended touch interaction has the potential to arouse strong affective responses in players which are qualitatively different to those in previous interpersonal touch games which focus on extreme force [25] or the use of touch patterns as discrete individual inputs directly analogous to gamepad buttons [6].

DIS 2017, June 10-14, 2017, Edinburgh, United Kingdom

ACM 978-1-4503-4922-2/17/06…$15.00
DOI: http://dx.doi.org/10.1145/3064663.3064727

Psychological and sociological research on interpersonal touch (e.g. [11,31,32]) often occurs in naturalistic environments, with the view taken that social and affective elements of interpersonal touch are unrealistically affected by laboratory settings [32]. In concordance with this work, we ran a long-term study of our game in a real-world videogame arcade, without researcher intervention. This year-long study provided us with a large amount of video recordings and gameplay logs which enable us to reach a deep understanding of how people play our game.

We analyse these video recordings and apply a thematic analysis [5] methodology, providing insight into player behaviour in the form of a set of explanatory codes arranged in three top-level themes:

- How players control touch sensing hardware.
- How players behave towards each other.
- How people around the players affect the game.

We follow this with a brief statistical analysis of how demographic variables (visually estimated age and gender) relate to higher or lower levels of some behaviours, for example showing that male/male pairs are less likely to show physical affection than pairs involving female players. These results are largely consistent with psychological research on interpersonal touch, so to us as game designers and researchers, they demonstrate that demographic variables have a real effect on players' experience of interpersonal touch.

We conclude with a discussion of what these results mean for the design of interpersonal touch games, in the form of 4 recommendations for game designers. In summary, the contributions of this paper are:

- Design of an **interpersonal touch game**.
- A **year-long in-the wild study** of our touch game.
- **3 themes** relating to how players play the game.
- **4 recommendations** discussing how to design interpersonal touch games.

PRIOR WORK

Experiences of social and affective interpersonal touch have been studied in a wide range of areas, both within HCI, and in wider social and psychological research fields.

Social Touch Gaming, HCI and Art

A small number of projects have directly explored interpersonal touch in entertainment situations. In particular, two projects explore the detection of hand to hand touch - gaming system *Sensation* [6] uses capacitive sensing to detect two person touch gestures, such as 'bro-fist' & '1 finger touch', which control a game in which players make the gestures together. *Enhancedtouch* uses bracelets which detect and measure human to human touch times [38], which are used to measure touch behaviours in games for children with autistic spectrum disorders. Performance work *Mediated Body* [17] also uses interpersonal touch sensing, with a private light and sound show controlled by touch between a performer and an audience member.

Several systems do not detect touch, but rather encourage forms of social touching: *Musical Embrace* [18] is controlled by a cushion between two players who hug to control a 3d game, creating a deliberately 'uncomfortable interaction' [4]. *Balance of Power* [25], encourages people to brutally force opposing players to move. *B.U.T.T.O.N* [41] gives players instructions such as 'the last player to let go of their controller button wins', designed to encourage players to use imaginative 'Brutally Unfair Tactics' for example to grab controllers off other players; similarly *Intangle* [13] uses shared controllers and instructions which encourage physical social interactions between players.

A key element of *Balance of Power* and *B.U.T.T.O.N.* which we aim to replicate here is that they create a system of rules and rewards but do not enforce particular mechanisms or specify player movements for game outcomes. We believe (after Gaver et al. [14]) that such deliberate use of ambiguity and lack of instructions inspires people to imaginatively explore the range of physical actions which will make a system respond in a desired fashion. In this research however, by creating something which responds to a wide range of inputs, we aim to make something which allows and responds to subtle differences in touch and gradation of control, in contrast to the extreme brutality of *Balance of Power* [25], the simple joypad sensing of *B.U.T.T.O.N.* [41], or the discrete gestures used by '*Sensation*' [6].

Mediated and Computer Generated Social Touch

Many HCI projects explore use of networked computer systems to create experiences of touch between remotely situated participants to communicate or induce affect. For example *move.me* [35] involved a pillow which senses pressure and actuates a remote pillow, aiming to allow remote intimacy. *Poultry Internet* even allows animal owners to stroke their pets remotely [8]. There is also work on the generation of synthetic social touch cues, such as *tactile jacket* [22], which generates tactile affective cues to accompany movies, and robots which aim to touch socially. While we focus here however on direct human-to-human touch, interested readers may wish to read van Erp and Toet's comprehensive review of social touch in HCI [10].

Social and Psychological Interpersonal Touch Research

Touch between people is interesting for game design because: "*tactile sensations elicited under ecologically-valid conditions that involve interpersonal interaction can have surprisingly powerful effects on people's behaviors and emotions* " [12]. Social and psychology work relating to touch also provides several useful insights into both how we experience touch, and what the potential effects of touch might be. Touch can be used in a discriminative nature, for feeling our surroundings, and can have strong emotional effects on those touched, both positive and negative [26]. Touch has also been shown to communicate emotion between two people [16], and alter social situations, such as tipping in restaurants [37] or selling second-hand cars [9].

How and where people are touched on their body is also important – with a key distinction being between hairy and non-hairy parts of the skin, with hairy skin often linked to more pleasurable touch sensations [26], although recent research suggests combinations of hairy and non-hairy touch can also be pleasurable [23]. Touch is also deeply social and interacts with many factors beyond the pure physical nature of contact – for example studies have shown differences in how effectively people in relationships can communicate emotions compared to strangers [40] and touch actions which would be identified as loving within an intimate relationship, are perceived as harassment within a working environment [21]. Touch can create different effects depending on the gender of the person giving [11] and receiving the touch [37]; a relevant corollary of this work is that in many touch situations there is a clear directionality as to who is doing the touching which is clearly relevant to gaming situations. Further to this, we note that cultural aspects of social behaviour also affect touch, with cultures often described as 'non-contact' (e.g. UK, USA) or 'contact' (e.g. Italy, Spain, Latin America) [15] depending on whether people from those cultures are comfortable with high levels interpersonal touch in general. As well as affecting underlying rates of touching, cultural differences intersect with other factors, affecting for example how comfortable people are with same sex touching or in what relationships they would consider kissing to be appropriate in [34:168].

As well as considering study results, social science research into touch is key to the design of our study. Social touch research often involves naturalistic studies, for example studying the effects of touching on positive appraisal of those doing the touching, done in a real library during checking out of a book [11], and study of touching by real waitresses in restaurant situations [37]. We take particular inspiration from Remland et al's work on proxemics and touch in different countries, which used video-recording of large numbers of subject interactions in situations chosen to be naturalistic and representative of the culture of the countries studied [31,32].

Figure 1. Touchomatic Arcade Cabinet

THE TOUCHOMATIC HARDWARE

The *Touchomatic* arcade cabinet is built around a standard two player sized arcade cabinet containing a standard PC and monitor, webcam, speakers, and a lighting board and LEDs to make the game name at the top of the cabinet flash pretty colours during the game. Instead of the joysticks, the control board contains just two large metal handles with arrows saying 'Player 1' and 'Player 2' next to each handle. An Arduino is connected to each handle using the circuit shown in Figure 2. All source code is linked at the end of the paper. The Arduino gathers data at 100hz using two types of sensing:

Capacitive Person Sensing:

Capacitive sensing is used to detect if anyone is holding each handle. This uses charge / release capacitive sensing on a single Arduino Analog pin connected directly to the handle (i.e. pin 3 or 4 on the diagram). Pins 1 & 2 are set as inputs which are for practical purposes disconnected. The sampling pin is first set as output and held low to discharge any residual charge. Then it is set to input mode and pulled high using the Arduino's built in pull-up resistor. The time this takes to return to 5v is proportional to the capacitance attached to the handle. The pin is sampled repeatedly to estimate speed of return of the pin voltage and hence the capacitive load. When a large capacitance is detected, the system reports that a person is touching the handle.

Resistive Circuit Sensing

Resistive sensing is used to detect whether and how strongly the two players are touching each other's skin. In resistive mode, pins 1 and 2 are set to zero to provide a weak pull-down resistor. The system then generates an oscillating signal on pin 3, by outputting a series of 1 and 0s, whilst reading from pin 4. The oscillating signal is received on pin 4 at a strength which varies depending on the overall resistance between the two player handles. Rather than measure the oscillating signal directly, we measure the variance of the received signal; this negates issues with delays caused by capacitance. For a given touch pose, such as finger to finger, resistance decreases as touch strength increases; this allows for detection of a smooth range of touch strengths (our system reports 512 different strengths).

After the each measurement cycle, Pins 3 and 4 are swapped and the same measurement is applied, to measure this resistance in the other direction. This should not in theory make any difference to measured resistance, but in practice it does, presumably due to differences in internal Arduino measurement circuitry; by swapping the direction of the sensing each measurement cycle, we ensure that the game is as symmetrical as possible.

The respective types of sensing are switched between at approximately 200hz, giving a full data rate of up 100hz.

Sensor Processing

The raw data from the two sensors gives us two basic pieces of information:

1) Is there a person or people holding each handle?
2) What is the resistance between the handles?

The raw sensor data is processed to obtain two further items of data, firstly by detecting moments where capacitive sensing detects a person touching both handles, yet resistive sensing does not detect a circuit, we can detect that there are indeed two people touching the handles, rather than one person touching both handles. We use this to enforce two person play in our games. Secondly, by sensing moments of no-touch followed by short moments of touch, we sense a high five gesture which is used for starting games etc.

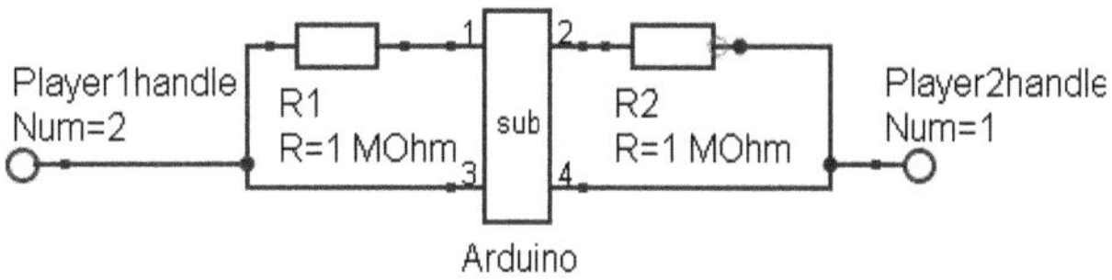

Figure 2. Touch-O-Matic Sensing Circuit

Figure 1. Two players of Astonishing Airship Adventures and game screen

ASTONISHING AIRSHIP ADVENTURES

We built a game called *Astonishing Airship Adventures* (*AAA*, Figure 3) to test *Touchomatic*, it is presented in sepia tone, with accompanying 1920s jazz music to match the bare wood aesthetic of the arcade cabinet. In *AAA*, players control an airship which is flying over a barren landscape. They must fly close to the ground to collect coins, whilst avoiding crashing. The balloon's height is controlled by the touch interaction, with stronger contact increasing the onscreen throttle gauge and making the ship fly higher. A new level occurs every 20 seconds – on higher levels the scenery becomes increasingly hilly (see Figure 5), making it harder to fly low and score, and more likely that players will crash.

Design Choices

When building *AAA*, we made several deliberate design choices to best support the Touchomatic:

- With the exception of text, the game and arcade cabinet is entirely symmetrical, the balloon flies away from the players and is directly between them. This was important as we wished to remove any cues that would imply one player was more important than the other player.
- The game is entirely controlled by touch, including starting the game, and consenting to the research video recording. We did not want players to be required to interact in any way other than interpersonal touching.
- The game starts off extremely easy, and gets difficult quite slowly, because we wanted to observe people playing for significant lengths of time, and wanted them to be able to explore the unfamiliar touch interaction without too much pressure to begin with.
- To encourage people to use the control in a nuanced way, getting a high score requires using detailed control interactions to fly very low.

Game Trajectory

Because the game must run unattended, we designed an overall experience for the pairs of players with all instructions coming from the game itself via a tutorial level.

Figure 4. Title screen

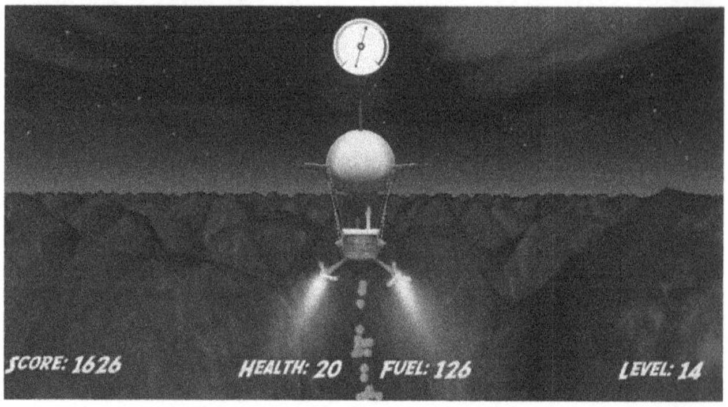

Figure 5. On higher levels, the terrain becomes more rugged.

The initial title screen begins with an instruction that two players must grab a handle each to play (Figure 4). Once the system detects both handles are touched, it checks that there is no connection between the two; this makes sure that it is two people, rather than just one person touching both handles. It then changes the text to "High five to play". Next, a video recording consent screen is shown, this shows the video camera image and notifies players that games are recorded, and to high five if they are happy to continue. The game starts with the airship landed and the instruction 'touch each other to fly'. As soon as the players touch, the ship takes off, and further instructions are shown ('the harder you touch the higher you fly' etc.). The player cannot crash in this section and can experiment with flight controls. After 10 seconds of instructions, the game proper begins and players can fly until they crash or run out of fuel. On achieving a high score, players are again shown the camera video, and a photo to be shown on the high score chart is captured when they do a high five.

STUDY

We installed *Touchomatic* at National Videogame Arcade (NVA), Nottingham, a public gaming arcade which showcases a wide range of classic and experimental gaming machines. Entry to NVA is by paid ticket, with game machines set to free-to-play. It is open 3 days a week normally and all week in school holidays.

This setting allowed us to study *Touchomatic* in the wild, in a real world setting, surrounded by other gaming machines, for example in the first half of the year, *Touchomatic* was installed in between the classic fighting game *Street Fighter II* [7] and Nintendo's *Duck Hunt* [27], and towards the end, when the arcade was reorganized, it was moved to be next to an early *Tetris* [29] arcade machine.

We left *Touchomatic* running for a full year, recording video of players, screen capture, and logs including data such as state of the touch input, score, level and player position. For privacy, we did not record player audio. In addition to venue consents and signage explaining that public video recording occurs in the arcade, players were specifically informed of *Touchomatic*'s video recording each time the game began, with a screen notifying that the game is recorded, showing them the view from the camera, and asking them to high five if they are happy to be recorded.

We had access 3 times over the year to maintain the machine and retrieve data, in between maintenance was performed by the arcade's in house team, who have significant experience of keeping game machines in playable state.

After running the game for a year, we retrieved all data from the game machine and performed a thematic analysis [5] on the data to explore how people actually played the game in this real world, in the wild setting.

Data availability and Ethical Approval

This study was approved by the School of [XXX] at the University of [XXX]. Video data from the *Touchomatic* is personally identifiable data which we do not have consent to share. Images shown here are blurred for privacy. Our coding dataset is included as supplementary materials.

Dataset Processing and Analysis

During the game's run, we had limited access to the machine, and maintenance was performed locally by the arcade staff. Their only priority was to keep the game itself working, for example by fixing loose game handles, replacing speakers which had been poked by children, cleaning screens etc. They were not interested in the game camera or network connection of the game. Because of this, there were some points in time were the camera was forcibly removed or where video capture software on the system failed, which we were unable to diagnose or fix for an extended period of time.

Players played a total of 3412 games, over 157 hours. We checked all the videos to recover games with full datasets including video. This gave us 93 hours of gameplay. For the purposes of practical analysis, we chose to analyse 500 games (27 hours of video) taken from the earliest and latest sets of games in the dataset; we did not observe any difference between early and late gameplay, probably due to the visitor attraction nature of the arcade meaning that there are few regular players, so most players will be experiencing the game on only one day, so we treat this as a single dataset representing typical play of *Touchomatic*.

From our initial set of 500 games, we initially briefly watched each video to check whether the gameplay video was usable, specifically noting whether: a) both players are visible, and b) the touch between players is visible. This gave us a set of 347 videos in which gameplay and players are visible. We also annotated each video with estimated demographic data, including a) estimated age for each player, as child (<12), teen (12-20), or adult (20+), and b) presenting gender of each player, male / female / uncertain.

Treating each gameplay video as a unit of assessment, we then analysed videos to identify player actions observed in the data and assign (potentially multiple) codes to each unit. We split this work between two researchers, who initially each independently watched half of the dataset and assigned their own set of codes describing actions of players in the games. We combined the two sets of codes and developed a shared code set around a set of themes, which we applied to the full dataset for the analysis described below.

DEMOGRAPHICS

Our dataset included 435 male players (63%), and 255 female (37%), 4 players were of uncertain gender. There were 179 same gender pairs, and 167 pairs of opposite gender players. We estimated 143 players (21%) were children, 195 (28%) teenagers and 353 (51%) were adults.

THEMATIC ANALYSIS

Our codes split into the three themes shown in Figure 6:

- Methods people use to **control** the touch sensing.
- **Interpersonal** interaction between players.
- **Social** interaction with people outside the game.

We describe these in the sections below. This is a primarily qualitative analysis, however where we make assertions of between-group differences relating to our codes, we apply appropriate statistical tests.

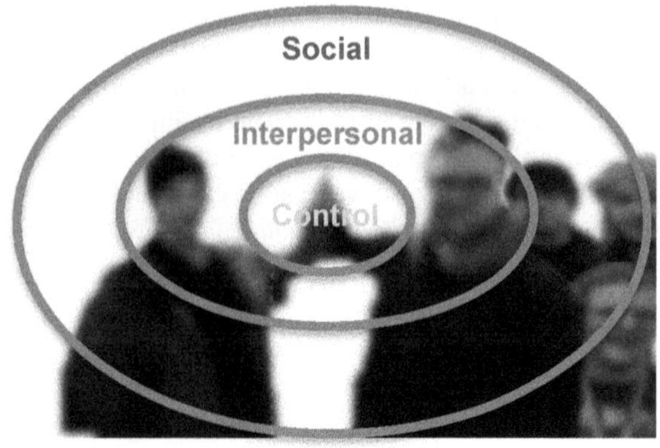

Figure 6. The three themes from our analysis

Theme 1: Methods to control the touch sensing

This theme relates to ways in which players move their hands and other body parts in order to actuate the touch sensing controls of *Touchomatic*. 358 of the 844 coded units are accounted for by this theme.

Whilst the start-up sequence of Astonishing *Airship Adventures* encourages players to do a high five, i.e. to use palm to palm contact, no direction is given in the rest of the game as to how to touch each other. We saw many examples of player pairs ***experimenting with ways of touching*** (86 units), for example by trying to touch through clothes, or touching heads together. Several pairs explored ***playful methods of touching*** (35 units), such as face touching, and even one pair who played the game by touching their heads together (Figure 7).

The touch detection hardware simply detects the quality of electrical connection between players, which, as long as players maintain the same type of physical connection, relates strongly to the overall pressure between players. The game does not change depending on how this pressure is applied. We observed several different approaches to controlling this pressure: many pairs of players began by adopting an approach of ***reciprocal touching*** (83 units), where both players adjusted their touch pressure at the same time. Pairs often however adjusted their play style to one in which ***one player takes control of the touch pressure*** (53 units), with the other player holding their hand or other body part still, often this involved an element of taking turns as to who was in charge. This was not always a simple negotiation as players did not always agree on who was in charge, we observed several ***moments of physical disagreement*** (22 units) where one player attempts to increase pressure and the other simultaneously moves their hand away to decrease pressure.

Touchomatic is designed to allow smooth, gentle analogue control. However, we noticed several players appeared to find modulating their touch levels difficult. Whilst some of these players simply ***failed to modulate touch pressure*** (14 units) and their airship oscillated wildly up and down, others found a work-around by treating the system as essentially a digital input, using a ***series of repeated taps*** (65 units) of greater or lower frequency depending on how high they wished their airship to go.

Figure 7. Players Bumping Heads and Touching Faces

Theme 2: Interpersonal interactions between players

This theme is concerned with ways in which players interacted together beyond purely controlling the touch sensing hardware, the 427 units in this theme provide insight into wider aspects of the interpersonal interaction between players.

One element of deploying this game in a real arcade which we had not anticipated or seen in deployments in research settings, was the very high incidence of ***play-fighting and forceful pushing*** (98 units), with players enjoying that they could slap each other in the face to control the game or use pushing the other player to the floor or punching fists together as part of their control strategy.

Figure 8. Right player hits left player in face.

Figure 9. Cuddling heads and faces together to control the game

Figure 10. Moment players realise they must touch each other

Players also made another use of interpersonal touch by controlling the system in ways that ***demonstrated affection*** (34 units), such as by hugging, kissing, or stroking the other player (Figure 9). Other players were clearly uncomfortable with the level of intimacy involved in human-to-human touch, and showed ***physical signs of feeling awkward*** (38 units), such as shying away from the other player's touch, refusing to play at all, and facial signs of awkwardness such as extreme grimaces and 'face-palming' as the player reads the instruction to touch the other player (Figure 10).

We also observed some distinctly contrasting styles of play – a large number of pairs were observed ***laughing constantly throughout*** (78 units), whereas a small number were observed to have adopted a ***highly focused play style*** (13 units), staring intently on the screen and focusing purely on the game (Figure 11 shows examples of both styles). We suggest that these two behaviours imply two differing conceptions of the computer game itself, by laughing players the game may be seen as stimulating a wider play situation, whereas the more focused players are not interested in what is going on around the game. Those who adopted the focused play style certainly had more success purely in the terms set by the game, lasting for longer before crashing (median=447 seconds) compared to the laughing group (median=143 seconds); a Mann-Whitney test indicated that this difference is significant, $U=159.0$, $p<0.001$

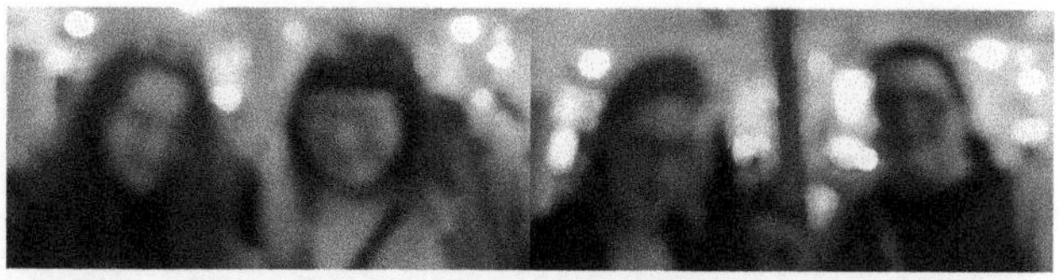

Figure 11. Contrasting play styles: laughing (L) vs focused (R)

One final aspect of social behaviour around the game which was observable in our video data is how players get bored and give up on the game. The difficulty level of the game was deliberately slightly low, plus for players who did not choose to collect coins and aim for a high score, it was possible to fly high for a large number of levels before fuel ran out. Because of this, 34% of players ***gave up playing before they crashed*** (120 units). This was in part made worse by the two player only nature of the game – unlike many arcade games, where if one player leaves, they drop to single player mode, if a player leaves the *Touchomatic*, whilst the single player left can grab both sticks and control it by releasing and touching one stick, much of the fun of the game is lost; evidence for this is seen in our analysis, where if ***one player leaves the game first*** (46 units), the other player is more likely to give up before crashing also, giving up 64% of the time (this difference is significant, Fisher's Exact Test, $p<0.001$).

Theme 3: Social interaction with people outside the game

Our final theme (59 units) relates to ways in which the game situation is affected by and affects people who are not directly involved in the game. Players using *Touchomatic* are often doing something which is visibly odd in a public gaming arcade, which attracts spectators. It was quite common to see situations where ***spectators advised or helped players*** (33 units), for example by physically gesticulating to demonstrate what players should aim to do, or by showing players that they had to keep their hands on the handles. We also saw several situations where a ***spectator enters the game*** (10 units), either taking the place of one of the players, or getting in between the two players to become part of the circuit between them (Figure 12).

The other way in which players interact with others via the game is through the pictures shown in the high score chart which are visible to future players and spectators. We saw that when this happened, players often took some time playing in front of the camera and ***composing their high score pictures*** (16 units), sometimes including bystanders also. Figure 13 shows some examples of high score poses.

Figure 2. Players pose for high score pictures.

Figure 12. Two players touching a third player's face

DEMOGRAPHIC DIFFERENCES

We analysed our coding results for differences in code distribution relating to our player demographic categories of age and gender. In this section, we present a discussion of codes where we found significant differences across demographic variables. We found no significant differences in distribution of any other codes relating to these variables. Analysis was done using IBM SPSS 22. The dataset and SPSS commands are provided as supplementary material.

Affection and Gender

We found that public displays of affection were strongly influenced by gender with 17% of female/female pairs showing affection towards each other, 14.3% of mixed gender pairs, and only 2.3% of male/male pairs. Chi-square tests for association showed that the difference is significant, $\chi^2(2)=14.976$, $p=0.001$; pairwise tests showed that this was only significant for male/male pairs compared to f/f ($\chi^2(1)=13.448$, $p=0.001$) and mixed pairs ($\chi^2(1)=12.944$, $p<0.001$). No significant difference was found between all female and mixed pairs, $\chi^2(1)=.271$, $p=.603$.

Awkwardness and Gender

All male pairs also showed significantly higher levels of behaviour indicating awkwardness, with 22% of m/m pairs displaying signs of discomfort, in comparison to 2% of f/f pairs and 5% of mixed pairs. Chi square tests again show significant differences between m/m and other pairs, $\chi^2(2)=25.429$, $p<0.001$. Again no significant differences were found between female and mixed pairs.

Play-fighting and Age (but not Gender)

We noted a strong association between *play-fighting and forceful pushing* and age. In pairs consisting of two non-adults, 39% of pairs engaged in some kind of forceful behaviour. Pairs with at least one adult were more restrained, with only 22% of players engaging in fighting play. A chi squared test showed this association to be significant, $\chi^2(1)=8.434$, $p=0.001$. We also found an association between fighting and whether the pairs had the same gender, however a logistic regression demonstrated that this was a side effect of different gender distributions in adult and child populations (with children more likely to play in same-sex pairs); showing significant effect, $p=0.032$ only of whether a pair included a child. We also found no significant differences between all female and all male pairs, child and/or teen pairs showed high incidences of play-fighting whether they were girls or boys.

Cultural Specificity of These Results

We note that whilst these show some interesting results, these are likely to be somewhat dependent on the cultural norms of the UK. Results on awkwardness and demonstrative physical affection are consistent with several studies from varying cultures around the world almost all of which demonstrate lower rates of male/male touching than female/female touching [36:219], which would suggest a likelihood for less comfort with touching amongst male/male pairs. We anticipate that results could be different in other societies as previous studies have demonstrated highly differing attitudes to touch and personal space between countries [12,31], for example studies in Mediterranean cultures have shown far greater social acceptability of touching and physical affection between all-male pairs compared to Northern European cultures [34:168].

DISCUSSION: 4 DESIGN RECOMMENDATIONS FOR INTERPERSONAL TOUCH

In this section, we present a set of design recommendations which distil our experiences and study of *Touchomatic* into practical recommendations for those designing other games which make use of interpersonal touch. Rather than provide a prescriptive how-to guide, we aim to guide designers in taking consideration of what our findings suggest are the most important factors, and provide sets of questions to sensitize designers to each recommendation.

R1: Highlight Controlling Interactions Between Players

In Jennet et al's discussion of the concept of immersion [20], their questionnaire suggests that for a game to be 'immersive' players should forget about the controls and should feel *separated from your real world environment.* Conversely, we believe that one of the key positive things that interpersonal touch has to offer over and above conventional controllers is the actual sensations of touch themselves, and that for such games we need a wider sense of the game environment, which includes the whole play situation. If one forgets about the control system in *Touchomatic*, we have essentially made a 3d version of the classic Flappy Bird game; without an awareness of the real world situation, we would also be unaware of the real world person standing next to us with whom we are touching to play the game. We believe that for this reason measuring immersion in this kind of game makes no sense, and that designing for immersion, i.e. for the interface to disappear, is a bad choice, and that designers should instead aim to highlight the interactions between those controlling, by considering the following questions:

How can we encourage players to focus on their touch senses?
Touchomatic is designed so players stand next to each other, and need to look at the screen. This encourages players to not look at each other while playing the game. Canat et al.'s *Sensation* [6] directly enforces this, by standing players on opposite sides of the screen. We might also consider games in which players are blindfolded, must wear headphones to block their hearing, or where touch occurs out of their sight.

How do we encourage nuanced control?
Touchomatic encourages players to vary their touch pressure gently and smoothly. To play effectively requires players to concentrate and collaborate in order to achieve this. Alternatively, as Canat et al.[6] suggest, we can consider subtleties in other dimensions of touch such as touch contact area shape or point of touch on the body.

How can the game be controlled with limited control dimensions?
The control of *Touchomatic*, is basically a single analogue value. In other touch systems such as [6,38] input is even more limited, being essentially constrained to a small number of discrete poses. There are many game models, especially from early games that fit such controls, from games such as *Pong* [2], which used a single rotary control, to *Flappy Bird* which is controlled by a single 'fly up' button. Many limited control games automate some common actions, for example *Super Mario Run* [28] automatically runs all the time, giving the player control only of 4 jumping actions.

R2: Encourage Interesting and Expressive Touch
For us, a key interest in using interpersonal touch is in the wide range of expressive possibilities which it affords. The following questions aim to help maximize the possibilities of interpersonal touch in games:

How does the game encourage interesting touch behaviour?
We found that a side effect of the way that we used the high-five to start the game was that players instantly understood that the game would respond not just to gentle hand-to-hand touching. We believe this encouraged people to explore a wider range of touch actions.

How can we allow for expressive latitude?
Benford et al discuss how sensing based systems involve ranges of actions that people are expected to perform, actions which can be sensed, and actions which are 'desired' to control an application [3], they argue that the fact some actions people will do cannot be sensed, allows opportunity for 'expressive latitude', where people express themselves in ways not sensed by the interface, in a way analogous to movements that pianists make around a piano keyboard, which the piano does not respond to, but can still be key to the pianists performance. *Touchomatic*'s simple sensing method allows for a wide range of expressive latitude, which we believe allows people to play with an interesting range of touch styles, and allows it to be played by people with highly differing touch preferences.

How does the physical interface support touching?
Touchomatic is deliberately built to be quite narrow, with the two handles approximately 50cm apart. Players typically grab the handle with their outside hand, and touch with the closer hand. This encourages people to stand quite close together and orient their bodies slightly towards each other. It ensures that players are almost always within each other's reach, and can easily reach a wide range of body parts on the other player. However, there are other ways to support touching, for example in *Balance of Power* [25] the freedom given by Kinect's non-contact sensing supports players to touch as each other as forcefully as they wish.

R3: Consider Demographics and Culture.
As we observed in our study, the interaction between players was strongly affected by gender and age effects. These effects are largely not discussed in previous HCI work relating to interpersonal touch interaction, perhaps due to sample size limitations in studies. Our study also showed effects consistent with wider research into the nature of touching in the UK, so although obviously we only studied in a single culture, we would also expect to observe different behaviour if we ran *Touchomatic* in other countries. When designing interpersonal touch gaming, assuming we have some idea of where the game is likely to be played, or by whom, we suggest that designers consider:

What kinds of touch will likely users be comfortable with?
We note that we may, as in *Musical Embrace* [19], actually wish users to experience uncomfortable touch interactions, which, as discussed in [4], can be appropriate as an active design choice.

What kinds of touch are players likely to spontaneously do?
According to Houmel and Flammia [34:168], in some cultures, it is common for greetings between two men to include kisses on the cheek, and seen as rude not to. Whereas in some cultures, even shaking hands is considered excessive contact between people who are not already intimate. We can expect that the level of touching which players perform by default will differ strongly between such cultures, and design accordingly. We also observed children in particular showing far more tendency to take part in play fighting and vigorous contact in our game, something which we might choose to discourage or encourage (as in [25]) if we built a game for a setting with a lot of child players.

How private should games be?
Psychological measures of extroversion show large differences across cultures [24]. Using interpersonal touch games such as *Touchomatic* is a visible and abnormal act. In some cultures it may be appropriate to create a level of privacy for players. Even in the UK, we wonder if we would have observed less awkwardness amongst male/male pairs in an environment which was less open to spectators.

Are there cultural restrictions on player demographics?
Interpersonal touch has strong valence in some cultures which will affect who players are able to touch. In many highly religious cultures, there are strong constraints on opposite sex touching [1], and in cultures with a high incidence of homophobia, men are likely not to want to touch other men [33].

R4: Design For Spectators

Two people playing a game by touching each other in public is something out of the ordinary and highly visible, especially if players choose to play with touching in funny places or slapping each other. We suggest designers should explore:

What should be visible to spectators?
Reeves et al. [30] discuss 4 approaches for exposing or hiding interface manipulations and outputs from computer systems to spectators. In *Touchomatic*, we take what Reeves calls an 'expressive' approach, of making sure that both the game and the interactions with the game are highly visible, mainly through our arcade cabinet layout, placement and audio. Performance work *Mediated Body* [17] in contrast uses headphones so that only the direct participants can hear the outputs of the system, whilst making the touch inputs highly visible. This 'suspenseful' approach highlights the touching to attract spectators by making them intrigued as to what is occurring for the participant. We could also envisage that in some games we may wish to make the touching not visible to spectators, a 'secretive' or 'magical' approach, for example if expected player demographics may not wish to be seen to touch in public.

What happens if spectators get involved in the game?
In *Touchomatic*, we observed moments when spectators took part in the game either by physically coming into the electrical loop between the two players, or by swapping places with players. We had not considered in designing *Touchomatic* that players would do this; in future designs we would explicitly consider how to facilitate likely spectator actions and whether they might transition to become additional players or replace existing players during a game. This could also aid with the inherent issue with two player games when one player becomes bored before the other.

CONCLUSIONS AND LIMITATIONS

In this paper, we present a large-scale analysis of hundreds of players through game recordings and logs. This has allowed us to answer the question: *how do people behave when presented with our interpersonal touch game*, and from it to draw wider design lessons.

We note that our approach of large-scale collection of gameplay logs and video allows us only to firmly answer the question of how people behaved. Whilst we believe that this is the most interesting question, we should be clear that with a study like this, we largely cannot evaluate factors such as the quality of our particular game or how much players enjoy playing it, beyond noting that a) players express themselves by laughing and smiling during the game, and b) the arcade have requested that we continue to leave the machine running indefinitely, something that has not been the case for previous research prototypes we have lent to them.

With this work, we have demonstrated that interpersonal touch has many interesting and expressive possibilities for game designers, and is highly practical to deploy in real world gaming environments. Readers wishing to build their own interpersonal touch systems may be interested in our source code and hardware designs. Code for *Astonishing Airship Adventures, Touchomatic* firmware & instructions for building the interface are available at https://github.com/paultennent/Flyer.

ACKNOWLEDGEMENTS

We would like to thank NVA and all our players for their help in this project, and Rich's Bartop Arcades for their work on our custom arcade cabinet. This work was supported by the Engineering and Physical Sciences Research Council (EP/M000877/1).

REFERENCES

1. Peter A Andersen. 2011. Tactile Traditions. In *The Handbook of Touch: Neuroscience, Behavioral, and Health Perspectives*, Matthew J. Hertenstein and Sandra J. Weiss (eds.). Springer, 351–369.
2. Atari. 1972. Pong.
3. Steve Benford, Bill Gaver, Andy Boucher, Brendan Walker, Sarah Pennington, Albrecht Schmidt, Hans Gellersen, Anthony Steed, Holger Schnädelbach, Boriana Koleva, Rob Anastasi, Chris Greenhalgh, Tom Rodden, Jonathan Green, Ahmed Ghali, and Tony Pridmore. 2005. Expected, sensed, and desired. *ACM Transactions on Computer-Human Interaction* 12, 1: 3–30. https://doi.org/10.1145/1057237.1057239
4. Steve Benford, Chris Greenhalgh, Gabriella Giannachi, Brendan Walker, Joe Marshall, and Tom Rodden. 2012. Uncomfortable interactions. *Proceedings of the 2012 ACM annual conference on Human Factors in Computing Systems - CHI '12*: 2005. https://doi.org/10.1145/2207676.2208347
5. Virginia Braun and Victoria Clarke. 2006. Using thematic analysis in psychology. *Qualitative Research in Psychology* 3, 2: 77–101. https://doi.org/http://dx.doi.org/10.1191/147808870 6qp063oa
6. Mert Canat, Mustafa Ozan Tezcan, Celalettin

Yurdakul, Eran Tiza, Buğra Can Sefercik, Idil Bostan, Oğuz Turan Buruk, Tilbe Göksun, and Oğuzhan Özcan. 2016. Sensation: Measuring the Effects of a Human-to-Human Social Touch Based Controller on the Player Experience. In *Proceedings of the 2016 CHI Conference on Human Factors in Computing Systems*, 3944–3955. https://doi.org/10.1145/2858036.2858418

7. Capcom. 1991. Street Fighter II: The World Warrior.
8. Adrian David Cheok. 2010. *Art and Technology of Entertainment Computing and Communication.* Springer-Verlag London. https://doi.org/10.1007/978-1-84996-137-0
9. Damien Erceau and Nicolas Guéguen. 2007. Tactile contact and evaluation of the toucher. *The Journal of social psychology* 147, 4: 441–444. https://doi.org/10.3200/SOCP.147.4.441-444
10. Jan B. F. van Erp and Alexander Toet. 2015. Social touch in human-computer interaction. *Frontiers in Digital Humanities* 2, 2: 1–14. https://doi.org/10.3389/fdigh.2015.00002
11. J D Fischer, M Rytting, R Heslin, J D Fisher, M Rytting, and R Heslin. 1976. Hands touching hands: affective and evaluative effects of an interpersonal touch. *Sociometry* 39, 4: 416–421. https://doi.org/10.2307/3033506
12. Alberto Gallace and Charles Spence. 2010. The science of interpersonal touch: An overview. *Neuroscience and Biobehavioral Reviews* 34, 2: 246–259. https://doi.org/10.1016/j.neubiorev.2008.10.004
13. Jayden Garner, Gavin Wood, Sandra Danilovic, Jessica Hammer, and Florian Mueller. 2014. Intangle: exploring interpersonal bodily interactions through sharing controllers. In *CHI PLAY '14: Proceedings of the first ACM SIGCHI annual symposium on Computer-human interaction in play*, 413–414. https://doi.org/10.1145/2658537.2661306
14. William W. Gaver, Jacob Beaver, and Steve Benford. 2003. Ambiguity as a resource for design. In *Proceedings of the conference on Human factors in computing systems - CHI '03*, 233. https://doi.org/10.1145/642611.642653
15. Edward Twitchell Hall. 1963. A system for the notation of proxemic behavior. *American Anthropologist 65*, 1003–1026. https://doi.org/10.1525/aa.1963.65.5.02a00020
16. Matthew J Hertenstein, Dacher Keltner, Betsy App, Brittany a Bulleit, and Ariane R Jaskolka. 2006. Touch communicates distinct emotions. *Emotion* 6, 3: 528–533. https://doi.org/10.1037/1528-3542.6.3.528
17. Mads Hobye and Jonas Löwgren. 2011. Touching a stranger: Designing for engaging experience in embodied interaction. *International Journal of Design* 5, 3: 31–48. Retrieved from http://www.ijdesign.org/ojs/index.php/IJDesign/article/view/976
18. Amy Huggard, Anushka De Mel, Jayden Garner, Cagdas "Chad" Toprak, Alan Chatham, and Florian "Floyd" Mueller. 2013. Musical Embrace: Exploring Social Awkwardness in Digital Games. In *Proceedings of the 2013 ACM International Joint Conference on Pervasive and Ubiquitous Computing* (UbiComp '13), 725–728. https://doi.org/10.1145/2493432.2493518
19. Amy Huggard, Anushka De Mel, Jayden Garner, Cagdas "Chad" Toprak, Alan Chatham, and Florian "Floyd" Mueller. 2013. Musical embrace. In *Proceedings of the 2013 ACM international joint conference on Pervasive and ubiquitous computing - UbiComp '13*, 725. https://doi.org/10.1145/2493432.2493518
20. Charlene Jennett, Anna L. Cox, Paul Cairns, Samira Dhoparee, Andrew Epps, Tim Tijs, and Alison Walton. 2008. Measuring and defining the experience of immersion in games. *International Journal of Human-Computer Studies* 66, 9: 641–661. https://doi.org/10.1016/j.ijhcs.2008.04.004
21. Josephine W. Lee and Laura K. Guerrero. 2001. Types of touch in cross-sex relationships between coworkers: perceptions of relational and emotional messages, inappropriateness, and sexual harassment. *Journal of Applied Communication Research* 29, 3: 197–220. https://doi.org/10.1080/00909880128110
22. Paul Lemmens, Floris Crompvoets, Dirk Brokken, Jack Van Den Eerenbeemd, and Gert Jan De Vries. 2009. A body-conforming tactile jacket to enrich movie viewing. *Proceedings - 3rd Joint EuroHaptics Conference and Symposium on Haptic Interfaces for Virtual Environment and Teleoperator Systems, World Haptics 2009*: 7–12. https://doi.org/10.1109/WHC.2009.4810832
23. Line S. Löken, Mika Evert, and Johan Wessberg. 2011. Pleasantness of touch in human glabrous and hairy skin: Order effects on affective ratings. *Brain Research* 1417: 9–15. https://doi.org/10.1016/j.brainres.2011.08.011
24. Richard Lynn and Terence Martin. 1995. National differences for thirty-seven nations in extraversion, neuroticism, psychoticism and economic, demographic and other correlates. *Personality and Individual Differences* 19, 3: 403–406. https://doi.org/10.1016/0191-8869(95)00054-A

25. Joe Marshall, Conor Linehan, and Adrian Hazzard. 2016. Designing Brutal Multiplayer Video Games. In *CHI '16 Proceedings of the SIGCHI Conference on Human Factors in Computing Systems*. https://doi.org/10.1145/2858036.2858080

26. Francis McGlone, Ake B Vallbo, Hakan Håkan Olausson, Line S Löken, Johan Wessberg, Line Loken, and Johan Wessberg. 2007. Discriminative touch and emotional touch. *Canadian journal of experimental psychology = Revue canadienne de psychologie experimentale* 61, 3: 173–183. https://doi.org/10.1037/cjep2007019

27. Nintendo. 1984. Duck Hunt.

28. Nintendo. 2016. Super Mario Run.

29. Alexey Pajitnov. 1984. Tetris.

30. Stuart Reeves, Steve Benford, Claire O'Malley, and Mike Fraser. 2005. Designing the spectator experience. In *Proceedings of the SIGCHI conference on Human factors in computing systems - CHI '05*, 741. https://doi.org/10.1145/1054972.1055074

31. Martin S. Remland, Tricia S. Jones, and Heidi Brinkaman. 1995. Interpersonal Distance, Body Orientation, and Touch- Effects of Culture, Gender, and Age. *Journal of Social Psychology* 135, 3: 281–297. https://doi.org/10.1080/00224545.1995.9713958

32. Martin S. Remland, Tricia S. Jones, and Heidi Brinkman. 1991. Proxemic and haptic behavior in three European countries. *Journal of Nonverbal Behavior* 15, 4: 215–232. https://doi.org/10.1007/BF00986923

33. Neal J. Roese, James M. Olson, Marianne N. Borenstein, Angela Martin, and Alison L. Shores. 1992. Same-sex touching behavior: The moderating role of homophobic attitudes. *Journal of Nonverbal Behavior* 16, 4: 249–259. https://doi.org/10.1007/BF01462005

34. Houman A. Sadri and Madelyn Flammia. 2011. *Intercultural Communication: A New Approach to International Relations and Global Challenges*. Continuum.

35. Thecla Schiphorst, Frank Nack, Michiel Kauwatjoe, Simon De Bakker, Lora Aroyo, Angel Perez Rosillio, Hielke Schut, Norm Jaffe, and Stock. 2007. PillowTalk: can we afford intimacy? *Tei 2007*: 23–30. https://doi.org/10.1145/1226969.1226975

36. Aron Wolfe Siegman and Stanley Feldstein (eds.). 1985. *Multichannel Integrations of Nonverbal Behavior*. Psychology Press.

37. Reneé Stephen and Richard L Zweigenhaft. 1986. The effect on tipping of a waitress touching male and female. *The Journal of Social Psychology* 126, 1: 141–142. https://doi.org/10.1080/00224545.1986.9713586

38. Kenji Suzuki, Taku Hachisu, and Kazuki Iida. 2016. EnhancedTouch: A Smart Bracelet for Enhancing Human- Human Physical Touch. In *Proceedings of the 2016 CHI Conference on Human Factors in Computing Systems - CHI '16*, 1282–1293. https://doi.org/10.1145/2858036.2858439

39. Stephen Thayer. 1982. Social touching. In *Tactual perception: A sourcebook*, William Schiff and Emerson Foulke (eds.). Cambridge University Press, 263–304.

40. Erin H. Thompson and James A. Hampton. 2011. The effect of relationship status on communicating emotions through touch. *Cognition & Emotion* 25, 2: 295–306. https://doi.org/10.1080/02699931.2010.492957

41. Douglas Wilson. 2011. Brutally Unfair Tactics Totally OK Now: On Self-Effacing Games and Unachievements. *Game Studies* 11, 1. Retrieved January 11, 2017 from http://gamestudies.org/1101/articles/wilson

Audience Participation Games: Blurring the Line Between Player and Spectator

Joseph Seering[1], Saiph Savage[3], Michael Eagle[1], Joshua Churchin[4], Rachel Moeller[1], Jeffrey P. Bigham[1], Jessica Hammer[1,2]

[1]Human-Computer Interaction Institute, Carnegie Mellon University
[2]Entertainment Technology Center, Carnegie Mellon University
[3]HCI Lab, West Virginia University
[4]Computer Science Department, University of Rochester
{jseering, hammerj, jbigham}@cs.cmu.edu, {meagle, rpmoelle}@andrew.cmu.edu, saiph.savage@mail.wvu.edu, jchurchi@u.rochester.edu

ABSTRACT
Audience Participation Games challenge traditional assumptions about gameplay by blurring the line between audience and player, allowing audience members to impact gameplay in a meaningful way. Their recent rise in popularity has created new opportunities for game research and development. To better understand this design space, we developed several versions of two prototype games as design probes. We livestreamed them to an online audience in order to develop a framework for audience motivations and participation styles, to explore ways in which mechanics can affect audience members' sense of agency, and to identify promising design spaces. Our results show the breadth of opportunities and challenges that designers face in creating engaging Audience Participation Games.

Author Keywords
Games and play; social media and online communities; entertainment

ACM Classification Keywords
H.5.3. Group and Organization Interfaces: Collaborative computing; K.8.0. General: Games

INTRODUCTION
Audience Participation Games (APGs) restructure the relationship between player, game, and game-watching spectators to allow audience members to have a meaningful impact on gameplay [19, 37, 45]. While APGs as a form of game are not new, they have grown in popularity in recent years due to the rise of livestreaming platforms such as Twitch, Youtube Gaming, and Hitbox, where users stream themselves playing games and can interact with a live audience [17, 22, 34, 47]. This form of games, coupled with the large numbers of viewers on platforms like Twitch, provides opportunities for exploring game characteristics such as transitory participation, massive simultaneous engagement, and improvisational performance, but also presents new challenges for design.

DIS 2017, June 10-14, 2017, Edinburgh, United Kingdom

DOI: **http://dx.doi.org/10.1145/3064663.3064732**

High-level conceptual decisions facing designers of APGs stem from the reshaping of the relationship between audience and player. Game designers have typically focused on the player, such as by offering them "a series of interesting decisions" that affect outcomes of play [1], and theories of player motivation have emphasized the experience of the player who directly manipulates the game [58]. Work studying game spectators, on the other hand, emphasizes the pleasures of observation rather than action [6].

Audience participants are neither fish nor fowl. Like players, they can influence the game's outcome through their participation, yet they have limited agency to take action in the game [22, 47]. Like spectators, they observe gameplay, yet with the potential to shift their role and intervene. Additionally, new technologies such as livestreaming allow audience participants to construct themselves as an audience through *mutual awareness*, rather than as distributed spectators who simply happen to be watching the same game.

In this paper, we seek to understand the experiences and motivations of audience participants in livestreamed APGs. We also explore participants' sense of *agency*, or how able they feel to meet their needs and achieve their experience goals. To accomplish this, we created custom-designed APGs, which we livestreamed on Twitch to use as probes with audience participants. While APGs can exist in many forms, an exploration of this relatively new form of APG can help us understand the design space more broadly and can inform design of both online and offline APGs.

Through our study we uncover five categories of motivations that describe the goals of audience participants in the livestreamed APGs we created. We also develop a framework to help clarify the relationship between mechanics and both individual and social engagement in livestreamed APGs. Finally, we discuss a series of potential design spaces within the full breadth of APGs, including Performable Gameplay, Asymmetric Information, and Audience Impact. We conclude by discussing challenges and future opportunities.

RELATED WORK

We begin by presenting a brief definition and history of APGs, providing examples of APGs from both before and after the rise of livestreaming, and highlighting their common elements. Next, we explore the literature on motivation in games, both as a player and as a spectator. Finally, we present agency as a concept that helps frame our lens for understanding the audience's ability to participate.

Defining APGs

We define Audience Participation Games as games that empower audience members to engage with and impact gameplay. In this section we elaborate on what "audience" and "participation" mean in this context, and comment on how this affects traditional definitions of what counts as a game. We note that due to our choice of Twitch livestreaming to explore APGs, we explore only a subset of the APG design space in this paper. For example, APG participation may be either synchronous or asynchronous, but in this paper we focus specifically on synchronous games and use examples of APGs built around livestreaming platforms to explore future possibilities for design.

Audience

Existing work on pervasive games [31, 55] and game spectatorship [6] frames players as being "on stage" and the audience as observers. But when audience members can also participate in gameplay, what does it mean to be in the audience? To answer this question, we turn to the concept of the "magic circle," Huizinga's framing of play as an activity that takes place outside ordinary life [21, 42]. Recent research shows that the magic circle can have a porous boundary [5, 7, 8]. Audience participants exist in this liminal space, with the ability to shift closer to and further from what is typically understood as "play." We therefore distinguish between the "audience" and the "player" primarily through *centrality* to play. A player in an APG serves as a coordinator, leader, or primary agent in gameplay, with a consistent and direct role. A player also typically establishes the time and conditions for play. The audience in aggregate can impact the gameplay, but no single member of the audience is required for the game to progress.

Additionally, we differentiate the notion of "audience" from that of "spectator." Spectatorship can be accidental, such as encountering a performance in public space [40]. Audiences, on the other hand, are typically understood to be intentional [44]. For example, the game *Cruel 2 B Kind* involves engagement with passersby who are not playing the game (or may not even be aware that it is being played), who in this definition would not be counted as members of an "audience" [29]. Spectatorship also does not imply mutual awareness between spectators; for example, viewers of the popular television show "American Idol" have the ability to impact the results of the show by voting, but have no coherent social structure or awareness of each other as a group [15]. In our definition of audience participation games, we consider audiences to be mutually aware and able to interact, which allows the construction of a group identity and goals [12].

Participation

We define "participation" in a game as the ability to produce an effect that plays out *within the magic circle of the game*, using game rules or mechanics. In the case of APGs, audience members might directly manipulate the game world, as in *Legend of Dungeon: Masters* [26]; they might change the powers or abilities available to the primary player, as in *Choice Chamber* [47]; or they might act as judges of whether the player wins or loses, such as in *Quiplash* [22]. While this definition may seem expansive, it excludes several types of audience behaviors that might at first seem like participation. For example, one channel on Twitch features audiences who place bets on the outcomes of an arcade-style fighting game while they react to the gameplay and discuss the results [43]. However, their actions have no impact on the course of the game. If the audience had no people in it, the game would proceed in exactly the same way. We also do not include audiences for traditional sports games; while the crowd at a baseball game might impact the game by energizing the home team with their cheers, this mechanism is not in any way formalized or incorporated into the rules of the game.

Games

Existing definitions of games can be extended to include audience participants. For example, Juul develops six themes common to definitions of games, such as "Player effort" and "Negotiable consequences" [25]. While audience participants may have different motivations for participation and different levels of agency from a more traditional player, audience participants can be understood as a particular case within these themes. While players and audience participants may have different modes of interaction, use different sets of game rules, or value outcomes differently, differentiation between player types is already a common pattern in game design. Examples include traitor-based board games like *Shadows over Camelot* and *Battlestar Galactica* where one player's secret goal is to make all other players lose [16, 33]. What makes these games distinct from other games is that Audience Participation Games must be watchable by an audience that is formed by gameplay and in turn forms gameplay, which emerges from the concepts of "audience" and "participation" as described above.

A Brief History of APGs

Pre-livestreaming APGs typically incorporated live gameplay with an in-person audience that was given clearly defined roles. Pausch, Seitz, and Maynes-Aminzade developed a set of games based on motion tracking where an audience in a movie-theater-style seating arrangement controlled content on a large screen, including a version of the classic game *Pole Position* where the car turned based on which way the audience leaned in their seats, and another game based on fans playing with beach balls at a concert [28]. The popular television show "Who Wants to be a Millionaire?" focused on a player advancing through a series of increasingly difficult trivia questions to win a cash prize. If the player needed help, they could choose to poll the studio audience for their opinions once per game. The audience would then vote by using a keypad device attached to their seat [10].

The increasing availability of social computing technologies facilitated a blending of online and offline environments in audience participation. "Uncle Roy All Around You" [3], an interactive experience mixing offline participation across London with online participation, explored the possibilities of creating engaging experiences. The authors found that it was challenging to involve online participants in the narrative in a meaningful way.

As livestreaming grew in popularity, existing games began to be adapted to the streamer/audience format. For example, Jackbox Games (formerly Jellyvision Games Inc.) originally created small-group party games such as the game-show-style trivia game *You Don't Know Jack*, in which one to four in-house players compete to answer humorous questions [23]. In 2014, Jackbox Games began to release games like *Quiplash* with Twitch integration [22]. In *Quiplash*, up to eight players answer a series of humorous questions, while any number of audience participants can join by voting on which answer is the best for each question. The audience participants watch the game on a Twitch stream and vote in a separate browser window. In this setup, only the streamer is required to own a copy of the game. Hamilton, Garretson, and Kerne note that streamers have also developed a variety of methods for allowing viewers to impact the stream, from informal conversations to formal polls [19].

Today, many APGs use structured forms of participation to incorporate massive audiences into gameplay, including voting games like *Quiplash*; games like *Choice Chamber* and *Legend of Dungeon: Masters* where audience participants influence mechanics and challenges; and games like *Twitch Plays Pokémon* and its offshoots where audience participants directly control play [22, 26, 27, 47]. Major streaming services are beginning to support and even develop APGs, from *Superfight* to *Breakaway*, to capture a segment of this rapidly growing market [36, 37, 45]. We are entering an era of widespread experimentation with the form of APGs and thus rich opportunities for research and design.

Related Literature

We draw on three areas of existing literature to inform our exploration of Audience Participation Games. First, we examine literature on motivations for play as a starting point for understanding potential motivations of audience participants. We next look at literature on game spectatorship, with the idea that motivations for audience participants might lie between motivations for direct play and motivations for spectatorship. Finally, we build on literature on agency in gameplay and theater to inform our investigations of audience participants' feelings of engagement with this form of games and potential methods for addressing challenges related both to the structure of Twitch and to general aggregation of different goals.

Motivations for Play

Prior work has classified a number of motivations for participation in games. Yee identified six motivations that drive interest in different types of gameplay: Immersion, Creativity, Action, Social, Mastery, and Achievement [56, 57, 58]. Metrics of engagement offer a slightly different perspective on player motivations by identifying factors associated with continued participation in a game. Engagement can result from persistent usage of particular features in a game [20], and in particular features that require some level of mastery of mechanics, but also from receipt of in-game rewards. Many games also make use of persistent avatars with which players identify to maintain engagement and motivate play [4]. The broader context for play is important both in shaping game features and in motivating particular categories of potential players [41]; for example, in Kinect games where players use their full bodies as game controllers, designers must consider players' motivations with regard to exercise and physical activity [30].

In this paper we argue that motivations and contexts for participation in APGs differ from those in traditional games. In APGs, audience participants are separated from game mechanics in a way such that they often impact the game as a member of a crowd rather than as an individual.

Game Spectatorship

Game audiences are communities of diverse participants, each member of which may be invested in watching the game for a different reason. Members can be classified within spectator personas such as bystander, pupil, assistant, commentator, and griefer, [6] which describe their relationship to other audience members and the players. Community-played games like Alternate Reality Games (ARGs) and esports communities often have a type of bystander called a "lurker" [18] who prefers to observe but still feels attached to the culture.

Spectators' social engagement with a game includes a connection to the streamer/player of the game, a connection to the other audience members, and social status within the audience community [12]. Inside jokes and sublanguages are common in these communities [35], as are metanarratives about the game constructed discursively by the player and audience [38, 39]. Spectator communities can congregate on their own forums outside of the esports arena or livestreaming sites, such as the *Twitch Plays Pokémon* subreddit, and build on this metanarrative [27]. In the case of livestreamed games, socially engaged communities can in turn boost the popularity of a streamer or a play style [49, 51] and foster mechanical engagement with the game being played.

In short, game spectatorship is a diverse and socially engaged experience. Because audience participants have the option of becoming spectators at any time, we seek to understand what audience participation offers over and above spectatorship.

Agency

In APGs, audience participants have limited control over the game. Both the structural features of Twitch and methods for aggregating input from large numbers of viewers, which are discussed in the section on livestreamed APG mechanics, challenge existing approaches to fostering a sense of agency within games. Literature on agency in gameplay and in other types of performance present possibilities for addressing these challenges.

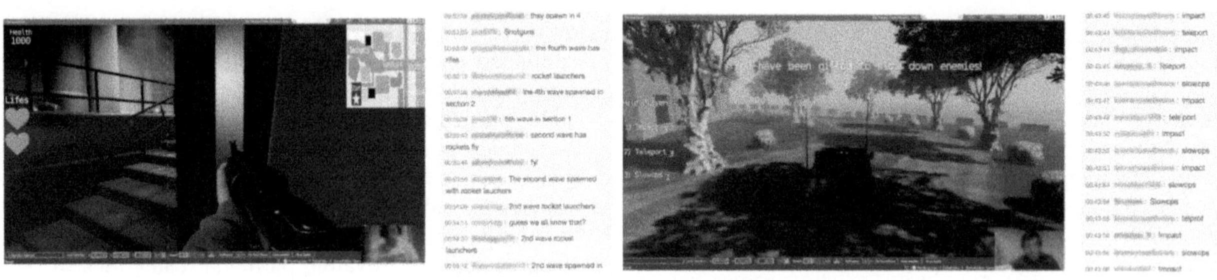

a) First Person Shooter Game with Adversary Version **b) Racing Game with Gifting Version**

Figure 1. Examples of the two games we made, showcasing different design versions. a) In the FPS APG we designed, audience participants gave gifts to or hindered the streamer while he tried to stay alive against waves of enemies. b) In the racing APG, audience participants helped the streamer win a race or made driving harder for him.

In games, concepts of agency have been described broadly in terms of the relationship between players, mechanics, and narrative [13, 48]. Evans describes agency as a contrast between users' control over a medium and a medium's control over users [13]. This aligns with one framing of agency within HCI: as the degree to which an interface allows users to complete desired actions, and the sense of ownership they feel about the consequences of those actions [9, 32]. Interface decisions such as the mode of input can have a substantial impact on agency, as can receiving help from an external source [9].

In single-player games such as *Achievement Unlocked* and *Progress Quest*, players are given intentionally limited or even meaningless options for engaging with a narrative [14, 24]. These games are nonetheless played and enjoyed, suggesting that the ability to take in-game actions is not the only relevant metric for agency; to date, *Achievement Unlocked* has been played more than 4.6 million times [24].This literature informs our examination of *individual agency*, which focuses on players' relationship with controls.

Other scholars emphasize interpretation and experience, both individual and social, as core to agency. Tanenbaum and Tanenbaum discuss agency as choice-making, but suggest that commitment to meaning and responsibility in a particular narrative may be a more meaningful metric [48]. In literature and in theater, observing and interpreting can be understood as actions [2]. While authors and actors create a fictional reality, audiences have the power to question, monitor, watch, spy, or bring to light through communication and interconnection [53]. This type of agency builds on social connections between audience members and performers, informing our concept of *social agency* [54].

PREPARING GAME DESIGN PROBES

To explore the nature of APGs and how audience participants engage with them, we developed games that allowed audiences to participate in gameplay. Our designs were informed by concepts from the literature, such as allowing for both individual and social agency in gameplay. We then probed the designs in live playtest sessions on Twitch to study how audiences engaged with particular design elements.

Prototype Design

For our design probes, we developed eight prototypes: two different games with four variants each. The two games we developed were:

1. A **first-person-shooter (FPS) game**, where the streamer was tasked with killing as many computer-controlled opponents as possible before being killed three times himself (see Figure 1.a).

2. A **racing game**, where the player raced a vehicle around a course against three other computer-controlled opponents (see Figure 1.b).

A single round of each game took between three and five minutes on average to complete. We selected these two genres of games because they offered clear ways for the audience participants to engage with the player. The goals of the streamer were obvious, and there were well-established mechanics with which the audience could interact.

Once we had clear ways that audiences could affect gameplay, we created four variants of each game that allowed us to explore social relationships between game participants (including the streamer), and gave audience participants different types of control. See Figure 2 for game versions. The *voting* and *message count* mechanics referenced in 2 were methods for aggregating chat influence, and are described in our section on livestreamed APGs mechanics.

1. In the **"Gifting"** version, audience participants could give the streamer various gifts by typing the associated phrases into the channel's chat.

2. The **"Adversary"** version allowed audience participants to vote to hinder the streamer by imposing various penalties.

3. The **"Combined"** version allowed audience participants to choose from all the options listed above, either giving the player gifts or imposing challenges or penalties. The audience could switch freely between gifting and penalizing.

4. The **"Oracle"** version involved a completely different mode of participation. Audience members were sent information that the streamer did not know about game conditions via Twitch direct message. They then chose whether

	Gifting	*Adversary*	*Combined*	*Oracle*
FPS Game (voting)	Ammo, health, speed boost	Slow motion, more enemies, forced knock-down	Choose from gifts and adversary options	Information about enemy locations and weapons
Racing Game (message count)	Teleport ahead, slow enemies, force enemies to crash	Shake screen, mix-up controls, slam brakes		Information about location of extra points

Figure 2. Matrix of game types vs conditions. In total, eight game versions were developed for audience participants to interact with - four modalities of interaction for each of two game types.

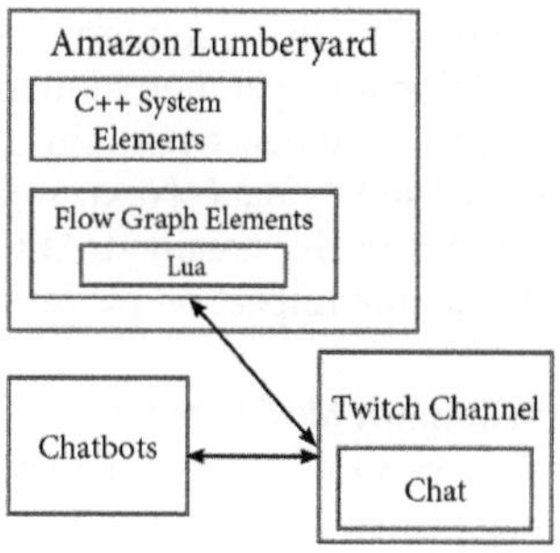

Figure 3. The games developed in Lumberyard were linked with the Twitch channel, while the chatbots collected data separately from chat.

to truthfully convey that information in the chat, to lie or "troll" the player, or not to engage at all.

"Gifting" only allowed the audience to help the player, "Adversary" only allowed the audience to hurt the player, and the "Combined" version gave audiences the power to control their relationship to the streamer by choosing whether to help or hurt. These three modalities of interaction already exist in livestreamed APGs on Twitch [47, 26]. The "Oracle" version was developed as a contrast to the above types of games; voting and spamming phrases in chat are very common existing mechanics in Twitch APGs [22, 27], but our "Oracle" prototype allowed for an exploration of what happens when the audience can interact with the player in an open-ended way.

Prototype Development

The game prototypes tested in this study were developed in Amazon's Lumberyard development environment, which allows for direct integration with Twitch. Lumberyard incorporates two programming languages, C++ and Lua, which work with a core feature called flow graphing. The primary Lumberyard engine uses C++, objects inside the engine are coded in Lua, and the flow graph system integrates directly with existing Twitch functionalities. This allows the connection of basic effects to keywords, as well as the incorporation of voting, scoring, and some Twitch API features. All connections to Twitch events developed for these games were incorporated within the flow graphs, with the exception of whispers which were sent via chatbot.

In addition to game development, data collection methods used two existing Twitch chatbots, one widely available and one developed for a previous study [59]. See Figure 3 for a visualization of the relationship between Lumberyard, Twitch, and the chatbots. Similar chatbots are already in use in existing APGs. *Choice Chamber* relies on a chatbot to broadcast polls to audience participants, mitigating issues associated with video feed delay [47].

Conducting Playtest Sessions

To study how the audience would engage with different game versions, we recruited audience participants to probe our game designs via emails to student lists, posts in public Facebook groups, and individual messages to interested gamers. Participants were assigned to one of four hour-long group sessions, which were scheduled at different times of the day and week. Prior to the study, participants were asked to fill out a pre-survey about their demographics, Twitch history, and gameplay preferences. These participants then logged on to Twitch at the scheduled time and joined the channel designated for use in the study. A total of 35 audience members participated.

We used the same streamer in all four playtesting sessions. We chose the primary developer of the game prototypes because of his familiarity with their mechanics. We also wanted all audiences to be exposed to only one type of streamer. Messages sent to the chat were captured by chatbots, and video of the stream was also recorded to capture gameplay events.

At the start of the study, the streamer began the first game and informed participants of how they could participate. The order of the two games was randomized for each session. One round of the first game was played, lasting approximately three to five minutes. When this round finished, participants were asked to fill out a short survey about their experiences with the game, which included questions about whether they collaborated with other audience participants or the streamer and how much control they felt over the outcome of the game. When all surveys were completed the streamer began the second game, again explaining the mechanics and then playing another single round. When the game finished, participants were asked to fill out a second short survey about their experiences with the game, as well as a longer survey with questions comparing the two games and asking for feedback about their overall experiences.

This format of brief engagement with the games limited our ability to observe development of players over the course of the life cycle of a stream, but did facilitate comparisons across different game types. Our analysis focused on users' initial reactions to a variety of mechanics, and as such was better served by multiple shorter sessions rather than a single longer-term observation. In addition, we elected to test these games as part of separate sessions run by a new streamer rather than through deployment in an established streaming community, but future tests in this area will certainly benefit from collaboration with such a community.

MOTIVATIONS AND MECHANICS

From data gathered during the playtests and experiences with prototype development, we developed a set of comparisons between traditional games and livestream-based synchronous

APGs. In this section we first compare audience participant motivations to traditional player motivations and define a new classification system for audience participant motivations that we derived from our survey data. Next, we explore mechanical differences between livestreamed APGs and traditional games and their potential impact on player agency.

1. Audience Participant Motivations

There are a variety of motivations for play and engagement within traditional games [4, 20, 30, 41, 56, 57, 58], and a number of motivations for engaging with Twitch streams [19]. While Audience Participation Games can incorporate many of the same themes and concepts that other games use, audience participants themselves exist in a liminal space between spectating and playing. Players are "on stage" or "in the magic circle", while audience participants are variably engaged but less central. Because of this distinction, we argue that the motivations of audience participants do not fit classification schemes traditionally used to group various types of players and require special investigation.

Method

In order to better understand the types of motivations for audience participants, we analyzed survey data gathered from post-surveys administered during playtesting sessions. One researcher began by coding categories of motivation from a set of randomly selected survey responses. Another researcher then analyzed and refined the list. Finally, the two researchers looked at a set of randomly selected responses and produced a final list of five mutually exclusive categories of motivations. Each audience member was coded into one of these categories based on their responses. We considered the hypothesis that these archetypes simply result from the limitations of the different affordances presented to players, but found that all of the types were represented in all conditions; players brought varying motivations to each of the game types.

Helpers

Regardless of whether the streamer's goal was to collect points, to survive another wave of enemies, or simply to win overall, "Helpers" devised techniques to help the streamer achieve the goal. As one participant stated, *"I wanted to help the player win [...] there were too many enemies in the match!"*

In this study, the majority of the "helpers" felt that they got what they wanted out of the game. However, most of these individuals did not feel connected to other audience members. They primarily interacted with the streamer, and felt that they had less power than the streamer over gameplay.

Power Seekers

"Power seekers" participated with the sole focus of having impact on the game, whether the impact they had was helpful or harmful to the streamer. As one "Power Seeker" explained, *"My goal was to have my input change the course of the game."*

In contrast to the "Helpers," the majority of these audience participants felt more powerful than the streamer, though in the end they still felt their influence was somewhat limited. Most of these participants focused on helping the streamer, not because they had an interest in seeing the streamer succeed, but rather because they felt they could have more impact through helping. These individuals also did not feel that they connected with others. They sought individual recognition, and felt that collaborating with others could diminish their individual impact on the game.

Collaborators

This user type had the highest proportion of individuals who stated that they collaborated with other audience participants and with the streamer. "Collaborators" also agreed most strongly that features of the game enabled them to do what they wanted; it is possible, however, that not having a clear goal in mind allowed them to be satisfied regardless of the outcome. Overall, these audience participants did not feel stronger than the streamer, nor did they feel they influenced the outcome of the game - *"...I didn't want to get anything out of the game [...] I saw the majority of the community in chat was helping, so decided to be helpful also."*

Solipsists

These participants focused on obtaining personal benefits from the game, such as learning how to use a new tool or meeting new people for networking opportunities: *"My goal was just to see the next generation of gaming [...] I also just wanted to be entertained"*. These individuals did not care about the player winning or losing, nor did they care about being entertaining to others or having impact on the game. They also felt they could influence the game and had more power than the streamer, but they did not choose to engage with the game to test this feeling and rarely collaborated with other audience participants or with the streamer.

Trolls

These audience participants focused on bullying and playfully harassing the streamer. In contrast to Helpers or Power Seekers, these participants assumed the role of Trolls mainly out of boredom - *"...then I kind of got sick of typing the same three things [to help the streamer]. I found it boring, so then i just wanted the game to end, so I switched to enemy mode..."*. While these participants seemed to get the most entertainment out of seeing the streamer suffer and provoking responses from other participants, they were able to switch back and forth between helping and hindering.

"Trolls" also felt more powerful than the streamer; while most did state that they wanted the streamer to succeed, they focused more on deriving enjoyment from any given situation regardless of whether their methods helped or hurt the streamer. One core characteristic that separated these participants from the others was that they were much more conscious about different roles they could take. This led them to devise more complex ways to collaborate and work with others. The majority of these participants felt more powerful than the streamer and also that they had substantial influence over the outcome.

In these categories, we see that audience participant motivations vary along two axes: the desire to engage with game mechanics, and the desire to engage with other audience members. First, player goals implied different levels of engagement with game mechanics, which some players wanted to use to affect the game's outcome. For example, Power Seekers wanted to use game mechanics to influence the game, regardless of the outcome. Second, there was a range of levels of engagement with the rest of the audience. For example, Collaborators cared a lot about other audience members and their behavior, while Solipsists did not.

We observed that the categories of participants who focused on working with or helping others felt they had the least ability to engage meaningfully with gameplay. People who focused on trolling or on entertaining their own personal goals felt that they had the most ability to attain their own personal goals in the game, but they also had less ability to connect with other audience participants. These differences suggest that audience participants' game satisfaction is not just about their personal motivation, but also about the degree to which there is a *fit* between their goals and the agency they experience. We therefore next consider the different types of agency available to players within APGs.

Though these categories emerged from limited playing time and a small subset of possible mechanical framings, they present a starting point from which game features can be linked to specific types of audience engagement or experiences. They also intersect in some ways with existing frameworks previously discussed. For example, within frameworks for spectatorship, Solipsists can be compared to a more engaged version of the 'bystander' archetype, while Trolls are similar to 'griefers' [6]. Engagement with meta-narratives [38, 39] emerged in the "Oracle" and "Combined" conditions across multiple player types. In individual motivations for play, these meta-narratives relate to both the 'immersion' and 'creativity' motivations [56, 57, 58]. Collaborators and Helpers fit with Yee's 'social' motivation, and Trolls and Power-seekers relate somewhat loosely to 'mastery'. These connections indicate that audience participant motivations relate both to motivations for spectatorship and motivations for play, but do not cleanly align with either. More work will be needed to clarify the nature of these relationships.

2. Livestreamed APG Mechanics

In exploring their role in the liminal space between spectatorship and play, audience participants in this study varied in the extent to which they sought control over game conditions and desired connection with other users. In our analysis, we divide agency into its individual and social components. Trolls and Power-Seekers wanted a high level of individual agency, where they could directly and personally control play. Collaborators, and to a lesser degree Helpers, sought social agency, which would allow them to build connections with other players and cooperate to achieve goals. Finally, Solipsists' goals rarely involved either manipulating gameplay or building relationships.

The distinction between individually-focused agency and socially-focused agency is important for APGs. While individual agency is core to many traditional games, where the player feels in control of game mechanics, this concept encounters significant problems when there are thousands of audience participants vying for control. Designers may consider granting participants social agency as an alternative or supplementary form of engagement, where collaboration leads to collective power and collective rewards. In this section we highlight factors in our playtest sessions that affected individual agency and social agency.

Individual Agency in Livestreamed APGs

In our study, we explored four types of audience-streamer interaction, ranging from "Adversary" to "Oracle". Among these, the two conditions that allowed audience participants to decide between helping and hindering the streamer, the "Combined" and "Oracle" conditions, led to qualitatively richer gameplay dynamics, matching observations in [19] where Twitch audience members desired both a positive connection with the streamer and impact on the progression of the stream. Audience participants in the "Combined" condition voted to help the streamer when he was behind in the racing game, but voted to hinder him when he got ahead. In the Oracle condition, users moved from conveying the information they had received to creating playful lies to tell the streamer. The narratives built from such interactions could, over time, help audience participants feel that they have agency in affecting the progression of the game [48].

Twitch incorporates a delay into streams in order to accommodate users with different internet connection speeds, the length of which varies across different users. This means that when the streamer responds to audience participants on stream, the response is seen between six and more than twenty seconds later. Both this delay and its variability across users are a challenge to mechanical responsiveness of games and to communication between audience participants and the streamer. In our study, this delay resulted in a time gap between when audience participants voted for particular options and when they saw their votes counted. For example, if an audience member voted to disrupt the streamer's controls in the racing game, they usually would not see their vote counted on screen until at least ten seconds later. This made it difficult to know whether their vote was important. The delay was even more impactful during the first-person shooter game, where votes were only totaled every thirty seconds. Due to variable delay, it was almost impossible for viewers to know whether their vote would count in the current thirty second cycle or the next one, directly reducing feelings of individual agency via control [9, 46]. Over time users might have adapted to this, as in the case of Twitch Plays Pokémon, but this did not occur in our playtests.

The presence of delay affects individual agency through separation of audience participants from the results of their actions, making it difficult for them to increase engagement and position themselves closer to the stage of play. Existing games have come up with novel methods for dealing with this, from Choice Chamber's use of chatbots to Quiplash's use of external browser pages [22, 47], but it remains a challenge that designers must contend with.

Social Agency in Livestreamed APGs

The development of feelings of social agency requires users to understand their role in the social network described by Copier [7, 8] and to strengthen bonds with other users. We encountered several core challenges to development of social agency both on Twitch and in our game designs.

We tested two different chat participation mechanics in each of the four interaction type conditions. We found that the different participation mechanics affected audience participants' ability and motivation to build social bonds. In the *message count* mechanism used in the racing game, a given effect occurred if the corresponding phrase was typed in chat a number of times equal to half of the number of active audience participants. This could include messages sent from one user or from multiple users working together. The *voting* mechanism used in the FPS game counted total votes every thirty seconds and imposed the single effect that had the most votes. In this condition, audience participants could have gained an advantage by trying to build blocs of users who voted in the same way. In theory, this meant that the mechanic encouraged strengthening of social bonds, but in practice this result was not achieved; they found it more advantageous to simply spam their vote instead. The *message count* condition also encouraged individual spam but did not in any way privilege the emergence of voting blocs- a single user with enough persistence could cause any effect to be achieved.

While the participatory game mechanics we built into these games allowed collaboration toward achieving certain effects, the games we created were not structured to allow social victories. The only possible outcomes were a victory or a loss for the streamer, for which audience participants might feel responsible. Mechanics that truly build social agency would provide incentives for users to collaborate and would formally scaffold the development of network bonds.

In the current state of Twitch, a scaffold for strengthening bonds must come from game design rather than the platform itself because identity signals are limited and formal mechanisms for social connections are limited. Absent in Twitch chat are identity markers common in games, such as avatars, character level, and guild tag. The linear presentation of participation (chat messages) on Twitch also makes it difficult to identify groups of users who are working together or who have established social connections because their messages are not separated out from the general flow of chat.

In our study, we directly observed this difficulty in forming social bonds. Users rarely conversed directly with each other; prior to and after games, a total of 10 conversational messages were sent between users, while during games no participants ever conversed with each other. Some participants in our study were familiar with the channel due to a pre-existing personal connection with the streamer, but we did not find any evidence that the display of this connection caused other users to treat them with any more deference.

Other possibilities outside the formal mechanics of the Twitch platform exist for developing identity signals. Some existing Twitch chat bots keep records of point totals associated with each audience member, which persist across streaming sessions [59]. These points indicate success in previous minigames or total time spent in the channel, and ranking users by points could help clarify social roles and encourage interaction. Some games also allow streamers to designate specific temporary or permanent social roles; in *Choice Chamber*, the game randomly selects a user from active audience participants to have extra powers [47]. Broadly, social identity tags that might enrich group dynamics and sense of social agency are sparse in Twitch chat, and additional tags can currently only be added through games, bots, and other external services.

The Twitch platform offers various. The most basic form is intra-chat text communication, where audience members send messages to each other in real time. While text-based messages have the advantage of simplicity, and many can be accommodated simultaneously, they can be insufficient to convey complex instructions or plan courses of action. Streamers can also communicate with individual viewers or the audience as a whole via speaking in stream, and while this medium can be significantly richer than text it suffers from asynchronicity due to stream delay. A third option for communication is private messaging, or "whispering" between individual users. In our study we used whispers to convey pieces of secret information about the games to audience participants. These modes of communication, while situationally effective, make it a challenge to work collaboratively toward a goal; feedback from the streamer is substantially delayed, individual messages in the chat can get lost in a sea of text, and whispers can be cumbersome and feel disconnected from gameplay.

While Twitch as a platform currently only offers interactions through chat, outside services have sprung up to fill this gap. For example, Discord is an external voice and text chat service that integrates with Twitch; it offers additional features such as multiple chatrooms and different tags for different user types. Development of new, richer modes of communication, both within games and on the Twitch platform itself, could substantially boost the development of feelings of social agency in gameplay both through ability to collaborate to achieve a goal and through feelings of commitment to the group [9, 48].

DISCUSSION: INFORMING DESIGN OF APGS

In the above sections we have focused primarily on Livestreamed APGs. Here we describe potential design spaces within APGs more generally and provide context for possible approaches based on our experiences in this study. We also touch briefly on additional areas that suggest interesting possibilities for design, but which were not explored in depth in this study.

Audience Impact on Gameplay

Traditional audiences are static, uniform, and often passive, but APGs give designers opportunities to subvert traditional roles by allowing audiences to impact gameplay both individually and as a collective. In this study we explored three modalities of impact: helping, hindering, or choosing between the two. We also looked at two modes of engagement with the game: spamming keywords in the chat, and posting open-ended descriptions of information in the chat. In both cases, players were more engaged when offered more complex interactions, whether by selecting their stance toward the the player, or by posting open-ended information rather than a simple keyword.

One approach to this finding is to make modalities of communication more complex and open-ended. Built-in mechanics such as map pings, and emergent mechanics such as jumping as a way of gaining attention, allow players to cooperate without explicit spoken or written discussion. Without these mechanics, audiences cannot, for example, easily refer to map positions or signify differences among apparently identical objects [52]. While our team was able to develop workarounds, such as making in-game objects different colors, workarounds come with their own sets of limitations.

Our findings also suggest that audience participants found open-ended interaction more satisfying because it gave them a deeper way to engage with play. This suggests that richer channels for interaction may not automatically meet audience participants' needs. To create a satisfying impact on gameplay, audience participants must be able to understand the game situation, how they might influence it, and how their actions affected the outcome. Richer communication channels, if not paired with careful design for accessibility, may increase the complexity of player interactions while decreasing their sense of impact. Designers must carefully balance audience impact on game conditions and outcomes with the technical affordances of different modes for engagement.

Creating Performable Gameplay

The success of Twitch streamers in large part depends on their ability to entertain the audience through narration and emotional expressiveness [19]. While it might seem that simply playing a game on stream is a performance, in our study we found that audience participation can directly impact streamers' ability to create a compelling narrative. The streamer chose to frame his relationship with the audience as an ongoing story, and to treat his interactions with the audience as narratively significant. For example, in the "Adversary" condition the streamer portrayed himself as at the mercy of the audience participants, and jokingly begged for leniency when they caused too many negative effects in a row. Audience members could participate in the narrative by causing negative effects; these effects became "performable moments," or game situations that allowed the streamer to advance the narrative and perform in emotionally expressive ways.

We observed that the streamer had increased flexibility in generating an engaging narrative when audience participants had the choice to help or hinder him. This effect was partly driven by audiences choosing to create dramatic tension in gameplay. For example, in the "Combined" condition's racing game, the streamer constantly narrated his position in the course relative to his opponents. When he talked about the game being easy because he was so far ahead, audience participants imposed penalties on him to make the race closer. When he fell behind as a result of these penalties, audience participants responded to the frustrations he expressed by giving him gifts to help him catch up. In other words, audience participants played a role usually taken by game systems: balancing player performance against that of opponents.

As this example illustrates, it is important to distinguish between how streamers perform through their *gameplay*, and how they perform through *narration*. Designers can enable both types of performance by allowing audiences to influence key game systems, and by ensuring that streamers can easily understand and summarize audience contributions.

Conveying Asymmetric Information

Asymmetric information can give streamers access to a wider repertoire of dramatic techniques, and can make the experiences of audience members more variable and individual [6]. Traditional audience members in a theater or sports game see more or less the same show, but this need not be the case in APGs; seeing only part of the show can add to the experience as other audience members and the streamer try to explain the parts that are missing.

In our study, we explored information asymmetrics as a way of generating interactions between players and streamer that were more complex than simply spamming keywords. In the "Oracle" condition, different audience participants had different pieces of information needed by the streamer. Because no one player had all the information, multiple audience members needed to contribute to the streamer's success; because the information was private, individuals could choose how truthful to be about the hidden information.

First, we discovered that audience participation rates affect this type of information asymmetry. Critical pieces of information can be left out of conversations, not because no one knows them, but because nobody who received them is participating. This problem is amplified in the Twitch context, which has a high rate of drop-in and drop-out, but applies to any scenario where audiences can participate at a range of levels of engagement.

Second, we found that the streamer identified individual participants and developed an evolving narrative about their honesty based on the information they shared. However, audience members did not collaborate with one another, even though they had mutually useful information. One difference between the two groups is that the streamer could test whether a piece of information was true by incorporating it in his gameplay, while audience participants could not. We conclude that engaging collaboration based on information sharing requires some method for discerning whether a piece of information is truthful; these interactions are not engaging if there is no way to differentiate between truth and lies.

Another consideration for testing the accuracy of information is the ability to predict outcomes. Can one determine whether a player is lying with greater than random chance? Existing designs on other platforms use systems for attaching a persistent reputation to a user that develops over time. They may also allow users to attach a social signal to their contribution that serves as evidence for its veracity [11]. The highly fluid nature of Twitch chat makes the former difficult, while the latter depends entirely on the structure of the game.

Future Design Explorations

Several other sources for design decisions that were not explored in this study are worth noting. First, in this study we defined five categories of audience participant motivations. Given that these categories emerged from playtesting, we did not design the games with the intention of accommodating these types of motivations. There is potential for designers to explore what it means to target games toward these different types of motivations, either individually or in combination. For example, games could be designed specifically to manage trolls - or to enable them.

Second, future designs could explore making more nuanced actions available to the audience. In our research prototypes, helpful actions were always helpful and harmful ones were always harmful. However, audience actions might use scarce resources, include both helpful and harmful consequences, or have a variable effect based on what the player is doing at the time. We can explore design spaces for APGs that incorporate richer choices, and we can examine how to make these choices accessible at a range of levels of engagement.

Third, while playtests performed for this study included between five and fifteen audience participants, which is a typical size for Twitch channels, audiences can also number in the thousands. It is important for designers to consider a variety of questions about how gameplay scales across different sized audiences. For example, is it possible to design an APG that is entertaining regardless of audience size? Should APGs be designed for a specific number of participants?

Finally, APGs allow innovation in financial models of game development and distribution. For example, if streamers expect to play a game with thousands of viewers on a consistent basis in a way that might generate revenue through donations, sponsorships, or increased ad viewership, they can justify spending a much larger amount of money on the game than most individual users would normally spend. This opens up possibilities for the development of games targeted toward a very small group of consumers (streamers) which make use of expensive peripherals, are site-specific, or are otherwise not accessible at mass scale. APGs allow for mass access to scarce real-world resources in play.

INFORMING FUTURE RESEARCH

This paper framed the context for APGs, the space of associated mechanics, and the motivations for contributing as an audience participant. A variety of research directions emerge from these frameworks.

First, while the motivation categories described here cover the motivations of participants in our playtests, work remains to be done to refine these categories to cover the motivations of participants across a wider variety of APGs. Research can explore the characteristics of members of these categories in greater depth and analyze the types of people that are likely to fall into each category.

Second, much of this study focused on the ways participants could impact gameplay. In traditional gameplay, much research has been done on the ways players respond to different types of mechanics, and on which types of mechanics contribute to different types of experiences. There is potential for a parallel arc of research for APGs that explores how different mechanics for engagement are differently satisfying for audience participants, and how different types of impact are more or less comprehensible to players. We suggest that mechanics that show clear evidence of an individual's contribution will be more likely to capture that individual's interest.

Third, we can explore the role of commitment to a community in feelings of agency. Our study explored a transient community of audience participants, and even in this situation some players demonstrated an agentic commitment to the group. Engaging players over weeks or months would allow us to investigate the different roles of control, choice, and commitment in agentic experiences during play.

Finally, while this study explored how audience participants impact gameplay, there remain many open questions about how gameplay impacts audience participants. Much literature exists on how games can teach players skills, increase bonds between players, and help to define players' identities [50, 51]. Corresponding research could explore how these effects translate to APGs. Can a skill be taught to ten thousand audience participants simultaneously via an APG? Can such games build solidarity within a community or increase participants' tolerance and empathy toward others?

CONCLUSION

In this paper we have defined APGs as games that have a *mutually-aware* group of audience members who participate in a way that has a *meaningful impact* on the game. They incorporate mechanics and deal with challenges to create feelings of social and individual agency that are not prevalent in other types of games.

We developed two prototype games and four different methods of audience-game interaction and collected data about audience engagement and agency. We identified five categories of audience participants: "Helpers", "Power-seekers", "Collaborators", "Solipsists", and "Trolls". The motivations for audience participants depended on their goals and on their individual and social agency. A distinction between individual and social agency emerged from playtest results and were further explored through an analysis of APG mechanics.

We highlighted several areas for future exploration in design including defining audience impact on gameplay, creating performable gameplay, and conveying asymmetric information. Study of APGs will further our understanding of player motivations, identify mechanisms affecting impact and visibility of mechanics, improve our understanding of agency, and define the ways in which games impact audiences.

ACKNOWLEDGMENTS

We would like to thank Amazon for their support of our work. We would also like to thank Chris Klug and Safinah Ali for their insights into APG research and design.

REFERENCES

1. Leigh Alexander. 2012. GDC 2012: Sid Meier on how to see games as sets of interesting decisions. *Gamasutra* (2012).
2. Roland Barthes. 2001. The death of the author. *Contributions in Philosophy* 83 (2001), 3–8.
3. Steve Benford, Martin Flintham, Adam Drozd, Rob Anastasi, Duncan Rowland, Nick Tandavanitj, Matt Adams, Ju Row-Farr, Amanda Oldroyd, and Jon Sutton. 2004. Uncle Roy All Around You: Implicating the city in a location-based performance. In *Proceedings of Advances in Computer Entertainment.*
4. Max V Birk, Cheralyn Atkins, Jason T Bowey, and Regan L Mandryk. 2016. Fostering Intrinsic Motivation through Avatar Identification in Digital Games. In *Proceedings of the SIGCHI Conference on Human Factors in Computing Systems.* ACM.
5. E Castronova. 2005. *Synthetic worlds: The business and culture of online games.* University of Chicago Press.
6. Gifford Cheung and Jeff Huang. 2011. Starcraft from the Stands: Understanding the Game Spectator. In *Proceedings of the SIGCHI Conference on Human Factors in Computing Systems.* ACM.
7. M. Copier. 2005. Connecting worlds. Fantasy role-playing games, ritual acts and the magic circle. In *Proceedings of DiGRA 2005 Conference: Changing Views Worlds in Play.*
8. M. Copier. 2007. *Beyond the magic circle: A network perspective on role-play in online games.* Utrecht University.
9. David Coyle, James Moore, Per Ola, Kristensson Paul, and C Fletcher Alan. 2012. I did that! Measuring Users' Experience of Agency in their own Actions. In *Proceedings of the SIGCHI Conference on Human Factors in Computing Systems.* ACM, 1903–1906.
10. Michael Davies. 2002. Who Wants to be a Millionaire? [ABC]. (2002).
11. Judith Donath. 1999. Identity and Deception in the Virtual Community. *Communities in Cyberspace* (1999), 27–58.
12. S. Drucker, L. W. He, M. Cohen, C. Wong, and A. Gupta. 2002. Spectator games: A new entertainment modality of networked multiplayer games. *Microsoft Research* (2002).
13. Elizabeth Evans. 2008. Character, Audience Agency and Trans-Media Drama. *Media, Culture and Society* 12 (2008). Issue 1.
14. Eric Fredricksen. 2002. Progress Quest. [In-Browser]. (2002). `http://progressquest.com/`.
15. S. Fuller. 2002. American Idol. Fox. (2002). FreemantleMedia North America.
16. Fantasy Flight Games. 2008. Battlestar Galactica: The Board Game. [Tabletop]. (2008). `https://www.fantasyflightgames.com/en/products/battlestar-galactica/`.
17. John Gaudiosi. 2016. Twitch Ups Its Game to Compete with YouTube Gaming. In *Fast Company.* "http://fortune.com/2016/02/26/twitchupsitsgameto-competewithyoutubegaming/".
18. Chris Georgen, Sean Duncan, and Lucas Cook. 2015. From Lurking to Participatory Spectatorship: Understanding Affordances of the Dota 2 Noob Stream. In *11th International Conference on Computer Supported Collaborative Learning.* ISLS.
19. William Hamilton, Oliver Garretson, and Andruid Kerne. 2014. Streaming on Twitch: Fostering Participatory Communities of Play within Live Mixed Media. In *Proceedings of the SIGCHI Conference on Human Factors in Computing Systems.* ACM.
20. Erik Harpstead, Thomas Zimmermann, Jose J Guajardo, Ryan Cooper, Tyson Solberg, and Dan Greenawalt. 2015. What Drives People: Creating Engagement Profiles of Players from Game Log Data. In *CHI PLAY.* ACM.
21. J. Huizinga. 1955. *Homo Ludens: A Study of the Play-Element in Culture.* Beacon Press.
22. Jackbox Games. 2015. Quiplash. [PC/Mac Computer, Xbox One, PS3, PS4, and Twitch]. (2015). `http://jackboxgames.com/project/quiplash/`.
23. Jellyvision Games Inc. 2011. You Don't know Jack. [PC Computer, Console, and Mobile]. (2011). `http://jackboxgames.com/games/`.
24. John. 2008. Achievement Unlocked. [In-Browser]. (2008). `http://armorgames.com/play/2893/achievement-unlocked`.
25. J. Juul. 2010. The game, the player, the world: Looking for a heart of gameness. *PLURAIS - Revista Multidisciplinar* 1 (2010). Issue 2.
26. Robot Loves Kitty. 2015. Legend of Dungeon: Masters. [PC Computer]. (2015).
27. Alex Leavitt. 2014. TwitchPlayedPokemon: An Analysis of the Experimental Interactive Phenomenon. Presentation. (2014). `http://www.gdcvault.com/play/1021438/TwitchPlayedPokemon-An-Analysis-of-the`.
28. Dan Maynes-Aminzade, Randy Pausch, and Steve Seitz. 2002. Techniques for interactive audience participation. In *Proceedings of the 4th IEEE International Conference on Multimodal Interfaces.*
29. J. McGonigal and I. Bogost. 2006. Cruel 2 B Kind. (2006). `http://www.cruelgame.com/`.
30. Ryo Mizobata, Chaklam Silpasuwanchai, and Xiangshi Ren. 2014. Only for Casual Players? Investigating Player Differences in Full-body Game Interaction. In *Chinese CHI.* ACM.

31. M. Montola. 2005. Exploring the edge of the magic circle: Defining pervasive games. In *Proceedings of Digital Arts and Culture*.

32. James Moore. 2016. What Is the Sense of Agency and Why Does it Matter? *Frontiers in Psychology* 7 (2016), 772–775. Issue 1272.

33. Days of Wonder Board Games. 2005. Shadows over Camelot. [Tabletop]. (2005). https://www.daysofwonder.com/shadowsovercamelot/en/.

34. Kevin Ohannessian. 2016. How Twitch Hooked 45 Million Viewers To Watch 13 Billion Minutes Of Gaming A Month. In *Fast Company*. "https://www.fastcompany.com/3027452/howtwitch-hooked45millionviewerstowatch13billionminutesof-gamingamonth".

35. Jedrzej Olejniczak. 2015. A Linguistic Study of Language Variety used on Twitch.tv: Descriptive and Corpus-based Approaches. In *Redefining Community in Intercultural Context*. 329–344.

36. Pipeworks. 2015. Superfight. [PC/Twitch, originally cards]. (2015). https://www.superfightgame.com/.

37. Luke Plunkett. 2016. Twitch Is Helping Build Games An Audience Can Play Too. In *kotaku*. http://www.kotaku.com.au/2016/03/twitchishelping-buildgamesanaudiencecanplaytoo/.

38. Daan Prujit. 2014. The game about the game: Metagaming in Twitchplayspokémon. Thesis. (2014). http://dare.uva.nl/cgi/arno/show.cgi?fid=550381.

39. Dennis Ramirez, Jenny Saucerman, and Jeremy Dietmeier. 2014. Twitch Plays Pokemon: A Case Study in Big G Games. In *DiGRA*. Digital Games Research Association.

40. S. Reeves, S. Benford, C. O'Malley, and M. Fraser. 2005. Designing the spectator experience. In *Proceedings of the SIGCHI Conference on Human Factors in Computing Systems*. ACM.

41. Chad Richards, Craig W Thompson, and T C Nicholas Graham. 2014. Beyond Designing for Motivation: The Importance of Context in Gamification. In *CHI PLAY*. ACM.

42. K. Salen and E. Zimmerman. 2004. *Rules of play: Game design fundamentals*. MIT Press.

43. Salty Bet. 2017. Salty Bet. [Twitch and PC Computer]. (2017). https://www.twitch.tv/saltybet.

44. Saiph Savage and Andrés Monroy-Hernández. 2015. Participatory Militias: An Analysis of an Armed Movement's Online Audience. In *Proceedings of the 18th ACM Conference on Computer Supported Cooperative Work & Social Computing*. ACM, 724–733.

45. Dennis Scimeca. 2016. Streamline could revolutionize the way we play games on Twitch. In *The Daily Dot*. "http://www.kotaku.com.au/2016/03/twitchishelping-buildgamesanaudiencecanplaytoo/".

46. Ben Shneiderman and Catherine Plaisant. 2004. *Designing the User Interface: Strategies for Effective Human-Computer Interaction*. Pearson Education.

47. Studio Bean. 2014. Choice Chamber. [PC Computer and Twitch]. (2014). http://www.choicechamber.com/.

48. Karen Tanenbaum and Joshua Tanenbaum. 2009. Commitment to Meaning: A Reframing of Agency in Games. In *Proceedings of the Digital Arts and Culture Conference*.

49. Ivan O. Jr. Taylor. 2015. Video Games, Fair Use and the Internet: the Plight of the Lets Play. *Journal of Law, Technology & Policy* (2015), 247–271.

50. T.L. Taylor. 2009. *Play between worlds: Exploring online game culture*. MIT Press.

51. T.L. Taylor. 2012. *Raising the Stakes: E-sports and the Professionalization of Computer Gaming*. MIT Press.

52. Zachary O. Toups, Jessica Hammer, William A. Hamilton, Ahmad Jarrah, William Graves, and Oliver Garretson. 2014. A Framework for Cooperative Communication Game Mechanics from Grounded Theory. In *CHI PLAY*. ACM, 257–266.

53. John Trimbur. 2000. Agency and the death of the author: A partial defense of modernism. *JAC* (2000), 283–298.

54. John Tulloch and others. 2002. *Television drama: agency, audience and myth*. Routledge.

55. A. Waern, M. Montola, and J. Stenros. 2009. The three-sixty illusion: designing for immersion in pervasive games. In *Proceedings of the SIGCHI Conference on Human Factors in Computing Systems*. ACM.

56. Nick Yee. 2006. Motivations for Play in Online Games. *CyberPsychology & Behavior* 9 (2006), 772–775. Issue 6.

57. Nick Yee. 2015. Gamer motivation model overview. Presentation. (2015). http://quanticfoundry.com/2015/12/21/map-of-gaming-motivations/.

58. Nick Yee, Nicolas Ducheneaut, and Les Nelson. 2012. Online Gaming Motivations Scale: Development and Validation. In *Proceedings of the SIGCHI Conference on Human Factors in Computing Systems*. ACM.

59. Zakery M. (Zelatko) and Alex (Phantomindex). 2016. PhantomBot. [PC/Mac/Linux Computer, Twitch]. (2016). https://phantombot.tv/.

AutoJam: Exploring Interactive Music Experiences in Stop-and-Go Traffic

Sven Krome, Joshua Batty, Stefan Greuter & Jussi Holopainen
RMIT University
Melbourne, VIC, Australia
{sven.krome, joshua.batty, stefan.greuter, jussi.holopainen}@rmit.edu.au

ABSTRACT
AutoJam is an interactive music listening experience played on an inactive steering wheel of an autonomous car. By designing *AutoJam*, our aim was to make in-car music interactive and align music creation with the progression of the traffic situation. Besides being a fun and creative activity for frustrating stop-and-go traffic, *AutoJam* helps to understand the building blocks of in-car performances. In order to explore the impact of *AutoJam*, we conducted an in-situ user study with 14 participants. From the findings, we constructed a map of experiential dimensions of *AutoJam* and found that player's experience, constitute itself through a continuous shifting between those dimensions. Reflecting on this process, we discuss four building blocks of in-car performances. Ultimately, this work aims to frame autonomous driving in difficult traffic as a creative and playful activity promoting situational awareness and musical expression.

Author Keywords
Autonomous Driving; Music; Games; Design; Improvisation

ACM Classification Keywords
H.5.m. Information interfaces and presentation (e.g., HCI): Miscellaneous.

INTRODUCTION
Music and sound has always played a central role as in-car entertainment. On-board sound systems can be perfectly tailored for the car's fixed seating arrangement and the spatial dimension to deliver a powerful and high-quality music listening experience. Moreover, the rhythms and movements of music and the movements and dynamics of driving a car can transform the driving situation into a unique emotional and self-expressive experience. In-car music not only emotionally enriches the driving experience, it also transforms the journey into a soundscape that matches the driver's mood and emotional constitution. As Bull noted, music transforms the car into a *sonic envelope* and the journey into an emotional *bridge*:

> *Drivers often describe the discomfort of spending time in their cars with only the sound of the engine to accompany them. Driving without the mediation of music [...] qualitatively changes the experience of driving* [3].

As long as driving a car required full operational control, listening to music was one of the few safe and accepted driver entertainment alternatives. With advancements in automated driving, new interactive forms of entertainment can be possible. However, as long as the autonomous driving system relies on a human driver as a supervisory control, the inactive driver should maintain situational awareness of the driving situation. As research shows, the reduction of active driving control to an inactive monitoring requirement, can also be experienced as a lack of autonomy and reduced competency [5].

To explore how interactive in-car music can create a pleasurable autonomous driving situation, we designed and tested *AutoJam*, an interactive in-car music game played on a touch-sensitive steering wheel. It combines rhythm gaming, creative improvisation and music listening and aligns those within the driving context of stop-and-go traffic. The design goal of *AutoJam* was the exploration of an interactive music experience that helps to reframe frustrating stop-and-go traffic into a context for fun and creative play. Furthermore, *AutoJam* should motivate the driver to keep situational awareness of the driving situation while the car is moving.

In this paper, we present the concept and design of *AutoJam* as well as an evaluation of the proof-of-concept prototype based on an in-situ user study with 14 participants. We categorize selected aspects of the user experiences into a descriptive experience map and propose four building-blocks of in-car performances. The *AutoJam* concept, as well as the identified building-blocks, contribute to the ongoing challenge to explore and design meaningful non-driving activities for autonomous driving contexts.

DIS 2017, June 10-14, 2017, Edinburgh, United Kingdom

ACM ISBN 978-1-4503-4922-2/17/06…$15.00
http://dx.doi.org/10.1145/3064663.3064758

RELATED WORK

Car-based music experience has been studied intensively as social phenomenon, as a safety and ergonomics issue as well as an entertainment opportunity.

Cunningham et al. have investigated the context of in-car music listening of a social group travelling together. Focusing on social music selection processes they suggest a collaborative playback system that dynamically selects musical content based on song characteristics and journey contexts [4]. Coming from a symbolic interaction perspective, Walsh demonstrates that in-car music and other sonic material is used to transform the car into an *habitable symbolic space* [18].

From an ergonomics/human factors perspective, researchers explored the effect of music and sound on driver vigilance. For example, Hasegawa & Oguri [9] investigated the impact of music characteristics on the driver's drowsiness. They conclude that music preference and tempo are effective factors for stimulating the driver's vigilance.

In the context of autonomous driving, sound has been explored as an information display facilitating a feeling of control, trust and location awareness. For example, Beattie et al. [1] investigated the effect of spatial auditory feedback on trust and situational awareness of autonomous and manual driving scenarios, concluding that auditory displays are a suitable method for enhancing trust and control of autonomous driving situations.

Despite the importance of music in the design space of the car and its impact on the driver's emotions, awareness and vigilance, there are surprisingly few explorative design studies that investigate the interactive potential of in-car music experiences. For example, Östergren [13] suggested and designed *SoundPryer*, a social music listening experience for brief traffic encounters. *SoundPryer* is a music sharing application that allows its users to tune into the music of cars in their proximity. The design rationale was that even short clips of other road user's music would add another social dimension to traffic encounters and therefore, makes it more fun and personal. Another example of collaborative music experiences among car passengers has been investigated by Eckholdt and Schulz [6]. In order to establish a social experience of relatedness among the car passengers, they implemented a drum kit into a car's interior. By exploration of the hidden instrument and coordination of their play, the passengers were invited to engage in a collaborative activity.

As seen, social engagement is the key focus of research looking at designing interactive music experiences. However, as Walsh [18] points out, music in cars is often a solitary experience that transforms the driving into an emotional private space. Our research on *AutoJam* explores the potential of connecting interactive and creative music gaming, as a constitutional factor of autonomous driving, as a mostly solitary experience.

THE *AUTOJAM* PROTOTYPE

We defined the autonomous driving technology as a future *traffic jam assistant* system [17] that is able to take over the complete driving operation below 60 km/h. In contrast to current driving automation systems, such as Tesla's *AutoPilot* [16], it will allow the driver to engage in various forms of non-driving activities. In this explorative research, we explicitly exclude safety related issues connected to those technologies.

We conceptualized the steering wheel as a key interface that would have a prominent role even in autonomous driving situations of the near future (such as when the steering wheel would turn "magically" by itself). Besides this, the steering wheel is already an important object for many non-driving activities such as drumming, stroking or tapping a rhythm. Based on this background, we initiated a contextual and iterative design process to explore interactive possibilities of the autonomous driving context.

Design Process

The design process of *AutoJam* was initiated and guided by the question, what interactions can be done on a stationary and inactivated steering wheel during an autonomous driving scenario?

Inspired by a contextual design approach [11], we intended to contextualize all phases and activities of the design process. For example, for ideating interactions and game ideas, we conducted a series of *car-storming* sessions [12]. In doing so, we mounted a second steering wheel on the passenger side of a test vehicle and drove into rush hour traffic as seen in Figure 1.

Figure 1: Car-Storming Session. In order to ideate and paper prototype in the context, we mounted a steering wheel on the passenger's dashboard and drove into rush hour traffic. The sessions were recorded for evaluation of the mockups.

The car-storming sessions were attended by various configurations of game and interaction designers, architects and computer scientists. Equipped with sticky notes, paper and pens, the sessions enabled ideation in context and an immediate *play-through* of ideas. These car-stormings provided a rich repository of possible concepts that were evaluated and documented based on the audio recordings and the prototyping material.

Concepts from the car-storming were selected for further lab-based development. The first iteration of *AutoJam* was an audio game in which the player has to repeat drum rhythms. The faster the car drives; the more instruments join the player. In a focus group, we found that the game's core interaction needed to be aligned with the driving phases in order to motivate situational awareness of the player. However, it also showed that music games are very promising in facilitating a feeling of progression and mastery in frustrating traffic. Based on these findings, the second iteration was focused on embedding the core-interactions with the driving phases in traffic.

Conceptual Design of *AutoJam*

Drumming on the steering wheel is a common activity when listening to music. *AutoJam* is based on a touch sensitive steering wheel cover as seen in Figure 2.

Figure 2: *AutoJam* prototype during in-lab development. The prototype consists of a modified steering wheel cover with three touch-sensitive pads. Each pad has a LED attached as a visual aid for the game interactions.

In an ideal version of a *AutoJam*-like music game, we envisioned that the players can choose they own music content of their favorite artists. The chosen songs are then dissected into three segments which are corresponding with the play-modes of the game: (1) The Drum-mode corresponds with the rhythm segments of the song i.e. the player practices the basic drum-rhythms of the song. (2) The Freeplay-Mode corresponds with the melodic segment of the original song i.e. the player is motivated to improvise with a typical instrument of the song. (3) The Progress-Mode plays the original song without modification so that the player can pre-listen to the song's musical content to get prepared for the upcoming challenges. In this mode, no interactions are required.

Each of these three game-modes are connected and triggered by three defined stages of driving a car in traffic: (1) the Idle-phase, when the car has stopped, (2) the Acceleration-phase, when the car drives at an inconsistent speed and (3) the Cruise-phase, when the car drives at a consistent speed for more than 15 seconds. Table 1 provides an overview on how the driving phases trigger the game-modes.

Table 1: *AutoJam* Modes. The three game modes are initiated by the driving phases.

Mode	Driving phases	Description	Scoring
(1) Drum	Idle-phase (0-5 km/h)	Repeat a one bar drum loop	Yes
(2) Freeplay	Acceleration / deceleration (5-60 km/h)	Improvise an instrument with car speed as input of the notes register	No
(3) Progress	Cruise (const. speed for 15 sec)	Song progresses	No

Game Design

For the proof-of-concept prototype of *AutoJam*, we chose the song *Chameleon* by Herbie Hancock as the musical content. From the song, we extracted nine simplified drum-rhythms and composed three instruments for the improvisation-phase; a synthesizer and two organs. Only when the car is standing still, the player can progress in the drum mode and level up. Every time the player has mastered three drum levels, he or she unlocks a new instrument which then becomes available during freeplay-mode.

Freeplay-mode was initiated when the car drives with inconsistent speed. In freeplay-mode, the player became the instrumentalist of the band and could improvise a solo with the unlocked instrument. Each of the three pads on the steering wheel triggers one note based on the song's harmonic scale. However, the register i.e. the pitch of the note was based on the speed of the car. The faster the car travels, the higher the register of the played note. We predicted that the player's creativity would be increased by the necessity to adapt the improvisation with the speed of the car.

Lastly, if the car drove at a constant speed for more than 15 seconds, the game triggered progression-mode. This mode did not require any interactions from the player. The original song progressed and the player can listen to upcoming challenges.

Technical Implementation and In-Car Setup

The technical implementation consists of three conductive pads mounted on the steering wheel cover that serve as trigger pads to play the music (Figure 2). Next to each of these drum pads, a LED-bar visually indicates the drum-patterns. Besides that, *AutoJam* does not require any further visual interface. Instead, all game instructions as well as information on progression and levels are audio based through music or verbal commands. The game is running on an *Arduino Touchboard* that is sending MIDI data to an external sound processor (*Ableton Live*) which contains the samples of the song. The car speed is synced with the *Touchboard* via an Arduino that is connected to the car's OBD-II interface.

Figure 3: *AutoJam* Setup. During the user study, the prototype was mounted on the stationary steering wheel on the dashboard of the passenger side.

To enable an in-situ user study, we mounted a second steering wheel with the *AutoJam* prototype on the passenger-side of the test vehicle, as seen in Figure 3. Even though the steering wheel could not be turned, it provided a realistic impression of a driving environment.

EXPLORATIVE IN-SITU STUDY

To investigate the impact of the *AutoJam* prototype on the driving experience, we conducted an in-situ user study with 14 participants. The *AutoJam* prototype was implemented on the passenger side of an Audi A8. The study took place during weekday city traffic in Melbourne. The traffic situation was busy to very busy with some intense stop-and-go phases which resulted in enough standing time to progress in the game. The durations of the *AutoJam* playtests were between 20-60 minutes (depending on the participant's motivation to keep playing). The test vehicle was occupied by the driving researcher and the test participant. All 14 participants were able to complete at least five drum levels i.e. they were able to unlock one extra improvisation instrument. Seven participants were able to complete the whole game.

Participants

All participants were recruited via social media channels or a mailing list from the *Audi Centre Melbourne*. To participate, an interested person had to complete an online registration form containing general demographic questions. From the pool of registrations, 14 were chosen based on demography and availability. The 14 participants (seven females; seven males) were between 26 and 47 years old (M=32.78, SD=6.79). All participants had a driving license and owned, or had previously owned a car. All test drives were scheduled during afternoon and early evening, in and around Melbourne CBD.

Study Procedure

The user study consisted of two stages. After consent and introduction to the *AutoJam* prototype, the test drive started. The participant could start the game as soon as the car stopped by touching the middle button on the steering wheel. This usually happened at the first traffic related stop. To stop the game, the participant needed to press the same button again. The participants could play the game as long as they wanted.

When the participant finished playing the game, the car was parked. We then conducted a semi-structured interview based on ten open questions on general feeling, the motivations to play, the perception of traffic, the autonomous driving scenario as well as a subjective evaluation of the situational awareness and the experience of improvising in collaboration with the car.

Both the playtesting, as well as the in-car interviews, were video recorded for analysis.

FINDINGS

Video recordings of the in-car interviews have been transcribed and analyzed through a thematic analysis approach [2]. Besides shared experiences, we focused on identifying unexpected aspects of the *AutoJam* experience. In the following, we report on the five most defining categories identified by the analysis. Each of the categories consist of several dimensions that describe one particular aspect of the overall experience.

A. Player experience

This category describes the overall player experience based on the three game-modes triggered by the car's speed. Since the cruise-mode was only initiated a few times, the drum-mode and the freeplay-mode had the strongest impact. The tension of the player experience ranges from a feeling of awkwardness to mastery.

Awkwardness of the situation. Resulting from the eye-catching setup of the steering wheel (P8) or resulting from the requirement of self-expression during freeplay (P9).

- *The other thing about being stopped was I became aware of other drivers looking at me and I was thinking, it makes me feel a bit, not embarrassed, but what are those people thinking about me doing this, ah, touching this funny steering wheel on the wrong side of the car, playing this game* (P8: media technician, 41, male).

- *Drumming makes me feel less awkward (laughs). When I was in freeplay [mode], I had to make it up [for] myself and that made me feel more uncomfortable. The amount of self-expression made me feel comfortable* (P9: project manager, 32, female).

Creative Performance. The eye-catching setup of *AutoJam* could also have a motivational impact on the creative performance based on the increased attention of other traffic participants.

- *It brings up self-esteem but this is because I'm a musician and performer. I like it a lot when people are looking strange. It's a fantastic tool for musicians* (P5: univ. lecturer/artist, 47, female).

Feeling of mastery and achievement. The drum-mode is experienced as a challenging and engrossing component resulting in feelings of success, mastery and achievement. It required a good timing and rhythm to proceed to another level.

- *It is more challenging and you're progressing, making it to another level, it's an achievement* (P1: analyst, 26, male).

B. Impact of driving and perception of car

This category describes the impact of *AutoJam* on the feeling of being driven and the perception of the car.

Controlled by the car. *AutoJam's* connection to the driving situation is based on the car speed. The game-modes, as well as the pitch of the improvisation instruments in freeplay, were directly controlled by the car leading to the perception of being under the car's control:

- *I felt more that the car was controlling me. The speed was controlling the options I had but the other way around of driving* (P10: PhD candidate, 29, female).

Accentuation of driving experience. On a more granular level, the connection of speed and music was experienced as a natural extension of the driving dynamics.

- *It is a natural connection between the car and the pitch of the sound. That makes sense and is very natural* (P12: PhD candidate, 28, male).
- *When we came around a corner and I felt the car speeds up while I was playing, I felt a connection in a way that it exaggerated the feeling [of moving], at least for some moments* (P13: R&D manager, 35, female).

Collaboration: car as instrument and actor. As expected, many participants described the car as being like an instrument. However, the car was also experienced as a band member or conductor that facilitates playful moments of music interactions.

- *It's a creative interaction but not like playing an instrument that you have to learn. More something that is motivated by collaboration with the car* (P6: media technician, 42, male).
- *The car is a part of the music experience, it's an actor* (P4: curator, 28, female).

C. Traffic and Progression

This category describes how *AutoJam* changed the perception of traffic and in particular, the feeling of progression.

Consistent progression. *AutoJam* facilitated consistent feelings of progression since either the game, the traffic, or ultimately the song and traffic (cruise-mode) was progressing.

- *Every stage of the drive gives me the opportunity to progress in the game, otherwise I progress in traffic and that provided a constant feeling of progression* (P14: safety engineer, 44, male).

Journey control through learning. Even though there was no clear indication of the expected arrival time or a representation of the progression of the overall trip, the learning and improvement facilitated a feeling of controlling the journey.

- *I didn't mind it. It wasn't too bad you just sitting there and playing the game. You're not getting frustrated with people in front of you. You're definitely feeling a connection between progressing in game and traffic as you are going along. You getting better in the game but you [are] also getting closer to where you're going. If you knew how many levels you have to finish before arriving, it would be much more accentuated* (P7: musician, 26, male).

Reframing Standstill. Connecting game-progression with the least desired element in traffic was one of the most effective ways to facilitate a new perception of the traffic situation.

- *It's funny because only in the stops you can progress and that makes them less threatening. Normally I hate stops but this gives me a chance to progress* (P2: architect, 32, female).

D. Situational Awareness

This category described the subjective evaluation of situational awareness facilitated by playing *AutoJam*.

Comfortable distraction. The level of traffic awareness was described as a comfortable distraction enabling a positive perception of traffic.

- *I think it's a good level of distraction because if you don't need to focus too much on the road you won't get angry. It positively influences the perception of traffic* (P9: project manager, 32, female).

Gameplay forced situational awareness. The challenges of the drum mode i.e. to complete the level before the car started driving again, motivated the participant to anticipate the stops. This was not an intended interaction but could be exploited as a mechanic to force traffic awareness.

- *There were a few of abrupt stops where the traffic was backed up, I was sort of interacting with that because I knew some tricky situations are coming up. Yeah I think I was aware about the traffic around* (P12: PhD candidate, 28, male).
- *I was watching the road as well as the wheel in both modes. Because the worst moment was when you progressed to four correct drum loops and then the car starts again. That's frustrating, so this is an additional challenge* (P3: artist, 32, female).

Awareness as a relation to others. Situational awareness was also described as an indirect result of the in-car performance. The other road participants are potentially the audience of the performance, making the driver more aware of them.

- *I was looking to other cars; I was relating to them even getting a bit aggressive toward them* (P5: University lecturer/artist, 47, female).

E. Freeplay motivations

This category describes dimensions of freeplay motivations. The freeplay-mode was arguably the most controversial part of the *AutoJam* experience. It challenged the player to be creative or explorative but did not provide any quantifiable feedback.

Self-expression. *AutoJam's* freeplay-mode was a platform for musical expression similar to an instrument that translates current feelings or mood into creativity.

- *I like the connection between music and car because you can express yourself. If you are tired you can react or if you are aggressive you can be violent* (P4: curator, 28, female).

Preparation to practice for drum-mode. Freeplay-mode showed some promising opportunities to be a place for relaxation and preparation. For example, enabling a moment of relaxation while still being connected to the car and the music (P3). Similarly: to make meaning out of the freeplay-mode in particular, with the changing register of the notes and practice for the upcoming drum-patterns (P14).

- *I was trying to get it and when I get the hang of the freeplay, that it gets higher when driving faster then it's much more enjoyable because I can relax between the levels. Like a break waiting for the car slows down* (P3: Artist, 31, female).
- *I could not really get a melody going because all the time I hit the button it was changing. So I was basically practicing the moves from the drumming parts while in freeplay* (P14: safety engineer, 44, male).

Useless since no goal. However, one participant struggled to make sense during freeplay-mode, in particular because the car was going again:

- *Because when the car was going I didn't see any point to do anything. There is no objective. I liked the drum mode much more. Freeplay was bit annoying in fact because I wanted to keep on playing* (P1: analyst, 26, male).

F. Improvisation Strategies

The creative character of the freeplay-mode required the participants to come up with improvisation strategies. To make meaning, they had to take different contexts as the source for their interactions.

Exploration of the connection speed and music. Initially, the exploration of the speed and pitch connection was the focus, and considered as an enjoyable connection of motion and music (P7). However, this exploration seemed to wear off after a while (P6).

- *It's an exploration of the music and speed that is always nice* (P7: musician, 26, male).
- *The pitch-shifting is going with the speed this is cool but after 10 minutes I want something new to be able to manipulate the sound and improvise. Another way to change the sound* (P6: media technician, 42, male).

Aligning with background music. After understanding the connection (the exploration phase) musical content became the focus of improvisation and the individual impact became secondary.

- *I was happy to groove with the background track and wasn't too much listening on my impact* (P13: R&D manager, 35, female).

Sonification of surrounding. Most interestingly, one participant (a professional musician) described a translation of the surroundings in relation to speed as the core of his interpretation strategy.

- *It was nice if it tuned up, so you were looking for a change. I was looking outside while improvising, take in the things around me. Much more than I thought I would. It is also a natural thing when you are driver. You won't look into the steering wheel when you do this* (P7, musician, 26, male).

BUILDING BLOCKS OF IN-CAR PERFORMANCES

Within the scope of this paper, we limited the findings to, what we believe, are the six most defining categories for

Table 2: *AutoJam* experience map. The categories and dimensions as identified from the semi-structured interviews. The individual experience of the player can be understood as a dynamic transition between the dimensions of the categories.

Player experience	Impact on driving exp.	Traffic and progression	Improvisation Strategies	Freeplay motivations	Situational awareness
Creative Performance	Accentuation of driving	Consistent flow	Exploration	Self-expression	Comfortable distraction
Mastery	Car as actor	Journey control	Backgrounding	Chance to practice	Forced by gameplay
Awkward Situation	Controlled by car	Reframing standstill	Sonification of surrounding	Useless	Relation to others

providing a detailed resolution of participants' experiences regarding the interplay between the in-car interactions, the outside world and the player's motivation.

Table 2 summarizes the six categories as a suggested experience map of 14 participants. Each column of Table 2 represents one of the mentioned categories. We assume that the individual experience of the *AutoJam* players can best be understood as a continuous process of swinging between different configurations (the dimensions of the experience map) depending on the dynamics of the game and the driving situation. Without doubt, the center of our investigations were the creative performances in the traffic context. This novel context for creative interactions enabled a new perspective, to frame future autonomous driving in dense traffic into a space of self-expression and improvisation.

To translate the dynamics of the experience map into a more generalized frame for in-car performances, we reflect the findings of the semi-structured interviews by discussing them as four elements of an (artistic) performance. As crucial building blocks of in-car performances we identified: (1) the stage, (2) the play, (3) the progression and (4) the roles/actors. In the following, we reflect on the dynamics of the experience map by suggesting an internal structure of those building blocks. Furthermore, we suggest implications for promoting or improving creative in-car performances through design.

(1) The Stage: a private / public play

The encapsulation by the car established a feeling of being protected from the outside. At the same time, the car is a genuine vehicle for (self-) presentation. The car situation, especially in stop-and-go traffic when exposed to other road users, is a public as well as a private space.

In the book *The presentation of self in everyday life* [8], Goffman analyzed everyday interactions as theatrical play. Following Goffman, the car is both the stage, as a space for public performance, and the backstage, a room for privacy. This ambiguity establishes not only tension between the car as a private space and the car as representation, but also frames the interaction. For some participants, the eye-catching setup motivated to great performances. For others, such as P8, the fancy setup resulted in awkward feelings of being exposed to other people's glances. In both instances, the situation was perceived as being exposed to an audience. Since tapping the steering wheel is a rather typical interaction when listening to music, we assume that this awkwardness resulted entirely from *AutoJam's* test setup of an additional steering wheel on the passenger side.

Nevertheless, according to Goffman [7], the frame is the definition of the situation and guiding principle, which organize the behavior and the subjective involvement of the actors. Situations where the actors have different frames may lead to awkwardness. For example, starting to sing an opera in a supermarket queue results in the actors (i.e. the singer and other shoppers) framing the situation differently, usually leading to mutual embarrassment. Appropriate cues, such as a costume and other stage props, can help, however, to frame the situation as a show. In the *AutoJam* setup, the car is not only stage and backstage, but also the costume and the stage props of the player. To prevent awkwardness, the props need to support and communicate the frame of the interaction, in our case the creative play.

In order to facilitate unconventional or even "awkward" non-driving activities, we propose that the framing of the situation has to be addressed; for example by communicating the element of play to the other road users. In the case of *AutoJam*, this could be realized by communicating elements of the creative play to the outside. Examples could be as simple as an LED strip or a windscreen display that would serve as visualization (such as equalizer-bars) or the casting of the music to the outside world.

(2) The Creative Play: Improvisation and situational awareness

In terms of creative play, the improvisations modulated and facilitated by the car's driving speed (i.e. the freeplay-mode) were the most crucial component. The freeplay-mode was designed to enable a heads-up experience; it was let by the assumption that the connection of music production and speed would motivate the player to creatively interact with traffic while maintaining a pleasurable situation awareness. The engagement in the playful interactions of *AutoJam* aimed at translating the mundane environment of traffic into creative content of musical interpretation, particularly mentioned by participants with musical background. Nevertheless, also non-musicians connected the interaction to the surroundings such as:

> *The things you are aware of are quite different than during usual driving. We feel the car differently, more from an aesthetical level. I think the car could be a very creative space* (P13: R&D manager, 35, female).

As the dimensions of the improvisation categories indicate, the motivation to engage in improvisation swings between an exploration of the relationship between speed and pitch of the note, the accentuation of background music, and the translation of the surroundings into musical expression. We propose that this motivational dynamic is a very productive way to promote creativity in driving situations. However, it also strongly influences the direction of situational awareness. Creative in-car activities benefit from motivating the player to engage in a transformation of the driving task into a creative product. In creative in-car games, the similarities between driving a car and playing an instrument can be exploited by phases of structure and improvisation. For P6, not only the driving situation resembles the structure of musical improvisation, also the driving interface (as well as the driving task) was interpreted from a musical perspective.

The *AutoJam* experience outlined a close relationship between creative improvisation strategies and situational awareness. These improvisation strategies appear to relate themselves on contextual factors: speed, music or surroundings. The design challenge for establishing situational awareness through improvisation was to make these contextual input factors playable.

(3) The dramatic Progression: the tension of stop-and-go

We designed *AutoJam* to facilitate a consistent feeling of progression despite of standing in heavy traffic. In doing so, progression should be experienced on three levels depending on the mode of play, i.e. the flow of traffic: (1) Progression in the game, i.e. advancing in the game and unlocking new instruments can only take place when the car has stopped. (2) Progression of the journey is experienced when the car starts or stops driving (i.e. accelerating or decelerating). Then, the players are exposed to the physical dynamics of driving and can express themselves by “jamming” with the unlocked instrument. (3) Progression of the music takes place when the car reaches consistent speed (cruise-mode). While in cruise-mode, the song progresses uninterruptedly in alignment with the driving.

From the interviews we learnt that the alignment of game and traffic progress resulted in a consistent feeling of progression in all three modes of play. By aligning the gameplay with the stop-and-go situation, the traffic literally became a playable element of the experience:

> *I was not paying too much attention to the progression of traffic because I was trying to progress in the game. I didn't realise the traffic but I internally worked through it* (P13: R&D manager, 35, female).

However, the feeling of progression comes with a trade-off: The tensions of stop-and-go traffic, even though translated into a challenge, afford a continuous switch between a gameful activity and a playful or creative activity. For some participants, this dialectic of instructions and improvisations became excessively demanding, as it would break the flow of the game. In contrast, the musician’s reported that this swing between the mindsets reminds them of playing in a band with phases of structured and freer parts.

> *I like the delineation between being stopped and moving. It sorts of makes me feel like playing music, like if you are in a band you have moments where you have to be really rigged with playing together and there are some parts where you can be free. That's music. It is a collaboration exercise* (P7: musician, 26, male).

This strong switch between mindsets of playful improvisation and instructive gaming could be relieved by an integration of the music, created in one mode, as a playable content of the other mode. Furthermore, gameful elements integrated into freeplay-mode could improve the motivation for creative, joyful improvisation. Recent research on the intersection of play and games such as [10,14,15] show promising results to facilitate creative activities by gameful mechanics.

(4) The Role of the car: play maker and instrument

As autonomous driving turns cars into transportation robots, the operational control of the car may shift toward a more collaborative driving activity. By designing and testing *AutoJam*, we also explored how a playful integration of the driving context (i.e. the speed of the car) can transform and motivate creative music production into a dialogue with the car and the driving situation.

The experience map indicates that the experience of being driven was swinging between an accentuation of the feeling of driving, a contribution to the driving task of the car, and even a feeling of being controlled by the car. While the last interpretation (the car as a playmaker) resulted most likely from the tensions between an instructive and creative play (as discussed before), we believe that the other experiences resulted from the implementation of speed as a game defining variable:

AutoJam, as a collaborative experience, was perceived as an addition to driving rather than a communication or even a dialogue with the car. Instead of being an independent actor, the car transformed into a medium for experiencing the driving situation from a musical perspective. This interpretation was reported as an experience of the driving context as an embodiment of music and the car:

> *I felt even closer to my car than usual because I'm playing with it. The car is the music, but the car and the music is also me because I'm contributing to it* (P5: univ. lecturer/artist, 47, female).

We assume that this embodiment, which connected the musical play with the car, also accentuated the experience of driving the car. As such, it established a feeling of control over the car and the experience of mastering frustrating stop-and-go traffic. This perception is also manifested in the participant's desire to incorporate the expected length of the trip into the game. The song progresses with the trip; whereas the car controls the play and is played at the same time. The *AutoJam* experience, therefore, highlights the importance of a journey-based perspective when designing for future in-car games. Metaphorically speaking, the role of the car in the *AutoJam* experience can be described as an embodied *play head* that connects the journey with a gameplay which unfolds in its progression.

LIMITATIONS AND FUTURE WORK

Designing for a future scenario such as an advanced autonomous driving situation, we made several design assumptions that require further discussion. First and foremost, we explicitly focused on the design, assuming that safety related aspects of a serialized implementation into a real autonomous driving context will require further thoughts. We assumed that future autonomous driving systems will resemble the current constrains of front-seat passengers, with the addition to maintaining situational awareness in case of a take-over request. The important question regarding response time and engagement in a non-driving task have not been taken into consideration during this explorative design and study work. Furthermore, in current autonomous driving systems, the steering wheel often serves as an interface for immediate take-over intervention of the driver. Drumming on the steering wheel would be a safety critical intervention. However, we designed *AutoJam* for a future, more advanced version of autonomous driving that require human take-overs only on request. This would enable new opportunities for interacting with the car's interfaces such as locking the steering wheel when in autonomous driving mode.

The user study focused on exploring the experiences of playing *AutoJam*. The findings are a qualitative evaluation of the users, that do not allow a conclusion regarding their actual situational awareness. In contrast, the findings reveal possible design strategies for establishing situational awareness through relating the inactive driver with the autonomous driving situation. The study provides a first conceptual understanding of the car's design space for motivating creative interventions in a frustrating traffic situation. Future research is required to guide a safe implementation in the autonomous driving context.

CONCLUSION

This paper presented *AutoJam*, the first conceptual understanding of designing creative, musical interventions to positively influence the perception of a frustrating traffic situation in an autonomously driven car. In doing so, we presented the concept of *AutoJam* and reported on the results of an explorative in-situ user study. From the user study, we extracted categories and dimensions of the most relevant user experience factors and articulated building blocks of in-car performances. This work informs future design activities by providing a frame for understanding the complexities of improvisational and creative activities in the context of future autonomous driving.

REFERENCES

1. David Beattie, Lynne Baillie, Martin Halvey, and Roderick McCall. 2014. What's Around the Corner? Enhancing Driver Awareness in Autonomous Vehicles via In-Vehicle Spatial Auditory Displays. *NordiCHI'14*, ACM, 10.
2. Virginia Braun and Victoria Clarke. 2006. Using thematic analysis in psychology. *Qualitative research in psychology* 3, 2, 77–101.
3. Michael Bull. 2004. Automobility and the power of sound. *Theory, Culture & Society* 21, 243–259. http://doi.org/10.1177/0263276404046069
4. Sally Jo Cunningham, David M Nichols, David Bainbridge, and Hasan Ali. 2014. Social music in cars. ISMIR, 457–462.
5. Kai Eckoldt, Martin Knobel, Marc Hassenzahl, and Josef Schumann. 2012. An Experiential Perspective on Advanced Driver Assistance Systems. *it - Information Technology* 54, 4, 165–171. http://doi.org/10.1524/itit.2012.0678
6. Kai Eckoldt and Benjamin N.N. Schulz. 2009. Das Auto als Musikinsturment: gemeinsames Trommeln als positives Erlebnis. *i-com* 1/2009, 1, 83–85.
7. Erving Goffman. 1974. *Frame analysis: An essay on the organization of experience.* Harvard University Press.
8. Erving Goffman. 1975. *The presentation of self in everyday life*. Penguin Book. http://doi.org/10.2307/258197
9. Chisa Hasegawa and Koji Oguri. 2006. The Effects of Specific Musical Stimuli on Driver ' s Drowsiness. ITCS'06, 817–822.
10. Jussi Holopainen and May Stain. 2015. Dissecting playfulness for practical design. *The Gameful World: Approaches, Issues, Applications*, 419.
11. Karen Holtzblatt and Hugh Beyer. 2014. Contextual

Design: Evolved. *Synthesis Lectures on Human-Centered Informatics* 7, 4, 1–91.

12. Sven Krome, William Goddard, Stefan Greuter, Steffen P Walz, and Angsgar Gerlicher. 2015. A Context-based Design Process for Future Use Cases of Autonomous Driving: Prototyping AutoGym. *AutomotiveUI 2015*.
13. Mattias Östergren. 2004. Sound pryer: Adding value to traffic encounters with streaming audio. *Entertainment Computing - Icec 2004* 3166, 541–552. http://doi.org/10.1007/978-3-540-28643-1_71
14. Miguel Sicart. 2014. *Play Matters*. MIT Press. http://doi.org/10.1017/CBO9781107415324.004
15. Jaakko Stenros. 2015. Playfulness, Play, and Games. A Constructionist Ludology Approach. Doctoral Dissertation, University of Tampere, Tampere, Finland.
16. The Tesla Motors Team. 2015. Your Autopilot has Arrived. *The Tesla Motors Team Blog*, 2015. Retrieved January 13, 2016 from https://www.teslamotors.com/en_AU/blog/your-autopilot-has-arrived
17. Viknesh Vijayenthiran. 2012. Autonomous Driving Traffic Jam Assistant Coming to Audi A8. Retrieved from http://www.motorauthority.com/news/1071685_autonomous-driving-traffic-jam-assistant-coming-to-audi-a8
18. Michael J. Walsh. 2010. *Driving to the beat of one's own hum: automobility and musical listening*. Elsevier. http://doi.org/10.1108/S0163-2396(2010)0000035015

Image-based Emotion Feedback: How Does the Crowd Feel? And Why?

David A. Robb[1] Stefano Padilla[1] Thomas S. Methven[1] Britta Kalkreuter[2] Mike J. Chantler[1]
[1]School of Mathematical and Computer Sciences, [2]School of Textiles and Design,
Heriot-Watt University, Edinburgh, UK. EH14 4AS
{d.a.robb, s.padilla, t.methven, b.kalkreuter, m.j.chantler}@hw.ac.uk

ABSTRACT
In previous work we developed a method for interior designers to receive image-based feedback about a crowd's emotions when viewing their designs. Although the designers clearly desired a service which provided the new style of feedback, we wanted to find out if an internet crowd would enjoy, and become engaged in, giving emotion feedback this way. In this paper, through a mixed methods study, we expose whether and why internet users enjoy giving emotion feedback using images compared to responding with text. We measured the participants' cognitive styles and found that they correlate with the reported utility and engagement of using images. Those more visual than they are verbal were more engaged by using images to express emotion compared to text. Enlightening qualitative insights reveal, surprisingly, that half of our participants have an appetite for expressing emotions this way, value engagement over clarity, and would use images for emotion feedback in contexts other than design feedback.

Author Keywords
Cognitive styles; affective computing; creativity; design feedback; crowdsourcing; perceptual and emotional feedback; image summarization.

ACM Classification Keywords
H.5.3 [Information Interfaces and Presentation]: Group and Organization Interfaces.

INTRODUCTION
The image-based emotion feedback method (IEFM) was developed to provide fashion and interior designers with visual feedback on the perceived mood of their designs. It was found in an evaluation to be popular with the designers receiving the feedback [47]. Those providing the feedback choose images from perceptually organized image browsers instead of using text. The motivation for the method was to allow designers in these domains to build large followings and engage them in visual co-design conversations around prototype designs and finished products. Images, rather than emoji, were used as it was important that the output be visually inspiring for the designer consumers and not too formulaic. Image summarization is used to allow designers to access the "wisdom of the crowd" [56] within the image feedback in a visually inspiring way analogous to their use of mood boards[1]. These thought provoking summaries are condensed from the massed image feedback. The algorithm used for this was validated in another experiment showing that the summaries effectively represented the totality of the feedback [48].

Those two investigations showed that, from the point of view of designers consuming the feedback, the method was viable. However, for the IEFM to work for designer users, crowd users would need to be attracted to giving feedback. A brief evaluation of the experience of those who gave the feedback consumed during the designer study was reported along with a demonstration of the software components [46]. It was noted that a proportion of the group of undergraduate participants involved did prefer using sets of images to express their emotional reaction to a design whereas others preferred text. It was speculated that individual differences including cognitive style, rather than simply personal taste, were a factor in this. Due to the narrow nature of that group of feedback-givers, generalizing beyond them was not possible.

Following that work we were motivated to discover what a wider sample of internet users would think of giving emotion feedback using the image browsers developed for the IEFM and the reasons underlying any preferences they expressed. Knowing why some people prefer using text or images for emotion feedback and whether they prefer particular types of images would be useful in formulating future image banks for use with the IEFM. This might also help understand why some people wish to comment using images rather than text in contexts outside design feedback.

In this paper we demonstrate for the first time that crowdsourced image-based design feedback engages a particular section of internet users. We describe a mixed methods study in which a gender balanced sample of 50

DIS 2017, June 10-14, 2017, Edinburgh, United Kingdom
ACM 978-1-4503-4922-2/17/06.
http://dx.doi.org/10.1145/3064663.3064665

[1] Mood boards are used to establish a perceptual and emotional theme when creating a design [16].

internet users, spread across a wide age range, contrasted two formats of image-based feedback with text in the context of giving their emotional reaction to interior designs. We measured participants' cognitive styles and correlated these with their experience of the formats. We show that those users who are, by nature, more visual than verbal in cognitive style, are more engaged by using images in the IEFM for emotion feedback compared to text. We hope that by demonstrating this empirically we will motivate the HCI community to further develop image-based response modes for emotion feedback. We argue that this will encourage inclusion of feedback from those who might previously have remained silent due to lack of an image-based mode of expression suiting their nature. Our study shows that internet users think that the IEFM, a medium for readily summerizable image-based emotion feedback, is applicable outside the realm of interior design feedback.

The rest of this paper is structured as follows. We examine other work forming the background to this paper. We describe our study and report the results. Finally we discuss the implications of our findings and draw conclusions.

BACKGROUND AND RELATED WORK

In this section we first situate image-based emotion feedback within the field of crowdsourced design feedback. We briefly review computer mediated emotion expression and then discuss the significance of emotion in design along with the use of images in accessing emotions. We then review the development of the visual and verbal cognitive styles construct which has culminated in the current instruments for measuring that aspect of individual differences.

Design Feedback from Crowds

Blogging or involvement in communities such as *Dribbble* [12] has given designers access to feedback from crowds. However, participation in such communities is limited due to the levels of commitment required [8]. In addition, tools have been created for crowdsourcing feedback using non-expert, paid, remote workers to provide supported, objective, critiques [27,69]. The image-based emotion feedback method (IEFM) has been developed to complement such systems by encouraging the participation of volunteer crowds, perhaps engaged through social media [11,70], in giving subjective, impressionistic, emotion feedback.

Computer Mediated Emotion Expression

Much of the area of Affective Computing is concerned with the sensing of emotions within users and with the expression of emotion by computer systems such that the user and the computer are to some degree in empathy with each other [38]. Studies in this area on the emotions that can be perceived in various forms of stimuli presented to participants have used multiple modes including sound and thermal stimuli as well as visual stimuli including animated shapes and color [4, 36, 50, 51, 52, 67, 68].

Work on person to person emotion communication mediated by computer systems has included visual modes and physicality such as gestures and squeezing of specially built input devices: In the *eMoto* studies, gestures along with squeezing on a modified mobile device stylus and selecting a colored animation have been used to allow users to express their emotions to accompany SMS messages [55]. Shape and the physicality of distorting a flexible surface have also been investigated [54]. Physicality and color (colored squeezable balls) were also used to gather the mood of a building's occupants in an in-the-wild study [14].

Emoji (pictographs represented by Unicode characters) are an important method of emotion expression. They have grown in popularity especially since the introduction of the iOS and Android Emoji keyboards (in 2011 and 2013). Although Emoji also depict non-emotion concepts their chief use is adding tone and emotion to text communication which they do with varying success [10, 30]. We believe that images offer a richer medium both for those expressing their emotions and for the inspiration of fashion and interior designers receiving feedback. In the next subsection we examine aspects of images as a feedback medium.

Emotion, Images and Design

Emotions play an important role in making purchasing and other decisions [26,58]. The emotions of users or consumers are acknowledged as being important in design [31,32]. The influence of emotion and images in design domains such as fashion is recognized in the design practice of mood boards (the arrangement of images and other materials to establish a perceptual and emotional theme for a planned design or work). It is this connection between emotions, designing, and the success of designs that led to the development of the IEFM. To avoid specific figurative connections affecting an individual's perception of a mood board abstract images are often used [16]. However, deliberately figurative images can access emotions in a more specific way than abstract images and such emotion imagery can be categorized by the emotions it evokes [25, 29]. The fact that people rapidly interpret the emotion content of images [20] indicates that images should work well for emotion feedback in fashion and interior design and possibly in other domains.

Cognitive Styles and Their Measurement

Images as a medium do have appeal for many and it is not unusual to hear people describe themselves as "visual" or indeed, "verbal". The idea that there are individual differences in the tendency of people to conceptualize in the form of mental imagery or in language has been considered and written about since Galton in the 19th century [15]. More recently psychologists developed this idea as a bipolar visual-verbal dimension - part of a larger construct of *cognitive styles* explaining individuals' differing preferences in the mental processing of information [e.g. 42, 35]. Cognitive styles are not to be confused with learning styles (or strategies) which are the particular strengths that individuals have in ways of learning and are recognized as a separate construct [49]. Models encompassing both describe cognitive styles as feeding into learning styles along with other factors including working memory, intelligence, and personality [43].

Riding & Cheema [44] reviewed cognitive styles and distilled the various constructs and terminology into two bipolar dimensions: *verbal-imagery*, and "*wholist-analytic*". Various methods of measuring cognitive styles were devised. Instruments to measure the visual-verbal dimension include Richardson's 15-item Verbalizer-Visualizer Questionnaire (VVQ), a pen and paper self-report questionnaire [42], and Riding's Cognitive Styles Analysis (CSA), a behavioral test administered on computer. The CSA also measured the "wholist-analytic" dimension [45]. By the early 2000's several other studies confirmed this two-bipolar-dimensional view of cognitive styles [7, 21, 22, 28, 64].

More recently, the validity of the bipolar visual-verbal dimension of cognitive styles was questioned [2, 23, 41]. A new model of *visual cognitive style* was proposed, based on the inconsistencies in the previous model and on neurophysiology [24]. That research included work showing that areas of the parietal lobes of the brain activated when participants imagined faces and colors whereas areas of the temporal lobe were activated when imagining a route map. The new model had two monopolar visual cognitive style dimensions: *object imagery* and *spatial imagery* and a new instrument to measure them, the Object-Spatial Imagery Questionnaire (OSIQ) [6]. The object imagery scale measured preferences for the representing and processing of "*colorful, pictorial and high resolution images of individual objects*" while the spatial imagery scale measured that for "*schematic images, spatial relations amongst objects and spatial transformations*". This was followed up with the Object-Spatial-Verbal cognitive style model measured by a three-subscale questionnaire. The Object-Spatial Imagery and Verbal Questionnaire (OSIVQ) measures those three monopolar dimensions [5]. An alternative three-subscale cognitive styles questionnaire was developed by Thomas & McKay [57] for a study on the design of teaching materials. However, that instrument has not been otherwise validated. The OSIVQ [5] was rigorously validated in the study which introduced it and has been used in other recent studies for measuring cognitive styles [e.g. 3, 17, 33]. The OSIVQ was therefore chosen to measure cognitive styles for our study.

STUDY

In this section we describe the aims and methods of the study in which we evaluated the feedback-giver view of the image-based emotion feedback method (IEFM).

Aim

Our aim was to find out what potential crowd users (feedback-givers) of image-based emotion feedback think about it in contrast to text, including their preferences and reasons for these preferences. Although *engagement* was our main focus we decided it was also important to probe *utility*, i.e. whether users felt able to express their emotions using the formats. We formulated these research questions:

RQ1 Do feedback-givers find image feedback formats more engaging or less engaging than text?

RQ2 Do feedback-givers feel able to express their emotions using image feedback formats?

RQ3 Are cognitive styles a factor in feedback-givers' experience of different feedback formats?

RQ4 Do feedback-givers prefer using images or text when describing their emotions and what is their reasoning for this?

Method

RQ1 and RQ2 were investigated in a repeated measures experiment. Participants rated the *engagement* and *utility* of two image-based feedback formats and text. RQ3 was addressed by measuring participants' cognitive styles and carrying out a correlation analysis against their *engagement* and *utility* ratings. RQ4 was probed in a questionnaire. The participants in our study did the following:

1) Completed a cognitive styles questionnaire.
2) Did a feedback task.
3) Completed a post-task questionnaire.

In the subsections below we describe a) the formation of our participant group, b) the measurement of their cognitive styles, c) the construction of the two image browsers which, together with text, would constitute three feedback formats for the task, d) the feedback task itself and finally, e) the post-task questionnaire.

Participants

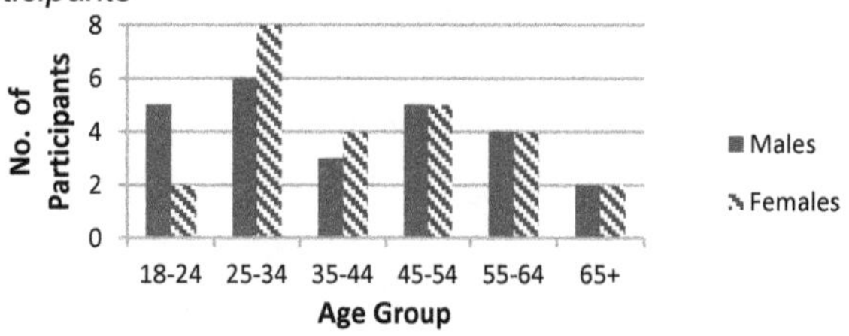

Figure 1. Participant gender and age group composition.

Participants were recruited by a combination of social media, email publicity, convenience and snowball sampling [66]. The target age profile was intended to reflect internet users in the UK [61, 62]. To achieve a gender balance and the desired age profile, purposeful sampling based on age and gender was used [37, 66]. We did not reach as many in the 35-44yrs and over-64s age groups as hoped and the sample had slightly more 25-34yrs and fewer over-64s than would be representative. The oldest was 77 and the youngest 19. (Figure 1). The final sample was 50 (25 male, 25 female). (A power analysis had indicated that this should be enough for the study's repeated measures experiment to expose a medium effect.)

Participants completed an online consent and demographics form. They were asked to report education level (Figure 2) and occupation. Occupations varied from electrician through admin assistant, police officer, occupational therapist, part-time event organizer, teacher, lawyer, stay-at-home mother and artist, and retired electrical engineer. They also included nine students (eight full-time and one part-time). The demographic data show that, while we made efforts to make our sample representative by age and gender, unskilled workers were under-represented and those more highly educated were over-represented. Eight (16%) were ethnic minorities (within 2% of UK average [60]). As a minimum, participants had to have English as a foreign language. They were required to have access to a computer or iPad with an internet connection as they would take part remotely. (It has been shown that reliable quality usability data can be gathered away from the lab [1, 59].) After it was established that they fit a gap in the age and gender profile for our sample, participants had a short screening interview by phone to ensure they understood their tasks. Participants were rewarded with a $20 shopping voucher.

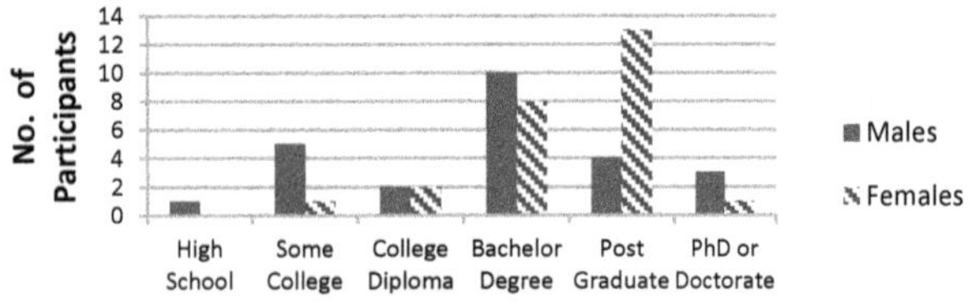

Figure 2. Education attainment level of the participants.

Cognitive Styles Measurement (OSIVQ)

The OSIVQ [5] was used. Each OSIVQ item is a 5 point Likert scale item. 45 items form three subscales. Participants completed the OSIVQ following its standard instructions and their responses were collated into three subscale scores (object, spatial and verbal). These are ratio data ranging between 1 and 5.

The Image Browsers for the Feedback Task

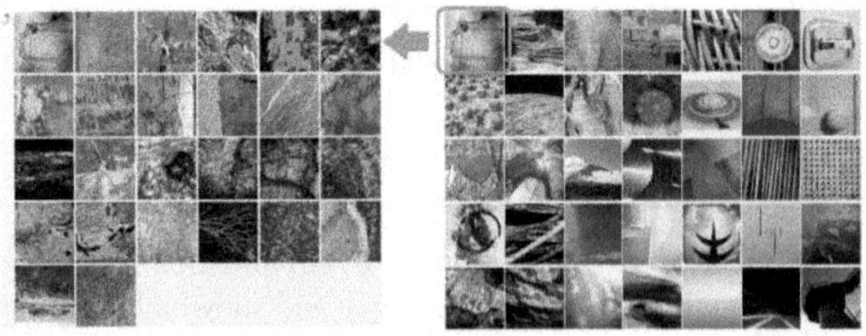

Figure 3. Screenshots from the abstract image browser. Right: the full array of stacks. Left: a stack from the array is shown opened. Each image occurs only once in the browser.

Two image browsers based on human perceptual data were built to provide intuitive browsing and two different styles of image for responses. One contains 500 abstract images in a self-organizing map (SOM) browser [63] based on similarity data from 20 lab-based and 200 paid crowdsourced participants. Its construction is described by Padilla et al. [34] and it provides a broad pallet of visually diverse images (Figure 3).

Figure 4. Screenshots from the emotion image browser. Top: the full array of stacks. Bottom: an opened stack.

To allow more specific emotion communication, a second browser was assembled (Figure 4). 2000 Creative Commons images were categorized by having 900 paid crowdsourced participants tag them with terms from the Plutchik emotion circumplex model [39]. As a result, each image has an emotion tag frequency profile representing the judgments of 20 different tagging participants (Figure 5).

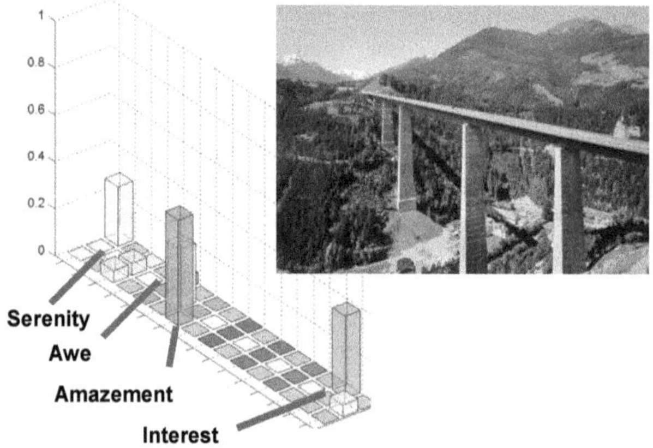

Figure 5. An image from the emotion image browser with its emotion profile. Labelled peaks correspond to popular tags for the image. The histogram shows the normalized tag frequencies laid out on the Plutchik emotion model [39]. Coloured and white spaces represent the model's 32 emotions. (Grey spaces are padding for chart layout purposes).

A subset of emotions was defined following a survey of 18 staff and students at a design institution in which respondents rated emotions for meaningfulness to design feedback. Based on this 19 out of the 32 emotions in the model were included in the browser. E.g. joy and sadness were included but ecstasy and grief were not. We aimed for a balanced coverage of the 19 emotions. The 2000 available tagged images were filtered to include 10 or 11 images with profiles best fitting each of the 19 emotions. The filtering algorithm took account of an image's highest emotion tag peak and the contrast between that and peaks for other emotions. For some of the emotions, there were no more than 10 images with clear profiles for those emotions and this limitation meant that the emotion image browser contained fewer images (204) than the abstract image browser (500). The images were arranged in a SOM browser defined by their emotion profiles (tag frequency vectors).

What makes a SOM browser intuitive to use is the organization of images in stacks. Tapping or clicking the top image of a stack reveals the full stack. Adjacent stacks contain similar images. Stacks far apart contain dissimilar images as defined by the human perceptual data. Tapping or clicking a thumbnail in an open stack displays the individual image at full size. 7 stacks by 5 was chosen as the size of the top-level grid for the SOM. This would allow it to be viewed on an iPad or small laptop screen and so place fewer limitations on the participant pool.

The Feedback Task

In itself the feedback task constituted a repeated measures experiment with three conditions. The measures were *Engagement* and *Utility*. The conditions were the three response formats: abstract images (AI), emotion images (EI), and text. Our participants were informed that they would a) see a series of designs by interior design students, b) for each design, be asked the question "How did the design make you feel?" and c) respond three times using three formats: two types of images and text. They were told that the student designers would each get three feedback summaries; one for each format used by all the anonymous participants when responding. Actually, as the focus of the study was on the feedback-givers themselves, it was not planned to show the feedback to the designers but it was necessary that participants believe their responses would go to the designers to ensure they approached the feedback task as a live exercise. In accordance with ethical guidelines the participants were debriefed about the true focus of the study later, after all data was collected.

Participants viewed a random selection of five interior designs from a pool of 12. For each they were asked "How did the design make you feel?", and they responded using the three formats: AI, EI and text. For each participant the format order was randomized. An image response consisted of three images chosen from the required browser. This was in case a combination of emotions was evoked by a design. A text response consisted of entering text into a text box. After each response to a design, participants were asked to rate that response format using visual analogue scale (VAS) items shown in Figure 6. VAS items were used as they yield high resolution interval data which is linear [18, 40] and ideal for correlating against the ratio data from participants' OSIVQ scores. The Engagement item was developed from an item used in Robb et al [46] which was based on items in a questionnaire by Webster & Ho [65]. The Utility item was that used in Robb et al [46]. Each raw VAS item rating ranged from zero to the length of the scale in pixels [40]. To aid understanding the ratings were normalized 0 to 100 by dividing by the pixel length of the scale and multiplying by 100. These were analyzed as follows. Each participant viewed five designs. For each design they provided two VAS ratings (Engagement and Utility) for each of the three answer formats: AI, EI and text. During the first design participants were familiarized with the experiment application, including the rating items, in relation to all three response formats. These ratings while responding to the first design were discarded and were not analyzed. Thus, for example, for text-Utility a participant would have four VAS ratings in total to be analyzed. The median of those four was taken to represent that participant's overall VAS rating for text-Utility; likewise for the other two formats and similarly for the Engagement item.

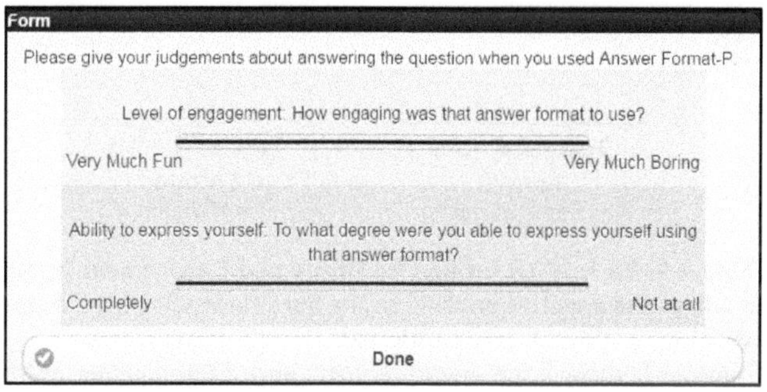

Figure 6. The rating items. On first click a 'draggable' cross appeared on the item scale. The answer formats were referred to by randomly chosen letters to avoid introducing preconceptions to the participants (e.g. *emotion images* were not called that during the task).

Post-Task Questionnaire

After finishing the feedback task the participants completed a questionnaire in which they were asked to rank the three answer formats (AI, EI and text) by overall preference. They were asked open questions as follows: *1) Please describe the reasons for the rankings you gave to the formats. 2) What do you think about using text to describe how the designs made you feel? 3) What do you think about using abstract images to describe how the designs made you feel? 4) What do you think about using emotion images to describe how the designs made you feel? 5) Please tell us anything else you feel is relevant about the idea of describing your emotions using images versus text. 6) Did you hold back (or consider holding back) from criticizing any designs in your responses to prevent hurting the designer's feelings? Whether or not you did, please comment about this stating which response format(s) you have in mind.* There was one closed question asking, "*For what other purposes do you think you would like to see image-based feedback as an option available for you to use?*" and giving a list of options including a negative option (detailed in Results). The questionnaire concluded with an open opportunity to comment. The open question responses were analyzed using a grounded theory approach with open, followed by axial coding [9, 53]. The open coding produced 73 codes in 22 categories during the first pass of the data. Overarching themes and subthemes were developed from this and, in a second pass, data was coded to these. There was a single coder (the lead author).

RESULTS FROM FEEDBACK TASK AND OSIVQ

In this section we report the results from the visual analogue scale (VAS) item ratings of the formats during the task and then correlations of those with the OSIVQ scores.

Utility and Engagement for the 50 Participants

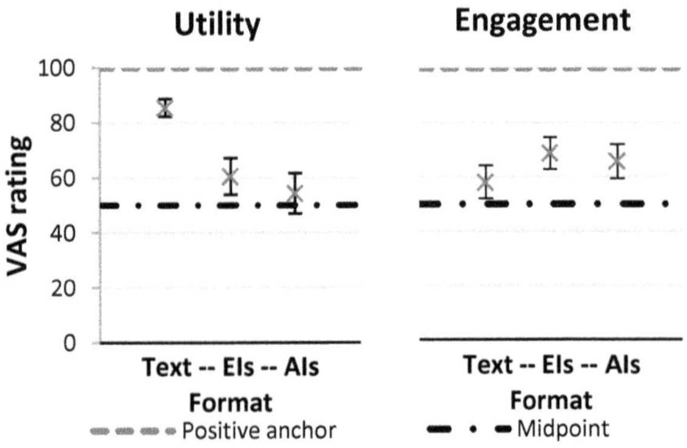

Figure 7. Mean VAS ratings for Utility and Engagement N=50. 0 marks the negative anchor. Error bars show 95% confidence intervals.

Figure 7 shows the mean *Utility* and *Engagement* VAS ratings for the 50 participants. It was clear from the chart for *Utility* that text was rated highest. For *Engagement,* emotion images (EI) appeared higher than text. VAS ratings are interval data, linear, and amenable to parametric tests [18]. A one-way repeated measures ANOVA was carried out on the *Engagement* scores. Greenhouse Geisser correction was used as sphericity was violated. *Engagement* was significantly affected by answer format, $F(1.54, 75.32) = 3.65$ $p<0.05$. However, post hoc tests using Bonferroni correction showed that, despite there being a statistical main effect of format on *Engagement* for the 3 formats (text, EI, and AI, M=58.0, M=68.6, and M=65.6 respectively), it was not possible to state which was statistically significantly greater than another at the 95% confidence level. However a difference was found when age was taken into account (see Age sub-section below).

Age

We split the participants into two groups at a point where there was a clear break in the ages and examined their ratings for *Engagement.* We took age groups 18 to 44 as the "Younger" group (N=28) and over-44s as the "Older" group (N=22). See Figure 8. (It happened that none were aged 40-44 so that is where we divided them giving two comparable sized groups and this was less arbitrary than splitting down the middle. We analyzed no other split.). It was clear from the chart that there was no difference between *Engagement* of the formats in the older group. A one way repeated measures ANOVA showed that *Engagement* in the younger group was significantly affected by the answer format, $F(2, 54) = 7.18$, $p < 0.05$. Post hoc tests using Bonferroni correction showed that, while there was no significant difference between *Engagement* for AI (M=67.3) and either EI (M=73.5) or text (M=53.2), *Engagement* for EI was significantly greater than for text in the younger group.

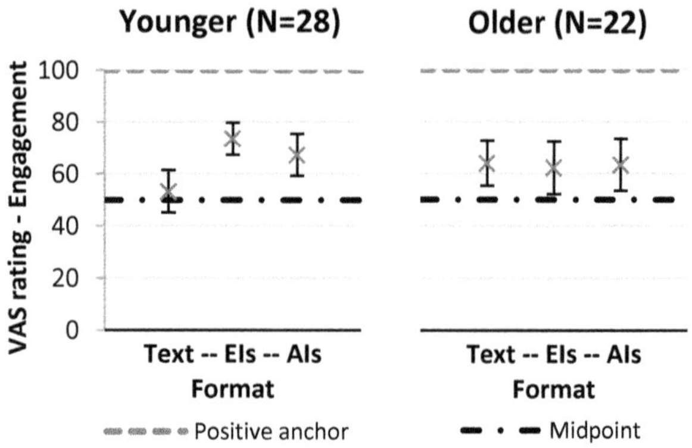

Figure 8. Mean VAS ratings for *Engagement* in younger and older groups. 0 marks the negative anchor. Error bars show 95% confidence intervals.

Correlation Analysis of Ratings with Cognitive Styles

It is a fundamental aspect of the monopolar dimensional model of visual and verbal cognitive styles that a person can be, for example, high on the verbal subscale and also high on the object imagery subscale. To gauge the degree to which a participant is more object visual than verbal we subtracted their verbal score (Vrb) from their object score (Obj) giving us the difference between their object and verbal scores (ObjVrbDif). We did the same with their spatial (Spt) and verbal scores obtaining their SptVrbDif. For these differences a low value indicated a participant more verbal than visual while a high value indicated one more visual than verbal. Paralleling this in the VAS ratings, we subtracted each participant's rating of *Engagement* for text from their rating of *Engagement* for EI (and similarly for AI) to gauge the degree to which they found EI (or AI) more engaging than text. The same was done with the *Utility* ratings. As we had earlier found a difference between ratings for *Engagement* between two age groups (Figure 8) we looked for a correlation between participants' age and ObjVrbDif. There was a significant negative correlation, $r = -.38$, $p < .01$(two tailed), meaning that, in our sample, the older the participant, the less object visual and more verbal they were likely to be. (There was no significant correlation between age and SptVrbDif.) In view of this when calculating correlations involving ObjVrbDif we controlled for age by using partial correlation [13]. Table 1 sets out these correlations. What

Table 1 shows is that when both *Engagement* and *Utility* VAS ratings for text were subtracted from those for the emotion images (EI) significant positive correlations existed with participants' ObjVrbDif (controlling for age). This means that the greater the degree to which a participant was more object visual than verbal in cognitive style the more likely it would be that the difference between their ratings of emotion images and text (for both *Engagement* and *Utility*) would be larger. We did the same for SptVrbDif (without the need to control for age) and found this only correlated significantly with *Engagement*.

VAS Rating Differences	Partial Correlation v.s. ObjVrbDif (Controlling for Age)	
	r	*p* (two-tailed)
Engagement EI –Text	**.34**	**< .01**
Engagement AI –Text	.23	-
Utility EI –Text	**.31**	**< .05**
Utility AI –Text	.02	-
VAS Rating Differences	**Bivariate Correlation v.s. SptVrbDif**	
	r	*p* (two-tailed)
Engagement EI –Text	**.31**	**< .05**
Engagement AI –Text	.20	-
Utility EI –Text	.24	-
Utility AI –Text	.10	-

Table 1. Participant VAS ratings for text subtracted from those for image formats correlated v.s. their OSIVQ verbal subtracted from OSIVQ object scores (ObjVrbDif) and spatial scores (SptVrbDif). Significant correlations are in bold.

RESULTS FROM POST-TASK QUESTIONNAIRE

Below we report quantitative and qualitative findings from the post-task questionnaire.

Format Preference Rankings

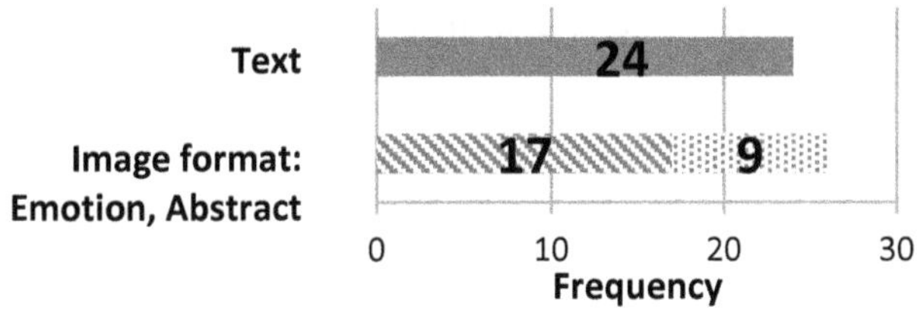

Figure 9. The frequency with which participants ranked each of the three formats top for overall preference.

Figure 9 shows the numbers of participants ranking a given format first for overall preference. Numbers preferring images (26 in total: 17, EI and 9, AI) and text (24) were roughly similar. While this is interesting, the reasons given by participants for the way they ranked the formats contribute enlightening insights in the themes below.

Themes from the Open Questions

Two overarching themes, *Engagement* and *Expression* arose from analysis of responses to the open questions and are described below.

Theme - Engagement

The abstract images engaged seven participants e.g. *"I have felt excited and interested in doing the evaluation this way"* [P3], *"...they were far more interesting to interact with. I also think some people will find it gamifies response and so might engage more deeply with it than words."* [P13]. For two their enjoyment of the abstract images was linked to the ability to express their feelings, e.g. *"I really enjoyed this. It was fun to see how much I was drawn to some over others and how satisfying it was to find one that fit how I felt. I might explore more abstract art now."* [P43]

The emotion image set was engaging for 15 e.g. *"Surprisingly easy and fun. [A] very interesting way to describe feelings"* [P32], "*It was fun to select emotion images, as many of them used facial expressions*" [P16], "*Fun and creative.*" [P38]. As with abstract images enjoyment was also linked to expression e.g. *"more exciting than just descriptions... and I liked exploring the images to find the right ones to use."* [P17].

Notably, no participant described text as being engaging or enjoyable despite equal opportunity to comment about text specifically. However, text was referred to negatively in terms of engagement by seven participants usually while linking this with expression e.g. "*Text box answers are boring and can become time consuming trying to describe how I felt*" [P15], and here although stating text was easy for expression it was still viewed negatively for engagement: *"[Text is] an, to me, easy way to express myself, though also boring."* [P19], *"Although I find the text option the least appealing, I do think I could describe how I felt about a design more accurately with the text option."* [P29].

These qualitative responses showed that many participants found the image formats enjoyable and for several their enjoyment was closely linked with the satisfaction of being able to express their emotions this way. No participants viewed text as engaging and some commented negatively about the engagement of text.

Theme – Expression

This theme was divided into a number of sub-themes.

Sub-Theme – Ease of Expression

23 participants expressed the view that text was an easy way to express how they felt, e.g. *"Text seemed much easier and quicker than trying to relate to an image to express an opinion."* [P45], *"... text is my comfort zone"* [P39], and *"I was able to immediately and easily find words to describe my feelings about the designs, but often struggled to find images which reflected my feelings about them"* [P37].

15 participants found the emotion images easy to use, e.g. *"I found this the easiest to do."* [P26], "*I enjoyed it - the images were nicely varied, and helped convey feeling and emotion well*" [P36], "*It was fun, and summarized the feelings more quickly than a text description would.*" [P43],

and "*I liked this because for me I find it easy to look at someone and think yeah you look exactly how I feel*" [P50]. Some did wish for more choice in the emotion images e.g. "*it was sometimes difficult to find a face/scene that conveyed my exact response, so I would have to settle for one that was closest*" [P20].

The abstract images were found to be problematic by 16 e.g. "*[These were] really hard, I couldn't 'match' the images to my feelings very well*" [P32], and "*[I was] frustrated. Some feelings [were] not in abstracts.*" [P47].

Sub-Theme – Clarity of Text

Text was pointed out as allowing clarity and precision by 17, e.g. "*[With text] Mostly, I felt I could pinpoint exactly what I thought and how I felt.*" [P46], "*Text allows a more accurate and succinct method of conveying feedback.*" [P45]. It was also pointed out, however, that vocabulary can be limiting e.g. "*Expressing emotions through text needs good vocabulary and a shared understanding of what that vocabulary actually means*" [P13].

Sub-Theme – Ambiguity of Images

The ambiguity of images was expressed as both a positive and a negative. Participants who appreciated the clarity of text thought the vagueness of images was a disadvantage e.g. "*You could pick images that expressed your own emotions but this still lacked the precision of language.*" [P10]. Conversely ambiguity was also seen as useful e.g. "*I felt that the Emotion images were a really good way of encapsulating how I felt about the designs, because much of the ambiguity in my response could be captured, in a way that can be missing when words are stripped of tone and context.*" [P41].

Sub-Theme – Images Worked Well for Emotions

18 participants expressed this theme in relation to the emotion images. e.g. "*[I] found it easier to ascribe my feelings to the emotion images especially those with faces or natural views*" [P1], and "*The emotion images felt like a truly efficient way of expressing how I felt about the design. I really enjoyed selecting a facial expression to match my emotion which I felt further helped me think of why I felt that way about the design.*" [P2]. Three stated abstract images were better for emotion expression, e.g. "*I preferred the abstract [images] the most, as it was easier to summarize an overall feeling*" [P43].

Sub-Theme – Freedom of Images

10 participants felt that images liberated them from language: "*Text is limited by my language and experience. Images give more freedom but I felt I needed familiar parameters so faces were easier than totally abstract.*" [P4] and about abstract images in particular: "*I think it allows you to have some freedom of thought, the abstract images can mean different things for different people and lets freedom of expression come through*" [P44]. In addition (for 6 participants) images, particularly the abstract images, were seen as requiring less consideration of the designers' feelings than text when offering criticism, e.g. "*[I] considered it, especially with the text format, but tried to be honest without being mean.*" [P47].

Sub-Theme – Communicating With Another Person

Four participants were explicit about considering how someone would understand what they were trying to communicate. e.g. "*The emotion images were by far the best way of expressing my emotional response to the designs. This wasn't because they were all a literal representation of my response but because I felt that the pictures had a shared understanding between myself and those looking at the results. I felt it more likely that my intention would be understood.*" [P38], and "*The abstract images could be interpreted in many different ways, and so I found it much more difficult to choose images that accurately reflected how I felt, and I worried that my answers would be likely to be misinterpreted*" [P41].

The *expression* theme showed that for many text offered clarity and was seen as an easy format to use. Finding images (particularly abstract images) to match emotions was problematic for some. For those who appreciated the precision of text, the ambiguity of images led to concern about misinterpretation. On the other hand images, particularly those from the emotion image browser, were seen as easy to use. Ascribing emotions to selections from the faces, people, and landscapes from that browser was often found to work well. Ambiguity in images was seen by some as a useful aspect of their responses. Some also appreciated the freedom from language that is afforded by images.

Use Beyond Interior Design Feedback

Participants were asked "For what other purposes do you think you would like to see image-based feedback as an option available for you to use?" and given a list of options. 15 participants chose the option, "I do not think image-based feedback should be an option for any other purpose". 35 chose at least one additional suggested purpose or specified another purpose of their own including: "*Product reviews, such as books, films*" [P19], and "*in response to TV or paper based advertising*" [P40]. Figure 10 shows the frequency with which options suggested in the question were chosen. The implications of this are examined in Discussion.

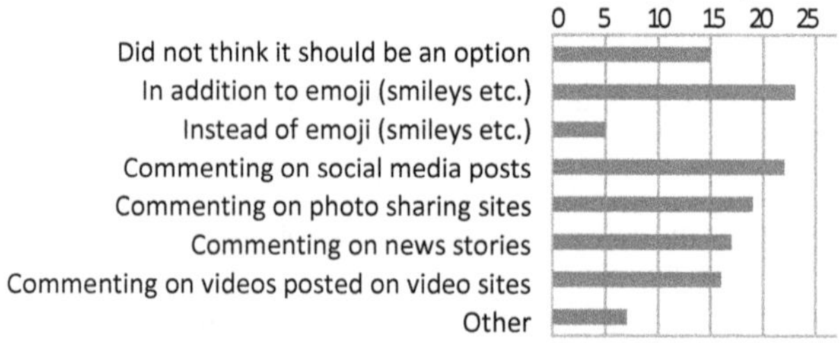

Figure 10. Suggested uses of image-based feedback. The bar chart shows the frequency with which participants chose the negative option or the additional suggested purposes.

DISCUSSION

Below we revisit the research questions posed in the study aims before widening the discussion. First we address RQs 1 and 3 and discuss cross cutting findings. Then we summarize findings for RQ2 and RQ4 before opening out our discussion to integrate the findings into the implications for the future of the IEFM and use of images for emotion feedback more generally.

RQ1 and RQ3

First we summarize the findings on the two questions and then we discuss the connection between them in our results.

RQ1 - Do feedback-givers find image feedback formats more engaging or less engaging than text?

In our sample, younger users (18-44yrs) found the emotion images significantly more engaging than text, whereas older users (over 44s) reported no significant difference in engagement. (Figure 8). See also RQ3.

RQ3 - Are cognitive styles a factor in feedback-givers' experience of different feedback formats?

Yes. a) For both engagement and utility the difference between participants' *object* and *verbal* style scores correlates significantly with the difference between their ratings for emotion images and text. b) Only for engagement (and not utility) did the difference between participants' *spatial* and verbal styles correlate significantly with the difference between their ratings of emotion images and text. (Table 1).

Age, Cognitive Styles and Generalizing Beyond Our Sample

Observing a correlation between age and OSIVQ object score in our sample raises a question over its representativeness. Riding [43] states that no significant correlation between age and cognitive style was observed. It is possible that the older participants in our sample could have non-typical OSIVQ scores and this might be contributing to our finding that younger participants are more likely to find images more engaging than older participants. i.e. the effects on engagement we observed due to age and cognitive style may just be down to the cognitive styles effect. To establish this definitively, a study with a larger sample, constructed using purposeful sampling beyond age and gender to include other demographic characteristics would be needed. Having said that, the partial correlations controlling for age did show that *even after taking age into account, cognitive styles were still a factor in the engagement ratings of image-based feedback compared to text.* (Table 1). This gives us confidence that it is safe to generalize about that finding beyond our sample.

RQ2 and RQ4

The findings directly relating to these two questions are briefly summarized here.

RQ2 - Do feedback-givers feel able to express their emotions using the image feedback formats?

On the whole participants reported while giving the feedback, that they were better able to express themselves using text. However, views in the questionnaire revealed this issue was more nuanced as described below.

RQ4 - Do feedback-givers prefer using images or text when describing their emotions and what is their reasoning for this?

In our sample approximately half (26/50) preferred images for this while the remainder preferred text.

The reasons participants gave for the preferences, set out in the themes from the questionnaire, were varied. In the sub-sections below, the different views expressed are integrated along with the other results into the discussion of the main implications arising out of the study.

Implications

Feedback-givers Valuing Engagement Over Clarity

Despite the reported superiority of text for clarity of expression, about half our sample still preferred image-based feedback over text. We interpret this as participants often valuing engagement over clarity. Does this mean that the IEFM might attract more but meaningless feedback for designers? We think that three issues come forward here. Firstly, the inspirational value of the visual feedback to designers will not depend on the exact communication of a specific message. According to Jakobsen's model of communication [19] a message can have its own inherent artistic quality. The fact that designers shown image-based feedback by Robb et al. [47] were inspired to make changes but were not so inspired by text feedback bears this out. Secondly, if designers can build a following by engaging people in feedback, the content of each message in the conversation need not be crucial. Again this reflects another aspect of the Jakobsen model i.e. the simple act of continuing the conversation in itself has value. In short, "it's good to talk". Thirdly, the idea that using images gives rise to inherently inaccurate feedback is countered by the popular sub-theme from the study that the emotion images were, in fact, good for expressing emotions. This included that ambiguity could be a desirable part of the feedback. The different qualities of the image feedback in regard to softening negative criticism compared to text were exposed particularly with regard to the abstract images. With the abstract image feedback, designers would have the opportunity of taking inspiration from feedback while avoiding the downsides of harsh criticism. Interestingly Emoji are also prone to ambiguity due to varying interpretations by users but also by variations in graphical rendering of Emoji characters [10, 30]. Emoji users, it seems, tolerate ambiguity; or at least those who are aware of it do. Perhaps some peoples' desire to express their emotions is greater than their desire to be fully understood?

Individual Differences

It is clear that a substantial proportion of internet users would prefer to use images rather than text when asked to express their emotional reactions. Equally, some prefer using text to express emotions but of course those users are already well catered for, and techniques such as text mining and topic modelling do exist for summarizing text. We have shown that important factors behind these preferences are individual differences including cognitive styles. The individuals expressing the preferences, although able to describe why they think they hold a given preference, also are behaving, in part at least, in line with deep individual characteristics. These may even go as deep as aspects of their neural anatomy and development [6]. The humble textbox in comment forums offers free rein to those who are more verbal than visual. The IEFM offers an alternative format, engaging, empowering, and embracing the strengths of users who are more visual than they are verbal.

A Summarizable Channel for Those More Visual than Verbal

Given that people's emotional reaction to potential products, services, or ideas is valuable information for their originators [26, 58], a channel encouraging the inclusion of input from people who are more visual than verbal in cognitive style is likely to be a benefit. The summarizable image-based emotion feedback method can fulfill this role. Its deployment alongside text-based feedback methods can serve to increase the overall amount of feedback available to designers by adding this new image-based strand.

Application Beyond Design Feedback

The 15 participants who did not wish image-based feedback as an option represent those users to whom using images this way clearly does not appeal. However, a majority of the participants could see that image-based emotion feedback would be useful outside design feedback and indeed would like to see that as an option. 23 wished to see it offered in addition to emoji, while five indicated they thought image-based feedback could be used instead of emoji. This implies that those participants see image-based feedback using browsers such as those in this study as possibly becoming a mainstream response option. The two participants who suggested it could be used for product reviews were indicating just the type of use that would exploit the capability of image selections from the IEFM browsers to be summarized. Large amounts of buyer feedback could be presented as a concise at-a-glance montage of images summarizing what users felt about a product. One notable aspect of the image banks for the IEFM is that they are controlled, unlike the user-sourced images in some comment forums which can require moderation when users post inappropriate content. The IEFM image banks might be useful as a comment medium outside design feedback resulting in a reduction in the moderation effort normally associated with allowing images in comments.

CONCLUSION

In order to find out whether and why image-based emotion feedback would be engaging for feedback givers we carried out a mixed methods study with 50 internet users from 19 to 77 years of age. Participants rated three feedback formats (abstract images, emotion images and text) for *engagement* and *utility*. We measured participants' cognitive styles. This allowed us to establish the degree to which each participant was more *object-visual* and *spatial-visual* than *verbal*. Significant correlations revealed participants more visual (both *object* and *spatial*) than they are verbal gave higher *engagement* ratings for emotion images relative to text. Those more verbal than they are visual gave lower ratings relative to text. Participants more *object-visual* than verbal also gave higher *utility* ratings for emotion images relative to text (and those more verbal than *object-visual* gave lower utility ratings relative to text). Overall text was rated best for utility (the clarity with which participants reported they were able to express their emotions). Additionally, we found that under-45s reported emotion images as being significantly more engaging than text but we remain cautious about generalizing beyond our sample about this particular age finding without further work.

Qualitative insights gathered from the participants showed that a substantial proportion (half in our sample) preferred one of the image formats over using text for expressing their emotions. It was common for engagement to be valued over clarity of expression. These expressed preferences, influenced by individual differences in cognitive styles, were accompanied by often cogent and revealing opinions of why images on the one hand, or text on the other, were good for expressing emotions. In cases where images were preferred reasons given included seeing ambiguity as an advantage (in that it can aid an ambiguous response) and seeing the selecting of images to represent feelings as being easier than trying to put their feelings into words.

As to which type of images (*abstract* or *emotion*) were preferred overall, considering all the evidence together, we conclude that while the *abstract* images do hold appeal for those who are particularly object-visual, it is the *emotion* images (faces, people in situations, and natural views) that resonate more with internet users the more visual they are than verbal (both object- and spatial-visual).

The qualitative data also showed that people (35/50 in our sample) wish to see image-based emotion feedback available as an option, for example, in comment forums for product reviews or for video posting sites. It was also seen as a useful addition alongside emoji and emoticons.

This style of image-based emotion feedback is designed to be summarized into a single montage of representative images making it useful for gathering and visualizing large volumes of impressionistic user feedback without the burden of content moderation. Our study shows that users who are more visual than verbal, giving feedback using this method, enjoy it and think it would be useful beyond interior design feedback.

ACKNOWLEDGMENTS

This work was assisted by Heriot-Watt University's CDI theme and EPSRC grant EP/L012626/1. Research data available in HWU repository (CC-BY). We gratefully thank Profs. Pat Thomas and Larry Katz for their correspondence on cognitive styles instruments. Creative Commons browser images are acknowledged here: bit.ly/tlab-ack.

REFERENCES

1. Chris Andrzejczak and Dahai Liu. 2010. The effect of testing location on usability testing performance, participant stress levels, and subjective testing experience. *Journal of Systems and Software*, 83(7), 1258-1266.
2. Alessandro Antonietti and Marisa Giorgetti. 1998. The verbalizer-visualizer questionnaire: A review. *Perceptual and Motor Skills*, 86(1), 227-239.
3. Ann Austin and Jose Abdelnour Nocera. 2015. So, Who Exactly IS The HCI Professional? In *Proceedings of the 33rd Annual ACM Conference Extended Abstracts on Human Factors in Computing Systems* (CHI'15), 1037-1042. http://dx.doi.org/10.1145/2702613.2732906
4. Pascal Belin, Sarah Fillion-Bilodeau and Frédéric Gosselin. 2008. The Montreal Affective Voices: A validated set of nonverbal affect bursts for research on auditory affective processing. *Behavior Research Methods*, 40(2), 531-539. http://dx.doi.org/10.3758/BRM.40.2.531
5. Olesya Blazhenkova and Maria Kozhevnikov. 2009. The new object-spatial-verbal cognitive style model: Theory and measurement. *Applied Cognitive Psychology*, 23(5), 638-663.
6. Olesya Blazhenkova, Maria Kozhevnikov and Michael A. Motes, 2006. Object-spatial imagery: a new self-report imagery questionnaire. *Applied Cognitive Psychology*, 20(2), 239-263.
7. Terry L. Childers, Michael J. Houston and Susan E. Heckler. 1985. Measurement of individual differences in visual versus verbal information processing. *Journal of Consumer Research*, 125-134.
8. Eric Cook, Stephanie D. Teasley, and Mark S. Ackerman. 2009. Contribution, commercialization & audience: *understanding* participation in an online creative community. In *Proceedings of the ACM Conference on Supporting Group Work (Group'09)*, 41-50. http://dx.doi.org/10.1145/1531674.1531681
9. Juliet Corbin and Anselm Strauss. 2008. *Basics of qualitative research: Techniques and procedures for developing grounded theory*, Sage.
10. Henriette Cramer, Paloma de Juan, Joel Tetreault. 2016. Sender-intended Functions of Emojis in US Messaging. In *Proceedings of the 18th International Conference on Human-Computer Interaction with Mobile Devices and Services (MobileHCI'16),* 504-509. http://dx.doi.org/10.1145/2935334.2935370
11. Steven Dow, Elizabeth Gerber, and Audris Wong. 2013. A pilot study of using crowds in the classroom. In *Proceedings of the ACM Conference on Human Factors in Computing Systems (CHI'13)*, 227-236. http://dx.doi.org/10.1145/2470654.2470686
12. Dribbble https://dribbble.com/ (Last accessed 16/1/2017)
13. Andy Field. 2009. *Discovering Statistics Using SPSS (3rd ed.)*. Sage.
14. Sarah Gallacher, Jenny O'Connor, Jon Bird, Yvonne Rogers, Licia Capra, Daniel Harrison, and Paul Marshall. 2015. Mood Squeezer: Lightening up the Workplace through Playful and Lightweight Interactions. In *Proceedings of the 18th ACM Conference on Computer Supported Cooperative Work and Social Computing (CSCW'15),* 891-902, http://dx.doi.org/10.1145/2675133.2675170
15. Francis Galton. 1883. *Inquiries into the human faculty & its development.* JM Dent and Company.
16. Steve Garner and Deana McDonagh-Philp. 2001. Problem interpretation and resolution via visual stimuli: the use of 'mood boards' in design education. *J Art Design Educ*, 20(1), Blackwell, 57-64
17. Erhan S. Haciomeroglu 2016. Object-spatial Visualization and Verbal Cognitive Styles, and Their Relation to Cognitive Abilities and Mathematical Performance. *Educational Sciences: Theory & Practice*, 16(3), 987-1003.
18. Joeri Hofmans and Peter Theuns. 2008. On the linearity of predefined and self-anchoring Visual Analogue Scales. *Br J Math Stat Psychol.*, 61(Pt 2).
19. Roman Jakobson. 1960. Closing statement: Linguistics and poetics. *Style in language*, 350, 377.
20. Markus Junghöfer, Margaret M. Bradley, Thomas R. Elbert, and Peter J. Lang 2001. Fleeting images: A new look at early emotion discrimination. *Psychophysiology*, 38(2), Cambridge Univ Press, 175-178.
21. Nancy H. Kerr, David Foulkes and Marcella Schmidt. 1982. The structure of laboratory dream reports in blind and sighted subjects. *The Journal of nervous and mental disease*, 170(5), 286-294.
22. John R. Kirby, Phillip J. Moore and Neville J. Schofield. 1988. Verbal and visual learning styles. *Contemporary educational psychology*, 13(2), 169-184.
23. Maria Kozhevnikov, Mary Hegarty and Richard E. Mayer. 2002. Revising the visualizer-verbalizer dimension: Evidence for two types of visualizers. *Cognition and Instruction*, 20(1), 47-77.
24. Maria Kozhevnikov, Stephen Kosslyn and Jennifer Shephard. 2005. Spatial versus object visualizers: A new characterization of visual cognitive style. *Memory & cognition*, 33(4), 710-726.
25. Peter J. Lang, and Margaret M. Bradley. 2007. The International Affective Picture System (IAPS) in the study of emotion and attention. *Handbook of emotion elicitation and assessment*, 29.

26. Jennifer S. Lerner, Deborah A. Small, and George Loewenstein. 2004. Research Report Heart Strings and Purse Strings Carryover Effects of Emotions on Economic Decisions. *Psychological Science*, 15(5), APS, 337-341
27. Kurt Luther, Amy Pavel, Wei Wu, Jari-lee Tolentino, Maneesh Agrawala, Björn Hartmann, and Steven P Dow. 2014. CrowdCrit: crowdsourcing and aggregating visual design critique. In *Proceedings of the ACM Conference on Computer Supported Cooperative Work & Social Computing (CSCW'14)*, 21-24. http://dx.doi.org/10.1145/2556420.2556788
28. Andrew L. Mendelson and Esther Thorso. 2004. How verbalizers and visualizers process the newspaper environment. *Journal of Communication*, 54(3), 474-491.
29. Joseph A. Mikels, Barbara L. Fredrickson, Gregory R Larkin, Casey M Lindberg, Sam J Maglio, and Patricia A Reuter-Lorenz. 2005. Emotional category data on images from the International Affective Picture System. *Behav Res Methods*, 37(4), 626-630.
30. Hannah Miller, Jacob Thebault-Spieker, Shuo Chang, Isaac Johnson, Loren Terveen, and Brent Hecht. 2016. "Blissfully Happy" or "Ready to Fight": Varying Interpretations of Emoji. In *Proceedings of the 10th International Conference on Web and Social Media, (ICWSM '16).*
31. Don Norman. 2002. Emotion & Design: Attractive Things Work Better. *Interactions*, 9(4), 36-42. http://dx.doi.org/10.1145/543434.543435
32. Donald A. Norman. 2005. *Emotional Design: Why We Love (or Hate) Everyday Things*: Basic books.
33. Valeria Occelli, Jonathan B. Lin, Simon Lacey and K. Sathian. 2013 Spatial imagery and cognitive style in blind individuals. *Multisensory Research*, 26(0), 186-186.
34. Stefano Padilla, Fraser Halley, David A. Robb, and Mike J. Chantler. 2013. Intuitive Large Image Database Browsing using Perceptual Similarity Enriched by Crowds. In *Proceedings of the 15th International Conference on Computer Analysis of Images and Patterns (CAIP'13)*, Springer, 169–176.
35. Allan Paivio and Richard Harshman. 1983. Factor analysis of a questionnaire on imagery and verbal habits and skills. *Canadian Journal of Psychology.* 37(4), 461.
36. Sébastien Paquette, Isabelle Peretz, Pascal Belin. 2013. The "Musical Emotional Bursts": a validated set of musical affect bursts to investigate auditory affective processing. *Frontiers in Psychology*, 4(509). http://dx.doi.org/10.3389/fpsyg.2013.00509
37. Michael Q. Patton. (1990). *Qualitative evaluation and research methods*. Sage.
38. Rosalind W. Picard. 1997. *Affective Computing*, MIT press Cambridge, Mass., USA.
39. Robert Plutchik. 2003. *Emotions and life : perspectives from psychology, biology, and evolution*, APA.
40. Ulf-Dietrich Reips, and Frederik Funke 2008. Interval-level measurement with visual analogue scales in Internet-based research: VAS Generator. *Behav Res Methods*, 40(3), 699-704.
41. Ali Reza Rezaei and Larry Katz. 2004. Evaluation of the reliability and validity of the cognitive styles analysis. *Personality and Individual Differences*, 36(6), 1317-1327. http://dx.doi.org/10.1016/S0191-8869(03)00219-8
42. Alan Richardson. 1977. Verbalizer-visualizer: A cognitive style dimension. *Journal of mental imagery.* 1(1), 109-125.
43. Richard J. Riding. 1997. On the nature of cognitive style. *Educational Psychology*, 17(1-2), 29-49.
44. Richard J. Riding and Indra Cheema. 1991. Cognitive Styles - an overview and integration. *Educational Psychology*, 11(3-4), Routledge, 193-215.
45. Richard Riding and Eugene Sadler-Smith. 1992. Type of instructional material, cognitive style and learning performance. *Educational Studies*, 18(3), 323-340.
46. David A. Robb, Stefano Padilla, Britta Kalkreuter, and Mike J. Chantler. 2015. Moodsource: Enabling Perceptual and Emotional Feedback from Crowds. In *Proceedings of the ACM Conference* Companion *on Computer Supported Cooperative Work & Social Computing (CSCW'15)*, 21-24. http://dx.doi.org/10.1145/2685553.2702676
47. David A. Robb, Stefano Padilla, Britta Kalkreuter, and Mike J. Chantler. 2015. Crowdsourced Feedback With Imagery Rather Than Text: Would Designers Use It? In *Proceedings of the ACM Conference on Human Factors in Computing Systems (CHI'15),* 1355-1364. http://dx.doi.org/10.1145/2702123.2702470
48. David A. Robb, Stefano Padilla, Thomas S. Methven, Britta Kalkreuter, and Mike J. Chantler. 2016. A Picture Paints a Thousand Words but Can it Paint Just One? In *Proceedings of the ACM Conference on Designing Interactive Systems (DIS'16),* 959-970. http://dx.doi.org/10.1145/2901790.2901791
49. Eugene Sadler-Smith. 2001. The relationship between learning style and cognitive style. *Personality and individual differences*, 30(4), 609-616.
50. Katri Salminen, Veikko Surakka, Jukka Raisamo, Jani,Lylykangas, Johannes Pystynen, Roope Raisamo, Teemu Ahmaniemi. 2011. Emotional responses to thermal stimuli. In *Proceedings of the 13th ACM International Conference on Multimodal Interfaces (ICMI'11)*, 193-196. http://dx.doi.org/10.1145/2070481.2070513

51. Katri Salminen, Veikko Surakka, Jukka Raisamo, Jani,Lylykangas, Roope Raisamo, Kalle Mäkelä and Teemu Ahmaniemi. 2013. Cold or Hot? How Thermal Stimuli Are Related to Human Emotional System? In I. Oakley & S. Brewster (Eds.), *Haptic and Audio Interaction Design: 8th International Workshop, (HAID'13)*, Springer, 20-29.
52. Marc Schröder. 2003. Experimental study of affect bursts. *Speech Communication*, 40(1–2), 99-116. http://dx.doi.org/10.1016/S0167-6393(02)00078-X
53. Anselm L. Strauss. 1987. *Qualitative analysis for social scientist,* Cambridge University Press.
54. Paul Strohmeier, Juan Pablo Carrascal, Bernard Cheng, Margaret Meban and Roel Vertegaal. 2016. An Evaluation of Shape Changes for Conveying Emotions. In *Proceedings of the ACM CHI Conference on Human Factors in Computing Systems (CHI'16),* 3781-3792. http://dx.doi.org/10.1145/2858036.2858537
55. Petra Sundstrom, Anna Stahl and Kristina Hook. 2005. eMoto: Affectively Involving Both Body and Mind. In *Extended Abstracts on Human Factors in Computing Systems (CHI '05)*, 2005-2008, http://dx.doi.org/10.1145/1056808.1057078
56. James Surowiecki. 2004. *The wisdom of crowds: why the many are smarter than the few and how collective wisdom shapes business, Economies, Societies and Nations.* Anchor.
57. Patrick R.Thomas, and Jacinta B. McKay. 2010. Cognitive styles and instructional design in university learning. *Learning and Individual Differences*, 20(3), 197-202.
58. Larissa Z. Tiedens, and Susan Linton. 2001. Judgment under emotional certainty and uncertainty: the effects of specific emotions on information processing. *Journal of Personality and Social Psychology*, 81(6), APA, 973.
59. Tom Tullis, Stan Fleischman, Michelle McNulty, Carrie Cianchette and Margaret Bergel. 2002. An empirical comparison of lab and remote usability testing of web sites. Paper presented at the *Usability Professionals Association Conference (UXPA2002)*.
60. UK Government. 2012. *Ethnicity and National Identity in England and Wales 2011.* Office for National Statistics.
61. UK Government. 2016. *Internet users in the UK: 2016, Statistical bulletin 20 May 2016.* Office for National Statistics.
62. UK Government. 2016. *Overview of the UK population: February 2016*. Office for National Statistics.
63. Johan H. J. Vesanto, Esa Alhoniemi and Juha Parhankangas. 1999. Self-organizing map in Matlab: the SOM toolbox. *Procedings of the Matlab DSP Conference*, 35–40.
64. Rick S. Warren and Glenn Good. 1979. The verbalizer-visualizer questionnaire: Further normative data. *Perceptual and Motor Skills*, 48(2), 372-372.
65. Jane Webster and Hayes Ho. 1997. Audience engagement in multimedia presentations. *SIGMIS Database: the DATABASE for Advances in Information Systems*, 28(2), ACM, 63-77. http://dx.doi.org/10.1145/264701.264706
66. Tom Wengraf. 2001. Qualitative research interviewing: *Biographic narrative and semi-structured methods,* Sage.
67. Graham Wilson, Dobromir Dobrev and Stephen A. Brewster, 2016. Hot Under the Collar: Mapping Thermal Feedback to Dimensional Models of Emotion. In *Proceedings of the ACM CHI Conference on Human Factors in Computing Systems (CHI'16),* 4838-4849. http://dx.doi.org/10.1145/2858036.2858205
68. Graham Wilson, Pietro Romeo, and Stephen A. Brewster. 2016. Mapping Abstract Visual Feedback to a Dimensional Model of Emotion. In *Proceedings of the ACM CHI Conference Extended Abstracts on Human Factors in Computing Systems (CHI EA'16)*, 1779-1787. http://dx.doi.org/10.1145/2851581.2892320
69. Anbang Xu, Shih-Wen Huang, and Brian P Bailey. 2014. Voyant: Generating Structured Feedback on Visual Designs Using a Crowd of Non-Experts. In *Proceedings of the ACM Conference on Computer Supported Cooperative Work & Social Computing (CSCW'14)*, 37-40. http://dx.doi.org/10.1145/2531602.2531604
70. Anbang Xu, Huaming Rao, Steven Dow, and Brian P. Bailey. 2015. A Classroom Study of Using Crowd Feedback in the Iterative Design Process. In *Proceedings of the ACM Conference on Computer Supported Cooperative Work & Social Computing (CSCW'15),* 1637-1648. http://dx.doi.org/10.1145/2675133.2675140

Designing for Self-Tracking of Emotion and Experience with Tangible Modality

Kwangyoung Lee, Hwajung Hong
School of Creative Design Engineering, UNIST
Ulsan, Republic of Korea
{dlight, hwajung}@unist.ac.kr

ABSTRACT
Self-tracking technologies have been developed to understand the self. Emotions are critical to understanding one's daily life; however, tracking the emotion is challenging due to the implicit form of data. In this paper, we introduce MindTracker, an approach for tracking emotion through a tangible interaction with plasticine clay. We explored the benefits and challenges of MindTracker via a two-week data collection study with 16 college students as well as via interviews with three clinical mental health experts. MindTracker is designed for users to craft a form that represents emotion using clay and to describe the experience that evokes the emotion using a diary. We found that the tangible modality of MindTracker motivated the participants to express various aspects of emotions. In addition, MindTracker's data collection and reflection process could have therapeutic properties, such as expressive therapy, self-soothing, and emotional self-regulation. We conclude this paper by discussing the design features of emotion-tracking tools and opportunities to use MindTracker to promote mental health.

Author Keywords
Self-tracking, emotion, mental health, MindTracker

ACM Classification Keywords
H.5.m. Information interfaces and presentation (e.g., HCI).

INTRODUCTION
Self-tracking tools ranging from diaries to wearable trackers have impacted the process of collecting and reflecting on personal information. The purpose of self-tracking is to gain self-knowledge through the reflection of gathered information [15]. The advent of self-tracking tools has allowed people to both automatically or manually log various aspects of their daily lives to improve their health and well-being [10]. Self-tracking tools produces a variety of personal health information, ranging from automated recorded fitness activities collected through embedded sensors (e.g., a pedometer, an accelerometer, or a GPS) to user-generated food and medication logs.

DIS 2017, June 10-14, 2017, Edinburgh, United Kingdom
© 2017 ACM. ISBN 978-1-4503-4922-2/17/06...$15.00
DOI: http://dx.doi.org/10.1145/3064663.3064697

Previous personal health informatics research has predominantly focused on physical activities that are often represented as explicit forms of data (e.g., steps counted, running distance, or calories burned). While there has been significant investment in self-tracking of physical activities, little is known about the methods for tracking one's emotional states (e.g., mood, stress, or depression), which are ambiguous but critical to understanding mental health. In this regard, we seek a deeper understanding of what an "emotion tracker" might be like. Research in this area is still new, with current technologies primarily targeted at assessing a person's mental health state using physiological parameters such as voice [16], or self-reported mood scale [17]. However, these deterministic and diagnostic tracking trends, in turn, reduce individuals' engagement with the data collection as well as self-reflection [21]. In this paper, we seek to design new ways of self-tracking technology that can engage users in the process of emotional data collection and reflection to better support mental well-being. To this end, we proposed to embed tangible modality—a mode that allows users to track their emotion through tangibly crafting an artifact—into the process of emotion tracking.

We begin by providing background on self-tracking practices for emotions. Also, we discuss the relation between form and emotion as well as the potential of tangible modality to express one's emotions. We then propose MindTracker, an approach to expressing invisible emotions by crafting a tangible clay form that represents one's state of mind. Focusing on college students' mental well-being, we examined the benefits and challenges of emotion data collection and reflection via MindTracker with 16 students and three mental health professionals. Our findings indicate that the novel data-creation method with tangible interaction engaged our participants in the activity of data collection and reflection, Meanwhile, our tracking approach provided therapeutic interventions such as expressive therapy and emotional self-regulation. Building upon these findings, we identify design properties of new types of emotion data tracking techniques as well as further design opportunities to employ the emotion tracking technique in a broad context—mental healthcare.

The contributions of this work include:

- The development of a novel emotion-tracking approach that adds a tangible modality to the data-collection process.
- An empirical study to validate the concept of MindTracker from the perspectives of students and experts.
- The identification of design features of emotion-tracking tools in general and opportunities for the use of MindTracker to promote mental health in a clinical setting.

RELATED WORK

Self-Tracking and Mental Well-Being

Self-tracking including sensing and tracking technologies has been widely developed with a desire of understanding oneself [7]. Many studies have been done in the fields of personal informatics and quantified self, to identify effective data-collection methods. Health-related self-tracking methods range from automated recording of physiological conditions to semi-automated or manual tracking [3]. Previous research in this area has predominantly focused on tracking physical activities. Understanding one's affective state, however, is as critical as understanding one's physical state for achieving in-depth understanding of oneself. Recent tendencies in health research represent the significance of mental well-being, especially dealing with depression, anxiety, and stress as the main topics [24]. For instance, Health Mashups [3] was built to integrate various sources of health and well-being data, including weight, sleep, step count, calendar data, location, weather, pain, food intake, and mood. The field study on Health Mashups revealed that contextual information supports data collection and reflection. The aforementioned mental health studies imply the importance of continuous monitoring of emotional states coupled with an individual's daily experience.

Approaches to Tracking Emotion

Recent efforts in HCI have emphasized tools to automatically monitor and assess a person's mental health state using physiological parameters (e.g., heartrate [18] voice [16], and face logging [25]). However, Rooksby et al [21] reported that such "diagnostic" data tend to be isolated from the lives that people lead. The tracking approach, in turn, reduces opportunities for proactive data collection and self-reflection. To address the remaining limitations in the traditional personal informatics model, researchers conceptualized personal tracking as "lived informatics" by highlighting the exploratory nature of data coupled with everyday life [9,10,21]. The playfulness of data creation is also considered a novel form of tracking. In this regard, our aim is to develop an approach that motivates people to engage with data creation and gain an understanding of data that are relevant to their emotional states.

A growing number of studies have highlighted that understanding the state of affect is necessary for mental well-being [2,3,16,24]. Affect is a broad range of feelings that people often experience in a form of emotions or moods. As defined by Santos et al [22], *emotions* are short-lived feelings that comes from contextual stimuli and can be mapped into diverse dimensions, while *moods* are longer lasting either positive or negative affect caused by unclear factors and that are comprised of multiple specific emotions. Self-reporting is a commonly used method of assessing the degree of affective state. One study monitored collective moods in workplaces to enhance managers' emotional intelligence through an interface for self-reporting [17]. Another study has investigated the self-assessment technique which is accessible via smart watch [11]. However, sustaining users' motivation to collect data is difficult with self-reporting, and it does not support users in expressing emotions that are ephemeral, subtle and subjective. There have been efforts to complement self-reporting by adopting technologies that automatically collect continuous emotional data [5,6,16] Although we can measure affective state and use the data for diagnostic approaches using these technologies, these technology-driven tracking approaches might reduce the chance of "exploration," which is a critical part of understanding oneself [21]. Enabling people to explore their emotions in a form of self-recognition and self-expression would significantly enhance their level of understanding about themselves. Thus, we propose that emotion tracking offers an invaluable opportunity to realize a more sophisticated form of self-understanding.

Emotion, Form, and Tangibility

In the domain of design research, a variety of work has linked visual dimensions of form to invisible properties such as emotion. To provide deeper understanding of the correlation between emotion and form, Isbister et al. created a set of biomorphic objects in clay (e.g., a bubbly form) that represent certain feelings such as happiness [12]. The participants of that study were asked to use the objects to express their emotions in the context of assessment and communication. Melcer et al. examined the embodiment of emotion in form and provided a taxonomy of affective dimensions of shape [20]. For example, sharp and spiky shapes convey frustration, while rounded shapes represent contentment. In this study, clay played a key for creative expression because it maintains fine-grained details of shape while it does not require highly skilled manipulation or tool use. This study reveals that expressing feelings with the objects increased engagement because doing so allowed for flexibility and tangibility—the sense of touch. Recent research has investigated the tangible modality as a tool for detecting stress via mindless gestural inputs such as squeezing, rocking, and rolling [1]. Tangible objects are also used to cope with stress [14] and increase mindfulness [23].

A conceptual breakthrough for MindTracker came during the ideation session, when we discovered the close relationship between emotion and form with tangibility described above.

To support the sophisticated form of self-understanding, we applied the properties of tangible modality to collect data about emotion. Existing self-tracking of one's mentality has largely depended on the self-reporting method, which has several limitations in producing a satisfactory outcome, as mentioned earlier. There have been subsequent attempts to track people's emotions in more indirect manners, but they do not seem to put much weight on physiological and behavioral sensing, which might isolate data from their context. Thus, we investigated ways of tracking and contextualizing emotions to improve mental health.

METHODS

In this section, we describe the process involved in the MindTracker study. We specify the design of the MindTracker Kit and the participation process. Then, we discuss the analysis process.

The Design of the MindTracker Kit

Our research goal was to design novel approaches for tracking emotion data. We began to imagine possible designs to make emotions visible. Specifically, we wanted to convert intangible forms of emotion into a tangible medium. Through our literature review, we realized that form creation with a flexible material such as clay would facilitate the realization of emotion. This initial insight led us to explore the opportunities of using tangible mobility to elicit and visualize emotion.

We propose the concept of a tool that allows people to log their emotions and experiences on a daily basis. Dubbed the MindTracker, this initial approach was intended to track emotions by having users keep reporting short-lasting feelings and emotion-provoking stimuli for a certain period. We designed a MindTracker study kit to investigate whether this approach is appropriate for documenting emotions, as presented in Figure 1. The MindTracker study consisted of three parts: (1) constructing a form of emotion with plasticine clay, (2) writing a detailed explanation about the form of emotion and the reason why the participant created it, and (3) charting the trend of emotion.

The MindTracker kit is simply composed of a box and a workbook. The box contained instructions informing the participant how to collect data, a chunk of plasticine clay, and a card for charting changes in the participant's mood over a two-week period. The workbook was designed for noting detailed descriptions of emotion to relate the actual meaning of the emotion to the clay forms. Specifically, the workbook provided a template for structured reporting. The template included a space for (a) placing a created clay form to take a picture, (b) naming a constructed form of emotion, (c) scoring the emotion on two scales (five-level) for positivity and negativity, respectively, and (d) describing the reasons or experiences that evoked the emotion. Using MindTracker in an empirical study, we sought to learn what emotions people decided to track, how they tracked the emotions, and how they perceived the logged data.

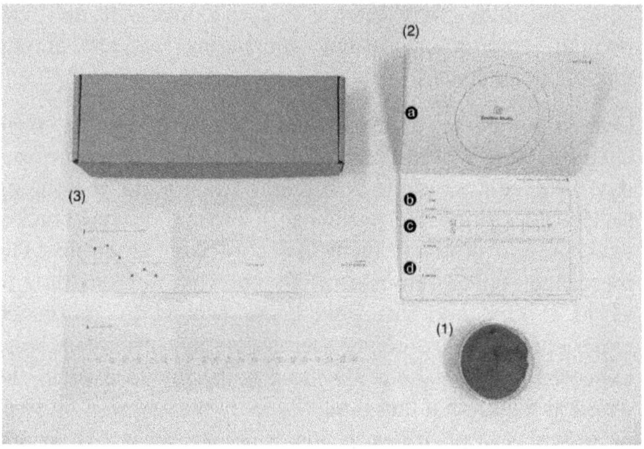

Figure 1. MindTracker Study Kit

The MindTracker Study

We conducted a two-week data collection study with 16 university students to understand their lived experience with MindTracker. At the end of the study, we conducted follow-up interviews with each participant to elicit feedback about MindTracker. To gain expert opinions about the validity of MindTracker, we organized a special focus group interview session with a psychiatrist, a clinical psychologist, and a counselor employed by a university healthcare center.

Recruitment

We wanted to explore the potential of MindTracker with people who have a need for tracking their emotions in their daily lives. Previous studies reported on the increasing mental health issues among young adults who are at risk for stress and academic pressure [19,26]. Thus, we decided to start with younger participants, such as college students, whose everyday lives are in some ways structured but also dynamic between studying and socializing.

The participants were recruited at a large university through flyers, word-of-mouth, and internal social media sites. While 22 students volunteered for the study at the initial screening phase, 16 (eight females and eight males, with a mean age of 23.1) finally confirmed their participation. Eight participants were undergraduate students, and the other eight students were graduate students. The participants had a variety of study majors, including Business, Chemistry, Design, Industrial Engineering, Material Science, and Physics. We launched a two-week study that included a week of final exams to introduce common variables that could incur emotion changes from students' day-to-day lives. For participating in the study, the participants were paid $50 for data collection with MindTracker during the two weeks and an additional $10 for participating in a follow-up interview.

Study Procedure

We held several informal meet-up sessions with participants just before starting the study to instruct them on how to collect data, what data to collect, and when to collect data. We then provided each participant with a MindTracker kit. To provide a prompt response to participants' questions about the study, we created a study account with the most popular smartphone instant messaging service among university students.

Over the course of two weeks, the participants were encouraged to record their emotions at least three times per day. We sent reminders through the mobile messaging service to remind the participants about the MindTracker study and to motivate them to record their emotions. The messenger sent a reminder at a somewhat random time to avoid similar emotions from being evoked by routinized experience. Upon receiving a reminder, the participants were expected to (1) make a 3D piece with clay to express the emotion they felt at that time, (2) score the emotion on five-point scales of positiveness and/or negativeness, (3) write a description of the clay piece in the notebook, and finally, (4) take a photo of the 3D clay piece and immediately send it to the study messenger account.

After the second week, each participant took part in a follow-up interview. The purpose of the follow-up interviews was to encourage the participants to reflect on their participation in the MindTracker study, expand on the context of specific clay pieces, and work through experiences pulled from the workbook. We asked them about their overall experience with MindTracker, the benefits of MindTracker for recording emotions, the practical and technical challenges of the study, and the effects of tracking their emotions for two weeks. The materials used during the follow-up interview included the pictures they sent and their workbooks. In this session, the participants also created a mood graph based upon the positive and negative scores they gave to each emotion.

Analysis

As a result of the MindTracker study, we collected a dataset of 616 forms of emotion with accompanying descriptions that contextualize each emotion. On average, each participant created 38.5 sets of emotion data over the two weeks (2.8 emotions per day), perhaps providing some evidence of their level of engagement in the MindTracker study. We discuss this theme in more detail in the next section. To ensure anonymity of the data, we eliminated any identifiable information from the raw data. We created a set of cards by translating handwritten scores and descriptions, which became our units of analysis. Each card contained a photo of a clay form, the affective score of the emotion, the description of the emotion, and further comments from the interview transcriptions.

We conducted a thematic analysis of our data [4] through a data workshop with eight students majoring in design. Our primary interests were in what kinds of emotion people chose to express using MindTracker, why they expressed the emotion with a particular clay form, and how they perceived the emotion. We proceeded by categorizing and coding the data based upon the primary interests. By doing this, we generated a taxonomy of the shape of the emotions across different participants. We finally presented the general trend of data to the three clinical experts, who provide mental healthcare services for students at the university where we conducted this study, to validate the quality of the data and to explore potential opportunities for designing emotion-tracking tools to serve clinical needs.

Figure 2. Affinity analysis of the 3D clay pieces and descriptions.

FINDINGS

With MindTracker, we wanted to uncover whether the approach we used motivates people to collect emotion data, what types of emotions people want to capture, how they embody emotion in forms, and how they interpret the logged data. In the following sections, we present examples and descriptions that best capture the core themes that emerged in analysis. We begin by describing the various motivations guiding participants' emotion data collection through the MindTracker study. We then highlight how the participants generated data, especially the mapping of emotion into a 3D form along with three approaches. Then, we present the taxonomy of forms representing emotions. We also discuss the value of MindTracker perceived by participants.

General Orientations

We were surprised by our enthusiastic participants who provided 616 emotion forms with scores and descriptions over the course of two weeks. We were concerned that the intensive schedule among the students during a week of final exams might affect the data collection. Most of the participants, however, constantly created data. For some participants, MindTracker itself was a pleasing experience. During the study period, three participants inquired if they could report emotions as many as they want. Two participants proactively reported emotions even before receiving the reminder. P7 reported, *"I was concerned that the [MindTracker] study might be burden on me because the schedule was overlapped with my final exam week. Surprisingly, I really enjoyed the study for two weeks, and it helped me recognize my emotion through crafting and writing."*

Clay as an Instrument for Creative Expression

The novelty of data collection—a combination of form and journal—acted as an engaging factor. Plasticine clay was a material with which most of the participants were familiar. During the instruction session for the MindTracker study, participants showed a positive reaction to the clay, and some immediately opened the box to touch the clay. One participant mentioned that clay reminded her of her childhood. P3 said, *"I made a lot of things with clay when I was young. It reminds me of how I liked this and how I was creative when I was young."*

The participants were able to construct the shape of an emotion without limitations because clay is a highly accessible material for artistic expression and improvisation. As P10 explained, *"I had no confidence in making at the beginning. I had no idea what to make over the first few days, so I decided to just play with clay and make random items around me, like flowers and cups."* He then described several benefits of clay: *"Clay is simple. There's no skill required. It is also flexible, which means I can make anything quickly. I especially love the feeling this clay gives me. It's soft and gentle, which makes me calm."*

Similar to the participant above, six other participants commented on the benefits of clay as a tool for expressing ideas. They commented that using the clay was better than drawing on paper to express their emotions freely. P2 said, *"Making a form using clay is different from drawing. It is reversible. I can destroy it if I don't like it and then make another one. If I were asked to draw my emotions, I couldn't do so."* This accessible nature motivated the participants to make a number of forms and seek sources of ideas. Making three-dimensional forms with clay allowed many of the participants to express what they felt and experienced without barriers.

Motivations: Dynamics of Emotion and Memorable Events

The motivations for recording emotions using MindTracker centered around two general themes: recognizing the dynamics of emotions at a glance and capturing short-lasting feeling with specific experience that stimulate the feeling. P15 explained his motivation for participating in the study: *"I am eager to look at how my emotion changes on these kinds of tough days. That's why I decided to participate in this study. I look forward to seeing the shapes of my emotion, especially when I am taking final exams."* P7 mentioned that final exam week was the most active period for her in recording her emotions: *"That period [finals] was stressful. Through what I made and what I wrote, I tried to know whether I was fine or not during that period."*

Motivated by the MindTracker study, P1 expressed that he would keep collecting his emotions and experiences after the study: *"MindTracker seems to me like mood journaling, and it's a great tool for daily logging. I wouldn't do that if I was doing only the written part of journaling, but making a form associated with my emotion and scoring the emotion made me do it three times a day. I will keep track of my feelings using this strategy."* The participants liked the idea of embodying emotion in a form and naming the form to describe the nuance of that emotion. When they browsed the workbook in the follow-up interview session, they felt proud of what they had created. P5 said, *"I wish I could upload all the pictures of my forms to my Instagram. I want to showcase them. [...] Also, I would like to see how others construct forms about similar emotions."*

Approaches to Constructing Clay Shapes

The vast majority of the data on MindTracker were related to emotions or experiences at the moment of creating the form. Our data workshop allowed us to establish a taxonomy of shapes to represent the intended emotions or experiences. We found that the participants embodied their emotions in forms in three distinctly different ways. First, an **abstract** form represented a nuance of emotion with a shape that was not accurately defined. The forms in the abstract category had a degree of independence from visual references in the world. Second, a **symbolic** form depicted a figure of a specific subject from the participant's surroundings to represent the intended emotion. Forms using metaphors are included in this category. Third, a **scene** form illustrated a specific situation, state, or experience that prompted the emotion. We categorized 610 constructed shapes, not including six situations in which the photo of the shape was not included. Of these 610 shapes constructed by the participants, 198 shapes (32.1%) were created in the abstract form; 309 shapes (50.2%) were created using a symbol; and 103 shapes (16.7%) were created using the scene format.

Abstract

We categorized the 198 *abstract* expressions of emotion into three subgroups: untitled or implicit shapes, geometric shapes, and shapes expressed by a gesture or a motion. The participants created 138 shapes using their own language that expressed how they feel and think about a particular emotion (see *Figures 3.a, 3.b, 3.c*). We could not completely understand these figures without supplementary explanation. For example, in *Figure 3.b*, P2 constructed a filled-in shape to express the emotion of satisfaction. The participants also created 24 geometric shapes, including basic 3D or plane models (e.g., a cube, sphere, rectangle, or circle; see *Figure 3.d*). The other 36 shapes employed a gesture (e.g., cutting, extending, grabbing, hitting, tearing, twisting) that participants used to show the emotion itself (see *Figures 3.e, 3.f, 3.g*). For example, in the case shown in *Fig 3.f*, P13 constructed a shape by grabbing, which was intended to express sickness. We focused in particular on the shapes created by gestures because the participants primarily used gestures to express negative feelings in 32 shapes (89%) of total 40 shapes created by gestures.

Symbol

For the emotions embodied using symbols, the participants constructed 309 shapes expressing a specific subject that could be discerned from their surroundings. The participants were often inspired by visual references in the real world. They expressed forms with a *symbol* when they wanted to explain the reason for an emotion or a medium that reminded them of other experiences. In comparison, the participants used 274 shapes to describe the exact shape of the subject (see *figures 3.h, 3.i, 3.j, 3.k*). For instance, in the case shown in *Fig 3.i*, P3 created a clock shape to express the feeling of time flying. Thirty-five other shapes were created with a transformed subject using other materials (*figures 3.l, 3.m, 3.n*) to express a more specific emotion (e.g., pouring water into clay, decorating the clay object with a real flower, or cutting off part of the clay). In the case of *Fig 3.m*, P5 added scissors to express a feeling that he or she wanted to cut tasks

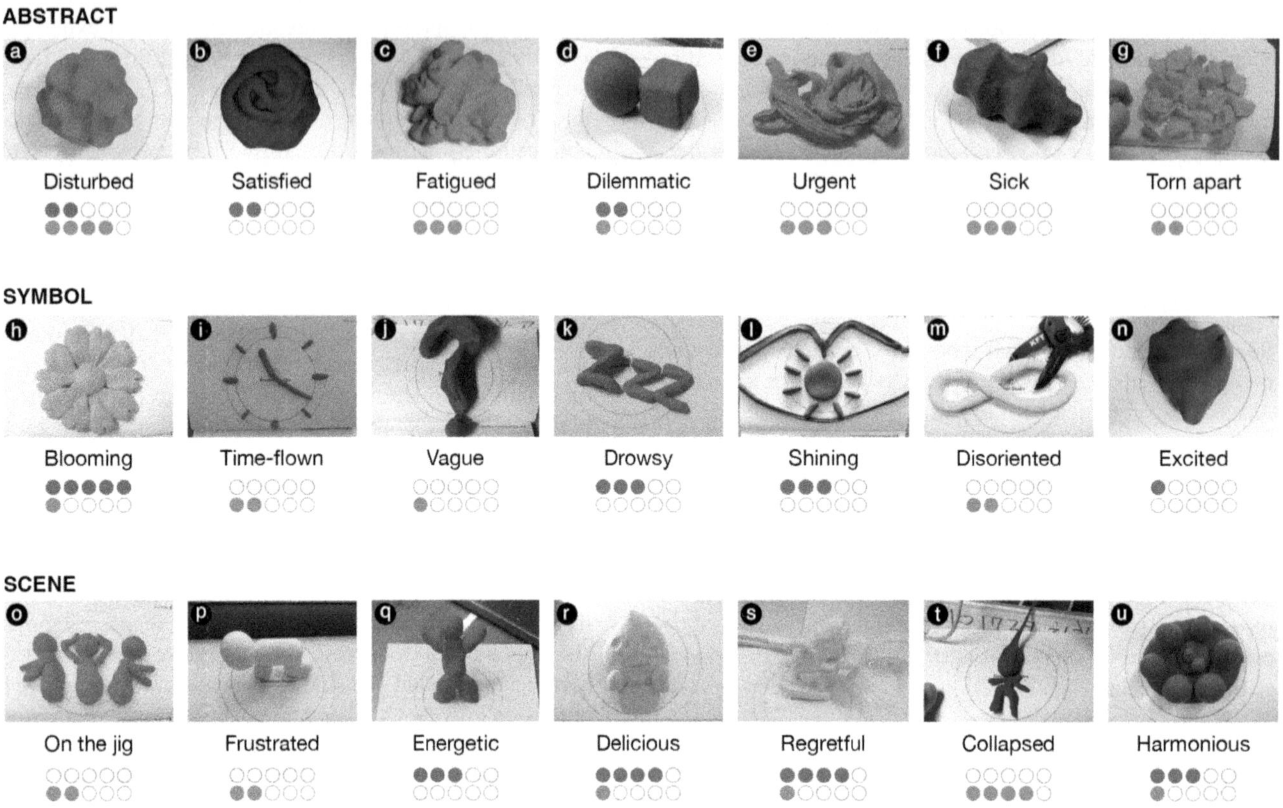

Figure 3. A taxonomy of three-dimensional shapes of emotions. Seven examples in each category.

that never seemed to end. Additionally, we found that the participants most often used a symbol to embody an emotion when they found it difficult to directly express their emotions. For example, P6 noted, *"I felt a limitation of creativity for constructing new shapes from day 3, so I started to find examples to express my emotion in my surroundings."* P2 said, *"When I had no idea about how to express, I searched for an image from Google with a keyword that was related to my emotion."*

Scene

As for the embodiment of an emotion through a scene, we found that 103 shapes were created to describe an emotional state or action. Fifteen participants explained their emotional state with a self-projected human-like figure. The scene forms were separated into three subgroups depending on how the participants described the self-projected figure. Fifty shapes described the participants themselves as a human figure explicitly *(figures 3.o, 3.p, 3.q)*, 27 shapes compared the participants to a symbolic subject that could express their situation more effectively, and 26 shapes simplified or exaggerated the figure. The following examples show differences among the subgroups using a scene to portray an emotion. In *Figure 3.o*, P3 used a human figure to represent himself. In *Figure 3.s*, P5 depicted an éclair exercising on a treadmill to express regret and compared himself to the éclair. Finally, in *Figure 3.u*, P8 represented people who ate dinner together, including herself, in the shape of a sphere.

Perceived Benefits of MindTracker

Our participants perceived several benefits while creating forms, observing the collected data, and interpreting data for insights to take action for their mental well-being.

Data Collection as an Expressive Therapy

We found that collecting emotional data had therapeutic properties which could provide an opportunity for interventions such as self-soothing and mindfulness. Several participants mentioned MindTracker as being a self-soothing tool that could enhance mindfulness. Our focus on touching clay to construct the shape of an emotion was helpful for relieving stress and provided comfort. P5 noted, *"I could relieve stress when I touched clay, so sometimes I spent time with the clay regardless of the experiment."*

Writing also can enhance self-awareness [13]. As P7 mentioned, *"The MindTracker was my emotional ventilation tool. I was mad at [my friend] because he canceled our dinner an hour before. I took out my MindTracker set to record my extreme anger, but I realized that I was quite relieved from the stress while making the shape and writing down the situation. I might need a cool-down time, and MindTracker offered me that chance."*

Goal Setting for Mood Management

A fitness tracker helps a user to set a specific goal, such as increasing step counts to maintain or improve health. We found that MindTracker might provide a similar opportunity for setting a specific goal related to emotions and mental health. The participants liked the idea of rating their emotions along the five-level scales of positivity and negativity. Checking the scale for the degree of the emotion and writing a detailed explanation of it could help the subjects recognize their emotional state objectively. P6 mentioned, *"I could recognize my accurate emotional state when I checked the scale and wrote the reason for the emotion."*

Charting their emotions helped the participants set a short-term goal for mood management. When they recognized negative or depressed feelings over a long period of time, they tried to formulate methods to overcome these feelings. P5 noted, *"I intentionally called my mother and friends to relieve stress and feel comfort when I realized I was depressed from the graph and MindTracker workbook."* P12 also said, *"When I recorded my emotions in the morning, I was able to tell today would not be good, so I set today's goal as overcoming my negative feelings until dinner by eating delicious food."* P2 mentioned, *"I had a lot of pressure from my final exams. When I recognized my negative mood, I tried to identify a reason for my stress. However, I realized that I couldn't get rid of the reason, which was final exams. The only way I could do so was concentrating on preparation. So, I came up with self-rewarding activities which I will do after the exams."* Through the participants' interviews, we determined that they tried to manage mood and unstable factors through self-rewarding, communicating with others, and increasing their productivity.

Summative Reflection

A fitness tracker showing analyzed and visualized data is an important motivator that encourages users to improve their lifestyles [7]. Similarly, we found that the participants in this study could reflect feedback from the results of the collected emotion data. The resulting graph played a key role in showing the flow of emotions during the experiment. When we reviewed the graph with the participants in their interview session, they could understand the trend of their emotion changes. Also, they could recognize triggers and contexts that affected this change. P1 noted, *"I could remind myself of the events that affected my emotions from the graph. I think final exams started this day and ended that day because I felt somewhat negative during that time period."*

Our participants were surprised by the unexpected graph results that differed from what they thought during experiment. P2 said, *"I guessed that I was entirely in the negative moods throughout last week, but I am surprised there are many positive feelings in this graph."* This process also allowed the participants to objectify their emotions. P14 answered, *"I could make myself more aware of my emotions through the graph that shows the entire flow of my emotion changes. I realized that I am a person with heavy mood swings through the graph, which shows a great change in mood."* Revising the data even after the completion of data collection is the foremost part of self-reflection. Therefore, the summarized data supported the participants to reflect on their emotions and encouraged self-awareness, while providing a key factor in the future design of an emotion tracker.

Expert Validation

We conducted semi-structured interviews to complement the study findings with expert perspectives. We interviewed three mental healthcare experts who worked in a university health care center to elicit feedback about the potential use of MindTracker in a clinical setting.

A psychiatrist (E1) stated that the MindTracker study could somewhat serve as an expressive therapy: *"Expressing emotion as itself has a natural effect of relieving stress. This [MindTracker] could allow your participants to understand themselves as they make, describe, and perform the situation stimulating the stress."* E1 also highly valued the use of soft clay to convey emotion. Compared to a drawing activity, constructing a clay form would be more accessible for those who are reluctant to express emotion: *"In our therapy sessions, we attempted to motivate our patients to express their feelings and describe the reason behind the feelings. To do this, we sometimes asked patients to draw something they want to express if they feel it is hard to say. However, they even felt pressure from drawing because they think they are not good at drawing and are afraid of being evaluated. But, the clay would help our patients easily initiate the expression.*

We were told that recognizing the current state of and reason for an emotion is an important factor for dealing with emotion data. As E2, a counselor, explained, *"Understanding the current state of an emotion is the first step to understanding myself. But, it is more important to figure out the reason why that emotion was evoked. I think the activity of writing a reason is necessary. I believe that, in many cases, this activity can provide a 'breathing space' for emotional self-regulation."*

A clinical psychologist (E3) remarked on the importance of continuous charting: *"It is very important to recognize and objectify emotions when we deal with mental health. Showing the entire emotional flow and reminding the subject of events triggering an emotion is a good method for objectifying the emotion."* According to E3, the emotion tracking could be similar to a self-regulation process that is comprised of expressing a short-lasting emotion through clay creation, recognizing the trend of mood through charting emotions, and taking an action.

All three experts suggested that the MindTracker kit could be used as a mediating tool for the period between making a reservation and treatment. There is a lag between a patient's first visit to make a reservation and the actual treatment—usually a week to four weeks, due to long waiting lists. E2 mentioned, *"Students should wait for at least one week. I am really concerned about students who need urgent care. I know many students are likely to visit this center when they feel completely devastated."* E2 suggested that the use of MindTracker on a regular basis could provide early intervention effect that might help patients overcome stress. Furthermore, patients who visit the health center are asked to fill out a 20-page self-reporting mental health assessment sheet at their first school's mental health clinic visit. Thus, MindTracker could be used as a field and long-term data-collection tool between clinical visits.

MindTracker was also depicted as a potential prevention method. The visual aspect of the clay forms could help clinicians easily detect disruptive signals at a glance. While reviewing data with the experts, E2 pointed to a photo of a clay form depicting a "hangman" with a five-point negative score and asked, *"Can you refer this participant to us or can you tell her or him to make an appointment with us? I really want to meet because this figure seems to say 'help me'."* Although we did not intend to design Mindtracker for examining or diagnosing an individual's mental health state, the clinical experts suggested further opportunities to recognize risk factors from the scan of clay forms with the aid of automation.

REFLECTIONS ON MINDTRACKER

The analysis of experiences with MindTracker presents the desire to keep track of emotions with personal experiences. Our participants engaged highly in the practice of tracking comprised of collection and reflection of emotion-related data with MindTracker. The process of making forms with soft and flexible material augments the ability of users to express themselves. MindTracker's tangible modality affords users an opportunity to embody their emotions in a variety of forms, including abstract, symbol, and scene forms. MindTracker also served as a self-healing tool by providing a moment of mindfulness and as an expressive therapy that supported the objectification of subjective experiences. Furthermore, visualizing emotions helps users to recognize their exact state of mind and to gain knowledge of themselves. Our participants also highly valued the moment of summarization, which allowed them to observe a trend in mood changes over two weeks. Our mental health expert participants suggested how MindTracker could support their clinical practices. In particular, MindTracker could serve a tool for gathering and tracking contextual data between clinical visits. We will now consider some wider reflections about the essential properties of MindTracker and how we can improve upon and employ the new emotion data-tracking technique in our daily lives as well as in the context of mental health care.

Properties of Emotion Tracker

We found that the properties of our emotion-tracking tool are similar to those of a fitness tracker, which collects user-generated data and shows analyzed visual data to the user. MindTracker allows for the collection of emotion and experience data and reflection on the results through visual data.

In this paper, we propose effective data-collection methods via recording materials with a tangible modality. The tangible modality feature is helpful for expressing emotions through shapes of things. However, it is not a technology for sensing emotions on an automatic level. Rather, MindTracker can motivate users to think about and recognize their emotions accurately by themselves. Motivation provides an important reason for using a tracking tool to record data continuously. Just as we can expect stress relief through touching a tangible modality, the beneficial effects of the compiled data will motivate users to record their emotion data continuously. Also, this method could have high accessibility for a broad range of age groups, as it can be used easily without needing highly skilled manipulation.

On the other hand, tangible modality has another benefit in that it provides sources of inspirations. Our participants reported that it would have been difficult to articulate how they feel if they did not have clay at hands. While playing with clay, they easily came up with ideas and created stories around the form they created. In addition, clay creation allows users to keep consistency of ways to reporting data, which are inherently subjective and varied in individuals. By scaffolding data types with clay, MindTracker could facilitate not only emotion tracking but also analysis of data being collected.

Considering that a workbook is used for providing detailed explanations, a recording tool for capturing the contexts triggering emotions is necessary to support exploring emotions which will lead to emotion regulation [27]. The process of emotion regulation includes: (1) recognizing the current state or event, (2) generating emotions from evaluating the state with the event, and (3) shaping an appropriate experiential, behavioral, and physiological response. The records of contexts by writing details and trends of mood change in graph represented by scoring could support users to objectify events that generate an emotion for managing future situations.

MindTracker to Promote Mental Health

Our study with students and clinical professionals shows that MindTracker can be used as a supporting tool to promote mental health. In this regard, we suggest three opportunities for the use of MindTracker by: (1) supporting data collection between clinical visits; (2) facilitating communication between clinicians and patients; and (3) supporting self-care to prevent disruptive moods from becoming chronic.

First, the MindTracker kit could be further developed as a lived data collection tool for the period between making a reservation and a treatment, which requires at most four weeks for interpreting the self-report survey and due to long waiting lists. The experts expressed a high demand for resources to tackle this issue because students are likely to visit the center when they need immediate services.

MindTracker could supplement the healthcare center's resources in various ways. First, by virtue of its self-tracking and awareness capabilities, MindTracker might empower an individual to be able to become her own counselor. Second, it could provide qualitatively improved data by overcoming the limitations of many self-report surveys that are not best for identifying latent problems among patients. In addition, the tangible interaction with a soft clay could be a type of emotional regulation activity that reduces nervousness, stress, or anxiety. Besides being used to collect data between clinical visits, MindTracker could also provide a chance for the preparation of the visit. Users could analyze the states of emotions and contributing experiences by themselves prior to the visit.

Second, the collected data could facilitate communication in treatment. A clinician and a patient suffering from mental health problems primarily communicate by talking. However, using only verbal communication prolongs the time needed to obtain a completed diagnosis of the patient, and the clinician may not be able to draw out sensitive issues. To overcome these limitations, clinicians often use expressive therapies (e.g., art therapy, sandplay therapy, music therapy, role-playing therapy) to open a patient's mind for detecting inner problems. Therefore, our participating experts suggested that the MindTracker study, which includes expressive therapy factors, can be an initiating tool for communication during diagnosis. The experts also imagined that the data from the patient's own experience including triggers and contexts would affect the likelihood of accepting the diagnosis. More importantly, MindTracker could be utilized to prevent stress from becoming chronic. As presented in our findings, an expert wanted to see the participating student who created a hangman figure and scored the emotion as five points negative. MindTracker provides an opportunity to monitor danger signals at a glance because it is visually represented. Previous studies on the relationship between form and emotion have suggested technologies for analyzing 3D shapes of form to understand emotion [20]. One can imagine an interactive system that automatically determines the emotion state by analyzing the shape of the emotion with visual recognition techniques. The system would be able to automatically classify data based upon a pre-defined model relating forms and emotions [20] or a machine learning algorithm that detects patterns of a vast amount of visual data being collected. In turn, it can notify users to visit a mental health care center when the expressed form signifies an extreme situation.

Finally, MindTracker could support self-care beyond clinical treatment. We found that the participants realized their emotional state by scoring the intensity of their emotions with scale and checking a graph that represents their overall changes. Then, they tried to set a goal to overcome their emotional state when they had negative feelings for a long time or in extreme negative feelings. They tried to refresh their situation through their own methods, like self-rewarding, communicating with others, and increasing productivity to evoke positive emotions. According to dialectical behavior therapy (DBT) [8], one strategy for regulating emotional vulnerability is accumulating positive emotions. Our experts also remarked that they had asked patients to keep thinking of positive experiences because emotions easily go away when they are no longer reinforced by positive consequences in action. Regarding the opportunity for interactive technology design, we could automatically obtain personal patterns of mood changes and keywords that trigger emotions using natural language processing (NLP) by digitizing the descriptions of experiences and scaled data. When depressive emotions or extreme mood changes are detected from a user, a system could provide a personalized reward to overcome the negative emotion by reminding them of experiences that evoke positive emotion.

POTENTIAL LIMITATIONS AND FUTURE WORK

Our study demonstrated some limitations and challenges. First, we recognized a variety of external factors that might affect the level of engagement with MindTracker and the validity of data participants reported. For instance, the reminding message we sent could be one of the contributing factors of participants' engagement throughout the study. Reporting emotions, however, was completely voluntary and had no additional incentives. As demonstrated in findings section, the total number of reported emotions indicated their willingness regardless a week of final exams, perhaps the busiest time of a semester. Also, participants reported they were highly motivated to track emotions because they wanted to understand how their emotions were affected by the stressful stimuli such as final exams.

Second, although participants were asked to report emotions they exactly felt at the moment of form creation, it is possible that the reported emotions might be affected by the practice of clay creations. Self-soothing effect is very encouraging, but quite unexpected because our primary focus was not on how the MindTracker can work as intervention, rather we were more interested in how participants express their emotions using the new type of emotion tracking tool. Nonetheless, we are excited to explore the effect of tangibility and expressiveness on emotional regulations in further studies.

We also recognized some practical challenges of the proposed emotion tracking approach. During the study period, participants were strongly encouraged to carry with clay and workbook and handwrite contextual information which might cause inconvenience. While our participants and clinical experts appreciated the value of manual input, we expect to reduce participants' physical burden by digitalizing input methods except clay construction when we develop interactive application built on the findings of this study.

CONCLUSION

We have explored the potential of technology to track one's emotions and experiences, which might be critical to mental health. We proposed MindTracker, an approach that asks users to express their emotions using clay and describe their experiences in the workbook. We confirmed that the participants were highly engaged in this study. We found that representing their emotional image with clay was a chance for them to express their reactions in creative ways by creating abstract, symbolic, and contextual forms. The tangible interaction during the data creation allows for self-soothing and emotional self-regulation. As mental health issues caused by emotional stresses are becoming severe in the contemporary world, emotion tracking would work as a great tool for approaching this problem. Just as self-tracking in the fitness area contributed to increased physical soundness among people, emotion tracking will do the same to the remaining half: mental soundness. We hope this study will guide others in designing interactive technologies that improve mental wellness.

ACKNOWLEDGEMENT

The final paper was greatly improved by the advice from the anonymous reviewers. We also thank all of our participants who made this study possible. This work was supported by the UNIST research fund (1.150125) of Ulsan National Institute of Science and Technology and Korea Institute of Design Promotion (KIDP) grant from Korea Ministry of the Trade, Industry & Energy (MOTIE) (N0001436, Promotion of Graduate School of Creative Design Engineering).

REFERENCES

1. Miguel Bruns Alonso, David V Keyson, and Caroline M Hummels. 2008. Squeeze, rock, and roll; can tangible interaction with affective products support stress reduction? In *Proceedings of the 2nd international conference on Tangible and embedded interaction - TEI '08*, 105. https://doi.org/10.1145/1347390.1347413
2. Steve Whittaker Artie Konrad, Vitoria Belotti, Nicole Crenshaw, Simon Tucker, Les Nelson, Honglu Du, Peter Pirolli. 2015. Finding the Adaptive Sweet Spot: Balancing Compliance and Achievement in Automated Stress Reduction. In *Proceedings of the 33rd Annual ACM Conference on Human Factors in Computing Systems - CHI 2015*, 3829–3838. https://doi.org/10.1145/2702123.2702512
3. Frank Bentley, Konrad Tollmar, Peter Stephenson, Laura Levy, Brian Jones, Scott Robertson, Ed Price, Richard Catrambone, and Jeff Wilson. 2013. Health Mashups: Presenting Statistical Patterns between Wellbeing Data and Context in Natural Language to Promote Behavior Change. *ACM Transactions on Computer-Human Interaction (TOCHI)*, 20, 5 (2013), 1–27. https://doi.org/10.1145/2503823
4. Virginia Braun and Victoria Clarke. 2006. Using thematic analysis in psychology. *Qualitative Research in Psychology* 3, 2: 77–101. https://doi.org/10.1191/1478088706qp063oa
5. Michael Brooks, Cecilia R. Aragon, Katie Kuksenok, Megan K. Torkildson, Daniel Perry, John J. Robinson, Taylor J. Scott, Ona Anicello, Ariana Zukowski, and Paul Harris. 2013. Statistical affect detection in collaborative chat. In *Proceedings of ACM Conferences on Computer-Supported Cooperative Work and Social Computing - CSCW 2013*, 317. https://doi.org/10.1145/2441776.2441813
6. Keng-hao Chang, Drew Fisher, John Canny, and Björn Hartmann. 2011. How's my Mood and Stress? An Efficient Speech Analysis Library for Unobtrusive Monitoring on Mobile Phones. In *Proceedings of Bodynets 2011*, 71–77. https://doi.org/10.4108/icst.bodynets.2011.247079
7. Eun Kyoung Choe, Nicole B. Lee, Bongshin Lee, Wanda Pratt, and Julie A. Kientz. 2014. Understanding Quantified-Selfers' Practices in Collecting and Exploring Personal Data. In *Proceedings of the 32nd Annual ACM Conference on Human Factors in Computing Systems*, 1143–1152. https://doi.org/10.1145/2556288.2557372
8. Pieter M A Desmet. 2015. Design for Mood : Twenty Activity-Based Opportunities to Design for Mood Regulation. *International Journal of Design*. 9, 2 (2015), 1–19.
9. Daniel A Epstein, An Ping, James Fogarty, Sean A Munson, Computer Science, and Human Centered Design. 2015. A Lived Informatics Model of Personal Informatics. In *UbiComp '15*, 731–742. https://doi.org/10.1145/2750858.2804250
10. Rebecca Gulotta, Jodi Forlizzi, Rayoung Yang, and Mark Wah Newman. 2016. Fostering Engagement with Personal Informatics Systems. In *Proceedings of the 2016 ACM Conference on Designing Interactive Systems - DIS 2016*, 286–300. https://doi.org/10.1145/2901790.2901803
11. Katrin Hänsel, Akram Alomainy, and Hamed Haddadi. 2016. Large scale mood and stress self-assessments on a smartwatch. In *Proceedings of the 2016 ACM International Joint Conference on Pervasive and Ubiquitous Computing Adjunct - UbiComp 2016*, 1180–1184. https://doi.org/10.1145/2968219.2968305
12. Katherine Isbister, Kia Höök, Michael Sharp, and Laaksoñahti Jarmo. 2006. The Sensual Evaluation Instrument: Developing an Affective Evaluation Tool. In *Proceedings of* ACM *Conference on Human Factors in Computing Systmes - CHI 2006,* 1163–1172. https://doi.org/10.1145/1124772.1124946
13. Adam N. Joinson. 2001. Self-disclosure in computer-mediated communication: The role of self-awareness and visual anonymity. *European Journal of Social*

Psychology 31, 2: 177–192. https://doi.org/10.1002/ejsp.36

14. Michael Karlesky and Katherine Isbister. 2016. Understanding Fidget Widgets: Exploring the Design Space of Embodied Self-Regulation. In *Proceedings of The 9th Nordic Conference on Human-Computer Interaction - NordiCHI 2016.* https://doi.org/10.1145/2971485.2971557
15. Ian Li, Anind Dey, and Jodi Forlizzi. 2010. A stage-based model of personal informatics systems. In *Proceedings of the 28th international conference on Human factors in computing systems CHI 2010*, 557. https://doi.org/10.1145/1753326.1753409
16. Hong Lu, Denise Frauendorfer, Mashfiqui Rabbi, Marianne Schmid Mast, Gokul T. Chittaranjan, Andrew T. Campbell, Daniel Gatica-Perez, and Tanzeem Choudhury. 2012. StressSense. In *Proceedings of the 2012 ACM Conference on Ubiquitous Computing - UbiComp 2012*, 351. https://doi.org/10.1145/2370216.2370270
17. Yuliya Lutchyn, Paul Johns, Asta Roseway, and Mary Czerwinski. 2015. MoodTracker: Monitoring collective emotions in the workplace. In *2015 International Conference on Affective Computing and Intelligent Interaction, ACII 2015*, 295–301. https://doi.org/10.1109/ACII.2015.7344586
18. Gloria Mark, Stephen Voida, and Armand Cardello. 2012. "A pace not dictated by electrons." In *Proceedings of the 2012 ACM annual conference on Human Factors in Computing Systems - CHI 2012*, 555. https://doi.org/10.1145/2207676.2207754
19. Gloria Mark, Yiran Department of Informatics Wang, Melissa Niiya, and Stephanie Reich. 2016. Sleep Debt in Student Life: Online Attention Focus, Facebook, and Mood. In *Proceedings of ACM conference on Human Factors in Computing System - CHI 2016*, 5517–5528. https://doi.org/10.1145/2858036.2858437
20. Edward Melcer and Katherine Isbister. 2016. Motion, Emotion, and Form: Exploring Affective Dimensions of Shape. In *CHI 2016 Late-Breaking Work: Designing Interactive Systems*, 1430–1437. https://doi.org/10.1145/2851581.2892361
21. John Rooksby, Mattias Rost, Alistair Morrison, and Matthew Chalmers Chalmers. 2014. Personal tracking as lived informatics. In *Proceedings of the 32nd annual ACM conference on Human factors in computing systems - CHI 2014*, 1163–1172. https://doi.org/10.1145/2556288.2557039
22. Ricardo Santos, Goreti Marreiros, Carlos Ramos, José Neves, and José Bulas-Cruz. 2011. Personality, emotion, and mood in agent-based group decision making. In *IEEE Intelligent Systems*, 26, 6: 58–66. https://doi.org/10.1109/MIS.2011.92
23. Anja Thieme, Jayne Wallace, Paula Johnson, John McCarthy, Siân Lindley, Peter Wright, Patrick Olivier, and Thomas D Meyer. 2013. Design to promote mindfulness practice and sense of self for vulnerable women in secure hospital services. In *Proceedings of the SIGCHI Conference on Human Factors in Computing Systems (CHI 2013)*, 2647–2656. https://doi.org/10.1145/2470654.2481366
24. Anja Thieme, Jayne Wallace, Thomas D Meyer, and Patrick Olivier. 2015. Designing for Mental Wellbeing : Towards a More Holistic Approach in the Treatment and Prevention of Mental Illness. In *Proceeding of BritishHCI'15*, 1–10. https://doi.org/10.1145/2783446.2783586
25. Rui Wang, Andrew T. Campbell, and Xia Zhou. 2015. Using opportunistic face logging from smartphone to infer mental health. In *Proceedings of the 2015 ACM International Joint Conference on Pervasive and Ubiquitous Computing and Proceedings of the 2015 ACM International Symposium on Wearable Computers - UbiComp '15*, 683–692. https://doi.org/10.1145/2800835.2804391
26. Rui Wang, Fanglin Chen, Zhenyu Chen, Tianxing Li, Gabriella Harari, Stefanie Tignor, Xia Zhou, Dror Ben-Zeev, and Andrew T Campbell. 2014. StudentLife: assessing mental health, academic performance and behavioral trends of college students using smartphones. In *Proceedings of the 2014 ACM International Joint Conference on Pervasive and Ubiquitous Computing*, 3–14. https://doi.org/10.1145/2632048.2632054
27. Thomas L Webb, Eleanor Miles, and Paschal Sheeran. 2012. Dealing with feeling: a meta-analysis of the effectiveness of strategies derived from the process model of emotion regulation. *Psychological bulletin* 138, 4: 775–808. https://doi.org/10.1037/a0027600

Designing Authentic Emotions for Non-Human Characters. A Study Evaluating Virtual Affective Behavior

Oliver Korn
Offenburg University
Offenburg, Germany
oliver.korn@acm.org

Lukas Stamm
KORION GmbH
Ludwigsburg, Germany
info@korion.de

Gerd Moeckel
SRH Hochschule Heidelberg
Heidelberg, Germany
gerd.moeckel@
hochschule-heidelberg.de

ABSTRACT
While human emotions have been researched for decades, designing authentic emotional behavior for non-human characters has received less attention. However, virtual behavior not only affects game design, but also allows creating authentic avatars or robotic companions.

After a discussion of methods to model and recognize emotions, we present three characters with a decreasing level of human features and describe how established design techniques can be adapted for such characters.

In a study, 220 participants assess these characters' emotional behavior, focusing on the emotion "anger". We want to determine how reliable users can recognize emotional behavior, if characters increasingly do not look and behave like humans. A secondary aim is determining if gender has an impact on the competence in emotion recognition.

The findings indicate that there is an area of insecure attribution of virtual affective behavior not distant but close to human behavior. We also found that at least for anger, men and women assess emotional behavior equally well.

Author Keywords
Emotion; emotion recognition; affective; games; design; perception; animation; facial expressions; body cues

ACM Classification Keywords
I.3.7 [**Computer Graphics**]: Three-Dimensional Graphics and Realism–Animation; H.1.2 [**User/Machine Systems**]: Human factors, Human information processing, Software Psychology; I.2.1 [**Applications and Expert Systems**]: Games; H.5.1 [**Multimedia Information Systems**] Evaluation/methodology

DIS 2017, June 10-14, 2017, Edinburgh, United Kingdom

ACM 978-1-4503-4922-2/17/06...$15.00
DOI: http://dx.doi.org/10.1145/3064663.3064755

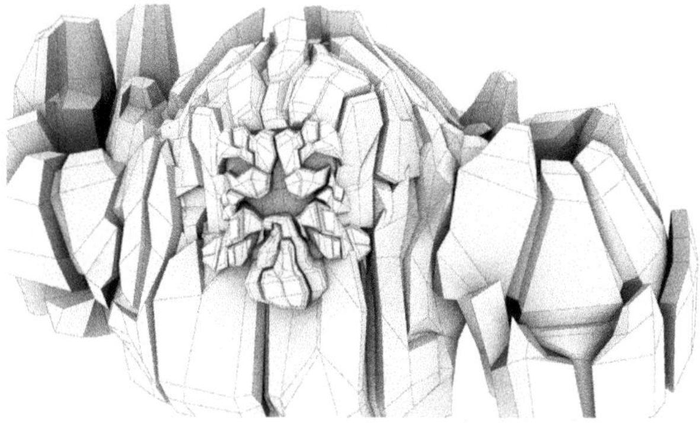

Figure 1. Designing "authentic" and recognizable emotions for virtual characters combines artistic skills and research.

INTRODUCTION
Games have become an integral part of popular culture and of the global entertainment market. With estimated global revenues of $ 91.5 billion already in 2015 [28] it probably has surpassed that year's film market revenues with estimated $ 88.3 billion [35]. However, not only digital immigrants but also a significant part of today's digital natives still consider games an "inferior" or "immature" form of art [4]. A reason for this skeptical attitude may be the gap between games and movies when displaying (and eliciting) emotions: as games use "a reduced spectrum of emotions, they are being perceived as emotionally shallow" [4]. This might also be the reason why most women play less and why they typically prefer different types of games. Indeed, the famous claim put forward by two Disney pioneers, that "in every art form it is the emotional content that makes the difference between mere technical skill and true art" [29], made games look artistically inferior for a long time.

This has changed. At least for humanoid characters and for top titles with the corresponding budget, advanced techniques of facial animation in combination with facial motion tracking [10] and body tracking today allow creating authentic behavior. The realistic display of emotional nuances in games like *L.A. Noire* (Rockstar Games, 2011) or *The Witcher 3: Wild Hunt* (CD Projekt RED, 2015) illustrates well the current technological possibilities.

In contrast, designing authentic emotions for non-human characters (Figure 1) remains complex, requiring both artistic skill and applied research. In consequence, most designers try to "humanize" such characters, so they can use human emotional behaviors with only little adaptation.

However, it is important to know more about the way we understand the emotions of non-human characters. This will not only improve game design, but also allow creating authentic avatars or robotic companions [16,33] which in many cases do not look like humans.

In the state of the art section, we briefly present models for human emotional behavior as well as standard techniques for creating authentic emotions in virtual humanoid characters. We then present a set of three characters with a decreasing level of human features and describe how established techniques for designing emotions can be adapted to create authentic emotional behavior for such non-human characters. For each character, seven animations illustrate the emotion "anger", resulting in 21 short animations. The choice of anger was a result of the co-operation with the game studio developing the characters.

These animations build the corpus of emotional behavior. In the study section, we use them to analyze how reliable users attribute emotional behavior if human features decrease. A secondary aim is determining if gender has an impact on the competence in emotion recognition.

STATE OF THE ART

For humans, emotions can be defined as "a coordinated set of response tendencies that facilitate adaptive responding" [13] based on a typical set of triggers. These responses will result in feelings (e.g. anger) as well as physiological changes (e.g. trembling) and potentially also elicit typical behaviors (e.g. attacking an aggressor). The underlying cognitive processes shaping these emotional responses have been described in previous work, for example by Gratch and Marsella [12,21]. However, for this work we will follow Hassenzahl and focus on emotions as "ephemeral" [15], that is a surface behavior rather than cognitive processes. Indeed, for virtual characters not embodied with artificial intelligence, the designers' main task is not to simulate but to mimic emotional responses as authentically as possible. This is relatively straightforward for humanoid characters.

Theories of Emotion and Models of Affect

In order for humans to "read" or interpret emotional behavior displayed by virtual characters, these need to share a comparable set of emotional responses. Indeed the dominant psychological theories of emotion since Tomkins' three-volume presentation on *Affect, imagery, consciousness* in the sixties [30] put forward the idea that humans share a discrete and limited set of basic emotions. However, since the 1990s this theory is questioned by other psychologists [20,23]. Currently many researchers think that the human emotional spectrum can be more adequately represented by the "circumplex model of affect" [24] as shown in Figure 2.

This neat two-dimensional model integrates the dimensions of valence (type of emotion, ranging from unpleasant to pleasant) and arousal (intensity of emotion). Thus, it offers a good orientation when emotional behavior needs to be adapted to contexts, e.g. by raising activation levels.

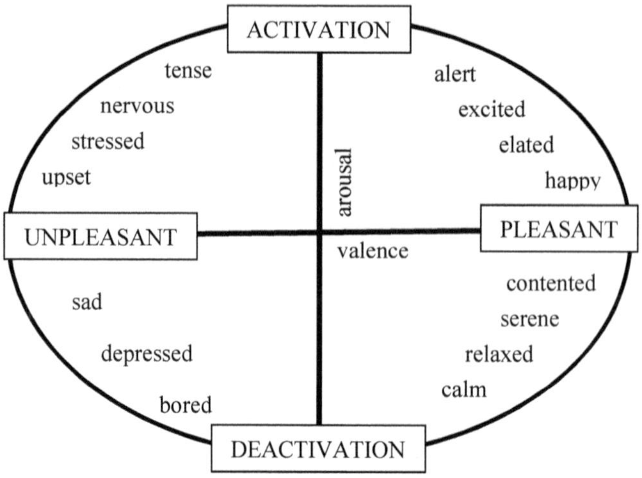

Figure 2. The circumplex model of affect, adapted from [24].

We will reference back to the models in the next sections. First, we will look at facial expressions to convey emotions, and then we will discuss the role body cues.

Emotions Conveyed in Facial Expressions

Although the circumplex model of affect is well established in psychology, many designers prefer a simpler approach: the set of basic emotions in the version presented by Ekman [8,9]. It lists six "universal" emotions: anger, disgust, fear, happiness, sadness, and surprise. Soon after its disclosure, Ekman and others used it as a basis to explore facial expressions and peripheral physiological responses to affective stimuli. They assumed that each basic emotion corresponds to a specific autonomic facial activation pattern [9].

Designers appreciate this model both for its simplicity (no dimensions but a discrete set) and for the seemingly direct relation between facial expression and emotions, as indicated by FACS, the facial action coding system [7]. Its "action units" (distinctive facial areas, e.g. Inner Brow Raiser) allow them to animate rigs accordingly (see example in Figure 3).

Figure 3. Rig of the human character "Violet" from the game *Space Battle Core* in agony. This and all other 3D images presented in this work were designed in Maya.

However, unlike in games or in drama, emotional patterns are far less obvious in everyday situations. Nevertheless the FACS model has also been influential in HCI, as computer scientists used the action units as a basis for applying pattern recognition algorithms [31]. Today, many emotion detection systems have "outgrown" the underlying theory and analyze more refined structures, e.g. by exploiting the "Minimum Description Length Principle" [17].

In designing characters for games, there are similar advances: at least in productions with a high budget, motion capturing systems are starting to replace manual artistic character rigging and animation. Real actors then provide the required facial expressions. This is particularly beneficial for displaying complex emotional processes. A good summary on using facial motion-capture systems is provided by [10].

However, what about all the fantastic creatures populating both classic and modern narrations? As described in the introduction, many designers adopt the successful Disney approach of "humanizing" non-human characters. Still, there are boundaries to this technique drawn by human physiognomy and the uncanny valley: the weird place where a character is almost human, but not quite – making it especially repulsive. Recent work examines how far faces can be altered to still be acceptable and how certain stereotypes ("the female villain") are reproduced by users [26].

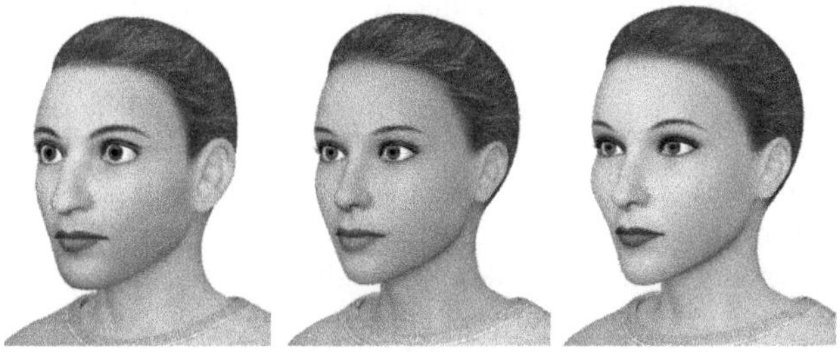

Figure 4. Female repulsive face (left), female hero (middle), female villain (right) as described in [26].

While this work already indicates the boundaries of the design space of facial adaptation, there are also inherent problems when focusing solely on facial expression. In the following section, we briefly present work on body cues as an important component of emotional expression.

Emotions Conveyed in Body Cues

When it comes to recognizing emotions, research focused on facial expressions for a long time. With the decreasing cost of whole-body sensing technology (especially after the release of the Kinect in 2010), human pose recognition from depth images converged into the technological mainstream [27]. This resulted into an increasing number of studies on affective body movement, of which Kleinsmith & Bianchi-Berthouse in 2013 provided an excellent overview [18].

The focus shift from face to body is very well exemplified by the influential 2012 *Science* paper from Aviezer et al., which illustrates this shift already in the title: "Body Cues, Not Facial Expressions, Discriminate Between Intense Positive and Negative Emotions" [1]. Emotion models postulating separate emotional categories (as Ekman's, [8,9]) like anger and fear predict that intense emotions activate maximally distinct facial muscles, increasing discrimination. Aviezer et al. show that facial expression do not suffice to convey positive and negative affective valence.

As figure 5 shows, especially intense positive and negative emotions look strongly alike. These finding correlates with neurobiological work, indicating that the opioid and dopamine systems modulate both pain and pleasure [34]. Accordingly, de Gelder [11] strongly highlights the importance of integrating bodily expressions in affective neuroscience. She even considers the "face centrism" a sociocultural phenomenon, as the "emphasis on the face is present in western culture and art but not, for example, in Islamic art". Fully in line with other affective researchers like Barret [2], de Gelder argues that the perception or even the recognition of bodily expressions partially is an automaticity and does not require full attention.

Figure 5. Images of players (1) losing or (2) winning a point and the same faces with incongruent-valence bodies such as (3) a losing face on a winning body and (4) a winning face on a losing body [1]. Copyright granted by The American Association for the Advancement of Science.

This is an advantage for designers, as they can use automated emotion recognition processes to convey emotional cues of ephemeral characters. So clearly, when designing authentic emotions for avatars or for artificial environments like games, both facial expressions and body cues have to be taken into account, as they are the result of the same underlying cognitive processes.

DESIGNING EMOTIONS OF NON-HUMANS

In this section, we describe how emotional behaviors for non-human characters can be designed. We took a three-step approach with a distinct character representing each step. In animation sequences, each character's arousal level is increased in seven steps, from indifference to anger to wild rage. At the same time, with each character, the extent of human features is decreased, deliberately taking a path of "dehumanization" as discussed by Moran [22] more than 30 years ago in the context of augmentation.

First, the designers need to be sure how anger manifests in humans conventionally. While this is well documented for facial expressions, the discussion in the section above shows that studies on affective body cues are more recent. In a meta-study, Kleinsmith & Bianchi-Berthouse [18] analyzed "Descriptions of Specific Body Features and How They May Be Attributed to the Recognition of Specific Affective States". Table 1 shows the major findings related to anger.

Table 1. Discriminating features of the anger state, adapted from Kleinsmith & Bianchi-Berthouse in [18]:

Study	Discriminating Features
Coulson 2004 [3]	Head bent back, no backward chest bend, no abdominal twist, arms raised forward & upward
De Meijer 1989 [6]	Bowed trunk & head, knees slightly bent, slow velocity, strong force, downward body movement, stepping backward, arms open frontally
Dahl & Friberg 2007 [5]	Both [musical] instruments: Large, very jerky, somewhat fast movements
Gross et al. 2010 [14]	High energy, expanded limbs, tense controlled flow
Kleinsmith et al. 2006 [19]	Head bent forward, elbows bent and laterally extended
Roether et al. 2009 [25]	Head bent forward, elbows bent

Artists developed these characters and designed their emotional responses based on the findings presented above as well as established techniques in game character design. In addition, the characters' emotional expressions were iteratively improved with the help of focus groups. These groups consisted of five expert video game players, defined as persons frequently playing more than 10 hours per week. The experts were recruited from the community of beta-testers. They especially paid attention to convey emotions both by the face and by body cues, which becomes more important with each step of dehumanization.

The first character served as a base line. While the "Pirate" has a small implant, its effects on facial expressions are minor. The second character called "Litho" was designed to be still humanoid, i.e. endowed with a kind of face and a body with arms, but completely different in material: stone. The third character "Bio" was designed to have no human features while still resembling some hybrid of animal and plant. In the following, we briefly portray the design processes.

Pirate Character

For the pirate character (Figure 6), the human physiognomy and body were the central reference. As common in state of the art modeling, the artists used knowledge of facial muscles and action units to create authentic facial structures.

Figure 6. The Pirate character with a facial prosthesis.

The only deviation from a standard face is the prosthesis – a reference to Moran's discussion of augmentation as a potential reduction of humans to machines [22]. While the prosthesis has no action units, it deliberately covers only a small part of the face. Thus, it primarily serves artistic purposes and does not distort recognizing facial expressions.

The pirate's body cues are straightforward: from indifference indicated by shrugging shoulders to threatening hand gestures like slitting the throat or hitting the observer, the level of aggression rises in seven steps. The cues used are universally understandable. Although shaking the head can mean "yes" in some cultures, the facial expressions accompanying the movement clarify the meaning.

Litho Character

For the Litho character (Figures 1; 7), human physiognomy again served as the main reference. However, the designers systematically replaced the action units by stone structures. An intermediate result (Figure 7, left) looks very humanoid.

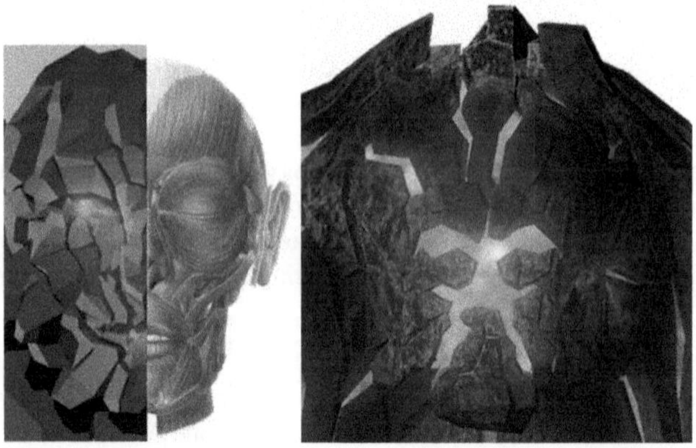

Figure 7. Detailed facial modeling of "Litho" based on human muscles (left) and abstracted finished model (right).

The designers then started to eliminate action units while still maintaining basic facial animation capabilities. The results were iterated in the focus groups to determine the level of detail required to still be able to discern the level of arousal. The overall design vision was a "living volcano".

The final character shows that it was possible to merge eyes, nose and mouth. As a result, cheeks, brows and mouth were the sole remaining parts. Still the impression of a face as well as animation capabilities could be preserved.

The body cues reach from slight head movements to pumping the chest and intense arm movements. In contrast to the pirate character, the designers did not employ cultural codes like slitting the throat. To compensate for the lack of action units and cultural body cues, the intensity of the lava glow provides a reliable indication of to the level of arousal.

Bio Character

When designing the Bio character (Figure 8) the aim was to create something, which is definitely not human, although clearly of biological origin (in opposition to "Litho").

Figure 8. The "Bio" character is the least human in the set. The only discernible "facial" feature is a mouth.

The intended result was a mix between a plant and an animal, combining buds with a throat resembling that of a turtle. In analogy to the Litho character with its stone and lava, hard and soft structures (here: green and cyan) were combined to make movement in the animation plausible.

The design iterations in the focus groups showed that for this character it was acceptable to leave out eyes, nose, cheeks and brows – with the mouth being the sole remaining facial feature. While there remains some vague resemblance to a face, it hardly contains any action units but essentially is just a large mouth, which opens by separating three segments.

For such a character to convey emotions, the body becomes much more important. As facial expressions are restricted to the degree of mouth opening, snake-like body movements are used to provide emotional cues. The increasing movement speed and the increasing degree of body inflection, could already indicate the rising arousal. However, the design iterations in the focus groups showed that in analogy to the lava glow of the Litho character, an additional cue was needed to compensate for the lack of action units inherent to an almost faceless creature.

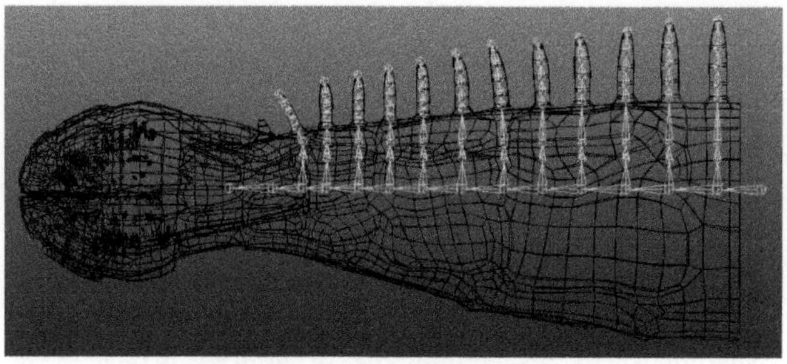

Figure 9. Rigged "Bio" spikes.

In case of "Bio", the designers created movable spikes on the back. These spikes, which are cyan-colored in both the model and the texture, "grow" from the spine (Figure 9). Technically, they are connected joints so movements reflect dynamically in their bending. As the character becomes more agitated and arousal increases, the spikes raise.

STUDY

The overall aim of the study was to evaluate, how users assess the emotional behavior of non-human characters. A secondary aim was to investigate, if there are differences in the competence of emotion recognition related to media preference, media consumption or gender.

To limit the scope, we focused on one emotion: anger. Thus, we could not investigate wrong attributions of valence, i.e. the type of emotion as described in [1]. However, we closely examined the dimension of activation by analyzing if users could attribute the level of arousal equally well for all characters. The naïve hypothesis is that the accuracy of emotion recognition decreases with dehumanization, i.e. users recognize emotional states worse from character 1 to 3.

Population

The test population consisted of 220 experienced video game players. They were recruited from the SRH Hochschule, a German university, so most users were students. 148 test subjects were male and 72 female. Although many users are young, for clarity and brevity we will refer to them as men and women when discussing gender aspects. The youngest user was 13 years old; the oldest user was aged 52. The mean age was $\bar{x}$ = 22.2 years (SD = 7.3 years). As the video game, where the animations are used, is rated PG-13, no ethical concerns did arise. Nevertheless, participants below 16 years of age did require parental consent.

Procedure

The study consists of two phases: a survey and an experiment. In the survey we collected data on relevant user attributes, for example the level of media consumption and the preference for emotional content in media. Responses were structured by a seven-point Likert-scale.

In the experimental section, the users were confronted with the animation sequences. In these sequences, each of the three character's level of anger is increased in seven steps, from indifference to wild rage. The 21 animations sequences showing these behaviors are added to this work.

The animations were presented to the users on a screen in randomized order. Their task was to rank them according to the intensity of the shown emotion. They could watch each animation multiple times to assess the details of the behavior and they could change their ranking until they were satisfied.

The independent variables in this experiment are the users' age, gender as well as the media preferences established in the survey section. The dependent variables are the users' assignments of the animations to arousal levels. If an animation was attributed a wrong level (e.g. 5 when it was in fact 3), we measured the error as the absolute difference to the correct value (in this example: 2). In the graphs (Figures 13-15), the aggregated errors result in a deviation from the ideal diagonal line. For inferential statistics, we used t-tests and ANOVA. When investigating correlations among all three characters, we applied Bonferroni correction.

Phase 1: Survey on Media Preferences

An important independent variable is experience with video games (Figure 10). The mean weekly playtime was $\bar{x} = 9.7$ hours. However, with some persons playing very few hours and others playing 30 or even 60 hours (!) there is a very high standard deviation (SD = 11.2 hours). Interestingly, the mean weekly playtime almost exactly equals the time spent with passive media (TV, films, internet video etc.) of $\bar{x} = 10.0$ hours (SD = 9.9 hours). In both cases, the high standard deviation shows that media preferences are still highly individual. In addition, with $r = -0.04$ there is no significant correlation between passive and active media use. Thus, the naïve hypothesis that participants who watch TV also play games is not supported ($p > 0.37$).

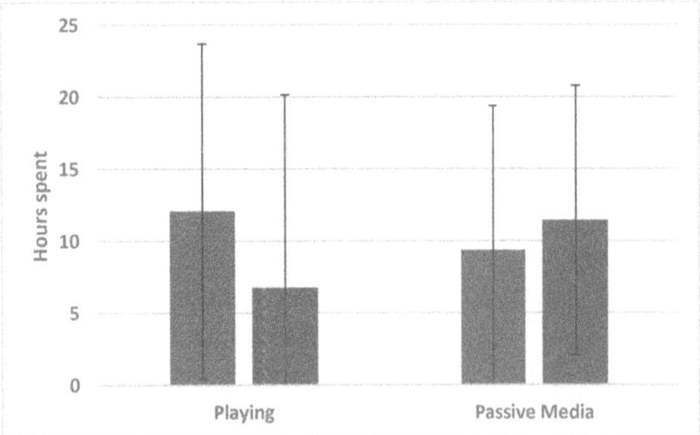

Figure 10. Time spent playing (left columns) and watching TV or videos (right columns) by men (blue) and women (red) with standard deviations.

With a mean playing time of $\bar{x} = 12.1$ hours (SD = 11.6 hours) for men and only $\bar{x} = 5.0$ hours (SD = 8.6 hours) for women, the stereotype that men play more than women is true for this population ($p < 0.01$; Figure 10). However, the passive media consumption is quite similar, with $\bar{x} = 9.4$ hours (SD = 10.0 hours) for men and $\bar{x} = 11.4$ hours (SD = 9.4 hours) for women. As the very high standard deviations show, both active and passive media consumption is highly individual.

We also inquired if there is a preference for emotions in media (Figure 11), as we expected that such a disposition might influence the overall ability to recognize emotions. Using a Likert scale from 1 to 7 we first asked "How important is it for you that characters in media show emotions?" In the next step, we separated between media types: "How important is it for you that characters in games show emotions?" We also asked the corresponding question for passive media: "How important is it for you that characters in TV programs or movies show emotions?"

The mean overall preference for emotions in media is $\bar{x} = 5.4$ (SD = 1.4). For men it is $\bar{x} = 5.6$ (SD = 1.3) and for women $\bar{x} = 5.1$ (SD = 1.6). This is interesting, as men are significantly ($p < 0.02$) more interested in emotions in media than women. This finding contradicts the stereotype that women are more interested in feelings than men are. It would be interesting to analyze this finding more closely in future work, e.g. one could hypothesize that male users favor only certain types of emotions.

The preference for emotions in games reinforces this observation: the overall mean preference here is $\bar{x} = 4.9$ (SD = 1.6). For men it is $\bar{x} = 5.1$ (SD = 1.5) and for women $\bar{x} = 4.5$ (SD = 1.6). Again, with $p < 0.01$ the difference is (highly) significant. Women seem to be less drawn to emotional content in media generally; this tendency is even stronger with games, i.e. interactive media.

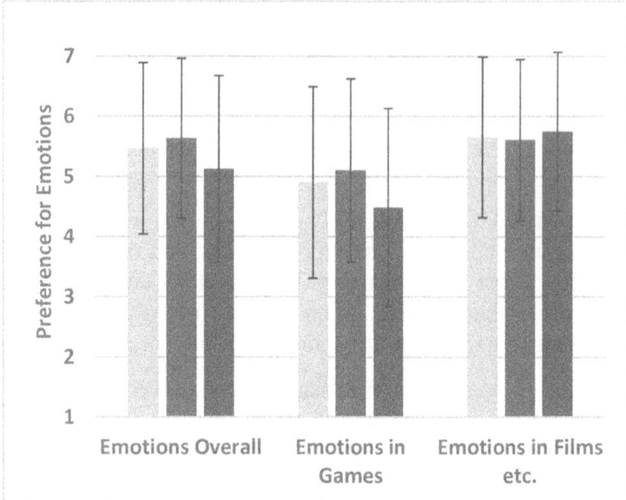

Figure 11. Preference for emotions: overall (all media), games and passive media like film and TV with standard deviations. Grey columns represent the overall population, blue columns men and red columns women.

However, the situation is different when we investigate passive media consumption. The overall mean preference for emotions here is $\bar{x} = 5.7$ (SD = 1.3). For men it is $\bar{x} = 5.6$ (SD = 1.3) and for women $\bar{x} = 5.7$ (SD = 1.3). Thus, in the established types of media, there is hardly any difference between the genders. In conclusion, (young) men enjoy emotions in both active and passive media while (young) women seem to prefer emotional movies, videos etc.

Phase 2: Experiment on Assessing Emotional Behavior

As described in the section 'Procedure', in this phase of the study the users' task was to rank animations showing emotional behavior (focusing on "anger") according to their intensity. In a preliminary step, we checked if the number of attribution errors is normally distributed. This should be the case, as the ability to recognize and assess emotions is a cognitive function. As Figure 12 illustrates, the errors indeed are normally distributed.

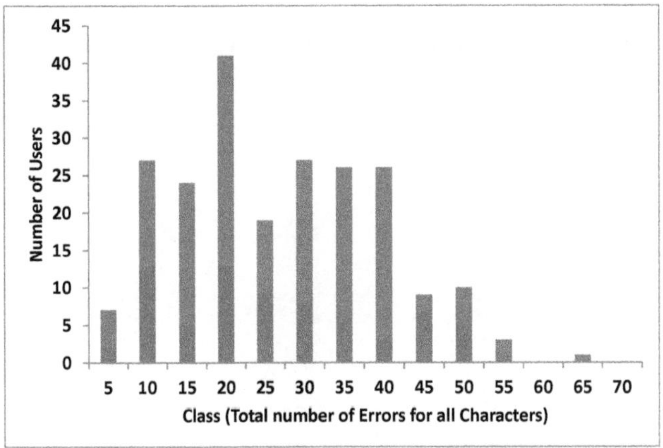

Figure 12. Histogram showing the distribution of attribution errors for women (red) and men (blue).

After the survey's findings on emotional preference in media, we first analyzed if the data support the stereotype that women surpass men in analyzing emotions. With a mean number of errors of $\bar{x} = 24.3$ (SD = 13.3) for women and $\bar{x} = 24.9$ (SD = 12.2) for men this is not the case ($p > 0.37$): men are not only generally more interested in emotions in media, their abilities in evaluating the emotion "anger" also equals that of the women. However, this might differ for other emotions: especially angry male faces are detected significantly faster by men than by women [32].

While there is no evidence for an effect of gender on the ability to recognize emotions (at least in this population for the emotion "anger"), the overall preference for emotions in media has a measurable effect: correlating the preference for emotional media with the number of attribution errors results in $r = -0.30$. The attitude towards emotional content in media shows a medium correlation (in Cohen terms) with the error rate. With $p < 0.01$, this correlation is highly significant.

In the next step, we take a closer look at how the users assessed the emotions of the individual characters. Figures 13-15 illustrate the mean attribution in relation to the ideal line (perfect attribution).

While this perspective results in an efficient visualization, it could also be misleading: errors are cancelled out, e.g. if anger state 3 is attributed '1' by user A and '5' by user B the mean attribution is '3'. However, Figures 16 and 17 illustrate the absolute number of errors and show that the visualization in Figures 13-15 is not misleading.

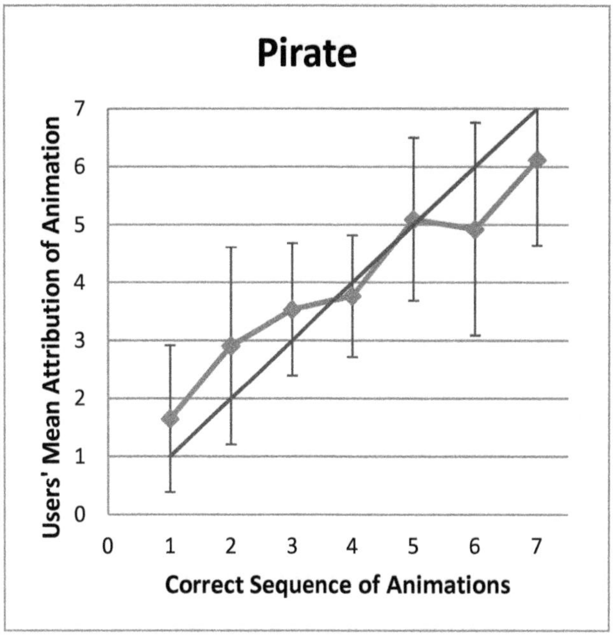

Figure 13. Attribution of Pirate animations (blue) with standard deviations in comparison to the ideal line (purple).

As hypothesized, most users attribute very well the human-like Pirate character's emotions as shown in the animations. The strongest deviation is observable with a high level of anger (animations 6 and 7).

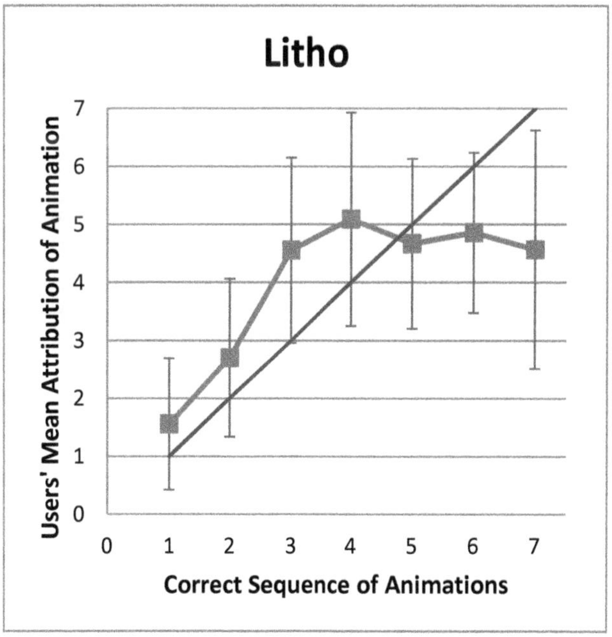

Figure 14. Attribution of Litho animations (red) with standard deviations in comparison to the ideal line (purple).

The attribution of the Litho character's emotions differs strongly from the precise attribution of the previous character. In animations 3 and 4 as well as in animations 6 and 7 the mean attribution highly deviates from the ideal line. While in animations 3 and 4 the emotions' intensity was over-rated, it was under-rated in the last two animations.

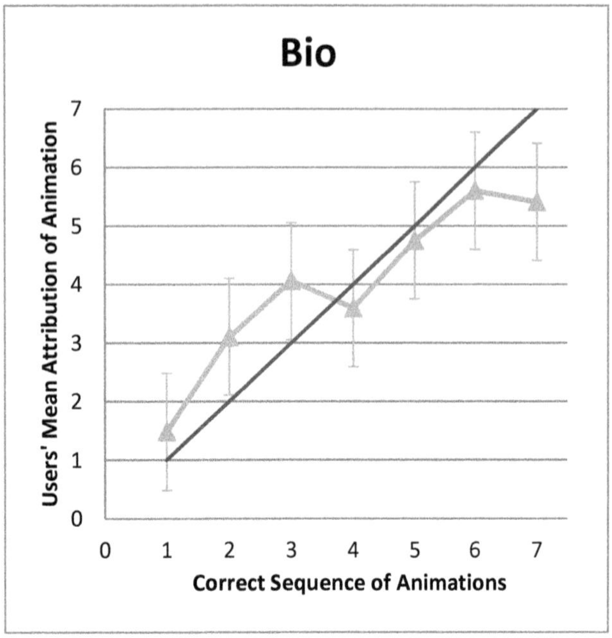

Figure 15. Attribution of Bio animations (green) with standard deviations in comparison to the ideal line (purple).

While the attribution of the Bio character's emotions does not fully match the very close attribution of the Pirate character, it still is close to the ideal line in many sequences, especially sequences 4 to 6.

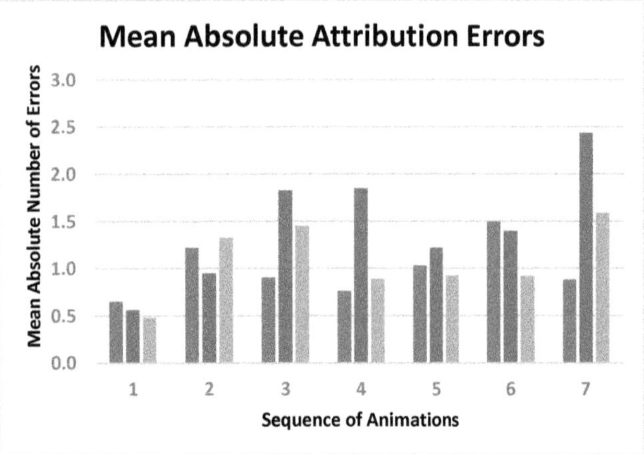

Figure 16. Mean absolute number of attribution errors for the characters Pirate (blue), Litho (red) and Bio (green).

As the diagram (Figure 16) shows, there is no striking difference between the mean attribution in relation to the ideal line (Figures 13-15) and the mean number of absolute errors. For example, the high number of attribution errors in the Litho sequences 3 and 4 becomes evident both in Figure 14 and in Figure 16.

Discussion

As indicated above, the naïve hypothesis is that the accuracy of emotion recognition decreases with dehumanization, so users would recognize emotional states worse with each character from 1 to 3.

For this reason, it was a surprising finding that the Litho character's emotional behavior was the most difficult for the users to interpret. The difficulty to attribute the displayed emotional behavior did not simply increase, the more "alien" and "dehumanized" a character was. In contrast to the naïve hypothesis, the highly aggregated view below (Figure 17) shows that there is no significant difference regarding the attribution of emotions between the Pirate and the Bio character while the Litho character evidently stands out.

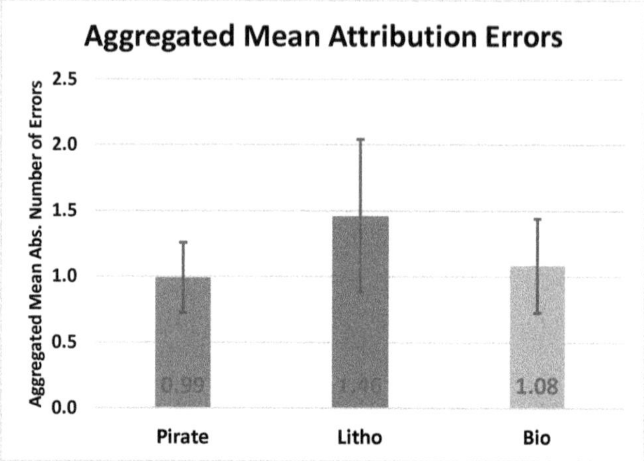

Figure 17. Aggregated mean absolute number of attribution errors for the three characters.

An ANOVA on the subset values (provided in Figure 16) shows that the attribution of emotions of the Litho character differs from the others with high significance ($p < 0.01$).

This is especially interesting, as the Litho design process of reducing facial action units (as described in the design section and illustrated in Figure 7) left many movement patterns of the human face intact. In addition, several body cues like shrugging the shoulders or shaking the head resemble human behavior. Nevertheless, the experimental data indicate that the result is emotionally ambiguous.

Our interpretation of that finding is that there is a sort of "uncanny valley of emotional attribution": if a character is very human-like but still different in some weird way, this might confuse the human capabilities of emotion recognition more than a character with completely alien features.

We are aware that this hypothesis requires more research with other virtual characters, as intense movements (like those of the Bio character) might convey emotions more efficiently than facial expressions and conventional body cues.

Nevertheless, there also is an explanation for the uncanny valley interpretation: for the Bio character, the users had a "clean slate" (assessing behavior by comparing it to the other sequences and building analogies from the animal world), but for Litho they seem to have activated the whole complex apparatus of human emotion recognition – and in doing so, they misjudged the behavior profoundly.

CONCLUSION

This work is an explorative first step on the way to a more systematic design and analysis of non-human characters emotions'. We first briefly discussed models for human emotional behavior and discussed the state of the art in designing emotional behavior, focusing of facial expressions and body cues.

The emotional evaluation is based on a set of three characters with a decreasing level of human features, both in the face and in the body, which were designed with the study in mind. We described how established techniques for designing emotions can be adapted to create authentic emotional behavior for such non-human characters. The three character models were used to create animation sequences with the arousal level increasing in seven steps, from indifference to anger to wild rage.

In phase 1 of a study with 220 participants, we examined the media preferences in a survey, especially with respect to emotions. In the phase 2, we conducted an experiment, using the video sequences to evaluate how the users assess the emotional behavior of non-human characters. We focused on the level of arousal in the emotion "anger". This systematic approach might prove helpful for researchers and designers who aim to calibrate the design of emotions – for better game design, the creation of authentic avatars or even the design of robotic companions.

Several of the survey findings illustrate the importance of gender when analyzing emotional media. Some of these findings were surprising: at least the young men in this population appreciate emotional content in media significantly more than the women – especially in games.

In the second phase of the study, when assessing the video sequences, we could not measure a significant effect of gender on the competence in emotion recognition. However, some readers may consider this a surprising result, too. Stereotypically, women are attributed the superior emotional competence. At least in this study, gender equality (in the area of emotion recognition) is a reality. As discussed above, this result might differ for emotions other than "anger" as men excel in the recognition of angry male faces. We also found that a high overall preference for emotional content in media correlates with a low error rate – thus, in this population, preference for affective content proved to be more important than gender for the competence in emotion recognition.

Finally, the data indicate that the emotional behavior of the "intermediate" or humanoid character was significantly more difficult to assess than the emotional behavior of an alien character. If validated in subsequent studies, this finding points to an "uncanny valley of emotional attribution": a virtual character, which has several human-like features but still differs in some weird way, confuses human emotion recognition more than an alien character.

LIMITATIONS AND FUTURE WORK

As mentioned before, this work represents an explorative first step on the way towards a more systematic design and analysis of non-human characters' emotions. While we were deliberately focusing on "anger", other emotions need to be addressed in subsequent studies. Such studies will also validate the findings, especially regarding the potential "uncanny valley of emotional attribution": this could be restricted to the emotion "anger" or a universal phenomenon.

To reduce the amount of required design work, such studies could build on the existing set of non-human characters. However, additional characters are required to cancel out the influence of the designers.

It will also be interesting to explore the gender aspects further. There is a surprisingly strong preference for emotional content by (young) male users in both active and passive media – we wonder if this is a universal preference (i.e. it covers the complete emotional spectrum) or if certain types of emotions are preferred.

Finally, an approach where the emotions of the users are measured directly through physiological responses (e.g. heart rate, facial expressions, galvanic skin conductance, and brain activity) would contribute a lot to the validity of this type of research. For example, this would allow determining if reduced emotional competence is accompanied by stress or high brain activity – or if certain emotions trigger different physiological responses in men and women.

ACKNOWLEDEGEMENTS

We thank the German game studio KORION for providing images (Figures 1, 3, 6-9) from their game Space Battle Core. We also thank the anonymous reviewers for their insightful comments which helped a lot to improve this work.

REFERENCES

1. Hillel Aviezer, Yaacov Trope, and Alexander Todorov. 2012. Body Cues, Not Facial Expressions, Discriminate Between Intense Positive and Negative Emotions. *Science* 338, 6111: 1225–1229. http://doi.org/10.1126/science.1224313
2. Lisa Feldman Barrett, K. N. Ochsner, and J. J. Gross. 2007. On the automaticity of emotion. In *Social Psychology and the Unconscious: The Automaticity of Higher Mental Processes*, John A. Bargh (ed.). Psychology Press, 173–217.
3. Mark Coulson. 2004. Attributing emotion to static body postures: Recognition accuracy, confusions, and viewpoint dependence. *Journal of nonverbal behavior* 28, 2: 117–139.
4. Rui Craveirinha and Licínio Roque. 2010. Looking for the Heart of Interactive Media: Reflections on Video Games' Emotional Expression. In *Proceedings of the 3rd International Conference on Fun and Games* (Fun and Games '10), 8–17. http://doi.org/10.1145/1823818.1823819

5. Sofia Dahl and Anders Friberg. 2007. Visual Perception of Expressiveness in Musicians' Body Movements. *Music Perception: An Interdisciplinary Journal* 24, 5: 433–454. http://doi.org/10.1525/mp.2007.24.5.433
6. Marco De Meijer. 1989. The contribution of general features of body movement to the attribution of emotions. *Journal of Nonverbal behavior* 13, 4: 247–268.
7. Gianluca Donato, Marian Stewart Bartlett, Joseph C. Hager, Paul Ekman, and Terrence J. Sejnowski. 1999. Classifying facial actions. *IEEE Transactions on Pattern Analysis and Machine Intelligence* 21, 10: 974–989.
8. Paul Ekman. 1992. An argument for basic emotions. *Cognition and Emotion* 6, 3–4: 169–200. http://doi.org/10.1080/02699939208411068
9. Paul Ekman. 1993. Facial expression and emotion. *American psychologist* 48, 4: 384.
10. Cathy Ennis, Ludovic Hoyet, Arjan Egges, and Rachel McDonnell. 2013. Emotion Capture: Emotionally Expressive Characters for Games. In *Proceedings of Motion on Games* (MIG '13), 31:53–31:60. http://doi.org/10.1145/2522628.2522633
11. Beatrice de Gelder. 2009. Why bodies? Twelve reasons for including bodily expressions in affective neuroscience. *Philosophical Transactions of the Royal Society B: Biological Sciences* 364, 1535: 3475–3484. http://doi.org/10.1098/rstb.2009.0190
12. Jonathan Gratch and Stacy Marsella. 2004. A domain-independent framework for modeling emotion. *Cognitive Systems Research* 5, 4: 269–306. http://doi.org/10.1016/j.cogsys.2004.02.002
13. James J. Gross. 1998. The emerging field of emotion regulation: An integrative review. *Review of General Psychology* 2, 3: 271–299. http://doi.org/10.1037/1089-2680.2.3.271
14. M. Melissa Gross, Elizabeth A. Crane, and Barbara L. Fredrickson. 2010. Methodology for Assessing Bodily Expression of Emotion. *Journal of Nonverbal Behavior* 34, 4: 223–248. http://doi.org/10.1007/s10919-010-0094-x
15. Marc Hassenzahl. 2004. Emotions Can Be Quite Ephemeral; We Cannot Design Them. *interactions* 11, 5: 46–48. http://doi.org/10.1145/1015530.1015551
16. Guy Hoffman, Shira Bauman, and Keinan Vanunu. 2016. Robotic Experience Companionship in Music Listening and Video Watching. *Personal Ubiquitous Comput.* 20, 1: 51–63. http://doi.org/10.1007/s00779-015-0897-1
17. Yelin Kim and Emily Mower Provost. 2015. Emotion Recognition During Speech Using Dynamics of Multiple Regions of the Face. *ACM Trans. Multimedia Comput. Commun. Appl.* 12, 1s: 25:1–25:23. http://doi.org/10.1145/2808204
18. A. Kleinsmith and N. Bianchi-Berthouze. 2013. Affective Body Expression Perception and Recognition: A Survey. *IEEE Transactions on Affective Computing* 4, 1: 15–33. http://doi.org/10.1109/T-AFFC.2012.16
19. Andrea Kleinsmith, P. Ravindra De Silva, and Nadia Bianchi-Berthouze. 2006. Cross-cultural differences in recognizing affect from body posture. *Interacting with Computers* 18, 6: 1371–1389. http://doi.org/10.1016/j.intcom.2006.04.003
20. Jeff T. Larsen, Gary C. Berntson, Kirsten Poehlmann, Tiffany A. Ito, and John T. Cacippo. 2008. The psychophysiology of emotion. In *Handbook of emotions* (3rd ed), Michael Lewis, Jeannette M. Haviland-Jones and Lisa Feldman Barrett (eds.). New York, NY, USA, 180–195.
21. Stacy Marsella and Jonathan Gratch. 2014. Computationally Modeling Human Emotion. *Commun. ACM* 57, 12: 56–67. http://doi.org/10.1145/2631912
22. Thomas P. Moran. 1981. Surveyor's Forum: Augmentation or Dehumanization? *ACM Comput. Surv.* 13, 4: 492–493. http://doi.org/10.1145/356859.356866
23. A. Ortony and T. J. Turner. 1990. What's basic about basic emotions? *Psychological Review* 97, 3: 315–331.
24. Jonathan Posner, James A. Russell, and Bradley S. Peterson. 2005. The circumplex model of affect: An integrative approach to affective neuroscience, cognitive development, and psychopathology. *Development and psychopathology* 17, 3: 715–734. http://doi.org/10.1017/S0954579405050340
25. C. L. Roether, L. Omlor, A. Christensen, and M. A. Giese. 2009. Critical features for the perception of emotion from gait. *Journal of Vision* 9, 6: 15–15. http://doi.org/10.1167/9.6.15
26. Valentin Schwind, Katrin Wolf, Niels Henze, and Oliver Korn. 2015. Determining the Characteristics of Preferred Virtual Faces Using an Avatar Generator. In *Proceedings of the 2015 Annual Symposium on Computer-Human Interaction in Play* (CHI PLAY '15), 221–230. http://doi.org/10.1145/2793107.2793116
27. J. Shotton, A. Fitzgibbon, M. Cook, et al. 2011. Real-time human pose recognition in parts from single depth images. In *Proceedings of the 24th IEEE Conference on Computer Vision and Pattern Recognition.*
28. Brendan Sinclair. Gaming will hit $91.5 billion this year - Newzoo. *GamesIndustry.biz*. Retrieved January 13, 2016 from http://www.gamesindustry.biz/articles/2015-04-22-gaming-will-hit-usd91-5-billion-this-year-newzoo
29. Frank Thomas and Ollie Johnston. 1995. *The illusion of life: Disney animation.* Hyperion.
30. Silvan S. Tomkins. 1962. *Affect, imagery, consciousness: Vol. I. The positive affects*. Springer, Oxford, England.
31. Michel Valstar and Maja Pantic. 2006. Fully automatic facial action unit detection and temporal analysis. In *Computer Vision and Pattern Recognition Workshop, 2006. CVPRW'06. Conference on*, 149–149. Retrieved April 12, 2016 from http://ieeexplore.ieee.org/xpls/abs_all.jsp?arnumber=1640595

32. Mark A. Williams and Jason B. Mattingley. 2006. Do angry men get noticed? *Current Biology* 16, 11: R402–R404. http://doi.org/10.1016/j.cub.2006.05.018
33. Tian (Linger) Xu, Hui Zhang, and Chen Yu. 2016. See You See Me: The Role of Eye Contact in Multimodal Human-Robot Interaction. *ACM Trans. Interact. Intell. Syst.* 6, 1: 2:1–2:22. http://doi.org/10.1145/2882970
34. Jon-Kar Zubieta, Joshua A. Bueller, Lisa R. Jackson, et al. 2005. Placebo effects mediated by endogenous opioid activity on mu-opioid receptors. *The Journal of Neuroscience: The Official Journal of the Society for Neuroscience* 25, 34: 7754–7762. http://doi.org/10.1523/JNEUROSCI.0439-05.2005
35. Topic: Film Industry. *www.statista.com*. Retrieved January 13, 2016 from http://www.statista.com/topics/964/film/

What Can Self-Reports and Acoustic Data Analyses on Emotions Tell Us?

Samaneh Soleimani
University of Leicester
Leicester, United Kingdom
ss887@le.ac.uk

Effie Lai-Chong Law
University of Leicester
Leicester, United Kingdom
lcl9@le.ac.uk

ABSTRACT
There are two approaches to measure people's experiences: memory-based and moment-based. Whereas the memory-based approaches are susceptible to the peak-end effect, the moment-based approaches appear to better reflect the experience of the present. In this paper, we propose that emotional assessment of think aloud verbalisations is a moment-based methodology for measuring UX. We conducted an empirical study with 46 participants in the domain of online shopping to evaluate their emotional experiences. Acoustic analysis of verbal data was used as the moment-based approach and self-report questionnaires as the retrospective or memory-based approach. Results of the study confirmed the previous finding that retrospective assessments did not reflect the actual experience. The results also suggested that retrospective evaluations of emotions were significantly correlated with the most frequently elicited emotion (i.e. modal emotion) during the interaction. In conclusion these results support the use of acoustic data analysis as an alternative approach to measuring UX.

ACM Classification Keywords
H.5.m. Information Interfaces and Presentation (e.g. HCI): Miscellaneous.

Author Keywords
User experience; evaluation; emotion; acoustic analysis.

INTRODUCTION
User experience (UX) is a broad and intriguing research area in the field of Human-Computer Interaction (HCI). Since the turn of the millennium, researchers have attempted to clarify this fuzzy notion by unpacking its major components and their interrelations. Among others, Hassenzahal [34] has defined UX as "momentary, primarily evaluative feeling (good-bad) while interacting with a product or service". From this definition three aspects can be inferred: First, UX as opposed to usability has extensively focused on the aspect of users' emotions. Second, these emotions are short-lived, and third they are triggered as the cognitive evaluation of events. These characterizations of emotions are consistent with those postulated by Russell [59], Bradley [8], Lang [41], Scherer [65, 63] and others scholars in psychological research on emotion and affect.

Although UX encompasses broader qualities than the usability metrics [42], the approaches to measuring UX have heavily relied on the traditional usability methods [69] such as subjective and retrospective self-reports through questionnaires and interviews. Whilst self-report methods can elicit the overall perception of an experience, they are not sufficient. Emotions as the integral part of UX are prone to memory bias such as the peak-end effect [39]. Typically retrospective evaluation cannot directly pinpoint when, which, how intense or how long a specific emotion is (or emotions are) experienced. Arguing along this line, the mapping between what users do and how they feel can be more reliable and valid when concurrent real-time measurements are taken [42].

To alleviate the aforementioned limitations, recent UX research has increasingly employed physiological measurements, which comprise both voluntary (e.g., facial expressions) and involuntary bodily responses (e.g., brain waves) in connection to human affects, emotions and moods [26]. In principle, a holistic understating of user experience can be obtained by triangulating objective physiological data with subjective self-reports [73]. Despite the advantages of using physiological measurements, there are several limitations associated with them. First, taking such measurements requires wearing sensors, some of which are obtrusive (e.g., headgear for electroencephalogram sensors) and some may cause discomfort such as tension and restraint, as some sensors are highly sensitive to movement [17]. Third, a robust approach enabling direct mapping of physiological data to specific emotions such as frustration is yet to be developed [2]. Moreover, employing physiological measurements involves additional expenses such as the purchase of special equipment and expertise that entails training [43].

On the other hand, recognising emotions from vocal cues has a long history in various fields of research, ranging from physiology to computer science and engineering. To detect emotions from voice, acoustic parameters of the speech signal are extracted for finding patterns of the vocal expressions of different emotional states [62]. With the advancement in audio analysis and pattern recognition techniques, the application

DIS 2017, June 10–14, 2017, Edinburgh, United Kingdom.

http://dx.doi.org/10.1145/X10.1145/3064663.3064770

of vocal expressions of naturally occurring emotions has been proposed in different HCI studies (e.g. [16]).

Nevertheless, the think aloud technique [27] is one of the most used methods in usability [46]. This technique has been applied in a handful number of studies (e.g. [49, 70]) to evaluate emotional experiences as well. Hence, we argue that utterances collected during thinking aloud can be analysed nonverbally and through vocal cues (such as intensity and pitch) to derive users' emotions. This approach can be used as an enhanced method for UX evaluation, where it is also consistent with the description that UX is a continuous self-talk and comprises constant pain and pleasure with different intensities [34].

This proposed approach has the advantage of flexibility because it does not require any sophisticated equipment and is also less invasive as compared to other physiological data collection approaches for identifying momentary emotions [77]. Moreover, collecting acoustic data for evaluating emotions in UX can be used to triangulate the validity and reliability of self-report questionnaires.

Most importantly, we envisage that our approach can contribute to enhancing usability and UX testing by enabling evaluators to have a good view of a user's dynamic emotional trajectory when interacting with technology, given real-time moment-by-moment measures. This fine-grained data can help understand which features of a product (including presentation, functionality, interaction and content [33]) trigger a specific emotion. Based on such enriched information (i.e. the emotionally annotated content), designers are enabled to find out what aspects of a product cause negative or positive experience and why [12]. Furthermore, processing and analysing data obtained from usability evaluations can be very expensive and tediously time consuming. However, if a participant's significant emotional changes at specific points of time during a user-based test (e.g. being irritated by a usability problem) can be detected automatically and marked as critical incidents in a recording medium, it can facilitate the process of data analysis by directing the evaluator's attention to those points of interest.

Moreover, contrary to memory-based assessments that are prone to the peak-end effect, where the most intense and/or last moment of emotional responses lead to the global evaluation of an experience, moment-based assessments draw on the measures of instantaneous experiences of pleasure and pain, a concept Kahneman referred to as experienced utility [38]. Experienced utility is anchored in the reality of occurring experience, not in erroneous reconstructions and evaluations of the past. According to Kahneman, the concept of well-being to which UX is strongly related [22] is constructed from the same building blocks as experienced utility: moments. Therefore, well-being is tightly linked to moment-based emotional experiences. Assuming this relationship, emotional experiences, when properly operationalised and measured, can account for and predict well-being.

In the new era of computing, digital technologies afford multiple forms of experiences in everyday life such as working, learning and communicating. Increasing attention has been shifted to understand how new technologies can be used to promote well-being to which positive user experience can contribute. To develop such a understanding, it is crucial to explore the nature of emotional experiences and how they can reliably be measured [15].

In this paper, we propose that the assessment of emotions in think aloud verbalisations is congruent with the moment-based approach, and can be utilised for understanding experience derived from the interaction with a product/system. Therefore, in this study we attempt to investigate two research questions (RQs):

> RQ1: Whether changes in emotions as expressed through think aloud verbalisations are sufficiently large to be measured/detected to indicate the corresponding changes in the quality of interaction with a product?

In addition, we address the following research question adapted from [34]:

> RQ2: How users' moment-by-moment emotions elicited when interacting with a product are integrated into their accumulated emotion and thereby attitude towards the product?

We have chosen online shopping as the domain to assess emotional experiences measured by our proposed moment-based approach. Typically, the success of online shopping hinges crucially on customers' emotions [45], as positive emotions stimulate the intention to purchase whereas negative emotions most likely result in avoiding a product purchase [21].

RELATED WORK

In this section, we first present the definition of emotion, current UX measurement methods, the role of emotions in online shopping activities and emotion analysis by acoustic data.

What are Emotions?

The definition of emotions has been widely discussed in psychology[40]. In this paper, we adopt the following definition of emotions from [63], in which emotions are cognitive responses toward a stimulus event; their duration is relatively short and lasts between seconds to minutes. Emotions differ from moods, which have longer duration, emerge without any apparent cause and are not necessarily linked to a specific event. While we are well aware of the ongoing debates on the differences between affect, emotion and mood [24, 74], we do not delve into details as it entails a separate exposition. Our work embraces the notion of emotion defined by Scherer [63] as involving cognitive and evaluative elements. In this work, similar to [53], the terms emotional state and affective state were used interchangeably. Both terms refer to the dynamic state when a person experiences an emotion.

Measurement Methods of UX

The most commonly used UX data collection methods include questionnaires, interviews, observation, focus groups, diaries and probes [3]. To measure emotions in UX, Self-Assessment Manikin (SAM) scale [8] is one of the most widely used instruments based on three independent dimensions: pleasure, arousal and dominance (PAD) [45]. Positive And Negative Affect Schedule (PANAS) [20] scale is another extensively used tool to measure emotions based on discrete descriptors. Despite the highly frequent use of both dimensional and discrete emotion measurements, the question whether emotional responses should be evaluated based on dimensional or discrete descriptors is still under debate [10] as each has its strengths as well as weaknesses. Nonetheless, it seems justifiable to utilise both approaches to gather data that are complementary as well as supplementary for evaluating momentary emotions.

Even though retrospective surveys can be used in large scale and are convenient, they have several drawbacks, as mentioned before. Likewise, retrospective evaluations do not reflect the reality of actual experience [42] and are fallible because of the memory bias [38]. To address these limitations, the think aloud technique can provide data about momentary emotional experiences [44]. In addition, to make sense of think aloud data, rigorous and lengthy processes such as content analysis are required [44]. This process can be made more efficient with the help of automatic acoustic data analysis to locate points of interest, as mentioned earlier.

A bulk of research studies in HCI has used physiological responses to measure emotions by placing sensors on participants (e.g. [10, 44]). The benefit of using physiological measurements is the ability to objectively capture changes in emotional states. For example, Galvanic Skin Response (GSR) has been found to have significant correlations with emotional arousal as well as cognitive activity [7]. Electromyography (EMG) has been used to differentiate between positive and negative emotions, and heart rate (HR) to indicate the emotional activity [44]. Physiological measurements can also be used alongside self-report questionnaires as an approach to check the reliability and validity of subjective responses [43]. Despite the increasing affordability and portability of the equipment for such physiological measures, the demanding data analysis processes and lack of standardised approaches to interpreting findings are some of the drawbacks. To circumvent them, some research has used motor expressions such as facial cues to identify emotions. To map facial expressions to emotions, Facial Action Coding System (FACS) [25] is a widely used approach in different research contexts (e.g. [60]). However, deploying FACS successfully requires exhaustive training and observation for coders to exploit it [76] and it is very time consuming [13]. These reasons have led to the position we have taken to investigate the feasibility of applying a new methodological approach making use of traditional methods as well as more recent ones for evaluating emotions.

Emotional Experiences in Online Shopping Environment

According to the basic research model of Mehrabian and Russel [45], environmental characteristics induce individuals' emotional responses. The premise of this model is that the atmospheric cues are the stimuli that influence people's cognitive and emotional reactions, which subsequently result in certain behaviours. In the domain of online shopping, this model has been widely used to explain the relationships between customers' emotions and their perception of the e-store's design attributes, including aesthetic and pragmatic features and their recognises toward the e-store (e.g. [53]).

To investigate emotional reactions in online shopping environments, the PAD framework [45] has been adopted by some studies (e.g. [53]). In the PAD framework, pleasure is the degree to which one feels happy or joyful, arousal is the degree to which one feels excited or stimulated, and dominance describes the level of control, autonomy or freedom. It has been stated that pleasure and arousal dimensions are adequate to represent the range of emotional states elicited in response to environmental stimuli [58]. However, dominance has been demonstrated as a reliable indicator for the controlling power over the environment in an online context [38]. Hence, we have considered all three dimensions of emotions in our study.

Acoustic Emotion Analysis

Research on emotional cues manifested in voices has a history of about 45 years, starting with the work of Williams and Steven in 1972 [75]. The theoretical idea behind vocal emotion analysis is that affective states have a specific effect on the somatic nervous system (SNS), which in turn changes the tension of musculature and thus influences the voice production. In other words, the characteristics of the vocal expressions at a particular time describe the effect of emotional changes on the SNS [61]. In this regard, research has shown that correlations exist between acoustic features such as intensity (loudness), energy, range, F0 (the acoustic feature known as pitch) and the vocal expressions of affective states such as stress, anger, boredom and sadness [61].

Based on this theoretical background, the study of vocal cues as indicators of emotions was investigated in different research and operationalised in varied applications. They include: voice emotion detection in negotiation systems to visualise feedback [47], tutoring applications to improve communication [51], entertainment and game programs [35], emotionally-intelligent car systems [67] and emotion tracking applications integrated in virtual agents [72].

In the work of Nowak [47], a single feature, median pitch was extracted by Praat (the phonetics software [5]) and used as an indicator of emotional arousal. However, the use of machine learning (ML) and classification techniques based on a set of features is another widely used approach for recognition of emotion from acoustic analysis (e.g. [51, 72]). The machine learning approach is coupled with choosing emotionally annotated corpora for training data, selection of the most important and optimal set of features related to emotions and the choice of classification algorithms to create models for recognition of unseen data. In this paper, we followed the procedure of machine learning approach for emotion detection in a user experience testing scenario. Details of the different choices made are given in the subsequent section.

VOICE EMOTIONAL ANALYSIS

In this section we explain the implementation methodology of voice emotion analysis that we followed in this study. It involves two key processes: Training and Recognition. The Training phase describes the details of developing an appropriate classifier (the left side of Figure 1). The Recognition

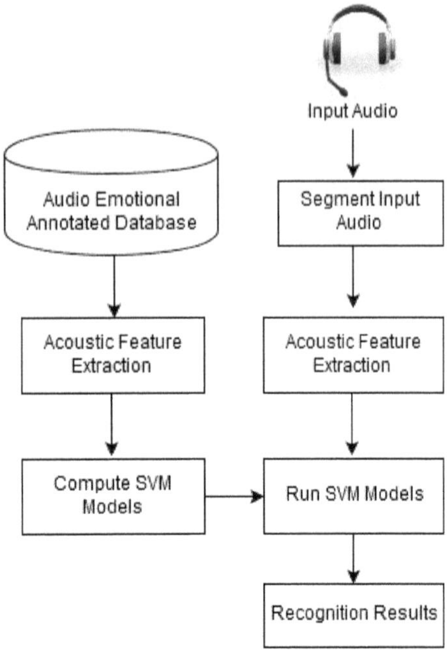

Figure 1. A flowchart of the functionality implemented for emotion recognition from acoustic features.

phase delineates the steps that are required to carry out for recognition of emotions on a dataset that is not emotionally annotated (the right side of Figure 1). Note that the classifier that is created during the Training phase is used for recognition of emotions in the Recognition phase.

Training Phase

Emotionally-Annotated Audio Database: IEMOCAP

The Interactive Emotional Dyadic Motion Capture (IEMOCAP) database was used as the training set for our emotion detection system. IEMOCAP is an audio-visual corpus generated by the Speech Analysis and Interpretation Laboratory (SAIL) at the University of Southern California [14]. This database includes approximately 12 hours of dyadic interactions from ten trained actors. In this database, actors performed scripted and spontaneous emotional scenarios designed to evoke specific types of emotions, namely: happiness, sadness, anger, frustration and neutral state. These emotion labels are the most common ones in the literature [52]. However, during the evaluation of this database by human evaluators, the emotional categories were expanded to include excitement, disgust, fear and surprise as well. In addition to the discrete emotional labels, this database was annotated with dimensional emotional descriptors arousal [1-calm, 5-excited], valence [1 negative-5 positive] and dominance [1 weak-5 strong] for each utterance.

In this database, emotion categories of fear, disgust and surprise comprised a very small number of utterances (e.g. 107 instances of 'surprise' out of a total of 10039 utterances). Since the large difference in the number of instances for each of these categories may cause the imbalanced dataset problem during the classification, in our work the utterances with these three labels were excluded from the training set. In addition, we combined the instances of emotion categories of happiness and excitement as one class - happiness, due to the reason that a significant overlap was also observed between human annotators' evaluations in annotating the IEMOCAP corpus [14].

In creating the IEMOCAP database, the actors were asked to perform scripted scenarios as well as improvised dialogs in spontaneous situations. While in acted emotions, it is expected that generic expressions of emotions can be achieved, there are some disadvantages related to them. For instance, acted emotions are not the same as spontaneous emotions elicited in realistic situations [66]. Therefore, having both acted and spontaneous emotions in a database is desirable, and this advantage enabled us to choose this database for emotion recognition.

Acoustic Feature Extraction

We used the openSMILE [29] feature extraction toolkit. OpenSMILE is an open source signal processing software that extracts acoustic features from voice signals. This software integrates voice activity detection algorithms to detect voice signals and then extracts multiple audio features from each signal. Hence, alongside the voice detection algorithms, a predefined acoustic feature set must be employed to extract those properties of the acoustic signal that best describes emotions. The INTERSPEECH Emotion Challenge 2009 is a predefined feature set in openSMILE that contains 384 acoustic parameters [68]. The reason behind using large-scale feature sets is the assumption that these sets most likely contain the right attributes for emotion recognition, yielding better performance in terms of mean accuracy of correctly recognised samples [68].

Apart from the best emotion describing selection of acoustic features, removing the weakly relevant and redundant features is an important step that improves the classification accuracy [1]. Consequently, we used Correlation-based Feature Selection (CFS) [32] algorithm to choose the most relevant features. This algorithm follows a heuristic-based approach with this assumption that relevant feature sets are highly correlated with the prediction class and uncorrelated with each other. After the feature selection stage, all the features were normalised to [-1, 1]. This is the setting that must be done to scale all attributes with small or large numeric values to the same range.

Classifier (Model) Creation

The classifier of choice for our work is the popular Support Vector Machines (SVMs) in the field of paralinguistics [28]. SVMs have shown higher accuracy in the field of voice emotion recognition than the other classifiers (e.g. [51]). SVMs work by constructing a high dimensional feature space or hyperplane based on the input space. The hyperplane is used to separate data into categories; each category includes data instances that best describe the desired class.

We used a linear classifier function for the SVMs using datamining software WEKA [31]. When using a linear SVM, the line between classes cannot be always drawn neatly. Therefore a margin is introduced around the lines between the classes to relax the constraint, allowing some instances to be mislabelled while allowing a better result in general. Consequently, it is required to evaluate a range of values in order to identify the most suitable value of the so-called margin or Complexity parameter (C).

In our work, a range of values of C was examined. The goal was to identify a good value of C so that the classifier can have the most optimised accuracy for recognition on unseen data. In addition, we applied the 10-fold cross-validation technique in which the training set is split into 10 folds with the same size; each fold is sequentially tested using the classifier parameterised with a value of C and trained on the remaining 9 folds.

Once the classifier with the best performance is computed, it is stored for recognition on the unseen or future data. By unseen data, we refer to the data that is not emotionally annotated by human evaluators. For example, in this work, think aloud verbalisations recorded during the study contain the unseen dataset.

Recognition

Segmentation

Emotion analysis of recorded audio data requires finding appropriate acoustic segments as units of analysis for emotion classification. There are different approaches to define the unit of analysis or segments. One approach is to automatically breakdown the audio input into units with a predefined length of duration (e.g. segments with 5 seconds length [55]). However, according to the literature, there is no clear consensus concerning the best length of duration for emotion analysis [56]. Another approach is to identify the meaningful units with varying lengths, for example, recognition on word or utterance level.

Nonetheless, we decided to manually segment audio recordings into meaningful utterances as the unit of analysis due to two reasons; First, each utterance is a well-defined linguistic entity which is emotionally consistent [72]. In this regard many studies have also used the utterance level for emotion analysis (e.g. [71]). Second, the IEMOCAP corpora, which was used as the training set in our study, was also emotionally annotated based on utterances.

In the process of recognition (Figure 1), the next step after segmentation is extracting acoustic features for each utterance. In this stage, the same procedure for feature extraction is followed, as it was explained in the previous section.

In the last step of the recognition phase, the classifier that has been developed during the training phase is run for each utterance to recognise its emotional descriptor.

Participants

Forty six participants (female=25, male=21) took part in this study. Thirty eight of the participants are native English speakers and the rest are very fluent in English. They were recruited through the authors' personal contacts. The sample consisted of university students from the undergraduate (n=26) to postgraduate level (n=17) and 3 participants were university academics or administrative staff. Most of the students participating in this study majored in computer science, followed by geography, law, physics, management, and chemistry. However, data of 7 participants were excluded from data analysis, because they were either incomplete or invalid (e.g., participants failed to follow the instructions).

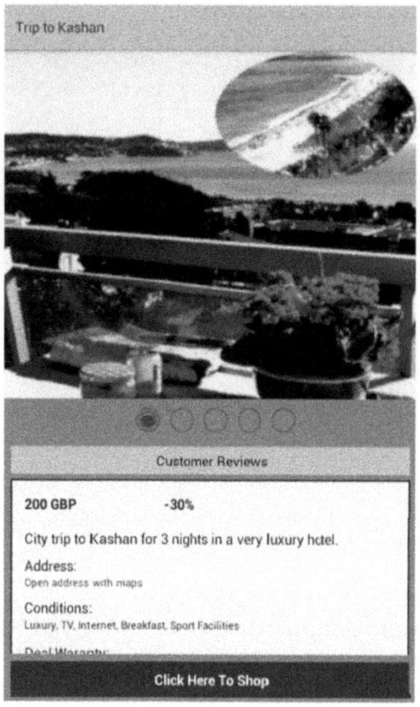

Figure 2. Second interface of HolidayFinder, the online shopping platform.

Equipment and Instruments

Hardware

The hardware that was used in this study included a tablet, 7 inches screen size, with the Android operation system and a laptop running Windows 7 equipped with an external microphone headset to capture the audio input and to filter out ambient noise.

Shopping Application

We developed an Android-based application, called HolidayFinder, as an online shopping platform that offered discounted travel recommendations. In this application, the selection of a service (the travel recommendation) was processed in three steps with each displayed in a user interface. The first interface contained details of the service, including multiple images and textual contents. The second interface included the checkout form to be filled in by the user. Finally the last interface contained the 'Thank You' message and a button to continue shopping (Figure 2).

We also created a Java-based application to record the audio data captured by the headset microphone at 44.1 kHz, 16bits as a wav file for each participant. This is the standard configuration that was used by the openSMILE software to process audio data.

Emotion-Aesthetic-Usability-Response Scale

We adopted the Porat & Tractinsky scale [53]. This scale includes sub-scales for measuring pleasure (5 items), arousal

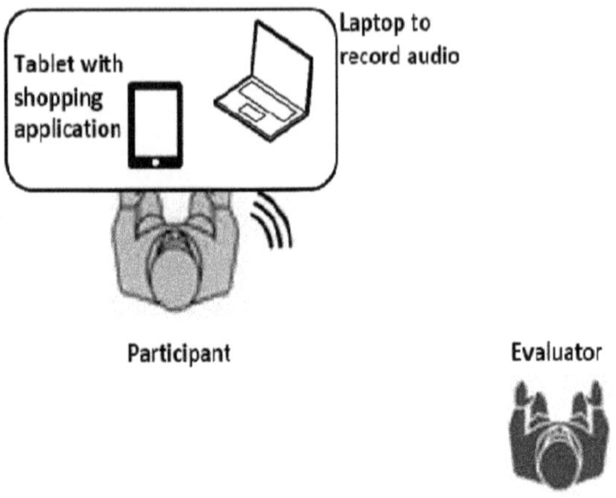

Figure 3. Experimental setup.

(six items) and dominance (six items). In addition, this scale has sub-scales for assessing Classical Aesthetics (four items), Expressive Aesthetics (four items), Usability (4 items) and Approach-Avoidance Response (5 items).

An online survey based on this scale was created by using the free version of the platform called Qualtrics. Specifically, the items of pleasure, arousal and dominance sub-scales were presented as bipolar statements in a 5- point range (e.g. 1 unhappy- 5 happy), and aesthetic, usability and approach-avoidance items were presented as statements with a 5-point scale with 'strongly disagree' as the leftmost anchor with the value 1 and 'strongly agree' as the rightmost anchor with 5. Demographic questions such as age, gender and current education level were added as a separate screen at the end of the survey.

Procedure

The study was ran as a series of lab-based sessions on an individual basis. In the beginning of each session the experimenter described the objectives of the study and procedures to the participant, including the think aloud protocol. Next, the session continued by a short think aloud trial phase where the participants were instructed to verbalise thoughts and feelings while interacting with the Amazon.com website. In addition, they were reminded that when they were carrying out the tasks with HolidayFinder, the experimenter would not interact with them except prompting them to keep on thinking aloud if they remained silent for 15 seconds.

After the introduction phase, the actual experiment began. In this phase, the participants were asked to complete a shopping process according to the following scenario and talk out loud their thoughts and emotions during their interaction, which were audiotaped:

> Your friend's wedding is coming in three days from today and you need to get him/her something as a gift. You are aware of his/her interest in taking pleasurable trips. There is an application in your tablet called HolidayFinder, which offers different holiday options. You find today a good time to buy a gift for your friend.

Utterances	Labels	P	A	D
It seems relatively straightforward to book.	Happiness	4	4	3
It wasn't really clear that was checkout being "click to shop"	Sadness	2	3	3

Table 1. Example of transcription of utterances. Note that the dimensions P (pleasure), A (arousal) and D (dominance) were recognised on the scale 1 (low)- 5 (high).

Upon the completion of the given task, the participants were asked to fill out the final questionnaire, which consisted of the Porat & Tractinsky scale. Finally at the end of session, participants were given time to provide optional feedback about the entire experiment and then they were thanked for their participation. Each participant was allocated a one-hour session. However, most of the sessions were completed before the planned time.

Audio Emotion Analysis

The audio records of all the sessions were manually transcribed and segmented into the utterance level as the unit of analysis to perform emotion recognition. To identify the meaningful utterances, two raters were involved in this task. One of the raters is an HCI researcher (the first author of this paper) and the other is an electrical engineer who is familiar with HCI work in general but was not involved in designing or running the empirical studies. The raters independently listened to the recorded audio files and segmented the related transcription into chunks where each chunk conveys distinct emotional information from the next chunk in the sequence of the verbalised content. In addition, to provide a clearer idea of what it was meant by a meaningful utterance, examples of earlier segmented transcriptions from the IEMOCAP corpus were given to the raters. To determine the level of agreements in the segmentation task between the two raters, inter-rater reliability was measured by Cohen's Kappa [30]. The value of Kappa was 0.74, which is a reasonable level of agreement [57].

Next, according to the process of emotion recognition that was explained in the previous section, the emotional state of each utterance was detected based on the discrete emotions and dimensional approach. As a result, for each utterance one emotion label (labels such as happiness, frustration, anger, sadness, and neutral) and three integer numbers (1: low, 5: high) corresponding to the level of pleasure, arousal and dominance were derived (Table 1).

In total 1499 utterances were segmented for emotion recognition (mean=39.4, SD=24.4 utterance per participant).

Human Validation

To check the validity of the recognised emotion values, the same two raters for the segmentations task were involved to assess the emotional attribute of each utterance based on the three dimensions of emotion - pleasure, arousal and dominance - on a 5-point integer scale, ranging from 1(low) to 5 (high). The Kappa value was computed to test the reliability of the evaluations between the two evaluators: Kappa pleasure= 0.51, Kappa arousal= 0.77 and Kappa dominance= 0.53, while the Kappa scores between 0.4- 0.6 are considered to be fair [57]. The rather low values of Kappa for pleasure and dominance can be attributed to the fuzziness in identifying emotions [23].

HYPOTHESES

Kahneman described the concept of total experience as the aggregation of moments with good or bad experiences [38]. Based on this concept, we assume that each utterance serves as a moment of experience that can be analysed along three dimensions of emotion. Hence, the total experience can be derived from accumulating the emotional values of all utterances of that particular participant. In addition, since the three dimensions are known to be independent, their corresponding values were accumulated independently [49]. Furthermore, Kahneman [38] also remarked that the retrospective evaluation of an experience should not be taken at face value. Accordingly, we hypothesise that the retrospective assessment of PAD dimensions is an erroneous estimate of total experience. This hypothesis (H) is formulated as follows:

> *H1.* Retrospective evaluation of PAD dimensions (pleasure, H1a; arousal, H1b; dominance, H1c) will not be significantly correlated to the total experience of PAD during the actual interaction as derived from acoustic analysis.

According to Scherer [63], there are a small number of emotions that are relatively frequently experienced, such as anger and joy. Scherer suggested calling these emotions *Modal Emotions*. In our study, we assessed the modal or most frequent occurring emotion that was detected by the emotion recogniser for each participant during his or her experiences. Anger was the most frequent emotional reactions recognised during the emotion analysis across all participants, followed by happiness and neutral. In our study, we were also interested to investigate whether and to what extent the modal emotions elicited during an experience could be inferred from the retrospective assessments, and formulated the following hypothesis:

> *H2.* The more positive the modal emotion is, the more positive the retrospective appraisal of the experience is; and vice versa.

DATA ANALYSIS

Normalising Total Experience

As explained previously, for each dimension of emotion, their corresponding values across all utterances of a particular participant were summed to obtain a value of total experience. However, due to individual differences in think aloud behaviours, the number of utterances could vary significantly from one participant to another.

To control this, the value of total experience was averaged based on the total number of utterances for each participant. In other words, for all participants, the value of dimensions - pleasure, arousal and dominance - were normalised to a number in a range from 1 to 5. Therefore:

Total Experience Normalised $_i$ = Total Experience Raw $_i$ / N_i

	P_R	P_{Ac}	P_M
Mean	3.31	2.14	2.22
SD	0.75	0.33	0.23
Max	4.8	4	3.6
	A_R	A_{Ac}	A_M
Mean	3.14	4.22	2.1
SD	0.62	0.44	0.35
Max	4.25	3.95	2.7
	D_R	D_{Ac}	D_M
Mean	3.33	2.01	2.25
SD	0.55	0.14	0.26
Max	4.42	2.35	2.89

Table 2. Descriptive analysis of PAD dimensions taken from retrospective questionnaire and moment-based emotion analysis assessed automatically using acoustic features and by human evaluators. The subscript R denotes Retrospective, Ac denotes Acoustic analysis and M refers to Manual assessment by the human raters.

Where N_i is the total number of utterances for the participant i.

Quantifying Modal Emotion

According to the circumplex model of affects [54], emotions can be categorized in a two-dimensional space defined by pleasure (P) and arousal (A). Thus, each emotion can be understood as the product of these two independent dimensions.

To obtain a comparable measure between the retrospective assessment of experience using the PAD dimensions and the modal emotions detected by the emotion recogniser, the following procedure was performed for each participant.

First, we assigned a value to each type of modal emotion. In this regard, happiness was assigned to 3 (most positive detected emotion), neutral to 2 and anger to 1 (most negative detected emotion). For instance, if for participant i the modal emotion was anger, value 1 represented this emotion category.

Next, the score $E=P*A$ from the self-reported retrospective assessment of pleasure and arousal dimensions was obtained. The score E was considered as the equivalent measure of the modal emotion derived from the retrospective assessment. As the results, it was expected to find a pattern that the highest scores of $P*A$ are associated with the positive modal emotion, which was happiness, the lowest scores of $P*A$ are associated with Anger and the medium scores of $P*A$ are associated with Neutral as the modal emotion.

RESULTS

Descriptive Statistics

Table 2 presents the mean, standard deviation and max values of the PAD dimensions taken from the retrospective questionnaire (which is designated as PAD_R), moment-based analysis of PAD collected during the experience and assessed using the acoustic-emotion analysis (which is designated as PAD_{Ac}) and manually by the human raters (which is denoted as PAD_M).

Three one-way ANOVAs were conducted, one for each of the three dimension- with pleasure, arousal and dominance being the dependent variables (DV) and the type of assessment

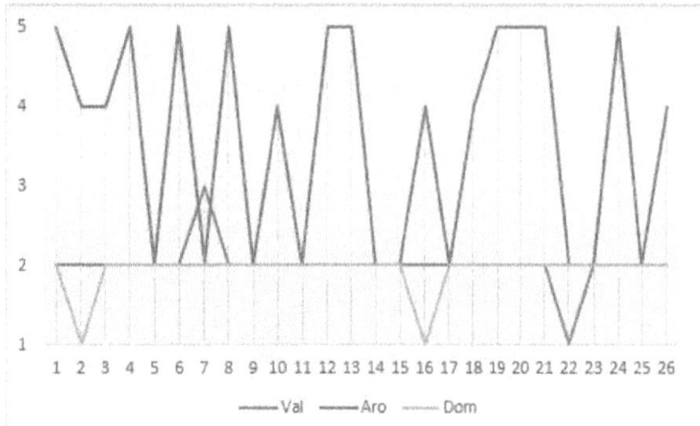

Figure 4. Example of emotional changes profile measured by acoustic analysis (participant 2).

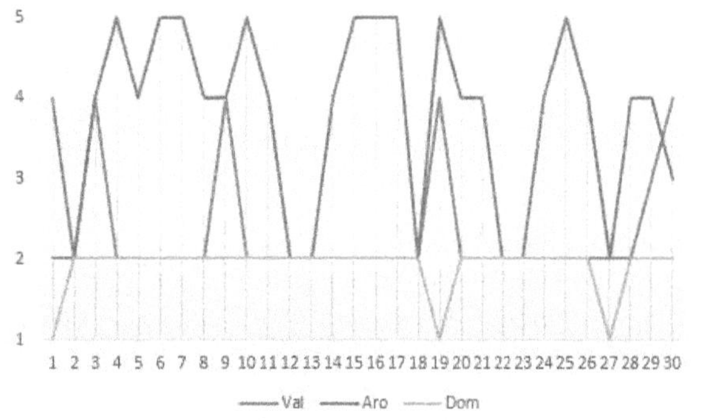

Figure 5. Example of emotional changes profile measured by acoustic analysis (participant 21).

method (Retrospective questionnaire, automatic Acoustic analysis and Manual assessment by human raters) as the independent variable (IV). Results of ANOVA revealed significant differences in measuring arousal across the three assessment methods (F (2, 98) = 132.4 $p < .001$). Acoustic assessment of arousal was significantly higher than Retrospective (t(37) = 8.74 $p < .001$) and Manual (t(37) = 20.31 $p < .001$) assessments. Retrospective assessment of arousal was significantly greater than Manual assessment (t(37) = 6.50 $p < .001$). In summary, the mean scores of arousal measured by the three approaches were in this order $A_{Ac} > A_R > A_M$.

In measuring pleasure, there was no significant difference between the Acoustic and Manual assessment. In contrast, the differences between Retrospective and Acoustic (t(37) = 8.77 $p < .001$) and between Retrospective and Manual (t(37) = 6.95 $p < .001$) were highly significant. Similarly, in measuring dominance, the significant differences were detected between Retrospective and Acoustic (t(37) = 15.92 $p < .001$) and between Retrospective and Manual (t(37) = 8.97 $p < .001$).

In addition, Figures 3 and 4 represent two participants' emotional changes during their interaction measured by acoustic analysis. They show that emotional arousal changes more quickly over time than emotional valence and dominance (see Discussion).

Correlations

H1: A Spearman's rank-order correlation was run to determine whether associations exist between the measures taken from the three assessment methods, including the use of questionnaire, audio-emotion analysis and human ratings in evaluating PAD dimensions. Results of the analysis showed no correlation in the measures of pleasure and arousal dimensions. However, positive and significant correlations were found for the Dominance dimension. The results showed that there were significant correlations between D_{Ac} and D_R ($r_s(39) = .432$, $p = .02$) and between D_M and D_R ($r_s(39) = .57$, $p = .04$). Therefore, we concluded that H1a and H1b were accepted, and H1c was not supported.

H2: Results of a Spearman's rank-order correlation test between the modal emotion and the *P*A* score derived from the retrospective assessment showed a statistically significant positive correlation ($r_s(39) = .339$, $p = .05$). Therefore, H2 was accepted.

DISCUSSION

Implications for UX Evaluation Practice

In this paper we proposed a methodological approach to measure UX using the think aloud technique and by emotional analysis of the acoustic features extracted from the think aloud data. While variations of thinking aloud protocols have been widely used to help identify usability problems (e.g. [11]), acoustic data obtained alongside the think aloud reports can be utilised for measuring emotional aspect of UX [50], as supported by the existing empirical research that acoustic characteristics of speech are reliable indicators for emotional responses [61].

The findings of our research study have further substantiated those of the previous work (i.e. that the retrospective measurements of experience were not consistent with the sum or average of real-time measurements of experience) [9, 18]. In addition, our work can contribute to the HCI community by providing some new insights into assessing users' emotional experiences momentarily and by utilising the advancement in machine learning techniques for real-time detection of emotions based on acoustic data. Overall, our proposed approach can make the better use of the think aloud technique, which is widely used in usability and UX assessments. Secondly, our proposed approach brings about this argument that how current usability and UX methods can be moved forward along with the improvements in other techniques. For example the advancements in the techniques for emotion recognition can result in a better analysis of verbal and non-verbal expressions, which can also be used as an alternative or complementary approach to self-report of emotions.

The data collection in this study was carried out in a laboratory setting with the presence of an experimenter, though out of the participant's sight. However, the quantity and quality of disclosure of emotions can differ depending on whether an audience is present or not [48]. Therefore, it would be intriguing to find out how our results would vary without the attendance of the experimenter in a test session.

Furthermore, as mentioned earlier, supporting well-being in relation to technology requires appropriate assessment methods [22]. One approach is to integrate multiple methods to evaluate varied expressions of emotions in multiple modalities, including text, audio (sound), visual (drawings), non-verbal facial expressions and body gestures, and others [15]. We addressed this goal by proposing a method to analyse emotional experiences from vocal expressions and self-report measures. Our future research will be extended to include the use of facial expressions and emotional analysis of verbal reports from the linguistic perspective [48] to find the relationships between different modalities.

Memory-based vs. Moment-based Assessments

In comparison between retrospective and moment-based assessments of the PAD dimensions, one significant correlation was found; positive correlation between D_{Ac} (moment-based evaluation of dominance through acoustic emotional analysis) and D_R (retrospective evaluation of dominance by the use of questionnaire). According to Kahneman [38], experience is characterized by the moments of good or bad (pleasure or valence) with different intensity from mild to extreme (arousal). Based on this conception, dominance or the level that a person feels in control of situation should not be considered as an attribute of the moment of experience. In addition, the reason for finding the significant correlation between D_{Ac} and D_R can be explained by the assumption that dominance is likely more stable over time, not as fluctuating as pleasure and arousal, which change from moment to moment (cf. Figures 4 and 5). As a result, the retrospective evaluation of the dominance dimension is correlated with that of the moment-based assessment reflected about this dimension. In addition, previous research has also argued that dominance reflects a more cognitive reaction and less of an emotional state [4]. This is another argument that can explain why there is no significant difference between memory-based and moment-based evaluations of dominance.

Previous research has shown that retrospective evaluations of past experiences are influenced by two moments, namely: the moment with the highest intensity (i.e. the peak) and the final moment (i.e. end) [37, 36]. Results of this study suggested that the overall evaluation of an experience could be predicted by the most frequently elicited emotion (i.e. modal emotion) during the experience. It can be argued that the most frequently evoked emotion has become the most remembered emotional response for an event (cf. the notion of rehearsal in the theory of memory [19]), and therefore this modal emotion correlates strongly with the retrospective evaluation, which also relies on memory. This observation is also linked to Kahneman's [36] arguments on 'experiencing self' versus 'remembering self', which in turn is closely related to psychological well-being. Nonetheless, the intricate relationships of these constructs entail more research efforts.

Acoustic Analysis for Emotion Recognition

This study suggested the use of acoustic analysis as a method to evaluate emotional experience. However, emotion recognition from acoustic features is a complex process due to number of reasons. Firstly, there is no general agreement regarding the best unit of analysis for emotion recognition. The length of the segmentation window to perform emotion recognition can vary from word level to sentence level or it can be defined based on various lengths (e.g. ranging from 0.48s to 6.24s [56]). While we opted for manual segmentation of audio recordings into utterance levels, different lengths should be examined to estimate which length performs best for emotion recognition.

Secondly, the most important step in acoustic analysis of emotion is the extraction of the most emotion-related feature set that is reasonably concise [66]. We addressed this issue by using INTERSPEECH 2009 feature set, which has been used in previous studies and resulted in good emotion recognition performance (e.g. [51]).

Thirdly, emotion recognition from speech is very dependent on the corpora that are used for training the classifier [6]. For example, whether the corpus contains acted or spontaneous emotions or both. On the other hand, with the introduction of multiple corpora, improvements to the performance can be expected [6]. This will be an empirical research question for our future work.

In this work, two human raters separately marked utterances based on the notion of 'emotionally consistent units' as the criterion [66]. The final speech signal files were then segmented, where both evaluators were in agreement. The process of segmentation took on average double the length of each audio recording, which introduced an additional cost of manual labor. A remedy to this problem could be automatic segmentation through objective measures; such as using predefined lengths for segmentation or pauses longer than a threshold. However, the reason for our choice relates to the fact that automatic segmentation has the possibility to span over more than one emotional unit, resulting in masking meaningful units [66]. Clearly, there is a trade-off between precision and human effort invested. This cost-effectiveness issue is largely dependent on the precision level that a particular application requires (e.g. analysing the emotions of a suspect's interview may demand a higher precision than a usability test participant's thinking aloud.)

Furthermore, previous research showed that emotional arousal changed more rapidly over time than emotional valence [56], this is the pattern that was observed in our data analysis as well (Figures 4 and 5).

Insights into the Two Research Questions (RQs)

Here we revisit RQ1 and RQ2 we posed in Introduction. Our results suggested fluctuations in emotional experiences during a course of interaction. These changes were observed between the verbalised contents by human raters and the analysis of acoustic features. In other words, the changes in emotions were large enough to be manifested in voice and therefore be detected. The answer to RQ1 is affirmative. This finding has laid the groundwork for our future research to evaluate the content of verbalisationd reports with higher emotional intensity against the quality of interaction, including instrumental and non-instrumental qualities, with a product or service.

Concerning RQ2, with the current work we attempted to propose a methodology that enables us to view UX with blocks of momentary emotions as well as from a retrospective perspective. In the procedure of this methodology, the momentary emotions with similar characteristics expressed in voice were classified into different emotion categories. The category with the highest number of occurrences or the modal emotion was hypothesise as a predictor for an attitude toward the product or service. Our study was exploratory in nature and the goal was to develop a practical approach in order to enable us to address this research question. One implication would be exploring how the momentary perceptions of a product/service's qualities evolve during the interaction.

LIMITATIONS AND FUTURE WORK

In this work, we used the think aloud technique and acoustic emotional analysis to measure emotional experience in the moment-based approach. These chosen techniques did not require any additional expenses or equipment. They are not intrusive and also deployable in everyday working environments. The use of other measures such as facial expressions can triangulate our findings, resulting in a deeper understanding of momentary emotional experiences. Specifically, previous research has shown that facial analysis performs better than acoustic analysis to recognise valence, whereas acoustic analysis performs better for arousal detection [35].

In addition, according to the model proposed by Scherer [64], emotions are multi-components processes. These components are subjective feelings, physiological reactions, motor expression, cognitive appraisal and behavioural tendencies. In this study, we investigated emotions by analyzing acoustic features. This is a measurement method related to the motor expression component, however, a combination of methods should be used to assess different components of emotional experiences.

The sample in this work consisted mainly of university students aged between 20 to 35 years old. Therefore, the generalisability of the results is restricted to university-educated people within this age group. Additionally, psychophysiological studies typically demand a large sample size to derive reliable conclusions, especially due to the large individual differences in emotional reactions.

Moreover, the application used in this study was able to evoke some changes in emotional reactions in our participants, albeit to a modest extent. Most of the participants had a rather flat pattern of emotional reactions. The range of emotional arousal that was detected in this study was from 2.2 to 3.95. Hence, the results of this study were limited to a few emotional categories with rather low intensities.

The current study investigated the concept of emotional experiences only in one domain of interactive application (online shopping). Thus, this undermines the generalisability of our findings to the other domains such as gaming, which is likely to elicit a (much) broader range of emotions. However, we envision the applicability of emotional analysis of vocal expressions in natural conversation settings such as learning, entertainment and consumer dialogue.

CONCLUSION

This paper presented an exploratory study based on Kahneman's theory of distinction between memory-based and moment-based approaches for measuring experience. In this regard, we proposed a moment-based approach based on the think aloud technique and emotional analysis of acoustic features extracted from think aloud verbalisations.

Previous research identified two dimensions, pleasure and arousal, as the characteristics of experience and therefore we used these two attributes in the construction of moment-based and memory-based assessments. In this study, in addition to the pleasure and arousal dimensions, we investigated the third dimension of the PAD model, dominance, as a construct of experience as well. Our results showed that there was no correlation between memory-based and moment-based assessments of pleasure and arousal. However a positive correlation was found between the two measurement approaches for the dominance dimension. We argued that the dominance dimension is relatively stable over time and therefore the memory and moment-based assessments are related. In addition, our results showed that the retrospective evaluation of experience was correlated with modal emotion during the experience. We tend to conclude that the more positive the modal emotion is, the more positive the retrospective assessment of the experience. However, more research needs to be carried out to substantiate the results of this study.

Overall, the main contribution of our work is to demonstrate the feasibility of deploying acoustic analysis to evaluate people's emotional experiences when interacting with a system, This alternative approach can better verbalise the traditional think aloud technique, benefiting usability and UX researchers and practitioners.

ACKNOWLEDGEMENTS

We thank Leandro L. Minku for his comments on the earlier version of this paper and all participants for their voluntary participation in this study.

REFERENCES

1. Halis Altun and Gökhan Polat. 2007. New frameworks to boost feature selection algorithms in emotion detection for improved human-computer interaction. In *International Symposium on Brain, Vision, and Artificial Intelligence*. Springer, 533–541.
2. Panagiotis D Bamidis, Christos Papadelis, Chrysoula Kourtidou-Papadeli, Costas Pappas, and Ana B Vivas. 2004. Affective computing in the era of contemporary neurophysiology and health informatics. *Interacting with Computers* 16, 4 (2004), 715–721.
3. Javier A Bargas-Avila and Kasper Hornbæk. 2011. Old wine in new bottles or novel challenges: a critical analysis of empirical studies of user experience. In *Proceedings of the SIGCHI Conference on Human Factors in Computing Systems*. ACM, 2689–2698.
4. Lisa Feldman Barrett and James A Russell. 1999. The structure of current affect: Controversies and emerging

consensus. *Current directions in psychological science* 8, 1 (1999), 10–14.

5. Paulus Petrus Gerardus Boersma and others. 2002. Praat, a system for doing phonetics by computer. *Glot international* 5 (2002).
6. Daniel Bone, Chi-Chun Lee, and Shrikanth S Narayanan. 2012. A Robust Unsupervised Arousal Rating Framework using Prosody with Cross-Corpora Evaluation.. In *INTERSPEECH*. 1175–1178.
7. Wolfram Boucsein. 2012. *Electrodermal activity*. Springer Science & Business Media.
8. Margaret M Bradley and Peter J Lang. 1994. Measuring emotion: the self-assessment manikin and the semantic differential. *Journal of behavior therapy and experimental psychiatry* 25, 1 (1994), 49–59.
9. Anders Bruun and Simon Ahm. 2015. Mind the gap! comparing retrospective and concurrent ratings of emotion in user experience evaluation. In *Human-Computer Interaction*. Springer, 237–254.
10. Anders Bruun, Effie Lai-Chong Law, Matthias Heintz, and Lana HA Alkly. 2016. Understanding the Relationship between Frustration and the Severity of Usability Problems: What can Psychophysiological Data (Not) Tell Us?. In *Proceedings of the 2016 CHI Conference on Human Factors in Computing Systems*. ACM, 3975–3987.
11. Anders Bruun and Jan Stage. 2015. An empirical study of the effects of three think-aloud protocols on identification of usability problems. In *Human-Computer Interaction*. Springer, 159–176.
12. Michael Burmester, Marcus Mast, Kilian Jäger, and Hendrik Homans. 2010. Valence method for formative evaluation of user experience. In *Proceedings of the 8th ACM conference on Designing Interactive Systems*. ACM, 364–367.
13. Brandon Burr. 2006. VACA: a tool for qualitative video analysis. In *CHI'06 extended abstracts on Human factors in computing systems*. ACM, 622–627.
14. Carlos Busso, Murtaza Bulut, Chi-Chun Lee, Abe Kazemzadeh, Emily Mower, Samuel Kim, Jeannette N Chang, Sungbok Lee, and Shrikanth S Narayanan. 2008. IEMOCAP: Interactive emotional dyadic motion capture database. *Language resources and evaluation* 42, 4 (2008), 335.
15. Rafael A Calvo and Dorian Peters. 2014. *Positive computing: technology for wellbeing and human potential*. MIT Press.
16. Ching Hau Chan and Gareth JF Jones. 2005. Affect-based indexing and retrieval of films. In *Proceedings of the 13th annual ACM international conference on Multimedia*. ACM, 427–430.
17. Akhilesh Chandra and Thomas Calderon. 2005. Challenges and constraints to the diffusion of biometrics in information systems. *Commun. ACM* 48, 12 (2005), 101–106.
18. Andy Cockburn, Philip Quinn, and Carl Gutwin. 2015. Examining the peak-end effects of subjective experience. In *Proceedings of the 33rd annual ACM conference on human factors in computing systems*. ACM, 357–366.
19. Fergus IM Craik and Robert S Lockhart. 1972. Levels of processing: A framework for memory research. *Journal of verbal learning and verbal behavior* 11, 6 (1972), 671–684.
20. John R Crawford and Julie D Henry. 2004. The Positive and Negative Affect Schedule (PANAS): Construct validity, measurement properties and normative data in a large non-clinical sample. *British Journal of Clinical Psychology* 43, 3 (2004), 245–265.
21. Pieter MA Desmet. 2012. Faces of product pleasure: 25 positive emotions in human-product interactions. *International Journal of Design* 6, 2 (2012).
22. Pieter MA Desmet and Anna E Pohlmeyer. 2013. Positive design: An introduction to design for subjective well-being. *International Journal of Design* 7, 3 (2013).
23. Sidney D'mello and Arthur Graesser. 2007. Mind and body: Dialogue and posture for affect detection in learning environments. *Frontiers in Artificial Intelligence and Applications* 158 (2007), 161.
24. Panteleimon Ekkekakis. 2013. *The measurement of affect, mood, and emotion: A guide for health-behavioral research*. Cambridge University Press.
25. Paul Ekman and Wallace V Friesen. 1978. *Manual for the facial action coding system*. Consulting Psychologists Press.
26. Paul Ekman, Robert W Levenson, and Wallace V Friesen. 1983. Autonomic nervous system activity distinguishes among emotions. *Science* 221, 4616 (1983), 1208–1210.
27. K Anders Ericsson and Herbert A Simon. 1980. Verbal reports as data. *Psychological review* 87, 3 (1980), 215.
28. Florian Eyben, Klaus R Scherer, Björn W Schuller, Johan Sundberg, Elisabeth André, Carlos Busso, Laurence Y Devillers, Julien Epps, Petri Laukka, Shrikanth S Narayanan, and others. 2016. The Geneva minimalistic acoustic parameter set (GeMAPS) for voice research and affective computing. *IEEE Transactions on Affective Computing* 7, 2 (2016), 190–202.
29. Florian Eyben, Martin Wöllmer, and Björn Schuller. 2010. Opensmile: the munich versatile and fast open-source audio feature extractor. In *Proceedings of the 18th ACM international conference on Multimedia*. ACM, 1459–1462.
30. Joseph L Fleiss and Jacob Cohen. 1973. The equivalence of weighted kappa and the intraclass correlation coefficient as measures of reliability. *Educational and psychological measurement* 33, 3 (1973), 613–619.

31. Mark Hall, Eibe Frank, Geoffrey Holmes, Bernhard Pfahringer, Peter Reutemann, and Ian H Witten. 2009. The WEKA data mining software: an update. *ACM SIGKDD explorations newsletter* 11, 1 (2009), 10–18.
32. Mark A Hall and Lloyd A Smith. 1999. Feature Selection for Machine Learning: Comparing a Correlation-Based Filter Approach to the Wrapper.. In *FLAIRS conference*, Vol. 1999. 235–239.
33. Marc Hassenzahl. 2003. The thing and I: understanding the relationship between user and product. In *Funology*. Springer, 31–42.
34. Marc Hassenzahl. 2008. User experience (UX): towards an experiential perspective on product quality. In *Proceedings of the 20th Conference on l'Interaction Homme-Machine*. ACM, 11–15.
35. Christian Jones and Andrew Deeming. 2008. Affective human-robotic interaction. In *Affect and emotion in human-computer interaction*. Springer, 175–185.
36. Daniel Kahneman. 2011. *Thinking, fast and slow*. Macmillan.
37. Daniel Kahneman, Barbara L Fredrickson, Charles A Schreiber, and Donald A Redelmeier. 1993. When more pain is preferred to less: Adding a better end. *Psychological science* 4, 6 (1993), 401–405.
38. Daniel Kahneman, D Kahneman, A Tversky, and others. 2003. Experienced utility and objective happiness: A moment-based approach. *The psychology of economic decisions* 1 (2003), 187–208.
39. Daniel Kahneman, Peter P Wakker, and Rakesh Sarin. 1997. Back to Bentham? Explorations of experienced utility. *The quarterly journal of economics* 112, 2 (1997), 375–406.
40. Paul R Kleinginna and Anne M Kleinginna. 1981. A categorized list of emotion definitions, with suggestions for a consensual definition. *Motivation and emotion* 5, 4 (1981), 345–379.
41. Peter J Lang. 1995. The emotion probe: Studies of motivation and attention. *American psychologist* 50, 5 (1995), 372.
42. Effie Lai-Chong Law. 2011. The measurability and predictability of user experience. In *Proceedings of the 3rd ACM SIGCHI symposium on Engineering interactive computing systems*. ACM, 1–10.
43. Irene Lopatovska and Ioannis Arapakis. 2011. Theories, methods and current research on emotions in library and information science, information retrieval and human–computer interaction. *Information Processing & Management* 47, 4 (2011), 575–592.
44. Regan L Mandryk, Kori M Inkpen, and Thomas W Calvert. 2006. Using psychophysiological techniques to measure user experience with entertainment technologies. *Behaviour & information technology* 25, 2 (2006), 141–158.
45. Albert Mehrabian and James A Russell. 1974. *An approach to environmental psychology.* the MIT Press.
46. Janni Nielsen, Torkil Clemmensen, and Carsten Yssing. 2002. Getting access to what goes on in people's heads?: reflections on the think-aloud technique. In *Proceedings of the second Nordic conference on Human-computer interaction*. ACM, 101–110.
47. Michael Nowak, Juho Kim, Nam Wook Kim, and Clifford Nass. 2012. Social visualization and negotiation: effects of feedback configuration and status. In *Proceedings of the ACM 2012 conference on Computer Supported Cooperative Work*. ACM, 1081–1090.
48. James W Pennebaker, Ryan L Boyd, Kayla Jordan, and Kate Blackburn. 2015. *The development and psychometric properties of LIWC2015*. Technical Report.
49. Helen Petrie and John Precious. 2010. Measuring User Experience of websites: Think aloud protocols and an emotion word prompt list. In *CHI'10 Extended Abstracts on Human Factors in Computing Systems*. ACM, 3673–3678.
50. Paolo Petta, Catherine Pelachaud, and Roddy Cowie. 2011. Emotion-oriented systems. *The Humaine Handbook, ISBN* (2011), 978–3.
51. Tomas Pfister and Peter Robinson. 2011. Real-time recognition of affective states from nonverbal features of speech and its application for public speaking skill analysis. *IEEE Transactions on Affective Computing* 2, 2 (2011), 66–78.
52. Rosalind W Picard and Roalind Picard. 1997. *Affective computing*. Vol. 252. MIT press Cambridge.
53. Talya Porat and Noam Tractinsky. 2012. It's a pleasure buying here: The effects of web-store design on consumers' emotions and attitudes. *Human–Computer Interaction* 27, 3 (2012), 235–276.
54. Jonathan Posner, James A Russell, and Bradley S Peterson. 2005. The circumplex model of affect: An integrative approach to affective neuroscience, cognitive development, and psychopathology. *Development and psychopathology* 17, 03 (2005), 715–734.
55. Tauhidur Rahman and Carlos Busso. 2012. A personalized emotion recognition system using an unsupervised feature adaptation scheme. In *Acoustics, Speech and Signal Processing (ICASSP), 2012 IEEE International Conference on*. IEEE, 5117–5120.
56. Fabien Ringeval, Florian Eyben, Eleni Kroupi, Anil Yuce, Jean-Philippe Thiran, Touradj Ebrahimi, Denis Lalanne, and Björn Schuller. 2015. Prediction of asynchronous dimensional emotion ratings from audiovisual and physiological data. *Pattern Recognition Letters* 66 (2015), 22–30.

57. Colin Robson. 2002. Real world research: a resource for social scientists and practitioner. *Adapting Open Innovation in ICT Ecosystem Dynamics References Real World Research: A Resource for Social Scientists and Practitioner* (2002), 270.

58. James A Russell. 1979. Affective space is bipolar. *Journal of personality and social psychology* 37, 3 (1979), 345.

59. James A Russell. 2003. Core affect and the psychological construction of emotion. *Psychological review* 110, 1 (2003), 145.

60. Andrew Ryan, Jeffery F Cohn, Simon Lucey, Jason Saragih, Patrick Lucey, Fernando De la Torre, and Adam Rossi. 2009. Automated facial expression recognition system. In *Security Technology, 2009. 43rd Annual 2009 International Carnahan Conference on*. IEEE, 172–177.

61. Klaus R Scherer. 1986. Vocal affect expression: a review and a model for future research. *Psychological bulletin* 99, 2 (1986), 143.

62. Klaus R Scherer. 2003. Vocal communication of emotion: A review of research paradigms. *Speech communication* 40, 1 (2003), 227–256.

63. Klaus R Scherer. 2005. What are emotions? And how can they be measured? *Social science information* 44, 4 (2005), 695–729.

64. Klaus R Scherer, Klaus R Scherer, and Paul Ekman. 1984. On the nature and function of emotion: A component process approach. *Approaches to emotion* 2293 (1984), 317.

65. Klaus R Scherer, Angela Schorr, and Tom Johnstone. 2001. *Appraisal processes in emotion: Theory, methods, research*. Oxford University Press.

66. Björn Schuller, Anton Batliner, Stefan Steidl, and Dino Seppi. 2011. Recognising realistic emotions and affect in speech: State of the art and lessons learnt from the first challenge. *Speech Communication* 53, 9 (2011), 1062–1087.

67. Björn Schuller, Gerhard Rigoll, Michael Grimm, Kristian Kroschel, Tobias Moosmayr, and Günther Ruske. 2007. Effects of in-car noise-conditions on the recognition of emotion within speech. *Fortschritte der Akustik* 33, 1 (2007), 305.

68. Björn W Schuller, Stefan Steidl, Anton Batliner, and others. 2009. The INTERSPEECH 2009 emotion challenge.. In *Interspeech*, Vol. 2009. 312–315.

69. Thomas Tullis, William Albert, Joseph S Dumas, and Beth A Loring. 2008. Measuring the User Experience: Collecting Analyzing, and Presenting Usability. (2008).

70. Asimina Vasalou and Tanja Bänziger. 2006. Using the *think aloud* for affective evaluations in the lab: a work-in-progress. (2006). http://emotion-research.net/projects/humaine/ws/wp10/presentation-materials/VasalouAsimina-BaenzigerTanja-UsingThinkAloudForAffectiveEvaluations.pdf.

71. Dimitrios Ververidis and Constantine Kotropoulos. 2006. Emotional speech recognition: Resources, features, and methods. *Speech communication* 48, 9 (2006), 1162–1181.

72. Thurid Vogt, Elisabeth André, and Nikolaus Bee. 2008. EmoVoice?A framework for online recognition of emotions from voice. In *International Tutorial and Research Workshop on Perception and Interactive Technologies for Speech-Based Systems*. Springer, 188–199.

73. David G Wastell and Michael Newman. 1996. Stress, control and computer system design: a psychophysiological field study. *Behaviour & Information Technology* 15, 3 (1996), 183–192.

74. Margaret Wetherell. 2012. *Affect and emotion: A new social science understanding*. Sage Publications.

75. Carl E Williams and Kenneth N Stevens. 1972. Emotions and speech: Some acoustical correlates. *The Journal of the Acoustical Society of America* 52, 4B (1972), 1238–1250.

76. Zhihong Zeng, Maja Pantic, Glenn I Roisman, and Thomas S Huang. 2009. A survey of affect recognition methods: Audio, visual, and spontaneous expressions. *IEEE transactions on pattern analysis and machine intelligence* 31, 1 (2009), 39–58.

77. Philippe Zimmermann, Sissel Guttormsen, Brigitta Danuser, and Patrick Gomez. 2003. Affective computing a rationale for measuring mood with mouse and keyboard. *International journal of occupational safety and ergonomics* 9, 4 (2003), 539–551.

Morse Things: A Design Inquiry into the Gap Between Things and Us

Ron Wakkary[1,2], Doenja Oogjes[1], Sabrina Hauser[1], Henry Lin[1], Cheng Cao[1], Leo Ma[1], Tijs Duel[2]
[1] Simon Fraser University, Surrey, British Columbia, Canada
[2] Eindhoven University of Technology, Eindhoven, Netherlands
{rwakkary, doogjes, shauser, hwlin, fuchengc, leo_ma}@sfu.ca, tijsduel@gmail.com

ABSTRACT
Applying a thing-centered, material speculation approach we designed the Morse Things to acknowledge and inquire into the gap between things and us. The Morse Things are sets of ceramic bowls and cups networked together to independently communicate through Morse code in an Internet of Things (IoT). We deployed the Morse Things in the households of six interaction design practitioners and researchers for six weeks. Following the deployment, we conducted a workshop to discuss the role of the Morse Things and ultimately the gap between things and people. We reflect on the nature of living with IoT things and discuss insights into the gap between things and humans that led to the idea of a new type of thing in the home that is neither human-centered technology nor non-digital artifacts.

Author Keywords
Things; Material Speculation; Internet of Things; Postphenomenology

ACM Classification Keywords
H.5.m. Information interfaces and presentation (e.g., HCI): Miscellaneous;

INTRODUCTION
The Morse Things project investigates the nature of living with everyday things that are networked together and communicate in what is commonly understood as the Internet of Things (IoT). In particular, we investigate IoT from a thing-centered perspective in order to explore the gap between things and us. We designed and fabricated six sets of networked ceramic bowls and cups (Figure 1) to be given to domain expert participants – professional designers and design researchers – to live with for several weeks.

In human-computer interaction (HCI) research there is a long trajectory of research beginning with ubiquitous computing [1] towards smart homes [23] to IoT in the home [3] to an extension of visions of ubiquitous computing [4].

DIS 2017, June 10–14, 2017, Edinburgh, United Kingdom.
© 2017 ACM ISBN 978-1-4503-4922-2/17/06...$15.00.
http://dx.doi.org/10.1145/3064663.3064734

Figure 1 A set of Morse Things and a single medium bowl

IoT promises to reconfigure our everyday environments by providing connectivity to and between things, buildings, the city and beyond [3]. IoT also imagines the disappearance of computing into our everyday lives and infrastructures [1].

The emergence of IoT has led to critical reflections on the relationship between technologies and humans. For example, De Roeck et al. point out that users "need to have the power and control over the creation and use of applications for smart environments" [11:170] in order for IoT to be more widely adopted. In another example, the IoT Design Manifesto [2] adopts a critical yet ultimately idealistic approach to IoT. The collective of designers and design researchers behind the manifesto advocates for key human principles to be brought to bear on the design of IoT systems. These examples reflect the vigilance of the human-centered orientation and the value the orientation brings to designing IoT systems [10,45,49]. In many respects, a human-centered approach aims to close the gap between humans and technologies in order for IoT to better serve human needs–a goal not being challenged here. Yet, what might a human-centered approach hide with respect to the relations we have with technology? Our adoption of a thing-centered approach in the Morse Things project begins with this question. Stated in the positive, what might be revealed in the relations we have with technology through a thing-centered approach to IoT?

Our generative approach with the Morse Things is an inquiry into the complexity of our relationship with things. In particular, we inquire about the gap between things and us. This gap results in somewhat of a conundrum that we simultaneously cannot understand what it is to be a thing, yet we would not be able to function in or comprehend our lives without things.

The contributions of this paper include an empirically derived description of experiencing the gap between IoT things and us. In particular, we describe the challenges of relating to things, new forms of attachment to technological things in our everyday lives, and a possible new type of thing in the home that is neither human-centered technology nor non-digital artifacts.

BACKGROUND

In the following sections we provide a background for the Morse Things. We position our thing-centered approach to connected artifacts as a way to investigate human-technology relations. We discuss related work in the area of IoT, and discuss related philosophies of technology and thing perspective research in HCI.

Internet of Things

The IoT is concerned with the design of internet-connected interactive artifacts enabled to collect and exchange data. The IoT development has emerged as an extension of ubiquitous computing [48] and pervasive computing [40] and is seen as a new way of thinking about connected technologies [31]. The IoT directly connects our physical world with computer-based virtual networks. Some examples include smart home devices (e.g. Philips Hue, Nest, Honeywell), wearables (e.g. Apple watch, Fitbit, Jawbone), smart cities, and connected cars.

However, concerns and critical thoughts have been raised about IoT. While the IoT broadens information access and empowers citizens, it also threatens privacy and autonomy and potentially enables social and political manipulation [24]. As the interactivity of IoT devices merges with or disappears within our everyday life and environments, we can witness an unawareness of users and subsequently users' loss of control and power. In terms of the design of IoT systems and devices, several scholars [15,16,30] mention the neglect of users' input and engagement in IoT developments. Desjardins et al. [16] further argues that while IoT aims to connect things with things by design it lacks the taking into account of the relations between IoT things and their lived-in environments, which include existing computational and non-computational things or systems. Crabtree et al. [13] propose building accountability into IoT models through specific HCI-oriented policies and procedures to better handle privacy issues.

Our view of IoT builds on the idea that IoT things will find themselves in the midst of complex configurations of human and non-human interactions or what we have elsewhere referred to as intersections and ensembles [33,46]. There is an inherent lack of stability and sharing of agency with non-human factors that as a consequence challenge the prescriptive reduction of things to functions and services all the while controlling human concerns like privacy and security. We therefore argue that there is a limit to the dominant human-centered perspective and that a better understanding of the nature of connected things would arise from a better understanding of the complex and ambiguous relations between things and humans.

Philosophies of technology

In many respects, our approach in Morse Things aligns with a particular strand in philosophies of technology known as postphenomenology. Briefly, postphenomenology as argued by Don Ihde and Peter-Paul Verbeek [26,43], understands technologies as mediators of human experiences and practices rather than functional and instrumental objects [39,43]. In a postphenomenological relationship between humans and technological artifacts, each mutually shapes the other through mediations that form the human subjectivity and objectivity of any given situation. Design is central to and bound up in a postphenomenological understanding of the world since digital technologies do not come to us in a "raw" form but in a form that is *designed.* In this respect, designed digital artifacts, or in our case *things,* manifest technologies and directly influence the mediation of our experiences and practices. Beyond postphenomenology, recent philosophical thinking like object-oriented philosophy [22] has adopted more radical thing-centered approaches that advance the position that things and artifacts bare knowledge in distinct and complex ways. While there are important differences in their own epistemological commitments, emerging theoretical notions such as Ian Bogost's *carpentry*, the construction of artifacts that do philosophy [8], Graham Harman's speculative realism that critiques anthropocentrism and the undermining of objects in philosophy [22], and Davis Baird's *thing knowledge* in which artifacts embody and carry knowledge prior to our ability to theorize or reason through language [5]—all offer intriguing perspectives that can be seen both as critical and generative mechanisms for thing-centered approaches to design.

Drawing on the philosophies and philosophers of technology such as Ihde, Verbeek, Albert Borgmann, and Bruno Latour [9,25,29,43,44] is not new to HCI research (see for example [17]). Recent research like Odom et al. [32] describe attachment as a key factor in human-technology relations for future design implementations. Pierce and Paulos [35–37] aim to describe the materializing of technologies and its implications from the material awareness of everyday things to embodied relations within technologies. Relatedly, Tromp et al. [42], reflect on the social consequences of mediated relations and argue that designers should make more informed decisions to design for socially responsible behavior. Our investigation similarly focuses on the role of the thing yet moves beyond materials, embodied interaction or moralizing behaviors to articulate the complex and ambiguous relationships that form between things and us.

Thing perspectives in HCI

Drawing on the philosophies of technology and object-oriented philosophy we can see that the notion of a *thing* is neither in reference to technologies nor simply artifacts in the physical sense. Things can be seen as non-human technological entities and artifact entities often bound together that are conditioned by humans and in turn shape what it means to be human. As such, they have a central importance to HCI as computational artifacts, systems, and processes that can be referred to as things.

Crabtree & Tolmie [13] explore a "day in the life" of things through analysing a series of mundane interactions within a household. It is an investigation of the challenges to the design of IoT things. This ethnomethodological study portrays a perspective of things in order to uncover the underlying "machinery" of interactions that tends to fade into the background yet governs the meaning of things in our everyday lives. This research provides a thorough but explicitly human view of things from third-person human perspectives.

Related research has taken more literal approaches to the notion of a thing-perspective. For example, the PetCam [28] BinCam [12] and FridgeCam [19] utilize small cameras embedded or attached to objects (and pets) to provide a visual perspective that is quite literally from the perspective of things. On the surface, these approaches appear to provide viewpoints unfamiliar to humans and in this light they reveal new insights and observations. For example, Giaccardi et al. [21] explicitly introduce things as co-ethnographers in a study that attaches cameras to household items like a kettle and cups to log a visual perspective on human actions and routines from the vantage point of artifacts. The Long Living Chair [38] by contrast does not set-out to observe human actions rather it embodies the relation to humans by detailing the day it was manufactured (i.e. its human age) and records and displays how many times it has been used. In contrast to our approach, these works adopt a thing-centered perspective of things that are in essence human-centered. The purpose and role of the things are purely focused on human actions and interactions whether to observe people or to embody and record human interactions.

Trojan Boxes [14] utilizes embedded cameras but turns its view to the lived experience of things that are mostly non-human encounters and show a world most people have not experienced. The Trojan boxes are mail parcels with a tilt-triggered camera inside to document the various stages in our global delivery system of goods. This work is similar to our approach in that it seeks to explore an existence of things independent of direct human action yet unlike our work and similar to others it relies on visual sensing as its main modality, a modality more common to humans than things. With the Morse Things, we instead intended to materialize the thing perspective of being on a network that manifests more broadly across perceptual modalities whether human or thing-based.

Summary

In contrast to the various approaches to IoT discussed in this section, our approach specifically builds on the idea that IoT things will become part of complex and contradictory configurations of human and non-human interactions. Further, we believe a thing-centered approach can complement the limits of human-centered approaches of IoT. We also build on postphenomenology in our investigation to focus on the role of the thing yet our emphasis is not on materiality, embodied interaction or moralizing behaviors but the ambiguous attachments that form and the emergence of new considerations for IoT that might result. As a matter of researching things we shy away from a thing perspective of human actions and routines and aim our observations and insights back onto the things themselves.

THE MORSE THINGS

The Morse Things are sets of ceramic bowls and cups that communicate solely to each other over an Internet connection. Over time, the conversation of the Morse Things and their degree of connectedness on the network can evolve in degrees of "awareness" from being alone, to being a pair of things, to being a group of things, to being part of a larger network of things. The Morse Things mostly sleep (computationally speaking) and wake at random intervals during the day at least once every eight hours. Upon waking a Morse Thing will send and receive messages to and from other Morse Things in its set. The messages sent by each Morse Thing are in Morse code and simultaneously expressed sonically and broadcasted on Twitter (Figure 2). The Morse Things can be used like any other bowl or cup for eating, drinking, and containing items, with the exception that they cannot be put in the dishwasher or microwave. We designed and fabricated six sets of Morse Things each including a large ceramic bowl, a medium bowl, and a cup. The form of each Morse Thing is made of ceramics that is shaped around the embedded electronics signaling the design intention to create a hybrid between an everyday and computational object.

Each Morse Thing is comprised of a Wi-Fi microcontroller, sleeping module, amplifier circuit, speakers and battery. When a Morse Thing wakes, it checks an Internet server for messages from other Morse Things in its set. The Internet server coordinates the messages sent and received by the Morse Things. Each Morse Thing has its own name based on its color (red, yellow or blue) and set. Each set has a unique name and color combination of bowls and cups. The

Figure 2 Excerpt of a conversation of one of the Morse Things sets on Twitter

Morse code we used is a combination of traditional and adapted Morse abbreviations. Next, we turn to giving insight into the many decisions in the process of crafting the Morse Things.

Designing the Morse Things, we adopted a material speculation approach to design research. Material speculation is the design of a counterfactual artifact that is experienced and lived with on an everyday basis over time as a way to ask certain types of research questions [47]. A counterfactual artifact is a realized functioning product or system that intentionally contradicts what would normally be considered logical to create given the norms of design and design products. Morse Things are counterfactual IoT artifacts for the home in that their digital capabilities are at the service of things rather than people. Their human functionality is of an everyday nature that already exists in homes today shifting the question from what they *do* to how they *are* in our homes. The Morse Things embody the proposition that our relationships with Internet enabled things is a matter of negotiation over time rather than predefined or prescribed as a service or functionality.

We chose to design ceramic bowls and cups because we wanted our Morse Things to readily fit with and be accepted like any other household object in order to perform the inquiry of a material speculation. The combination of technological and non-technological identities within the Morse Things underscored our use of *defamiliarization* as a technique common to speculative design (see for example [7]). To defamiliarize is to make the familiar strange as a way to call into question the usual interpretations of everyday or known things.[1]

We purposely limited the communications of the Morse Things to communicating with each other and to affirming their individual or group existences on a network. The aim here was to foreground a thing-centered approach. In a sense, we designed the Morse Things to ask the question what is it like to be a thing on a network? We exaggerated the thing-centered approach by designing computational technological functions of the Morse Things to the exclusion of people, to have the objects computationally exist in their own world independent of human action. While they can be used as any other bowl or cup for eating, drinking and containing items, this use does not impact their communication or "awareness" nor are these interactions with the Morse Things sensed or data logged. We constrained the computational technologies to be solely at the service of the Morse Things. These strategies are combined as a way to both acknowledge and inquire upon the gap between things and us.

Enforcing the gap between technological things and us was important however it was equally important to design links and reminders of the potential relations between the things and us despite this gap. The physical form of the Morse Things was aimed to keep present the idea that the bowls and cups were also technological objects although the electronics were hidden. The form of the bowls and cups protrude in odd shapes (unlike other ceramic bowls) revealing where the electronics fit between inner and outer ceramic shells (Figure 1). Similarly, we chose to make the communication between the Morse Things potentially intelligible to people yet still thing-centered by having them in Morse code, sonically expressing the messages, and translating the messages on Twitter. We chose Morse code as both potentially familiar yet an outmoded form of communication that is for human communication yet designed for the mechanical and electronic properties of non-human things. Twitter was chosen as the Morse Things' communication platform because it was easily integrated into our system, enabled participants to monitor the communications easily, and is reminiscent of other IoT things on Twitter (see for example @mytoaster [50]).

OUR STUDY

With the main goal of exploring a deeper understanding of the gap between things and humans we applied a relatively unique methodological approach. Our study adopts a material speculation approach as discussed earlier (see The Morse Things). In material speculation the first step is the design and making of a counterfactual artifact(s) that embodies a proposition and research question, and is robust enough to be deployed in everyday settings for long periods of time. In the second step of deploying the counterfactual artifacts we adopted a unique approach to deployment studies that is in keeping with the particularities and challenges of the research questions we are asking. A key motivation in our approach was the desire to deepen our

Figure 3 Participant photos of Morse Things in their homes

[1] Defamiliarization is originally a literary theory device (see [41] to have readers examine their assumed interpretations of known and familiar experiences. The literary critic, Frederic Jameson cited in Bleeker [7] succinctly characterizes the aim "defamiliarize and restructure our experience of our own present..." [27]. Bleecker is one account of utilizing defamiliarization in design fictions and others have argued for it as a critical inquiry approach within HCI and domestic contexts in particular (see [6]).

investigation by including a wider range of experts that have the design expertise to perceive and investigate the nuanced and challenging notions of thing-centeredness. In order to do so, we set out to sensitize–through lived experience–a group of *domain expert participants* [18] to our thing-centered approach by deploying the Morse Things in their households for several weeks. In the context of this study, we see this deployment as a priming exercise. Data from the lived-with experiences with the Morse Things was collected (Figure 3) however our main interest was to engage in a workshop with our expert participants to discuss the relationship between things and us after they had the lived experience of the Morse Things. In what follows, we describe the individual steps of our methodological approach focusing on the deployment and workshop given that the methods of material speculation have been previously published in detail [47].

Deployment

We deployed the Morse Things for six weeks with six domain expert participants who were engaged in interaction design professional practice and research. After the novelty period of about one week the Morse Things eventually became part of the daily lives of the household. All expert participants lived with other household members and in what follows we describe in detail the households beginning with our primary participants and mentioning who participated from the households in the workshop. All participants are given pseudonyms:

Olivia (30) holds a PhD in interaction design (IxD) research and a bachelor's degree in industrial design. She is a professor in Interaction Design at a university in a nearby city. Her partner Noah (32) holds a degree in landscape architecture and has been working in landscape architecture for over eight years. Both participated in the workshop.

Ethan (47) holds a PhD in media arts, has several years of experience in research and art practice and currently holds a chair position as an art and design research faculty member at another local university. His wife Emily (32) is an experienced social science researcher and media professional holding degrees in anthropology and cinematic arts. The also have a 4-year old son Edwin. All three household members attended the workshop.

Hannah (31) is a senior Experience Designer and Digital Strategist with over six years of work experience at leading design agencies and consultancies in North America. She holds an undergraduate degree in interaction design. She participated in the workshop.

Ella (47) is a senior design faculty member, with years of design experience, and a special interest in textiles and wearables. She holds a bachelor's and master's degrees in design. Her husband Mike (53) is a scientist operating in the field of endocrinology and molecular biology. They have two children, Heather (20) a third-year communication design student, and Tim (18) a professional water polo player. Only Hannah participated in the workshop but shared some of her entire family's experiences.

Figure 4 The Morse Things as they were delivered to the participants.

Spencer (37) is a practicing interaction designer specializing in the production of interactive installations and creative applications with over 10 years of work experience and his own company. He holds an undergraduate degree in interaction design and a master's degree in Interface Culture. His wife Mel (35), who is an independent art curator and art history PhD candidate, and their 2-year old (Marvin) did not participate in the workshop.

Toby (34) is a senior interaction designer with 10 years of work experience and his own company in the field. He holds an undergraduate degree in interaction design. His partner Sandra (30) works as a library assistant. She holds an undergraduate degree in photography and has some work experience in the telecommunication industry. Only Toby attended the workshop.

As we mentioned earlier, we see the deployment of the Morse Things as a priming method for the workshop that followed. Through the deployment we aimed to spur our participants' engagement with the Morse Things. For each household, we provided a set of Morse Things (each included a large bowl, medium bowl, and cup plus a Wifi hub and a set of instructions) encased in a wooden box (Figure 4). The box also contained an information sheet specifying the messages that Morse Things send, how they translate, and when they occur and how to access the messages on Twitter. Participants were asked to live with the Morse Things and to document the experience in response to a question and task we provided: *Describe what it is like to live with the Morse Things from the perspective of the Morse Things*? And *Design an artifact, system, or service to co-exist with the Morse Things.* It was left up to the participants as to the form of their response and the form of the concepts they generated. While living with the Morse Things our participants gathered photos, video, and text entries from diaries, as well as sketches of concepts. Across all participants we gathered 233 photos, approximately 30 minutes of video, 34 days of diary entries, and 18-20 sketches of concepts. For the purpose of this study, this rich data is part of the priming of our participants, however, it still informed workshop activities and discussions. We aim to analyze this deployment data to a larger extent in future research.

Workshop

At the end of the deployment, we organized a workshop with all of the domain expert participants and family members with our own team of three researchers to discuss the role of the Morse Things and ultimately the idea of the gap between things and humans. During the workshop, which lasted approximately six hours, the expert participants were asked to first present individually their experiences of living with the Morse Things and give special attention to the deployment question about the experience of the Morse Things from the perspective of the things. In a second round of presentations, participants presented their individual concepts of things designed for the Morse Things. Then, participants were divided into two groups and engaged in a group activity of designing things for the Morse Things as a group. Throughout these workshop activities we engaged in in-depth discussions with our domain expert participants that was as lively as it was informative. We gathered audio and video recordings of the workshop.

DATA ANALYSIS

After conducting the deployment and the workshop, we set out to analyze the collected data. The data included: text, images and videos collected from participants during the deployment and workshop data including presentations given in response to our deployment activities (see Deployment) and design concepts generated during the workshops; and lastly our videos and audio transcriptions from the workshop. Our method for analyzing data was done collaboratively by us, the researchers. Data was analyzed into themes through grounded theory techniques of open, axial and selective coding [11].

FINDINGS

In analyzing the data from the deployments and workshop we found three main themes: 1) searching for humanness; 2) thing-centeredness; and 3) tensions in making sense of the gap between things and us. Our analysis is organized to reflect the shift in thinking of our participants from viewing things as human-related to then thing-related and lastly the tension of holding these two positions simultaneously.

Searching for humanness

Projecting human qualities onto the Morse Things

Participants projected human emotions and experiences on the Morse Things. For example, Hannah translated the messages of the Morse Things into more human language. She also considered the "emotional life" of Morse Things like feeling lonely, frustrated, bored, forgetful, restless and ignored. Olivia described the reactions of the Morse Things to events in their 'lives'. For example, she thought the Morse Things would be happy with their new home, and as the Morse Things made sounds when she and Noah entered the house, she imagined them to be happy to see them: *"they were here and they spoke a little bit and then we went out for dinner [...] we came back [...] and as we entered the door, someone, one of them was like bipbipbip, and I was like, Oh! He's so happy to see us!"*

Comparing Morse Things to family members and pets

Along the same line of analysis, the Morse Things were compared to humans and animals. For example, Olivia described the Morse Things as a family that stayed together as a set. The Morse Things were compared to children in different instances. Noah described them as young children that were learning and evolving. In their presentation during the workshop, Ethan and Emily emphasized that their son Edwin could most easily relate to the Morse Things because *"he is already in that space, making Lego and doing things."* Most of Spencer's concepts were inspired by children's toys motivated by a desire to maintain the abstract and playful aspects of the Morse Things. Both Ella and Emily compared the Morse Things to teenagers, as well as to cats thinking of them as going their own way: *"I think what they do is make us aware that there's other things going on that we have no idea about, like with the teenagers. [...]. I don't know what the cat is doing when I'm sleeping or what my kids are doing."*

Morse Things being aware of humans

In responding to our request to document the experiences of the Morse Things from the perspective of the things, the Morse Things are described as thinking of and being aware of the people in the house. Spencer describes conversations between the bowls and their thoughts of humans, which in his account they call 'strange giants': *"I get used the most in the morning. But, not the way I expect. The big one usually puts some sugar and milk in me before the warm brown liquid. Which is strange, because it does it the other way with those stupid mugs."*

Ella also describes, in a short-sentenced robotic way, the Morse Things' awareness of the people in the house: *"Human number four only heard us once...; Human number two has been waiting for a ...; Human number one is remaining objective. ; Human number three can't count our attempts to connect. "*

Control and feedback modalities for humans

In their concepts, participants indicated a desire to better connect with the Morse Things. For example, when the

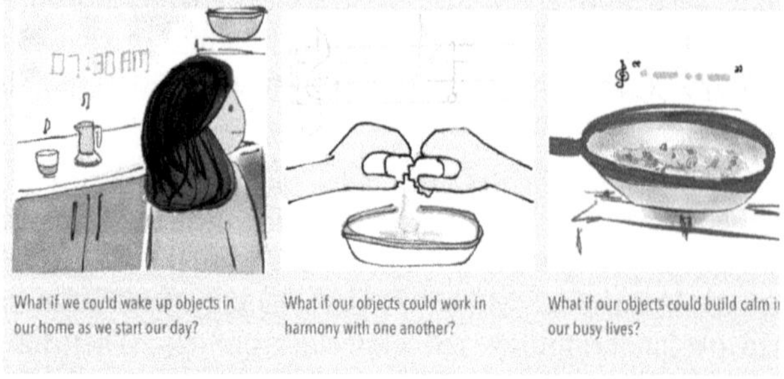

Figure 5 Hannah's concept of Morse Things as part of daily routines.

Morse Things would make a sound, Spencer tried to keep track of which Morse Thing was saying what, but always found himself too late to distinguish and locate the sound: *"Maybe an LED in the rim or something, which got brighter every time there was some activity, and then faded out over time to give you some indication of how active they had been relative to each other."* Participants' concepts also included giving the cups and bowls personalities which could reflect in the aesthetics of interaction, for example sound and light. Hannah was specifically looking for added feedback modalities motivated from a more empathetic standpoint in which she mainly wanted to make sure the communicating cups and bowls were finding each other: *"I thought that if one was seeking, another could vibrate".* This empathy with the perceived struggle of the Morse Things connecting to each other was also reflected in the concept of another participant who envisioned a device that would manage the timing of their messages, enabling the Morse Things to be "awake" and communicating at the same time.

Connecting to human practices

The desire to connect the Morse Things to human practices emerged too: *"If they could detect us through motion, or maybe just by touch, if we pick them up and all of a sudden they vibrate or they spoke or they can feel us touching them."* Beyond direct interaction, participants were envisioning ways in which the Morse Things could work themselves into daily human routines (Figure 5). Ethan's concept positioned the Morse Things as use-logs that would remind you of your last activity with them 24 hours later, to recall or even dictate routines, where Hannah's concept argued for having the Morse things as melodic, harmonious companions providing moments of reflection in everyday mundane things: *"They would wake up with us, as we are starting our day. So if I walk past a cup, and maybe a coffee maker, it would just chime as I walk by it, and as I do more it becomes a bit more musical."*

Thing-centeredness

Learning the Morse Things' language

While the Morse Things were often approached from a human centered perspective, on many occasions a more thing-oriented projection came through. Participants felt like they themselves needed to learn more about being a thing to understand the Morse Things. Noah mentioned that it might take more time to understand the Morse Things: *"Maybe it's a process that takes a longer time to really see. Because, like everything takes time to evolve and change, and maybe the speed of that discussion is like that. Maybe not a computer speed evolution, more like a human evolution. More slow basically, versus technology going really fast."*

Noah and Olivia also talked about learning Morse code to understand the Morse Things' conversation. Sandra, Toby's partner, wanted to tell them apart: *"I continue to keep trying to grab the bowls while they are "tweeting." I don't know why I'm doing this, because I can just wait and check Twitter to see which bowl it was ... guess I feel like I might be able to learn if they have different sounds? Maybe I'll be able to tell them apart eventually."*

Things with other things

In our expert participants' concepts, the Morse Things were often connected to other objects in their environment. Concepts included the Morse Things as eavesdropping bowls that listen in to you and your devices, and the Morse Things as silent ethnographers informing a social tablecloth that keeps track of the activity in a coffee shop. Other concepts looked at possibilities of how the Morse Things could include other things in the house on their network, for example Olivia proposed the idea that the Morse Things could "hack" into other things in the home like televisions to join their network (Figure 6).

Comparing to other things and new type of thing

In understanding the Morse Things, expert participants compared and related them to other existing things. Ella compared them to lost socks: *"I was also thinking that the home that you live in sort of contains these lost things. It contains a lot of lost socks, they are somewhere. The bowls are in the same way sort of contained."* (Figure 7) She continued this comparison in explaining why the bowls were useful and useless to her at the same time: *"[...] those are things that are in our homes and they are just, they're there. I suppose that's why I went to that space because although we think of bowls functioning in a particular way, we put things in it, as another type of entity that has a digital life, it wasn't functional. It was like the lost socks. We have an object that actually functions, physically, but we have an object that is just there. So you are playing with our assumptions."*

Noah did not see the Morse Things as different than other cups and bowls, and compared them to the Nest thermostat: *"To me, there's technology in it, but I look at it as a thermostat. I don't see it as being a new everyday complex thing. I look at that thing and I look at the Nest thing, and it's the same thing for me. So the same with the bowl, I look at that bowl and I look at the other bowl in the cupboard: same thing."* He also compares the Morse Things' conversation to playing a Compact Disc (CD) or running a script on which he has no impact: *"It feels like it's a CD that plays on a loop. It plays that and it just keeps going."*

Figure 6 Olivia imagined the Morse Things could hack into other things to join their network

Figure 7 Ella's concept for finding and containing things

Toby introduces the idea of the Morse Things being a new class of object and positions them between a digital product and a puzzle or a painting: *"It's kind of a new class of object. I was thinking is there any non-digital object in my house that is actively disrupting the environment for its own pleasure, [...] just to please itself. And there isn't really. Sometimes you'll have like a puzzle or an object you misread, like maybe you got a painting and you still haven't really figured out what it is, what it means. But that's different, because it's passively there, and you choose when to engage with it and you get to make some meaning. You're not really trying to put it to any purpose, whereas the bowl...sometimes you are trying to put it to purpose and than it just interrupts you and is like hey, figure me out."*

Tensions in making sense of the gap between things and us

The tensions in making sense of what the Morse Things were and what role they could play in everyday life was very present throughout the study. While Olivia *"loved imagining"* that the Morse Things talked and cared for her and her partner, she realized that *"that's not what they're saying at all, and they don't care about us at all"*. Emily described a situation in which she was not home, but saw on Twitter that the bowls had been making sounds. She continued with her comparison to cats and teenagers: *"And there is something kind of nice about not knowing, [...] but with a bowl, that's where it sort of gets strange."* Ella recognized this friction, and attributed it to the fact that the bowls are not conscious beings: *"If my kids are going out and they have a relation and they are talking with each other – I don't know what's going on but I know they're doing it – I at least know that they are conscious and aware of it. With these bowls I know that they are not. That's why it seems like [...] why are we doing that for them if they are not conscious or something going on."*

Continuing with his comparison of the Morse Things to a CD or script, Noah wondered whether the experience of the Morse Things is actually ours or the designer or researchers who made and programmed them. This friction in what the Morse Things are or should be continued in participants' concepts. Where some participants' concepts added explicit functionality to the Morse Things, for example Toby's concept of them as part of a system in which they would function as both a WiFi repeater and a plant watering reminder system (Figure 8), while Spencer was very clear in his desire to avoid making it useful, as he wanted to keep thinking of them as an abstract, playful thing, rather than something utilitarian. Hannah mentioned that she did not need the Morse Things to have more functions: *"It doesn't need to have a specific use, I like that they are just there and kind of in their own world and speaking in their own language, and sometimes my interactions with them impact them."*

Should things exist for us?

In the discussion at the end of the workshop, the participants were divided in their opinions on whether the Morse Things should exist for us, as Ella argued *"if it can talk, allow it to talk to us. If it's communicating than we want to have a conversation"*, or whether they should exist on their own as Spencer says *"that's why I like the idea of something else, let them be themselves. Other stuff is going on that we're just totally unaware of and it doesn't matter."*

DISCUSSION

The discussion that follows represents an answer to the question we posed at the outset of our paper: what might be revealed in the relations we have with technology through a thing-centered approach to IoT? Aspects of the answer include the withdrawal of things from our human understanding and perception that contributes to the gap between things and us, the ability to form attachments with things despite this gap, and lastly the notion of a new type of thing between thing-centered and human-centered technologies in the home.

These insights contribute to our discussion of human-technology relations in the context of IoT (See Background). Specifically we extend related IoT research that raises issues of human and non-human agency alongside a shift away from human-centered concerns [15,16,30,47]. Our insights reflect and engage through design, the thing-centered philosophical inquiries of post-phenomenology Ihde and Verbeek [26,43] and object-oriented approaches of Harman [22] and Bogost [8].

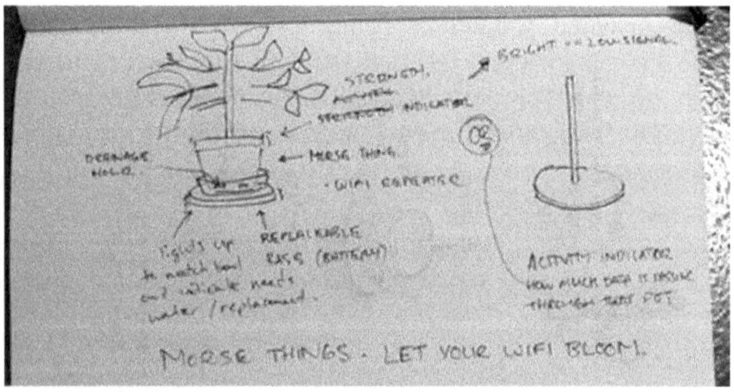

Figure 8 Spencers concept of having the Morse Things as a WiFi repeater and watering system

Withdrawal of things from human understanding

Understanding experience from the perspective of things is a difficult task for humans. We tend to relate to non-humans as surrogate humans, that is we anthropomorphize non-humans. Philosophically speaking, non-human perspectives "withdraw" from human understanding into a non-human world that we can neither fully comprehend nor articulate [8,43]. In addition, non-human worlds are formed in a configuration of materials and performances rather than language [5]. This naturally poses inherent difficulties in adopting thing-centered perspectives.

This challenge was confirmed in our study as our domain expert participants readily described the Morse Things as having human qualities like an "emotional life" (Hannah) or belonging to a family (Olivia). In imagining the perspective of the Morse Things, participants gave them language and forms of agency. For example, Spencer saw the Morse Things as human-like characters that perceived humans as 'strange giants'. Ella described the Morse Things similar to how one might describe robots that express themselves like humans but through logic and without emotions.

It is important though that these interpretations were not resolute and our participants knowingly held contradictory views of the Morse Things. These knowing contradictions acknowledge the gap between what we imagine of things and how they actually exist. Referring again to comments made by Olivia (see Tensions in making sense of the gap between things and us), she said that despite the fact that she "loved imagining" that the Morse Things talked and cared about her she knew they did not care at all about her.

Our study gave details on experiencing the gap between things and us but also revealed the more nuanced idea of how things withdraw from our understanding, as has been expressed by [8,43] and others. It is important that while much of the experience of things is beyond our grasp, this perspective is not entirely invisible to us. Rather we establish many commonalities and reliable interactions that form the foundations for the fundamental and ubiquitous relations we have with things. This relationship to things in the context of their withdrawal emerged clearly in our study. For example, we reported on how Ethan and Emily believed Edwin, their 4-year old son could best relate to the Morse Things since he spent his day playing in an imaginary world of things. Ella and Emily throughout our workshop compared the Morse Things to pets and teenagers signaling familiar relationships that at times are very unfamiliar if not inaccessible to us.

Attachment with things we don't understand

Despite this gap between things and us it was evident in our study that participants formed attachments with the Morse Things. After the initial curiosity subsided the Morse Things were momentarily forgotten or ignored but later became part of the daily lives of the homes. This was clear in the reports and images sent to us during the deployment (see Deployment). In addition, the Morse Things' messages were routinely checked on Twitter and participants spoke about taking care of their set. In one incident, two sets were accidentally swapped during a maintenance check and both households immediately demanded their own set back (each set is a unique combination of colors). Lastly, at the end of the deployment, nearly all participants wanted to keep the Morse Things. This attachment with the Morse Things was not necessarily a foregrounded experience but rather one in which the Morse Things faded into the background of everyday living to on occasion surface in ways that caused reflection, new considerations and even pleasure and comfort. Toby's comment on his experience of "rediscovering" a Morse Thing speaks well to a type of attachment that was common in the study: "*finally heard a bowl! It's been a week. I didn't expect that I would be as surprised or excited as I ended up being. Had a pretty good rhythm to it. Dah-do-dah-do-do-dah-dah-do-dah-dah ... or something like that.*"

The attachment to the Morse Things was also described in ways that acknowledged that the relationship was with things that could not be fully understood–that the relationship could be more thing-centered than human-centered. Noah commented on how it may take time to fully develop a relationship with things that in the case of the Morse Things would be at a slow evolutionary speed rather than computer speed observing the difference between things, humans, and computers. Noah and Olivia also discussed learning Morse code to better to understand the Morse Things from their perspective. Lastly, Ella elaborated that the attachment was a matter of things that function on some level (being a bowl) but digitally they are "just there" in our home.

A new type of thing in the home

We propose that the Morse Things can be viewed as a new type of thing in the home that is neither a human-centered nor thing-centered. The Morse Things are not typical everyday artifacts like other bowls or cups in the home but you can just as easily use them like a typical bowl or cup. They are also not digital devices like mobile phones or smart thermostats, however they are Internet enabled and connected.

Toby was explicit and most insightful about the possibility of a new type of thing. He considered Morse Things to be a "new class of object" that he compared to artifacts like a painting. One does not fully understand a painting yet one forms a special relationship that spurs ongoing reflections and interpretations despite knowing these can never be resolved. However, unlike paintings, Morse Things have autonomy and "interrupt" or emerge into our lives on their own accord. This is the crux of the new type of artifact, one that we are ambiguously attached to in our daily life and is in many respects independent of our actions and desires. This notion of a new type of thing opens IoT approaches to consider IoT things that form attachments with people through qualities other than human driven functionality or explicit services. Ambiguity in this sense is a resource [20] that adds dimensionality and complexity that is more commensurate with human-technology relations; Verbeek reminds us that technologies are mediators of human experience and practices rather than functional and instrumental objects [43].

Ambiguity or ambivalence in relation to this new type of thing is important to recognize. In keeping with the complexity of our relations to things it is not clear why these relations should be resolved or satisfying in order to maintain an attachment. Maintaining relations while not knowing is critical to future possibilities and alternate meanings that ultimately sustain our relationships with things. In our study, this ambivalence with the attachment to Morse Things emerged. Ella, in her comparison of the Morse Things with teenagers makes the point that they are "conscious and aware" as opposed to the Morse Things that "are not conscious" and yet we are concerned for them in ways similar to our complex relationships with teenagers.

In existing IoT systems we see glimpses of non-human agency and thing-centeredness in systems that automate updates of mobile operating systems and applications or service and maintenance notifications of appliances and automobiles. However, these are human-centered in their orientation, focused on automating human tasks. An overlooked example but one that is more relevant may be the accidental relationships that form between digital things and other things. For example, audio speakers that unintentionally convert nearby cellular radio transmissions of mobile phones into sound that can reveal incoming data or phone calls. This unintentional thing-to-thing interaction reveals independent but intelligible thing-centered interactions. In other research we have discussed the idea of *ensembles* [33,46] in which over time things configure into relations *seemingly* on their own. Examples of this include complex arrangement of objects and furniture in your apartment or home, or how keys always find themselves in a bowl on a table near the front door. Human actions co-mingle with non-human qualities to form ensembles that demonstrate the thing-centered relations that would be typical of the new type of thing our Morse Things suggest.

CALL FOR FUTURE RESEARCH

Morse Things may manifest a new type of thing in the home despite the fact that they are not intended as a viable or commercial product. Morse Things are a counterfactual artifact produced to perform a research inquiry into new IoT possibilities [34,47]. They disclose alternatives that set the stage for further research and development of a thing-centered IoT.

In support of pursuing a thing-centered IoT research agenda, we also see the need for methodological innovations. For the Morse Things we decided to pursue a different methodological approach that asked domain experts to be study participants that co-speculated with us in our inquiry. Furthermore, we relied on generative activities that infused each step of our method that together with our expert participants navigated this new space of thing-centeredness. Giaccardi et al. [21] invokes things as co-ethnographers, Pschetz and Banks [38] embody human relations into crafted artifacts, and Davoli and Redstrom [14] engage in thing *sousveillance* as methods to thing-centered understandings. If we look to enable designers to design a new type of thing for the home that is situated between human-centered and thing-centered orientations, new vocabularies, practices, and methods are required. As a matter of including philosophical work into design, new concepts and language will need to be worked through and become manifest in both design processes and artifacts. This is in the spirit of Bogost's *carpentry* in which through the making of things we do philosophy [8].

This work leads us to invite researchers to contribute to a thing-centered IoT and interaction design research agenda. We also invite further future work in tackling methodological issues better suited to investigate human-technology relations and thing-centered approaches.

CONCLUSION

In this paper, we presented our design inquiry into the gap between things and us in our Morse Things project. We employed a material speculation approach to this investigation that led to the design of counterfactual artifacts in the form of ceramic bowls and cups as IoT things networked together and independently communicating through Morse code. We described our deployment of the Morse Things in the households of six interaction design practitioners and researchers for six weeks as domain expert participants. We analyzed the data gathered from our deployment and a workshop to reflect deeply on the nature of living with IoT things and discuss insights into the gap between humans and things. Our findings and discussion led to the idea of a new type of thing in the home that is neither human-centered technology nor non-digital artifacts. Lastly, we suggest future research to pursue things that are between human and thing-centered considerations and the need for new methodological experimentation for both thing-centered and human-technology relations related to design research.

ACKNOWLEDGMENTS

We thank our expert participants for their generosity and effort and those from the Everyday Design Studio and Material Matters who helped with this project. Funded by NSERC and SSHRC.

REFERENCES

1. Gregory D. Abowd. 2012. What Next, Ubicomp?: Celebrating an Intellectual Disappearing Act. In *Proceedings of the 2012 ACM Conference on Ubiquitous Computing* (UbiComp '12), 31–40. https://doi.org/10.1145/2370216.2370222
2. Afdeling Buitengewone Zaken, Beyond.io, Frolic Studio, and The Incredible Machine. 2015. IOT Design Manifesto. Retrieved January 16, 2017 from

https://www.iotmanifesto.com/wp-content/themes/Manifesto/Manifesto.pdf

3. Luigi Atzori, Antonio Iera, and Giacomo Morabito. 2010. The Internet of Things: A survey. *Computer Networks* 54, 15: 2787–2805. https://doi.org/10.1016/j.comnet.2010.05.010
4. Matthew P. Aylett and Aaron J. Quigley. 2015. The Broken Dream of Pervasive Sentient Ambient Calm Invisible Ubiquitous Computing. In *Proceedings of the 33rd Annual ACM Conference Extended Abstracts on Human Factors in Computing Systems* (CHI EA '15), 425–435. https://doi.org/10.1145/2702613.2732508
5. Davis Baird. 2004. *Thing Knowledge: A Philosophy of Scientific Instruments*. University of California Press, Berkeley, Calif.
6. Genevieve Bell and Paul Dourish. 2007. Yesterday's Tomorrows: Notes on Ubiquitous Computing's Dominant Vision. *Personal Ubiquitous Comput.* 11, 2: 133–143. https://doi.org/10.1007/s00779-006-0071-x
7. Julian Bleeker. 2009. *Design Fiction: A Short Essay on Design, Science, Fact and Fiction.* Retrieved April 6, 2017 from http://drbfw5wfjlxon.cloudfront.net/writing/DesignFiction_WebEdition.pdf
8. Ian Bogost. 2012. *Alien Phenomenology, or What It's Like to Be a Thing*. Univ Of Minnesota Press, Minneapolis.
9. Albert Borgmann. 1987. *Technology and the character of contemporary life: a philosophical inquiry.* University of Chicago Press, Chicago.
10. Donghoon Chang. 2015. Tuesday Keynote: UX Design in the IoT Era. In *Proceedings of the 33rd Annual ACM Conference Extended Abstracts on Human Factors in Computing Systems* (CHI EA '15), 807–808. https://doi.org/10.1145/2702613.2725423
11. Kathy Charmaz. 2014. *Constructing Grounded Theory.* SAGE.
12. Rob Comber, Anja Thieme, Ashur Rafiev, Nick Taylor, Nicole Krämer, and Patrick Olivier. 2013. BinCam: Designing for Engagement with Facebook for Behavior Change. In *Human-Computer Interaction – INTERACT 2013: 14th IFIP TC 13 International Conference, Cape Town, South Africa, September 2-6, 2013, Proceedings, Part II*, Paula Kotzé, Gary Marsden, Gitte Lindgaard, Janet Wesson and Marco Winckler (eds.). Springer Berlin Heidelberg, Berlin, Heidelberg, 99–115. https://doi.org/10.1007/978-3-642-40480-1_7
13. Andy Crabtree and Peter Tolmie. 2016. A Day in the Life of Things in the Home. In *Proceedings of the 19th ACM Conference on Computer-Supported Cooperative Work & Social Computing* (CSCW '16), 1738–1750. https://doi.org/10.1145/2818048.2819954
14. Lorenzo Davoli and Johan Redström. 2014. Materializing Infrastructures for Participatory Hacking. In *Proceedings of the 2014 Conference on Designing Interactive Systems* (DIS '14), 121–130. https://doi.org/10.1145/2598510.2602961
15. Dries De Roeck, Karin Slegers, Johan Criel, Marc Godon, Laurence Claeys, Katriina Kilpi, and An Jacobs. 2012. I Would DiYSE for It!: A Manifesto for Do-it-yourself Internet-of-things Creation. In *Proceedings of the 7th Nordic Conference on Human-Computer Interaction: Making Sense Through Design* (NordiCHI '12), 170–179. https://doi.org/10.1145/2399016.2399044
16. Audrey Desjardins and Ron Wakkary. 2016. Living In A Prototype: A Reconfigured Space. In *Proceedings of the 2016 CHI Conference on Human Factors in Computing Systems* (CHI '16), 5274–5285. https://doi.org/10.1145/2858036.2858261
17. Daniel Fallman. 2011. The New Good: Exploring the Potential of Philosophy of Technology to Contribute to Human-computer Interaction. In *Proceedings of the SIGCHI Conference on Human Factors in Computing Systems* (CHI '11), 1051–1060. https://doi.org/10.1145/1978942.1979099
18. Brian Frey, Kate Rosier, Caleb Southern, and Mario Romero. 2012. From Texting App to Braille Literacy. In *CHI '12 Extended Abstracts on Human Factors in Computing Systems* (CHI EA '12), 2495–2500. https://doi.org/10.1145/2212776.2223825
19. Eva Ganglbauer, Geraldine Fitzpatrick, and Rob Comber. 2013. Negotiating food waste: Using a practice lens to inform design. *ACM Transactions on Computer-Human Interaction* 20, 2: 1–25. https://doi.org/10.1145/2463579.2463582
20. William W. Gaver, Jacob Beaver, and Steve Benford. 2003. Ambiguity As a Resource for Design. In *Proceedings of the SIGCHI Conference on Human Factors in Computing Systems* (CHI '03), 233–240. https://doi.org/10.1145/642611.642653
21. Elisa Giaccardi, Nazli Cila, Chris Speed, and Melissa Caldwell. 2016. Thing Ethnography: Doing Design Research with Non-Humans. In *Proceedings of the 2016 ACM Conference on Designing Interactive Systems* (DIS '16), 377–387. https://doi.org/10.1145/2901790.2901905
22. Graham Harman. 2010. *Towards Speculative Realism: Essays and Lectures*. Zero Books, Winchester, UK.
23. Richard Harper (ed.). 2003. *Inside the Smart Home.* Springer-Verlag, London. https://doi.org/10.1007/b97527
24. Philip N. Howard. 2015. *Pax technica: how the internet of things may set us free or lock us up*. Yale University Press, New Haven□: London.
25. Don Ihde. 1990. *Technology and the Lifeworld: From Garden to Earth.* Indiana University Press.
26. Don Ihde. 1993. *Philosophy of Technology: An Introduction.* Paragon House Publishers, New York, NY, USA.
27. Fredric Jameson. 1982. Progress versus Utopia; Or, Can We Imagine the Future? (Progrès contre Utopie,

ou: Pouvons-nous imaginer l'avenir). *Science Fiction Studies* 9, 2: 147–158.
28. Chris Keeney. 2014. *PetCam: The World Through the Lens of Our Four-Legged Friends*. Princeton Architectural Press, New York.
29. Latour, Bruno. 1992. Where are the missing masses? The sociology of a few mundane artifacts. In *Shaping technology/building society: studies in sociotechnical change*, Wiebe E. Bijker and John Law (eds.). MIT Press, Cambridge, Mass, 225–258.
30. Jessica Lingel. 2016. The Poetics of Socio-Technical Space: Evaluating the Internet of Things Through Craft. In *Proceedings of the 2016 CHI Conference on Human Factors in Computing Systems* (CHI '16), 815–826. https://doi.org/10.1145/2858036.2858399
31. Susan S. Lukesh. 2014. The internet of things. *ACM Inroads* 5, 3: 60–60. https://doi.org/10.1145/2659002
32. William Odom, James Pierce, Erik Stolterman, and Eli Blevis. 2009. Understanding Why We Preserve Some Things and Discard Others in the Context of Interaction Design. In *Proceedings of the SIGCHI Conference on Human Factors in Computing Systems* (CHI '09), 1053–1062. https://doi.org/10.1145/1518701.1518862
33. William Odom and Ron Wakkary. 2015. Intersecting with Unaware Objects. In *Proceedings of the 2015 ACM SIGCHI Conference on Creativity and Cognition* (C&C '15), 33–42. https://doi.org/10.1145/2757226.2757240
34. William Odom, Ron Wakkary, Youn-kyung Lim, Audrey Desjardins, Bart Hengeveld, and Richard Banks. 2016. From Research Prototype to Research Product. In *Proceedings of the 2016 CHI Conference on Human Factors in Computing Systems* (CHI '16), 2549–2561. https://doi.org/10.1145/2858036.2858447
35. James Pierce. 2009. Material Awareness: Promoting Reflection on Everyday Materiality. In *CHI '09 Extended Abstracts on Human Factors in Computing Systems* (CHI EA '09), 4459–4464. https://doi.org/10.1145/1520340.1520683
36. James Pierce and Eric Paulos. 2011. A Phenomenology of Human-electricity Relations. In *Proceedings of the SIGCHI Conference on Human Factors in Computing Systems* (CHI '11), 2405–2408. https://doi.org/10.1145/1978942.1979293
37. James Pierce and Eric Paulos. 2013. Electric Materialities and Interactive Technology. In *Proceedings of the SIGCHI Conference on Human Factors in Computing Systems* (CHI '13), 119–128. https://doi.org/10.1145/2470654.2470672
38. Larissa Pschetz and Richard Banks. 2013. Long living chair. 2983. https://doi.org/10.1145/2468356.2479590
39. Robert Rosenberger and Peter-Paul Verbeek. 2015. A Field Guide to Postphenomenology. In *Postphenomenological investigations: essays on human-technology relations*, Robert Rosenberger and Peter-Paul Verbeek (eds.). Lexington Books, Lanham, 9–41.
40. Mahadev Satyanarayanan. 2001. Pervasive computing: vision and challenges. *IEEE Personal Communications* 8, 4: 10–17. https://doi.org/10.1109/98.943998
41. Viktor Borisovic Shklovskij. 1991. *Theory of prose*. Dalkey Archive Press, Elmwood Park, Ill.
42. Nynke Tromp, Paul Hekkert, and Peter-Paul Verbeek. 2011. Design for Socially Responsible Behavior: A Classification of Influence Based on Intended User Experience. *Design Issues* 27, 3: 3–19. https://doi.org/10.1162/DESI_a_00087
43. Peter-Paul Verbeek. 2005. *What things do: Philosophical reflections on technology, agency, and design*. Pennsylvania State University Press, University Park, Pa.
44. Peter-Paul Verbeek. 2011. *Moralizing Technology: Understanding and Designing the Morality of Things*. University Of Chicago Press, Chicago□; London.
45. Stephen Viller, Peter Worthy, Marie Bodén, Jason Weigel, Geraldine Fitzpatrick, Tom Rodden, and Ben Matthews. 2016. IoT: Designing for Human Values. In *Proceedings of the 2016 ACM Conference Companion Publication on Designing Interactive Systems* (DIS '16 Companion), 61–64. https://doi.org/10.1145/2908805.2913019
46. Ron Wakkary, Audrey Desjardins, and Sabrina Hauser. 2015. Unselfconscious Interaction: A Conceptual Construct. *Interacting with Computers* 28, 4: 501–520. https://doi.org/10.1093/iwc/iwv018
47. Ron Wakkary, William Odom, Sabrina Hauser, Garnet Hertz, and Henry Lin. 2015. Material Speculation: Actual Artifacts for Critical Inquiry. In *In Proceedings of The Fifth Decennial Aarhus Conference on Critical Alternatives (AA '15)*, 97–108. https://doi.org/http://dx.doi.org/10.7146/aahcc.v1i1.21299
48. Mark Weiser. 1991. The Computer for the 21st Century. *Scientific American* 265, 3: 94–104. https://doi.org/10.1038/scientificamerican0991-94
49. Peter Worthy, Ben Matthews, and Stephen Viller. 2016. Trust Me: Doubts and Concerns Living with the Internet of Things. In *Proceedings of the 2016 ACM Conference on Designing Interactive Systems* (DIS '16), 427–434. https://doi.org/10.1145/2901790.2901890
50. mytoaster (@mytoaster) | Twitter. Retrieved April 7, 2017 from https://twitter.com/mytoaster?lang=en

Towards Commoditised Near Infrared Spectroscopy

Simon Klakegg[1], Jorge Goncalves[2], Niels van Berkel[2], Chu Luo[2], Simo Hosio[1], Vassilis Kostakos[2]
[1]Center for Ubiquitous Computing, University of Oulu
[2]School of Computing and Information Systems, The University of Melbourne
simon.klakegg@oulu.fi, jorge.goncalves@unimelb.edu.au, n.vanberkel@student.unimelb.edu.au,
chul3@student.unimelb.edu.au, simo.hosio@oulu.fi, vassilis.kostakos@unimelb.edu.au

ABSTRACT
Near Infrared Spectroscopy (NIRS) is a sensing technique in which near infrared light is transmitted into a sample, followed by light absorbance measurements at various wavelengths. This technique enables the inference of the inner chemical composition of the scanned sample, and therefore can be used to identify or classify objects. In this paper, we describe how to facilitate the use of NIRS by non-expert users in everyday settings. Our work highlights the key challenges of placing NIRS devices in the hands of non-experts. We develop a system to mitigate these challenges, and evaluate it in a user study. We show how NIRS technology can be successfully utilised by untrained users in an unsupervised manner through a special enclosure and an accompanying smartphone app. Finally, we discuss potential future developments of commoditised NIRS.

Author Keywords
Near Infrared Spectroscopy; sample identification; sensor accessibility; user-induced errors; pharmaceuticals; user study; gluten detection.

ACM Classification Keywords
H.5.m. Information interfaces and presentation (*e.g.*, HCI): Miscellaneous.

INTRODUCTION
As can been seen in consumer electronics, sophisticated hardware is becoming cheaper and more accessible to the modern customer (*e.g.*, smartphones), this includes Near Infrared Spectroscopy (NIRS) scanners. NIRS has the ability to penetrate the surface and traverse the physical structure of an object. It allows for the retrieval of information about the inner composition of a sample in the form of a spectrum, which acts as a proverbial fingerprint [48] of the sample. Thus, it enables accurate and detailed object identification.

While NIRS scanners have been used in research laboratories for decades [38], only recently has the technology matured enough to allow for end-user hardware which is both small and robust enough to be carried around, while still capable of producing reliable results. The NIRS device used in our study (DLP NIRscan Nano [15]) costs under 1000 US dollars at the time of writing and weighs just 80 grams – a fraction of the price and weight of high-end NIRS hardware. These numbers can be expected to continue to decline, which in turn encourages researchers to start considering everyday scenarios for this technology. For the first time, we argue, it can plausibly be placed in the hands of consumers. The main objective of our work is to explore the improvement of the accessibility of these devices for non-experts.

Coupling NIRS hardware with commodity devices (*e.g.*, tablets, smartphones) opens a range of exciting research avenues to explore. An *in situ* scanner placed at supermarkets could enable classification of products while they are being weighted, and report to the users the current state of the product (*e.g.*, the level of ripeness of a fruit [45]). In a home scenario, augmented shelves can detect the food being stored, and even determine if it has gone bad [3]. In a domiciliary health scenario, a user can scan a pill or medicine to confirm that this pill is the correct one to take at that moment [9]. There are a vast number of potential use cases for an everyday device that can identify objects based on their physical composition and ingredients.

The contribution of our work is three-fold. First, we explore the challenges in obtaining reliable scanning results, namely the impact of user-induced errors on scan accuracy. This is an unexplored territory in the context of miniaturised NIRS scanning. Second, we map the complexity and required knowledge to carry out a full sample analysis [27]. Third, we design and evaluate a set of mechanisms to address these issues and make NIRS more accessible and usable to non-experts. Our design consists of a custom enclosure to physically guide the user in the scanning process, and a mobile application to assist the user, inform of scanning errors during usage, and encapsulate the sample analysis process. We evaluate our design in a user study to collect feedback and ideas for future improvements. Our findings show that non-experts can successfully use this technology when both *physical* and *procedural* guides are in place.

RELATED WORK

Making Sensors Accessible
Sensors play an increasingly larger role in consumer electronics. Today, consumers' personal devices are

DIS 2017, June 10-14, 2017, Edinburgh, United Kingdom

ACM 978-1-4503-4922-2/17/06…$15.00
DOI: http://dx.doi.org/10.1145/3064663.3064738

embedded with a plethora of different hardware sensors, such as accelerometer, gravity, gyroscope, light, and magnetic [47]. Beyond providing benefits to the users themselves, these sensors have proven to be valuable tools when conducting research in fields such as traffic management [5], HCI [41], localisation [10], and healthcare [32]. While these electronic components are now commoditised and embedded as an integral part in a variety of products, they were originally much larger standalone devices. For example, the first accelerometer weighted almost 0.5 kg and measured 1.90 x 4.76 x 21.59 cm in size [53]. The size, weight, and cost of the accelerometer was eventually reduced, while the use cases expanded [53]. Initially, the accelerometer was used mostly in industry, but now benefits end-users with service enhancement in numerous applications. Further, smart devices do not only serve as a host for embedded sensors, but frequently act as control points for smaller and mobile sensors. This, combined with the widespread nature of smartphones [42], allows for innovative services. For instance, smartphones can be connected to portable medical devices (*e.g.*, blood pressure, glucose, and pulse oximeter) to process, analyse, and present biohealth data [22,31]. It is increasingly feasible for end-users to self-monitor their health, without the need for trained healthcare personnel. In essence, the development of these sensors and their increased accessibility help bridge the gap between end-users and advanced medical equipment.

In another example, Samsung's Galaxy Note 7 includes an infrared iris sensor, which allows biometric authentication on consumers' devices for security and access control [43]. Similarly, while until recently only a few devices came with fingerprint sensors [19], this technology has become increasingly more accessible for end-users. Goel *et al.* [20] showcase how a hyperspectral sensor, previously used for research, can assist in a wider set of use cases. Using *functional* Near-Infrared Spectroscopy (fNIRS) for Brain–Computer Interfaces (BCI) has begun to proliferate in the HCI community [30,33,40,51]. Strait *et al.* [52] investigate the reliability of fNIRS in BCI through a user study, and highlight some of the obstacles. Yuksel *et al.* [54] develop a system that automatically adjusts musical learning tasks based on the user's cognitive workload measured by fNIRS. In our work, we take initial usability steps towards facilitating the use of NIRS scanners by non-experts and by using smartphones as a control point.

Near Infrared Spectroscopy

NIRS sends near infrared light into a sample and measures the absorbance at various wavelengths, thus allowing for object identification [7]. Because of the characteristics of the NIR band (780 nm to 2500 nm), it can penetrate objects up to several millimetres. This enables quick and accurate analysis of the inner composition of samples (*e.g.*, analysing if a food product contains gluten), something that cannot be attained using computer vision. NIRS has been shown to be a useful technique in research across many different fields [16,17,49]. One of the more popular use cases of NIRS is to verify the quality of food. Sinelli *et al. [49]* used NIRS to analyse the freshness of minced beef. By comparing scans taken at different times, they were able to accurately determine the expiry date of the product. Others have explored NIRS as a way of developing a non-destructive solution for analysing fruit quality [28]. NIRS methods can reveal information about the inside of the fruit, something impossible to achieve solely through visual inspection. The reflected spectra contain the information used to infer the fruit's maturity, pH factor, solid content, and flesh elasticity. Another distinct feature of NIRS is the possibility to scan an item with no manipulation or pre-treatment applied to the object itself [6]. For this reason, NIRS has also gained popularity in the pharmaceutical industry [4]. This industry is heavily regulated, with a need for fast and safe quality control. NIRS can also help to address the challenge of counterfeit drugs. It is estimated that around 7% of the pharmaceuticals sold in the world are fake [13]. These counterfeit drugs are typically defined as drugs that have active substances which have been modified [13]. Similarly, in textile industries there is a need to verify the fibres of clothes at different stages in the production and recycling. However, many of the current methods for textile classification are both time consuming and involve dangerous chemicals. Cleve *et al.* [12] report how they accurately identified fabrics using NIRS. Durand *et al.* [16] argue that NIRS can replace existing methods and report an identification accuracy of over 96% for textiles. The aforementioned use cases (*i.e.*, food, pharmaceutical, textile) provide realistic real-world usage scenarios and are suitable for testing in a miniaturised NIRS context.

Miniaturised Near Infrared Spectroscopy

Most of the previous examples rely on heavy desktop NIRS equipment or larger portable devices. Given their success, miniaturised versions for field use have recently been developed. For instance, a mobile NIRS device has been used to detect tomato's pathogen [1]. By scanning the fruit just before it is harvested, it is possible to avoid large losses of fruit being rejected in quality control. Instead of sending the sample to a lab and waiting for a report, results can be obtained *in situ* in a matter of seconds. Unlike many of the current *in situ* chemical approaches, NIRS is also a non-destructive method. However, farmers reported that they considered the equipment to be both too expensive and too difficult to use [13].

Recently, cheaper and smaller devices have entered the market. However, there is a lack of research that investigates the effects of user-noise and usability when the device is placed in the hands of non-expert. Specifically, the effect of device motion [26], sample distance [46], sample angle [35], sample surface [36], sample interference [56], and ambience [50] have not been tested in the context of end-user miniaturised NIRS usage. Therefore, in this paper we investigate the effect of these parameters and consider ways to overcome the challenges they may impose. Furthermore, we propose a non-expert assistance for end users.

CHALLENGES OF NIRS SCANNING

There are two main challenges that users face when utilising NIRS technologies: 1) the impact of user-induced errors on the reliability of the results, and 2) the complexity of the sample analysis process. The effect of the former is exacerbated when NIRS devices are placed in the hands of non-experts. The latter is a challenge pertaining to commoditising this technology, since we expect that everyday users lack the skills to extract, analyse, and interpret the output generated by the device. Next, we describe in detail the impact of both these challenges on the reliability of the results.

Challenge 1 – User-Induced Errors

We experimentally investigate the limitations of NIRS technology in terms of user-induced errors in a scanning scenario with everyday materials. When a user interacts with the device (*e.g.*, place an object, hold the device), the user may introduce some noise to the system that can degrade scan accuracy. This could for example be caused by improper sample placement or an (unintended) shaking motion. To support non-expert NIRS usage, we have to identify the magnitude of the various types of user-induced errors. Moreover, based on the data from these test, we can inform the design of our non-expert assistance.

To showcase the impact of each type of user-induced error, we chose three different sample types (fruit, pharmaceutical, textile) with varying characteristics, as shown in Table 1. In some cases, we used different items from the same sample type for a more appropriate evaluation of each parameter. For example, when testing sample surface, it would not make sense to test a round object with no edges or varying texture. A NIRS scan was deemed inadequate when it produced values that are significantly different from the values obtained under ideal conditions (significance tested through Wilcoxon signed-rank tests).

Sample	Properties	Test(s)
100% Cotton	Area (Square): 196 cm Height: 2,5 cm	1 - 6
Omega 3	Brand: Möller Weight: 1200 mg	2, 5, 6
Multivitamin Plus M	Brand: Orion Pharma Weight: 250 mg	1, 3, 4
Banana	Uncut Diameter: 20 cm Weight: 120 g	1 - 5
Apple	Uncut Diameter: 6 cm Weight: 80 g	5, 6
Grape	Uncut Diameter: 2 cm Weight: 5 g	5

Table 1. Selected samples, properties, and respective tests.

Scan setup and configuration

Our scan setup consists of a NIRS scanner (DLP NIRscan Nano [15]) and a camera tripod. We use a custom-built aluminium plate and the tripod's spirit level to align the scanner with the scanned object. We use a separate spirit level to ensure both an overall alignment and the incident beam hitting the sample orthogonally. Figure 1 depicts the scan setup. Our scan setup was installed in a room with controlled light conditions, and a lux meter was used to detect the amount of light visible in the room. The lux meter detects wavelengths within the visible light range (400-700nm). Fluorescent lamps, such as the ones in our testing room, mainly radiate within the same spectra [18]. Therefore, the level of stray light interference can be measured by the lux meter.

The DLP NIRscan Nano software allows the user to configure and calibrate the device before starting a scan. A reference scan was set using a labsphere Spectralon Diffuse Reflectance Standard. This calibration tool reflects up to 99% of incoming light, allowing the machine to adjust to changing hardware performance. The configuration during all experiments used the whole available NIRS wavelength range (900-1700nm). The resolution of the hardware describes the smallest spectral features that it is able to detect. In our case the hardware has an optical resolution of 10nm. The digital resolution can be increased at the cost of decreasing the Signal-to-Noise Ratio (SNR). The lowest setting with the manufacturer's software is 7.02nm without receiving warnings about degrading performance. Therefore this setting was chosen as literature suggests that a higher resolution helps to detect all spectral features [12,21,37]. The manufacturer ships the device with four typical scan configurations [15]. For a digital resolution of 7.02nm, it is suggested that the spectra should be sampled approximately 228 times, meaning that it will be oversampled by 2 to satisfy the Nyquist-Shannon Sampling Theorem [8].

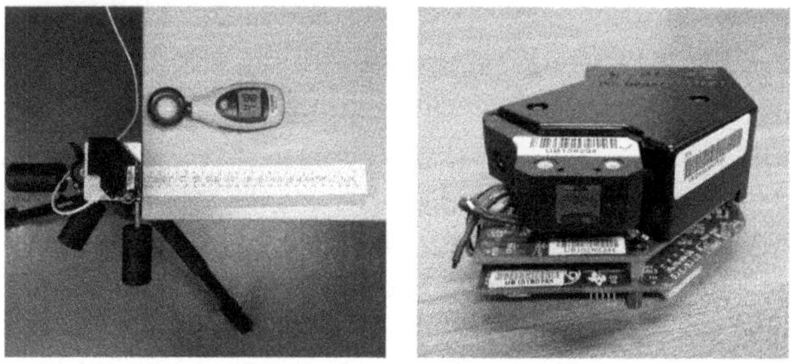

Figure 1. Left: Scanning platform with the DLP NIRscan Nano mounted and the lux meter. Right: DLP NIRscan Nano.

Specifically, the spectral bandwidth being sampled is 800nm (*i.e.*, 1700nm-900nm). With a digital resolution of 7.02nm, we need 114 (*i.e.*, 800nm / 7.02nm) patterns to sample the whole spectra. A common way to increase the SNR while sampling is by signal averaging [23]. We scan each object six times, as advised by the manufacturer. Each sample is recorded in the same manner, and all are averaged to increase the SNR. Each data point in Figure 2 – 7 represents the average mean absorbance of six individual scans.

There are two available scan methods for the device, which determine how the wavelengths are scanned: Hadamard scan and Column scan. Hadamard multiplexes several wavelengths together and decodes individual wavelengths. Noise in the incident signal is distributed evenly over the spectrum to minimize the effect. This method also collects more light and provides a greater SNR than the Column scan [15], and was therefore chosen for our study.

Test 1: Device Motion

The device could be used either as a handheld point and scan device (*e.g.*, baggage scanner) or as a stationary device (*i.e.*, mobile, but placed on a table when scanning). We investigated the effect of device motion on scan quality. If even small movements from events such as hand tremor cause inadequate scans, then the latter positioning technique would be the best solution when using these devices.

Movement of the NIRS while scanning can cause the lens window to lose contact with the sample. This may lead to unwanted reflections, distortion of the signal, and exposure to ambient light [26]. To explore the effect of device motion on scan accuracy, we scan each sample while the device is under three different levels of motion. First, we scan the sample with the device placed on the table. Second, we scan the sample while holding the device (*i.e.*, light movement). Lastly, we conduct scans with moderate motion to reflect careless usage.

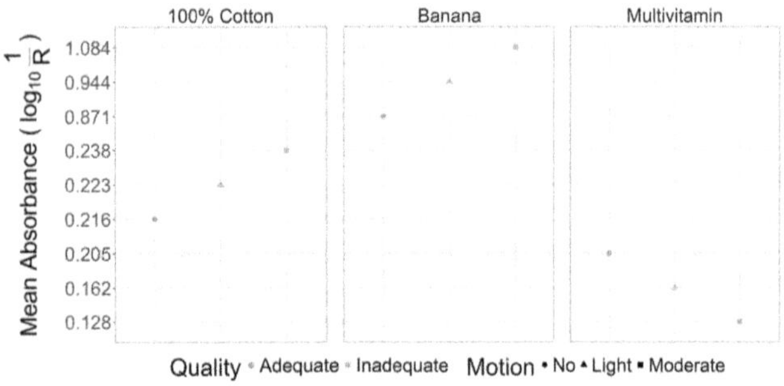

Figure 2. Mean absorbance of objects with different levels of device motion.

Figure 2 shows how the quality of the scans degrades when motion is applied to the NIRS when scanning. The absorbance also increases for both the 100% cotton and the banana sample, meaning less light is reflected. The multivitamin experiences a decrease in absorbance, likely caused by an increase in the lens exposure to ambient light.

Test 2: Sample Distance

Device positioning depends on the sample distance range for which it can deliver adequate results. Typically, lower ranges yield more accurate results, and in such cases the scanner should ideally be positioned upwards to enforce that the samples are directly on top of the lens window. However, a larger range would facilitate a more flexible design. The two lens-end broadband tungsten filament lamps in the NIRS hardware emit light through the device's sapphire window. Both the light source paths and the vision cone of the receiving lens intersect directly in front of the window. The further away the sample is positioned, the less light the system is able to collect because of path loss [44]. In addition, the reflected signal contains less information and is more prone to noise. NIRS scanners assume that all light which is not reflected has been absorbed, even though it may have radiated through or around the object. While different objects absorb at varying rate, lower absorbance (*i.e.*, a higher reflectance) often indicates that the object is closer and more ideally positioned. In addition, a sample positioned at close range will ensure less stray light entering the spectrometer, thereby increasing accuracy [46].

To test the accuracy of our scans over different distances, we attached a ruler to the table. Each sample was then measured from 0cm to 3cm with increments of 1mm. The effect of the distance on the absorbance is shown in Figure 3. All of the curves display a similar characteristic, with the main difference seen in the level of object absorbance (dependent on the chemical composition of the sample). We can see that pure cotton reflects back more light back than the omega-3 sample. This is because the omega-3 is transparent, with the majority of incoming light being scattered in multiple directions.

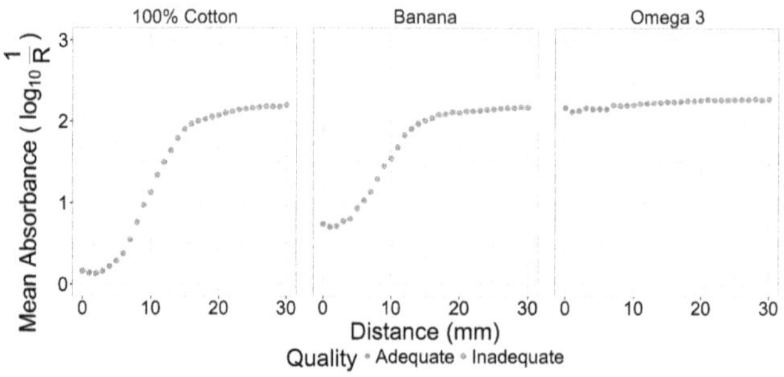

Figure 3. Mean absorbance of objects over different distances to the scanner

Test 3: Sample Angle

To design an appropriate sample holder for the hardware, we identify the sample angle range in which the device delivers adequate result. The holder needs to hold the sample flat down if the range is limited. With adequate results in a larger range, the design could be more universal with less focus on holding the sample in a certain angle.

For scans to be of high quality, the scanner needs to collect as much of the reflected light as possible. Ideally, the incident wave should hit a flat surface with an angle of 0°, following the law of reflection [35]. To measure the effects of scanning an item at various angles, we scan samples from 0° to 90° with increments of 15°. Figure 4 shows the effect of object angle on absorbance levels. For every increment of 15°, the quality deteriorates rapidly. While 0° is the optimal angle to retain all the spectral properties, small items (*e.g.*, multivitamins) reflect an adequate amount of light up to 15° (as shown in Figure 4) because of the illumination angle of the device.

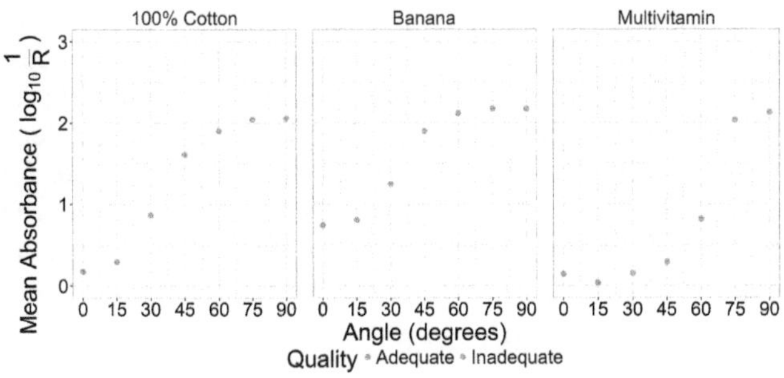

Figure 4. Mean absorbance of objects over different scanning angles.

Test 4: Sample Surface

The sample may have a surface with varying texture. It is crucial to know if the different textures will affect the scan accuracy. If the texture degrades scan accuracy significantly, the non-expert user should be instructed on how to correctly place the item to scan the most appropriate surface. A flat surface can reflect the signal in one direction, whereas a rough surface may cause signal scattering [36]. To investigate the consequences of scanning at various areas, we scanned the same samples from 3 reference points and 3 uneven surfaces. The reference scans are taken at 0mm distance and at a 0° angle at a flat surface covering most of the lens. The uneven surfaces consist of parts of the object that have edges or are rugged.

In Figure 5, we can observe that all the reference scans are of adequate quality and have little variance between them. In contrast, just one out of the nine uneven samples is of adequate quality. The uneven cotton samples also have a large variance compared to the rest. Since the cotton samples were placed unfolded in front of the lens, they had a varying thickness when we were scanning the three uneven samples.

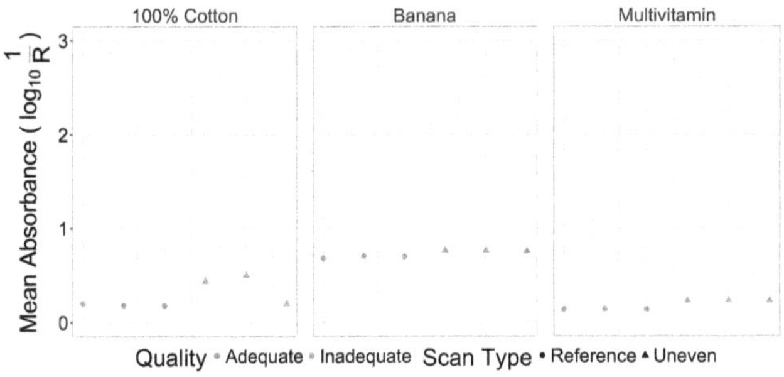

Figure 5. Mean absorbance of objects with different surface evenness

Test 5: Sample Interference

When scanning a sample, nearby objects may be a source of interference. If the magnitude of this noise causes inadequate scans, then the user should be instructed on correct scan behaviour (*i.e.*, only scan one sample at a time). Furthermore, this may also further encourage a stationary design, where the object is placed on a sample holder. The ratio of the NIRS waves that is reflected, absorbed, or passed through the scanned object depends on the object characteristics. Fruits [29], textiles [56], and pharmaceuticals [11] all have different penetration properties. Furthermore, a secondary object placed directly behind the sample might also reflect some light and affect the resulting spectra. To inspect the effects of this potential source of interference, we placed one object to be scanned in an ideal position while a secondary object was positioned directly behind the scanned object, moving up to 5cm away from the primary object at increments of 2mm.

Figure 6 shows how the distance of a secondary object to the scanned object can affect the quality of the signal. For the first and second graph, there was only one instance of interference when the secondary object (*i.e.*, apple, banana) was placed directly behind the sample (*i.e.*, cotton, grape). Finally, the level of interference from cotton on the omega-3 decreased in magnitude from 0mm to 37mm. This is because the omega-3 is transparent and therefore light is transmitted through the object and hits the cotton. It is then reflected back to the lens, causing the resulting spectra to be distorted.

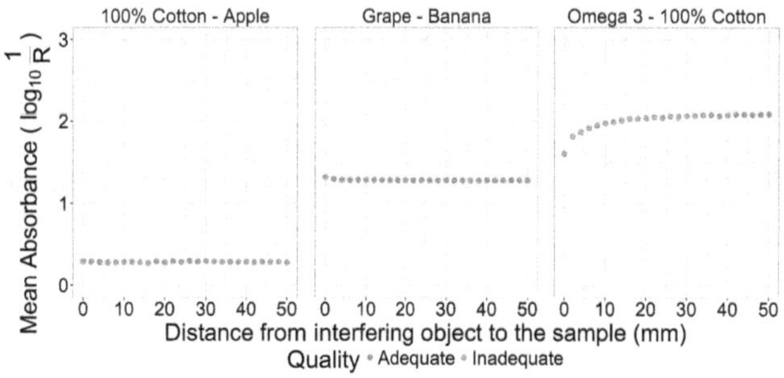

Figure 6. Mean absorbance of objects over different distances of interfering objects to the main object

Test 6: Ambience

The user may add noise to the spectrum by conducting scans with the NIRS in a context with unsuitable levels of ambient light, humidity, or temperature. We focus on light, as humidity and temperature's effect on the NIR spectra is limited in non-extreme climates [55]. The user should be instructed through the interface if the ambient light can cause the scan quality to drop significantly.

Radiation from nearby light sources can affect the accuracy of the NIRS [50]. The level of interference depends on the magnitude of the illuminance and the distance between scanner and sample. We use a 120W halogen lamp as an interference source and a lux meter to measure its illuminance. As the halogen lamp transmits on wavelengths beyond the lux meter's range, not all the light was detected. However, we still obtained a good indication of the illuminance level. We measured the effect of five different lux levels: 500 (bright office), 800, 1200 (daylight), 1600, and 2000 lux (shop window) [14]. The measurements were taken at four distances: 0, 10, 20, and 30mm. The effect of increased illuminance on SNR can be observed in Figure 7. The graphs are divided into bins. Samples in the same bin were taken at equal distance. Cotton and apple were unaffected by higher amounts of lux at 0mm range, while cotton showed varying results at 10, 20, and 30mm. For the apple, the scan contained substantial noise when increasing the lux beyond 0mm range. Omega-3 was affected more by stray light than the other two samples. Readings became noisy when the measured lux was above 500. This was expected as omega-3 is transparent and the interfering light can easily penetrate and cause noise.

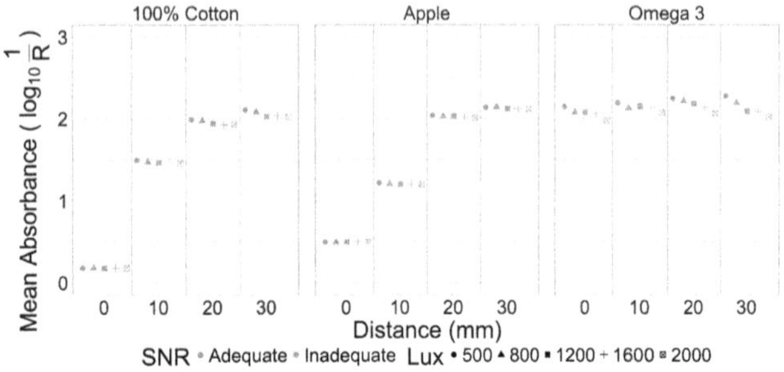

Figure 7. Mean absorbance of objects over different lux levels

Challenge 2 - Complexity of the Sampling Process

In addition to the challenges associated with user-induced errors when using NIRS, interaction with the scanning device is another important aspect. To facilitate novice end-user interaction with NIRS, a graphical user interface is required [27]. Figure 8 shows a procedural overview of the steps a user has to complete when using a NIRS device. The first two columns contain the steps and their respective descriptions. The third column indicates whether a user has to conduct that step when using a default NIRS device.

STEP	DESCRIPTION	ORDINARY NIRS USER INVOLVEMENT
Phone	UI Interaction	No
NIRS	SW / HW Interaction	Yes
Spectrum	Extract Raw Data	Yes
Analysis	Filtering Machine Learning	Yes
Results	Interpretation	Yes
Phone	Presentation	No

Figure 8. Necessary steps a user needs to complete with a typical NIRS device. Adapted from [26].

First, users have to operate the instrument through typically complex software (and sometimes hardware) operations. Current NIRS systems require users to configure the device, set scan parameters, and navigate complex menus. Following these steps, the user also has to handle information produced by the device. A major challenge for non-experts is that data is usually returned in a raw format, not revealing much information to the end user. To extract the data and turn it into understandable knowledge, analysis methods (*i.e.*, chemometrics) have to be applied to the dataset. This involves pre-processing the data when needed, and using multivariate analysis to classify the information [34]. Furthermore, a reference library is required to serve as training data for the classification model. The whole process hinders non-experts without strong analytical capabilities to interpret the information produced by the instrument. Consequently, training and education is a prerequisite for personnel wanting to utilise this technology in its present state. Our work is a step towards a future where users are not required to perform complex steps that require specific skills.

NON-EXPERT ASSISTANCE

To overcome the challenges related to scanning and identifying samples, we adopt a combined hardware-software approach. We address potential user-induced errors and the procedural complexities through a 3D printed enclosure and by guiding the user through a smartphone application capable of automating the required analysis.

Physical Assistance: Enclosure

We designed a 3D printed enclosure to both protect the scanner, reduce the effect of user-induced errors, and facilitate the scanning process. The design of our enclosure is informed by the findings of our tests. The design consists of a modular approach (protective casing and two different sample holders), which can be replaced by the user. The sample holders are distinctive in both shape and size to allow for different types of objects to be scanned. Figure 9 shows the final iteration of the enclosure and sample holders.

Figure 9. Enclosure and sample holders. The smaller sample holder contains two walls for small samples to be held in place.

The enclosure is formed to be positioned on the table, which removes the chance for device motion noise during operation. It is also pointing upwards, guaranteeing that object placement is within close proximity of the lens. This increases the accuracy as discovered in the sample distance test. Furthermore, it also the reduces the interference from ambient light, as the object is now covering the lens. The holder ensures that items are by default positioned at an even sample angle. In addition, our design prevents users from accidentally placing another object behind the scanned object, affecting the scan results (sample interference). Two arrows were placed on each platform to guide the user as to where the sample should be positioned.

The larger sample holder has a dimension of 20 x 20 cm. The considerable surface area enables comfortable placement of samples, without concern for the sample falling off. The smaller sample holder consists of two small walls placed at an incline, allowing for small samples to be held securely in place. This addition can be seen more in detail in Figure 12. The walls are covered using insulating tape with IR absorbing characteristics, to reduce light scattering and to shield from interference caused by any nearby objects. The base of the walls are positioned at the edge of the lens, so that any item positioned between the walls is covering the lens. The final setup as described above is the result of three iterations of design, 3D printing, and testing.

Procedural Assistance: Software

We developed a smartphone application to allow end-users to interact with the NIRS device. The application provides a single interaction point. Furthermore, it provides the user with instructions and warnings regarding scan quality issues in order to reduce the effect of user-induced errors. The software also automates and encapsulates all the complex analysis stages, thus reducing the burden for the user. Figure 10 displays the various screens of the application.

Figure 10. Top row from left: Initial screen, settings, example of scanning instructions. Bottom row from left: Example of sample identification result, example of scan result warning about the presence of a component, example of scan result regarding the absence of a component.

The home screen allows users to adjust the settings or start a new scan. In the settings screen, the user selects the type of sample that will be scanned. Instead of having to adjust a long list of parameters for the scan, the user can choose a pre-determined category. Based on this configuration, the scan screens will adjust to show the relevant instructions, guiding the user in correctly scanning the sample. For example, the text instructs the user to position an even surface down and only scan one sample at a time. These guidelines were based on our tests investigating user-induced errors. After a scan is completed, the application displays the results. We utilise the built-in lux sensor of the phone to infer the level of illuminance in the area. Lux is measured in luminous flux per square metre, so while the phone and sensor are not in the exact same position, it can still be used as a baseline for how much light is reaching the NIRS. The lux measurement (top right corner of scan screen) changes from green, to yellow, to red, depending on the level of illuminance based on our ambient light tests.

When the user presses the scan button, the button becomes disabled and a progress bar appears together with a text field describing the stage (*i.e.*, scanning, analysis, or processing). The whole process takes around 20 seconds (approximately 10 seconds for scan, 5 seconds for analysis, and 5 seconds for processing) to complete. Upon completion, the application will display the results and also vocalise the results using text-to-speech. The current version of the application has the ability to identify pharmaceuticals and detect whether a bread contains gluten. While the application could be implemented for a vast number of scenarios, we focus on the two aforementioned scenarios in our user study.

Communication (*e.g.*, starting a scan, receiving scan results) between the smartphone and the NIRS device occurs over Bluetooth Low Energy. When the application receives the scan results, they are sent to a server for processing (*e.g.*, filtering, classification, regression). After the sample is analysed, the results are sent back to the smartphone and presented to the user. In addition, there are four scenarios in which the application will display a warning message to the user. While the warnings are active (10s), the scan button is greyed out and disabled. This is to ensure that the user reads it and does not accidently press the scan button again. After ten seconds, the button becomes active again. Warnings are intended to correct scan behaviour and limit the effect of user-induced errors, and are displayed in Figure 11. The thresholds for triggering these warnings were informed by the user-induced errors tests.

Figure 11. Warnings 1 - 4 from top left to bottom right.

Warning 1. If insufficient light is reflected back to the receiver, this is interpreted by the software as the object being misplaced.

Warning 2. If substantial noise is detected in the resulting spectra, this can be caused either by object transparency or uneven surfaces.
Warning 3. When the illuminance is larger than 800 lux, the text turns yellow and the user will be informed that the accuracy of the scans might be inaccurate.
Warning 4. When the illuminance is larger than 1200 lux, the text turns red and scanning is temporarily disabled until the user can find a darker location.

Evaluation

To evaluate our proposed software and physical guides, we conducted a user study with participants who had no prior experience with NIRS technology. The main goal was to investigate whether non-experts are able to successfully conduct the scanning procedure without training. We investigated how people interact with the technology through a scanning experiment, and conducted a semi-structured interview to capture their opinions and feedback. Thus, our objective here is to explore the practical usability and perceived usefulness of the developed solution.

Participants and Procedure

We recruited 15 people using mailing lists of our university (9 males, 6 females; ages: 20-34 years old, M=26.6). Participants had a diverse range of educational backgrounds (*e.g.*, Finance, Biology, Anthropology, and Computer Science). We carried out the experiments with each participant individually. The experiment duration was approximately 30 minutes per participant. Participants were rewarded for their participation with a movie voucher. After a short introduction to the experiment, participants were asked to scan a set of objects placed on the table before them using the NIRS scanner within the enclosure and a provided mobile phone running our application. The study was divided in two parts: 1) sample identification using 10 different pharmaceuticals, and 2) gluten detection using 10 pieces of bread. Both parts had items with varying characteristics (*e.g.*, shape, size, texture, and transparency) to thoroughly test our non-expert assistance. We counterbalanced the scanning order.

Participants did not receive any instructions on how to use the devices, as we wanted to assess the usability of our proposed solution in a realistic setting (*e.g.*, the user would encounter this device in a supermarket without additional guidance from the staff). The participants were asked to report the scan results to the observing researcher. During the experiment, we recorded the participants' answers and how they interacted with the non-expert assistance, as well as any comments from the participants while they scanned the objects. In addition, we also recorded any warning messages that were displayed by the application, for which object this warning message was displayed, and the user's reaction. After all scans were completed, we conducted a semi-structured interview in which we asked participants to comment on the application (*e.g.*, usage, instructions, warnings, results), the enclosure, and the technology in general. The interview was structured as follows.

Age, gender, occupation, background.

Statements ranked on a 5-point Likert scale.

- The scan time was acceptable.
- The instructions/warnings/results (asked individually) were easy to understand.
- The instructions/warnings (asked individually) had enough details.
- It was easy to understand where to place the object.
- It was easy to place the object in the correct position.
- I felt comfortable when I used the device.
- I would trust this type of technology.
- I can see myself using this technology daily.

Open-ended questions.

- What is your overall experience using our solution?
- Did you have any issues understanding how to use the application?
- Did you make any adjustments when you received the warnings?
- What steps would you take upon receiving a warning?
- What is your impression of the accuracy of the device?
- What type of information would you like to receive with the result?
- What features did you like on the enclosure?
- What features did you not like on the enclosure?
- What features would you change on the enclosure?
- What would you scan with a device like this?

Since not all the warnings were shown during the scans, we printed them on paper and showed them individually during the interview in order to collect feedback. We asked participants to envision receiving the warnings and describing their subsequent actions. In addition, we asked the participants what additional information they would like to receive in scenarios besides the two we presented. The main focus of the study was to investigate whether novice end-users would be able to successfully utilise a NIRS device using our design. We were also interested in collecting opinions on our design and the technology in general.

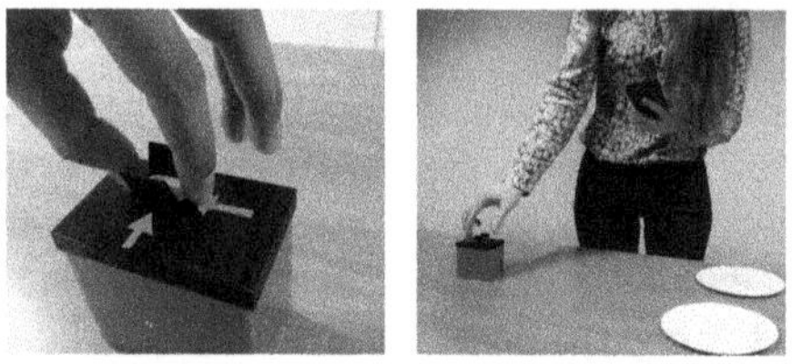

Figure 12. Left: Object placement on small sample holder. Right: Participant during the user study.

Results

Perceptions

The majority of participants (N=14) immediately understood the instructions and started using the application with no notable problems. One participant (P07) tried scanning the object by holding the phone towards it instead of placing the object on the platform. The participant quickly corrected his behaviour and explained that the confusion was due to having used several applications that rely on the camera. Participants strongly agreed that the instructions were easy to understand (M = 4.53, SD = 1.06), and also agreed that the instructions they were provided with by the smartphone were of sufficient detail (M = 4.40, SD = 0.91). Some participants commented that the instructions could be presented in a stepwise fashion, allowing for a more legible presentation: "I *would like stepwise instructions, where you swipe to show the next instructions. It would allow for bigger pictures and text.*" (P09). None of the participants reported having any issues with using the application and generally agreed that the scan time was acceptable (M = 3.80, SD = 0.68). Context was also deemed an important factor: "*A user in the supermarket would not be able to wait that long*" (P01).

Warnings

A few warnings were caused by participants pressing the scan button before positioning the sample, triggering Warning 1. In these cases, the users quickly recovered. There were also events in which transparent samples (omega-3) generated Warning 2. We showed each individual warning to the participants, and they generally agreed that they were understandable (M = 4.34, SD = 0.80) and contained enough details (M = 4.41, SD = 0.85). P04, P09, P11, and P12 commented that the icon for Warning 2 did not correlate with the text in the warning. "*The icon in Warning 2 does not indicate transparency*" (P04). P05 recommended more visual instructions, instead of text. P06 requested more information about the lux range and more distinct difference for the icons in warning 3 and 4. Regarding the actions they would take upon receiving a warning, the answers were in line with the steps we envisioned a user would take (*e.g.*, reposition object, place flat surface down, shade the machine from interfering light, or move to a darker area).

Scan Presentation

Participants strongly agreed that the results were easy to understand (M = 4.87, SD = 0.35). When questioned about what additional information participants would like to have included with the results, most answers were related to more nutritional information (*e.g.*, protein, carbohydrates, fats, sugar) but also other allergens (lactose). We received positive comments for the pharmaceutical results, such as "*I really like the vitamin feedback. It is cool that it tells you what it contains. Reminds me of a video game, where you can inspect items and see their stats*" (P05).

Physical Enclosure

Multiple participants positively commented on the enclosure, with comments such as, "*It's small, light, and portable*" (P04), and "*The large surface area makes it easy to position the bread*" (P01). Participants strongly agreed that it was easy to understand where to place the sample (M = 4.67, SD = 0.72). "*I liked the arrows and colour indications on the box*" (P05). They also agreed that it was easy to place the item in the correct position (M = 4.20, SD = 0.86). When asked about potential improvements to the enclosure, a few remarks about aesthetics were noted. "*Would change the package a bit, make it less bulky and more flat.*" (P08). Another participant believed the scanning process of smaller items could be improved with a redesign of the enclosure, "*Make the box so that you put the item inside and scan it, and change the platform to be a bowl, so the item falls to the middle.*" (P10).

Future Use

The participants reported being comfortable when using the device (M = 4.47, SD = 0.64), and the general consensus was that they would use the technology on a daily basis (M = 4.47, SD = 0.74). In addition, participants stated they would trust this type of technology (M = 4.53, SD = 0.64), "*I think it was accurate and made correct identifications. I trust this machine more than my own judgement or some labels*" (P12). However, a couple of participants expressed the importance of getting the scans right in certain situations, "*False classifications could potentially be dangerous for the user. In those cases, accuracy is really important.*" (P04).

When probed about potential scenarios where they would use this technology, several participants mentioned food, pharmaceuticals, textiles, and various chemicals. Three participants proposed creative ways of using the technology: "*It would be interesting to scan makeup to look for micro plastic. I don't use makeup that can potentially damage the nature.*" (P05). "*I would like to scan food products for gelatine. We Muslims don't eat products that contain it.*" (P12). "*It would be nice to have a survival scanner that could detect if food found in the nature (e.g., berries and mushrooms) are poisonous or safe to eat.*" (P13).

Typical information to look for could be nutritional content, Active Pharmaceutical Ingredient (API) percentages, allergens, and item quality. Multiple users would like to have the machine in a supermarket, to scan products and retrieve information about their quality (*e.g.*, fruit ripeness). "*Putting it in the supermarket would be really helpful, I can see a lot of people using it.*" (P12). "*It would be useful for dementia patients. Pharmaceuticals can look the same, but have strongly different effects.*" (P04). Several participants envisioned that in the future, NIRS could be a helpful sensor embedded in their smartphones. Multiple participants also expressed their desire to have such a device in their home for a number of different reasons. Throughout the study, people were enthusiastic about the technology, and commented positively on its potential.

DISCUSSION

Towards End-User Near Infrared Spectroscopy

Previous work on portable NIRS has mainly been concerned with testing performance under ideal conditions with domain experts [2,28,39]. However, there is a scarcity of research that highlights the potential use cases, design challenges, and solutions to enable non-experts to use NIRS. The effect of user-induced errors on NIRS can pose significant challenges, particularly for untrained users. Users currently have to operate the instrument through complex software and require knowledge about advanced analytical methods to understand the result. We argue that in order to make the technology more accessible and still produce reliable results, the scanner and its software/hardware controls must be designed to guide the user and avoid problematic scanning conditions. In this paper, we report and evaluate a hardware-software design that proved successful in guiding and facilitating the scanning process for non-expert end users.

Our application provided simplified instructions for users with no previous contact with the technology. The warnings were designed to help users overcome probable scanning errors, and were shown to help them overcome sample misplacement. Our design effectively provides an interactive way to train users of the equipment, and our user study shows that participants were able to quickly start using the technology reliably without any verbal instructions.

Furthermore, the 3D printed enclosure and sample holder enabled, for the most part, correct scanning behaviour by facilitating optimal object placement. Participants felt that the enclosure effectively guided them in correctly placing the samples, while at the same time protecting the device. One element of the scanning process that was rated slightly lower than others was the scanning time ($M = 3.80$, $SD = 0.68$). One potential reason for this is that the technology is quite new - it is possible that users have not yet formed an opinion on how long a scan should take. The scan time depends on the scan configuration (*e.g.*, resolution, width, and SNR). By increasing the precision or reliability of the scan, it takes a longer time to complete. Some configurations are more appropriate, depending on the nature of the analysis and the scanning environment. Ultimately, what constitutes a feasible and acceptable scan time will depend on the scenario (*e.g.*, supermarket, home) and the analysis requirements (*e.g.*, allergens, API, nutrition, ripeness, poisonous).

Moreover, one important challenge for end-user NIRS is the collection of reference scans. With our system, users have to indicate the type of objects that they are scanning so that the application can optimise the scanning configuration. This then loads the appropriate model depending on the user's choice. We envision that in the future, devices will come pre-loaded with models for commonly scanned objects. In addition, crowdsensing communities [24] can emerge to establish a shared repository of sample fingerprints to facilitate object identification. Furthermore, methods that enable use of existing knowledge-bases built by benchtop instruments can be used with acceptable performance [21].

Implications for Practice and Research

We tested a relatively cheap and miniaturised NIRS device on a wide set of everyday objects. We have shown how the device performs when scanning various objects with different physical characteristics. By better understanding these parameters, it is possible to design enclosures and applications that facilitate the correct usage of the technology. This would allow for a smartphone to be turned into an advanced scientific instrument by simply installing an application and coupling it to a NIRS device. As a result, even novice users would be able to conduct experiments, earlier limited only to trained lab personnel. For instance, farmers can be better informed on the best time to harvest their crops without relying on expensive or time-consuming methods. About 125,000 people die every year due to medication mismanagement and the estimated cost is around $300 billion [25]. Miniaturised NIRS could be implemented to help nurses or the users themselves (*e.g.*, old adults) administer medicine. Furthermore, a number of interesting use cases that we did not envision were identified by our participants, highlighting the potential of the technology for a wide variety of everyday scenarios. For researchers, our study opens multiple avenues to explore. Due to the small form factor, our solution can be carried around by the user for *in situ* sample analysis. Furthermore, a multitude of everyday objects, from cups and dishes to shelves and refrigerators can begin to be instrumented with NIRS hardware to identify objects. Ubiquitous scanning stations where the NIRS is bundled with tablets could be installed in public locations and serve a broad group of users. As NIRS devices decrease in size and price, it may become possible to bind them to smartphones in the future. This could create a range of opportunities for scanning "in-the-wild" without having to carry around an additional device.

Limitations

The work presented in this paper has several limitations. First, we conducted the user-induced errors experiments using visual alignment. While both careful precision and measuring tools were used to align the samples, there may still exist some human error. Second, we did not compare participant usage of the technology with and without our solution. It would be unreasonable to give the hardware with its default elements and expect a participant to be able to conduct any given step of the scan and analysis process. Also, discussion about classification models is considered to be out of scope for this paper. Finally, we only utilise one NIRS scanner in this paper. While our findings can be used as guidelines for a larger array of hardware, it would be interesting to test multiple devices from different vendors for a more thorough investigation.

CONCLUSION

Our work has systematically investigated the effect of user-induced errors and the complexity of the sampling process in the context of an affordable and miniaturised NIRS. We subsequently investigated the magnitude of these parameters to derive their potential impact on scanning quality and usability. Previous work has taken for granted that the instrument is used under ideal conditions by trained personnel. We show that NIRS can be successfully used by novice end-users, if the challenges explored in this paper are taken into consideration. This is validated through a user study where non-expert users test a NIRS equipped with a 3D printed enclosure and smartphone application. The results indicate that the accuracy and user experience when using NIRS for object detection and analysis is adequate when use is facilitated with our proposed non-expert assistance. In our ongoing work, we intend to deploy an *in situ* scanner in a variety of different scenarios.

REFERENCES

1. Nawaf Abu-Khalaf. 2015. Sensing tomatos pathogen using Visible/Near infrared (VIS/NIR) spectroscopy and multivariate data analysis (MVDA). *Palestine Technical University Research Journal* 3, 1: 12-22.
2. T. Akinaga, Munehiro Tanaka and Sheishi Kawasaki. 2008. On-tree and after-harvesting evaluation of firmness, color and lycopene content of tomato fruit using portable NIR spectroscopy. *Journal of food, agriculture & environment.*
3. Dimitris Alexandrakis, Gerard Downey and Amalia G. Scannell. 2012. Rapid non-destructive detection of spoilage of intact chicken breast muscle using near-infrared and Fourier transform mid-infrared spectroscopy and multivariate statistics. *Food and Bioprocess Technology* 5, 1: 338-347.
4. Katherine A. Bakeev. 2010. *Process analytical technology: spectroscopic tools and implementation strategies for the chemical and pharmaceutical industries.* John Wiley & Sons.
5. Ravi Bhoraskar, Nagamanoj Vankadhara, Bhaskaran Raman and Purushottam Kulkarni. 2012. Wolverine: Traffic and road condition estimation using smartphone sensors. In *2012 Fourth International Conference on Communication Systems and Networks (COMSNETS 2012)*, 1-6.
6. M. Blanco and I. Villarroya. 2002. NIR spectroscopy: a rapid-response analytical tool. *TrAC Trends in Analytical Chemistry* 21, 4: 240-250.
7. L. Bokobza. 1998. Near infrared spectroscopy. *Journal of Near Infrared Spectroscopy* 6: 3-18.
8. Emmanuel J. Candès and Michael B. Wakin. 2008. An introduction to compressive sampling. *IEEE signal processing magazine* 25, 2: 21-30.
9. A. Candolfi, R. De Maesschalck, D. L. Massart, P. A. Hailey and A. C. E. Harrington. 1999. Identification of pharmaceutical excipients using NIR spectroscopy and SIMCA. *Journal of pharmaceutical and biomedical analysis* 19, 6: 923-935.
10. Zhenghua Chen, Han Zou, Hao Jiang, Qingchang Zhu, Yeng C. Soh and Lihua Xie. 2015. Fusion of WiFi, smartphone sensors and landmarks using the Kalman filter for indoor localization. *Sensors* 15, 1: 715-732.
11. Fiona C. Clarke, Stephen V. Hammond, Roger D. Jee and Anthony C. Moffat. 2002. Determination of the information depth and sample size for the analysis of pharmaceutical materials using reflectance near-infrared microscopy. *Applied spectroscopy* 56, 11: 1475-1483.
12. E. Cleve, E. Bach and E. Schollmeyer. 2000. Using chemometric methods and NIR spectrophotometry in the textile industry. *Analytica Chimica Acta* 420, 2: 163-167.
13. Anil K. Deisingh. 2005. Pharmaceutical counterfeiting. *Analyst* 130, 3: 271-279.
14. David L. DiLaura, Kevin W. Houser, Richard G. Mistrick and Gary R. Steffy. 2011. The lighting handbook: Reference and application.
15. DLP® NIRscanTM Nano EVM User's Guide. Retrieved 21/03/2016 from http://www.ti.com/lit/ug/dlpu030f/dlpu030f.pdf
16. A. Durand, O. Devos, C. Ruckebusch and J. P. Huvenne. 2007. Genetic algorithm optimisation combined with partial least squares regression and mutual information variable selection procedures in near-infrared quantitative analysis of cotton-viscose textiles. *Analytica Chimica Acta* 595, 1: 72-79.
17. M. Dyrby, S. B. Engelsen, L. Nørgaard, M. Bruhn and L. Lundsberg-Nielsen. 2002. Chemometric quantitation of the active substance (containing ≡ N) in a pharmaceutical tablet using near-infrared (NIR) transmittance and NIR FT-Raman spectra. *Applied Spectroscopy* 56, 5: 579-585.
18. Christopher D. Elvidge, David M. Keith, Benjamin T. Tuttle and Kimberly E. Baugh. 2010. Spectral identification of lighting type and character. *Sensors* 10, 4: 3961-3988.
19. Ming Gao, Xihong Hu, Bo Cao and Dianxin Li. 2014. Fingerprint sensors in mobile devices. In *2014 9th IEEE Conference on Industrial Electronics and Applications*, 1437-1440.
20. Mayank Goel, Eric Whitmire, Alex Mariakakis, T. S. Saponas, Neel Joshi, Dan Morris, Brian Guenter, Marcel Gavriliu, Gaetano Borriello and Shwetak N. Patel. 2015. HyperCam: hyperspectral imaging for ubiquitous computing applications. In *Proceedings of the 2015 ACM International Joint Conference on Pervasive and Ubiquitous Computing*, 145-156.
21. C. V. Greensill and K. B. Walsh. 2000. Optimization of Instrumentation Precision and Wavelength Resolution for the Performance of NIR Calibrations of Sucrose in a Water-Cellulose Matrix. *Applied Spectroscopy* 54, 3: 426-430.
22. Mathew J. Gregoski, Martina Mueller, Alexey Vertegel, Aleksey Shaporev, Brenda B. Jackson, Ronja M. Frenzel, Sara M. Sprehn and Frank A. Treiber. 2012. Development and validation of a smartphone heart rate acquisition application for health promotion and wellness telehealth applications. *International journal of telemedicine and applications* 2012: 1.
23. G. M. Hieftje. 1972. Signal-to-noise enhancement through instrumental techniques. II. Signal averaging, boxcar integration, and correlation techniques. *Analytical chemistry* 44, 7: 69A-78a.
24. Simo Hosio, Jorge Goncalves, Niels van Berkel and Simon Klakegg. 2016. Crowdsourcing Situated &

Subjective Knowledge for Decision Support. In *International Joint Conference on Pervasive and Ubiquitous Computing Adjunct*, ACM, 1478-1483. http://dx.doi.org/10.1145/2968219.2968591.

25. Is Mom Taking Her Medicine? An Entrepreneur Takes On A $300 Billion, Life-And-Death Challenge. Retrieved 02/01/2017 from http://www.forbes.com/sites/elizabethmacbride/2016/09/27/is-mom-taking-her-medicine-an-entrepreneur-takes-on-a-300-million-life-and-death-challenge/#210eb96054b3
26. Meltem Izzetoglu, Ajit Devaraj, Scott Bunce and Banu Onaral. 2005. Motion artifact cancellation in NIR spectroscopy using Wiener filtering. *IEEE Transactions on Biomedical Engineering* 52, 5: 934-938.
27. Simon Klakegg, Chu Luo, Jorge Goncalves, Simo Hosio and Vassilis Kostakos. 2016. Instrumenting Smartphones with Portable NIRS. In *International Joint Conference on Pervasive and Ubiquitous Computing Adjunct*, ACM, 618-623. http://dx.doi.org/10.1145/2968219.2971590 .
28. Jeroen Lammertyn, Bart Nicola, Kristine Ooms, V. De Smedt and Josse De Baerdemaeker. 1998. Non-destructive measurement of acidity, soluble solids, and firmness of Jonagold apples using NIR-spectroscopy. *Transactions of the ASAE* 41, 4: 1089.
29. Jeroen Lammertyn, Ann Peirs, Josse De Baerdemaeker and Bart Nicola. 2000. Light penetration properties of NIR radiation in fruit with respect to non-destructive quality assessment. *Postharvest Biology and Technology* 18, 2: 121-132.
30. Kristiyan Lukanov, Horia A. Maior and Max L. Wilson. 2016. Using fNIRS in usability testing: understanding the effect of web form layout on mental workload. In *Proceedings of the 2016 CHI Conference on Human Factors in Computing Systems*, 4011-4016.
31. Chu Luo, Angelos Fylakis, Juha Partala, Simon Klakegg, Jorge Goncalves, Kaitai Liang, Tapio Seppänen and Vassilis Kostakos. 2016. A Data Hiding Approach for Sensitive Smartphone Data. In *International Joint Conference on Pervasive and Ubiquitous Computing Adjunct*, ACM, 457-468. http://dx.doi.org/10.1145/2971648.2971686.
32. David Luxton, Russell A. McCann, Nigel E. Bush, Matthew C. Mishkind and Greg M. Reger. 2011. mHealth for mental health: Integrating smartphone technology in behavioral healthcare. *Professional Psychology: Research and Practice* 42, 6: 505.
33. Horia A. Maior, Matthew Pike, Sarah Sharples and Max L. Wilson. 2015. Examining the reliability of using fNIRS in realistic HCI settings for spatial and verbal tasks. In *Proceedings of the 33rd Annual ACM Conference on Human Factors in Computing Systems*, 3039-3042.
34. Desiré L. Massart, B. G. M. Vandeginste, S. N. Deming, Y. Michotte and L. Kaufman. 1988. Chemometrics: a textbook.
35. D. A. McNamara, C. W. I. Pistorius and J. A. G. Malherbe. 1990. The Uniform Geometrical theory of diffraction. *Artech House, London.*
36. Shree K. Nayar, Katsushi Ikeuchi and Takeo Kanade. 1991. Surface reflection: physical and geometrical perspectives. *IEEE Transactions on Pattern Analysis & Machine Intelligence* 7: 611-634.
37. Bart M. Nicolai, Katrien Beullens, Els Bobelyn, Ann Peirs, Wouter Saeys, Karen I. Theron and Jeroen Lammertyn. 2007. Nondestructive measurement of fruit and vegetable quality by means of NIR spectroscopy: A review. *Postharvest Biology and Technology* 46, 2: 99-118.
38. Brian G. Osborne and Thomas Fearn. 1986. *Near infrared spectroscopy in food analysis.* Longman.
39. Andrew J. ONeil, Roger D. Jee, Gad Lee, Andrew Charvill and Anthony C. Moffat. 2008. Use of a portable near infrared spectrometer for the authentication of tablets and the detection of counterfeit versions. *J. Near Infrared Spectrosc* 16: 327.
40. Evan M. Peck, Daniel Afergan, Beste F. Yuksel, Francine Lalooses and Robert J. Jacob. 2014. Using fNIRS to measure mental workload in the real world. *Advances in physiological computing*: 117-139.
41. Ling Pei, Robert Guinness, Ruizhi Chen, Jingbin Liu, Heidi Kuusniemi, Yuwei Chen, Liang Chen and Jyrki Kaistinen. 2013. Human behavior cognition using smartphone sensors. *Sensors (Basel)* 13, 2: 1402-24. http://dx.doi.org/10.3390/s130201402.
42. Quarter of the world will be using smartphones in 2016. Retrieved 29/08/2016 from http://www.telegraph.co.uk/technology/mobile-phones/11287659/Quarter-of-the-world-will-be-using-smartphones-in-2016.html
43. Kiran B. Raja, Ramachandra Raghavendra, Vinay K. Vemuri and Christoph Busch. 2015. Smartphone based visible iris recognition using deep sparse filtering. *Pattern Recognition Letters* 57: 33-42.
44. Theodore S. Rappaport. 1996. *Wireless communications: principles and practice.* Prentice Hall PTR New Jersey.
45. Sirinnapa Saranwong, Jinda Sornsrivichai and Sumio Kawano. 2004. Prediction of ripe-stage eating quality of mango fruit from its harvest quality measured nondestructively by near infrared spectroscopy. *Postharvest Biology and Technology* 31, 2: 137-145.

46. T. W. L. Scheeren, P. Schober and L. A. Schwarte. 2012. Monitoring tissue oxygenation by near infrared spectroscopy (NIRS): background and current applications. *Journal of clinical monitoring and computing* 26, 4: 279-287.
47. Sensors Overview | Android Developers. Retrieved 04/03/2014 from http://developer.android.com/guide/topics/sensors/sensors_overview.html
48. Heinz W. Siesler, Yukihiro Ozaki, Satoshi Kawata and H. M. Heise. 2008. *Near-infrared spectroscopy: principles, instruments, applications.* John Wiley & Sons.
49. Nicoletta Sinelli, Sara Limbo, Luisa Torri, Valentina Di Egidio and Ernestina Casiraghi. 2010. Evaluation of freshness decay of minced beef stored in high-oxygen modified atmosphere packaged at different temperatures using NIR and MIR spectroscopy. *Meat science* 86, 3: 748-752.
50. Walter Slavin. 1963. Stray Light in Ultraviolet, Visible, and Near-Infrared Spectrophotometry. *Analytical Chemistry* 35, 4: 561-566.
51. Erin T. Solovey, Audrey Girouard, Krysta Chauncey, Leanne M. Hirshfield, Angelo Sassaroli, Feng Zheng, Sergio Fantini and Robert J. Jacob. 2009. Using fNIRS brain sensing in realistic HCI settings: experiments and guidelines. In *Proceedings of the 22nd annual ACM symposium on User interface software and technology*, 157-166.
52. Megan Strait, Cody Canning and Matthias Scheutz. 2014. Reliability of NIRS-Based BCIs: a placebo-controlled replication and reanalysis of Brainput. In *CHI'14 Extended Abstracts on Human Factors in Computing Systems*, 619-630.
53. Patrick L. Walter. 2006. The History of the Accelerometer: 1920s-1996 - Prologue and Epilogue. *Sound & Vibration 41*, 84-90.
54. Beste F. Yuksel, Kurt B. Oleson, Lane Harrison, Evan M. Peck, Daniel Afergan, Remco Chang and Robert J. Jacob. 2016. Learn piano with BACh: An adaptive learning interface that adjusts task difficulty based on brain state. In *Proceedings of the 2016 CHI Conference on Human Factors in Computing Systems*, 5372-5384.
55. Ying Zhou, Xiaping Fu and Yibin Ying. 2006. Influence of humidity on spectral performance for near-infrared detection of fruit. In *Optics East 2006*, 638119-638119. http://dx.doi.org/10.1117/12.686542.
56. M. Zoccola, N. Lu, R. Mossotti, R. Innocenti and A. Montarsolo. 2013. Identification of wool, cashmere, yak, and angora rabbit fibers and quantitative determination of wool and cashmere in blend: a near infrared spectroscopy study. *Fibers and Polymers* 14, 8: 1283-1289.

"Proof in the Pudding": Designing IoT Plants for Wellbeing

Sarah Martindale◆, Ben Bedwell◆, Robert Phillips○, Micaella Pedros○

◆Horizon Digital Economy Research,
The University of Nottingham,
Nottingham, United Kingdom
{sarah.martindale, benjamin.bedwell}
@nottingham.ac.uk

○Royal College of Art,
Design Products
London, United Kingdom
robert.phillips@rca.ac.uk,
micaella.pedros@network.rca.ac.uk

ABSTRACT
This paper contributes a participatory design case study that used workshops and ideation frameworks to scaffold a conceptualisation of 'user data-actuated' plants. The framework combines ideation cards, worksheets and facilitated co-design, guiding non-experts to conceptually connect personal data, health/wellbeing goals, plants and people. We demonstrate how the framework enabled participants to envisage 'connected' plants, linking personal data outputs with inputs to actuated growing environments, creating biofeedback.

From the results of design work carried out by participants, we synthesise and present four themes. The themes provide a spectrum of values that participants embedded in their connected plants, and in the act of gifting their connected plants to other people. The results of these workshops sign-post a new design space for personal data embodied in plants that could be taken forward by the DIS community.

Author Keywords
Internet-of-things; IoT; plants; growing; wellbeing; health; participatory design; ideation.

ACM Classification Keywords
H.5.m. Information interfaces and presentation (e.g., HCI): Miscellaneous; H.5.2. User interfaces: User-centered design.

INTRODUCTION
An ever-increasing range of Internet-of-Things (IoT) products aim to enrich our personal environments by collecting, representing and repurposing personal data. Wearables (e.g. Fitbit), our mobiles (especially through frameworks such as HealthKit), and our homes (e.g. when enhanced with ecosystems such as SmartThings) provide an ecosystem of sensors and feedback devices than can be embedded and connected by non-technical users. However, the creation of a homogeneous environment where we are sensed everywhere and have access to data everywhere, may reduce our opportunities to retreat from persistent pressures, restore our stamina, and make positive plans.

Many IoT products are sold with the promise of revealing insights into the user's activity through quantified measurement and informatics [2,32]. Allied to this data collection capacity, these devices also make the promise of helping to change users' behaviour for the better [22,25]. However, the successful conversion of information and intention into positive action relies on confluence with contextual and social factors. Thus, some products attempt to capitalise on social effects to improve the potential for IoT to change behaviour.

Our research focuses on the potential to use plants as a new interface for personal data. Plants are already integrated into our private and public environments, and growing is shown to improve mental health [4,10,11,24,44] and provide tangible rewards in the form of aesthetically pleasing plants and healthy food [18]. Linking the wellbeing of plants to streams of personal data has the potential to make plants salient in non-"green" settings, abstract data into organic forms, and move our relationship with plants towards one that is more explicitly symbiotic, i.e. where positive behaviour generates positive data, which is mapped to positive growing conditions, and where negative behaviour creates negative growing conditions.

In this paper, we present a case study of co-designing concepts for 'connected' plants using a design framework to explore the possibility of closely coupling plants to personal data and wellbeing. The research questions we set out to investigate through this process were threefold: 1) what data would users appropriate to quantify their wellbeing goals; 2) would they see value in connecting those goals to the growth of plants; and 3) how could that new interaction be meaningful in their social contexts?

The participatory design framework was created specifically to enable members of the public without experience of growing or IoT to generate design concepts. Based on our experience of running participatory design workshops we present an emerging design space for personal data embodied in plants, representing new user-

DIS 2017, June 10-14, 2017, Edinburgh, United Kingdom

ACM 978-1-4503-4922-2/17/06…$15.00
DOI: http://dx.doi.org/10.1145/3064663.3064743

oriented opportunities to motivate health behaviours and increase a sense of connectedness. We end by reflecting on our method, and opportunities for future work.

BACKGROUND AND RELATED WORK

Our research focuses on the potential for plants to allow end-users - members of the public who produce and consume personal data - to appropriate personal data in ways that enable positive changes to their wellbeing. In particular, we approach this as an opportunity to design systems that place human values, not technology, at the heart of behaviour change. In this section we consider how our three research questions relate to existing work.

Personal data and wellbeing goals

There are many examples of readily available IoT products that seek to enrich environments, changing the way we track our physical activity (e.g. Fitbit[1], HealthKit[2]), shop (e.g. Amazon Dash[3]), and customise our surroundings (e.g. SmartThings[4]). Some of these are designed with the aim of improving health and wellbeing by self-monitoring physical activity (e.g. number of steps), biorhythms (e.g. heart rate), and consumption (e.g. calorific intake), and feeding back this personal data to the user. As a result, the notions of Quantified Self (QS) and Personal Informatics (PI) have emerged [2,32]. Design issues around current IoT devices are well-known, e.g. how to easily connect them to infrastructures [17], but the key challenges have moved up the stack, from low-level device development towards how to present personal data so that it is intelligible and actionable.

Personal IoT devices can generate huge amounts of data, but on-screen visualisations that provide great detail and accuracy may not be best suited to representing personal behaviour: it can be difficult for users to understand numerical data and graphs and to separate the data from its context [39]. More abstract representations of personal data in "natural" form have been explored: Roo et al. present *Inner Garden* - an ambient artefact that provides a representation of the user's mood [33]. The artefact is data-driven yet organic and speaks to some of the same values as small-scale growing: the user can invest effort in tending their garden, or leave it to evolve in response to data. Others also note that physical naturalistic embodiments of personal data may be better placed than numerical visualisations to encourage users to self-reflect [3]. Studies have also demonstrated that infrequent reflections on health data can be effective and reduce the chance of data "fatigue" associated with more detailed persistent feedback [31]. Aipperspach et al. argue for considering strategic and sparing placement of feedback technology in the home to create heterogeneous, restorative environments [1]. We believe that there is a compelling opportunity to explore plants as a particular class of abstract interface to personal data, offering naturalistic representations of complex data that are well integrated into home settings and demand occasional rather than persistent attention.

Fundamental behavioural challenges have also become salient, in particular how IoT devices can effectively help users to move from "good intentions" to actually taking positive action (the value-action gap). Research has shown that users can change their behaviour as a result of recording their behaviour [22] or by becoming more self-aware [25], but IoT devices have been criticised for building on "naïve change theory" [14 p.251]: relying on individual users making rational decisions (e.g. smart meters and in-home displays [38]) with a focus on utility [27], or assuming users as "data scientists" [34]. There is evidently value in generating and collecting personal data that can be related to wellbeing goals, but research shows that some people may struggle to positively appropriate 'rational' quantifications of their behaviour. In practice, a range of contextual and social factors, not least social pressure by our family, friends and community, influence decisions about our behaviour. Our participatory design method caters for 'rational' and social motivations, encouraging participants to generate designs that include private and social feedback loops of personal data.

Connecting plant growth and personal wellbeing

In the previous section we identify plants as a potentially valuable naturalistic representation of personal data. However, we approach plants and growing as a site for new design, not as professional growers or horticulturalists. To this end we build on existing understandings of the links between plants, growing and wellbeing drawn from health and environmental psychology.

Growing processes, e.g. gardening and farming, have been the site of previous research by the sustainable HCI movement, e.g. [26], which has sought to address environmental as well as social concerns, such as health and wellbeing [9,13]. Traditionally, small-scale growing has played an important role in food production around the world. In an organised fashion, allotments and community gardens were at one time vital in providing the poor with fresh produce in Europe and North America [16], and were re-characterised as "victory gardens" following WW2, providing food security and physical activity for returning soldiers and their communities. In the UK there are currently estimated to be over 300,000 allotments [30], with long waiting lists in many cities [7].

Our interest is in the relationship between contemporary small-scale growing and health and wellbeing, and in bringing these positive effects into the design of new products. From a physical health point of view, obesity and

---

[1] https://www.fitbit.com/

[2] https://developer.apple.com/healthkit/

[3] http://www.newyorker.com/culture/culture-desk/the-horror-of-amazons-new-dash-button

[4] https://www.smartthings.com/

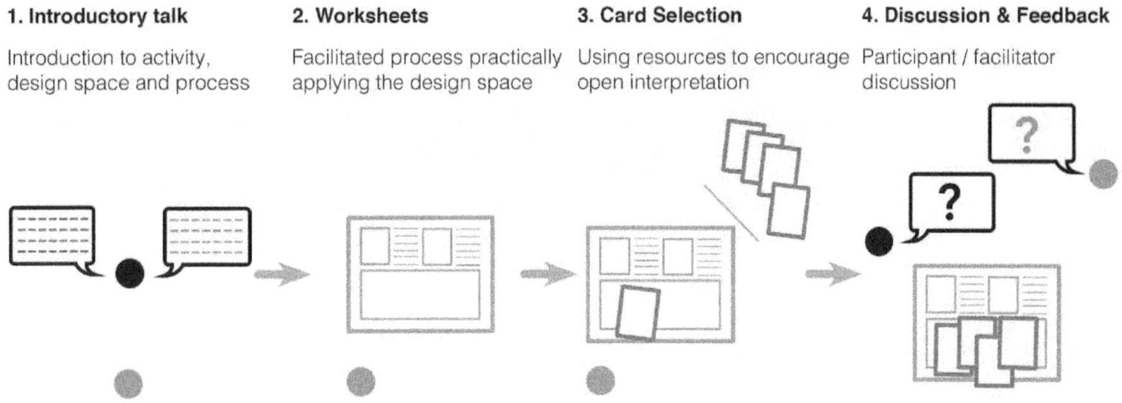

Figure 1. PD workshop process

related illnesses such as diabetes have been linked with increasing consumption of processed foods over fresh foods [36]. The physical health benefits of including "grow your own" produce in our diet, as well as the exercise involved in growing, are well established [18] yet only a small proportion of the population engage in small-scale growing. This can be partly attributed to the spread of urban space and a lack of private gardens [8], and to a fear of the risks of "non-professional" food production [18].

Beyond the physical benefits, plants and the process of growing play an important role in a holistic view of wellbeing. The particular qualities of plant-person relationships promote a closely coupled relationship with the grower's environment and their subjective wellbeing [11]. Steiner et al. have explored ways to interface with plants through natural language to allow plants and humans to have a heightened, possibly more harmonious understanding of their shared environment[5]. Studies in Europe have demonstrated the inclusionary value of community gardening for older people, as a place for growers to develop new social connections [24] as well as an opportunity for physical activity [5]. Others have shown that sessions spent caring for plants provide a positive "antidote to urban living" and to the work day [10], with growers exhibiting less depression and fatigue and more vigour [44]. Even very short amounts of "green exercise" - tending to plants or green spaces - provide significant benefits to mental health [4].

We see opportunities in design that makes key qualities of plants and growing more salient, to encourage people to reflect on and act on their wellbeing. Literature points to qualities of the plant-person relationship that we are interested in surfacing: the achievement and self-esteem associated with caring for a living plant, and the sense of connectedness with the environment and others that can emerge by growing with or for others.

[5] https://msrstudio99.wordpress.com/2015/11/05/project-florence/

IoT devices as socially embedded artefacts

In order to bridge the value-action gap and incorporate the benefits of the plant-person relationship, we believe that the design of connected plants should account for and be adaptable to users' values and circumstances. Ohlin & Olsson reflect on the tendency for QS and PI to focus on utility and call for HCI researchers to draw on their traditions of postphenomenology to design IoT that fits with and responds to the "whole life-world context" of users [27], pointing towards the community's "maturing confidence in human-centred design" [40].

Previously, design research had to make "insider tools" that enabled designers to view through the participant's eyes; whilst this is still relevant, it is easier to include users in the design process [ibid.]. Empathetic or co-design is a process of "getting people personally, emotionally engaged so they can reflect on a process they are designing for" [42]. Co-design helps designers gather "information about the contexts of people's interactions with products" to understand how these could be adapted or simplified [ibid.]. The practise of co-design is often built around "tools that create a fluency" and engagement [37]. Whilst very "few high-street designers will have the time to engage in these sorts of activities", they are important for getting wider perspectives from, or with, intended audiences [19]. Co-design is a means to understand people's "behaviours and perceptions" placing them centrally in the design process [40]. The process of co-design can "be creative for all stakeholders involved" if there is targeted involvement and a clear strategy [19]. The practice implies that users can act as idea creators but also be involved as "detectors of value-in-context" [43].

Traditionally, participatory design (PD) has involved users in "evaluative research: testing existing products or prototypes of developed concepts" [42]. PD is different to co-design as it has more "open-ended outputs to look for [design] opportunities" [6]. The often-non-linear process of PD explores users' either "existing or possible contexts of use, aiding the design team to have a more empathetic approach" [6].

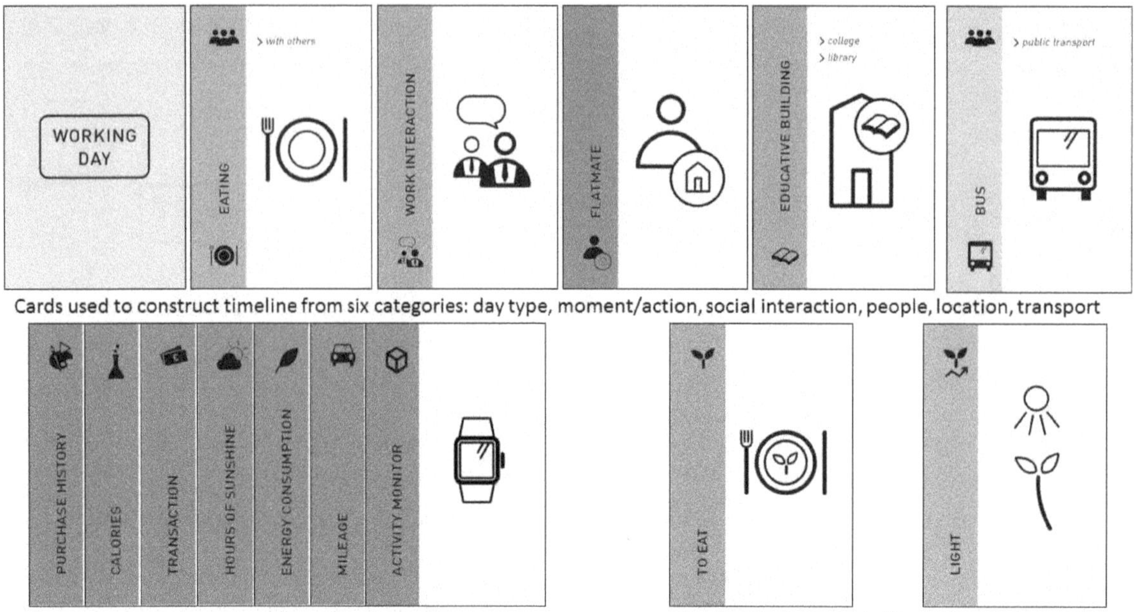

Cards used to construct timeline from six categories: day type, moment/action, social interaction, people, location, transport

Seven categories of data cards: cultural, scientific, financial, weather, environment, transport, object

Cards to indicate desirable quality of plant and output to be controlled by the data

Figure 2. A selection of the PD workshop ideation cards

This practice can often create a "rich setting" to discuss and work within [6]. The PD process should take participants through "small steps" of a process, without overwhelming them [42]. Including users in PD processes should situate audiences in a "context, actively involving [them to] try things" [40]. Our intention was to use PD to clearly create a place for people to have a conversation about how they could make interaction with plants as IoT devices engaging, rich and applicable to themselves.

METHODOLOGY

To help end-users understand the new concept of appropriating their data in the form of plant growth, a workshop was designed involving a four-stage process (Figure 1). Workshop resources comprised worksheets and a flexible ideation card system[6]. The two worksheets guided participants through a thirteen-step task. Worksheet A collected some background information (step 1) then invited participants to use ideation cards to consider their own daily routines (steps 2-5) and the data that they generate - purposefully and incidentally - associated with those patterns of behaviour (steps 6 & 7). Worksheet B provided a framework for imagining, step-by-step, how a connected growing system embedded in the user's social context could support them to achieve a goal. Participants were asked to identify: one aspect of the day they mapped that could be changed to improve their health and wellbeing (step 8); data to measure progress (step 9); a type of plant to connect (step 10); the effect of data on the plant (step 11); a person to whom the plant could be given (step 12); and the impact of giving the plant to that person (step 13). To aid completion of the worksheets participants could utilise a bespoke deck of 96 pictogram cards that represented daily interactions, types of personal data and attributes of a connected plant (Figure 2). Participants used the worksheets and cards in combination to complete the workshop process (Figures 3 & 4). This section describes firstly how the workshop method was designed and implemented on 2 occasions and secondly how PD was documented and subsequently analysed in this case.

Design Method

As highlighted in the related work, we expected our participants to have differing responses to personal data, and differing goals and motivations. The "key to running successful [workshops] is preparation" so our resources directed participants and stakeholders [21]. The inclusion of end-users within design workshops can develop either "convergent conversation[s], narrow[ing] discussion or divergent conversation[s], expand[ing] discussion by allowing for a multiplicity of perspectives" [12]. To create effective design outputs, "designers must have an understanding of the characteristics and diversity of those" they design for [23], and so while the worksheets directed the participants the cards offered flexibility. This combination encourages convergent and divergent thinking, ultimately offering new but appropriate designs.

The worksheets and cards drew inspiration from the noun project[7], a repository of pictograms. These pictograms communicate complex activities through visual representation, and are nondescript so they still encourage convergent and divergent thinking, because they are open to

[6] https://www.horizon.ac.uk/project/growing-data/

[7] https://www.thenounproject.com/

interpretation. The team built on their previous experience of design projects [28], open design principles [41] and running workshops for understanding [29]. If the team had created a prototype or physical technology response it could have steered the participants, resulting in either approval or complete lack understanding and alienation. It was also the goal of the design team to scope the area, and too early to use a Research Through Design approach.

To challenge the participants and develop their understanding of the connected plant concept they needed to be facilitated. To help make this concept understandable to a lay audience the process involved storyboarding. Storyboarding is the act of documenting scenarios "illustrating a character-rich story line describing the context of use for a product or service", as scenarios can "help to communicate and test the essence of a design idea within its probable context of use" [15]. Storyboarding helps participants to contextualise and get "a grip on context and time by forcing them to attend to diverse aspects, integrate these aspects and confront the implications that could be postponed with abstract considerations" [20]. The worksheet and cards built on Sampaio et al's scenario constructing techniques to "enhance a situation with a concrete and precise goal inside a scenario and provide a means of communicating among stakeholders" [35]. Scenario building helps users perceive situations beyond their existing knowledge or perception, highlighting "possible features, functions or design attributes" [15]. The structure of the resources (worksheets and cards) provided a framework for the participants to work within and expand from.

Workshop 1

The Victoria and Albert Museum in London annually hosts a 'digital design weekend', coinciding with a major design festival. As one of the largest museums in the capital, this is a vibrant space to attract technology minded participants that are already motivated to engage in design. The theme in 2016 was *the future of engineering and making*. Members of the public visiting the museum could interact with installations and hands-on activities delivered by invited artists, designer, engineers and technologists. A free publication about the work presented was also distributed at the event (and subsequently online[8]). In total across Saturday and Sunday 24,487 people visited the festival.

During the two days of the event 151 members of the public took part in our workshop; 26 completed the PD process using our worksheets and ideation cards. Some participants enrolled through an online platform, but were also supplemented by passers-by. Because of the open nature of the event it was necessary to offer several levels of engagement for participants. The entry-level introduction offered on arrival was a description (with supporting images to illustrate) of the basic design space being explored: the potential to actuate a controlled indoor growing system using some form of personal data. At the next level, participants (especially those with children) were invited to engage with the idea of growing plants indoors, using household materials and open source 3D printed components[9] to make a simple hydroponic system to take away. Finally, those visitors who could invest more time in exploration of the design concept could undertake our full PD process.

All those who undertook the PD task gave their informed consent to form part of our research. Working through the two worksheets was a relatively contemplative activity for individual participants, although researchers were on hand to offer explication or advice about the ideation process itself, and to probe decisions at different stages. Some participants were content to work through the sheets independently, examining and choosing cards that represented their experiences with minimal prompting and support; while others enjoyed verbalising their thought processes for the benefit of researchers. In either case, a facilitator would re-join a participant at the end of the process and ask to be guided through the completed worksheets (e.g. Figures 3 & 4). As the activity was largely self-directed, the amount of time participants devoted to it was variable; although all devoted their sustained attention for a period of between 15 and 30 minutes.

Workshop 2

Shortly after the London workshop, members of the research team ran another workshop elsewhere in the UK to gather additional responses from an alternative audience. For the second workshop, we deliberately set out to recruit participants with an established interest in growing plants, but not necessarily in design and technology innovation. To do this we worked with an existing research partner – a large allotment association in the UK Midlands - utilising their visitor centre and connections with communities of local growers. The much smaller sample size (5) from workshop 2 is unsurprising given the relatively small pool of potential participants available from the locality at a given time on a weekday. Like workshop 1 at the museum, participants were self-selecting volunteers and the process of the sessions was identical.

Because all participants at workshop 2 undertook the PD activity simultaneously, there was opportunity for group discussion and feedback; unlike at the museum workshop, where participation took place on an ad hoc basis over the course of two days. Nevertheless the common aim in both workshops was to enable participants to step through the worksheets based on their individual circumstances, considering the value of data about their everyday lives and

[8] https://lguariento.github.io/Engineering-the-Future/

[9] https://www.3dponics.com/wiki/download-parts-3dponics-mini/

how that could be harnessed for their own benefit through the design of a data-driven plant.

Analysis

In London 26 people completed the PD process using our worksheets and ideation cards. We asked all participants to provide some basic demographic information, from which we learned that most of the museum sample were female (16/22), living in an urban environment (21/25) and in the age range 25-35 (13/25). Workshop 2 involved 5 participants. Like those in London, most of the participants were female (4/5) and city-dwelling (4/5), but they were distributed across a wider age range, with 2/5 participants in the over 55 year-old category. In the following section, results from both workshops are presented together. The results do not compare groups of participants but consider the variety among responses to the ideation activity.

All participants' contributions were carefully documented in situ at the workshops through overhead photographs of completed worksheets, because these were transient artefacts, which had to be disassembled so that participants could return the cards to the decks for use by others. Photographs from both workshops were subsequently collated, transcribed and analysed as a data set. This analysis attended to the particularities of each individual response and also sought to identify emergent themes that applied across the data set. The first stage of analysis involved quantifying information about the participants and their use of the workshop resources. Next all the qualitative data participants provided about their goals, connected plants and plant recipients were coded. Once coding of the entire data set was complete, data were grouped into emergent themes. Codes and thematic groupings were checked for interrater reliability by members of the research team. A characterisation of each theme was then produced based on the underlying data. Finally the team selected two exemplars to illustrate the themes expressed in participants' conceptual designs for connected plants.

RESULTS

In this section, we report the results of this PD study, describing how the resources were utilised in the workshops. Firstly, we present an overview of participant responses to the ideation process and observable patterns within those responses. Secondly we draw out emergent themes from the workshop materials, in terms of the participants' design goals and the values embodied in the products they envisaged. Finally, we look in detail at some exemplars to illustrate how the PD process worked as a scaffolded, sequential task producing conceptual designs.

Worksheet A

In step 1 of the PD process we asked participants for a couple of free text responses to the general subject of growing and wellbeing, in addition to demographic information. In general, participants expressed an abstract concept of growth as development and change, rather than a literal association with plants and the natural world. However, perhaps unsurprisingly, 3/5 participants at workshop 2 specifically associated the concept of growth with the cultivation of edible plants. Taken as a whole, participants' statements about wellbeing acknowledge both physical and psychological aspects.

Prior to any product design, worksheet A foregrounded individual contexts of use: the initial choice for participants was whether to focus on a working day or a day off. Overwhelmingly, our participants focused upon their activities during a working day: only 5/31 participants concentrated on leisure time. Participants also made quite extensive use of the ideation cards in constructing their timelines, on average selecting 13/48 activity cards available for this purpose. In terms of the types of features detailed in the timelines, cards relating to people and actions were more prominent than those relating to space and movement. When asked to indicate personal data associated with the activities depicted in their timeline, participants on average identified 12/39 different types of data depicted on cards. The data cards were split into 7 categories: financial, cultural, scientific, weather, transport, object and environment data. Participants selected data types from across these groupings, on average utilising data cards from more than 4 of the categories.

Worksheet B

The design of worksheet B allowed for cards used previously to be transferred into this second stage of the process. However, 90% of participants described the underpinning objective in their own words. Participants were more likely to make use of the cards to specify the data input used to calculate their achievement, but two thirds of those who completed the task still jotted down ideas without reference to the cards, tailoring the parameters of their system per the circumstances they had in mind. Some indicators unanticipated by the ideation deck included a sewing machine being switched on, silence and free (i.e. unscheduled) time. 4 ideation cards were provided to highlight qualities of plants that users might appreciate: fragrance, visual appeal, tactility and edibility. These seem to have encompassed the opinions participants wanted to express, as they were utilised by all bar one. Where a few participants added to the resources it was to specify a plant, thus providing additional insight into the characteristics of value to them, e.g. the aroma when lemon verbena is rubbed. Many of the participants appreciated multiple qualities of plants: averaging across the sample, participants wanted their plant to exhibit more than 1 desirable feature.

Emergent themes

Bringing together data of participants from the two workshops revealed four high level themes. Imagined affordances of a connected plant as a living product are intrinsic to all four of the themes. Quotes are taken directly from notes and sketches on the worksheets.

Caring for yourself

Understandably, many of the changes that participants wanted to make in their lives related to taking better care of themselves. What was interesting was the variety of ways in which participants wanted to go about achieving an improvement in their wellbeing. In some cases, the focus was on physical changes: taking exercise (p10, p14, p16, p24, p26, p29), playing sport (p12, p13, p15) and/or eating a healthier diet (p5, p6, p8, p10, p25, p29). Others focused instead on steps to support their mental wellbeing by: being more organised about work commitments ("do less things but better" p30); pursuing hobbies ("more personal creative time" p22); relaxing ("more me-time" p11) and resting ("get more sleep" p31). One participant (p6) pointed out that "fun" might be another reason to interact with the growing system. Despite the introspective starting point, almost all participants situated the goal embodied by their plant in wider social contexts; only one person couldn't see the value in giving the plant to someone else ("because I'm the only one that matters, right?" p25). In direct contrast, another participant (p10) identified that concern for the plant's health might be more motivating than personal wellbeing: "maybe I'll be responsible to take care of the plant, and indirectly care for my health". Here the incorporation of effect on another organism into an IoT system explicitly influences interaction. Coding participants' responses revealed that self-care was often discussed in conjunction with tangibility, connection and discovery. Most obviously, participants identified how a virtuous development cycle would be established between their behaviour, the plant's health and the experience of the plant by others: "It will make our space prettier. A happy home is going to improve my wellbeing" (p26).

Tangible feedback

The physical presence of the plant within a space as a tangible reflection of their behaviour was something that participants considered from several perspectives. As an organic object the plant provides a visual status update and its existence within an environment provides constant feedback about progress ("it is a tangible indication of my goal each day" p14). Good progress can be translated into a uniquely botanical outcome that serves as a reward for good behaviour: "every time I engage with people [by messaging old friends], the plant will shake to liberate the smell" (p9). For two of the growers who participated in workshop 2, the intrinsic value of plants as plants took precedence over any symbolic or embodied connection to a user. One of these participants focused on plants within a natural ecosystem in terms of the benefits "to help bees and pollinators to survive and continue" (p27). The other participant saw the system as an opportunity to "assist" and "benefit" someone else, who would otherwise be unable to grow plants, "a stranger who lives in a flat with no outside space" (p30). This brings us back to the idea of a virtuous cycle from behaviour, to growth, to shared experience. For several participants, the ultimate outcome of the cycle was tied to the possibility of coming together for a meal of healthy, home-grown produce. For example, p7 imagined giving her plant to a friend who then "has some vegetables" which taste "more delicious" and "we can eat together".

(Re)connecting people

The idea that connected plants would draw on and/or reinforce a significant bond between people was common among participants, for several reasons, many of which revolve around additional levels of meaning. This might be creating a sense of proximity to "a foreign friend" through the plant, which "will keep communication alive - even if we don't have time to catch up each day, progress is visible" (p28). In this example the two friends are working in tandem towards "similar goals" and monitoring/ supporting each other's efforts, and other participants likewise expressed the value of being made "more

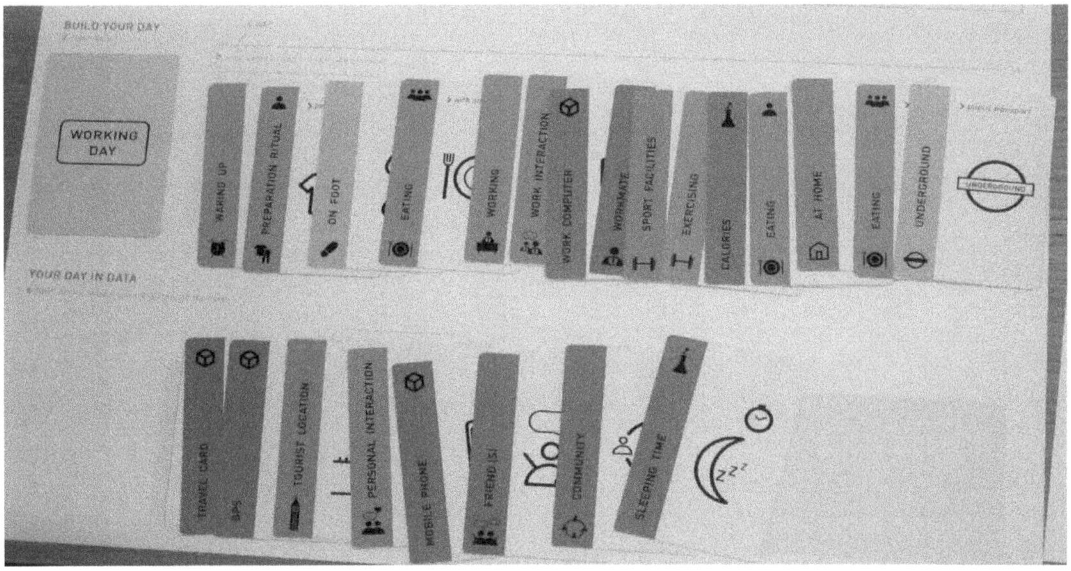

Figure 3. P20's worksheet A showing interspersed activity and data cards

accountable with each other's activities" (p19). One participant felt the plant could serve to reaffirm the love between partners - "I love her and she loves plants" (p23) - meaning that the goal is pursued as a gesture of care for both something and someone else. Similarly, the goal could be used to demonstrate that another person's views are being taken seriously, e.g. p29, who would give the plant to a brother who "lives far away and is passionate about healthy living". Some participants also emphasised the trust placed in the custodian of the plant, who is in a powerful position of supervision: "we will hate/love him" but ultimately want "to please, and get him a good taste with the plant" (p4). In some cases, when participants would give the plant to family the choice was apparently motivated by convenience, rather than deeper meaning, because they live together (p13, p15). However, in other cases, the plant was identified as a simple mechanism for assuaging worry among family: "My sister always worries about me! If she had the plant, she might not check in with me so much! Perhaps our contact with each other would evolve beyond a checklist of 'how are you?'!" (p16).

Discovery

All of which indicates that participants' decision to share their plant and its significance with someone else is bound up in considerable socio-cultural complexity. In the process of thinking through this complexity a couple of participants envisioned negative consequences. One mother who would entrust the plant to her kids, could foresee that they might nag her to achieve a better growth rate for the cabbage, which "could be annoying" (p12). Under these circumstances, the participant felt that her motivation "may not last"; with the conceivable consequence that the cabbage would wither like any other neglected houseplant, giving the children even greater ammunition against her.

A different participant, who chose a flatmate as "convenient" recipient of the connected plant, acknowledged that this might in fact be an unwanted gift: "he's gonna complain because the plant will be in his room" (p11). For some other participants, however, the novel interpersonal challenges posed by giving a data-driven plant to someone else were opportunities, which could serve a valuable forcing function to stimulate and maintain behaviour change. Some goals listed were exploratory, such as "seeing new places and meeting people" (p2). This participant described the plant as a potential conversation starter because its fruit could be given to or shared with others. P21 had a similar idea that the act of gifting the plant could instigate a new relationship with an "unknown person". One participant saw the plant as a more roundabout route to new social interactions because it would improve her relationship with her best friend and consequently build her self-confidence to make new friends too: "feeling secured with good friends helps me to go for more interaction with different people" (p18).

Exemplars

To demonstrate how the themes overlapped and interconnected for individual participants, we briefly work through two exemplars of designs produced by p20 & p24.

"Reclaiming home" plant

P20 - a marketing assistant - mapped out her working day using worksheet A resulting in a routine that contained only 6 data cards, but - unlike all other participants - interspersed these into her timeline (see Figure 3). The emphasis in her map is on actions and places, and the map demonstrates that she spends only the briefest moment at home in between work, fitness and social activities.

Reflecting on this routine, her health and wellbeing goal stated on worksheet B focused on carving out more time from this packed schedule for "personal projects", e.g. "artwork; reading; meditating", and conceived a plant that

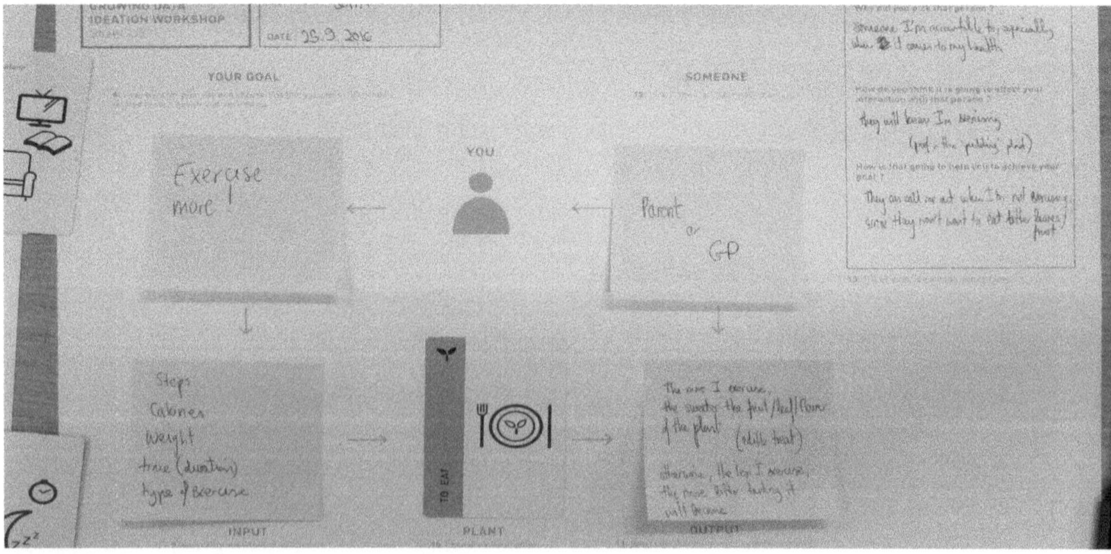

Figure 4. P24's worksheet B, showing connections between goal, data, output and relationships in conceptual design

will receive light whenever she spends time at home, becoming more attractive as home time increases (*tangible feedback*). This inwards-facing goal is typical of the *caring for yourself* theme, but developed as the participant translated it to her plant: in notes on the worksheet, the participant suggests that she would gift her plant to her mother. In doing so, the plant provides social value: on one hand knowing that her child is spending more personal time at home would "be good for her [the mother's] peace of mind" (*connecting people*), and on the other it would encourage the participant to visit her mother more often to see the plant ((re)*connecting people*). In this way, "my mum and I could help each other to achieve my goal".

"Proof in the pudding" plant

P24 - a customer experience consultant - used many data cards when mapping her working day, and split these into two rows on the worksheet to express both the data she is "using now" and data she would "like to have".

Having reflected on her day, the participant focused on the physical goal to "exercise more" (*caring for yourself*). From her existing and desired pool of generated data the participant specified 5 data types, from number of steps to her weight, which would be fed to her plant. Her connected "proof in the 'pudding' plant" would then produce *tangible feedback* in the form of sweeter fruit in response to her physical activity or bitter fruit from lack of activity (see Figure 4). To increase the chance of this motivating her, she suggested that the plant could be given to her parent or doctor ("someone I'm accountable to"; *connecting people*).

These exemplars are not outliers compared to other concepts from the workshops, but demonstrate how the worksheets and cards allowed participants to produce rich, contrasting designs. While participants' designs shared common features - motivating healthy behaviour, nourishing people and enhancing the living environment - the mechanisms selected were idiosyncratic. Both exemplars align with *caring for yourself*, however p20's design promotes wellbeing in terms of relaxation and peace of mind - physical activity is already part of her mapped daily routine - while p24's design focuses on bringing more physical activity into her day. Although both exemplars are designed to foster *connectedness*, p24 conceptualises the possible benefits of "accountability" to an external authority figure (her doctor), as well as (like p20) to a parent.

DISCUSSION

Reflecting on the results presented above, there appear to be three broad positive conclusions that we can make about personal data embodied in plants as a new design space. These points relate to our original research questions: 1) what data would users appropriate to quantify their wellbeing goals; 2) would they see value in connecting those goals to the growth of plants; and 3) how could that new interaction be meaningful in their social contexts? Although our reflections relate to connected plants as a particular novel case of IoT, our results also sign-post wider issues of interest to the DIS community.

Appropriating personal data

Firstly, participants were able to envisage ways in which data derived from their everyday routines could be repurposed in order to measure progress towards a desired life change. These data might come from diverse sources and might not, taken in isolation, have any obvious connection with the goal being pursued. Secondly, participants could conceptualize a connected indoor actuated environmental system that used the data they specified to control the growing conditions of a plant. They liked the idea that this plant would provide tangible feedback about their behavior through its physical presence, and its natural development and vigor, which would result in sensory reward (flower, scent, fruit). In summary, our results suggest that participants without technical or plant growing experience can appropriate personal data as a component of a value-driven design process.

When IoT is sold as a concept to a public still unsure what the term means and what the technology has to offer, the examples of products often illustrate an instrumental connection between sensing capability, data collected by those sensors, and automated processes triggered by those data. In terms of IoT products to promote health and wellbeing the underpinning paradigm is quantified self, the longitudinal collection of physiological information in order to identify patterns and changes, with the potential to introduce an element of comparison between users. Our PD approach, however, started with a human goal and encouraged participants to leverage the value inherent in that goal to determine what data would be collected and how it would be utilized. The data that participants chose do not necessarily have an obvious causal relationship with their goal. For example, in our study p11 would use silence as an indicator of caring for yourself. Establishing a link between an individual and another living organism complements both the personal character of the data and the underlying health and wellbeing goal. This promotes meaningful interaction that fits naturally with the user's established daily routines.

Designing embodied remote presence/healthcare

The value in the connected plants concept is revealed in our participants' designs, which often overlapped with a concept familiar to the interaction community: remote presence. In this case, the medium – growing plants – is novel. Additionally, the designs point to an interesting variety of external situations in which the plant might use personal data to create presence, including some that are particularly sensitive such as medical or insurance providers. We believe that the connected plants concept has particular value when considering opportunities for new products in remote wellbeing and healthcare. From a design perspective this application area presents product, service and system opportunities and challenges, not least how personal data can be revealed to a third party in a way that is informative, but privacy-preserving. Ode[10] is a dementia product designed for sensitive communal environments – care homes – that releases food aromas to coincide with the ideal mealtime schedule of a resident to help stimulate appetite. Like our connected plants, Ode is designed to fade into the environment such that it draws attention only from those intended to be influenced, and is an abstract representation of personal data, in this case hiding the precise details of the resident's meal plan. Remote wellbeing and healthcare design applications demand sensitivity around personal data: secure and abstract representations of data in the form of naturalistic interfaces – such as connected plants – are ideally suited to underpin such opportunities.

Making personal data public

Participants negotiated the final imaginative leap in the process, which we had anticipated might present a challenge, identifying circumstances in which it might be valuable to entrust the plant (and its personal significance) to someone else. In making their choices of recipient, participants considered how interactions with the plant would intertwine with interpersonal interactions, in ways that might allow them to reinforce existing close relationships or form meaningful new bonds.

Although our worksheets encouraged participants to consider whether they would benefit by sharing their connected plant, the resources did not suggest whom they might share it with. In practice - except p25, who did not want to share their plant - participants decided on a broad range of recipients, including close social connections (e.g. family and friends) and acquaintances (e.g. doctors), as well as unknown recipients. The participants easily created gifts for these recipients from the combination of personal data and plants. In some cases the personal data *enhanced the plant*, making it a more interesting, surprising or emotive artefact; in other cases, the plant *enhanced the personal data*, putting it in a form that would be attended to (not ignored) or be more meaningful.

In most cases, the data chosen by the participants was sensitive, including a variety of health indicators and home presence. Given the focus of our workshops on creativity rather than critique, it is unsurprising that issues of trust, privacy and security were rarely raised. Instead, some participants did focus on accountability, i.e. the ability of their plant to reveal just enough of their data to the recipient to embarrass or encourage them to work towards their goals. Worksheet B enabled participants to pick and choose how explicitly and precisely their plant responded to data, and participants designed biofeedback that ranged from the abstract and continuous (fruit flavor changes as behavior indicators) to discrete (plants that move when behavior occurs). We believe that our results implicitly highlight valuable qualities of plants as privacy-preserving data interfaces: in comparison with digital devices plants respond more slowly to stimuli (at least at the level where the results are perceivable by the human owner), hence plant feedback is a cumulative, delayed representation of the underlying data in which individual data points are lost. Unless grown in a tightly controlled environment, plants are also susceptible to a range of other environmental stimuli – sometimes serendipitous (e.g. draughts or shade), sometimes deliberate (e.g. intervention by the owner and other passers-by). Generally speaking, plants offer potential for a representative, yet imprecise and organic view of personal data that might be gifted to others to reveal a representation of self that does not compromise personal privacy and security.

[10] http://www.myode.org/

Reflection on method

This study was conducted at a small scale in two different places with self-selecting participants available at the workshop time. The participants' responses were guided by the ideation tools provided, although they always had the opportunity to substitute cards with notes of their own devising. In the main, participants used the cards for Worksheet A, but expressed more of their own ideas when completing Worksheet B. The authors would repeat the activity with an actual artefact/prototype to see impact and insights over time. The work did yield the validation of its users through the process and therefore, we believe, warrants this design space as something of value.

CONCLUSION

In this paper we presented a participatory design process in which 31 participants without technical backgrounds designed new forms of biofeedback - plants driven by personal data - with the aim of motivating themselves to achieve a health and wellbeing goal. We demonstrated how our worksheets, ideation cards and step-by-step method allowed the participants to creatively tackle a challenging design task, appropriating personal data and producing a range of "connected plant" concepts. This process demonstrated that incorporating living products into IoT systems could create affordances for self-care, tangible feedback, social connection and discovery. Our findings suggest that biohacking to connect IoT sensors with digital hydroponics would produce new opportunities for meaningful forms of tangible and embedded interaction.

We believe that this is a fruitful design space, and sign-post ways that the DIS community can take this exploration forward. Our participants' designs show how value-driven IoT can allow designers to break out of the "rational" constraints of quantified self and utilitarian actuation applications; they also demonstrate that plants can be a useful form of privacy-preserving, socially embedded feedback for sharing and representing personal data. With this in mind, we suggest "connected plants" may have a valuable role in embodied remote presence and healthcare.

ACKNOWLEDGMENTS

The research was supported by "From Human Data to Personal Experience" (Research Councils UK grant EP/M02315X/1). The team wishes to thank Dr Michael Brown, Irini Papadimitriou, Kate Green and Qing Li for their input.

REFERENCES

1. Ryan Aipperspach, Ben Hooker, and Allison Woodruff. 2008. The heterogeneous home. In *Proceedings of the International conference on Ubiquitous computing (UbiComp '08)*. ACM, New York, NY, USA, 222-231.
2. Manal Almalki, Kathleen Gray, and Fernando Martin Sanchez. 2015. The use of self-quantification systems for personal health information: big data management activities and prospects. *Health Information Science and Systems* 3, 1: 1–11.
3. Ilhan Aslan, Hadrian Burkhardt, Julian Kraus, and Elisabeth André. 2016. Hold my Heart and Breathe with Me: Tangible Somaesthetic Designs. In *Proceedings of the Nordic Conference on Human-Computer Interaction (NordiCHI '16)*. ACM, New York, NY, USA.
4. Jo Barton and Jules Pretty. What is the best dose of nature and green exercise for improving mental health? A multi-study analysis. *Journal of Environmental Science Technology* 10, 3947: 55.
5. Agnes E van den Berg, Marijke van Winsum-Westra, Sjerp de Vries and Sonja ME van Dillen. 2010. Allotment gardening and health: a comparative survey among allotment gardeners and their neighbors without an allotment. *Environmental Health* 9, 74.
6. Erling Björgvinsson, Pelle Ehn, and Per-Anders Hillgren. 2010. Participatory design and "democratizing innovation". In *Proceedings of the Biennial Participatory Design Conference (PDC '10)*. ACM, New York, NY, USA, 41-50.
7. Campbell M, and Campbell I. 2013. *Allotment Waiting Lists in England 2013.* Transition Town West Kirby and The National Allotment Society.
8. Department for Communities and Local Government (DCLG). 2010. *English Housing Survey*. London: Crown, 1999.
9. Carl DiSalvo, Phoebe Sengers, and Hrönn Brynjarsdóttir. 2010. Mapping the landscape of sustainable HCI. In *Proceedings of the ACM Conference on Human Factors in Computing Systems (CHI '10)*. ACM, New York, NY, USA, 1975-1984.
10. Marion Ericsson Nolan. 2012. *Allotments, health and well-being.* Doctoral dissertation, University of Essex.
11. Jon Fieldhouse. 2016. The Impact of an Allotment Group on Mental Health Clients' Health, Wellbeing and Social Networking. *British Journal of Occupational Therapy* 66, 7: 286-296.
12. Derek Greenly and Colin Carnall. 2010. Workshops as a technique for strategic change. *Journal of Change Management* 2, 1: 33-46.
13. Tad Hirsch, Phoebe Sengers, Eli Blevis, Richard Beckwith, and Tapan Parikh. 2010. Making food, producing sustainability. In *CHI '10 Extended Abstracts on Human Factors in Computing Systems (CHI EA '10)*. ACM, New York, NY, USA, 3147-3150.
14. Huang, M.L. and Huang, W. 2013. Innovative Approaches of Data Visualization and Visual Analytics. IGI Global.
15. IDEO. 2013. Design Thinking for Educators. Available via http://www.designthinkingforeducators.com/toolkit [accessed 1/15/17].
16. Seana Irvine, Lorraine Johnson, and Kim Peters. 1999. Community gardens and sustainable land use planning: A case study of the Alex Wilson community garden. *Local Environment* 4, 1.
17. Michael O. Jewell, Enrico Costanza, and Jacob Kittley-Davies. 2015. Connecting the things to the internet: an evaluation of four configuration strategies for wi-fi devices with minimal user interfaces. In *Proceedings of the International Joint Conference on Pervasive and Ubiquitous Computing (UbiComp '15)*. ACM, New York, NY, USA, 767-778.
18. Jonathan R Leake, Andrew Adam-Bradford, and Janette E Rigby. 2009. Health benefits of 'grow your own' food in urban areas: implications for contaminated land risk assessment and risk management? *Environmental Health* 8(1), 6.
19. Yanki Lee. 2008. Design participation tactics: the challenges and new roles for designers in the co-design process. *International Journal of CoCreation in Design and the Arts* 4, 1: 31-50.
20. Corrie van der Lelie. 2006. The value of storyboards in the product design process. *Personal and Ubiquitous Computing* 10, 2: 159-162.
21. Vicky A Lofthouse and D. Lilley. 2006. What they really, really want: user centred research methods for design. In *Proceedings of International Design Conference*. Dubrovnik.
22. Alessandro Marcengo and Amon Rapp. 2014. Visualization of Human Behavior Data: The Quantified Self. In *Innovative Approaches of Data Visualization and Visual Analytics*, Mao Li Huang. and Weidong Huang (Eds.). IGI Global, Hershey, PA, 236-265.
23. Chris McGinley and Hua Dong. 2011. Designing with Information and Empathy: Delivering Human Information to Designers. *The Design Journal* 14, 2: 187-206.

24. Christine Milligan, Anthony Gatrell, Amanda Bingley. 2004. 'Cultivating health': therapeutic landscapes and older people in northern England. *Social Science & Medicine* 58, 9: 1781-1793.

25. Raymond G. Miltenberger. 2008. *Behavior modification: Principles and procedures* (4th ed.) Wadsworth, Belmont, MA.

26. William Odom. 2010. "Mate, we don't need a chip to tell us the soil's dry": opportunities for designing interactive systems to support urban food production. In *Proceedings of the ACM Conference on Designing Interactive Systems (DIS '10)*. ACM, New York, NY, USA, 232-235.

27. Fredrik Ohlin and Carl Magnus Olsson. 2015. Beyond a utility view of personal informatics: a postphenomenological framework. In *Adjunct Proceedings of the ACM International Joint Conference on Pervasive and Ubiquitous Computing and ACM International Symposium on Wearable Computers (UbiComp/ISWC'15 Adjunct)*. ACM, New York, NY, USA, 1087-1092.

28. Robert Daniel Phillips, Jesse Michael Blum, Michael A. Brown, and Sharon L. Baurley. 2014. Testing a grassroots citizen science venture using open design, "the bee lab project". In *CHI '14 Extended Abstracts on Human Factors in Computing Systems (CHI EA '14)*. ACM, New York, NY, USA, 1951-1956.

29. Robert Phillips, Dan Lockton, Sharon Baurley, and Sarah Silve. 2013. Making instructions for others: exploring mental models through a simple exercise. *Interactions* 20, 5: 74-79.

30. Tanja Pless-Mulloli, Vivienne Air, Catherine Vizard, and Phillip Hartley. 2004. The legacy of historic land-use in allotment gardens in industrial urban settings: Walker Road allotment in Newcastle upon Tyne, UK. *Land Contamination and Reclamation* 12: 239-251.

31. Nithya Ramanathan, Dallas Swendeman, W. Scott Comulada, Deborah Estrin, Mary Jane Rotheram-Borus. 2013. Identifying preferences for mobile health applications for self-monitoring and self-management: Focus group findings from HIV-positive persons and young mothers. *International Journal of Medical Informatics* 82, 4: 38–46.

32. Amon Rapp, Federica Cena, Judy Kay, Bob Kummerfeld, Frank Hopfgartner, Till Plumbaum, and Jakob Eg Larsen. 2015. New frontiers of quantified self: finding new ways for engaging users in collecting and using personal data. In *Adjunct Proceedings of the ACM International Joint Conference on Pervasive and Ubiquitous Computing and International Symposium on Wearable Computers (UbiComp/ISWC'15 Adjunct)*. ACM, New York, NY, USA, 969-972.

33. Joan Sol Roo, Renaud Gervais, and Martin Hachet. 2016. Inner Garden: an Augmented Sandbox Designed for Self-Reflection. In *Proceedings of the International Conference on Tangible, Embedded, and Embodied Interaction (TEI '16)*. ACM, New York, NY, USA, 570-576.

34. John Rooksby, Mattias Rost, Alistair Morrison, and Matthew Chalmers. 2014. Personal tracking as lived informatics. In *Proceedings of the ACM Conference on Human Factors in Computing Systems (CHI '14)*. ACM, New York, NY, USA, 1163-1172.

35. Julio Cesar Sampaio do Prado Leite, Graciela D. S. Hadad, Jorge Horacio Doorn, and Gladys N. Kaplan. 2000. A Scenario Construction Process. *Requirements Engineering* 5, 1: 38-61.

36. Jac Smit, Annu Ratta, Joe Nasr, G. Shabbir Cheema. 1996. *Urban Agriculture: Food, Jobs, and Sustainable Cities*. United Nations Development Programme (UNDP), New York, NY.

37. Pieter Jan Stappers. 2006. Creative connections: user, designer, context, and tools. *Personal and Ubiquitous Computing* 10, 2: 95-100.

38. Yolande Strengers. 2011. Negotiating everyday life: The role of energy and water consumption feedback. *Journal of Consumer Culture* 11, 3: 319-338.

39. Hariharan Subramonyam. 2015. SIGCHI: Magic Mirror - Embodied Interactions for the Quantified Self. In *CHI'15 Extended Abstracts on Human Factors in Computing Systems (CHI EA '15)*. ACM, New York, NY, USA, 1699-1704.

40. Jane Fulton Suri. 2003. The Experience of Evolution: Developments in Design Practice. *The Design Journal* 6, 2: 39-48.

41. James Tooze, Sharon Baurley, Robert Phillips, Paul Smith, Edwin Foote, and Sarah Silve. 2014. Open Design: Contributions, Solutions, Processes and Projects. *The Design Journal* 17, 4: 538-559.

42. Kirsikka Vaajakallio and Tuuli Mattelmäki. 2007. Collaborative design exploration: envisioning future practices with make tools. In *Proceedings of the ACM Conference on Designing Pleasurable Products and Interfaces (DPPI '07)*. ACM, New York, NY, USA, 223-238.

43. Lars Witell, Per Kristensson, Anders Gustafsson, and Martin Löfgren. 2011. Idea generation: customer co-creation versus traditional market research techniques. *Journal of Service Management* 22, 2: 140-159.

44. Carly J. Wood, Jules Pretty, and Murray Griffin. 2016. A case–control study of the health and well-being benefits of allotment gardening. *Journal of Public Health* 38, 3: 336-344.

Fruit Are Heavy: A Prototype Public IoT System to Support Urban Foraging

Carl DiSalvo
Georgia Institute of Technology
Atlanta, GA, USA
cdisalvo@gatech.edu

Tom Jenkins
Georgia Institute of Technology
Atlanta, GA, USA
tom.jenkins@gatech.edu

ABSTRACT
Smart cities are one area of interactive systems design where the technologies and services of the Internet of Things (IoT) have the potential to serve public interest. In this paper we present a design research project that explores the use of IoT technologies—specifically environmental sensing—to support urban foraging. We describe the design of a simple proof-of-concept sensing platform to monitor the relative ripeness of fruit in trees, and reflect upon its potential effectiveness for urban foraging. From the project, we draw out themes for designing in the context of smart cities, including questioning the presumed "smartness" of IoT systems, and highlight issues in designing to support diverse community economies.

Author Keywords
Foraging, Public IoT, Public Design, Participatory Design, Diverse Economies, Community Economies, Smart Cities, Digital Civics

ACM Classification Keywords
H.5.m. Information interfaces and presentation (e.g., HCI): Miscellaneous.

INTRODUCTION
Sensors, data, and networks are components of the so-called Internet of Things (IoT) that—when coupled with machine learning and analytics—are offered as promising opportunities for shaping our lives in the early 21st century. Our research is concerned with understanding how these technologies might comprise a kind of civic media [30] and support the multiple and varied ways we live together. We use the term "Public IoT" to describe this broad domain of inquiry. By Public IoT we refer to the technologies of sensing that are common to the Internet of Things. In this case, though, rather than being oriented towards supply chain management or other industrial concerns, it is instead oriented towards facilitating social relations: aiding the formation and sustaining of communal and shared attachments and commitments. One common example of this in both popular culture and academic research is the trope of the smart city, which proffers the integration of an array of technologies, ostensibly to improve cities along multiple registers, including sustainability, efficiency, and in some cases equity [35, 35, 65].

DIS 2017, June 10-14, 2017, Edinburgh, United Kingdom

ACM 978-1-4503-4922-2/17/06…$15.00
DOI: http://dx.doi.org/10.1145/3064663.3064748

Much of the promise of the smart city remains mere rhetoric—arguments for the development and deployment of systems, platforms, and infrastructure. Much of this rhetoric is oriented towards the makers of these components and services and to municipal governments. In order to explore the potentials and issues of Public IoT—to investigate the capabilities these technologies might offer for communities to address their matters of concern and care [10, 11, 36, 42]—we have chosen to collaborate with communities that are engaged in collectivism and cooperation. In this paper we present a design research project with one such community, an urban foraging group, and our effort to prototype a proof-of-concept sensing system to aid their work. In what follows we first provide a general background to this project and set the context in urban foraging. We then describe the design and deployment of a proof-of-concept system to sense the relative ripeness of fruit as a way to mitigate one of the more onerous aspects of foraging: fruit monitoring. From this we draw out insights specific to both designing interactive systems for smart cities, and designing to support diverse community economies.

BACKGROUND
This research is situated at the intersection of three domains: smart cities, diverse community economies, and participatory design. Initially, we did not describe our work in the context of smart cities. In its place, we used the term "Public IoT." The term Public IoT serves as shorthand for an assemblage of technologies and services that comprise the Internet of Things, and as a description of the context and purpose of that assemblage. More specifically, what is of interest to us is how IoT technologies and services work to both serve public interest and contribute to the formation

of publics [2, 4, 11, 14, 44]. While there is no shortage of design research into IoT, little of that research is concerned with the public-ness of the technology and services. Instead it is more often focused on either industrial or domestic environments [8, 13, 63].

Outside of design research but within smart cities discourses and projects, we find many visions, explorations, and critiques of how IoT technologies and services might be integrated into the context of urban life. This includes research on governance and civics [6], devices, systems, and infrastructure [7, 56], work [4, 54], civil society [42, 44, 45, 47] and recreation [16]. Alongside the research advancing smart cities, there is also a significant amount of scholarship questioning smart cities [34, 35, 39, 40] and in particular the implications of smart cities for equity and privacy [1, 23, 28, 53, 64, 66], including concerns about the increasing encroachment of an algorithmic culture into government, civics, and our public lives [9, 28, 31, 39, 40].

Our exploration of IoT technologies and services in smart cities is grounded in the context of diverse economies. The term diverse economies is drawn from a body of research in economic geography, specifically from the work of J.K Gibson-Graham [24-27] and researchers who have extended and built upon the theories of Gibson-Graham [55]. A fundamental aspect of the work on diverse economies is the idea that "the market" is more varied than is often recognized. So, while discussions of the market tend to assume free-market competitive capitalism, the market economy also includes many other forms of labor and exchange, such as bartering, informal lending, and self-provisioning. This occurs not just among the gainfully employed but also children, the unemployed, those employed illegally, and in a range of contexts that also include the street, within families, and in schools. These community economies provide sites for researching everyday practices in contemporary society that are often overlooked, particularly in design. There *is* some work in design that is specifically oriented towards diverse economies [17]. But more generally, diverse economies connect to work in design research that explores practices such as simple living [32, 33], cohousing and other forms of intentional communities [38, 48], community organizing [2], and other 'alternative lifestyle practices' [36]. What the diverse economies literature provides is a theoretical frame drawn from empirical research, which in turn can be generative for design.

Finally, our work is situated within the theories and methods of participatory design. Although we do not reflect upon the implications of this project for advancing participatory design research in this paper, we believe it is important to acknowledge that our approach is grounded in participatory design. Using a participatory design approach to research and engage in issues of smart cities and diverse economies aligns with both the history of participatory design, and its current practice. Diverse economies are a kind of work, a mode of labor. From its origins, participatory design has been explicitly concerned with work and with supporting skilled labor. The activities of diverse economies are most certainly skilled and, from the perspective of participatory design, warrant attention, respect, and the involvement of those who do that labor in the design of tools and systems that they might use. Diverse economies are also an example of the expanding notion of work that concerns participatory design, which increasingly involves various forms of informal work such as making in community contexts [4, 14, 15 58, 59]. Our research employs participatory design methods that strive to simultaneously contribute to invention and to produce opportunities for exploring new modes of togetherness enabled through making [58, 59]. Thus, the goal is not just to collaboratively produce proof-of-concept systems but also to collaboratively explore the feasibility and desirability of different configurations of social forces and conditions [5, 11, 22].

SETTING THE CONTEXT: URBAN FORAGING

Foraging is a canonical example of a diverse community economy, often characterized as a form of self-provisioning [55]. Foraging is the collection of naturally growing food in the wild [21, 41, 46, 50, 51, 55]. By "naturally growing food," we mean items such fruits, vegetables, nuts, and funghi that are not prepared or processed. By "in the wild," we mean from sites other than farms or orchards, places other than those intended for cultivating food. Although this distinction may seem a bit awkward, it is important to understand what foraging is and is not, and to appreciate the distinct challenges inherent to foraging. For instance, foraging is different from gleaning, which is the collection of leftover foodstuffs from farms or orchards or food providers such as restaurants or grocery stores. Gleaning could include the recovering of day-old bagels from a dumpster, or the donation of leftover sandwiches from a catered event, or the gathering of corn crop remains from a field after that field has been harvested. In contrast, examples of foraging include collecting pears from trees on a golf course, or garlic from an abandoned lot, or mushrooms from under a log in the park. With foraging, the foodstuffs grow and are collected opportunistically, in an ad-hoc manner.

From the perspective of diverse economies research, these distinctions are important for several reasons. First, there are different regulations that come into play between different modes of gathering and distributing food. In some places, it is illegal to give away or otherwise distribute pre-made food items once they have left the market (for instance, to give away unsold bagels or uneaten sandwiches). Second, there are different kinds of labor involved in these different modes of gathering and distributing food. These regulations and modes of labor affect the work of foraging, and thereby affect designing for foraging.

Image 1. Concrete Jungle volunteers at a single persimmon tree along a city street

One key factor to understand about foraging, in order to appreciate its practice, is that is it decidedly **not** farming. Farming almost exclusively involves a dedicated site, a space that is intentionally developed and maintained to grow food. In contrast, foraging is distributed. The fruits, vegetables, and other foodstuffs are scattered across the city, and grow voluntarily instead of being planned. Moreover, the spaces in which they grow are not nurtured in the same way as farmland. Certainly, pear trees growing in a park or fig trees in a front yard may benefit from purposeful watering, or perhaps even soil fertilizing; however, that care is not usually taken with the express intention of supporting the productivity of the trees that bear pears or figs. The spatial distribution of these trees, bushes, and other plants means that the work of tending to and harvesting the food is also distributed in space. The work of foraging is therefore significantly different than the work of farming. These distinctive qualities of the work of urban foraging comprise one of the motivating factors of our design research—how to design systems and services to support the work of foraging.

Concrete Jungle

Over the past four years we have collaborated with Concrete Jungle, an urban foraging collective in Atlanta, Georgia. Concrete Jungle has one paid staff member but is otherwise an all-volunteer, organization. There is a core of 3 founding members, a board comprised of approximately 10 members who take on significant work in running and sustaining the organization, and 100 or so volunteers who participate in fruit picks throughout the year. Concrete Jungle has been active in Atlanta since 2009, though they only became a registered 501c3 organization in 2016. Their primary objective is to gather fruit growing wild across the Atlanta Metro region and donate it to local social service providers. These social service providers range from large organizations, such as the Atlanta Community Food Bank, to smaller programs, such as women's shelters that sit within community centers and churches.

Image 2. Concrete Jungle volunteers at a grove of persimmon trees in a city park

Each year, Concrete Jungle organizes dozens of picks to collect fruit from wild trees, and from these picks, amass thousands of pounds of fruit (in 2016, over 12,000 pounds of fruit and vegetables were collected). Much work goes into foraging at this scale. For instance, in addition to organizing picks and donations, Concrete Jungle is constantly looking to discover and document new fruit trees, so as to increase the amount of fruit they can provide to those in need. Most of the trees they collect from are on public property. Some are on private property, but these picks are negotiated with the property owners. As part of the effort to track forage-able food in the city, Concrete Jungle maintains a digital map of food sources that is public, as well as a more elaborate private database that tracks the approximate ripening dates of individual trees and bushes and their yearly yield. Currently, Concrete Jungle tracks approximately 2,700 fruit trees and bushes in the metro area.

Fruit Monitoring as Key Concern

One key concern for Concrete Jungle is fruit monitoring: knowing when fruit is ripe so that they can organize picks and donations. Keeping track of the ripeness of the fruit across all of the trees and bushes is incredibly time consuming. Not all of the fruit ripens at once, and the climate in Atlanta supports a long growing season. Moreover, the location of the fruit is widely distributed. These factors contribute to the significant time commitment required to walk, bike, or drive around the city, keeping track of when each plum, apple, or pear tree is nearing the time to pick.

The key reason to know when the fruit is ripe is to know when to schedule a fruit pick and the subsequent donation of the fruit. These picks tend to be labor intensive. Even a small tree will often take a team of four people with a ladder, and larger trees and groves of trees can require much larger teams for a pick (see Image 1 & Image 2). Scheduling a pick tends to involve rallying and organizing volunteers (sometimes 10 or more), so planning the timing of that pick is important. If it is too early, the volunteers will arrive and there will be nothing to actually do. If it is too late, the fruit may have already fallen to the ground and been stepped on or eaten by insects. Finally, given the amount of fruit picked, transportation for the fruit needs to be arranged, and in some cases short-term storage must also be arranged until the fruit can be donated. All of which is to say, timing is important and that timing depends upon the ripeness of the fruit.

It is for these reasons that our collaboration with Concrete Jungle over the past several years has focused on exploring methods for remotely monitoring fruit trees. Specifically, we are collaboratively exploring how digital technologies and computational media might be appropriated or designed to support foraging. While this might at first seem amusing, the idea is not entirely outlandish. As already noted, there is a growing body of research on the smart cities technologies. There are also a substantial amount of existing products and services oriented towards so-called precision agriculture: the use of sensing and data technologies to streamline farming. This difference in scale and practice between precision agriculture and farming has been, for us, an opportunity for invention [12].

Of course, other approaches for fruit monitoring are possible, such using mobile phones for crowdsourcing images of fruit trees or even just assigning volunteers to regularly check individual trees. While we are exploring such approaches with Concrete Jungle, in this paper we report on our research into sensing technologies. With regards to use of technology in general and the specific choices of technology in this project, it is important to note that these decisions are not made by the academic researchers on our own, but rather in close collaboration with Concrete Jungle.

The Structure of Our Collaboration with Concrete Jungle

Our work with Concrete Jungle has been framed as a collaborative design research project from the start. Indeed, it was Concrete Jungle who first approached the academic researchers about the possibilities of developing a mobile mapping application and later proposed the notion of using drones for foraging. Concrete Jungle is not only interested in improving their capacity for foraging right now but also in exploring how technologies might aid and amplify their work in the near future. In part, this stems from the fact that one of the founding members has a background in engineering and has worked in multiple startups, contributing to a predisposition to technological experimentation. In part, it also due to the fact that Concrete Jungle recognizes that foraging itself is a playful practice. While the issues of hunger and food security that Concrete Jungle work to address are serious, part of the mission of the organization is to “promote fun and intriguing ways to provide fresh produce to those who need it.” Exploring the role of technologies to support foraging becomes another means of achieving this mission.

We work together with Concrete Jungle in multiple ways. First, we participate in all almost all aspects of their volunteer efforts, including fruit monitoring and picks. In terms of the design research, we collaboratively define approaches to problems. That is, Concrete Jungle may present us with a general problem, such as fruit tree monitoring, and then we work together to discover the range of possibilities to address that problem. In this way, our activities—what we choose to research and to make—are collaboratively articulated. Many aspects of the design process itself also involve collaboration. For instance, in the proof-of-concept system described below, we regularly drew upon the engineering insights of one of the Concrete Jungle members to make design decisions. This extends to all aspects of the design, from the industrial design of housing, to the user experience design, to the optimization of the hardware and software. In short, members of Concrete Jungle are integrated into our design research. In describing the design and deployment in the following sections, the “we” usually includes the authors, student designers who work on the project, and members of Concrete Jungle.

FROM DRONES TO DISTRIBUTED SENSORS

Earlier work with Concrete Jungle involved a mobile mapping application and the exploration of drone use in the context of urban foraging. It was, in fact, the design research with drones that led us to work with sensors [12]. Although drones have the potential to be useful in remotely monitoring fruit trees around the city, there are two fundamental problems. The first problem is battery life. No affordable drone has enough battery life to support the flight distances that would make the use of the drones worthwhile. While there are some cases for using drones that do not require long flight distances—for instance, checking the condition of fruits in hard to reach places such as in roadway medians or inside of gated apartment complexes—these scenarios are rare, and in and of themselves do not make enough of an impact on the workload of fruit monitoring. The second problem is regulatory. During our initial work with drones, federal policy concerning unmanned aerial vehicles (UAVs) use was being debated and the status at the time made our envisioned use of drones, if not outright illegal, within a grey area of regulations that was untenable for our ongoing experiments.

In line with the general notion of appropriating the tools and techniques of precision agriculture for foraging [12], the use of sensors in trees was a logical next step in our exploration and experimentation. Using sensors to detect ripened fruit is an active area of research in agricultural engineering. The majority of the research is oriented towards using gas sensors to detect the presence and concentration of specific organic compounds that are emitted from fruit as it ripens [3, 60]. Other sensing techniques include the use of computational vision to detect visual changes in the fruit (usually color) [57, 62], and ascertaining the acoustical qualities of fruit, which in some cases can also change as fruit ripens [20, 61]. While many of these techniques offer the promise of high-fidelity monitoring, many of them are prohibitively expensive, and almost none of them are feasible for field deployment.

The insight into the system we developed came through our co-design work with Concrete Jungle. In the process of discussing the fruit spotting and monitoring processes and brainstorming possible uses of mobile phone cameras as sensors, one of the foragers commented that, *at a certain point, it becomes easy to see that a tree is full of ripe fruit.* When we asked how, they replied, *the trees droop, a lot, enough that you can see the droop from a ways away.* We quickly began considering options for using mobile phone cameras to compare images of a given tree at multiple points in a growing season. In the process of this brainstorming, it dawned on us that sensing the droop of a branch directly should be a relatively easy and inexpensive affair. This insight sparked the development of the *Fruit Are Heavy* sensing system.

DESIGNING THE *FRUIT ARE HEAVY* SENSING SYSTEM

Drawing on the insight that tree branches bend as fruit ripens, we developed the *Fruit Are Heavy* sensor system. The system is a prototype; it is not entirely functional. As a prototype, it is intended to allow us to explore the conditions and potentials of using a sensing system to support of the work of urban foraging.

The *Fruit Are Heavy* sensor system measures the bend of fruit tree branches as a proxy for tracking the ripeness of the fruit on those branches. The system is comprised of three primary components. The first is the platform hardware and software, which utilizes a custom board and software to monitor the sensor (see Image 3). The second component are the sensors. To date, we have prototyped the system with two different methods for sensing the bend in a tree branch: a bend sensor and a stretch sensor. The third and final component is the housing for the sensor platform, which both provides protection and lets the platform attach to the tree. In order to be of value in monitoring the relative ripeness of fruit, the sensor platform needs to be deployed for a minimum of a month, to detect the progressive bend in the branch that corresponds to the growth of the fruit. As such, making the system robust enough to last for full deployment was a primary concern throughout the design process.

Sensor System Design

Early testing found that a standard Arduino board would drain the battery too quickly to support an extended deployment. At idle, a standard Arduino board draws around 200 milliamps. Even with the largest capacity battery we could find, holding 6,000 milliamp hours, a stock Arduino would run for only 30 hours. This current draw comes from a combination of the LED indicating that

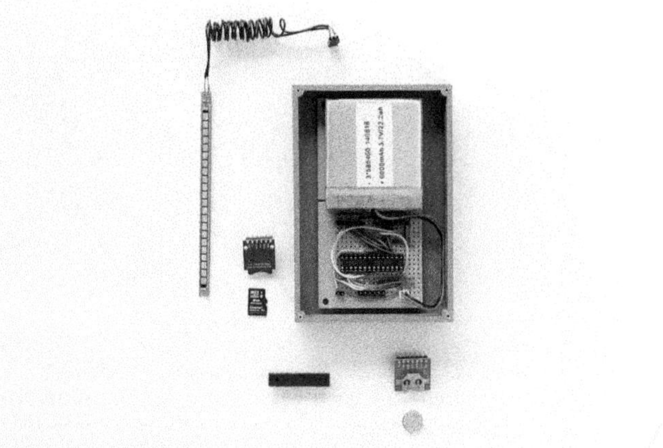

Image 3. Custom electronics and stock parts for the sensing platform.

regulators, oscillators, and a USB controller. In order for the batteries on these sensor platforms to last an entire month, we designed a custom board. This board design takes advantage of several techniques to minimize current draw during the deployment period.

To make our board use as little power as possible, our custom version strips away all unnecessary components. Instead of including USB connectivity on-board, we use an FTDI cable to program the boards directly, meaning we can omit USB controllers entirely while still leaving the boards simple to program via the Arduino IDE. To remove the external 16Mhz oscillator from the board design, we flash the microcontroller's default firmware with replacement firmware so that uses the microcontroller's internal 8MHz oscillator instead. This firmware was originally designed for the Arduino Lilypad, and the low-power mode that is helpful in wearable computing is also useful in our application. Finally, we do not include any LEDs to indicate power status, saving a constant 40 milliamp draw.

The hardware design is only part of energy savings. The software, too, needed to be optimized to reduce energy use. Initially, the microcontroller itself would still draw a constant ~80 milliamps of current. The best way to reduce that current draw is to set the device to sleep when it is not actively reading sensor data or writing that data to the microSD card. Because we are already using a real-time clock (RTC) to keep track of the day and time during data collection, it is relatively straightforward to use it to wake the microcontroller up when it is time to take a new reading. Every 24 hours, the RTC module sends an interrupt to the microcontroller. It in turn wakes up, takes the current sensor reading, writes it to the SD card, and then go back to sleep. In this way, we can dramatically extend the battery life of the sensor platform.

Data Transmission and Storage

Data transmission was, in many ways, fundamental to the system design. In order for the system to achieve the objective of reducing the work of fruit tree monitoring, the sensors need to be able to send the data on a regular basis to

Image 4. Experimenting with forms and mechanism for sensor and platform attachment.

Image 5. Another experiment with forms and mechanism for sensor and platform attachment.

foragers. Data transmission, however, was elusive in our system design. In our initial iterations of the platform design, we explored using cellular communication—having the platform send text data over a cellular network.

However, the cost of the additional electronic components together with the cellular network subscription cost was prohibitive. In a subsequent iteration, we explored the use of WiFi. Unfortunately, no open WiFi was available in our test locations. Rather than shelving the project, in a compromise collectively reached between the researchers and foragers, we decided to pursue the development of the prototype system in the absence of data transmission. Recording data, however, was still necessary as part of the proof-of-concept for the sensing mechanism. Our solution was to equip the sensor platform with microSD card for storing sensor readings. Although this solution was far from ideal, it was a trade-off we deemed reasonable in order to produce a prototype system.

Sensor Housing Design

The custom boards are designed to be placed alongside the batteries in boxes that are 3D printed with laser-cut lids. The boxes provide a substantial amount of protection from the elements, as well as providing a sturdy shell that protects the electronics. However, we were unsure if the boxes alone would be enough to withstand the regular, and

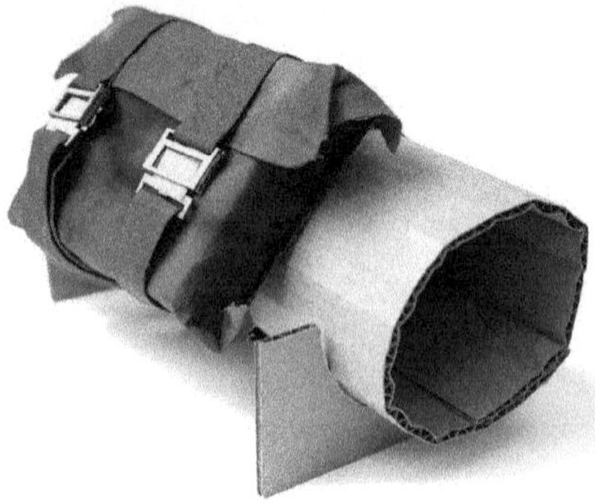

Image 6. Early material and functional prototype of backpack form and clip mechanisms for housing.

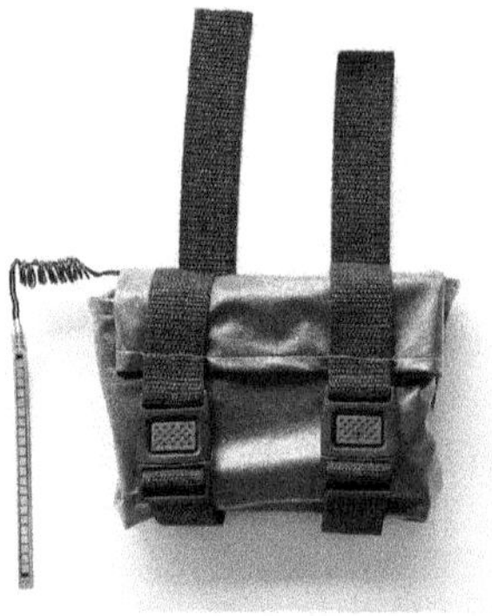

Image 7. Final design of housing with sensor platform placed inside and sensor extending out.

sometimes torrential, summer rains. Moreover, we needed a way to attach the sensors onto the trees. So, in parallel with iterations on the sensor board designs, we began researching and prototyping custom housings that would provide additional protection from the elements and enable the foragers to easily attach the sensors to the trees.

We began our design exploration by collecting examples of existing products that served similar functions. We quickly realized that products designed to carry things on the human body were a good analogy for the functionality that we needed, including the capacity to strap on to a range of sizes and angles. So, for example, we experimented with the straps and buckles mechanism used by fanny-packs as well as armbands for holding mobile phones while exercising. Placing these in situ while using simple cardboard mockups for the sensors allowed us to quickly prototype and iterate through a variety forms and mechanisms (see Images 4 & 5) for both holding the sensor platform to the tree and for connecting the sensors to branches. At multiple points in the design process, a partner from Concrete Jungle provided feedback as informal assessment of the proposed housings, sharing insights and suggestions based upon his experiences of foraging. We finally settled on a backpack-like form with clips that would allow for a range of adjustments to accommodate a

Image 8. Bend sensor attached to branch

Image 9. Stretch sensor attached to branch

variety of thicknesses of tree trunks and branches (see Images 6 & 7). The two straps wrap around a sturdy branch, tightening around both the sensor box and the tree.

From the box, snaked under a flap in the backpack, wire leads connect to the sensor placed in the tree. The simplest solution we found for attaching the sensors themselves to the tree branch was to use plastic ties. The backpack is made from a cloth material used in DIY diaper (or nappy) making. We happened upon this fabric in our material exploration as we were searching for something that was water resistant, inexpensive, and easy to sew. When it is time to recover the sensors, it is as simple as cutting the zip ties and detaching the backpack's straps. From there, the backpacks are easily opened and the microSD cards removed from the sensor boxes.

SENSOR PLATFORM IN USE

We currently use two different kinds of sensors to approximate ripeness. Each of these sensors use the bend of the branch as a proxy to tell when the fruit is ready to be picked by Concrete Jungle volunteers. The first of these is a flex sensor that is placed on a branch to read the bending of the branch directly (see Image 8). The second is a stretch sensor. In this case, one end of that sensor is placed on the bending branch, and the other on the trunk or nearby stable limb of the tree. In this case, the branch bending away from the stable end will stretch the sensor (see Image 9).

In either case, the first step in using the system is to locate a tree that is in the earliest stages of growing fruit. Apples, pear, plum, and fig trees work best because the fruit is heavy enough to produce a significant bend in the branch. Citrus trees would likely also work well. This system, however, would not work well with blueberry bushes or trees where the fruit is not heavy.

Once a tree is identified, and a branch found that will likely bend is selected for the sensors, the forager then finds a stable branch or place on the trunk to secure the sensor platform. Next, she unscrews the lid on the sensor box, turns the platform on from the switch on the board, attaches the sensor leads into the screw terminals for the sensor, and reseals the box. Then the box goes into its backpack to be attached to the tree.

In the case of the flex sensor, zip ties are used to attach the sensor along the parts of the branch that seem most likely to bend. To figure out where it will bend, we hold the fruiting branch where the fruit is growing and bend it manually. In the case of the stretch sensor, one end is zip-tied to a secure, immobile portion of the tree, like a limb near to the trunk, and the other is attached to as near as possible to where the where the fruit is growing.

Two Test Deployments

We conducted two test deployments of the sensor systems over two summers—one in the summer of 2015 and other in the summer of 2016. In both cases we used the same tree: a pear tree that is on private property where we know the owners, and thus could have regular access to platforms with less concern about them being tampered with or stolen. In both cases, we deployed the sensor system together with a partner from Concrete Jungle, who assisted in identifying the best branches to use for testing, and hung the sensor system in the tree.

In both of the test deployments, the sensor platforms operated for approximately five weeks without interruption. In fact, in each case, the platform was still operating when we collected it from the field. This suggests that our design should support at least five weeks of monitoring, and we estimate it may actually support between six and seven weeks. Also, in each case, the housing was successful at both protecting the boxes and securing them to trees. The boxes remained in the trees in the precise location where they were initially attached, as did the sensors themselves. Moreover, despite sustained high humidity, occasional torrential rains, and regular drizzle (as is common in Atlanta), the sensor platforms remained dry and continued to operate consistently.

At the end of the five weeks, we removed the backpacks from the trees, ejected the microSD card, and reviewed the

Image 10. Concrete Jungle member and design collaborator deploying the sensor platform.

data. In both test deployments with the bend-branch sensor (2015 and 2016), there was a clearly discernable change in the sensor reading over the course of month. With the stretch-branch sensor, there was minimal change in the data (the sensor data is publicly available to view on Github at https://github.com/PublicDesignWorkshop/foraging-platform/tree/master/data). Despite some noise in the data, the bend-branch sensor seems to capture the drooping of the branch, with the most dramatic change occurring in the last week of the data collection. This suggests to us that the bend-branch sensor shows potential for use. We are unsure of the stretch-branch sensor—the minimal change in the sensor reading suggests that perhaps some change in the branch's droop is being detected, but certainly not enough to claim that it works. For this sensor, another round of testing is warranted.

DISCUSSION

The *Fruit Are Heavy* project allows us to explore one way of using IoT technologies to support a collective and public endeavor. Working together with community partners, we were able to design and prototype a system that serves a public interest and contributes to the work of a public in addressing its concerns [11]. In this case, this happened to be a public of urban foragers broadly concerned with providing food for those in need, and more narrowly concerned with mitigating the work of that endeavor. Regarding the work of fruit monitoring, the prototype platform suggests that a finished platform based on similar engineering and design principles could do the monitoring work necessary to alleviate the need for foragers to check fruit trees regularly. This could reduce their total labor, enabling foragers to direct those efforts elsewhere in the organization, such as increasing the number of trees that they monitor—thereby increasing the amount of fruit donated—or simply put, taking less time and effort to achieve the main goal of providing for others.

Of course, as a prototype, this system is partial, and has issues that could be improved upon. Most glaring is the issue of data transmission. We do not view this issue as a design flaw so much as an issue of context and infrastructure, and we address that in the following section. Some modifications to the housing are also in order. In particular, all of the control mechanisms were placed inside of the box to limit exposure of the electronics to the elements. With a more refined and robust design, those controls could be made accessible without having to open the boxes during each deployment and recovery. In addition, we believe there are improvements we could make directly to the bend-branch sensor. Currently we are using a pre-made sensor, approximately 15 centimeters in length. If we custom-built our own bend sensor, of a significantly longer length, we should be able to capture more of the bend in the branch and provide a better reading of the overall droop.

More than the informing the design of the platform, sensors, or housing, the *Fruit Are Heavy* project was intended to provide an opportunity for research into the potentials and issues of designing Public IoT in the context of smart cities and practices of diverse economies. Next, we discuss insights and implications for designing interactive systems within these contexts and practices.

Broader Insights Into Design and Use in the Context of Smart Cities

Our research into supporting urban foraging through the appropriation of the techniques of precision agriculture has led us to develop insights relevant for smart cities. This is perhaps not surprising, given that the uses of data, geographic information systems, drones, and distributed sensing comprise the visions of both smart cities and precision agriculture. What we have found is that urban foraging offers an example of existing and vibrant community practice that could indeed actually benefit from the infrastructures, systems, and services proffered by smart cities initiatives. Examining how those technologies might be designed and used *now* thereby provides empirical insights into the design and use of near-term smart cities infrastructures, systems, and services by communities. In what follows, we identify and discuss three insights, moving from basic technical concerns, to policy concerns, to design concerns about the "smartness" of smart cities.

Ubiquitous Connectivity: The base, but often absent, condition for a smart city

Perhaps the fundamental issue in deploying community-driven sensing is a lack of network connectivity. This is a problem that could be easily solved through the development of free and open civic Wi-Fi networks. In fact, in some cities where such networks exist, connectivity would cease to be an issue. Without such an already-existing network, however, the transmission of data remains a critical issue. Cellular is an option for transmission, for example, meaning that the sensor would send data via text message. However, cellular options increase the cost of the device, add a cost to data transmission, and increases the battery cost as well. Together, these costs mean that cellular connectivity becomes prohibitively expensive and ceases to be a viable option. The most promising alternative would be the use of various low-power and long-range networking technologies. This, too, introduces cost and complexity into the system, but, in the absence of a free and open Wi-Fi network, seems like the most viable near term solution to the problem of connectivity.

Are We Really Allowed to Do This?: Policies for community sensor deployment

Another crucial issue is the lack of policies for community deployment of sensors. There have been enough serious repercussions from various "suspicious" electronic gadgets and projects left in public spaces that it is naïve to think that a community could choose to strap their own sensors on neighborhood trees (or light posts, street signs, or mailboxes) without causing a stir that could have significant and costly legal consequences. If drones are any indication, the policies for the use of such emerging technologies will be slow and faltering. There are real concerns with the public deployment of sensing systems that include safety concerns and privacy concerns. In our deployments, we utilized spaces where we both knew resident-owners and that were off the beaten path to avoid these issues as best as we could. If communities develop significant interest to experiment with various kinds of sensor systems, it will be imperative to develop guidelines and policies around experiments like this, and researchers should take an active role in supporting communities and municipalities in the development of those guidelines and policies.

Maybe We Don't Need To Be So Smart: Re-scaling smartness in the smart city

The overarching theme of smart cities is that sensor systems together with machine learning and data analytics will provide more and more precise evidence and acumen for civic decision-making. This is the "smartness" of smart cities. What the *Fruit Are Heavy* system demonstrates is that there is value in systems that are low-fidelity, high-latency, and carrying only few bits of data. This is a constitution of the smart city that is different from the more familiar visions of high-bandwidth, always on, precise data streams. This is not to say one vision should take precedence over another, but rather, that when we conceptualize and design smart city infrastructures and services, we should appreciate that there may be real and immediate value in infrastructures and services that offer simpler modes of connectivity and awareness.

In a sense, *Fruit Are Heavy* is a Public IoT service that shifts the scale of intelligence in the smart city. *Fruit Are Heavy* is intended to operate at the human scale—its "smartness" is not an insight that is only made possible through big data analytics, but also an insight that is possible for any individual human to make. What the system provides is a familiar move to delegate awareness for the sake of saving effort.

Perhaps social media is an analogy for considering these design implications. While there is value in systems that enable real time synchronous video and audio from multiple sources (such as conferencing software), there is also value in systems that are constrained to a single image, 140 characters, or six seconds of video. It is not that one form of media is more "social" than another, but rather, that they provide different modes for sociality. Perhaps we should consider smart cities technologies and services similarly—that while there is value in fast and rich data, there is also value in minimal data, and correspondingly, value in the kinds of minimal computing needed to produce that data.

Sensing Technologies in the Context of Designing to Support Diverse Community Economies

This work is situated within a broader domain of practices concerned with diverse community economies. Within this literature, there is a significant amount of work on foraging [21, 41, 46, 50, 51, 55]. However, little of that research addresses the intersection of technology with foraging, or even more generally, the role of technology in diverse community economies. As such, this research provides an opportunity for reflection on what might be key themes at the intersection of fields and practices. Here, we address two of those themes.

Does Sensing Technology Affect Commoning: Are we distancing ourselves from an element of practice?

Commoning is an important notion within diverse community economies—it is a descriptor for how togetherness is created and experienced [17, 24, 26, 59] Commoning often occurs through shared activities and knowledge. In foraging, the activities of fruit monitoring themselves, of going out into and around the city to know the trees, is a prime example of commoning. As we design technologies and services that mediate some of our knowledge practices and delegate some of our activities, we have wondered if we are, in fact, undermining rather than supporting a fundamental quality of community economies.

Future work will explore the question of whether the use of sensing technologies, or even more generally, the use of data as an intermediary to direct sensory knowing affects the commitment to the practices of foraging. If we look to scholarship on other contexts and practices of environmental sensing, there is no clear answer [17, 18, 49]. Following from work that explores how sensing technology constructs hybrid—more than human—assemblages of knowledge and action [17, 18, 19, 37, 52], we hypothesize that while sensing technologies certainly affect what and how we know, they do not necessarily inhibit practices of commoning. Indeed, within the research on diverse economies that looks specifically at foraging, some authors note that one of the characteristics of foraging is that it sensitizes foragers to recognizing and appreciating the limits of human agency and the different forms of agency expressed through human/nonhuman encounters, which includes trees and bushes and also the multiple factors of the built environment that affect foraging [51]. So, it would seem adding sensors into the mix might simply diversify these agencies, making them different but not necessarily "better" or "worse." Rather than avoiding sensing technologies in practices of commoning, what is needed is careful attention to how they configure experience and agency, and perhaps, imagine ways they might in fact contribute to an even richer understanding of nonhumans in diverse economies.

Diverse Economies is Work: Considering automation in community economies

Building on the concern of whether mediation negatively affects commoning, we have come to realize that understanding and appreciating the significant work required to sustain diverse community economies is crucial to designing for community economies. Though it may be volunteer-based, and though it operates outside of and in parallel to mainstream markets, there is still significant labor that goes into activities such as foraging. Precisely because this work is informal, contingent, and demanding, sensing (and other) technologies may be of particular value.

Abstracting beyond the immediate context of the practices of foraging, it would seem that there is a lesson to be learned about "smartness" and automation. Sensing and other techniques of producing, analyzing, and acting upon data are part of automation in the 21st century. These technologies work to systemize and proceduralize work. There is real concern with regards to automation, in agriculture and food systems, and in work more generally. Perhaps projects such as *Fruit Are Heavy* provide another way to conceptualize and undertake these sorts of data practices without capitulating to rhetoric and techniques that undermine community agency. Automation may have its place in diverse economies, but it is imperative that it be developed from the perspective of the worker. It is for this reason that participatory design, with its tradition of acknowledging work as a skilled activity and including workers in the design of systems they will use, is relevant.

CONCLUSION

In this paper we presented the *Fruit Are Heavy* system as an example of a proof-of-concept IoT system designed to serve a public interest—in this case, to aide in the work of urban foraging. Foraging, as practiced by our collaborators Concrete Jungle, is a mode of provisioning and care that operates in parallel to more mainstream practices of providing food for those in need. While the system we designed was a prototype, our deployments suggest that the design has promise as an approach to remote fruit tree monitoring that could alleviate some of the work of foraging.

But more important that the specifics of the electronics, sensors, or housing, we believe the research we have presented in this paper is valuable, especially as we move from the vision to the design to the implementation of smart cities. By undertaking design research to explore how environmental sensing can support urban foraging, we have demonstrated the viability of an alternative approach to designing technologies and services in the context of smart cities. This approach is not inherently or explicitly critical of other approaches, but it emphasizes the potential value of low-fidelity sensing and offers a notion of "smartness" that functions at the human-scale. We also demonstrated the potential of designing IoT services to support diverse economies, to support a kind of parallel social and civic practice. This continues a long line of research in design and human-computer interaction that has explored alternative forms of social organization and everyday life and argued for the value of attending to these practices [32, 33, 36, 63, 64, 67].

For future work, we plan to continue the exploration of the use of IoT technologies and services for diverse economies generally, and for foraging specifically. This includes the continued development of sensing systems, as well as exploring the integration of sensor data into geographic information systems and other techniques for data analysis. We also plan to address how projects such as this provide the opportunity to experiment with new models of participatory design in the context of smart cities and Public IoT, expanding our notion of how we work together with communities of practice to shape not only technical systems, but also informal civics and systems of care. [10, 11, 36].

ACKNOWLEDGMENTS

Thank you to Concrete Jungle, in particular Craig Durkin for ongoing partnership. Thanks also to Catherine Meschia for the design of the sensor backpacks, and Sean MacKay for photographing the sensor platforms. Finally, thank you to Daniela Rosner, Sarah Fox, and James Pierce for ongoing collaboration around Public IoT and Amanda Meng and Cookie Nguyen for exceptional feedback. This work was supported in part by the Intel Science and Technology Center for Social Computing, and the National Science Foundation grant #1523562.

REFERENCES

1. Ricardo Alexandre Afonso, Kellyton dos Santos Brito, Clóvis Holanda do Nascimento, Vinicius Cardoso Garcia, and Alexandre Álvaro. 2015. Brazilian smart Cities: Using a maturity model to measure and compare inequality in cities. In *Proceedings of the 16th Annual International Conference on Digital Government Research* (dg.o '15). ACM, New York, NY, USA, 230-238. DOI=http://dx.doi.org/10.1145/2757401.2757426
2. Mariam Asad and Christopher A. Le Dantec. 2015. Illegitimate Civic Participation: Supporting Community Activists on the Ground. In *Proceedings of the 18th ACM Conference on Computer Supported Cooperative Work & Social Computing* (CSCW '15). ACM, New York, NY, USA, 1694-1703. DOI: http://dx.doi.org/10.1145/2675133.2675156
3. M. Benady, J. E. Simon, , D. J Charles & , G. E Miles. 1995. Fruit Ripeness Determination By Electronic Sensing Of Aromatic Volatiles. *Transactions of the ASAE*, 38(1), 251-257.
4. Thomas Binder, Giorgio De Michelis, Pelle Ehn, Giulio Jacucci, Per Linde, and Ina Wagner. *Design Things*. MIT Press, 2011.
5. Erling Björgvinsson, Pelle Ehn, and Per-Anders Hillgren. 2010. Participatory Design and "Democratizing Innovation". In *Proceedings of the 11th Biennial Participatory Design Conference* (PDC '10). ACM, New York, NY, USA, 41-50. DOI=http://dx.doi.org/10.1145/1900441.1900448
6. Manuel Pedro Rodríguez Bolívar. 2016. Mapping Dimensions of Governance in Smart Cities: Practitioners versus Prior Research. In *Proceedings of the 17th International Digital Government Research Conference on Digital Government Research* (dg.o '16), Yushim Kim and Monica Liu (Eds.). ACM, New York, NY, USA, 312-324. DOI: https://doi.org/10.1145/2912160.2912176
7. M. Castro, A.J. Jara, & A.F. Skarmeta, 2013. Smart Lighting Solutions For Smart Cities. In *Proceedings Of The 27th International Conference On Workshops Of Advanced Information Networking And Applications* (WAINA), 2013, IEEE, 1374-1379.
8. Andy Crabtree and Peter Tolmie. 2016. A Day in the Life of Things in the Home. In *Proceedings of the 19th ACM Conference on Computer-Supported Cooperative Work & Social Computing* (CSCW '16). ACM, New York, NY, USA, 1738-1750. DOI: http://dx.doi.org/10.1145/2818048.2819954
9. Kate Crawford. 2015. Can An Algorithm Be Agonistic? Ten scenes from life in calculated publics. *Science, Technology & Human Values*, 41(1), 77-92.
10. Maria Puig de la Bellacasa. 2011. "Matters of Care in Technoscience: Assembling neglected things." *Social Studies of Science* 41, No. 1, 85-106.
11. Carl DiSalvo, Jonathan Lukens, Thomas Lodato, Tom Jenkins, and Tanyoung Kim. 2014. Making public things: how HCI design can express matters of concern. In *Proceedings of the SIGCHI Conference on Human Factors in Computing Systems* (CHI '14). ACM, New York, NY, USA, 2397-2406. DOI=http://dx.doi.org/10.1145/2556288.2557359
12. Carl DiSalvo . 2016. The Irony of Drones for Foraging: Exploring the Work of Speculative Interventions. In *Design Anthropological Futures*, eds. Kjærsgaard, M. G., Halse, J., Smith, R. C., Vangkilde, K. T., Binder, T., & Otto, T. Bloomsbury, 139-152.
13. Audrey Desjardins and Ron Wakkary. 2016. Living In A Prototype: A Reconfigured Space. In *Proceedings of the 2016 CHI Conference on Human Factors in Computing Systems* (CHI '16). ACM, New York, NY, USA, 5274-5285. DOI: https://doi.org/10.1145/2858036.2858261
14. Pelle Ehn. 2008. Participation in Design Things. In *Proceedings of the Tenth Anniversary Conference on Participatory Design 2008* (PDC '08). Indiana University, Indianapolis, IN, USA, 92-101.
15. Pelle Ehn, Elisabet M. Nilsson, and Richard Topgaard, eds. *Making Futures: Marginal notes on innovation, design, and democracy*. MIT Press, 2014.
16. Shane B. Eisenman, Emiliano Miluzzo, Nicholas D. Lane, Ronald A. Peterson, Gahng-Seop Ahn, and Andrew T. Campbell. 2010. BikeNet: A mobile sensing system for cyclist experience mapping. *ACM Trans. Sen. Netw.* 6, 1, Article 6 (January 2010), 39 pages. DOI=http://dx.doi.org/10.1145/1653760.1653766
17. Fabio Franza & Bianca Elzenbaumerb. Commons & Community Economies: Entry points to design for eco--social justice? 2016. In *Proceedings of DRS 2016, Design Research Society 50th Anniversary Conference.* Brighton, UK, 27–30 June 2016.
18. Jennifer Gabrys. 2014. A Cosmopolitics Of Energy: Diverging materialities and hesitating practices. *Environment and Planning A*, 46(9), 2095-2109.
19. Jennifer Gabrys. 2014. Programming Environments: Environmentality and citizen sensing in the smart city. *Environment and Planning D: Society and Space*, 32(1), 30-48.
20. N. Galili, I. Shmulevich, & N. Benichou. 1998. Acoustic Testing Of Avocado For Fruit Ripeness Evaluation. *Transactions of the ASAE*, 41(2), 399.
21. R. E. Galt, L.C. Gray, & P. Hurley. 2014. Subversive And Interstitial Food Spaces: Transforming selves, societies, and society–environment relations through

urban agriculture and foraging. *Local Environment*, 19(2), 133-146.

22. P.A. Hillgren, A. Seravalli & A. Emilson. 2011. Prototyping And Infrastructuring In Design For Social Innovation. *CoDesign*, 7(3-4), 169-183.
23. David Gibbs, Rob Krueger, and Gordon MacLeod. 2013. Grappling With Smart City Politics In An Era Of Market Triumphalism. *Urban Studies* 50, No. 11, 2151-2157.
24. J.K. Gibson-Graham.1996. *"The" End of Capitalism (as We Knew It): A Feminist Critique of Political Economy*; with a New Introduction. U of Minnesota Press.
25. J.K. Gibson-Graham. 2003. An Ethics of the Local. *Rethinking Marxism*, 15(1), 49-74.
26. J.K. Gibson-Graham. 2006. *A Postcapitalist Politics*. U of Minnesota Press.
27. J.K. Graham & G. Roelvink. 2010. An Economic Ethics for the Anthropocene. *Antipode*, 41(s1), 320-346.
28. J. Ramon Gil-Garcia, Theresa A. Pardo, and Armando Aldama-Nalda. 2013. Smart Cities And Smart Governments: Using Information Technologies To Address Urban Challenges. In *Proceedings of the 14th Annual International Conference on Digital Government Research* (dg.o '13). ACM, New York, NY, USA, 296-297. DOI=http://dx.doi.org/10.1145/2479724.2479728
29. Tarleton Gillespie. 2014. The Relevance of Algorithms. *Media Technologies: Essays on communication, materiality, and society*, MIT Press, 167-194.
30. Eric Gordon & Paul Mihailidis, eds. 2016. *Civic Media: Technology, Design, Practice*. MIT Press.
31. Adam Greenfield. (2013). *Against the Smart City: A Pamphlet*. Do projects.
32. Maria Håkansson and Phoebe Sengers. 2013. Beyond being green: simple living families and ICT. In *Proceedings of the SIGCHI Conference on Human Factors in Computing Systems* (CHI '13). ACM, New York, NY, USA, 2725-2734. DOI: http://dx.doi.org/10.1145/2470654.248137
33. Maria Håkansson, Gilly Leshed, Eli Blevis, Lisa Nathan, and Samuel Mann. 2012. Simple, Sustainable Living. In *CHI '12 Extended Abstracts on Human Factors in Computing Systems* (CHI EA '12). ACM, New York, NY, USA, 2795-2798. DOI: http://dx.doi.org/10.1145/2212776.2212723
34. Robert Hollands. 2015. Critical Interventions Into The Corporate Smart City. 2015. *Cambridge Journal of Regions, Economy and Society* 8, no. 1, 61-77.
35. Robert Hollands. 2008. Will The Real Smart City Please Stand Up? Intelligent, Progressive Or Entrepreneurial? *City*, 12(3), 303-320.
36. Lara Houston, Steven J. Jackson, Daniela K. Rosner, Syed Ishtiaque Ahmed, Meg Young, and Laewoo Kang. 2016. Values in Repair. In *Proceedings of the 2016 CHI Conference on Human Factors in Computing Systems* (CHI '16). ACM, New York, NY, USA, 1403-1414. DOI: https://doi.org/10.1145/2858036.2858470
37. Tom Jenkins, Christopher A. Le Dantec, Carl DiSalvo, Thomas Lodato, and Mariam Asad. 2016. Object-Oriented Publics. In *Proceedings of the 2016 CHI Conference on Human Factors in Computing Systems* (CHI '16). ACM, New York, NY, USA, 827-839. DOI: https://doi.org/10.1145/2858036.2858565
38. Tom Jenkins. 2017. Living Apart, Together: Cohousing as a Site for ICT Design. In *Proceedings of the 12th Conference on Designing Interactive Systems* (DIS '17). https://doi.org/10.1145/3064663.3064751
39. Rob Kitchin. 2014. "Making sense of smart cities: addressing present shortcomings." *Cambridge Journal of Regions, Economy and Society*, 8(1), 131-136.
40. Rob Kitchin. 2014. "The Real-Time City? Big data and smart urbanism." *GeoJournal* 79, no. 1, 1-14.
41. N. Larder, K. Lyons, G. Woolcock. 2014. Enacting Food Sovereignty: Values and meanings in the act of domestic food production in urban Australia. *Local Environment,* 19(1), 56-76.
42. Bruno Latour. 2004. "Why Has Critique Run Out Of Steam? From Matters Of Fact To Matters Of Concern." Critical inquiry 30, no. 2, 225-248.
43. Airi Lampinen, Victoria Bellotti, Coye Cheshire, and Mary Gray. 2016. CSCW and the Sharing Economy: The Future of Platforms as Sites of Work Collaboration and Trust. In *Proceedings of the 19th ACM Conference on Computer Supported Cooperative Work and Social Computing Companion* (CSCW '16 Companion). ACM, New York, NY, USA, 491-497. DOI: http://dx.doi.org/10.1145/2818052.2855527
44. Chris Le Dantec. 2016. *Designing Publics*. MIT Press.
45. Christopher A. Le Dantec, Mariam Asad, Aditi Misra, and Kari E. Watkins. 2015. Planning with Crowdsourced Data: Rhetoric and Representation in Transportation Planning. In *Proceedings of the 18th ACM Conference on Computer Supported Cooperative Work & Social Computing* (CSCW '15). ACM, New York, NY, USA, 1717-1727. DOI: http://dx.doi.org/10.1145/2675133.2675212
46. R.J. McLain, P.T., Hurley, M.R. Emery & M. R. Poe. 2014. Gathering "Wild" Food In The City: Rethinking the role of foraging in urban ecosystem planning and management. *Local Environment*, 19(2), 220-240.

47. Taewoo Nam and Theresa A. Pardo. 2011. Conceptualizing smart city with dimensions of technology, people, and institutions. In *Proceedings of the 12th Annual International Digital Government Research Conference: Digital Government Innovation in Challenging Times* (dg.o '11). ACM, New York, NY, USA, 282-291. DOI=http://dx.doi.org/10.1145/2037556.2037602
48. Lisa P. Nathan. 2008. Ecovillages, Values, And Interactive Technology: Balancing sustainability with daily life in 21st century america. In *CHI '08 Extended Abstracts on Human Factors in Computing Systems* (CHI EA '08). ACM, New York, NY, USA, 3723-3728. DOI=http://dx.doi.org/10.1145/1358628.1358920
49. Patrick Olivier and Peter Wright. 2015. Digital Civics: Taking a local turn. *interactions* 22, 4 (June 2015), 61-63. DOI=http://dx.doi.org/10.1145/2776885
50. M.R. Poe, R. J. McLain, M. Emery & P. T. Hurley. 2013. Urban Forest Justice And The Rights To Wild Foods, Medicines, And Materials In The City. *Human Ecology*, 41(3), 409-422.
51. M.R. Poe, J. LeCompte, R. McLain, & P. Hurley. 2014. Urban Foraging And The Relational Ecologies Of Belonging. *Social & Cultural Geography*, 15(8), 901-919.
52. Helen Pritchard. 2013. Thinking With The Animal Hacker, Articulation In Ecologies Of Earth Observation. *APRJA: Back When Pluto Was A Planet: The reinvention of research as participatory practice.*
53. Tim Regan, David Sweeney, John Helmes, Vasillis Vlachokyriakos, Siân Lindley, and Alex Taylor. 2015. Designing Engaging Data in Communities. In *Proceedings of the 33rd Annual ACM Conference Extended Abstracts on Human Factors in Computing Systems* (CHI EA '15). ACM, New York, NY, USA, 271-274. DOI=http://dx.doi.org/10.1145/2702613.2725432
54. J. Rifkin. 2014. *The Zero Marginal Cost Society: The internet of things, the collaborative commons, and the eclipse of capitalism*. Macmillan.
55. G. Roelvink, ed. 2015. *Making Other Worlds Possible: Performing Diverse Economies*. University of Minnesota Press.
56. Daniela K. Rosner, Margaret E. Morris, Ariel Duncan, Sarah E. Fox, Kathi R. Kitner, Ankur Agrawal, and Mei J. Chen. 2016. Designing for Movement in Public Life with Itinerant Probes. In P*roceedings of the 2016 ACM Conference on Designing Interactive Systems* (DIS '16). ACM, New York, NY, USA, 1072-1082. DOI: https://doi.org/10.1145/2901790.2901913
57. N. Sarkar, & R.R. Wolfe. 1985. Feature Extraction Techniques For Sorting Tomatoes By Computer Vision. *Transactions of the ASAE*, 28(3), 970-0974.
58. Anna Seravalli. 2012. Infrastructuring for opening production, from participatory design to participatory making? In *Proceedings of the 12th Participatory Design Conference: Exploratory Papers, Workshop Descriptions, Industry Cases - Volume 2* (PDC '12), Vol. 2. ACM, New York, NY, USA, 53-56. DOI=http://dx.doi.org/10.1145/2348144.2348161
59. Anna Seravalli. 2014. *Making Commons: Attempts at composing prospects in the opening of production.* PhD Dissertation, Malmö University.
60. J. E. Simon, A. Hetzroni, B. Bordelon, G. E. Miles, D. J. Charles. 1996. Electronic Sensing Of Aromatic Volatiles For Quality Sorting Of Blueberries. *Journal of Food Science*, 61(5), 967-970.
61. M. Soltani, R. Alimardani, & M. Omid. 2010. Prediction Of Banana Quality During Ripening Stage Using Capacitance Sensing System. *Australian Journal of Crop Science*, 4(6), 443.
62. K. Tanigaki, T. Fujiura, A. Akase, & J. Imagawa. 2008. Cherry-Harvesting robot. *Computers and Electronics in Agriculture*, 63(1), 65-72.
63. Alex S. Taylor and Laurel Swan. 2005. Artful systems in the home. In *Proceedings of the SIGCHI Conference on Human Factors in Computing Systems* (CHI '05). ACM, New York, NY, USA, 641-650. DOI=http://dx.doi.org/10.1145/1054972.1055060
64. Alex S. Taylor, Siân Lindley, Tim Regan, David Sweeney, Vasillis Vlachokyriakos, Lillie Grainger, and Jessica Lingel. 2015. Data-in-Place: Thinking through the Relations Between Data and Community. In *Proceedings of the 33rd Annual ACM Conference on Human Factors in Computing Systems* (CHI '15). ACM, New York, NY, USA, 2863-2872. DOI: http://dx.doi.org/10.1145/2702123.2702558
65. Anthony Townsend. 2013. *Smart Cities: Big data, civic hackers, and the quest for a new utopia*. WW Norton & Company.
66. Vasillis Vlachokyriakos, Clara Crivellaro, Christopher A. Le Dantec, Eric Gordon, Pete Wright, and Patrick Olivier. 2016. Digital Civics: Citizen Empowerment With and Through Technology. In *Proceedings of the 2016 CHI Conference Extended Abstracts on Human Factors in Computing Systems* (CHI EA '16). ACM, New York, NY, USA, 1096-1099.
67. Ron Wakkary and Karen Tanenbaum. 2009. A sustainable identity: the creativity of an everyday designer. In *Proceedings of the SIGCHI Conference on Human Factors in Computing Systems* (CHI '09). ACM, New York, NY, USA, 365-374. DOI=http://dx.doi.org/10.1145/1518701.1518761

The Rise of Bots: A Survey of Conversational Interfaces, Patterns, and Paradigms

Lorenz Cuno Klopfenstein
cuno.klopfenstein@uniurb.it

Saverio Delpriori
saverio.delpriori@uniurb.it

Silvia Malatini
silvia.malatini@uniurb.it

Alessandro Bogliolo
alessandro.bogliolo@uniurb.it

Department of Pure and Applied Sciences
Piazza della Repubblica 13, 61029 Urbino
University of Urbino "Carlo Bo" — Italy

ABSTRACT
This work documents the recent rise in popularity of messaging bots: chatterbot-like agents with simple, textual interfaces that allow users to access information, make use of services, or provide entertainment through online messaging platforms. Conversational interfaces have been often studied in their many facets, including natural language processing, artificial intelligence, human-computer interaction, and usability. In this work we analyze the recent trends in chatterbots and provide a survey of major messaging platforms, reviewing their support for bots and their distinguishing features. We then argue for what we call "Botplication", a bot interface paradigm that makes use of context, history, and structured conversation elements for input and output in order to provide a conversational user experience while overcoming the limitations of text-only interfaces.

ACM Classification Keywords
H.5.2 Information Interfaces and Presentation: User Interfaces

Author Keywords
Conversational UI; mobile UI; botplication; bots; messaging

INTRODUCTION
The reach of third-party applications for mobile operating systems—usually marketed as "apps"—has grown dramatically over the last years. A decade after the launch of the *App Store* for iPhone in 2008, the number of apps available to smartphone users now reaches into the order of millions. Their reach, impact, and economic significance cannot be ignored.

However, recent statistics have shown that users frequently make use of a limited set of popular apps. Moreover, most smartphone owners are accustomed to installing nearly zero new apps on their devices on a monthly basis [8]. For app developers it has become more and more difficult to make their products visible in an already crowded application store, where competition is harsher than ever.

Instant messaging (IM) and social network applications consistently take up the top spots among the most used applications. IM apps in particular have shown tremendous growth over the last years, recently taking over the lead in terms of number of users, growth, and user engagement [35]. Messaging platforms are getting immense attention and—as their success depends on the network effect of their users—ferociously compete for market share.

Starting in 2014, many messaging systems have introduced support for so-called "bots": enhanced conversational agents that can chat with users, right inside the messaging app itself. These bots live inside a very familiar place: in a conversation thread, right next to private conversations with friends and relatives, which is increasingly the most used feature of a user's smartphone. Most users in fact use messaging apps several times a day and have a well-rounded understanding of their interface and manner of working.

Instead of trying to attract people to new apps, bots provide an incredibly convenient way for services and developers to engage with users where they already are, making use of the existing conversational paradigm. Even if the conversation follows the familiar and recognizable conventions of a messaging system, the exchange does not need to be text-based. Thanks to the richness of the development frameworks made available by many messaging platforms, bots can also exchange information using complex messages and UI primitives, which allow the conversation to be more efficient.

Bots are growing fast in number and many IM platforms have started offering *bot stores*, just like mobile OS platforms do for apps. In fact, the robustness of the messaging ecosystem—encompassing its existing user base and distribution channels—make bots the perfect bridgehead to transform instant messaging systems into software delivery platforms. This could be a lucrative endeavor for messaging apps, bringing them into competition with the mobile platforms on which they operate.

However, to the best of our knowledge, a thorough and detailed appraisal of this phenomena is still missing.

DIS 2017, June 10–14, 2017, Edinburgh, United Kingdom.

ISBN 978-1-4503-4922-2/17/06.

DOI: http://dx.doi.org/10.1145/3064663.3064672

Contribution
Our work examines this trend with a history of existing chatbots and a survey of popular IM platforms. We then propose the definition of "Botplications": conversational agents designed to follow a set of guidelines that can serve as functional replacements of apps. The distinguishing characteristics of such agents are identified, including differences and advantages over traditional applications. We then speculate about the future trends of these technologies and conversational interfaces.

HISTORY OF CONVERSATIONAL INTERFACES
The idea of building a computer—or better, a program—able to talk with humans, giving the illusion of a true human-to-human interaction, can be dated back to the '50s, when Alan Turing proposed his seminal "Imitation Game" [31]. Better known as the *Turing test*, it aims to determine if a machine can give the impression to other humans of being human itself. Today the Turing test is still used as a test for evaluating to which extent a program, a *bot*, is human-like: the Loebner Prize is annually assigned to the best computer system pretending to be human.

Chatterbots
One of the first examples of such a program was *ELIZA*, created by Weizenbaum in 1966 [34]. ELIZA did simply answer all the user's utterances with other vague questions, giving a rough impression of a Rogerian psychotherapist. Weizenbaum's first example of a so-called "chatterbot", and its crude attempts at fooling users into believing they were interacting with another human, laid the foundations for chatterbots and bots in the following 50 years, until today.

Another example of a popular and more recent chatbot is *ALICE* (Artificial Linguistic Internet Computer Entity), which won the Loebner prize in 2000, 2001, and 2004. It was developed by Wallace in 1995, inspired by ELIZA. ALICE relies on a simple pattern-matching algorithm: it uses pattern templates to represent input and output and makes use of recursive techniques to apply different rules [33]. The underlying intelligence is based on the Artificial Intelligence Markup Language (AIML), which makes it possible for developers to define the building blocks of the bot's knowledge [32].

Personification
From the initial attempts with ELIZA and ALICE, to the ambition of developing "intelligent" agents able to fully converse with humans using natural language, bots have been increasingly employed in many fields with a discrete success, yet with limited spread. They have been applied in e-commerce applications [17], like *Nicole*, a virtual assistant with customer service tasks, or *Anna* by IKEA; in education, like CHARLIE [23], a bot that lets students communicate with the online learning platform INES, or TQ-bot [10], dedicated to student tutoring and evaluation; information retrieval [26, 29], and e-government services [21]. Most of those bots are based on AIML and ALICE [27, 30].

Along with chatterbots, supported by the evolution of Automatic Speech Recognition (ASR) systems in the '80s, Spoken Dialog Systems (SDS) started drawing the attention of academics and the industry [22]. The conversation did move from a textual to a spoken channel, as a presumably easier and more natural interface for humans. ATIS [13] was a telephone-based flight reservation system, funded by DARPA, developed in 1990, in the USA; in the same years, SUNDIAL was developed in Europe [25], with the same aim of giving information about flights via telephone. The latter system was able to understand between 1.000 and 2.000 words in four different languages. Mercury was a similar, more recent, undertaking in this field [28]. These systems addressed several difficult technological issues, including speech recognition, understanding the user's requests, and giving the system the means of offering satisfactory answers.

A further step toward the "personification" of intelligent systems has been achieved with the development of Embodied Conversational Agents (ECA) [22], in the late '90s. Animated characters, with human features, able to simulate emotions with facial expressions and gestures, have been employed in different fields to interact with humans. They seem to be perceived as more trustworthy and agreeable, and are thus employed with the hope of being more readily accepted in everyday life applications than simple textual or spoken interfaces. Cassell et al. developed REA (Real Estate Agent) [4], a humanoid expert in real estates, that interacted with users and could sense them by means of cameras. Kopp et al. give another example of an ECA that has been used as a museum guide, in order to engage visitors and to interactively chat with them. In a real world study it was observed that users were inclined to use human-like communication strategies and that they perceived the agent as being sociable [19].

Instant messaging
After the success of browser chats at the beginning of the '90s, like IRC (Internet Relay Chat), the end of that decade has seen the spread of instant messaging services, such as AOL Instant Messaging (known as AIM), Yahoo! Messenger, and MSN Messenger. Many of these platforms allowed users to add bots to their contact lists as if they were real people: they could then exchange simple text messages and receive different kind of information [17]. A famous example of such a bot was *SmarterChild*, that could converse about breaking news and the weather.

Virtual Private Assistants
Only few years ago, "smart assistants" have started drawing the attention of the greater public. According to McTear et al., different reasons have influenced this new success of conversational interfaces [22]: the progresses in artificial intelligence assistive technologies, like speech and image recognition; the emergence of the semantic web; the increasing availability of connectivity and improvements in device hardware; and the renewed interest of big technology players. Apple's *Siri* (generally considered to be the the first public voice-enabled Virtual Private Assistant), Microsoft's *Cortana*, *Google Now* and *Google Assistant*, Amazon *Alexa*, and Samsung *S Voice* are the main actors of the last five years in the field of conversational interfaces.

Most notably, the reasons of the growing success of VPAs could also be explained by the many differences in respect to older personal assistants. First of all, smartphones have become pervasive in everyday life and are perceived as more personal than any other device. The same goes with the assistants, which are always present for the user. Modern assistants are perceived as more flexible: they are not limited to a very narrow task, but are able to interact with a plethora of applications, internal and external to the device [3]. The interaction is more "human-like", using simple, yet impressive tricks: the effort made to provide direct answers, in integrated and often spoken dialogs; improvements to the inference of the user's intents and the correction of ambiguities; better interpretations of the input's semantics; the capability of answering sassy questions, giving the illusion of a synthetic and likable personality. All these factors have probably made the luck of modern VPAs and the failure of older ones, like for instance *Wildfire*, a VPA of the mid '90s, multi-modal and phone based, but with poor human-like interaction capabilities [15].

Even though basic services of the aforementioned personal assistants are somewhat similar (including web search capabilities, event planning, voice calls and messaging, music playback, personalized notifications, weather information retrieval, etc.), some peculiar aspects can differentiate them. Siri and Cortana are the more similar ones, acting as personal assistants with a well defined "personality" that transpires in many of their answers. Google Now is also similar to these first two, but lacks a well defined personality and pulls information directly from the user's online Google Account, possibly raising some privacy questions. Samsung S Voice is probably the more "classical" one among the others and may not be perceived as personal like the other ones. Lastly, Amazon Alexa is going in a somewhat different direction: developed for Amazon Echo, a smart speaker, it brings the Internet of Things (IoT) closer to everyday life and it can be integrated with different other devices and services, especially in regard to home automation and entertainment.

It is also worth mentioning the IBM statistical responding agent called "Watson" [9], which stepped into the limelight in 2010 for participating in the "Jeopardy" television program. In that occasion Watson beat both his two human competitors only relying on an off-line database of unstructured contents. In more recent years, IBM further developed Watson, turning it into a powerful Artificial Intelligence (AI) assistant employed in health-care and custom-care scenarios. Watson can also be exploited as a cloud-based cognitive services of composable AI building blocks [37]. Developers can train the Watson AI to answer to answer questions posed in plain natural language about particular intent, and use it to build applications like chatbots.

The Rise of Bots

In the last couple of years a new approach to conversational interfaces has been reclaiming prominence: an apparent return to the classic *chatterbot* texting interfaces has been observed, with the main difference that these new bots have gained additional capabilities and now "live" in the cloud.

Starting in 2014, many online messaging systems (like Kik, Telegram, and WeChat) have opened up to third-party developers, offering the means to building bots and programmatically exchanging messages with users through their platforms. Application Programming Interfaces (APIs) for bots expose high level services (messaging, payments, bot directory, authentication, etc.) and UI elements (buttons, locations, images, etc.) giving developers the possibility of implementing innovative services through a conversational user experience.

Services offered by these new bots are of a higher level than the ones offered by their predecessors. Bots often feature access to other services that have utility in everyday life, such as ordering food, managing an e-commerce purchase, booking restaurants, ordering a cab, and so on. Examples include health care bots such as *Nombot* [11], a bot helping users to track their daily food consumption on Telegram; educational bots, like the one by Chaniago et al. that let parents track their children's presence at school [5]; educational help, like *MOOCBuddy* that proposes MOOC courses over Messenger [14].

It is also of note that the possibility of building more helpful and practical bots is in good part due to the increased availability of service APIs open to third-parties and the rise of the "platform" business model [7]. The recent decade has seen a growing attention to *open data* as well, which is increasingly made available by governments or administrative entities, also providing a useful foundation for many bots.

Since data and services are more and more accessible through programmatic interfaces, and given that bots often offer a simpler development platform than apps in terms of development and maintenance efforts, the task of offering access to such services through a conversation interface is very approachable.

Many of the major messaging platforms lately have started offering *bot directories*: repositories similar to app stores, listing the available bots that can be accessed through the platform.

Beyond "Chatbots"

In light of the recent resurgence in popularity of chatbots, we argue for a new and more significant taxonomy of autonomous conversational agents.

Firstly, the very nature of the term "chatbot" sets certain expectations about the agent's interactions: users may assume that a chatbot will be able to "chat" with them using natural language, but only a subset of autonomous agents are designed to simulate natural conversations. Agents that are not will inevitably fall short in their understanding of humans, who have been generally shown to tend to impatience when interacting with software agents [16, 3].

In fact, the "chat" verb trivializes the potential of bots, leading back to chatterbots as silly novelties with which to exchange messages on a command-line, mimicking human idiosyncrasies without any further purpose, just like with the aforementioned ELIZA chatterbot. Instead, as we discuss in the next section, bots have the potential to be a powerful and efficient software platform, only incidentally accessible through text messages.

BOTPLICATIONS

Among the plethora of new and old conversational interfaces, we identify a category of conversational agents that, having been designed according to principles of simplicity and effectiveness, can serve as functional replacements of mobile applications.

We call them "Botplications".

A Botplication is an agent that is endowed with a conversational interface accessible through a messaging platform, which provides access to data, services, or enables the user to perform a specific task.

In particular, a Botplication is generally characterized by the following distinguishing features.

Thread as app

Botplications are stepping stones in the evolution from an *app-centric* mobile OS experience—where the whole user experience of the device is concentrated in mostly independent applications that serve as an enclave of unique services and functions—to a *thread-centric* experience. That is, a user experience where services and information are provided as streams of messages and notifications, presented using a coherent and consistent set of interface paradigms.

Messaging threads are independent conversations that enclose personal relationships. Exchanging messages is in fact the primary method for users of a mobile OS to keep up relations with other people, in a very natural and intimate way. These personal conversations and relations can be naturally extended to services and businesses.

Each one of these threads is an entity that can send updates and notifications to the user, even in multiple parallel conversations, while taking advantage of the built-in facilities of the messaging system.

Among these facilities, for instance, the ability of users to retain total control over each single thread: they can chose to reply, mute the conversation, or even to permanently delete the thread. Also, threads have the capacity of keeping track of read/unread status and message drafts on multiple devices or platforms. The user has the ability to search for a message across all open threads, instead of having to remember in which particular app or service the information is hidden. Incoming messages on any thread are notified to the user in a familiar way.

Most modern messaging apps are in fact presented as a threaded "inbox", automatically grouping messages from the same sender and surfacing recently updated conversations that may be of interest. Instead of having new information dispersed across a number of isolated apps, each with its own custom interaction modes, users can rely on the fact that frequently or recently used services are automatically promoted to a visible position.

A user's "inbox" acts as a replacement for the app-centric homescreen of a mobile OS, where the most recent threads serve the same purpose of a dynamic list of favorite apps.

Conversation threads make it easy to provide integrated tools and services that make it easy to accomplish regular tasks, but in a recognizable and familiar place: a personal relationship developed through the exchange of text messages.

History awareness

Just like mobile apps, Botplications are designed to solve a specific and circumscribed issue. However, unlike most apps, Botplications inherently keep an exhaustive chronological log of past interactions with the user in their thread.

This ingrained feature of a thread of messages allows the user to explore past information in a familiar way, by scrolling through a timeline or by using built-in temporal search. Users can approach the service with more confidence, since past state appears frozen in previous messages and data does not unexpectedly vanish.

History can only change with familiar and explicit user actions, deep-seated in muscle memory for the majority of users used to receive and send text messages. New messages are appended to the history in a predictable and well-known way, while past interactions can be deleted through explicit action of the user.

History also serves as guidance to users, since past commands (and the results they generated) can be easily used as a template for future requests.

Also, past history provides the context in which all future interactions can be evaluated. Information collected by a Botplication *should* be maintained and used in order to streamline requests, skipping questions and automatically disambiguating between different choices if possible. A conversation is a natural and effective way to collect personal information, interests, purpose, and preferences of the user, all of which can be employed in order to improve the quality and accuracy of the service.

Enhanced UI

Despite the fact that Botplications derive from chatterbot-like conversational interfaces, their UI does not *have* to consist of mere plain text messages.

Modern messaging platforms support a variety of messages, including pictures, "stickers" (preset or custom images that convey emotion), videos, and audio. Most platforms also allow the transmission of packaged data, as in the case of geo-locations or contact information, in addition to generic data files. While these platforms of course do not offer the graphical capabilities of apps, it is important to make use of the features available and to exploit the conventions of the messaging platform. For instance, instead of printing out a raw URL, some platforms may display links as nicely formatted cards with a preview.

Moreover, on many messaging platforms even plain text messages can be enriched with a limited subset of rich text formatting. Bold, italic, and embedded links are the most common formatting options, available through markup languages such as a subset of HTML or Markdown. Unicode-encoded *emoji* characters can also be used to efficiently transmit additional meaning or to convey emotion.

Typing should be reduced to a minimum: ideally it should be limited to very short and concise commands and replies, of few characters. A fitting comparison can be done with UNIX commands, which are an example in terseness, as they were designed to efficiently work over teletypewriters—the primeval example of text-based interfaces—and reward users with powerful functionalities through very little typing.

Even if it can be argued that younger generations are getting more accustomed to typing on touch-based soft keyboards, the practice of shortening common words or using abbreviations in everyday messaging by itself demonstrates why full-fledged and verbose conversations should be avoided if possible. Interactions with Botplications should follow linear conversation routes and avoid complicated branching or multiple complex dialogs: anything that cannot be accessed through a couple of taps on the screen will become tiresome to most users. In a user study by Azenkot et al. the average text entry for all participants on a popular mobile OS keyboard was of 41.01 Words per Minute (WPM) [1]. Also, the theoretical maximum typing rate predicted by MacKenzie et al. was of 43.2 WPM for expert users on QWERTY keyboards [20], which is of course far lower to what can be achieved by expert typists on a physical keyboard [12]. Text interactions for mobile users should therefore be kept short and precise.

Many messaging platforms also feature advanced structured message forms, which can further enhance the flow of conversation. Structured messages may, for instance, contain buttons for preset "canned" replies, show different alternatives in a rich representation, or show a list of available commands. Examples of such messages are shown in the next section. The advantages of structured messages are manifold: (1) They constrain the conversation into a limited number of expected outcomes, reducing the possibility of users feeling trapped in a dead end where they have to "guess" their way out. (2) They push the user to use the service, suggesting how the conversation can continue. They also reduce the need for the users to "explore" the interface, making it easier to learn and use. (3) Buttons and quick replies reduce interactions to a single tap instead of requiring complex typing. (4) The service can be implemented more easily.

Botplications try to fill the gap between plain conversational interfaces—which are inherently inefficient to use and offer little way in terms of user experience customization—and the world of the full graphical interface.

Limited use of Natural Language Processing (NLP)

Given the aforementioned rising interest in Virtual Private Assistants (VPAs), voice appears to be a natural fit for conversational interfaces. However, to the best of our knowledge, existing bots on messaging platforms avoid voice processing and choose digital text as the most direct and unambiguous form of communication, possibly adopting NLP systems in order to extract commands and intent from the user's messages. Even if natural language understanding is getting progressively more advanced [3], in many scenarios complex dialogs break down because of simple misunderstandings, because of unexpected turns of phrase (human language shows incredible variation and rarely follows a script), or because the user's context cannot be fully elicited from the conversation [22, 2].

Botplications should not attempt to provide the complex experience of a full VPA. Instead, in keeping true to the principles of simplicity and effectiveness, Botplications should almost completely avoid natural language where possible. At the scale of a single bot, going after AI is mostly excessive and counterproductive, when the same results can be obtained with simple text commands using a limited structured language.

Botplications should in fact not pretend to be human: except in cases where this is desirable (e.g., for customer support or as a barrier before an actual conversations with a human operator is activated), it should be clear to users that they are talking to a machine. Even if artificial delays or "is typing" indicators can be used in order to make the conversation more familiar to the user, faking human responses risks to increase the perceived distance between service and user instead of decreasing it. Texting a computer that doesn't understand what the user is saying can be a frustrating experience, in particular when the computer hides its failures inside a dialog that is artificially kept "natural" and "human-like". This hides failure points in the conversation and makes the user feel less in control of the interaction.

However, this does not imply that bots shouldn't show a personality or take advantage of humor and emotional responses to provide a charming and likable interaction with users.

Botplications should rely on the limited—but accurate—interaction tools the messaging platform makes available, while NLP frameworks can optionally be employed to accommodate unforeseen user requests. AI and deep human-like dialogs are red herrings in the current development of conversational interfaces: Botplications should be about accessing services efficiently, a command-line-like interface to cloud-based APIs, not talkers.

Message self-consistency

Each single message sent by a Botplication should contain the full context of the conversation and should embody what a single UI screen represents for mobile apps. Users should not have to browse through their conversation history in order to figure out what they are attempting to do and what the service is expecting. Each message has an atomic meaning and stands on its own.

The scope of each message must be clear, its intent must be explicit, and what action must be taken by the user—if any—must be explicit and unequivocal. Indeed, a message delivered by a Botplication should be conceptually seen as a *micro application*, while the conversation is a timeline of past application screens. As mentioned before, structured forms of messages, which include buttons or commands, should be used where appropriate.

Some messaging platforms have, in fact, the ability to alter messages after they have been delivered. In that case, messages can be changed based on the availability of new data or other changes in state, giving the impression of a living view on the service.

Table 1: Features of major messaging platforms that support bots (as of October 2016).

Platform	MAU†	Groups	Mentions	Message types	Buttons	Carousel	Quick reply	Payment
Messenger	800 M			Picture, video, file, voice.	✓	✓	✓	✓
	Persistent menus, several message templates (Airline trip, Buy, Receipt, Web link, etc.).							
WeChat	700 M		✓	Picture, video, sticker, voice, location.			✓‡	✓
	Deep-links through QR codes, Rich media and Music messages. Integrated web views§.							
Skype	300 M			Picture, video.	✓	✓		
	Several message templates (Hero image, Thumbnail, Receipt, Sign-in, etc.), phone call support.							
Line	220 M	✓		Picture, video, sticker, voice, location.	✓	✓		
	Imagemap message template (picture with multiple hot-spots).							
Telegram	100 M	✓	✓	Picture, video, sticker, file, voice, location.			✓	
	Persistent commands. Deep-links to conversations.							
Kik	80 M	✓	✓	Picture, video, sticker, voice.			✓	
	Kik code identifiers, browser integration via Javascript.							
Slack	$\gtrsim$ 3 M	✓	✓	File.	✓			

† Monthly Active Users, based on most recent quarterly report published at the end of 2016. Numbers for Slack are an approximation based on known Daily Active Users.
‡ In the form of custom defined menus shown in the conversation UI.
§ WeUI, HTML/Javascript library that provides web-based UI elements coherent with the WeChat app: `https://weui.io/0.4.x/`.

Guided conversation

An important part of an application's user experience is based on user guidance and, likewise, the same care should be applied when designing conversational interfaces through text messages. In fact, because of the free-form nature of the medium, it is easy for bot users to get lost and not to be certain of what commands or what exact syntax is required to perform the desired action.

A successful Botplication guides the user through a task in order to avoid this impasse. The service proactively suggests actions that are likely to follow up after the current interaction, offers alternative choices when needed, and generally offers a framework in which user interactions feel reliable. This can be achieved using the same UI enhancements mentioned before, that is through the use of buttons, formatted messages, or built-in menus that offer interface guard rails to the conversation.

Also, notice that when starting the first interaction with a bot, many messaging platforms offer a way to show a welcome message to the user. The design of the onboarding experience must take into account the initial user guidance and ensure that all functionalities are readily available.

TECHNOLOGICAL SURVEY

In this section the most popular messaging platforms that support bots through their APIs will be taken into exam, describing distinguishing features of each one.

All of the platforms mentioned allow third-party developers to register an identity for a virtual agent and to programmatically receive messages from any user of the platform, either by accessing an API end-point (*pull* mode) or by being called back by the platform itself using a "web-hook" (*push* mode). All platforms, in any mode, make use of the HTTP protocol.

The *Kik* messenger service launched in 2010 and introduced bots in 2014. On April 2016 the platform launched a "bot-shop", which includes a directory of available service bots. *WeChat* is a popular IM system in China, first launched in 2011, that always included more features than simple messaging. The platform includes support for "Official accounts", which can provide services to users. It includes a payment system that allows the exchange of monetary gifts, known as "red envelopes". *Telegram* published its bot support API on July 2015, further expanding it with the 2.0 API in April 2016. *Line* also launched its first messenger API in 2015, while Facebook's *Messenger* and *Skype* joined the game only later, including support for bots in April 2016. The former also added support for payments in September 2016.

Given the rising interest in bots, most platforms are rapidly iterating and evolving their APIs and services to third-party developers. This survey is updated to March 2017.

In Table 1 the platforms considered in this study are listed, firstly reporting the amount of *Monthly Active Users* (MAU), which gives an approximation of the relative popularity of each system. Furthermore, the table shows whether the platform supports *group messaging* (i.e., if one or more bots can be added to a group conversation between real users) and *mentions* (i.e., if bots can be "called into" a conversation using a special combination of characters). Both of these features allow bots to be used in order to perform specific tasks for a group of users instead of only one. The table also reports the different *message types* supported by the platform (including pictures, voice, video, stickers, and structured messages, discussed in the next section) and other significant features.

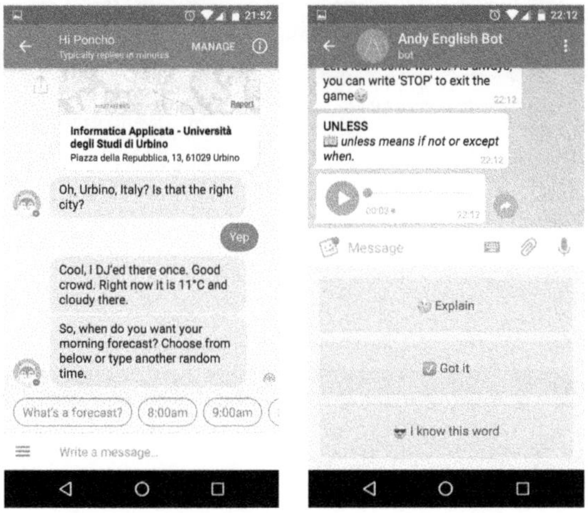

(a) (b)

Figure 1: Features that allow users to pick suggested replies. (a) *Quick replies* on Messenger. (b) *Button keyboard* on Telegram.

Interface features

Messaging platforms distinguish themselves not only for their underlying technical aspects, but also because of the different user interface elements they offer to bot developers and, ultimately, to the end-users. While sending and receiving text and basic multimedia messages is a common feature, more structured messages are available only on some platforms and often differ in key aspects.

Many platforms offer a way to suggest canned replies, which can be sent with a single tap. For instance, on Messenger bots may display a selection of *quick replies* that appear on the bottom of the conversation and remain valid for one interaction, as shown in Figure 1a. On Telegram and Kik, bots have the ability to replace the keyboard with suggested responses, as shown in Figure 1b.

While these preset replies can change in the course of the conversation, other UI features can immutably be added to the chat. In Figure 2a a list of *commands* are shown. On Telegram, like on Slack, commands are characterized by starting with a '/' character and are always available to the user to perform tasks in a command line-like experience. A similar system, but with a hierarchical structure, is shown in Figure 2b: WeChat allows developers to add a fixed menu to the chat interface, showing a maximum of 3 first-level options and several second-level ones. The same system has been also adopted by Messenger in March 2017. Commands and menus alike give direct access to a bot's main features.

Other UI features are not bound to the overall conversation, but are instead tied to a specific message. For instance, *carousel* messages shown in Figure 3a make it possible to include multiple rich cards, provided with an image, a description, and a button, and make them horizontally scrollable to the user.

In Figure 3b a message with *embedded buttons* is shown: in this case the actions provided to the user are not persistent throughout the conversation, but are limited to one single interaction. Both message formats allow bot developers to show available alternatives to the user, providing a well defined path for the conversation.

Several other message formats are available to specific platforms, among which messages including a "Buy" link for shopping-oriented bots, messages with music support in WeChat, and flight travel itinerary messages on Messenger.

In terms of making bots interoperate with external systems, it is noteworthy that several messaging platforms have included support for QR Codes or variations thereof. On WeChat, code scanning can be used internally to the system in order to send payments of a preset value to a given contact, which makes the platform compelling for sellers of physical goods as well. On the other hand, Skype, Telegram, and Messenger allow web sites and apps to launch conversations through the use of a specially marked URL. Such URLs include a custom data payload that is sent to the bot in order to track user entry points or to invoke specific actions. This mechanism—also known as "deep linking"—can be used to embed bots in innovative and complex workflows [18].

Advantages of Bots for users

Instant availability

Bots do not need to be downloaded and installed: they are immediately up and running as soon as a conversation is started inside the messaging app. Device storage capacity, installation, and complex configuration steps are not required. This makes bots fast and lightweight, if compared to traditional mobile apps.

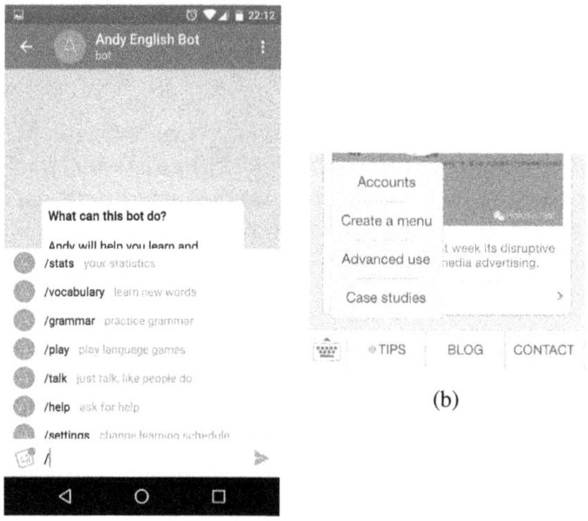

(a) (b)

Figure 2: Structured commands available during the whole conversation. (a) *Commands* on Telegram. (b) *Custom defined menu* (with an open second-level menu) on WeChat.

"Instant Apps", a technology for Android still in development, will bring a similar experience to apps as well, making them instantly available to users without installations[1].

Gentle learning curve

Texting has been used since the dawn of mobile phones and this makes it quite natural for users of any skill level. Provided that the bot provides adequate guidance through its features, learning how to interact with it is never an outlandish experience.

Since all bots on the same messaging platform rely on the same UI building-blocks (such as buttons, carousels, quick-replies, and so forth, down to the basic text messages), all bots share a common UI vocabulary. Knowledge in the use of one bot can easily be transfered to the usage of other bots.

Notifications

Many mobile applications implement their own notification system, used as a mean to re-engage inactive users. Instant messaging applications however already include an efficient and functional push notification system, which is available by default without any additional implementation effort.

According to statistics by Localytics[2], more than 50% of users find push notifications annoying. However, receiving notifications through the messaging apps could be perceived as being less invasive.

Social graph and contacts

Users are already accustomed to voluntarily sharing and storing contact information in messaging apps. In fact, as soon as a bot conversation is initiated, the bot automatically receives the user's basic personal data. When participating in a group conversation with multiple users, bots also gain access to the contact information of all participants.

Moreover, all contents generated by an interaction with the bot exist in the form of messages, which can be directly forwarded and shared with friends. Thus contact to the bot can be spread through a user's social graph, without leaving the messaging app or installing new applications.

Platform independence

Bots live inside instant messaging applications without having to worry about which mobile platform they are running on. This makes bots independent from the underlying host operating system: each bot is inherently available on all operating systems the messaging app supports, without any graphical or functional adjustment.

On the contrary, native mobile applications must be adapted or rewritten for each mobile operating system, often with great effort. Users sometimes perceive the same application as being different if they are using it on different operating systems, which can frustrate user engagement. Also, mobile applications must be frequently updated in order to keep up with upgrades to the host system and its features.

[1] `http://developer.android.com/topic/instant-apps/`

[2] `http:/info.localytics.com/blog/the-inside-view-how-consumers-really-feel-about-push-notifications`
Accessed: 2016-10-10.

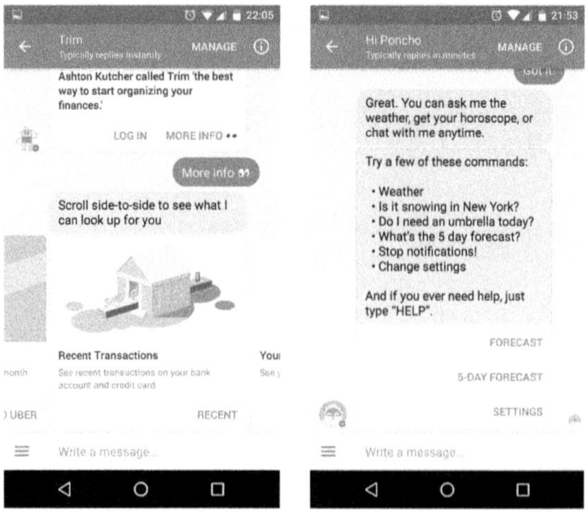

(a) (b)

Figure 3: Structured message templates in Messenger. (a) *Carousel* presenting multiple choices through horizontal scrolling. (b) *Message buttons* embedded in a message.

Authentication

Usually, for each new application or service, users need to register and go through the steps of creating a new account. This is a known obstacle to user onboarding, who notably dislike long registration processes and often do not remember new account credentials.

In contrast, user authentication is not needed in bots. The hosting messaging platform already provides and guarantees the user's identity reliably. Users are uniquely identified by default and they do not have to create additional accounts and passwords in order to interact with the service.

Payment support

Some of the analyzed platforms include payment services, integrated in the messaging system. Often users will have already connected their credit cards or bank accounts to such services, allowing bots to use the existing payment methods in a safe and reliable manner, for both user and developer. In contrast, for each brand new app requiring payment capabilities, users have to re-connect their payment accounts and have to trust the newly installed app.

Discoverability

As seen previously, discoverability is a very real problem for mobile application on application stores: fierce competition and very small economic margins often make it very hard to compete and gain visibility. The same issues exist for bots. Even if many messaging platforms offer "bot stores" with a selection of available bots, emerging and gaining a solid user base remains one of the main development issues. However, bots have some advantages considering that they can be easily integrated in group conversations or shared just like any other contact.

Asynchronicity

Exchanging instant messages is an asynchronous task: after sending a message, users do not have to wait for a reply. Conversation threads store the context, letting user free of leaving a conversation and going back to it later, picking up the dialog from the very last interaction. Multiple conversations can be easily carried forward in parallel.

Limited data requirements
Downloading a new app can have a sizable impact on a limited mobile data plan, whereas starting to use a new bot only requires to initiate a new thread in an existing messaging app, with a negligible impact in terms of data traffic. The data size of exchanged messages in an instant messaging app is limited and usually more predictable. This makes bots very attractive for users with limited data plans or in countries with less developed technological infrastructure [24]. In fact, Facebook recently developed "Lite" versions of its applications, specifically targeted at emerging markets, where limited data plans are more common [36].

Advantages of Bots for developers

Communication reliability
Instant messaging applications are naturally designed for fast and efficient message delivery. They are capable of dealing with all kinds of network issues, automatically retrying transmissions and ensuring that the message is either delivered or that failure is handled adequately or correctly reported to the user. Security and privacy of transmitted messages are also guaranteed by many platforms.

On the other hand, mobile applications must implement most of these networking features independently, incurring in the likely risk of bugs or security issues. These issues are multiplied in case of multi-platform applications.

Fast iteration
Since a bot's logic is implemented server-side and no code must be deployed onto user devices, deployment is effectively effortless. Similarly to what happens for web pages or web apps, bot updates are also almost immediately propagated to all users. This form of deployment also completely avoids issues with app stores, for instance due to rejections or delays during application review. This allows for fast and uncomplicated development iterations.

Lack of version fragmentation
The immediate propagation of updates to all users also means that no user risks staying stuck with an old version of a mobile application: just like web apps, bots are always updated to the latest version.

Limited design efforts
Bots heavily rely on the instant messaging application UI and usually have quite limited possibilities of graphical customization. This reduces the interface design time, limiting it to minor customizations of interface elements and focusing on a rich user experience using few simple building-blocks.

Development ease
As seen in the previous sections, several important and demanding services are already implemented by the messaging platform. Services such as user authentication or payments normally require major efforts and attention by mobile app developers. Bots however already include many of these services, which are ready to use through developer APIs.

Moreover, having a generally smaller API surface—which can be used through any development platform and language—developing a bot is generally cheaper and less time demanding than the development of a mobile application.

DISCUSSION

As previously examined, the mobile device ecosystem has been characterized by the popularity of mobile apps and app stores as a software distribution platform in the last decade. Recent statistics have however shown that users tend to rely almost exclusively on a very restricted set of consolidated, preferred apps, instead of trying out new ones, leading the number of new downloaded apps nearly to zero in the short-medium period [8]. Moreover, a 2014 report has also shown the surprising overtake of online messaging platforms usage over social network apps [35].

Bots on instant messaging platforms have recently started gaining widespread interest. As discussed above, not only do bots rely on very popular messaging apps, they also eschew many of the difficulties of mobile app development and distribution. In fact, bots can increasingly be considered as a novel approach to the software distribution problem.

From this point of view, bots show many similarities with mobile web apps, as a distribution system competing with native mobile applications [6]:

1. they allow the development of multi-platform services using a commonly available platform (messaging apps or the web),
2. they are partly limited in terms of what features of the mobile device they have access to (this is particularly true for bots, which however have a different usage paradigm with different expectations from users),
3. the "look and feel" is different from a native app (however, while the user experience of mobile web apps may be different from what users are accustomed to, bots offer a very familiar interface that feels native to the messaging app at least),
4. both approaches favor developers in terms of development, distribution, and maintenance efforts, however bots also ensure a high ease of use to end-users.

These advantages notwithstanding, there are different drawbacks to bots that must be taken into consideration when evaluating their merits as a software platform.

In the first place, not every application is well suited for conversational interfaces. There are several tasks that are inherently more convenient to be tackled by means of a dedicated app, with access to local computational resources and data storage, instead of a remote bot. Other tasks simply work better with a rich visual interactions that goes beyond what a conversational interface can offer.

Even if bot development is very approachable by developers and offers many advanced features at essentially very little effort, a bot is tightly bound to its messaging platform, which may lead to design constraints. There are, very noticeably, inherent limits to the customization of UI elements, the look and feel, and finer details of the user experience.

Bots require an active Internet connection in order to work (in contrast to modern mobile web apps, which may provide an offline experience). This can create discontinuities in service availability and negatively affect the bot's perceived reliability, in case of lacking network coverage or limited data plans, especially in growing markets [24].

Despite the appearance of "bot directories", discoverability is still a crucial issue that must be tackled both by developers and bot platforms. Also, the risk of an overpopulation of bots that hinders the discovery of new services, like for app stores, is equally likely.

Many recent efforts in the field of bots have made use of natural language processing in order to create a generic conversational interface, supporting natural human-like interactions. There is however an inherent distinction between conversational virtual assistants (such as Amazon *Alexa* or Apple's *Siri*), which are well-suited to interactions through spoken natural language, and service-oriented bots, that currently benefit from structured input. While the first kind of bots may provide a more convenient, and in some cases instinctive, interface, the latter can focus on providing a more efficient and lean experience. Also, NLP capabilities are presently not always sufficient to fulfill natural-feeling conversations and they still impose a learning curve on users [3, 2].

Even though some of these issues can be addressed and mitigated in the near future, there are inherent limitations to what bots can offer, which limit how far they can serve as a replacement to native and web apps.

The relative novelty of bots must also be taken into account: the first roots for the spread of bots have been put down, but we are still in the very early days of this new era. A "killer application" for bot platforms, which goes "viral" and fully justifies the rising interest by clearly showing the full potential of bots, is yet to be seen.

Conclusions

In this work the spread of the new generation of bots on messaging platforms has been discussed, describing how the concept of "bot" has changed from its very first stages to the present days.

A definition of *Botplications* has been given, as a conversational agent living on existing messaging platforms, that follows a set of principles of simplicity and purposefulness in providing access to services and data.

Features and limitations of the most prominent messaging platforms have been presented and compared. A technological survey, depicting in detail the peculiar available user interface mechanisms, and advantages of bots, for both users and developers, were discussed in detail.

In conclusion, even if bots will not substitute the whole mobile application ecosystem in the near future, close attention must be paid to the "rise of bots", as a new software platform for delivering services and data to users.

REFERENCES

1. Shiri Azenkot and Shumin Zhai. 2012. Touch behavior with different postures on soft smartphone keyboards. In *Proceedings of the 14th international conference on Human-computer interaction with mobile devices and services*. ACM, 251–260.
2. Emanuele Bastianelli, Daniele Nardi, Luigia Carlucci Aiello, Fabrizio Giacomelli, and Nicolamaria Manes. 2016. Speaky for robots: the development of vocal interfaces for robotic applications. *Applied Intelligence* 44, 1 (2016), 43–66. DOI: http://dx.doi.org/10.1007/s10489-015-0695-5
3. Jerome R Bellegarda. 2014. Spoken language understanding for natural interaction: The Siri experience. In *Natural Interaction with Robots, Knowbots and Smartphones*. Springer, 3–14.
4. Justine Cassell, Timothy Bickmore, Mark Billinghurst, Lee Campbell, Kenny Chang, Hannes Vilhjálmsson, and Hao Yan. 1999. Embodiment in conversational interfaces: Rea. In *Proceedings of the SIGCHI conference on Human Factors in Computing Systems*. ACM, 520–527.
5. Muhammad Benny Chaniago and Apri Junaidi. 2016. Student Presence Using RFID and Telegram Messenger Application. 8th Widyatama International Seminar on Sustainability (WISS 2016), Widyatama University and IEEE.
6. Andre Charland and Brian Leroux. 2011. Mobile Application Development: Web vs. Native. *Commun. ACM* 54, 5 (May 2011), 49–53. DOI: http://dx.doi.org/10.1145/1941487.1941504
7. Sangeet Paul Choudary, Marshall W Van Alstyne, and Geoffrey G Parker. 2016. Platform revolution: How networked markets are transforming the economy–and how to make them work for you. (2016).
8. comScore. 2014. The U.S. Mobile App Report. URL https://www.comscore.com/Insights/Presentations-and-Whitepapers/2014/The-US-Mobile-App-Report. (2014). Accessed: 2016-10-10.
9. David Ferrucci, Eric Brown, Jennifer Chu-Carroll, James Fan, David Gondek, Aditya A Kalyanpur, Adam Lally, J William Murdock, Eric Nyberg, John Prager, and others. 2010. Building Watson: An overview of the DeepQA project. *AI magazine* 31, 3 (2010), 59–79.
10. FA Fonte, Juan Carlos, Burguillo Rial, and Martín Llamas Nistal. 2009. TQ-Bot: an AIML-based tutor and evaluator bot. *Journal of Universal Computer Science* 15, 7 (2009), 1486–1495.
11. Bettina Graf, Maike Krüger, Felix Müller, Alexander Ruhland, and Andrea Zech. 2015. Nombot: simplify food

tracking. In *Proceedings of the 14th International Conference on Mobile and Ubiquitous Multimedia*. ACM, 360–363.

12. Nathan Green, Jan Kruger, Chirag Faldu, and Robert St. Amant. 2004. A Reduced QWERTY Keyboard for Mobile Text Entry. In *CHI '04 Extended Abstracts on Human Factors in Computing Systems (CHI EA '04)*. ACM, New York, NY, USA, 1429–1432. DOI: http://dx.doi.org/10.1145/985921.986082
13. Charles T Hemphill, John J Godfrey, and George R Doddington. 1990. The ATIS spoken language systems pilot corpus. In *Proceedings of the DARPA speech and natural language workshop*. 96–101.
14. Adrian Iftene and Jean Vanderdonckt. 2016. MOOCBuddy: a chatbot for personalized learning with MOOCs. In *RoCHI–International Conference on Human-Computer Interaction*. 91.
15. Philippe Jeanrenaud, Greg Cockroft, and Allard VanderHeidjen. 1999. A multimodal, multilingual telephone application: the wildfire electronic assistant.. In *EUROSPEECH*.
16. Henry Kautz, Bart Selman, Michael Coen, Steven Ketchpel, and Chris Ramming. 1994. An experiment in the design of software agents. In *AAAI*. 438–443.
17. Ian R Kerr. 2004. Bots, babes and the californication of commerce. *University of Ottawa Law and Technology Journal* 1, 1-2 (2004), 20004.
18. Lorenz Cuno Klopfenstein and Alessandro Bogliolo. 2017. The Quiz-Master Bot: a persistent augmented quiz delivered through online messaging. In *INTED2017 Proceedings (11th International Technology, Education and Development Conference)*. IATED, 9806–9811. DOI: http://dx.doi.org/10.21125/inted.2017.2328
19. Stefan Kopp, Lars Gesellensetter, Nicole C Krämer, and Ipke Wachsmuth. 2005. A conversational agent as museum guide–design and evaluation of a real-world application. In *International Workshop on Intelligent Virtual Agents*. Springer, 329–343.
20. I Scott MacKenzie, Shawn X Zhang, and R William Soukoreff. 1999. Text entry using soft keyboards. *Behaviour & Information technology* 18, 4 (1999), 235–244.
21. RP Mahapatra, Naresh Sharma, Aakash Trivedi, and Chitransh Aman. 2012. Adding interactive interface to E-Government systems using AIML based chatterbots. In *Software Engineering (CONSEG), 2012 CSI Sixth International Conference on*. IEEE, 1–6.
22. Michael McTear, Zoraida Callejas, and David Griol. 2016. *The Conversational Interface*. Springer.
23. Fernando A Mikic, Juan C Burguillo, Martín Llamas, Daniel A Rodríguez, and Eduardo Rodríguez. 2009. CHARLIE: An AIML-based Chatterbot which Works as an Interface among INES and Humans. In *EAEEIE Annual Conference, 2009*. IEEE, 1–6.
24. San Murugesan. 2013. Mobile apps in Africa. *IT Professional* 15, 5 (2013), 8–11.
25. Jeremy Peckham. 1991. Speech Understanding and Dialogue over the telephone: an overview of the ESPRIT SUNDIAL project.. In *HLT*.
26. Antonella Santangelo, Agnese Augello, Antonio Gentile, Giovanni Pilato, and Salvatore Gaglio. 2006. A Chat-bot based Multimodal Virtual Guide for Cultural Heritage Tours.. In *PSC*. 114–120.
27. Md Shahriare Satu, Md Hasnat Parvez, and others. 2015. Review of integrated applications with AIML based chatbot. In *2015 International Conference on Computer and Information Engineering (ICCIE)*. IEEE, 87–90.
28. Stephanie Seneff and Joseph Polifroni. 2000. Dialogue Management in the Mercury Flight Reservation System. In *Proceedings of the 2000 ANLP/NAACL Workshop on Conversational Systems - Volume 3 (ANLP/NAACL-ConvSyst '00)*. Association for Computational Linguistics, Stroudsburg, PA, USA, 11–16. DOI: http://dx.doi.org/10.3115/1117562.1117565
29. Abu Shawar, Eric Atwell, and Andrew Roberts. 2005. FAQchat as in Information Retrieval system. In *Human Language Technologies as a Challenge for Computer Science and Linguistics: Proceedings of the 2nd Language and Technology Conference*. PoznanÌĄ: Wydawnictwo PoznanÌĄskie: with co-operation of Fundacja Uniwersytetu im. A. Mickiewicza, 274–278.
30. Bayan Abu Shawar and Eric Atwell. 2007. Chatbots: are they really useful?. In *LDV Forum*, Vol. 22. 29–49.
31. Alan M Turing. 1950. Computing machinery and intelligence. *Mind* 59, 236 (1950), 433–460.
32. Richard Wallace. 2003. The elements of AIML style. *Alice AI Foundation* (2003).
33. Richard S Wallace. 2009. The anatomy of ALICE. In *Parsing the Turing Test*. Springer, 181–210.
34. Joseph Weizenbaum. 1966. ELIZA - a Computer Program for the Study of Natural Language Communication Between Man and Machine. *Commun. ACM* 9, 1 (Jan. 1966), 36–45. DOI: http://dx.doi.org/10.1145/365153.365168
35. Will McKitterick. 2015. *The Messaging App Report: How instant messaging can be monetized*. Technical Report.
36. Susan P. Wyche, Sarita Yardi Schoenebeck, and Andrea Forte. 2013. "Facebook is a Luxury": An Exploratory Study of Social Media Use in Rural Kenya. In *Proceedings of the 2013 Conference on Computer Supported Cooperative Work (CSCW '13)*. ACM, New York, NY, USA, 33–44. DOI: http://dx.doi.org/10.1145/2441776.2441783
37. Mengting Yan, Paul Castro, Perry Cheng, and Vatche Ishakian. 2016. Building a Chatbot with Serverless Computing. In *Proceedings of the 1st International Workshop on Mashups of Things and APIs*. ACM, 5.

Real-Fictional Entanglements: Using Science Fiction and Design Fiction to Interrogate Sensing Technologies

Richmond Y. Wong
BioSENSE Lab, UC Berkeley
School of Information
Berkeley, California, USA
richmond@ischool.berkeley.edu

Ellen Van Wyk
UC Berkeley
School of Information
Berkeley, California, USA
ejvw@berkeley.edu

James Pierce
UC Berkeley, Jacobs Institute
for Design Innovation
Berkeley, California, USA
pierjam@berkeley.edu

ABSTRACT
We present a set of design fiction proposals related to sensing and tracking technologies, inspired by the 2013 science fiction novel *The Circle*. By creating design proposals that explore connections between the novel's imagined world and our present and future realities, we show that we are able to explore, expand, and articulate a range of social, technical, and legal configurations of the future. This paper contributes a set of design fiction proposals and a case study of a design project that uses design fiction inspired by a science fiction text to engage issues of privacy and surveillance. The paper also provides a new approach to creating design fiction, by using science fiction texts as a starting point.

Author Keywords
Design fiction; science fiction; privacy; design workbooks;

ACM Classification Keywords
H.5.m. Information interfaces and presentation (e.g., HCI): Miscellaneous;

INTRODUCTION
Emerging sensing and tracking technologies often seem like something straight out of science fiction, although their implications for the future can be very unclear. Our work aims to better understand the privacy implications of emerging and near-future sensing technologies. Many such technologies are developed and studied by HCI researchers, such as detecting heartbeats from a distance [1], image analysis [11,23], or wearable sensors [21,49]. Social issues (including privacy) related to these technologies are often explored through technical research or user studies. Here, however, we engage with these technologies and issues by adopting a design approach involving the creation of design fictions in order to explore near-future scenarios.

DIS 2017, June 10-14, 2017, Edinburgh, United Kingdom

ACM 978-1-4503-4922-2/17/06...$15.00
DOI: http://dx.doi.org/10.1145/3064663.3064682

Figure 1. A screenshot of early design ideas and references, shared among the authors on a tumblr blog.

Inspired by fictional sensing technology products from the 2013 fiction novel *The Circle*, this paper uses a design workbook to develop variations of visual design fiction proposals, exploring privacy and surveillance implications of sensing technologies. This work develops and deploys design fictions in a novel way: by explicitly adapting written science fiction we tap into an author's existing richly imagined world, rather than creating our own imagined world from scratch or being implicitly inspired by ideas from science fiction. Adapting fictional worlds from literature allows researchers who are not professional fiction writers to engage in creating design fictions. This helps us engage ideas in the cultural imagination, forging a bridge between popular speculative fiction and research.

This paper provides three main contributions. First it contributes a workbook of visual design fiction proposals; second it presents a case study addressing how researchers can understand and make use of cultural representations of new and emerging technologies to interrogate their privacy implications; third it points towards a design approach for creating design fictions by using science fiction texts as a starting point. In the following sections, we review prior work and discuss why we find *The Circle* a useful starting point for our work. We next present our designs and analyze them through a privacy framework. We then step back and reflect more broadly on our design approach.

ENGAGING FICTION IN PRIOR WORK

Researchers, particularly in design and HCI, have engaged with fiction in a number of ways which contribute to our approach. Bleecker provided one of the first discussions of "design fiction," placing it as an authorial practice that exists in the space between science fiction and science fact, using yet-to-be-realized design concepts to understand, explore, and question possible alternative futures [4]. Bleecker and Kirby describe "diegetic prototypes," noting that design fiction objects exist within a narrative or story world [4,22]. Other authors expand on how these diegetic design fiction "props" help imply or create a fictional world in which they exist [9,25].This suggests that design fictions must be considered in relation to sociocultural contexts.

In the design research community, design fiction has been predominantly deployed in one of two ways. First, a line of work uses the process of making design fictions as a method of inquiry. Blythe has used fictional abstracts to interrogate the genre of research papers [5], expanded upon by Lindley and Coulton who use fictional research papers to examine and critique practices in the HCI community [27]. Design fictions have increasingly taken non-textual forms, including textual-visual artifacts studying the roles of "counterfunctionals" [36], videos exploring sustainability futures [19], and creating material artifacts as design fictions [7,48]. These bring attention to the exploratory and critical roles the process of *making* design fictions can play. A second line of work uses the lens of design fiction to analyze diegetic practices and narratives, including the practices of steampunk communities [46] or concept videos that portray corporate futures [52]. Tanenbaum et al.'s analysis of the film *Mad Max: Fury Road* [45] and Lindley et al.'s analysis of *Her* [28] suggest considering science fiction films as design fictions. These authors use design fiction as an *analytical lens* to interrogate fictional worlds created by others, particularly ones in popular culture.

We bring these lines of work together by creating new design fictions to both analyze an existing fictional world from a novel, and to ask and explore new questions about privacy. Instead of using science fiction media as objects of analysis, we use a science fiction text as a starting point to create our own design fiction artifacts.

Our work builds on past connections drawn among design, research, fiction, and public imagination [29]. For researchers and designers, science fiction has helped shape the field of ubiquitous computing [13] and inspired interface and interaction design [37]. Pastiche scenarios use characters from fiction in design scenarios to flesh out personas [6]. Sturdee et al. explicitly find inspiration in the sci-fi film *Blade Runner* to create design fiction [42], while Dunne and Raby's "United Micro Kingdoms" Train design fiction [14] appears implicitly inspired by the film *Snowpiercer*. Literary scholars note how science fiction has garnered more literary respect in recent years and how literature engages technology in complex (and not purely adversarial) ways [16]. Fictional representations of technology also take hold in the public imagination, such as the vernacular use of "big brother" from George Orwell's dystopian novel *1984* or the popularity of the speculative fiction anthology show *Black Mirror*. Public processes of imagination are facilitated in part through cultural and media production, including advertisements [18,52] and films [45]. Design fictions and speculative designs appear to hold similar potential, such as Superflux's *Drone Aviary* [43] and Matsuda's *HYPER-REALITY* [30] videos which have been viewed by hundreds of thousands of people. Our work contributes to understanding the 'infrastructuring' of new technologies [40] by using design fiction as a bridge between technical and design research, and popular culture representations of future technologies.

CREATING DESIGN WORKBOOKS FROM FICTION

Our design work draws from the fictional world of *The Circle*, a 2013 novel by Dave Eggers. Set at an unspecified time in the near-future, the novel focuses on Mae, a new employee at The Circle, the most powerful internet company in the world. The Circle (the company) provides services like social media, email, and personal finance, and creates hardware devices like cameras and health-monitoring bracelets. In the story, consumers are encouraged to share more and more details of their lives online in the name of transparency and knowledge building. The Circle uses its power to limit users' desire and ability to opt out of its systems. Though critical of technology, the novel is not dystopian. Rather it employs a dark humor, as throughout the story new technologies and services are introduced in the name of providing greater user value, though to the reader they may seem increasingly invasive.

The Circle (the novel) presents an opportunity to look at a contemporary popular depiction of sensing technologies, and reflects timely concerns about privacy and increasing data collection. We have no interest here in assessing the literary or cultural quality of the novel. Rather we were drawn to the novel as it was a New York Times bestseller, and thus a noteworthy part of the public discourse about the social, political, and ethical implications of new sensing technologies. We were also drawn to news that a film adaptation of the novel was in production, suggesting that the story will play a larger role in the public imagination after its release.[1] *The Circle* can be viewed as science fiction, defined broadly, using a near-future narrative to explore social issues related to fictional technologies that have a discernible basis in what is being developed today.

While prior design fictions incidentally touch on privacy (such as gestures towards data collection concerns in "Game of Drones" [26] and the "Future IKEA Catalogue" [10]), we wanted to use design fiction to explore a space of

[1] Our designs were created before the film adaptation's release in 2017 and represent our visual interpretation of the novel's world.

possible futures involving sensing technologies' potential privacy implications. We turned to design workbooks as our method to open this space, and to a privacy framework to analyze and map the breadth of our explorations.

We follow the design workbook method to create a set of design fiction proposals. Design workbooks are collections of design proposals or conceptual designs, drawn together to investigate, explore, reflect on, and expand a design space; they purposely lack implementation details, allowing designers and workbook viewers to reflect, speculate, and generate multiple stories of possible use [17]. Grounded in our readings of *The Circle*, we chose a set of sensing technologies that might be interesting to explore variations upon. Our goal was to create a set of proposals to open a design space of possible futures that would both include and expand beyond the future described in the book. We also wanted to see what new themes might emerge over time. Designs were primarily brainstormed and created by the second and first authors, shared among all authors through a blog (Figure 1), and periodically all three authors would discuss the design ideas to reflect on what questions and themes arose from the designs. The first author worked on a separate but related project using surveys to explore respondents' reactions to technologies from *The Circle*. Qualitative responses from that project's pilot survey were shared with the authors to provide design inspiration.

Our designs make use of two design genres: "interfaces," and "products and services." Our interface designs imagine what these technologies' user interfaces might look like. Product and service designs play on the genres of Amazon product pages, or websites for startups, products, and services. These genres help us think about the designs as everyday objects and imagine how they might be situated in the world. To create the interfaces we used Photoshop, Illustrator, and Sketch. To create the product and service pages we adapted HTML and CSS from websites including Amazon.com and getbootstrap.com. We included a variety of public domain stock images, hand drawn illustrations, and photos that the second author staged and shot as assets.

Given our interest in privacy and surveillance concerns, we looked to privacy literature, finding that contemporary approaches view privacy as *contextual* [32]; that is, the same technologies can preserve or violate privacy in different social contexts. Furthermore, Mulligan et al.'s privacy analytic framework suggests that rather than attempting to discuss privacy under a single definition (which can be debated endlessly, e.g.[38,39,50]), it is more productive to map how various *dimensions* of privacy are represented in *particular situations* [31]. Their dimensions include: theory (why there should be privacy), protection (who and what is being protected by privacy), harm (actions and actors who violate privacy), provision (what mechanisms provide privacy protection), and scope (how broadly does privacy apply) [31]. This review of the literature led us to focus on creating variations on our designs by placing them into new contexts and new social situations to change the values of these dimensions.

We began our first set of designs by trying to visually imagine the technologies described in *The Circle*, staying as close to the textual descriptions as possible. We then discussed privacy themes emerging from the designs. We did two more rounds of design iterations to explore new combinations of privacy dimensions creating variations on our first set of designs. In these iterations, we used new social contexts, put the technologies in the hands of different users, or integrated Eggers' fictional technologies with real-world contexts and technologies. After each round of iteration, we evaluated how our collection of designs mapped onto Mulligan et al.'s dimensions. We ended our iterations after finding we explored a wide variety of combinations of privacy dimensions, suggesting that we had opened and broadened our design space.

USING TECHNOLOGIES FROM *THE CIRCLE*

Our design fiction proposals draw from three technologies presented in *The Circle*. While reading the novel, we noted that the story reminded us of several non-fictional technologies. To diversify and blend our design work with non-fictional technologies, some proposals are based on a fourth real technology currently being developed but could fit into the novel's story world. We provide a brief summary of Eggers' three technologies from *The Circle* and a description of the fourth non-fictional technology.[2]

SeeChange

SeeChange is the most prominent technology introduced in the novel. It is described as a small camera, about the size of a lollipop, which wirelessly records and broadcasts live high-definition video. Its battery lasts for 2 years without recharging. It can be used indoors or outdoors and can be mounted discreetly. Live video streams from the cameras can be shared with anyone online. The story introduces the cameras as a way to monitor outdoor sports locations, share video streams for entertainment, or monitor spaces to prevent crimes. Later in the story, SeeChange becomes ubiquitous: they are placed in Mae's parents' house while they undergo medical treatment; worn continuously by elected officials to ensure democratic transparency; and eventually worn by Mae to promote The Circle to consumers through a constant live personal video stream. Below is a short excerpt from the novel which takes place during SeeChange's product launch, in which a lead executive from The Circle publicly demos the product.

SeeChange Excerpt from The Circle

"I set up that camera this morning. I taped it to a stake, stuck that stake in the sand, in the dunes, with no permit, nothing. In fact, no one knows it's there. So this morning I turned it on, then I drove back to the office, accessed Camera One, Stinson Beach, and I got this image. Actually, I was pretty busy this morning. I drove

[2] **Spoiler alert:** Several descriptions of these technologies include mentions of major plot points from the novel.

around and set up one at Rodeo Beach, too. And Montara. [...]" With each beach Bailey mentioned, another live image appeared, each of them live, visible, with perfect clarity and brilliant color.

[...] "Now imagine the human rights implications. Protestors on the streets of Egypt no longer have to hold up a camera, hoping to catch a human rights violation or a murder and then somehow get the footage out of the streets and online. Now it's as easy as gluing a camera to a wall. Actually, we've done just that."

[...] "imagine any city with this kind of coverage. Who would commit a crime knowing they might be watched any time?"

[...] Live shots from all over the world filled the screen, and the crowd erupted again. Now Bailey cleared the screen again, and new words dropped onto the screen:

ALL THAT HAPPENS MUST BE KNOWN. [15]

ChildTrack

In the novel, ChildTrack is introduced as an ongoing project at The Circle. It is a small chip that can be implanted into the bone of a child's body, allowing parents to know their child's location at all times. In the story, ChildTrack starts as a pilot program involving the insertion of location chips into children's wrists to prevent kidnapping. This leads to the problem of criminals knowing where the chips are located, and removing them from children. The solution is to embed the chips into children's bones, making it harder for criminals to extract. Later in the story, The Circle uses the same chips to store data about a child's educational records which parents can access "in one place." It is speculated that there eventually would be a complete record of a student's every academic activity, including every word ever read and every math problem ever completed.

NeighborWatch

NeighborWatch is introduced as a product pitch to The Circle within the novel. It is a neighborhood watch service utilizing SeeChange cameras placed throughout a neighborhood, so that residents can identify suspicious persons. People in the neighborhood register their data and biometrics with NeighborWatch to identify them as residents. Via a screen-based interface users can see an outlined-version of the inside and outside of nearby homes. Residents of the neighborhood or known visitors are displayed as blue figures. Unknown people are displayed as red figures, triggering a notification to residents. It is speculated in the story that other sources of data, such as criminal records, can be further used to color-code people.

Vital-Radio

Vital-Radio is a real life prototype developed at MIT which uses radio waves to wirelessly detect a user's breathing and heart rate. It can monitor users up to 8 meters away and in separate rooms [1]. Adib et al. note that Vital-Radio is limited to monitoring users who stay in-place and can only monitor three people simultaneously. We imagined a future version of Vital-Radio that could monitor more than three people simultaneously while moving. We also imagined that users could see and interact with their heart rate data as well as their stress levels, emotional states, and other extrapolated information. In order to imagine how Vital-Radio might exist in the world of *The Circle*, we composed a short fiction passage in the style of Eggers depicting a launch and demo event for Vital-Radio by Victor, our own made up executive at The Circle.

Our Vital-Radio Fan Fiction

Mae watched as Victor held a sleek black box, about the size of a small DVD player. He turned to the audience and smiled.

"My grandma's eighty-seven. Last year she broke her hip and I've been concerned about her. Last week, while she was napping-"

A wave of laughter rippled through the audience.

"Forgive me! Forgive me!" he said, "I had no choice. She wouldn't have let me do it otherwise. So I snuck in, and I installed Vital-Radio in her bedroom and the living room. It can see through walls up to twenty five feet, so with just two of these boxes I can cover her whole house. She won't notice it."

"And of course," Victor continued "all that data is stored in the cloud, and in your tablet, anywhere you want it. It's always accessible, and is constantly updated. So if you fall, hit your head, you're in the ambulance, the EMTs can access everything about your vitals history in seconds. And it's not just healthcare. Imagine your home adapting music and lighting based on your vital signs and your mood. Or getting customized assistance based on your stress level at a Vital-Radio kiosk in an unfamiliar airport. Imagine the possibilities!"

DESIGNS

We present a sample of our design workbook proposals that show the progression of our design explorations, the breadth of design ideas inspired by the four technologies, the varying genres we used, and different ways we were inspired by the novel. (See supplementary materials for additional detail on these proposals.)

Design Round 1: Adapting *The Circle*

Our first designs adapt the technologies from the novel's textual descriptions. As there are no illustrations in the novel, these designs realize our interpretation of the novel's world, in which these technologies were sold as consumer products by a large technology company.

SeeChange Beach (Figure 2) interprets SeeChange's interface based on its introduction in *The Circle*, when Bailey, one of the company's executives, reveals live SeeChange footage. This design highlights the features of the fictional camera by juxtaposing two languages—glossy stock photos, and a security camera overlay that usually accompanies grainy, low resolution footage. This design felt surprisingly believable after we made it, and slightly creepy as it put us in the position of feeling like we were surveilling people when looking at the design.

ChildTrack UI (Figure 3) interprets the book's description as an interface. Since ChildTrack is a complicated system that tracks children's location and academic records, its look is borrowed from Facebook's design patterns to make the concept easier to consume. A contrast is presented between presumably benign, user-friendly design, and the reality that The Circle has an extensive knowledge of their users that goes beyond individual posts and photos.

ChildTrack builds more 'meaningful' profiles by aggregating feed data over time, which is represented in the "overview" tab. This design puts the viewer in the position of a parent, able to see all of their child's information.

Grandma's Data (Figure 4) is an interface for Vital-Radio which realizes the description from our own *Circle*-like fiction passage. This design focuses on the presentation of the device's data and the visual design is kept to a wireframe stage. The data present a narrative of grandma's day and raise questions about how the data are related and how "emotion" and "stress" are classified and quantified.

Figure 2. SeeChange Beach cameras

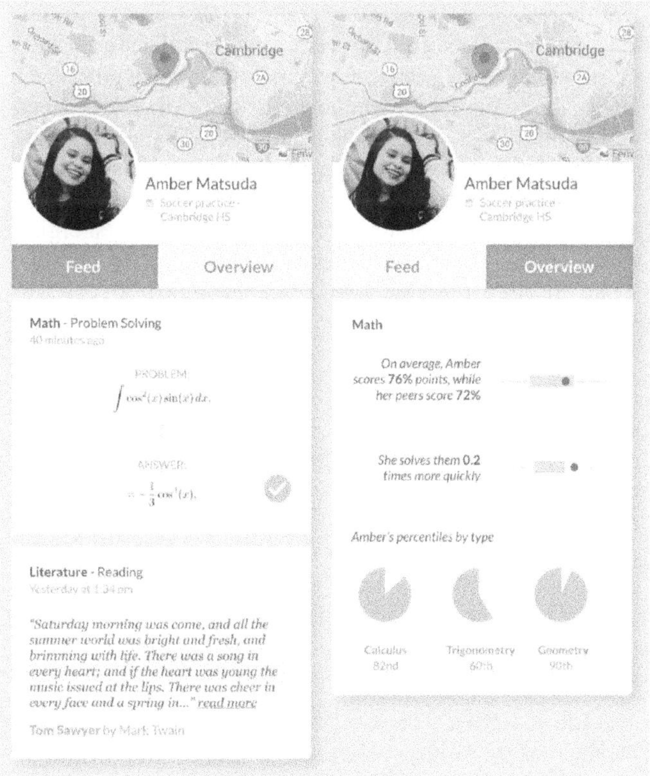

Figure 3. ChildTrack UI

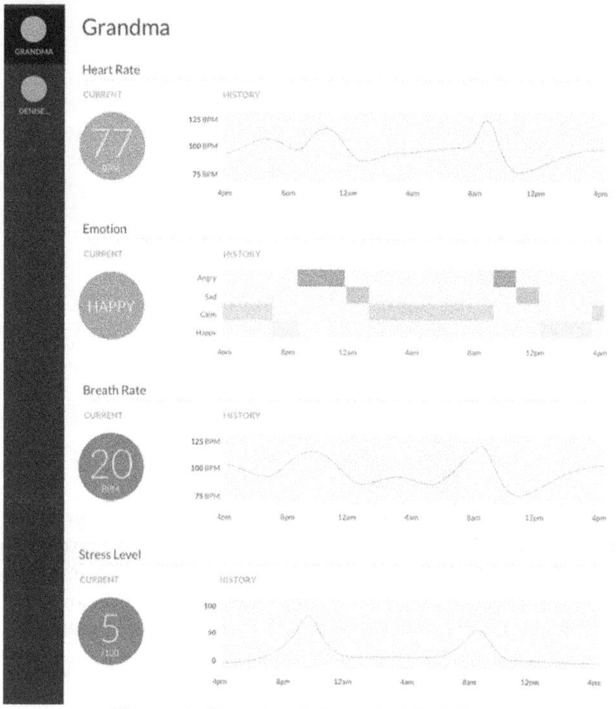

Figure 4. Grandma's Data in Vital-Radio

Design Round 2: *The Circle* in New Contexts

After our initial set of designs adapting technologies from their descriptions in *The Circle* (and our Vital-Radio fiction passage), we discussed how our first set of designs reflected potential privacy concerns. We began thinking about how the same set of technologies might be used in other situations within the world of the novel, but not depicted in Eggers' story, and how that might lead to new types of privacy concerns [31,32]. This second set of designs goes beyond the textual descriptions in the novel by taking the same technologies and re-imagining them for new sets of users or for use in new social contexts, but could still exist and be sold in the fictional world presented in *The Circle*.

The **SeeChange Amazon pages** present the SeeChange camera being sold as three different products to user groups not discussed in *The Circle*. First is SeeChange as a **police body camera** (Figure 5a). Second is SeeChange framed as a small, hidden, wearable **camera for activists groups** like PETA (Figure 5b). Third is SeeChange marketed "**For Independence, Freedom, and Survival,**" to be used by people suspicious of the government who may want to monitor government movements (Figure 5c). The latter was inspired by a pilot survey respondent's worry that SeeChange could be used by "right-wing activists harassing liberal groups" in the U.S. Our design frames SeeChange as a product that might seem valuable and useful to a person who might want to hide the camera with the desire to watch government employees for perceived abuses of power. This set of designs interrogates which surveillance concerns stem from SeeChange's technical capabilities and which come from concerns about who SeeChange's users or subjects are. We play on this question by writing in the body camera's product description "Provides OBJECTIVE evidence of wrongdoing," leaving ambiguity about whether it is recording the police officer's or citizen's wrongdoing.

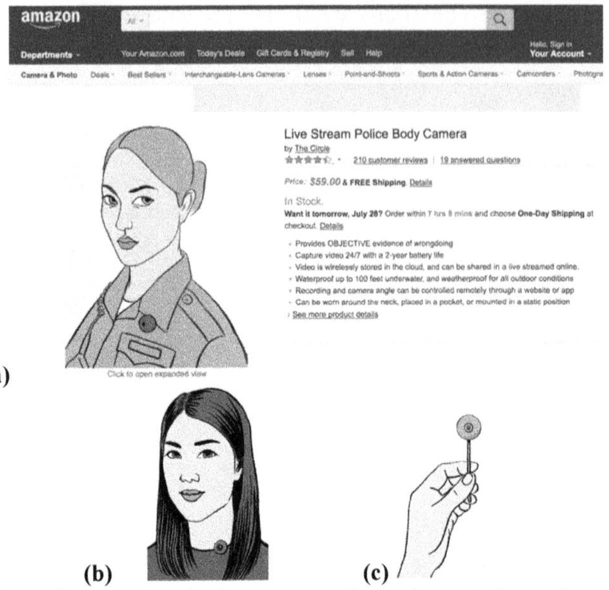

Figure 5. Amazon wireframe pages. Swapping out the product name and image, we show SeeChange as (a) a "live stream policy body camera", (b) a small wearable version for activists, and (c) SeeChange "For Independence, Freedom, and Survival", small enough to hide and monitor the government.

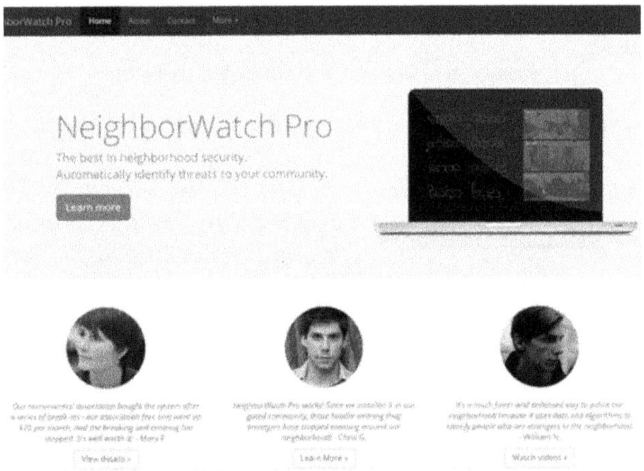

Figure 6. NeighborWatch Pro website

Figure 7. SeeChange Angles

NeighborWatch Pro (Figure 6) uses a product website to market a version of NeighborWatch. While presented in the book as a service that any community could use, a pilot survey participant expressed concerns that only "wealthy closed communities" would use it. Our design imagines an "enhanced" automated version of NeighborWatch which intentionally caters to those communities, raising questions about racial and socioeconomic biases reflected by users, datasets, and algorithms utilized by the system.

SeeChange Angles (Figure 7) was inspired by our thinking about the implications of ubiquitous SeeChange cameras always recording and broadcasting. On one hand, it might be nice to be able to automatically (re)watch sports and special events from multiple angles. Conversely, it might be creepy to use many multiple angles to watch a person doing daily activities. To explore this use case, the second author took photos of a subject from multiple angles inside and outside a room, and added a security camera overlay. The high quality and large quantity of photos suggest what may be possible with many high-definition SeeChange cameras.

Design Round 3: New Fictions and New Realities

After our second round of designs and thinking through the privacy analytic, we began thinking about privacy concerns that were *not* particularly present in *The Circle* or our existing designs, such as government surveillance (instead of surveillance by web companies), or how advertisers or other third parties might benefit from this expanded collection of data. We also began to realize that many of the design ideas we were thinking about reflected non-fictional products being researched or developed. We wanted to more tightly integrate fictional and real emerging technologies through our proposals. The following designs, while inspired by *The Circle*, are imagined to exist in worlds beyond the novel's.

Airport Security (Figure 8) depicts an imagined use of NeighborWatch and SeeChange, where an airport surveillance system automatically assigns threat statuses to people by color-coding them. Rather than focusing on consumer technologies like in the novel, we re-imagine these as government technologies. The user interface is omitted in this design in order to invite questions about how the system classifies people, and what each of the colors mean. One interpretation is that it uses computer vision or machine learning techniques to classify people (instead of the manual database entry technique in the novel).

The **License Plate Tracker** (Figure 9) also puts SeeChange in the hands of the police or government intelligence agencies. It is presented in a low fidelity mockup where the

Figure 8. Airport Security, inspired by NeighborWatch. Images adapted from [35,51] under CC BY-SA 2.0

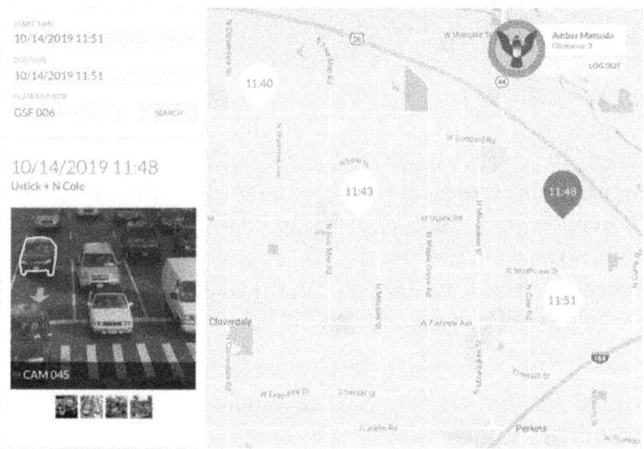

Figure 9. License Plate Tracker, inspired by SeeChange

UI elements help describe system's context and capabilities. For instance, the imagined user is a government official who can easily see anybody's location history and traffic camera images using the search feature, without restriction.

TruWork (Figure 10) re-imagines ChildTrack as an implantable tracking device for employees that employers use to keep track of their whereabouts and work activities, as employer surveillance is not critically addressed in the novel. Our design presents a product website targeting employers, using language like "Know the truth" about your employees. While presented positively, the lack of employee viewpoints raises questions about power, and how employees may try to resist or game these systems.

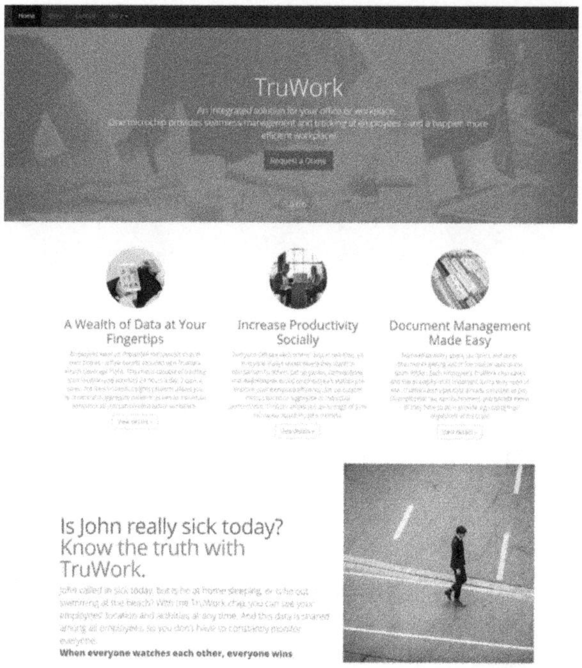

Figure 10. TruWork website, inspired by ChildTrack

The next set of designs employs the visual language of startup companies and their products and services. For example, onboarding tutorials or advertising often include cute, simple cartoons explaining the use of a product. **Vital Radio Match** (Figure 11a) extends the real-world Vital Radio to be used as an online dating service by matching people's "compatible" heart rates. The visual language draws comparisons to other dating applications, and provokes questions about the persuasive power of algorithmically generated results. **CoupleTrack** (Figure 11b), based on ChildTrack, allows adult couples to use implanted chips to continuously track each other's location and activities. **ChildTrack for Advertisers** (Figure 11c) allows advertisers, who are never discussed in *The Circle*, to leverage a child's location data to individually target them with advertisements, or for things that children with a "similar profile" like. Together these designs interrogate the relationship between privacy and personal data from the viewpoints of different stakeholders.

Amazon Echo with Vital-Radio combines the real Amazon Echo—a hands-free speaker, smarthome controller, and virtual assistant—with Vital Radio, presented as a product for sale by Amazon (Figure 12). Our design proposal uses a person's heartbeat patterns to adjust a home's lighting and temperature settings, and automatically buys items from Amazon.com that it thinks will suit the user's current mood, raising questions about what types of third parties have access to a user's data.

ANALYZING PRIVACY DIMENSIONS IN OUR DESIGNS

Using Mulligan et al.'s privacy analytic [31] to interpret our design fictions after each round of designs, we ended our iterations after finding we explored a wide variety of combinations of privacy dimensions, allowing us to explore

(a)

(b) (c)

Figure 11. Product diagrams depicting (a) Vital Radio Match, (b) CoupleTrack, (c) ChildTrack for Advertisers

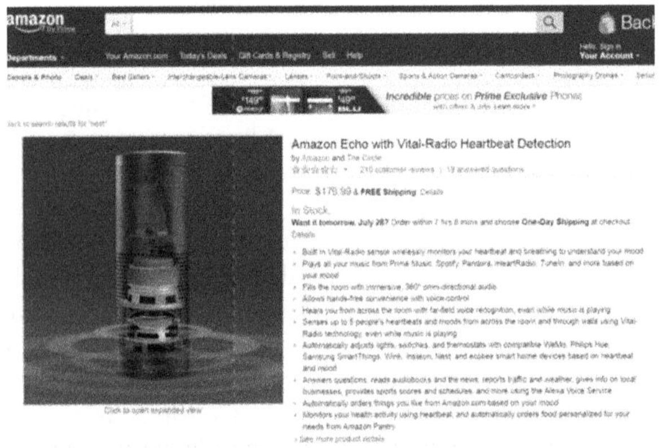

Figure 12. Amazon Echo with Vital-Radio

a broad space of privacy issues in and beyond *The Circle*. We present a brief analysis and interpretation of our design fictions using the privacy analytic dimensions (theory, protection, harm, provision, and scope) before discussing some broader reflections on our design process.

First looking at the issues arising from our initial round of designs (SeeChange Beach, ChildTrack UI, Grandma's Data), the main theory of privacy employed is that privacy protects individuals' personal information. What is being protected is individuals' data and their image or likeness (in SeeChange). Privacy harms stem from other individual consumers who buy and use these technologies. The novel does away with mechanisms that might provide privacy protection: laws and social norms that require consent before collecting information or embedding devices in someone's body do not exist in this fictional world; and new technical abilities that make it easier to hide or disguise sensing technologies. The scope of these privacy issues is broad, encompassing both public and private spaces. Our design fiction proposals in subsequent rounds of design vary or provide more specifics to these dimensions of privacy, to think about issues not present in the Eggers novel. Each of these dimensions is outlined below:

Theory. Our designs go beyond conceptualizing privacy as merely keeping data secret. NeighborWatch Pro and Airport Surveillance both conceive privacy as protecting adults' personal autonomy from surveillance. SeeChange Angles shows another conception of privacy focused on maintaining the sanctity of private space.

Protection. ChildTrack UI, CoupleTrack, and TruWork are imagined to use the same technology, but identify new specific groups being protected by privacy. ChildTrack UI violates a child's privacy; CoupleTrack explores privacy in the context of an adult relationship; TruWork explores employers violating employees' privacy.

Harm. Our designs identified privacy harms caused by actors beyond consumers and users. TruWork identifies employers as causing privacy harms, while License Plate Tracker and Airport Surveillance imagine government institutions using sensors to violate privacy. Amazon Echo with Vital-Radio and ChildTrack for Advertisers raise questions about privacy harms caused by data-sharing with third parties. NeighborWatch Pro and Airport Surveillance suggest that computer vision coupled with algorithmic decision making could also cause privacy harms.

Provision. Understanding why a design fiction violates privacy helps us understand what mechanisms currently protect privacy. For instance, ChildTrack would likely be illegal in the U.S. due to child privacy laws, highlighting legal privacy protections. It is also currently not technically possible to make a consumer camera as small as SeeChange with such high resolution and streaming capabilities or make a GPS transmitter as small as ChildTrack, highlighting technical limitations that help provide privacy protection [44]. And as of today, many people do not feel comfortable embedding digital technologies in their bodies, excepting small groups of body hackers and artists (e.g. [3,47]), surfacing social norms that help protect privacy.

Scope. Many designs help us understand potential privacy violations that could occur in public space (e.g. Airport Surveillance, License Plate Tracker), or private space (e.g. Grandma's Data). However, scope is not limited to physical spaces. SeeChange Angles helps us understand a scope of scale – the privacy violation of nine cameras in one room is different than a violation caused by one camera in the room.

This analysis suggests that design fictions can be designed for and analyzed using frameworks created for specific empirical topics, such as privacy. Design fictions can be used as examples for analysis, and perhaps help refine the frameworks themselves (e.g., creating borderline cases).

REFLECTIONS

Real-Fictional Entanglements

After creating our proposals, we found that several designs similar to our design fictions have been made or are in the process of being implemented by companies. Some of these we were aware of beforehand, such as wireless security cameras. Yet we were surprised to find that some products we had imagined as fiction were close to being realized as 'real,' such as a smart employee badge similar to TruWork [20]. One interpretation of this might be that our proposals are design fictions while similar commercial designs are not; that is design fiction is based on intent—indeed some have distinguished between "intentional" and "incidental" design fictions [24]. However we find it useful to blur those boundaries, instead using our design fictions to interrogate the inherent entanglement between fictional representations of technologies and their material realities.

Here we are inspired by Barad's feminist philosophy, who conceptualizes phenomena in the world as emergent through the "mutual construction of entangled agencies" rather than as external, pre-existing things to be defined and observed [2:33]. Rather than viewing the real and fictional as separate pre-defined realms, we view them as inherently entangled and mutually co-constructive, questioning the clear distinction between them. This comes through in a tension that arises in our designs, as we try to make them seem like realistic everyday products in order to suspend disbelief, yet also present them as a way to explore fictional futures or realities. The blurring of boundaries allowed our designs to exist in a liminal space, situated among *The Circle*, our imaginations, other fiction and non-fiction technologies, and real-world debates about privacy. For example, our SeeChange-inspired designs reflect uses similar to those of life logging cameras and traditional closed-circuit surveillance cameras. These designs relate to established products and services such as smartphone cameras, GoPro cameras, or Facebook Live streaming. They also relate to experimental and emerging ideas such as Google Glass or smart-eye implants. SeeChange links to cameras in other media, including Telescreens which receive and transmit what people are doing in Orwell's *1984*, the *Big Brother* reality television show where viewers watch live streams of people living in a house, or predictive policing from *Minority Report*. The SeeChange-inspired Police Body Camera design places a fictional technology in the midst of current sociopolitical debates in the U.S and other countries about surveillance and police conduct.

We often felt a strong affective response while making and reflecting on our designs, particularly when it was not clear whether designs were fictional or real. By putting designs into the form of a product page with images and copy, they felt like they could be real products from the near future. This made several designs feel especially creepy, providing us with a useful starting point to explore norms, values, and expectations that have a bearing on privacy.

Our exploration of the space between real and fictional helped us chart relationships between technologies that are existing and nascent, emerging and experimental, and fictional and speculative. Rather than viewing science fiction as an external force that influences technological research and development, through design we highlight how the real and fictional are integrally connected and entangled. In that sense, our design proposals act as boundary objects [41]. They highlight the interconnections and blurred boundaries between real and fictional, between the imaginary, research, and commercial development.

Strategies for Using Science Fiction in Design Fiction

Choosing a Science Fiction Text for Complex Engagement

Given design fiction's focus on creating artifacts that exist within a fictional world, a benefit of starting with a science fiction text is that we do not have to create that world from scratch. Rather, we can build on a professional author's already richly imagined world. This allows designers and researchers without story-writing experience new opportunities to engage in making design fiction.

Choosing a piece of *popular* fiction allowed us to play with and develop concepts and ideas that are already part of the public cultural imagination. Popular fiction does not emerge from a vacuum, but rather reflects real desires, urges, or needs. *The Circle*, as a New York Times bestseller and being adapted into a movie, signals that it has a broad resonance. Furthermore, the novel's subject matter matched our interest in asking research questions about privacy.

We purposely avoided using an overtly dark dystopian novel. We find that one of Egger's key insights upon which he builds his novel is that the user-friendliness and convenient functionality of pervasive technology products belie their darker implications. We translate this insight into our design fictions, which also shed light onto the nature of currently available technologies. We describe TruWork as "an integrated solution" where "one microchip provides seamless management...and a happier, more efficient workplace!" CoupleTrack, ChildTrack for Advertisers, and Vital Radio Match use cartoon figures similar to the design genre of infographics. We took inspiration from Eggers' approach, which critiques technologies by framing them in an extremely positive and technologically deterministic way, parodying current technologies. This provides an alternative approach to engaging darkly serious and autocratic dystopian science fiction, such as *1984* or *A Clockwork Orange*, such as in Blythe and Wright's pastiche scenarios [6]. We find that using non-dystopian narratives can also be productive, in our case to explore the role of positive advertising in framing invasive products.

Using Design Workbooks for Design Fiction

We used the design workbook method to create a set of design fiction proposals. Creating visual design fictions in the form of a workbook allows for a moment of pause that one might not get in other media, such as film, or a user test of a digital or physical artifact. The static nature of the designs allows us to take our time to interrogate or reflect upon a design. Our use of a design workbook is similar to the speed dating design method [12,34] in that it provides a low-cost and rapid way to broaden the design space and explore multiple potential future designs. However, while our design engagement is not able to explore questions related to the material construction of or lived experiences with these design products, we find that the workbook does important work without building a physical artifact. Using a fictional world can also explore designs that are difficult to produce technically, socially, or legally in our world (such as CoupleTrack's or TruWork's implanted GPS trackers).

Visually our proposals lie between rough hand-drawn sketches and glossy mockups to allow us to present our designs as real enough to attract attention, but leave enough openness and ambiguity to encourage interrogation and questioning. Keeping designs open-ended as to how they would function led us to ask interesting questions about their technical underpinnings. For instance, we wondered how the Airport Security system would categorize people into different threat colors. Might it use probability-based algorithms, computer vision, metadata, or existing no-fly lists? What types of biases might emerge? For License Plate Tracker, we asked what would happen if SeeChange collects metadata from people as well as images? What types of processing could be done on the images if combined with collected metadata? Metadata surveillance issues go beyond Eggers' largely vision-based surveillance scenarios. Our design fictions thus explore issues that Eggers does not sufficiently engage. Beyond research, it is possible that design fiction in the form of workbooks can be used as a rhetorical tool that is more widely accessible than academic papers and can engage broader audiences such as speculative fiction enthusiasts, or designers and cultural producers looking to create alternative designs.

Using Design Fiction to Blur Real and Fictional

Our designs helped uncover entanglements between real and fictional technologies and social worlds. We used design language from commercial webpages and interfaces, and adopted copy language that focuses on positive user propositions. Using this language, we convey that our imagined products have the potential to be highly invasive, but exist in a world where consumers willingly purchase them. This helps us envision these (rather invasive) designs as everyday objects and makes them more affectively striking. In this sense, our approach is useful in bridging real technological trends with an often satirical critique of emerging technologies' privacy implications, or what Blythe and Encinas term design fiction's "Scientific Highlands" and "Great Plains of Irony" [8]. Despite the designs' similarity to some real products, we do not intend for these to be mass produced objects. However, it may be possible for some of these to be realized as research products in the future, as built objects that live in a person's everyday life to explore a set of questions and ideas [33].

Utilizing External Frameworks to Investigate Empirical Research Questions

Because our designs explored privacy issues, we reviewed the privacy literature and analyzed our designs using a privacy analytic framework. This framework helped us conceptualize and map the breadth of our exploration of the design space. Utilizing external frameworks can help design fiction bridge the languages, concepts, and ideas of design and other areas of empirical research. Design fictions can also be used to provide examples for frameworks, or explore a framework's limits. We believe our approach can also be utilized by non-expert designers, such as privacy researchers or non-designers in the HCI community who want to explore the social and ethical dimensions of systems, products, or artifacts they are creating.

CONCLUSIONS

This paper contributes a set of design fiction concepts in the form of a workbook, a case study of a project using design fiction to interrogate emerging sensing technologies to explore empirical privacy research questions, and presents an approach to creating design fiction artifacts by using science fiction texts as a starting point. We see potential further uses for our design fictions, as tools to broaden the design space for people who make decisions affecting the creation and use of sensing technologies. In further research, they could be used as interview probes with policymakers thinking about social and legal issues of emerging sensing technologies, or used in design or engineering ethics courses to quickly create and explore many different scenarios.

Pragmatically, explicitly tapping into an existing fictional universe provides a concrete starting point to begin design exploration; we did not have to start from scratch, making the process more accessible. This provides a new approach to creating design fiction that lies between creating a fictional world from scratch and implicitly being inspired by science fiction. Design fiction helps broaden the design space (or prevent a 'failure of imagination') to explore more possibilities. Exploring many possibilities will also help us find bad ones, problematic ones, and dark ones that we might otherwise ignore or not think about. Exploring positive and negative possibilities is important to better understanding the design space, and in informing choices about what to design. By engaging in real-fictional entanglements, design fiction can be used generate design ideas that explore and reflect on futures which might otherwise go unnoticed.

ACKNOWLEDGEMENTS

We thank Deirdre Mulligan, John Chuang, and the BioSENSE and Berkeley Social Science Matrix groups for their support and feedback, and we thank the reviewers for their valuable comments. This work was supported in part by the UC Berkeley Center for Long Term Cybersecurity, and the National Science Foundation Graduate Research Fellowship Program under Grant No. DGE 1106400. Any opinions, findings, and conclusions or recommendations expressed in this material are those of the authors and do not necessarily reflect the views of the NSF. Figures 5,7,11 © Ellen Van Wyk.

REFERENCES

1. Fadel Adib, Hongzi Mao, Zachary Kabelac, Dina Katabi, and Robert C Miller. 2015. Smart Homes that Monitor Breathing and Heart Rate. In *Proceedings of the 33rd Annual ACM Conference on Human Factors in Computing Systems (CHI '15)*, 837–846. http://doi.org/10.1145/2702123.2702200
2. Karen Barad. 2007. *Meeting the Universe Halfway: Quantum Physics and the Entangelement of Matter and Meaning*. Duke University Press, Durham.
3. Dann Berg. 2012. Body Hacking: My Magnetic Implant (12 March 2012). Retrieved September 20, 2016 from http://www.iamdann.com/2012/03/21/my-magnet-implant-body-modification
4. Julian Bleecker. 2009. *Design Fiction: A Short Essay on Design, Science, Fact and Fiction.*
5. Mark Blythe. 2014. Research through design fiction: Narrative in Real and Imaginary Abstracts. In *Proceedings of the SIGCHI Conference on Human Factors in Computing Systems (CHI '14)*, 703–712. http://doi.org/10.1145/2556288.2557098
6. Mark A. Blythe and Peter C. Wright. 2006. Pastiche scenarios: Fiction as a resource for user centred design. *Interacting with Computers* 18, 5: 1139–1164. http://doi.org/10.1016/j.intcom.2006.02.001
7. Mark Blythe, Kristina Andersen, Rachel Clarke, and Peter Wright. 2016. Anti-Solutionist Strategies: Seriously Silly Design Fiction. In *Proceedings of the 2016 CHI Conference on Human Factors in Computing Systems (CHI '16)*, 4968–4978. http://doi.org/10.1145/2858036.2858482
8. Mark Blythe and Enrique Encinas. 2016. The Co-ordinates of Design Fiction: Extrapolation, Irony, Ambiguity and Magic. In *Proceedings of the 19th International Conference on Supporting Group Work (GROUP '16)*, 345–354. http://doi.org/10.1145/2957276.2957299
9. Torie Bosch. Sci-Fi Writer Bruce Sterling Explains the Intriguing New Concept of Design Fiction. *Slate.com*. Retrieved September 20, 2016 from http://www.slate.com/blogs/future_tense/2012/03/02/bruce_sterling_on_design_fictions_.html
10. Barry Brown, Julian Bleecker, Marco D'Adamo, et al. 2016. The IKEA Catalogue: Design Fiction in Academic and Industrial Collaborations. In *Proceedings of the 19th International Conference on Supporting Group Work (GROUP '16)*, 335–344. http://doi.org/10.1145/2957276.2957298
11. Rafael Calvo, Sidney D'Mello, Jonathan Gratch, Arvid Kappas, Nadia Bianchi-Berthouze, and Andrea Kleinsmith. 2015. Automatic Recognition of Affective Body Expressions. In *The Oxford Handbook of Affective Computing*. Oxford University Press. http://doi.org/10.1093/oxfordhb/9780199942237.013.025
12. Scott Davidoff, Min Kyung Lee, Anind K Dey, and John Zimmerman. 2007. Rapidly Exploring Application Design Through Speed Dating. In *International Conference on Ubiquitous Computing (UbiComp 2007)*, 429–446.
13. Paul Dourish and Genevieve Bell. 2013. "Resistance is futile": reading science fiction alongside ubiquitous computing. *Personal and Ubiquitous Computing* 18, 4: 769–778. http://doi.org/10.1007/s00779-013-0678-7
14. Anthony Dunne and Fiona Raby. 2012. Train - United Micro Kingdoms. Retrieved April 7, 2017 from http://www.unitedmicrokingdoms.org/train-comments/
15. David Eggers. 2013. *The Circle*. McSweeny's Books, San Francisco.
16. Peter Freese and Charles B. Harris. 2004. Introduction: The Holodeck in the Garden. In *The Holodeck in the Garden: Science and Technology in Contemporary American Fiction*, Peter Freese and Charles B. Harris (eds.). Dalkey Archive Press, Champaign, Illinois, ix–xxviii.
17. William Gaver. 2011. Making spaces: how design workbooks work. In *Proceedings of the SIGCHI Conference on Human Factors in Computing Systems (CHI '11)*, 1551–1560. http://doi.org/10.1145/1978942.1979169
18. Ellie Harmon and Melissa Mazmanian. 2013. Stories of the Smartphone in everyday discourse: conflict, tension & instability. In *Proceedings of the SIGCHI Conference on Human Factors in Computing Systems (CHI '13)*, 1051. http://doi.org/10.1145/2470654.2466134
19. Sabrina Hauser, Audrey Desjardins, and Ron Wakkary. 2014. Sfuture: envisioning a sustainable university campus in 2065. In *Proceedings of the 2014 companion publication on Designing interactive systems (DIS Companion '14)*, 29–32. http://doi.org/10.1145/2598784.2602774
20. Thomas Heath. 2016. This employee ID badge monitors and listens to you at work — except in the bathroom. (7 September 2016). *The Washington Post*. Retrieved September 20, 2016 from https://www.washingtonpost.com/news/business/wp/2016/09/07/this-employee-badge-knows-not-only-where-you-are-but-whether-you-are-talking-to-your-co-workers/
21. Javier Hernandez, Daniel McDuff, and Rosalind Picard. 2015. BioWatch: Estimation of Heart and Breathing Rates from Wrist Motions. In *Proceedings of the 9th International Conference on Pervasive*

Computing Technologies for Healthcare. http://doi.org/10.4108/icst.pervasivehealth.2015.259064

22. David Kirby. 2010. The Future is Now: Diegetic Prototypes and the Role of Popular Films in Generating Real-world Technological Development. *Social Studies of Science* 40, 1: 41–70. http://doi.org/10.1177/0306312709338325
23. Mohammed Korayem, Robert Templeman, Dennis Chen, David Crandall, and Apu Kapadia. 2016. Enhancing Lifelogging Privacy by Detecting Screens. In *In Proceedings of the 2016 CHI Conference on Human Factors in Computing Systems (CHI '16)*, 4309–4314. http://doi.org/10.1145/2858036.2858417
24. Joseph Lindley. 2016. A Pragmatics Framework for Design Fiction. In *11th EAD Conference Proceedings: The Value of Design Research.* http://doi.org/10.7190/ead/2015/69
25. Joseph Lindley and Paul Coulton. 2015. Back to the Future: 10 Years of Design Fiction. *Proceedings of the 2015 British HCI Conference (British HCI '15)*: 210–211. http://doi.org/10.1145/2783446.2783592
26. Joseph Lindley and Paul Coulton. 2015. Game of Drones. In *Symposium on Computer-Human Interaction in Play (CHI PLAY '15)*, 613–618. http://doi.org/10.1145/2793107.2810300
27. Joseph Lindley and Paul Coulton. 2016. Pushing the Limits of Design Fiction: The Case For Fictional Research Papers. In *Proceedings of the 2016 CHI Conference on Human Factors in Computing Systems (CHI '16)*, 4032–4043. http://doi.org/10.1145/2858036.2858446
28. Joseph Lindley, Dhruv Sharma, and Robert Potts. 2015. Operationalizing Design Fiction with Anticipatory Ethnography. In *Ethnographic Praxis in Industry Conference*, 58–71.
29. Conor Linehan, Ben J. Kirman, Stuart Reeves, et al. 2014. Alternate endings: using fiction to explore design futures. In *CHI '14 Extended Abstracts on Human Factors in Computing Systems (CHI EA '14)*, 45–48. http://doi.org/10.1145/2559206.2560472
30. Keiichi Matsuda. 2016. HYPER-REALITY. Video. (16 May 2016). Retrieved September 20, 2016 from https://vimeo.com/166807261
31. Deirdre K. Mulligan, Colin Koopman, and Nick Doty. 2016. Privacy is an essentially contested concept: a multi-dimensional analytic for mapping privacy. *Philosophical Transactions of the Royal Society A: Mathematical, Physical and Engineering Sciences* 374, 2083. http://doi.org/10.1098/rsta.2016.0118
32. Helen Nissenbaum. 2009. *Privacy in Context: Technology, Policy, and the Integrity of Social Life.* Stanford University Press, Stanford, California.
33. William Odom, Ron Wakkary, Youn-kyung Lim, Audrey Desjardins, Bart Hengeveld, and Richard Banks. 2016. From Research Prototype to Research Product. In *Proceedings of the 2016 CHI Conference on Human Factors in Computing Systems (CHI '16)*, 2549–2561. http://doi.org/10.1145/2858036.2858447
34. William Odom, John Zimmerman, Scott Davidoff, Jodi Forlizzi, Anind K. Dey, and Min Kyung Lee. 2012. A fieldwork of the future with user enactments. In *Proceedings of the Designing Interactive Systems Conference (DIS '12)*, 338–347. http://doi.org/10.1145/2317956.2318008
35. Pelican. 2013. Sendai airport. Image. (17 May 2013). Retrieved September 4, 2016 from https://www.flickr.com/photos/pelican/8767376807/
36. James Pierce and Eric Paulos. 2014. Some variations on a counterfunctional digital camera. In *Proceedings of the 2014 conference on Designing interactive systems (DIS '14)*, 131–140. http://doi.org/10.1145/2598510.2602968
37. Nathan Shedroff and Christopher Noessel. 2012. *Make it So: Interaction Design Lessons from Science Fiction.* Rosenfield Media, Brooklyn, New York.
38. Daniel J. Solove. 2002. Conceptualizing privacy. *California Law Review* 90: 1087–1155. http://doi.org/10.1145/1929609.1929610
39. Daniel J. Solove. 2003. A Taxonomy of Privacy. *University of Pennsylvania Law Review*, 477: 477–560.
40. Susan Leigh Star and Geoffrey C. Bowker. 2002. How to Infrastructure. In *The Handbook of New Media*, Leah A. Lievrouw and Sonia Livingstone (eds.). Sage, London, 230–245.
41. Susan Leigh Star and James R. Griesemer. 1989. Institutional Ecology, `Translations' and Boundary Objects: Amateurs and Professionals in Berkeley's Museum of Vertebrate Zoology, 1907-39. *Social Studies of Science* 19, 3: 387–420. http://doi.org/10.1177/030631289019003001
42. Miriam Sturdee, Paul Coulton, Joseph G. Lindley, Mike Stead, Haider Ali, and Andy Hudson-Smith. 2016. Design Fiction: How to Build a Voight-Kampff Machine. In *Proceedings of the 2016 CHI Conference Extended Abstracts on Human Factors in Computing Systems (CHI EA '16)*, 375–386. http://doi.org/10.1145/2851581.2892574
43. Superflux. 2015. Drone Aviary. Video. (7 April 2015). Retrieved September 20, 2011 from https://vimeo.com/124292043

44. Harry Surden. 2007. Structural Rights in Privacy. *SMU Law Review* 60: 1605–1629.
45. Joshua Tanenbaum, Marcel Pufal, and Karen Tanenbaum. 2016. The Limits of Our Imagination: Design Fiction as a Strategy for Engaging with Dystopian Futures. In *Proceedings of the Second Workshop on Computing within Limits (LIMITS '16)*. http://doi.org/10.1145/2926676.2926687
46. Joshua Tanenbaum, Karen Tanenbaum, and Ron Wakkary. 2012. Steampunk as design fiction. In *Proceedings of the SIGCHI Conference on Human Factors in Computing Systems (CHI '12)*, 1583. http://doi.org/10.1145/2207676.2208279
47. Oliver Wainwright. 2015. Body-hackers: the people who turn themselves into cyborgs. (14 August 2015). *The Guardian*. Retrieved September 20, 2016 from https://www.theguardian.com/artanddesign/architecture-design-blog/2015/aug/14/body-hackers-the-people-who-turn-themselves-into-cyborgs
48. Ron Wakkary, William Odom, Sabrina Hauser, Garnet Hertz, and Henry Lin. 2015. Material Speculation: Actual Artifacts for Critical Inquiry. *Proceedings of The Fifth Decennial Aarhus Conference on Critical Alternatives (AA '15)* 1, 1: 97–108. http://doi.org/10.7146/aahcc.v1i1.21299
49. Chen Wang, Erik N. Geelhoed, Phil P. Stenton, and Pablo Cesar. 2014. Sensing a live audience. In *Proceedings of the 32nd annual ACM conference on Human factors in computing systems (CHI '14)*, 1909–1912. http://doi.org/10.1145/2556288.2557154
50. Alan Westin. 1967. *Privacy and Freedom*. Atheneum, New York.
51. Stan Wiechers. 2007. Taipei Airport. Image. (6 August 2007). Retrieved September 4, 2016 from https://www.flickr.com/photos/whoisstan/1035746340/
52. Richmond Y. Wong and Deirdre K. Mulligan. 2016. When a Product Is Still Fictional: Anticipating and Speculating Futures through Concept Videos. In *Proceedings of the 2016 ACM Conference on Designing Interactive Systems (DIS '16)*, 121–133. http://doi.org/10.1145/2901790.2901801

Apply Now! Fictional Job Postings as an Instrument to Discuss Interactive Futures of Work

Verena Fuchsberger, Thomas Meneweger, Daniela Wurhofer, Manfred Tscheligi
Center for Human-Computer Interaction
University of Salzburg, Austria
firstname.lastname@sbg.ac.at

ABSTRACT
Design fiction provides us with a variety of ways to explore potential interactive futures. In order to reflect on the future of workplaces, we created fictional job postings for the context of production facilities. This context is characterized by many constraints, which are often hard to overcome when envisioning the future of interactive practices in such environments. With the fictional job postings, we triggered discussions with stakeholders from a production site and with the public – which both resulted in highly controversial debates. In this note, we present the evolution of an exemplary job posting and the reactions it evoked. We then discuss our learnings (e.g., that the degree of fiction is essential) and conclude by reflecting on how this instrument facilitates the exploration of prospective interactive practices at work.

ACM Classification Keywords
H.5.m. Information Interfaces and Presentation (e.g. HCI): Miscellaneous

Author Keywords
Design fiction; work places; computer-supported practices.

INTRODUCTION
Interaction Design is about exploring possible futures, sometimes also in collaboration with "future users" [22]. Some scholars argue that working with future users is difficult, if not impossible, since they actually do not exist (e.g., [13]). Nonetheless, involving individuals in design (research) has been valuable in various settings, including work contexts (e.g., via participatory design [9]), even if designers and users may face realities that are hard to negotiate and change. Complex organizational structures, for instance, constrain possibilities to make a difference in practice [8]. In our own research in organizations we found similar issues, i.e., the discussion not only with users, but also with stakeholders of various organizational levels is very much influenced by their realities, making it difficult to create visions beyond the instant actuality.

In order to "peak into a possible future" [15, p. 71], we developed an instrument that facilitates individuals' participation in envisioning the future of work, i.e., of work places and computer-supported work practices. Our approach has been inspired by *design fiction*, aiming to develop a format that is at the same time known and unknown, including real and fictional components: we created *fictional job postings*.

This approach was influenced by the current, intense discourse on forms and values of design fiction (e.g., [18]). Design fiction has promisingly been used for various purposes, for instance, as a means to design research (e.g., [2, 20]), as a means to counteract solutionism [3], or as an instrument in participatory design [26]. We found it specifically compelling to explore future, fictional realities for an organization, which in our work is a large-scale production facility in central Europe, as an alternative that allows to escape existing constraints. Furthermore, by using job postings, we were able to work with a very contextually focused instrument, one that is specifically targeting work, and that foregrounds the question of whether oneself would want to have such a job, or apply for it, and, consequently, is expected to be individually relevant and engaging.

Our aim was to provoke discussions about potential futures in production facilities. We created fictional job postings for future workers, which show that fiction is not absolute; it is relational to a specific context, such as an organization. We applied them twice, one time in a stakeholder discussion at the production plant, and another time at a public event. The main learnings were that the fictional job postings led to immediate resistance and, thereby, triggered intense and controversial discussions, and that presence and future need to be combined to collaboratively create pictures of prospective work in highly technological contexts. In this note, we describe how the fictional job ads contribute a novel way of engagement with possible interactive futures of work places and practices.

DESIGN FICTION
The idea of design fiction was first mentioned in 2005[1], pursuing earlier discussions about the value of science fiction for

[1] A historical overview can be found in [19].

DIS 2017, June 10–14, 2017, Edinburgh, United Kingdom.
Copyright © 2017 ACM ISBN 978-1-4503-4922-2/17/06 ...$15.00.
http://dx.doi.org/10.1145/3064663.3064750

HCI (e.g., [23, 24]). Science fiction was considered to bring "powerful visions of future technology and the society in which it is embedded" to the community [24, p. 95]. However, it was only in 2009, when Bruce Sterling wrote his seminal article on design fiction [27], that it was considered a research method and design approach in its own right, though an inherently ambiguous one [19]. This ambiguity seems to be arising from its flexibility, which can only be faced by clearly communicating the purpose of the design fiction for a specific project and particular task, its appearance and potentials [19].

According to Sterling, design fiction may be considered as designing "prototypes that imply a changed world" [28], it "attacks the status quo and suggests clear ways in which life might become different" [28]. Design fiction may take various forms, such as *imaginary abstracts* [2], which are a means to research. Those abstracts summarize findings of papers that do not exist, which report about non-existing prototypes. They can be used to explore possible user interactions, for instance, regarding an artificial intelligence system [4], and have already been extended towards fictional research papers, challenging "norms and conventions in academic research" [20, p. 4041]. Other manifestations are the illustration of research findings, such as advertisements for products and services that do not exist [7], the creation of alternate endings to research papers in order to "envision long-term consequences of contemporary HCI projects" [21, p. 45], or fictional characters in pastiche personae to disrupt designers' prior assumptions [5].

Recently, Blythe and Encinas presented "broad patterns and family resemblances between fictions" [6, p. 346] in order to categorize the increasing number of forms of design fiction. By means of literary analysis of a variety of design fiction examples, they arrive at a map of *fictional lands*. This map shows that the majority of design fictions are residents of *scientific highlands*, with more or less closeness to the *great plains of irony*. Less inhabitants are in the *fields of magic*, and there is "wide space of future undiscovered countries" [6, p. 352]. We locate our work in the well-inhabited scientific highlands, which are characterized by extrapolations of current trends, a search to make predictions, and an attempt to be plausible [6].

Design fiction has also already been described regarding its value for academia-industry cooperation. Brown et al. [10] have created a "future IKEA catalogue", combining wholesome scenes of contemporary catalogues with possible subversions. They argue that design fiction can be a 'boundary object', allowing to escape "the limitations of a lengthy academic paper or specific technical prototype" [10, p. 335]. It might facilitate speculative or innovative thinking, since (among others) it is not necessarily perceived as a comment on current products or practices. Design fiction may also be an appropriate form of critique; however, finding the right degree of criticality is challenging, one that does not run the risk of immediate rejection, but results in positive impact [10].

THE FICTIONAL JOB POSTINGS

In all the aforementioned forms of design fiction, their function of envisioning possible futures has been described to work well, either as a research tool or a communicative means to engage users or the public. For the work at hand, this communicative aspect was the main reason for adopting design fiction, since our research aim was to facilitate a dialogue both with stakeholders of the production plant and the public on how the future of work might look like. In contrast to many other design fiction formats, we rather aimed to address computer-supported practices [17] than specific artifacts or interactions. Therefore, we considered job ads as appropriate, as they commonly focus on practices, including spatial, technological, and social conditions. Another rationale for this format (instead of using scenarios, for instance) was that it provides familiarity for many people in how it is constituted and what it aims for.

Research Aims

The objectives of fictional job postings were (a) to establish an instrument that allows to deliberately neglect existing realities of specific contexts and (b) to provoke discussions about potential futures to make assumptions visible that are usually hidden in organizational or public status-quo discussions. For creating fictional job postings, we needed to describe an ecosystem of humans' factory work, including tasks and activities, technologies, social settings, etc. We based these descriptions on our experiences gained in previous studies – we had collaborated with the production facility for seven years, leading to detailed knowledge about the context and its characteristics[2].

Example: A Future Operator in A Smart Factory

In total, we created three job postings for the roles of future operators, maintainers, and engineers. For this note, we chose to depict the example of the future operator. Figure 1 illustrates the ingredients of the fictional job postings. The concrete manifestations of job duties and qualifications were primarily inspired by our own findings regarding computer-supported practices in the very context. For instance, the job ad says: "You are invited to contribute your ideas for improvements or developments of processes, products, and services and will be granted sufficient time, space, and equipment to do so." This is based on a study we did on innovation within the company, where we identified that workers' participation in innovation efforts is highly constrained to non-existing [16]. Another example: "You coordinate activities of your co-workers, i.e., of human and non-human colleagues on the shop floor" is a result of previous research on workers' experiences with robots, where we found the need of humans to adapt to robots, which, briefly said, led them to feel inferior to robots [25].

The job ad was furthermore informed by related work. For instance, the assumed future of industrial labour, as depicted in [14], may follow a complementary automation concept, where tasks are distributed *between* humans and machines; this may even result in human-machine *integration*, the vision of a "symbiotic relationship in which humans and software act with autonomy" [11], which is slowly coming true.

Furthermore, we have tried to stay close to usual formats of job ads, including the use of (maybe shallow, but characteristic) buzz words, such as efficiency, flexibility, or mobility.

[2]We decided against describing the context in more detail, since the job postings are required to function without any further information in their role as job posting, i.e., they tell about the context themselves.

We are hiring! Operator in smart factory

Location: Central Europe **Start Date:** 2020/01/01

We live an active cooperation between humans and machines. In order to create an optimal balance, we, a future-oriented production facility, are looking for a committed employee in the area of machine monitoring.

We provide you with the possibility to work in a highly technologized environment in a multinational company. You will be a member of a heterogeneous team – humans and machines are equal, collaborating actors in the production of goods. Adaptivity, flexibility, and mobility are of major importance. You will have the opportunity to contribute your ideas, and you will have the choice between stationary and mobile work. There will be times when no activity is required, and you can fully make use of this time for education or relaxation.

Job duties
- Our highly effective and efficient shop floor requires you to work in shift operation
- You are responsible for monitoring equipment and robots, and for organizing quick maintenance in case of breakdowns
- You coordinate activities of your co-workers, i.e., of human and non-human colleagues on the shop floor
- You are required to share your knowledge within and outside the company
- You are invited to contribute your ideas for improvements or developments of processes, products, and services and will be granted sufficient time, space, and equipment to do so

Qualification
- You have an affinity to, expertise for, or experience with highly technological environments
- You have solid computer skills and solid social skills
- You are able to take responsibility, prefer flexibility over routines and have fun to work together in heterogeneous and interdisciplinary teams

To apply please send a link to your CV and/or portfolio to: office@fiction.com

Figure 1. Fictional job posting for the position of a future operator, including the position's label, location and start date, a description of the work environment, job duties, required qualifications, and application mode. The versions for maintainers and engineers were similar in their overall structure; in terms of content, the maintainer ad included details on the spatial and temporal flexibility of work, and visions of international cooperation and connection via technology; the version for engineers focused on interdisciplinary computer-supported work, including user- and innovation-oriented tasks. All versions used were paper-based, deliberately designed plain and simple to concentrate on the content rather than on the layout; we also refrained from using the company's corporate identity since we wanted to detach it from the existing reality.

Here, we decided for easy touch points rather than academic sensitivity that would have required to fully represent the complexity and subtlety of factory work. We deliberately accepted this trade-off in order to quickly initiate discussions in a language spoken by researchers, practitioners, and the public alike. A paradoxon inherent to this fictional job posting is that its elements are not fictional per se, since each is supposedly realized in some company somewhere. However, in this specific cultural environment this job is non-existing. For instance, the explicit offer to choose between stationary and mobile work is not revolutionary; however, even if job crafting is an increasingly well-known concept that argues for workers to proactively design their jobs (e.g., [29]), it is rarely implemented. We will discuss shortly how provocative the job ad had been perceived, though it might not seem far off at first.

APPLICATION 1: STAKEHOLDER DISCUSSION

The first application was a group discussion [12] with stakeholders of the production facility. The participants of this discussion were one human resources employee and two engineers of an automation department, as well as three HCI researchers, who were familiar with the production plant. Since this cooperation had been established earlier, all discussants knew each other, i.e., our role and research aims had been clear to all participants. We had planned for the discussion to take one hour, and started with describing design fiction and how we implemented it to talk about the workplace of the future, a topic that was of importance to that production plant. Then, we distributed the three job postings (operator – as depicted in Figure 1, maintainer, and engineer) to all participants. Since we did not use the fictional job postings before, we did not pre-structure the discussion, but were flexible in how it would develop. The following overview of themes is based on the notes that the researchers took during that session. The notes were sorted (i.e., ordered based on their (dis-)similarity) and interpreted in regards to what they reveal about the instrument.

After everyone had read the fictional job ad, the discussion started without the need to pose a question. It was interesting to see how the illustration of human-machine hybrids in the future factory led to immediate resistance, and resulted in a controversial debate of whether this is a *desirable* future. The participants also discussed how *visionary* the job postings would be; a major element thereby was the indication of a start date; this sets the temporal tone of how close the vision is, with different requirements (the farer, the more visionary the participants expected the job ads to be). While some components seemed to be visionary, others were assessed to be reality anyway (e.g., monitoring machines, coordination responsibilities, shift work), resulting in questioning the *degree of fiction* in those job postings. Furthermore, the participants created *alternative visions* of other job roles or activities, such as considering a novel integrated job role for an all-round employee. Finally, the instrument itself was reflected upon during the discussion: in a large-scale factory, communication between employees is critical; the fictional job ads were considered a valuable means to *communicate visions* of how the factory will evolve in the coming years also within the company.

APPLICATION 2: PUBLIC DISCUSSION

The discussion with the stakeholders resulted in a very intense dialogue about the future of workplaces on the shop floor, so we aimed to broaden this dialogue beyond the factory towards the public, since job postings are manifest in public discourses. In a public university event that aimed to facilitate scientific communication, we displayed the fictional job ad for the position of the operator and asked the visitors about their opinion. The event took place during an evening in April 2016, with heterogeneous visitors (varying age, professions and degrees of formal education). We also prepared a feedback opportunity (a fourfold table to position a sticker within) for quantitatively assessing visitors' opinions on two dimensions: whether the job postings showed a positive / negative development, and whether the job ad was realistic. However, since the event did not allow us to collect any further data about those making use of that feedback mechanism, we refrained from analyzing the data quantitatively. By asking the visitors why they assessed the job postings in a certain way, we also gathered qualitative, anecdotal feedback, which we collected by taking notes after talking to approx. 50 visitors of the event. We analyzed the data in the same way than in application 1.

The visitors' feedback also mainly focused on one or few statements of the fictional job ads, wherein some wordings highly *polarized*. For instance, "active cooperation between humans and machines" or "humans and machines are equal, collaborating actors" led visitors to question whether this vision is *desirable*. The idea that humans monitor machines, but, at the same time, are considered equal co-workers, was perceived as *ambiguous*. One reading of this notion is that the perspective of humans and non-humans being co-workers had been considered realistic, while monitoring and co-working seem to clash. Some visitors were *skeptical*, even *hostile*, towards how the job was described, with older people notably being more skeptical than younger visitors. Visitors also *emphasized the opportunities* that arise, such as getting rid of boring or exhausting work. Overall, opinions ranged from "this will be the future anyway", "that's in part already reality" to "this won't happen". The main finding was that visitors were immediately able to *make sense* of the job ads, though only some had earlier contact with production facilities or complex machines.

OPPORTUNITIES & CHALLENGES

The two applications of the fictional job postings were not set up to gather generalizable results; rather, they were explorative to find out whether this instrument is valuable to trigger discussions and reflections. The anecdotal findings revealed that the job postings worked well to discuss possible futures:

Controversial discussions: Several times, the job postings led to immediate resistance and, thereby, triggered intense and controversial discussions with stakeholders and the public. Different arguments were provided in discussions, many of which were normative, e.g., discussing whether the described future workplace was desirable. The job ads worked as 'boundary objects' in that they provided enough information about the context to reflect on them without requiring first-hand experiences; but they also contained enough details for the industrial stakeholders to be believable.

Alternative visions: Although the main mechanism of the fictional job postings was to discuss the visions that were represented by the job postings, alternatives were created by the discussants. For instance, they argued for other visions to be more likely to be true (e.g., there won't be a human operator at all) or to be more desirable.

Degree of fiction: Combining current and future aspects of workplaces allowed to collaboratively create pictures of future practices. Integrating existing components (e.g., required computer or social skills) with fictional ones (e.g., equality of human and non-human team members) was successful in providing sufficient familiarity to immerse into the context, while, at the same time, challenging it.

This design fiction format, thus, facilitated questioning existing norms and believes, and supported the establishment of a critical discourse with different stakeholder and the public about how to design (for) future computer-supported work practices. However, we also experienced challenges: Not only is it difficult for stakeholders and the public to envision the future, but also for us as researchers. The most difficult part in this work was detaching ourselves from the reality that we had researched for several years. The question remained what would be fictional anyway; this question was representative for the whole process, and later on posed by the stakeholders and the public as well.

Coming back to the argument provided in the beginning of this note, even if "future users" do not exist, it might also be beneficial to discuss the job postings with current workers in a next step. Similarly, the layout might be varied: our plain paper-based version might not be a future-oriented format, which is likely to be purely digital (as it is most of the times nowadays already). Consequently, when creating fictional job postings for the distant future, we need to reconsider how to present them, including appearance, layout, branding, and, especially, possibilities for interactivity. Further variations might focus on the "start date", i.e., varying them in temporal distance to today, which will impact the *degree of fiction* tremendously. Based on our findings we hypothesize that the farer in the future the job will be, the more controversial the discussion will unfold. Similarly, creating a variety of (opposed or complementary) job roles may also fuel such debates.

Design fiction plays with defamiliarization for the purpose of productively upsetting things to examine new possible forms, styles, and experiences [1]. It "happens when you tie together fact and fiction and play comfortably and happily in the between" [1, p. 25]. In our work we also found that fact and fiction are entangled, that defamiliarization requires familiarity; we add to the discourse that focusing on practices instead of single interactions or artefacts is also a valuable perspective for design fiction. While we have specifically looked at production, a larger picture involves all kinds of interactive future work practices; and even further, all kinds of future computer-supported practices. While job postings will only be a suitable instrument for work contexts, the underlying mechanisms might be the same – playing with *contextual* familiarity, alternative visions, and speculations in variably distant futures.

CONCLUSION

Anticipating or envisioning interactive futures of work practices is a challenging task. Therefore, we developed an instrument that is able to act as a communicative means; the aim was not to develop *a* future, but to explore different possibilities in order to learn for the design of future workplaces, a topic that is currently much-debated in industrial, public, and scientific discourses. Taking design fiction as a starting point, we showed in this paper that fictional job postings are a promising instrument to trigger discussions about work places and practices with diverse stakeholders as well as with the public. The job ads were a form of provocation, independent from whether three different job ads were presented, as in the first case, or only one, as in the second case; they enabled an increasingly necessary dialogue not only on how we collaborate with machines, but also how we, as researchers, communicate, discuss, and design for and with industry and the public. A variety of further research is, however, still to be done – from applying fictional job ads in further contexts to in-depth studies that provide knowledge about the scope of the ads (whether they function for discussing a specific technology as well), their relation to participatory design, to critical design, etc.

REFERENCES

1. Julian Bleecker. 2009. Design Fiction: A short essay on design, science, fact and fiction. *Near Future Laboratory* 29 (2009).
2. Mark Blythe. 2014. Research Through Design Fiction: Narrative in Real and Imaginary Abstracts. In *Proceedings of the SIGCHI Conference on Human Factors in Computing Systems (CHI '14)*. ACM, New York, NY, USA, 703–712. DOI: http://dx.doi.org/10.1145/2556288.2557098
3. Mark Blythe, Kristina Andersen, Rachel Clarke, and Peter Wright. 2016. Anti-Solutionist Strategies: Seriously Silly Design Fiction. In *Proceedings of the 2016 CHI Conference on Human Factors in Computing Systems (CHI '16)*. ACM, New York, NY, USA, 4968–4978. DOI: http://dx.doi.org/10.1145/2858036.2858482
4. Mark Blythe and Elizabeth Buie. 2014. Chatbots of the Gods: Imaginary Abstracts for Techno-spirituality Research. In *Proceedings of the 8th Nordic Conference on Human-Computer Interaction: Fun, Fast, Foundational (NordiCHI '14)*. ACM, New York, NY, USA, 227–236. DOI:http://dx.doi.org/10.1145/2639189.2641212
5. Mark Blythe and Andy Dearden. 2009. Representing Older People: Towards Meaningful Images of the User in Design Scenarios. *Univers. Access Inf. Soc.* 8, 1 (March 2009), 21–32. DOI: http://dx.doi.org/10.1007/s10209-008-0128-x
6. Mark Blythe and Enrique Encinas. 2016. The Co-ordinates of Design Fiction: Extrapolation, Irony, Ambiguity and Magic. In *Proceedings of the 19th International Conference on Supporting Group Work (GROUP '16)*. ACM, New York, NY, USA, 345–354. DOI:http://dx.doi.org/10.1145/2957276.2957299
7. Mark Blythe, Jamie Steane, Jenny Roe, and Caroline Oliver. 2015. Solutionism, the Game: Design Fictions for Positive Aging. In *Proceedings of the 33rd Annual ACM Conference on Human Factors in Computing Systems (CHI '15)*. ACM, New York, NY, USA, 3849–3858. DOI: http://dx.doi.org/10.1145/2702123.2702491
8. Tone Bratteteig and Ina Wagner. 2016. What is a Participatory Design Result?. In *Proceedings of the 14th Participatory Design Conference: Full Papers - Volume 1 (PDC '16)*. ACM, New York, NY, USA, 141–150. DOI: http://dx.doi.org/10.1145/2940299.2940316
9. Ole Broberg. 2010. Workspace design: a case study applying participatory design principles of healthy workplaces in an industrial setting. *Int. Journ. of Technology Management* 51, 1 (2010), 39–56. DOI: http://dx.doi.org/10.1504/IJTM.2010.033127
10. Barry Brown, Julian Bleecker, Marco D'Adamo, Pedro Ferreira, Joakim Formo, Mareike Glöss, Maria Holm, Kristina Höök, Eva-Carin Banka Johnson, Emil Kaburuan, Anna Karlsson, Elsa Vaara, Jarmo Laaksolahti, Airi Lampinen, Lucian Leahu, Vincent Lewandowski, Donald McMillan, Anders Mellbratt, Johanna Mercurio, Cristian Norlin, Nicolas Nova, Stefania Pizza, Asreen Rostami, Mårten Sundquist, Konrad Tollmar, Vasiliki Tsaknaki, Jinyi Wang, Charles Windlin, and Mikael Ydholm. 2016. The IKEA Catalogue: Design Fiction in Academic and Industrial Collaborations. In *Proceedings of the 19th International Conference on Supporting Group Work (GROUP '16)*. ACM, New York, NY, USA, 335–344. DOI: http://dx.doi.org/10.1145/2957276.2957298
11. Umer Farooq and Jonathan Grudin. 2016. Human-computer Integration. *interactions* 23, 6 (Oct. 2016), 26–32. DOI:http://dx.doi.org/10.1145/3001896
12. Helen Finch and Jane Lewis. 2003. *Qualitative research practice: A guide for social science students and researchers*. London: SAGE publications, Chapter Focus groups, 170–198.
13. Lars Hallnäs and Johan Redström. 2006. *Interaction design: foundations, experiments*. Textile Research Centre, Swedish School of Textiles, University College of Borås and Interactive Institute.
14. Hartmut Hirsch-Kreinsen. 2016. Digitization of industrial work: development paths and prospects. *Journal for Labour Market Research* 49, 1 (2016), 1–14. DOI: http://dx.doi.org/10.1007/s12651-016-0200-6
15. Henrik Korsgaard, Clemens Nylandsted Klokmose, and Susanne Bødker. 2016. Computational Alternatives in Participatory Design: Putting the T Back in Socio-technical Research. In *Proceedings of the 14th Participatory Design Conference: Full Papers - Volume 1 (PDC '16)*. ACM, New York, NY, USA, 71–79. DOI: http://dx.doi.org/10.1145/2940299.2940314
16. Alina Krischkowsky, Verena Fuchsberger, and Manfred Tscheligi. 2014. Revisiting Corporate Social Media: Challenges and Implications from a Long-Term Study. In *Proceedings of the 18th International Conference on Supporting Group Work (GROUP '14)*. ACM, New York, NY, USA, 157–166. DOI: http://dx.doi.org/10.1145/2660398.2660411
17. Kari Kuutti and Liam J. Bannon. 2014. The Turn to Practice in HCI: Towards a Research Agenda. In *Proceedings of the SIGCHI Conference on Human Factors in Computing Systems (CHI '14)*. ACM, New York, NY, USA, 3543–3552. DOI: http://dx.doi.org/10.1145/2556288.2557111
18. Joseph Lindley. 2015. Crypto Heater: A Design Fiction. In *Proceedings of the 2015 ACM SIGCHI Conference on Creativity and Cognition (C&C '15)*. ACM, New York, NY, USA, 355–356. DOI: http://dx.doi.org/10.1145/2757226.2757367
19. Joseph Lindley and Paul Coulton. 2015. Back to the Future: 10 Years of Design Fiction. In *Proceedings of the 2015 British HCI Conference (British HCI '15)*. ACM, New York, NY, USA, 210–211. DOI: http://dx.doi.org/10.1145/2783446.2783592

20. Joseph Lindley and Paul Coulton. 2016. Pushing the Limits of Design Fiction: The Case For Fictional Research Papers. In *Proceedings of the 2016 CHI Conference on Human Factors in Computing Systems (CHI '16)*. ACM, New York, NY, USA, 4032–4043. DOI: http://dx.doi.org/10.1145/2858036.2858446

21. Conor Linehan, Ben J. Kirman, Stuart Reeves, Mark A. Blythe, Joshua G. Tanenbaum, Audrey Desjardins, and Ron Wakkary. 2014. Alternate Endings: Using Fiction to Explore Design Futures. In *CHI '14 Extended Abstracts on Human Factors in Computing Systems (CHI EA '14)*. ACM, New York, NY, USA, 45–48. DOI: http://dx.doi.org/10.1145/2559206.2560472

22. Jonas Lowgren. 2013. Interaction design - brief intro. In *The Encyclopedia of Human-Computer Interaction, 2nd Ed.* The Interaction Design Foundation, Aarhus, Denmark.

23. Aaron Marcus, Donald A. Norman, Rudy Rucker, Bruce Sterling, and Vernor Vinge. 1992. Sci-fi at CHI: Cyberpunk Novelists Predict Future User Interfaces. In *Proceedings of the SIGCHI Conference on Human Factors in Computing Systems (CHI '92)*. ACM, New York, NY, USA, 435–437. DOI: http://dx.doi.org/10.1145/142750.142892

24. Aaron Marcus, Elliot Soloway, Bruce Sterling, Michael Swanwick, and Vernor Vinge. 1999. Opening Pleanary: Sci-fi @ CHI-99: Science-fiction Authors Predict Future User Interfaces. In *CHI '99 Extended Abstracts on Human Factors in Computing Systems (CHI EA '99)*. ACM, New York, NY, USA, 95–96. DOI: http://dx.doi.org/10.1145/632716.632775

25. Thomas Meneweger, Daniela Wurhofer, Verena Fuchsberger, and Manfred Tscheligi. 2015. Working together with industrial robots: Experiencing robots in a production environment. In *Robot and Human Interactive Communication (RO-MAN), 2015 24th IEEE International Symposium on.* 833–838. DOI: http://dx.doi.org/10.1109/ROMAN.2015.7333641

26. Sebastian Prost, Elke Mattheiss, and Manfred Tscheligi. 2015. From Awareness to Empowerment: Using Design Fiction to Explore Paths Towards a Sustainable Energy Future. In *Proceedings of the 18th ACM Conference on Computer Supported Cooperative Work & Social Computing (CSCW '15)*. ACM, New York, NY, USA, 1649–1658. DOI: http://dx.doi.org/10.1145/2675133.2675281

27. Bruce Sterling. 2009. COVER STORY: Design Fiction. *interactions* 16, 3 (May 2009), 20–24. DOI: http://dx.doi.org/10.1145/1516016.1516021

28. Bruce Sterling. 2013. Patently untrue: fleshy defibrillators and synchronised baseball are changing the future. (2013). http://www.wired.co.uk/article/patently-untrue

29. Maria Tims and Arnold B. Bakker. 2010. Job crafting: towards a new model of individual job redesign. *SA Journal of Industrial Psychology* 36 (01 2010), 1 – 9. http://www.scielo.org.za/scielo.php?script=sci_arttext&pid=S2071-07632010000200003&nrm=iso

Tiles: A Card-based Ideation Toolkit for the Internet of Things

Simone Mora, Francesco Gianni and Monica Divitini
Department of Computer Science
Norwegian University of Science and Technology
Sem Sælandsvei 7, 7491-Trondheim (Norway)
{simone.mora, francesco.gianni, monica.divitini}@ntnu.no

ABSTRACT
The Internet of Things (IoT) offers new opportunities to invent technology-augmented things that are more useful, efficient or playful than their ordinary selves, yet only a few tools currently support ideation for the IoT. In this paper we present Tiles Cards, a set of 110 design cards and a workshop technique to involve non-experts in quick idea generation for augmented objects. Our tool aims to support exploring combinations of user interface metaphors, digital services, and physical objects. Then it supports creative thinking through provocative design goals inspired by human values and desires. Finally, it provides critical lenses through which analyze and judge design outcomes. We evaluated our tool in 9 ideation workshops with a total of 32 participants. Results show that the tool was useful in informing and guiding idea generation and was perceived as appealing and fun. Drawing on observations and participant feedbacks, we reflect on the strengths and limitations of this tool.

Author Keywords
Design tools; card tools; Internet of Things; IoT; augmented objects.

ACM Classification Keywords
H.5.2 Information interfaces and presentation (e.g. HCI): User interfaces—Theory and methods

INTRODUCTION
The Internet of Things (IoT) holds huge promise to change the way we work, play and learn. The core idea of the IoT is that a huge variety of things will be augmented with technology in order to become interactive and connected to the Internet, yet maintain elements of their traditional physical appearance. Examples include a paintbrush that samples colors from surfaces and uses them as a drawing palette in a computer program [30], a water faucet that lights up in colors to display daily water consumption data [22] and wood bricks that can be used by children to create computer programs [15]. Technology can be used either to augment an existing purpose of an object, making it more useful, playful or engaging than usual, or to add new functions that are controlled using the object's affordances; at the extreme, the object may look magical or enchanted [28]. Although this vision is shared by long-established research in ubiquitous computing, by putting the emphasis on connectivity the IoT promotes the development of applications that make use of ecosystems of connected things that leverage and interact with online services [20].

IoT research has concentrated mainly on two ends: the technical, solving technological challenges such as connectivity and security; and the theoretical, following up on visions, e.g. [36] [13] of how computers integrated into the fabric of the physical world can serve human needs. Compared with these two goals, an exploration of the IoT from an HCI point of view is in its infancy [20]. As consequence, the user experience provided by several IoT devices is often unsatisfactory, at least when compared to traditional software products.

As noted by Rowland et al. [29], interaction design for connected things is different from, and in some aspects more complex than, traditional computer products. Functionalities can be distributed among multiple devices offering varying input/output capabilities, form factors, and purpose. User interface elements often leverage tangible interaction themes [16,19], such as direct manipulation and physical representation of data. Despite such a large paradigm shift, design tools for the IoT are mostly based on traditional methodologies that emerged in the pre-IoT era. Very few products provide specific design tools and methods, e.g. [9,16,17].

The aim of our research is to investigate how to foster human-centered design of novel IoT user experiences by providing tools to engage *non-experts* in idea generation. Non-expert participation in design is a long-established practice in human-centered design. With the term 'non-expert' we mean users without formal training in design techniques or previous knowledge in IoT or ubiquitous computing: for example, researchers and students, makers,

DIS 2017, June 10-14, 2017, Edinburgh, United Kingdom
 ISBN 978-1-4503-4922-2/17/06…$15.00
DOI: http://dx.doi.org/10.1145/3064663.3064699

and children. Our approach is inspired by a *thing-oriented* vision of the IoT [see 2] and uses *object augmentation* [21 pag.254] as a design strategy.

This paper contributes to this strand by presenting the *Tiles Ideation Toolkit* (hereafter abbreviated as *Tiles*), a card-based ideation tool for Internet of Things user experiences. Ideation—the formulation of initial ideas and thoughts as both personal and collaborative processes—is an essential step in design methods [10]. Tiles comprises a set of 110 cards and a workshop technique to engage non-experts in idea generation. *Tiles cards* provide a source of inspiration for ideas by: (i) suggesting a set of technology primitives to describe the IoT design space, (ii) providing triggers for divergent and creative thinking, and (iii) offering criteria for reflecting on and evaluating the ideas generated. *Tiles workshop* structures the use of the cards in ideation workshops with step-by-step guidance, support for collaboration and by complementing the cards' use with traditional design thinking techniques and artifacts.

The cards and workshop materials are released under a Creative Commons license and available for download at http://tilestoolkit.io/cards.

We evaluated the usefulness of our tool in informing and guiding idea generation during nine workshops with a total of thirty-two participants. We discuss which features of the tool facilitated or hindered idea generation. In closing, we outline directions for future work.

RELATED WORK

Characteristics of cards-based design tools

Research projects have found card-based tools effective in supporting idea generation in design workshops [34]. Cards are useful for presenting theoretical constructs and making the design practice more engaging and playful, thus enlarging the group of people that take part in designing new systems. They can be an effective vehicle for transferring knowledge between theory and practice [9], for example to convert theoretical frameworks to guidelines that can be manipulated by designers [9]. Card-based tools help keep people at the center of the design process [18,24] and facilitate creative dialogue and shared understanding. Cards can be a source of inspiration to steer a discussion when it becomes unproductive [17], for example by proposing provocative questions to unlock thinking [27]. Cards can also be used to evaluate, rate or bookmark ideas generated during design sessions [17,24].

Cards facilitate collaborative and divergent thinking by providing a medium for conversation between stakeholders and designers [7,14,24]; furthermore, they allow externalizing ideas and ensuring that a design space is investigated from different points of view. Card play adds game mechanics helpful in exploring design alternatives in a playful manner [5,24], empowering users and engaging multiple stakeholders [34]. Game rules add constraints that may improve design outcomes [5] and foster creativity. For example turn-taking helps ensure that everyone is involved in the process [17] and role-taking help smooth power relations and conflict among participants [5]. From this perspective, cards act as physical props to externalize thoughts and help structure common grounds to which everybody can relate [5], helping them take risks within the framework of a game.

To summarize, the characteristics of card-based tools we aim to embrace with our tool are: (i) informative: helping to describe complex concepts to non-experts, (ii) inspirational: helping trigger and guide brainstorming and idea generation, (iii) collaborative: engaging users by helping collaboration and creative dialogue.

Applying card-based tools to IoT ideation

Card-based design tools have been applied to the design of technology for a wide range of domains related to IoT, including embodied interfaces [17], tangible interfaces for learning games [9] and exertion games [27]; to design for playfulness [24] and for influencing behaviors [23]. Recently a few card-based tools have specifically targeted IoT ideation [1,8,12].

Similarly to *Exertion Cards* [27] and *Tango Cards* [9], Tiles offers provocative questions that trigger creativity. Like *Plex cards* [24], it provides dimension to evaluate and judge the outcome idea generation. Yet these tools have a much broader domain than Tiles: for example, design for playfulness, where "*potentially any activity can be approached and performed in a playful manner*" [24] or learning games [9]. Similarly to *Know-cards* [1], our tool describes the components of IoT technology in a language accessible to novices, yet the former doesn't provide triggers for creativity or reflection. *Thingclash* [8] provides a structured ideation technique similar to that of Tiles. Yet rather than supporting ideation, Thingclash focuses on critical analysis of actual IoT products with the aim of finding friction points at the technological, societal, economic and policy levels. *IoT Service Kit* [12] shares with Tiles a goal of ideating IoT scenarios by merging physical objects, digital services and interaction metaphors. Interestingly enough, they provide objects as tiny 3D models rather than as drawings on cards, yet their focus is on involving tech professionals from different backgrounds rather than non-experts. Analogously to *Envisioning Cards* [11] and *Picking up artifacts* [35], Tiles provides "create your own" cards that can be freely customized by the user. The envisioning cards also present other similarities to our tool, like the focus on a specific group of stakeholders and criteria to facilitate reflection. Likewise with Tiles, some of the card tools are meant to be used in design workshops [3,7] but a defined and repeatable workshop structure is not reported. Finally, most of the tools reviewed are freely available, e.g. [9,24], or licensed under a Creative Commons license that allows for the tools' adaptation and customization, e.g. [8,12].

Augmentation as a design strategy for the IoT

Successful IoT product design requires one to take into consideration multiple, sometimes seemingly unrelated, criteria at once. This spans the spectrum from physical attributes, such as form factors and technical components, to intangible concepts, such as interaction patterns or user values. Rather than thinking up the mix of factors from scratch, a possible design strategy leverages starting from a non-digital, everyday object, preserving its broad purpose, and adding computation capabilities on top of it. Kuniavsky [21] motivates enriching everyday objects as a design strategy. He claims that augmentation leverages the advantages of using user-familiar shapes and functionalities: "Augmentation is most successful when it keeps what the target audience perceives as the core of the experience of an object intact, enhancing it without changing its perceived key attributes" [21 pag.262]. Because people are familiar with everyday affordances, technology needs only to extend those and can build on existing use patterns since "the more familiar is the tool the less effort it takes to learn it."

As with most of tools reviewed, Tiles adopts cards as a participation and learning tool. Yet based on the need found in previous work, e.g. [27] for more guidance in the process that cannot simply be provided by the cards *per se*, we aim to complement the card use with a structured process as well as design artifacts to support the process' adoption. Besides the fact that a structured process might restrict freedom during workshop supervision or facilitation, this comes at the interest of facilitating a broader adoption of the tool. The characteristics of our tool can be summarized in: (i) specific focus on IoT user experiences, (ii) ideation workshop with a repeatable structure and guidelines, (iii) can be specialized towards specific domains (iv) oriented to non-experts, (v) use object augmentation as a design strategy.

TILES IDEATION TOOLKIT

Tiles has been created to inspire ideas for IoT user experiences by fostering both divergent and convergent thinking. With Tiles, we aim to investigate how to facilitate human-centered, creative, and reflective idea generation by engaging users without expertise in design techniques and IoT.

Toolkit composition

Tiles comprises a set of 110 cards (Tiles Cards) and a workshop technique that makes use of the cards together with supporting design methods and artifacts (Tiles Workshop).

Tiles cards have descriptive and inspirational roles. Five sets of *primitive cards* (Decks 1-5, Fig. 1) inspire combinations of IoT components like everyday things, user interface elements, sensors, and services. Divergent thinking is supported by *themes cards* (Deck 6), suggesting a set of provocative design goals to provide creativity triggers. Finally, *criteria cards* (Deck 7) help converging and formalizing ideas by providing arguments to reflect and evaluate design outcomes.

Providing non-experts only with a set of cards can be overwhelming and confusing. Browsing the cards without any guidance or constraints might not be a sufficient stimulus for creative and collaborative thinking [17]. For these reasons, the Tiles workshop provides an ideation technique and workshop-related tools: (i) a cardboard that scaffolds use and placement for the card, storyboarding, and reflection, (ii) a playbook to guide the users step-by-step in the ideation process, (iii) integration with user-centered design artifacts, such as personas and scenarios to address specific problem domains.

Following on from the descriptive framework by Atzori et al. [2], we look at the IoT from a "things-oriented" perspective. Several elements of their framework influenced our tool: (i) the foreseeing of internet nodes to reside in every object, like food packages, furniture, paper documents, and more, (ii) the concept of *spime*, defined as an object that is tracked throughout its lifetime and that will be sustainable, enhance-able, and uniquely identifiable [32], (iii) IoT as an architecture of independent federated services and applications, characterized by a high degree of autonomous data capture, event transfer, network connectivity, and interoperability. The focus on idea generation and design was also inspired by the work of Atzori et al. [2], who assess the lack availability of IoT applications, despite the potential the technology already offers.

Toolkit extendibility

Tiles has been designed as a flexible tool, adaptable to ideate augmented things for a variety of application domains. On the other hand, which *thing* to augment and how to intervene with technology is often related to the needs and values of specific user groups and contexts. Although Tiles does not provide tools to investigate a specific domain, insights can be gathered using user research methods borrowed from ethnography [4], including interviews, user diaries, or surveys. User research outcomes formalized in artifacts like *Personas* and *Scenarios* can be used in a Tiles Workshop to focus ideation toward a specific domain, problem, or need for a specific user group. Furthermore, because Tiles is licensed under Creative Commons, the set of cards can be extended by domain experts, adding cards related to a specific domain, for example, making adaptations of our work such as *Tiles for smart cities* or *Tiles for serious games*. Finally, although the cards have been developed in conjunction with the workshop technique, they can also be used with different ideation or brainstorming techniques or game mechanics.

The development of Tiles has been undertaken in three iterations, in collaboration with a design studio. The process benefitted from having direct access to designers' experience in workshop facilitation and participatory

Figure 1: Tiles Cards decks.

design. The contents of the cards and the workshop structure have been refined according to feedback gathered during focus groups with experts and formative evaluations with design students. In this paper, we focus on the final version of the toolkit and its evaluation. The initial design of the tool and a pilot study is described in [26].

In the following two sections, we describe the rationale behind the creation of the different decks of cards and the workshop technique.

TILES CARDS

The 110 cards are sized 9x6cm and shaped with rounded corners arranged in seven categories (decks) (Figure 1). All decks are color-coded to be easily discernible from one another.

The front side of each card explains its role and the deck to which it belongs. The back side provides content specific to each card. The object or concept for each card is illustrated with graphics and a short text. The contents on the cards have been chosen for understandability, not requiring any background in design or technology. The cards have a unique ID printed on the bottom right corner to simplify data collection and logging during design workshops.

For each deck, we provide blank cards that can be personalized by players. In this way, we expect to free participants' creative impulses and allow for out-of-the-box thinking. Popular user-designed cards can also be included in future versions of the tool.

In the remainder of this section, we describe the cards by grouping them according to their roles.

Description of IoT components

To help non-experts navigate the space of opportunities offered by the IoT, we created five groups of primitive cards. The cards help to deconstruct and explain IoT elements, such as data sources and user interface metaphors, in a simple language, hiding unnecessary complexities.

The Atzori et al. framework [2] has been adopted as a source of inspiration to simplify IoT characteristics in a set of primitive cards that can be used pragmatically for brainstorming. The heterogeneity of the groups of cards reflects their vision of systems composed of many subsystems, with extremely different characteristics. These cards are grouped in five categories: *things, human actions, feedback, connectors, and data channels.*

Things cards (deck 1) suggest a set of everyday, low-tech things that can be enhanced by technology. Objects depicted on cards belong to the following categories: the home (e.g. fridge, stove), the office (e.g. desk, pen), clothing (e.g. shoes, watch), outdoors (e.g. sporting equipment, plants) and transportation (e.g. bike). We included both objects meant for personal and shared use. We excluded objects that are relevant only to particular groups of people, such as work tools or weapons, or those that are already technology augmented, such as smartphones.

Figure 2: Group A playing with cards during a Tiles workshop. Cards, Board and Playbook are visible.

Human Actions cards and Feedback cards (deck 2-3) propose several interaction metaphors that can be composed to design the user interfaces of an augmented object. *Human actions* describe how the user can trigger a digital input via a physical action, such as approaching an object, manipulating it, or moving it. *Feedback* describes how the object communicates back to the user, for example via visual, audio, or haptic feedback. These interaction styles, popular in the field of tangible interaction, can be quickly prototyped using technology toolkits like Arduino [25] and Little Bits [3], facilitating complementing design explorations with prototypes. Conversely, because IoT devices usually don't feature a large screen or input peripherals, we excluded elements of GUI metaphors, such as menus or windows.

Connectors cards (deck 4) list logical relations among objects to be used to define their *interusability* [29 pag.340]. Those include logic operators common to programming languages, such as *if/then,* temporal operators like *while*, and spatial operators like *together.* Connectors make it easier to design user experiences that span an ecology of things orchestrated to show a coherent behavior, for example, when an action or a sequence of actions performed on an object triggers an output on another object. Their abstract nature helps combine physical things with digital services.

Data channels cards (deck 5) list popular internet services, social networks, and sensor devices that provide or store information accessible via public APIs, e.g. Twitter, traffic warnings, or cloud documents. They inspire the design of augmented objects acting as avatars for digital services. For example, a data channel card can be combined with a thing and a feedback card to design a device that visualizes data in a tangible way, e.g. a keychain that vibrates when a traffic alert is issued. Likewise, an association of a thing card and a human action card can define an object that provides a physical affordance to control a remote data source.

Support for creative thinking

Combining things, user interface metaphors, and data channels has the potential to turn individual components into meaningful combinations. Yet those combinations might not necessarily describe an augmented object that is novel, useful, or user-friendly. Without triggers for creative thinking and constraints in the design process, users of our tool could fall into designing artifacts that resemble existing products and make use of mainstream user interface metaphors. The following two decks of cards have been created to avoid these issues.

Themes (deck 6) help to engage users in creative thinking by providing twenty provocative design goals. Those triggers aim to support the generation of divergent ideas and creating a conversation momentum among participants. Example of themes are: "Sixth-Sense: Create an object that gives its owner some kind of superpower, like new types of senses, perceiving new information, etc." and "Trojan Horse: Create a concept that seemingly does one thing, but where the intention is to produce another, deeper effect."

Theme cards are centered on human behaviors and desires; they have been inspired by David Rose's *Enchanted Objects* [28] and the *perceptual lenses* of the *Design with Intent* toolkit [23]. Each card briefly describes a specific design theme and provides examples of how the theme can be implemented in an augmented object.

Support for reflection on generated ideas

After a number of ideas are generated, *Criteria cards* (deck 7) help participants to reflect on and evaluate their design outcomes by looking at their ideas through a set of nine critical lenses. Examples of criteria cards are: "Creativity: Ideas that solve a problem in a clever and unusual way"; and "Feasibility: Ideas that solve a problem in a plausible manner, and that seem realistic to develop."

The criteria act as triggers for collaborative reflection. While themes cards foster divergent thinking, criteria support refining ideas toward converging on a concept that satisfies one or more criterion. Criteria encourage trade-off discussions and enable finding inspiration for future design iterations. Criteria could be also used in the early phases of idea generation, for example, by discarding ideas that are evaluated as not innovative enough or feasible to prototype.

To summarize: primitive cards enable quick exploration of multiple combinations of physical things, user interface metaphors, and data channels. Themes cards introduce triggers to help re-frame ideas toward certain users' goals and values. Criteria cards provide lenses through which to reflect, evaluate, and select ideas, and to inform new design iterations.

TILES WORKSHOP

To provide guidance for collaborative ideation using the Tiles Cards, we developed a workshop technique to be used in sessions with 2-6 participants facilitated by professionals. The technique reflects the structure of the creative design process as defined by Schön [31], which iterates between problem analysis, problem framing, generation of potential solutions, and critical reflection on ideas generated.

The technique guides the use of the cards and complements it with traditional design activities, such as sketching and storyboarding and with user research artifacts, such as Personas. The activities of the workshops are supported by a *playbook* and a *cardboard.*

The playbook describes seven design actions the users must accomplish in a limited amount of time and according to certain rules, e.g. limiting the number of cards that can be used in a design session. The cardboard offers visual affordances to support the actions and rules described in the playbook. It guides the user in combining different type of cards and incentives, sketching, and note-taking. By adding constraints to the use of the cards, we expect to increase the creativity and number of ideas generated, as discovered by [5]. In the remainder of this section, we further detail the playbook and cardboard.

Playbook

The playbook guides workshop participants in designing an augmented object with a seven-step process. Although the ideation technique is meant to be supervised by professionals, the playbook helps keep the design process visible and minimizes the need for supervision.

The activities participants are asked to perform are the following:

1. *Select a user and a context you agree to design for* – it helps define the boundaries of the design space. A user and a context, formulized as persona, scenario or problem elaboration, are to be provided by workshop organizers to steer design efforts to a specific domain.
2. *Browse Things cards and select one or more objects that are central for a given user. Use Connector cards to define the relationships among the objects, as needed* – it defines what object(s) will be augmented by technology. It enables participants to start generating ideas leveraging their native knowledge of how everyday objects work, using technology to improve upon their original affordances and capabilities.
3. *Define which actions trigger the things by browsing Human Actions and Data Channels cards* – it allows users to define how humans and third-party services interact with the selected objects.
4. *Define how the things respond when triggered by browsing Feedback and Data Channels cards* – it allows users to define how the selected objects communicate back to the user, either via user interface feedback or via sending information over a data channel.
5. *Flesh out ideas on the storyboard section* – it allows participants to focus on one idea by sketching how the augmented object is used and what values it brings to the users.
6. *Use Themes cards to find ways to challenge one's idea, then go back and refine the storyboard contents.* – it provides triggers to diverge by iteratively modifying and expanding previous ideas.
7. *Look through the Criteria cards and discuss how well one's idea scores on each criterion* – it helps collaborative reflection and trade-off discussion.

Participants are expected to be given a limited amount of time to complete each step. A time constraint is added to the process in the attempt to avoid participants' getting stuck or converging too early on an idea before having explored different cards. Collaboration in the group is left informal; cards can be freely browsed and chosen according to the persona and scenario for which the group is designing. When needed, some strategies could be enforced to guarantee that everyone takes part in the discussion, for example, asking participants to draw and discuss one card each in turns or introducing rules to foster competition among participants.

Cardboard

A cardboard (Figure 2) is provided as scaffolding. It consists of four areas, to be used in sequence to scaffold the design activities in the playbook:

- *Ideas* helps outline the augmented things. It guides users in combining cards by suggesting grouping cards as *things*—the *things* to be augmented by technology, *triggers*—the set of *human actions* and *data channels* that initiate some interactive behavior of the thing(s), and *responses*—the kind of *feedback* and *data channels* the things use to communicate back to the user.
- *Storyboard* allows the sketching of the user experience with the augmented things in six blank frames. It facilitates moving from a static representation of several augmented things into a dynamic view of how people interact with the things.
- *Themes* allows for placement of *Themes* cards that are selected as relevant to the current idea and provides space for annotating how the themes have been used and discussing trade-offs.
- *Reflection* allows for the placement of *Criteria* cards and provide space for annotating strengths and weakness of an idea with respect to selected criteria.

By framing the cards in use during a design session, the board provides a conversation medium to foster collaborative brainstorming. Because of its large size, the board enables 3-4 people to sit shoulder-to-shoulder. Furthermore, the use of cards and cardboard recalls playing board games, an activity familiar to many.

USER STUDY

We conducted user studies to understand how Tiles was useful in informing and guiding ideation for the IoT. We focused on the following aspects:

1. Informing about IoT: as the capability to transmit knowledge and awareness of IoT basic components to non-experts
2. Creativity: intended as sparking design thinking and idea generation
3. Reflection: as the ability to change perspective and refine ideas in a critical way
4. Guidance: as the ability to support participants in idea generation

We do not aim to evaluate the contents of the cards, but rather their use as part of the workshop technique.

Participants

Participants (n=32) were a convenient sample of graduate and undergraduate students from a local university, high-school students, and one researcher in IT. Some of the participants had basic experience in programming, but none of them declared themselves to have experience in design topics or techniques. High-school students were aged 15 and 16; they were not mixed with university students or researchers when attending the workshop. University students came from the Computer Science and Architecture departments. The researcher was also from the Computer Science department, but not involved in IoT or design research. A movie-ticket raffle was used as an incentive for participation. The premise for the participation was to learn about the IoT.

Evaluation process

Participants used the Tiles Cards during Tiles Workshops organized in multiple sessions. Groups of two to four participants were formed according to their availability. Each participant attended one workshop only. Each workshop was supervised by two researchers and lasted for about 1 hour and 30 minutes.

The goal of each workshop was to design an IoT application to support sustainable behaviors in smart cities, a topic that has been considered interesting for a general audience. A set of sample *personas* and *scenarios* related to the domain were provided to the participants.

Participants were welcomed with a five-minute presentation about the IoT, followed by a brief description of Tiles. Participants were then asked to start an idea-generation session following the rules reported in the playbook, which was provided as a reference during the workshop. Participants were given about five minutes to complete each of the playbook's seven steps, resulting in sessions that lasted between 35 and 45 minutes. After the ideas were finalized, each group presented their outcomes in a short pitch. Participants were then asked to respond individually to a questionnaire about their experience in the workshop. A five-point Likert scale was used to assess the results. Each session ended with a 10-to-25 minute group interview, where participants were asked to provide feedback about the tool and the process and encouraged to comment on any detail they considered relevant. The interview was also meant to confirm the data collected by the questionnaires.

Data collection and analysis

Video and audio of each group session was captured. Researchers also observed and took notes and photos during idea generation and interviews. The videos were replayed later and a transcript was produced from them. Data from the questionnaires were aggregated and analyzed using spreadsheet software. Consent forms were signed by all participants.

The analysis of collected data was guided by the Strauss and Corbin process [33] and by the guidelines in [6]. We focused on patterns of actions that involved participants and elements of the Tiles workshop, especially in connection to the research questions. Observations were also meant to spot and discover the process, intended as unexpected usage of the toolkit or pre-defined procedures supported by the workshop. Transcripts of videos and free-entry comments from questionnaires were coded using the focus criteria of the evaluation. Quotations reported in the following sections are from the unmodified transcript of user feedback mainly collected through video recording.

RESULTS

Example of ideas generated

We first present one of the ideas generated during the workshop to exemplify the type and complexity of ideas that can be achieved with a ~40-minute ideation session using Tiles. We chose this idea because the participants rigorously followed all the steps in the playbook. The idea demonstrates everyday object augmentation well; special attention was also given by the participants to critical reflection and refinement of the idea.

The idea, developed by group C, describes "The Small-Talk Bench": a technology-augmented public bench to promote social interaction among the elderly. The augmented object is a public bench to be placed in a park. The bench is activated when one or more people are sitting. When only one person is sitting, the bench provides breaking news, bus schedules, and other useful information. When two or more people are sitting, the bench also has an "ice-breaker" function, asking questions to those sitting (with a synthesized voice) about popular topics in politics and science, such as "What do you guys think about the upcoming elections?" The goal of the *Small-Talk Bench* is both to act as a simple interface for the elderly to stay informed and to encourage social interaction among strangers by proposing small-talk topics.

Ideating the small-talk bench, group C choose to work with the Theme cards *Omniscience* (TM-18), *Safekeeping* (TM-19), *Social Interaction* (TM-5), and *Enjoyable Objects* (TM-6). They critically reflected upon and improved the idea using the Criteria cards *User-friendly (C-8), Utility (C-4), and Market Potential (C-9).*

Roles of the tool

Data from the questionnaires suggest that Tiles was perceived as useful. More than 90% of the participants agreed at least partially with the statements in Figure 3. Almost 90% agreed that the visual design was appealing and more than 90% agreed at least partially that the cards were easy to understand and that the design process provided guidance to develop new ideas. In the following section, we report results for each evaluation goal.

Informing participants about IoT components

Observations and data from the questionnaires show that the tool was useful in helping users navigate through the IoT design space. The mind-opening capabilities and the possibility for non-experts to understand what IoT has to offer emerged from interviews and observations: *"This process shows you a lot of possibilities for IoT we haven't thought about", "I read a lot about IoT before, but the cards are more structured and made easier to remind and recall the concepts", "The process was also helpful to understand what the possibilities are", "I like that data channels are used both for triggers and output, that helped to see what the possibilities were."*

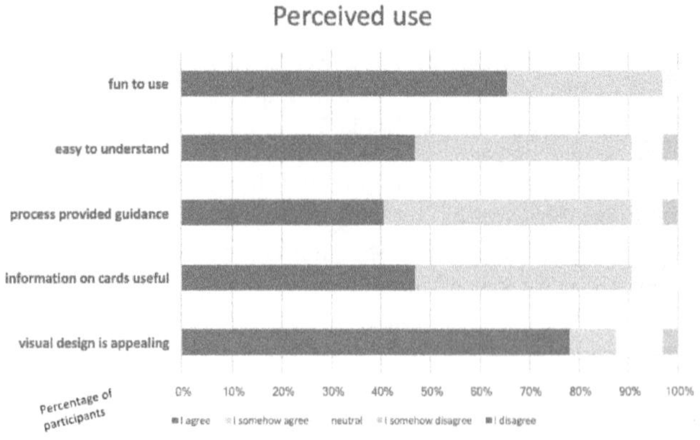

Figure 3: Use of the tool.

Primitive cards describing user-interface metaphors were considered particularly useful. From the questionnaire, more than 85% of the participants agreed or partially agreed that the Human Action and Feedback cards helped to understand the opportunities provided by IoT technologies. Participants stated that the Things cards were useful in connecting IoT technology with everyday objects: *"Things cards are useful because you can understand which everyday objects you can augment."*

The overall experience with the tool contributed to inform and introduce participants to the IoT field: *"I didn't have a clue of what IoT was before, now I feel I have a better knowledge", "I have a better understanding of IoT and I think it's more useful. I see IoT now more as a process than a network of objects."*

Support for creativity

Questionnaires show that Tiles was useful in sparking creativity. Almost 70% of the participants agreed or partially agreed that they had ideas they would not have had without the cards (Figure 4). Participants also agreed at least partially that *Themes* cards helped them to be creative and that it was easy to design interactive objects using the cards.

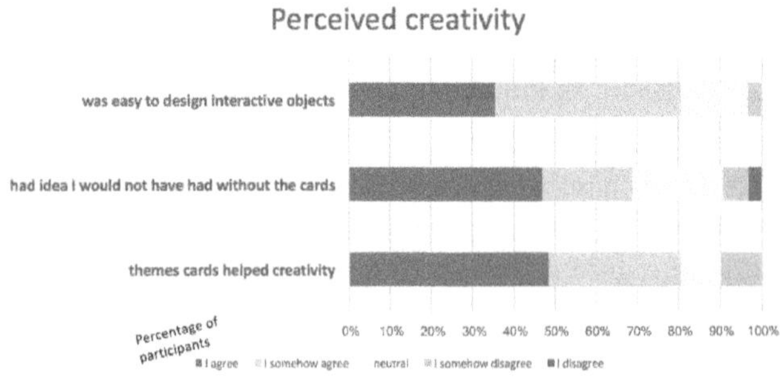

Figure 4: Perceived creativity support in using the cards.

Not everybody agreed on through which step creativity was best expressed and encouraged: *"For me the Things section was the grounding of the idea, it's where my mind worked more and I was more creative"*, one participant said, while others pointed to the Themes cards: *"Themes category made us more creative, made us come up with new ideas for the product we already have."* Some participants declared that the *triggers* and *response* areas of the board contributed best to creativity, while others assigned some credits also to the context or the storyboard: *"A scenario like this can be used for a lot of things depending on your creativity"*, *"We were most creative on the storyboard, we didn't choose a specific idea and object before the storyboard, we could make up whatever we want."*

Mixed opinions were also collected about diverging or converging on generating ideas: *"If you think about a problem maybe you only think about related objects, but this tool opens your mind and force you to evaluate objects that are not necessarily related"*, *"The cards show a vast array of possibilities, opens your mind a lot."* On the other hand, some participants suggested the addition of constraints to the process: *"Better to have a context but not choose freely the card: can help to generate more unique ideas"*, *"I think it's divided in two parts: left part of the board more opening your mind, right side more narrowing down."*

Cards were a source of inspiration for many: *"Cards were useful at the beginning to trigger the initial idea, a lot of possible different combinations"*, *"What are you thinking when I say plants? Maybe is related to sustainable behavior…."*

Finally, some participants suggested improvements of the ideation process: *"Maybe a rule to restrict the number of events or objects, to narrow down more efficiently"*. It is interesting that participants felt the need for more constraints to be more creative. This is in line with results from other card-based tools, e.g. [17,27].

Support for reflection

When interviewed about the support for reflection the tool provided, participants commented that they were able to reflect on the idea they generated: "*The reflection section is pushing you to think why you do it in the first place*", *"I learned more with criteria and themes: you get back on the idea, the rationale of the idea, you reflect on the idea Themes raise awareness, evaluate the idea under a different point of view."*

When asked whether *Criteria* cards helped to reflect and evaluate ideas, more than 80% of the participants agreed or partially agreed with the statement. Indeed, we observed participants reflecting on the idea while browsing Criteria cards: *"[looking at criteria C-2 Innovation] Innovative? The idea is probably out there but it's not of common use, it's the right direction"*, *"[group while browsing cards] I think we need to focus on the social aspect because if not what's the difference between staying home watching the news and sitting on this bench watching the news?"*

Support for guidance

More than 90% of the participants agreed at least partially that the tool provided guidance to develop new ideas. The interviews confirmed that participants were glad to have a clear structure to rely on and some sort of guidance: "*Normally [in IoT] everything is mixed, but it is useful to have a structure and to think about data channel, things and feedback, separately"*, *"I think the cards guided me to a point, that was like [just] watching them, I was able to make the story."* Yet the high number of cards provided (110 cards in 7 decks) made some participants feel overwhelmed: *"At the beginning we struggle to understand, to pick up things"*, *"Too many cards, too many possibilities."*

Analyzing the role of cardboard and playbook in guidance, we gathered mixed opinions. Comments were not positive regarding the role of the cardboard in supporting the ideation process: *"We followed some steps, but when we reached the end it was like what's now? Do we have an idea now?"* Many declared that the board was not explicit enough: *"I didn't really know what cards I have to connect"*, *"We need a more specific guide on the board."* Because the board design was not immediately understood nor well accepted, it led participants to spread the cards all over it (see Figure 2), ignoring the card placeholder, hiding important sections, and adding to confusion. This is confirmed by the interviews, where users declared *"Didn't use the board, didn't get the vertical alignment of trigger-things-feedback"*, *"I didn't notice the boxes [cards placeholder] on the board."* Participants were more positive about the guidance provided by the playbook: *"This is better than traditional brainstorming"*, *"We need to move to the following step, it say 15 minutes here on the board!"*. The playbook was often used as a support when getting stuck, as participants skipped to the next listed step to continue working.

DISCUSSION

The Tiles Card workshop proved to be an effective process to support design and idea generation for the IoT. Results show that in a very limited amount of time, participants were able to:

- Design one or more augmented objects;
- Use the augmented objects in a user story addressing a specific problem and scenario; and
- Reflect upon and improve the idea, looking at the problem from different perspectives.

In this section, we reflect on the strengths and limitations of our approach, identifying which elements played a role in facilitating or hindering idea generation. These reflections can be considered as useful guidelines for the design of similar IoT ideation tools.

Strengths of the tool

A structured process facilitated ideation outcomes

The design process was guided by the instructions reported on the playbook area of the board. This was an element of novelty compared to previous works that chose to not provide prescriptive guidelines about how to use the cards, e.g. [14,17,27], and it came at the risk of obstructing the creative nature of design work. Surprisingly, workshop participants called for even more constraints in the process rather than fewer. This might be justified by the process leaving room for freedom and to tweak the process as needed. For example, we did not put any constraints on the number of cards to be used and participants could always re-do or revisit previous steps if new information or ideas arose. Like the workshop technique in [14], we did not set up rules for roles or turn-taking.

Yet the strategy adopted by the groups was more articulated than we expected. The initial choice of the domain context drove the selection by the participants. Things cards were then excluded if not relevant for a certain context. During steps 3 and 4 of the playbook, participants were pushed to think about how to connect triggers and feedback to things and were advised by the playbook to use multiple cards for the same object. Despite the playbook's focus on triggers and feedback, participants continued referring to selected *context*, *user* and *things* to get inspiration. Sketching the storyboard forced participants to discuss a detailed scenario to use, while cards were added and/or removed and the idea was usually refined and improved, resulting in a more robust version. There was much more happening during this step than simply writing down a developed idea. Themes cards also helped participants to gain confidence in their idea: they were relieved to find that their idea fit one or more themes.

Driven by the progressive discovery of new cards, participants were often excited to include a specific card into an idea. If the card explicitly clashed with the core of the idea, it was easy for other group members to prevail in the argument, quickly discard the unnecessary card, and continue in the design process.

Given the novelty of the field, it was critical to support the user when exploring new paradigms. When allowed a great deal freedom, users tend to revert to what they already know. To avoid allowing this to happen, the process is delegated to support and point the user in the pursued direction. The Tiles Workshop succeeded in preventing the users from coming up with ideas that involved mainstream concepts and classical interfaces like screens, pointers, etc., which are not strictly connected to the IoT.

Finally, a structured process support by a playbook given to participants as a design artifact also helped to reduce the help given by professionals in workshop supervision. This can reduce the risk of adding the personal bias of workshop facilitators to the ideas generated by the groups, an issue that limited other projects [27].

Creativity permeated the whole ideation process

Divergent and convergent thinking were observed and sometimes even suggested by participants in relation to the cards. Some converging elements like Scenario and Criteria cards served the purpose of sparking creativity, but some participants wished for a more constrained approach, for example when dealing with the Things cards. Others, on the other hand, appreciated the diverging and mind-opening experience of getting to know the possibilities offered by the IoT. We believe that, given the novelty of the field, allowing participants to discover a wide design space can be more beneficial than restricting them to a limited set of cards randomly chosen—for example, enforcing turn-taking. This would also introduce the risk of pushing participants to generate an idea at all costs, losing sight of user and context, or the problem that drives the design.

Idea generation was a creative process that permeated the whole workshop, regardless of the specific phase. Participants continued adding to and refining the fundamental core of the idea during every phase of the workshop. In some cases, they added significant details not discussed before, even during the final pitch of the idea.

Intra-group coordination naturally occurred

Although not explicitly enforced by the workshop technique, group discussions and collaboration naturally occurred while taking decisions or developing ideas. Discussions were often triggered by the cards: *"[Browsing theme cards] Is there something we could change in the sequence here?", "Should we work on the social interaction card or we drop it?", "Should we change anything? Improve anything over here? [point at cards on the board]"*

We observed many groups splitting card decks among all the participants, who browsed and selected relevant cards to be evaluated collectively in a second step. A suggestion in this direction also came from the interview: *"Introducing game rules like turn based can help involve everybody. We split the deck so everybody was involved in the decision."* Due to the high number of cards provided, this has also been a way to divide tasks and speed up the card-selection process. Only one person browsed the cards in only a couple of groups, asking the others whether they agreed on the selection.

Sketching storyboards was an activity central to promoting discussion and collaboration. Even in groups where a clear leader emerged, all the participants contributed in some way to the storyboard. Groups didn't start sketching immediately: every step of the storyboard was discussed and elaborated upon, contributing to the development of the idea. Collaboration was also observed whenever different groups of cards had to be connected. In several groups however, a leader prevailed in the choice. To prevent this from happening, it could be useful to introduce a mechanism to actively involve every participant in the process, like turn-taking.

Limitations of the tool

Session hijacking

In some groups a single user assumed the role of the leader, "driving the show" without involving the other group members much. Introducing some game mechanics, like turn-based contribution and card drawing, could help preventing this to happen, assuring more fairness in the process.

Effectiveness of the board

Several points of improvement to the board design were suggested. Some users struggled to understand how the cards were intended to be placed on the board or how the board was meant to be used. The fact that some groups randomly placed many cards on the board added to confusion: important sections of the board were hidden, hindering guidance and preventing the users from following the playbook. A more effective board design could have allowed for better guidance. Consistency in the design between the cards and the board could help to mitigate the observed issues. Research in board game design could also be used as a source of inspiration.

Evaluation process

So far, the Tiles Workshop has only been presented and run by the authors. Consequently, we cannot draw conclusions about the adoption or use of the tool by other researchers on the level of supervision needed. Because we did not attempt to evaluate or rank the ideas generated, we also cannot draw conclusions about their novelty. Finally, comparing the results from the workshop was limited by the participants having different levels of expertise and the groups consisting of both researchers and students. More user studies are needed in order to better focus the evaluation process towards possible criticalities.

CONCLUSIONS AND FUTURE WORK

The Tiles Ideation Toolkit aims to support explorations of the IoT design space and provide triggers for creative reflective ideation of augmented objects. We developed a set of 110 cards grouped in 7 categories and a workshop technique providing step-by-step guidance to involve non-experts in idea generation. The toolkit is extendible and can be customized to direct ideation efforts toward specific domains. During our user studies, the toolkit has been useful in informing and guiding non-experts in quickly generating ideas for augmented objects by supporting creative thinking and critical analysis of design outcomes. Furthermore, the toolkit facilitated articulate thinking and collaboration strategies among participants.

Future work point at multiple directions. We are revising the cards' contents, the board, and the playbook based on the findings from the user study. Furthermore, we plan to evaluate the use of the cards with different workshop techniques and with other user groups in order to understand the entry barriers to the adoption of the tool. We aim to explore how the addition of mechanics borrowed from traditional card and board game play, as well as computer interactivity, can improve the fun and user-engagement aspects. We will also provide guidelines to extend the tool and templates for the design of new cards. Finally, we are interested in investigating how to complement ideation with prototyping. We will integrate Tiles with hardware tools and digital manufacturing techniques in order to support the rapid prototyping of the ideas generated.

ACKNOWLEDGMENTS

The work in this paper has been co-funded by the Norwegian Design and Architecture Centre. We are grateful to Nice Industridesign for the insights they brought to the development of Tiles Cards and to NTNU Technology Transfer for their feedback. Finally, we thank all the people who took part in the evaluation of our tool.

REFERENCES

1. Tina Aspiala and Alexandra Deschamps-Sonsino. Know-cards. Learn. Play. Collect. Retrieved January 5, 2017 from http://know-cards.myshopify.com/
2. Luigi Atzori, Antonio Iera, and Giacomo Morabito. 2010. The Internet of Things: A survey. *Computer Networks* 54, 15: 2787–2805.
3. Ayah Bdeir. 2009. Electronics as material: littleBits. *Proceedings of TEI*: 397–400. http://doi.org/10.1145/1517664.1517743
4. J Blomberg and M. Burrell. 2009. An ethnographic approach to design. *Human-computer interaction: Development process*: 71–94.
5. Eva Brandt and Jörn Messeter. 2004. Facilitating collaboration through design games. *Proceedings of Participatory Design Conference* 1: 121–131. http://doi.org/10.1145/1011870.1011885
6. R B Burns. 2000. *Introduction to Research Methods*. SAGE Publications.
7. Gabriela Carneiro and Zhu Li. 2011. i|o Cards: A Tool to Support Collaborative Design of Interactive Objects. *Proceedings of DESIRE*: 357–2. http://doi.org/10.1145/2079216.2079268
8. Changeist. Thingclash. *thingclash.com*. Retrieved January 6, 2017 from http://thingclash.com
9. Ying Deng, Alissa N Antle, and Carman Neustaedter. 2014. Tango Cards: A Card-Based Design Tool for Informing the Design of Tangible Learning Games. *Proceedings of DIS*: 695–704. http://doi.org/10.1145/2598510.2598601
10. Robert A Fowles. 1979. Design methods in UK schools of architecture. *Design Studies* 1, 1: 15–16. http://doi.org/10.1016/0142-694X(79)90022-X
11. B Friedman and D Hendry. 2012. The Envisioning Cards: A Toolkit for Catalyzing Humanistic and Technical Imaginations. *Proceedings of CHI*: 1145–1148. http://doi.org/10.1145/2207676.2208562

12. Futurice. IoT Service Kit. *iotservicekit.com*. Retrieved January 6, 2017 from http://iotservicekit.com
13. Adam Greenfield. 2010. *Everyware: The dawning age of ubiquitous computing*. New Riders.
14. K Halskov and P Dalsgård. 2006. Inspiration Card Workshops. *Proceedings of DIS*: 2–11. http://doi.org/10.1145/1142405.1142409
15. Michael S Horn and Robert J K Jacob. 2007. Tangible Programming in the Classroom with Tern. *Proceedings of CHI Extended Abstracts*: 1965–1970. http://doi.org/10.1145/1240866.1240933
16. Eva Hornecker and Jacob Buur. 2006. Getting a grip on tangible interaction. ACM Press, 437–446. http://doi.org/10.1145/1124772.1124838
17. Eva Hornecker. 2010. Creative Idea Exploration within the Structure of a Guiding Framework: The Card Brainstorming Game. *Proceedings of TEI*: 101–108. http://doi.org/10.1145/1709886.1709905
18. IDEO. 2003. IDEO Method Cards: 51 Ways to Inspire Design. Retrieved from https://www.ideo.com/post/method-cards
19. Robert J K Jacob, Audrey Girouard, Leanne M Hirshfield, et al. 2008. Reality-based interaction: a framework for post-WIMP interfaces. *Proceedings of TEI:201-210.* http://doi.org/10.1145/1357054.1357089
20. Treffyn Lynch Koreshoff, Toni Robertson, and Tuck Wah Leong. 2013. Internet of things: a review of literature and products. *Proceedings of OzCHI*: 335–344. http://doi.org/10.1145/2541016.2541048
21. M Kuniavsky. 2010. *Smart Things: Ubiquitous Computing User Experience Design*. Elsevier Science.
22. Stacey Kuznetsov and Eric Paulos. 2010. UpStream: Motivating Water Conservation with Low-Cost Water Flow Sensing and Persuasive Displays. *Proceedings of CHI*: 1851–1860. http://doi.org/10.1145/1753326.1753604
23. Dan Lockton, David Harrison, and Neville A Stanton. 2010. *Design with intent: 101 patterns for influencing behaviour through design*. Dan Lockton.
24. A Lucero and J Arrasvuori. 2010. PLEX Cards: A Source of Inspiration When Designing for Playfulness. *the 3rd International Conference*: 28–37. http://doi.org/10.1145/1823818.1823821
25. D Mellis, M Banzi, D Cuartielles, and T Igoe. 2007. Arduino: An Open Electronic Prototyping Platform. *Proceedings of CHI Extended Abstracts*.
26. Simone Mora, Jonas Asheim, Anders Kjøllesdal, and Monica Divitini. 2016. Tiles Cards: a Card-based Design Game for Smart Objects Ecosystems. *Workshop on Smart Ecosystems cReation by Visual dEsign. CEUR Proceedings*. Retrieved from http://ceur-ws.org/Vol-1602/
27. F Mueller, M R Gibbs, F Vetere, and D Edge. 2014. Supporting the Creative Game Design Process with Exertion Cards. *Proceedings of CHI*: 2211–2220. http://doi.org/10.1145/2556288.2557272
28. D Rose. 2014. *Enchanted Objects: Design, Human Desire, and the Internet of Things*. Scribner.
29. Claire Rowland, Elizabeth Goodman, Martin Charlier, Ann Light, and Alfred Lui. 2015. *Designing Connected Products: UX for the Consumer Internet of Things*. O'Reilly Media.
30. Kimiko Ryokai, Stefan Marti, and Hiroshi Ishii. 2004. I/O brush: drawing with everyday objects as ink. *Proceedings of CHI*: 1–8. http://doi.org/10.1145/985692.985731
31. D A Schon. 1987. *Educating the Reflective Practitioner: Toward a New Design for Teaching and Learning in the Professions*. Wiley.
32. B Sterling. 2005. *Shaping Things*. MIT Press.
33. A Strauss and J M Corbin. 1998. *Basics of Qualitative Research: Techniques and Procedures for Developing Grounded Theory*. SAGE Publications.
34. Kirsikka Vaajakallio and Tuuli Mattelmäki. 2014. Design games in codesign: as a tool, a mindset and a structure. *CoDesign* 10, 1: 63–77. http://doi.org/10.1080/15710882.2014.881886
35. Shahtab Wahid, Stacy M Branham, Lauren Cairco, D Scott McCrickard, and Steve Harrison. 2009. Picking Up Artifacts: Storyboarding as a Gateway to Reuse. Proceedings of *INTERACT:* 528–541. http://doi.org/10.1007/978-3-642-03658-3_57
36. Mark Weiser. 1991. The Computer for the 21 st Century. *Scientific american*. http://doi.org/10.1038/scientificamerican0991-94

De-emphasizing Content to Study the Relationship between Meaning, Messages, and Content in IM Systems

Bin Xu
Information Science
Cornell University
bx55@cornell.edu

Yang Qin
Information Science
Cornell University
yq93@cornell.edu

Dan Cosley
Information Science
Cornell University
drc44@cornell.edu

ABSTRACT

The design of most instant messaging (IM) tools focuses on exchanging content as the meaning and process of communication, a convention that equates content with meaning in a way counter to modern theories of interpersonal communication. We critique these conventions in designing a mobile messaging application, *BubbleQ*, which de-emphasizes message content and defamiliarizes interaction flows by forbidding users to send content directly. Instead, users send empty "bubbles", blank messages that recipients can fill and return to the sender. Messages are also presented not as per-user threads, but as an aggregation of bubbles across all conversational partners; they are also given a physical form to interact with to further violate common IM design conventions. Interviews with 28 college students who used *BubbleQ* for two weeks show that these design twists made room for negotiating other meanings, supported playful, mundane interaction, and provided resources for deepening relationships. Further, the aggregate bubbles view led people to reflect holistically on interactions. Together, these findings suggest that IM designers should spend more time addressing the meanings, embodiments, embedding, and cost of messages.

Author Keywords

Messaging; content; daily communication; prototyping.

ACM Classification Keywords

H.5.m. Information interfaces and presentation (e.g., HCI): Miscellaneous.

INTRODUCTION

Traditional Instant Messaging (IM) tools tend to emphasize the role of content in conversations. This emphasis is reflected in several common design conventions: a message is composed using explicit contents like texts, pictures, videos or even locations, while conversations are conducted through exchanging these contents. Further, the representations are quite literal: the message is simply the content, usually with an included timestamp; the conversation is simply a chronological series of messages, with some indicator of the sender such as left or right justification in a window.

Taking an interactional perspective, we regard these conventions as a manifestation of an underlying default assumption about human interaction that equates *meaning* with *content*. We critique this default as neglecting the multiplicity of ways and kinds of *meanings* people communicate. Many of these meanings are not dependent on semantic content in everyday interaction, and some of them are harmed or marginalized when content is in focus. We aim to explore designs that violate these assumptions and break these conventions in order to make room for other meanings and to stimulate designers' thinking about alternatives to focusing on content.

Some messaging applications already have design elements that reduce this emphasis on content. The early design of the Yo app de-emphasized content by not providing affordances for generating content: it only allowed users to send two characters "yo" to each other. Yet the app still gained quick popularity [3] and supported the negotiation of meaning in part through its ambiguity and lack of semantic content. Snapchat takes a different approach to de-emphasizing content by limiting content saving and retrieving: the app deletes message content by default after it is viewed. Doing this reduces concerns about self-presentation and encourages relational rather than informational interactions [2, 32], and it has managed to acquire high user engagement [26].

Inspired by these and related interfaces, we identify the "de-emphasis of content" to be an intentional design effort that attempts to surface the meaning in communication without the heavy dependence on exchanging content. To illuminate this idea, we designed and developed our own IM tool called *BubbleQ* that explicitly de-emphasizes content by restricting how people exchange messages: *BubbleQ* users cannot directly send a message containing content; instead, they can send empty "bubbles", containers that are displayed on the recipient's homepage. Recipients are allowed, but not required, to fill the bubbles with text, custom emojis, or short videos; filled bubbles are returned to the sender, who can then view the content but, as in Snapchat, only once. Using *BubbleQ* as a probe, we aimed to understand how people

DIS 2017, June 10-14, 2017, Edinburgh, United Kingdom

ACM 978-1-4503-4922-2/17/06…$15.00
DOI: http://dx.doi.org/10.1145/3064663.3064719

would use such a design and what meanings they would develop.

We conducted a two-week trial of using *BubbleQ* for daily use with 28 college students, who we interviewed after the trial. Results show that de-emphasizing content in *BubbleQ* interactions encouraged participants to have more mundane talk with others, that users negotiated various meanings for empty bubbles in the process of intention expression and interpretation, and that the embodiment of using bubbles to represent messages helped users to reflect on their interactions with others. Together these findings demonstrate the value of deeper thinking about just what the "message" in IM systems is about, beyond content: the *meanings* and intentions people have in IM; the *embodied* nature of messages in terms of their content, visual form, and relation to other messages; the *embedding* of messages in a wider ecology of communication practices, tools, and goals; and how these design choices balance the benefits with the *costs* and risks of using IM systems.

BACKGROUND

Our interest in de-emphasizing content is rooted in ideas about where meaning comes from in communication, and issues around the process by which communication takes place. Our goal is to highlight, and question, two conventions common to IM systems: that messages always have content, and that conversations are initiated by content-ful messages.

Content, Form, Function, Messages and Meaning

To design for messaging, it is important to think about *what is a message*. In the early development of communication systems based on Shannon's information theory [27], a *message* was considered as a piece of information represented by a set of semantic symbols (like a sequence of letters *a b a c a c a c a b* in Shannon's original paper.) This notion has shaped how IM applications are designed: despite the variety of interfaces and interaction flows in Snapchat, SMS, and other IM tools, one consistent design convention is that a *message* is almost always represented as semantic content: words, pictures, videos, audio, etc.

This assumption that the message is equivalent to its content has been questioned in interpersonal communication research. Regarding interpersonal communication as a way to accomplish social goals, Burleson conceptualized *messages* as behavior expressions to exchange *meanings*, "the internal states (thoughts, ideas, beliefs, feelings, etc.) that communicators seek to express or convey in a message and interpret a message as expressing or conveying. (page 150)" [6] In this notion, "a message is more than symbols that compose words and sentences; a message is fundamentally a *speech act*—the performance of an action through the expression of words and gestures. (page 151)" [6] In a way, the *act* of messaging itself is a performance that has meanings, as suggested in [30] and experienced in our daily life. We sometimes do not communicate through words: we may just nod heads at each other when we pass in the hallway, or have eye contact when we sit nearby.

This perspective leads to questions about IM applications' focus on content, as not being sufficient to convey—and perhaps hindering the conveyance of—important meanings that are not strictly about the content of the exchange. In fact, content can pose risks: part of Snapchat's appeal comes from the fact that ephemeral content reduces identity threats [32].

A natural next step is to de-emphasize content entirely. For instance, in the Yo messaging app [3], the only message content is the string "yo". In the Shannon sense this has zero information content, but users still exchanged meanings like greeting and connecting to fulfill relationship maintenance goals [33]. Similarly, Kaye et al. developed a Virtual Intimate Object (VIO) that only allowed a user to send their partner a one-bit message by offering a virtual circle they could tap; the partner's corresponding circle would become bright red and fade over time [18]. Users thought this communication without explicit content offered values in connecting to remote partners and maintaining intimacy. In both cases, the meanings exchanged were achieved not from the content of the message, but rather from their mutual interpretation of the fact of receiving a message.

Content, Intention, and Initiation of Conversations

The second design convention is that conversations are both initiated and continued via messages with explicit content. Taking an interactional perspective, the process of conversation is established by a structure constituted through reciprocal expression and interpretation of *intentions* of the interactants [6]. In some cases, the *intention* does not require the exchange of explicit content. For example, in face-to-face situations, sometime we do not need words to start a conversation; instead, being approached by another person raises awareness that that person might want to talk to you, and vice versa [10]. Likewise, conversations often end implicitly rather than through explicit goodbyes: others walk by, bodies shift, we glance at a clock or attend to the external environment, and so on.

The typical IM representation of conversations as a chronologically ordered sequence of content-ful messages does not support managing intentions around conversation very well. When available, people do employ a wide variety of tools—some provided by the system such as away messages, availability indicators, and typing indicators, some by the social-technical context such as network glitches, whether real or made up to support plausible deniability [13])—to help negotiate intentions around interaction and attention management. However, these tools are not always available, and we see opportunities for representing conversation and structuring interaction in ways that smooth these transitions into and out of conversation.

Designing not Just for Messages, but for Meanings

Seeing the goal of *messaging* as to achieve shared *meanings* constituted by a set of acts initiated and ended with *intentions*, we critique these default IM system designs as narrowing the multiplicity and expressiveness of communication.

In particular, we argue that design conventions like messaging with required content and the flow of interaction based on exchanging content shape the kinds of meaning that can be easily and naturally made. People have a wide variety of instrumental goals in communication: entertaining, connecting, supporting, information, persuading. Content in messages supports some goals well, and others less so. For instance, although participants in Kaye et al.'s one bit intimacy work could also use much 'richer' channels like SMS and Email, participants reported that the simple one-bit tapping message without content was better for maintaining intimacy than using these tools that afforded 'rich' content [18]. This suggests that designing only with content exchange in mind probably misses opportunities to serve communication goals that are not well suited to symbolic exchanging.

Sharing meanings through content also requires effort to either generate or capture the appropriate content to convey the expected meanings. A simple "yo" that took seconds to send might be at least as good for keeping in touch with people as explicitly conducting a conversation starting with "how are you". As we will see, creating this content can impose costs and risks on communicators.

THE DESIGN OF BUBBLEQ

Our critical assessment of the default choice related to the role content plays in messaging encourages us to explore the design space by creating a world that de-emphasizes content. For the first convention that messages rely on content, we seek a message format that reduces the role of content; for the second convention that conversation is conducted by exchanging content, we seek a flow that allows intentions to be expressed without explicit content. By creating a world like this, we hope to provide both a critical lens for thinking about assumptions around the role of content in messaging and specific insights about what the de-emphasis of content means to users and how it might be employed by users. Here, we describe how our IM system *BubbleQ* evolved over three iterations, focusing on how the role of content and the interaction flow evolved through users' reactions.

Initial Design: Eliminate Content Entirely

There are several ways to design a form of message with the absence of explicit content, as in the Yo and VIO prototypes described earlier. Our initial design was somewhere between these: similar to the homepage in final design (Figure 1.a), by pressing the "+" button in the middle, users could send a message to one of their contacts (Figure 1.b); the contact then received a circle ("bubble") only with its sender's username on it (in this design there were no user pictures). These "given" bubbles were presented on the homepage, and users could interact with them by dragging them around the homepage, and the bubbles had a simulated magnetic force to the center of the homepage as well as to each other, using physical collision simulation so that bubbles could bump but not overlap. We applied these physical elements with the goal of engaging users. Users could also delete bubbles by tapping them. We named this prototype *BubbleQ* to illumine its *bubble* body of message without explicit contents.

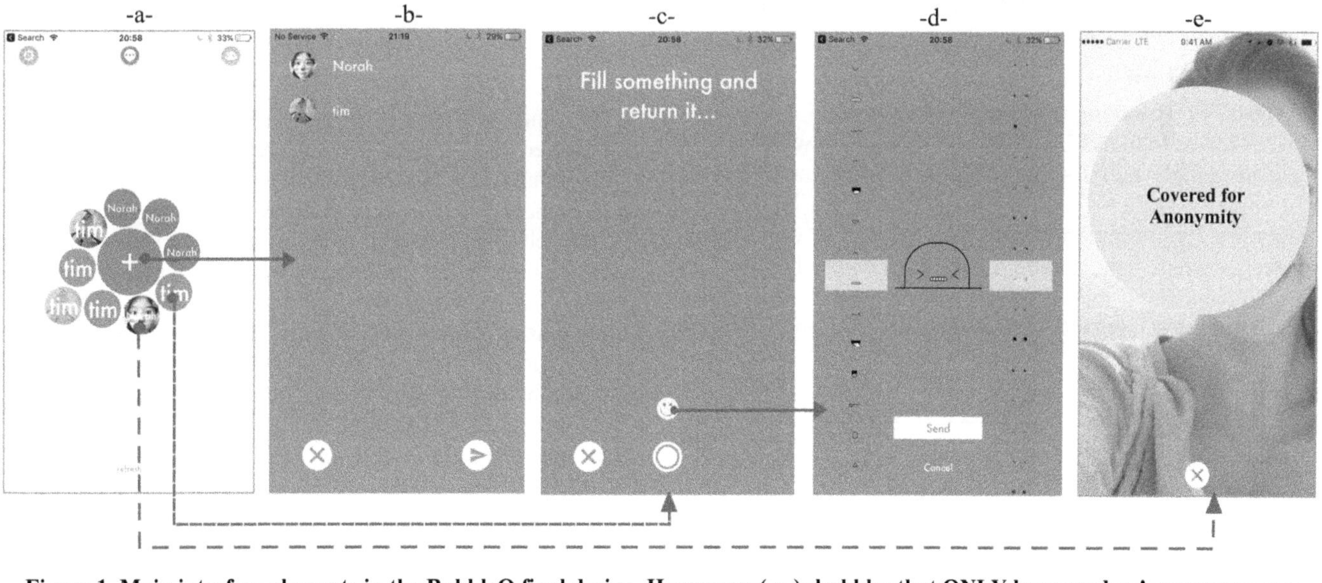

Figure 1. Main interface elements in the BubbleQ final design. Homepage (-a-): bubbles that ONLY have senders' usernames are empty bubbles, and others with user pictures are filled bubbles with contents, among which color-decayed filled bubbles are read ones. By tapping the "+" button users go to -b- to select to whom they want to send an empty bubble, and then by tapping the send button (right bottom in -b-) an empty bubble will appear on the recipient's homepage. Tapping an empty bubble such as the "tim" blue bubble will lead user to the message composing window (-c-), where users choose to fill the bubble with text by taping the placeholder text, video by tapping the middle bottom round button, or emoji by tapping the emoji button. -d- shows the emoji composing page, and by tapping the send button a filled bubble will appear on "tim"'s homepage. When the user taps an unread filled bubble like the one with "Norah"'s username and picture, it pops up the message viewing window (-e-) to show content.

We showed this first design to eight of our friends and asked them to test it for a week in June 2016. Pilot participants reported that even though they found the bubble to be an interesting format, they considered "bubbling" to be like "tickling" each other (c.f., Facebook Pokes). They quickly lost interest as it supported few communicative meanings.

Second Try: Optional Content Was Not Actually Optional

Based on these reactions we created a second design that offered users options between sending empty bubbles or bubbles with content. After tapping the "+" button they choose a recipient (as in the first design), however, after tapping the send button as in Figure1.b, another window popped up (similar to Figure 1.c, but with the instruction "*fill in something or just leave it blank*") asking them to either fill it with text or just leave it blank and then send it. On the receiver's homepage (same as Figure 1.a), filled bubbles would have the sender's profile image and username while empty bubbles would only have the username. Filled bubbles could be read by tapping, while empty bubbles could not be opened. Read bubbles were shown in washed-out colors to distinguish them from bubbles that hadn't been read yet. And, since bubbles take space on the homepage, we allowed users to delete them by double-tapping.

The same group of people used the new version for several days. They reported that although they had the option to send either empty or filled bubbles, they felt obliged to send filled ones because it was perceived as inappropriate to "tickle" people without saying anything. We found it interesting that the affordance of sending content appeared to create a norm that it *should* be sent, defying our assumption that offering alternatives was enough, and frustrating because this meant we couldn't learn about the effects of empty bubbles.

Third Try: Breaking the Content Convention

This led us to think about designs where users were required to use empty bubbles. Considering two choices of bubbles (empty vs. filled) and two places to create bubbles and content (conversation initiation vs. reply), we came upon a design where senders could only send empty bubbles, and recipients could then fill them with content in reply. Users can always send empty bubbles but can only send content by filling a bubble they received. When user A sends an empty bubble to user B, B can fill the bubble or save it for later; when A sends a filled bubble, B can read its content immediately or save it for later. This design was appealing as we hadn't seen other applications that used this idea, and also clearly violated the second convention we aimed to break around normal IM interaction flows. Figure 2 shows the different messaging flows among the three iterations.

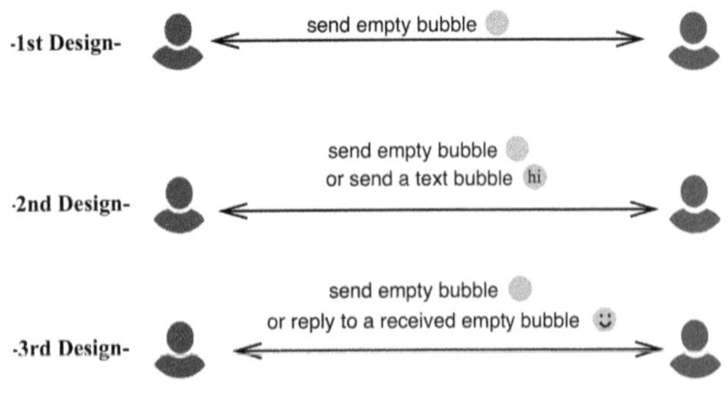

Figure 2. *BubbleQ* interaction flow in each design iteration.

Participants who used the second version strongly suggested adding the ability to fill bubbles with more than just text. Therefore in this version, users could also take a short video and optionally apply filters (the middle bottom button on Figure 1.c); some participants appropriated this feature by taking extremely short videos they used more like pictures. We also built an interface for users to generate simple custom emoji by choosing a combination of the eyes (from 30 given shapes) and the mouth (from 30 more shapes) as shown in Figure 1.d. Our intent was still to de-emphasize content; the idea of light videos was borrowed from Snapchat, and the emojis were designed to be as much for creativity and fun as for expressing specific content or emotions.

To further de-emphasize content, we adopted ephemerality from Snapchat, allowing filled bubbles to only be opened once. Note that neither the opened content (Figure 1.e shows the screenshot of a filled bubble with video) nor the homepage shows when a bubble was filled, or in what order; this choice was made to address the chronological sequencing aspect of standard IM interfaces. Users could delete read bubbles by double-tapping them, but we did not allow them to delete empty bubbles, in order to better probe their effect on communicating intention and structuring interaction.

One other theme the emerged from the pilots was that testers expected the app to be fun and playful, even though playfulness was not our initial design goal; pilot participants liked the way bubbles could be moved by dragging them and thus felt like physical bubbles. Respecting this sense of playfulness, in this third design we made bubbles move when users shake their phones and added animations of opening and closing when users interacted with specific bubbles. We also allowed users to assign colors to their contacts that would be displayed with their bubbles, both for playfulness and to help people distinguish bubbles from different senders (as illustrated in Figure 1.a).

In summary, different from most IM designs that represent messages as a threaded conversation, *BubbleQ* used a metaphor of free-moving bubbles to represent two kinds of messages: empty bubbles were blank messages without any content, and filled bubbles are messages with text, video, or emoji content. Users could either send empty bubbles or fill empty bubbles they had received, but not send content directly; content can only be used in replies, and conversations must be initiated with an empty bubble.

Technical details

BubbleQ mobile client was developed as an iOS native app using Swift 2.3. *BubbleQ* had a Node sever for user registration, Mango database, passing messages and delivering notifications. The server was hosted on the cloud deployment service Heroku.com. The connections between client and server were SSL-encrypted.

As an iOS messaging application, *BubbleQ* also supported mobile push notifications: when users received a bubble (empty or not), they also received a push notification delivered to their iPhone notification center, just as when they receive SMS. A red circled badge number also appeared on the *BubbleQ* app icon showing whether users had unread filled bubbles and if yes how many. We chose to only show number of unread filled bubbles on badge in order to be consistent with the design thinking that empty bubbles were supported to reply to rather than read.

THE FIELD TRIAL

Considering *BubbleQ* as a technology probe [17], we conducted a field trial to examine how its de-emphasizing of content affected communication. We chose this method because we wanted users to experience *BubbleQ* by using it in a relatively natural communication setting.

Procedure and Participants

We recruited participants from a study recruitment system at a university located in New York State. We explained that participants would need to download and use a mobile messaging application for two weeks, then participate in a semi-structured interview. After signing up, participants were invited to the lab to meet the research team and to be introduced to *BubbleQ* and the study. We showed them the app and explained how to use it, and (if willing) they signed the consent form and agreed to *BubbleQ*'s terms of use.

After consenting, we asked participants to download the app from the App Store and create an account. Each participant was asked to find at least two people they could use *BubbleQ* with. Some participants signed up as pairs or groups, and they were encouraged to add each other as contacts on *BubbleQ*. We asked them to use it in ways that made sense to them, and did not require them to use it instead of other messaging applications. However, we did ask them to use it frequently with the other *BubbleQ* users they found, aiming for at least 15 bubbles between them and each contact every day to let them fully experience the application. We also sent them reminders to use the app every three days. These reminders and usage levels were set with the goal of increasing the chance participants would have a solid experience of the interaction and interface without sacrificing too much ecological validity through forced use.

After two weeks, participants returned to the lab for a follow-up interview. Through pilot interviews, we developed an interview guide with questions about their general use frequency; their thoughts on the interface and interaction; their messaging patterns such as when and to whom they sent empty bubbles; when, to whom, and with what they replied to empty bubbles; and the goals or motivations they both had and inferred about others when using *BubbleQ*. We also asked them to compare it to other messaging applications, to reflect on the values and disadvantages of using *BubbleQ*, and to offer any other suggestions they had.

Participants who finished the two-week trial and the interview were given either seven participation (SONA) credits they could use to fulfill course requirements for research participation, or $35. A total of 28 people participated, all U.S. citizens, aged between 18 and 26 (average 20), with 6 males and 22 females.

In addition to the 28 recruited participants, another 53 people used *BubbleQ*, either invited by our participants when we asked them to add *BubbleQ* contacts, or who happened to find *BubbleQ* on the App Store. We did not advertise the app publicly, so we expect that most were friends of participants. When they registered their *BubbleQ* accounts, these users also agreed to the terms of use, which explained that they were participating a research project and what data we would collect and use later.

Data Collection and Analysis

Data collected included the 28 participants' interview data and all 81 users' message metadata logged by the system, which was later anonymized by removing user ids. Interviews were audio recorded, transcribed to text, and anonymized (referenced below as P1 through P28). Transcripts were imported into the Dedoose.com qualitative data analysis tool and divided into meaningful units. We used a grounded theory inspired method [28] to analyze our data. As a study focusing on exploring design insights rather than building of theories, we chose not to invest efforts on coding reliability to fulfill theoretical validation, and the lead author conducted the analysis. This author first wrote memos at the initial reading of all transcripts and created memos consistently during all phases of analyses to highlight key themes about relationships in the data, to help refine categories as a part of an open-coding process [7, 12] to code distinct concepts and categories in the data. An initial codebook of categories was developed, and a full coding of the interviews was conducted, iterating both through the codes and the codebook as an axial coding process [7]. Lastly, selective coding [7] was conducted to illuminate themes and categorize the results.

FINDINGS

Across the 81 users, 9548 empty bubbles were sent during the first two weeks. Of these, 7269 were filled with content: 874 (12%) with videos, 1830 (25%) with customized emoji, and 4565 (63%) with texts. Texts ranged from 1 to 493 characters, with a mean of 32 and a median of 18 ($SD = 35$).

Next we present findings based on the analyses of interview data. We start with an account of how people learned to interact in *BubbleQ* and the meanings people attached to bubbles, messages, and interactions. We then present users' perceptions of the physicality and playfulness of the interface, and how they saw *BubbleQ* compared to other IM tools.

Filling Versus Sending Encourages Mundane Talk

Getting Used to the Process

BubbleQ forced users not to send content directly, but to reply to empty bubbles they received. Some participants experienced "*a learning curve* (P6)" to understand and get used to this process; though one that could be "*pretty fun, um, because it's just like this kind of explore. And then like once you figure out, I think it's like easy to use* (P2)". To help make sense of it, they made parallels how they would communicate with paper: "*it's as if you're giving me a blank piece of paper and then I have to fill it out, and then I could send it back to you* (P7)", or more succinctly, "*like passing notes in class* (P19)".

This new interaction flow required effort and raised potential frustrations. People often "stored" bubbles, or sent stores of bubbles to others, even though they were not looking to talk at that moment: "*to make sure my friend could respond cause then that's how, she can't respond to me if I don't have, if she doesn't have any bubbles. So I just made sure to send a few (empty bubbles) every day* (P9)". This, however, did not address times when a sender wanted to initiate a conversation; in those cases, people sent extra bubbles: "*so hopefully they see it and then they'll like reply to* (P2)".

Participants would also sometimes ask for more empty bubbles during conversation, reminding the other person to send empties to keep the conversation flowing. When this failed and conversations lapsed because one party forgot to send empty bubbles, they would sometimes repair through other channels: "*it happened a few times where I didn't know when she ran out of bubbles for me and she messaged me (on my phone): hey send me more bubbles* (P12)".

The necessity of having empty bubbles to send content also altered the way conversations ended. In many messaging applications, participants reported using explicit endings such as "butler lies" [14] to terminate a conversation (for example P3 said he normally said "*I need to do something*" to the other person). In *BubbleQ* participants felt the conversation did "*keep going*" and "*there is no need to end to it* (P4)" as they saw not sending new empty bubbles as an implicit way to end conversations rather than explicitly terminating them.

Participants also saw the need to have empty bubbles to chat and the ability to ignore them as a way to prevent unwanted interaction: "*with Snapchat and the way other messaging apps work is that a lot of people get unwarranted messages. I feel like this happened in middle school and high school at times. You are friend with a guy and suddenly he just wants to like talk to you all the time. He just keeps texting you, texting you, texting you, keep messaging you. And like with this app, it definitely doesn't allow that. You have to want to talk to them. You have to ask, 'Hey, come talk to me' before they talk to you. So you wouldn't really get any of that (spamming)* (P7)". And although sending many empty bubbles to other people could be spam in its own right, users did not spontaneously reflect on this possibility.

Light, Mundane Talk for Connection

Participants reported that this kind of process was more suitable to conduct light conversations rather than "*intense*" and "*in-depth*" conservations: "*before cellphones, people would just like pass notes in class or whatever to talk to people. So I'm just saying like, not necessarily in class but something like small like that, like little things that you might want to say, and those are kind of just fun* (P19)".

Following Duck's categorization of communication into superficial talk, informal talk, task talk, and deep talk [9], the conversations in *BubbleQ* mostly fell into the category of superficial talk, covering topics of limited depth with the purpose of passing time: "*I feel like I pretty much just used to like tell them like something funny that happened during the day or like what I'm doing right now. Not really informational stuff, not really stuff they like necessarily need to know or not really stuff that they would need to write down somewhere or they would need to like look back on. Just like a funny picture or I was walking through the quad and I saw a dog and I would send them a picture of it. Or be like, 'Hey, look who I just saw'* (P17)".

One main motivation of such superficial talk was to greet or quickly catch up: "*just like saying, 'Hi, how's it going?' And then like talking maybe for a little, and then going on with your day. Um, just like something casual, nothing like super in-depth that you would talk about. Something just short and friendly* (P2)". Another was entertainment; besides "funny" short texts and visual messages, 1/4 of filled bubbles were filled with customized emojis that served not just to communicate emotion but also as playful, fun act: "*I kind of thought of the little like emojis as like little like Mr. Potato heads that you could like change them up and you're always trying to like make them look funny. So my friends and I would try to send real ones, but sometimes we'd like try to find like the best combination of like funny ones I guess* (P7)".

Presenting messages as bubbles rather than a chronologically ordered thread also led participants to use *BubbleQ* less for deeper talk because the lack of order affected grounding: "*Some of my friends have sent me (back) three or four (filled bubbles) at a time. I would have to go through them and sometimes I'd pick the third bubble at first, and the first bubble last. And then I'd have to think about it, so I cannot follow that conversation easily* (P12)".

This focus on light content was perceived to potentially reduce users' pressure in capturing appropriate contents for their communicative goals: "*I would use BubbleQ if I'm just trying to be playful (then I) send a cute little emoji or just say hey or something. With Snapchat, ... I'll send my friends like a picture of something that I saw somewhere else that I thought that they would like; or they were looking for something and I found it so I just send them, oh my gosh look I found what you were, what you were talking about* (P19)".

Overall, this process in *BubbleQ* which twisted the initiation of conversations through requiring content to be sent as a reply to an empty bubble introduced some cognitive costs and occasionally induced frustration when the bubbles ran out. However, this filling rather than sending mechanism made conversation easier to end and reduced unwanted interaction. Participants also tended to use this type of interaction for superficial talk in daily communication with a goal of quick sharing of mundane events in life to stay connected and entertain each other.

Empty Bubbles, Full Meanings

In addition to being a mechanism for conversation, participants attached a number of meanings to the intentions behind empty bubbles, depending on their history and relationship with a given person.

Negotiating Attention and Interaction

Sending an empty bubble was generally seen as a way to request attention: "*sending bubbles is ... really easy to get a person's attention. Especially because you can send, literally 20 bubbles at one time. So if someone did send me 20 bubbles, I would know that they're trying to get my attention* (P4)". It was seen as a lightweight mechanism that reduced the effort needed to get attention, "*a little bit more conservative than writing a message* (P18)", because it eliminated the need to create content: "*It's easier (to get attention) because you just press the button, you send them a bunch of bubbles, and then, they just pop up. But, like pictures you have to actually physically take the picture* (P4)".

Often, the reason for requesting attention was to invite the empty bubble's recipient to reply and start a conversation: "*It's kind of, like, poking someone, like, 'Hey, I want you to talk to me.'* (P6)" This is straightforward, as the process of replying to an empty bubble defined that the default response to empty bubbles was to fill them with messages to conduct conversations, even though it did not explicitly tell when, how, and why to do this.

Recipients of empty bubbles talked about the need to interpret the sender's intention, and whether they should reply right away, in part based on the number of bubbles: "*if I had like, a couple empty bubbles around it (the center button), then you're like, 'Okay, like whatever, she sent me two or three.' But if you see that it takes up like half the screen, you're like, 'Oh, like I should look at it'* (P7)", and in part based on a particular partner's practices: "*if my cousin or my friend back home sent it to me, I would have to respond if they sent me empty bubbles, they were for a response, but my friend here, if she sent me empty bubbles, it was just like I could bubble her back whenever I wanted* (P7)".

A Good Interaction for Deepening Relationships?

As described earlier, *BubbleQ*'s interaction style (as with Snapchat [32]) was seen as effective for supporting superficial talk between people who already have a close relationship. Participants also saw potential for *BubbleQ* to help in developing new relationships.

Sending empty bubbles was seen as a subtle way to express interest in someone, especially if they "*were acquaintances and wanted to become a better friend or maybe someone that you kind of have like a crush on and you wanted to get to know better* (P19)". Sending empty bubbles, as a lightweight and somewhat playful invitation, was a comfortable way to ask to talk: "*for developing friendships, relationships, I think it's kind of hard to, or people are nervous about maybe starting a conversation or with and, they are unsure what to do, I think BubbleQ was helpful cause it was fun, it (sending empty bubbles) lightened up the situation if you wanted to get to know someone better and have like, a way to prompt them to let you know that you wanted to talk to them. So I think it was just easier* (P9)". As with the earlier quote from P4 about not having to find a picture to take, the sending of empty bubbles reduced the cost and concern for senders, especially in newer relationships with less history.

This passed both power and responsibility on to recipients. Power, because as described earlier, it's easier to ignore empty bubbles than unwanted interactions: "*it works in the dating applications. Basically, it's a dating website, and you don't want unknown people to be messaging you a lot. So, BubbleQ would work out in that situation because, well they're only sending you an empty message, if you don't want to talk to them you don't have to talk to them* (P12)". Responsibility, because the cost of knowing what to say could be passed to receivers: "*I feel like if someone text me, say I have like a crush on someone, or me and my boyfriend first start dating, if he texts me something saying, 'Hey,' with a smiley face, I feel like I would feel more confident that he wants to talk to me, versus, if he just sends me a bubble, because then that, then I would feel like, I don't know exactly what he wants me to say* (P18)".

These meanings of sending empty bubbles were enabled in part by the ability to reply to them and conduct conversations. Empty bubbles alone might not support these meanings, as expressed in this comparison to Facebook pokes (where people can poke their friends or friends of friends on Facebook, and poked ones only get a notification saying being poked): "*The difference with the poke is when you poke someone, there's no room for interpretation, that's like 'Oh,' or 'you poked me,' and that's about it. But, for an empty bubble, if you sent me an empty bubble, then I can respond, like, 'want to grab pizza?' There could be an explicit thing that I ask, or I might just reply with something really minimal like 'Hi,' or something really dumb. But if you poked me, the only thing I can do back is either be like, 'Okay,' or poke you back, and nothing else.* (P6)" In principle, the recipient of a poke could switch to other Facebook communication tools, but in practice, *BubbleQ*'s provision of both lightweight, empty bubbles and ways to follow them up and add meaning to them made it easier for participants to negotiate intentions and meanings, as well as to support common relational goals.

Bubble: A Physical Body of Messages

In previous sections, we presented findings around the content de-emphasis through twists on the messaging process and de-emphasizing content. *BubbleQ* also differs from other IM tools in that, rather than threaded conversations presented as text and grouped by contact, it presented messages as a collection of interactive bubbles, and this affected how people thought about their interactions.

First, the ability to interact with bubbles gave people a different experience of messages beyond just reading them. Some participants reported they played with the bubbles by dragging them around the homepage or shaking their phone to see bubbles bumping when they were waiting for others to respond, seeing this as "*aesthetically pleasing* (P11)" and "*kind of cool to play with* (P4)". This led them to see bubbles as a physical, embodied representation of the messages: "*I felt like it gave it more of like a physical aspect. It felt like I was holding a bunch of things in my hand, like holding like a box of letters or something like papers that you could just like move around* (P7)". This interaction also fostered a feeling of playfulness: "*The form in BubbleQ is kind of more playful. ... where you fill it, um, as opposed to just like maybe a square of text, in regular messaging* (P20)".

The physicality of bubbles and their occupation of space also emphasized the aggregation of messaging beyond individual messages or conversations: "*having the bubbles kind of made you realize how many messages you actually got, because it would fill up, like, space, instead of just having a number, it would fill up a space* (P4)". It encouraged them to think about their overall interaction patterns with others in a way that other messaging interfaces don't: "*in Snapchat, it just shows up as Joe sent you a bunch of messages, but it's just like that red square. You don't know how many they sent you. But then with this (BubbleQ homepage), you could be like, 'Wow, they sent me this one and this one and this one.' And it is like the spatial relation of it versus this person sent me a message. For example, my cousin would have sent me two (bubbles), but then my friend here would have sent me like six of them. So it just looks so much bigger in comparison and like makes it feel more important I guess* (P7)". It let users "*see who you talk to the most* (P2)" and view "*a web of people and like how often you talk to them, like how often they want to talk to you* (P8)". This could also have negative effects, however: "*having a good amount of bubbles is good to keep conversation going, and it looks nice. Having too few bubbles is kind of sad, because they're mostly empty* (P11)".

Overall, giving messages a body of "bubble" with some materialized physical sense led people to see messages not just as exchanged content but as interactive virtual objects with a certain playfulness. Further, like CrystalChat [29], as a visualization of historical conversation, the homepage containing these bubbles impacted users' perception and reflection on their interactions with others as well as their own communicative performance.

Limitations

Before moving on to further discuss these findings, we would like to call out several limitations to the study. First, having females as the majority of participants (22 vs. 6) potentially introduced a gender bias in the findings. The ratio is not so different from the underlying balance in this participant pool, and we didn't see obvious differences between genders in our interview results or use logs. Still, it may be that *BubbleQ* appealed more to females than males on average, or that our results apply more to women than men.

Participants also had on average a small number of close contacts. Users could only add contacts if they knew their *BubbleQ* username or account email, and we also asked participants to find contacts manually. Thus, people mostly used *BubbleQ* with close ties rather than acquaintances (though, people still saw potential value for more distant relationships, notably, early-stage friendships and romantic relationships). The small number of contacts also means we don't know how the interface would scale. We suspect "badly", although it would be straightforward to have multiple homepages that reduce this problem by dividing contacts into meaningful groups or highlighting particularly important individuals.

Another limitation is that participants were compensated to use the app, told to send a minimum number of messages daily, reminded to use the app every three days, and only used it for two weeks. Although we consciously made these choices to balance experiencing the interaction with naturalness of use, it means we know little about unconstrained, long-term patterns of use or norms that would emerge.

Finally, log analysis shows that most participants stopped using *BubbleQ* after the study. Although they saw interesting advantages versus other tools, including Snapchat, they also saw a number of disadvantages, including questions about its ability to capture enough users to make it meaningful to use alongside other tools, expectations of long term support, privacy and security risks of a new tool, and problems with the interface (notably, the idea of capturing short videos as pictures was not obvious). More generally, participants found it hard to explain the interaction flow to friends and wanted a tutorial, as well as a way to more easily find and invite friends than through exchanging *BubbleQ* usernames. Some of these flaws—notably, the ability to take pictures and their difficulty in explaining *BubbleQ* to their friends—likely did impact how people used and perceived the system, and thus our results.

DISCUSSION: WHAT'S IN A MESSAGE?

Despite these limitations, our design and deployment of *BubbleQ* led to useful insights about the relationship between a message's content and meaning in messaging systems. As we argued in the Background section, equating the notion of a message's meaning and its content is common in messaging systems, partly because of convention and partly because the content is usually the dominant feature in the interface. However, this emphasis risks reducing attention to meanings of conversation that are not explicitly encoded in the content.

BubbleQ breaks the inherited conventions of emphasizing content by using empty bubbles both as a message and to initiate conversation, and demonstrates its influence on users' practices in daily communication conducted through the design, their interpretations of messages and the meanings associated with them. Participants felt the design supported some communication goals over others (notably, mundane and playful interaction, as has been found for Snapchat, which also breaks these design conventions through ephemerality [32]). The design also encouraged them to reflect on the meaning and intention around conversations. Participants interpreted the intentions behind sending empty bubbles based on their relationship and history with other communication partners. Further, the interactivity of and occupation of space by bubbles on the homescreen encouraged participants to reflect on the amount and nature of their communication with other people, as well as enhancing the impression of playfulness many participants expressed. Though participants did not add *BubbleQ* to their everyday repertoire of IM tools, many of them found these features interesting and potentially valuable, especially in developing relationships.

These findings give weight to our main contention that de-emphasizing content is an interesting and generative design move, and we encourage designers to add it to their toolbox. Below, we give some thoughts about why, when, and how to use this move through synthesizing our findings and argument into four key concerns that can be overlooked when thinking of messaging systems primarily as ways to exchange content: the *meaning*, *embodiment*, *embedding*, and *cost* of messages.

Messages serve multiple goals and meanings

We found that when contents were not emphasized nor well supported, participants still managed to flexibly express and interpret conversational intentions and meanings. For example, sending empty bubbles could represent a desire for attention, a way to express interest, an invitation (or demand) to talk, an opportunity for future interaction, or a mechanical requirement to continue a conversation in the *BubbleQ* interaction flow.

These intentions might also be achieved with explicit content such as "I want to talk to you" or "Let me know if you'd like to chat later?" or "How are you doing?" or even P18's "Hey :)". However, there is value in subtle, negotiated, ambiguous meanings that support interpretation of social interaction (e.g., plausible deniability [5], butler lies [14])—and de-emphasizing content is one way to enable this negotiation. Like Yo and the Virtual Intimate Object, *BubbleQ* users were able to make space and make sense for their conversation needs with almost no semantic content.

Beyond the negotiation of interaction, people have a wide variety of motivations for conversation: to exchange information, to support, to impress, to achieve intimacy, to entertain, and so on. This is a semi-automatic and complex process to achieve these goals through communication [19] as goals are many times mixed together [10] and people are not always consciously aware of them [22].

Design choices will make some goals easier and some harder, depending on how the message structures support representation and interpretation of meanings as well as the how the message process shapes the interactions through which people convey them. For instance, participants found *BubbleQ* (and Snapchat [32]) to be effective for playful and mundane talk, but much less suited for Duck's task talk and deep talk; the short, informal, ephemeral nature of communication in them encourages perceptions of play, but their de-emphasis of content and conversational history in both systems reduces people's ability to refer to and ground in the past.

Note that this is not an argument to stuff all potential meanings into a system by providing a vast array of content features and interaction styles. Rather, it's a call for designers to ponder what intentions and meanings they aim to support and how their design choices can match those intentions and meanings.

Message embodiments foreground particular goals

In particular, we see potential in alternatives to the standard representation of messages as a conversation that consists of separate content-ful turns, chronologically ordered, and grouped by conversational partner. This is a fine representation for many communication goals that involve exchanging information, and people routinely appropriate the format for other goals as well. But alternate designs can foreground alternate values: the reduction in impression management concerns afforded by ephemeral content [2, 32]; the playfulness encouraged by mobile, colorful bubbles or drawing on pictures; the focus on interaction and relational rather than informational goals created by de-emphasizing content.

Beyond de-emphasized content, our participants saw value in the aggregation and spatial embedding of messages. As with other types of visualization, aggregation of interaction behaviors can de-emphasize specific content and provide overviews that support meaning-making above the level of individual messages and conversations. Somewhat like the CrystalChat prototype that represented conversation histories in a spatial visualization [29], the *BubbleQ* homescreen's spatial embedding provided a tool for thinking about the history of one's interactions both with specific individuals and across their circle of friends. The spatial embedding of the messages—also used to good effect in Chat Circles to support proxemics, grouping, and playfulness [31]—also enabled this kind of meta-meaning making through direct visual comparison, as well as enabling the playful motion-based aspects of interacting with the bubbles.

So, parallel to face-to-face messages being a rich set of behavioral expressions [22], we pose that IM systems should take this stance as well, and think more explicitly about the visual presentation of messages. Whether a linear set of balloons as Facebook Messenger and most of the other IM systems do, a collection of bubbles as in *BubbleQ*, a set of spatially embedded conversation lines as in Chat Circles, animated texts as in the Kinetic Instant Messanger [4], or a pinboard of virtual postcards or collection of virtual objects that might be created in future IM interfaces, we encourage designers to spend more time trying out alternate embodiments to support alternate meanings.

Messages and meanings are embedded in practices

Another point to consider is that both individual messages and messaging systems fit into a larger picture of people's communication practices. Communication theories that highlight the factors that affect people's media choice, such as media multiplexity [15, 16, 21] and media richness [1, 8], provide a general set of lenses for thinking about these relationships; our results provide several concrete examples of design choices that worked well for embedding message form and structure with communication needs.

For instance, participants described Facebook Pokes as limited for making meanings because it was hard to build on them despite the availability of other channels in Facebook for the communication. *BubbleQ*'s empty bubbles are similar to Pokes, but the affordance of returning them filled with content allowed both senders and receivers to build richer meanings than Pokes. A tight but separated coupling of intentions around and content of communications worked well here.

Another example that highlights the importance of embedding is participants' perception of *BubbleQ* as a tool not just for conversation, but also for reflection on conversation. A number of systems, including CrystalChat [29], iSpace [20], PieTime [23], and TheMail [11], aim to help people visualize past interactions with others. Those systems, however, decouple the analytical interface from the conversation system itself, while in *BubbleQ*, the aggregate interface *is* the homepage and is intimately integrated into the process of messaging. We did not explicitly design the interface with reflection in mind, but we suspect that this natural interleaving of aggregate view and detailed interaction encouraged people to perceive this possibility through their practice of messaging in *BubbleQ*.

Messages and content impose costs

The final point that we want to emphasize is that messages and content creation impose costs and risks. Our participants described the experience of costs both in *BubbleQ* and in other systems: uncertainties in how to respond to others, the fear of spam, the time spent to create messages, the pressure of making interesting content. Other, more general costs and risks—impression management, context collapse, harmful social comparison, harassment—have been outlined in a number of studies of social media and CMC tools.

We emphasize cost because designers could disregard the downsides of their choices, and because those choices can affect these costs through how they support the creation, exchange, presentation, and even destruction of messages. In *BubbleQ*, enforcing the sending of empty messages eased some costs around initiating conversation, imposed others around the mechanics of maintaining a supply of bubbles, and shifted still others from senders to receivers, such as the burden of crafting a content-filled reply. This last, and more general concerns about not knowing what to say, was arguably eased somewhat by the ability to respond with a customized emoji, allowing people to be creative and entertaining "on the cheap" when the capture of an entertaining video or creation of a meaningful text became difficult. Snapchat's auto-deletion of messages to make them ephemeral was perceived a way to make space for more mundane conversations while reducing self-presentation concerns—though norms about the value of producing interesting, funny photos and videos arose that increase the costs [32].

It's hard to prescribe general strategies to anticipate and address costs, because the design moves, costs, and values at play will vary depending on context. Still, finding sweet spots that maximize meanings and value while reducing cost and risk is a worthy design goal; to that end, we encourage designers to attend explicitly to the meanings, embodiments, and embedding of messages in people's communication practices.

CONCLUSION

This paper has three main contributions: first, based on a dissection the notion of message, we gave a critique of IM design conventions that emphasize content over other message properties such as meanings and intentions. Secondly, we developed a messaging prototype to illustrate one design that breaks these conventions, conducting a field trial to understand how such a design affects communication and why. Last, based on the findings we extend our discussions on the meaning, embodiment, embedding, and cost of messages to offer constructive implications for designing messaging applications.

ACKNOWLEDGMENTS

This work is supported in part by the National Science Foundation (IIS-0910664 and IIS-1405634). We acknowledge the support of the BubbleQ users, especially the early users, as well as helpful comments on previous versions of this document from anonymous reviewers and the Associate Chair.

REFERENCES

1. M S Balaji, and Chakrabarti Diganta. 2010. Student interactions in online discussion forum: Empirical research from 'media richness theory' perspective. *Journal of Interactive Online Learning* 9, 1: 1–22.
2. Joseph B. Bayer, Nicole Ellison, Sarita Y. Schoenebeck, Emily B. Falk. 2015. Sharing the Small Moments: Ephemeral Social Interaction on Snapchat.

Information, Communication & Society, 1–22. DOI=http://dx.doi.org/10.1080/1369118X.2015.1084349

3. Alyssa Bereznak. 2014. Developers Have Hit a Yo Point with This Terrible New App. Yahoo! Tech. 2014. Retrieved January 2 2017 from https://www.yahoo.com/tech/developers-have-hit-a-yo-point-with-this-terrible-new-89277145724.html
4. Kerry Bodine and Mathilde Pignol. 2003. Kinetic typography-based instant messaging. In *CHI '03 Extended Abstracts on Human Factors in Computing Systems* (CHI EA '03). ACM, New York, NY, USA, 914–915. DOI=http://dx.doi.org/10.1145/765891.766067
5. Erin Bradner and Gloria Mark. 2001. Social presence with video and application sharing. In *Proceedings of the 2001 International ACM SIGGROUP Conference on Supporting Group Work* (GROUP '01), Clarence (Skip) Ellis and Ilze Zigurs (Eds.). ACM, New York, NY, USA, 154–161. DOI=http://dx.doi.org/10.1145/500286.500310
6. Brant R. Burleson. 2010. The Nature of Interpersonal Communication: A Message-Centered Approach. In *The Handbook of Communication Science,* Charles R. Berger, Michael E. Roloff, and David R. Ewoldsen (eds.). Sage, Thousand Oaks, CA, 145–163.
7. Juliet M. Corbin and Strauss Anselm. 1990. Grounded theory research: Procedures, canons, and evaluative criteria. *Qualitative sociology* 13, 1: 3–21.
8. Alan R. Dennis and Susan T. Kinney. 1998. Testing media richness theory in the new media: The effects of cues, feedback, and task equivocality. *Information systems research* 9, 3: 256–274.
9. Steve Duck, Deborah J. Rutt, Margaret H. Hurst, Heather Strejc. 1991. Some evident truths about conversations in everyday relationships: All communications are not created equal. *Human Communication Research* 18, 2: 228–267
10. James Price Dillard. 2008. Goals-plan-action theory of message production. In *Engaging theories in interpersonal communication: Multiple perspective,* Dawn O.Braithwaite and Paul Schrodt (es.). Sage, Thousand Oaks, CA, 65–76.
11. David B. Gerritsen, Dan Tasse, Jennifer K. Olsen, Tatiana A. Vlahovic, Rebecca Gulotta, William Odom, Jason Wiese, and John Zimmerman. 2016. Mailing Archived Emails as Postcards: Probing the Value of Virtual Collections. In *Proceedings of the 2016 CHI Conference on Human Factors in Computing Systems* (CHI '16). ACM, New York, NY, USA, 1187–1199. DOI: https://doi.org/10.1145/2858036.2858541
12. Barney G. Glaser. 1965. The constant comparative method of qualitative analysis. *Social Problems* 12, 4: 436–445.
13. Rebecca E. Grinter, Leysia Palen, and Margery Eldridge. 2006. Chatting with teenagers: Considering the place of chat technologies in teen life. *ACM Trans. Comput.-Hum. Interact.* 13, 4 (December 2006), 423–447. DOI=http://dx.doi.org/10.1145/1188816.1188817
14. Jeff Hancock, Jeremy Birnholtz, Natalya Bazarova, Jamie Guillory, Josh Perlin, and Barrett Amos. 2009. Butler lies: awareness, deception and design. In *Proceedings of the SIGCHI Conference on Human Factors in Computing Systems* (CHI '09). ACM, New York, NY, USA, 517–526. DOI=http://dx.doi.org/10.1145/1518701.1518782
15. Caroline Haythornthwaite. 2002. Strong, weak, and latent ties and the impact of new media. *The information society* 18, 5: 385–401.
16. Caroline Haythornthwaite. 2005. Social networks and Internet connectivity effects. *Information, Community & Society* 8, 2: 125–147.
17. Hilary Hutchinson, Wendy Mackay, Bo Westerlund, Benjamin B. Bederson, Allison Druin, Catherine Plaisant, Michel Beaudouin-Lafon, Stéphane Conversy, Helen Evans, Heiko Hansen, Nicolas Roussel, and Björn Eiderbäck. 2003. Technology probes: inspiring design for and with families. In *Proceedings of the SIGCHI Conference on Human Factors in Computing Systems* (CHI '03). ACM, New York, NY, USA, 17–24. DOI=http://dx.doi.org/10.1145/642611.642616
18. Joseph 'Jofish' Kaye, Mariah K. Levitt, Jeffrey Nevins, Jessica Golden, and Vanessa Schmidt. 2005. Communicating intimacy one bit at a time. In *CHI '05 Extended Abstracts on Human Factors in Computing Systems* (CHI EA '05). ACM, New York, NY, USA, 1529–1532. DOI=http://dx.doi.org/10.1145/1056808.1056958
19. Kathy Kellermann. 1992. Communication: Inherently strategic and primarily automatic. *Communications Monographs* 59, 3: 288–300.
20. Da-jung Kim and Youn-kyung Lim. 2012. iSpace: interactivity expression for self-expression in an online communication environment. In *Proceedings of the Designing Interactive Systems Conference* (DIS '12). ACM, New York, NY, USA, 210–219. DOI=10.1145/2317956.2317989 http://doi.acm.org/10.1145/2317956.2317989
21. Andrew M. Ledbetter and Joseph P. Mazer. Do online communication attitudes mitigate the association between Facebook use and relational interdependence? An extension of media multiplexity theory. *New Media & Society* 16, 5: 806–822.

22. Michael T. Motley. 1990. On whether one can (not) communicate: An examination via traditional communication postulates. *Western Journal of Communication* 54, 1: 1–20.
23. Tiffany Ng, Ou Jie Zhao, and Dan Cosley. 2011. pieTime: Visualizing Communication Patterns. In *Proceedings of the Privacy, Security, Risk and Trust (*PASSAT*) and 2011 IEEE Third Inernational Conference on Social Computing* (SocialCom '11), 720–723. DOI=http://dx.doi.org/10.1109/PASSAT/SocialCom.2011.90
24. Robert B. Cialdini. 1993. *Influence: The psychology of persuasion.* New York: Morrow.
25. Robert E. Kraut, Susan R. Fussell, Susan E. Brennan, Jane Siegel. 2002. Understanding effects of proximity on collaboration: Implications for technologies to support remote collaborative work. *Distributed work*: 137–162.
26. Rob Price. 2016 Almost 10 million Brits use Snapchat every day. *Business Insider*. Retrieved January 1 2017 from http://www.businessinsider.com/snapchat-has-nearly-10-million-daily-users-in-uk-dau-2016-5.
27. Claude Elwood Shannon. 2001. A mathematical theory of communication. *SIGMOBILE Mob. Comput. Commun. Rev.* 5, 1: 3–55. DOI=http://dx.doi.org/10.1145/584091.584093
28. Anselm L. Strauss, 1987. *Qualitative analysis for social scientists*. Cambridge University Press.
29. Annie Tat and Sheelagh Carpendale. 2006. CrystalChat: Visualizing personal chat history. In *Proceedings of the 39th Annual Hawaii International Conference on System Sciences (HICSS '06)*, 58c–58c.
30. Karen Tracy and Jessica S. Robles. 2013. *Everyday talk: Building and reflecting identities.* Guilford Press.
31. Fernanda B. Viégas and Judith S. Donath. 1999. Chat circles. In *Proceedings of the SIGCHI conference on Human Factors in Computing Systems* (CHI '99). ACM, New York, NY, USA, 9–16. DOI=http://dx.doi.org/10.1145/302979.302981
32. Bin Xu, Pamara Chang, Christopher L. Welker, Natalya N. Bazarova, and Dan Cosley. 2016. Automatic Archiving versus Default Deletion: What Snapchat Tells Us About Ephemerality in Design. In *Proceedings of the 19th ACM Conference on Computer-Supported Cooperative Work & Social Computing* (CSCW '16). ACM, New York, NY, USA, 1662–1675. DOI: http://dx.doi.org/10.1145/2818048.2819948
33. Yo app: what is it and why is it popular? In *The Week Business*. 2014. Retrieved January 12 2017 from http://www.theweek.co.uk/technology/59094/yo-app-what-is-it-and-why-is-it-popular.

Soil, Rock and Snow: on Designing for Information Sharing in Outdoor Sports

Paweł W. Woźniak[1], Anton Fedosov[2], Eleonora Mencarini[3], Kristina Knaving[4]
[1]University of Stuttgart, Stuttgart, Germany, pawel.wozniak@vis.uni-stuttgart.de
[2]Università della Svizzera italiana (USI), Lugano, Switzerland, anton.fedosov@usi.ch
[3]University of Trento & FBK, Povo (TN), Italy, mencarini@fbk.eu
[4]University of Gothenburg, Gothenburg, Sweden, kristina.knaving@ait.gu.se

ABSTRACT
While outdoor sport activities keep gaining popularity as part of a global trend to maintain a healthier lifestyle, current technology offers limited support for activity-specific needs. Therefore, a greater understanding of information sharing behaviours is necessary in order to build comprehensive, socially-embedded sports applications. To this purpose, we interviewed 46 practitioners in three outdoor sports: trail running, climbing, and skiing. Our qualitative study investigates how participants share information in the context of outdoor sports and how current technology supports this practice. Through thematic analysis, we derived five themes that describe the current information sharing practices: nature, risk and planning, content selection, audience selection, and privacy. Based on these themes, we present five recommendations for design that can inform, inspire and refine future sharing technologies for outdoor sport.

Author Keywords
Information sharing; skiing; climbing; trail running; communication; qualitative study.

ACM Classification Keywords
H.5.m. Information Interfaces and Presentation (e.g. HCI): Miscellaneous

INTRODUCTION
Participating in outdoor sports activities is becoming an integral part of daily routines in western societies[1]. Nevertheless, in her keynote at CHI 2010 [3], Genevieve Bell argued that Human-Computer Interaction (HCI) pays much less attention to sports than the majority of the population. In fact, although there is a considerable number of papers presenting systems that support training, HCI still lacks a systematic knowledge of the lived practices and experiences within this domain. Sportspeople often rely on the motivational support of their friends and families to keep up with their demanding training routines [2]. Nevertheless, current tracking devices and apps on the market do not fully address the social and emotional demands of sportspeople. Workout statistics, competition performance or training routes can be shared widely via social media or selectively to followers within an application ecosystem. However, apps like Runkeeper, Endomondo, Nike+ do not address some of the social needs of outdoor sports, like finding training partners or sharing the information needed to achieve athletic goals. In these situations, extra effort is required to manage the preparation of the information they want to share and the target audience [31], hence it may result in decreased motivation or reduced social connection. On the other hand, researchers in Communication Sciences (e.g. [17]) have demonstrated that sharing not only facilitates creation and maintenance of social ties, but also promotes egalitarianism, mutuality, openness and trust within a community; particularly when it comes to sharing personal emotions and feelings, which are common in sports [21]. In conclusion, current designs do not reflect the social character of sports, and an increased understanding of the information sharing practices of amateur sportspeople is needed to build technology that will improve their sport experience and sustain their motivation.

To that end, we took a closer look at how sportspeople currently share information using technology in the context of three outdoor disciplines, namely skiing, climbing, and trail running. Outdoor sports are interesting because people practise them widely in western societies; not just to get fit or to experience the 'game' aspect of team sports, but to measure themselves against natural elements and challenge their skills. All the sports we considered require the participants to immerse themselves in nature and challenge themselves by facing a natural element (steep slopes, high mountains, long distances on uneven trails), however they differ in the degree of social interactions in which they are performed (groups, pairs, individuals). Therefore, by investigating and comparing them we aimed to gain an overview of insights relevant to outdoor sports in general.

[1]The number of physically active individuals in the EU is increasing according to Eurostat cf. `http://appsso.eurostat.ec.europa.eu/nui/show.do?dataset=hlth_ehis_pe2e&lang=en`

DIS 2017, June 10-14, 2017, Edinburgh, United Kingdom

ACM 978-1-4503-4922-2/17/06...$15.00
DOI: http://dx.doi.org/10.1145/3064663.3064741

We contribute to the HCI for sports community by outlining five themes resulting from interviews on three different outdoor sports practised in three different countries (NATURE, RISK AND PLANNING, AUDIENCE SELECTION, CONTENT SELECTION and PRIVACY) and five recommendations for designing socially-embedded technology for information sharing in outdoor sports. By conducting in-depth interviews, we aimed to explore the existing information sharing practices and to discuss the relation between content, audience, and timing of the sharing. Our findings highlight that sportspeople expect to be offered extended means to easily manage content and audience. The analysis also shows that sports technology needs to embrace the intricate issues of timing to facilitate outdoor sharing practices.

The paper is organized as follows: in the next section, we discuss previous HCI works exploring designing for sports and information sharing research in general. We then provide the details of our study and analysis, and our five themes of information sharing in outdoor sports resulting from this analysis. We conclude the paper with design recommendations for future sport technology that can help designers create engaging socially-embedded experiences.

RELATED WORK

In this section, we review past research efforts that influenced our study. First, we provide the broader context of our inquiry in the domain of HCI for sports. Later, we look at past inquiries into information sharing and collective content creation beyond the context of sport.

Designing technology for supporting sportspeople

Sports as an application area is an emerging topic in the HCI community [28]. Part of HCI research in this domain has focused on understanding motivation mechanisms and on designing systems aimed at persuading users less involved in sports to engage in regular activity. Knaving et al. [21] endeavoured to understand the motivational factors that influence amateur runners. Byrne and Mueller [4] proposed a comparison between the motivations of climbers to practise the sport derived from literature and the technology for climbing developed by HCI research with the purpose of highlighting the mismatch between theory and practice. Reynolds et al. [37] investigated how beginner and experienced sportspeople react to gamified physical activity features present in the game Wii Fit. Further, Purpura et al. [35] presented a critical design view on the ethical and sociocultural consequences of an interactive system designed to convince people to reduce obesity.

A different strain of research focused on improving the individual sport experience, both during training and competition. Tholander and Nylander [41] explored how technology can influence the experience of sport, concluding that the role of technology can be two-fold; on the one hand, it should be instrumental since it helps to measure the performance, and on the other it should be experiential and support reflecting and remembering the felt experiences. Among the works presenting technology to support the effectiveness of training, we note de Oliveira and Oliver [8] who developed and evaluated TripleBeat; a mobile application for helping runners maintain pace. Schneegaß and Voit [40] investigated in-run interaction using a wearable gesture device on the runner's hand. Hasegawa et al. [16] presented an application to support beginner skiers to adjust their centre of gravity through sonification and consequently to assume a correct posture. Past research has also recognised and addressed the need for increased playfulness of the sport experience: Dunlop et al. [10] proposed to interactively visualise data while skiing and Kajastila and Hämäläinen [18] offered new dynamic challenges to climbers by designing and developing a projection-augmented climbing wall.

More recently, researchers became more interested in the social aspects of sport and investigated the issues of temporal and spatial displacement between the different parties involved in the sport experience, such as team mates, sports buddies or supporters. In particular, Mueller et al. [29] presented Jogging over a distance, a system for enhancing the feeling of social connectedness of remote runners, and Woźniak et al. [47] investigated how technology can allow family and friends to support runners during long-distance performances. Similarly, Romanowski et al. [38] used drones to mediate cheering during running races. These works, however, focused on remote users, and did not address the needs of co-located sportspeople or supporting groups.

Co-located interaction was explored by Mauriello et al. [25], who explored spontaneous interactions prompted by wearable displays during running races, and Walmink et al. [46], who observed the reactions to a cyclists heart rate being displayed on her helmet. Mencarini et al. [26] outlined suggestions to use wearable devices for augmenting the communication between climber and belayer in order to enhance the experience and reduce the negative emotions of an ascent. Desjardins et al. [9] reflected on the design of avalanche beacons to facilitate collaborative rescue operations. This strain of research explored on-the-spot reactions and simple information processing, while a few works explored also complex two-way information exchange in the sport context. For example, Fedosov et al. [12] engaged in a co-design activity with a group of backcountry skiers to meet their information sharing requirements before, during and after the descent. Based on collected requirements they developed SkiAR, the augmented reality system to support decision making within group of skiers through sharing personalized virtual content on panoramic resort maps [13].

The papers above are motivated by the fact that sportspeople's needs are not yet fully understood by HCI research nor by the market, and thus demonstrate the purposefulness of our work. So far, little work has addressed the question of which needs are sport-specific and which are true for the larger context of physical activity. We assume that a thorough understanding of sportspeople's needs is a prerequisite to develop new successful sport technologies. We believe that experience, sociality and motivational factors are intertwined in an eclectic gestalt (much like Dalsgaard et al.'s participation gestalt [7]) of sports systems. Our work answers to an emerging challenge of understanding how the social dimensions of everyday sports influence the user's perception of the sports experience.

Understanding information sharing practices

In order to study information sharing practices effectively, we reviewed past work that explores how users share information not only in the context of sports, but in other domains as well. Following research of Communication scholars such as John [17], we explore sharing as an act of *communication* in the context of sport. Although the logic of sharing as an act of *distribution* is also an interesting opportunity, it requires a separate inquiry outside of the scope of this study.

A large number of works has studied sharing focusing on personal digital data, for example personal data files [45], photos [1], or videos [22]. Olsson et al. [33] investigated what motivate users to create collective content. They observed how sports fans, scouts, online group chatters and fishing enthusiasts created shared repositories of online media. In a follow-up study, Olsson [32] showed that collective content could be described by the community's contribution, the relevance of the content and the level of sharing. Our work is inspired by Olsson's considerations and provided us with guidance for creating scripts for user interviews. Similarly, Leitner et al. [23] investigated the reasons for users joining online communities. They concluded that a key motivation was the access to a pool of shared information. Our work investigates whether similar information practices take place in the case of sports and, like Leitner et al., we relied primarily on semi-structured interviews to build our understanding of information sharing practices.

Past research also explored some aspects of the social setting of sports. Ojala and Saarela [31] summarized motivations for tracking and sharing details of training routines and physical exercises in online sports communities. Among the most frequent reasons to share to online communities based on previous research they outline four: (1) to get feedback and guidance; (2) to create and maintain social ties (e.g. through finding a running partner); (3) to build an attractive social profile; and finally (4) to compete among peers. Prior work confirmed that social sharing contributes not only to the overall user experience and enjoyment of workouts [29, 3, 30], but it could be also a powerful motivator for physical activity itself [42]. Curmi et al. [6] discovered that sharing real-time physiological data (e.g., heart rate) can create bidirectional social connection between sportsmen and their supporters. Consolvo et al. [5] with their deployment of Houston, a mobile application that encourages opportunistic physical activity by sharing step count within small group of friends, identified that competitiveness and social pressure are areas of influence for physical exercising. Nevertheless, the study conducted by Lin et al. [24] found that sharing physical activity through a chat with strangers is not always motivating and can be uncomfortable.

Previous work also looked at privacy concerns [20], associated risks [36] and preferences [34] regarding the tracking (and potentially sharing) of personal health data. Common concerns about sharing are (1) fear of appearing boring or boastful; (2) consequences of oversharing; and (3) insufficient support received from the community [30]. Informed by the rich insights of factors that support and inhibit sharing activity of personal exercise data, we aim to understand how interactive artefacts can better support social activity in outdoor sports. Our goals are also similar to those of Ahtinen et al. [2] who investigated how mobile applications can be improved to better support wellness through design-based research. Guided by the design framework for social sharing in personal informatics [11], we especially emphasise the importance of audience and content selection for designing technology across three distinct sports disciplines. Consequently, we conducted an interview study with participants practising running, climbing and skiing.

METHOD

Our study consisted of three qualitative inquiries into three different sports. For each of the disciplines we conducted a series of semi-structured interviews with amateur sportspeople practising regularly. Since we conducted our investigations in different moments and in different countries, we agreed on a common ground of tools and methods to guide the investigation, such as the research questions, the use of semi-structured interviews, and the topics to be investigated during the interview. Beyond these guidelines, each researcher was free to conduct the study as s/he deemed appropriate. Therefore, the composition of the participant groups, the recruitment methods and location, and the interviewing techniques were adjusted to best match the specific qualities of the three sports. We collected data from the one-on-one interviews with skiers and runners, and from the focus group interviews with climbers and skiers. Given that climbing and skiing usually have higher levels of social interaction in comparison to runners and that social dynamics were a matter of interest for the scope of this research, we deliberately employed a focus group format for these two sports.

Participants

Our study not only spans multiple sports, but also multiple nationalities. Runner interviews were conducted primarily in Sweden, but included also runners from Poland and the United States; climbers were recruited in Italy; the skiing resorts where skier/snowboarder interviews took place were located in Austria and France.

Runners

We recruited trail runners for semi-structured interviews by contacting a local running club and also spontaneously at a local well-known running spot. A total of 12 participants (2 females), aged 24 – 74 (M = 42 yrs.) took part in the study. The majority of the interviews were conducted individually, but we also interviewed one pair and one group of three senior citizens. The interviews were always conducted in conjunction with a running-related activity (sometimes during organised races), so we interviewed participants directly post-run. Total interview time was 256 minutes.

Climbers

We recruited 15 climbers (4 females), aged 27 – 43 (M = 22 yrs.) through the snowball sampling technique. We divided participants into two groups according to their availability and then we conducted two focus groups. Focus group was chosen as investigation method due to the great difference in the participants level of experience (years of practice $M = 6$, the highest-grade climbed leading ranging from 4b to 7b[2]). By adopting this interviewing method, we aimed at considering and comparing all the possible different points of view on the topics investigated. During the discussion, we encouraged all participants to participate by actively inviting them to express their opinions. The focus groups were conducted at a researcher's workplace located in a well-known climbing area of Italy, and lasted approximately 90 minutes each.

Skiers

We recruited 12 skiers/snowboarders (3 females), aged 22–34 (M = 32 yrs.) with various levels of skiing experience both on and off-piste. Each semi-structured interview lasted 30 – 45 minutes and was conducted after a full skiing day in a resort in the Alps. This way, we strived to make it easier for the participants to reflect on their day of skiing. The participants were recruited through snowball sampling. Additionally, we conducted a focus group with 7 participants (3 females) aged 25 – 31 (M = 26 yrs.). These were experienced backcountry skiers and snowboarders spending a week together in an alpine resort. The focus group was organized through a peer, conducted after a skiing day, and lasted 60 minutes.

Interviews

All the interviews focused on information sharing habits in relation to the sport practiced. Primarily, we asked what data they shared and what technical means they used (e.g. specialized apps or hardware). Examples of the opening questions include "How would you describe the ingredients for a good climbing/skiing day", "What information do you share about your running/skiing activity? With whom? Why?" We also inquired about their chosen audience and if they had any privacy concerns. Further questions focused on when information was shared in relation to the activity. The physical context of the sharing practices was important to us as well — we inquired whether particular surroundings elicited specific sharing behaviours. Finally, we asked the participants to reflect on the social dimension of information sharing in sports, and on the role information played in their sport groups. Having common interview questions allowed us to understand descriptively the commonalities and the differences among those sports. All the interviews were audio recorded and then transcribed. Moreover, during each interview we took field notes and reviewed them immediately after. Travelling back and forth between prior research findings, our field notes and the interview transcripts allowed us to quickly find emergent patterns in the collected data, and subsequently establish common themes between different disciplines.

Analysis

As the original data was in four different languages (English, Swedish, Polish and Italian), relevant passages representing the three sports in equal parts were later translated into English so that all authors could compare results and reflect on the differences and similarities of each data set. We established a coding tree by translating about 10% of the data set to English with equal parts representing the three sports. All four authors coded the data independently using thematic analysis [27]. Next, in two code-adjustment meetings, we iteratively reached agreement on the final coding tree that was later used to code the entire data set. The tree contained the five top-tier themes that are presented below. Finally, in order to reduce the language differences further, we created a data synopsis for each of the sports, which we linked to the most relevant quotes from our participants to support emerging empirical categories. The data reported below was derived from the synopses. These practical considerations enabled us to conduct a study spanning multiple sports and nationalities without the need for professional translators and language-level analysis.

[2]French grading system.

THEMES

In this section, we present the themes that emerged across the three sports. Through these it was possible to identify the common and different attitudes that participants practising the different sports exhibited towards technology and information sharing. We chose to present the data separately for the three sports to highlight the differences and the commonalities.

Nature

Nature, or "the great outdoors", is the common thread in the three sports we considered. Skiing is inevitably an outdoor activity, and although running can be done in cities and climbing is practised worldwide thanks to indoor gyms, all our participants preferred to practise their sports outdoors, outside city areas.

Runners

All the participants have a developed relationship with nature:

'I love the freedom in running in the forest.'

They also exhibit strong a preference for exercising in non-city environments, which is not always possible:

'Unfortunately, there is not much you can do in the city, route-wise.'

One often-cited reason for preferring nature is the experience of being alone with oneself. Other reasons include the possibility to explore new places, to see how nature changes throughout the year, and the need for an environment that contrasts with an intensive work life. When asked about their ideal running routes, participants would mention the mountains, hilly forests, and other scenic environments.

Climbers

Climbers have an extremely direct relationship with nature; they move up the rock by grasping it with bare hands and pushing with their feet, while continuously searching for balance and the most effective movements. In particular, the tactile sensations climbers get from the rock influence their sense of self-confidence, performance, and enjoyment.

'In mountain climbing, (what makes a good day) is the kind of rock, the kind of movements required by the wall...'

Isolation, together with immersion in nature, is considered positive. For example, to have the possibility to explore nature without other people except the climbing partners is considered a great privilege:

'SM: In my opinion, the environment matters a lot. For example, climbing on mount Sella is unpleasant because you can hear the motorbikes racing at the foot of the mountain.
DC: Being isolated is pleasant. (...)
SM: Yes indeed, to have someone climbing above you that makes stones fall is not pleasant at all. (...) I enjoy also the time spent approaching the start of the route. I prefer to spend two hours bringing the ropes in the backpack and climb a shorter route in an environment that is far from busy roads; it's more like an adventure!'

Part of the beauty of being immersed in the nature is also due to the challenges it provides. This aspect is reflected in the words of one participant addressing the proposal of another participant about having a system of augmented reality to show the route while climbing a mountain:

'Alpinists would assault you if you create something like that. You should know the path by yourself, that's the sense of going mountaineering.'

Skiers

Similarly, nature plays a profound role in skiers experience:

'I love quiet untouched slopes with a lot of powder, maybe some nice ways through the forest... where you have 20 minutes of a great ride.'

While, for some participants, skiing is about performance and getting the best out of the day:

'I love going skiing just for myself. So, I really like this independence. With great snow, I do hours of skiing, lunch on the lifts.'

For others, it is a social activity built around spending time outdoors with a group of people:

'I think (skiing as) the social construction where you can do something together without really being together is quite, I think, attractive. You have synchronization points where you are basically in a cable car or in the lift, you have the chance to talk to people for quite a while and mainly without much disturbance.'

Risk and planning

Safety and risk are important concerns in outdoor sports. Risk is a combination of environmental factors, personal conditions and self-confidence, and coordination between sport partners. Therefore, in the disciplines we explored, sportspeople often seek additional information prior to the activities to increase their safety and comfort. In particular, weather conditions and information about the area are searched as both affect outdoor practices significantly. However, the need for planning differs naturally between the sports; while backcountry skiers and mountain climbers go for longer trips, where careful planning is needed in order to mitigate risk and make the time investment count, runners often noted that one of the best aspects of running is that it can be done with minimal preparation. These attitudes were repeated during the activity, when the need for sharing in order to minimise risk is higher for backcountry skiers and mountain climbers - who always practise their sport in pairs or larger groups, and thus have to be coordinated - and lowest for the runners, where the majority of people prefer to run solo.

Runners

The runners used a variety of strategies for planning the run and integrating it into daily routines. Some made the decision on where to run during the day, indicating that they had already explored the nearby environment and were versed in the possible routes. Notably, discovering new routes and consulting with others on the matter was perceived as a labour-intensive task that could not be done properly using just a mobile phone. Some runners mentioned explicitly that they obtained simple weather information directly preceding a run:

'Before a longer run, I look at the weather forecast to see if a downpour is about to start.'

Furthermore, two runners highlighted that the choice of route and surface was often dictated by the specific training format one had planned for a given day. This, however, was also subject to change as perceived rates of exertion may have affected the final training format for the day. Another precaution that runners tend to take is staying in touch with friends and family:

'(regarding using the phone to orient oneself) I think there should exist better ways (in the app) to — well, it happens that you are out in the forest and hurt yourself, for example — that you would be able to quickly send your position to, well, your boyfriend or family or anyone, really — purely out of a safety perspective.'

Climbers

Information retrieval and accurate planning are especially important for this sport because climbing entails various types of risks. Climbers can be caught by thunder storms, rain showers, go out of the climbing route, fall, etc. Therefore, it is fundamental for them to have very accurate updates and reliable information.

'That's why is so important to know when a route was created. If you go to France and you find a 5th grade route but it was bolted in the 80s, you risk serious falls.'

Climbers are highly dependent on weather and the challenges posed by the chosen route. Consequently, they need to know a number of parameters that are solely controlled by nature:

'(we need to know) the time required to approach the route/crag, the difficulty grades, the weather, how slippery the rock is...'

Generally, to get this kind of information climbers rely on the Internet, guide books, or directly on friends who know the spot. Smartphone apps were not used often. Our participants affirmed to have used mobile applications for a while, but to have stopped later because the applications' primary focus was skiing or hiking. They ascribed a lot of importance to the source of information, which they needed to trust. For example, almost all of our participants relied upon a few websites known to be reliable, but they preferred receiving information from friends rather than from strangers.

'DC: Well, I think that the word of mouth plays an important role. Climbers use much more the word of mouth than... of course on Google you can find the report, but...
MF: Or 5 different reports
DC: (laughing) or 5 different reports, together with variants!'

Another user was reluctant towards information obtained from internet forums:

'If someone has completed the same route, I ask him: how is it? Are there falling rocks? I try to get some hints about the situation so that I know what to expect. (...) I do not trust forums at all. There, it's all a competition between who is cooler and braver. It's very likely that they tell you 'sure, it's so easy and well-protected!' And then you find a bolt every pitch.'

During the ascent, communication between climbing partners was perceived as fundamental for managing risk. Apart from the need for coordination in joint actions that can be performed either verbally or non-verbally (e.g. by pulling the rope), there is also a decision-making process involved.

'Seeing the weather changing and taking a decision with your climbing partner like "Ok, we are a pitch away from the top but we need to turn back", being able to take such a decision and going back home alive, is not a trivial matter.'

The relevant things to be communicated in those cases are personal conditions (tiredness, loss of self-confidence, difficulties in climbing, etc.), and evaluation of external factors (e.g. weather change). This communication usually happens when climber and belayer meet at a belay station; otherwise they have to solve their difficulties on their own since environmental noise and distance hamper the communication. A new trend is to use walkie-talkies, but our participants considered these as tools for inexperienced people and not very efficient because the signal is disturbed by the many communications using the same channel. In case of extreme need, they would use their smartphones, but they do not really rely on them because mobile signal coverage is spotty in mountain areas. Smartphones were used primarily for taking pictures, to have a backup of the report of the route (while the main one is always on paper) and for security reasons, i.e. to make a phone call in case of need.

Skiers

Similarly to climbers, the skiers' experience was also highly affected by current weather. Snow conditions are important factors to get the best out of a skiing holiday. The amount of fresh snow at the resort, visibility, temperature, wind, condition of the slope and precipitation on the mountain were among the factors that influence the decision to choose where to ski the next day.

'I did not plan to go skiing there, I just saw one day before that prediction of 1 metre snow. So I call this friend of mine at the evening at 10pm: "What are you doing tomorrow? — Not so much. Do you have time until 2-3pm? So let's go there at 8-8.30 and ski for 5 hours."'

As backcountry skiing is known to be a high-risk sport, those practising the discipline develop a number of risk management measures. First, skiing groups have clearly defined roles. The lead, an experienced skier, chooses the path and the stops and provides immediate feedback to the rest of the group. Followers are mid-pack skiers that form the core of the group. Another experienced skier is at the end of the group and provides support to anyone struggling with the route. The skiers strive to keep the lead within their line of sight:

'The lead chooses a safe place and the rest follow. [...] it is important not to overload the slope.'

The route of descent is chosen by the group members collaboratively during every second stop and depends on the skills of the group members. Safety is a primary concern and it is the central element of group communication.

Audience selection

Participants in all three groups had thought about with whom they shared sports activities.

Runners

All the runners were conscious of whom they shared their running data with. Some communicated solely (or almost solely) with other runners:

'I don't seek out friends on Runkeeper. These (my Runkeeper friends) tend to be people I've run in the past with.'

The users either became members of established groups (e.g. Facebook running groups) or established their own well-defined groups in which they conducted regular sharing. The data varied from automatic sharing via Garmin and Runkeeper to more elaborated explicit forms e.g. direct messaging or taking screenshots of apps. Events or especially successful runs were given extra attention and intensified sharing. One user mentioned how they had posted their race result on Facebook and received multiple likes and comments which heightened the experience of achievement. Two runners were explicitly concerned about supplying too much content:

'When I noticed how I was spamming the wall, I stopped doing it.'

These runners endeavoured to limit the amount of data available publicly to not spam their followers with too many run reports. They also reflected on the days when they had been beginners and noted that they tended to share less over time.

Climbers

Climbers usually did not share their experiences publicly, despite their strong need for self-expression:

'(If you don't tell stories), why go in the mountains?!'

They preferred to share their experiences with friends or acquaintances who share their same passion, so that they could understand their commitment, effort, and satisfaction. This kind of sharing was done both as diary keeping and as a repository of known places, so that other people could ask information about a place they had been recently. This was mostly achieved through media with restricted access like Dropbox, closed groups on Facebook, or Whatsapp. It is worth noticing that within these groups reciprocity was expected:

'I usually put the routes on Facebook. I put one picture, the name of the route, the place... because I have these (closed) groups of friends, and I know the others will do the same.'

More general sharing on social networks was used almost solely for special achievements like climbing a certain route for the first time. Otherwise, sharing with bigger groups or even publicly happened when climbers had some role in the wider community, e.g. being route setters or alpine guides. For example, a participant mentioned a closed but crowded group on Facebook where members shared news and equipment reviews. Thus, we could say that the more public the sharing is, the more it acquires a value-driven purpose. In fact, climbing may also be used to communicate other values; for instance, a participant mentioned a blog of mountaineering girls who shared their achievements with the intent of being role-models and spreading feminist values.

Skiers

In the case of skiing, the primary sharing audience is the current skiing group on a given day. Location-based content is used extensively to coordinate skiing activities and set up meeting points when the group splits. Most of the sharing activities occur when the skiers are not directly engaged with skiing activity itself, e.g. during the breaks or in the cable car.

Users reflected that they did not want to overwhelm their social media audience with skiing pictures. Consequently, they used other means of sharing:

'I don't want to share it on Facebook with everybody, but (just) with the people who were in the picture. I usually send it immediately, because if I don't do it more or less immediately it's never going to happen.'

Another audience for skiers was friends who could possibly be skiing with them. They were hoping the friends could join next time, but careful not to elicit negative feelings:

'I share the track with friends I kind of like I guess to show them that you were there and sometimes you can even say like 'Hey, you should have joined!' or maybe sometimes you can make people jealous.'

Finally, backcountry skiers expressed a need for companion apps to have a comprehensive view of snow and road conditions to reach places with untouched powder. However, drawing on the excitement and exclusivity of discovering less known places, skiers did not want to share all the knowledge beyond their group to avoid bringing crowds to specific spots at the resort.

'For all of us would be great whether an app would show how to get to certain point in mind (to the bus, to the track), how many cm of snow in a desired location, track including a map, but then the ski resort will be too popular among others, and an exclusivity of such this small village we are in right now will be lost.'

Content selection

Depending on where and with whom the content was shared, participants had different sharing strategies. Practicalities, self-representation, and privacy were important, but also understanding that friends and acquaintances were not necessarily interested in all data.

Runners

Two runners noted that they were conscious that extended data (e.g. physiological measurements or gait features) may be meaningful only to those who have extensive experience running, and shared data (e.g. running routes or uphill run difficulty) explicitly for the purpose of helping other runners. One participant mentioned they only shared location data with established training partners they had met face-to-face. One participant also mentioned that other apps were already collecting location data in the background, so perhaps his concerns about running apps were unreasonable. Some relied on the default setting of the chosen running app for choosing what to share:

'I do the automatic sharing: that shares my average time, my heart rate, my elevation change... whatever, I'm not so concerned with that.'

One runner reflected that the content they shared evolved over time. As they gained more experience they appreciated subjective feedback more:

'I figured out I missed out on making notes. I should have taken notes on how tiring the run was early on.'

Climbers

We realized that climbers registered data primarily for their personal memory, as a form of diary keeping. It has to be noticed that very few applications for climbers are available on the commercial market. None of the climbers with whom we spoke used dedicated means for ascent tracking; they used generic tools or kept no record at all:

'R: Do you keep trace of your improvements in climbing and, if yes, what do you use?
LT: I remember the beautiful days, where I was, and what I did. Also the bad ones. But just in my mind.
R: So you don't use any device, not even a paper diary... Did you used to once? What did you used to write?
EM: I used to write down the routes I accomplished.'

The focus of attention on what to record depended strictly on the motivation for practising climbing and on whether one was a beginner or not. Usually, beginners are enthusiastic about their new experiences and sensations, and they achieve new results more often:

'At the beginning, you really want to share what you are doing, but then, after a while, you focus more on the practice and less on documenting.'

For more experienced climbers, some suggested leveraging on competitiveness to keep motivation high:

'Nowadays I don't climb so much anymore, but I'd like to have an app like Strava for climbing. The coolest thing Strava offers you is the comparison with the people you know. I know that Moon is currently trying to do something similar with the Moonboard.'

Moreover, our participants distinguished between the needs of people who climb for fun and those who train with the goal to improve or to take part in competitions:

'If you climb for fun but you want to have a track of your improvements it is enough to know how many routes you climbed (...) if you train seriously you might need to keep a more accurate track of what you do.'

Skiers

The skiers in our study shared a wide variety of data types. Sharing personal and group information during a day out skiing often included details such as location, photos and videos. Skiers share location primarily to coordinate activities on the slope. Smartphones or walkie-talkies are used to instantly communicate one's position. A location on a digital map is often sent through an instant message service, which may be followed by subsequent voice communication. Similar patterns may be used to manage the group composition:

'If we have some people who want to split, we give them the walkie-talkie and keep in touch.'

Aside from coordination, backcountry skiers also frequently document their descents: they create large amounts of content to review after the activity. They often carry high-performance equipment to record high quality video such as GoPro cameras or DSLRs. The equipment is used to stage particularly exciting moments (e.g. jumps). One skier reported that usually multiple members of the group would carry recording equipment, however only one would volunteer to maintain a coherent account of the activity and to create a final video clip.

'When DM was at home, he had all the footage and made a great video cut about the trip.'

One group established a data policy where footage was synced to a single external hard drive:

'(At the end of the day) it is actually a great way to agree on transferring media [...] while we are still here.'

Privacy

Many respondents expressed privacy concerns, not only in relation to sports data but also regarding other sensors and apps that their smartphones were equipped with. Consequently, there was an understanding that this was unlikely to be solved within sports alone, but that sports apps should conform to a more comprehensive personal data privacy management.

Runners

While most users shared different forms of data, many established boundaries of what could be shared. Photos and playlists were considered easy to share and unlikely to pose a risk. In contrast, many users expressed concerns about sharing location data widely. They cited the fact that not only it affected them, but also their friends and family, and thus they did not feel entitled to decide on other people's privacy. Interestingly, one runner reflected on the need to balance risk-taking and privacy:

'I found a Swedish website that was doing just that (ID bracelets), but they actually stored the information. And then I felt: No, I don't want that.'

On the other hand, some users expressed the possibility of trading some privacy for good reasons. For instance, one user wanted to promote a local running location he enjoyed, so he was willing to publicly share routes from that location:

'I tell people about Skats to make them understand they should run here. I want to advertise Skats, it is fantastic.'

Climbers

Climbers' privacy concerns were related to the careful selection of the audience that they had to perform in order not to create conflict with other people. An example is offered by a participant who told about realizing the consequences of sharing on Facebook and adjusting their behaviour accordingly:

'I used to share a lot on social networks and I enjoyed having chats with climber friends that I did not see often, but then other people were envious or started to annoy me. I felt invaded in my privacy and I took everything off. Then, I restarted sharing because I wanted to share with friends I cant meet anymore, but now I put some limits (to who can see what I share).'

The need to pay attention to the people with whom they share information could explain also why climbers often retain facts to share them only face to face:

'Sure, face to face. At the bar, in the evening.'

Secondly, climbers' tendency to limit digital sharing was also linked to the dynamics of secrecy and competition. Providing certain information or experience could have simplified achievement for competitors or have made lose exclusivity to certain crags. Thus, climbers were wary not to share too much.

Skiers

Skiers differ from the previous two groups since performing the activity in a publicly available ski resort already implies a privacy trade-off. Modern ski resorts use RFID cards that trace lift usage, which is then available online, albeit in anonymous form. This is a compulsory service required for all skiers in the area. The skiers in our study reflected that they understood this data enabled the ski resort to run the facilities more efficiently, despite the fact that several concerns were raised that collected data should not be linked to a skier's identity. When it comes to the tracked activities using apps, the users expressed the desire to be fully in control on what events were shared:

'I think the system automatically posted something on Facebook, which I disabled, because, I mean, you don't always want other people to know where you are or what you were doing. So, I mean, I want to decide by myself what I want to share and what I want to keep private.'

As for sharing the extended footage backcountry skiers are likely to create during a trip, the photos and videos were considered private to the group. While the skiers recognised that uploading the content to the cloud would simplify sharing, they were determined to keep the footage exclusive to a closed group:

'Great if you could create a group page about the trip, which would include only people who were skiing there.'

RECOMMENDATIONS FOR DESIGN

Having reviewed our themes, we present the recommendations for design that emerge from the user needs evidenced in our qualitative analysis. By doing so, we aim to inspire future systems exploring gaps in current sports technology. Our five recommendations can also be used as entry points for specific design inquiries in the three sports. We link each recommendation with the themes above for clarity. While some aspects of the recommendations may apply to more than just technology for running, skiing and climbing, designers should use them with caution in case of other sports. We imagine that the five recommendations below may function as a checklist for designers to ensure the information sharing aspects of their sports-oriented application are addressed thoroughly.

Augment, not obstruct the outdoor experience

The participants in our study felt a personal connection with the great outdoors, as shown in the NATURE theme. Irrespective of the discipline, the users were both motivated by the possibility of experiencing nature and concerned of being exposed to its forces (e.g. their activities were heavily affected by weather conditions). Future technologies should embrace this complicated balance and strengthen the connection with nature. This appears to be especially challenging as we have observed that the experience of nature often blends with the sense of achievement and creating personal memories. On one hand, we saw the users taking extensive footage of their activities (with backcountry skiers being the extreme case), while on the other hand, we observed that users tended to limit the number of devices they took with them to experience the mountains better and that technology interface in most cases is not designed for usage while involved in such physical activities (this was especially evident for climbers [26]).

We believe that future systems should offer a large degree of freedom in terms of how many sensors to use and how one experiences nature. There appears to be a need for both minimalistic, unobtrusive tracking (e.g. through wearables) and extensive visible tracking (e.g. drone-mounted cameras). We learned that designers need to tread carefully as designs should balance the need for using technology with the need for experiencing nature without the filter of technology. Designing for periodic use [14] and relating to non-use [39] are design concepts that appear to be applicable in this case. Incorporating these aspects in future designs should be fundamental to augmenting, not superseding, the nature experience that motivates these users.

Provide explicit support for planning

A common feature shared by all three sports in our study was the need for planning. Also in trail running, which appears to be a more spontaneous discipline, participants often conducted preparatory activities. Our results show that current technology provides little to no support for planning activities in outdoor sports. The interviewees used generic tools both to obtain the necessary information and coordinate within groups. It also appears that social media provides little support as most users reported obtaining information from generic search engines. Coordination was also conducted through generic means such as e-mail, instant messaging or phone calls.

We see the lack of support for planning as a significant gap in current sport technology. Our participants did not use a tool to keep all the required information in a single space and resorted to alternative means. We envision that future outdoor sport support systems should easily be able to gather information such as geographical location, weather and group composition in a single interface. In the RISK AND PLANNING theme, we saw how users consider planning to be central to their safety and their enjoyment of the outdoor activities. It is worth noting that all three sports are constrained spatially by the accessible parts of the surroundings, available ascents, and lifts. Users require efficient means to negotiate those constraints and communicate their decisions. Finally, those who have more experience need ways to communicate their advice to novices already in the planning phase, which is now difficult. Consequently, designers should empower users to effectively contact their activity groups and coordinate plans prior to heading into the outdoors.

Incorporate risk management features

In our study, we observed that users often needed to reach consensus within the group to balance possible enjoyment and risk. They needed to consider their skills, personal plans for the day and external factors to decide on a course of action that would be safe and most enjoyable. Current technology offers little support for risk management. As a consequence, we saw users appropriate generic technologies to accomplish that task.

In the RISK AND PLANNING theme, we saw that users often required external information to fully assess risk. Weather information and opinions from others are often basic requirements to decide on a safe course of action. Yet given that risk management is often carried out across a group, there is the risk of some information being omitted and the assessment being wrong. Future technology should strive to minimise that possibility. We envision future applications that integrate multiple sport-specific information sources. For instance, climbers would benefit from weather, ascent rating and rescue service alerts being integrated. A dedicated system could also account for the intrinsic risks of the event such as weather and the ascent conditions. Users in our study often collected data manually, and out-of-date information may pose an additional risk that could be mitigated by group risk-assessment discussions. In summary, it appears that choosing a safe route is a sensemaking task, so we recommend that designers use the experiences of past sensemaking systems (e.g. [15, 19]) to build extensive support for risk management in outdoor sports applications.

Support multiple informal groups

Users were especially careful about with whom they shared their sport-related information. In the AUDIENCE SELECTION, we observed how users chose to share with different audiences at different times. All three sports benefit from a system of clubs and informal groups to maintain the users' motivation. Furthermore, we see an emergent need for future technology to empower users to quickly and efficiently select audiences for sharing sports data (e.g. [11]). Privacy control was discussed in the PRIVACY theme, with the conclusion that sport enthusiasts should be able to easily select the right target audience for a given piece of content, in order to prevent unwanted access. These findings are related to unwanted audience concerns in social media [43].

Prior research in personal sensing identified privacy concerns [20], especially when it comes to conversation logs or data that describe private psychological states [36]. For instance, in our study, skiers were not highly concerned about sharing data with the resort that would eventually support their descents through lift operations, presuming anonymity. More frequently, they shared various digital content describing the overall activity within the group, where privacy restrictions are rather relaxed. On the whole, the need to differentiate between multiple groups most likely arises from the different purposes of sharing for sportspeople ranging from peer support [42] through self expression [31] to competitiveness [5]. The AUDIENCE SELECTION theme showed that many of our participants were part of small, informal cliques where they fully trusted their closest sports friends. Consequently, we believe that future sharing applications in sports should offer extensive tools for audience selection that consider the intricacies of cliques, bragging, privacy and competition. These applications should allow users to quickly and efficiently select audiences for sharing sports data (e.g. [11]), otherwise this may lead to hindering the enjoyment of the outdoor activities for competitive users.

Enable multiple levels of content selection

Our last recommendation is closely tied to the CONTENT SELECTION and PRIVACY themes. We observed that most users differentiate between the kinds of data they share in different moments. Some relied on automated sharing and were unaware of what exactly was shared (e.g. runners) while others took great care in gathering and creatively modifying content before sharing (e.g. backcountry skiers). In line with the *Post Content* design dimension from the social sharing framework in personal informatics [11], we observed how different levels of control over information were required to allow users to effectively curate the content generated during sport activities. The need for an accurate content selection is often caused by the users different purposes for sharing in the social environment. Content is often adjusted to suit particular audiences. For instance, we saw users trying to convince others to join them at a precise location. This required simple information sharing without extensive exercise-related statistics. On the other hand, climbers may want to share the exact route and ascent time to gain recognition in their community. We observed that content often helped negotiate group status, future plans or training schedules. These social agreements may require data that may be considered confidential.

All in all, we believe that future systems for outdoor sports should offer more control over content; users need to be given the ability to explicitly share chosen aspects of their activities at particular moments with the cluster of people they want. In addition, content obfuscation strategies identified in prior research in personal informatics [11] such as restricting or abstracting the disclosure of temporal context [36] can be also explored in designing for sharing in outdoor sports since those strategies mitigate users' privacy concerns. Finally, providing awareness or restrictions about the data retention policies employed by tracking devices and applications, and providing visibility and control over the sensed data may contribute to the adoption of continuous tracking [20], hence potential sharing of personal content. Future research could also explore the impact and relation of personal content sharing generated from sport activity to social media platforms taking into consideration context collapse [44] and users' disclosure strategies [43] employed when posting content online.

LIMITATIONS

Our inquiry spans multiple sports and countries, but we still see a number of limitations inherent to our study. Firstly, all but one of our participants live in urban areas of Western Europe; this introduces a cultural bias. We see that especially the perception of the great outdoors in our study may be distinctively European. Hence, results should be interpreted with caution and account for racial and cultural peculiarities. The choice of the outdoor sports in our work is also somewhat subjective. We chose the three disciplines based on their widespread popularity and the fact that they all leverage the connection with nature. We can only wonder how different our study would be had we chosen other sports, yet we believe that the commonalities (i.e. usually practised in hilly regions and characterized by a strong relation between athlete and nature) and differences between them (i.e. the level of risk-taking attitude, overall safety concerns, different social settings of each activity) are generalizable across a wider range of sports and therefore provide a useful proxy.

Finally, we are also aware that language issues might have affected the outcome of our analysis, as it depends on the translations of source texts to English by the authors. We hope that any shortcomings and bias resulting from this are outweighed by the benefits of a study spanning multiple social environments.

CONCLUSION AND FUTURE WORK

In this paper, we described an inquiry into the intricacies of information sharing practices in three sports: trail running, climbing and skiing. Through extensive interview studies in multiple countries, we obtained a rich data corpus that we then analysed using thematic analysis. We discussed the five emerging themes: the relationship with the greater outdoors, the need for risk management, selecting with whom to share information, choosing what information to share and maintaining privacy. Based on our analysis, we elaborated five recommendations for the design of future systems that aim to support sharing in outdoor sports. With our work, we tried to build actionable insights that can be reused by designers to build future socially-embedded sport systems. We believe our inquiry can serve as a starting point for designing both tailormade technologies as well as designing sports-supportive features for already existing social platforms. We suggest that future designers embrace the whole outdoor experience in their design to minimise the risk of disrupting the holistic experience of practising outdoor sports. We also see an emergent need for systems that support planning and coordination prior to outdoor activities, as well as risk-management during the activity. Finally, we have provided recommendations to support the complex informal social constructs that emerge around outdoor sports practices by helping users to manage the content they share with different audiences. In our view, the natural unfolding of the work presented here would be a participatory design process based on the recommendations we elicited.

REFERENCES

1. Shane Ahern, Dean Eckles, Nathaniel S. Good, Simon King, Mor Naaman, and Rahul Nair. 2007. Over-exposed?: Privacy Patterns and Considerations in Online and Mobile Photo Sharing. In *Proceedings of the SIGCHI Conference on Human Factors in Computing Systems (CHI '07)*. ACM, New York, NY, USA, 357–366. DOI: http://dx.doi.org/10.1145/1240624.1240683
2. Aino Ahtinen, Minna Isomursu, Muzayun Mukhtar, Jani Mäntyjärvi, Jonna Häkkilä, and Jan Blom. 2009. Designing Social Features for Mobile and Ubiquitous Wellness Applications. In *Proceedings of the 8th International Conference on Mobile and Ubiquitous Multimedia (MUM '09)*. ACM, New York, NY, USA, Article 12, 10 pages. DOI: http://dx.doi.org/10.1145/1658550.1658562
3. Genevieve Bell. 2010. Messy Futures: Culture, Technology and Research. In *Proceedings of the SIGCHI Conference on Human Factors in Computing Systems (CHI '10)*. ACM, New York, NY, USA, Article 5. DOI: http://dx.doi.org/10.1145/1753326.2167157
4. Richard Byrne and Florian 'Floyd' Mueller. 2014. *Designing Digital Climbing Experiences through Understanding Rock Climbing Motivation*. Springer Berlin Heidelberg, Berlin, Heidelberg, 92–99. DOI: http://dx.doi.org/10.1007/978-3-662-45212-7_12
5. Sunny Consolvo, Katherine Everitt, Ian Smith, and James A. Landay. 2006. Design Requirements for Technologies That Encourage Physical Activity. In *Proceedings of the SIGCHI Conference on Human Factors in Computing Systems (CHI '06)*. ACM, New York, NY, USA, 457–466. DOI: http://dx.doi.org/10.1145/1124772.1124840
6. Franco Curmi, Maria Angela Ferrario, Jen Southern, and Jon Whittle. 2013. HeartLink: Open Broadcast of Live Biometric Data to Social Networks. In *Proceedings of the SIGCHI Conference on Human Factors in Computing Systems (CHI '13)*. ACM, New York, NY, USA, 1749–1758. DOI: http://dx.doi.org/10.1145/2470654.2466231
7. Peter Dalsgaard, Kim Halskov, and Ole Sejer Iversen. 2016. Participation Gestalt: Analysing Participatory Qualities of Interaction in Public Space. In *Proceedings of the 2016 CHI Conference on Human Factors in Computing Systems (CHI '16)*. ACM, New York, NY, USA, 4435–4446. DOI: http://dx.doi.org/10.1145/2858036.2858147
8. Rodrigo de Oliveira and Nuria Oliver. 2008. TripleBeat: Enhancing Exercise Performance with Persuasion. In *Proceedings of the 10th International Conference on Human Computer Interaction with Mobile Devices and Services (MobileHCI '08)*. ACM, New York, NY, USA, 255–264. DOI: http://dx.doi.org/10.1145/1409240.1409268
9. Audrey Desjardins, Carman Neustaedter, Saul Greenberg, and Ron Wakkary. 2014. Collaboration Surrounding Beacon Use During Companion Avalanche Rescue. In *Proceedings of the 17th ACM Conference on Computer Supported Cooperative Work & Social Computing (CSCW '14)*. ACM, New York, NY, USA, 877–887. DOI: http://dx.doi.org/10.1145/2531602.2531684
10. Mark D Dunlop, Brian Elsey, and Michelle Montgomery Masters. 2007. Dynamic Visualisation of Ski Data: A Context Aware Mobile Piste Map. In *Proceedings of the 9th International Conference on Human Computer Interaction with Mobile Devices and Services (MobileHCI '07)*. ACM, New York, NY, USA, 375–378. DOI: http://dx.doi.org/10.1145/1377999.1378040
11. Daniel A. Epstein, Bradley H. Jacobson, Elizabeth Bales, David W. McDonald, and Sean A. Munson. 2015. From "Nobody Cares" to "Way to Go!": A Design Framework for Social Sharing in Personal Informatics. In *Proceedings of the 18th ACM Conference on Computer Supported Cooperative Work & Social Computing (CSCW '15)*. ACM, New York, NY, USA, 1622–1636. DOI: http://dx.doi.org/10.1145/2675133.2675135
12. Anton Fedosov and Marc Langheinrich. 2015. From Start to Finish: Understanding Group Sharing Behavior in a Backcountry Skiing Community. In *Proceedings of the 17th International Conference on Human-Computer Interaction with Mobile Devices and Services Adjunct (MobileHCI '15)*. ACM, New York, NY, USA, 758–765. DOI: http://dx.doi.org/10.1145/2786567.2793698
13. Anton Fedosov, Evangelos Niforatos, Ivan Elhart, Teseo Schneider, Dmitry Anisimov, and Marc Langheinrich. 2016. Design and Evaluation of a Wearable AR System for Sharing Personalized Content on Ski Resort Maps. In *Proceedings of the 15th International Conference on Mobile and Ubiquitous Multimedia (MUM '16)*. ACM, New York, NY, USA, 141–152. DOI: http://dx.doi.org/10.1145/3012709.3012721
14. William W. Gaver, John Bowers, Andrew Boucher, Hans Gellersen, Sarah Pennington, Albrecht Schmidt, Anthony Steed, Nicholas Villars, and Brendan Walker. 2004. The Drift Table: Designing for Ludic Engagement. In *CHI '04 Extended Abstracts on Human Factors in Computing Systems (CHI EA '04)*. ACM, New York, NY, USA, 885–900. DOI: http://dx.doi.org/10.1145/985921.985947
15. Nitesh Goyal, Gilly Leshed, and Susan R. Fussell. 2013. Effects of Visualization and Note-taking on Sensemaking and Analysis. In *Proceedings of the SIGCHI Conference on Human Factors in Computing Systems (CHI '13)*. ACM, New York, NY, USA, 2721–2724. DOI: http://dx.doi.org/10.1145/2470654.2481376

16. Shoichi Hasegawa, Seiichiro Ishijima, Fumihiro Kato, Hironori Mitake, and Makoto Sato. 2012. Realtime Sonification of the Center of Gravity for Skiing. In *Proceedings of the 3rd Augmented Human International Conference (AH '12)*. ACM, New York, NY, USA, Article 11, 4 pages. DOI: http://dx.doi.org/10.1145/2160125.2160136

17. Nicholas A John. 2013. The social logics of sharing. *The Communication Review* 16, 3 (2013), 113–131.

18. Raine Kajastila and Perttu Hämäläinen. 2014. Augmented Climbing: Interacting with Projected Graphics on a Climbing Wall. In *CHI '14 Extended Abstracts on Human Factors in Computing Systems (CHI EA '14)*. ACM, New York, NY, USA, 1279–1284. DOI: http://dx.doi.org/10.1145/2559206.2581139

19. Aniket Kittur, Andrew M. Peters, Abdigani Diriye, Trupti Telang, and Michael R. Bove. 2013. Costs and Benefits of Structured Information Foraging. In *Proceedings of the SIGCHI Conference on Human Factors in Computing Systems (CHI '13)*. ACM, New York, NY, USA, 2989–2998. DOI: http://dx.doi.org/10.1145/2470654.2481415

20. Predrag Klasnja, Sunny Consolvo, Tanzeem Choudhury, Richard Beckwith, and Jeffrey Hightower. 2009. Exploring Privacy Concerns About Personal Sensing. In *Proceedings of the 7th International Conference on Pervasive Computing (Pervasive '09)*. Springer-Verlag, Berlin, Heidelberg, 176–183. DOI: http://dx.doi.org/10.1007/978-3-642-01516-8_13

21. Kristina Knaving, Paweł Woźniak, Morten Fjeld, and Staffan Björk. 2015. Flow is Not Enough: Understanding the Needs of Advanced Amateur Runners to Design Motivation Technology. In *Proceedings of the 33rd Annual ACM Conference on Human Factors in Computing Systems (CHI '15)*. ACM, New York, NY, USA, 2013–2022. DOI: http://dx.doi.org/10.1145/2702123.2702542

22. Patricia G Lange. 2007. Publicly private and privately public: Social networking on YouTube. *Journal of Computer-Mediated Communication* 13, 1 (2007), 361–380.

23. Michael Leitner, Peter Wolkerstorfer, and Manfred Tscheligi. 2008. How Online Communities Support Human Values. In *Proceedings of the 5th Nordic Conference on Human-computer Interaction: Building Bridges (NordiCHI '08)*. ACM, New York, NY, USA, 503–506. DOI: http://dx.doi.org/10.1145/1463160.1463230

24. James J Lin, Lena Mamykina, Silvia Lindtner, Gregory Delajoux, and Henry B Strub. 2006. FishnSteps: Encouraging physical activity with an interactive computer game. In *International Conference on Ubiquitous Computing*. Springer, 261–278.

25. Matthew Mauriello, Michael Gubbels, and Jon E. Froehlich. 2014. Social Fabric Fitness: The Design and Evaluation of Wearable E-textile Displays to Support Group Running. In *Proceedings of the 32Nd Annual ACM Conference on Human Factors in Computing Systems (CHI '14)*. ACM, New York, NY, USA, 2833–2842. DOI: http://dx.doi.org/10.1145/2556288.2557299

26. Eleonora Mencarini, Antonella De Angeli, and Massimo Zancanaro. 2016. Emotions in Climbing: A Design Opportunity for Haptic Communication. In *Proceedings of the 2016 ACM International Joint Conference on Pervasive and Ubiquitous Computing: Adjunct (UbiComp '16)*. ACM, New York, NY, USA, 867–871. DOI: http://dx.doi.org/10.1145/2968219.2968539

27. Matthew B Miles and A Michael Huberman. 1994. Qualitative data analysis: A sourcebook. *Beverly Hills: Sage Publications* (1994).

28. Florian Mueller, Rohit A. Khot, Alan D. Chatham, Sebastiaan Pijnappel, Cagdas "Chad" Toprak, and Joe Marshall. 2013. HCI with Sports. In *CHI '13 Extended Abstracts on Human Factors in Computing Systems (CHI EA '13)*. ACM, New York, NY, USA, 2509–2512. DOI: http://dx.doi.org/10.1145/2468356.2468817

29. Florian Mueller, Frank Vetere, Martin R. Gibbs, Darren Edge, Stefan Agamanolis, and Jennifer G. Sheridan. 2010. Jogging over a Distance Between Europe and Australia. In *Proceedings of the 23Nd Annual ACM Symposium on User Interface Software and Technology (UIST '10)*. ACM, New York, NY, USA, 189–198. DOI: http://dx.doi.org/10.1145/1866029.1866062

30. Sean A Munson and Sunny Consolvo. 2012. Exploring goal-setting, rewards, self-monitoring, and sharing to motivate physical activity. In *2012 6th International Conference on Pervasive Computing Technologies for Healthcare (PervasiveHealth) and Workshops*. IEEE, 25–32.

31. Jarno Ojala and Johan Saarela. 2010. Understanding Social Needs and Motivations to Share Data in Online Sports Communities. In *Proceedings of the 14th International Academic MindTrek Conference: Envisioning Future Media Environments (MindTrek '10)*. ACM, New York, NY, USA, 95–102. DOI: http://dx.doi.org/10.1145/1930488.1930508

32. Thomas Olsson. 2009. Understanding Collective Content: Purposes, Characteristics and Collaborative Practices. In *Proceedings of the Fourth International Conference on Communities and Technologies (C&T '09)*. ACM, New York, NY, USA, 21–30. DOI: http://dx.doi.org/10.1145/1556460.1556464

33. Thomas Olsson, Hannu Toivola, and Kaisa Väänänen-Vainio-Mattila. 2008. Exploring Characteristics of Collective Content: A Field Study with Four User Communities. In *CHI '08 Extended Abstracts on Human Factors in Computing Systems (CHI EA '08)*. ACM, New York, NY, USA, 2967–2972. DOI: http://dx.doi.org/10.1145/1358628.1358792

34. Aarathi Prasad, Jacob Sorber, Timothy Stablein, Denise Anthony, and David Kotz. 2012. Understanding Sharing Preferences and Behavior for mHealth Devices. In *Proceedings of the 2012 ACM Workshop on Privacy in the Electronic Society (WPES '12)*. ACM, New York, NY, USA, 117–128. DOI: http://dx.doi.org/10.1145/2381966.2381983

35. Stephen Purpura, Victoria Schwanda, Kaiton Williams, William Stubler, and Phoebe Sengers. 2011. Fit4Life: The Design of a Persuasive Technology Promoting Healthy Behavior and Ideal Weight. In *Proceedings of the SIGCHI Conference on Human Factors in Computing Systems (CHI '11)*. ACM, New York, NY, USA, 423–432. DOI: http://dx.doi.org/10.1145/1978942.1979003

36. Andrew Raij, Animikh Ghosh, Santosh Kumar, and Mani Srivastava. 2011. Privacy Risks Emerging from the Adoption of Innocuous Wearable Sensors in the Mobile Environment. In *Proceedings of the SIGCHI Conference on Human Factors in Computing Systems (CHI '11)*. ACM, New York, NY, USA, 11–20. DOI: http://dx.doi.org/10.1145/1978942.1978945

37. Lindsay Reynolds, Victoria Schwanda Sosik, and Dan Cosley. 2013. When Wii Doesn'T Fit: How Non-beginners React to Wii Fit's Gamification. In *Proceedings of the First International Conference on Gameful Design, Research, and Applications (Gamification '13)*. ACM, New York, NY, USA, 111–114. DOI: http://dx.doi.org/10.1145/2583008.2583027

38. Andrzej Romanowski, Sven Mayer, Lars Lischke, Krzysztof Grudzien, Tomasz Jaworski, Izabela Perenc, Przemysław Kucharski, Mohammad Obaid, Tomasz Kosiński, and Paweł W. Woźniak. 2017. Towards Supporting Remote Cheering during Running Races with Drone Technology. In *Proceedings of the 2017 CHI Conference Extended Abstracts on Human Factors in Computing Systems (CHI EA '17)*, ACM Press (Ed.). ACM. DOI: http://dx.doi.org/10.1145/3027063.3053218

39. Christine Satchell and Paul Dourish. 2009. Beyond the User: Use and Non-use in HCI. In *Proceedings of the 21st Annual Conference of the Australian Computer-Human Interaction Special Interest Group: Design: Open 24/7 (OZCHI '09)*. ACM, New York, NY, USA, 9–16. DOI: http://dx.doi.org/10.1145/1738826.1738829

40. Stefan Schneegass and Alexandra Voit. 2016. GestureSleeve: Using Touch Sensitive Fabrics for Gestural Input on the Forearm for Controlling Smartwatches. In *Proceedings of the 2016 ACM International Symposium on Wearable Computers (ISWC '16)*. ACM, New York, NY, USA, 108–115. DOI: http://dx.doi.org/10.1145/2971763.2971797

41. Jakob Tholander and Stina Nylander. 2015. Snot, Sweat, Pain, Mud, and Snow: Performance and Experience in the Use of Sports Watches. In *Proceedings of the 33rd Annual ACM Conference on Human Factors in Computing Systems (CHI '15)*. ACM, New York, NY, USA, 2913–2922. DOI: http://dx.doi.org/10.1145/2702123.2702482

42. Tammy Toscos, Anne Faber, Shunying An, and Mona Praful Gandhi. 2006. Chick Clique: Persuasive Technology to Motivate Teenage Girls to Exercise. In *CHI '06 Extended Abstracts on Human Factors in Computing Systems (CHI EA '06)*. ACM, New York, NY, USA, 1873–1878. DOI: http://dx.doi.org/10.1145/1125451.1125805

43. Zeynep Tufekci. 2008. Can you see me now? Audience and disclosure regulation in online social network sites. *Bulletin of Science, Technology & Society* 28, 1 (2008), 20–36.

44. Jessica Vitak. 2012. The impact of context collapse and privacy on social network site disclosures. *Journal of Broadcasting & Electronic Media* 56, 4 (2012), 451–470.

45. Stephen Voida, W. Keith Edwards, Mark W. Newman, Rebecca E. Grinter, and Nicolas Ducheneaut. 2006. Share and Share Alike: Exploring the User Interface Affordances of File Sharing. In *Proceedings of the SIGCHI Conference on Human Factors in Computing Systems (CHI '06)*. ACM, New York, NY, USA, 221–230. DOI: http://dx.doi.org/10.1145/1124772.1124806

46. Wouter Walmink, Danielle Wilde, and Florian 'Floyd' Mueller. 2013. Displaying Heart Rate Data on a Bicycle Helmet to Support Social Exertion Experiences. In *Proceedings of the 8th International Conference on Tangible, Embedded and Embodied Interaction (TEI '14)*. ACM, New York, NY, USA, 97–104. DOI: http://dx.doi.org/10.1145/2540930.2540970

47. Paweł Woźniak, Kristina Knaving, Staffan Björk, and Morten Fjeld. 2015. RUFUS: Remote Supporter Feedback for Long-Distance Runners. In *Proceedings of the 17th International Conference on Human-Computer Interaction with Mobile Devices and Services (MobileHCI '15)*. ACM, New York, NY, USA, 115–124. DOI: http://dx.doi.org/10.1145/2785830.2785893

Applying Real-Time Text on Instant Messaging for a Rapid and Enriched Conversation Experience

Chang-Min Kim[1], Hyeon-Beom Yi[1], Ji-Won Nam[1], Geehyuk Lee[2]
[1]Department of Industrial Design, KAIST
[2]Department of Computer Science, KAIST
291 Daehak-ro, Yuseong-gu, Daejeon 34141, Republic of Korea
{peterkim12, roetry, joseph3553, geehyuk}@kaist.ac.kr

ABSTRACT
Despite the advantages of instant messaging (IM) such as simple and fast messaging, IM cannot be as effective as face-to-face conversation. The current message-by-message interface shows a gap with actual conversation in terms of temporal structure and information channel. Our study investigated the real-time text-displaying interface as a way of reducing this gap. A comparative user study was conducted with three types of IM interfaces to compare and analyze the duration of silence (short pause when nobody types through the IM) quantitatively. Varying chatting experiences for each IM interface were qualitatively analyzed through a focus group interview. We report the study results in terms of the reduced duration of silence, non-verbal expression channel and new texting techniques found in the real-time text interface. We also discuss design implications for improving the conversing experience for IM interfaces.

Author Keywords
Real-Time Text; Instant Messaging; CMC; Turn-Taking; Discourse Analysis; Comparative Study

ACM Classification Keywords
H.5.2 User Interfaces: Interaction styles.

INTRODUCTION
Instant messaging (IM) is a fast and simple way of communication. Currently, for most IM clients, text-based messages are typically transmitted bi-directionally between users when each user chooses to complete a message and press the "send" button. This method of transmitting messages via sending completed messages by pushing an enter/return key is categorized as a message-by-message interface and is being used as a chatting application standard for the industry. Despite the advantages of IM, such as offering simple and fast messaging, IM cannot be as effective as face-to-face conversation. Structurally, the communication differs in the chronological order, which makes IM very different from actual conversation.

DIS 2017, June 10-14, 2017, Edinburgh, United Kingdom
© 2017 ACM. ISBN 978-1-4503-4922-2/17/06…$15.00
DOI: http://dx.doi.org/10.1145/3064663.3064679

The interactors of IM are not actually speakers and hearers. They are writers and readers of textual messages [7]. In oral conversation, the construction of speech and the hearing process occur simultaneously. However, with IM, message reception occurs separately from message production. The pause, and hence the delay that the IM creates during the textual communication is the disadvantage of IM and message-by-message interfaces [6]. Eventually, the delay generates differences in communication in terms of turn-taking and communication intervals for IM compared to an actual conversation.

Previous cases sought to overcome the disadvantages of message-by-message interfaces. For systems that are intended to provide unique communication that greatly differ from message-by-message interfaces, there are real-time text interfaces, such as Unix Talk, WYSWIS (What You See is What I See), and older versions of ICQ, which transmit each character of a message in real time. For the stability of protocols and the efficiency of writing and receiving messages, the real-time text interface was depreciated in the industry, and the message-by-message interface was chosen as the standard communication method. The real-time text interface was preferred only in special applications such as the telecommunications device for the deaf (TDD), teletypewriter (TTY), and live television captioning.

Nevertheless, recently, new light has been shed on real-time text and its values. Not only special purposed applications but also applications for mainstream users are emerging. Accessibility groups such as Real-Time Text [13] have summarized the protocol and usage examples for the standardization of real-time text. Etherpad [5] has provided real-time text editing tools to support such collaborative works. These emerging applications try to simulate a text communication experience similar to an actual conversation using real-time texting. Still, it is necessary to study the differences between communication experiences of the message-by-message interface and real-time text interface. Furthermore, comparing IM interfaces to actual conversations and understanding the differences between them will contribute to improving the IM conversing experience.

In this paper, we report the results of a study in which we compared the real-time texting approach and message-by-message approach in IM. Specifically, we studied the duration of silence (short pause when nobody types through the IM). It was discovered that the duration of silence significantly decreased in the real-time text interface. We also elaborate on non-verbal expression channel, enabled by reflecting the typing process, and new texting techniques for real-time text at IM, which were identified based on interview data. Based on the study findings, we discuss the design implication for improving the conversing experience with IM.

RELATED WORKS

Turn Taking in Computer Mediated Communication

All interfaces for computer-mediated communication (CMC) presuppose a particular theory of social interaction, that is, turn taking: One study [12] reported the improved efficiency of conversation when CMC users took turns in their communication. Another study found that users preferred the turn-taking format instead of simultaneous collaboration [14] in CMC. Based on actual conversations, users naturally learn and apply the turn-taking pattern in CMC. Users take turns typing a message and then wait for a reply. However, unlike an actual conversation, the waiting phase in the CMC turn-taking structure may sometimes be unpleasant and silent. Real-time text can be one of the options for minimizing the duration of such silence. However, a structured comparison study between actual conversation and real-time text has yet not been conducted.

Message-By-Message Interface vs. Real-Time Text

Studies on developing a new type of IM interface with novel features are well discussed, but comparison studies of different IM interfaces are not yet mature. When comparing different IM interfaces, it is challenging to find an objective measure from the case-specific discourse log data; the data varies depending on the partners involved in the conversation and the topic of interest.

Studies on turn-taking in CMC [2, 11] have compared the discourse structure and task performance of different text-display interfaces. Unfortunately, the results were inadequate to conclude which type of interface was better in terms of efficiency. Campbell [8] tried to decompose the basic elements of IM in sequential order to build a framework for understanding IM usage through quantitative measures. However, the results showed a degree of dependency on the types of tasks and participants. Research on speaking through text [7] has used various types of data (i.e., number of deletions made, key strokes per second, time spent typing, etc.) to clarify the differences between real-time text and message-by-message communication. However, excluding some data, both interface styles showed no significant differences. Therefore, to fully understand the values of real-time text, it is necessary to find an objective measure for comparing message-by-message IM and real-time text IM.

STUDY GOAL

We reveal the limitations of the currently used message-by-message interface by comparing it with the real-time text interface in terms of the temporal structure and information channel.

Temporal Structure

We have identified the need to find an objective measure that can be interpreted as representative data for both IM interfaces. By referring to the study of the theory on the process of actual conversation [3] and the sequential framework of IM [8], we designed a diagram to explain the differences of person A's and B's communications at different interfaces in IMs (Figure 1).

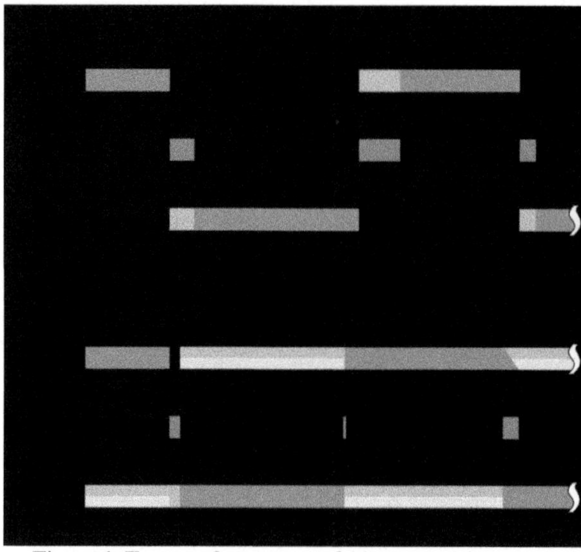

Figure 1. Temporal structure of (a) message-by-message interface and (b) real-time text (RTT) interface

In actual communication, the construction of speech and the listening to the spoken words occur simultaneously. However, in IM, message production occurs separately from message reception. Until the typing of the message is complete and the message is sent, the recipient remains in silence. We defined the duration of silence as the short pause when nobody types through the IM interface (Figure 1, mapped as 'silence'). Figure 1 illustrates the chance of the real-time text interface having a shorter duration of silence compared to the message-by-message interface. Since an actual conversation involves continuous interactions between the speaker and listener, a shortened duration of silence in IM will likely simulate the similar experience of an actual conversation.

Information Channel

In actual conversations, speakers and listeners interact "moment-by-moment" to ensure that what is being said is also being understood [6]. During a conversation, the speaker and listener constantly and simultaneously provide feedback to indicate their comprehension of what is being communicated [2]. These feedbacks in actual conversation not only include the speech itself but also non-verbal expressions, such as facial expressions or gestures. Speakers and listeners share information in these multi expression channels. However, communicated information in IM is restricted to a single text channel compared to face-to-face conversation. What the writer intends to deliver is crammed in a limited line of text, unintentionally excluding contextual cues in the process. No situational context of the message is delivered, unless explicitly described in text [1]. Previous researches have explored fonts and text sizes [9] as well as animated typographies [10] to extend the information channel for text communication. Real-time text can carry contextual information regarding the way in which the message was formed. We explore the potential of using the typing process as a new channel of expression for text communication in our study.

USER STUDY

We conducted a user study with three types of IM interfaces to compare the duration of silence quantitatively and analyze varying chatting experiences qualitatively.

IM Client Design

We implemented a real-time text interface into the standard IM client by differentiating the color of the message boxes (Figure 2). The orange-colored message box shows when the partner starts typing and delivers the whole typing process in real time. When the transmitter finishes typing and presses the return key, the orange-colored message box changes to a white box and the message appears as received (Figure 2). In our study, we applied the real-time text interface into the IM client with two different versions: real-time text based on characters, and real-time text based on words. Our prototype can also serve as the conventional message-by-message interface by suppressing the real-time text feature.

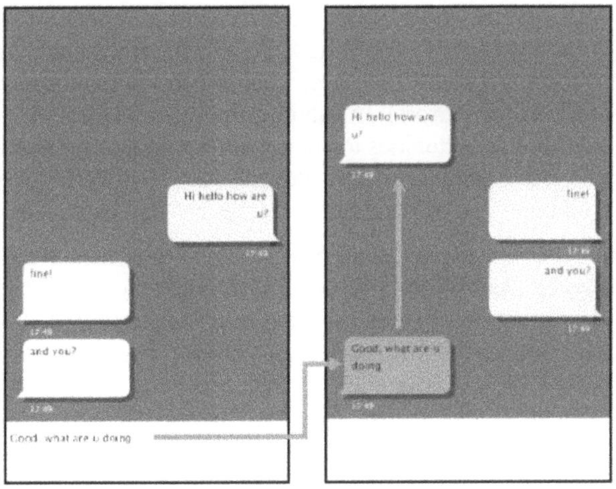

Figure 2. Real-time text IM client Design

Procedures of the Study

To understand and compare the unique texting experience of the real-time text, we have conducted a comparative user study with three types of chatting: message-by-message, real-time text based on characters, and real-time text based on words. A total of 4 participants (2 male, 2 female, average age 25.5) participated in the experiment and they all conversed with each other in pairs (total 12 distinct conversation dialogues). Each conversation was guided in a structured manner: for every paired chat, participants experienced 3 different types of IM interfaces for 7 minutes (total 21 minutes per paired participants). Every duration of silence in the conversation was measured in millisecond units. In addition, to prevent the errors in measured silence caused by awkwardness or lack of activity in the conversation, participants talked to their paired partners in person before chatting for 2 minutes. Lastly, when the chat sessions ended, users gathered and participated in a focus group interview session with the study moderator. The FGI were later analyzed using a bottom-up affinity diagram.

STUDY FINDINGS

We report our study findings from three perspectives: 1) reduced duration of silence, 2) non-verbal expression channel, and 3) new texting techniques.

Reduced Duration of Silence

A total of 966 durations of silence were gathered from the user study. In the study, we considered the individual differences such as typing speed and chatting style of participants. To eliminate these individual tendencies, we standardized the durations data based on each participant's standard deviation of durations. After standardizing each participant's duration data into a z-score table, we conducted a within group one-way ANOVA on three types of IM interface using SPSS. For each IM interface, standardized 300 durations of silence were randomly selected for comparison.

The results imply that the type of IM interfaces influenced the duration of silence, $F(2, 598) = 10117.33$, $p < 0.05$. Further, the results of the Bonferroni post-hoc test show that there are significant differences between the real-time text based on words, real-time text based on characters and message-by-message interface ($p = 0.00 < 0.05$ from all pair comparison). Figure 3 summarizes the results of the post-hoc test. Estimated marginal means show that the real-time text and message-by-message interface have significant differences for the duration of silence and that real-time text has significantly shorter duration of silence. The tests of within subject contrasts showed that the character version and the word version of the real-time text showed a significant difference as well ($F(2, 598) = 241.061$), but it was not as effective as the comparison above ($F(2, 598) = 17510.75$).

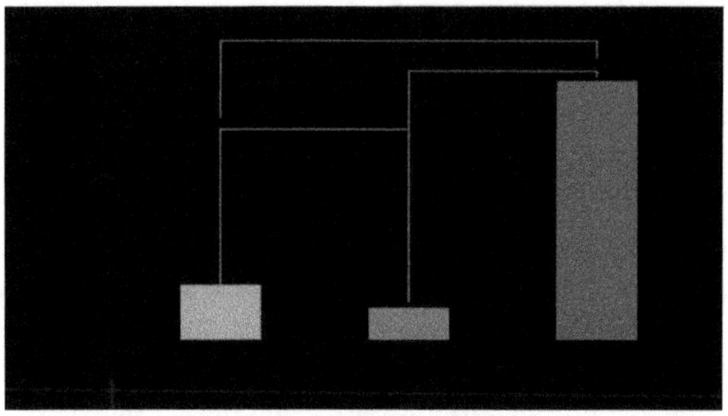

Figure 3. Post-hoc analysis result of different IM interfaces

Non-Verbal Expression Channel

The use of real-time text as a non-verbal expression channel was found in the study. P1 commented that the non-verbal expressions (i.e., gesture, facial expression) that are usually present in actual conversations were also perceived in real-time text. P2 added that messages that include typing speed and delay serve as an extra channel of communication and add richer information to the meaning of written text. P2 said, "They helped me to understand intentional and unintentional non-verbal expressions of my partner, such as hesitation, humor, confusion, and even attentiveness."

The unique effect of non-verbal expression was a sense of remote presence. P3 mentioned, "Sometimes when both sides were laughing through real-time text client, laughing expressions were not exchanged by turn-taking, but those occurred simultaneously and actively." Participants agreed that, although they were chatting in different places, they felt like they were conversing together in a virtual space; remote presence enabled by non-verbal expression channel contributed to bridging the gap between the IM communication and the actual conversation.

New Texting Techniques

By analyzing the examples of real-time text usages found in the focus group interviews, we were able to discover some novel texting techniques. These techniques are the unique expressions of real-time text that are not possible in the message-by-message interface.

Commonly observed techniques are:

- Writing 'A' first then writing a contrary 'B' content so that the process of writing real-time text reveals ironic meanings;
  i.e., *"I ~~don't~~ (delete) really like (rewrite) that idea"*
- Intentional delay expressed as animation;
  i.e., *". (delay) . (delay) . (delay) let's say yes to that"*
- Instantly reacting positively or negatively toward the message while the partner is writing. i.e.,
  A : *"I haven't had my dinner because ~"*
  B : *"~oh...~"*
  A : *"~I thought I might be late for this study"*

These expressions demonstrate that including the process of typing could add new expression capabilities to textual messages. Whereas the interactions are limited to a single point of time (sending/receiving) in the message-by-message interface, giving access to a continuous stream of messages in real-time enabled IM users to converse using richer expressions.

DISCUSSION AND FUTURE WORK

Based on the findings and interview results, we identified several issues and implications that need further discussion.

Value of Typing Process

Based on the study results, we can suggest that real-time text makes differences not only in terms of silence but also in terms of reflecting the typing process within the message. While a message-by-message interface delivers the information solely based on what is written, real-time text adds contextual meanings about how the text is written. These expressions, enabled by reflecting the typing process, open up a new way to demonstrate one's unique intentions and emotions aside from using emoticons or explicitly describing one's emotions. This uniqueness is possible because users can either explicitly design a typing process as an animation or naturally let the real-time text embed his or her texting process. This indicates that non-verbal components such as typing speed or delay can be integrated as part of the message. Therefore, real-time text can allow for an extension of the expression channel and can make the conversation more enriched at IM, while its scope remains intact within the textual communication range.

Applying Real-Time Text on Instant Messaging

Due to the lack of efficiency of turn-taking and the stability of the communication protocol, real-time text was neglected and even abandoned in early stage of the development of IM industries. However, we have discovered a new potential that could help applications based on real-time text re-emerge. Thus, it is time to re-evaluate the value of real-time text as an IM interface. Participants were also curious about what our prototype would look like at a commercial level when integrated with the messaging applications they use daily. Based on usability comments on the study, we suggest a few recommendations that can be referenced to when developing an actual real-time text IM service.

- The color of the text box is an effective method to differentiate messages that are confirmed and sent as permanent messages by pressing enter key, and messages that are real-time texts that are currently being written.
- Although the sense of remote presence was reported to be more dominant in the character-based interface compared to the word-based interface, it tended to reveal too much (such as typo errors). In contrast, the word-based interface provided opportunities to correct one's mistake and remain efficient in conversations. Nevertheless, it tended to give the impression of 'legging' or 'buffering' to the receiver.
- For further improvement of usable real-time text, we can suggest usability options such as providing the following: a skip animation button, on/off button, fast-forward button, and delete without showing buttons. These functions would be necessary if the real-time text were to be integrated within the existing commercial messaging service as a hybrid add-on.

CONCLUSION

In our study, we have compared a message-by-message interface and real-time text interfaces both quantitatively and qualitatively. We found that real-time messaging brings more rapid and enriched IM conversation experience in terms of reducing the duration of silence, non-verbal expression channel and novel texting techniques. Our contribution is an exploration of the potential of real-time text for IM to understand what is lacking in IM compared to an actual conversation.

REFERENCES

1. Amy Voida, Wendy C. Newstetter, and Elizabeth D. Mynatt. 2002. When conventions collide: the tensions of instant messaging attributed. In Proceedings of the SIGCHI Conference on Human Factors in Computing Systems (CHI '02). ACM, New York, NY, USA, 187-194. DOI=http://dx.doi.org/10.1145/503376.503410
2. Bruce Phillips. 2000. Should we take turns?: a test of CMC turn-taking formats. In CHI '00 Extended Abstracts on Human Factors in Computing Systems (CHI EA '00). ACM, New York, NY, USA, 341-342. DOI=http://dx.doi.org/10.1145/633292.633497
3. Clark, H. H. 1996. Using language. Cambridge: CUP.
4. David Vronay, Marc Smith, and Steven Drucker. 1999. Alternative interfaces for chat. In Proceedings of the 12th annual ACM symposium on User interface software and technology (UIST '99). ACM, New York, NY, USA, 19-26. DOI=http://dx.doi.org/10.1145/320719.322579
5. Etherpad. Retrieved December 13, 2017, http://etherpad.org/
6. Garcia, Angela Cora, and Jennifer Baker Jacobs. 1999. The eyes of the beholder: Understanding the turn-taking system in quasi-synchronous computer-mediated communication. Research on language and social interaction, 32(4), 337-367.
7. Jacob Solomon, Mark Newman, and Stephanie Teasley. 2010. Speaking through text: the influence of real-time text on discourse and usability in IM. In Proceedings of the 16th ACM international conference on supporting group work (GROUP '10). ACM, New York, NY, USA, 197-200. DOI=http://dx.doi.org/10.1145/1880071.1880105
8. Jeffrey D. Campbell. 2004. Instant messages: a framework for reading between the lines. In Proceedings of the 2004 ACM conference on Computer supported cooperative work (CSCW '04). ACM, New York, NY, USA, 519-522. DOI=http://dx.doi.org/10.1145/1031607.1031693
9. Jodi Forlizzi, Johnny Lee, and Scott Hudson. 2003. The kinedit system: affective messages using dynamic texts. In Proceedings of the SIGCHI Conference on Human Factors in Computing Systems (CHI '03). ACM, New York, NY, USA, 377-384. DOI=http://dx.doi.org/10.1145/642611.642677
10. Joonhwan Lee, Soojin Jun, Jodi Forlizzi, and Scott E. Hudson. 2006. Using kinetic typography to convey emotion in text-based interpersonal communication. In Proceedings of the 6th conference on Designing Interactive systems (DIS '06). ACM, New York, NY, USA, 41-49. DOI=http://dx.doi.org/10.1145/1142405.1142414
11. Laurie P. Dringus. 1992. A Study of Delayed Time and Real Time Text-Based Computer-Mediated Communication Systems on Group Decision Making Performance. Ph.D. Dissertation. Nova University, Fort Lauderdale, FL, USA. UMI Order No. GAX92-14990.
12. McKinlay, A., Procter, R., Masting, O., Woodburn, R., & Arnott, J. 1994. Studies of turn-taking in computermediated communications. Interacting with computers, 6(2), 151-171.
13. Real-Time Text. Retrieved December 2, 2017, from http://www.realtimetext.org/
14. Siegel, J., Dubrovsky, V., Kiesler, S., & McGuire, T. W. 1986. Group processes in computer-mediated communication. Organizational behavior and human decision processes, 37(2), 157-187.

TransPoint: Real-Time Remote Lecturing via Adaptive Transparency

Jiwon Nam
KAIST
Daejeon, South Korea
joseph3553@kaist.ac.kr

Tek-Jin Nam
KAIST
Daejeon, South Korea
tjnam@kaist.ac.kr

ABSTRACT
Conventional ways of delivering lecture slides and lecturer scenes for synchronous remote lectures have several challenges in terms of resource and attention management. We present TransPoint, a lightweight remote lecturing system that combines lecture slides and lecturer scenes via adaptive transparency. The natural teaching behavior of the lecturer and contextual cues are used to selectively adjust the overlaid transparency of the slides. We conducted a comparative user study with 3 ways of delivering lecture slides and lecturer scenes: (1) TransPoint, (2) Picture-in-Picture, and (3) Total Shot. We found that TransPoint could coordinate remote students' attention according to the lecture contexts and improve real-time interaction between the lecturer and remote students. Based on the results, we discuss system design implications for synchronous remote lectures.

Author Keywords
Synchronous Remote Lecture; Transparency; Dynamic Lecture; Contextual emphasis.

ACM Classification Keywords
H.5.m. Information interfaces and presentation (e.g., HCI): Miscellaneous.

INTRODUCTION
Synchronous remote lectures are in high demand, as they overcome the limited space of the collocated class while providing real-time interaction between the lecturer and remote students. Nevertheless, challenges remain with the method of delivering lecture slides and the lecturer video capture. Conventional ways of delivering lecture slides and lecturer scenes for synchronous remote lectures are fixed and separated during synchronous remote lectures in most cases. Thus, these approaches disperse remote students' attention by having a skewed emphasis on either the lecture slides or the lecturer. In cases where switching between lecture materials and the video capture of the lecturer is possible in real time, costly resources, such as a video editing station and supporting staff, are required. Also, remote students tend to be less motivated to participate in the class. According to the Media Richness Theory by Daft and Lengel [2], remote students receive less information compared to collocated students.

Several attempts have been made to improve remote lectures. Previous researches either automated the traditional video editing process [15] or automatically combined core lecture components [9, 10]. Nevertheless, these approaches cannot be used for real-time editing during synchronous remote lectures. Previous researches focusing on synchronous remote lectures utilized an avatar robot [13], a human proxy [4], or a conjoined classroom [14] to assist with remote student participation. While they contributed in supporting remote students' participation, these synchronous remote lecture systems require costly resources and may have intrusive components compared to the collocated classroom.

We propose using adaptive transparency to combine lecture slides and lecturer scenes. Previous researches have applied the association between transparency and information in UI for public shopping, collaboration work, and navigation contexts [6, 7, 8]. Nevertheless, the association between transparency and information has not been applied to educational contexts. Also, previous research [5] has revealed potential for overlaid images, yet dynamic overlaid images with transparency could enable even richer expressions.

The contributions of our research are as follow: 1) a novel concept of applying adaptive transparency to integrate lecturer scenes with lecture materials and a working prototype that allows easy usage and installation with minimal addition to the existing system for synchronous remote lecturing; 2) comparative user study results revealing that TransPoint improved remote students' attention and interaction between the lecturer and remote students; and 3) design implications for remote lecture systems.

TRANSPOINT SYSTEM
TransPoint is a lightweight system for synchronous remote lectures that combines lecture slides and lecturer scenes via adaptive transparency and allows real-time interaction

DIS 2017, June 10-14, 2017, Edinburgh, United Kingdom

DOI: http://dx.doi.org/10.1145/3064663.3064691

between the lecturer and remote students. The adaptive transparency maps different lecture contexts to different ratios of transparency for lecture slides and lecturer scenes. The adaptive transparency enables compatible and intuitive expression by using only two necessary resources: lecture slides and lecturer scenes. Previous research has shown that users prefer the lecturer to be included on the lecture screen instead of having only lecture materials presented [11, 12]. Adaptive transparency could allow intuitive emphasis on the lecturer with the system's visual outcome (Figure 3); the resulting scene delivers the lecture contexts along with the intentions of the lecturer so that remote students' learning experiences are supported.

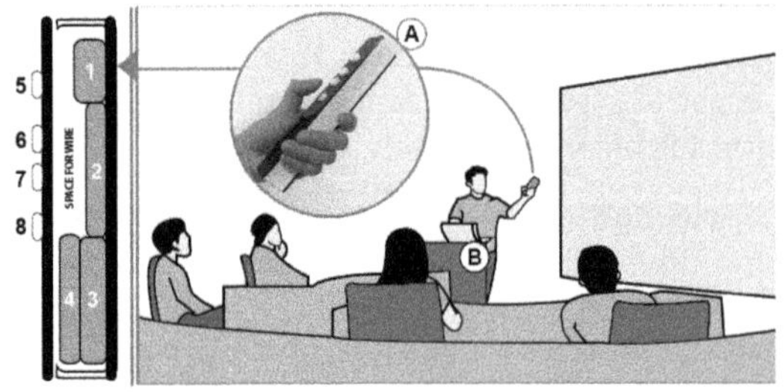

Figure 1. The figure shows system settings for the collocated lecture room. Components include A) TransPoint controller and B) laptop / components of A: A-1) gyroscope sensor, A-2) microprocessor, A-3) battery, and A-4) Bluetooth device.

The system is lightweight so it can be integrated into existing lecture room settings. The TransPoint system does not require any costly equipment or professional skills, allowing easy installation and usage. Only a standard laptop and TransPoint controller need to be added. By using the TransPoint system, the lecturer can manage both collocated lecture rooms and remote lecture rooms by him- or herself. Normal lecture slides are projected on the projector screen of a collocated room while video-mixed scenes with adaptive transparency are delivered to the remote classroom.

TransPoint Controller

The TransPoint controller (Figure 1.A) was prototyped as a means for the lecturer to interact with the system during the lecture. It was intended to replace a laser pointer, which is a conventional tool for lecturing and emphasizing lecture materials. The control settings are as follow: Figure 1.A_5 – highlight function, which puts the laser pointer icon over the video-mixed scenes for the remote classroom and moves the icon by a tilting behavior in 8 directions; Figure 1.A_6 – previous slide function, which synchronously changes slides for a collocated room and video-mixed scene for a remote classroom; Figure 1.A_7 – next slide function, which also triggers a synchronous change of lecture slides; and Figure 1.A_8 – manual transparency shift function, which changes the transparency state of video-mixed scene for the remote classroom to Figure 3.a, Figure 3.c, or Figure 3.e.

Software

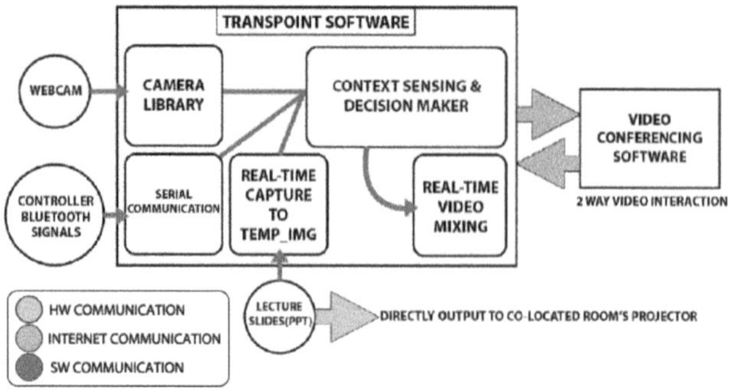

Figure 2. Software flow of the TransPoint system.

As shown in Figure 2, the TransPoint software integrates lecture slides from off-the-shelf presentation tools (e.g., Microsoft PowerPoint) and lecturer scenes from a camera either manually by using the controller or automatically by sensing lecture contexts. The resulting video-mixed scene is then broadcasted to standard video-conferencing software (e.g., Skype), which allows the lecturer to see and talk with remote students in real time during the lecture.

Usage Scenarios

There are several lecture contexts wherein different degrees of adaptive transparency are mapped. The transparency ratio visually indicates the ratio of importance between lecture slides and the lecturer. Current ratios of adaptive transparency combinations include Figure 3.a) 100% focus on the lecturer, Figure 3.b) 90% focus on the lecturer and 10% on the lecture material, Figure 3.c) 50% focus on the lecturer and 50% on the lecture material, Figure 3.d) 10% focus on the lecturer and 90% on the lecture material, and Figure 3.e) 100% focus on the lecture material. Only 5 combinations exist to prevent visual distraction caused by ambiguous and slow changes of transparency, and the combinations were pruned through iterative prototyping to allow meaningful visual expressions.

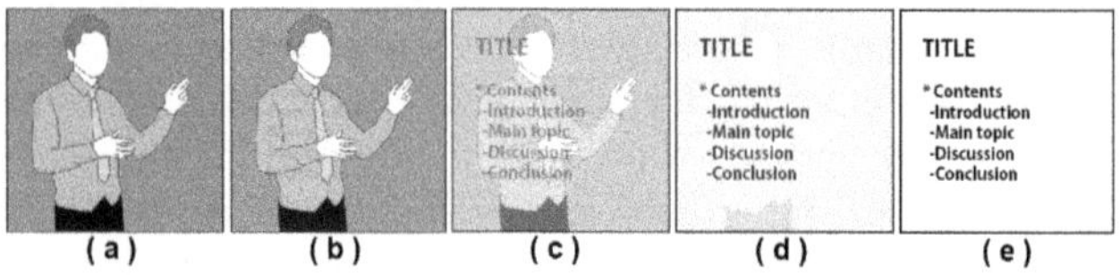

Figure 3. Transparency states: a) emphasizing lecturer, b) transitional state, c) default state, d) transitional state, and e) emphasizing lecture slides.

General Situation

When both the lecture slides and the video capture of the lecturer need to be delivered with equal importance, Figure 3.c is used.

Intentional Emphases

When the lecturer wants remote students to focus on him- or herself, or wants to show real objects or gestures, the first state is used (Figure 3.a). In contrast, when the lecturer wants remote students to focus solely on the lecture material for note-taking or memorization, the fifth state

(Figure 3.e) is used. Also, the highlight function of the TransPoint controller can be used to emphasize a particular section of the video-mixed scene. These three scenarios are manual, and intentional emphases are triggered by using the controller (Figure 1.A) with teaching cognitions.

Vocal Emphases

When the lecturer raises his or her voice while using the highlight function, the transparency state shifts to the fifth state (Figure 3.e) to naturally emphasize lecture materials. In contrast, when the lecturer raises his or her voice when the highlight function is not in use, the transparency state shifts to the first state (Figure 3.a) to emphasize the lecturer, considering voice raising as an action of appeal for attention. Voice threshold detection is processed by the TransPoint software (Figure 1.B).

Contextual Emphases

When the lecturer moves the slide, the fourth state (Figure 3.d) is activated temporarily, and then the transparency state slowly shifts to the third state (Figure 3.c) over 3 seconds. When a new slide is presented, it is important for remote students to notice and read the new slide. Also, it is equally important to shift their focus to the lecturer after they have read the content of the slide. Therefore, the transparency change was designed to guide remote students' flow of attention.

USER STUDY

In order to study whether TransPoint's dynamic way of delivering lecture slides and lecturer scenes improves remote students' learning experiences, especially in terms of coordination of remote students' attention and interaction between the lecturer and remote students, a comparative user study was conducted. We also sought to test whether our design rationales for usage scenarios were appropriate.

Lecture Formats Compared

TransPoint (Figure 4.a), which was the only dynamically edited lecture format in the study, and two other conventional and fixed lecture formats were compared in the user study. The two other formats were Picture-in-Picture (Figure 4.b) and Total Shot (Figure 4.c).

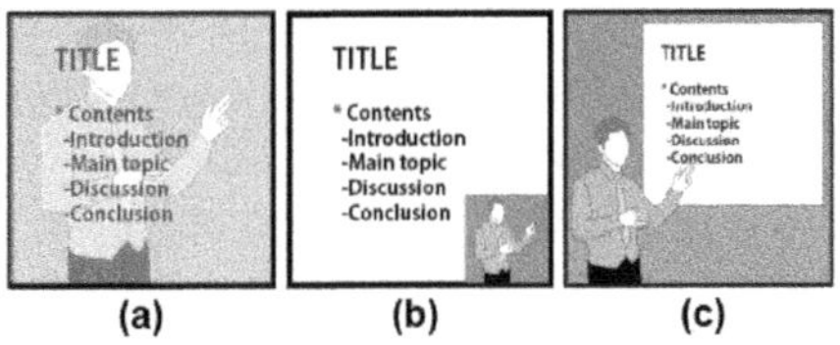

Figure 4. Three lecture formats compared.

Picture-in-Picture presents the lecturer in a corner box while displaying the lecture slides as the background. Total Shot is a direct camera capture of the lecturer and projected screen on the wall. While TransPoint and Picture-in-Picture require minimal resources, Total Shot requires more costly resources such as a high-definition camera, a camera man, and camera settings such as lighting, camera positioning, and secured angles.

Participants

A total of 16 undergraduate and graduate students (10 males and 6 females) who were familiar with remote lectures participated in the comparative user study as remote students.

Method

Four sessions were held, and each session included 1 lecturer and 4 remote students. TransPoint, Picture-in-Picture, and Total Shot formats were used in random order for each session, which respectively had 3 series lecture parts. The lecturer and the lecture materials were identical for all sessions. All formats during the study used standard video-conferencing software; thus, the lecturer was always able to see and talk with remote students.

After the 3-part lecture session, individual interviews and group interviews were conducted. Until the debriefing session, no specific explanations about TransPoint were given to the remote students to test the appropriateness of the design rationales for it. Individual interviews were conducted for specific evaluation of TransPoint's usability and compatibility, while group interviews were used to compare the three lecture formats extensively. During the individual interviews, participants gave a score ranging from 1 to 5. The question for quantitative comparison of the lecture formats was "*Rate how much this lecture format motivated you to participate in the lecture.*" We used self-reporting for evaluating perceived motivations to participate in terms of the lecture format [1]. The quantitative responses were analyzed with one-way ANOVA, and the qualitative responses were analyzed via a bottom-up affinity diagram [3].

RESULTS

Lecture Format	N	Average	SE	Average Difference	P Value
TransPoint	16	4.17	0.32	-	-
Picture-in-Picture	16	3.08	0.19	-1.09	**0.02***
Total Shot	16	3.42	0.26	-0.75	0.13

Table 1. Quantitative responses to motivation to participate. Average difference indicates difference from TransPoint.

The feedback from the participants shows that TransPoint highly motivated remote students to participate compared to Picture-in-Picture. While both lecture formats required minimal resources, TransPoint was more motivating in terms of participation. Although TransPoint did not show a significant difference from Total Shot, Total Shot required more costly resources than TransPoint.

Dynamic Format for Synchronous Remote Lectures

Among the remote students, 69% preferred the dynamic lecture (i.e., TransPoint), whereas 31% preferred the fixed lectures. Users mainly preferred the dynamic lecture because it alleviated boredom: G1-M2 said, "*Because the screen continues to change, it is less boring, and it helps concentration.*" Also, the adaptive transparency was evaluated as an appropriate medium for the dynamic lecture.

G3-M2 said, "*Because both lecture slides and lecturer scenes are on the largest scale, it helps to bring awareness when the transparency changes*"; similarly, G1-F1 said, "*I can fix my gaze at one place and still see both the lecture slides and the lecturer* (at Figure 3.c)."

Coordinating Remote Students' Attention

According to remote students' comparative evaluation, TransPoint was able to deliver an acceptable combination of lecture slides and lecturer scenes at proper moments.

Attention Management for the Lecturer

For TransPoint, the lecturer was able to gain attention from remote students when needed. G3-M3 stated, "*I looked at the lecturer when overlapped with lecture slides because I was done reading the slide.*" Likewise, G4-F1 commented, "*When suddenly just the lecturer appears (at Figure 3.a), I look at his (her) facial expressions and gestures.*" For the Picture-in-Picture format, the small size and the position of the lecturer scene distracted the remote students' attention. G3-M1 said, "*I cannot see the gestures or facial expressions of the lecturer. I tend to ignore and just watch the lecture materials and listen.*" Total Shot delivered the lecture scene holistically but was less effective at emphasizing the lecturer. As G4-F2 commented, "*The direct camera capture gives more sense of the place, but the lecturer seems blended in the scene.*" Thus, it can be said that TransPoint was more effective at emphasizing the lecturer when needed.

Attention Management for Lecture Slides

For TransPoint, the lecture materials were emphasized at proper moments. As G1-M1 commented, "*I paid more attention to lecture materials because the screen changed when the lecturer was explaining them.*" Because the lecture materials were always visible in the Picture-in-Picture format, the availability of lecture materials was high. G4-F1 said, "*I could clearly see the contents and can look at them whenever I want. But it tends to get boring.*" In contrast, Total Shot had comparatively low resolution for lecture slides, and they did not stand out from the screen. G3-M2 stated, "*Compared to other formats, I tended to lose focus on the lecture materials. They looked like part of the scene.*" Thus, for distinctive emphasis of lecture slides, TransPoint was most effective.

Real-Time Interaction with More Awareness

Among the three lecture formats, TransPoint was evaluated as most appropriate for real-time interaction by the participants. Because the lecturer was emphasized when the lecturer wanted attention, remote students were able to focus on the lecturer during real-time interaction; dynamic switching by the adaptive transparency corresponded when remote students presented an answer or asked questions. The awareness also made remote students feel like extra care was being given to them. As G1-F1 stated, "*I felt like the lecturer was watching me, so I paid more attention*"; similarly, G2-M1 said, "*Thinking that the lecturer could see me, I felt like making eye contact.*"

Specific Evaluation of TransPoint's Design Rationales

The users evaluated the design rationales for the TransPoint system as appropriate. When debriefed, 100% agreed that the design rationales for the usage scenarios were reasonable and plausible. For remote students, 94% said yes to the question "*Did you pay more attention to the* lecturer's *gestures or facial expression in the first ratio* (Figure 3.a)?"; 100% of participants agreed that lecture slides and the lecturer were visible in the third state (Figure 3.c). In addition, 100% of the participants said they could understand that the lecturer was emphasizing lecture materials when the transparency state shifted to the fifth state (Figure 3.e). Finally, 75% of remote students understood the intentions of contextual emphases. Still, 4 users commented on the need for explanation about transparency change.

DISCUSSION AND CONCLUSION

We presented TransPoint to improve synchronous remote lectures and demonstrated its value through a comparative user study. The user study showed that lecture contexts can be mapped to the adaptive transparency by using the natural lecturing behavior of the lecturer, enabling intuitive expressions with contextual meanings. With TransPoint, synchronous remote lectures could be more integrative, coordinated, and motivating.

The user study results suggest several design implications for remote lecture systems. There are clear needs for assisting remote students in terms of interaction and psychological awareness. Dynamic lectures are more fitting for synchronous remote lectures than fixed lectures because they are able to assist with various lecture situations. Interactivity that uses the natural teaching behavior of the lecturer and lecture context is positively understood by remote students. Lastly, various transparency animations with contextual meanings are possible with adaptive transparency.

Constant visual changes can alleviate remote students' boredom and motivate them to participate more. Therefore, TransPoint can be synergetic for long lectures and discussion-heavy lectures. Also, the system can include more students with a larger remote room or with multiple remote rooms when the group call function of standard video-conferencing software is used. Additionally, TransPoint can be integrated as a recorded asynchronous remote lecture whereby students would have the authorship to control interactivity with the adaptive transparency. During a synchronous remote lecture, there is no clear way to allow multiple students to control a shared and broadcasted screen.

Lastly, TransPoint has areas for improvement. The highlight function of the controller could be smoother if it really worked like a laser pointer. Furthermore, tutorials on transparency changes could be given to ensure that remote students are aware of the contextual meanings of transparency changes.

REFERENCES

1. William Albert, and Donna Tedesco. 2010. Reliability of Self-Reported Awareness Measures Based on Eye Tracking. In *Journal of Usability Studies, 5(2), 50-64.*
2. Richard L. Daft, and Robert H. Lengel. 1983. *Information richness: a new approach to managerial behavior and organizational design*, Straw and L. Cummings (eds.). Research in Organizational Behavior. Department of Management, Texas A&M University, TX.
3. Karen Holtzblatt and Hugh Beyer. 1998. Affinity Diagram. In *Contextual Design: A Customer-centered Approach to Systems Design* (1st. ed.). Morgan Kaufmann, San Fransico, 24-27.
4. Clarissa Ishak, Carman Neustaedter, Dan Hawkins, Jason Procyk, and Michael Massimi. 2016. Human Proxies for Remote University Classroom Attendance. In *CHI 16 Proceedings of the 2016 CHI Conference on Human Factors in Computing Systems*, 931-943. http://dx.doi.org/10.1145/2858036.2858184
5. Hiroshi Ishii. 1990. TeamWorkStation: towards a seamless shared workspace. In *Proceeding CSCW '90 Proceedings of the 1990 ACM conference on Computer-supported cooperative work*, 13-26. http://dx.doi.org/10.1145/99332.99337
6. Heesun Kim, Bo Kyung Huh, Seung Hyen Im, Hae Youn Joung, Gyu Hyun Kwon, and Ji-Hyung Park. 2015. Finding Satisfactory Transparency: An Empirical Study on Public Transparent Displays in a Shop Context. In *CHI'15 Extended Abstracts, Apr 18-23, 2015, Seoul, Republic of Korea. ACM 978-1-4503-3146-3/15/04.* http://dx.doi.org/10.1145/2702613.2732844
7. David Lindlbauer, Toru Aoki, Robert Walter, Yuji Uema, Anita Höchtl, Michael Haller, Masahiko Inami, and Jörg Müller. 2014. Tracs: transparency-control for see-through displays. In *UIST '14 Proceedings of the 27th annual ACM symposium on User interface software and technology,* 657-661. http://dx.doi.org/10.1145/2642918.2647350
8. David McGookin, Inti Herteleer, and Stephen Brewster. 2011. Transparency in mobile navigation. In *CHI EA '11 CHI '11 Extended Abstracts on Human Factors in Computing Systems,* 1903-1908. http://dx.doi.org/10.1145/1979742.1979891
9. Rajiv Ratn Shah, Yi Yu, Anwar Dilawar Shaikh, Suhua Tang, and Roger Zimmermann. 2014. ATLAS: Automatic Temporal Segmentation and Annotation of Lecture Videos Based on Modelling Transition Time. In *MM '14 Proceedings of the 22nd ACM international conference on Multimedia,* 209-212. http://dx.doi.org/10.1145/2647868.2656407
10. Hijung Valentina Shin, Floraine Berthouzoz, Wilmot Li, and Frédo Durand. 2015. Visual Transcripts: Lecture Notes from Blackboard-Style Lecture Videos. In *ACM Transactions on Graphics (TOG) - Proceedings of ACM SIGGRAPH Asia 2015. 34(6).* 240. http://dx.doi.org/10.1145/2816795.2818123
11. Jaspal Subhlok, Olin Johnson, Venkat Subramaniam, Ricardo Vilalta, and Chang Yun. 2007. Tablet PC Video based Hybrid Coursework in Computer Science: Report from a Pilot Project. In *SIGCSE '07 Proceedings of the 38th SIGCSE technical symposium on Computer science education,* 74-78 http://dx.doi.org/10.1145/1227310.1227339
12. Lalida Sritanyaratana, Kizilcec Rene, and Karthryn Papadopoulous, and Lalida Sritanyaratana. 2014. Showing face in video instruction: effects on information retention, visual attention, and affect. *CHI '14 Proceedings of the SIGCHI Conference on Human Factors in Computing Systems.*

    http://dx.doi.org/10.1145/2556288.2557207
13. Morita Tomoyuki, Kenji Mase, Yasushi Hirano, and Shoji Kajita. 2007. Reciprocal attentive communication in remote meeting with a humanoid robot. In *ICMI '07 Proceedings of the 9th international conference on Multimodal interfaces,* 228-235. http://dx.doi.org/10.1145/1322192.1322232
14. Weikai Xie, Yuanchun Shi, Guangyou Xu, Runting Shi, Enyi, Chen, Yanhua Mao, and Fang Liu. 2003. The smart classroom: Merging technologies for seamless tele-education. *In IEEE Pervasive* Computing, 2(2), 47-55.
15. Cha Zhang, Yong Rui, Jim Crawford, and Li-Wei He. 2008. An automated end-to-end lecture capture and broadcasting system. In *ACM Trans. Multimedia Comput. Commum,* 6(23). http://dx.doi.org/10.1145/1324287.1324293

FutureSelf: What Happens When We Forecast Self-Trackers' Future Health Statuses?

Saeyoung Rho, Injung Lee, Hankyung Kim, Jonghyuk Jung, Hyungi Kim, Bong Gwan Jun, Youn-kyung Lim
KAIST (Korea Advanced Institute of Science and Technology)
Daejeon, Republic of Korea
{saeyoung.rho, edndn, hkkim31, jonghyuk101, roy83kim, bonggwan, younlim}@kaist.ac.kr

ABSTRACT
The adoption of self-tracking services to improve health-related behavior is increasing. Although psychologists claim that thinking about the future has a motivational impact on current behavior and cognition, few studies have explored using future forecast in self-tracking services. In this paper, we explore how future forecast information can be used in the design of self-tracking services. We conducted a four-week study that qualitatively investigated 11 participants' perceptions of and practices with future forecast information. Participants used the FutureSelf app that we developed, which forecasts dieters' future weights and expected goal achievement rates based on their current behavior. The findings reveal that predicting future weight based on prior performance induced participants to imagine their future selves and reminded them of their ultimate goals. In fact, the predictions became the participants' primary source of motivation. We also suggest design implications for self-tracking services that forecast users' future statuses.

Author Keywords
Consequence Information; User Experience; Design; Health; Activity Tracker; Self-Tracking; Personal Informatics.

ACM Classification Keywords
H.5.m. Information interfaces and presentation (e.g., HCI): Miscellaneous.

INTRODUCTION
As Ebenezer Scrooge says after seeing the Ghost of Christmas Yet to Come in the novel ***A Christmas Carol***, "*Men's courses will foreshadow certain ends, to which, if persevered in, they must lead, but if the courses be departed from, the ends will change. Say it is thus with what you show me* [9]." After being visited by ghosts showing his future, Scrooge realizes that he will meet with a tragic end if he continues to be cold and miserly, and it transforms him into a changed man. He compares his future image as shown to him by ghosts to what he actually wants to be. The difference between these two images acts as a new stimulus, persuading him to change his behavior. This phenomenon was already studied by psychologists; they report that considering possible futures influences an individual's current cognitive/emotional state and goal-setting behavior [17].

Designers in the human-computer interaction (HCI) field have studied how to design self-tracking services to better induce, improve, and maintain health behavior change. One popular approach is to express self-tracking data in a more understandable and actionable way for users. Since thinking about the future affects motivation, predicting the future can be a viable approach to helping health behavior change. Self-tracking services also offer the potential to predict the future of the user. Self-tracking services store a wealth of personal health data that can be used to generate predictions by adopting advanced medical understanding. However, the information provided by current services is mainly related to past performance, not allowing people to imagine the future.

To explore how people's experiences with self-tracking services change as they gain access to predictive information, we devised a study in the form of a four-week weight-loss program and recruited 11 people who wanted to lose weight. Participants were asked to track their activities and food intake using a wearable activity tracker and to use the FutureSelf app, which forecasts the future consequences of continuing current behavior by analyzing the collected data. Interviews and journaling were employed to qualitatively probe participants' experiences both with and without future consequence information with respect to how they set and changed goals, how they planned strategies to satisfy these goals, and what motivated them to engage in certain behavior to achieve their goals. As a result, we determined that forecasting future weight based on current self-tracked data motivates users to change their behavior.

This paper makes following contributions: First, we suggest a new type of information to represent self-tracked data, which we term *consequence information*, i.e., the predicted future information based on collected data. Second, we reveal that this type of information can help increase users' motivation to engage in healthy behavior through in-depth qualitative user studies, and propose several points to consider when designing such type of information.

DIS 2017, June 10-14, 2017, Edinburgh, United Kingdom

ACM 978-1-4503-4922-2/17/06…$15.00
DOI: http://dx.doi.org/10.1145/3064663.3064676

RELATED WORK

Potential of Imagining the Future in Behavior Change

Psychologists have already sought to bridge the gap between people's conceptions of the future and their current statuses. There are two different ways that people conceive their futures. One way is to imagine possible selves, conjecturing how they might act, look, or feel in the future [7]. People may construct positive (want to achieve) or feared (want to avoid) selves, and individuals' knowledge, moods, and expectations affect the construction of those possible selves. In this process, people who imagine the future more explicitly are more confident that the future event will happen and tend to do more things that can catalyze it [1, 30]. In addition, people felt more motivated when a fictional future story was described from the third-person perspective rather than from the first-person perspective [35]. Additionally, Oettingen et al. distinguished expectation from fantasy, verifying that expectation has a greater motivational impact [21]. These studies imply that a conception of the future based on more objective criteria can better motivate people.

The second way that people can imagine their futures is to be reminded of their goals. When people set a goal, they fabricate several possible futures, select the one they most prefer, and conceive a plan to achieve that end state [3, 20]. Thus, a goal is a representation of a desired future and can motivate people, guide their behavior, and elicit better performance [2, 11]. "*The future, as represented by goals, exerts a major influence on current behavior* [17, p. 595]." Based on the potential of predicting people's future behavior changes, we suggest that the investigation of how people's experience is influenced when images of their futures are conceived in an objective and unbiased manner is important.

Limitations in Self-Tracked Data Interpretation

A large number of self-tracking services are available in the form of activity trackers and diet logging apps that help people collect and reflect on their personal information to foster health behavior changes. However, limitations exist regarding how people interpret self-tracked data. Although the ultimate goal of health behavior change occurs over the long term, self-tracked data are currently employed with reference to short-term goals and decision-making [29]. In addition, people cannot fully exploit the data to gain insights—not due to a lack of collected data, but because they lack the methodology for proper interpretation [8].

Providing people with the expected consequences of continuing their current behavior based on self-tracked data may eliminate the limitations in interpreting the data. If we forecast a dieter's future weight, that forecast can be connected to a long-term goal (to lose weight), rather than to a short-term goal (to have salad for lunch). Additionally, people do not need to contemplate their self-tracked data to conjecture the consequences of their current behavior; instead, the system can analyze the self-tracked data and make predictions for them.

Forecasting the Future in Current Self-Tracking Services

Although many self-tracking services help users set and attain their goals, current self-tracking services do not attempt to forecast a user's future status based on his or her current behavior. A few services provide some futuristic information; however, they do not reflect the consequences of users continuing their current behavior. "Noom Coach (https://www.noom.com/about/)", which is a smartphone app for dieters intended to help them develop better eating habits and lose weight, provides a tailored plan for users to follow after they set a goal weight. The plan includes suggestions such as how many steps to walk. The app tells users that if they stick to the plan, they will be able to reach their goal. However, it does not predict the future based on a user's current behavior.

Another application is "UP by Jawbone (https://jawbone.com/up)", which is a smartphone app that gathers data from users' fitness trackers to analyze and display information. It offers a "Smart Coach" function that provides personalized advice to help users make better choices. For instance, the Smart Coach might say "It's almost time for bed. Getting ready now will help you get in bed by your 23:15 bedtime." Smart Coach analyzes a user's current behavior to deliver the best advice and meaningful insights but delivers it more as a suggestion than as a predicted consequence of a user's behavior.

Suggesting healthier behavior can be helpful, but many scholars in the HCI field have discussed the subject of user autonomy in ubiquitous technology. Rogers has pointed that we are becoming more dependent on technology; thus, we need to design new technologies to encourage people to be proactive in their lives [28]. Forecasting future consequences has the potential to provide users with opportunities to set their own goals; rather than assigning a goal, the technology provides information to aid users' own goal setting. Forecasting benefits from technology being able to predict the future, but leaves the goal-setting process to the individuals.

DEFINITION OF CONSEQUENCE INFORMATION (CI) AND PERFORMANCE INFORMATION (PI)

To clarify what we have termed "the future consequence", we define Consequence Information (CI) as follows:

- CI: Information showing a consequence of an anticipated activity, measured from the average speed of an activity observed from the past up to the present.

As opposed to the concept of CI, we refer to the user performance data accumulated from the past up to the present, which is the most common method for reporting self-tracked data in existing services, as Performance Information (PI) and define it as follows:

- PI: Information showing a person's performance of an activity completed from the past to the present.

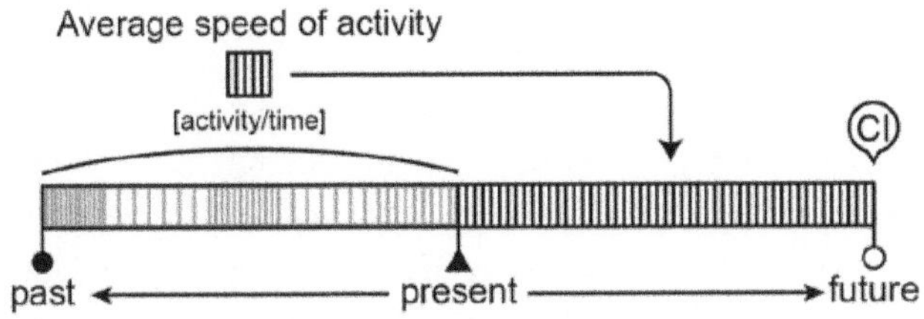

Figure 1. Definition of Consequence Information (CI)

The average speed of an activity (e.g., walking 10,000 steps per day) means the pace at which behavioral data have been accrued—such as a person's number of steps per day or daily caloric intake—from a past timepoint to the present (Figure 1). This value is used as a base to predict one's future activity; we assume that a user will maintain the same speed of activity up to a certain moment in the future. Given this information, we can obtain CI by predicting the future consequences based on the speed of the expected activities.

Consider Sarah (female, 60 kg), who tracks her step count. She walked between 7,000 and 12,000 steps each day, and her average step count per day over the past week was 10,000 steps per day. Thus, if we assume that Sarah will maintain the same speed of activity, she will walk 70,000 steps during the next week. A variety of consequences can be expected from this prediction: 1) she will reach 70% of her weekly step goal if her goal was to walk 100,000 steps in a week; 2) she will burn approximately 3,000 kcal if she maintains a pace of 5 km/h [16]. She can obtain different types of CI by tracking diverse health-related data. By defining CI in this manner, we can predict individuals' possible futures that are grounded in self-tracked data. CI is not a lie; it is a probable future state that can act to amplify the effect of a person's past performance. The future prediction length is adjustable to vary the size of amplification.

STUDY DESIGN

We devised a study to probe how the participants interact with CI; the study focused on the *weight-loss-related behavior* of dieters. CI can be clearly expressed for weight loss because people trying to lose weight tend to quantify their desired weight goals (e.g., 50 kg). Furthermore, a wearable activity tracker can provide adequate information to predict future weight, e.g., caloric intake and burn data. The FutureSelf app was developed as an example of how a self-tracking service can provide CI to dieters. The FutureSelf app accesses a user's personal data, generates messages based on these data and sends the messages to users. By adopting the FutureSelf app, the study was devised as a one-month weight-loss program, and people who wanted to lose weight by tracking their daily activity and food intake were recruited. During the study, journaling and five semi-structured interviews were conducted. And a year after the study, one follow-up interview was conducted in order to enable the participants to provide more objective reflection of their experience of this concept.

FutureSelf App Development

In the FutureSelf app system, the activity tracker Fitbit Flex was employed to log the participants' daily activities and food intake using built-in functions, and the messaging app Telegram was employed to send messages (Figure 2). First, users manually input their age, gender, current weight, height, goal calorie intake/burn, and wakeup/bedtime information to the FutureSelf app. Next, the FutureSelf app connects to the user's Fitbit server to collect caloric intake/consumption data. Then, it generates messages based on those data. To contrast experiences with and without CI, the FutureSelf app produces not only the CI messages but also messages that report only the accumulated user performance data (e.g., caloric intake). It sends the messages to users at designated times. To reduce bias from visual elements or a nuance, information was delivered as short text messages in a neutral tone, without any compliment or criticism.

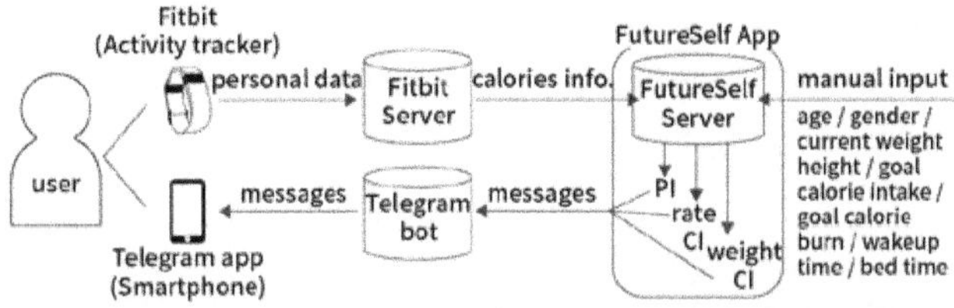

Figure 2. Data flow diagram of the FutureSelf app

To obtain PI, we need to select a certain point of time in the past. For instance, if we choose the timepoint as 00:00 today, PI corresponds to what Sarah has completed from 00:00 up to the present. If she walked 7,000 steps during that interval, her performance can be described as follows: 1) Sarah has walked 7,000 steps so far; and 2) she has achieved 70% of her daily step goal if her goal was to walk 10,000 steps a day.

The FutureSelf app generates PI and two types of CI (Figure 3). The PI describes caloric intake/consumption because this information is a fundamental factor with regard to weight loss. Since we initially did not know how CI would work, we created two types of CI and aimed to explore how the participants experience two types of CI: goal achievement rate CI (Rate CI) and future weight CI (Weight CI). Rate CI is calculated by comparing a user's goal for caloric intake/consumption to that user's expected future caloric intake/consumption. This calculation assumes that a user will make a linear progression during waking hours. Weight CI is produced using the weight-loss calculator, which predicts future weight by modeling the correlations between people's weight changes and information about age, gender, current weight, height, and calorie reductions/increases [34].

The FutureSelf app sends push notifications 30 minutes before sending PI and CI to induce manual logging (Figure 3) [4]. The FutureSelf app creates its messages based on users' updated Fitbit data, and the time lag between the actual behavior and the logging is reduced to avoid recall bias and produce more accurate data [6].

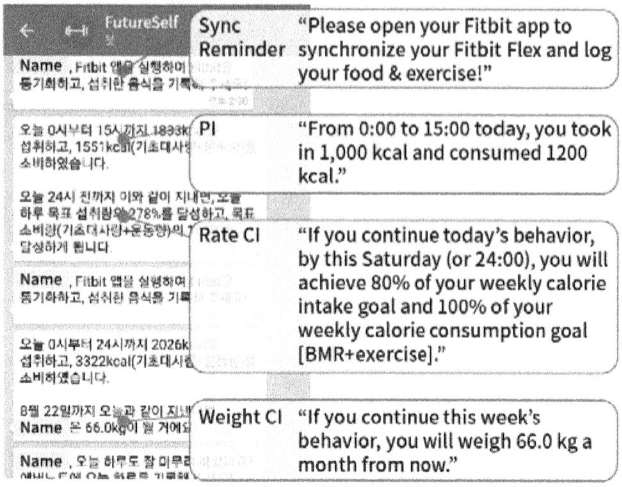

Figure 3. Examples of FutureSelf app message (screenshot)

Participant Recruiting

To observe various situations in which CI is addressed, we aimed to recruit participants with diverse qualities in terms of current weight, body mass index (BMI), and weight-loss goal. Five selection conditions were imposed on participants by conducting a preliminary survey. First, people who were already on a diet were excluded because time factors may affect people's engagement levels of weight loss [33]. Second, people who require clinical support were excluded since the goal was to observe how people manage their health behavior using their volition. Thus, people with a BMI that exceeded 25 were not selected because they were recommended to consider clinical support [10, 33]. Third, people with a BMI less than 18.5 after achieving their goal weight were not selected because the prediction tool that we employed did not offer predicted weight values for BMI values less than 18.5, which indicates that a person is underweight. Fourth, people in approximately the same age range were selected since physical condition can affect weight-loss performance. Last, people with similar lunchtimes and bedtimes were selected since message receiving times may affect the use of information.

This study was advertised on online communities where many local people spend time. All the participants were required to accomplish and adhere to four major tasks; 1) track daily activity and food intake using Fitbit, 2) check all messages from the FutureSelf app, 3) complete a short diet journal using online notes, and 4) participate in five weekly interviews. As a reward, those who completed the study received the activity trackers we provided for the study. Six men and six women in their twenties were recruited from among 110 applicants and were divided into two groups with even distributions of age, gender, and BMI (Table 1). However, one participant dropped out due to lack of active participation; therefore, the final analysis included data for 11 participants. The average BMI was 22.3 in Group A (SD=1.62) and 22.4 in Group B (SD=1.81).

Group	P#	Age, gender	BMI (Weight)	Weight-loss goal
Group A	P1	23, M	22.34 (78.3 kg)	-1.0 kg
	P2	23, F	20.60 (54.4 kg)	-2.0 kg
	P3	25, M	23.20 (77.7 kg)	-4.7 kg
	P4	23, F	22.73 (58.2 kg)	-3.0 kg
	P5	29, M	24.49 (74.9 kg)	-5.0 kg
	P6	23, F	20.22 (56.6 kg)	-1.6 kg
Group B	P7	22, M	21.40 (67.8 kg)	-1.0 kg
	P8	28, F	20.73 (51.1 kg)	-1.0 kg
	P9	28, M	24.18 (70.7 kg)	-1.0 kg
	P10	25, F	21.33 (54.6 kg)	-1.5 kg
	P11	27, M	24.58 (65.3 kg)	-5.0 kg

Table 1. Participants' information

Study Setup

In the beginning of the study, we planned to observe two weeks first, and then change into the most suitable settings to inquire design implications for CI. Participants were divided into two groups in order to clearly understand how the experience of CI is different from the experience without CI. During the first three weeks of the study, we provided CI only to Group B and concentrated on comparing the experience between Groups A and B to find out the unique potential of CI. After two weeks of observation, we found that the participants experienced Weight CI and Rate CI in profoundly different ways. Weight CI led participants to believe that their weight-loss goal was more attainable and, thus, motivated them, whereas Rate CI did not show such an impact: *(P10, week 1; CI provided) "I liked the percent value (Rate CI), but, it seemed natural after few days. However, after seeing this digitized value (Weight CI), I thought, oh, really? Can I lose weight if I continue this? No, but, no I didn't agree, I doubted it, but I became strong-minded. I was very motivated to do so."*

Thus, in the third week, we changed the CI setup to better investigate in what ways Weight CI motivated the participants to keep exercise and control diet. In the last week, Group B stopped receiving CI, whereas Group A started to receive CI. Each group's interview results of the 4th week were compared to the interview results of that same group's first three weeks, rather than making a comparison between Groups A and B. In this way, all participants were able to experience both situations—both with and without CI. We asked participants in Group B what they missed most in the last week without CI and asked Group A what they found most interesting in the last week with CI.

Message Generation (CI setup)

The FutureSelf app sends push notifications to users four times a day; twice (15:00 and 24:00) to provide PI and/or CI and twice (14:30 and 23:30) to request Fitbit synchronization and manual logging. These times were selected by considering participants' normal routines; all participants typically went to bed after midnight, had lunch between 12

PM to 2 PM, and did not eat a regular breakfast. Thus, we aimed to have them check the first message after finishing lunch and the second message before going to bed. The CI included in messages varied between weeks and the time at which the messages were sent (Table 2).

In the first two weeks, we sent Rate CI from Sunday to Friday because we assumed no large differences among the Weight CI if we provided it every day. Messages sent at 15:00 predicted participants' daily goal achievement rates, and messages sent at 24:00 predicted their weekly goal achievement rates. By doing this, we expected participants to plan the remainder of their day at 15:00 and to plan the rest of the week at 24:00. On Saturdays, we sent Weight CI messages, which predicted participants' future weights at the end of the study. These weights were calculated on the assumption that the participant would repeat the same performance as during the past week.

In the last two weeks, we decided to focus on Weight CI because we found that Weight CI has greater motivating power than Rate CI. Thus, we sent Weight CI at 24:00 every day to predict a person's weight at the end of the study based on their performance for this day. To investigate the influence of time represented in Weight CI on the user experience, we provided Weight CI predicting body weight two months after the start date based on this week's performance on Saturday.

Journaling, Interviews, and Data Analysis

We conducted six personal semi-structured interview sessions per participant: five during the study and one a year after the study. The first five interviews were conducted at one-week intervals. The first interview was conducted face-to-face on the day before the program began. Participants were asked to measure their body composition and bring the result sheet to this interview. A moderator asked the participants questions about their previous experiences with weight loss, other health-related self-tracking services that they had used, and why they wanted to lose weight. Then, each participant set a calorie intake/burn goal with the moderator's help based on their body composition data.

During the four weeks, participants were asked to write a short diet journal at the end of each day using a shared online notebook (Evernote) so that we could conduct interviews based on the journal entries. In the journal, participants were asked to write down the most impressive FutureSelf messages, their daily diet/workout goal, their strategy to meet that goal, and reasons for each response. In the three subsequent interviews, which were conducted by phone, we asked what the participants did after they checked the messages, how they utilized the information in the messages, whether they instituted any changes in their way of thinking or their lives due to the messages, what metaphors they would use to describe their impressions of the FutureSelf app, if they encountered any changes in their goals and diet plans, and how satisfied they were with their previous week's performance.

In the fifth face-to-face interview, in addition to asking the same questions as in the previous telephone interviews, we requested participants to compare the experiences of weeks 3 and 4 regarding their confidence, motivation, and pictured future self-image. We conducted a generative session to discuss redesigning FutureSelf messages to investigate participants' underlying needs for another type of CI or their preferences for message settings.

The final interview took place one year after the discontinuation of the FutureSelf app. This follow-up interview was conducted in the summer, just like the main study, so participants were considering diet. Through this interview session, we investigated how participants were affected by their previous CI experience when they were not exposed to CI. We also observed the participants' objective responses to their CI experience. Ten of the 11 participants responded to the interview request, and each interview lasted approximately 30 minutes.

Audio recordings were made of all interviews (27+ hours), and the recordings were transcribed within 2 days of each interview session. We separately analyzed the data collected when CI was provided and the data when CI was not provided, and extracted the influence of CI on weight-loss-related behavior by comparing those two groups of data. Our data were iteratively open and axial coded until we had clearly identified the issues that emerged. Affinity diagramming was also conducted to categorize those issues. Three of the authors who conducted the interviews were mainly responsible for analyzing the data; after individual analysis, the three interviewers analyzed all the data together.

Week	Time	Time period selected to calculate the average speed of activity	Future timepoint represented in CI	Type of CI (unit)
Week 1&2	15:00	15 hours	24:00 (the end of the day)	Rate CI (%)
	24:00	A day	Saturday (the end of the week)	
	24:00, Sat.	A week	A month after the start date	Weight (kg)
Week 3&4	15:00	15 hours	24:00 (the end of the day)	Rate CI (%)
	24:00	A day	A month after the start date	Weight (kg)
	24:00, Sat.	A week	2 months after the start date	

Table 2. How we generated CI

FINDINGS

We determined that Weight CI was imperative for dieters; one participant who was not given CI messages during the first two weeks tried to calculate his CI from PI: *(P1, week 3; CI not provided) "Every day, my caloric intake is 400 calories less than caloric burn, and if I assume only carbohydrates burn, I'm supposed to lose 100 g. That will be 3 kg in a month. I don't think that's accurate, but I think I will lose at least 1 kg."*

In the following section, we present findings from the interview analysis regarding how Weight CI, Rate CI, and PI were utilized during self-management of health behavior.

Weight CI Makes Participants Imagine the Future Self

Motivational impact of Weight CI originated from the participants' imagination of their future selves. Since Weight CI directly shows the weight (kg), participants were able to easily create their future self-images when Weight CI was given. Since participants did not have to translate or re-calculate given information, participants were able to acquire their future self-images in a concrete manner compared with when they had to estimate how their body would change based on information other than Weight CI. This imagination led participants to be more confident in their ability to lose weight and resulted in increased motivation. This finding is consistent with previous research findings, which indicate that people who explicitly imagine the future are more confident that the future event will occur and tend to do things that can catalyze it compared with people who do not explicitly imagine the future [1, 30]: *(P6, week 4; CI provided: commenting on Weight CI) "This week's alarm was much more helpful than the one from week 3 (CI was not provided). When I step on the scales, I see kg, not calories. [...] I can picture detailed images and I feel more likely that I will really lose weight. I also thought I should work out more, and become more determined."*

Accordingly, some of the participants mentioned that having their weight forecast too far into the future may not be desirable because of the many possible variables that can influence events during that time. Those variables disrupt the clear envisioning of future self-images: *(P9, week 3; CI provided: commenting on Weight CI) "I'm not certain of what will happen in two months. Thus, I think predicting [weight] a month later [but not two months] is most appropriate since I can plan my schedule and imagine that I will lose some weight if I continue what I've done last week."*

Weight CI Reminds Participants of Their Ultimate Goal

In addition, because Weight CI represents information related to the dieters' ultimate goals, it naturally evoked participants' thoughts about their ultimate goals. What P6 conceived in the aforementioned quote corresponds to the ultimate goal (to lose weight) rather than a means to an end (to restrict calorie intake). After receiving Weight CI, participants tried to imagine their changed body, which spontaneously sparked recall of their ultimate goals. Remembering one's goal is important as a starting point in the cognitive process of behavior change; *"Thinking begins with goals and cannot move without them"* [31, p. 19].

Therefore, participants also wanted to be able to personalize the forecast date based on their goal dates. In this case, it was reasonable to forecast weight after a month because at the beginning of the study we asked participants to set a weight-loss goal for a month later. Likewise, participants wanted to be able to get specific forecasts targeting a specific goal date they had in mind: *(P4, wrap-up interview: commenting on Weight CI) "The weight forecast should tell me my future weight on my goal date, not on some arbitrary date such as three months from the start. Let's say I'm on a diet for my wedding. I'm going to be interested in my weight on my wedding day, not other days!"*

Accordingly, participants wanted CI to predict something related to their ultimate goal, not necessarily limited to weight (kg) information. Although the ultimate goal of all the participants was to lose weight, they approached it from different aspects: some wanted to reduce body fat, while others aimed to fit into smaller jeans. Participants perceived that CI directly refers to their ultimate goal to be more intuitive: *(P8, week 3; CI provided: commenting on Weight CI) "The weight forecast was useful, but it may also be good to forecast my clothing size. [...] Saying 'you will be able to fit into your size 24 jeans!' will make me say 'wow!' and I will diet even harder."*

The Use of Weight CI Depends on the Individual's Ultimate Goal

The impact of Weight CI on participants' experience differed according to their ultimate goals. Weight CI was more important for participants who wanted to lose weight than participants who wanted to maintain their current weight. In the follow-up interviews, some participants' diet goal was not to reduce but to maintain current weight. In this case, Weight CI was not as influential as it was during the diet program. Since they were not expecting a change in the value, to step on a scale every day and confirm that their weight was within the acceptable range was an easier way to manage their weight. If a person's goal is to "maintain" a certain value, CI is not the best form to present this value: *(P1, follow-up interview: commenting on Weight CI) "Now my goal is to maintain this weight, not losing or gaining too much. [...] There is a scale at the gym, and it shows my weight if I step on it. [...] So, information that I will be xx kg in the future is not really relevant to me. I can check my weight right now, so there is no need to know my weight a week later."*

P6 wanted to incorporate Weight CI in her daily life, even when she is not on a diet to ensure that she is alerted before she gains weight. She regarded weight as a simple indicator to keep an eye on her health. Thus, after she stopped using the FutureSelf app, she tried to use her knowledge from Weight CI to calculate her Weight CI each day. However, since her weight changed, she could not use this knowledge anymore. Therefore, she wanted Weight CI to act as an alarm clock to warn her that she needed to be careful: *(P6, follow-*

up: commenting on Weight CI) "I want FutureSelf to exist in my usual life, not only for a diet but for checking my health condition before it actually goes bad. Like an alarm clock. If I skip exercise or sleep less, then I have to change my lifestyle, and FutureSelf can predict the consequences of that and alert me to control my habits."

When the participants' ultimate goal is to lose weight, Weight CI predictions that are closer to the goal weight tended to boost their confidence. Weight CI close to the goal weight convinced participants that they would lose weight as long as they continued the same behavior, which motivated them to meet their sub-goals. This is in accord with Locke's description: people's commitments to goals increase with the belief that those goals are attainable [19]: *(P1, week 4; CI provided: commenting on Weight CI) "The forecast said 77 kg and I thought I could reach that goal. Just 1 kg more to go. It was too vague at first, but after I got the messages [containing Weight CI] in Week 4, I became confident. All I had to do was just to keep going."*

However, Rate CI Is Not Construed as a Prediction

Participants discovered that Rate CI was less easy to imagine in the future perspective. After receiving Rate CI at 15:00, some participants divided the number in half and tried to construe it as an "achievement rate so far". Other participants perceived that they had done 120% of the activity amount that should be done by 15:00 when their Rate CI value was 120%. This representation of achievement rate can hardly be regarded as a prediction for the future: *(P8, week 2; CI provided: commenting on Rate CI) "But, when I tried to understand the achievement rate prediction, if it said 80%, I divided it in half and thought I did about 40% so far. But I don't know why I did so. It doesn't make sense."*

Goal achievement rate information (%) was preferred to kcal information since percent value has a standard to be compared. However, no participant wanted this information to be presented in the future perspective; they all wanted to know "what percentage of the goal they have achieved so far". This observation demonstrates that the goal achievement rate indicated by Rate CI is consumed not in the future perspective but in the present perspective. The goal achievement rate represents the activity amount, and thus it is utilized while making a decision on how much more/less to do a certain activity. Therefore, when participants received Rate CI, they had to somehow translate it into "achievement rate so far" to use the information to plan their activities.

Weight CI and PI Collaborate with Each Other

Weight CI motivated the participants, but it did not provide enough information to plan detailed strategies to meet their goals; it did not indicate how much more to exercise or how many calories to intake. Thus, participants needed information regarding "activity" to organize a weight-loss plan and set sub-goals to hit the ultimate goal. For example, one day, P3 received Weight CI predicting that he would meet his weight-loss goal, and he tried to repeat that day's activity. However, he could not acquire enough information from CI, so he checked Fitbit to find more detailed information to plan his strategy, how he should behave to lose weight. The information he found in Fitbit can be regarded as PI: *(P3, week 4; CI provided) "My goal for this week was to eat the same as on Monday and Tuesday. On Monday and Tuesday, I received a forecast saying that I would be 74 kg. So I thought I was doing well. I checked the data on those days on Fitbit and set them as a standard."*

We observed two types of collaboration between Weight CI and PI. First, as you can see from the example above, Weight CI served as a criterion that helped people evaluate their current performance. This is beneficial because taking a subjective view of health-related symptoms is risky and easily biased [27]. People may notice their obesity only after they have already become obese, without having a chance to prevent it. Thus, it is important to be vigilant to health-related symptoms and to take an objective view of them. Using Weight CI as an objective criterion, participants reinterpreted PI to set a sub-goal; this phenomenon was observed in every case, whether the predicted weight was higher or lower than the participants' goal weight:

(P9, week 3; CI provided: commenting on Weight CI) "One day I ate so little and my forecast said 60 kg. I thought that was too small, so I planned to eat more."

(P2, week 4; CI provided: commenting on Weight CI) "It was shocking. I am participating in a one-month diet program and I am hardly losing any weight. I thought I ate a bit much that day and decided to change my diet the next day."

Second, PI acted as evidence of CI. Providing both PI and CI together helped P8 imagine how CI was calculated; therefore, CI seemed more plausible and credible. This perception is important because it is difficult to trust questionable data, and distrust may decrease the impact of data on behavior change [13]: *(P8, wrap-up: commenting on CI) "Starting a report with a fact is very convincing. Saying 'You did this, and you did that [PI]' before telling me the important information [CI] was like an introduction."*

Consequently, through gradual learning, participants were able to discover whether they would gain or lose weight from a certain behavior. Participants who were initially clueless about caloric information became able to estimate their caloric intake or consumption as they repeatedly synchronized and checked the Fitbit app. Additionally, they began to compare the difference between their caloric intake and their consumption each day with the Weight CI predictions to calculate how large the difference should be to achieve their goal weight. As a result, participants learned to judge whether they were losing or gaining weight: *(P9, week 4: commenting on Weight CI received in week 3) "Now I have my own way of estimating calories while eating. It's like, 'I feel like I'm going to get fat because I ate this much,' or, 'eating this much is okay.' It's embodied cognition."*

Tolerance for Imperfect Prediction of Weight CI

Participants' attitude toward the prediction accuracy of CI differed greatly depending on the type of CI. When participants were asked in the follow-up interviews if they would use the FutureSelf service again, most of them did not want to receive Rate CI since it includes an irrational assumption: people do not repeat their daily experiences. Although this assumption is also made in the prediction of Weight CI, all participants indicated in the follow-up interviews that they wanted to receive Weight CI.

Three participants mentioned that they distrusted Rate CI because the prediction assumes that they will repeat their experiences at the same rate in the future, which is not guaranteed. Because goal achievement rate information is employed in the present perspective, the prediction of Rate CI, which inevitably entails reducing the credibility of information, was not necessary. Even if prediction accuracy was increased by adopting a personalized prediction algorithm with machine-learning technology, the participants continued to reject Rate CI: *(P1, follow-up: commenting on Rate CI) "I think I am not going to use it [Rate CI] even if it adopts deep learning. Prediction quality may become better than before, but I don't think my lifestyle is that predictable."*

Five participants questioned the prediction algorithm of Weight CI; in this case, however, they gained confidence and motivation. For instance, P5 became so skeptical that he tried to find the calculation algorithm, but was unable to find the right answer. Although he remained doubtful, he continued to be impacted by Weight CI: he believed that he could lose weight when he saw the Weight CI. This phenomenon was shared by another participant, P3, who regularly (3 times per week) weighed himself. He said that the gap between measured weight (76 kg, measured on Monday) and predicted weight (74.4 kg, his Saturday forecast, received on Monday) was so large that he could not trust the forecast, but he still gained hope and confidence from it.

As these two examples show, participants tended to understand the technical limitations of the weight forecast. To benefit from the positive impact of Weight CI, they were willing to tolerate some inaccuracy: the participants wanted to feel hopeful and maintain a positive attitude rather than focus on exact numbers. However, they still wanted CI to be more credible. Thus, we consider that the participants tolerated inaccuracy as compensation for positive impacts rather than preferring low accuracy. In particular, P6 described this feature of forecast as a "fortune teller:" *(P6, week 4; CI provided: commenting on Weight CI) "Predicting my weight was amazing but not that credible. It was like a fortune teller. [...] But my future self-image changed along with kg. Last week [CI was not provided], I thought I would 'probably' lose weight. But this week [CI was provided], I could really imagine my future image specifically."*

DESIGN IMPLICATIONS AND DISCUSSION

Based on these findings, we discuss several points that designers should consider when producing and delivering CI in self-tracking services.

What Type of Information Should CI Indicate to Stimulate Future Envisioning?

When people receive CI that illustrates activity amount data, such as Rate CI, they have difficulty imagining what CI actually means in the future perspective because activity amount data are consumed in the present perspective: first, to analyze what they have done so far, and second, to plan detailed strategies to satisfy sub-goals (e.g., how to satisfy the daily goal before the end of the day). Thus, if activity amount data are presented in the future perspective, as in CI, people have to reinterpret the future perspective in the present perspective. Since this reinterpretation process may confuse users, we should avoid presenting activity amount data as CI.

By contrast, when people receive CI that illustrates status change data, such as Weight CI, they can easily imagine their future body state. Because this type of CI helps people delineate the future self-image more explicitly, people become more confident and more inclined to meet their goals [1, 30]. Consequently, they begin to believe that their goal is attainable, strengthen their self-efficacy, and gain motivation. These changes in a user's attitude are difficult to achieve but are required to produce sustainable behavior change, as previous research findings illustrate [22].

Therefore, we should design CI to *indicate status change data rather than activity amount data* to help users change their attitudes and maintain changes in their behavior. As an example, if a user's workout goal is to increase muscle, workout hours could be used as an example of activity amount data, and muscle mass could be used as an example of status change data. If we present workout hours in the form of CI, it will be "if you continue your workouts, you will have worked out for 100 hours in one month". Users cannot intuitively understand what this sentence means, and since it is not construed in the future perspective, there is no impact as CI. However, if we illustrate muscle mass in the form of CI, it will be "your muscle mass will be 40 kg in a month." This CI causes users to conjecture their changed future self-images and subsequently gain hope and confidence.

The same data can be transformed into various types of information, resulting in various types of CI. Some types of data become more negative when presented as CI, whereas other types of data can produce new positive impacts that were not observed when the data were not presented as CI. These impacts align with previous research findings, which indicate that the form in which data are presented is crucial in behavior changes since it impacts how users understand the data [25]. Recently, S Health by Samsung provided estimated active minute information to users, which corresponds to Rate CI. Although providing a novel type of information is a good attempt, this information would not have been construed in the future perspective. Thus, designers should carefully select the type of information presented in CI.

How Can We Design a CI System to Better Assist Users in Recalling Their Ultimate Goals?

CI with forecast content, which directly refers to users' ultimate goals, intuitively sparked recall of their ultimate goals. This finding is important in behavior changes since reminding people about a goal can motivate people [17]. Conversely, when people receive CI that does not directly correspond to their ultimate goals, they are forced to reinterpret the information to compare their ultimate goals with the provided forecast. Therefore, designers should *carefully select forecast content of CI that is related to users' ultimate goals*. Many types of status change data, from which we should choose data that represent users' ultimate goals, are possible.

Content and the time represented in CI should be personalized based on users' goal dates. Although the app can be designed to predict CI for any future date, people with a specific goal date are particularly stimulated by CI that targets this date. Thus, we recommend designing CI to *forecast the future regarding the fixed goal date*. In this way, people can better observe their progress toward the specific goal date. Furthermore, if we do not provide CI prediction for the user's goal date, the user may have to reinterpret the given CI to guess the CI on the goal date, which is an unnecessary and inaccurate process.

However, if the goal of a user is too distant, she or he may have difficulty conjecture the future self-image even though the prediction is personalized to the user's ultimate goal. Since the motivational impact of CI is attributable to the imagination of future selves, the time represented in the CI should be in the foreseeable future. People often had stable schedules within a one-month period, but there were too many variables over a two-month period. They found it easier to imagine a future only one month away and therefore preferred one-month forecasts to two-month forecasts. The ideal prediction timeframe can differ from individual to individual; however, the bottom line is that *CI should predict an imaginable future that is not too far away*.

To bolster motivational impacts of CI, we can design a system to help users divide a distant goal into several short-term goals. If a user's goal date is too distant to imagine, the system can break down the distant goal into several time points. For example, if the goal date is one year from now, we can split one year into twelve individual months and assign twelve monthly goals that the user should achieve to satisfy the goal. In this case, the inclusion of CI prediction both on the original goal date and the newly formulated goal date is recommended because the imagination of the future self on the goal date is still needed.

However, we need a different approach for users whose goal is to maintain their current statuses rather than to make a behavior change. For these users, CI is not the best method for making them imagine their future selves and reminding about ultimate goals. In this case, CI can be designed to notify users of seemingly benign symptoms that they neglected. Specifically, CI can act as objective criteria to alert users that they have to be careful by amplifying the consequence of a small change that users would have ignored. This action may enable CI to be used even when no specific goals are established.

How Can We Create an Actionable CI System?

To make CI actionable, we need to consider not only CI but also the whole system delivering CI. To be specific, we should provide PI that shows the raw data for the prediction along with CI in the system. Specifying the PI used to predict CI has two consequences. First, an environment in which both CI and PI exist creates a synergistic effect of CI and PI: CI is utilized as a reminder of ultimate goals, and the PI is utilized in setting sub-goals. Second, PI acts as evidence of CI, making CI more credible.

Create a Synergistic Effect of CI and PI

By providing PI that shows base material for CI prediction, we can inform users about the most important behaviors for changing CI. PI indicating raw data for the prediction corresponds to *Factors*, which is defined as what influences behavior over a long period of time by Li et al. [18]. Li et al. expounded on the importance of knowing factors since it allows people to assess those factors to change their behavior. Thus, providing PI that illustrates *Factors* of CI helps users understand what behavior they have to control.

In this way, we can *design PI to be useful in setting sub-goals and planning detailed strategies*. In addition, *well-designed CI can support motivation and remind users of their ultimate goals*. Consequently, we can create an environment in which CI and PI collaborate to create a synergy effect. Since a person that is motivated by CI will check their PI, we can use *CI as a trigger to promote PI exploration*. This environment can be interpreted using Fogg's model [14]. Fogg explains that while people must have both enough *motivation* and the *ability* to perform a specific behavior, they need a *trigger* to spark a behavioral change. When both CI and PI are provided, CI will increase *motivation* and PI will provide information to help people find out what they need to do to reach their goal, increasing their *ability*. While analyzing PI, CI may act as an objective criterion for evaluating performance and planning strategies. Additionally, CI can act as a *spark as a trigger,* to motivate people by eliciting hope and fear. Hence, CI designed to motivate people and PI designed to be easily exploited for sub-goal setting will create a persuasive service environment.

Current research on self-tracking services focuses on how people engage with their sub-goals but is less concerned with their ultimate goals [18, 29]. We surmise that the reason for this focus is that the information provided by the current self-tracking services is primarily composed of PI. However, if we adopt both PI and CI in self-tracking services, we will be able to impact not only people's sub-goals but also their ultimate goals.

Increase the Credibility of CI

Since questionable information may reduce the impact of this information on behavior changes, the information should be designed to be defensible [13]. This is particularly important in producing CI because CI may arouse user's questions on how it is predicted, which may result in low credibility of the information. One certain way to produce believable CI is to improve the quality of prediction by increasing the prediction accuracy, such as by developing a better weight-loss model or personalizing the prediction algorithm. Although these solutions require additional studies, we can make CI more credible by designing the presentation of CI to users to include the base materials employed for predicting CI.

By simultaneously providing both CI and PI, we can adumbrate how CI was predicted. PI that illustrates raw material for CI prediction serves as evidence of CI and enables users to assume the prediction algorithm. This finding makes the black-box prediction system more guessable and consequently increasing the credibility of CI to some degree. This adumbration is also important since users can be motivated to adopt misguided workarounds when the calculation algorithm is unclear [36]. Thus, CI should be accompanied by sufficient explanation to help users unveil the CI prediction process.

CONCLUSION AND FUTURE WORK

This paper proposed the concept of predicting the future weight of a dieter. By exploring how people experience and interact with these predictive information, we presented design considerations that can practically help designers use this information in their self-tracking service design. Findings from the 4-week study and follow-up interviews revealed that the forecasts of users' future weight based on their current behavior had unique impacts: it made participants imagine their future selves, reminded them of their ultimate goals, gave them hope that they could reach their goals, and motivated them to be more conscientious in making that future come true. Based on these findings, we suggested design implications to bolster these impacts: the consequences should represent status change data rather than activity amount data and refer to an individual's ultimate goal. We hope this research will be a step toward the next generation of self-tracked information representations that will change people's attitude toward their health behavior.

However, there are still unsolved questions around generating CI. In this study, all participants received reduced future weights because the participants were actively engaged in a diet program. This result may simply show that CI was successful in keeping the participants working hard to reduce their weight. However, it also means this study had no chance of discovering how people would have behaved if they received a negative forecast that predicted a weight gain rather than a weight loss. In changing health behavior, both positive and negative feedback have different impacts [12]. Thus, the question remains whether we should provide CI when the forecast is negative.

In addition, the selection criteria imposed on the participant recruitment may have affected the results. First, we observed the motivational impact of CI, but it is unclear whether the participants had previous issues related to motivation. Second, participants may have already had a fairly positive self-image because their weight loss goals were not too bold. This modest goal also indicates that participants do not need to guess a self-image that is very different from the current image. Thus, the process of imagining their future self could have been quite pleasurable and easy. Thus, future iteration of this study with different group of people will be necessary.

Furthermore, CI may have different impacts on different individuals due to individual differences in susceptibility to the consideration of future consequences. People differ in their degree of sensitivity to distant behavioral outcomes. Strathman et al. assessed this as the Consideration of Future Consequence (CFC) Scale [32]. An individual's tendency to value the immediate or distant outcomes of behaviors can interfere with the use of CI [23]. Thus, we still have to investigate whether CI is beneficial across the CFC Scale.

There is also the question of how the impact of CI will differ when users do not have a specific goal. Most people who adopt self-tracking services to become healthy have specific health-related goals [8]. However, the system can also be employed as a tool for preventive healthcare, as one of the participants commented. In this case, we need to investigate differences in how CI influences users and, consequently, how it should be designed when users do not have specific goals because the production of CI was strongly related to users' ultimate goals. Thus, our future research will investigate how CI influences users without specific health-related goals.

We glimpsed opportunities to provide CI using more concrete methods or metaphors but the design of CI requires careful consideration since the manner in which we present CI may influence its impact. Previous research suggests an avatar as an effective method for communicating risk [24]. Visual representation enables users to communicate with the information in a concrete manner. Therefore, CI could be delivered in various forms such as avatars, caricatures or realistic images. However, we could not conclude whether providing more detailed descriptions of CI in the form of images and avatars is superior to providing weight values and maintaining the imagination gap. Such presentation techniques warrant further study.

ACKNOWLEDGEMENT

We thank all the participants of the study for their active engagement in every task. This research was supported by "High Risk High Return Project" Funded by KAIST (N10150037).

REFERENCES

1. Craig A. Anderson. 1983. Imagination and expectation: the effect of imagining behavioral scripts on personal influences. *J Personal Soc Psychol* 45, 2: 293-305.
2. James T. Austin, Jeffrey B. Vancouver. 1996. Goal constructs in psychology: structure, process, and content. *Psychol Bull* 120, 3: 338-375.
3. Albert Bandura. 1990. Self-regulation of motivation through anticipatory and self-reactive mechanisms. In *Perspectives on Motivation: Nebraska Symposium on Motivation* 38: 69-164.
4. Frank Bentley, Konrad Tollmar. 2013. The power of mobile notifications to increase wellbeing logging behavior. In *Proceedings of the SIGCHI Conference on Human Factors in Computing Systems* (CHI '13), 1095-1098. DOI: 10.1145/2470654.2466140
5. Frank Bentley, Konrad Tollmar, Peter Stephenson, Laura Levy, Brian Jones, Scott Robertson, Price, Richard Catrambone, Jeff Wilson. 2013. Health mashups: presenting statistical patterns between wellbeing data and context in natural language to promote behavior change. *ACM. Trans Comput-Hum Interact* 20, 5: 30.
6. Gordon D. Brown and Nick Chater. 2001. The chronological organization of memory: common psychological foundations for remembering and timing. In *Time and Memory: Issues in Philosophy and Psychology.* Christoph Hoerl and Teresa McCormack (eds.). Clarendon Press, Oxford. 77-110.
7. Nancy Cantor, Hazel Markus, Paula Niedenthal, Paula Nurius. 1986. On motivation and the self-concept. In *Handbook of Motivation and Cognition: Foundations of Social Behaviour*. Guilford, New York, NY, 96-121.
8. Eun Kyoung Choe, Nicole B Lee, Bongshin Lee, Wanda Pratt, Julie A Kientz. 2014. Understanding quantified-selfers' practices in collecting and exploring personal data. In *Proceedings of the SIGCHI Conference on Human Factors in Computing* (CHI '14), 1143-1152. DOI: 10.1145/2556288.2557372
9. Charles Dickens. 1843 *Christmas Carol*. Chapman & Hall, Boca Raton, FL.
10. Pamela A. Dyson. 2010. The therapeutics of lifestyle management on obesity. *Diabetes Obes Metab* 12, 11: 941–946.
11. Andrew Elliot, Mandy M. Shell, Kelly Bouas Henry, Markus A. Maier. 2005. Achievement goals, performance contingencies, and performance attainment: an experimental test. *J Educ Psychol* 97, 4: 630-640.
12. Ayelet Fishbach, Tal Eyal, Stacey R. Finkelstein. 2010. How positive and negative feedback motivate goal pursuit. Soc Personal Psychol Compass 4, 8: 517-530.
13. B. J. Fogg. 2002. Persuasive technology: using computers to change what we think and do. Ubiquity December: 89-120. DOI: 10.1145/764008.763957
14. B. J. Fogg. 2009. A behavior model for persu asive design. In Proceedings of the 4th International Conference on Persuasive Technology (Persuasive '09) Article 40, 7 pages. http://doi.acm.org/10.1145/1541948.1541999.
15. Thomas Fritz, Elaine M Huang, Gail C Murphy, Thomas Zimmermann. 2014. Persuasive technology in the real world: a study of long-term use of activity sensing devices for fitness In *Proceedings of the SIGCHI Conference on Human Factors in Computing Systems* (CHI '14), 487-496. http://doi.acm.org/10.1145/2556288.2557383
16. M. Jetté, K. Sidney, G. Blümchen. 1990. Metabolic equivalents (METS) in exercise testing, exercise prescription, and evaluation of functional capacity. *Clin Cardiol* 13, 8: 555-565.
17. Rachel Karniol, Michael Ross. 1996. The motivational impact of temporal focus: thinking about the future and the past. *Annu Rev Psychol* 47, 1: 593-620.
18. Ian Li, Anind Dey, Jodi Forlizzi. 2011. Understanding my data, myself: supporting self-reflection with ubicomp technologies. In *Proceedings of the Conference on Ubiquitous Computing* (UbiComp '11), 405-414. DOI: 10.1145/2030112.2030166
19. Edwin A. Locke, Gary P. Latham. 1990. A Theory of Goal Setting & Task Performance. Prentice-Hall, Inc., Upper Saddle River, NJ.
20. Edwin A. Locke. 1996. Motivation through conscious goal setting. Appl Prev Psychol 5, 2: 117-124.
21. Gabriele Oettingen, Doris Mayer. 2002. The motivating function of thinking about the future: expectations versus fantasies. *J Personal Soc Psychol* 83, 5: 1198–1212.
22. Harri Oinas-Kukkonen. 2013. A foundation for the study of behavior change support systems. *Personal Ubiquitous Comput.* 17, 6 (August 2013), 1223-1235. http://dx.doi.org/10.1007/s00779-012-0591-5
23. Sheina Orbell, Marco Perugini, and Tim Rakow. 2004. individual differences in sensitivity to health communications: consideration of future consequences. *Health Psychol* 23, 4: 388-396.
24. Perry Parks, Rosanna Cruz, Sun Joo Grace Ahn. 2014. Don't hurt my Avatar: the use and potential of digital self-representation in risk communication. International Journal Robots, *Education and Art* 4, 2: 10.
25. Bernd Ploderer, Wolfgang Reitberger, Harri Oinas-Kukkonen, and Julia Gemert-Pijnen. 2014. Social interaction and reflection for behaviour change. *Personal Ubiquitous Comput.* 18, 7 (October

2014), 1667-1676. http://dx.doi.org/10.1007/s00779-014-0779-y

26. James O Proschaska. 2013. Transtheoretical model of behavior change. In *Encyclopedia of Behavioral Medicine.* Springer Verlag, New York, NY, 1997-2000.
27. Rebecca M. Puhl,Corinne A. Moss-Racusin, Marlene B. Schwartz, Kelly D. Brownell. 2008. Weight stigmatization and bias reduction: perspectives of overweight and obese adults. *Health Educ Res* 23, 2: 347-358.
28. Yvonne Rogers. 2009. The changing face of human-computer interaction in the age of ubiquitous computing. In *HCI and Usability for e-Inclusion.* Andreas Holzinger, Klaus Miesenberger (eds.). Springer Verlag, Berlin, 1–19.
29. John Rooksby, Mattias Rost, Alistair Morrison, Matthew Chalmers Chalmers. 2014. Personal tracking as lived informatics. In *Proceedings of the SIGCHI Conference on Human Factors in Computing Systems* (CHI '14), 1163-1172. http://doi.acm.org/10.1145/2556288.2557039.
30. Steven J. Sherman, Richard B. Skov, Esther F. Hervitz, Caryl B. Stock. 1981. The effects of explaining hypothetical future events: from possibility to probability to actuality and beyond. *J Exp Soc Psychol* 17, 2: 142-158.
31. Herbert A. Simon. 1994. The bottleneck of attention: connecting thought with motivation. *Nebr Symp Motiv* 41: 1-21.
32. Alan Strathman, Faith Gleicher, David S. Boninger, C. Scott Edwards. 1994. The consideration of future consequences: weighing immediate and distant outcomes of behavior. *J Personal Soc Psychol* 66, 4: 742-752.
33. The Korean Society for the Study of Obesity. 2012. *Guidelines for Managing Overweight and Obesity.* KOSSO, Selangor, Malaysia.
34. Diana M. Thomas, Dale A. Schoeller, Leanne A. Redman, Corby K. Martin, James A. Levine, Steven B. Heymsfield. 2010. A computational model to determine energy intake during weight loss. *Am J Clin Nutr* 92, 6: 1326-1331.
35. Noelia A. Vasquez, Roger Buehler. 2007. Seeing future success: does imagery perspective influence achievement motivation? *Personal Soc Psychol Bull* 33, 10: 1392-1405.
36. Rayoung Yang, Eunice Shin, Mark W. Newman, Mark S. Ackerman. 2015. When fitness trackers don't 'Fit': end-user difficulties in the assessment of personal tracking device accuracy. In *Proceedings of the Conference on Pervasive and Ubiquitous Computing* (UbiComp '15), 623-634.

Designing Documentary Informatics

Chris Elsden[1], Abigail C. Durrant[2], David Chatting[1], David S. Kirk[2]

Open Lab, Newcastle University[1]
Newcastle-upon-Tyne, UK
{c.r.elsden; david.chatting}@ncl.ac.uk

Northumbria University[2]
Newcastle-upon-Tyne, UK
{abigail.durrant; david.kirk}@northumbria.ac.uk

ABSTRACT

In this paper we describe a Research through Design inquiry about a speculative wedding documentation service, in the mode of the Quantified Self. We reflect on our design research, which included design ethnography, interviews, enactments of parts of the service, and the production of a concept brochure. In so doing, we explore the design of personal tracking as a documentary activity, one intended for longer-term self-expression and remembering – rather than simply to monitor, regulate and motivate a data-driven life. Developing the Lived Informatics discourse, we use our design-led inquiry to propose 'Documentary Informatics' as an alternative and longer-term design perspective on self-tracking tools.

Author Keywords

Documentary Informatics; Data-Driven Life; Quantified Self; Speculative Methods; Remembering; Weddings;

ACM Classification Keywords

H.5.m. Information interfaces and presentation

INTRODUCTION

As a 'data-driven life' [55] is increasingly possible, researchers in Human Computer Interaction (HCI) have, of late, looked beyond 'extreme users' [8] to consider the lived and socio-cultural experience of quantified lifestyles [18,19,29,38,50,53]. Rooksby et al. set out the foundations for this experiential perspective as 'Lived Informatics' [45], and critique 'technology-centric' stage-based models of personal informatics [34] that prioritize behavior change. Adopting a phenomenological perspective, Lived Informatics [45] describes the diverse *styles* and idiographic meanings that emerge from the interweaving of self-tracking and quantified data in people's everyday lives.

Our work in this paper is concerned with one particular 'style' reported by Rooksby et al. – '*documentary tracking*'. In this style, participants *"were interested in documenting their activities rather than changing them."* [pp. 1167, 43]

Figures1, 3-7: ©Chris Elsden. Figure 2: ©Chris Elsden, David Green.

DIS 2017, June 10-14, 2017, Edinburgh, United Kingdom
 ISBN 978-1-4503-4922-2/17/06…$15.00
DOI: http://dx.doi.org/10.1145/3064663.3064714

Despite focusing on behavior change, Li et al. [34] also report documentary uses of quantified data to reminisce or to manage their affairs. In our own prior work (herein Elsden et al. [17]), we interviewed long-term trackers about their 'quantified past', as an emerging personal record.

Rooksby et al. emphasize that most tracking, documentary or otherwise, is a prospective and promissory activity, focused on the very recent past, present and near-future [45] – few participants in their study showed interest in *long-term* documentary tracking. Elsden et al. also note that only half of their participants had deliberately looked back on their historical data [17]. One interpretation we posit here is the extraordinary extent to which the current research and design of data-driven tools is focused on present and short-term goals – simply becoming 'fitter, happier, and more productive' [19]. Perhaps then, it is unsurprising that self-tracking is approached as a present-focused activity.

Viewed only through stage-based models of behavior change (e.g. [21,34]), data risks being viewed as simplistic, and one-dimensional. However, the quantified data that can now be collected on the body, in the home, in places of work and on the street, is often much more descriptive. Put another way, 10,000 steps is never just 10,000 steps. It is also a commute, a hike, or sightseeing in a foreign city. Lived Informatics hints at this broader relationship with data, which is derived from and unavoidably tangled up in diverse aspects of our everyday lives. Elsden et al. contend that whatever the initial motivation for self-tracking – the instrumental use for data at the time – this data has the potential to document people's lives over time [17].

Taking these observations as our departure point, this paper asks: 'what would it mean to prioritize these *documentary uses of data,* in the design of personal informatics tools? How might we reconfigure the design of data-driven services for longer-term self-expression and remembering, rather than only to monitor, regulate and motivate?'

This paper presents a Research through Design (RtD) [25,57] project, which turns to speculative methods to frame and address these questions. The basis of our project was to speculate about the design of a 'wedding datagraphy' service (as a parallel to wedding *photo*graphy) to professionally capture and curate meaningful and evocative data from a wedding. Though unique events, weddings provide an intriguing documentary context in which data might support experiences of sharing and remembering one's wedding, rather than optimizing it.

To investigate this speculation, the project pursued multiple strands of design-led inquiry. This initially involved: design ethnography; the use of design workbooks; interviews; and the design and deployment of promotional materials. These strands culminated in two 'speculative enactments' [14] in which two engaged couples met a wedding 'datagrapher' to discuss data they could document about their wedding. Both couples were then featured in a 'real wedding' style article describing their experience of wedding datagraphy. We designed, laid out and professionally printed these articles as a fictional brochure, promoting Abacus, our proposed wedding datagraphy service. In this paper, we critically reflect on the process and multiple outcomes of these design-led engagements with research participants.

By working in a speculative context prioritizing long-term self-expression and remembering, we propose that our exploration of wedding datagraphy contributes a foundation for the design of a new class of personal tracking tools: *'Documentary Informatics'*. We suggest that coining this new class of tool takes seriously the documentary potential of quantified data, with opportunities for alternative and longer-term uses of personal tracking.

RELATED WORK

Documenting Everyday Life with Quantified Data

Rooksby et al. [45] describe *documentary tracking* in terms of a personal interest to document activities rather than change them, and the authors offer several examples. They suggest that some people document *"out of interest"*; for example, nurses who wonder how far they walk in their working day. Documentary tracking is frequently pursued out of more than just curiosity, and is used to "*underline effort"* or commitment. Others are reportedly tracking "*to work out information about their routine activities"*; for example gaining a sense of their average speeds cycling to work (ibid. pp. 1167). These practices resonate with Lazar et al.'s [33] described use of trackers for *"curiosity"*; once a satisfactory answer has been found, continued tracking is no longer necessary. Lastly, Rooksby et al. [45] describe how participants use trackers "*to document pleasurable experiences, and couples using trackers on special walks"* (ibid. pp1167). Such tracking enhances the activity at the time, but appears to be valued in the longer term as well. In all these cases, people are appropriating trackers to use them in a documentary way, often as a means to tell stories about themselves, usually in the here and now.

However, Kim et al. [32] note that even after tracking has finished or stagnated, many people sought to keep or control access to their data. Lazar et al. [33] report on those who continued tracking, hoping for future potential use of their data, even when it was no longer useful for them. Indeed, *"this expectation for future benefit led participants to stop using devices that did not store data"* (pp. 641).

Anticipating this future use and reflection on data as a quantified past, Elsden et al. [16,17] report examples of the ways in which self-tracking data could be valued for documenting one's past. Participants reflecting on long-term data *remarked on changes* and transitions in their lives. Places they used to live and commute from; recovery from injuries; leaving university. Participants could easily recount different *periods of their life* – intense busyness, moving home, or dieting. The tracked data prompted reminiscence about these times, as well as specific events, such as a music festival or winning a triathlon. Equally, however, data could sometimes appear anonymous, or routine, and by itself, of limited documentary interest.

These studies suggest that users of personal tracking devices are aware of the potential value – or at least the implications of – the long-term storage of data that documents their daily activities. As such, while much *documentary tracking* reported by Rooksby et al. is largely focused on the present time; it appears that quantified data can have documentary potential beyond its original capture. As a supplementary point, it is important to recognize the communicative and social role of documentary tracking. Rooksby et al. [45] emphasize how their study was suffuse with the telling and reflection of *"something akin to a life story"* (pp. 1171). Elsden et al. position their inquiry [17] alongside recent work on digital possessions [40] and technology heirlooms [3,39], which emphasizes a socio-cultural perspective on remembering [4,36]. From this perspective, remembering is a reconstructive and collective achievement; memory is a 'resource-for-action', rather than simply 'something-in-the-head' [30].

Through this related work, we are building a position that documentary tracking is not simply a way of creating copies or impressions of reality, but is also a means of communicating personal narrative, identity and a felt sense of self (selfhood). Elsden et al. suggest that 'objective' quantified data is made personally meaningful through contextualization or '*data work'* [17]. Davis [9] suggests: *"narratives and subjective interpretations are the mechanisms by which data morphs into selves"*. Verisimilar accounts of everyday life emerge from the interweaving and appropriation of data with personal accounts.

Quantified Data as Identity, Narrative and Selfhood

Useful parallels can be drawn between data and practices and orientations towards photography. Van House et al. describe the daily *communicative* uses of photographs [52]. Miller and Edwards emphasize a transition from telling stories *about* photographs, to telling stories *with* photographs [37], as a form of social communication [10,47]. Equally, we could consider more communicative and social uses of data, something a variety of researchers, designers and artists have begun to explore as a way of *"seeing ourselves"* [43].

Epstein et al. [20] describe the challenges and some of the awkwardness of sharing data on social media as impression management. However, Sharon [49] paints a particularly nuanced portrait of self-trackers in the Quantified Self movement, who, more than simply data-fetishists, have complex relationships with their data, using it to enact a kind of authenticity. *"Rather than a numerical and constraining understanding of the self, as critics decry, this may point to an open-ended aesthetic one, where identity is constructed and curated, the product of quantitative and qualitative piecings together"* [p23, 33]

The self as a product of these 'piecings together' was the subject of our recent Metadating project [18]. Singles were invited to create a 'data profile' about themselves, and use this to talk about themselves at a speed dating event. Crucially, this work emphasized how talking about and 'performing' one's data was distinct from analyzing it, with implications for the style, presentation and detail required.

The work of artists and designers pushes the boundaries of data as a documentary material. Graphic designer Nicholas Felton has produced ten annual 'Feltron reports' [24], which detail many aspects of his life in data, from daily activities, to personal communication and media consumption. At the time, they were an exercise in self-awareness and annual reflection. They are now remarkable documents of his life. Stefanie Posavec and Giorgia Lupi also focus on everyday phenomena (e.g. their wardrobes, thankyous, swearwords and greetings), by exchanging 52 weekly self-portraits of hand-drawn data postcards for a year [42]. Lastly, Mimi Onohua's *"data storytelling project"* Pathways [41] presents interactive stories about four families based on passively collected mobile messaging and geo-location data. These are brief, but instructive, examples that emphasize the documentary potential of quantified data and the way that it can become imbued with a sense of personal identity and humanity.

Towards Documentary Informatics

These social and performative uses of data are integral to Lived Informatics, and suggest the potential for a less goal-oriented relationship with quantified data. Herein we contend that much of this relationship turns on the inevitably descriptive and documentary nature of a data-driven life. The related work captured here suggests that new kinds of documentary are an inevitable by-product of a data-driven life, which can support identity construction and narrative expression with quantified data. Nonetheless, despite identifying this documentary potential of a data-driven life, very little work in HCI has explicitly considered the *design* of what we term Documentary Informatics.

WEDDING DATAGRAPHY AS A DESIGN-LED INQUIRY

We have described how the driving paradigm of a Quantified Self is short-term, goal oriented, focused on self-optimization and behavior change, rather than documentary. Speculative RtD approaches (e.g. [5,13]) have been appropriated by HCI as a way to critique and explore 'alternative presents' [1] and near futures, which break from such existing paradigms of technology use. Hence, we turned to speculation to configure a design space that shifts potential values of personal informatics towards long-term self-expression and remembering; specifically, services for recording one's wedding with quantified data. This was used to foster empirical engagement around possible documentary interactions with data in a possible social reality that we constructed for both our research team and our research participants to explore. In such a context, our participants, and we as researchers, could have tangible, performative and real-life engagements with the proposition of long-term documentary tracking. In this way, we pursued a *design-led inquiry*: that is, an HCI study that is led by creative design practice. A combination of RtD methods were brought to the design of a number of linked empirical studies. We now describe these studies, in chronological order of how they were conducted. In practice, the studies were overlapping and mutually informing.

The Wedding Datagraphy Concept

The concept of wedding datagraphy – to professionally produce evocative data from a wedding – emerged from an ideation exercise undertaken with colleagues to develop design briefs for services to support remembering with data. We understood a wedding to be a particularly significant life event, where great importance is placed on personal expression and shared remembering through the careful recording and documenting of the day. In a rich description of existing technology use at weddings, Massimi et al. [35] highlight how photographs, video and treasured mementos are used to reassert the 'magic' of the day. Most importantly, we felt that weddings would be far removed from more goal-oriented notions of behaviour change, and would support an explicit focus on documentary styles of tracking. Although weddings are exceptional, rather than everyday events, they provide a context that many people can evocatively and excitedly relate to. As an initial exploration of the potential of documentary informatics, we sought to play with this prosaic cultural setting.

Design Ethnography

Our inquiry began with Design Ethnography [46], through which we sought opportunities to document quantified data about a wedding. We referred to wedding magazines extensively, visited a wedding fair, and clipped online material from popular wedding blogs and wedding vendors' websites. Initial clippings were photocopied and annotated, or gathered in the Evernote tool. We were particularly attentive to idealized wedding aesthetics, diverse modes of documentation, and the rhetoric, process and representation of wedding photographers. We produced three design workbooks [27] to elaborate and share initial ideas and concepts from this ethnographic work. These became a frequent source of reference, and directly fed into a number of the subsequent design activities. An initial output was the design of a brand for our datagraphy service: 'Abacus'.

Abacus Data Cards

Through our design ethnography, we considered different approaches and structures to the overall conceptual service design. We focused mainly on examples of documentary data, setting aside any immediate technical or practical barriers to the data collection. Examples were identified as prose statements (e.g. 28 steps down the aisle; Your guests travelled 2,374km; 13:01 – Your first kiss). We attended to the form of the data, and the language used to present it. From this study we realized the need to develop a playful, flexible way to introduce the wedding datagraphy concept to others (e.g. research participants or potential clients). To this end, we developed a deck of 52 Abacus Data Cards [Fig. 1], which rapidly communicated the breadth of quantified data forms we were interested in. These were partly inspired by the wealth of existing card-based ideation tools [e.g., 21]. These cards became our go-to method for introducing and explaining the service.

Figure 1: Abacus Data Cards.

Interviews

We conducted 12 semi-structured interviews (P1-P12, 7M, 5F). This was a convenience sample, including two wedding photographers, eight recently married individuals, one married couple, and one engaged individual. At interview, we invited participants to describe their own wedding. We probed in particular about their efforts to document the day, and their use of photographs, video, mementos and social media. We asked the photographers to describe their role and practice on the day, seeking opportunities to ground the role of the *data*grapher.

In the second half of each interview, we gave participants a pack of Abacus Data Cards and asked them to pick out data that they would have found compelling to record about their wedding. As a twist, we asked them to choose five cards for themselves, and five cards for their partner, and any cards they found inappropriate. Their choices scaffolded a broad conversation about the kind of data that could be captured from a wedding, and its personal, historical value. These interviews extended initial insights from our design ethnography, and in particular insights into actual practices of wedding documentary, particularly around photos. The interviews, augmented by the cards, allowed us to pilot a way of speaking about the speculative service in a plausible and appealing manner.

Speculative Enactments

Rather than deploying the proposed wedding service in full, we focused on developing one feature of it in-depth, as a Speculative Enactment. Speculative Enactments are an RtD approach proposed by Elsden et al. [14,15], to design consequential and social circumstances in which participants are invited to *act amidst* and *experience* speculation. Speculative Enactments hence invite empirical analysis as part of a speculative design-led inquiry.

For an enactment of the quantified wedding service we envisioned, we were drawn to the meetings that engaged couples have with their photographer to discuss and plan their wedding photography. At this stage of planning, couples are already excitedly imagining, disagreeing on and deciding how to document their big day. We sought to connect with these kinds of interactions in the context of our speculative datagraphy service.

Figure 2: Promotional image of 'meeting a datagrapher'.

We created and staged a competition for two engaged couples to meet with an Abacus datagrapher. We did this through the design of an Abacus website, advertised through social media and local wedding vendors:

Come and imagine the future of wedding recording with us. We are seeking TWO engaged couples, to feature in a concept brochure for Abacus. We want to imagine and tell the story of your future wedding, as it would be captured with data. Our chosen couples will meet exclusively with an Abacus Datagrapher to discuss their wedding, and how they would capture and represent it with data. Our datagrapher will then produce a four-page feature article on your imagined wedding, featuring data and mementos from the day. They will share this with you for a final edit, before publishing in a 12-page concept magazine about wedding datagraphy.

We hoped to attract imaginative couples who would enjoy speculating on the possibilities of the service. We were not intending to deploy a datagrapher at their wedding – we felt this was technically and ethically beyond what we could achieve. Instead, we proposed writing a 'real-wedding' article about them: as a tangible outcome; intended as a valued memento for the couple; and as promotional material for the concept. We recruited two Scottish couples. Annabelle & Calum were to be married in Edinburgh just two months after our meeting. Annabelle would arrive at her wedding in a big red bus that would later take guests on a tour of the city. Rowan & Julia were to have a 'rustic and relaxed' wedding the following summer (eight months later) in the grounds of stately home in Yorkshire, with tepees and a hog roast.

Each couple was sent the Abacus Data Cards as a Cultural Probe [26]. As before, they were invited to choose cards for themselves and for their partner, but keep this secret until our meeting. The lead author, in the role of a wedding datagrapher/researcher, visited each couple twice at their homes. Both meetings were audio-recorded. The first of these discussed their upcoming wedding, and then their choice of data cards, which served as a kind of data catalogue. This scaffolded an open-ended conversation about the meaning and value of different kinds of data.

We responded to this initial conversation and drafted a 500-word article imagining the couple's experience of wedding datagraphy. This incorporated a large portrait photo, and images of three fictional 'data artifacts', imagined to be produced after their wedding. The draft article was sent to the couple in advance, and the second meeting focused on editing and discussing it. These conversations allowed the couples to identify and represent themselves through the data, and speculate about its prospective use – both as an *imagined* artifact and as the *actual* brochure to be published. In this respect, couples were engaged both in speculation about the service, but more immediately in impression management, with the datagrapher and through the article. Finally, both couples were posted the published wedding brochure [Fig. 7], delivered inside 'Rock & Roll Bride', a popular UK wedding magazine.

Data Artifacts

Images of the data artifacts formed the centerpiece of the articles. These were a bespoke design response, part of a dialogue between the couple and their datagrapher. They were proposed as mementos to represent their data, which we wanted the couples to see as reflecting them and their wedding. These artifacts were portrayed in print, through the brochure. There were three for each couple, who refined the data they displayed at the second meeting.

Annabelle & Calum

For Annabelle and Calum, their central artifact was an infographic printed onto the side of a big red bus [Fig. 3]. This included mainly aggregate data, such as the number of wedding guests, a graph of dance floor activity, and the total bar spend. (Remarkably, Annabelle still had a hotel receipt from her parents' 1971 wedding). In discussion with the datagrapher, the couple envisaged the bus as a large print to be displayed in their living room. They even asked for the original image so that they could rework it after their wedding with data they anticipated they could capture, a request demonstrating the depth of the couple's engagement with the artifact and the scope of a Datagraphy service.

A second data artifact was a set of coasters [Fig. 4], overlaid with the path of the couple's first dance, as well as turns and holds. Annabelle and Calum warmed to the coasters as playful and ambiguous. They imagined them as a conversation starter, around which tales could be spun.

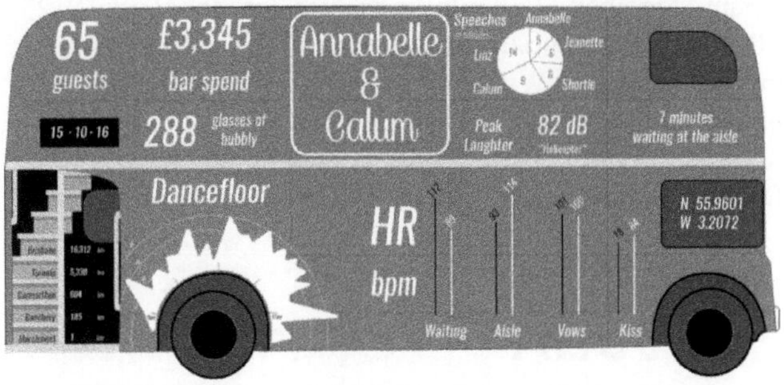

Figure 3: Annabelle & Rowan's bus infographic.

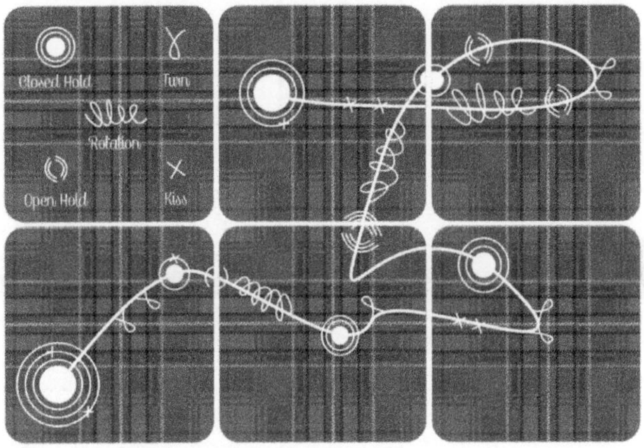

Figure 4: Coasters decorated with the pattern of a first dance.

Lastly, they were presented with a playing card declaring the precise time of their first kiss. The couple had actually included decorative playing cards in their invitations to their guests. During the enactment, the couple felt the exact time would become a ritual on their anniversary, as they would playfully recreate the moment. In design terms, it is notable how simple and memorable this data point is, it does not require elaborate representation. Like one's time of birth perhaps, this would be something that was simply known and remembered, rather than necessarily on display.

Julia & Rowan

Julia and Rowan envisaged a timeline of their day, not only of traditionally important events, but also amusing, unique or infelicitous moments that could index their character and the 'style' of the day [Fig. 5]. In many of our interviews, participants were curious about, and extraordinarily grateful for, the travel of their guests. Julia and Rowan imagined an interactive map that would (like a video) play out the trickle of guests arriving to their venue. As many guests knew each other, the couple anticipated this being of interest to their guests as well as to themselves.

Julia's sister is a florist, so the flower arrangements for their outdoor reception would be a significant and shared part of the event. The couple felt this could somehow be captured with data. Rowan and Julia imagined data about the quantity and variety of the flowers being bound up with photos of the flowers themselves [Fig. 6], perhaps in an album together. Felton's examples of 'photoviz' [23] illustrate the potential of this visual mixing of photographic images and data. Within the scope of this paper, we offer brief, bespoke examples that are limited to what we may represent in print. These illustrate the possible opportunities for valuable representations of documentary wedding data.

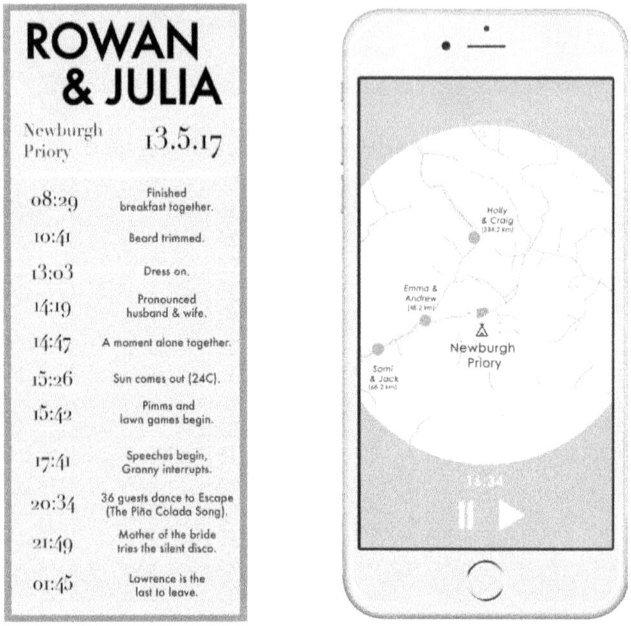

Figure 5: For Julia & Rowan, an alternative timeline of the day, and an interactive map of the arrival of their guests.

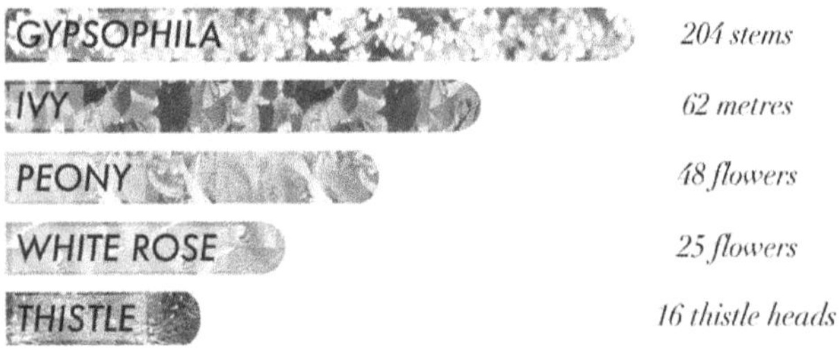

Figure 6: An infographic of the flowers at their wedding.

Brochure

The final 16-page, B5 brochure [Fig. 7] consists of: a front and back cover; an introduction to the Abacus service; and two 'real-wedding' stories. Its design mimics pullouts commonly found inside magazines, and is printed on glossy paper. The introduction gives a broad suggestion of a service in three parts; 'Collection; Processing; and Curation'. A datagrapher supports couples in deciding what data they could collect, capture and process, presenting numerous options for representing and sharing this data.

The immediate role of the brochure was as a boundary object, between the datagrapher and participating couple, as well as to give some consequential outcome to the enactment. Ultimately, the brochure functions as a Design Fiction artifact [5]; it communicates a possible world in which Annabelle & Calum, and Julia & Rowan, were married with Abacus Datagraphy. It is important to note that the couples were not anonymized in the design research process – the brochure would be for them to keep, and perhaps reflect on, later. They were aware that the brochure would be published and used to promote future articulations of the concept, at wedding fairs or even in the media.

Analysis

The many outcomes from these activities – i.e. design workbooks, interviews, cards, brochures, enactments, design artifacts – are each available to many analytic lenses. Within the scope of this paper, we perform a higher-level analysis, reflecting both on our engagement with the speculation, as designers and reflective practitioners [48], as well as our participants' responses to it. Practically, we have reflected on many field notes, our design workbooks, and interviews, as well as the resulting design artifacts – the Abacus Data Cards, the data artifacts, and the brochure.

In pursuing 'Lived Informatics' [45] our perspective is phenomenological and experience-centered [56]; we attempt to convey the felt experience of documentary tracking, and the way this speculation became interwoven with people's lives. We first describe our understanding of the central values and motivations in documenting a wedding with data, drawn primarily from interviews and enactments with the Abacus Data Cards. Secondly, we reflect on the design of the Abacus service and data artifacts to elicit design considerations for documentary tracking.

Figure 7: The wedding brochure. (Left to right) Annabelle and Calum; Julia and Rowan; an introduction to Abacus' services.

WHY DOCUMENT A WEDDING WITH DATA

Through early interviews, and especially the enactments, our participants presented a range of values for documenting their wedding with data. In general terms, our interview participants painted a picture of their wedding as a wonderful but overwhelming experience. Those already married described how the event flew by so quickly; it took a long time to appreciate and make sense of the day. Over time, memories of the day settled into a series of anecdotes about key moments, and photographs were framed or collated in albums. There are desires to relive parts of the day, but this unfolds slowly, in the months and years following the wedding, with friends and family.

In these accounts, data was variously approached as a means to gain some purchase on the bewildering day: to create a new perspective; to highlight particular events; to acknowledge the event as a set of achievements; to show people having fun celebrating. Throughout, participants engaged with the prospect of documentary data quite *playfully*. Data did not seem to carry the same 'weight' as official or formal posed photographs might. This was not *"scientific collection"* but often more *"anecdotal funny"* data (P12). This lightness was perhaps a reaction to data that might be too determinative, jarring with the 'magic' [35], which people seek to reconstruct after the event.

But while much data would be something *"fun to know"* at the time, it was not always anticipated as something to really remember. Numbers can matter immensely in the successful planning of the day, but quickly fade from view. Data that might be valued longer term tended to do what we might call *'wedding work'* for a couple, in three main ways. 1) It represented their experience; 2) It represented the wedding itself; 3) It played a social role. Clearly, photos, videos and mementos are the main outlet for this work. But these illustrate ways in which participants were able to transpose the values and experiences of wedding documentary onto quantified data.

Representing their personal experience as a couple

Participants often personally related to data that had a particular likeness to their own experiences, or invited them to tell specific stories from their day. '*Nine minutes alone together'* rang true for several individuals. Participants weren't clear that they would explicitly set out to record such data, but on reflection, it was evocative when it aptly defined a felt experience. "*The heels thing's hilarious because I took mine off instantly after I got out of the ceremony.*" [P3] Relatedly, participants identified data that expressed their personal touches. '*19:29, the 12 minute cigar'* stood out to one participant, for whom cigars were "*a big thing"* [P3] in her groom's family. In this case, the data itself is perhaps less significant than the topic of cigars. The data is used to signify that cigars are something that matter, and are worthy of record. Annabelle & Calum's bus is a 'data portrait' [12] that signifies and calls out all of their interests. "*We love the bus, big time. Like an image of that for us to keep would be great.*" For well travelled couples, a map of where their guests had arrived from was almost universally appealing. Such a map in itself says much about the couples' own identity and geography.

Representing the wedding day

Data could be reflective of a wedding's thematic styling; Julia and Rowan felt their timeline reflected the rustic and relaxed feel they hoped for their wedding. Other data highlighted distinctive or highly personalized parts of the day, which often had become part of the telling. For a couple married on a cold February day, the weather, and temperature were significant. *"It's something that we remember about the day, that it was really cold, but it was a really nice day. It'd be just quite nice to have some figures associated with that... it shaped quite a few things"* [P8]. Seeking to capture data about a first kiss, or steps down the aisle was often simply another way of marking the importance of these moments, rather than an intense curiosity about whether one walked 28 or 32 steps.

Data can have an aggregating quality, providing totals and summaries. In documenting a wedding, this was imagined to *show the achievement* of the wedding day itself. The extent of guests' travel, the total number of glasses of champagne, the numerous handshakes, the time everyone finally went to bed: these all speak of that unique 'piecing together' [49] of things and the collective efforts of many people to make the wedding happen.

Social roles of data

Many sought data that would become a *"talking point"*. Heart rate might playfully reveal who was the most nervous or excited. Rowan imagined telling his future children *"Do you know how long your mum took to get ready? I was left waiting for 45 minutes!"*. Records, such as the bar bill, or the longest confetti line [P3] were anticipated as details to be raised with friends. Others sought to use data to recognize significant roles that others played in the day – such as time spent with bridesmaids [P1], creating flower settings together [Julia], or making a playlist [P5].

Sharing wedding data was conceived in the same way as sharing wedding photos. For example, some considered incorporating data *"as a really nice thing to put in thank you letters"* [P1]. However, there was awareness of data that could be contentious or sensitive, particularly relating to the expense of a wedding, or revealing of family politics.

DESIGN REFLECTIONS

Though it is important to underline the potential motivations for documenting a wedding with data in the first place, our focus in this paper is primarily on the *design* of services and technologies to support this.

Documentary data as a resource for action

Harper et al. [30] describe memory-as-a-resource-for-action. In line with the socio-cultural study of memory, this perspective emphasizes that *remembering* is not simply the recall, or record of events (as suggested by lifelogging).

Instead, remembering entails the inevitably social and cultural ways in which the past is incorporated, and brought to bear on the present [30,36]. As a parallel, Frohlich et al. [47] suggest, *"photos operate not as copies of reality but as statements people can make about themselves"*.

Our point is that **the purpose of documenting a wedding is *not* to obtain a complete, unerring record of the day, but as a resource for particular kinds of remembering.** Everything that is captured – video, photos and mementos – are inevitably, and subjectively, edited down, and very often stored away. Photographers do not promise clients 'the most accurate record of your wedding', nor do they produce 'evidence'. Many see their documentary photography as an art – producing just one possible representation of the day. One photographer we spoke to described his role as *"taking the whole wedding, and breaking it down into small little moments, which together make the entire wedding"* [P2]. Another prioritized taking *"one killer image"* [P11].

Indeed, some couples eschew too much documentation, lest it diminish the experience *as remembered* or disturb their own *"holistic memory"* [P1]. The choices couples face – about which photographer to hire, for how long, whether or not to also record video, or to record the speeches, and so on – are oriented towards accomplishing remembering that couples anticipate being important for them. Our effort through this inquiry has been to explore the qualities of data *as a documentary medium* in order to consider how our participants, and our own design work, could appropriate data as a new resource with which to do 'wedding work'.

Designing poetic data

Quantified data connotes scientific precision and objectivity. Yet, it is clear that a precise record is rarely a valued a way of remembering a wedding. For weddings in particular, people tend to want to remember the magic, and not necessarily all the details [35]. Further, there is a contrast between naturally reconstructive human remembering [4] and the kind of certainty offered by data-driven descriptions of the world [11]. This presents a fundamental design challenge for data as a personal documentary medium. In wedding datagraphy, it has meant playing with what one participant called *"a poetic response"* [P1]. This is not only to romantically propose *data as art*: rather, to highlight the way data can succinctly distil some essence of the experience. Masses of data could be constructed as 'true', but evoke almost nothing of the experience, hence meaning little in this context.

Cartier-Bresson, French master of candid photography, describes his search for the *"decisive moment"* to take a photograph, which recognized *"the significance of an event as well as of a precise organization of forms which give that event its proper expression."*[6]. The wedding datagrapher is not then a scientist or a technician: just as the job of a wedding photographer and a police photographer are utterly different. Part of the datagrapher's presumed skill is being able to capture and present data that *"give that event its proper expression"*. Massimi et al. emphasize the recording of *"special moments of spectacle that act as indices into the event"* [33]. The forms of data chosen for Annabelle and Rowan's bus seek to do this. Like a collage, we imagine a new detail drawing attention at each glance.

In our inquiry, we have been more concerned with the experience of remembering than with its precise recall – with those memories that bring joy, comfort, or a shared sense of identity, even if the details might become hazy, or change over time. Hence representations of data that seem to aptly sum up a couple, or that chime with visceral experience-as-remembered, became more valuable than even data that gives a more 'accurate' picture of the day.

Data as an alternative lens

As we have described, weddings are momentous events. They make for overwhelming personal experiences. Part of the role of documenting a wedding is to grapple with, and to at least partially pin down, defining experiences from it. Datagraphy offered further hooks into remembering, understanding, and reconstructing experience. On occasion, we found data could express context or details – e.g. distance, heart rate, playlists – that other media lacked. Like the effort of guest's travels: *"photographs, it doesn't capture that at all"* [P6]. But more often, data provided another focus on significant details already captured by photo or video - the exact moment of marriage, the colors of the day, or one's steps down the aisle. In this way, data acted as an alternative lens that was valued because it might offer another viewpoint on particular special moments. Presentationally, data was frequently imagined alongside photographs – either as context, or as an artifact or index that would encourage seeking out other mementos.

This is an approach to documentary recognizing that a complete representation of the entire wedding is inevitably beyond reach. The experience is always unfinalized, and is continually open to being made sense of by others, from a multitude of perspectives that may change over time [2, 56]. The playfulness of the events represented on Rowan & Julia's timeline suggests an alternative to the official schedule, or expected milestones of the day. We became aware of avoiding data that has a totalizing effect or presenting things as unequivocally so. One participant rejected the idea of an exact transcript of his speech, but imagined keywords or word counts as a more ambiguous alternative, open to interpretation: *"...enough that if you were there it would be a prompt, a reminder of that story but it didn't give away the details" [P12].*

Data, Photos and Video

In the course of our speculation, datagraphy was rarely presented or interpreted as competing with other media. Of course in practice, in terms of a couple's budget, space and time on the day, this may not be so. Nonetheless, a lot of attention in this project concerned the differing qualities of video, photo and data as documentary media.

Video appears to divide opinion, with many couples not stretching to the expense, or only recording specific parts of the day, such as the ceremony or the speeches. Video requires performance [44] and dedicated attention to sit down and watch it. One photographer described video as "*impressive – it impresses emotion on to you*" [P11]. By contrast, he suggested photography was more extractive, and candid photography allowed people to remember being in a particular moment. A number of others reflected this sentiment – that photographs, especially candid ones, could "*stretch a moment out*" [P2], and generated an imaginative space around them, which invited reflection.

Our instinct was to imagine data that worked in a similar extractive way. From a poetic standpoint, data can be remarkably compact and pointed, inviting opportunities to imaginatively contextualize around the data. This resonates with findings from the Metadating event [18] emphasizing the discursive value of ambiguity around data. Presenting only the time of a first kiss invites remembering of that moment, and for Annabelle and Rowan, subsequent ritual on their anniversary. Data could expansively be used to document every moment of the couples whereabouts on the day – but we would suggest this is not its documentary power. Instead **it can deeply and succinctly cut through to particular aspects of the experience** which mediate valued remembering. As the datagrapher, we sought data that provoked imagination, ahead of providing explanation.

Designing for social remembering

Remembering weddings is particularly collective. These are not just personal experiences. While the couple is the centre of attention, many people share and participate in the documentation and remembering of the day. Yet, as personal informatics, Elsden et al. [17] note that data can appear particularly ego-centric. A challenge of wedding datagraphy was to make data sociable.

We found interest in producing representations of data, such as the coasters of a first dance: left at hand and easily encountered, drifting in and out of attention. These were available as *"talking points"* for guests in the home. In this way, the ambiguity of Annabelle & Calum's 'first dance' coasters, supported a social curiosity. Aggregate data, to which all the guests had contributed, or within which they could identify themselves also appealed. A photographer described making a 'wedding wall'. He photographed every guest individually against a wall, and then stitched the individual images together to create a large print showing every guest at the wedding. Reportedly guests try and find themselves in the picture, appreciating their place at the wedding. We considered how Rowan & Julia's interactive guest map might have a similar inviting effect.

Curating Documentary Data

Within the Quantified Self movement, it is widely acknowledged that the challenge is no longer just gathering 'enough' data; it is about being able to make sense of it. This goes beyond simply making the data digestible. In the wedding context, curation concerned marking things out as worthy of recording in the first place; such choices already invest meaning and expectation in the data.

Media curation takes place throughout: in the decisions made beforehand about what to record (perhaps by the datagrapher on the day); and subsequently in the choice of means to represent the data. Perhaps most interestingly, the project raises questions about who plays this curatorial role. A photographer is usually trusted to take, and curate the best few hundred photos, but as Julia suggests: "*Our photographer is just going to give us loads of photos... Because I would choose the ones I want myself.*" Arguably, people are much more literate in the use and curation of photos than data. So what then are the boundaries for curation and authorship of data? If the couple were to have the raw data, what form would this take? A dashboard? A CSV file or spreadsheet?

Summary

We have located the roots of our speculative inquiry in Rooskby et al.'s 'documentary style' of personal tracking, and the use of quantified data towards remembering and self-expression. Though weddings are a special case for documentary, they are nonetheless a prosaic concern, broadly experienced and relatable, providing a crucible for us to explore the potential of Documentary Informatics. Further work should certainly explore the degree to which the documentary practices of a wedding might translate to the documentary of 'day-to-day' life connoted as 'Lived Informatics'. Still, we suggest that these Design Reflections are foundational for a new documentary approach to the design of data-driven tools that prioritize documenting one's activities rather than changing them.

OPPORTUNITIES FOR DOCUMENTARY INFORMATICS

Below, we suggest a series of opportunities and challenges, in an effort to advance the design and research of Documentary Informatics tools.

Snapshot Datagraphy

Support the crafting of spontaneous 'snapshots' with data, as distinct from documenting pre-conceived activities.

Through the design of the Abacus service, and particularly the enactments, it became apparent that preparing to capture data about the wedding event often required anticipating things that would happen. Couples told us that cigars were important, or that they were interested in the activity on the dance floor. Practically, these would need to be attentively set up for measurement or observation.

Akin to Cartier-Bresson [6], the roving candid wedding photographer is attentive to key moments, but also able to pivot, and capture events as they unfold. These impromptu moments – like grandad playing with his grandson – are often some of the most valued. In contrast, the datagrapher seems constrained. Whereas photos can be conceived of, and taken in an instant, data capture seems to occur over a much longer period of time.

Leading from this, can we imagine new ways in which one might take spontaneous 'snapshots' with data? What tools might a datagrapher carry on the day? Wilkens [54] designed a 'weather camera' device for example. Fundamentally, we imagine these might be tools to rapidly count with; ways of making categories; means of following movement, perhaps. Nicholas Felton's app 'Reporter' [22] offers a highly customizable reporting interface to regularly quantify things people care about, in self-defined terms. What might a more real-time, in the moment, approach to such applications offer? Data analytics and graphics company Chryon Hego employ analysts to capture live data from sports events using Xbox controllers [7]. The latest GoPro wearable cameras now overlay telemetry data in real-time [28]. This sort of functionality, channeled through a smartphone app, could create intriguing new possibilities for 'snapshot' datagraphy.

Providing new orientations to traditional media

Data could significantly shape alternative orientations to photography.

Another way to read our design efforts here would be as an exploration into whether or not quantified data could take on some of the documentary qualities of photography. We do see a lot of value in this inquiry, but the dominant role of photography as a technology of memory [51] is clear. A fitting role for data could be in supporting different orientations to photography, and possibly video as well. The use of 'smart journal' applications, combining multiple media and data streams already hints at this possibility [16].

In the first instance, this requires ways of linking representations of data to media – for example, Rowan imagined the interactive guest map as an alternative platform for guests' photos. While there may always be a traditional chronological narrative to one's photo album or wedding video, documentary informatics could provide a non-linear mapping through vast media records.

Physicalizing as curating a fixed form

Giving data a fixed form forces active curation and meaning making.

The nature of designing a printed brochure with our engaged couples saw the curation of data mainly by giving it physical form. This also fitted with expectations of printing and framing wedding photos, and displaying mementos in the home. On reflection, we find that the physical nature of the bus infographic, the timeline, and the coasters created a fixed form for data. Committing to these physical forms contrasts with digital representations of data, which are highly malleable, and subject to frequent transformations and inter-connection. As a design opportunity, we suggest committing to a more fixed form enhances the long-term value of the representation. Not only is the data at hand, developing a sense of possession; but by making choices about their data's embodiment, couples invested it with meaning and personality. Data can then *settle in place* [50] as part of the rituals and anecdotes, which develop in the couple's practices of remembering their wedding. Documentary informatics tools might encourage these sort of curatorial and framing exercises.

New editorial roles

Data can require extensive editing and curation, opening up new editorial roles.

One trend from our inquiry has been our participants' preferences for certain specifics and particulars around which remembering could be oriented. As such, the data that could document a wedding requires extensive editing and curation. The Abacus service suggests that a datagrapher takes on much of this work. Photographers and videographers agree broad instructions, but are then trusted to capture and edit the highlights of the day as they choose. Our participants were quite directly involved in deciding the data that would be captured and represented. As a service, we imagined differing degrees of engagement, from bespoke design with couples, to pre-selected package products. Documentary Informatics should address the nature of these editorial roles, whether automated in places, or divided between individuals and services.

CONCLUSIONS AND FUTURE WORK

Given our speculative framing, we were unconcerned with technical implementations of a wedding datagraphy service. Still, the prospect of documenting a wedding with quantified data was entirely plausible, and welcomed by our participants. Through this speculation, we have been able to explore the values and design considerations for materials, tools and services that prioritize documentary uses of quantified data. Just as Rooksby et al. find users sometimes appropriating existing personal trackers in a 'documentary style', we have sought to demonstrate here the case for the explicit design of Documentary Informatics tools. Our exploratory findings and the design opportunities we describe in this paper are first steps, providing impetus and opportunity for future work within the DIS and broader HCI community. We might turn to the rich history of documentary studies as a discipline, to consider how many different modes of documentary may translate, or be represented with, quantified data. A wedding is a very particular event to document, after all. Beyond speculation, we might develop functioning design artifacts or mobile apps, for design-led and empirical studies of Documentary Informatics in the day-to-day. We hope through our own investigation of wedding datagraphy, we have been able to inspire future work in this direction.

ACKNOWLEDGMENTS

We would like to thank all of the many colleagues and participants who we engaged in this speculative work, but especially our two engaged couples Annabelle & Calum, and Julia & Rowan, without whom this work would not have been possible. Thank you also to the thoughtful anonymous reviewers. The second author was supported by The Leverhulme Trust (ECF-2012-642) and the third and fourth authors by the EPSRC (EP/N005848/2).

REFERENCES

1. James Auger. 2013. Speculative design: crafting the speculation. *Digital Creativity* 24, 1: 11–35.
2. Mikhail Bakhtin. 1981. *The dialogic imagination: Four essays*. University of Texas Press.
3. Richard Banks. 2011. *The future of looking back*. O'Reilly Media, Inc.
4. Frederic C. Bartlett. 1932. Remembering: An experimental and social study. *Cambridge: Cambridge University*.
5. Julian Bleecker. 2009. Design Fiction: A short essay on design, science, fact and fiction. *Near Future Laboratory* 29.
6. Henri Cartier-Bresson. 2014. *The Decisive Moment*. Simon & Schuster.
7. Matthew Champion. 2015. Here's what the man with an Xbox controller at St James' Park was actually doing. Retrieved April 4th, 2017 from https://www.indy100.com/article/heres-what-the-man-with-an-xbox-controller-at-st-james-park-was-actually-doing--Zk5NjoxLBg
8. Eun Kyoung Choe, Nicole B. Lee, Bongshin Lee, Wanda Pratt, and Julie A. Kientz. 2014. Understanding Quantified-selfers' Practices in Collecting and Exploring Personal Data. In *Proceedings of the SIGCHI Conference on Human Factors in Computing Systems* (CHI '14), 1143–1152. https://doi.org/10.1145/2556288.2557372
9. Jenny Davis. 2013. The Qualified Self. Retrieved April 4th, 2017 from http://thesocietypages.org/cyborgology/2013/03/13/the-qualified-self/
10. José van Dijck. 2013. *The culture of connectivity: A critical history of social media*. Oxford University Press.
11. José van Dijck. 2014. Datafication, dataism and dataveillance: Big Data between scientific paradigm and ideology. *Surveillance & Society* 12, 2: 197–208.
12. Judith Donath, Alex Dragulescu, Aaron Zinman, Fernanda Viégas, and Rebecca Xiong. 2010. Data portraits. In *ACM SIGGRAPH 2010 Art Gallery*, 375–383. http://dx.doi.org/10.1145/1836786.1836793
13. Anthony Dunne and Fiona Raby. 2013. *Speculative everything: design, fiction, and social dreaming*. MIT Press.
14. Chris Elsden, David Chatting, Abigail C. Durrant, Andrew Garbett, Bettina Nissen, John Vines, and David S. Kirk. 2017. On Speculative Enactments. In *Proceedings of the 2017 CHI Conference on Human Factors in Computing Systems* (CHI '17), Forthcoming. http://dx.doi.org/10.1145/3025453.3025503
15. Chris Elsden, Abigail C. Durrant, David Chatting, David Green, and David S. Kirk. 2017. Abacus Datagraphy: A Speculative Enactment. In *3rd Biennial Research Through Design Conference. 2017.* https://figshare.com/articles/Abacus_Datagraphy_A_Speculative_Enactment/4746961
16. Chris Elsden, Abigail C. Durrant, and David S. Kirk. 2016. It's Just My History Isn't It?: Understanding Smart Journaling Practices. In *Proceedings of the 2016 CHI Conference on Human Factors in Computing Systems* (CHI '16), 2819–2831. https://doi.org/10.1145/2858036.2858103
17. Chris Elsden, David S. Kirk, Abigail C. Durrant. 2016. A quantified past: Toward design for remembering with personal informatics. *Human–Computer Interaction*, *31*(6), 518-557. https://doi.org/10.1080/07370024.2015.1093422
18. Chris Elsden, Bettina Nissen, Andrew Garbett, David Chatting, David S. Kirk, and John Vines. 2016. Metadating: Exploring the Romance and Future of Personal Data. In *Proceedings of the 2016 CHI Conference on Human Factors in Computing Systems* (CHI '16), 685–698. https://doi.org/10.1145/2858036.2858173
19. Chris Elsden, Mark Selby, Abigail C. Durrant, and David S. Kirk. 2016. Fitter, happier, more productive: what to ask of a data-driven life. *interactions* 23, 5: 45–45. https://doi.org/10.1145/2975388
20. Daniel A. Epstein, Bradley H. Jacobson, Elizabeth Bales, David W. McDonald, and Sean A. Munson. 2015. From "Nobody Cares" to "Way to Go!": A Design Framework for Social Sharing in Personal Informatics. In *Proceedings of the 18th ACM Conference on Computer Supported Cooperative Work & Social Computing* (CSCW '15), 1622–1636. https://doi.org/10.1145/2675133.2675135
21. Daniel A. Epstein, An Ping, James Fogarty, and Sean A. Munson. 2015. A Lived Informatics Model of Personal Informatics. In *Proceedings of the 2015 ACM International Joint Conference on Pervasive and Ubiquitous Computing* (UbiComp '15), 731–742. https://doi.org/10.1145/2750858.2804250
22. Nicholas Felton. 2014. Reporter App. Retrieved April 4th, 2017 from http://www.reporter-app.com/
23. Nicholas Felton. 2016. *Photoviz*. Gestalten.
24. Nicholas Felton. 2014. *2014 Feltron Annual Report*. Retrieved April 4th, 2017 from http://feltron.com/FAR14.html
25. Christopher Frayling. 1993. Research in art and design.

26. Bill Gaver, Tony Dunne, and Elena Pacenti. 1999. Design: cultural probes. *interactions* 6, 1: 21–29. https://dx.doi.org/10.1145/291224.291235

27. William Gaver. 2011. Making Spaces: How Design Workbooks Work. In *Proceedings of the SIGCHI Conference on Human Factors in Computing Systems* (CHI '11), 1551–1560. https://doi.org/10.1145/1978942.1979169

28. GoPro. Telemetry and GPS Add New Layers to Your GoPro Story. Retrieved April 4th, 2017 from https://gopro.com/news/New-Telemetry-Feature-Quik-Desktop-App

29. Nanna Gorm and Irina Shklovski. 2016. Sharing Steps in the Workplace: Changing Privacy Concerns Over Time. In *Proceedings of the 2016 CHI Conference on Human Factors in Computing Systems* (CHI '16), 4315–4319. https://doi.org/10.1145/2858036.2858352

30. Richard Harper, David Randall, Nicola Smyth, Carwyn Evans, Lisa Heledd, and R. Moore. 2008. The past is a different place: they do things differently there. In *Proceedings of the 7th ACM conference on Designing interactive systems* (DIS '08), 271–280. http://dx.doi.org/10.1145/1394445.1394474

31. IDEO. 2003. Method Cards. Retrieved April 4th, 2017 from https://www.ideo.com/post/method-cards

32. Da-jung Kim, Yeoreum Lee, Saeyoung Rho, and Youn-kyung Lim. 2016. Design Opportunities in Three Stages of Relationship Development Between Users and Self-Tracking Devices. In *Proceedings of the 2016 CHI Conference on Human Factors in Computing Systems* (CHI '16), 699–703. https://doi.org/10.1145/2858036.2858148

33. Amanda Lazar, Christian Koehler, Joshua Tanenbaum, and David H. Nguyen. 2015. Why we use and abandon smart devices. In *Proceedings of the 2015 ACM International Joint Conference on Pervasive and Ubiquitous Computing*, 635–646. http://dx.doi.org/10.1145/2750858.2804288

34. Ian Li, Anind Dey, and Jodi Forlizzi. 2010. A stage-based model of personal informatics systems. In *Proceedings of the SIGCHI Conference on Human Factors in Computing Systems* (CHI '10), 557–566. http://dx.doi.org/10.1145/1753326.1753409

35. Michael Massimi, Richard Harper, and Abigail J. Sellen. 2014. "Real, but Glossy": Technology and the Practical Pursuit of Magic in Modern Weddings. In *Proceedings of the 17th ACM Conference on Computer Supported Cooperative Work & Social Computing* (CSCW '14), 854–865. https://doi.org/10.1145/2531602.2531682

36. David Middleton and Steven D. Brown. 2005. *The social psychology of experience: Studies in remembering and forgetting*. Sage.

37. Andrew D. Miller and W. Keith Edwards. 2007. Give and take: a study of consumer photo-sharing culture and practice. In *Proceedings of the SIGCHI Conference on Human Factors in Computing Systems* (CHI' 07), 347–356. http://dx.doi.org/10.1145/1240624.1240682

38. Dawn Nafus. 2016. *Quantified: Biosensing technologies in everyday life*. MIT Press.

39. William Odom, Richard Banks, David Kirk, Richard Harper, Siân Lindley, and Abigail Sellen. 2012. Technology heirlooms?: considerations for passing down and inheriting digital materials. In *Proceedings of the SIGCHI Conference on Human Factors in Computing Systems* (CHI' 12), 337–346. http://dx.doi.org/10.1145/2207676.2207723

40. William Odom, John Zimmerman, and Jodi Forlizzi. 2014. Placelessness, spacelessness, and formlessness: experiential qualities of virtual possessions. In *Proceedings of the 2014 conference on Designing interactive systems* (DIS '14), 985–994. http://dx.doi.org/10.1145/2598510.2598577

41. Mimi Onohua. 2015. Pathways. Retrieved April 4th, 2017, from http://www.nationalgeographic.com/pathways/

42. Stefanie Posavec and Giorgia Lupi. 2016. *Dear Data*. Penguin.

43. Jill Walker Rettberg. 2014. *Seeing ourselves through technology: How we use selfies, blogs and wearable devices to see and shape ourselves*. Palgrave Macmillan.

44. Sean Rintel, Richard Harper, and Kenton O'Hara. 2016. The Tyranny of the Everyday in Mobile Video Messaging. In *Proceedings of the 2016 CHI Conference on Human Factors in Computing Systems*, (CHI '16), 4781–4792. https://doi.org/10.1145/2858036.2858042

45. John Rooksby, Mattias Rost, Alistair Morrison, and Matthew Chalmers Chalmers. 2014. Personal Tracking As Lived Informatics. In *Proceedings of the 32nd Annual ACM Conference on Human Factors in Computing Systems* (CHI '14), 1163–1172. https://doi.org/10.1145/2556288.2557039

46. Tony Salvador, Genevieve Bell, and Ken Anderson. 1999. Design ethnography. *Design Management Journal (Former Series)* 10, 4: 35–41.

47. Risto Sarvas and David M. Frohlich. 2011. *From snapshots to social media-the changing picture of*

domestic photography. Springer Science & Business Media.

48. Donald A. Schön. 1983. *The reflective practitioner: How professionals think in action*. Basic books.

49. Tamar Sharon. 2016. Self-Tracking for Health and the Quantified Self: Re-Articulating Autonomy, Solidarity, and Authenticity in an Age of Personalized Healthcare. *Philosophy & Technology*: 1–29. https://doi.org/10.1007/s13347-016-0215-5

50. Alex S. Taylor, Siân Lindley, Tim Regan, David Sweeney, Vasillis Vlachokyriakos, Lillie Grainger, and Jessica Lingel. 2015. Data-in-Place: Thinking through the Relations Between Data and Community. In *Proceedings of the 33rd Annual ACM Conference on Human Factors in Computing Systems* (CHI' 15), 2863–2872. https://doi.org/10.1145/2702123.2702558

51. Nancy Van House and Elizabeth F. Churchill. 2008. Technologies of memory: Key issues and critical perspectives. *Memory Studies* 1, 3: 295–310.

52. Nancy Van House, Marc Davis, Morgan Ames, Megan Finn, and Vijay Viswanathan. 2005. The uses of personal networked digital imaging: an empirical study of cameraphone photos and sharing. In *CHI'05 Extended Abstracts on Human Factors in Computing Systems*, 1853–1856. http://dx.doi.org/10.1145/1056808.1057039

53. Peter West, Richard Giordano, Max Van Kleek, and Nigel Shadbolt. 2016. The Quantified Patient in the Doctor's Office: Challenges & Opportunities. In *Proceedings of the 2016 CHI Conference on Human Factors in Computing Systems* (CHI '16), 3066–3078. https://doi.org/10.1145/2858036.2858445

54. Kjen Wilkens. 2010. Sensor Poetics. Retrieved April 4th, 2017 from http://www.di10.rca.ac.uk/kjenwilkens/

55. Gary Wolf. 2010. The data-driven life. *The New York Times* 28. Retrieved April 4th, 2017 from http://www.nytimes.com/2010/05/02/magazine/02self-measurement-t.html

56. Peter Wright and John McCarthy. 2004. *Technology as experience*. MIT Press.

57. John Zimmerman, Jodi Forlizzi, and Shelley Evenson. 2007. Research through design as a method for interaction design research in HCI. In *Proceedings of the SIGCHI Conference on Human Factors in Computing Systems*, (CHI' 07), 493–502. http://dx.doi.org/10.1145/1240624.1240704

Digital Systems and the Experience of Legacy

Rebecca Gulotta[1], Aisling Kelliher[2], Jodi Forlizzi[1]
[1]Human-Computer Interaction Institute, Carnegie Mellon University,
{rgulotta, forlizzi}@cs.cmu.edu
[2] Computer Science, Virginia Tech, aislingk@vt.edu

ABSTRACT

As people generate large quantities of heterogeneous data across their lifetimes, there is an opportunity to consider how we might build digital systems that leverage this information to help people communicate aspects of their life for which they would like to be remembered without the need to directly assign or pass on this information to another person. We present a study that leverages existing research and the use of an online design probe to explore how people think about how they'll be remembered, and how digital systems and information might help shape how people look back on and interpret people's lives after they've passed away. Findings from this work articulate specific challenges and opportunities for building systems to support people's ability to engage with experiences and memories through their digital materials.

Author Keywords

Digital systems; legacy; memory; remembrance; family; design research; experience design; death and dying

ACM Classification Keywords

H.5.m. Information interfaces and presentation (e.g., HCI): Miscellaneous

INTRODUCTION

When a person dies, they leave behind digital information and media generated over the course of their life. As with physical artifacts, these digital representations of a person's experiences exist as a way that people may interpret, reflect on, and communicate aspects of a person's life, even long after they have passed away. Though digital materials may not change the fundamental desire to be remembered in a particular way or have a particular impact on future generations, the affordances, capabilities, and limitations of digital materials do influence how and when people engage in legacy-oriented or commemorative practices.

Our work seeks to understand how digital information and digital systems can communicate the various things that make up a person's legacy or remembrance without requiring that people directly assign a recipient or steward for their digital information. This work builds on existing work in HCI that has focused on the specific mechanisms of owning, managing, and passing on digital materials. Systems like Facebook's Legacy Contact and Google's Inactive Account Manager serve a valuable purpose ways to pass on specific accounts and permissions, but there is a need to understand how systems can support the many informal and unstructured ways that people engage with legacy and remembrance through the broader collections of heterogeneous digital materials left behind by other people. As a part of this work, we draw from participant's descriptions of how they experience aspects of the lives and legacies of people who have passed away.

Building on literature from death and dying studies [21, 25, 30, 40], the first part of this work investigates the particulars of what people want to pass on to future generations, how they want to be remembered, and how they think about the legacy they'll leave behind after they pass away. The second part of this work bridges death and dying studies and human-computer interaction to investigate how digital systems might engage with information that hasn't been assigned to another person or directly passed down. To investigate these questions, we developed a multi-methods study that consisted of four open-ended interviews interspersed within a 9 week deployment of an experimental website developed as a design probe. The "Retrospect" website used data from participants' Facebook accounts to explore the content and form of an individual's digital legacy and was used as a starting point for discussions about diverse types of digital information people share online.

Findings from this work reveal insights into how to approach building of digital systems can make use of digital information of the deceased to shape how a person will be remembered and to provide other people with the ability to engage with the lives of people who have passed away.

PRIOR WORK

This research draws on prior work that describes goals and obstacles associated with the creation of a legacy, articulates the ways that people deal with death and its implications online, and argues for the potential benefits of creating systems that sensitively engage with lifetimes or generations of digital materials. We provide an overview of

DIS 2017, June 10-14, 2017, Edinburgh, United Kingdom

ACM 978-1-4503-4922-2/17/06...$15.00
DOI: http://dx.doi.org/10.1145/3064663.3064731

that work below and where appropriate, in other sections of the paper. In doing so, we provide context for our work and identify areas where our research extends and contributes to existing knowledge. As our research work spans a number of genres, the content below is not exhaustive. Instead, this work was selected to highlight the ideas that influence and contextualize the work in this paper.

Before the review of prior work we feel that it's important to acknowledge that, in this paper, discussions about death, dying, legacy, and remembrance are most deeply influenced by Western perspectives and writings on those topics.

Legacy and life stories

This work is grounded, in part, in an understanding of the steps people take to shape how (and by whom) they'll be remembered. As people age, they are often motivated to consider and shape the impact their life has on the lives of others [40]. This process can have many parts, all of which contribute to the larger goal of leaving behind an impactful or enduring legacy [21, 36, 40]. For some people, the process of establishing a legacy involves passing on one's values to their children, friends, and communities [11]. For others, there is a desire to increase the longevity, size, or reach of one's impact on the world. To do so, people take steps to highlight meaningful aspects of their life and experiences through activities such as telling stories, accumulating objects, making donations to cultural or educational institutions, and by giving away symbolic objects to other people [25, 40].

However, the desire to be remembered or to have a particular impact on the world after one's death is not an entirely straightforward process. A legacy, like the performance of identity during a lifetime, is interpreted by the people to whom it is communicated. When a person passes away, people who mourn their death may integrate aspects of their life into their own [42]. A person's hopes for how they'll be remembered, however, may not align with how other people interpret or look back on their life. Instead, each person is influenced by their own values, memories, and perceptions of the deceased.

Dealing with death online

Though our work is focused on a multigenerational timeframe, it is also influenced by work from a variety of disciplines that examines the role that digital systems play directly before and after a person's death.

Before death, digital systems are sometimes used to help the dying find support and to share information about their experiences with death and terminal illness [39, 43]. Going beyond finding support and information, some digital systems also offer people the ability to record their wishes for post-mortem concerns, such as end-of-life care or funeral arrangements [13]. Caregivers also use online resources, like forums, to connect with people who can offer information and emotional support [45]. These services can be a valuable resource for the dying and their caregivers, family, and friends.

Post-mortem, digital platforms like social networks offer a space where people can share details about a person's life, grieve, and seek support from others [4, 23, 28]. Research in this area has demonstrated how online platforms have extended the groups of people who can participate in mourning a person's death and has made elements of this experience more public. The bereaved also use digital spaces to memorialize the dead [13, 32]. Doing so provides them with a way to connect with other people, share information about the deceased, create a space for people to grieve, and create an enduring reflection of a person's life.

After a person passes away they leave behind a vast assortment of digital materials [27, 34]. These materials differ for each person, but often include social media accounts, photographs, financial information, and emails, and may be spread across a variety of different accounts, websites, and devices. Digital resources are also used to help people gather materials, like photographs and quotes, that can be used as a part of a funeral service [31].

Multigenerational systems

Looking beyond the period of time directly before or after a person's death, researchers have discussed the potential significance of intentionally creating systems designed to span generations. This work does not often focus directly on the subject of legacy or experience, but describes systems that serve similar purposes using similar types of digital materials.

This research on multigenerational systems suggests that such systems would make use of information created in the near and distant past for a variety of purposes: helping people unpack and address complex issues like war and genocide, helping people better understand their own lives, and mediating more meaningful interactions with digital materials and the physical world [2, 13]. Research in this area also raises concerns regarding the design of such systems, particularly the difficulty of finding meaningful content in larger archives, questions regarding the ownership of these digital materials beyond a person's lifetime, and the difficulty of engaging with large collections of digital materials [7, 12, 26]. These concerns are significant and reflect how the standard, well-understood challenges of managing personal digital information are further complicated by death and dying.

A synthesis of this literature reveals that there is an opportunity to design systems that have functionality to support death-related practices and needs. Much of the current research in this space has focused on system services like Facebook's Legacy Contact [11] that support the direct transmission of specific accounts or pieces of digital media from one person to another [5]. This work is significant (and likely meaningful for the many families who make use of those features). However, as we argue in this paper, it is important to consider how future systems might make sense of digital materials that are not managed in this way. Systems like Legacy Contact [11], Google's Inactive Account Manager [16], or beneficiary systems used by financial institutions will help people make plans for particularly meaningful accounts, but after that that there is a need for a different kind of system – one that can help people engage with the broader landscape of digital materials that people leave behind when they pass away.

One potential avenue for this work is the development of automated or assistive systems that curate large collections of digital information [16]. Such systems, the algorithmic precursors of which already influence the content people see online [10, 37], might someday be employed to help convey meaningful representations of another person's life and experiences, even after their death. In this paper, we explore how emerging computational capabilities of digital systems can help communicate legacy oriented ideas and materials. We also discuss ethical implications stemming from the development of such systems.

METHOD

We used a multi-methods approach for this research. Participants were asked to use Retrospect, a design probe we developed and populated with their data, for nine weeks and to participate in four interviews over that time period. Prior to developing Retrospect and collecting data from participants, we spent several months designing the system and corresponding interview protocols to ensure that each piece would help elicit information relevant to the goals of our work. In the sections below, we first describe the design and development process for Retrospect and the tasks that participants completed using that system. Our desire to describe the process of designing and developing Retrospect was influenced by work by Boehner et al. [3] that noted that this work is not often shared in research papers. We hope that this information will be useful for people interested in similar design research methods. After discussing Retrospect, we then describe the interview protocols and the information we set out to collect from participants through those interviews.

RETROSPECT SYSTEM DESIGN

After identifying that we were interested in learning about how people engage with the lives of people who have passed away and about their own understanding of how future generations of people will interpret what they leave behind, we began to design a probe that could use a person's digital information to facilitate and support conversations about the information that is captured and made visible by digital systems. In addition to addressing our research questions, we had several high-level goals for this system. First, we wanted the system to provide an engaging experience for participants to support their continued participation in this nine-week study. Second, it was important that the website be robust and able to handle potential issues with gathering and presenting user data over the duration of the study since participants would be using the system unsupervised at home.

Designs went through a number of iterations, but started with an analysis of the probes we'd developed as a part of prior research projects [17, 18]. This review highlighted the ongoing need for research that investigates how people and digital systems can collaboratively communicate important aspects of a person's life in the context of death and legacy. In addition, our design process for Retrospect was inspired, at a high level, by Wallace et al.'s work on personalized probes [41] and by Khovanskaya's work on probes using digital traces [22]. A critical decision we made at this stage was to create a digital probe that lived on the internet. There were a number of factors behind this decision: we wanted to create a system that could easily and flexibly make use of a participant's digital materials and we wanted a create a system that participants could use on their own outside of interview sessions.

We then set out to identify what information the probe would use. We explored the types of data that could be collected from the APIs provided by different websites including the US Census, social media sites like Facebook and Twitter, and location-based services like Google Maps and Yelp. Figure 1 and Figure 2 depict some early designs that we developed during this phase of the project.

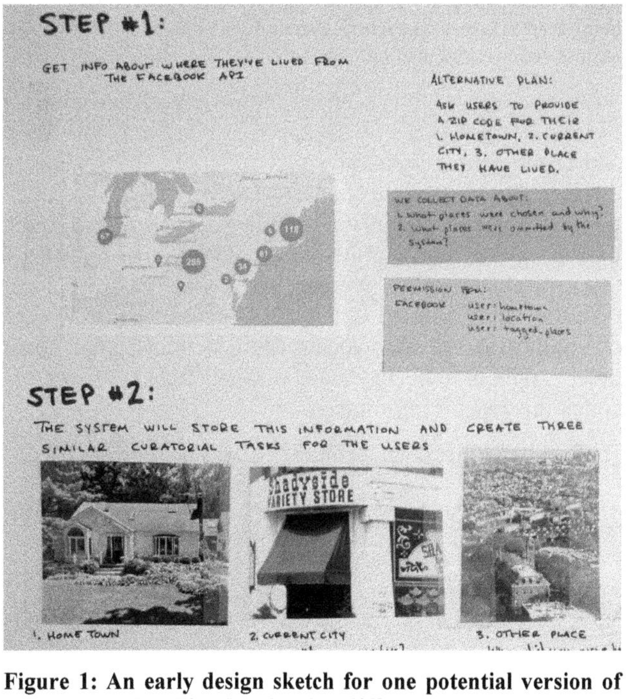

Figure 1: An early design sketch for one potential version of Retrospect. In this sketch, the different data sources we considered can be seen along with notes about how design decisions would allow us to ask particular research questions.

After reviewing our preliminary design work and the available data sources, we decided to build the probe using Facebook's API. We chose to use Facebook data for a number of reasons. Their API is well documented and there was a large group of developers using the API (which turned out to be immensely helpful when we ran into issues developing the probe). In addition, the popularity of Facebook allowed us to recruit from a larger, more diverse pool of potential participants than if we'd used services with fewer users or that were primarily used by tech savvy people. Finally, Facebook captures a wide range of information about different aspects of people's lives and we felt as though it would be a good way to foster conversations about people's digital information in general.

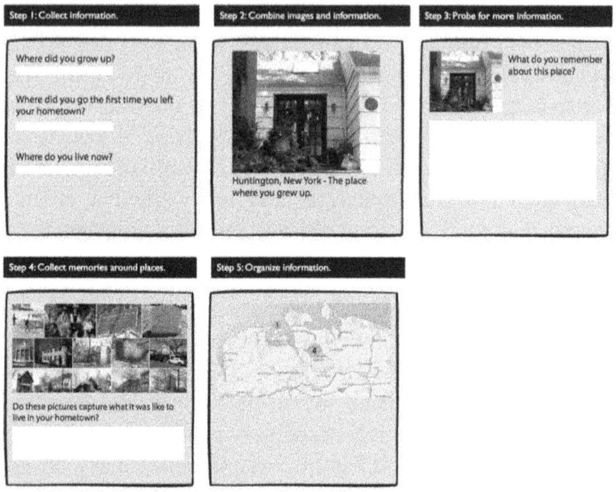

Figure 2: Another potential design for Retrospect. This design combined information from several data sources to help people curate information about places from their past.

After choosing to focus on information available through Facebook's API, we took the many designs we'd developed and experimented with ways that we could adapt some of these designs to make use of information available through the API while still addressing the larger goals of the study. Our work was also influenced by institutional guidelines that governed what information could be displayed, solicited, and captured about third parties, which limited our ability to ask participants detailed information about other people or to display materials that might inadvertently solicit this type of information.

Our probe, Retrospect (Figure 3), was a product of this iterative, exploratory process. At each stage in the design process we assessed how changes to our design might help us elicit more useful information both from and for our participants. At the end of this process, we produced a probe that gathered information from a participant's Facebook account and then used that information to prompt them to reflect on different aspects and stages of their life using their profile pictures, information about places they'd been, and information about different personal milestones with work, education, and relationships.

This information was used as the basis for nine tasks in three different categories: *place, milestone,* and *gallery* tasks. Participants were asked to complete three of each of these types of tasks (for a total of nine). For the place task, participants were asked to reflect on (1) what it was like to live in their hometown, (2) what motivated their decision to come to their current city, and (3) a place they'd been in the past that had been significant to them in some way. For the milestone task, participants were asked to reflect on what it was like to (1) attend and graduate or leave a school they'd attended, (2) work at some job they'd had, and (3) be a part of a relationship with another person. For the gallery tasks, participants were shown two profile pictures from different times and were asked to write about how their life had changed between the times when the photographs were taken. Participants had the option to refresh the page to get two new photos if they weren't interested in the photos that were being displayed.

As an important note, although Retrospect asked participants to reflect on aspects of their life, we were not formally interested in making any primary contributions to research on reflection [1, 38] and reminiscence [8]. Instead, in Retrospect we used reflection to help participants consider what information is available about them online, and how that accessible data aligns with their understanding of important aspects of their life and experiences.

Retrospect was developed using the Python programming language and was translated to the web using Flask, a framework for building and deploying websites using Python and a host of related services including SQLite3, a

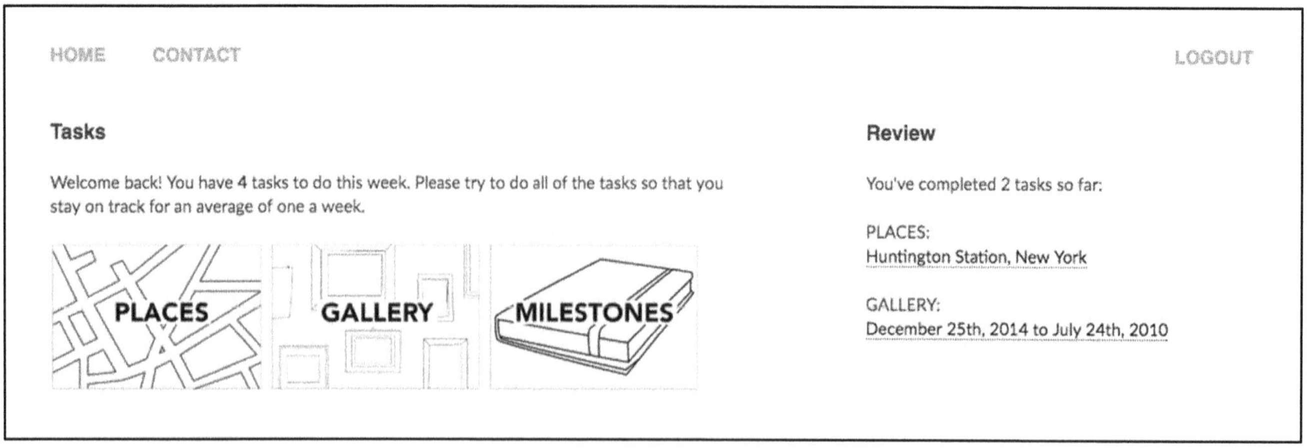

Figure 3: The Retrospect homepage. New tasks were shown on the left and completed tasks were available for review on the right.

data management tool. The website was hosted on the Python Anywhere platform which offered secure hosting and an appropriate level of functionality for a small website.

Each participant had a unique account on the Retrospect website that they set up during the first interview session by picking a username and password, and by authorizing Retrospect to access some of the information in their Facebook account. As a part of that authorization, Retrospect collected the following data from participants:

1. Their 50 most recent profile photos. For participants with less than 50 photos, the system simply collected however many they had.
2. Location information, including a person's hometown, current city, and any location they had tagged in a photograph or post.
3. Information about milestones or major events. This included a person's work history, education history, and relationship status.

Participants were not screened or excluded from the study based on the information they had in their Facebook profiles. As a result, the system did not always have all of the information that was used to build tasks for participants. When information was missing, participants were asked to supply that information. For example, if information was missing for a place or milestone task, participants were invited to choose a relevant milestone or location that had some significance to them and to answer the questions based on what they'd chosen. They also had the option to skip tasks for which they did not want to provide information.

All of the Facebook data used during the entire course of the study was stored in Retrospect's database as it was collected from the Facebook API during setup, which meant that the system did not have any information that was shared to a person's Facebook account after the start of the study. As a result, participants were welcome to rescind their Facebook authorization for Retrospect after this setup process had been completed. This helped streamline the process of using the Retrospect website, avoiding repeated user re-authorizations and reducing potential errors connecting to Facebook during the 9-week deployment. The Retrospect website also contained standard functionality to assist with common issues experienced using websites over time, including the ability for users to reset their passwords, send messages to the researchers from within the website, and access information about the study and the researchers (including a copy of the consent form). The Retrospect website was extensively tested before the main participant study through a series of pilot studies aimed at screening for possible errors and potential security issues.

INTERVIEWS

In addition to being asked to use Retrospect to complete a reflective task each week on their own time, participants participated in four interviews over the course of the nine week study.

First Session

The first session with each participant marked the start of nine weeks participating in the study. During the first interview session, we talked with participants about the goals and components of the project. After confirming that they still wanted to participate, we helped each participant set up their account on the Retrospect website, answered any questions they had about authorizing the website to access their Facebook data, and explained our institution's policy on participant data management and security. We then showed them the different types of tasks they'd be asked to do over the course of the study and showed them how to access parts of the website they could use to report errors, reset their password, and send us a message.

We also explained our use of Retrospect as a design probe. That is, we did not build Retrospect as a prototype, nor did we intend to use it outside of the study itself. Instead, we built it to better understand the aspects of a person's past that are shared online, to investigate how people perceive the value and impact of that information, and to ground, prompt, and guide discussions during the interview sessions.

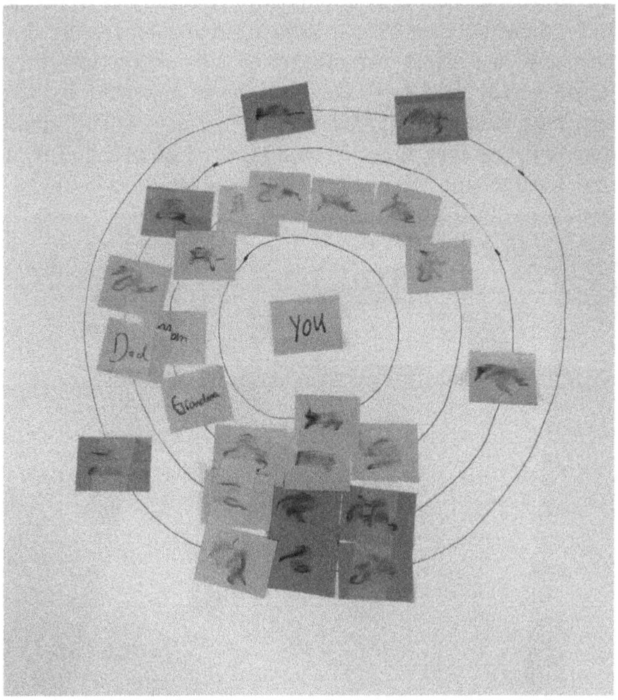

Figure 4: A participant's participant-aided sociogram. The names have been blurred to protect participant privacy.

We then conducted a short interview, lasting between 15 to 30 minutes, in which we asked each participant to give a brief overview of their life, to talk about the different websites they visit online, to talk about their experience using websites to revisit older content, and to describe their interest in reflecting on their own life. We also had participants complete a participant-aided sociogram [1], which are simple graphical representations useful for displaying, reflecting on, and interpreting social relationships. Following [1], participants wrote out the names of all of the people with whom they had 'very close' and 'somewhat close' relationships and then arranged them on concentric circles, positioning people relative to themselves and to each other. After the participant completed their sociogram, we asked them to describe their relationships with the people they'd included. Figure 4 shows a sociogram created by one of the participants.

Second Session

We scheduled a second interview with participants 2-3 weeks after the first interview. In this interview, we talked to participants about their experience using Retrospect and we then asked them to answer questions about their experiences making end of life plans (such as creating a will), their experiences talking to their parents or relatives about their deaths, their experience inheriting things from people who have passed away, and any recent or significance experience they'd had with the death of someone who was close to them. These interviews lasted about an hour.

Third Session

The third interview was scheduled for week 6 or 7 of the study, depending on the participant's schedule. During this interview, we asked participants to talk about how they define legacy and how they had been impacted by the legacy or memory of other people. We also talked about their sense of how their life and legacy had changed over time. On average, these interviews lasted about an hour.

Figure 5: For each participant, we created a booklet that contained excerpts of the information they shared with Retrospect. We gave these booklets to participants in the fourth interview session.

Fourth Session

We scheduled a final interview with each participant after 9 weeks. During this interview, we asked them to talk about the experience of using Retrospect. As a memory aid, we gave each participant a custom booklet containing excerpts of the responses they'd contributed to Retrospect so far. This booklet, an example of which is shown in Figure 5, reflected our interest in exploring how we might give participants access to the information they provided to the design probe. In the interview session, the physical format of the booklet provided an easy way for the researchers and the participants to review the information that a participant had contributed. Prior to creating and then looking through the booklet with each participant, we did not review the information they had contributed to the system. Because we did not intend to analyze the information participants wrote using Retrospect, we made the decision to give the participants the opportunity to share this information as it pertained to the interviews.

We also asked the participants to talk about their experiences researching their family history. Finally, we interviewed them about the different ways in which they document their life online and offline. These interviews lasted about an hour.

PARTICIPANTS

We recruited 10 adults to participate in the study through a local email list. Participants were selected that were diverse in age, stage of life, technological proficiency, family size and situation, gender, and socioeconomic status. To participate in this study, participants had to be at least 18 years old, have a tablet, laptop, or desktop computer in their home that could access the internet, and have a Facebook account. They also had to be comfortable with sharing their Facebook data with the Retrospect system, with participating in in-home interview sessions, and with joining a study that was designed to take place over nine weeks. Because we were collecting personal information from people's Facebook accounts, we provided potential participants with detailed information about these aspects of the study so that they could make an informed decision about whether or not they'd like to participate.

Of the 10 participants, 5 were men and 5 were women. The age of participants ranged from 23 years old to 52 years old, with an average age of 33.8 years old. 7 of the participants were married and 5 of the participants had children. Participants had a wide range of occupations, including a small business owner, a professor, and a nurse. In addition, participants varied with regards to their interest in and proficiency with computers, though all had some means of connecting to the internet, a presence on Facebook, and an email account. Participants also had a wide range of life experiences. For example, nine of the ten participants were not originally from the local area but had moved there at different stages of their life for work, to go to school, or to move closer to friends and loved ones. They also had varying experiences thinking about death, legacy, and end-of-life care. Several had recently experienced the death of a family member, friend, or classmate.

Interviews took place primarily in participants' homes, but also took place in an office at Carnegie Mellon when that was more convenient for a participant. Participants were paid a total of $80 for their involvement in the entire study. They were paid $20 after the first interview, $10 for the second interview, $15 for the third interview, and $35 for completing the fourth and last interview. All of the participants completed all four interviews and did at least one task for each of the three task types. Six participants did all nine tasks; participants completed an average of 8.2 tasks.

DATA ANALYSIS

For each participant, we had three recorded interviews (the first interview was mostly a preliminary session and was not recorded) in addition to many pages of notes and documents created and collected by the researchers. Each of these three interviews was transcribed directly after the interview session.

After the study was complete and all of the recordings were transcribed, we analyzed the data using an iterative, open coding process drawn from the methods used in grounded theory [6]. We began by reading through each of the interviews to get a better sense of the connections between the information provided by each of the participants. From there, we created a collection of codes that described the data and that connected the information we'd collected with the larger goals of the study. The codes changed as we continued to review the transcripts. After several revisions, this coding scheme contained 80 codes distributed among 10 higher-level categories. Once a final set of codes was developed, we re-coded each interview and began to formally identify meaningful findings from the study data.

It is important to note here that the information contributed by participants to Retrospect via their task activities was not included in our analysis. Within our research, Retrospect was used to accomplish several clear and related goals: 1) to get a better sense of the aspects of a person's past that are shared as information online, 2) to draw out examples of how people use digital systems, like social networks, in ways that might not be apparent to curatorial systems, and 3) to scaffold conversations with participants about how their shared online information might shape how they're viewed after their death. The information collected and then surfaced in Retrospect helped us explore these ideas with participants and elicited a rich set of examples drawn directly from participants' experiences using and thinking about the Retrospect website.

FINDINGS

Below, we present a collection of findings, which describe 1) the need for systems that engage with materials that are and will be left behind (and not directly passed down), 2) comparisons between how a person wants to be remembered and the digital materials they think they'll leave behind, and 3) the potential for systems to support the ability for people to engage with the experience of legacy. Afterwards, we discuss these findings and examine how designers and developers could build systems that engage with the large, heterogeneous collections of digital materials that people leave behind when they pass away.

Systems for passing down and leaving behind

A key aspect of this work was to better understand the role that different types of systems can play in how people engage with a person's digital materials over time and across generations. Prior research in this area [5, 35] has described considerations for systems that allow for the assignment or stewardship of particular accounts or pieces of digital information (*i.e. things that are passed down).* Though that work has elicited valuable contributions, the findings from our work focus on a distinct, but related vein of inquiry: how people engage with information that is not directly or deliberated handled using such features (*i.e. things that are left behind*). Our findings build on this work and describe how digital systems can represent and adapt to the ways in which a person's legacy may change over time and the ways in which a person's interest in another person's life may change over time.

While features like Facebook's Legacy Contact and Google's Inactive Account Manger are valuable, none of the participants in our study had used post-mortem account management features. Furthermore, only about half of the participants had a will (though many noted the value of creating such documents). This situation highlights the opportunity to learn from how people handle the many physical or financial things that people leave behind, but do not formally pass on, when they die. That is, although a significant percentage of the population of US adults do not have a will [14], the bereaved are often still able to make decisions about what should happen to possessions that are left behind after that person has passed away. This is based, in part, on their understanding of a person's life and on existing norms and practices. This finding articulates the importance of two complementary aims: 1) encouraging companies to develop services that facilitate passing on particularly important aspects of a person's digital materials, and 2) creating systems that help survivors and future generations of people engage with the rest of a person's digital materials without their direct instruction, assignment, or stewardship.

Participants expressed mixed feelings about using features like Facebook's Legacy Contact. Some were open to using these features if it would have value to their partners or relatives, saying things like "*I don't really care what happens to my Facebook page after - if they want to keep it up and running or not, same idea*" (P4). Others expressed questions and concerns about using those features, such as *"What happens? I guess it just stays, does it ever go away, after several years of inactivity?"* (P1) and *"I'm not personally a fan of that. I would rather just have it shut down and I think if people need to say something they can just send a prayer or call my parents or something. there's other avenues for showing support other than writing on the wall of someone who's never going to read it."* (P7). This evidence serves as another reason to consider the development of systems that manage legacy information without direct instruction or assignment. In keeping with existing research [23, 33], participants did, of course, name digital materials that they hoped would endure, including photos of significant events, like weddings and trips, and photos that depicted significant family members and friends. However, participants also questioned 1) the value of maintaining a digital presence after their death, 2) whether digital information would have value many years in the future, and 3) the effort that would be required from the person assigned to manage some account or information.

Despite this uncertainty, participants in the study also identified a number of potential benefits of systems that would help people engage with their digital materials (whether passed down or left behind). Of the ten participants, five (P2, P3, P7, P8, P9) felt as though their children might find value in the digital information they'd leave behind both because of what is captured in that information and because of what it conveys about a person's life and values. P9, talking about a picture of his daughter he'd recently shared on Facebook through the Facebook 'On This Day' feature said *"Yesterday there was like the, you know, [Facebook] memories. So yesterday there were a whole bunch [of photos]– I changed my profile picture to my daughter when she was two weeks old and I was like 'oh that's really cool'... She could potentially see that kind of thing in the future and my son could potentially see that kind of thing in the future. Oh, look at what I looked like or look at what I did. So I think that's really cool."*

Conveying important aspects of one's life

During conversations with participants we discussed the different ways that aspects of participants' lives could be passed down or left behind after their deaths. In line with existing literature [29, 21], participants described that they wanted to 1) pass on their values to future generations, 2) have a positive impact on future generations, and 3) ensure the continuation of particular traits, values, and traditions. Given that focus, we asked participants to consider the extent to which information about those things could be found in, or understood through, their digital materials.

Retrospect played a large role in this line of inquiry – the website asked people to reflect on pieces of their digital information as a part of every task on the site. In the second, third, and fourth interview sessions we used Retrospect tasks as a jumping off point for conversations about the different types of digital materials participants generate and how that relates to important aspects of their life. Participants did not always feel a strong connection to the people, places, and things that populate their digital accounts. For example, nearly all of the participants had their hometown listed on their Facebook account but several participants were not interested in reflecting on it as a part of the place task, or in talking about it as one of the important parts of their life. Providing information about one's hometown, high school, or college serves a logistical function within systems as a way for people to identify and connect with other users. While this information describes some aspect of a person's life, it may not be as meaningful to a person as other information that is not documented in the same way.

Discussions with participants about the different ways they use system functionality to accomplish their own goals also highlighted opportunities for systems to capture potentially meaningful aspects of a person's life. For example, P3 talked about changing her profile picture to a photo of the deceased actor Philip Seymour Hoffman when he died, saying *"I wrote a tiny bit about Phillip Seymour Hoffman, because that was one of the photos that came up today. It was that and this other one... [I thought] wow I posted this picture on the day that he died, in my favorite role of his."* Many people choose profile pictures that feature a place, object, or different person as a way for people to demonstrate their connection to that thing and to foster conversations about it. Similarly, several participants described occasions in which they updated their profile picture to be an old photo of themselves, such as a photo of when they were a child. In these cases, it is clear to see how the metadata about those photos (such as the date they were posted relative to a person's age) could help surface or convey some meaningful or interesting content from a person's life.

There is a great variety in how people perceive the value (in both the short term and long term) of the information they share online. Though it is easier to prioritize or privilege structured data, it is important to consider the implications for doing so and to look for opportunities to find and highlight other, meaningful aspects of a person's life.

Experiencing legacy

Interviews with participants elicited information about how they engage with legacies and memories that other people have left behind. Seven of the participants reported that they'd inherited things from people who had passed away; five had inherited money, one had inherited jewelry, and one had inherited a treasured possession from her grandfather. Participants also described objects that they had been given or had claimed after the death of a loved one. These objects weren't inherited directly from the person who had passed away, but were instead given to the participant by an intermediary (such as a parent) or were taken as a part of organizing and giving away a person's possessions as they reached the end of their life (as has been described in research work such as [25]). This included a set of gloves and a brooch from a participant's great-aunt and a jacket a participant's grandparent had worn. Though the participants appreciated the money they'd inherited, people seemed to be more deeply impacted by objects that reminded them of people who had passed away.

Participants also engaged with memories of other people through their everyday experiences. These experiences, which rarely involved any valuable, old, or rare objects, instead focused on specific memories people had about people who'd passed away. P1 illustrated this idea by describing one of the ways in which she is reminded of her grandmother *"Every time I see a red cardinal we always say 'That's grandma!' because she loved red cardinals. We have so many cardinals in my backyard, we say 'Hi Grandma!!' So things in that way I think is kind of a legacy because the red cardinal was insignificant until grandma made it something. That's something, like, our whole family does now. I guess that's kind of a legacy, it's just a bit of her that we remember even though she's been gone for several years now."* Nearly all of the participants were able to provide an example of this type of remembrance. P6, for example, also shared a way he is reminded of his deceased grandfather: *"[My grandfather] really enjoyed walking. A lot. He used to – whenever we'd visit, or whenever he visited here when we first moved out to America, he would... leave the house and then just go start walking and then he'd be back like 5 hours later. We'd be like where'd you go? and he'd be like I just walked until it ended. Anytime I go on like long walks or hikes I guess it's a little bit [like] mini reminders [of him]."* As with these two examples, many of these remembrances were connected to nature in some way.

It's unlikely that digital information would form the basis for this type of remembrance; many of these examples resulted from a person internalizing some memory about a loved one. There is, however, the potential that digital information could be used to trigger the process of remembering and experiencing some aspect of a person's legacy in a similar way. Just as seeing a red cardinal evokes memories of P1's grandmother, there is an opportunity to build systems that foster mundane or everyday reminiscence about people who have passed away. Though these systems would need to be sensitive to potential harm that could result from reminding a person about a deceased loved one, such systems could also provide people with a new way to connect with treasured memories and experiences.

Another important consideration for how people experience and engage with other people's legacies is the idea that a person's understanding of another's person's life will change over time. In one of our interview sessions, P5 discussed how raising a child had changed how she understood her mother's life and her mother's interest in elementary education, saying *"I think all of her mothering went into her students, pupils - into the kids. But she would talk to me sometimes about what happened at school and I took on certain attitudes about early childhood through her that have served me very well as a mother."* Several participants described family traditions, traits, and memories they hoped to instill in the next generation of their family. Creating a legacy is a process that is undertaken, in part, because a person wants to establish some form of enduring remembrance of their life. Digital systems operating in this space should account for the ways in which a legacy can change over time as it is interpreted and reinterpreted by new generations. For example, a system might allow a person to select and integrate particular aspects of another person's digital information into their existing accounts or profiles.

DISCUSSION

In this section we describe several potential avenues for system development, including the opportunity to leverage information about a person's life to identify aspects of that life that might be worth reflecting on or sharing post-mortem, the opportunity to guide people through the process of learning more about their ancestors, and the opportunity to help people better understand information created in the past by placing that information into context.

Opportunities for analytical systems

As illustrated by this work and other related research [18, 27, 31], there is an opportunity to understand how we can use digital information, and the digital systems that capture and hold that information, to help people communicate important aspects of their life post-mortem. One way of doing this is to develop systems (or features for existing systems) that facilitate this process by leveraging what systems know about a person's preferences, hobbies, and personality to organize content around those topics in formats that can be easily shared with other people. Most social networks have an internal assessment of a user's personality, hobbies, and interests, and this information can help systems identify meaningful representations of a person's life in their digital materials. For example, if a system observes that a person has an interest in travel, they might generate a slideshow of travel-related content that they can reflect on and share. Creating an assessment of one's life relative to one's broader digital materials may not be entirely feasible at this point in time, but the ability for systems to analyze and make judgments about digital content continues to develop.

A concern here is the degree to which such systems might influence a person's understanding of their own life or the lives of others. Though prior research indicates that people are interested in this type of system [18], work by Warshaw et al. emphasizes that people felt uncomfortable making corrections to a system's analysis of their personality traits [44]. Systems that curate and synthesize found digital information need to be cognizant of how their rendering of a person's life and experiences may impact how they are remembered.

Finding experience in large archives

If people are interested in engaging with information about a person's life, systems can help with this process in much the same ways that they help people make sense of their own digital information. One way to do so is for systems to offer people the ability to get a quick sense of a large amount of information. For example, a system might analyze the content from an old online diary and present the viewer with a mediated summary of the contents. This information could include topics covered in the posts, the names that are mentioned, any photographs that were posted, or the dates when the service was used. This information could then help a person decide whether they'd like to explore that account more deeply. The ability to provide this type of information might be coupled with broader analytical capabilities. Prior work has illustrated the value of this technique [9], and there is an opportunity to understand how we might apply it to lifetimes of digital information.

Another way to address this issue would be to develop systems that search directly for content relevant to particular supported queries. Participants in this study who had conducted family history research described being particular interested in a small set of questions such as what was a person's life like, or how did a particular person make important decisions? Finding content related to specific questions could help people initially approach or become interested in researching their family history using digital information (which might otherwise be a daunting task). There is a great opportunity for future work to leverage the ways that people investigate their family history to inform the design of future systems that engage with information left behind when people pass away.

Communicating context

If future generations of people are interested in digging deeper into a person's digital materials, a major challenge to a person's ability to understand that information is that the norms and practices that influence the use of digital systems will likely have changed over time. This has happened many times already with online social networks (including once prominent sites like Friendster, Orkut, and Myspace which no longer operate in the same contexts). Norms for the content and format of what people share has also changed on websites that are currently popular. Similarly, changes to people's understanding of audience have shaped how individuals engage in identity presentation and management on these websites. The potential difficulty of understanding the context of some piece of digital information and media is not unique to digital things, but the scale and format of digital things exacerbates this issue.

As a result, there is an opportunity to build system features that allow people to explore how websites were used in the past. One could imagine, for example, a feature that allows a person to roll back their own Facebook or Twitter feed to see what the experience of using the site was like a decade ago. This feature could be built into existing functionality, such as Facebook's security-based 'View As' feature, which allows people to see what their profile looks like from the perspective of other people.

Advancing the probes method

Finally, there is an opportunity to extend the use of design probes in HCI research, and to better understand how we might engage in participatory work with probes. A number of papers have outlined how researchers build and utilize probes, and how the results of that process might (or might not) be analyzed [3, 15]. Building on that work, we believe that there is a need to understand how probes like Retrospect can demonstrate that the contributions made by participants are valued and allow those participants to lead discussions about what they've shared.

In this study, we assembled each participant's data into booklet and gave it to the participant in the final interview. Prior to that interview, we did not review the information participants had written in Retrospect. By allowing participants to control the process by which we looked through and learned about the information they provided, we hoped to communicate our respect for their experiences and their contributions to our work. This procedure was also a way for us to allow participants to decide what to share with us, and how and when to share that information. This is only one of many different potential options for expressing these ideas, and we look forward to future variations on utilizing probes to collect sensitive or personal information from participants.

CONCLUSION

This study explored how people might communicate aspects of their life, relative to the stores of digital information that they have collected, once they pass away. We presented a mixed-methods study that involved an online design probe which investigated how digital systems and information might help shape how people look back on and interpret people's lives after they've passed away. We hope that findings from this work will guide the design and development of systems that work with large found and unassigned archives of digital information to surface meaningful aspects of a person's life and legacy after they've passed away.

ACKNOWLEDGEMENTS

Thank you to all of our friends and colleagues at Carnegie Mellon, Virginia Tech, and elsewhere, for their support of this work. Thank you as well to the people who participated in this study, we are truly grateful for the time you spent sharing your perspectives and experiences; your contributions had a tremendous impact on this work and our own understanding of what makes life meaningful. Finally, thank you to the reviewers who provided valuable feedback that helped refine this work.

REFERENCES

1. Eric P.S. Baumer, Vera Khovanskaya, Mark Matthews, Lindsay Reynolds, Victoria Schwana Sosik, and Geri Gay. 2014. Reviewing reflection: on the use of reflection in interactive system design. *DIS 2014,* 93 – 102.
2. Gordon Bell and Jim Gemmell. 2007. A digital life. *Scientific American.*
3. Kristen Boehner, Janet Vertesi, Phoebe Singers, and Paul Dourish. 2007. How HCI interprets the probes. *CHI 2007*, 1077 – 1086.
4. Jed R. Brubaker and Gillian R. Hayes. 2011. "We will never forget you [online]": An empirical investigation of post-mortem Myspace comments. *CSCW 2011,* 123 – 132.
5. Jed R. Brubaker and Vanessa Callison-Burch. 2016. Legacy contact: Designing and implementing post-mortem stewardship at Facebook. *CHI 2016,* 2908 – 2919.
6. Kathy Charmaz. 2006. Constructing grounded theory. SAGE Publications.
7. Mary Czerwinski, Douglas W. Gage, Jim Gemmell, Catherine C. Marshall, Manuel A. Pérez-quiñonesis, Meredith M. Skeels, and Tiziana Catarci. 2006. Digital memories in an era of ubiquitous computing and abundant storage. *Communications of the ACM* 49, 1: 45 – 50.
8. Dan Cosley, Victoria Schwanda Sosik, Johnathon Schultz, S. Tejaswi Peesapati, and Soyoung Lee. 2012. Experiences with designing tools for everyday reminiscing. *Journal of Human-Computer Interaction* 27, 1-2: 175 – 198.
9. Daragh Byrne, Aisling Kelliher, and Gareth J.F. Jones. 2011. Life editing: third-party perspectives on lifelog content. *CHI 2011,* 1501 – 1510.
10. Motahhare Eslami, Aimee Rickman, Kristen Vaccaro, Amirhossein Aleyasen, Andy Vuong, Karrie Karahalios, Kevin Hamilton, and Christian Sanvig. 2015. "I always assumed that I wasn't really that close to [her]": Reasoning about invisible algorithms in news feeds. *CHI 2015,* 153 – 162.
11. Facebook Legacy Contact. Retrieved from: https://www.facebook.com/help/1568013990080948
12. Andrew Fitzgibbon and Ehud Reiter. 2003. Memories for life: Managing information over a human lifetime.
13. Batya Friedman and Lisa Nathan. 2010. Multi-lifespan information system design: A research initiative for theHCI community. *CHI 2010*, 2243 – 2246.
14. Gallup Poll – Last Wishes: Half of Americans Have Written Wills. 2005. Retrieved from: http://www.gallup.com/poll/16660/last-wishes-half-americans-written-wills.aspx
15. William Gaver. 2012. What should we expect from research through design? *CHI 2012,* 937 – 946.
16. Google's Inactive Account Manager. Retrieved from: https://support.google.com/accounts/answer/3036546?hl=en
17. Rebecca Gulotta, William Odom, Jodi Forlizzi, and Haakon Faste. 2013. Digital artifacts as legacy: Exploring the lifespan and value of digital data. *CHI 2013,* 1813 – 1822.
18. Rebecca Gulotta, Alex Sciuto, Aisling Kelliher, and Jodi Forlizzi. 2015. Curatorial agents: How systems shape our understanding of personal and familial digital information. *CHI 2015,* 3453 – 3462.
19. Rebecca Gulotta, David B. Gerritsen, Aisling Kelliher, and Jodi Forlizzi. 2016. Engaging with death online: An analysis of systems that support legacy-making, bereavement, and remembrance. *DIS 2016,* 736 – 748.
20. Bernie Hogan, Juan Antonio Carrasco, and Barry Wellman. 2007. Visualizing personal networks: Working with participant-aided sociograms. *Field Methods* 19, 2: 116 – 144.
21. Elizabeth G. Hunter and Graham D. Rowles. 2005. Leaving a legacy: Toward a typology. *Journal of Aging Studies* 19, 3: 327 – 347.
22. Vera Khovanskaya, Eric P.S. Baumer, Dan Cosley, Stephen Voida, and Geri Gay. 2013. "Everybody knows what you're doing": A critical design approach to personal informatics. *CHI 2013,* 3403 – 3412.
23. David S. Kirk and Abigail Sellen. 2010. On human remains: Values and practice in the home archiving of cherished objects. *TOCHI* 17, 3.
24. Jessa Lingel. 2013. The digital remains: Social media and practices of online grief. *The Information Society* 29, 3.
25. Jean-Sébastien Marcoux. 2001. The 'casser maison' ritual: Constructing the self by emptying the home. *Journal of Material Culture* 6, 2: 213 – 235.
26. Catherine C. Marshall, Sara Bly, and Francoise Brun-Cottan. *2006.* The long-term fate of our personal digital belongings: Toward a service model for personal archives. *Archiving Conference.*
27. Michael Massimi and Andrea Charise. 2009. Dying, death, and mortality: Towards thanatosensitivity in HCI. *Proceedings of CHI 2009 Extended Abstracts.*
28. Michael Massimi and Ronald M. Baecker. 2011. Dealing with death in design: Developing systems for the bereaved. *Proceedings of CHI 2011,* 1001 – 1010.
29. Dan P. McAdams, Ed de St. Aubin, Regina L. Logan. 1993. Generativity among young adults, midlife, and older adults. *Psychology and Aging* 8, 2: 221 – 230.
30. Dan P. McAdams. 2001. The psychology of life stories. *Review of General Psychology* 5, 2: 100 – 122.

31. Wendy Moncur, Jan Bikker, Elaine Kasket, and John Troyer. 2012. From death to final disposition: Roles of technology in the post-mortem interval. *CHI 2012,* 531 – 540.
32. Wendy Moncur. 2014. An emergent framework for digital memorials. *DIS 2014,* 965 – 974.
33. William Odom, James Pierce, Erik Stolterman, and Eli Blevis. 2009. Understanding why we preserve some things and discard others in the context of interaction design. *CHI 2009,* 1053 – 1062.
34. William Odom, Richard Banks, Richard Harper, David Kirk, Siân Lindley, and Abigail Sellen. 2012. Technology heirlooms? Considerations for passing down and inheriting digital materials. *Proceedings of CHI 2012,* 337 – 346.
35. Raquel O. Prates, Mary Beth Rosson, Clarisse S. de Souza. 2015. Making decisions about digital legacy with Google's Inactive Account Manager. *INTERACT 2015,* 201 – 209.
36. Linda L. Price, Eric J. Arnould, and Carolyn Folkman Curasi. 2000. Older consumers' disposition of special possessions. *Journal of Consumer Research* 27, 2: 179 – 201.
37. Emilee Rader and Rebecca Gray. 2015. Understanding user beliefs about algorithmic curation in the Facebook news feed. *CHI 2015,* 173 – 182.
38. Corina Sas and Alan Dix. 2009. Designing for reflection on experience. *Proceedings of CHI Extended Abstracts,* 4741 – 4744.
39. Barbara F. Sharf. 1997. Communicating breast cancer on-line: Support and empowerment on the internet. *Women and Health,* 26, 1.
40. David R. Unruh. 1983. Death and personal history: Strategies of identity preservation. *Social Problems* 30, 3: 340 – 351.
41. Jayne Wallace, John McCarthy, Peter C. Wright, and Patrick Olivier. 2013. Making design probes work. *CHI 2013*, 3441 – 3450.
42. Tony Walter. 1996. A new model of grief: Bereavement and biology. *Mortality* 1, 1: 7 – 25.
43. Tony Walter, Rachel Hourizi, Wendy Moncur, and Stacey Pitsillides. 2012. Does the internet change how we died and mourn? Overview and analysis. *Omega* 64, 4: 275 – 302.
44. Jeffrey Warshaw, Tara Matthews, Steve Whittaker, Chris Kau, Mateo Bengualid, Barton A. Smith. 2015. Can algorithms know the 'real you'? Understanding people's reactions to hyper-personal analytics systems. *CHI 2015,* 797 – 806.
45. Lia Willis, George Demiris, and Debra Parker Oliver. 2007. Internet use by hospice families and providers: A review. *Journal of Medical Systems,* 31, 2: 97 – 101.

The Autobiographical Design and Long Term Usage of an Always-On Video Recording System for the Home

Yasamin Heshmat, Carman Neustaedter, Brendan DeBrincat
School of Interactive Arts and Technology, Simon Fraser University
Surrey, BC, Canada
{yheshmat, carman; bdebrinc}@sfu.ca

ABSTRACT
Photo and video capture is currently dominated by the use of digital cameras, often in the form of smartphones. Yet there is easily the chance that one can miss capturing a precious moment. We explored the idea of automated video recording in the home as a form of memory collection and display for families through the autobiographical design of Moments, an always-on video recording system. We iteratively designed Moments and it was used by one of the researchers and his family over a two-year period. The family found potential for the system in capturing moments that would have otherwise been forgotten in time, where they especially valued seeing 'big changes' and minute details of their life. Yet tensions existed around the family's inabilities to access specific points in time, commitment to keeping the system running, and privacy. We use these benefits and concerns to suggest future research directions for always-on video recording in the home.

Author Keywords
Photos and video; families; surveillance; memories; slow technology.

ACM Classification Keywords
H.5.2. [Information interfaces and presentation]: User Interfaces – Evaluation/methodology

INTRODUCTION
Many people capture copious amounts of photos or videos of their family members and their activities [34]. Yet there is typically a requirement that someone is present and ready to capture a desired moment [23]. This is easily challenging to do amidst the everyday busyness of life. As such, we were inspired to explore the idea of automated video capture of cherished family moments in the home. Past research has looked at the automatic recording of family moments by capturing of images based on ambient sound [23]. Life logging technologies similarly attempt to capture everyday moments using wearable cameras [48].We build on this work by exploring the idea of always-on video recording in the home. Studies have looked at reactions to video recording in the home as a data collection tool [44]; however, we have yet to see user reactions to always-on recording when it provides them with the benefits of family memory collection. We also see a variety of research focused on always-on video that is shared live between two or more homes [28,29,35]; what we are proposing is quite different where video is recorded and accessible within a single home, not shared across homes.

Naturally, the idea of always-on video recording in home provokes many questions. While it offers potential to capture and replay significant family moments, including developmental milestones of children, celebrations, and changes in people over time, there is certainly the risk of familial privacy concerns around video surveillance. There are also a range of design questions around what locations and angles are best suited for always-on recording, when and how recorded videos should be made accessible, whether video recording should indeed be *always*-on, what moments families value most when it comes to replaying their past experiences, and what privacy concerns are evoked through always-on video recording.

We recognized that answering these questions would be difficult. They would require a large corpus of family life to be captured and then replayed, in the order of months to years, and extensive buy-in would be needed from family members in order to keep a recording system active, with the willingness to have the family's privacy at risk. This meant that traditional lab-based user studies would not suffice because they would not capture 'real' activities. Field deployments in participant homes would be ideal but problematic for such long durations of time and it would likely be difficult to get family commitment. Typically, deployments of home technologies last in the order of several weeks to one or two months because of their complexity, difficulty in running, and level of commitment from participant families [4,30]. Only in rare cases and for particular types of technology have field deployments been in the order of a year or more (e.g., [42,46]). As such, we realized we needed an alternative design and evaluation method outside of what is typically used in present-day HCI research if we were going to uncover the benefits and challenges of such a system during longitudinal usage.

Here we turned to autobiographical design, a design

DIS 2017, June 10-14, 2017, Edinburgh, United Kingdom
© 2017 ACM. ISBN 978-1-4503-4922-2/17/06…$15.00
DOI: http://dx.doi.org/10.1145/3064663.3064759

research method drawn from the field of computer science as a reflexive practice [1] and more commonly used in the early days of the field of CSCW as a means to deeply explore systems design research [38]. Autobiographical design involves extensive self-usage of a technology throughout its design process and is valuable for collecting longitudinal data on technology usage [38]. It has been shown to be particularly valuable in situations where it is difficult to deploy technologies in real situations given their frailty and incorporation of ubiquitous technologies [37,38]. It is also useful in situations where researchers want to "put themselves in harm's way" first with a potentially risky system before knowing how it should be designed and presented to other users more broadly [37,38]. In this way, it is a test case to understand what is important in the design, what should be refined, and what should be left out. The goal of autobiographical design is certainly not to generalize usage behavior to broader populations; instead, it is meant as a means to deeply understand a design area to suggest research direction [37,38].

Our research involved designing an always-on video recording system called Moments and using it over a period of two years. Our design draws from slow technology design principles [20,42] as a means to create anticipation and reflection around the reveal of past family memories. At the 21-month mark of usage, we had a second researcher, independent from the family, conduct interviews and design activities with the family members to understand the effect of Moments on the family's life. Our paper describes and reflects on this long-term usage to reveal key themes related to the value of media content and aspects of presence, commitment, and privacy with video recording systems. We use these lessons to step back and explore the broader implications from our work for the design of always-on video recording systems in home environments.

RELATED WORK

Photo and Video Capture and Sharing

Traditionally, families and friends shared photos with each other in a collocated setting using printed photographs [9,34]. This social act was highly desirable and people's preferred mode of viewing [9,17] as it allowed family members and friends to reminisce and tell stories about their experiences [13,17]. As digital photos and videos became widespread, the amount of work needed to manage them became large [31]. Given the popularity of collocated photo sharing, a variety of prototype systems have been designed to support such practices around digital media. For example, these have focused on photo viewing and reminiscing around a digital table [24,49] and the design of domestic objects to support collective memory amongst family members [51], conversation, and reminiscing [5].

There have also been systems designed with an emphasis on automated or ubiquitous capture of video, similar to Moments. The Other Brother [23] captured unplanned or spontaneous photos in the home based on ambient sound. Studies found that family members appreciated the capture of surprising moments [23]. Initially family members had privacy concerns, but, over time, they noticed the recording device much less. TIMELINE provided the recording and rapid review of video from multiple workspaces [40]. Participants could watch each other work in real time, or see recorded footage from earlier. SenseCam was designed as a lifelogging camera to capture images throughout one's day [7,8] and has been shown to allow people to connect to their past as well as aid memory during challenging health situations, e.g., Alzheimer's disease [7,26,48].

Slow Technology

Researchers have recognized that technologies designed for settings outside of the workplace need to move beyond efficiency to other forms of meaning and connection where people might draw different understandings from their media or data and its consumption [20]. To this end, slow technologies aim to create a more meaningful connection between people and computational artifacts through designs that take time for users to learn how they work and why they work in a particular way [20,42]. For example, GoSlow was a slow technology for mobile devices that periodically prompted users to reflect on their mood [10]. Postulater let users share photos or videos with family by sending media to a specific date and time in the future [21,22]. A field study showed that these features created valuable reflection [22]. The PhotoBox was a slow technology that randomly printed out Flickr photos for household members as a means to reconnect them to their past [42]. This created additional interest in users' photo archives [42]. We build on these ideas to explore how principles from slow technology design might be used with always-on video recording to create user reflection.

Always-On Communication Systems

Always-on video for communication has been explored in domestic settings as a means to connect multiple homes together. The VideoProbe [12,27] shared still images between homes based on user movement. Users enjoyed capturing humorous moments and being playful, but sometimes had privacy concerns [12]. RoomLink focused on shared audio between two household; however, focus groups revealed privacy concerns over streamed audio [25]. The Family Window connected two homes and provided 'time shifted' video that could be recorded and played back. Participants liked the idea of having the option of recording events since it meant they would not likely miss special moments [28]. Family Portals connected three households together with always-on video [29]. Users valued the sense of connection, however, there was increased privacy risk by having more people connected [29]. Our work is similar, however, we look at only recorded video rather than live video streaming between homes.

Surveillance and Video Recording

Ubiquitous surveillance involves the "unilateral collection of data on people with sensors embedded in their everyday environment" [44]. A day reconstruction study on video recording in environments such as offices, malls, and public spaces found that people were concerned with notification and consent to be recorded, improper access to video, and unauthorized use [39]. Using a similar method, Massimi et al. [33] found that people use visual cues in their environment to determine if they are being surveilled (e.g., the presence of cameras). O'Donnell et al. [41] found that surveillance is more accepted when performed by a group with whom one identifies. A survey by Choe et al. [11] that asked people to speculate about their reactions to ubiquitous recording in their home found that they were concerned about being recorded when partially clothed or during intimate or socially awkward acts [11]. They were also concerned about audio being captured, including talking to oneself, child rearing, and arguments [11].

As can be seen, most studies of ubiquitous video recording focus on speculations of usage with few exploring actual usage and reactions to recording in the moment. A notable exception is the Helsinki Privacy Experiment, a study of ubiquitous surveillance *within* families' homes over a period of six months [44]. The idea was to explore a 'worst case scenario' where a large amount of data would be logged without any particular benefit to users. Some surveillees grew accustomed to having their lives logged, while others grew increasingly concerned or changed their behaviors to reflect the fact that their activities were being recorded and logged. The most disturbing sensors to participants were video and audio recording along with Internet activity logging. Our research builds on this study by more deeply exploring video recording in the home, in particular, when the family has potential to receive benefits from the recorded footage (e.g., family memory collection).

The Human Speechome Project (HSP) is also similar to our study of Moments. In the HSP, video cameras continuously capture a single home in an effort to understand and map children's speech development patterns [47,52]. While also focused on recording *one* family's activities, the HSP has not studied the family's reactions to continuous capture.

AUTOBIOGRAPHICAL DESIGN AS A METHOD

Our research draws from autobiographical design as a design research method. Autobiographical design is "design research drawn from extensive, genuine use by those creating or building the system" [38]. It draws its roots from practices in the 1980s by computer scientists who designed for themselves as a *reflexive user* where they would imagine themselves as future users [1]. In the early days of the field of CSCW, media space researchers used a similar self-usage approach to design and study their systems [3,15,32]. Since then, it has been periodically used and published as a design research technique (e.g., [16] in 1996, [18] in 2006, [28] in 2010, [14] in 2016]). Yet what happens often is that researchers use the method but are hesitant to publish their results from it because of potentially negative reactions from peer reviewers [38].

Autobiographical design is similar to design requirements elicitation methods such as ethnography and technology probes, yet differs in observations and understanding of usage, which are tied with an initial period of design iteration [37]. Usage is then tracked long term over periods of months to years to provide detailed longitudinal data situated in aspects of 'real life' [37]. HCI and CSCW expert researchers who have used the method described it being a valuable design research method for early design when little is known about a design space and when it is difficult to deploy a technology to external users or where it may not make sense to do so [38]. However, they cautioned that autobiographical design needs to ensure its own sense of rigor as is the case with all research methods in the field of HCI [38]. Rigor for autobiographical design means careful and critical reflection on one's work including, *"an extensive period of genuine, intensive use, measured in months or years; surprises in usage that lead researchers to rethink or develop initial design conceptions; improvements to design driven by specific, documented incidents of use; and careful articulation of the impact of design decisions on experiential qualities of the system."* [38]

By following these tenets, autobiographical design supports fast tinkering with an idea, reveals 'big effects' from usage, and provides detailed and experiential understanding, not often available from other research methods [38]. Of course, autobiographical design does not produce generalizable results, and nor should this be expected [38]. In the subsequent sections, we describe how we employed an autobiographical design approach to create and study always-on video recording in the home.

Figure 1: The Moments camera near the roof of the kitchen.

Figure 2: A Moments iPad on the kitchen counter.

THE DESIGN OF MOMENTS

Moments is an always-on video recording system with an interface designed to help families revisit memories. The system is designed to be used within the home. A Kinect camera is placed in one location and connected to a computer that records video continuously (Figure 1). A web application runs on a tablet and has access to play back the recorded video (Figure 2, bottom right), with constraints that are described in subsequent sections. The goal is to help families collect and reflect on past moments and experiences that took place in certain areas of the home.

Design Need and Iteration

Moments was designed to capture everyday spontaneous moments that occurred within a family's home. Due to the study being longitudinal and privacy intrusive, the research started with one of the author's family containing himself, his wife, and his three young children (aged 1, 6, and 8 at the onset of the project). The idea was to be able to capture the growth and development of each family member, especially the kids in the family, as well as the 'special moments' that might occur in home. These special moments might include, for example, a child's first steps or family celebrations. There was a particular interest in the changes that might occur within these moments over a long period of time, for example, seeing a pattern of who sits down to eat together at mealtimes and how this might change. Many of these moments were either missed or difficult to capture. That is why the researcher thought about a more automated approach for such capture.

Over a period of four months, an undergraduate research designer iteratively created Moments through a series of brainstorming, sketching, and prototyping activities, in consultation with the researcher. During this time, Moments was placed in the researcher's home in a home office and recreation room to explore the design ideas as they were developing. This represented a period of 'fast tinkering' with the design, which is common in autobiographical design and one of the benefits of the method [38]. After four months, the design reached a stable point where the researcher and designer felt the system met the primary needs of the family. Development ceased and the family began using Moments more permanently in the main living space of their home, a kitchen/living room.

Usage Constraints

As we designed and built Moments we recognized that we wanted to purposely include a number of usage constraints in an effort to make the system more focused on family moments and less on surveillance. Our ideas were inspired by slow technology designs where notions of time and relevance can be brought to the surface by allowing a design to slowly reveal itself, its contents, and its value to the user [20,42]. For example, content from the past could be revealed to the user at particular moments in time in an effort to make a past moment more memorable or valuable than it might otherwise be if it was more easily accessible [22,42]. Existing systems such as the PhotoBox [42] and Postulater [21,22] used this technique to bring forward photographs from the past to the user in present day where the technique created valuable user anticipation and reflection; we extended this idea to video recording.

Location

First, in order to watch recorded video, the user must be located in close proximity to the capturing camera. For example, Figure 3 shows Moments displaying video on an iPad located on a kitchen counter. Directly above it is the recording camera. Clicking on a 'settings' icon on the Moments display causes a calendar to appear that family members can use to select a date that they would like to review for that camera. When a date is picked, video plays for that day. Thus, family members can set the iPad on the counter (with the screen set to permanently stay on) and video will be shown of the selected day continuously. In this way, it can act as a glanceable display into the family's past. The idea of glanceable displays in the home builds on prior work on digital family calendars [36] and messaging systems [43] which show that families find value in being able to walk by and glance at content on a display with ease. Previous research also suggests that playing the video back in the same location it was recorded in can help create an emotional connection to the video [45].

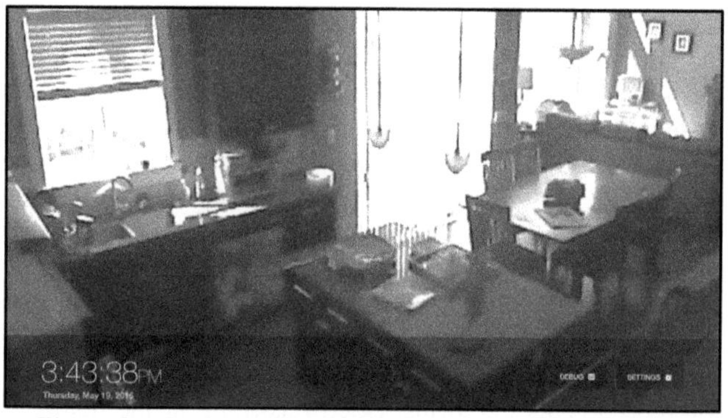

Figure 3: Moments showing video from one year earlier.

Timing

We also constrained the timing of the video that could be replayed. Video is only ever played from the selected day at the present time. Thus, when selecting video to play on a display, if one were to select yesterday as a date, and it was presently 1:00 pm, the device would play video from yesterday at 1:00 pm. For example, if a person wants to see video of children opening up presents on Christmas morning, she/he would need to think about what time of day that occurred at, and then wait until the next day to see it, if the time had already passed today. The intention was to use the time delay to generate anticipation much the same way that slow technologies have been successful in creating anticipation around the reveal of time-delayed photographs [21,22,42]. We also felt that by bounding video replay by three elements—time, date, and location—we could ease the burden that might come with having a large video archive and being unsure of what to review.

This type of viewing contrasts nearly every present day photo or video-sharing application where usage includes letting people easily access recorded videos and replay them at any point in time. Despite this ease-of-access, researchers have, somewhat ironically, found that people do not often view their saved videos/photos once they are placed in an archive [17]; thus, in some ways, we wanted to see the effect of an 'opposite' style of design. We also recognized that by limiting playback, family members would not be able to replay any moment at any point in time, as well as re-watch moments in short succession. This might be more akin to scrubbing recorded video from surveillance systems, which was not our intended use of Moments. Of course, there are many ways to design a system such that it does not feel and act like a video surveillance system. We chose but one route that seemed promising and reflected the desire to create anticipation with the revealing of past moments.

Audio

Moments does not record audio due to privacy concerns and the desire to not resurface 'bad' memories (e.g., arguments) from the past, which might be more easily noticed with audio. Previous research on always-on video media spaces in the home has found the transmission of audio to be more privacy-invasive than video [28,29]. Prior research has also shown large concerns over audio recording and streaming [11,25]. By capturing audio, we would be more likely to record family arguments or negative conversations about other people, which might be much less desirable. On the other hand, video of such events would likely appear somewhat mundane. We also did not want to alter conversations in the home, which was found by researchers studying audio recording [44].

Implementation

Moments works with two applications. The first runs on a Mac mini connected to a Microsoft Kinect camera and continuously polls the camera for images at a resolution of 640 x 480. Images are stored in a database running on a local server computer within the home. Thus, there is no concern over access to the images from outside of the home. We deliberately chose low-resolution images to reduce storage consumption. Video is also captured at a low rate of up to 5 frames per second (fps). Computer vision techniques are used to detect how many people are present in the room. If nobody is present, we captured video at a rate of 1 fps in order to capture changes in the ambiance of the room (e.g., lighting changes). The user interface to replay video is implemented as a web application that can run on any tablet, computer, or smartphone device when connected to the home's intranet. When a date is selected, images are retrieved from the database and concatenated together to playback video from the time period. Video continues to play as long as the web page is open.

EVALUATION METHOD

Moments was used by the researcher and his family for a period of two years. Throughout this time, the researcher recorded periodic confessional videos of himself and his children that described their usage of Moments and their thoughts about the system. These videos represented the thoughts and reflections from a trained researcher in HCI. This brings the added value of having a researcher as a participant where the researcher is trained to observe, critique, and reflect on the family's usage with extensive knowledge of the related literature and continuous access to observe the home environment and see nearly all of the effects of the technology. Such 'all day, everyday' observations are not usually possible in field studies.

We wanted to augment this data and understand the family's usage from an external perspective as well as bring additional rigor to the analysis by having a second researcher, independent from the family, perform data collection and analysis. Our goal was to have an unbiased, third-party researcher understand the family's experience and analyze, describe, and document it. This person was brought on to the project and she conducted semi-structured interviews with family members at the 20-month mark of usage. The confessional videos were used as an entry point to think about how the interviews should be structured and what focal points would be interesting to explore.

Interviews

Interviews with the two parents focused on topics such as usage patterns, views of the recorded video, location of the camera and privacy. For example, the invited researcher asked, "When do you most often look at Moments?", "What do you look for?", "Tell me about the most surprising usage you found for Moments". The two oldest children (aged 7 and 9 at the time) performed a design activity that involved drawing Moments, how they thought it worked, and what they would like to add to it, if anything. For example, the invited researcher asked, "Can you draw what you would like to add to the Moments system?" After the activity, the children were interviewed about their drawing and thoughts on Moments. The interview focused around their knowledge of the system, details of what they saw interesting in the system, and possible privacy concerns. For example, they were asked, "Can you tell me about a time you tried to look at the display very closely to see what was happening back then?" The third child (2-years old) was not interviewed.

Data Collection and Analysis

Interviews were audio-recorded and transcribed for data analysis purposes. The independent researcher performed open coding on the data to draw out the important findings and then axial coding to group them into categories. Selective coding was used to draw out and summarize the key findings into themes. These are discussed in the following sections and relate to aspects of commitment, screen attention, reflecting on moments, time constraints, and privacy. Throughout our results, we refer to the family members as the father (researcher), mother, oldest son (age 9), the daughter (age 7), and youngest son (age 2).

GENERAL USAGE

After the initial four months of Moments' design and development, it was setup within the family's home in the kitchen on the main floor. A Kinect camera was placed on top of the cupboard in the corner of the kitchen. Figure 1 shows the camera's placement and Figure 3 shows the view from the camera. Both parents wanted to capture the family's everyday comings and goings, activities around the dining room table, and play that might occur in the adjacent living room. In contrast, placement of the camera on a kitchen counter may cause it to change viewpoints fairly frequently or be blocked by items. On the counter below the camera, the father placed an iPad, which was meant to continuously show Moments on a selected day (Figure 2). The goal was to make the video viewable at-a-glance when they walked by, such that they might be drawn into looking at it more closely if something interesting appeared. This location was never changed during the family's usage, which reflects the value of the location and its mapping to the family's needs. Family members described glancing at the Moments display when they were in the kitchen area getting dishes or food, or while on their way to the garage. The related literature on photo sharing suggests that family members might move the design to a area like the kitchen table for shared viewing [24,49]; however, this never happened with their use of Moments.

For the first year, Moments was set to show yesterday by default. Sometimes family members would change the date (described later), but this was infrequent. After the family had used Moments for a full year, the design was modified so that by default it showed video from exactly one year before. This created a straightforward way of knowing what Moments was displaying; it was always exactly one year ago. This display configuration continued to the end of their usage when the equipment was removed for use in other projects. Throughout the remainder of the results, we describe the way in which the family used Moments and their reactions to the system.

SEEING BIG CHANGES (OR A LACK OF)

The family was most often drawn into looking at the Moments display when they would glance at it and see 'big' changes in the video compared to present day. For example, they noticed dramatic appearance changes such as someone having long hair vs. short hair, the changing ways in which a toddler sat at the kitchen table (in a high chair vs. a regular chair), as well as large changes in clothing styles, such as might occur on a special occasion.

"We notice when somebody has super long hair compared to super short hair." –Father

"There are times that I pass it and I'll be holding [my youngest son] and I yell for [my oldest son], or [my husband], or [my daughter] to come and see, 'Look how small he was!' He is the one you can tell the greatest difference in because he was a baby and he was in my arms and now he's a toddler running around." –Mother

Family members were also drawn in to looking more closely at Moments when there was a *lack* of big changes. For example, a family member might notice that someone was wearing the same shirt today as they did a year ago, recognizing that the shirt was now likely 'getting old.'

Family members repeatedly talked about times when they noticed guests in their home on the Moments display. Seeing only their immediate family members on the display was fairly typical, yet seeing an extended family member or friend on Moments was rare and so it tended to spark curiosity. This curiosity led one or more family members to congregate around the corner of the kitchen and look more closely at the display to inspect who was there and ponder over the reasoning. This was typically a conversation-starter amongst family members if multiple people were around.

"I think the most surprising would probably be when you see somebody on there that's not a part of the house. And you have to remember back to ... like I'll see my mom on there and I'll be like, 'Hey! My mom was visiting us last year at this time? What was she doing out here?'" –Mother

THE IMPORTANCE OF 'THE DETAILS'

The entire family was keen to be able to see past moments that were tied to birthdays and special seasonal celebrations, such as Christmas or Easter. For the first few months of usage (December through March), because the system had not been recording for a very long time, when the family purposely selected dates to look at, they often focused around the recent Christmas.

As time progressed, family members would notice the replay of birthdays, holidays, and other special celebrations that had occurred in the home. Yet what was surprising was *exactly what* they found interesting in those moments. Rather than enjoying the re-creation of the event per se, both parents and the children found it interesting to look at the details of what was going on. Thus, the value of the video was not in seeing a replay of the overall event. Instead, value was found in knowing the specific details of the day, regardless of how mundane they might seem. For example, the parents liked to see what item was prepared for a meal, what show was playing in the background on the television, what shirt each person was wearing, how the house was decorated, or what time of day people were awake and eating breakfast. In addition, family members said that the preparation for important celebrations was interesting to see. Normally this was not something they would capture on photo or video.

"Say it was Christmas and I looked back at last year's Christmas... What was cool is, each year we change our tree. Change where our tree is. The stockings are usually different. When we set the decorations you can see it on Moments, which is really cool." –Oldest Son

The father distinguished such usage of Moments from the way that they routinely used photos and videos within the family. With Moments, memories were about a broader, more detailed view of life.

"It's more about a way to capture this higher level sense of our existence, whereas I think with a photo or a video, you're catching a very specific instance of your life. This is not that. It's about, what was life like for me at that point in time?... it's all these mundane things that we do." –Father

Although the time constraints of the system added a sentimental value to it, they also caused burdens in terms of its usage. Sometimes the mother and father wanted to see a special moment but they did not know what day or time it happened at. Instead, they remembered details of the activity and their feelings associated with it. This led to less targeted usage with the system (e.g., looking at a specific moment of interest) than the parents had anticipated.

"You have to know exactly what time the memory happened in order to go back and use it....So, that's why I think it's less useful for me because even on birthdays and stuff, unless I know what time we had the cake, I have to keep periodically checking it every couple hours in order to go back and get that memory." –Mother

THE PURPOSEFUL CREATIONS OF MOMENTS

While much of the moments that the system captured were spontaneous, there were instances when family members would do certain actions for the sole purpose of Moments capturing them. For example, throughout the first few weeks of usage, while the novelty of the system was still in effect, the children and father would occasionally perform silly actions such as waving at the camera or performing dance moves. The hope was that they would see them again at some point in the future. The children, in particular, liked seeing themselves on the screen.

"Me and [my sister] would usually dance. We'd dance in front of it and then go see what was happening when we'd hide behind the couch and just pop up." –Oldest Son

While this behavior mostly happened during the design's early usage, the behavior periodically resurfaced when guests were over and Moments was explained to them.

On another occasion, Moments was used by the father to purposely capture information for his children, to be seen at a later point in time. The father was going out-of-town to a conference and so he created a scavenger hunt for his children to do while he was gone. The father recorded himself in front of the camera making a particular gesture with his arms. He recorded the date and time of this event on a piece of paper representing the clue. Then, when he was out-of-town and the children were doing the scavenger hunt, they had to view the associated video in order to see what their father had done as part of the clue. This required them to wait until the next day at just the right time to see the father's visual message.

Reviewing these purposefully-created moments was easy in the above instance because it was carefully planned. However, the difficulty in knowing when past events occurred meant that the humorous clips that the children recorded rarely resurfaced because they did not carry a significant date with them that was easily remembered.

LONG TERM PRESENCE AND COMMITMENT

Moments was designed to provide automated capture in an almost unobtrusive form. That is, it was expected that video would simply be recording without the requirement for intervention, or, perhaps, even knowing that the system was recording. Yet usage was far from this ideal. Instead, the system had somewhat of a continuous presence in the home. For example, the father described Moments as a 'friend that was always around.' The computer made a soft humming sound as it processed and recorded video, which meant that it was easy to notice it was running. The father also described somewhat of a continuous sense in his head that Moments was running and needed to be attended to in order to ensure it stayed running. These thoughts came up often when he was near the system. For example, the father talked about always ensuring the cupboard door near Moments was closed because if it was left open, it would partially obscure the camera's view.

"If something is capturing you all the time, you develop this sense that you need to help it capture you and you're not going to block its view. Now I'm its friend and I have to help it out and make sure it can see all the time." –Father

The children liked to routinely use the Moments iPad to play video games. This occurred in the morning before school and during intermittent periods of time after school. The challenge was that every time the iPad was used to play games, it had to be returned to displaying Moments when the play was done. The children were initially told to do so by the father and then it eventually became a habit. Again, this represents act of commitment to ensure the technology was running.

The mother talked about easily noticing when Moments was not working, e.g., the video display was blank. During these times, she felt compelled to tell her husband that it was not working, such that he could either restart it or find out the problem. This was ongoing and, again, represents a sense of commitment to the technology.

Over time, both the parents and children grew accustomed to the presence of Moments. This helped entrench the feeling that it was 'part of' the family and a representation of their life together for the father. He described his desire for the presence of the system and his commitment to it to persist longer term such that it could then act as a type of family heirloom that could be passed on from generation to generation. This was despite the work needed in order to ensure it was always running and recording the family.

"It is useful as a family heirloom, which is weird because I never expected it to be like that...[With Moments] it's just this comforting thing that you see on the counter." –Father

PRIVACY

Family members had several concerns when it came to privacy. Initially, the father was concerned that he would forget that the camera was recording and be recorded partially clothed (e.g., first thing in the morning). Yet this concern went away with time as the idea that his life was being captured became 'routine'. The mother had concerns about being recorded while breastfeeding her baby. Her concern was not with being partially clothed though. Instead, she sometimes worried that the video might resurface when guests were around and they would have issues with 'breastfeeding in public.' Thus, while breastfeeding her baby, it felt similar to breastfeeding in a public place. In this way, she said her home was momentarily transformed from being a private dwelling to one where she had to concern herself with public perceptions of breastfeeding and whether others would be offended. Despite the concerns, this type of video recording never happened to appear when guests visited, yet the potential for such an instance to occur still existed.

"I think the only thing is when I nurse [my youngest son]. Because it happens wherever, whenever. So there's no real time for it. I don't really care, but then I wonder if people are over at the house... " –Mother

In addition, the mother periodically worried about her husband's perceptions of her as a stay-at-home mother. She was concerned that her husband might look at Moments and see what she was doing during the day, and judge her as 'not doing enough.' She also worried that sometimes bad memories might be captured of her or her husband getting upset with their children for misbehavior.

The daughter (age 7) described Moments in a way that was similar to a surveillance system (e.g., cameras watching you) though she was not bothered by it and enjoyed that she could "*see people easier*." The son (age 10) did not have any concerns about privacy when asked.

Given their privacy concerns, both parents talked about how Moments caused them to create a mental representation of what was a 'private zone' in their home. By private zone, they referred to places in the living room and kitchen (or adjoining rooms) that could not be seen on-camera. They said that, because Moments' had a fixed location, it was easy to create this mental model.

"I know the privacy zones... And I know if I go further this way into the living room, then it's more blurry." –Mother

"I think because of the fixed viewpoint, I have a really good sense of what is on camera and what isn't. Because it never changes...I guess I'm always in my head remembering what that zone of the house is." –Father

Both parents were concerned about guests to the home and whether they would be comfortable with Moments capturing them. Guests included periodic visits from friends and stays of several days by grandparents. Both parents said that they routinely told the guests about the system as part of conversation and, initially, the guests appeared uncomfortable where the guests described the system in terms of surveillance. This is likely because they did not receive any benefit from it. Guests also did not have the advantage of knowing what regions were visible on camera given their limited usage. Thus, unlike the family members, they were not able to develop a mental model of the system longer term. Despite these concerns, the parents said that, later in their visit, guests looked as though they had 'eased' into having Moments going or likely had forgotten about it.

When each family member was asked whether there was a time that they wanted to delete footage, their answers were all negative. They said they usually forgot that Moments was recording so they would not know what was recorded.

"I honestly can't think of a moment that I would want deleted because I sometimes forget it's recording. So, I wouldn't know unless I went through every day, every hour, if there was something I would want deleted." – Mother

The father said that there were some recorded moments that he did not want his children to see at present time, For example, he noted that Moments had recorded the parents placing Christmas presents from Santa Claus under their tree on Christmas Eve and, if the kids saw this footage, it would ruin the idea that Santa Claus was real. Seeing the video at a later point in time once the children had learned about the true nature of Santa Claus would be fine.

DISCUSSION

Our paper explored the autobiographical design of an always-on video recording system for the home. Given our focus on the researcher's family, like other autobiographical design studies [37], our goal is not to generalize the usage of the system to other families. Instead, we now focus on several key takeaways from the family's usage that suggest further design investigations in this research space and raise important research questions.

What is Valuable to Record?

First, we found that Moments challenged our assumptions of what might be considered valuable to record in the home. This raises design questions about what is important to capture in video recording systems and what family members may find valuable to see during playback. As expected, the family did indeed value seeing changes over time. Yet what was surprising was the level of detail they valued seeing and how such details pertained to everyday mundane things. This is because the details became forgotten and prompted the family, in a quizzical fashion, to think about and question their past. These findings are similar to the mundane details that prior work has found to be valuable when sharing always-on video between homes [28]. Now we see that such information is also valuable within large collections of recorded video, when one might seemingly expect a person to focus only on 'big' life moments and changes, given the sheer volume of data.

The challenge is that it could be difficult to know what people are interested in seeing a priori, which speaks to the value of always-on video recording. By 'capturing everything,' one has the option and the ability to gather whatever sort of details they might find interesting to review after the fact. However, capturing everything may not always be an option, given the pragmatic realities of long-term capture with always-on video recording (e.g., disk storage). Thus, determining what is worthy of capture ahead of time would certainly be useful. The most interesting moments for the family tended to revolve around situations where more than one person was present, including everyday situations as well as holidays and celebrations, as well as points in time where a non-family member was present. These types of situations are relatively straightforward to detect with computer vision techniques (e.g., counting people). This suggests value in future design research that explores the automatic capture and replay of such situations. However, family members also valued seeing the 'unremarkable stuff' that might be more difficult for a machine to detect. This raises the question of whether or not technology could understand what might be thought of as 'unremarkable' or mundane, in order to periodically capture and resurface it. This design tension should be explored.

Our study also revealed a desire to specifically tie together time periods through a form of asynchronous communication where family members would purposely do something in front of the camera for their future selves. This is intriguing as we have yet to see designs for families that purposely allow them to do this in the home. Research prototypes have supported the random reveal of past media content [42], but none that we know of have allowed one to specify a future point in time for content to 'reveal' itself. Designs have done this for mobile device usage [21,22]; our research suggests the expansion and exploration of these ideas for situated displays in the home. Research should explore how this type of system might alter the future of family narratives and collective memories associated with events. For example, there is the chance that 'bad memories' resurface and how designs deal with such situations remains an open question. Should an individual be allowed to remove such data? And, if so, how, when, and by whom since the interpretation of memories may be different for different family members.

Tensions with Slow Reveal

Second, our study reveals new ideas around the design and long-term use of slow technologies. Past research on slow technologies shows that users can face a tension between a lack of control over the reveal of content and the enjoyment they receive from its slow and random reveal [42]. Yet in past research, users have had other options for accessing their media content (e.g., an existing communication system [20], a Flickr archive [42]) outside of the slow technology, if they wanted. In our case, users could *only* access their content through a slow technology. This created frustration because users had control over what was viewed, but they did not necessarily know where to look to see content they were interested in. They could also not look at other systems to see their content; they were forced to have Moments reveal it to them. This raises design questions around what amount of control a slow technology should provide users. Should a slow technology only ever provide content in a way that reveals itself slowly over time? Or should there be hybrid approaches where content is also made more accessible to users? What is the appropriate level of control and access? Will additional levels of control take away from the benefits of slow reveal?

Given these questions, we see benefits in exploring always-on video recording systems that might remind people of when particular events of significance occurred (e.g., birthday parties or celebrations) to provide a greater sense of control, while still allowing the system to reveal content to family members. For example, systems could provide visual indicators in a calendar of how many people were present at particular moments in each day; a large number of people might mean it was a family gathering. Designers may also want to explore ways to allow family members to flag or highlight days of importance shortly after interesting moments occurred by, for example, interacting with a display to 'tag' days or times. In both of these situations, family members might still be able to gain the benefit of anticipation by waiting for a time of day to play, yet now they would have a stronger sense of what days to look at.

We also recognize that family members may want to purposely block the availability of certain moments and restrict access to them. This may be permanently or for shorter durations of time. For example, the parents wanted to hide videos of them acting as Santa Claus until a later point in time. This raises questions around how designers may want to allow users to include or exclude content from appearing where it may be available at different times (e.g., when children have reached a certain age) and not others. Again, it raises the question, who should have control over such access and settings?

Commitment over Long Periods of Time

Third, we recognize that there are important considerations to be made about the level of commitment that an always-on video recording system creates. Moments created an ongoing sense of presence in the home for itself and with this presence came the creation of work and commitment by family members. Even though the system was meant to be autonomous and passive in its recording of the family's life, it still required work. Certainly some of the work came from the fact that the system was still a research prototype. Yet it is also likely the case that if always-on video recording systems are placed in homes more broadly, the users will not be as technically proficient as the family members who used Moments (e.g., the researcher) or perhaps as committed. Thus, even in a possible 'best case' (the researcher's family using his own design), commitment is a major concern. Systems like Moments would likely create additional work for family members just like it did for the researcher's family.

Such ideas need to be thought through if designers are to consider the broader exploration of always-on video recording. Always-on system in some ways means that it must be always thought about, or frequently attended to. Unlike past slow technology research where designs could be hidden or not worried about, if desired [42] The pragmatic challenges of large amounts of data from always-on recording means that such systems can be difficult to forget about. Cloud-based servers may provide a storage solution, but they pose the risk of having one's data stored outside of the home. This raises design questions around how such systems could be created to relieve user commitment while still ensuring usage continues long term. How does one design for device placement such that 'good' views of family life are always available? How can technical issues be attended to by users in a manner that requires as little attention and commitment as possible?

Privacy

Lastly, there are questions and challenges around privacy. Always-on video recording caused the parents to create a mental representation of what was on camera in their home where fixed camera locations made it easy to develop such mental models. This is similar to how location was critical for always-on video sharing between homes in prior work [35] only with Moments video is recorded and not ephemeral. With video streaming between homes, privacy intrusive moments may come and go quickly because they are streamed and not recorded.

Guests did not have the advantage of easily knowing what was on or off camera and nor did they receive benefit from the system, unless it was valuable to them that they be recorded as part of a family moment. This raises questions around how guests can be easily told about recording devices or have recording zones presented to them in an understandable manner. The use of an always-on recording system can become unremarkable to family members over long periods of time, and, after prolonged use, they may not want the constant reminder that the system is recording, despite the value of the feature for guests. How can designs create a balance between warning people about always-on recording and not being obtrusive in the presentation of this information? Design suggestions from the media space literature across the years [6] present some possibilities from workplace settings (e.g., feedback displays), however, this requires testing and exploration in home contexts since domestic life can be much different than work.

We also found interesting issues arise around gender politics and what is acceptable to be captured and replayed, and the various views people may have about it. This arose around topics such as women's roles in domestic life. Such issues did not come up in past research on always-on video streaming between homes [28,29,35] or ubiquitous capture of domestic life [11,44]. Again it raises questions around who should have access to the recorded video and at what points in time. Even within a single household, it may not be the case that family members want everyone in the home to be able to see everything, all the time. Should a person only be allowed to see the moments that they were apart of? Or should they only be allowed to watch video of others if everyone in the video is present and watching together? would these ideas be seen as being overly restrictive? One challenge is that people and their perceptions change over time. For example, young children may be comfortable in having video recorded, but this is not to say they will share the same views when they are teenagers or adults and videos of their past are resurfaced. This raises further questions around control and access.

Limitations

Our study is limited in that we did not explore the reactions of guests to the system. Future work should certainly explore this broader set of stakeholders for always-on video recording. At this stage, we can only speculate about their reactions, based on comments from the primary users of Moments. Currently the system is not running at the home anymore since Moments was required for another project. We used autographical design as a research method to accomplish a long-term study in the field for two years. A study of this length is very rare within the field of HCI and interaction design. While utilizing external families as part of a deployment would have been valuable, we felt it was most appropriate to test this type of technology on ourselves first to understand the likely impact before trying out similar design ideas with other families. This was because of the potential privacy risks associated with always-on video recording. This allowed us to understand the risks that might occur with such systems so they can be specifically designed for before future studies, or future studies could directly watch for them in order to circumvent negative situations.

CONCLUSION

We studied the design and use of an always-on video recording system called Moments. Through this process, we identified several themes of behaviours and routines around one family's long-term usage of the system. On the positive side, the family was able to gain a valued perspective on their life and be reminded of their past experiences, sometimes in great detail. However, the design of Moments raised important design questions around how past moments should be made accessible while still creating anticipation; and, how always-on video recording systems can be designed such that they do not create new commitments around their maintenance and ongoing care as well as privacy concerns. This raises important design questions for future research to explore that build on our autobiographical design experiences.

ACKNOWLEDGMENT

We thank our participants for their time and long-term efforts, and NSERC for funding this study.

REFERENCES

1. Bardini, T., Horvath, A., Summer, 1995. The Social Construction of the Personal Computer User. Journal of Communication. 45 (3).
2. Louise Barkhuus and Jennifer A. Rode. 2007. From Mice to Men - 24 Years of Evaluation in CHI. In Proceedings of the SIGCHI Conference on Human

Factors in Computing Systems (CHI '07). ACM, New York, NY, USA, 10, pages.

3. Sara A. Bly, Steve R. Harrison, and Susan Irwin. 1993. Media spaces: bringing people together in a video, audio, and computing environment. *Commun. ACM* 36, 1 (January 1993), 28-46.
4. A.J. Brush, Brian R. Meyers, and James Scott. In-Home Deployments. *Studying and Designing Technology for Domestic Life: Lessons from Home*. Morgan Kaufmann.
5. Martijn ten Bhömer, John Helmes, Kenton O'Hara, and Elise van den Hoven. 2010. 4Photos: a collaborative photo sharing experience. In Proceedings of the 6th Nordic Conference on Human-Computer Interaction: Extending Boundaries (NordiCHI '10). ACM, New York, NY, USA, 52-61.
6. Michael Boyle and Saul Greenberg. 2005. The language of privacy: Learning from video media space analysis and design. ACM Trans. Comput.-Hum. Interact. 12, 2 (June 2005), 328-370.
7. Niamh Caprani, Noel E. O'Connor, and Cathal Gurrin. 2013. Experiencing SenseCam: a case study interview exploring seven years living with a wearable camera. In *Proceedings of the 4th International SenseCam & Pervasive Imaging Conference* (SenseCam '13). ACM, New York, NY, USA, 52-59
8. Niamh Caprani, Paulina Piasek, Noel E. O'Connor, Cathal Gurrin, Kate Irving, and Alan F. Smeaton. (2013). Identifying motivations for life-long collections and their implications for lifelogging. Irish HCI.
9. Richard Chalfen, *Snapshot Versions of Life*, Popular Press (1987).
10. Justin Cheng, Akshay Bapat, Gregory Thomas, Kevin Tse, Nikhil Nawathe, Jeremy Crockett, and Gilly Leshed. 2011. GoSlow: designing for slowness, reflection and solitude. In *CHI '11 Extended Abstracts on Human Factors in Computing Systems* (CHI EA '11). ACM, New York, NY, USA, 429-438.
11. Eun Kyoung Choe, Sunny Consolvo, Jaeyeon Jung, Beverly Harrison, and Julie A. Kientz. 2011. Living in a glass house: a survey of private moments in the home. In Proceedings of the 13th international conference on Ubiquitous computing (UbiComp '11). ACM, New York, NY, USA, 41-44.
12. Stéphane Conversy, Nicolas Roussel, Heiko Hansen, Helen Evans, Michel Beaudouin-Lafon, and Wendy Mackay. 2003. Sharing daily-life images with videoProbe. In Proceedings of the 15th Conference on l'Interaction Homme-Machine (IHM '03), Thomas Baudel (Ed.). ACM, New York, NY, USA, 228-231.
13. Andy Crabtree, Tom Rodden, and John Mariani. 2004. Collaborating around collections: informing the continued development of photoware. In Proceedings of the 2004 ACM conference on Computer supported cooperative work (CSCW '04). ACM, New York, NY, USA, 396-405.
14. Audrey Desjardins and Ron Wakkary. 2016. Living In A Prototype: A Reconfigured Space. In Proceedings of the 2016 CHI Conference on Human Factors in Computing Systems (CHI '16). ACM, New York, NY, USA, 5274-5285.
15. Paul Dourish, Adler, A., Bellotti, V., Henderson, A., 1996. Your Place or Mine? Learning from Long-Term Use of Audio-Video Communication. J. CSCW 5 (1). Kluwer Academic Publishers.
16. Thomas Erickson. 1996. The design and long-term use of a personal electronic notebook: a reflective analysis. In Proceedings of the SIGCHI Conference on Human Factors in Computing Systems (CHI '96), Michael J. Tauber (Ed.). ACM, New York, NY, USA, 11-18.
17. David Frohlich, Allan Kuchinsky, Celine Pering, Abbe Don, and Steven Ariss. 2002. Requirements for photoware. In Proceedings of the 2002 ACM conference on Computer supported cooperative work (CSCW '02). ACM, New York, NY, USA, 166-175.
18. W. Gaver. 2006. The video window: my life with a ludic system. Personal Ubiquitous Comput. 10, 2-3 (January 2006), 60-65.
19. Saul Greenberg and Bill Buxton. 2008. Usability evaluation considered harmful (some of the time). In Proceedings of the SIGCHI Conference on Human Factors in Computing Systems (CHI '08). ACM, New York, NY, USA, 111-120.
20. Lars Hallnäs , Johan Redström, Slow Technology – Designing for Reflection, Personal and Ubiquitous Computing, v.5 n.3, p.201-212, August 2001.
21. Dan Hawkins, Jason Procyk, and Carman Neustaedter. 2014. Postulater: slowing the pace of media sharing. In Proceedings of the 2014 companion publication on Designing interactive systems (DIS Companion '14). ACM, New York, NY, USA, 89-92.
22. Daniel Hawkins, Carman Neustaedter, and Jason Procyk. 2015. Postulater: The Design and Evaluation of a Time-Delayed Media Sharing System, Proceedings of Graphics Interface New York, NY, USA, ACM.
23. John Helmes, Caroline Hummels, and Abigail Sellen. 2009. The other brother: re-experiencing spontaneous moments from domestic life. In *Proceedings of the 3rd International Conference on Tangible and Embedded Interaction* (TEI '09). ACM, New York, NY, USA, 233-240.
24. Otmar Hilliges and David Stanley Kirk. 2009. Getting sidetracked: display design and occasioning photo-talk with the photohelix. In Proceedings of the SIGCHI Conference on Human Factors in Computing Systems (CHI '09). ACM, New York, NY, USA, 1733-1736.

25. Debby Hindus, Scott D. Mainwaring, Nicole Leduc, Anna Elizabeth Hagström, and Oliver Bayley. 2001. Casablanca: designing social communication devices for the home. In *Proceedings of the SIGCHI Conference on Human Factors in Computing Systems* (CHI '01). ACM, New York, NY, USA, 325-332.
26. Steve Hodges, Lyndsay Williams, Emma Berry, Shahram Izadi, James Srinivasan, Alex Butler, Gavin Smyth, Narinder Kapur, and Ken Wood. 2006. SenseCam: a retrospective memory aid. In Proceedings of the 8th international conference on Ubiquitous Computing (UbiComp'06), Paul Dourish and Adrian Friday (Eds.). Springer-Verlag, Berlin, Heidelberg, 177-193.
27. Hilary Hutchinson, Wendy Mackay, Bo Westerlund, Benjamin B. Bederson, Allison Druin, Catherine Plaisant, Michel Beaudouin-Lafon, Stéphane Conversy, Helen Evans, Heiko Hansen, Nicolas Roussel, and Björnn Eiderbäck. 2003. Technology probes: inspiring design for and with families. In *Proceedings of the SIGCHI Conference on Human Factors in Computing Systems* (CHI '03). ACM, New York, NY, USA, 17-24. DOI=http://dx.doi.org/10.1145/642611.642616
28. Tejinder K. Judge, Carman Neustaedter, and Andrew F. Kurtz. 2010. The family window: the design and evaluation of a domestic media space. In *Proceedings of the SIGCHI Conference on Human Factors in Computing Systems* (CHI '10). ACM, New York, NY, USA, 2361-2370.
29. Tejinder K. Judge, Carman Neustaedter, Steve Harrison, and Andrew Blose. 2011. Family portals: connecting families through a multifamily media space. In *Proceedings of the SIGCHI Conference on Human Factors in Computing Systems* (CHI '11). ACM, New York, NY, USA, 1205-1214.
30. Tejinder K. Judge and Carman Neustaedter. 2014. Conducting Field Trials with Multiple Connected Households. *Studying and Designing Technology for Domestic Life: Lessons from Home*, Morgan Kaufmann
31. David Kirk, Abigail Sellen, Carsten Rother, and Ken Wood. 2006. Understanding photowork. In Proceedings of the SIGCHI Conference on Human Factors in Computing Systems (CHI '06), Rebecca Grinter, Thomas Rodden, Paul Aoki, Ed Cutrell, Robin Jeffries, and Gary Olson (Eds.). ACM, New York, NY, USA, 761-770.
32. Marilyn M. Mantei, Ronald M. Baecker, Abigail J. Sellen, William A. S. Buxton, Thomas Milligan, and Barry Wellman. 1991. Experiences in the use of a media space. In Proceedings of the SIGCHI Conference on Human Factors in Computing Systems (CHI '91), Scott P. Robertson, Gary M. Olson, and Judith S. Olson (Eds.). ACM, New York, NY, USA, 203-208.
33. Michael Massimi, Khai Truong, David Dearman, and Gillian Hayes. 2010. Understanding Recording Technologies in Everyday Life. IEEE Pervasive Computing 9, 3 (July 2010), 64-71.
34. Andrew D. Miller and W. Keith Edwards. 2007. Give and take: a study of consumer photo-sharing culture and practice. In Proceedings of the SIGCHI Conference on Human Factors in Computing Systems (CHI '07). ACM, New York, NY, USA, 347-356.
35. Carman Neustaedter. 2013. My Life With Always-On Video, Electronic Journal of Communication: Special Issue on Video Conferencing, 23.38.
36. Carman Neustaedter, A. J. Bernheim Brush, and Saul Greenberg. 2007. A digital family calendar in the home: lessons from field trials of LINC. In Proceedings of Graphics Interface 2007 (GI '07). ACM, New York, NY, USA, 199-20. DOI=http://dx.doi.org/10.1145/1268517.1268551
37. Carman Neustaedter, Tejinder K. Judge and Phoebe Sengers. 2014. Autobiographical Design in the Home. *Studying and Designing Technology for Domestic Life: Lessons from Home*, 135. Morgan Kaufmann
38. Carman Neustaedter and Phoebe Sengers. 2012. Autobiographical design in HCI research: designing and learning through use-it-yourself. In Proceedings of the Designing Interactive Systems Conference (DIS '12). ACM, New York, NY, USA, 514-523.
39. David H. Nguyen, Aurora Bedford, Alexander Gerard Bretana, and Gillian R. Hayes. 2011. Situating the concern for information privacy through an empirical study of responses to video recording. In Proceedings of the SIGCHI Conference on Human Factors in Computing Systems (CHI '11). ACM, New York, NY, USA, 3207-3216.
40. Michael Nunes, Saul Greenberg, Sheelagh Carpendale, and Carl Gutwin. "What did I miss? Visualizing the past through video traces." In *ECSCW 2007*, pp. 1-20. Springer London, 2007.
41. Aisling T. O'Donnell, Yolanda Jetten, and Michelle K. 2010. Who is watching over you? The role of shared identity in perceptions of surveillance, European Journal of Social Psychology, Vol. 40(1), 135-147.
42. William T. Odom, Abigail J. Sellen, Richard Banks, David S. Kirk, Tim Regan, Mark Selby, Jodi L. Forlizzi, and John Zimmerman. 2014. Designing for slowness, anticipation and re-visitation: a long term field study of the photobox. In Proceedings of the SIGCHI Conference on Human Factors in Computing Systems (CHI '14). ACM, New York, NY, USA, 1961-1970.

43. Kenton O'Hara, Richard Harper, Axel Unger, James Wilkes, Bill Sharpe, and Marcel Jansen. 2005. TxtBoard: from text-to-person to text-to-home. In CHI '05 Extended Abstracts on Human Factors in Computing Systems (CHI EA '05). ACM, New York, NY, USA, 1705-1708.

44. Antti Oulasvirta, Aurora Pihlajamaa, Jukka Perkiö, Debarshi Ray, Taneli Vähäkangas, Tero Hasu, Niklas Vainio, and Petri Myllymäki. 2012. Long-term effects of ubiquitous surveillance in the home. In Proceedings of the 2012 ACM Conference on Ubiquitous Computing (UbiComp '12). ACM, New York, NY, USA, 41-50.

45. Jason Procyk and Carman Neustaedter. 2014. GEMS: the design and evaluation of a location-based storytelling game. In Proceedings of the 17th ACM conference on Computer supported cooperative work & social computing (CSCW '14). ACM, New York, NY, USA, 1156-1166.

46. Jim Rowan and Elizabeth D. Mynatt. 2005. Digital Family Portrait Field Trial: Support for Aging in Place. In Proceedings of the SIGCHI Conference on Human Factors in Computing Systems (CHI '05). ACM, New York, NY, USA, 521-530.

47. Deb Roy, Rupal Patel, Philip DeCamp, Rony Kubat, Michael Fleischman, Brandon Roy, Nikolaos Mavridis, Stefanie Tellex, Alexia Salata, Jethran Guinness, Michael Levit, Peter Gorniak. (2006). The Human Speechome Project. Proceedings of the 28th Annual Cognitive Science Conference.

48. Abigail J. Sellen, Andrew Fogg, Mike Aitken, Steve Hodges, Carsten Rother, and Ken Wood. 2007. Do life-logging technologies support memory for the past?: an experimental study using sensecam. In Proceedings of the SIGCHI Conference on Human Factors in Computing Systems (CHI '07). ACM, New York, NY, USA, 81-90.

49. Chia Shen, Neal B. Lesh, Frederic Vernier, Clifton Forlines, and Jeana Frost. 2002. Sharing and building digital group histories. In Proceedings of the 2002 ACM conference on Computer supported cooperative work (CSCW '02). ACM, New York, NY, USA, 324-333.

50. Thacker, C.P., 1988. Personal Distributed Computing: The Alto and Ethernet Hardware. In: Goldberg, A. (Ed.), A History of Personal Workstations. ACM Press, New York, NY, pp. 267e289.

51. Daisuke Uriu, Naruhiko Shiratori, Satoru Hashimoto, Shuichi Ishibashi, and Naohito Okude. 2009. CaraClock: an interactive photo viewer designed for family memories. In CHI '09 Extended Abstracts on Human Factors in Computing Systems (CHI EA '09). ACM, New York, NY, USA, 3205-3210.

52. Soroush Vosoughi and Deb Roy. (2012). A longitudinal study of prosodic exaggeration in child-directed speech. Proceedings of the 6th International Conference on Speech Prosody. Shanghai, China.

Author Index

NOTES

NOTES

NOTES

NOTES

NOTES

NOTES

NOTES

NOTES

www.ingramcontent.com/pod-product-compliance
Ingram Content Group UK Ltd.
Pitfield, Milton Keynes, MK11 3LW, UK
UKHW051419290926
15471UKWH00009B/1691

9 781450 356015

ISBN 978-1-4503-5601-5
90000
9 781450 356015